VOLUME **2**

**African Literature
and Its Times**

World Literature
and Its Times

Profiles of Notable Literary Works and the
Historical Events That Influenced Them

Joyce Moss • Lorraine Valestuk

GALE GROUP

Detroit
New York
San Francisco
London
Boston
Woodbridge, CT

World Literature and Its Times

Profiles of Notable Literary Works and the Historical Events That Influenced Them

VOLUME 2

African Literature and Its Times

JOYCE MOSS • LORRAINE VALESTUK

STAFF

Lawrence J. Trudeau, *Production Editor*

Maria Franklin, *Permissions Manager*
Edna Hedblad, *Permissions Specialist*

Dorothy Maki, *Manufacturing Manager*
Wendy Blurton, *Senior Buyer*

Mary Beth Trimper, *Manager, Composition and Electronic Prepress*
Evi Seoud, *Assistant Manager, Composition Purchasing and Electronic Prepress*

Cynthia Baldwin, *Art Director*
Pamela Galbreath, *Cover and Page Designer*

Michael Logusz, *Graphic Artist*
Randy Bassett, Image *Database Supervisor*
Robert Duncan, *Imaging Specialist*
Pamela A. Reed, *Imaging Coordinator*
Dean Dauphinais, *Senior Image Editor*
Robyn V. Young, *Senior Image Editor*
Kelly A. Quin, *Image Editor*

ISBN 0-7876-3727-0

Printed in the United States of America
10 9 8 7 6 5 4 3 2

Library of Congress Cataloging-in-Publication Data

Moss, Joyce, 1951-
    African literature and its times: profiles of notable
literary works and the historical events that influenced them
/ Joyce Moss, Lorraine Valestuk.
    p. cm. — (World literature and its times; v.2)
    Includes bibliographical references and index.
    ISBN 0-7876-3727-0 (hardcover: alk. paper)
    1. African literature—History and criticism. 2. Literature and history—
Africa. 3. Africa—History—Miscellanea. I. Valestuk, Lorraine, 1963- II. Title. III. Series.
    PL8010 .M65 2000
    809'.896—dc21
                                                                    00-024488
                                                                    CIP
                                                                    Rev.

Contents

General Preface

The world at the turn of the twenty-first century is a shrinking sphere. Innovative modes of transmission make communication from one continent to another almost instantaneous, encouraging the development of an increasingly global society, heightening the urgency of the need for mutual understanding. At the foundation of *World Literature and Its Times* is the belief that within a people's literature are keys to their perspectives, their emotions, and the formative events that have brought them to the present point.

As manifested in their literary works, societies experience phenomena that are in some instances universal and in other instances tied to time and place. T. S. Eliot's poem *The Wasteland,* for example, is set in Europe in the early 1920s, when the region was rife with the disenchantment of the post-World War I era. Coincidentally, Juan Rulfo's novel *Pedro Páramo,* set in Latin America over a spread of decades that includes the 1920s, features a protagonist whose last name means "bleak plain" or "wasteland." The two literary works, though written oceans apart, conjure a remarkably similar atmosphere. Likewise André Brink's novel *A Dry White Season* concerns the torture of political prisoners in South Africa in the 1970s while Isabelle Allende's *House of the Spirits* portrays such torture in Chile during the same decade. A close look at the two instances, however—and the two wastelands referred to above—exposes illuminating differences, which are tied to the times and places in which the respective works are set.

World Literature and Its Times regards both fiction and nonfiction as rich mediums for understanding the differences, as well as the similarities, among people and societies. In its view, full understanding of a literary work demands attention to events and attitudes of the periods in which the work takes place and the one in which it is written. The series therefore examines a wide range of novels, short stories, biographies, speeches, poems, and plays by contextualizing a work in these two periods. Each volume covers some 50 literary works that span a mix of centuries and genres. Invariably the literary work takes center stage, with its contents determining which issues—social, political, psychological, economic, or cultural—are covered in a given entry. Every entry discusses the relevant issues apart from the literary work, making connections to it when merited and allowing for comparisons between the literary and the historical realities. Close attention is also given to the literary work itself in the interest of gleaning historical understandings from it.

Of course, the function of literature is not necessarily to represent history accurately. Nevertheless the images promoted by a powerful literary work—be it José Hernandez's poem *The Gaucho Martín Fierro* (set in Argentina), Isak Dinesen's memoir *Out of Africa* (Kenya), or William Shakespeare's play *Macbeth* (Scotland)—leave impressions that are commonly taken to be historical. In taking literature as fact, one risks acquiring mistaken notions of history. In the process of describing life in Africa, for example, various European novels of the early to mid-twentieth century evoked an image of its people as generally barbarous and simple-minded. Succeeding these novels were works that showed this image to be false, such as Chinua Achebe's *Things Fall Apart,* which reveals the ethnic richness of life among the Igbo of Nigeria, evoking a sophistication that belies stereotypes in the earlier, European fiction. In fact, many of the works covered in this series upset longstanding stereotypes, from Bartolomé de Las Casas's *A Short Account of the Destruction of the Indies* (mid-1500s Latin America) to Ferdinand Oyono's *Houseboy* (mid-1900s French Cameroon).

Beyond upsetting stereotypic images, literary works broaden our understanding of history. They are able to convey more than the cut-and-dried record by portraying events in a way that captures the fears and challenges of a period, or by drawing attention to groups of people who are generally left out of standard histories. This is well illustrated with writings about women in different societies—from Rosario Ferré's short story "The Youngest Doll" (Puerto Rico), to Flora Nwapa's novel *Efuru* (Nigeria), to Mary Wollstonecraft's essay *A Vindication of the Rights of Woman* (England). Taken together, the entries present a cross-section of perspectives and experiences of women and others in the societies of a region in a manner that begins to do justice to their complexity.

Nonfiction too must be anchored in its place and times to derive its full value. Octavio Paz's essay *The Labyrinth of Solitude* explains the character of contemporary Mexicans as a product of historical experience; the entry on the essay amplifies this experience. Another entry, on Albert Memmi's *The Pillar of Salt,* uses the less direct genre of biography to depict the life of an Arab Jew during the Nazi occupation of North Africa. A third entry, on Frantz Fanon's essays in *The Wretched of the Earth,* considers the merits of violence in view of the ravages inflicted on the colonized in places such as Algeria.

The task of reconstructing the historical context of a literary work can be problematic. An author may present events out of chronological order, as Carlos Fuentes does in *The Death of Artemio Cruz* (Mexico), or may feature legendary heroes who defy attempts to fit them neatly into an exact time slot (such as the warrior Beowulf of Denmark, glorified in England's epic poetry; or the Manding hero Sunjata, who founds the empire of Mali). In the case of Fuentes's novel,

World Literature and Its Times unscrambles the plot, providing a linear rendering of events and associated historical information. In the case of the epics, the series profiles customs particular to the respective cultures, arming the reader with details that inform the heroes' adventures. The approach sheds light on the relationship between fact and fiction, both of which are shown to provide insight into the people who generated the epic. As always, the series takes this approach with appreciation for the beauty of the literary work independent of historical facts, but also in the belief that ultimate regard is shown for the work by placing it in the context of pertinent events.

Beyond this underlying belief, the series is founded on the notion that a command of world literature bolsters knowledge of the writings produced by one's own society. Long before the present century, fiction and nonfiction writers from different locations influenced one another through trends and strategies in their literatures. In our postcolonial age, such cross-fertilization has quickened. Latin American literature, influenced by French and Spanish trends, in turn influences African writers of today. This is well illustrated by the Moroccan novel *The Sand Child,* one of whose characters resembles Argentine author Jorge Luis Borges. Likewise, Africa's literary tradition has affected and been affected by France's, and the same relationship holds true for the traditions of India and Great Britain. The degree of such literary intermixture promises only to multiply in our increasingly global society. In the process, world literature and its landmark texts gain even greater significance, attaining the potential to promote understanding not only of others, but also of ourselves.

The Selection of Literary Works

The works chosen for *African Literature and Its Times* have been carefully selected by professors at the universities detailed in "Acknowledgments." Keeping the literature-history connection in mind, the team made its selections based on a combination of factors: how frequently a literary work is studied, how closely it is tied to pivotal events in the past or present, and how strong and enduring its appeal has been to readers in and out of the society that produced it. Attention has been paid to all regions of the continent. There has also been a careful effort to represent female as well as male authors, to cover a mix of genres, and to include a number of precolonial works available in English, though they are far scarcer than the current century's offering. Also for colonial and postcolonial works, the selection was limited to those that are presently available in English. However, recognizing that much of Africa's finest literature was written in other languages, a careful effort has been made to include translations of works that first appeared in Arabic, French, Portuguese, or a local African language as well as those that first appeared in English.

Format and Arrangement of Entries

The volumes in *World Literature and Its Times* are arranged geographically. Within each volume, entries are arranged alphabetically by title of the literary work. The time period in which the work is set appears at the beginning of an entry.

Each entry is organized as follows:

1. **Introduction**—identifying information in three parts:

    The literary work—specifies the genre, the place and time in which the work is set, the year it was first published, and, if applicable, the year in which it was first translated; also provided, for translations, is the title of the literary work in its original language.

    Synopsis—summarizes the storyline or contents of the work.

    Introductory paragraph—introduces the literary work in relation to the author's life.

2. **Events in History at the Time the Literary Work Takes Place**—describes social and political events that relate to the plot or contents of the literary work. The section may discuss background information as well as relevant events during the period in which the work is set. Subsections vary depending on the literary work. Taking a deductive approach, the section starts with events in history and telescopes inward to events in the literary work.

3. **The Literary Work in Focus**—summarizes in detail the plot or contents of the work, describes how it illuminates history, and identifies sources used by the author. After the summary of the work comes a subsection focusing on an aspect of the lit-

erature that illuminates our understanding of events or attitudes of the period. This subsection takes an inductive approach, starting with the literary work, and broadening outward to events in history. It is followed by a third subsection specifying sources that inspired elements of the work and discussing its literary context, or relation to other works.

4. **Events in History at the Time the Literary Work Was Written**—describes social, political, and/or literary events in the author's lifetime that relate to the plot or contents of a work. Also discussed in this section are the reviews or reception accorded the literary work.

5. **For More Information**—provides a list of all sources that have been cited in the entry as well as sources for further reading about the different issues or personalities featured in the entry.

If the literary work is set and written in the same time period, sections 2 and 4 of the entry on that work ("Events in History at the Time the Literary Work Takes Place" and "Events in History at the Time the Literary Work Was Written") are combined into the single section "Events in History at the Time of the Literary Work."

Additional Features

Whenever possible, primary source material is provided through quotations in the text and material in sidebars. The sidebars include historical details that amplify issues raised in the text, and anecdotes that provide a fuller understanding of the temporal context. Every effort has been made in both the sidebars and the text to define in context unusual or locally nuanced terms. There are timelines in various entries to summarize intricate series of events. Finally, historically relevant illustrations enrich and further clarify the information.

Comments and Suggestions

Your comments on this series and suggestions for future editions are welcome. Please write: Editors, *World Literature and Its Times,* Gale Group, 27500 Drake Road, Farmington Hills, Michigan 48331-3535.

Acknowledgments

*A*frican Literature and Its Times is a collaborative effort that evolved through several stages of development, each of which was monitored by experts in North, South, East, and West African literatures. A special thank you goes to Emmanuel Obiechina of the University of Nigeria, Roger Beck of Eastern Illinois University, Julia Clancy-Smith of the University of Arizona, Chris Ehret of the University of California, and Ernest N. Emenyonu of Southern Connecticut University for their enthusiastic guidance at every stage in the process.

For their incisive participation in selecting the literary works covered in the volume, the editors extend deep appreciation to the following professors:

Ned Alpers, University of California at Los Angeles, Department of History

Roger Beck, Eastern Illinois University, Department of History

Ali Behdad, University of California at Los Angeles, Department of English

Julia Clancy-Smith, University of Arizona, Department of History

Donald Cosentino, University of California at Los Angeles, Department of World Arts and Culture

Chris Ehret, University of California at Los Angeles, Department of History

Ernest N. Emenyonu, Southern Connecticut State University, Department of English

Mona Mikhail, New York University, Department of Middle Eastern Studies

Emmanuel Obiechina, University of Nigeria, Department of English

Olakunle George, University of Oregon, Department of English

The following professors carefully reviewed the entries to insure accuracy and completeness of information. Sincere gratitude is extended to these professors:

Hédi Abdel-Jaouad, Skidmore College, Department of Foreign Language and Literatures

F. Odun Balogun, Delaware State University, Department of English/Communications

Roger Beck, Eastern Illinois University, Department of History

Ali Behdad, University of California at Los Angeles, Department of English

Elleke Boehmer, University of Leeds, School of English

Donald Cosentino, University of California at Los Angeles, Department of World Arts and Cultures

Ross Dunn, San Diego State University, Department of History

Chris Ehret, University of California at Los Angeles, Department of History

Ernest N. Emenyonu, Southern Connecticut State University, Department of English

Acknowledgments

Samba Gadjigo, Mount Holyoke College, Department of French

Russell G. Hamilton, Vanderbilt University, Department of Spanish and Portuguese; Dean of the Graduate School

Françoise Lionnet, University of California at Los Angeles, Chair, Department of French

Mona Mikhail, New York University, Department of Middle Eastern Studies

Barbara Moss, Clark Atlanta University, Department of History

Emmanuel Obiechina, University of Nigeria, Department of English

Olakunle George, University of Oregon, Department of English

John Voll, Georgetown University, Department of History

Richard Watts, Tulane University, Department of French and Italian

For their painstaking research and composition, the editors thank the contributors whose names appear at the close of the entries that they wrote. A complete listing follows:

Adeleke Adeeko, Associate Professor, University of Colorado at Boulder

Faisal Azam, B.A., University of California at Berkeley; professional writer

Anne-Lancaster Badders, Ph.D. candidate, University of California at Los Angeles

Kimberly Ball, M.A. candidate, University of California at Berkeley

Clarissa Burt, Assistant Professor, American University in Cairo

Donald Cosentino, Professor, University of California at Los Angeles

Julia Clancy-Smith, Associate Professor, University of Arizona

Terri DeYoung, Associate Professor, University of Washington

Mary Dillard, Ph.D. candidate, University of California at Los Angeles

Susan Douglass, M.A., Georgetown University; professional writer

Ernest N. Emenyonu, Professor, Southern Connecticut State University

John Erickson, Professor, University of Kentucky

Laura Franey, Assistant Professor, Millsaps College

Jeff Jung, Instructor, El Camino College

Jamil Khader, Instructor, Bilkent University, Ankara, Turkey

Jacob Littleton, Ph.D. candidate, University of California at Los Angeles

LaShonda Long, Ph.D. candidate, University of California at Los Angeles

Pamela S. Loy, Ph.D., University of California at Santa Barbara; professional writer

Mildred Mortimer, Professor, University of Colorado at Boulder

Joyce Moss, M.Ed., University of Southern California; professional writer

Iyunolu Osagie, Associate Professor, Pennsylvania State University

Dwight F. Reynolds, Associate Professor; Chair, Department of Islamic and Near Eastern Studies, University of California at Santa Barbara

John Roleke, M.A., Indiana University; professional writer

Victoria Sams, Ph.D. candidate, University of California at Los Angeles

Samah Selim, Assistant Professor, Princeton University

Richard Serrano, Assistant Professor, Rutgers University

Brian P. Thompson, Ph.D., University of California at Los Angeles; professional writer

Carolyn Turgeon, M.A., University of California at Los Angeles; professional writer

Lorraine Valestuk, Ph.D., University of California at Davis; professional writer

Allison Weisz, M.Phil, Cambridge University; Instructor, Convent of the Sacred Heart

Sherifa Zuhur, Associate Professor, American University in Cairo

Deep appreciation is extended to Larry Trudeau of the Gale Group for his deft editing of the entries and to Deborah Morad of the Gale Group for her painstaking research and compilation of the illustrations. Anne Leach indexed the volume with great sensitivity to both readers and subject matter. Lastly, the editors express their gratitude to Peter Kline for his photographic research, and to Hallie Jones for her proficient word processing and organizational management.

Introduction to African Literature and Its Times

African literature first gained world renown in the 1950s and '60s, in large part because of World War II. The racism of the Axis powers before and during this war raised global consciousness about subject peoples everywhere. In Africa, members of colonized societies had put their lives on the line for the Allies against Germany and Italy, and those nations' racist pretensions to superiority. Now, in the postwar period, Africans refused to tolerate the racism that still raged on their own home ground. From Ghana in West Africa, to Algeria in North Africa, Kenya in East Africa, and Zimbabwe in southern Africa, nationalist leaders organized independence movements or fought life-and-death guerrilla campaigns to wrest themselves free from European domination. One after another, the groups achieved their goal, in some cases at horrific costs. In Kenya, the death toll climbed to 20,000; in Zimbabwe, to 30,000; in Algeria, to more than one million. Often the struggle called for enormous sacrifice, but it was a heady time nonetheless, one full of promise as well as uncertainty about what lay ahead and how Africans could best define themselves in the contemporary world. For nearly 70 years, since the last two decades of the nineteenth century, Africa's rich array of ethnic groups had suffered an era of intensified colonial rule. European powers vied for control of the continent, then often brutally imposed their colonial policies and cultures on its peoples. In the process, older, African political systems and ways of life were disrupted or undermined, a course of events that in many cases did severe damage to separate African senses of identity.

As the Nigerian novelist Chinua Achebe explains, the decades of European rule had an amnesic effect on Africa. They swept its peoples "out of the current of their history into somebody else's history," transformed them from major into minor players in their own lands, turned their saga into the saga of alien races in Africa, and obliterated "the real history that had been going on since the millenia ... especially because it was not written down" (*Conversations with Chinua Achebe* [Ed. Bernth Lindfors. Jackson: University Press of Mississippi, 1997], 157). The reference here is to a rich foundation of oral literature—of proverb, song, folktale, and legend—that preceded the European invasions and has survived to the present day. In the early 1200s, poet-historians in the empire of Mali, for example, told and retold the story of their origins, the *Epic of Son-Jara* (or Sunjata), which in the 1950s found its way onto paper, the core of the story remarkably preserved for 700 years.

From the seventh into the eleventh century, Arab peoples mounted a series of invasions of North Africa that brought the Muslim religion to the continent. By the mid-1300s, when Ibn Battuta wrote his *Rihla* (see *Ibn Battuta in Black Africa*) Islam had penetrated into East and West Africa, as shown in his book of travels, the world's only existing eyewitness account of life in these areas during the fourteenth century.

Next came the first Europeans to venture south of the Sahara Desert, the Portuguese, who settled in coastal areas of the region during the fifteenth century and trafficked heavily in slaves. Over the next few centuries, other European powers became involved in the slave trade, abducting a total of perhaps 12 million Africans, among them a ten-year-old Igbo boy from West Africa, Olaudah Equiano. Kidnapped and sold into English slavery, Equiano later published his memoirs (*The Interesting Narrative of the Life of Olaudah Equiano or Gustavus Vassa the African*) to promote abolition, thereby initiating African protest literature, which would rear its defiant head on behalf of other pressing causes in the twentieth century. Meanwhile, in South Africa, the 1780s saw the birth of the Zulu chief Chaka, who would amass a kingdom that endured for much of the nineteenth century (1816-79), until the last two decades, when European nations embarked on a scramble for control of almost all of Africa. Apart from battling Africans, these nations competed with one another. In South Africa, on Chaka's home ground, the British waged war against descendants of the Dutch for territorial control. Elsewhere the Germans vied with the French, the Portuguese with the Germans, and the Italians with the English, the French, and the Turks. From the 1880s to the 1920s, most of Africa became subject to one European nation or another.

With the rush of colonizers came missionaries and their educational systems, which led to the emergence of an African literature written in European languages. Also affected were works in Arabic, a language long used in Africa for writing. The continent's literature evolved from the early through the mid-twentieth century into a vigorous collection, including novels, short stories, plays, poems, memoirs, and essays, most of them politically tinged. To a great extent, literature in Africa is a medium of expression that aims to serve the inhabitants: it has taken on the challenge of coming to grips with what happened to them under and after colonization, of creating stories whose intention is to aid people in the daily struggle of life. In a sense, as Achebe explains about his own separate novels, the various works all tell the same story, the story of Africa in today's world, of its relationship to Europe, of the issues that confront its people in the present, which can be understood only by examining their past, their particular histories, which literature passes on from one generation to the next. Africa is a huge continent, characterized by diversity; to do it justice one must view the whole picture, its multiplicity of issues, and from different angles. "You don't," argues Achebe, "stand in one place to see it, you move around the arena and take different perspectives . . . . [T]o get it right you have to circulate the arena and take your shots like a photographer from different positions" (*Conversations with Chinua Achebe*. [Ed. Bernth Lindfors. Jackson: University Press of Mississippi, 1997], 156). It is to this end that the mix of works has been selected for inclusion in *African Literature and Its Times*.

Colonial rule was at first confusing. With it came benefits, like the advantages of education, and liabilities, like forced labor, the seizure of indigenous lands, and legal double standards for the colonizers and the colonized. Astutely, Africans learned to sort out the benefits from the liabilities, as evident in their coming-of-age stories. Literatures around the world feature such stories, or bildungsromans; there is a difference, though, to these tales in Africa. Stories of growth here have involved an extra dimension, an expanding consciousness of the hypocrisy inherent in colonialism, which professed to benefit the same peoples that it so profoundly oppressed. The growing awareness of this reality produced an additional type of "coming-of-age" story in African literature. In the first place, there were tales of passage into adulthood that involved finding one's place in a bifurcated world of traditional and European forces (as reflected in Taha Husayn's *An Egyptian Childhood* (Egypt) and Camara Laye's *Dark Child* (French Guinea). In the second, less obvious, place, the growth process involved a dawning awareness of being denigrated and exploited because of one's race, and, in the case of women, because of one's gender. These recognitions manifest themselves in novels from different reaches of the continent—in Ngugi wa Thiong'o's *Weep Not, Child* (Kenya), for example; in Ferdinand Oyono's *Houseboy* (Cameroon Republic); and in Tsitsi Dangarembga's *Nervous Conditions* (Zimbabwe). In some respects, the identity crises in such novels are unique to a specific environment; in other respects, similar by virtue of being African.

Along with these coming-of-age threads, from the canon of literary works in Africa one can extract mutual concerns about other issues as well. There are works about polygamy and the stress colonialism placed on marriages, about colonialism's abuses, and about its failure to acknowledge the validity of precolonial customs—issues that surface, respectively, in *Song of Lawino and Song of Ocol* (Uganda), *We Killed Mangy-Dog and*

Other Stories (Mozambique), and *Death and the King's Horseman* (Nigeria). A host of additional issues surface in works set around the continent, as evident in the sampling below:

- **African defiance**—*God's Bits of Wood* (Senegal and French Sudan), *Mine Boy* (South Africa), *Things Fall Apart* (Nigeria)

- **Idealism**—*Cry, the Beloved Country* (South Africa), "Farahat's Republic" (Egypt), *When Rain Clouds Gather* (Botswana)

- **Intra-African generation gap**—*The Joys of Motherhood* (Nigeria), *Valley Song* (South Africa)

- **Interethnic conflict**—*Chaka* (South Africa), *The Last Duty* (Nigeria), *The Pillar of Salt* (Tunisia)

- **Parental and extended family devotion**—*The Oil Man of Obange* (Nigeria), *Nervous Conditions* (Zimbabwe)

- **Fusion of the worldly and supernatural**—*The Famished Road* (Nigeria), *The Dark Child* (French Guinea)

- **Traditionalism versus colonialism**—*Mission to Kala* (Cameroon), *Midaqq Alley* (Egypt)

- **Official torture**—*Houseboy* (Cameroon Republic), *Waiting for the Barbarians* (South Africa)

- **Violent liberation**—*The Wretched of the Earth* (Algeria), "The Rivonia Trial Speech" (South Africa)

- **Women's rights and roles**—*Fantasia* (Algeria), *Efuru* (Nigeria), *The Sand Child* (Morocco)

More issues and illustrative literary works exist. Unique among them is apartheid, in effect in South Africa from 1948 to 1994. As apartheid's architects saw it, South Africa consisted of distinct nations, each of which ought to live in its own separate area, or homeland, with blacks entering the white homeland only for work. In theory, the policy promoted the idea of separate development. In reality, it served as the basis for all manner of abuses, protested in literature by blacks and whites alike. Peter Abrahams's *Mine Boy* and Nadine Gordimer's *Burger's Daughter* are novels in this vein, while Nelson Mandela's "Rivonia Trial Speech" tackles the issue through rhetoric. Like the rest of the continent, though, South Africa was much more than a black-and-white, one-issue society. There was the experience of the coloured, or mixed-race, minority to consider (see Alex La Guma's *A Walk in the Night*), and of the white minority that acted against apartheid (see André Brink's *A Dry White Season*). Of course, divisions in white South African so-

ciety were nothing new; they had already surfaced in nineteenth-century literature, as shown in distinctions made between Afrikaner and British characters in Olive Schreiner's *Story of an African Farm.*

These and other works covered in *African Literature and Its Times* begin to convey the complexity of African societies, although space and the primarily historical focus preclude a comprehensive coverage. Postcolonial life, for example, gave rise in the 1970s and '80s to works about internal strife and to works by women writers. In keeping with these developments, the volume covers Isidore Okepwho's *The Last Duty,* about internal friction in a border town during the Nigerian Civil War, and Mariama Bâ's *So Long a Letter,* about women in transition in Senegal. But the rigors of selection preclude coverage of *Labyrinths,* a posthumous work by the Igbo poet Christopher Okigbo, a martyr in Nigeria's Civil War, or of *The Beggar's Strike,* a Senegalese novel by Aminata Sow-Fall about the marginalized group identified in the title.

On the other hand, the volume does include not only a mix of perspectives and experiences from all regions of the continent, but also stories that rise above the issues of the moment to convey the integrity of a culture apart from its encounter with colonialism. Two cases in point are Wole Soyinka's play *Death and the King's Horseman* and Chinua Achebe's novel *Things Fall Apart.* In the first instance, colonialism is a convenient excuse that allows a character to escape his duty to observe a difficult custom—to disastrous effect; the Yoruba, not the colonial view, takes precedence in the play. Similarly, in Achebe's novel, the protagonist lets his individual inclination overpower that of the group and the results are just as disastrous. Again the work rises above the colonial factor to reveal an indigenous truism, in this case of sanctioned behavior among the Igbo people.

The character, and beauty, of the literature surfaces not only in what it says but also in how it tells its stories. Most of the writers covered in this volume generate their works in a European language or in Arabic, in many cases Africanizing the language and genre, tailoring them to indigenous society. Achebe infuses his novel with elements of his own traditional folklore, as do Amos Tutuola (*The Palm-Wine Drinkard and His Dead Palm-Wine Tapster in the Deads' Town*), Flora Nwapa (*Efuru*), and Kateb Yacine (*Nedjma*). Likewise Soyinka incorporates into the dialogue of his play traditional proverbs and the type of

English spoken by Africans in the colonial power structure. In his short story "Farahat's Republic," Yusuf Idris breaks new ground by digressing from standard Arabic and including dialogue that reflects the dialects genuinely spoken in mid-1900s Egypt.

Lastly, African writers have shaped their literature by portraying in it a unique set of heroes, sometimes tragic heroes, but heroes nonetheless. In Soyinka's play an educated African dies to preserve the Yoruba world view. In *God's Bits of Wood,* Wolof (or Djolof) railway workers go on a deadly strike to protest unequal labor conditions. *Fantasia* highlights the role of rural women in Algeria's war for independence. In *A Dry White Season,* an African janitor and a white schoolteacher lose their lives to unmask the truth about an instance of official torture. In fact, the authors of all this literature are themselves heroes, for daring to generate literary works that have exposed or contradicted those in power. Some of these works were banned in their country of origin (*Burger's Daughter*—South Africa; *Woman at Point Zero*—Egypt). In other places, the works startled official versions of history by introducing an African perspective on European conquest (*Things Fall Apart*), by portraying the colonizer rather than the colonized as savage (*Yaka*), or by exposing forms of postcolonial oppression and corruption (*Sweet and Sour Milk*). Perhaps most important, though, has been the portrayal for Africans, and the rest of the world, of everyday heroes. In Nigeria there is a novel, *The Oil Man of Obange,* in which a father, despite hardship after hardship, literally works himself to death so that his sons and daughter can afford an education. An unsung hero, he is one of many who make Africa's heart beat.

Chronology of Relevant Events

African Literature and Its Times

~

FROM AFRICAN EMPIRES TO THE FIRST COLONIZERS

South of the Sahara Desert, medieval Africa was largely dominated by the rise of three inland empires—Ghana, Mali, and Songhai. Other cultures developed as well, including the Yoruba and Igbo in today's Nigeria, the Wolof (or Djolof) in Senegal, and the Shona in Zimbabwe. Early trade with Mediterranean countries fostered the spread of Christianity to some African kingdoms, most notably to Axum in Ethiopia, while other kingdoms, such as Mali, were converted to Islam by the teachings of Muhammad after Arab invasions of the continent. Meanwhile, trade continued, over north–south and east–west routes that linked Africa to the Arabian peninsula, India, and the Mediterranean countries and enabled Africans to participate in international culture. Traders journeyed by land and sea to traffic in goods and slaves, their activity increasing after European explorers, led by the Portuguese, ventured into African territory. By the end of the seventeenth century, the Portuguese, British, French, and Dutch were poised to begin a competition for domination in Africa that would last for more than two hundred years.

Historical Events	Related Literary Works
350–550 C.E. In Ethiopia, Axumites convert to Christianity as a result of Mediterranean contact	
400–1100 Empire of Wagadu (ancient kingdom of Ghana) flourishes in the western Sudan	
500 c. 570 The prophet Muhammad is born in the Middle East in Mecca	
600–1300 Height of Nubian Christian kingdoms in eastern Sudan	
620 Muhammad preaches his revelations	

	Historical Events	Related Literary Works
	632 Death of Muhammad	
	640–1000 Islamic faith and culture spread throughout North Africa	
	800–1000 Rise of Swahili town-states along East African coast	
1000	1000s Spread of Islamic religion into the western Sudan; Wagadu is a powerful center of trade, with gold from the south exchanged for salt and other goods from the north	
	1000–1500 Igbo people spread widely through southeast Nigeria, continuing to set up many town-states	*The Concubine* by Elechi Amadi
	1067–68 Cordoban geographer al-Bakri compiles detailed account of kingdom of Wagadu	
	1100s Yoruba people organize inland city-states in West Africa; Susu Empire briefly replaces Wagadu as major power in western Sudan	*The Palm-Wine Drinkard and His Dead Palm-Wine Tapster in the Deads' Town* by Amos Tutuola
	1230 Sumamru, king of Kaniaga, rebels against Wagadu, conquers empire	
	1235 Sunjata king of Kangaba, defeats Sumamuru at Battle of Krina, founds empire of Mali	*The Epic of Son-Jara* as told by Fa-Digi Sisòkò
	late 1200s–early 1500s East African city of Kilwa becomes powerful trading center, linking Zimbabwe, Mogadishu, Persia, and India	
	1230s–40s Rise of Great Zimbabwe empire in southeastern Africa; rise of Kisalian kingdom on the upper Kongo River	*African Laughter* by Doris Lessing
1300	1300s Height of Mali Empire, under ruler Mansa Musa (1312-37); first large state, Kitara, arises inland in East Africa; fall of Nubian Christian kingdoms in eastern Sudan	
	1324 Mansa Musa makes pilgrimage to Mecca	
	1329–31 Ibn Battuta visits East Africa; Great Zimbabwe culture achieves growing prosperity	*Ibn Battuta in Black Africa* by Abu Abdalla ibn Battuta
	1352–53 Ibn Battuta visits West Africa	*Ibn Battuta in Black Africa* by Abu Abdalla ibn Battuta
	1360 Decline of Mali empire begins with splitting off of the Wolof (Djolof) kingdom of Senegambia region	
	1370 Establishment of Solomonic dynasty in Ethiopia	
1400	1400s Wolof empire establishes itself in Senegal; end of Zimbabwe empire and rise of Mutapa and Torwa kingdoms in its place; rise of kingdom of Kongo	
	1415 Prince Henry the Navigator leads Portuguese conquest of Ceuta, a city in Morocco, inaugurating Portuguese efforts to extend trade down western coast of Africa	
	early 1440s The Atlantic trade between Europe and West Africa gets underway; slave trade by sea begins when Portuguese take captured Africans to Lisbon	
	1448 Portuguese establish first European trading post in West Africa	
	1450 Height of kingdom of Benin in West Africa; period of complex flow of influences among Yoruba, Benin, and Igbo cultures begins	
	1451–1601 About 367,000 Africans are taken from the continent by the Atlantic slave trade	
	1464–1591 Songhai kingdom on the bend of the Niger River establishes itself as an empire, with Sonni Ali as its ruler	

Historical Events	Related Literary Works
1471 Portuguese arrive in West African coastal region west of the Volta River, which they name the Gold Coast (today's Ghana)	
1481 Portuguese emissaries visit court of the king of Benin, establish commercial ties	
1482–84 Diogo Cão, Portuguese explorer, reaches mouth of Congo River and establishes relations with the kingdom of Kongo	
1487 Portuguese navigator Bartolemeu Días voyages around Cape of Good Hope	
1498 Portuguese explorer Vasco da Gama sails around Africa to reach India from Europe; vigorous trade begins	
1500 1500s Rise of the Yoruba empire of Oyo in Nigeria; Portuguese threaten the independence of Swahili town-states and try to control Indian Ocean trade; rise of Sinnar kingdom in eastern Sudan	*Death and the King's Horseman* by Wole Soyinka
1518 First direct delivery of slaves from Guinea coast to West Indies	
1550–1600 Dutch traders reach Benin kingdom in West Africa; Portuguese trade on African coast is threatened by the Dutch, who build their first trading post on the Gold Coast	
1600 1600–1650s British build their first fort in West Africa on St. James Island; French, British, Dutch, and Portuguese trade with Niger Delta peoples; rise of Asante empire inland from the Gold Coast	
1652–1795 The Dutch East India Company builds refreshment station at the Cape of Good Hope; descendants of Dutch settlers (the Afrikaners) expand into South African interior	
1660s–90s British capture Dutch forts on Gold Coast; French capture Dutch stations in Senegal; Omani Arabs replace the Portuguese as dominant outside power in the affairs of the Swahili city- states	

EGYPT AND THE SUDAN: FROM ARAB CONQUEST TO REPUBLICS

Muslim Arab armies swept into Egypt in the seventh century, initiating the spread of Islam into the area, a religious legacy that persists to this day. By contrast, European interest in Egypt ignited fairly late, after French troops led by Napoleon invaded in 1798, only to be ignominiously driven out in 1801 by troops of the British and Ottoman Turks. Soon after, Egypt began its own rise to power, under the leader Muhammad 'Ali who conquered the Sudan and introduced numerous reforms. Fearing the presence of a strong state in the Mediterranean Sea, Great Britain moved to limit 'Ali's power base and establish its own. In 1882, after the 'Urabi rebellion and a series of riots directed at Europeans, British forces occupied Egypt, which officially became a British protectorate in 1914. Protests by the increasingly vocal Egyptian nationalist movement prompted Britain to grant Egypt nominal independence in 1922. After World War II, Egypt voted to dissolve treaties that made it a virtual colony of Britain. Greater changes were introduced in 1952, when a group of Egyptian army officers overthrew and abolished the monarchy, paving the way for Egypt to become an independent republic.

	Historical Events	Related Literary Works
600	639–42 C.E. Muslim Arabs conquer Egypt; Roman-Byzantine rule ends; Islam starts spreading into North Africa	
800	800s Rise in Egypt of Sufism, a mystical branch of Islam	
900	969–1171 Fatimid dynasty governs Egypt	
	972 Mosque and college of al-Azhar opens in Cairo	
1500	1517 Ottoman Turks invade and conquer Egypt	
	1798–1801 Napoleon conquers Egypt, but is ultimately driven out by British and Ottoman troops	
1800	1805–49 Muhammad 'Ali, a Turkish Army officer, establishes himself as khedive ("ruler") of Egypt, introduces educational and agricultural reforms with mixed success	
	1820 Egyptian ruler Muhammad 'Ali sends his forces to invade the Sudan	
1825		
1850	1856–69 French- and British-owned Suez Canal Company constructs canal, using thousands of Egyptian peasants to do manual labor; 20,000 die during construction	
	1863–79 Isma'il, Muhammad 'Ali's grandson, rules Egypt, amasses huge personal and state-related debts; he is ultimately deposed, exiled, and replaced by his son, Tawfiq	
	1870s *Othello* becomes first Shakespearean play to be performed in Middle East	*Season of Migration to the North* by Tayeb Salih
	1871–79 The preacher Jamal al-Din al-Afghani helps revive conservative Islam in Egypt until he is expelled	
1875	1880s Egypt's Native Courts are reformed	*The Maze of Justice* by Tawfiq al-Hakim
	1881–82 After presenting a list of grievances, Egyptian officers, led by Colonel Ahmad 'Urabi, are arrested by Tawfiq; Egyptian troops loyal to 'Urabi march on the palace, demanding his release; Tawfiq accedes, appointing 'Urabi Minister of War; unrest continues	
	1881–85 Muhammed Ahmad, a Sudanese holy man, declares a *jihad*—holy war—against the Egyptians, who, despite superior numbers and weapons, are driven from the Sudan	
	1882–1914 After anti-European riots in Alexandria, the British occupy Egypt, beginning period of "Veiled Protectorate"; 'Urabi and other mutineers are exiled to Sri Lanka	
	1885–98 Period of Sudanese independence	
	1890s Egypt regains financial solvency, but the British remain, despite an earlier pledge to depart; strikes and demonstrations are staged to protest British occupation	
	1896 Anglo-Egyptian army marches into the Sudan	
	1898 Sudanese are defeated in Battle of Omdurman, which ends independence; the Sudan will be ruled jointly by England and Egypt until 1956	
1900	1900–10 Approximately 4,500 village schools operate in Egypt	*An Egyptian Childhood* by Taha Husayn
	1907 Formation of Wafd ("the organization") marks birth of Egyptian nationalist movement	
	1908 Egyptian University opens	
	1914 Britain formally declares Egypt a protectorate	

Historical Events	Related Literary Works
1918 Egyptian delegates are not permitted to attend World War I Versailles Peace Conference	
1919 Egyptian nationalists rebel against British rule	
1922 Egypt gains formal but nominal independence from Great Britain	
1923 Founding of the Egyptian Feminist Union; feminists Huda Sha'arawi and Saiza Nabarawi cast off their face veils in public	*Woman at Point Zero* by Nawal El Saadawi
1924 Sir Lee Stack, British commander in chief of Anglo-Egyptian army, is killed by Wafdist agents; British demand heavy indemnities from Egyptian government; first Egyptian parliament convenes	
1930s–40s Worldwide depression exacerbates crime in Egypt; political unrest leads to new political parties, banking and insurance industries become more "Egyptianized"	*The Maze of Justice* by Tawfiq al-Hakim
1936 British and Egyptian governments sign agreement restricting British military occupation to Canal Zone	
1938–41 Postsecondary schools are established in the Sudan, but it has no university	*Season of Migration to the North* by Tayeb Salih
1939–45 Egyptian government allows Britain additional military bases in Egypt because of World War II; 140,000 British troops in Cairo in 1941	*Midaqq Alley* by Najib Mahfuz
1940s Rise of Arab nationalism in Egypt; massive Allied buildup in Egypt stimulates industrial development; feminist movement gains momentum in Egypt and presses for reforms	
1944 Egyptian Wafdist government, led by Prime Minister Mustafa al-Nahhas, is forced to resign; Egyptian Feminist Union hosts the Arab Feminist Conference	
1945 After Egypt declares war on Germany, Egyptian Prime Minister Ahmad Mahir is assassinated by Nazi sympathizer; formation of the Arab Feminist Union	
1946 Demonstrations by students and workers protest unresponsive Egyptian politicians and continued British presence in Egypt	
1951 Egypt reasserts sovereignty, abrogates treaties that made it a virtual colony of Great Britain	
1952 Free Officers, led by Gamal Abdul Nasser (Jamal 'Abd al-Nasir), overthrow monarchy, exiling King Faruq; all political parties are banned; Revolutionary Command Council provides transitional government, with General Muhammad Naguib (Muhammad Najib) as prime minister; British evacuate Egypt	"Farahat's Republic" by Yusuf Idris
1953 Egypt officially abolishes monarchy and becomes a republic	
1953–54 Power struggle between Nasser and Naguib ends with Naguib's arrest for attempted assassination of his rival	
1954 Nasser negotiates treaty with British requiring their withdrawal from Canal Zone by June 1956	
1956 The Sudan gains independence; Nasser is elected president of Egypt; Israeli, British, and French forces invade Egypt at Suez; after United Nations pressure, they withdraw	*Season of Migration to the North* by Tayeb Salih
1958–61 Egypt and Syria form United Arab Republic, which ultimately dissolves	
1960–68 Aswan High Dam is constructed in Egypt; Egypt and Israel fight June (1967) War	

1925

1950

Historical Events	Related Literary Works
1968–70 War of Attrition with Israel on Suez Canal results in heavy Egyptian losses	
1970 After Nasser dies, Anwar al-Sadat becomes president of Egypt	
1975 1979 Sadat's regime enacts Personal Status Code reforms, giving women new divorce and other rights	*Woman at Point Zero* by Nawal El Saadawi
1981 Sadat is assassinated; Hosni Mubarak succeeds him as president	
1985 Egyptian government revokes rights accorded to women in 1979	
1989 Sudan torn by internal conflicts, civil war between North and South	
1990s Violence by Islamic fundamentalist extremists in Egypt leads to many arrests and executions	
1990–91 Egypt opposes Iraq's invasion of Kuwait, participates in Persian Gulf War	

MOROCCO, TUNISIA, AND ALGERIA: COLONIZATION AND INDEPENDENCE IN THE MAGHREB

While European nations vied to gain footholds in the western and southern regions of Africa, the Ottoman Turks loosened their control over Tunisia and Algeria, which were semiautonomous by the early nineteenth century. The French invasion of Algeria in 1830 touched off decades of conflict, during which the inhabitants rebelled against their European colonizers. Ultimately the struggle was resolved in a bloody, eight-year war of independence. By contrast, the French conquests of Tunisia and Morocco were less destructive of local institutions and societies. The French colonizers even permitted the ruling family of Tunisia to remain on the throne. Nonetheless, colonial inequities led to the rise of Moroccan and Tunisian nationalist movements in the 1920s and 30s. After World War II, during which Tunisia was occupied by Nazi troops, these movements gained momentum, finally realizing their goal. Tunisia and Morocco were granted independence in the mid-1950s, within a year of each other. Meanwhile, Algeria battled its colonists until 1962, finally achieving independence when French president Charles de Gaulle committed himself to ending the war, despite terrorist attempts to keep France fighting.

	Historical Events	Related Literary Works
600	c. 670 C.E. Arab-Islamic conquests of North Africa begin	
1400	1400–1600 In wake of the *Reconquista* (Reconquest) of Spain and Portugal by Christian forces, Spanish Jews arrive in North Africa, augmenting its existing Jewish population	
1500	1500s–1830 Ottoman Turks establish borders of Algeria between Morocco and Tunisia; Turks rule Algeria through indigenous tribal leaders and urban aristocratic families	
1700	1700–1800 Italian Jews from Livorno move to Tunisia, serving as commercial arbitrators between Europe and the Tunisian elite	
1800	1830 The French invade Algeria	*Fantasia: An Algerian Cavalcade* by Assia Djebar
	1830s–43 'Abd al-Qadir, controlling two-thirds of Algerian land, leads Muslims against the French; he is forced to flee to Morocco	
	1834 Algeria officially becomes a French colony	

Historical Events	Related Literary Works
1840s Northern Algeria is divided into three departments of metropolitan France; southern Algeria is designated a military zone	
1850 1857 French win final campaign against Berbers of Kabylia area in Algeria	*Nedjma* by Kateb Yacine
1871 Second Muslim uprising in Algeria; French quash rebellion, respond by seizing a million acres of Muslim land and implementing a rigorous *indigénat* (law code for subjects)	
1874–95 Reign of Sultan Mawlay Hassan in Morocco; Hassan's leadership and skill at manipulating European nations forestalls colonization for many years	
1875 1881 France invades Tunisia, which becomes a French protectorate, with ruling family allowed to remain on throne	
1883 French colonial authorities in Tunisia create Directorate of Public Education, which establishes a school system for French, European, and Tunisian students	
1900 1908–11 Young Algerians movement demands improved civil rights and the granting of full French citizenship to Muslims	
1912 Morocco becomes subject to French and Spanish protectorates, its territory divided between France and Spain	
1917–18 Pogroms against Jews are carried out in several Tunisian cities	
1919 Jonnart Law increases number of Algerians with the vote to 425,000	
1920s–40s Jewish and Muslim intellectuals in Tunis establish Jewish-Muslim Alliance as part of cooperative nationalist project; Alliance is later undermined by World War II Holocaust and postwar Zionism	*The Pillar of Salt* by Albert Memmi
1925 1927 First call for Algerian independence by Paris-based group Star of North Africa; movement is hastily driven underground	
1930s Rise of Tunisian nationalist movement; Algeria becomes third-largest wine-producing country in the world after France and Italy	
1936 Muslim Congress in Algiers lobbies for educational and electoral reforms but effort is squelched by colonials	
1937 Former Star of North Africa leader, Ahmed Messali Hadj, founds Parti du Peuple Algérien	
1939–45 Jewish population in Tunisia peaks at between 71,000 and 85,000	
1940–42 French colonial officials try to limit anti-Semitic laws in Tunisia after France falls to Germany	
1942 Tunisia is occupied by German and Italian troops; 5,000 Tunisian Jews are forced into Nazi labor camps	*The Pillar of Salt* by Albert Memmi
1943 Algerians present French colonists with "Manifesto of Algerian People," thereby airing grievances regarding land and political rights; in response, French grant citizenship to 60,000 additional Muslims; Tunisia is liberated by the Allies; May 8— armed clash between Algerian Muslims and French police in Sétif results in heavy casualties and imprisonment of nearly 6,000 Algerian men	*Nedjma* by Kateb Yacine
1948–70 40,000 Tunisian Jews emigrate to Israel	
1950 1954–62 Algerian war for independence, in which women fight alongside men	*Fantasia: An Algerian Cavalcade* by Assia Djebar; *The Wretched of the Earth* by Frantz Fanon

Historical Events	Related Literary Works
1955 Tunisia gains independence; Habib Bourguiba becomes president, adopts goal to bring women out of seclusion; armed nationalist revolts erupt in Morocco	
1956 Morocco becomes independent; Muhammad V is restored to throne	*The Sand Child* by Tahar Ben Jelloun
1958–61 Army-led revolt topples French government; de Gaulle regime opens negotiations with Algerian nationalists	
1960s–70s Tunisia unsuccessfully experiments with socialism under Ahmed Ben Salah; Ben Salah ultimately flees to France to live in exile	
1961 Hassan II succeeds to the throne of Morocco; his oppressive regime lasts until his death in 1999	
1962 Algeria gains independence from France; European settlers flee Algeria	*The Wretched of the Earth* by Frantz Fanon
1963 Ahmed Ben Bella, rebel leader, becomes first president of Algeria, which he declares a socialist state	
1965–78 Houari Boumedienne overthrows Ben Bella, begins program of rapid economic development in Algeria	
1974–75 Habib Bourguiba is elected to an unprecedented fourth term as president of Tunisia	
1979 Defense Minister Chadli Bendjedid is elected president of Algeria after Boumedienne's death, devotes resources to production of agricultural and consumer goods, reelected in 1984 and 1988	
1984 New family code in Algeria says wife owes obedience to husband; continued segregation and seclusion of women in Morocco	*The Sand Child* by Tahar Ben Jelloun
1989 Revised Algerian constitution results in formation of additional political parties, including Islamic Salvation Front (FIS)	
1991–92 Violent protests in favor of FIS in Algeria; FIS is ultimately banned in wake of multiparty election debacle; Bendjedid resigns as Algerian president	
1996 Algerian constitution bans political parties based on religion, sex, language, or regional differences	

(Note: "1975" appears in the left margin beside the 1979 entry.)

EAST AFRICA: FROM COLONIALISM TO POSTCOLONIALISM

As in North Africa, the predominant influence in East Africa during the early centuries of exploration and conquest was Arabic. Although Portugal raided and sacked various East African city-states during the 1500s, the Arabs regained power in the region during the 1600s, driving the Portuguese from most of their holdings north of Mozambique. Arabic and Portuguese influences were mostly concentrated on the coast, having little impact on inland areas. During the European scramble for control in the late nineteenth-century, Britain explored and laid claim to territories in the East African interior. First Uganda, then Kenya and Tanzania—united as British East Africa—became British protectorates. The British also competed for control over the coastal territory of Somalia, which they ultimately divided with the Italians. However, two world wars and growing nationalist movements weakened Europe's hold over East Africa. Most colonies and protectorates in this region gained independence in the 1960s.

Historical Events	Related Literary Works
700 700s C.E. Arabs establish settlements along the East African coast, then conduct trade with indigenous people in the interior	*Ibn Battuta in Black Africa* by Abu Abdalla ibn Battuta
800 800–900s Somalis move into area south of Gulf of Aden, interact with Arab and Persian settlers on Indian Ocean coast	
1100 1100s Somalis are converted to Islam	
1500 1500s Portuguese wrest control of East African coast from Arabs	
1600 1600s Arabs defeat Portuguese and regain control of the area	
1800 1850–1900 Arab traders arrive in Buganda, a powerful kingdom with a large army and highly developed system of government	
1860s–70s British explorers and missionaries arrive in Buganda	*Song of Lawino and Song of Ocol* by Okot p'Bitek
1875 1880s Gikuyu (Kikuyu) people move into Ngong Hills in Kenya	
1880s–90s British take over much of northern Somalia, which becomes British Somaliland; Italians control Indian Ocean coast, move inland towards Ethiopia, establishing Italian Somaliland	*Sweet and Sour Milk* by Nuruddin Farah
1886 Britain stakes claim on Kenya, then called British East Africa	
1888 British government entrusts new land to Imperial British East Africa Company to develop for trade	
1890s British engage in trade with the Gikuyus, support certain lineages against others in exchange for loyalty to British government; Maasai people become allies of the British against other local groups	
1894 Buganda (future Uganda) becomes British protectorate	
1895 British East Africa becomes a protectorate	*Out of Africa* by Karen Blixen
1895–1914 British government organizes military expeditions to quell local resistance; railroad constructed between Mombasa and Lake Victoria (completed 1901)	
1900 1900s Indigenous Kenyans suffer land seizures by British; influx of Europeans to Kenya; Somali nationalists fight British, Italian, and Ethiopian forces	
1902 British government imposes "hut tax" on Gikuyu, obligating them to sell their labor to white settlers	
1904 Maasai people are confined to reserves	
1915–18 British ordinance decrees all Kenyan males between 18 and 45 can be conscripted into military in World War I; famine results from lack of manpower on Kenyan farms	
1919 Ex-Soldiers Settlement deprives local Kenyans of land, which is bestowed upon British war veterans	
1920 British East Africa officially becomes colony of Kenya	
1921 British adopt new currency, which invalidates pay of Kenyan soldiers and military porters, sparking resentment	
1925 1931 Jomo Kenyatta, a Kenyan, travels with a delegation to England to air African grievances	
1936 Italy conquers Ethiopia, making it and Italian Somaliland part of Italian East African Empire	
1940–41 Italy captures British Somaliland but is driven out by the British	

Historical Events	Related Literary Works
1944 Kenyatta and 32 other Kenyans form Kenya African Union (KAU) to make British give Kenyans a larger share in colonial government	
1946 Kenyatta returns to Kenya a hero after 15 years in England	*Weep Not, Child* by Ngugi wa Thiong'o
1947 Kenyatta is elected president of KAU	
1950 1950 United Nations rules that Italian Somaliland be placed in Italy's care for 10 years, then given independence; inhabitants of British Somaliland demand self-government	
early 1950s Mau Mau guerrilla war begins in Nairobi, Kenya, ultimately claims 20,000 lives; Ugandans take increased role in own government, which sparks independence movement	*Weep Not, Child* by Ngugi wa Thiong'o
1952 187 suspected Mau-Mau leaders are arrested on October 20, including Jomo Kenyatta	
1957 Mau Mau leader Dedan Kimathi is captured and executed, ending the Kenyan rebellion	
1960 British agree to restructuring of Kenyan government, giving Africans majority rule; British and Italians grant independence to Somali territories, which unite to become independent Somalia	*Sweet and Sour Milk* by Nuruddin Farah
1961 Jomo Kenyatta is released from prison	
1962 Uganda gains independence; Apollo Milton Obote becomes prime minister	
1963 Kenya gains independence; Jomo Kenyatta becomes prime minister	
1967 New constitution makes Uganda a republic and abolishes traditional kingdoms	*Song of Lawino and Song of Ocol* by Okot p'Bitek
1969 Military coup in Somalia; Major General Mohammad Siyad Barre seizes control of government	
1970s Siyad Barre brings Somali land, schools, transport, banks, and medical services under government control; crippling drought occurs	*Sweet and Sour Milk* by Nuruddin Farah
1971 Ugandan Army overthrows Obote, sets up military government	
1971–79 Major General Idi Amin Dada becomes president of Uganda, orders 40,000 to 50,000 Asians (who dominated Uganda's economy) from the country, kills or imprisons Ugandans who oppose his policies; Tanzanian troops and Ugandans depose Idi Amin	
1974–88 Fighting erupts between antigovernment Somali rebels and Ethiopian forces; both sides sign peace agreement in 1988	
1975 1978 On Kenyatta's death, Vice President Daniel T. Arap Moi becomes president of Kenya	
1991 Kenya's constitution is amended to allow for multiparty system; United Somali Congress (USC) overthrows Somalia military regime, but fighting continues among USC factions	
1992 Starvation claims 270,000 Somali lives; United Nations sends armed forces to distribute food	
1993 U.N. troops clash with Somalia clan leader, Mohammed Farah Aidid	
1994–97 Peace agreement signed in Somalia, but fighting among factions continues	

WEST AFRICA: BRITISH COLONIALISM
TO POSTCOLONIALISM

For much of the seventeenth and eighteenth centuries, Great Britain concentrated its colonization efforts in West Africa, founding its first colony, Senegambia, in 1765. In 1783, the Treaty of Versailles obligated Britain to cede several African territories to France, including the colonized area that would become part of modern-day Senegal. Nonetheless, the British maintained a firm foothold in West Africa, especially in Nigeria and the Gold Coast (Ghana). In the late nineteenth century, five European nations—Britain, France, Portugal, Germany, and Italy—competed for wealth, land, and prestige in Africa. Spurred on by tiny Belgium's establishment of the Congo Free State in 1879, the five nations engaged in a frantic "scramble" for control of the continent. British troops and missionaries poured into West Africa, subduing indigenous peoples by force or religious conversion. Generally the British sought to implement a policy of indirect rule, that is, of governing their colonies through African rulers whom they had defeated. After World War II, the growth of African nationalism prompted Britain to rethink its position on colonialism. It granted independence to its territories in this region in the 1950s and 60s.

	Historical Events	Related Literary Works
1700	1700s About 42,000 West Africans per year become victims of the slave trade	
	1700–1750s Abolition movement grows gradually in England	
1750	1756 Igbo boy Olaudah Equiano is captured by slavers at age 11	*Equiano's Travels* by Olaudah Equiano
	1765 Senegambia (maritime Senegal and Gambia) becomes first British African colony	
	1772 Somerset case abolishes slavery on English soil	*Equiano's Travels* by Olaudah Equiano
	c. 1775 Abiodun becomes last ruler of Yoruba empire of Oyo; under his rule Oyo empire reaches its height	*Death and the King's Horseman* by Wole Soyinka
	1783 British cede Senegal and some other West African territories to French	
	1787 Sierra Leone, a colony for freed slaves, is founded	
1800	1807 England outlaws slave trade	
1825	1834 Great Britain outlaws slavery in its colonies	
	1840s Christian missionary work begins in Abeokuta, Nigeria, hometown of Yoruba writer Amos Tutuola	*The Palm-Wine Drinkard and His Dead Palm-Wine Tapster in the Deads' Town* by Amos Tutuola
	1844 Fante people on the Gold Coast enter into treaty negotiations with British, hoping for trading partners and military allies	
1850	1857 Protestant Church Missionary Society founds its first mission in Igboland	
	1860s Fante Confederacy unsuccessfully attempts to oust British from territory after British try to control local law	
	1861 Founding of Lagos Colony in Nigeria marks beginning of British colonial rule here	
	1874 The Gold Coast (later Ghana) becomes a British colony	
1875	1880s Christian missionaries expand into central Igboland	*Things Fall Apart* by Chinua Achebe
	1890s British conduct military actions throughout southwestern Nigeria, gaining control over Ijebu, Oyo, Benin, and Yoruba states	*Death and the King's Horseman* by Wole Soyinka

Historical Events	Related Literary Works
1897–1920s Aborigines' Rights Protection Society is founded to help African elite defend indigenous lands; the group later evolves into National Congress of British West Africa	
1898 Igbo peoples form Ekumeku movement to resist missionaries and European rule, fight first battle under this banner	*Things Fall Apart* by Chinua Achebe
1900 1900s British proclaim Northern and Southern Nigeria to be individual protectorates; Frederick Lugard is appointed high commissioner of Northern Nigeria, establishes policy of indirect rule	
1901 British annex large Asante territory in the Gold Coast	
1904–09 British take control of 16,000 square miles in southern Nigeria	
1910-20s Various missionary movements in Nigeria establish schools, churches, and health facilities	*The Oil Man of Obange* by John Munonye
1912–26 Construction of two railroads in Nigeria	
1914 Protectorates of Northern and Southern Nigeria unite with Lagos colony to form colony of Nigeria	
1920s Political parties form in Nigeria; African American Marcus Garvey starts Back-to-Africa movement	*Dilemma of a Ghost* by Ama Ata Aidoo
1925 1929 "Women's War"—African women in eastern Nigeria protest rumors of taxation by colonial government	*The Joys of Motherhood* by Buchi Emecheta
1937 Gold Coast Youth Council, devoted to achieving independence, is founded by Joseph Boakye Danquah	
1940s Nigerians are encouraged by British to enlist and fight in World War II; nationalist parties form in postwar period	*The Joys of Motherhood* by Buchi Emecheta
1944 Oyo king (Siyanbola Ladigbolu) dies; his Master of Stables fails to observe Yoruba rite that requires him to commit suicide	*Death and the King's Horseman* by Wole Soyinka
1946 Richards Constitution divides Nigeria into three regions associated with main ethnic groups—the North (Hausa-Fulani), West (Yoruba), and East (Igbo)	
1947 Gold Coast Youth Council merges with United Gold Coast Convention (UGCC); strikes, demonstrations, and civil unrest against British follow; Joyce Carey's *Mister Johnson*, a British novel about life in Nigeria, is published	*Things Fall Apart* by Chinua Achebe
1949–51 Kwame Nkrumah breaks from UGCC and establishes more radical Convention People's Party (CPP), which mounts strikes and boycotts; British government revises Gold Coast constitution to extend voting rights	
1950 1950s Nigeria adopts three-tiered education system similar to Great Britain's; economy grows with the help of peanuts, palm oil, and other agricultural products; independence movement results in new constitutions	*Efuru* by Flora Nwapa; *The Oil Man of Obange* by John Munonye
1956 Petroleum is discovered in eastern Nigeria	
1957 Ghana becomes first African nation to gain independence; Kwame Nkrumah becomes Ghana's prime minister; western and eastern Nigeria attain self-government; rivalry abounds between regions	
1958 About 8,000 women in Lagos, Nigeria, engage in trade, outnumbering the city's male traders	*Jagua Nana* by Cyprian Ekwensi; *The Joys of Motherhood* by Buchi Emecheta
1959 Northern Nigeria attains self-government	
1960 Nigeria achieves independence	

Historical Events	Related Literary Works
1964 Nigerian political elections are marred by violence and corruption; Kwame Nkrumah outlaws opposition parties in Ghana	*The Famished Road* by Ben Okri
1965 First independent Nigerian government suffers discord— alliance of the NPC (Northern People's Congress) and NCNC (National Council of Nigerian Citizens) dissolves	
1966 Nigerian army officers stage coup, deposing parliamentary democracy; General Yakubu Gowen attains power; massacre of Igbos in North; Igbos flee eastward; in Ghana, military coup overthrows Kwame Nkrumah	*Jagua Nana* by Cyprian Ekwensi; *The Beautyful Ones Are Not Yet Born* by Ayi Kwei Armah
1966–91 Nigeria experiences a series of bloody military coups	
1967–70 Nigerian Civil War—in wake of pogroms targeting Igbos, most of eastern Nigeria attempts to secede and form its own country, the Republic of Biafra, but 30 months later secessionists are defeated	*The Last Duty* by Isidore Okpewho
1969 Second Republic succeeds period of military rule in Ghana	
1971 Nigeria provides more than 50 percent of world's trade in palm oil	*The Oil Man of Obange* by John Munonye
1975–76 Coup in Nigeria deposes Gowon, puts Murtala Muhammed in power; Muhammed is assassinated; his second-in-command, Olusegu Obasanjo, becomes head of state	
1979–83 Nigeria returns to brief period of civilian rule under Shehu Shagari	
1980s Market women's associations organize mass protests and demonstrations in Nigeria	
1981 64 percent of Nigerian girls attend school	*The Oil Man of Obange* by John Munonye
1983–98 Series of military rulers in Nigeria	
1999 Nigeria returns to civilian rule under retired army general Olusegu Obasanjo	

1975 (margin, aligned with 1975–76 row)

WEST AFRICA: FROM FRENCH COLONIALISM TO POSTCOLONIALISM

The French presence in West Africa dates back to the end of the seventeenth century, when trading posts appeared in the area of today's Senegal. More than a hundred years later, in 1817, Europe fought the Napoleonic Wars, which prompted Great Britain to acknowledge French supremacy in part of West Africa. Thereafter, the region saw pivotal new developments: mission schools and then public schools; an infrastructure that permitted exploitation of natural resources; and a system of governance that encouraged local African political and religious leaders to collaborate with French rule. By 1895 Senegal and other West African territories were formally recognized as French colonies. Unlike the British, the French viewed some Africans as potential citizens and so instituted a limited policy of assimilation, encouraging a small number of the colonized to educate themselves in order to qualify as "black Frenchmen." World War II brought changes in the French colonial strategy. During the postwar period, growing nationalist movements and a bloody war for independence in Algeria prompted France to reconsider its policies and ultimately to grant independence to most of its West African colonies.

1600

1638 First French establishment in West Africa appears at St. Louis in Senegal

	Historical Events	Related Literary Works
1700	1701–1800 French merchant ships engage in Atlantic slave trade, participating in removal of 6,133,000 Africans from continent	
	1758–79; 1807–17 British seize French-controlled areas, which are definitively returned to the French in 1817	
1800	1800s–50s Various Roman Catholic orders found mission schools in region of French West Africa	
	1817 French prohibit slave trade	
1850	1854 Louis Faidherbe is appointed French governor of Senegal; helps establish school system for Africans as well as Europeans	
1875	1884 African chiefs of Cameroon sign treaties ceding their sovereignty to Germany, which renames the territory "Kamerun"	
	1886 French occupy Ivory Coast	
	1889 Germans establish first Christian mission in Kamerun	
	1891 Colony of French Guinea is formed	
	1895 Senegal, along with Mauritania and French Sudan, are formally recognized as colonies of French West Africa	
	1895–1946 Policies are implemented throughout French West Africa to educate a small black African elite on the French model	
1900	1903–44 French Federal School System founds a number of preparatory and elementary schools in French Guinea	*The Dark Child* by Camara Laye
	1914–18 400,000 West Africans perform military duty for France in World War I	
	1918 German colony of Kamerun becomes a mandate governed by Britain and France, with France receiving five-sixths of the territory	
	1918–60 France establishes government schools to accompany mission schools in Cameroon	*Mission to Kala* by Mongo Beti
	1920s–30s Inception and rise of African trade unions in French West Africa	
1925	mid-1930s In Paris, Léopold Senghor and friends begin Négritude movement, promoting pride in one's heritage	
	1938 Railway strike in Thiès, Senegal, leads to gunfire and the deaths of 6 strikers	*God's Bits of Wood* by Ousmane Sembène
	1939–44 Nearly a million Africans serve in the French military in World War II	
	1944 Population of Conakry, capital of French Guinea, swells to 26,000; "Free French" colonial governors hold conference at Brazzaville, condemn *indigénat,* the separate legal code for unassimilated Africans	*The Dark Child* by Camara Laye
	1945 Repatriated African troops, who demonstrate against conditions at Camp de Thiaroye, Senegal, are killed by French soldiers	
	1945–48 Wave of general strikes in Senegal as militant African laborers battle discrimination in workplace	*God's Bits of Wood* by Ousmane Sembène
	1946 The indigénat is formally abolished; French citizenship is extended to entire population of French West Africa as part of the Union Française, which includes French colonies around the world; Cameroon becomes U.N. trusteeship	*Houseboy* by Ferdinand Oyono
	1947–48 Négritude movement spreads to Africa	

Historical Events	Related Literary Works
1948–59 Union des Populations du Cameroun (UPC) is founded in 1948 by Ruben Um Nyobé, a trade-union organizer; a guerrilla war led by Nyobé ends with his death; UPC splinters and is replaced by less radical Union Camerounaise (UC); UC leader Amadou Ahidjo negotiates for fixed date for independence	
1950s Schools in Senegal are expanded and refurbished, enrollment increases; scholarship program for study abroad is established	
1952 New Labor Code grants Africans in French West Africa a reduced work schedule (a 40-hour week), paid holidays, and overtime pay	
1956 The *loi-cadre* ("enabling act") reforms lead to universal suffrage in Senegal and broaden powers of the 12 territorial assemblies of French West Africa	
1957 In Senegal, University of Dakar (now called University of Cheikh Anta Diop) is founded	
1958 Senegal and the former French Sudan form Mali Federation	
1960 French Cameroon and Senegal achieve independence; Senghor becomes Senegal's first president	
1961 British Southern Cameroons becomes part of new Republic of Cameroon; British Northern Cameroons becomes province of Nigeria	
1974 Growing women's movement in Senegal; new legislation says marriages can be dissolved only through divorces granted in court	*So Long a Letter* by Mariama Bâ
1981 Abdou Diouf succeeds Senghor as president of Senegal	
1982–89 Senegal and Gambia form Senegambia Confederation to strengthen economic ties and unite armed forces; disputes lead to dissolution of confederation seven years later	

(Timeline markers: **1950**, **1975**)

CENTRAL AND SOUTHERN AFRICA: FROM PORTUGUESE DECLINE TO POSTCOLONIAL RULE

Despite Portugal's impressive gains over the years following its initial contact, by the mid-seventeenth century its dominance in Africa was in eclipse, threatened by the rising power of the Dutch and the Omani Arabs. Even Portugal's active involvement in the slave trade could not offset its losses—by 1700, the Imam of Oman had forced the Portuguese from many of their holdings in East Africa, including Kilwa and Mombasa. In the late-nineteenth-century scramble for control in Africa, though, Portugal was able to carve out "spheres of influence" in both Mozambique and Angola. Repressive policies of the Portuguese government—especially of the Salazar regime—stimulated anticolonial activity in the 1950s, which led to the formation of several aggressive independence movements and decades of armed struggle.

Historical Events	Related Literary Works
1600–1650s Rise of Luba and Lunda empires in Central Africa	
1600–1800 Portugal engages in unrestricted slave trade, selling some 4 million Angolans into slavery	

(Timeline marker: **1600**)

Historical Events	Related Literary Works
1650–1700 Portuguese are in eclipse—Dutch wrest control of Indian Ocean trade from them; Imam of Oman seizes Kilwa, Mombasa, Pemba, and Zanzibar from Portugal, leaving it with a few African holdings in Angola and Mozambique regions	
1700 early 1700s Luba and Lunda conduct raids to capture slaves and ivory for trade	
1800 1842 Portugal accepts treaty with Britain to enforce ban on slave trade	
1850 1850s–1918 Portuguese consolidate their control in areas of Africa	
1875 1875 Formal abolition of slavery in Portuguese colonies	
1875–1900 Protestant missionaries travel into Angolan interior	
1880s Portuguese try to claim vast area including Angola, Rhodesia, Malawi, Zambia, and part of southern Congo; thwarted by Britain, they settle for Angola	
1899 Portuguese law obligates local peoples to provide forced labor	
1900 1902 Bailundo Rebellion attempts to oust Portuguese from Angola, but is ultimately suppressed	*Yaka* by Pepetela
1907 Portuguese establish colonial administration in Mozambique	
1913 Formation of *Liga Angolano*, an association to obtain full rights for indigenous Angolans	
1925 1925 Portuguese complete colonial occupation of inland Angola and Mozambique	
1927 Portuguese government implements assimilationist policies in overseas territories	
1929 Formation of Associação Regional dos Naturais de Angola to obtain rights for indigenous Angolans	
1930 Colonial Statute, written by Dr. António de Oliveira Salazar, defense minister of Portugal, proclaims Portugal and overseas territories interdependent	
1932–68 Salazar is elected prime minister of Portugal, encourages colonial production of Portuguese goods and emigration of whites to Mozambique	*We Killed Mangy-Dog* by Luís Bernardo Honwana
1950 1950s–60s Anticolonial political organizations are founded by Angolans in exile; independence movements form in Mozambique	
1956 Angolan Communist Party and Popular Movement to Liberate Angola (MPLA) are formed in exile	
1961 MPLA forces launch full attack on Luanda, Angola's largest city, beginning 14-year armed struggle for Angolan independence	
1962 FRELIMO (Front for the Liberation of Mozambique) is formed from three prior liberation movements; FNLA (Frente Nacional de Libertação de Angola) is formed from two prior groups; FNLA establishes Revolutionary Government of Angola in Exile (GRAE) in Leopoldville	*We Killed Mangy-Dog* by Luís Bernardo Honwana
1964 FRELIMO soldiers attack Portuguese outpost of Chai, beginning organized armed struggle against colonial regime; rift in GRAE government prompts Foreign Minister Jonas Savimbi to leave FNLA and start rival movement	

Historical Events	Related Literary Works

	Historical Events	Related Literary Works
	1966 Savimbi helps form União Nacional Para a Independencia Total de Angola (UNITA), a populist movement with socialist leanings	
	1974 Military coup in Portugal overthrows dictatorship, which stimulates Angolan independence movements	
1975	1975–76 Mozambique and Angola gain independence; fighting erupts between FNLA, MPLA, and UNITA, leading to mass exodus of white settlers; South African and Zairean troops invade Angola but are defeated by MPLA, backed by Cuban forces and Soviet aid	*Yaka* by Pepetela
	1984 Mozambique and South Africa sign treaty not to aid guerrillas, but fighting continues between FRELIMO and RENAMO (National Resistance Movement)	*African Laughter* by Doris Lessing
	1990–95 MPLA renounces Marxism, legalizes all political parties; charges of election fraud result in more civil strife between MPLA and UNITA in 1992; MPLA and UNITA sign peace agreement, overseen by U.N. peacekeeping force in 1995	
	1992 FRELIMO and RENAMO sign peace treaty; new political parties register in Mozambique	
	1994 First multiparty election in Mozambique results in FRELIMO victory for the party and its leader Joaquim Chissano, who becomes president	

SOUTH AFRICA: FROM THE PRECOLONIAL TO THE POSTAPARTHEID ERA

Beginning in the seventeenth century, there was fierce competition between the Dutch and the British for possession of South Africa. The Dutch had settled in the Cape Colony many years earlier. Once the British arrived, a rivalry ensued that rapidly intensified after the British seized the region from the Dutch in 1795. For over a century, the British and Dutch battled indigenous peoples and each other for control of South Africa. The nineteenth-century discovery of diamonds and gold in the Transvaal region raised the stakes even higher. The ongoing tensions between British settlers and descendents of the Dutch, known as Afrikaners, culminated in the South African War (1899–1902), from which the British emerged victorious. Afterwards the disparate regions of South Africa were united under the British flag. The Afrikaners, though defeated, would regain power later in the century. There was a resurgence of Afrikaner nationalism in the post-World War II period, as shown by the formation of the National Party. After attaining power in the 1948 elections, this Afrikaner political party implemented "apartheid"—a policy of rigid racial segregation that would dominate South African politics until 1994.

	Historical Events	Related Literary Works
300	300 C.E. Ancestors of Bantu-speaking Africans settle in southernmost Africa, joining ancestors of the Khoisan, who have already dwelled in the region for centuries	
1600	1652 Dutch settlers led by Jan van Riebeeck arrive in the Cape area of South Africa	
	1652–1795 Dutch descendants (Afrikaners, or formerly "Boers") expand settlement, conquer Khoisan, import slaves from Indonesia, India, Ceylon, Madagascar, and Mozambique	
1700	1709 First pass laws require Cape Colony slaves to carry passes to distinguish them from free Africans	
	1795 British take Cape Colony from the Dutch	

Historical Events		Related Literary Works
1800	1803 Dutch regain Cape Colony by treaty	
	1806 British reconquer Cape Colony	
	1811–12 British expel Africans from territory west of Fish River	
	1816–28 Chaka (Shaka) establishes Zulu Kingdom	*Chaka* by Thomas Mokupu Mfolo
	1820 4,000 British immigrants settle in the Zuurveld region of South Africa	
1825	1828 Cape Colony repeals pass laws; Cape governor Richard Burke passes Ordinance 50, making the free people of color equal to whites	
	1834–36 Xhosa people are defeated by British and colonial forces	
	1834–38 Cape Colony slaves are emancipated	
	1835–40 The Great Trek—5,000 Afrikaners travel from Cape Colony into the South African interior	
	1843 Britain annexes area of Natal	
1850	1852–54 Britain recognizes independent Afrikaner republics of Transvaal and Orange Free State	
	1867 Diamonds are discovered near the confluence of the Vaal and Harts rivers	*The Story of an African Farm* by Olive Schreiner
	1868 Britain annexes Lesotho ("Basutoland")	
	1870 Larger deposit of diamonds is discovered near the future town of Kimberley; schools and seminaries are founded in Cape area	
1875	1877 Britain annexes the Transvaal	
	1879 Anglo-Zulu War begins with slaughter of British forces at Insandlwana, ends with British capture of Zulu leader Cetshwayo	
	1880s Cecil Rhodes acquires control of De Beers and Kimberley diamond mines	
	1886 Gold-mining begins on the Witwatersrand in South Africa; city of Johannesburg grows up around mining camps	
	1887 Zululand is incorporated into British colony of Natal	
	1888 King Lubengula of the Matabele signs treaty with John Moffat, which puts Matabeleland and Mashonaland under British power (future colony of Rhodesia)	*African Laughter* by Doris Lessing
	1889 Cecil Rhodes lobbies for monopolist charter from British government over Shona lands for his British South African Company	
	1890 Cecil Rhodes becomes prime minister of Cape Colony; British South Africa Company begins to govern area of future Rhodesia	
	1891 De Beers Consolidated Mines establishes monopoly over diamond production in region	
	1896–97 In Rhodesia, Matabele and Shona rise against British in First Chimurenga, or war of liberation; Africans are defeated with difficulty	*African Laughter* by Doris Lessing
	1899–1902 South African War between Afrikaners and British—Orange Free State and Transvaal become British colonies	
1900	1900 British South Africa Company subsidizes mission schools in Rhodesia to educate Africans to work for European minority	*Nervous Conditions* by Tsitsi Dangarembga

Historical Events	Related Literary Works
1900-48 Racial segregation policy is enforced in South Africa	*Cry, the Beloved Country* by Alan Paton
1910 Cape Colony, Natal, the Transvaal, and Orange Free State form Union of South Africa; South African Police (SAP) is established	
1911 Mines and Work Act earmarks skilled jobs for whites	*Mine Boy* by Peter Abrahams
1912 Formation of national African organization, the African National Congress (ANC)	
1912–62 Authorities forbid Europeans to sell alcohol to Africans, who are themselves prohibited from buying or selling alcohol; shebeens and unlicensed saloons flourish	
1913 Natives Land Act sets aside reserves of land for Africans, limits their landownership to the reserves	*Cry, the Beloved Country* by Alan Paton
1914 General J. B. M. Hertzog forms new National Party to champion Afrikaner interests	
1920 Communist Party of South Africa is established	
1923 Southern Rhodesia becomes self-governing colony under nominal British control, implements segregationist policies favoring whites	
1924–31 National Party forms alliance with British Labour Party; J. B. M. Hertzog becomes prime minister of coalition government	
1925 1930s–40s Mass migration of South Africans from rural to urban areas, especially Johannesburg and Cape Town; government uses pass laws to limit black migration to cities; housing shortage leads to rise of shantytowns and squatters' camps	*Cry, the Beloved Country* by Alan Paton
1931 1,370 South African miners suffer tuberculosis and other lung ailments	
1933–66 19,000 gold miners, mostly Africans, are reported killed in mining accidents	*Mine Boy* by Peter Abrahams
1936 Natives Representation Bill eliminates black representation in House of Assembly; blacks lose right to vote in Cape Province	
1939 South Africa enters World War II on British side, angering Afrikaners	
1941 African Mine Workers' Union (AMWU) and Council of Non-European Trade Unions (CNETU) is formed	
1943–44 Bus boycotts in Alexandra, an African-occupied suburb of Johannesburg, result in lower fares and formation of Public Utility Transport Corporation	
1944 Lansdown Commission investigates conditions in South African mines; antipass campaign begins but ultimately fails; Congress Youth League (CYL) is created within ANC, attracts members such as Oliver Tambo and Nelson Mandela	
1946 70,000 to 100,000 African gold miners strike for higher wages but are driven back to mines by police troops	*Mine Boy* by Peter Abrahams
1948–94 National Party comes to power in South Africa; Prime Minister D. F. Malan implements apartheid policy	
1950 1950 Group Areas Act authorizes zoning of neighborhoods in South Africa according to race; Population Registration Act differentiates between light- and dark-skinned coloureds (mixed-race) inhabitants	*A Walk in the Night* by Alex La Guma
1952 CYL and ANC launch Defiance Campaign of nonviolent resistance to laws of apartheid	

Historical Events	Related Literary Works
1953 Public Safety Act allows South African government to declare state of emergency when public order cannot be maintained; act weakens Defiance Campaign	
1955 Alliance of groups in South Africa draws up Freedom Charter calling for abolition of apartheid	
1956 Ruling families of Botswana renounce kingship rights, fostering new spirit of democracy	
1956–61 Treason trial—156 African rebels are arrested and accused of treason, including Nelson Mandela; all are acquitted in 1961	
1958–59 ANC splits; Pan-African Congress (PAC) forms	
1960s Thousands of Africans flee from South Africa to Botswana to escape apartheid; freedom-fighting movements gather momentum in Southern Rhodesia	*When Rain Clouds Gather* by Bessie Head; *African Laughter* by Doris Lessing
1960 Police kill 69 antipass-law demonstrators at Sharpeville, prompting more protests and passbook burnings; ANC and PAC are outlawed and forced underground	
1961 South Africa secedes from British Commonwealth, becoming an independent republic; Zimbabwe African People's Union forms in Southern Rhodesia	
1961–63 Umkhonto we Sizwe, a military wing of ANC, carries out sabotage operations through South Africa, brought down by police after 19 months; Rivonia trial ensues	
1962 Sabotage Act allows South African justice minister to ban potential terrorists; Nelson Mandela is arrested for his Umkhonto involvement	
1963 Northern Rhodesia, renamed Zambia, obtains independence; Nelson Mandela is sentenced to life in prison	"Rivonia Trial Speech" by Nelson Mandela
1965 Prime Minister Ian Smith issues Unilateral Declaration of Independence, proclaiming Southern Rhodesia an independent state; white elite assumes control	*African Laughter* by Doris Lessing
1966 South African government declares District Six, Capetown's most populous coloured neighborhood, an all white district; Botswana and Lesotho (Bechuanaland and Basutoland) gain independence from Britain; War of Liberation (Second Chimurenga) erupts in Rhodesia	*African Laughter* by Doris Lessing; *A Walk in the Night* by Alex La Guma; *When Rain Clouds Gather* by Bessie Head
1968 Swaziland gains independence from Britain	
1970 Southern Rhodesia becomes a republic	
1970s Black Consciousness Movement in South Africa rejects white involvement in antiapartheid struggle; black townships deteriorate, housing shortage ensues; 30 percent of African population in Southern Rhodesia is illiterate	*Burger's Daughter* by Nadine Gordimer; *Nervous Conditions* by Tsitsi Dangarembga
1974 Government declares Afrikaans official language of South Africa	
1976–77 Confrontations between Africans and police in Soweto and other South African townships leave at least 575 dead; Stephen Biko, leader of Black Consciousness Movement, is beaten to death in prison (1977)	*A Dry White Season* by André Brink; *Burgher's Daughter* by Nadine Gordimer; *Waiting for the Barbarians* by J. M. Coetzee
1980 In Southern Rhodesia (renamed Zimbabwe), Smith's government capitulates to guerrilla pressure; Zimbabwe gains independence; general elections result in ZANU victory, with Robert Mugabe becoming prime minister	
1980–81 Many whites leave Zimbabwe	*African Laughter* by Doris Lessing
1985 In South Africa, Nelson Mandela rejects offer of conditional release from prison	

1975

Historical Events	Related Literary Works
1989 National Party begins to dismantle apartheid in South Africa	
1990 Nelson Mandela is freed; Mugabe is reelected president of Zimbabwe	
1993 Mandela and F. W. de Klerk receive Nobel Peace Prize	
1994 First multiracial elections in South Africa; ANC wins by a landslide; Nelson Mandela becomes president; apartheid ends	*Valley Song* by Athol Fugard
1996 South Africa adopts new constitution with broad bill of rights; Mugabe is reelected president of Zimbabwe	
1997 Mandela steps down as head of ANC, replaced by Thabo Mbeki	
1999 Mbeki succeeds Mandela as president of South Africa	

Contents by Title

Contents by Title

Contents by Author

Contents by Author

Photo Credits

Robert Mugabe with F. W. de Klerk, Gaborone, Botswana, 1994, photograph. AP/Wide World Photos. Reproduced by permission. —Doris Lessing, photograph. © Jerry Bauer. Reproduced by permission. —Open boats along shore of Gold Coast, British West Africa, c. 1890-1910, photograph. © Corbis. Reproduced by permission. —Kwame Nkrumah, photograph. © Bettmann/Corbis. Reproduced by permission. —Sharpeville Massacre aftermath, March 21, 1969, photograph. © Hulton-Deutsch Collection/Corbis. Reproduced by permission. —Abraham, Fischer, Pretoria, South Africa, 1966, photograph. AP/Wide World Photos. Reproduced by permission. —Shaka Zulu, 19th century, color lithograph. The Granger Collection, New York. Reproduced by permission. —Zulu king Cetewayo, with some of his wives, Port Durnford, Zululand, South Africa, 1879, wood engraving by Commander Crawford Caffin, R.N. © Corbis. Reproduced by permission. —Nigerian wedding party, photograph by Kerstin Geier. Corbis. Reproduced by permission. —Igbo refugee women, Owerri, Biafra, Nigeria, 1970, photograph. AP/Wide World Photos. Reproduced by permission. —Residents outside shacks in slum of Sofiatown, Johannesburg, South Africa, 1954, photograph. UPI/Corbis-Bettmann. Reproduced by permission. —Alan Paton, photograph. Archive Photos, Inc. Reproduced by permission. —Roof thatching, Loma Village, Southern Guinea, photograph. © Bettmann/Corbis. Reproduced by permission.

—Camara Laye, photograph. —Egungun festival, Porto Nuovo, West Africa, photograph by Caroline Penn. © Caroline Penn/Corbis. Reproduced by permission. —Wole Soyinka, photograph. Archive Photos, Inc./Trappe. Reproduced by permission. —W. E. B. DuBois, photograph. © Corbis. Reproduced by permission.

Rioting in Soweto, South Africa, 1976, photograph. © Hulton-Deutsch Collection/Corbis. Reproduced by permission. —André Brink, photograph by Jerry Bauer. © Jerry Bauer. Reproduced by permission. —Igbo men thatching roof, Nigeria, 1920, photograph. © Bettmann/Corbis. Reproduced by permission. —Market vendors, photograph by Paul Almasy. © Paul Almasy/Corbis. Reproduced by permission. —'Abbas II, Khedive of Egypt, sepia photograph by J. Heyman. © Hulton-Deutsch Collection/Corbis. Reproduced by permission. —Muslim mud mosque, Mopti, Mali, photograph by Charles Lenars. © Charles & Josette Lenars/Corbis. Reproduced by permission. —Slave ship stowage layout, line drawing. The Library of Congress. —Olaudah Equiano, photograph. The Library of Congress. —Abubakar Tafawa Balewa, London, 1958, photograph. AP/Wide World Photos. Reproduced by permission. —Ben Okri, London, 1991, photograph. AP/ Wide World Photos. Reproduced by permission. —Inspection of Algerians soldiers, photograph. UPI/Corbis-Bettmann. Reproduced by permission. —Algerians with their hands on their heads being herded, photograph. UPI/Corbis-Bettmann. Reproduced by permission. —Suez Canal crisis, 1956, photograph by Bill Johnson, II. © Bettmann/Corbis. Reproduced by permission. —Gamal Abdel Nasser, 1956, Egypt, photograph. © Bettmann/Corbis. Reproduced by permission. —Ousmane Sembène, photograph. Caroline Penn/Corbis. Reproduced by permission. —Leopold Senghor, photograph. AP/Wide World Photos. Reproduced by permission.

Cameroonian youngsters pushing water cart, photograph. AP/Wide World Photos. Reproduced by permission. —Malian clay fortification, photograph. Picture Collection, The Branch Libraries, The New York Public Library. —Minaret in Timbuktu, Mali, photograph by Wolfgang Kaehler. © Wolfgang Kaehler/Corbis. Reproduced by permission. —Old district of Lagos, Nigeria, photograph by Paul Almasy. © Paul Almasy/Corbis. Reproduced by permission. —Biafran War soldier, Nigeria, 1968, photograph. © Hulton-Deutsch Collection/Corbis. Reproduced by permission. —Crowds celebrating cease-fire from Nigerian Civil War, 1970, photograph. © Bettmann/Corbis. Reproduced by permission. —Sugar cane harvest along the Nile, Egypt, 1993, photograph by Richard T. Nowitz. © Richard T. Nowitz/Corbis. Reproduced by permission. —Al Azhar Square and Al Azhar Mosque, photograph by Owen Franken. © Owen Franken/Corbis. Reproduced by permission. —Allied officials drafting Versailles Treaty, December 2, 1918, photograph. © Bettmann/Corbis. Reproduced by permission. —Men working in Sallies Gold Mine, 1948, photograph. © Bettmann/Corbis. Reproduced by permission. —Women protesting outside Cato Manor Beer Hall, Cato Manor, South Africa, 1959, photograph. © Hulton-Deutsch Collection/Corbis. Reproduced by permission. —Germans taking possession of Cameroon, 1881, photograph. © Bettmann/Corbis. Reproduced by permission.

Algerian rebel army in training, photograph. © Bettmann/Corbis. Reproduced by permission. —Ian Smith, signing proclamation, Rhodesia, Africa, 1965, photograph. AP/Wide World Photos. Reproduced by permission. —Students at University of Zimbabwe, photograph by David Reed. © David Reed/Corbis. Reproduced by permission. —Shoppers in outdoor market, Nigeria, 1973, photograph by Owen Franken. © Owen Franken/Corbis. Reproduced by permission. —Girl at desk, Lagos, Nigeria, 1986, photograph by Jerry Cooke. © Jerry Cooke/Corbis. Reproduced by permission. —Kikuyu women, Samburu National Reserve, Kenya, 1980s, photograph by David Bartuff. © David Bartuff/Corbis. Reproduced by permission. —Theodore Roosevelt, photograph. © Bettmann/Corbis. Reproduced by permission. —Yoruba men, Nigeria, 1973, photograph by Owen Franken. © Owen Franken/Corbis. Reproduced by permission. —British troops advancing on Tunisian front, c. 1943, photograph. © Hulton-Deutsch Collection/Corbis. Reproduced by permission. —Segregated restrooms, photograph. United Nations. —Nelson Mandela, South Africa, 1994, photograph. AP/Wide World Photos. Reproduced by permission. —Outdoor market, Marrakech, Morocco, 1990, photograph by Owen Franken. © Owen Franken/Corbis. Reproduced by permission. —Woman walking in front of archway, Morocco, photograph by Cory Langley. Reproduced by permission. —Sudanese woman near Nile River, Sudan, 1970, photograph by Jonathan Blair. © Jonathan Blair/Corbis. Reproduced by permission.

Muslim woman on beach, Senegal, 1978, photograph by Owen Franken. © Owen Franken/Corbis. Reproduced by permission. —Schoolchildren, Dakar, Senegal, 1978, photograph by Owen Franken. © Owen Franken/Corbis. Reproduced by permission. —Vatusi men, Uganda, photograph by Fulvio Roiter. © Fulvio Roiter/Corbis. Reproduced by permission. —Open diamond mine, Kimberley, South Africa, c. 1888, photograph. © Hulton-Deutsch Collection/Corbis. Reproduced by permission. —African Zulus, photograph by Carl Van Haoffman. Corbis-Bettmann. Reproduced by permission. —Woman and child during drought in Somalia, photograph. © Bettmann/Corbis. Reproduced by permission. —Burial in Las Dhure Refugee Camp, Somalia, 1981, photograph by Kevin Fleming. © Kevin Fleming/Corbis. Reproduced by permission. —Igbo women, Nri, Nigeria, 1988, photograph by Margaret Courtney-Clarke. © Margaret Courtney-Clarke/Corbis. Reproduced by permission. —Graduation in Lagos, Nigeria, photograph by Paul Almasy. © Paul Almasy/Corbis. Reproduced by permission. —White South Africans demonstrating against release of Nelson Mandela, Pretoria, South Africa, 1990, photograph by Peter Turnley. © Peter Turnley/Corbis. Reproduced by permission. —Karoo region, South Africa, 1996, photograph by Charles O'Rear. © Charles O'Rear/Corbis. Reproduced by permission. —Stephen Biko, photograph. AP/Wide World Photos. Reproduced by permission. —J. M. Coetzee, photograph by Jerry Bauer. © Jerry Bauer. Reproduced by permission. —Children in District Six,

African Laughter:
Four Visits to Zimbabwe

by

Doris Lessing

~

Doris Lessing was born in 1919 in Persia to British parents. In 1925, the family moved to the British colony of Southern Rhodesia in Africa, where her parents became unsuccessful farmers. Twenty-four years later, after two unhappy marriages and the philosophical and personal turmoil of being involved in Marxist politics, Lessing left Africa for London, where she quickly established herself as a promising novelist, becoming known among other works for her series *Children of Violence,* about Martha Quest, a character who grows up in Africa and settles in England. Lessing returned to Southern Rhodesia in 1956 to find herself a "prohibited immigrant" because of her politics; she was at this point officially exiled from the country, a ban that was not lifted until 1982. Finally the Marxist government of Robert Mugabe allowed her to return to a transformed land. She entered the newly founded nation of Zimbabwe, born after a decade of civil war between whites and blacks in the former British colony. *African Laughter* records Lessing's joyous, painful reunion with the land and people (white and black) of her youth, now so greatly changed.

Events in History at the Time of the Memoir

Background: Chimurenga. *African Laughter* examines the social and political aftereffects of the civil war (called the "Bush War" or, more properly, "Zimbabwe's Liberation War") that transformed the former British colony of Southern

THE LITERARY WORK

A memoir set in Zimbabwe between 1982 and 1992; published in English in 1992.

SYNOPSIS

Doris Lessing returns to the homeland from which she was exiled some 30 years earlier and contemplates Zimbabwe's past, present, and future.

Rhodesia into the rebel state of Rhodesia, the temporary state of Zimbabwe-Rhodesia, and then into the new nation of Zimbabwe. The war, which left an estimated 30,000 people dead, is also known as "the Second Chimurenga"—a word that means "war of liberation." The First Chimurenga took place a century earlier, when European settlers made a concerted land grab in the territory of the Shona people, who had occupied what is now Zimbabwe for at least 1,500 years, and of the Ndebele (or Matabele) people, who had moved north to the area from present-day South Africa in the early 1800s.

On February 11, 1888, J. S. Moffat, a British official in Bulawayo, made an agreement with the Ndebele king, Lobengula; apparently there is some contention over whether Lobengula actually signed such a document or if he knew what it was he was signing. In any case, the king promised not to enter into land agreements with other foreigners without British sanction. Later

TIMELINE: THE FIRST AND SECOND CHIMURENGAS

The history of race relations in Zimbabwe encompasses little more than a century but is nevertheless complicated. The following dates provide a quick overview of some key events leading up to the Second Chimurenga.

1890: "Pioneer Column" of British South African settlers and soldiers arrives in the area; by British royal charter, the area is governed by Cecil Rhodes's British South Africa Company until 1923.

1893: Under Lobengula, the Ndebele people rebel in protest of land encroachment; British settlers loot Bulawayo, Lobengula's royal village.

1894: The British set up first Reserves for black Africans (hereafter simply called Africans) in Matabeleland (home of the Ndebele; reserves will be set up in Mashonaland in 1898).

1895: May 3—The British South Africa Company renames Matabeleland "Rhodesia."

1896: Shona and Ndebele protest land encroachment; known as the "First Chimurenga," their rebellion rages on in Mashonaland until October 1897.

1923: British government holds referendum to see whether Rhodesians would rather be self-governing or join South Africa; white settlers vote for self-government; indigenous peoples are not consulted.

1930: Land Apportionment Act divides Southern Rhodesia racially, giving finest land to Europeans.

1948-49: African Voice Association sponsors strike of African municipal workers, and protests government removal of Africans from their land.

1951: At All African Convention, Africans oppose proposed Federation of Southern Rhodesia, Northern Rhodesia (now called Zambia), and Nyasaland (now Malawi). Federation lasts from 1953 to 1960, then dissolves.

1957: Africans found the Southern Rhodesia African National Congress (ANC), a nonviolent organization for government reform of race laws.

1959: Southern Rhodesia government declares a state of emergency, bans ANC, and enacts a barrage of antiblack race laws.

1960: Africans found National Democratic Party (NDP), which demonstrates for radical political change; 11 protestors die; government passes Law and Order (Maintenance) Act, giving police unlimited power against NDP.

1961: Britain calls Constitutional Congress, which preserves minority white rule; Africans receive token 15 of 65 seats in legislature; Southern Rhodesia bans NDP; birth of Zimbabwe African People's Union (ZAPU).

1962: ZAPU is banned; racist right-wing Rhodesian Front comes to power.

1963: Britain grants independence to Northern Rhodesia (renamed Zambia).

1964: Africans form Zimbabwe African National Union (ZANU), which opts for armed struggle against racist regime; the union is banned.

1965: Southern Rhodesian government rejects mandate to implement majority African rule; declares independence from Britain in Unilateral Declaration of Independence (UDI). UDI deemed illegal by United Nations.

1966: April 28—Second Chimurenga begins as ZANU forces meet whites at Battle of Sinoia.

that same year representatives of Cecil Rhodes, a British mining magnate based in Cape Town, South Africa, concluded the Rudd Concession with Lobengula; Rhodes won mineral rights—but no land concessions—within all of Lobengula's kingdom. Yet Rhodes, who may or may not have understood that Lobengula's kingdom did not in fact extend the length and breadth of Zimbabwe, immediately set about colonizing the land. On September 12, 1890, a band of British mercenaries and adventurers arrived in Harare (which they called Salisbury), set up the Union Jack, and declared themselves at home. By 1895, 4,863 Europeans had settled in Zimbabwe (Uwechue, p. 1644). They set aside special pockets of land on which the original inhabitants would be permitted to live, gradually earmarking the rest for European use. Unsurprisingly, this situation led to unrest and rebellion on the parts of the Shona and Ndebele. In Mashonaland (home of the Shona) the battle that would become famous as the "First Chimurenga" claimed the lives of one tenth of the white settler population (450 lives) (Uwechue, p. 1645). The battle ended with the help of a negotiated settlement and the British remained, but the war raged on in the imaginations of black and white Rhodesians for the next 100 years.

The War of Liberation erupted in 1966, initiated by blacks in Rhodesia (as the former Southern Rhodesia was now known). Outraged by a century of racial discrimination that left them economically, politically, and socially powerless—but most importantly, deprived of their ancestral land—the rebels began an armed struggle against the white minority government. Under Ian Smith, this government had declared itself independent of Britain in 1965 in order to insure its continuing rule over Rhodesia. The United Nations Security Council judged the break to be illegal. Beginning in 1967 the U.N. imposed economic sanctions, which ultimately isolated Rhodesia from the international community. Other nations were not allowed to export goods to Rhodesia, to import Rhodesian goods, or to have financial dealings with the nation. Even air travel to and from the nation was banned. The British blockaded the Mozambiquan port of Beira, from which Rhodesia had run an oil pipeline, pressing the Rhodesian government to come to the bargaining table. Under these harsh conditions, the War of Liberation escalated in violence and scale. In 1971 the British government stepped up pressure on the illegal Rhodesian government, and succeeded in hav-

ing Smith agree to review racist legislation, and to prepare for majority African rule around the year 2035. This agreement was put to the Rhodesian people (under a British-sponsored body known as the Pearce Commission) and was rejected. Meanwhile, the war raged on. It is important to understand that the War of Liberation was not just a struggle for political independence. It was also a struggle to escape vicious, sometimes life-threatening discrimination and poverty, and to obtain basic amenities like education and healthcare.

- The Land Tenure Act of 1969 alloted 45 million acres (out of 96.4 total) to black Rhodesians, who made up 96 percent of the population.
- In 1969 only 10 percent of black dwellings had electricity.
- When the War of Liberation broke out, 60 percent of the national income was earned by the 4 percent white minority.
- In 1977 the average income for a white Rhodesian was Z$513/month; the average income for a black was Z$49/month.
- In 1976 only 14.6 percent of black Rhodesians were employed.
  (Tungamirai, pp. 36 and 38; Weiss, p. xxi)

In 1974 the Portuguese were driven from their former colonies in Mozambique and Angola. Mozambique, directly east of Rhodesia, gave the armed black struggle in Rhodesia a huge boost—both in morale and in the more practical form of arms, training, and safe haven from which to launch attacks on the government. Suddenly the rules of the game looked a lot different. In November 1974 Smith released the imprisoned leaders of ZANU and ZAPU, and agreed to begin negotiations. In December the ANC—which, though banned, remained operative outside Rhodesia—agreed with Smith to a cease-fire, the beginning of negotiations, and the Rhodesian government's release of its political prisoners. The government, however, broke its word—the cease-fire was not observed, prisoners were not released, and the murder of a ZANU leader led straight to the government's door. The mood of the time is best captured in the inability of both sides to agree even on a place to hold negotiations—Smith insisted on Rhodesia, while the ANC argued for somewhere outside Rhodesia (in part because Smith threatened to arrest certain ANC leaders if they set foot on Rhodesian soil). The parties finally agreed to meet in train cars on a bridge over Victoria Falls (on the Rhodesia-Zambia border), but this meeting did not go well, nor did the next, nor the next.

In 1978 Smith contacted leaders on the fringes of the black liberation movement and reached an agreement with them, one that would still concentrate most power in the hands of whites. Elections in April 1979 saw one of these black leaders, Bishop Abel Muzorewa, a long-time activist and former head of ANC, establish a government. The country's name became "Zimbabwe-Rhodesia." All of this was essentially a show on Smith's part designed to convince the international community that sanctions should be lifted from the economically crippled Rhode-sia; it did not work. As the war continued, it became clear that the black liberation forces would win. By the end of 1979 Smith showed his readiness to negotiate for real. Rhodesia's government was placed in the hands of Britain's Lord Soames, the Muzorewa government was dissolved, a constitution was written, and elections were scheduled for February 27-29, 1980. Robert Mugabe, head of ZANU, became prime minister on March 14, and Canaan Banana, the new president of Zimbabwe, opened Parliament on May 14 of that year.

Learning a lesson: Mozambique. Lessing's narrative is peppered by explosions on the Mozambique border, where RENAMO (Resistencia Nacional Mocambicana, or Mozambique National Resistance), a white-financed terrorist organization, is blowing up the pipeline that brings petroleum to Zimbabwe. A landlocked nation, Zimbabwe depends on nearby ports, such as Beira or Maputo in Mozambique. Mozambique had been a Portuguese colony. When the Portuguese settlers were forced to concede power in the early 1970s, they chose to leave rather than take part in a multiracial government. The sudden and complete departure of the nation's political and technological experts played havoc with Mozambique's economy and infrastructure. Robert Mugabe, the first prime minister of Zimbabwe, had lived in Mozambique as head of ZANU for many years; the specter of total economic collapse that he witnessed there influenced his own decision to make peace with the white community in Zimbabwe.

"Rhodies." On the other side of the War of Liberation in Zimbabwe were Rhodesia's white settlers. In 1969 they were outnumbered by black Rhodesians by a ratio of 21:1. Less than half had been born in Rhodesia; at least half had dual citizenship in some other country; one third had arrived in the country within the last eight years (Godwin and Hancock, pp. 16-17). Many of them resided in the city of Salisbury (renamed Harare after independence) and a smaller but still sizeable number, including Lessing's brother, lived in rural areas. They ranged widely in class and ethnicity, with Jews, Greeks, and Afrikaners forming their own close communities, bound, it seems, less by cultural similarities than by their collective need as a tiny minority to segregate from the blacks among whom they lived. Most of these white Rhodesians enjoyed a high standard of living, made possible by the exploitation of black labor.

THE WARRIORS

African Laughter, like most works that deal with recent events in Southern Rhodesia/Zimbabwe, refers to a dizzying array of armies, movements, military and government agencies, and to the men who led them. In the following table are some of the most important of these:

Ian Smith: Known among white Rhodesians as "good old Smithy"; leader of Southern Rhodesia as it evolved into the rebel state of Rhodesia and then to Zimbabwe.

ZAPU: Zimbabwe African People's Union; operated out of Zambia; supported by the Soviet bloc; most active and influential in the 1960s; its forces were called ZIPRA (Zimbabwe People's Revolutionary Army).

ZANU (PF): Zimbabwe African National Union (Patriotic Front); operated out of Mozambique; supported by China; its forces were called ZANLA (Zimbabwe African National Liberation Army); formally abandoned Marxism-Leninism in 1991; most influential as of 1972.

Joshua Nkomo: Leader of ZAPU; former leader of the African National Congress in Southern Rhodesia.

Robert Mugabe: Leader of ZANU (PF); prime minister of Zimbabwe.

Bishop Abel Muzorewa: Bishop of the United Methodist Church; former leader of African National Congress in Zimbabwe; later leader of United African National Council, which formed the "Zimbabwe-Rhodesia" government that was Ian Smith's brainchild.

FRELIMO: Front for the Liberation of Mozambique; anti-Portuguese movement based in Mozambique.

RENAMO: Mozambique National Resistance; started by Smith government to destabilize FRELIMO and black Zimbabwe rebels; after Zimbabwean liberation, RENAMO was flown out of Zimbabwe by South African security forces.

As soon as the war was over and the new Republic of Zimbabwe had been declared, whites left in droves. During the time that Lessing was visiting Zimbabwe, she reports hearing many white people speak of moving elsewhere; statistics show that in 1979 there were 232,000 white citizens of Rhodesia, whereas in 1990 there were only 80,000 (Godwin and Hancock, p. 314). Those who stayed, however, learned that it was still possible to live a good life in Zimbabwe. Inflation soared, government propaganda flooded the airwaves, bureaucratic ensnarlments were legendary, and it became difficult to procure parts for automobiles and tractors—but the basic pattern of their lives was not disrupted. This is not to say that the white Zimbabweans were overjoyed with their new situation—most historians, and certainly Lessing herself, note that the white population spent the first few years of Zimbabwean independence grumbling derisively about the ineptitude and corruption of the new black government.

White farmers, among whom Lessing grew up, were protected from land expropriation for ten years under the British-sponsored transition to black majority rule, and they lived their postwar lives much as they always had. They had the best land and the technology with which to farm it most productively—and were thus vital to the well-being of the entire nation. After independence some white farmers, like Lessing's friend "the Coffee Farmer," became advisers to the new government, keeping an eye on black agricultural efforts to make sure that all was going well. Agriculture, always among the nation's most important industries, remained so after the war.

One of the most trying aspects of transition for all concerned was the resettlement of black Zimbabweans on land appropriate for farming. The three-year Transitional National Plan (1982-85) stated that 162,000 black Zimbabwean families were to be resettled on some 9 million hectares of land. However, the Plan did not work out well; by 1989 less than a quarter of these people had been resettled on only 2 million hectares. Many others simply squatted on land owned by whites. Of course, this caused significant tension, even among people of different races who were trying to get along. The Land Acquisition Act of 1992 exacerbated tensions, allowing the government to purchase whatever land it desired, at a fair price, with no appeal possible from the white owners. Lessing notes the effect that this policy was having on the white farmers of Zimbabwe:

Robert Mugabe

"GIVING UP"

Lessing recounts the many rationales of people who have flooded out of Zimbabwe, for one reason or another. In a characteristic effort to provide a balanced view, she notes these snippets of conversation:

"I moved house. I put up a dura wall around the garden." (A type of cement fencing.) "All day in the department I hear, 'So you've put up a dura wall, just like a white. . . . All I hear is the whites this, the whites that. I've had enough of this racism. It's getting worse. I'm off."

A scientist left because, having many times applied unsuccessfully for some laboratory equipment, refused on the grounds of shortage of foreign exchange, he stood at the airport watching "Dozens of these damned [black leaders] off to one of their conferences somewhere. There's always enough money for that."

The last straw for another was a new history book for use in schools, designed to correct the errors of the white version of African history. . . .

But: the man who left because of the fence is black. . . .

(Lessing, *African Laughter,* pp. 418-19)

A new law provides for the taking of land without appeal from white farmers in certain designated areas. The perennial threats to do this means [sic] that a productive part of the agricultural economy is kept in a state of uncertainty, farmers beginning to refuse to invest in their farms, and trying to put money into movables. Meanwhile the government has large areas of land still not allocated. It is being said that this law is designed to distract the attention of the Povos [the poor] from the government's mistakes.

(*African Laughter*, p. 434)

Ngangas. Sprinkled throughout *African Laughter* are references to the *ngangas* (now spelled *n'angas*), the traditional healer-diviners whose role in Shona society is to communicate with the spirit world. Sometimes they act as mediums for ancestral spirits or for spirits that, for example, make rain. They diagnose and cure illnesses that are physical and individual, as well as communal ills that are metaphysical, political, and social. At the end of 1989 it was estimated that there was one n'anga for every 257 Shona. By contrast, in 1984, there was one "Western" doctor for every 6,700 Shona (Reynolds, pp. xxvi-xxvii). As respected counselors in the Shona communities the n'angas served as advisers to the black fighters in the War of Liberation; n'anga approval of the African soldiers went a long way toward legitimizing their actions and confirming the validity of their struggle to reclaim their ancestral land. Not all n'angas approved of the war, of course, but they did what they could to provide healing and reconciliation to the community. When the war ended the n'angas filled perhaps their most important ritual function, cleansing people of evil, internally and externally, with the help of plants, animals, and dream interpretation.

Education. When the War of Liberation erupted in the early 1970s, the black guerillas closed many rural schools, in part to encourage children to join the freedom fighters. And, in fact, the children did join up in massive numbers, usually because of forced recruitment or abduction. By the end of the decade more than a thousand schools had been closed. Lessing reports throughout *African Laughter* on the efforts of the Zimbabwean government to reinstall education as the primary pursuit of the nation's youth; new schools were going up, albeit on a shoestring budget, and teachers, both Zimbabwean and foreign, were struggling to improve the quality of education in the new nation. In 1980 the Mugabe government made primary education free and compulsory. The number of schools skyrocketed, as did enrollments, and the government made education a priority in its budget. But there was a dearth of teachers, materials, buildings, and, perhaps more important, a lack of prospects for those students who did manage to graduate:

In 1982 I met teachers radiant with exhaustion and idealism, who said they worked in schools converted from barns, shacks, shops—anything, and there might be two or three shifts of pupils in a day.... Parents helped to build schools, giving time, skills, and money, often going without necessities. Secondary education was the key to their children's future, and there was no sacrifice too great.

Eight years since Liberation.... Zimbabwe is now covered with secondary schools. But there are not enough teachers, textbooks, let alone—often—electricity, or even clean water. ... The teaching staff in these schools never stay long, they are always on their way to somewhere better.... The children at these schools believe they are being given a future....

This situation is dangerous, a classic for revolution: numbers of young people who have been promised everything, have made sacrifices and are in the end disappointed.

(*African Laughter*, pp. 192-93)

The Memoir in Focus

Contents summary. *African Laughter* is made up of a rich and wide-ranging series of vignettes, dealing with everything from the public health ramifications of the Blair toilet, to the state of Zimbabwean hospitals, to farming techniques and government corruption, to black novelists and the disappearance of the Zimbabwean

---

FROM A CHIMURENGA SONG

∼

The air is still
But they who watch
Know that their children
Fight for their land.

Spirits of the ancestors
Lead us, protect us,
We die for you
For our land.

(Weiss, p. 13)

wilderness. Throughout its pages are discussed various gaps—between races, nationalities, genders, generations. And, in "The Monologue," the rote series of complaints voiced by white farmers against the black government—to Lessing's mind, ad nauseam—emerges the most important of gap of all: the geographic "Gap" through which white Zimbabweans threaten to pass forever into South Africa. Lessing pastes these vignettes into a sort of scrapbook about her travels in Zimbabwe during the troubled period when the new nation was struggling to define itself.

The memoir is divided into four sections: "Then" (1982), "Next Time" (1988), "And Again" (1989), and "And Again, In Passing" (1992). The last is the shortest section, comprising a sort of coda to the themes worked out in the previous three. These three share certain continuities that shape the work. For example, subsections entitled "Air Zimbabwe" appear at or near the beginning of all three, and foreshadow the condition of the nation that Lessing is about to visit. In 1982 the black air hostesses are defensive and reserved, the passengers are almost all white, and the atmosphere is tense and uncomfortable. Lessing finds her seatmate, a white racehorse owner, to be peevish and prejudiced, aghast at what he sees as the clumsiness of Zimbabwe's new black government. At Immigration she is greeted by a shy, inexperienced black officer. In 1988, by contrast, the hostesses are confident and firm; the plane is filled with black businessmen, government representatives, and celebrities; and the customs officials are as confident as the cabin crew. In 1989 Lessing sits next to a *chef*—one of the new class of black Zimbabwean government officials who have somehow managed to reconcile their official Marxist philosophy with personal economic rapaciousness. The immigration official is sarcastic and hostile, and gives her problems because she is a writer and journalist—"thus proving how thoroughly Zimbabwe has entered the modern world" (*African Laughter,* p. 324). These three "Air Zimbabwe" pieces trace the memoir's progression through Zimbabwe's early hopeful promise, ebullient confidence, and eventual decline into cynicism and despair.

In 1982 Lessing is filled with a sense of discombobulation—she is back in "the streets of the town that was once my big city" and nothing is as it once was—the physical and psychological effects of the war are still visible in the land and in the faces of people, white and black, she meets (*African Laughter,* p. 15). Immediately, she is plunged into nostalgic reverie, and recounts

episodes from her childhood days with her family (mother, father, brother) camping in the vast bush that spread across so much of Rhodesia. Her return surprises her in this regard: "When I returned to Zimbabwe . . . I expected all kinds of changes, but there was one change I had not thought to expect. The game had mostly gone, the bush was nearly silent. Once, the dawn chorus hurt the ears" (*African Laughter,* p. 23).

THE DISAPPEARING BUSH

During her 1988 visit Lessing speaks to a young African schoolteacher who likes to walk in the "bush" by himself. She realizes with shock that, although their experiences are separated by only some 50 years, the change in the bush has been immense—what he considers bush she considers a denuded landscape.

"When I was a girl in Banket the bush was full of koodoo, sable, eland, and all the smaller buck, particularly duiker. There were stem buck and bush buck, anteaters and porcupines and wild cats and monkeys, and baboons and wild pig. There was every kind of bird. There were still leopards in the hills. . . ."

"Did you live in a game park?" he asked.

"No. That was how the bush was then. Everywhere. In every part of the country. . . ."

"You say that wasn't a safari park?"

(*African Laughter,* p. 344)

Lessing is also confronted by the years that have passed when she meets, for the first time in nearly two decades, her younger brother, Harry. Harry has never shared his sister's "funny ideas" about race relations and communism. He is outraged by the still-fresh transition to power of the black Marxists, by the fact that President Canaan Banana lets chickens run in the gardens of Government House and by Prime Minister Mugabe's habit of traveling in an armed motorcade. He concludes his tirade with "they're inferior to us, and that's all there is to it" (*African Laughter,* p. 43). This is Lessing's first exposure to "The Monologue," the antigovernment rant that springs to the lips of many white Zimbabweans. But the rapid social transformation is disorienting not only to white Zimbabweans: a young black hitchhiker fired from his new job in Harare weeps in Lessing's car; blacks who were promised land at the war's end, only to discover that this land was to be communal, not private, become stubborn squatters on white-owned farmland; the French wife of an unemployed black writer finds herself waiting on her husband and his friends according to "African custom" (*African Laughter*, p. 112).

In 1988 Lessing returns to a nation that has teetered for six years on the brink of another civil war, this time between rival black factions. A year earlier Prime Minister Mugabe became convinced that Zimbabwean stability was being threatened by South African-supported ZAPU forces under Joshua Nkomo, and Mugabe took action. He entered into the Unity Agreement of 1987, which drew Nkomo's troops out of the bush—who turned out to be less numerous than feared—and brought Nkomo into the Mugabe government. Meanwhile, in the six years since Lessing first visited Zimbabwe, corruption has run rampant in government, now at least partly in the hands of the chefs, the new black elite:

> A United Nations official remarked . . . "it is not exactly unknown for the victorious side in a civil war to line their pockets, but Zimbabwe is unique in creating a boss class in less than ten years and to the accompaniment of marxist [sic] rhetoric."
>
> (*African Laughter*, p. 146)

Nevertheless, what Lessing herself has learned through "reading newspapers from Zimbabwe, letters from Zimbabwe, [and] listening to travellers' tales . . . [is] vitality, exuberance, optimism, enjoyment" (*African Laughter*, pp. 146-47). This visit is marked by paradox, contradiction, and irony. Lessing notes the passion with which people discuss politics, build schools, teach, struggle to improve healthcare and women's rights, form collective farms and help former "terrorists" reintegrate into society; she notes also people's disillusionment with the government, like this tirade by a Zimbabwean:

> I expected a period of incompetence. I expected every kind of mess and muddle. I knew nothing would work for a time. How could it when they didn't have the trained people? But what I didn't expect was that these bastards would get into power and then not care about anything but feathering their own nests. . . . Do you imagine they care about those poor bastards out in the Reserves—yes, they are still the reserves, you can give them a new name if you like, but. . . .
>
> (*African Laughter*, pp. 154-55)

In 1989 Lessing returns to a grumbling, crumbling Zimbabwe. It is not yet the bitter Zimbabwe

she will see in 1992, but it is grappling with an AIDS epidemic, an out-of-control black elite, a corrupt commercial class, the further disappearance of the bush, entrenched suspicions between the races, and the political disillusionment of young men and women who fought a war seemingly only to change the white elite for its black twin. To encapsulate this feeling, Lessing reproduces a poem by S. J. Nondo, written in protest of the black elite:

The Vengeance of the Poor Man

In your sumptuous house
I toil and sweat for you,
Yet in the heart of Harare
You see a stranger in me.
When I am dead and buried,
Your deeds will tear your heart.

In hotels that glitter,
On fatty steaks you dine,
Honey your tongue with oozy puddings
and sink your frame on cozy beds.
When I am dead and buried,
Your deeds will tear your heart. . . .

(*African Laughter*, p. 375)

The final section, which takes place in 1992, is brief, erratic, and bitter; it records the demise of hope in Zimbabwe. Lessing reports tiny fragments of information, sometimes only a sentence or two, on the order of: "In Zimbabwe they are not saying, 'Why doesn't Mugabe . . . ?' 'Mugabe should . . .' The people have given up hopeful expectation" (*African Laughter*, p. 431). Or: "A letter: when I think of our dreams at independence I want to cry for Zimbabwe" (*African Laughter*, p. 436). The memoir concludes with a brief overview of the history of Zimbabwean agriculture and the place of Zimbabwe in southern Africa.

Women's rights in Zimbabwe. Throughout *African Laughter*, Lessing notices women—poor, badly fed, pregnant—who go unnoticed by the men around her. She obtains firsthand access to their world. In 1988 Lessing has "that stroke of luck travellers dream of, which we cannot plan, expect, order, or foresee: I was invited to go with a team of people making instructional books for use in the villages" (*African Laughter*, p. 236). She travels through rural Zimbabwe in the company of a "Book Team" of three Zimbabwean women and a Zimbabwean man on a cultural mission. This team and others like it spread out in groups of four or five across the nation, and speak with large gatherings of women and men, trying to discern and address the sociological and political concerns of average (i.e., rural) Zimbabweans. They are to publish their findings in a book, hence the name of the team. Several such books have in fact been produced, including one on basic economics (how to open a bank account, etc.). The project that Lessing is invited to join is devoted to women's issues. The Zimbabwean government had promised women—who had fought in the bush alongside men—equality in law and in the workplace. A series of laws suggested that it would deliver on this promise:

- In 1980 the Minimum Wages Act mandates that there be a minimum acceptable wage paid even for unskilled workers, a group that overwhelmingly includes women.
- Also in 1980, Equal Pay Regulations stipulate that men and women be awarded equal wages for equal work.
- In 1984 the Labour Relations Act gives women three months of maternity leave and forbids employment discrimination on the basis of gender.
- In 1985 female Public Service workers are given the same pension benefits as their male counterparts.

As one women's publication has observed, however, "the implementation of these laws to the benefit of women is a different story" (Getecha and Chipika, p. 111). Traditional beliefs, which dictate that women are inferior, have been entrenched in both black and white Zimbabwean society. Lessing reports, for example, the plight of a white Zimbabwean women in the mid-1980s who had to obtain the permission of her ex-husband before a doctor would perform a sterilization procedure upon her.

The book team project of which Lessing writes is not the only women's rights publication to be issued in post-liberation Zimbabwe. The journal *Tauri* or "Speak Out," for example, is a bilingual (English and Shona) magazine put out by the Women's Action Group in Harare. It deals with such issues as sexual discrimination, domestic violence, what to do if arrested, and how to avoid contracting AIDS. In 1995 the Zimbabwean Women's Resource Center and Network published *Zimbabwe Women's Voices*, a collection of information on equal rights legislation, poetry, interviews, and essays on such subjects as "Violence against Women," "Women, Land, and the Environment," and "Women and Education." Aiding in the effort are such organizations as the Zimbabwe Women's Bureau, Women and Law in Southern Africa, Association of Women's Club, and the Global Fund for Women. Their participation—in fact, their very existence—demonstrates that at least in some circles women's rights in Zimbabwe have been the focus of considerable activism.

Sources and literary context. "Every writer has a myth country," asserts Lessing at the beginning of *African Laughter*. "This does not have to be childhood" (*African Laughter*, p. 35). In her case, however, it is. Lessing returns to Zimbabwe, despite everything. Not only did the government brand her with "Prohibited Immigrant" status, but she has also been alienated from her family there—she left behind two ex-husbands and two children. Her return nevertheless has an air of the inevitable about it. In Part 1 of her autobiography, *Under My Skin,* composed about the same time that she was finishing *African Laughter,* Lessing writes: "A few weeks ago—1992—I was in the bush not far from where I was brought up.... I might not ever have left it, this is where I belonged" (Lessing, *Under My Skin,* pp. 111-12). Her brother, Harry, traumatized by World War II and by the recent War of Liberation, cannot remember large portions of their shared childhood, so from the dialogue in *African Laughter* we learn only scraps here and there. In her autobiography, however, Lessing writes more fully of her childhood adventures in the wilderness that surrounded her parents' farm:

AIDS

~

Like many African nations, Zimbabwe suffers from a severe AIDS epidemic. In 1992 Lessing writes that "the government says [AIDS] will kill at least a million people by the year 2000, in a population of nine million.... In an urban clinic recently one out of four babies was HIV positive. Most men refuse to wear condoms" (*African Laughter,* p. 435). The grief that Lessing feels in recounting these statistics is the keener for her having noticed on two previous trips the government's offhand way of dealing with the crisis. In 1988 she writes:

In every conversation these days, sooner or later, AIDS appears. Not in government offices: officially Zimbabwe is not supposed to have a problem with AIDS. The Minister of Health has just announced publicly that talk of AIDS is put about by ill-wishing whites to destroy the infant tourist industry.

(*African Laughter,* p. 234)

Doris Lessing

There is a memory, a most particular and special memory.... [F]or years, knowing how little my brother and I agreed on, or shared, I would think: I wonder if he remembers that day, but as it turned out, he did not....

We knew that buck liked to spend the hot daytime hours in the shade of antheaps where there is thick cover.... We found a high place on a rock, shielded by branches.... We waited. It was about six in the morning, and the sun had just got up. Not easy for a nine-year-old, or ten-year-old ... to sit absolutely still.... We heard small sounds, and then there he was, a male koodoo, slowly picking its way up through the drapes of Christmas fern, the boulders.... We could see liquid dark eyes, dark lashes ... we sat scarcely breathing, stiff with the effort not to make a sound.... We had never been so close to a living koodoo.... We were seeing how the beast experienced its life ... always on the watch for enemies, always wary, listening, turning its head this way and that.

(Lessing, *Under My Skin*, p. 114)

From scenes such as this are fabricated a "concentration of truth" that makes up Lessing's myth-country, Zimbabwe (*African Laughter*, p. 35). It is against these childhood perceptions that Lessing's adult experiences of Zimbabwe are measured.

Reviews. *African Laughter* has been well received in the United States and internationally. Describing the book as "a saddening tale of the forfeit of possibility," Vincent Crapanzano praises Lessing for offering "a jagged but brilliant report of her . . visits to the new country of Zimbabwe" (Crapanzano, p. 18). Robert Oakshott of the *Spectator* stresses the laughter as well as the sadness of this "marvelous" work, calling it "delightful and profoundly moving by turns, and frequently both at the same time"; Lessing's "subject matter" is so various "as sometimes to defy classification" (Oakshott in Chapman and Jorgensen, p. 272). Some critics—for example, as does Richard Stengel in the *Los Angeles Times Book Review*—have preferred to read *African Laughter* as an autobiographical portrait of the artist: "In this elegant and elegiac memoir, Lessing not only returns to her native land but to her earliest themes as a writer.... While the book recounts her travels during four trips to Zimbabwe, it is really a Proustian journey to the past, a search for the fountainhead of her own artistic sensibility" (Stengel in Chapman and Jorgensen, p. 272). Others however, have focused more heavily on the historical and political merits of Lessing's book: "Lessing gives us one of the most penetrating and evenhanded critiques of Zimbabwe as a new nation," writes P. Mathabane; her depiction "is without stereotype or sentimentality" (Mathabane in Chapman and Jorgensen, p. 272). While positive about Lessing's depiction of the area's white settlers "and what has become of them," K. Anthony Appiah expresses a reservation, related to the limitations of her perspective as a white outsider: "Lessing shows us only the exterior of the black Zimbabweans.... The best of this book is the white man's story" (Appiah in Chapman and Jorgensen, p. 272).

—Lorraine Valestuk

For More Information

Barber, James. *Zimbabwe's Regional Role: Prospects for a Land-Locked Power*. London: Research Institute for the Study of Conflict and Terrorism, 1991.

Bhebe, Ngwabi, and Terence Ranger, eds. *Society in Zimbabwe's Liberation War*. Portsmouth, N.H: Heinemann, 1996.

Chapman, Jeff, and John D. Jorgensen, eds. *Contemporary Authors New Revision Series*. Vol. 54. Detroit: Gale, 1992.

Crapanzano, Vincent. "This Home Can Never Be Home." *The New York Times*, 18 October 1992, p. 13.

Getecha, Ciru, and Jesimen Chipika, eds. *Zimbabwe Women's Voices*. Harare: Zimbabwe Women's Resource Centre and Network, 1995.

Godwin, Peter, and Ian Hancock. *"Rhodesians Never Die": The Impact of War and Political Change on White Rhodesia, c. 1970-1980*. Oxford: Oxford University Press, 1993.

Kriger, Norma J. *Zimbabwe's Guerilla War: Peasant Voices*. Cambridge: Cambridge University Press, 1992.

Lessing, Doris. *African Laughter: Four Visits to Zimbabwe*. New York: HarperCollins, 1992.

———. *Under My Skin: Volume One of My Autobiography, to 1949*. New York: Harper Collins, 1994.

Reynolds, Pamela. *Traditional Healers and Childhood in Zimbabwe*. Athens: Ohio University Press, 1996.

Tungamirai, Josiah. "Recruitment to ZANLA: Building up a War Machine." In *Soldiers in Zimbabwe's Liberation War*. Ed. Ngwabi Bhebe and Terence Ranger. Portsmouth, N.H.: Heinemann, 1995.

Uwechue, Raph, ed. *Africa Today*. 3rd ed. London: Africa Books, 1996.

Weiss, Ruth. *Zimbabwe and the New Elite*. London: British Academic Press, 1994.

The Beautyful Ones Are Not Yet Born

by

Ayi Kwei Armah

THE LITERARY WORK

A novel set in Ghana in 1965-66; published in English in 1968.

SYNOPSIS

A young civil servant struggles with political corruption, family pressures, and disillusionment in postcolonial Ghana.

Born in Ghana in 1939, Ayi Kwei Armah participated in the events that took Ghana from British colony to independent country. His first novel, *The Beautyful Ones Are Not Yet Born* established him as a writer of world renown. The work, whose title has an intentional misspelling taken from an inscription on a bus, portrays both the euphoria of independence and the disillusionment that followed in Ghana. It was a sobering period, in which the early promise of freedom gave way to economic malaise, political corruption, and continued financial dependence on Europe. Since 1968 Armah has generally lived outside Ghana, and occasionally outside Africa, though remaining a vital figure in African literature. His subsequent novels have continued to address the issues of modern African culture. A vocal proponent of pan-African unity, Armah has proposed the adoption of Swahili as an African *lingua franca*, championed African literatures past and present, and deplored the continued cultural domination of Europe and the United States.

Events in History at the Time the Novel Takes Place

Traces of colonialism. In 1471 the Portuguese became the first Europeans to arrive in what is now Ghana. Traders, not colonists, they named the area the Gold Coast, after the commodity they prized above all others; the region would later be renamed Ghana by its native inhabitants. Soon British, Dutch, Swedish, and Danish traders were competing with the Portuguese for the traffic in gold and other raw materials.

European interest in Ghana took a new, vicious turn with the development of the plantation system (and its demand for slaves) in North and South America. Between 1650 and 1800 the Gold Coast lost about 10,000 people a year to the slave trade that fueled American plantations. The slave trade promoted strife and instability among different African peoples. When African kingdoms warred against each other, the victor took captives. Slave traders made it profitable for victors to sell their vanquished foes to the Europeans. Europe was also deeply interested in profiting from economic ties to the area. Europeans cast a covetous eye on the raw materials that could be extracted from West Africa, and sought also to exploit it as a market for manufactured goods. Such a relationship was firmly established 200 years before Ghanaian independence. This basic pattern of exchange—raw natural wealth for more expensive finished prod-

The Gold Coast shoreline circa 1900, when the country that would become Ghana was still a British colony.

ucts—would characterize the period of colonialism proper.

In the Gold Coast this period of colonialism began in the middle of the nineteenth century. Before then, the formal British presence was limited to coastal forts. To protect their interests, the British would occasionally intervene in wars between different African kingdoms. This trend led, in 1844, to the "Fante Bond": chiefs of the coastal Fante people, who with British help were fighting the inland Asante, conceded to England the right to administer justice. The Asante (occasionally aided by the Dutch) resisted vigorously, posing a continual threat to British trade and government until they were subdued in 1900.

The colonial territory of the Gold Coast assumed its final shape in 1901, when the large Asante territory was annexed: 55 years later, this combined territory would become the free country of Ghana. The British mostly employed indirect rule—instead of sending British citizens to govern the territory, they formed alliances with certain native chiefs and elders, and influenced society, politics, and the economy that way. Various councils, composed mostly of British colonists, supervised and supported the native rulers and judges. These councils had final say over any decision made by the Africans; however, the British were fairly permissive unless trading interests were involved. There were a number of exceptions to the policy of indirect rule. Asante territory was one such exception; here the British ruled directly in an attempt to avoid any future rebellion.

Two consequences of the British mode of colonialism directly affected the society depicted in *The Beautyful Ones Are Not Yet Born*. First, the British system tended to create a native elite. A very small percentage of Africans were given European education and power (supported by British guns); the rest were left, powerless, to toil in the cocoa fields and gold mines. The existence of this new elite, and the premium they placed on all things European, proved to be durable facts of life, even after the colonial era ended. As Armah notes with bitterness, many in the postcolonial power structure remained obsessed with European lifestyles and luxury goods. Second, the economic structures of British colonialism systematically removed natural resources from Ghana, retarding the growth of native manufacturing and industry. When the British withdrew they left an infrastructure that made it easy to send raw material to the coast but difficult to make anything with those raw materials in Ghana. Armah's hero, a railway employee, oversees his country's underdevelopment. He coordinates the trains whose cars are filled with resources from the interior for export.

Traces of resistance. Another saga takes place alongside the history of British colonialism in Ghana: this is the story of how the peoples of Ghana resisted European domination. The Asante, as mentioned, staunchly opposed the British; it took four separate wars for the colonizers to subdue them. Even the Fante, who initially welcomed the British as allies against the Asante, eventually turned against the Europeans, forming the popular Fante Confederacy and attempting throughout the 1860s to oust the British from the country. Although these insurgencies failed to stop British advances, they inspired later, more successful protests.

In the first decades of the twentieth century African resistance to colonialism began with the native elite, those Africans trained by the British themselves. This seeming paradox is simply explained: while the masses of the colonized may have resented the British, they lacked the power or the voice necessary for effective protest. At this point only the elite were positioned to defend their native lands. The first organized effort, the Aborigines' Rights Protection Society, was founded in 1897; it evolved into the National Congress of British West Africa in the 1920s. This organization, while often sharply critical of the British, hoped to transform colonialism rather than eradicate it altogether. Members agitated for more European education in the Gold Coast, and more places for Africans on the British-dominated colonial councils. Such appeals were clearly grounded in the interests of the elite class and made no attempt to represent the mass of Africans.

In the 1930s more radical organizations began to appear as Britain's political strength waned. First the Great Depression (1929-34) and then World War II (1939-45) weakened Britain, as they did all the European powers, making an end to colonialism inevitable. Furthermore, Britain's defense of antiracist principles in opposition to Adolph Hitler appeared increasingly hypocritical in light of the institutionalized racism pervasive throughout the British empire. In 1937 Joseph Boakye Danquah spearheaded the creation of the Gold Coast Youth Council, an organization explicitly dedicated to freeing the Gold Coast. In 1947 Danquah's group merged with others like it to create the United Gold Coast Convention (UGCC). Civil unrest, strikes, and demonstrations were

the order of the day. It was clear that the British would leave—the questions to be answered were when and how; by some British estimates, it would take another 60 to 80 years. The British had come to accept the need for substantial change in their governance of the Gold Coast: first the Watson Commission and then the Coussey Committee attempted to satisfy native agitators by allowing Africans more self-gover-

---

PAN-AFRICANISM: AN UNFULFILLED IDEAL

From the inception of the twentieth century, anticolonial activists were possessed by the idea of a "Black Nation"—unity for African people everywhere. This Pan-African ideal was most forcefully expressed in the 1920s by the West Indian Marcus Garvey, who recommended that African Americans return to the homelands from which they had been abducted. He envisioned Africa as a single country, unified by pride in African culture.

Garvey's ideas, while extreme, exerted a profound influence both in the United States and in Africa: two Africans deeply affected by these ideas were Ayi Kwei Armah and Kwame Nkrumah. For anticolonialists it seemed that, because Africa had been carved up among various European countries, the key to independence would be unification: by joining forces, the colonies would have the strength to cast off their separate oppressors. Looking back at the origins of colonialism, they realized that the Europeans had exploited strife between kingdoms, first to gain slaves and then to gain direct control. Nkrumah knew that, as long as the Fante remained suspicious of the Asante, his country would never achieve independence. Further, on a transnational level, he doubted that the Gold Coast could sustain its independence or become economically self-supporting if it were hostile to its neighbors. "[Nkrumah] argued that while nationalism is necessary for gaining independence, it cannot be a final solution, because . . . only a united Africa can effectively resist the pressures of neocolonialism" (Afari-Gyan, p. 170).

In the end, however, Pan-Africanism remained no more than a dream. As each colony gained its independence it set up its own government and its own traditions, and sometimes old tribal hostilities reemerged. However, the Pan-African vision is an enduring ideal that Armah, for one, continues to espouse, advocating the adoption of Swahili as a universal African language.

Kwame Nkrumah, prime minister of Ghana, in a triumphant pose in 1957, when his country
achieved independence from Great Britain. Armah's novel is set in the turbulent months leading up
to the 1966 coup that deposed Nkrumah.

nance. Ironically the very willingness of the
British to make concessions to Africans ended
up splintering the African opposition. Danquah
and the UGCC, tending to trust the British,
wanted gradual change and an orderly progression to eventual independence. But by 1948, the
mood of the people was more radical, and the
masses were not inclined to trust the British nor
to be satisfied with the concessions to self-governance that the colonial power gave them. Danquah and his group, which had initiated the
modern anticolonial movement in the Gold
Coast, ended up seeming like conservatives, or
even antipatriots: they are the "yessir men," the
English-loving traitors, ridiculed in Armah's
novel. At this point, a new type of leader was
needed, and the Gold Coast found one in Kwame
Nkrumah.

Kwame Nkrumah. It is difficult to overstate the
importance of Kwame Nkrumah in Ghanaian history. A master politician and a visionary, he advocated Pan-African unity and economic self-sufficiency. Most important, he understood that
building a nation required the participation and
consent of the masses, and could not be accomplished by isolated elites. He was never universally beloved, and his government was over-

thrown by a military coup in 1966, but he is the
key figure in the history of Ghana.

In 1947 Nkrumah was simply a London-
based political activist in the Pan-African movement. Late that year the UGCC invited him to
return home to become their secretary-general.
Fearing that their base of support was limited to
the educated elite and prospering urban businessmen, they hoped Nkrumah could mobilize
popular support for their organization. Discontent was spreading through the country, as reflected in incidents of civil unrest: the people
wanted more daring and flamboyant leadership
than that of the rather conservative UGCC.
Nkrumah filled this role, to a degree that probably exceeded the wishes of the UGCC. In 1948
he began to act independently of the organization; he started publishing a newspaper (the *Accra Evening News*) and set up an organization (the
Committee on Youth Organization) that was responsible to him alone. Nkrumah was receptive
to the mood of the general public and toured the
country extensively, drawing into his fold the
rural farmers previously overlooked by the
UGCC.

In 1949 Nkrumah formally broke from the
UGCC and established the more radical Con-

vention People's Party (CPP). The UGCC did not disband, although many of its members followed Nkrumah into the CPP; for the next decade, the UGCC would be Nkrumah's most significant political opponent. Both of these parties set out to rid the land of the British but the CPP employed more radical tactics. In 1950 the CPP organized a campaign of civil disobedience, called Positive Action, which used strikes and boycotts of imported goods to increase pressure on the British. Nkrumah and many of his followers were jailed, but Positive Action had beneficial results. The new constitution (1950-51) extended voting rights and called for a black majority on the colonial councils. In the first elections after this constitution was enacted, the CPP emerged victorious, and Nkrumah was released from jail to become the leader of the African government. He had been arrested in 1948 after a widespread riot that neither he nor the other jailed scapegoats had instigated.

At this point, in 1952, the Gold Coast was functionally independent. The British would not fully withdraw, however, until 1957 whereupon Nkrumah became prime minister. In less than a decade Nkrumah had risen from being an unknown activist to leading the first free country of postcolonial Africa. His fame spread worldwide. His tactics of mass action provided a model for independence movements elsewhere, heartening Africans in other colonies. Within Ghana, his actions and sayings were followed reverently. He would pilot his country for 15 years, until his regime was toppled by a coup in 1966. For good or bad, Nkrumah put his stamp on every aspect of life in Ghana. By the mid-1960s economic stagnation, official corruption, and political strife had tarnished his image. In the euphoric atmosphere of 1952, however, his administration seemed full of promise.

The Novel in Focus

Plot summary. *The Beautyful Ones Are Not Yet Born* takes place in 1965 and 1966, one of the darkest periods of Ghana's history. It opens in the final months of Kwame Nkrumah's regime and closes with the coup that ousted him on February 24, 1966. The early promise of independence had given way to profound disillusionment, as poverty ran rampant and the economy, overdependent on foreign goods and capital, stagnated. Nkrumah was perceived to have withdrawn from the people and his Convention People's Party, which during the 1950s was the voice

of the masses, was now seen as serving only the interests of its own bureaucrats. Corruption and bribery were ubiquitous. As one historian writes, "It was with a shock that this country realized that a nation might dance its way to freedom, but might not dance its way through the thorny problems of self-government" (Hagan, p. 187).

The unnamed hero of *The Beautyful Ones Are Not Yet Born* has been thoroughly disillusioned by his country's decline. A high school-educated civil servant for the national railroad, he is torn between two contradictory desires. On the one hand, he wants to provide a comfortable life for his wife and children; on the other, he is repulsed by what is required to get rich in Ghana: participation in the bribery and corruption that accompany almost every public transaction. He refuses to surrender to fraud and corruption but, because this decision hurts his family, he cannot even feel proud of his own honesty.

The novel begins slowly. Its first half follows the protagonist through a day and a half of his life. Nothing extraordinary happens, which is precisely the point: Armah depicts the everyday life of a man in deep mental distress. He portrays the decaying urban landscape in pictorial detail: trash cans, outhouses, and crumbling buildings are lavishly described. Alongside such depictions runs a description of the interior life of the protagonist as he reflects on his predicament. He is torn between his desire to believe that life is beautiful and his fear that corruption and decay are inevitably a part of the human condition. In short, he represents the condition of Ghana in the mid-1960s—a country still young enough to remember the elation of independence but quickly succumbing to greed and self-interest.

In the course of the protagonist's day it becomes clear that corruption is everywhere. The first chapter begins with a description of a bus conductor who systematically steals from his passengers by giving them too little change. In Chapter Two the protagonist banters with a messenger who has just won the lottery, and who will have to bribe someone just to get his hands on his prize money. In Chapter Three the protagonist encounters corruption directly. While working alone in the railway office, he receives a visit from a timber contractor, Amankwa. Amankwa wants to bribe someone to ensure that his cut timber finds a place on the trains and is carried to port. Trying to conduct his business honestly, he has been told there is no space on the trains, even though he sees empty trains leaving for port every day. The protagonist steadfastly refuses to accept the bribe, incurring Amankwa's wrath. Though he has done nothing more than behave honestly, the protagonist feels like a criminal: "Everyone said there was something miserable, something unspeakably dishonest about a man who refused to take and to give what everyone around was busy taking and giving" (Armah, *The Beautyful Ones Are Not Yet Born*, p. 31).

SOMETHING ROTTEN

One of the most notable features of *The Beautyful Ones Are Not Yet Born* is the narrator's interest in waste, human and otherwise. The first chapter alone provides a detailed picture of an overflowing garbage can and a two-page philosophical treatise on the various types of grime on a banister. The outhouse in particular seems to fascinate the narrator. The protagonist's bowel movements are frequently and explicitly described; when Koomson visits the protagonist's house, he is shocked by an unnamed neighbor's violent diarrhea; and at the novel's climax, the narrator and Koomson must squeeze through the filthy drain of a communal latrine.

This aspect of the novel received a great deal of attention from reviewers. Some applauded it: "It calls for no small gift to expound on excreta and neither offend nor bore. . . . Armah brings it off" (Miller, p. 25). Others deplored it: "Armah's belief that realism comes only by spelling out every crude action, by rubbing the reader's nose in every vile smell, makes it impossible to recommend the book generally" (Herrick, p. 93).

Why does Armah devote so much attention to filth? First, it physically represents the novel's themes of decay, corruption, and waste—Ghana, it seems, is a figurative cesspool. More importantly, it provides a literary register for the protagonist's disgust at his surroundings. He finds using the bathroom a nauseating, but necessary, ordeal, as is negotiating the needs and expectations of his peers.

On his way home from work the protagonist encounters the central embodiment of official dishonesty: his classmate Koomson, who has risen through the CPP to a position of prominence. The protagonist sees Koomson in his luxury car, buying fruit and bread from a street vendor who gives him the honorific nickname of "white man." Koomson is the protagonist's foil; while the latter has been paralyzed by a desire to do right, the former has achieved great success

by his willingness to do anything. Before they part ways, Koomson announces that he and his wife will have dinner with the protagonist next Sunday night.

At home, the protagonist must face his wife, Oyo. Although they love each other, their marriage is strained to the breaking point because Oyo wants security and comfort, and cannot understand her husband's desire for honesty. She interprets his integrity as cowardice or stupidity. In a brief conversation, they quarrel about Koomson, about participating in corruption, and about the timber contractor. Oyo wants a toilet and other conveniences for her home. At the most elemental level, she wants a clean life like Estella Koomson's; the protagonist counters by saying, "Some of that kind of cleanness has more rottenness in it than the slime at the bottom of the garbage dump" (*Beautyful Ones*, p. 44). But for Oyo this is just cowardice: she likens her husband to the proverbial chichidodo, a bird that eats only maggots but is too fastidious to dig through the excrement where maggots live.

To escape the tension of this home life the protagonist goes to visit a friend, the Teacher, to whom he pours out his problems. The Teacher provides an uneasy sort of comfort—although he does not dispute his friend's right to remain honest, he also presents Oyo's plight sympathetically. In short, he clarifies the protagonist's sense of his own dilemma.

With Chapter Six the novel takes a turn. The narrative is interrupted by a long, first-person reminiscence by the Teacher, who provides the protagonist with an impressionistic account of the Teacher's own life. He speaks of the anger and frustration of his young manhood and of the violence and poverty of the final years of the colonial regime. He condemns the "old lawyers" and "yessir men" who first struggled for independence, claiming they were so infatuated with European ways that they failed to understand that this cultural worship merely ensured their continuing powerlessness: "How could they understand that even those who have not been anywhere know that the black man who has spent his life fleeing from himself into whiteness has no power if the white man gives him none?" (*Beautyful Ones*, p. 82). These pathetic creatures are briefly contrasted with the young Nkrumah, a poor man who spoke in the language of the people and did not base his authority on his relationship with the British. The Teacher and his friends were inspired, and they helped him to achieve Ghana's independence. But in the final irony, Nkrumah, who realized power by refusing to mimic those from whom he took power, ended up no different from the British or their African yessir men: "He was good when he had to speak to us, and liked to be with us. When that ended, everything was gone. . . . It [this degeneration] has happened to those around him, those who were not always there for the simple sake of the power they could find" (*Beautyful Ones,* p. 88). The Teacher's narrative ends with a long condemnation of Koomson, who began as a dock worker but, by learning to mouth the slogans of Nkrumah's CPP, rose through the bureaucracy by corruption and hypocrisy.

The Teacher's memories provide no answers for the protagonist's plight, but they do connect his individual predicament with the larger trends of Ghana's history. In the first half of the novel the protagonist feels he is alone, separated by his integrity from those around him, even his wife. The Teacher does not contradict that feeling of loneliness, but he does remind the protagonist (and the reader) that corruption is not an inevitable fact of life in Ghana. In a novel dominated by despair, this brief glimpse of a happier time provides a benchmark for optimism: it makes the protagonist's honesty noble rather than perverse.

After the Teacher's digression the plot of the novel quickens, moving to the night on which Koomson and his wife, Estella, visit the protagonist and Oyo. They are joined by Oyo's mother, a narrow-minded woman who despises her son-in-law. It turns out that Koomson has a proposition for his old friend. He wants to buy a yacht but is forbidden by government regulations from owning one himself, so he wants to register the boat in the protagonist's name. Although Koomson promises nothing more than an occasional gift of fish in return, Oyo and her mother are convinced that agreeing will win his favor, opening up further opportunities for wealth. The protagonist agrees to the plan, although skeptically.

This scene and the next one, in which the protagonist and Oyo go to Koomson's luxurious house, critique the European habits of Ghana's ruling class. Koomson and his wife prefer imported liquor and refuse to use the protagonist's humble outhouse; their own house boasts British-style silver and a German stereo. Koomson even mispronounces his own servant's name, speaking in the way of white men, "trying to pronounce African names without any particular desire to pronounce them well, indeed deriving that certain superior pleasure from that inability"

(*Beautyful Ones,* p. 147). At the last minute the protagonist refuses to sign the ownership papers for the boat, although he allows his wife to: this moral fastidiousness is joined to his certainty that Koomson will do nothing for the couple.

As it turns out, the man is right: they get nothing more than fish. However, the boat figures prominently in the next and final episode of the novel—the military coup that overthrows Nkrumah in 1966. At work the protagonist hears of the coup but refuses to participate in the celebratory processions. Only when he returns home is he forced to play a part in the drama, as he discovers Koomson, now facing arrest as a member of the ousted government, hiding in his bedroom. Out of common decency rather than political loyalty, the protagonist helps Koomson escape from approaching soldiers—ironically, by squeezing through the very outhouse the bureaucrat had earlier refused to use. They make their way to the dock and, after bribing the night watchman, escape on Koomson's yacht. Once Koomson is safely headed out of Ghana, the protagonist swims back to shore, where he falls asleep in exhaustion.

When he awakes he walks to a bus stop, witnessing the subsiding chaos that has followed the coup. In the final moments of the novel, he sees the graffiti from which the novel takes its name:

> The green paint was brightened with an inscription carefully lettered to form an oval shape:
>
> THE BEAUTYFUL ONES
> ARE NOT YET BORN
>
> In the center of the oval was a single flower, solitary, unexplainable, and very beautiful.
> (*Beautyful Ones,* p. 183)

This logo inspires him, but only briefly. He trudges home, all his despair returning as he realizes that nothing in his life has changed.

Lost illusions. Although the novel paints the Nkrumah regime as irredeemably corrupt, it is careful to avoid celebrating the new rulers of Ghana. In fact, it insists on the hypocrisy of those who participate in the overthrow. Unimpressed by the new leaders, the protagonist watches a demonstration from his desk:

> Through the window the sounds came: old songs with the words changed from the old praise for Nkrumah to insults for him. So like the noises of the Party when all the first promise had been eaten up and it had become a place

where fat men found things to swell themselves
up some more.

(*Beautyful Ones*, p. 158)

In the final chapter of the book the protagonist witnesses three acts of bribery and extortion
by officials of the new regime. Clearly, Ghana's
problems run deeper than a single bad leader or
a single corrupt party.

It seems that the root of the problem lay deep
in the independence movement itself. When he
began, Nkrumah created a broad-based popular
movement that could encompass Ghanaians
everywhere. Although the CPP often faced stiff
competition, this was usually limited to specific

CULTURAL COLONIALISM

One of the most significant intellectual influences on Ayi
Kwei Armah is the psychiatrist Frantz Fanon, who, though
born in Martinique, allied himself with the Algerian independence movement in the 1950s. In his **The Wretched of the
Earth** (also covered in *African Literature and Its Times*), Fanon
expounds a psychologically based theory of colonialism, arguing that decades of dependence on European decisionmak-
ers impoverished native African culture because leaders of the
newly independent countries were afraid to break free from
foreign advice and foreign aid. Because they had been trained
to see European culture as supreme and African culture as backward, success to them meant imitating European ways and acquiring European goods. In brief, they had an inferiority complex. According to Fanon, along with breaking free of economic
and political impediments to real independence, Africans must
learn once more to trust their own culture and history.

The applicability of this analysis to *The Beautyful Ones Are
Not Yet Born* cannot be denied. The government official Koomson, his wife, and even the protagonist's family are focused on
what Armah calls "the gleam": beautiful, highly processed, and
artificial foreign goods. Estella Koomson even complains that
Ghanaian drinks don't "agree with her constitution," as if she
were from somewhere else (*Beautyful Ones*, p. 131). Armah
makes it clear that Koomson's dereliction of duty springs from
an acquired dislike of the very people he is supposed to be
serving. One might argue that Armah eventually saw, in his
own following of European literary traditions, a subtler version
of the same cultural inferiority complex. Thus, his later novels
deal with, for example, African revolution (*Why Are We So
Blest?*) and Asante history (*The Healers*).

regions concerned about a single issue—for instance, wealthy cocoa farmers in the north disliked his agricultural policy. In the first years
sweeping opposition to Nkrumah was mostly
limited to the remnants of the old UGCC.

However, as the years passed the party that
had unified Ghana began to separate itself from
the nation. As Nkrumah's regime became more
authoritarian, the CPP became a culture unto itself, less concerned with promoting Ghana's general interest than with enriching and empower-
ing its own members. As the novel's Koomson
demonstrates, rising through the CPP ranks was
not so much a matter of effective service as it was
of cultivating the right relationships, ignoring the
corruption of one's peers, and keeping an eye out
for "unofficial" opportunities. The common
Ghanaian must have had the impression that the
CPP was a kind of parasite on society, little better than the British, except that now Africans
were doing the exploiting. To make matters
worse, economic failure and growing dissent led
Nkrumah to sponsor repressive measures, and to
cement his hold on power by outlawing opposition parties in 1964.

As the novel notes, the bitterest part of this
failure was that it represented a complete re-
versal of Nkrumah's original principles. Ghana
was not only oppressed, it was betrayed, and
the traitor was the very man who had promised
an end to oppression. The coup itself did nothing to change that basic fact. It later came to
light that Nkrumah was not particularly corrupt
himself; he had not rooted out the wrongdoing
of others around him, but neither had he exploited his position for personal profit. In the
long run, however, Nkrumah had overseen the
creation of a national political culture marked
by hypocrisy, greed, and naked self-interest. As
Armah intimates, it did not matter who filled
the seats of government and bureaucracy, or
what slogans they mouthed. Whether socialist
or capitalist, army or civilian, the real business
of government was to steal and squander the
wealth of the nation.

Sources and literary context. The most important contexts of *The Beautyful Ones Are Not Yet
Born* are political—the struggle for African freedom and the subsequent disappointment in the
realities of independence. Armah belongs to the
first generation of postcolonial African writers
and has been heavily influenced by the heady
mixture of political, economic, and cultural ideologies at play in the struggle to end colonialism. His career has encompassed journalism, let-

ter campaigns, and pedagogical theory as well as fiction.

Aesthetically, however, *The Beautyful Ones Are Not Yet Born* owes as much to European as to native traditions. It has little to do with the African proverbial and folkloric elements that energize other African novels of the time, such as Chinua Achebe's **Things Fall Apart** and Ngugi wa Thiong'o's **Weep Not, Child** (both also covered in *African Literature and Its Times*). The novel's portrayal of an alienated and confused individual has elicited comparisons to the existential novels of French writers Jean-Paul Sartre and Albert Camus; its lengthy passages of psychological description and its difficult syntax mark it as an heir to the works of European modernists such as James Joyce, Virginia Woolf, and D. H. Lawrence. At one point, Armah appears to have thought of himself as just a writer, not a distinctly African writer (Achebe, p. 41). He seems later to have revised this view, informing the African American poet Gwendolyn Brooks that his first novel was, in essence, too Eurocentric: "Future books, he assures us, will have an African focus, an absolutely African focus" (Brooks, p. 127). His subsequent novels have abandoned the existential and modernist style that characterize his first.

Events in History at the Time the Novel Was Written

After the coup. Although Nkrumah's regime (called, in retrospect, "the First Republic") was widely disliked and the coup that toppled him greeted with genuine warmth, the usurping government turned out to be incapable of reversing the slide into malaise that had made the coup inevitable in the first place. Despite the fact that the new leaders, members of the National Liberation Council (NLC), were capitalist rather than socialist, they shared many of the CPP's methods and attitudes. The NLC began by outlawing the CPP and arresting many of its members. Less than a month after taking power, the NLC issued a decree authorizing detention without trial: "The new leaders thus revealed their hypocrisy about democratic values as they repeatedly condemned Nkrumah's dictatorial inclinations, in practice using largely the same means" (Petchenkine, p. 35). In spite of the NLC's hostility to the CPP, many of Nkrumah's former aides found their way into the new government, ensuring that certain practices would be carried over. Although the NLC planned to return the government to civil-ian hands, and actually scheduled supposedly free elections for 1969, it was so afraid that Nkrumah might seize power that it interfered in the election from beginning to end. It outlawed the more socialist parties, harassed individual candidates, and continually changed the rules of procedure to give conservative candidates the advantage. Thus, when the period of military rule gave way to the Second Republic in 1969, not even the rosiest optimist would have heralded this change as a return to democracy. Most must have felt, as Armah felt, that while the names of the leaders had changed, their destructive and corrupt methods had not.

Reviews. *The Beautyful Ones Are Not Yet Born* received generally favorable, and often glowing, reviews. With this one book, Armah established himself as a writer with a worldwide reputation. One reviewer wrote, "This is a brash and powerfully colorful novel, and if it amounts to doing the laundry in public, we can only say *What a laundry!* and *What an heroic job at the scrub board!*" (Davenport, p. 1121). The critic Charles Miller added, "This is a valid and uncommonly arresting view of the abuse of power" (Miller, p. 51).

Although the novel was widely celebrated, it was also criticized by various African writers. The famous Nigerian novelist Chinua Achebe took Armah to task for insufficient respect for Africa:

> Armah is clearly an alienated writer complete with all the symptoms. Unfortunately Ghana is not a modern existentialist country. It is just a Western African state struggling to become a nation. So there is enormous distance between Armah and Ghana. . . . A man is never more defeated than when he is running away from himself.
>
> (Achebe, p. 40)

Charles Nnolim seconded this idea: "The first novel [*The Beautyful Ones Are Not Yet Born*] has nothing essentially Ghanaian about it: no specifically Ghanaian mannerisms or special brand of politics, no language in the local idiom of the people" (Nnolim, p. 109). To some extent, one may assume that Armah himself partly concurred with these objections, as his later work draws inspiration more consistently from sources in African culture.

—Jacob Littleton

For More Information

Achebe, Chinua. "Africa and Her Writers." In *Morning Yet on Creation Day*. New York: Anchor Press, 1975.

Afari-Gyan, K. "Nkrumah's Ideology." In *The Life and Work of Kwame Nkrumah*. Ed. Kwame Arhin. Trenton: Africa World Press, 1993.

Armah, Ayi Kwei. *The Beautyful Ones Are Not Yet Born*. London: Heinemann, 1968.

Brooks, Gwendolyn. *Reports from Part One*. Detroit: Broadside Press, 1972.

Davenport, Guy. "Old Tunes and a Big New Beat." *National Review*, 5 November 1968, pp. 1120-21.

Fraser, Robert. *The Novels of Ayi Kwei Armah*. London: Heinemann, 1980.

Hagan, George. "Nkrumah's Leadership Style." In *The Life and Work of Kwame Nkrumah*. Ed. Kwame Arhin. Trenton: Africa World Press, 1993.

Herrick, M. D. Review of *The Beautyful Ones Are Not Yet Born*. *Library Journal* (July 1968): 93.

Miller, Charles. "The Arts of Venality." *Saturday Review*, 31 August 1968, pp. 434-36.

Nnolim, Charles. "Dialectic as Form: Perjorism in the Novels of Armah." *African Literature Today* 10 (1979): 200-13.

Pellow, Deborah, and Naomi Chazan. *Ghana: Coping With Uncertainty*. London: Gower, 1986.

Petchenkine, Youry. *Ghana: In Search of Stability, 1957-1992*. London: Praeger, 1993.

Burger's
Daughter

by
Nadine Gordimer

Born in 1923 in the small mining town of Springs, South Africa, Nadine Gordimer is a white South African of Jewish descent. Her father, Isidore Gordimer, immigrated from Lithuania to escape the pogroms there, and her mother, Nan Myers Gordimer, was of English extraction. Nadine Gordimer was raised South Africa's white suburbs. She attended a convent school and, briefly, the University of the Witwatersrand in Johannesburg. Only slowly, she explains, did she gain a political awareness: "When you're born white in South Africa you're peeling like an onion. You're sloughing off all the conditioning that you've had since you were a child" (Gordimer in Malinowski, p. 204). Gordimer went on to write short stories, novels, and essays, winning the Nobel Prize for literature in 1991. Her works have explored the devastating effects of apartheid on her society. *Burger's Daughter* was her first extended portrayal of white revolutionaries in South Africa.

Events in History at the Time of the Novel

Before apartheid. At the turn of the twentieth century, the area now known as South Africa was embroiled in a war between the country's two prominent groups of white rulers. There were the descendants of seventeenth- and eighteenth-century European (mostly Dutch) settlers—named Boers (the Dutch word for "farmers"), then renamed Afrikaners—who sought to preserve the independence of their settler states. And there

THE LITERARY WORK

A novel set in Johannesburg, South Africa, and in the south of France in the 1970s; published in English in 1979.

SYNOPSIS

A young Afrikaner woman struggles to define her own identity and political stance against the legacy of her famous revolutionary father, who died in prison after a life spent fighting for the liberation of black South Africans.

were the descendants of the British, who sought complete dominance over the region they had partially occupied since the late eighteenth century. The British emerged victorious from the South African War (also called the Boer War; 1899-1902). By war's end, they had destroyed 30,000 Afrikaner farmsteads, razed whole villages, and placed thousands of Afrikaners in concentration camps. The defeat portended decline and assimilation for the Afrikaners, but they resisted absorption into the British empire, setting up private schools that relied on the Dutch as well as the English language, and generally promoting Afrikaner consciousness. Several years later, with only a few thousand British immigrants and a resistant Afrikaner population in the region, conditions improved for the Afrikaners. A new Liberal government in London granted South Africa's two Afrikaner states—the Transvaal and the Orange Free State—the right to self-government. In 1910 the Union of South Africa was formed, the hope being that the Afrikaners and British would resolve their differences and forge a single South African nation. The two Afrikaner states joined the two British territories of Cape Colony and Natal on a less-than-equal footing. Under the 1910 constitution, all four areas were bound by the will of the British Crown.

Many Afrikaners supported reconciliation, including the former Afrikaner generals Louis Botha—the new prime minister—and Jan Smuts, Minister of Defence and future leader of the United Party. At the same time, the Afrikaner fear of British domination was strong, provoking a group led by General J. B. M. Hertzog to form a new National party in 1914 to champion Afrikaner interests. When Botha and Smuts led South Africa into World War I, many viewed them as traitors to Afrikaner interests and in retaliation raised arms against the government. Though the uprisings were quickly put down, many Nationalist martyrs emerged, and in 1924 the National Party won more government seats than any of the other parties. It formed a brief alliance with the English-speaking Labour party, and Hertzog became prime minister of a coalition government, fighting hard over the next eight years for the Nationalist Afrikaner cause. A new flag was approved, consisting of small replicas of the former Afrikaner state flags along with the Union Jack; Afrikaans became an official language; and, in 1931, South Africa was freed from formal British control. Though Hertzog was satisfied with these gains, a more strident group of Nationalists began to organize against him, marshalling support from Afrikaners who faced poverty because of disorienting economic changes.

As more and more Afrikaners were forced by economic conditions to move to the nation's towns and gold fields, and to live in squalor among nonwhites—which, in their view, led to a "debasing [of] the entire Afrikaner stock"—Afrikaner leaders grew alarmed (Meredith, p. 17). A widespread prejudice of the day held the Afrikaners to be inferior to the British, which helped create an environment in which Afrikaners were now forced into competition with cheap black labor. Though Hertzog initiated a "civilized labour" policy that forced employers to privilege white workers over black workers wherever possible, such measures were not enough to counter the increasing poverty levels among the Afrikaners flooding South Africa's cities and towns. "Facing social upheaval and finding themselves ... at the mercy of British commerce and culture," Afrikaners began forming groups to preserve their own culture (Meredith, p. 19). One of these groups, the Broederband, developed a powerful, extensive, clandestine network of influence throughout the country. Initially formed to promote Afrikaner culture, the group slowly came to define its goal as total Afrikaner domination of South Africa.

In 1932 Hertzog joined Smuts in forming the United Party and the two entered into a coalition known as the "fusion government." Their aim was to unite all of white South Africa. At this point Afrikaner nationalists feared that Hertzog no longer represented their interests. In 1933 the Gesuiwerde National Party (GNP), heralded as a more pure, staunch, and "true" Afrikaner national party, was formed by a former preacher of the Dutch Reformed Church, Dr. Daniel Malan. Though the GNP made little impact initially, the Broederband steadily gained power and enfolded the new party into its ranks. Influenced by European fascism, Broederband intellectuals created theories and myths proclaiming, among other things, that the Afrikaners were a "chosen people" meant to fulfill a divine destiny in South Africa. Such ideas sparked the popular imagination and Afrikaner loyalty. The GNP gained some decisive victories during and after World War II, which South Africa entered after Smuts's prowar followers outvoted those of the antiwar Hertzog, prompting Hertzog's resignation.

Most Afrikaners were outraged at being forced to fight what they saw as Britain's war, and in the 1943 election the GNP won two-thirds of the Afrikaner vote, though it lost the election. Meanwhile, as the nonwhite urban population increased, threatening to equal that of whites, the "native question" became pressing. Smuts's policy had been vague; although, like most Afrikaners, he believed in white superiority and supported segregation, he offered no concrete solutions or resolute actions. In this respect the virulent GNP had the advantage over him. In 1948 Malan's National Party was voted into power, under the new campaign slogan *apartheid*. The slogan would crystallize into the notion that South African society consisted of distinct nations, each of which must live in its own separate area or homeland, and that blacks should be able to enter the white homeland only temporarily, as workers.

From segregation to apartheid. From the beginning, "the history of white colonization [in Africa] was one of conquest, plunder, and dispossession of the indigenous Black peoples and societies" (Harsch, p. 15). Only in the twentieth century, however, was the ideology of segregation perfected, in response to the unsettling effects of modernization and industrialization. In contrast to many colonies in the Americas, in South Africa the native populations suffered no great demographic losses, and were able to satisfy the white settlers' need for a labor force. Cheap black labor created the enormous wealth of the diamond and gold mining operations, constructed buildings and roads, and provided various domestic and commercial services within the expanding white population. It is true that most of white South Africa regarded blacks as barbaric, desired separation to preserve white "purity," and feared being submerged within the "black masses." However, the wealth enjoyed by many whites was gained through the exploitation of black workers, which made complete separation impractical. The result was "myriad laws, ordinances, and regulations that govern[ed] Black life" to insure white profit (Harsch, p. 13). The Union of 1910 had brought together South Africa's two dominant white groups—British and Afrikaner—at the expense of 80 percent of its population; from this union emerged one of the most pervasive systems of racial separation in the twentieth century.

Historians of South Africa usually distinguish between segregation, operative from 1900 to 1948, and apartheid, in effect from 1948 to 1990. Segregation was based on a number of laws that restricted nonwhites in almost every sphere. These laws included the 1911 Mines and Works Act (segregating workers); the 1913 Natives Land Act (segregating the races in rural settings and prohibiting land purchases by nonwhites); the 1923 Natives Urban Areas Act (segregating the races in urban settings); the 1936 Representation of Natives Act (completely abolishing the African franchise); and the 1936 Native Trust and Land Act (expanding the 1913 Natives Land Act). As a result of these laws, black South Africans were forced to leave their own lands, live on cramped reserves, enter the labor market, carry pass cards, and work for extremely low wages. Blacks could neither strike nor take jobs reserved for white workers. As Smuts explained to parliament in 1945, "all [white] South Africans are agreed . . . except those who are quite mad . . . that it is a fixed policy to maintain white supremacy in South Africa" (Smuts in Harsch, pp. 54-55).

In many ways apartheid was an extension and elaboration of segregationist measures; what was distinctive was the ideology and moralizing accompanying it. Whereas segregation had become more difficult to justify in a world that placed an increasingly high value on racial equality, apartheid claimed to divide ethnic groups vertically, making them equal but separate. One cabinet member described apartheid as the separation of "heterogeneous groups . . . into separate socioeconomic units, inhabiting different parts of the country, each enjoying in its own area full citizenship rights" (Eiselen in Le May, p. 208). Daniel Malan explained the policy in similarly euphemistic terms: "[L]ike a wire fence between two neighboring farms, [apartheid] indicates a separation without eliminating necessarily legitimate contacts in both directions, and although it places reciprocal restrictions on both sides it . . . serves as an effective protection of one another's rights" (Malan in Le May, p. 208). But, while most supporters presented apartheid as an ideal, equality-based solution to South Africa's racial problems, in effect it legislated and provided a morality for continued white domination over South Africa.

FROM A 1948 NATIONAL PARTY ELECTION MANIFESTO

We can act in only one of two directions. Either we must follow the course of equality, which must eventually mean national suicide for the white race, or we must take the course of apartheid through which the character and the future of every race will be protected. . . . [The National Party] therefore undertakes to protect the white race properly and effectively against any policy, doctrine or attack which might undermine or threaten its continued existence. At the same time, the Party rejects any policy of oppression and exploitation of the non-Europeans by the Europeans as being in conflict with the Christian basis of our national life. . . .

(Le May, p. 202)

When Malan's National Party came into power in 1948, it became the first South African government to consist of only Afrikaners. The party proceeded to "right" what it perceived as past wrongs against Afrikaners by releasing Afrikaner prisoners, privileging Afrikaners over the British in the workplace, and lengthening the process by which British immigrants could attain South African citizenship. At the same time, the Nationalists turned their attention to the "native problem," constructing "an apparatus of laws, regulations and bureaucracies" that would develop into "the most elaborate racial edifice the world had ever witnessed" (Meredith, p. 54). Interracial marriages, as well as sexual acts between the races, were banned; different racial groups were compelled by law to use separate restaurants, post offices, theaters, buses, and so on, or to use separate entrances and seats in public buildings. As residential areas for each racial group were demarcated, whole communities were uprooted to effect widespread racial sepa-

ration. Regarding this last piece of legislation (which became known as the Group Areas Act) in 1950, the Minister of the Interior explained:

> We believe that if we remove the points of contact that cause friction, then we will remove the possibility of that friction and we will be able to prevent the conflagration which might one day break out. This is what the Bill stands for. . . . Its object is to ensure racial peace. . . . It has been . . . designed to preserve White South Africa while at the same time giving justice and fair play to the Non-Europeans in this country.
> (Meredith, pp. 54-55)

Though apartheid rhetoric promised separation but equality, the areas demarcated for nonwhite South Africans, who were by far the country's majority, represented only a small percentage of the country's total land mass; as a result of this act, many nonwhites had no alternative but to build makeshift shantytowns on the outskirts of white-populated cities. In fact, overwhelming inequality was a standard feature of the ostensibly "equality-driven" apartheid legislation. Between 1948 and 1971, 151 racial laws were enacted, affecting every aspect of daily life—three times the number of racial laws enacted in the four decades preceding the National Party's reign, which would last until 1990.

Communism and antiapartheid liberation movements. Apartheid and the segregation measures preceding it were not met without resistance by either nonwhite or white South Africans. The African National Congress (ANC) was the first of several local organizations to become involved in the struggle for black political rights. Founded in 1912, the ANC was conservative in nature and composed primarily of prominent, Christian black men.

For the most part, African nationalist groups like the ANC saw communism as antithetical to their purposes. They generally condemned its class analysis approach as a strategy on the part of communists to limit the strength of control by Africans while using government channels to promote the Communist Party.

When the white National Party came to power in 1948, the relationship between black African nationalists and the mostly white CPSA altered significantly. Common opposition to apartheid brought the CYL (still part of the ANC) and the CPSA into cooperation, through their mutual goal of developing mass resistance to government oppression. This willingness to cooperate was more practical than ideological, however. When

SOUTH AFRICAN POLITICAL FACTIONS

ANC—African National Congress: Founded in 1912, the ANC is the oldest of South Africa's liberation movements. It provided black Africans with their first opportunity to join a political organization devoted to their interests.

CPSA—Communist Party of South Africa: The CPSA was devoted to socialist revolution in South Africa. Established in 1920, the CPSA was the first serious attempt to form a revolutionary party in South Africa.

CYL—Congress Youth League: The CYL was formed in 1944 by young men impatient with the conservativism of the ANC. Primarily an ANC pressure group, the CYL attempted to invigorate and hasten the struggle for black liberation.

COD—Congress of Democrats: Set up in 1953 by radical whites, many of whom belonged to the CPSA before it was banned, the COD was a multiracial dissident group that later became a key part of the Congress Alliance of 1955.

PAC—Pan-African Congress: Formed in 1959, the PAC set itself in opposition to the more conservative ANC. Its goal was black domination of South Africa, and its methods were more militant than the older group's.

SAP—South African Police: Formed at the 1910 Act of Union, the SAP was responsible for enforcing racial segregation and apartheid, and for putting down all resistance.

BOSS—Bureau of State Security: Formed after Balthazar Johannes Vorster came to power in 1966, BOSS was a privileged and powerful agency devoted to state security. Along with the SAP, BOSS was the dominant force in the intelligence community.

FRELIMO—Mozambique Liberation Front: In 1974 Portuguese rule collapsed in Mozambique and Angola—both neighbors to South Africa—and Frelimo came to power. Frelimo's victory inspired South Africa's black population; the group is mentioned often in *Burger's Daughter*.

South African Police survey the aftermath of a demonstration that ended with police firing upon the crowd.

the CPSA was outlawed in 1950, the ANC remained unaffected by communist ideas, but because of this banning and intensified government opposition against both groups, communists and black African nationalists strengthened their alliance. In the 1950s, when racist legislation was further bolstered by the new Minister of Native Affairs, Hendrik Verwoerd, the ANC was forced to become more strident. It was in this decade that "the young lions" like Nelson Mandela, Walter Sisilu, Oliver Tambo, Potlako Leballo, and Robert Sobukwe came to the fore—all "educated men who were unwilling to wait, as their elders had done, for some indefinite future when white men should have experienced a change of heart" (Le May, p. 215).

In June 1955 what came to be known as the "Congress Alliance" was formed among several different revolutionary groups, including the ANC, the South African Indian Conference, the National Union of the Organization of Coloured People, and the Congress of Democrats (COD), a white organization with communist connections. The Congress Alliance produced the Freedom Charter, a document demanding the abolition of apartheid and calling for universal suffrage, land redistribution, and other rights for nonwhites in South Africa. The government responded with a series of police raids in which papers were seized and people arrested, and, a

year later, it accused 156 revolutionaries of high treason. Stating that "South Africa belongs to all who live in it, black and white," the Freedom Charter anchored the nonracial revolutionary tradition of the Congress Alliance in a founding document (Lazerson, p. 2). Despite and because of these nonracial ideals of peace and brotherhood, relationships remained racially charged.

In other cases, there was overt hostility to white reformers. In 1959 the ANC split, and the PAC was formed. The argument between the ANC and PAC mainly concerned the role of nonblacks in the African nationalist struggle, as well as the widespread influence of communism within the Congress Alliance. Unlike the ANC, the PAC devoted itself to totally replacing rule by the white minority with rule by the black majority. The PAC's sentiments in this regard would also characterize the Black Consciousness Movement (BCM) that emerged in the early 1970s under the slogan "Black man you are on your own!" Indeed, as Rosa Burger discovers in *Burger's Daughter,* the white presence in antiapartheid liberation movements was often fraught with tension.

Enforcing apartheid—the South African Police. The South African Police (SAP) "were always in the front line in the enforcement of apartheid" (Cawthra, p. 1). Formed by the 1910

Act of Union, the SAP retained the features of the colonial military units preceding it—units such as the Cape Mounted Police and the Natal Mounted Rifles, which had helped conquer the black populations. The SAP was responsible for enforcing pass laws (which required black Africans to carry identification cards permitting and recording their entry into white areas), liquor laws (prohibiting blacks from drinking certain kinds of alcohol), and other restrictive, racially based edicts. It was also responsible for putting down any type of resistance. Consisting mostly of Afrikaner men by the 1940s, SAP became increasingly political as black militancy grew more widespread. For the most part, policemen saw nothing unusual in being placed in political positions and countering antigovernment threats. Their approach to the black population was "essentially authoritarian and confrontational"; by 1947 almost half of all prosecutions were for racially based crimes (Cawthra, p. 12). When Malan's National Party took office in 1948, the new government viewed the SAP as its first line of defense and increased the size of the force.

When, in the 1950s, the ANC began a program of noncooperation and civil disobedience—in 1952, for instance, Mandela led his followers in a passive resistance campaign—the police responded by jailing thousands of protesters. A series of violent confrontations between the SAP and antiapartheid protesters led the government to enact more repressive laws and to declare a state of emergency. The 1950 Suppression of Communism Act gave the SAP license to detain and imprison hundreds of mostly white revolutionaries, who were not always communists. Revolutionary forces fought back, engaging in the "cloak-and-dagger stuff" Rosa Burger describes in *Burger's Daughter* (Gordimer, *Burger's Daughter*, p. 141). In the first half of the century, the SAP had set up a Detective Branch to counter political "agitators"; in the second half this branch evolved into the Security Branch, or political police, who monitored and interrogated everyone suspected of antigovernment activity. Through intelligence efforts, the Security Branch was able to crack ANC and PAC underground networks, imprisoning hundreds of black nationalists.

In the 1960s—when Balthazar Johannes Vorster served as South African minister of justice and then as prime minister—the police acquired even more power. Vorster believed that decisive action was needed to counter increasing revolutionary activity, and "steered through parliament a string of laws which increased the

state's powers to banish, restrict and detain its opponents" (Cawthra, p. 15). By broadly defining what constituted terrorism or subversion, these laws allowed police to detain people indefinitely without trial and made it easier for the courts to convict political prisoners. Torture of detainees became routine. By the middle of the decade, the security police had put down most armed resistance but continued to hunt down potential enemies of the state. The police "stamped on the merest flickers of opposition," forcing potential enemies out of the country or placing them under house arrest (Cawthra, p. 15). When Vorster became prime minister in 1966, he created the Bureau for State Security, or BOSS. Along with the SAP, BOSS became one of South Africa's main intelligence forces. South Africa had effectively become a police state, with executions occurring so often that one scholar estimated that nearly half of the world's executions at the time were taking place in South Africa (Cawthra, p. 16).

Two of the SAP's most notorious acts occurred in 1960 and 1976; the levels of police brutality shocked the international community. In 1960 the PAC declared a nonviolent campaign in which large crowds would appear at police stations to surrender their pass cards and demand arrest. Thousands of unarmed blacks showed up at police stations nationwide and still more stayed home from work. Shooting into the crowds, police killed 87 and wounded 27 others in Sharpeville; in Langa they killed 17 more and wounded another 46. Their violence provoked a storm of criticism abroad and inspired massive protests across South Africa. Initially the government made concessions to blacks, temporarily allowing them to travel without pass cards, but in the long run little changed; as one historian puts it, "Sharpeville was the turning point where nobody turned" (Le May, p. 221). In 1976 another mass protest ended in police violence. When the government insisted that Afrikaans be used along with English for secondary school instruction, 15,000 blacks took part in an illegal protest march in Soweto. The police again opened fire, and this time the violence lasted a year, as protesters burned schools, attacked apartheid collaborators, and rioted in various locations across the country. Descriptions of the long, devastating Soweto Revolt appear at the end of *Burger's Daughter*:

> The School riots filled the hospital; the police
> who answered stones with machine-guns and

patrolled Soweto firing revolvers at any street-corner group of people encountered, who raided High Schools and picked off the targets of youngsters escaping in the stampede, also wounded anyone else who happened to be within the random of their fire. The hospital itself was threatened by a counter-surge of furious sorrow that roused the people of Soweto to burn and pillage everything the whites had "given" them in token for all, through three centuries, they had denied the blacks.

(*Burger's Daughter*, p. 342)

The Novel in Focus

Plot summary. *Burger's Daughter* opens with a flashback: a young Afrikaner schoolgirl, Rosa Burger, carrying an eider-down quilt and a red hot-water bottle, waits outside the prison in which her mother is being detained. As a witness remembers, "the child was dry-eyed and composed, . . . an example to us all of the way a detainee's family ought to behave" (*Burger's Daughter,* p. 12). On that day Rosa's father, Lionel Burger, had put the plight of others before his own, "going from police station to police station, trying to establish for helpless African families where their people were being held"; he knew "that his schoolgirl daughter could be counted on in this family totally united in and dedicated to the struggle" (*Burger's Daughter,* p. 12). Rosa's mother and father were famous white communist revolutionaries who dedicated their lives to the struggle for a free and equal South Africa. Constant surveillance, clandestine meetings, and prison stays were parts of their everyday existence. The magnitude of their cause was so great that Rosa, now 27, with both parents dead (her father having died a hero in prison), has had her own identity subsumed within that of her famous parents, and most potently within that of her father. When her father, who had been a doctor, served his final, lengthy prison sentence, Rosa was obligated to visit him twice a month, bringing him books and coded messages from the outside world. As she herself remarks,

My mother is dead and there is only me, there, for him. Only me. My studies, my work, my love affairs must fit in with the twice-monthly visits to the prison, for life, as long as he lives—if he had lived. . . . I have no passport because I am my father's daughter. People who associate with me must be prepared to be suspect because I am my father's daughter. And there is more to it, more than you know—what I wanted was to take a law degree, but . . . I had to do

something else instead, anything, something that would pass as politically innocuous. . . .

(*Burger's Daughter*, pp. 62-63)

The bulk of *Burger's Daughter* takes place after the death of Rosa's parents (about a year after the death of her father), and centers on her search for an identity and a life outside of her parents' world. The narration shifts between first and third person. When the narrative is presented in her voice, Rosa addresses an ex-lover, her father's first wife, and her father. Set in South Africa, Part One concerns the hidden political worlds in which her parents circulated. Most of the people with whom Rosa has contact at this point are her parents' friends and colleagues, their children, and various hangers-on; through flashbacks as well as the efforts of one of Lionel Burger's biographers, the reader learns of the Burgers' past, and the events surrounding Lionel's trial, imprisonment, and death. Being under constant surveillance, the daughter of political agitators, Rosa has learned to keep secrets, speak in codes, relay sensitive messages, and mask her feelings—"cloak-and-dagger stuff," as she wryly calls it (*Burger's Daughter,* p. 141). Rosa attempts to explain such a life to an ex-lover:

If Lionel and my mother . . . if the concepts of our life, our relationships, we children accepted from them were from Marx and Lenin, they'd already become natural and personal by the time they reached me. D'you see? It was all on the same level at which you—I—children learn to eat with a knife and fork, go to church if their parents do, use the forms of address by which the parents' attitudes—respect, disapproval, envy, whatever—towards people are expressed. I was the same as every other kid.

(*Burger's Daughter*, p. 50)

It was a life marked by both exhilaration and tragedy. The Burgers' house was open to people of all races and to revolutionaries whose families became entwined with their own. Intense political discussions took place around the swimming pool, the same pool in which Rosa's brother later drowned as a child. One black revolutionary's son, called "Baasie," or "little boss," lived with the family because his father, a member of the African National Congress, moved around too much to be able to care for him. On the rare occasion when both of Rosa's parents were in prison at the same time, Rosa was sent to her aunt and uncle's country hotel, while Baasie was sent to his grandmother; Rosa's relatives were traditional Afrikaners embarrassed by Lionel's politics and at the same time proud to be associated with someone so famous and respected. Indeed, throughout the novel Rosa will encounter those who thrill to be in the presence of one who seems so politically dangerous and upright—people who always define Rosa through the legend that was her father.

A year after her father's death, however, Rosa attends a gathering in which, for the first time in the novel, she encounters a "new political factor" that suggests her father's "political relevance is almost over" (Daymond, p. 60). During a long debate, a young black revolutionary, Duma Dhladhla, speaks of her father in less than reverential terms: "He knows what he was doing in jail. A white knows what he must do if he doesn't like what he is. That's his business. We only know what we must do ourselves" (*Burger's Daughter,* p. 160). Later Dhladhla explains:

> White liberals run around telling blacks it's immoral to unite as blacks, we're all human beings, it's just too bad there's white racism, . . . we must work out together the solution. . . . Whites don't credit us with the intelligence to know what we want! We don't need their solutions.
>
> (*Burger's Daughter,* p. 160)

Shortly thereafter Rosa starts arranging her departure from the country. Because of her political associations, she is under constant surveillance and is denied a passport. She has to rely on an influential Afrikaner to finally obtain one for her. Her reason, as the Afrikaner man understands, is clear: "*I want to know somewhere else. The mother, the father; their destination, here or anywhere, did not have to be hers*" (*Burger's Daughter,* p. 185). At a decisive point during these preparations, Rosa witnesses a brutal scene: a drunk black man is beating a donkey violently with a whip, an act that to Rosa at that moment seems "the sum of suffering" (*Burger's Daughter,* p. 210). Though she realizes that, as a white woman, she could easily stop the donkey's suffering, she does nothing:

> I drove on. I don't know at what point to intercede makes sense, for me. . . . I drove on because the horrible drunk was black, poor, and brutalized. If somebody's going to be brought to account, I am accountable for him, to him, as he is for the donkey. Yet the suffering—while I saw it it was the sum of suffering to me. I didn't do anything. I let him beat the donkey. The man was a black.
>
> (*Burger's Daughter,* p. 210)

It is this scene that finally compels Rosa to leave South Africa—"after the donkey," she says, "I couldn't stop myself. I don't know how to live in Lionel's country" (*Burger's Daughter,* p. 210).

Part Two of *Burger's Daughter* takes place mainly in the south of France, where Rosa stays with Katya, her father's first wife, whom she'd seen only in photographs. Her new life is strikingly different from the one she has left behind: sensual, languorous, filled with sunbathers and lovers, people living for present pleasures rather than the distant, intangible "Future" that had driven her father and his colleagues (*Burger's Daughter,* p. 264). Here Rosa relaxes in the company of Katya and her circle, in a place where she is recognizable only as a foreigner, an English speaker—"nobody could see me, there, for what I am back where I come from"—and where she can stay in a room made for "a girl, whose sense of existence would be in her nose buried in flowers, peach juice running down her chin" (*Burger's Daughter,* pp. 229-30, 231). When she tells a young man that her father had died in a prison in South Africa, he responds by explaining that his father had collaborated with Nazis, and had been sent to prison also. "We have to forget about [our fathers]," he says. "It's not our affair. I'm not my father, êh?" (*Burger's Daughter,* p. 243).

Rosa does seem to forget, for a while; from Katya, who had recognized "'a whole world' outside what [Lionel] lived for," Rosa attempts to learn how to "defect from [her father]" (*Burger's Daughter,* p. 264). She meets and begins a passionate affair with a married French academic, Chebalier. The affair brings her into a new awareness of herself as a sensual being, who, as Bernard Chebalier's mistress, "isn't Lionel Burger's Daughter; [and is] certainly not accountable to the Future" (*Burger's Daughter,* p. 304). Soon Rosa is planning to live permanently in Paris, in an apartment Chebalier will find for her and with working papers that he, through various contacts, will obtain for her. First, however, she goes to London, where Chebalier will join her for a romantic vacation. While she waits there, Rosa is befriended by a young Indian couple, who take her to a party where she encounters other South Africans. Afterwards, and for the first time since she left South Africa, Rosa begins attending political gatherings and allowing herself to be known as Lionel Burger's daughter. At one of these meetings she recognizes her childhood playmate, Baasie.

To Rosa's surprise, Baasie is aloof and disdainful. He is offended when she calls him by his childhood nickname, and informs her that his given name is Zwelinzima Vulindlela. That night he calls her and, despite her sleepy protests, makes her hear him out.Echoing the earlier sentiments of Duma Dhladhla, he says he did not like the way she had spoken that night about her father:

> Everyone in the world must be told what a great hero [Lionel] was and how much he suffered for the blacks. Everyone must cry over him and show his life on television and write in the papers. Listen, there are dozens of our fathers sick and dying like dogs, kicked out of the locations when they can't work any more. Getting old and dying in prison. Killed in prison. It's nothing. I know plenty of blacks like Burger. It's nothing, it's us, we must be used to it, it's not going to show on English television.
> (*Burger's Daughter*, p. 320)

Rosa is sickened by Zwelinzima's contempt for her. Immediately after his phone call and apparently without telling Chebalier that she is leaving, Rosa returns to South Africa in the novel's brief third part. "I can't explain to anyone," she narrates, "why that telephone call in the middle of the night made everything that was possible, impossible" (*Burger's Daughter*, p. 328). Despite her happy, passion-filled sojourn in France, Rosa decides that she "cannot be other than a creature of her time and place . . . cannot be other than Lionel's child" (Daymond, p. 168). She takes a job at Baragwanath Hospital and begins working with crippled black children there, whose numbers increase when the Soweto revolt sends them in droves, shot and otherwise wounded, to the hospital.

> No one can defect.
>
> I don't know the ideology:
>
> It's about suffering.
>
> How to end suffering.
>
> And it ends in suffering. Yes, it's strange to live in a country where there are still heroes. Like anyone else, I do what I can. I am teaching them to walk again, at Baragwanath Hospital. They put one foot before the other.
> (*Burger's Daughter*, p. 332)

On and after October 19, 1977, a number of people are detained, arrested, or banned in South Africa, including Rosa, who "was taken away by three policemen . . . waiting at her flat when she returned from work on an afternoon in November" (*Burger's Daughter*, p. 353). In prison she encounters some women she knows, including the beautiful, black Marisa, who sings hymns that

"the other black women took up and harmonized" (*Burger's Daughter*, p. 355). Because she has a spinal ailment, Marisa is allowed to visit Rosa's cell twice a week for therapy, and during these visits "laughter escaped through the thick diamond-mesh and bars of Rosa's cell" (*Burger's Daughter*, p. 355). One day Katya receives a letter from Rosa that includes a reference to a water-mark of light entering her cell every sundown—something Lionel Burger had once mentioned about his cell. On this note the novel ends.

SOUTH AFRICAN FREEDOM SONGS

In jail the novel's Marisa sings ANC freedom songs and a hymn by Miriam Makeba—a popular, exiled black singer of South Africa (*Burger's Daughter*, p. 355). Freedom songs were an important part of African resistance in the 1950s and thereafter. The songs included defiant lyrics such as those below, taken from protest tunes of the times:

- "We Africans! We cry for our land and they took it. Europeans must let our country go"
- "Jan van Riebeek has stolen our freedom" (referring to the Dutch founder of the first white community in South Africa)
- "Hey Malan! Open the jail doors. We want to enter. We volunteer. . . ."

(Anderson in Byerly, p. 223)

Black consciousness and white revolutionaries. In *Burger's Daughter* Rosa Burger witnesses a shift in relations between blacks and white revolutionaries fighting for a new South Africa. Whereas Lionel Burger had been able to work closely with the black revolutionaries of the ANC, by the time Rosa reaches adulthood, Black Consciousness has become a powerful political movement. The Black Consciousness Movement (BCM) and the man who became known as its father, Stephen Biko, viewed whites—and particularly white liberals—as irrelevant in the South African national liberation struggle. The presence of whites in almost every black political organization was interpreted by the BCM's leaders as supreme arrogance, an implication by whites that blacks could work only with white leadership and guidance. Biko argued that blacks, accustomed to oppression and feelings of inferiority, could acquire strength only by distancing themselves from whites and by building black consciousness. In *Burger's Daughter* these ideas influence Duma Dhladhla and Zwelinzima Vulindlela, both of whom suggest that there is no place for Rosa in their revolution.

The question of the white role in the South African struggle vexes the novel's Rosa Burger; it also affects Nadine Gordimer, a white woman and writer living in South Africa. Discussing the complex relationship between races in South Africa before apartheid ended, Gordimer explains:

> There are vast areas of actual experience—rubbing shoulders with blacks, having all kinds of relationships with blacks.... It's not as simple as it sounds ... all kinds of conflicts, of a very special nature ... arise between black and white. ... I do believe that when we have got beyond the apartheid situation—there's a tremendous problem for whites, unless whites are allowed in by blacks, and unless we can make out a case for our being accepted and we can forge a common culture together, whites are going to be marginal, because we will be outside the central entities of life here....
>
> (Gordimer in Bazin and Seymour, pp. 168-69)

BRAM FISCHER—THE REAL LIONEL BURGER

~

As an Afrikaner, Bram Fischer was fairly rare among South Africa's white revolutionaries. Fischer was born in 1908 in the Orange Free State, where his grandfather had been prime minister and his father president of the Orange Free State Supreme Court. In fact, Fischer's grandfather had been responsible for the enactment of the 1913 Natives Land Act, one of the first laws to ensure the dispossession of blacks in South Africa. By aligning himself with the black cause, Bram Fischer rejected his heritage even more forcefully than other white revolutionaries—all of whom, given apartheid's rules, at some level had to abandon (and be abandoned by) their own people for the sake of a nonracial social ideal. In the 1940s Fischer helped the ANC draft a new constitution and also served on the CPSA's Executive Committee; he became an advocate for political prisoners too, whom he defended in South African courts. For his various political activities Fischer was arrested in 1964, but he fled during his trial in order "not to remain a spectator, but to act" (Fischer in Lazerson, p. 101). Captured in 1966, Fischer was sentenced to life in prison. He was diagnosed with cancer in 1974 and died shortly after being released to go live with his brother.

In 1982 Gordimer published an article, "Living in the Interregnum," in which she identifies herself with that part of the white South African population struggling to understand how they might offer themselves to a new South Africa. She discerns that "blacks must learn to lead and whites to follow, blacks to talk and whites to listen" (Daymond, p. 170). Gordimer offers a more optimistic view of the role of white South Africans in the nation's political struggles, and records "a black friend's encouraging comment, 'whites must learn to struggle.'" To her it conveys a faint hope that whites will be able to 'look for some effective way, in the living of their own personal lives, to join the struggle for liberation from racism'" (Daymond, p. 170).

Sources and literary context. In the first chapter of her collection of essays, *Writing and Being,* Gordimer describes the moment in which the inspiration for *Burger's Daughter* came to her:

> I was waiting outside a prison to visit a friend detained for political interrogation, and there was the schoolgirl daughter of [an anti-apartheid activist friend of mine], presented to me, as it were, in the group of prison visitors....
>
> What was she thinking?
>
> What was her sense of a family obligation that *chose for her* to stand there among the relatives of thieves and murderers?
>
> She was in a gym frock and blazer of a conventional private school for young ladies; how did her genteel bourgeois teachers and classmates receive a girl whose father was in prison for treason against the State that protected their white privilege?
>
> (Gordimer, *Writing and Being,* p. 8)

Gordimer had long been interested in the lives of white South African revolutionaries—writing, for instance, about Bram Fischer, the Afrikaner revolutionary on whom Lionel Burger is based. *Burger's Daughter* is Gordimer's first piece of fiction to center upon such a figure, prompting one critic to ask: "What has made it possible for Gordimer to finally write *Burger's Daughter*?" (Daymond, p. 60). M. J. Daymond argues that Gordimer, like Rosa, was able to begin this process of self-questioning only after the age of Lionel Burger had ended—when the confidence of white revolutionaries had shifted to self-consciousness, and when the vigilance of the Black Consciousness Movement signaled that whites might no longer have a secure place within a future South Africa.

Reviews. Initially banned in South Africa, *Burger's Daughter* consequently gained a wide

Bram Fischer, shown with his daughter, Ilse, was the Afrikaner revolutionary upon whom Gordimer based the character of Lionel Burger.

and receptive international audience. Those protesting the ban included Heinrich Böll (*The Lost Honor of Katharina Blum*), Paul Theroux (*The Great Railway Bazaar*), and John Fowles (*The French Lieutenant's Woman*), as well as the Association of American Publishers, the Freedom to Write Committee, and the PEN American Center. In response to this outcry, South Africa's Publications Control Board appointed a special literary committee to report on the novel. The committee judged the book to be biased and even called its literary integrity into question.

Critics elsewhere in the world had a different opinion. In the *New York Times Book Review* Anthony Sampson called *Burger's Daughter* Gordi-

mer's "most moving novel, going to the heart of the racial conflict in South Africa" (Sampson, p. 1). A. J. Mojtabai complimented Gordimer on the novel's universality:

> Miss Gordimer . . . living in the thick of real trouble, is subdued, sober, very sober, indeed. She scarcely raises her voice, yet her voice reverberates over a full range of emotion. Her precision is very fine, her discriminations are reflective and subtle, her mind marvelously awake. She remains stubbornly in place, linked to the earth and to recognizable inhabitants and institutions of the earth. She is not a regionalist—or, if she is, her region includes ours, wherever we may be.
>
> (Mojtabai, p. 7)

According to Nadine Gordimer herself, the strongest praise came from the actual schoolgirl who, standing among a group of prison visitors, initially inspired the character of Rosa Burger. Before the novel's publication, Gordimer sent a copy of the manuscript, along with a long letter, to the now-adult schoolgirl. The woman did not respond for several weeks. One afternoon she came, unannounced, to Gordimer's house, carrying the manuscript.

> She said, "This was our life."
>
> And nothing more.
>
> I knew this was the best response I should ever have to that novel. Perhaps the best I should ever have in respect of any of my fictions....
>
> For she was not speaking of verisimilitude...; she was conceding that while no one can have total access to the lives of others ... the novelist may receive, from the ethos those lives give off, a vapour of the truth condensed, in which, a finger tracing upon a window-pane, the story may be written.
>
> (Gordimer, *Writing and Being*, p. 12)

—Carolyn Turgeon

For More Information

Bazin, Nancy Topping, and Marilyn Dallman Seymour, eds. *Conversations with Nadine Gordimer*. Jackson: University Press of Mississippi, 1990.

Byerly, Ingrid Bianca. *The Music Idaba: Music as Mirror, Mediator, and Prophet in the South African Transition from Apartheid to Democracy*. Ph.D. diss., Duke University, 1996.

Cawthra, Gavin. *Policing South Africa: The SAP and the Transition from Apartheid*. London: Zed Books, 1993.

Daymond, M. J. "*Burger's Daughter*: A Novel's Reliance on History." In *Momentum: On Recent South African Writing*. Ed. M. J. Daymond, J. U. Jacobs, and Margaret Lenta. Pietermaritzburg, South Africa: University of Natal Press, 1984.

Gordimer, Nadine. *Burger's Daughter*. London: Jonathan Cape, 1979.

———. *Writing and Being*. Cambridge, Mass.: Harvard University Press, 1995.

Harsch, Ernest. *South Africa: White Rule, Black Revolt*. New York: Monad Press, 1980.

Lazerson, Joshua L. *Against the Tide: Whites in the Struggle Against Apartheid*. Boulder, Colo.: Westview Press, 1994.

Le May, G. H. L. *The Afrikaners: An Historical Interpretation*. Cambridge, Mass.: Blackwell, 1995.

Malinowski, Sharon, ed. "Nadine Gordimer." In *Contemporary Authors New Revision Series*. Vol. 28. Detroit: Gale Research, 1990.

Meredith, Martin. *In the Name of Apartheid: South Africa in the Postwar Period*. London: Hamish Hamilton, 1988.

Mojtabai, A. G. "Her Region is Ours." *New York Times Book Review*, 24 August 1980, p. 7.

Sampson, Anthony. "Heroism in South Africa." *New York Times Book Review*, 19 August 1979, p. 1.

Chaka

by
Thomas Mofolo

> **THE LITERARY WORK**
>
> A semi-biographical novel set in Zululand from circa 1780 to 1828; completed in 1909; published in Sesotho in 1925, in English in 1931.
>
> **SYNOPSIS**
>
> Chaka of the Zulus achieves kingship and great power at the price of his humanity.

Almost half a century after the death of Chaka, the founding ruler of the Zulu kingdom, Thomas Mofolo was born in Basutoland, a small country known today as Lesotho, surrounded on all sides by the nation of South Africa. The Basuto people came to Basutoland as refugees in the early 1820s during a period of great turmoil caused in part by Griqua raids and in part by Zulu military expansion under Chaka, the great Zulu leader. *Chaka,* the first novel written in an African language to achieve an international readership, is the last of Mofolo's three published novels and is considered to be the author's greatest work. In *Chaka,* Mofolo, a missionary-educated Christian, broke with the proselytizing style of his earlier novels and wrote of traditional pre-Christian African culture. Some considered the novel a dangerous encouragement of pagan superstition, and Basutoland's sole missionary-run publishing company did not release *Chaka* until many years after its completion. Perhaps due to the frustration of this experience, after *Chaka,* Mofolo left Basutoland and stopped writing, turning his attention to business ventures. He died in poverty in 1948 after being deprived of his property under a South African law limiting black ownership of land. The subject of his novel, the Zulu warlord Chaka, remains a character of intense debate.

Events in History at the Time the Novel Takes Place

Zululand and the Zulu. At the time of Chaka's birth in the 1780s, the Zulu were a small chiefdom of cattle herders living in the hilly grasslands between the Indian Ocean and the Drak-ensberg Mountains that parallel Africa's southeastern coast. The Zulu were but one of many little chiefdoms and kingdoms of the Nguni, the cultural and linguistic group inhabiting this region. The country in which the Nguni dwelt provided ample grazing for huge herds of cattle, which played an important part in the Nguni economy and culture. Due, however, to a series of droughts, these grasslands began to fail in the late eighteenth century, and the resulting competition for pastures drove the Nguni to war against each other. Two kingdoms gained dominance during this period—the Ndwandwe under their leader, Zwide, and the Mthethwa under their leader, Dingiswayo, to whom the Zulu allied themselves in exchange for protection.

Nguni peoples of the period lived in villages that housed extended families or clans. The Nguni practiced polygyny, with a single homestead consisting of a circular thatched house for the patriarchal head of the family and a separate circular house for each of his wives and their respective children. The houses were arranged around a central cattle pen and surrounded by a sturdy wall. A typical village consisted of several such family homesteads, representing different branches that shared common descent from a hereditary chief, or *inkosi*. According to oral tradition, the common ancestor of the Zulu people was a man named Zulu, who established a village in a valley considered to be the Zulu homeland, or Zululand, today known as KwaZulu.

Nguni chiefs held power in both this world and the world beyond. They served as commanders of armies, judges of disputes, and chief emissaries to the spirit world of the ancestors. Chiefdoms passed from father to son, but in polygynous Nguni society the firstborn son of a nuclear family was not necessarily considered the rightful heir. Rather, the first son born to the chief's first wife inherited his father's chiefdom. The king employed the services of various male age-grade guilds, or *amabutho*. Young men would join the amabutho around the age of 17, with an *ibutho* (singular of amabutho) being comprised of young men born a year or two apart. The amabutho served their chief until they were dismissed at his will to pursue marriage. Before that time, amabutho hunted, herded, farmed, built structures, and, importantly during the time of the droughts, engaged in warfare.

Traditionally, warfare among the Nguni was highly ritualized and had more to do with shaming one's opponent than killing him. Warriors would stand a good distance apart from one another and hurl insults as often as they hurled spears. The light Nguni spears often did not cause much more damage than the insults, and could be easily parried with the stout Nguni shields. During the late eighteenth-century droughts, all this changed; oral history imputes the changes (discussed below) to the influence of Chaka.

Zulu belief and medicine. Traditional Zulu belief posits a first being, *uMvelinqangi*, who lives "above" with the "Princess of the Sky," *inkosazana yezulu*. The Zulu do not have immediate recourse to uMvelinqangi or inkosazana yezulu, who are conceived of as remote deities; the people can, however, petition them through the ancestors, the spirits of the dead of one's clan. The ancestors are believed to retain the personalities they had in life and to continue their lifestyle beneath the earth, where they herd cattle and raise crops. Ancestors are keenly interested in the welfare and behavior of the descendants whom they have left behind. If the ancestors approve of a descendant's actions, they can provide that person with protection against misfortune and disease. Thus,

when good things happen, Zulus say "the ancestors are with us." In order to honor the ancestors and gain their protection, Zulus sacrifice goats and cattle. The ancestors need these sacrifices in order to be integrated into the realm of the dead; prior to sacrifice on their behalf, the newly dead lead a lonely existence in a sort of limbo that is separate both from the world of the living and the spirits of the ancestors. If an ancestor is displeased by a descendant's bad behavior or failure to sacrifice, he or she can cause illness, crop failure, or general bad luck. Thus, when bad things happen, Zulus say "the ancestors are facing away from us."

The bad things that can happen when the ancestors turn away are linked to the Zulu concept of *isifo*, or disease, which refers not only to physical ailments, but also to general misfortune and susceptibility to misfortune. Isifo may be caused by the ill will of the ancestors or by harmful substances that occur naturally in the environment or are deliberately placed there by one's enemy. An example of a natural substance that can cause disease is *umkhondo*, an invisible trace left behind by people and animals in places where they have been. A person becomes infected with harmful umkhondo, such as that of wild animals or new mothers, through physical contact, through inhalation, or simply by stepping over tracks.

Closely related to the Zulu concept of disease is the Zulu concept of medicine, or *umuthi*, which refers to substances with the power to heal or cause good, as well as to substances with the power to harm or cause ill, depending upon the intentions of the user. Umuthi is for the most part herbal, though it sometimes contains animal matter, and takes the form of powders, pastes, teas, and the like. There are two kinds of umuthi: that which works independently and that which works only in the context of ritual. Because of harmful umuthi that may be used against a person and the abundance of natural isifo-causing substances in the environment, positive, strengthening umuthi is frequently used to fortify the individual. In the novel, Chaka receives such strengthening umuthi from his doctors.

As in the novel, Zulu medical practitioners can be either male or female. Male practitioners are *inyanga* and learn their trade through apprenticeship to other inyanga. Female practitioners are *isangoma*, or "diviners," and gain their skills through the ancestors, who bestow upon them clairvoyant powers. A patient generally goes to an isangoma to receive a diagnosis, and then may seek treatment either from an isangoma or an inyanga, or, in modern times, from a Western-trained doctor. An isangoma uses various methods to learn the cause of her patient's isifo: she may simply listen to the voices of her ancestors; her ancestors may speak directly to the patient; or she may throw bones and read the cause of her patient's ailment from the bones' positions. Those who use umuthi primarily to harm are known as *umthakathi,* or "night-sorcerers," of whom more will be said later.

Chaka. Sometime in the 1780s, a son named Chaka was born to Prince Senzangakhona of the Zulu and a woman named Nandi of the Langeni. Chaka grew up with his mother among the Langeni, who neighbored the Zulu. Eventually mother and son left the Langeni and came to reside among the Mthethwa, so that when Chaka grew old enough to join an ibutho, he fought under the Mthethwa leader Dingiswayo, and not under the Zulu leader, his father, Senzangakhona.

Various sources account for Chaka's estrangement from his father in different ways. Some African informants claim that Chaka's parents never married, and even that Chaka's birth was hidden from his father. Other African sources claim that Chaka's parents did marry, but not until after Chaka was conceived, adding that the hasty marriage led to tension within the family. A number of sources cite Nandi's fierce temperament as the reason for her expulsion from her home with Senzangakhona; elsewhere it is suggested that the pressures of drought and a diminishing food supply sent Nandi, as Senzangakhona's youngest and least powerful wife, back to her parents' home. In any case, Chaka apparently grew up in unusual circumstances that led to a difficult childhood in which his peers tormented him, treatment to which he responded with a violence that caused his mother and himself to be cast out of her homeland. Another explanation sometimes given for their departure from the Langeni is the need to stay on the move in search of food and water in those troubled times.

In his service under Dingiswayo, Chaka quickly gained a reputation as a great warrior. While fighting in Dingiswayo's amabutho, Chaka is credited with designing a new shorter spear, the *assegai,* to be used specifically for stabbing in hand-to-hand combat—an innovation that allowed the Mthethwa to gain further ascendancy in warfare. In return, Chaka gained the love and support of Dingiswayo in the matter of Chaka's succession to Senzangakhona's kingship when

Chaka (or Shaka) Zulu, the great warrior and first ruler of the Zulu kingdom.

Senzangakhona died at a young age. According to some accounts, Dingiswayo treated Chaka with medicines to give him a "'magical' ascendancy" over his father, and as a result Senzangakhona grew ill and died, whereupon Chaka took his place (Hamilton, p. 60). Others claim that Senzangakhona died of natural causes, but that Chaka wrested the kingship from Sigujana, another son of Senzangakhona, who had been appointed by his father as the rightful heir. In any case, Chaka became Zulu chief in the year 1816.

Reports indicate that, as Zulu chief, Chaka continued his military innovations. He made his troops discard their clumsy sandals and harden their feet by treading on thorns so that they could run barefoot into battle. He is remembered as a crafty tactician and a harsh disciplinarian who executed his soldiers for any show of cowardice or disobedience. Shortly after Chaka's accession to chieftaincy, his mentor, Dingiswayo, was captured and killed by a rival king, Zwide of the Ndwandwe, whereupon Chaka is reported to have cried out, "Zwide has killed my father!" (Knight, p. 20). The close connection between Dingiswayo and Chaka perhaps allowed Chaka to claim the Mthethwa kingship. As leader of the

Mthethwa, Chaka commanded all the chiefdoms that owed allegiance to this powerful community, who now owed allegiance to Chaka's people, the Zulu.

Seeking to expand the limits of his power, Chaka established a new royal Zulu village named Buluwayo, "the place of killing," and began to war against neighboring chiefdoms. Chaka consolidated his power by requiring that the young men of all the peoples under Zulu dominion come to serve under him in the Zulu amabutho. Chaka thus promoted a sense of unity among the hundreds of clans under his power, who came to regard themselves as Zulu. Accounts of this period of Zulu expansion, known as the *mfecane,* or "crushing," characterize it as a time of great violence and devastation. Chaka is depicted by his enemies as a power-mad warlord whose armies massacred entire peoples, burning their lands and plundering their cattle, reducing the few survivors to starvation or cannibalism. Another possible explanation is that drought-induced famine turned the various chiefdoms and kingdoms against each other in increasingly desperate competition for disappearing resources. More recently, some historians have suggested that Chaka's brutality was fabricated by European slavers of the nineteenth century to conceal the true cause of the mfecane: their own depredations. Debate over the true origins of the mfecane is ongoing.

The coming of the Europeans. Although Europeans had already established colonies in other parts of southern Africa, by the mid-1820s the only white people who had strayed into Nguni land were a handful of shipwrecked sailors whom the Nguni regarded as pathetic. Eventually word spread to the residents of the British Cape Colony (now part of South Africa) of a powerful king named Chaka, and this news piqued interest in his wealthy and as yet uncontacted African kingdom. In 1824 British Lieutenant Francis Farewell led an expedition to establish trade in ivory with the powerful king. Farewell's party eventually made it to Buluwayo where Chaka graciously entertained them and expressed an interest in their firearms. The party asked Chaka to sign a document granting them title to the strategic port of Natal where their ship had landed and Chaka, unfamiliar with European notions of land ownership, granted their request. Nguni society had no concept of land ownership by individuals; a king might control the land for a time, but only as a function of his power, not as a legal right.

It seems that Chaka regarded the Natal party's request for land as he would the request of any small chiefdom or people for a place in the Zulu kingdom. They would be a subject clan occupying the land at Chaka's pleasure, owing the king allegiance when required. The Farewell party, like any other subject clan, were induced to fight in Chaka's battles, and it has been suggested that this experience changed their view of Chaka. Whereas the party's previous accounts of the king had emphasized his goodwill and hospitality, later accounts described Chaka as a dangerous savage. Perhaps Farewell's party saw a side of Chaka in battle that was not evident in daily life, or perhaps, as some historians suggest, Farewell found it expedient to portray Chaka as a scoundrel in order to secure support from British authorities, which he needed to expand trade.

While hunting elephant with members of the Farewell party in 1827, Chaka received word that his mother was gravely ill. He immediately marched his hunting party to Nandi's residence several miles away; Nandi died of dysentery soon after her son's arrival. Chaka's reaction was extreme, and his hysteria is reported to have been shared by the Zulu. Thousands died in the week following Nandi's death, reported Henry Francis Fynn of the Farewell party, some from the customary abstention from food and water in times of mourning, others by killing their neighbors in a frenzy of grief. Those who did not appear to be sufficiently mournful were executed at Chaka's command.

In 1828 Chaka sent a group of Zulu ambassadors to Cape Colony. These were accompanied by two members of Farewell's party who wished to establish an overland trade route to the Cape. Simultaneously, Chaka launched an attack against the Mpondo peoples settled along the trade route that the Englishmen wished to establish. Chaka's ambassadors arrived in Cape Colony at a time of political upheaval and were denied an official audience. Instead, they were detained and questioned and suspected of being spies before they were allowed to leave. Members of the Farewell party said Chaka felt the Cape colonists had made a fool of him.

Death of Chaka. Chaka was assassinated on September 22, 1828, stabbed to death outside his own house by his two brothers, Dingane and Mhlangana, sons of Senzangakhona by other wives. Whether these two were driven by a desire to free the Zulu from a bloodthirsty despot or a desire merely for personal power is unknown. They struck while Chaka's armies were away on campaign; by the time the armies returned, Dingane had murdered Mhlangana and succeeded to Chaka's kingship. Perhaps the people were glad to be rid of Chaka; perhaps the returning armies, who had been defeated, were happy to be spared his customary punishment for failure. In any case, the people accepted Dingane as ruler, and unceremoniously cast Chaka's body into the fields to feed the hyenas. Eventually, it is believed, his corpse was buried in an old grain pit, and today a stone monument marks the place where Chaka's body is said to lie.

The Novel in Focus

Plot summary. Senzangakhona is a king without an heir. None of his wives has yet borne him a son, and he has begun to worry that his wealth and his kingship will be lost to his lineage when he dies. Therefore, Senzangakhona decides to take another wife. At a dance, he notices a beautiful and dignified young woman named Nandi to whom he is instantly attracted. She, in turn, is attracted to him, and agrees to a private meeting with the king. Senzangakhona asks Nandi to engage in sexual intercourse with him and, despite the fact that out-of-wedlock pregnancy is punishable by death, Nandi agrees. When she becomes pregnant, Senzangakhona hastily marries her, and he soon gains the male child, named Chaka, for whom he has longed. Senzangakhona sends word to the Mthethwa king Jobe, to whom the Zulu owe allegiance in exchange for protection, that Chaka will be his successor.

At first, Nandi's co-wives are pleased that the newcomer has provided an heir for the family. Soon, however, the other wives bear sons of their own and, since Zulu royal succession does not follow seniority of the king's children but rather the seniority of the king's wives who bear the children, the wives claim that their sons supersede Chaka as heirs to the kingship. Senzangakhona, who is fond of Chaka and his mother, refuses to revise the order of succession. Therefore, the senior wives employ a sorcerer to turn the king against Nandi and her son. The wives also threaten to reveal the circumstances of Chaka's conception until Senzangakhona finally agrees to change the order of succession and to exile Nandi and her child from his kingdom.

Mother and son seek refuge in Nandi's homeland, but gossip has spread that Chaka is a "child of sin" who should never have been born, and the boy is subjected to torment by his peers (Mo-

folo, *Chaka,* p. 11). Other boys, with whom Chaka herds calves, gang up and beat him regularly, at times nearly killing him, and Chaka never understands why. Through experience, he grows strong and becomes adept at combat. In addition, Nandi takes Chaka to a doctor who gives the boy special medicines to make him strong, fearless, and eager to fight. This doctor informs Nandi that "the events that will take place around the life of this child are of great importance," and instructs Chaka to bathe in a river at dawn at the time of each new moon (*Chaka,* p. 14).

THE "REAL" CHAKA

"That man used to play around with people. A man would be killed though he had done nothing, though he had neither practiced witchcraft, committed adultery, nor stolen."
(Baleka ka Mpitikazi, Zulu informant, in Knight, p. 28)

"[Chaka was] a savage in the truest sense of the word, a monster, a compound of vice and ferocity without one virtue to redeem his name from the infamy to which history will consign it."
(Nathanial Isaacs, British visitor to Chaka's kingdom, in Knight, p. 9)

"[Chaka,] to do him justice, is for a savage the best-hearted of his race."
(James King, Port Natal trader, in Hamilton, p. 41)

"King Shaka rose like a colossus in his day and age to make KwaZulu a place of Zulus. . . . He made one people out of many peoples. . . . King Shaka . . . was the greatest visionary of his time."
(Zulu king Zwelithini, Shaka Day speech, September 24, 1992, in Hamilton, p. 11)

While still a child, Chaka demonstrates his courage and strength by killing a lion that has been menacing his village. Through this act, he incurs the resentment of the village men, who all fled from the lion in fear, but he gains the respect of the village women, who sing his praises and mock his enemies. Nandi's co-wives and their sons hear of the insults directed against them and their hatred of Chaka increases. Many people would like to see him dead.

Early one morning as Chaka bathes according to the doctor's instructions, an enormous water serpent raises its head out of the black water. It approaches Chaka, who neither fights nor flees because the doctor has enjoined him not to do so, "no matter what may appear" (*Chaka,* p. 23). The serpent comes face to face with him, sticks out two long tongues that wrap around Chaka's head, and then proceeds to coil its body entirely around Chaka's. After licking every inch of Chaka's body, the snake withdraws and disappears into the dark waters. From a patch of reeds, disembodied voices prophesy in song a brilliant future for Chaka. After these events, Chaka's mother is anxious to consult her doctor to learn of their significance, presently to no avail. The doctor has died but has sent for another doctor to attend Chaka.

Soon thereafter Chaka rescues a girl from a hyena that stole her from the house where she was sleeping. None of the other young people in the house, nor indeed any of the adults in the village, makes any attempt to save the girl; hyenas are regarded as familiars, or animals in the service of witches, and are thus extremely feared. Chaka's brother Mfokazana, senior to him in succession to his father's throne, happens to be visiting Chaka's village and sleeps in the young people's house next to the girl, who is regarded as his sweetheart, yet even he does nothing to help her. When Chaka slays the hyena, he again arouses admiration and resentment in equal parts, the latter particularly in Mfokazana, who is now disgraced. Determined to kill his rival, Mfokazana attacks his brother, and a general melee ensues with some villagers taking Chaka's side, some Mfokazana's. When Senzangakhona arrives on the scene and demands Chaka's death, it is too much, and after breaking his spear in battle, Chaka flees, determined to never return again. In the face of such injustice, he decides that "from that day on, he would do just as he pleased, and that, whether a person was guilty or not, he would simply kill him if he so wished, for that is the law of man" (*Chaka,* p. 35).

While wandering the land as an outcast, Chaka falls asleep one day underneath a tree and awakens to find a strange man confronting him. From his unkempt appearance and the many pouches he carries, Chaka knows at once that the man is a doctor. This man, named Isanusi, seems to know all about Chaka. Apparently the man is the doctor for whom Nandi's doctor sent. Before he will help Chaka, Isanusi demands that Chaka obey him absolutely, and Chaka agrees. Isanusi

asks Chaka what he wants and Chaka replies that he wants his father's kingship. Isanusi responds by offering Chaka a kingship that will surpass all others and to which all other kings will owe allegiance. Chaka eagerly accepts the offer.

Isanusi treats Chaka with various powerful medicines to make him invincible. Together the two make their way to the village of Dingiswayo, successor to Jobe and the king to whom Senzangakhona now owes allegiance. Dingiswayo has heard of Chaka's brave feats, and welcomes the young man into his household and into his army. Nandi is already with Dingiswayo, to whom she has fled for protection after the events surrounding the hyena attack. Chaka soon proves himself through valorous fighting. In short order, he advances to the rank of commander of one of Dingiswayo's best regiments. Much to his pleasure, Chaka finds that his abilities do not produce resentment but rather admiration among Dingiswayo's men, who prize a brave fighter above all else. Dingiswayo himself comes to love Chaka like a son.

Isanusi, meanwhile, has left because of old animosity between himself and Dingiswayo, but sends two of his servants to help Chaka. These are Malunga, "a beautiful and refined young man" whom Dingiswayo instantly recognizes as evil, and Ndlebe, a seeming half-wit (*Chaka,* p. 57). Dingiswayo forbids Malunga to remain in his village, but Ndlebe is allowed to stay and serves Chaka by unobtrusively observing everything and reporting the news back to Chaka. Malunga meets up secretly with Chaka during battles beyond the village boundaries and suggests tactics that increase Chaka's renown as a warrior. Meanwhile, Chaka never speaks of Isanusi to either his mother or Dingiswayo, promotes the misconception that Ndlebe is a half-wit, and lies outright when asked about his relationship with Malunga.

Senzangakhona dies and Mfokazana assumes his father's kingship, but Dingiswayo refuses to recognize Mfokazana as Senzangakhona's rightful heir. Senzangakhona never informed Dingiswayo or his father, Jobe, of any change in the order of succession since the initial message that Chaka would be heir to the kingship. With the backing of Dingiswayo, Chaka battles his brother for the kingship and wins. Chaka further strengthens his ties to Dingiswayo through engagement to Dingiswayo's favorite sister, Noliwa, a woman whose physical and moral perfection are the earthly image of "the beauty and profound love of [the] Creator" (*Chaka,* p. 71).

Soon thereafter, Dingiswayo is captured and held prisoner by an enemy king. Chaka hears of this and sends messengers to offer Dingiswayo's captors anything they want in return for Dingiswayo's life. But before these messengers reach the royal village, Malunga and Ndlebe spread the false rumor that Dingiswayo is already dead. Upon hearing this, the messengers abandon their mission, and as a result, Dingiswayo truly is killed. The people of Dingiswayo's kingdom unhesitatingly offer the kingship to Chaka in return for his protection from the attacking armies of the enemy king. Chaka accepts and vanquishes the invading troops, his success due in part to the order he gives his troops to use their spears for stabbing instead of throwing.

With Dingiswayo out of the way, Isanusi returns to Chaka's side and asks him if he is now satisfied or if he desires a kingship still greater than the one he currently has. Chaka replies that he desires the greatest kingship possible, though it be obtainable only through the terrible medicine that Isanusi claims it requires. This medicine is the blood of the person whom Chaka loves best, Noliwa. Chaka readily agrees to sacrifice his beloved, remarking that "in this world there isn't anything I love other than kingship, war, and commanding armies" (*Chaka,* p. 102). Chaka himself must kill Noliwa for the medicine to be effective. He commits this deed in her house, as he caresses her by the fire, suddenly stabbing her in the armpit with a knitting needle. When her body is found, drained of blood, Chaka accuses Noliwa's serving women of sorcery and has them executed, whereupon "the last spark of humanity remaining in him [is] utterly and finally extinguished in the terrible darkness of his heart" (*Chaka,* pp. 127-28).

In pursuit of greatness Chaka builds a royal city in which he institutes new customs and laws. On Isanusi's advice Chaka shuns marriage and instead keeps a harem of women in his royal compound. He proceeds to have the children they bear him murdered so that there will be no heirs to challenge his kingship. He also forbids his troops to marry until they prove themselves with unusual bravery in battle or they reach middle age. Chaka leads his armies in attacks against neighboring kingdoms, capturing cattle and killing all the inhabitants. Among Chaka's own soldiers, those who lose their spears, fail to capture an enemy spear, or flee the scene are mercilessly slaughtered when they return to the royal village. This is the means by which Chaka encourages bravery in battle. He goes on a violent rampage, attacking chiefdoms and villages without cause, spreading his kingdom as far as he can. Those who flee Chaka's notorious armies descend upon neighboring villages in their flight, fighting the inhabitants for food and shelter. Mass migrations result and, as Chaka's troops burn fields and steal cattle, mass starvation as well. Whole peoples are wiped out, and some turn to cannibalism as a result of the scourge of Chaka.

Eventually Chaka returns to manage the affairs of the royal city, and commands his troops to push the limits of his kingdom ever further. Without battle to satisfy his bloodlust, Chaka turns his aggressions against his own people, whom he kills for the slightest semblance of an infraction. Meanwhile, his troops begin to chafe under the harsh restrictions. Some defect to different kingdoms; others plot to overthrow the despot. As he observes these developments, he takes to executing anyone who seems to be overly popular among his troops. This injustice further fuels resentment against him. Nandi, who desires a grandchild, abducts a pregnant member of Chaka's harem and hides the young woman until she gives birth. Although Nandi conceals the child from Chaka, he soon finds the infant, and when Chaka's shadow falls upon his son, the child dies. Furious, Chaka murders his mother in the same manner as Noliwa.

Despite Chaka's constant killing, the medicine within him cries out for more blood. To satisfy it, Chaka begins to murder his own people in droves, looking for any excuse to kill. Finally, he takes some troops just beyond the village and, through contrivance, manages to get them to kill one another. But even this is not enough. Chaka is plagued by horrible dreams and visions of the people he has killed. When he is in this weakened state his younger brothers, Dingana and Mhlangana, who have been plotting against Chaka for some time, attack him, stabbing their brother to death. Before he dies, Chaka tells his brothers that they will be thwarted in their desire for kingship when he is dead because "*umlungu,* the white man, is coming, and it is he who will rule you, and you will be his servants" (*Chaka,* p. 167). Chaka is not buried but left in the open fields for the wild beasts to devour. Even these, however, shun him; finally Dingana orders the intact corpse to be buried, lest Chaka rise again.

The individual vs. the collective in *Chaka.* In the novel, Chaka uses various strengthening medicines in the pursuit of power. As discussed above, such strengthening umuthi are an integral part of traditional Zulu medicine, in which they are used to counteract the many harmful substances that threaten to cause isifo, or disease. Zulus believe, however, that care must be taken that people who live together are strengthened at the same time, for if one comes into contact with someone who has been strengthened to a greater degree than oneself, one can become sick. Thus power, specifically an imbalance of power, is regarded by the Zulu as dangerous.

CHAKA'S PRAISES

~

. . . They said Shaka [Chaka] would not rule,
Would not be king
Yet that was the very year Shaka inherited a life of comfort.

Ferocious one of the armies of Mbelebele
Who unleashed his fury within the large villages
So that till dawn the villages were tumbling over each other.

Fire of the dry tinder, of Mjokwane of Ndaba,
Fire of the dry tinder scorches fiercely. . . .

(From *Ushaka* by Chakijana, Son of Msenteli,
Zulu praise-singer in *Chaka*, p. 119)

Umthakathi is a Zulu word for "power," and it is also the word for "sorcery," or the pursuit of power by harming others through magical means. Anyone can practice umthakathi, the most common method of which is the hiding of harmful umuthi in the environment of one's intended victim. Those who practice sorcery only against their enemies or rivals are considered to be decent members of society in good standing— only their victims would regard them as evildoers. There are those, however, who are believed to practice umthakathi against everyone indiscriminately and without cause. These are known as "night sorcerers," and they are born, according to Zulu belief, "with an evil heart" (Ngubane, p. 31). Night sorcerers are always men, and their umthakathi consists of hiding harmful substances in people's homes as well as scattering them indiscriminately in public places. Those regarded as night sorcerers in Zulu society tend to be unusually successful and hence powerful men with a reputation for arrogance and selfishness.

Traditional Zulu society, and indeed traditional Nguni society, is highly cooperative. The institution of polygyny ensures that families are large, and that the individual exists within a web of relations to whom he is obligated and who are obligated to him. Nguni religion reinforces the value of community in its emphasis on pleasing the ancestors through behavior that furthers the survival and well-being of the group. The cooperation of age guilds to carry out the work of the group brings members of a generation together, and the marriage custom of *lobola,* wherein the groom's family gives cattle to the family of the bride, creates a bond between pastoral clans because, as explained in Thomas Mofolo's novel, "a head of cattle is a great uniter of people" (*Chaka,* p. 90).

Inevitably tensions arise between people, and in a collective culture in which everyone must cooperate, such tensions can be devastating. The Nguni regard antisocial behavior as the most egregious crime, and exile as the most extreme form of punishment. In this culture where seemingly nothing is achieved without a group effort involving both the living and the dead, it is no wonder that individual power is equated with sorcery and that individuals with power who also exhibit selfishness are regarded as evil. Power, like strengthening umuthi, must be shared or else it destroys the individual and the group. These attitudes towards power appear in *Chaka.* The key method Chaka employs in his pursuit of power is sorcery. Isanusi, a character invented by Mofolo, can be likened to a night sorcerer whose influence on Chaka is diabolical. Isanusi's medicines strengthen Chaka, but Chaka can be strong only through the destruction of others, most notably Noliwa.

When Thomas Mofolo wrote *Chaka* in the early 1900s, his country of Basutoland was host to Christian missionaries who taught not only reading and writing but also Christian and European values—values that conflicted in many ways with the traditional values of the Basuto who are, like the Zulu, a Bantu people. The conflict was between a primarily individualistic culture and a primarily collective culture. Traditional Basuto religion, like traditional Zulu religion, focuses on pleasing the ancestors, whereas Christianity's focus is salvation of the individual soul. Similarly, Basuto economic structure was based on barter and cooperation between members of large extended families while European economic structure was based on individual competition for monetary gain. In ad-

Cetshwayo, Chaka's nephew and one of his successors, was captured and imprisoned by the British in 1879. Here, Cetshwayo and some of his wives, under the orders of Commander Crawford Caffin, board a small boat bound for the H.M.S. *Natal* anchored offshore Zululand.

dition, the missionaries in Basutoland actively opposed certain collectivity-promoting African practices such as polygyny, age guilds, and ancestor veneration. Thus the unity of the Basuto people was being undermined at just the time when, as colonial powers laid claim to African territory, the Basuto most needed to present a united front.

The figure of Chaka, who helped exacerbate the tendency of chiefdoms to turn on one another, even as he turned troop against troop at the end of Thomas Mofolo's novel, can be seen as emblematic of the disruptive forces threatening southern Africa at this time. He exemplifies the pursuit of personal power at society's expense, a value promoted by Europeans in Africa and also evident in the African figure of the night sorcerer. Chaka's pursuit of power brings the people together as "Zulus," but this same power turns the people against one another in flight from Chaka's depredations, even reducing them to the ultimate antisocial behavior, cannibalism. Chaka's pursuit of power also allows him to achieve a great kingship, but it is a power very much identified with sorcery. Ultimately the power destroys him.

Mofolo's Chaka is an outsider. Driven from his father's clan, driven from his mother's clan, he meets his end outside the walls of the village he himself built. In his outsider status Chaka resembles the Europeans, outsiders to African culture, who promoted among Africans the pursuit of individual power exemplified by Chaka and so inimical to the collectivity valued in traditional African society.

Sources and literary context. In the introduction to *Chaka*, Thomas Mofolo speaks about the novel's relationship to fact: "I am not writing history, I am writing a tale, or I should say I am writing what actually happened, but to which a great deal has been added, and from which a great deal has been removed" (*Chaka*, p. xv). Though not a history, *Chaka* is a text woven with strands of historical tradition, both written and oral. Mofolo, who was born to Christian Basuto parents and educated in missionary schools in his native tongue, Sesotho, as well as in French, had access to several published histories of the Zulu, and much of *Chaka* tallies with the accounts in such works as *The Diary of Henry Francis Fynn*, written by a member of the Farewell trading party. In addition, before writing *Chaka*, Mofolo bicycled through Zululand, where he consulted the Zulu praise singer Chakijana, quoted in *Chaka*. He probably discussed the great Zulu king with other informants in Zululand as well. Mofolo must have also heard accounts of Chaka from the Basuto people of his community, for whom Chaka was an important historical figure; the novel follows recorded oral traditions about Chaka in many regards.

THE LEGACY OF CHAKA

~

Since the early 1970s, September 24, the day of Chaka's death, has been celebrated as "Shaka Day" in the KwaZulu-Natal region of South Africa, former Zululand, where the memory of Chaka is evoked as a symbol of Zulu identity. On this day the current Zulu monarch addresses his subjects in speeches promoting Zulu nationalism.

In 1986 the South African television miniseries *Shaka Zulu* aired to millions of viewers. It told the story of Chaka's interactions with the Farewell party, and was criticized by one reviewer as being "Shaka through White Victorian eyes" (Hamilton, p. 173). In 1988 a successful African hotel-chain established Shakaland, a "living museum to Zulu culture" built around one of the sets created for *Shaka Zulu* (Hamilton, p. 187). In Shakaland, visitors become guests in a re-creation of the homestead of Chaka's father, Senzangakhona, where they are introduced to Zulu history and culture by actors portraying members of a traditional Zulu household.

Through the purely fictional elements of *Chaka*, one can trace the profound influence of Mofolo's novel on subsequent treatments of the story of Chaka in poetry, drama, and fiction. For example, Mofolo invented the character Isanusi and his servants, Malunga and Ndlebe, as well as Chaka's sacrificed beloved, Noliwa; Isanusi subsequently appeared in the Sengalese writer Léopold Sédar Senghor's 1956 drama *Chaka*, in the Malian writer Seydou Badian's 1961 *The Death of Chaka*, and in the Guinean writer Djibril Tamsir Niane's 1971 *Chaka*. Some of the later African treatments of Chaka present a more favorable picture of the Zulu king, depicting him as the hero of the Zulu people who brought together the scattered clans. Other African treatments focus, as Mofolo's novel does, on the corruption of power and ambition.

Events in History at the Time the Novel Was Written

Moshoeshoe and Basutoland. In *Chaka*, the Basuto chief Moshoeshoe is a minor character, a subject king who manages to stay on good terms with Chaka by sending him gifts of crane feathers. The real Moshoeshoe is a cultural hero who led his Nguni people to safety in the time of the mfecane, and established a haven for other people fleeing Chaka's soldiers on the fortresslike slopes of Thaba Bosiu, the "Mountain of the Night." In the early 1830s Moshoeshoe invited French Christian missionaries to come and educate his people, who would as a result become the most literate African people in southern Africa. Later, when Basutoland faced encroachment by Boer farmers (whites mainly of Dutch descent, now called Afrikaners), Moshoeshoe sought the protection of the British, who proclaimed Basutoland to be British territory in 1868. Basutoland, however, maintained its sovereignty in that the British followed a policy of "protection without control" (Spence, p. 15). The Basuto government was still in the hands of Basuto chiefs when Thomas Mofolo was writing *Chaka* in the early 1900s.

The French missionaries had, perhaps, a more profound influence on the Basuto than did the British government. They introduced writing and eventually established newspapers in the Basuto language, Sesotho. They set up schools throughout Basutoland, where, as discussed above, European values and the principles of the Christian faith were taught alongside reading and writing. The schools trained missionary-educated youths like Thomas Mofolo who became in some sense alienated from the culture of their ancestors but also became those who could most effectively challenge European encroachment on European terms.

Zululand and Chaka's successors. Meanwhile in Zululand, the Zulu kingship had passed from Chaka's brother Dingane to another son of Senzangakhona, Mpande, who in turn passed the kingship to his son, Cetshwayo. There were two groups of white settlers to contend with: those from Great Britain and the Boers. Under Dingane in 1838-39 the Zulu lost control of lands south of the Tukela River to the Boers, but remained a strong independent kingdom north of that river under first Mpande and then Cetshwayo. The British took over the colony of Natal from the Boers in 1845 and employed a policy of minimal interference in the Zulu kingdom's affairs. After diamonds were first discovered in Africa in 1868, the British authorities began to push for a wider unification of the various southern African territories. To create a pretext for intervening in the Zulu kingdom, the British in 1878 made demands that an independent kingdom could not be expected to accept, culminating in the requirement that the Zulu military be dismantled. Cetshwayo refused. The Zulu troops, who possessed a minimal number of outdated firearms, managed to repel the first British attack, but were ultimately defeated in 1879. The British took Cetshwayo prisoner, disbanded his troops, and transferred control of the Zulu to a group of puppet chiefs who answered to the British. Cetshwayo managed to get his kingship back through a public-relations visit to London, but in exchange he would henceforth answer to British authorities. Soon thereafter, civil war erupted between different Zulu chiefdoms and clans during which King Cetshwayo died.

Cetshwayo's son, Dinuzulu, succeeded his father and reigned from 1884 to 1913. Dinuzulu made an unsuccessful alliance with a group of Boer adventurers against the British. Captured by the British in 1887 and imprisoned for ten years, he was afterward demoted to district chief, though the Zulus still honored him as their unofficial king. During this period, drought and locusts combined to destroy some 90 percent of Zulu crops, while rinderpest, a livestock disease, killed some 90 percent of Zulu cattle. Then, between 1902 and 1904, the British government opened nearly half of what remained of Zululand to white settlement and use, and instituted a tax on the African population. Such pressures resulted in Zulu uprisings from 1906 to 1908, in which thousands of Zulus were killed and Dinuzulu was once more arrested and imprisoned. It may have been the witnessing of these events that inspired Thomas Mofolo to explore the beginnings of the Zulu nation that in the early 1900s was suffering so greatly.

Reception. The first printing press was established in Lesotho in 1861 by Christian missionaries, and missionaries still controlled Lesotho publishing in 1925, when *Chaka* was published. The reason for the lapse between the completion of *Chaka* in 1909 and its publication in 1925 is unknown, but given Thomas Mofolo's sudden departure from Lesotho in 1910 and the reactions of some of the missionaries to the novel when it was eventually published, it seems that the author had some difficulty getting approval for *Chaka*. One missionary described *Chaka* as "an apology

for pagan superstitions," and exhorted his fellow missionaries to remember that "the literary value of a work should not make us forget the pernicious effects it can have" (Paris Evangelical Missionary Society in Lesotho, in Molema, p. 24). A similar critique appears in a letter to the editor of a Lesotho newspaper, which describes *Chaka* as "poison among the nation" that contains "fabrications" and reinforces the "misconceptions of people in darkness" (Thoahlane in Swanepoel, p. 151). Another Lesotho reader of *Chaka,* however, praised the book's presentation of fact and found it to be "unforgettable even when one goes out to the fields" (Khoachele in Swanepoel, p. 152). This sentiment was echoed by a second Lesotho reader, who described *Chaka* as "a fine book, one that is entertaining, written with skill and with wide knowledge," and who argued, "there is not the slightest danger that this book can cause to the nation" (Potsane in Swanepoel, p. 152).

Upon its translation into English in 1931, *Chaka* received praise principally for what one review described as "genuine insight into the mind and traditions of the African peoples as they were before the coming of the white man" (*Times Literary Supplement* in Knight, James, and Brown, p. 739). Reviewers of the time considered the literary value of the novel only secondarily, though in favorable terms, such as those in a review that proclaimed *Chaka* "a work of art" characterized by "virile and eloquent" writing (*New Republic* in Knight, James, and Brown, p. 739). It is perhaps this same "virile" quality that yet another review refers to as "crudity," deeming the novel, nonetheless, to be "a work of genius" (*New Statesman and Nation,* in Knight, James, and Brown, p. 739).

—Kimberly Ball

For More Information

Ballard, Charles. *The House of Chaka.* Durban: Emoyeni Books, 1988.

Hamilton, Carolyn. *Terrific Majesty: The Powers of Shaka Zulu and the Limits of Historical Invention.* Cambridge, Mass.: Harvard University Press, 1998.

Knight, Ian J. *Warrior Chiefs of Southern Africa.* Dorset: Firebird Books, 1994.

Knight, Marion A., Mertice M. James, and Dorothy Brown, eds. *The Book Review Digest 1931.* New York: H. W. Wilson, 1932.

Malaba, Mbongeni. "The Legacy of Thomas Mofolo's *Chaka.*" *English in Africa* 13, no. 1 (May 1986): 61-69.

Mofolo, Thomas. *Chaka.* Trans. Daniel P. Kunene. Oxford: Heinemann International, 1981.

Molema, Leloba Sefetogi. *The Image of Christianity in Sesotho Literature: Thomas Mofolo and His Contemporaries.* Hamburg: Helmut Buske Verlag, 1989.

Ngubane, Harriet. *Body and Mind in Zulu Medicine.* London: Academic Press, 1977.

Spence, J. E. *Lesotho: The Politics of Dependence.* London: Oxford University Press, 1968.

Swanepoel, C.F. "The *Leselinya Letters* and Early Reception of Mofolo's *Chaka*." *South African Journal of African Languages* 9, no. 4 (November 1989): 145-53.

The Concubine

by

Elechi Amadi

THE LITERARY WORK

A novel set in a remote Nigerian village at an unspecified mythical time; published in English in 1966.

SYNOPSIS

A beautiful, virtuous woman unwittingly brings death and destruction to all men who desire her.

Elechi Amadi was born near Port Harcourt in eastern Nigeria in 1934. Educated at Government College, Umuahia, and University College, Ibadan, Amadi received a degree in mathematics and physics. He taught science and mathematics from 1960 to 1963 in Merchants of Light School, Oba, before joining the Nigerian army. After three years Amadi left the army to teach and begin a writing career. His first novel, *The Concubine,* received accolades for its vivid depictions of Nigerian village life and remained highly popular in subsequent decades. Amadi went on to write more novels as well as plays and works of nonfiction, including an autobiographical account of his experience in Nigeria's civil war (*Sunset in Biafra,* 1979) and a book of his philosophical ideas (*Ethics in Nigerian Culture,* 1982). Basic to all his works is the concept of life as an ongoing struggle. "There is a rather ironic contradiction between Amadi's philosophy about man's insignificance and ultimate impotence in the hands of the gods, and the fact that his characters struggle to the very end, irrespective of obstacles and threats even from the gods," as demonstrated in *The Concubine* (Eko, p. 1).

Events in History at the Time of the Novel

Igbo society. Although Amadi never specifies that the characters in *The Concubine* are Igbo (or Ibo), they are supposed by critics to belong to Igbo society. The Igbo reside primarily in southeastern Nigeria. Amadi's fictional term for them is "Erekwi"; a little shuffling of the letters produces "Ikwere," the ethnic group to which Amadi himself belongs. The Ikwere speak a distinct language within the Igbo language cluster, and they are a riverine people, which helps explain the appearance in their pantheon of a sea-king deity, who enters into the plot of *The Concubine.*

The traditional Igbo lived in small self-governing villages, each comprised of kin who traced their origins to a mutual ancestor. They did not base their society on a centralized government or supreme political authority, such as a king or chief. Rather the Igbo vested power in the people themselves or in a council of elders. These elders, drawing on the wisdom of the ancestors, settled land disputes and other fractious or crucial matters. There were public forums, too, at which the poor, the rich, and the young, as well as the old could voice opinions before decisions affecting the whole village were made. In the novel the village of Omokachi corresponds closely to this model. It has no single leader; instead the villagers themselves govern their community, giving particular weight to the judgment of the elders. At one point, the protagonist Ihuoma reminds her greedy neighbor Madume that a land dispute between him and her late husband, Emenike, has been decided in Emenike's favor by the village elders. At another juncture, the domestic disputes of the unhappily married Ekwueme and Ahurole are arbitrated by the elders of Omokachi and of Ahurole's home village, Omigwe.

Gods and mortals. Polytheism—the worship of many gods—was characteristic of precolonial Igbo society. However, this did not preclude the belief in a supreme deity. Once close to people, the supreme being, Chukwu, was thought to have withdrawn from direct intervention in their affairs.

> Igbo mythology is replete with examples illustrating the fact that this supreme being used to be close to individuals, and in fact used to intervene in the affairs of individuals and communities, until it was annoyed by the aberrant behaviour of some individuals, women especially, who transgressed one overriding code or the other. . . . From all accounts, it appears that the supreme being having decided to abscond from intervention in the day to day activities of human beings decided to vest some of His powers on beings with lesser and localized powers.
>
> (Opata, p. 150)

There was no equivalent of Satan, or the devil, in the precolonial faith. While the Igbo ascribed one evil or another to various deities in the pantheon, no single spirit was thought to embody all evil. Likewise, the precolonial faith did not include a concept of hell.

The traditional Igbo appear to have preoccupied themselves most often with their own guardian spirit. "The supreme being is nominally supposed to be in charge of all things. At the individual level, however, the *chi,* variously interpreted as the guardian angel or the personal spiritual guardian of every individual, appears to play a more active role in the affairs of any individual" (Opata, p. 150). The belief was that a person's chi had a direct hand in his or her affairs. Igbo ideas of destiny and free will were bound up with chi. "Each individual," taught the Igbo, "has a destiny ascribed to his life" and his personal god controls his destiny (Opata, p. 151). The proverb "if one attempts to run in front of one's chi, the person would run himself to death"

alludes to the power of destiny; in order to succeed, one's objectives for oneself must be aligned with those of one's own chi. Other proverbs allude to free will, and taken together the two types of proverbs (on destiny and on free will) reflect the duality in Igbo thought. The belief was that everyone had hidden powers, supplied by his or her chi. A person had only to make use of these powers to score achievements in life. In other words, one can affect one's own destiny, or, as a proverb says, "if a man wills, his personal chi wills also."

A man and his chi were not thought of as perennially tied together. "There are areas of life in which one must struggle to achieve something by oneself, with or without the active support and collaboration of one's *chi*" (Opata, p. 162). It was, however, believed that a man must at all times be on good terms with his chi, so that when called upon, it would come to his support. When someone failed "to mobilise his *chi* to support a particular undertaking," the spirit was commonly said to be asleep or away (Opata, p. 163). In the *Concubine,* Emenike, despite his prowess as a wrestler, suffers serious injuries in a fight with the less skillful Madume, a circumstance attributed to his god's neglect of him: "a man's god may be away on a journey on the day of an important fight and that may make all the difference. This was clearly what had happened in the last fight between Madume and Emenike" (Amadi, *The Concubine,* p. 7). By the end of the novel, however, it becomes clear that more may be going on here. Another supernatural force may have had a hand in the failure—namely, the Sea-King, whom the novel reveals to be the husband of the beautiful, seemingly mortal woman that Emenike has married. Jealous, this sea god bears deadly ill will for his wife's human husbands, Emenike included.

In Igbo society, when an individual fell victim to an accident or illness for no discernible reason, it was frequently believed that he had offended a god, who then had to be appeased by ritual offerings and sacrifices, often of goats and chickens. This inclination to assuage the supernatural entities manifested itself often in Igbo households. Villagers turned to sacrifice as a way—in fact, the only way—to escape the evil intentions of a given spirit. A priest of the god in question, known as a *dibia* ("medicine man"), would perform the sacrifice, acting as an intermediary between the human and spirit worlds. It was the duty of the dibia to inform the people when to sacrifice, either as tradition dictated through the year or to meet an individual need. The dibia also specified the type of sacrifice to be made. In the novel, the villagers of Omokachi are grateful for the services of Nwokekoro, priest of Amadioha (god of thunder), and Anyika, a medicine man of considerable reputation. It is Anyika who divines the truth of the beautiful Ihuoma's origins—that she is the human incarnation of the Sea-King's wife—and discovers the threat that she unwittingly poses to all her suitors.

Gender roles. Because Igbo society was both male-dominated and patriarchal, gender roles tended to be very traditional. Men supported their families by farming and hunting; they were also expected to contribute to public festivals, honor sacrificial obligations, and defend their communities in times of war. Women led largely but not solely domestic lives, learning to carry out household chores from early childhood. Once women were married, their primary duties included cooking, raising children, and otherwise maintaining an orderly household. They also took part in fieldwork, planting and harvesting crops of their own. Margaret M. Green writes, "Husbands and wives both have crops, the men having chiefly yam and the women having cocoyam and cassava and often a certain amount of yam. . . . It is the women who provide the lion's share of the normal family food, buying such extras as salt out of their own money" (Green, p. 170). Women likewise did the lion's share of buying and selling at the marketplace, with men sponsoring wives and daughters who conducted trade. In *The Concubine*, the polarization of men and women into gender-specific spheres is readily observable. The male villagers, including Emenike, Madume, and Ekwueme, spend their days farming and hunting while the women cook, clean house, and tend the needs of the men. Adaku, Ekwueme's mother, waits devotedly upon her husband and son and has trained her daughter, Nkechi, to do the same. Similarly, Ihuoma, Emenike's wife, is considered a paragon by her village because of her attentiveness to her husband.

Courtship and marriage. Although love might be a factor in an Igbo marriage, it was not necessarily the sole reason for the union. After marriage a woman's husband attached a value to her along with the other property of his household. In the man's eyes, the best possible bride was one who could bring him material wealth and bear him healthy children. Each Igbo family inhabited

A Nigerian wedding ceremony.

a compound of closely grouped houses, and a new wife had to adjust to living in the compound. Expected to fit into her husband's family, she became more than his wife. She took her place as a member of his clan, entitled to belong to it and obligated to share in everything that affected it. A bride's best interests were in adapting to the ways of her new relatives, among whom she would be living.

A man might select his own bride and then acquire his parents' consent to the match. Otherwise the marriage might be arranged by two families when a woman reached marriageable age (around 16 years old) or when she and her prospective husband were still children. In this case, both sets of parents would conclude the childhood betrothal, then enter into marriage negotiations when the girl reached the appropriate age. An intermediary of the groom's family would initiate the process, visiting the bride's family with a present of palm wine. Later, visits between the families ensued, more gifts were exchanged, and a bride price—payment from the man's to the woman's family—was agreed upon. Meanwhile, the couple became better acquainted with each other. The girl, in particular, was expected to spend time in what would be her future home with her future family. On her first stay, she remained four Igbo weeks (16 days). While her prospective husband's family welcomed her, the bride-to-be would also be subject to criticism. Her new family would size her up, so to speak, judging how well she measured up to their standards and how smoothly she would fit into the day-to-day workings of the extended family household.

There was no fixed interval between the time of betrothal and the actual marriage, which was left to the discretion of the families. The final wedding festivities—which included a marriage feast—lasted seven days, at the end of which the bride would be escorted to her new home, at night, by her female companions. In the novel, the marriage preparations of Ekwueme and Ahurole follow just such a pattern. Betrothed when Ekwueme was five years old and Ahurole only eight days old, they have little contact until their parents start marriage negotiations, a circumstance complicated by their living in different villages. Their budding relationship is further strained by Ahurole's immaturity and Ekwueme's preference for the widowed Ihuoma, who has refused him. Nonetheless, the young couple attempts to obey the strictures of tradition. Ekwueme dutifully calls on his betrothed, and Ahurole pays an extended visit to her prospective in-laws in Omokachi.

DIVORCE, IGBO STYLE

In Igbo society, dissolving a marriage tended to be less complicated than formulating one. A man could divorce his wife simply by ordering her to leave his compound. If she resisted, he could drive her out. She was entitled to take nothing with her, save her cooking pot and a few personal possessions, which were usually thrown after her in a symbolic gesture of repudiation. Their children remained with her husband. Since the man had paid a bride price, he treated his wife as his possession. But women were not without some rights of their own. They could initiate divorce proceedings in an unsatisfactory or abusive marriage by running away from their husbands. A man who was so abandoned might demand his wife's return or, if he agreed to the divorce, a refund of what he had paid for her. The bride price, however, was not likely to be refunded unless she remarried, in which case her new husband would reimburse his predecessor. In the novel, the conscience-stricken Ahurole runs away after Ekwueme seemingly goes mad from a love potion she gave him. The marriage is thus dissolved; Ahurole's embarrassed father even refunds the bride-price.

Pride and polygyny. Among the Igbo, polygyny—the practice of having more than one wife—was not merely an accepted fact but was considered a sign of prestige and prosperity. Igbo men typically showed an interest in acquiring an increasing number of wives until old age discouraged them from doing so. The more wives they had, the higher their social status was in Igbo society. Under native law and custom, however, a man's first wife enjoyed certain privileges; she was head of the womenfolk in the family compound. Subsequent wives were considered secondary to the first wife or "headwife" in all respects. Igbo women themselves were often proponents of polygyny, because of the added social status their husbands acquired after marrying again. It was humiliating to be a man's only wife, for such a status intimated that the husband was a poor man. If, on the other hand, one was a first wife in charge of several other women, one gained status with the position. A headwife frequently found the women who later joined her husband's household to be a source of companionship and domestic assistance. In the novel, Madume schemes to acquire the recently widowed Ihuoma as his second wife. Not only does Madume's wife, Wolu, refrain from contesting this plan, she even argues that Ihuoma should be appointed first wife over her because Ihuoma is "better than I" (*The Concubine*, p. 70).

Women took an active role in their relationships with men in other ways too. Especially in the polygynous family with a great many wives, it was not uncommon for a woman to have a discreet affair (concubinage) outside her marriage. This practice figures in *The Concubine*, whose female protagonist is already married, although for much of the novel she does not know it. As indicated by the events that transpire, she may therefore become the concubine of another male with impunity, but his wife only at his peril. Of course, not all Igbo marriages were polygynous. There were husbands who had only one wife, as Emenike does in the novel. After he dies, his family continues to regard his widow as part of their unit and expects her to take care of her late husband's property, although his brother steps in as head of her family.

The Novel in Focus

Plot summary. The novel begins with a forest encounter between Emenike, a young man of Omokachi village, and Madume, a fellow villager with whom he has recently quarreled over land.

The two men brawl, but their fight ends when Madume throws Emenike on top of a jagged tree stump, knocking him unconscious. Madume flees the scene, while the injured Emenike comes to and limps home.

The day after the brawl it becomes apparent that Emenike's injuries are very serious. His wife, Ihuoma, a beautiful and virtuous woman, sends for Anyika, the village medicine man, who performs purification rites to banish evil spirits and speed Emenike's recovery. Meanwhile, Madume lies low, nursing his resentment over the more popular Emenike's prosperity, envying him both his lands and his wife, whom Madume courted unsuccessfully before her marriage. Nonetheless, Madume hopes no one in Omokachi will hold him responsible should Emenike die.

At first Emenike appears to recover, especially after Nwokekoro, priest of Amadioha, the god of thunder, offers a sacrifice on his behalf. But the young man eventually succumbs to an illness known as "lock-chest," ostensibly caused by his working too long in the rain. Now a grieving widow with three children, Ihuoma wonders how she will handle all her new responsibilities, which include running Emenike's farm and looking after the family compound in which she lives. Visits from her mother, Okachi, and a young male neighbor, Ekwueme, however, bring her some consolation. After returning to his own family compound, Ekwueme finds himself thinking wistfully of Ihuoma's beauty and grace.

A year after Emenike's death, Ihuoma carries out a final mourning ritual, sacrificing some of her livestock and holding a feast for the villagers in her late husband's honor. Eight days after this ceremony, Ihuoma lays aside her sackcloth mourning clothes and dresses as she did before. As she regains her looks and spirits, men begin to admire her again. One day, while Ihuoma visits her parents in the neighboring village of Omigwe, her mother suggests that she might remarry and mentions Ekwueme as a possible suitor. But Ihuoma becomes upset and refuses to consider the matter.

Before the rainy season begins, Ihuoma's brother-in-law, Nnadi, and some of his friends, including Ekwueme, volunteer to thatch her leaky roof. Ihuoma gratefully accepts their help and cooks a large meal for the roofers. Ekwueme lingers after the others have left for the night and tries to speak to Ihuoma of his growing feelings for her, but she seems distant and aloof. Discouraged by her lack of response, a moody Ekwueme returns to his own family compound.

That night he has a strange dream about Emenike, Ihuoma's dead husband, who tries to drag him across a dark stream. On hearing of the dream, Adaku, Ekwueme's doting mother, persuades him to visit the medicine man Anyika for a protective charm. Later, despite Ihuoma's apparent indifference to him, Ekwueme enlists the assistance of Nnenda, one of Ihuoma's friends, to further his courtship. Adaku, however, grows concerned about her son's infatuation with Emenike's widow and decides that it is time for him to marry.

MOURNING RITUALS

The Igbo, especially the women, responded to the death of a loved one with loud weeping and lamentations. The widow or mother of the newly deceased would often be surrounded by friends and family lest she do herself an injury while deranged with grief. The speedy burial of the deceased—along with some emblems of his life and work, like his favorite tools and weapons—was accompanied by sacrifices and purification rites. A new widow was expected to weep copiously for her dead husband during the four or five days immediately following her loss. She would then move to a secluded house in the family compound, where no man could see or speak to her for three Igbo weeks (12 days). For seven Igbo weeks (28 days), a widow was prohibited from bathing or combing her hair. Her sole occupation during that time was to mourn for her dead. After an unspecified length of time, however, a "second burial" ceremony was held for the deceased. Unlike the original burial, this ritual was far more festive, a feasting rather than a grieving time, the occasion in which the deceased received a celebratory goodbye before leaving for the spirit world. The deceased's family spared no expense in honoring the memory of the departed—besides feasting, the second burial often featured singing and dancing. In the novel, Emenike's friends stage a mock-wrestling bout to honor their late comrade's prowess as a wrestler.

Meanwhile, Madume, Emenike's greedy neighbor, has also begun to think about Ihuoma again. Although Madume already has a wife and four daughters, he wants to take a second wife in hopes of siring a son. Madume's wife, Wolu, is not upset by his interest in Ihuoma, whom she admires, but her husband's indifference to their own children distresses her. Hoping to ingratiate himself with Ihuoma, Madume pays her a visit but cuts his foot badly while he is at her compound. Beset by vague fears, Madume consults Anyika, who divines that the gods are behind Madume's injury because they want him to leave Ihuoma alone. Anyika tells Madume to make a series of complicated sacrifices to appease these angry spirits. Madume performs these rites and reluctantly decides to renounce Ihuoma as a prospective second wife. He remains determined, however, to claim the land over which he and Emenike once quarreled. Sneaking over there at night, Madume is surprised by Ihuoma, who orders him to leave her husband's property alone. Madume lays rough hands on Ihuoma while restraining her and makes her cry. Ihuoma's friends and neighbors come to her defense, but a defiant Madume insists on claiming what he feels is his. He starts to cut down a huge plantain tree, but seconds later, he is blinded by the venom of a spitting cobra hiding among the leaves. Despite an elaborate sacrifice and the application of various remedies, Madume remains totally blind.

SUICIDE, A TABOO

~

In the past, certain acts were considered abominations, which called for elaborate sacrifices and purification rituals. Suicide, an offense committed by Madume in the novel, was one such act. The belief was that no one had the right to reject the gift of life, which came from Chukwu, so suicides were spiritual outcasts. The Igbo subscribed to the existence of two worlds—the human world in which they lived and the spiritual one in which the ancestors dwelled. Suicides were not given decent burials because they were not allowed to return to the world of the ancestors. Neither did they belong in the human world, according to Igbo thought. Instead they were carried into a part of the forest to prevent pollution of the earth and ward off evil spirits.

Although Wolu ministers to her husband devotedly, Madume grows increasingly irrational and angry. Terrified, Wolu and her daughters steal away one night, returning to find that Madume has hanged himself in their absence. The body is cut down and taken to the forest "into which bodies rejected by the earth were thrown" (*The Concubine*, p. 98).

Ekwueme continues to visit Ihuoma who, despite her growing fondness for the young man, tries not to encourage his pursuit. When Ekwueme finally declares his love and expresses a desire to marry her, Ihuoma reminds him that he has been betrothed since childhood to Ahurole, a young girl from Ihuoma's own native village of Omigwe. Despite Ekwueme's protestations, Ihuoma insists that he honor his prior commitment. Meanwhile, Ekwueme's parents, alarmed about their son's attentiveness to Ihuoma, decide to accelerate plans for his marriage to Ahurole. Ekwueme informs his parents that he wants to marry Ihuoma instead. His father, Wigwe, tries to dissuade him, reminding him that Ihuoma's first loyalties belong to her children and Emenike's property, but Ekwueme remains obdurate. Wigwe and Ekwueme then pay a late-night visit to Ihuoma's compound, during which Wigwe asks Ihuoma if she will marry his son. Mortified by the sudden proposal, Ihuoma refuses outright. Ekuewme's betrothal to another, along with the unexpectedness of the proposal, prompt her to reject him. Now convinced that Ihuoma does not reciprocate his feelings, the young man agrees to marry Ahurole.

After six months of negotiations and visits to his bride-to-be in Omigwe, Ekwueme marries Ahurole and brings her to live in Omokachi. The young couple encounters marital difficulties almost immediately. Young and beautiful, Ahurole is prone to moodiness and frequent tearful outbursts. Ekwueme grows impatient with his wife's capriciousness and wishes she were calmer and more mature, like his mother or Ihuoma. One night, during a quarrel, Ekwueme strikes Ahurole and she runs back to her parents' house. The couple reunites after elders from both villages arbitrate their dispute, but their reconciliation is short-lived: "[Ekwueme's] resentment and resignation deepened. He tried to ignore his wife as much as possible. In retaliation she avoided him. They spoke to each other in monosyllables and only on inevitable topics like eating. Gradually the gulf widened between them" (*The Concubine*, p. 187).

As Ekwueme's marriage founders, his interest in Ihuoma revives. Unwilling to cause greater problems between Ekwueme and Ahurole, Ihuoma tries again to keep the young man at arm's length. Nonetheless, Ahurole soon learns of her husband's attraction to Ihuoma and seeks the advice of her mother, who suggests she purchase a love potion. Ahurole visits Anyika but he refuses to give her what she asks for because in the long run it might harm Ekwueme: "I am sure you have seen active and intelligent men suddenly become passive, stupid and dependent. That is what a love potion can do" (*The Concubine*, p. 207). Undeterred, Ahurole's mother goes to a medicine man in the neighboring village of Chiolu and obtains the potion for her daughter. Ahurole hides the drug in Ekwueme's food; the young man then begins to suffer from a variety of physical complaints, including dysentery, boils, and muscle aches. Although these ailments eventually subside, Ekwueme grows lethargic, then oddly restless and moody, alarming his family. One day he becomes completely irrational and bolts out of the compound. Encountering Ahurole on one of the paths, Ekwueme chases his terrified wife through Omokachi until his fellow villagers catch and restrain him. That night Ekwueme escapes and flees into the forest. The younger men of the village team up to search for him; Ahurole, too ashamed to admit her part in Ekwueme's madness, runs away.

Meanwhile, Anyika realizes that Ekwueme is suffering from the effects of a love potion and hurries to concoct an antidote. In the morning Ekwueme is still missing but eventually his friends find him, armed with a club, sitting in a tree. The villagers try unsuccessfully to talk him down. Ekwueme suddenly asks for Ihuoma, who is hurriedly summoned. To everyone's surprise, he listens to reason and descends from the tree at her request.

Back at the compound Ekwueme regains his senses after Ihuoma persuades him to take Anyika's antidote. Once recovered, he starts visiting Ihuoma frequently, this time with his family's blessing. Informed of Ahurole's flight and the impending dissolution of Ekwueme's marriage, Ihuoma at last admits her love for the young man and agrees to marry him. Anyika, however, opposes the marriage after divining that Ihuoma is the human incarnation of a favorite wife of the Sea-King, "the ruling spirit of the sea" (*The Concubine*, p. 253). Because of the Sea-King's jealousy, Ihuoma cannot marry without great harm befalling her mortal husbands. Anyika reveals to Ekwueme's parents that water-spirits were present at the deaths of Emenike, Ihuoma's late husband, and Madume, who hoped to make Ihuoma his wife. Terrified for their own son, Adaku and Wigwe relate Anyika's warning to the young man but he remains determined to wed Ihuoma. Ekwueme also decides not to make Ihuoma aware of her identity for fear that she will back out of their impending marriage.

Although Anyika claims there is no way around the Sea-King's curse, Ekwueme and Wigwe visit Agwoturumbe, a famous medicine man in the village of Aliji. Agwoturumbe divines the same truths about Ihuoma's identity, but he believes the Sea-King can be prevented from harming Ekwueme by a powerful sacrifice. Reassured, Ekwueme and his family agree to Agwoturumbe's plan and begin to make preparations for the sacrifice, which requires, among other things, a brightly colored male lizard. Agwoturumbe comes to Omokachi to conduct the ceremony, while Nwonna, Ihuoma's young son who prides himself on his archery, is enlisted to catch the lizard. Ekwueme tells the curious Ihuoma an edited version of the truth about her connection to the spirit world, leaving out the fact that her human husbands face grave danger. The young couple looks forward to years of happiness together. But, just before the ceremony, tragedy strikes: an arrow from Nwonna's bow, targeted at a red lizard on the wall, accidentally hits Ekwueme as he emerges from his room. Despite Agwoturumbe's ministrations, Ekwueme dies just after midnight.

The mythological and the mundane. Emmanuel Obiechina attributes the success of *The Concubine* to Amadi's skillful depictions of a traditional society and its inhabitants, observing, "In this society, human beings are in close contact with the world of gods, spirits, and ancestors. The close interplay of the natural and supernatural, of the physical and the metaphysical, and of the secular and the spiritual provide a strong backdrop to the drama played out by the characters" (Obiechina, p. 50). Fact mingles with spiritual beliefs and customs to create the reality of Amadi's characters, as evidenced by their account of how different villages came to exist:

> Igwe, the founder of Omigwe, was forced to leave Omokachi when one of his babies cut its upper teeth first. This was a terrible omen signifying that Igwe had done something very wrong, though no one seemed to remember exactly the nature of the offence. . . . Whatever it was, the sacrifices needed for absolution were too involved and costly. . . . Igwe could not collect these things and to ward off the wrath of the gods the villagers ejected him from the village. But he prospered (some say he performed the sacrifices later) and founded Omigwe.
>
> (*The Concubine*, p. 18)

Myth and legend are the tools that the inhabitants of Omokachi use to explain their

Igbo women processing food items for the market.

lives. They ascribe unforeseen and mysterious occurrences—such as the death of a neighbor—to the will of the gods, an interpretation frequently borne out by the divination rites of their dibia, Anyika. By making offerings and carrying out sacrifices to appease angry spirits, they restore a sense of order and control to the community.

Another village legend gradually takes shape around Ihuoma, a beautiful, virtuous woman who is the pride of Omokachi but whose life is marred by tragedy. Ihuoma's mature beauty and distinctive allure seem to possess a magical quality, drawing men irresistibly towards her. One suitor, Ekwueme, declares to his father, "I really cannot help wanting to marry Ihuoma," as though external forces are partially to blame for his attraction to her (*The Concubine,* p. 139). However, the inexplicable misfortunes that befall the men who desire Ihuoma—her husband, Emenike; her greedy neighbor, Madume; the lovestruck Ekwueme—soon cast a sinister light upon her charms. After divining Ihuoma's supernatural origins as the wife of the jealous Sea-King, Anyika remarks, "Look at her. . . have you seen anyone quite so right in everything, almost perfect. I tell you only a sea goddess—for that is precisely what she is—can be all that" (*The Concubine,* p. 254). Other villagers are quick to concur with Anyika's assessment, though Ihuoma

protests when told of her link to the spirit world, "I certainly don't feel like a daughter of the sea" (*The Concubine,* p. 261). Indeed, Ihuoma becomes a victim of her own myth, when her betrothed, Ekwueme, is killed during preparations for a sacrifice intended to disempower the Sea-King so she can safely remarry. Ekwueme's death is punishment for his defying the Sea-King's jealousy by courting Ihuoma.

The accuracy of Amadi's portrayal of Igbo/Ikwere perspectives on myth and religion is corroborated by other sources. Scholars have commented on the integral nature of mythical beliefs in the daily life of traditional Igbo. Juliet I. Okonkwo observes that "[t]o those who appreciate the potency of [supernatural] forces in traditional societies, [Amadi's] extensive use of them merely reinforces the authenticity of his presentation" (Okonkwo, p. 151). Ebele Eko, however, notes that Amadi employs a "double perspective" in his writings, depicting the supernatural element meticulously, yet allowing for the possibility of rational explanations for the apparently inexplicable: "[Amadi's] aim is to draw attention to the integrity, beauty and wisdom of traditional culture, without hiding from the rational modern mind its rigidity, restrictions, limitations and potentials for suppressing and even stagnating originality in some characters" (Eko, p. 8).

Sources and literary context. Although *The Concubine* takes place in an unspecified area at an indeterminate time, Amadi draws upon the culture and history of his own people to establish the novel's setting. The inhabitants of Omokachi and its neighboring villages are designated as "Erekwi," which, as mentioned, is a transposition of "Ikwere," the ethnic group to which Amadi belongs. The major deities in *The Concubine* are part of the Ikwere pantheon—Amadiaoha, god of thunder; Ojukwu, god of smallpox; and the jealous Sea-King. The novel also shares a common thread with certain Igbo folktales, in which it is suggested that beautiful women are "a danger to the authority or even the lives of their husbands," an attitude that "also underlies the *Ilu* [proverb] 'He who marries a beauty, marries trouble'" (Arndt, p. 205).

Elechi Amadi's novels have earned him a significant place in Nigerian literature. Along with Chinua Achebe, Wole Soyinka, and Camara Laye (see ***Things Fall Apart, Death and the King's Horseman,*** and ***The Dark Child,*** all covered in *African Literature and Its Times*), Amadi has contributed to a literary renaissance that called for a renewed respect for African traditions and culture. Eko writes: "As a reaction to colonialism, early African novelists were not only concerned with recreating life's ideals for man in the society but they also assumed a definite aggressive posture in defense of African culture against foreign detractors by asserting its wholesomeness, its dignity, and its rights to exist" (Eko, pp. 5-6). Amadi's major contribution to this literary movement is his vivid recreation of life in traditional African society.

> Amadi has intricately woven the minutiae of daily existence of the people among whom his novels are set. More than even Achebe, he is able to evoke authentic village life. . . . His descriptions of sacrifices, dances, hunting, farming, and even cooking are so woven into the stories as not to obtrude.
>
> (Okonkwo, pp. 150-51)

Reviews. *The Concubine* received mostly favorable reviews when it first appeared in 1966. An anonymous reviewer in the *Times Literary Supplement* praised it as a work of "considerable quality and promise" (*Times Literary Supplement,*

p. 281). Some critics objected to plot contrivances that, they felt, weakened the novel's artistry. Theo Vincent, writing for *Black Orpheus,* complained, "Not much artistic quality can be expected from a plot that is entirely worked out by supernatural machinations. . . . Everything is predictable and the plot seems to jog-trot along under the impulse of a good tale" (Vincent, p. 62). He conceded, however, that "Amadi has a fine ear and eye for details. His descriptions and dialogues are vivid" (Vincent, p. 62). Others found Amadi's blend of mythology and realism compelling. Richard Mayne, writing for *New Statesman,* declared the novel to be "a highly sophisticated measured treatment" of a basic theme, "the fatal loves of a woman in an East Nigerian village. Written in a grave and simple style, it . . . reveals its author . . . as a fine writer ruminating on a past already turning into legend" (Mayne, p. 389).

—Pamela S. Loy

For More Information

Arndt, Susan. *African Women's Literature: Orature and Intertextuality.* Trans. Isabel Cole. Bayreuth African Studies 48. Bayreuth, Germany: Bayreuth University, 1998.

Amadi, Elechi. *The Concubine.* London: Heinemann Educational Books, 1966.

Basden, G. T. *Niger Ibos.* London: Frank Cass, 1966.

Eko, Ebele. *Elechi Amadi: The Man and His Work.* Lagos: Kraft, 1991.

Green, Margaret M. *Igbo Village Affairs.* London: Frank Cass, 1964.

Mayne, Richard. Review of *The Concubine. New Statesman,* 18 March 1966, pp. 388-90.

Obiechina, Emmanuel. "Elechi Amadi." In *Dictionary of Literary Biography.* Vol. 117. Eds. Bernth Lindfors and Reinhard Sander. Detroit: Gale, 1992.

Okonkwo, Juliet I. "Elechi Amadi." In *Perspectives on Nigerian Literature: 1700 to The Present.* Vol. 2. Ed. Yemi Ogunbiyi. Lagos: Guardian Books Nigeria, 1988.

Opata, Damian U. *Essays on Igbo World View.* Nsukka, Nigeria: AP Express, 1998.

Review of *The Concubine,* by Elechi Amadi. *Times Literary Supplement,* 7 April 1966, p. 281.

Vincent, Theo. Review of *The Concubine. Black Orpheus* 21 (1967): 62-63.

Cry, the Beloved Country

by

Alan Paton

~

Born in Pietermaritzburg, South Africa, in 1903, Alan Stewart Paton was educated at Maritzburg College and the University of Natal, graduating with a degree in science. As a young man, he taught mathematics and chemistry for several years at Ixopo High School, an institution for white children, before joining the staff of Maritzburg College. After a bout with enteric fever in 1934, Paton decided to change careers. In 1935 he moved to Johannesburg to become principal of the Diepkloof Reformatory for African Boys (that is, black African boys). During his ten years there, Paton wrote several articles on crime, punishment, and penal reform and became deeply interested in race relations. In 1946 he took a leave of absence to study penal and correctional institutions in Europe, the United States, and Canada. His interest in race relations meanwhile led to his writing *Cry, the Beloved Country,* which he began while traveling through Norway. Paton's depiction of the tragedy that engulfs two families—one black, one white—brought South Africa's race relations problems to worldwide attention.

Events in History at the Time of the Novel

Urban migration. "All roads lead to Johannesburg," the omniscient narrator of *Cry, the Beloved Country* frequently observes (Paton, *Cry, the Beloved Country,* p. 10). The historical truth of this declaration is borne out by the mass migration of black and white South Africans from rural

THE LITERARY WORK

A novel set in the South African province of Natal and the city of Johannesburg in the 1940s; published in English in 1948.

SYNOPSIS

The lives of a Zulu parson and a wealthy white farmer intertwine when an encounter between their sons ends in tragedy.

to urban areas in the 1930s and 1940s. Black farmers, bound by such legislation as the Natives Land Act (1913)—which prohibited them from purchasing or leasing land from non-Africans outside of the colonial reserves set aside for blacks—were most affected by drought and soil erosion. Unlike white farmers, black farmers had no access to the advanced technology and irrigation techniques that would revitalize their land and make it productive again:

> By the 1920s, some of [the reserve land] was already carrying such a heavy concentration of people and livestock that the original vegetation was disappearing, streams and waterholes were drying up, and soil erosion was spreading. In the years that followed, the African reserves continued to deteriorate.
>
> (Thompson, p. 164)

In the novel, the Zulu farmers in Ndotsheni village struggle to eke out an existence in the midst of a crippling drought and too many cat-

A slum in Sophiatown, Johannesburg, before 1957.

tle. However, the plantation of white farmer James Jarvis, which is located above Ndotsheni, flourishes because of his knowledge of irrigation and production techniques, a knowledge that he later shares with the black farmers.

The decreasing profitability of subsistence farming drove many Africans to seek their fortunes in large cities such as Johannesburg and Cape Town. By 1936, out of a population of close to 3.5 million, 447,000 nonwhites—most of them able-bodied males between 15 and 50 years old—had left the reserves to work on a white farm or in a white town.

Percentage of Ethnic Group in South African Urban Areas, 1904-60

	Blacks	Coloureds	Whites	Indians
1904	10%	51%	53%	37%
1936	17%	54%	65%	66%
1960	32%	68%	84%	83%

(Adapted from Wilson and Ramphele in Thompson. p. 244)

People designated as "coloured" refer to descendants of mixed unions (some combination of whites, Khosian, African slaves, and slaves from southeast Asia). By 1946, the year *Cry, the Beloved Country* takes place, the coloured, like every other major ethnic group in South Africa,

had a growing percentage of its population living in towns.

The government tried to limit the influx of black workers to the towns, imposing complicated pass laws that restricted the amount of time blacks could spend seeking jobs in the city. Government-issued permits stating the bearer's identity, racial classification, and the nature of his or her business in the city or town were to be produced on demand. Blacks who failed to show their passes when questioned by an official could be jailed or expelled from the town. Despite these pass laws and the failure of anti-pass campaigns to abolish them, the urban black population in the cities continued to grow. Competition among whites and blacks for jobs was fierce and many who could not find legitimate employment turned to crime. In the novel, Reverend Kumalo is robbed of his bus fare by a young Zulu-speaking street hustler within minutes of his arrival in Johannesburg, and his son Absalom is arrested for killing Arthur Jarvis during a robbery attempt.

From segregation to apartheid. In 1910 the two Boer states of the Transvaal and the Orange Free State were linked to the two British territories of Cape Colony and Natal to form the Union of South Africa. Institutionalized racial discrimination began soon after—blacks were permanently barred from voting in the Transvaal and the Orange Free State. More legislation limiting the social and political rights of blacks followed.

Legislation	Year	Effect
Native Labour Regulation Act	1911	Made it a criminal offense for a black to break a labor contract
Mines and Works Act	1911	Reserved skilled jobs for whites
Natives Land Act	1913	Limited black ownership of land to governmental reserves
Native Urban Areas Act	1923	Authorized segregation in urban areas
Native Trust and Land Act	1936	Expanded amount of land in reserves from 7 to 11.7 percent; still prohibited blacks from purchasing land outside reserves
Representation of Natives Act	1936	Eliminated black representation in the House of Assembly

Also in 1936 blacks lost the right to vote in Cape Province, the only area in which they had previously retained the privilege.

During the 1940s—the decade in which *Cry, the Beloved Country* takes place—segregation became an established policy. After World War II, the National Party, comprised of white Afrikaners (who were descended from early European, mainly Dutch, settlers) increased in size and popularity. The British-influenced United Party's decision to enter the war on the Allied side had antagonized Afrikaners, many of whom sympathized with Nazi ideas about a white master race: "nearly all believed that the state should do more to maintain white supremacy and the 'purity' of the white 'race'" (Thompson, p. 185). In the 1948 general election, the National Party united rural and urban Afrikaners by appealing to their racial attitudes as well as to their economic interests and won the election. The new government, led by Prime Minister D. F. Malan, swiftly implemented *apartheid* (derived from the Afrikaner word for "apartness"), a policy that completely separated the races. Apartheid rested on the notion that South African society consisted of separate nations that ought to live in their own distinct homelands within South Africa. Nonwhites could enter the white homeland only as temporary workers. Behind the policy was a conviction that whites and nonwhites had separate destinies, which could be fulfilled only by isolating the races.

The Zulu community. In the novel, Reverend Stephen Kumalo and his family live in the village of Ndotsheni, near the Natal border, a region inhabited by the Zulu people. During the eighteenth century, Zulu society included a large number of Nguni-speaking chiefdoms north of the Tugela river. Traditionally, Zulu households consisted of an extended polygamous family, largely self-sufficient, with labor divided according to gender. Men defended the homestead, cared for the cattle, and built weapons and dwellings, while women handled domestic responsibilities and raised crops. All Zulu households, however, were under the control of chiefs, who received tribute or taxes from their subjects, commanded large armies, and sometimes conquered other chiefdoms (see *Chaka,* also covered in *African Literature and Its Times*). In the nineteenth century the Zulu empire weakened, especially after the Anglo-Zulu war, when Zululand was invaded by British forces and in 1887 incorporated into the British colony of Natal.

SQUATTERS' CAMPS AND SHANTYTOWNS

Mass migration to the cities caused a large-scale housing crisis. While incoming Africans were permitted to settle in black suburbs, like Sophiatown, Alexandra, and Pimville near Johannesburg, those who could not find rooms or afford houses were forced to build squatters' camps and shantytowns. Black migrant workers constructed crude shacks of corrugated tin, cardboard boxes, newspaper, and wood in these makeshift settlements. During the latter half of the 1940s, from 60,000 to 90,000 blacks inhabited such dwellings just outside Johannesburg. Living conditions were abysmal, yet it was not unheard of for the inhabitants to establish a sense of community through their common experience of hardship and disillusionment with the government's failure to deliver on its promise of housing.

In the novel, the Zulu population and way of life has been fragmented. Although the inhabitants of Ndotsheni retain some sense of ethnic and cultural identity, they also recognize that their traditional way of life is vanishing, and the departure of so many able-bodied men to the city has weakened the Zulu people even further. There is still a Zulu chief but he must defer to the authority of the white magistrate who presides over the region. Reverend Kumalo's brother, John, a Johannesburg resident, scornfully dismisses the chief as "an old and ignorant man, who is nothing but a white man's dog," his only purpose being "to hold together something that the white man desires to hold together" (*Cry, the Beloved Country*, p. 35). Stephen Kumalo still hopes, however, to contribute to the rebuilding of his people by bringing his wayward sister, son, and nephew back to Ndotsheni, though he will be only partly successful in this effort. From the outset, Reverend Msimangu warns him that "the white man has broken the tribe. And it is my belief . . . that it cannot be mended again" (*Cry, the Beloved Country*, p. 25). After his son is sentenced to death and his sister returns to a life of dissolution, Kumalo salvages what family he has left in the city—his nephew, his son's new wife, and her unborn child—before returning to the country.

Gold-mining in South Africa. Gold-mining has been a major South African industry ever since huge deposits of gold were discovered in Witwatersrand (commonly known as "the Rand") in

1886. A settlement of crude shacks and canvas tents—called "Johannesburg" in honor of the president of the Transvaal and the Director of Mines, both named Johannes—sprang up around these early mining operations. Ten years later, Johannesburg had grown into "an American-style city with straight, intersecting streets, parks, gardens, a residential district away from the city centre and a business quarter with Stock Exchanges, clubs and offices that emptied every evening" (Lacour-Gayet, p. 159). At the time of the novel, Johannesburg had become a sprawling metropolis, characterized by both great affluence and grinding poverty.

During the 1930s and 1940s, the gold-mining industry remained "the backbone of the South African economy" (Thompson, p. 167). In 1939 the mines employed 364,000 workers: 43,000 whites and 321,000 blacks. Working conditions in the mines were "arduous, unhealthy, and dangerous," marked by intense heat and *stopes* (or steplike excavations) so narrow that the miners had to work from a crouching position (Thompson, p. 168). Black miners, barred from the skilled-labor positions reserved for whites, often became victims of this brutal work environment; many died in accidents or contracted tuberculosis or other serious lung diseases. Their wages were meanwhile significantly lower than those of whites—after 1920 whites continued to earn 11 times more than blacks. In 1939, just before the time of the novel, white miners also received paid leaves and pensions, benefits denied to black miners. In the novel, after gold is discovered in Odensdaalrust, John Kumalo speaks out against the wage discrepancy between black and white miners: "We are asking only for more money from the richest industry in the world. This industry is powerless without our labour. Let us cease to work and this industry will die" (*Cry, the Beloved Country*, p. 185). But despite a brief strike by miners in Driefontain—quickly suppressed by the police—the financial situation does not change: "African miners are simple souls," says a spokesman for the mines, "hardly qualified in the art of negotiation, and an easy tool for unscrupulous agitators. And in any event, everyone knows that rising costs would threaten the very existence of the mines and the very existence of South Africa" (*Cry, the Beloved Country*, p. 189).

THE MINERS' STRIKE OF 1946

On August 12, 1946, 73,000 mine workers—predominantly black—launched a four-day strike at the Witwatersrand gold mines, protesting low wages and hazardous working conditions. Production ceased completely in ten mines and was significantly affected in others. The government responded with brutal swiftness—its police arrested strike leaders, killed 12 men, and injured more than 1,200 others while suppressing the strike. The Chamber of Mines refused all demands for higher wages and better working conditions, on the grounds that trade-unionism was beyond the comprehension of the black workers. The leaders of the African Mine Workers' Union who organized the strike were tried under stringent wartime regulations and the union itself was seriously crippled. As in the novel, no positive change resulted.

The Novel in Focus

Plot summary. Book One of the novel begins on an autumn day in 1946 when a child delivers a letter to Reverend Stephen Kumalo, parson of Ndotsheni Village in Natal, from a Reverend Theophilus Msimangu, a fellow Anglican minister living in Sophiatown, Johannesburg. The letter informs Kumalo of his sister Gertrude's illness and urges him to come to Johannesburg, offering him lodgings at Msimangu's mission house in Sophiatown. Kumalo and his wife are disturbed by this report, all the more so because their only son, Absalom, went to Johannesburg some time ago and they have heard nothing from him. The Kumalos quickly scrape together what money they have for the reverend's journey.

Kumalo boards the train, entering the compartment for "non-Europeans" (*Cry, the Beloved Country,* p. 13). As the train travels across the country, Kumalo is overwhelmed by the increasing signs of urbanization that he sees. Arriving in Johannesburg, he is disoriented by the crowds, noise, and "great high buildings" (*Cry, the Beloved Country,* p. 17). He is almost immediately robbed by a young Zulu-speaking man at the bus station, after which an elderly man escorts Kumalo to Msimangu's mission house in Sophiatown.

Msimangu informs Kumalo that Gertrude is not physically sick, but spiritually ill: she has become a prostitute and seller of liquor and currently lives in Claremont, a slum area in Johannesburg. Deeply saddened, Kumalo confides in Msimangu about his other missing relations, his brother, John, and son, Absalom. Msimangu tells Kumalo that John has become a politician; he has no news of Absalom, but he offers to help Kumalo search for his son. The next day Kumalo tracks down his sister and finds her and her son living in squalor. After an emotional confrontation, Gertrude confesses her sins, breaks down, and agrees to return with Kumalo to Ndotsheni. Heartened, Kumalo takes Gertrude and her son back to Sophiatown, confident that he will succeed in reuniting his whole family.

With Gertrude settled in the mission house, Kumalo and Msimangu visit Kumalo's brother, John, at his shop, hoping for news of Absalom. Kumalo finds that John has become "a man of some importance" in Johannesburg, and a powerful orator against the growing apartheid movement (*Cry, the Beloved Country,* p. 35). Disgusted by the racial inequality in South Africa, and spiritually and politically disillusioned, John has abandoned the Church and will not consider returning to Ndotsheni. He grows uncomfortable and evasive when Kumalo asks about Absalom, but reveals that his own son and Absalom had gone to work for a factory in Alexandra.

Setting off for Alexandra, Kumalo and Msimangu learn from another activist, Dubula, that there is a bus boycott going on to protest higher fares. Agreeing to help the cause, the reverends set out for Alexandra on foot. In Alexandra they learn that the young Kumalos left their lodgings a year ago and that they kept bad company while living there. Further investigation leads Kumalo and Msimangu to a shantytown in Orlando, where Absalom had been staying before he was arrested for theft and sent to the local reformatory. A worker at the reformatory informs Kumalo that Absalom left a month ago and is now living in a Pimville housing project with a local girl whom he impregnated. The worker then takes Kumalo and Msimangu to meet the girl, who despondently tells them that Absalom has gone away and she does not know if he will return. The reverends agree to let the reformatory worker handle the search, and go back to Sophiatown. That evening, at the mission house, one of the priests shows Kumalo a headline in the *Evening Star,* reporting the murder of Arthur Jarvis, a white city engineer shot by black intruders. Kumalo reveals that he knows the victim's father, who has a farm above Ndotsheni. On further reflection, Kumalo suddenly experiences nameless fear and dread. Later, his worst fears are confirmed: Absalom, along with his cousin and an acquaintance, has been arrested and charged with murder.

BUS BOYCOTTS

Paton based his fictional depiction of the Alexandra bus boycott on real-life incidents. Two bus boycotts—one in 1943, the other in 1944—took place in Alexandra, a well-populated black suburb of Johannesburg, in response to fare increases levied by private bus companies. The first bus strike lasted nine days, during which thousands of workers walked to their jobs. The fare was reduced. The second boycott, which lasted seven weeks, resulted in the government's establishing and subsidizing the Public Utility Transport Corporation to keep fares down.

When Reverend Kumalo and his brother visit their sons in the penitentiary, Absalom—who has admitted to firing the gun—is sullen and withdrawn, unable to answer his father's anguished questions. Meanwhile, John Kumalo plans to engage a shrewd lawyer to get the charges against his own son dismissed. The next day Kumalo learns that Absalom's pregnant girlfriend wishes to marry his son and live in Ndotsheni. The reverend moves the girl into his own lodging-house in Sophiatown. The girl and Gertrude become friendly, but the landlady, Mrs. Lethebe, fearing Gertrude's influence on the younger woman, advises the girl to keep her distance and the friendship cools.

While visiting his son in prison again, Kumalo learns that Absalom's accomplices have deserted him and plan to deny any involvement in Jarvis's murder. Father Vincent, a friendly priest at the mission house, introduces the Kumalos to a lawyer who will handle Absalom's case *pro deo* ("for God"). The reverend is moved by this act of kindness and hopes Absalom may yet be saved.

The second book of the novel begins when James Jarvis, Arthur's father, receives news of his son's tragic death and, with his wife, hurries to Johannesburg. Knowing little of his son's life in the city, the elder Jarvis is startled to learn from Arthur's in-laws, the Harrisons, of Arthur's humanitarianism and passionate advocacy of black rights. Jarvis, a wealthy farmer, has had little personal contact with black Africans and until now has unquestioningly accepted the segregation of races in South Africa. But spurred by the desire to know more about his only son, Jarvis visits Arthur's house and combs through his books and papers. He learns of Arthur's admiration for Abraham Lincoln, of the clubs and organizations to which he belonged, and of the speeches he was to deliver at these meetings. Arthur's writings reveal his devout Christianity, sympathy for the oppressed blacks, and belief that black crime often stems from corrupt white leadership and abuses of power. Jarvis is deeply affected by what he reads and begins to rethink his own position on the "native question." At Arthur's funeral, Jarvis observes that his son is mourned by blacks as well as whites, and, for the first time in his life, shakes hands with native Africans.

Meanwhile, Absalom Kumalo's trial begins, though the proceedings attract little attention because of the recent discovery of gold in Odendaalsrust. Absalom admits to shooting Arthur Jarvis but swears that he did not shoot to kill him. The other two defendants, Matthew Kumalo and Johannes Pafuri, plead not guilty. After court is adjourned on the first day of the trial, Reverend Kumalo catches sight of James Jarvis in the courtroom and trembles in fear and remorse. During a court recess, the two men encounter

each other by chance. Kumalo nervously blurts out his identity and Absalom's responsibility for Arthur's death. Jarvis is stunned by this disclosure but assures Kumalo that he is not angry. After learning that they are neighbors after a fashion, Kumalo and Jarvis bond briefly over their shared grief.

Elsewhere in Johannesburg, John Kumalo gives a fiery speech demanding higher wages for black miners, while white policemen grimly watch and assess how great a threat he represents. A miners' strike at the Driefontein is quickly suppressed after three black miners are killed. In Sophiatown, Mrs. Lethebe warns Gertrude about her heedlessness, advising her not to cause greater heartache for Reverend Kumalo. Ashamed and contrite, Gertrude considers leaving her son with her brother and becoming a nun.

At the conclusion of the trial, Absalom is convicted of murder and sentenced to death, but his two accomplices are acquitted. Reverend Kumalo is devastated but rallies to arrange the marriage between Absalom and his pregnant girlfriend. The father and son share a painful parting, as Absalom breaks down in tears when the guards come to escort him to prison in Pretoria. Kumalo exhorts his son to have courage and promises to look after the girl and the baby. Back in town, Kumalo visits his brother John, intending to warn him about the dangers of being corrupted by power. But grief and anger overwhelm him and the brothers quarrel bitterly. Turning back to apologize, Kumalo finds John's door barred against him. That night, at Mrs. Lethebe's, Msimangu hosts a going-away party for the Kumalos. Msimangu tells Kumalo that he is retiring into a religious community and forsaking all his worldly possessions, so he bequeaths what money he has saved to the older man to help the village of Ndotsheni. The next morning, Kumalo wakes his family for their journey to Ndotsheni, but finds that Gertrude has disappeared, leaving her child behind.

Book Three takes place back in Ndotsheni, as Kumalo introduces his wife to her nephew and new daughter-in-law and receives a warm welcome from his parishioners. The drought, Kumalo notices, is taking a heavy toll on the village, drying up the streams and parching the maize crop. Determined to find a way to restore Ndotsheni, Kumalo meets with the Zulu chief and voices his concerns about the land and the villagers, many of whom have fallen ill because of the drought. The chief listens intently, then promises to speak to the magistrate about what can be done.

In Ndotsheni Kumalo is visited by a young white boy—Arthur Jarvis's son—who wants to learn Zulu from him. The boy is sobered to learn that a village child is dying from lack of milk. That very night, one of Jarvis's employees arrives in Ndotsheni with a cart full of milk cans and instructions that Kumalo is to ration the milk to the children. More changes rapidly follow—a black agriculturist comes to help the villagers care for their land, and a dam is built to ensure a water supply for the cattle. Meanwhile, the boy continues to visit Kumalo for Zulu lessons, reinforcing the growing bond between the Kumalo and Jarvis families. Jarvis himself comes to Ndotsheni and has another encounter with Kumalo as they take refuge in the dilapidated church during a rainstorm. Jarvis asks if there will be mercy for Absalom but Kumalo informs him that there will be none. The two bereaved fathers again unite in their sorrow, and Jarvis promises to remember the day of Absalom's execution.

On the day before Absalom's execution, Kumalo packs some provisions and heads towards the mountain of Emoyeni. Towards dusk, he meets Jarvis out riding. The two men speak again of their shared plans for Ndotsheni and Jarvis vows to continue the work he has started in memory of his son. Alone, Kumalo climbs the mountain, then kneels down to pray for everyone who has been touched by the tragedy of Arthur and Absalom. Towards morning, when the hour of execution approaches, Kumalo removes his hat and stoically faces the dawn of Absalom's death.

A plea for racial harmony. In the novel the election of 1948—which will officially introduce apartheid—is still two years away, but black and white South Africans are aware of the ongoing struggle to coexist and the difficulty of finding solutions to this problem:

> And some cry for the cutting up of South Africa without delay into separate areas, where white can live without black, and black without white. . . . But what does one do, when one cries this thing, and one cries another? Who knows how we shall fashion a land of peace where black outnumbers white so greatly?
> (Cry, the Beloved Country, p. 78)

Paton's own hopes for better relations between white and black South Africans are mirrored in the parallel journeys of Stephen Kumalo and James Jarvis, whose lives intersect after Kumalo's son kills Jarvis's son.

Alan Paton

Although Kumalo and Jarvis have lived in the same rural area for many years, they have been only vaguely aware of each other's existence. The tragedy, however, brings them abruptly into contact with each other and with a changing world. In Johannesburg, both men are brought face to face with the racial issues that divide South Africa. While seeking Absalom, Kumalo witnesses the interaction between whites and blacks during a bus boycott, observes crime and poverty in a shantytown, and listens to his brother John's incendiary speeches against racial discrimination. Reverend Msimangu, Kumalo's new friend in Sophiatown, has an even greater impact on his views. Having observed the same societal injustices as Kumalo for many years, Msimangu contends that "there is only one thing that has power, and that is love," adding, "I see only one hope for our country, and that is when white men and black men desiring neither power nor money, but desiring only the good of their country, come together to work for it" (Cry, the Beloved Country, pp. 39-40). Jarvis undergoes a similar epiphany when he journeys to Johannesburg after Arthur's death. While many whites, including Arthur's father-in-law, admit to distrusting and fearing blacks, Jarvis encounters a different perspective when he reads his son's unfinished writings. In one manuscript, Arthur expresses sentiments similar to those of Msimangu about the white man's responsibility for the black man's plight: "[The blacks'] simple system of order and tradition and convention has been destroyed . . . by the impact of our civilization. Our civilization has therefore an inescapable duty to set up another system of order and tradition and convention" (*Cry, the Beloved Country*, p. 146). Moved by his son's words, Jarvis dedicates his own resources to helping the blacks in Ndotsheni. The growing sympathy between Jarvis and Kumalo is a microcosmic realization of Msimangu's hopes for cooperation between whites and blacks. Ironically, *Cry, the Beloved Country* was published in 1948, the year in which the Afrikaner Nationalists came to power and implemented the policy of apartheid. The novel's promotion of understanding, faith, and love as the best solutions to racial divisiveness seems all the more poignant given these real-life developments.

Sources and literary context. In his "Author's Note" to *Cry, the Beloved Country*, Paton writes: "No person in this book is intended to be an actual person . . . nor in any related event is reference intended to any actual event" (*Cry, the Beloved Country*, p. vii). Paton describes his account of such incidents as the boycott of buses, the discovery of gold in Odendaalsrust, and the miners' strike as "a compound of truth and fiction" (*Cry, the Beloved Country*, p. vii). Despite such disclaimers, however, Paton did take his inspiration for events in the novel from similar real-life occurrences. Likewise, several of Paton's characters are composites of people he knew or admired. For example, Stephen Kumalo was based on a clergyman who used to visit his son in the Diepkloof Reformatory, while Arthur Jarvis shared many of Paton's own traits and interests.

Like Olive Schreiner's **The Story of an African Farm** (also covered in *African Literature and its Times*), *Cry, the Beloved Country* occupies a pivotal place in South African literature. Paton's novel recreates, with painstaking accuracy, the problems of South Africa in the 1940s, while introducing readers to a country unfamiliar to many of them. The South African Nobel laureate Nadine Gordimer (see **Burger's Daughter**, also covered in *African Literature and Its Times*), declared that South African literature "made a new beginning with *Cry, the Beloved Country*. . . . It was a book of lyrical beauty and power that moved the conscience of the outside world over racialism and, what's more, that of white South Africa as no book had done before" (Gordimer in Callan, p. 10).

Reviews. Paton received some hate mail about *Cry, the Beloved Country*, from Afrikaners who felt that he had betrayed his own heritage by advocating black rights and portraying the Kumalos so sympathetically. At best, the novel met with a mixed reception in South Africa. Black writers generally respected Paton's social scrutiny, but "the countrified Parson the Revd Stephen Kumalo . . . was regarded as an embarrassment" by journalists, whose own personas and agendas tended to be more radical than the novel's (Chapman, p. 239).

Critics abroad embraced *Cry, the Beloved Country*. Richard Sullivan, writing for the *New York Times*, declared that "this is a beautiful novel, a rich, firm and moving piece of prose" (Sullivan in James and Brown, p. 6). U.S. journals, in contrast to the criticism cited above, praised the novel's characterization—in the *New Republic*, James Stern predicted that Reverend Kumalo would become "an immortal figure" in literature, adding "if there is a man who can read the tragedy of Kumalo's life with eyes dry, I have no desire to meet him" (Stern in James and Brown, p. 26). Adrienne Koch of the *Saturday Review* concurred, calling Paton's characters "utterly credible" (Koch in James and Brown, p. 14).

Recognizing Paton's didactic intent, other critics commended his restraint in handling the inflammatory race issue. O.D. Hormel, writing for the *Christian Science Monitor*, called the novel "a rare and beautiful instance of that 'singleminded attempt to render the highest kind of justice to the visible universe,' which has been called the requisite of a true work of art" (Hormel in James and Brown, p. 15). And in the *Yale Review*, Orville Prescott wrote that *Cry, the Beloved Country* "lacks entirely the bitterness, dogmatism and exaggerated melodrama which disfigure most fictional treatments of race relations. . . . There is a generosity of spirit here which is as rare as it is beautiful and moving" (Prescott in James and Brown, p. 573).

—Pamela S. Loy

For More Information

Alexander, Peter F. *Alan Paton: A Biography*. Oxford: Oxford University Press, 1994.

Byrnes, Rita M., ed. *South Africa: A Country Study*. Washington, D.C.: Federal Research Division, 1997.

Callan, Edward. *Cry, the Beloved Country: A Novel of South Africa*. Boston: Twayne Publishers, 1991.

Cameron, Trewella, ed. *A New Illustrated History of South Africa.* Johannesburg: Southern Book Publishers, 1986.

Chapman, Michael. *South African Literatures.* London: Longman, 1996.

Fage, J. D. *A History of Africa.* 3rd ed. London: Routledge, 1995.

James, Mertice M., and Dorothy Brown, eds. *Book Review Digest 1948.* New York: H. W. Wilson, 1949.

Lacour-Gayet, Robert. *A History of South Africa.* Trans. Steven Hardman. London: Cassell, 1977.

Leach, Graham. *South Africa: No Easy Path to Peace.* London: Routledge & Kegan Paul, 1986.

Paton, Alan. *Cry, the Beloved Country.* New York: Charles Scribner's Sons, 1948.

Thompson, Leonard. *A History of South Africa.* New Haven, Conn.: Yale University Press, 1990.

The Dark Child

by

Camara Laye

amara Laye wrote *The Dark Child* while he was a student in France, to ease his homesickness by recalling his youth in West Africa. Laye was born January 1, 1929, in Kourassa, French Guinea, and became the eldest son of 12 children fathered by Camara Komady, a leading blacksmith in the region. At 15, Laye traveled to the colonial capital, Conakry, to study at a technical college, and four years later left his homeland on a scholarship to study in France. When his scholarship was not renewed, he found work in France. He took a job at the Simca auto factory and with the French railroad, pursuing his studies in night classes. It was during this period that Laye wrote *The Dark Child*: "Living in Paris, far from my native Guinea, far from my parents . . . I bore myself in thought a thousand times to my country, close to my people . . . and then, one day, I began to write" (Laye in King, p. 14). The resulting memoir recounts his youth from the early 1930s to the late 1940s. A seminal work in African literature, *The Dark Child* was the first to convey in French to European readers the experience of growing up in Malinke society in colonial Guinea.

Events in History at the Time of the Memoir

Malinke society. The Malinke are a subgroup of the larger Mande people who dwell in lands by the Upper Niger River, including those around the Guinea-Mali border. The area featured in the memoir, known as Upper Guinea, lies in the

---

> ## THE LITERARY WORK
>
> A memoir set in French Guinea during the 1930s and 1940s; published in French (as *L'enfant noir*) in 1953, in English in 1954.
>
> ## SYNOPSIS
>
> A Malinke recalls his youth and the choices he faced between the traditional and colonial paths to adulthood.

Mande heartland. The Mande count among their ancestors the legendary Sunjata Keita (see *Epic of Son-Jara*, also covered in *African Literature and Its Times*), who early in the thirteenth century established the Mali empire through a series of conquests. Sunjata's forefathers are thought to have immigrated to the Mande region from the Ghana empire, and to have found there a number of small societies, including the Camara, Traore, and Kone clans.

According to Laye, the political, social, and religious framework of the Malinke society existed largely unchanged from Sunjata's day through French colonial times. In religion, the Mande practiced a mix of Islam and their own indigenous faith. Society allowed men to marry more than one wife. The traditional household consisted of a polygamous compound, or "concession," as it is called in the memoir. There was a separate, circular thatched structure for each adult (circumcised) male and for each married

A village in French Guinea.

woman; all others shared the house of their mother or closest relative. Artisans like Laye's father might even have apprentices living in the concession; the average concession housed 18 or so people. The size of a town varied from perhaps 20 concessions in a small community to 100 or more. Aside from the capital of Conakry, however, the large town was more a cluster of villages around an administrative and commercial core than it was a modernized urban area. Within the compound, or concession, women tended children, prepared food, drew water, raised crops, washed, and gathered firewood. Meanwhile, men raised cattle and sheep, farmed, or pursued a craft. Contrary to popular opinion, says Laye's memoir, which holds the African woman to be "ridiculously humble," in his country her role "is one of fundamental independence, of great inner pride" (Camara, *The Dark Child,* p. 69).

Mande society in general long consisted of three groups—nobles, specialized professionals, and the defunct subdivision of slaves. The nobles consisted of farmers, who grew rice, millet, and garden vegetables for subsistence; from their clans came the political leaders. Their lives were intertwined with those of the specialized profes-

sionals, known as *nyamakala.* The nyamakala inherited the spiritual means to perform and be protected from the consequences of their trades, which were thought to unleash *nyama,* energizing force. Divisions of nyamakala were blacksmith (*numu*), leatherworker (*garanke*), musician and historian (*jeli*), and Qur'anic praiser/genealogist (*fune, fine*). The blacksmiths fashioned hoes, saddles, wooden plates, statues, rifles, and amulets; their trade was fraught with potential danger. Some were healers too. Among the most hazardous acts a blacksmith performed was circumcision, a rite Laye undergoes in the memoir.

> A blacksmith is born into a caste which enables him to smelt iron ore, to transform the iron, earth, and wood, and to survive the forces unleashed by his transformation.... The means or powers required to perform an act are referred to as *dalilu.* All acts and their associate instruments have *nyama* [energizing force]....
> The inherent dalilu of the *nyama-kala* [nyama caste] affords protection against the nyama they release.
>
> (Bird and Kendall in Charry, p. 52)

The farmer nobles were obligated to provide for the nyamakala—recompense for the goods they crafted and the services they furnished. Apparently blacksmiths ranked high in the nyamakala hierarchy; they were obligated to furnish lower-ranking nyamakala such as the professional musician/oral historian (the jeli, or, in French, the *griot*) with gifts, as Laye's father does in *The Dark Child.* In the memoir, a jeli serves as an intermediary for a woman who wants Laye's blacksmith father to fashion a gold trinket. The jeli, a hired voice, appeals to the pride of the blacksmith, recalling the lofty deeds of his ancestors in couplets, while plucking the *kora,* a 21-stringed harp unique to the Mande. According to Laye, the jeli exceeded his mercenary status—"he was no longer ... a man whose services anyone could rent. He was a man who created his song out of some deep inner necessity" (*The Dark Child,* p. 39). The explanation touches on a negative image under which the jeli labored: often he was looked down upon, perceived as a "yes" man whose praises were less than heartfelt and resented for the money he managed to amass. In fact, a debate rages today about the status of the nyamakala in general. Historians long thought them an inferior caste, but recent scholarship suggests that relationships were more complex, and in the memoir, Laye's father certainly commands a great deal of respect. While nyamakala could not own land or hold public office in Mande society, political leaders would not make a decision without first consulting a senior blacksmith. Clearly there were many facets to the status of nyamakala.

From age 10, apprentices worked by a blacksmith's side, learning to harness their innate power. Born into a blacksmith family themselves, these apprentices were believed to possess the heretofore untapped power as their birthright, and older blacksmiths kept it intact by marrying among themselves. In *The Dark Child,* Laye's mother's father was a blacksmith too. Those born into such families could leave the trade, as do Laye's uncles (one is a farmer in Tindican; another, a businessman in Conakry). However, only children born into such a family could pursue the craft. It should be noted that there were farmers and tradespeople who also engaged in sideline businesses. A farmer, for example, might sell surplus produce while not preoccupied with planting or harvesting, while a blacksmith might raise crops in his spare time.

Education. For most Malinke, education was dispensed by parents, especially the mother, who imparted traditional knowledge in the form of songs, tales, and proverbs. On-the-job training came from other family members too, who had children help at herding cattle, chasing birds from crops, and harvesting rice, the way Laye does in the memoir. At one point in his memoir, Laye wonders whether he would have been better off had he been schooled in his father's workshop instead of the classroom. Vocational education, as suggested by the discussion of apprentices above, was a matter of learning by experience. A youth would be apprenticed to a master; as maturity approached, these apprentices were taught not only the necessary practical skills, but also the trade's spiritual secrets: its chants, its rituals, and its taboos.

Before Guinea's independence in 1958, formal schooling was limited to a minority of Malinke children. Islam demands a basic knowledge of the Qur'an and the teachings of Mohammed, so Qur'anic schools were always widespread and well attended; however, for a child destined to labor in the fields or at a forge, until European colonialism this was all the classroom experience parents thought children needed.

As late as 1949 only about 6 percent of the school-age population in French West Africa attended European-style centers of learning. Village schools were sparse, and secondary education was limited. Between 1903 and 1944 the French Federal School System founded a number of elementary and preparatory schools, which emphasized basic instruction, assuming that most students would not go on to secondary schools. For the most part, higher education focused on vocational training—Laye attends a technical school in the capital—and was reserved for the especially gifted or well disciplined. The French aimed to create an indigenous elite, a small class that could govern the colony effectively. The cream of the elite—those who excelled in the French schools of West Africa—might be rewarded with a scholarship to a school in France. However, this "reward" often came at considerable cost. In France, Guinean students found their African degrees to be all but meaningless: their education had not prepared them for the rigors of French schools, and their diplomas were disrespected. On top of these disadvantages, they coped with new experiences of racism in a predominantly white society and with inner pangs of homesickness. By 1954 some 512 West African students held such scholarships, and perhaps as many financed their own way to France (Hargreaves, p. 151). It is into this tiny fraction that Camara Laye falls.

LAYE CAMARA—CAMARA LAYE

There is an ongoing dispute among critics about how to use the author's name. Critics generally refer to him as "Laye" rather than "Camara," even though the latter is his real last name. The discrepancy arises from the fact that, during his schooling, French teachers required students to put their family name first, followed by the given name, which prompted the switch from Laye Camara to Camara Laye.

Colonial society. In Conakry, Laye lives with Uncle Mamadou, whose family occupies one house, not separate dwellings as in Kourassa, although each wife and circumcised male inhabits separate quarters, observing the law if not the letter of custom. Although the specter of French colonial authority hardly appears in Laye's memoir, there was some agitation in Guinea at the time and a proper appreciation of the memoir's context demands awareness of it.

Not in the memoir, but important for understanding its backdrop, is the fact that the post–World War II years, when Laye attends technical school in Conakry, saw the rise of vigorous nationalism in French West Africa. World War II inspired movements for social and political reform that would lead to independence. In 1944 (at the Brazzaville Conference) France reaffirmed its commitment to empire, not the independence of its colonies, but its leaders also promised reforms in the colonies, which were ultimately enacted. France's 1946 constitution entitled its African territories to their own elective assemblies and to representatives in the French national legislature. Perhaps most significantly, the colonized changed from "subject" to "citizen," though their new status remained only vaguely defined. Nevertheless, it freed Africans from the most oppressive features of colonial rule—forced labor and discriminatory law. Africans themselves had a hand in bringing about these reforms. In 1946 they banded together to form a movement (the *Rassemblement Democratique Africain*) that agitated for constitutional guarantees of their rights, and in 1947 an arm of this movement (the *Parti Democratique de Guinée*) was established in Guinea. All these reforms suggested that perhaps France would finally implement a policy that so far it had invoked only as

cant: full assimilation, which African activists demanded just after the war. At the same time, many called for a peaceful end to the colonial system throughout Africa. Laborers in Guinea started to marshal support from the population at large—youths as well as women and farmers. (The majority of Africans continued to live in villages and to practice subsistence agriculture in the 1940s.) In Laye's memoir, the French colonizers make almost no appearance; their imprint is reflected only in his education. Given that the movement, initiated by workers, was still in its infancy at the close of his memoir, it may have not yet reached students like Laye or his uncle, an executive in a French firm in Conakry.

Conakry. When the French formed the colony of French Guinea in 1891, they chose for their capital the small fishing village of Conakry. Conakry sat on an island called Tombo, from which the French built a thousand-foot causeway to the mainland. By 1944 the population of Conakry had swelled to 26,000, and the city was by far the most important place in the colony.

Laye is overwhelmed by his initial experience of the city. His own village had a population of just over 6,000, so the sheer number of people shocks him. On top of that, the majority speak a language (Susa) he does not understand, and the climate is oppressively humid compared to that of his inland home. Finally, Conakry is planned like a modern city, with straight, tree-lined streets, and, as mentioned, single homes instead of concessions. But perhaps most amazing to the youth from the interior is a novelty that has nothing to do with school, city, or colony at all: his first glimpse of the Atlantic Ocean. It is this type of emotional reaction that makes *The Dark Child* such a unique mix of particular (Malinke) and universal (human) experience.

The Memoir in Focus

Contents summary. *The Dark Child* unfolds as a series of sentimental recollections of Camara Laye's childhood and adolescence. The narrator expresses his longing for his lost natal community by remembering the joy and wonder experienced by his younger self. Less a continual narrative than a grouping of thematically distinct chapters, *The Dark Child* moves at a leisurely pace from Laye's earliest memories to the day he leaves for France. The first eight chapters center on life in the Camara compound, Laye's trips to visit his mother's family, his life at school, and initiation ceremonies. In these chapters, Laye appears to

---

THE RAILROAD

Built between 1902 and 1914, the railroad in French Guinea connected the interior (and the products found or grown there) to coastal Conakry and, through that port, to European manufacturers and consumers. The rail lines made concrete the essential fact of colonialism: that it was designed to send physical and human wealth to the European capital, in this case, Paris. In the colony, all advancement is found in Conakry; and the only way to get to Conakry is by rail. Camara recalls that the railway passed so close to his family's compound that, during the months of dryness, children had to be ready to extinguish the fires that the sparks of passing trains set off on the compound's thatched fence. Every day of his life, the sight of the railway provided Camara with a visual reminder of the colonial power that would shape his life. When he is ready to go to school in the capital, it is a train that carries him away. In short, the railroad encapsulates the changing world of the Malinke; in moving from Kourassa to Conakry, Camara moves from a cozy life bound by tradition and enchantments to a colder and harder society governed by the kind of technology that the train represents.

---

be just another boy in a loving family—a happy Malinke youth, living in the manner of his forefathers. Only in the last four chapters, in which he recalls his experiences in Conakry, does he take on a more distinct identity. His life there cannot follow a customary model; when he returns to Kourassa on holidays, he realizes that he is slowly changing, and his mother recognizes it too, adding European touches to his dwelling. These changes become official when he accepts his headmaster's offer of a scholarship in France.

In the memoir's opening scene, a very young Camara is playing with a snake that, unbeknownst to him, has a deadly venom. One of his father's apprentices jerks the child to safety as another apprentice kills the snake. In this way the boy learns about the dangers of snakes. One day he spots a small black snake slithering into his father's workshop. He prepares to kill it, but fortunately does not: it is his father's totem animal. His father feeds and houses it and, in return, the snake's spirit comes to the father in dreams and imparts foreknowledge that helps him plan his business, his financial affairs, and his family life.

The memoir moves on to describe his father's work at the forge, a job that requires not only manual dexterity, but also mastery of chanting, cleansing, and ritual. This spiritual dimension is contrasted to the less quantifiable, but no less powerful, magic of his mother, whose totem is a crocodile. Not only is she safe near crocodiles, but she appears to have power over animals. Whenever a farmer finds his horse or mule unwilling to move, he appeals to Laye's mother, because animals listen to her direction.

Laye spends the next two chapters on his youthful vacations with his mother's family in the small village of Tindican, describing his twin uncles, the care his grandmother takes in bathing him, the joy and arduous work of the rice harvest. He describes his days at Tindican as ones in which he is pampered, examined, made much of; his grandmother plies him with dish after dish, convinced that he does not eat enough in Kourassa. And of course he is taken around to all her friends, who call him her "little husband" and stuff him even fuller. However, his time at Tindican is not idle; besides helping the whole village during the December rice harvest, he aids other children of the village in whatever tasks their parents have set them to achieve. In these chores, he is hampered by the school clothes he wears. His less citified playmates are fascinated by, if not envious of, these fine, strange clothes, but he is less enchanted: "I envied their freedom of movement. My city clothes . . . were a great nuisance, for they might become dirty or torn" (*The Dark Child,* pp. 52-53).

School life presents the boy with a different set of problems. Laye devotes a chapter to describing the bullying the young children receive at the hands of the older children in the schoolyard. The youngsters are teased and forced to do manual labor that the teachers dole out to the older children as punishment for misbehavior. The younger students bear the abuse quietly until one of Laye's friends and then Laye himself break down and tell their fathers. Incensed, the fathers see to it that a bully himself is thrashed and Laye's takes a swing at the school headmaster. The situation nearly comes to a breaking point, until the headmaster is fired, and security at the school grows tighter.

Following this episode, Laye describes, in vivid and emotional detail, his participation in the rite of Kondén Diara and in circumcision. Having being taught that Kondén Diara is a "lion that eats up little boys,'" Laye and the other initiates are taken to the forest to spend the night near the lair of the alleged lion (*The Dark Child,* p. 94). He describes the stages involved in this rite, as he does later for circumcision. In these two events, Laye comes as close as he ever will to being a full participant in the customary life of his people. At the dance that precedes the circumcision, mothers hold aloft the implements of their son's future profession: A future peasant's mother holds a hoe; Laye's "second mother" (his father's other wife) holds aloft a notebook and pen, bragging about her half-son's status as a scholar. To the extent that scholastic success was the key to advancement in colonial society, Laye's diligence and intelligence are highly respected. However, these same qualities are tragic, in that they remove Laye from his native environment, and eventually into the cold northern foreignness of France.

When he has completed elementary schooling in Kourassa, Camara wins acceptance to a technical school in the capital. Of all his classmates, he is the only one so honored. In Conakry, he lives with his father's brother, Mamadou. Mamadou is among the first wave of the indigenous colonial elite; French-educated, he serves as head accountant with a French firm in the city. Mamadou encourages his nephew to persevere, even though Laye finds city life difficult and his schoolwork initially boring and simplistic. Although Laye underplays the extent of his unhappiness, Conakry's humidity and the long hours spent standing in the school's workshop combine to give him horrible ulcers on his feet. A month or two after his arrival, he is hospitalized, and he remains in the hospital for the whole school year—miraculously healing as school ends and he can return to Kourassa for the summer.

The next term he finds that the school has been reorganized. Now he is challenged and engaged by the curriculum, and further stimulated by the presence of Marie. A close friend of Uncle Mamadou's family, she and Laye themselves become intimate, if platonic, friends. Even though they never declare their love for each other, Laye calls her friendship one of the sustaining forces of his life in Conakry. After three years in which he flourishes as a scholar, he places first on the final proficiency exam and is told by the headmaster that he has been offered a scholarship in France. He accepts without thinking; not until he returns to Kourassa does he realize that he failed to consult his parents.

The final chapter describes the pain his decision brings to himself and his family. Reluctantly his father agrees: "Yes, I want you to go to France. I want that now, just as much as you do. Soon we'll be needing men like you here" in Guinea (*The Dark Child*, p. 182). Laye's mother flatly rejects the possibility of her eldest son leaving her, perhaps forever. She wonders if the French even have families, since they are so eager to destroy hers. Together, father and son prevail upon Laye's mother, who finally accepts, though tearfully, the inevitable. In the last moment of the memoir, Laye is on the plane bound for Paris with Marie, who will be dropped off to finish her studies in Dakar. He thinks sadly about all he is leaving behind, then sticks his hand in his coat pocket and discovers a map of the Paris subway system.

Sleeping with the enemy? Laye's book drew criticism from many African intellectuals. They felt he had idealized village life, presenting Africans as happy, superstitious primitives, and totally ignoring the devastation wreaked on African cultures by the colonial system. Europeans embraced the memoir. But given the era's rise in African self-consciousness and anticolonialism, the early 1950s was seen by many Africans as the wrong time for a mostly apolitical treatment of African life. The memoir's popular success in Europe would serve only to exacerbate such criticisms.

However, neither the purpose nor the effect of the book is as simple as Laye's critics made it out to be. The memoir's popularity in France proves little; it is as likely that French readers misunderstood Laye's deeper intent as that he intended to pander to them. And the success of 1950s works by such writers as Chinua Achebe (see *Things Fall Apart*, also covered in *African Literature and Its Times*) demonstrate that European readers had a taste even for works that criticized colonialism. Laye himself asserted that the book attacked colonialism indirectly, by speaking of African civilization and culture sympathetically and by countering the stereotypes of missionaries and anthropologists with insights that promoted true understanding. Clearly the book's statements on the nature of African culture deserve a close look.

Admittedly the evils of colonialism are not one of the memoir's themes; the only part approaching a direct criticism of the French regime is Laye's dissatisfaction with the curriculum at his technical school during his first year. However, the memoir itself is shaped by a contradiction that is essential to the African critique of colonialism: the dilemma of educated Africans, seized by Europeans from the heart of their own traditions, who are not rewarded with a full place in the European world or given a philosophical outlook that satisfies them as fully as the outlook of their people satisfies their family and less-educated friends. From an early age, Laye stands slightly apart even from his closest friends: at his grandmother's village, he must refrain from the roughest play to avoid ruining his expensive school clothes. Laye is a natural scholar, and his family pushes him to excel; but every success takes him farther from Kourassa.

The French aimed to create an African elite of well educated local people; but this elite would be estranged from the home life of their own culture. In this context, the absence of European characters from the book takes on a new, more sinister significance. Colonial policy dictated that children as smart as Laye be removed from the village environment, but it did nothing to assuage the loneliness and isolation that result from this separation. All the education in the world cannot make Laye French, or give him a community to replace the one he loses when he leaves Kourassa. In this regard, *The Dark Child* presents a powerful, if submerged, critique of the logic of colonialism.

This same tension between African and European understandings appears in one of the most sensitive aspects of Laye's work: his treatment of Malinke spirituality. Writing in a European language for a largely European audience, Laye is well aware that he cannot flatly assert that his father's small black snake actually appears in dreams and tells his father the future. To do so would be to court the ridiculous in the eyes of European readers. At the same time, he refuses to reject the beliefs of his people outright. Laye finds two solutions for this potential dilemma. First, and more frequently, he shows the rationality and logic behind what may seem to be mere superstitions. The paradigmatic example is his treatment of the night of Kondén Diara. The monstrous lions who terrify the initiates are manufactured, not real. To anyone not brought up in Malinke society, this solution to the "mystery" may appear obvious. But, had Laye acknowledged that fact as he wrote his description, he would have risked making the whole event seem ludicrous. To avoid this, he insistently returns to the point of view he had as a boy. He recounts his father's advice not to be afraid, and vividly repaints his own fear in all its aspects and details. The reader may never believe in the reality of Kondén Diara; but he or she will certainly finish the book with a deep sense of how real it is to the youthful initiates. Then, when Laye pulls back the veil to reveal what readers may have suspected, they can understand why such events are so important, how sophisticated in fact these rituals are. On this night, Camara and the other boys are not simply being tormented; they are being tested. Their courage, their obedience, and perhaps most of all, their trust, are measured. After all, it is no easy thing, when supposedly a few feet away from very real-sounding howling lions, to remember that your father has assured you that you will not be harmed. The unstated assertion is that, while the vehicle may look like superstition, the content is social genius, no more worthy of scorn than practices that initiate European youths into their adult society. Laye's respect for Malinke beliefs results in his portraying them not as superstitions of an exotic, primitive people, but as cultural manifestations of a particular time and place, as valid for their circumstances as the ways of the French are for France.

Laye also has another tool at his disposal, although he uses it more sparingly: the weapon of belief. He never mocks or satirizes even those aspects of the traditional faith that have become somewhat suspect to him in his later years. More commonly, he implies that he still believes there is some truth to much of it, refusing to discount his native traditions simply because his Western education has told him to do so. He remains

the stubborn empiricist. Commenting on his mother's supernatural skills with animals, Laye says, "They seem to be unbelievable; they *are* unbelievable. Nevertheless, I can only tell you what I saw with my own eyes" (*The Dark Child*, p. 70). Even after he learns there is trickery behind Kondén Diara, he half suspects a supernatural hand in aspects for which he does not know the exact explanation. He learns the lion's roars are false, and that, in a later part of the ritual, streamers are attached to houses and small trees with long poles. But how on earth did such streamers get to the thorny tops of the bombax trees? Slings? For better or worse, Laye is removed from his village before he learns this se-

FROM MALINKE TO MUSLIM BELIEFS

While Islam is widespread among the Mande peoples, the Muslim faith never completely displaced the older, animistic religion of the group. The nature of the combination of the two beliefs varies greatly from person to person. One of Laye's uncles is a devout Muslim, but Laye's own father teaches him a basically traditional faith under an Islamic superstructure. As animists, the Malinke believe in the existence and power of spirits in every object. These spiritual powers must be propitiated by rites, sacrifices, and ceremonies. Methods of propitiating the spirits structure daily life. Laye recalls that his father performed secret ablutions every morning, the belief being that without this ritual cleansing his work with gold and other metals would be unsanctified and unsuccessful. Furthermore, people of certain lineages, like Laye's mother, are thought to have mysterious powers of a mystical nature.

Rigid Muslim practice is closely associated with city life. Laye's uncle in Conakry is the most devout Muslim in the book. Kourassa, though a smaller town, has a large Muslim population too. At any rate, no Malinke sees a contradiction between the two types of spirituality. Indeed, one good-luck potion consists of water and honey mixed with the chalk washed from the boards of Qur'anic scholars—the holier the scholar, the luckier the potion. That the Malinke see no contradiction between Muslim faith and more traditional practices is proved by the ease with which they combine observances from the two faiths. The traditional rite of initiation for males, Kondén Diara, is performed on the eve of the Muslim holiday Ramadan. The people of Kourassa slide smoothly from observance of the first festival into the next.

Camara Laye

cret. Laye shares too his own conviction in connections between the Muslim faith and the practical world. Before his final exam in college, he has his mother visit *marabouts* (Muslim religious teachers) for good luck. In reporting the results, Laye attributes some of the outcome to the energy of the religious leaders: "Finally the examination came. It lasted three days. Three days of agony. But the marabouts must have given me all the help they could. Of the seven candidates who passed I was first" (*The Dark Child*, p. 167).

LOST IN TRANSLATION

Some recent criticism has focused on the problems of translation in *The Dark Child*. Early readers of the English version denigrated Laye's stylistic abilities, not understanding that the flaws belonged to the translation, not the work. The English version loses the qualities of alliteration and repetition that Laye uses to excellent effect. Even worse, early translators made a few gross errors. One of the most famous mistranslations is "canari." A "canari" is a water pitcher, but an early translator rendered it as "canary," and then had to contort the rest of the sentence to maintain logic. Also detracting from Laye's art is the fact that some translations simply omit entire sentences.

Sources and literary context. Though gifted as a storyteller and a prose stylist, Laye was not trained in literature but as an engineer. His main source for *The Dark Child* are his memories of the cultural life of the Malinke people among whom he was raised. A subscriber to Malinke beliefs might also say he was born into a nyamakala family, and as such possessed creative power of his own. In any case, *The Dark Child* can be situated within the African literature of his time. In an introduction to the memoir, Philippe Thoby-Marcelin writes, "We are eager to know the rest—his life as a poor student in Paris, and most of all the return to his native land" (Thoby-Marcelin, p. 13). The statement alludes to Laye's connection to a larger cultural pattern: the African scholar in the colonizing country. This ties him perhaps most importantly to the "negritude" movement. Founded by Aimé Césaire, Léopold Senghor, and Léon Damas, African students in Paris in the 1930s, the movement gained prominence in the postwar period. In 1947 it produced a journal, *Présence africaine,* whose aim was to revise colonial stereotypes about African life by celebrating the brilliance of its cultures and artistic expression. Along these lines, *The Dark Child* may be said to present the deep logic behind aspects of Malinke culture that may have seemed bizarre to Europeans, such as the faith in spirits and the night of Kondén Diara. Others associated Laye with negritude, and he himself said, "if Negritude is considered the expression of the life of black people," then his writing falls into that category (Laye in Egejuru, p. 86).

Early readers assumed that *The Dark Child* was simple memoir, which, to a large extent, it is. However, Laye does not merely relate his life events; he transposes them "into a fictional system" (Wynter, p. 44). His memoir is thus comparable to other, slightly later semiautobiographical works of African literature, such as **Weep Not, Child** by Kenya's renowned novelist Ngugi wa Thiong'o (also covered in *African Literature and Its Times*).

Laye's prose style owes less to the traditional African tale than it does to the slow-moving, carefully crafted sentence of the European novelists. He cites Gustave Flaubert as a primary influence on his method of composition; like the famously fastidious French novelist, Laye continually reworked his own writing—*The Dark Child* went through six drafts before Laye had it published.

Reviews. *The Dark Child* met with both acclaim and criticism when it was first published. In France, the work was praised for its stylistic and thematic excellence and simplicity. Unfortunately, it played into French stereotypes about the primitive, superstitious African. French readers saw the book as an African idyll, not perceiving the cultural angst that undergirds Laye's memoir. He was praised for maintaining optimism in the face of pain, and for not renouncing his cultural heritage. The popularity of Laye's work in France is indicated by the fact that it won the Prix Littéraire Charles Veillon in 1954.

African readers were often less enchanted; many felt Laye was pandering to the taste of the French colonists for exotic tales of simple, contented Africans. Most objectionable, for such critics, is the complete absence in the memoir of the pressure and terrors levied on Africans by French colonialism, exposed a few years later in novels from West Africa like **Houseboy** by Ferdinand Oyono, and **Mission to Kala** by Mongo Beti (both also covered in *African Literature and Its Times*). The critics claimed that Laye had missed his great chance to present an indictment of colonial rule. Particularly strident was the criticism from Mongo Beti, who described Laye's book as *littérature rose*—literature written through rose-colored glasses. For Beti, this was a false Africa, one that ignored the harsh realities of colonialism; Laye failed to meet his ethical responsibility to present his village not as he remembered it, but as it was—full of pain as well as joy.

More recently, critics have revised the harshness of these initial rejections. Léopold Senghor, the Senegalese poet and politician, himself a driving force behind the negritude movement, has questioned critiques that assume there is a single right way to present Africa. He has defended Laye's right to be faithful to his own vision of life, and his own vision as a writer (Senghor, p. 155). Nigeria's Wole Soyinka has concurred, adding his own line of defense—that "a reader could be so gracefully seduced into a village idyll is a tribute to the author" (Soyinka, p. 387).

—Anne-Lancaster Badders

For More Information

Beti, Mongo. "Afrique noir, littérature rose." *Presence africaine* 1-2 (April-July 1955): 133-45.

Camara Laye. *The Dark Child*. Trans. James Kirkup and Ernest Jones. New York: Noonday Press, 1994.

Charry, Eric S. *Musical Thought, History, and Practice Among the Mande of West Africa*. Ph.D. diss., Princeton University, 1992.

Egejuru, Phanuel Akubueze. *Towards African Literary Independence: A Dialogue with Contemporary African Writers*. Westport, Conn.: Greenwood Press, 1980.

Hargreaves, John D. *West Africa: The Former French States*. Englewood Cliffs, N.J.: Prentice Hall, 1967.

King, Adele. *The Writings of Camara Laye*. London: Heinemann, 1980.

McNaughton, Patrick R. *The Mande Blacksmiths: Knowledge, Power, and Art in West Africa*. Bloomington: Indiana University Press, 1988.

Sellin, Eric. "Islamic Elements in Camara Laye's *L'enfant noir*." In *Faces of Islam in African Literature*. Ed. Kenneth W. Harrow. Portsmouth, N.H.: Heinemann, 1991.

Senghor, Léopold. *Liberté I: Negritude et humanisme*. Paris: Seuil, 1964.

Soyinka, Wole. "From a Common Black Cloth: A Reassessment of the African Literary Image." *The American Scholar* 32, no. 3 (summer 1963): 387-96.

Thoby-Marcelin, Philippe. "Introduction to *The Dark Child*, by Camara Laye." Trans. Eva Thoby-Marcelin. New York: Noonday, 1994.

Wynter, Sylvia. "History, Ideology, and the Reinvention of the Past in Achebe's *Things Fall Apart* and Laye's *The Dark Child*." *Minority Voices* 2, no. 1 (1978): 43-61.

Death and the King's Horseman

by

Wole Soyinka

~

W ole Soyinka, one of the best-known playwrights in the English-speaking world, was born in Abeokuta, Ogun State, Nigeria, in 1934. He attended St. Peter's School in Abeokuta, where his literary-minded father was the headmaster. At the prestigious Government College, a high school in Ibadan, Soyinka nurtured his literary interests by participating in the school's artistic and cultural activities and by reading extensively in the school's library. After high school Soyinka studied English at the University of Ibadan, and drama and theater at Leeds University in England. He went on to write and produce more than 20 plays, several films, two novels, three volumes of autobiography, and one prison memoir, among other works. Soyinka received the Nobel Prize for literature in 1986. His literary works and real-life political engagements show a consistent commitment to the freedom of the human spirit. Soyinka's uncompromising stance on this principle has made him a target of repressive governments in Nigeria. Because of his opposition to the Nigerian civil war, he was imprisoned from August 1967 to October 1969, spending many of these months in solitary confinement. Soyinka subsequently published an account of his prison experience (*The Man Died*), then went into self-imposed exile from 1972 to 1976, returning after the overthrow of military head-of-state Yakuba Gowon. In 1994 he went into exile again because an even harsher dictatorial government became uncomfortable with his criticisms of its human rights infractions. He had, in fact, been

THE LITERARY WORK

A play set in Oyo, the capital of the colonized Oyo kingdom in Nigeria, during World War II; published in English in 1975.

SYNOPSIS

Tragedy results from the failure of a traditional chief, Elesin Oba, the Master of the King's Stables, to commit ritual suicide on the last day of the funeral rites of his king, the Alaafin of Oyo.

expressing such criticism for years; *Death and the King's Horseman* can be read as commentary on the behavior of certain Nigerian rulers during and after the country's civil war.

Events in History at the Time the Play Takes Place

Yoruba royal funeral rites and worldview. Historians speculate that the first Oyo king in verifiable Yoruba history probably reigned about the end of the fifteenth century, and that the expanding kingdom reached its height in the early eighteenth century. Internal rivalries led to its decline in the early nineteenth century, a decline aggravated by British colonial penetration in the mid-nineteenth century. Oyo's centralized control dissolved completely; the Yoruba reorganized themselves around local sites, in some cases around former "seats of traditional kings," like Oyo (Fage, p. 342). Their power meanwhile continued to wane, given the spread of British colonial authority in the mid-to-late 1800s.

Late in 1944, Siyanbola Ladigbolu, the political, spiritual, and cultural leader of Nigeria's Oyo kingdom, died (or "ascended into the rafters," to use a Yoruba idiom). Until the mid-nineteenth century several of the closest family members, aides, advisers, and ministers of a deceased king were compelled to commit "honorable suicides" on the last day of the month-long royal funeral rites. These aides, it is believed, provided the king with the level of service he needed to function adequately in the ancestral realm into which he was transported at death. Politically, the deaths of the former king's advisors allowed the incoming ruler to assume office with his own trusted officials and to rule without worrying about ambitious officers of the previous regime. At the time of Ladigbolu's death, after more than 80 years of Britain's colonial subjugation of Oyo, only a few of those who would traditionally have died with the king were still required to do so. Among the officials attached to the king's person, the Master of the Stables was one of those still mandated to follow the king to the other world. At the end of Ladigbolu's funeral, his Master of the Stables, Jinadu, refused to kill himself as tradition required, in spite of his having enjoyed all the benefits of the office. In his place, Jinadu's oldest son, who deemed his father's refusal insufferable, took his own life. This is the historical event that inspired Soyinka's play. The events and the furor they caused have also been the subject of two plays in the Yoruba language: Duro Lapiipoo's *Oba Waja* and Moses Oylaiya's *Abobaku.*

To understand the trouble created by the king's final rites both in the play and in history, knowledge of the worldview that gives meaning to the practice is required. In the Yoruba society of the play, as in most other African cultures, there are three interrelated states of existence: the ancestral plane of the dead, the earth of the living, and the unformed world of the unborn. A newborn is believed to be an incarnation of returning ancestors, the living person is an ancestor-in-waiting, and the ancestors minister unseen to the living and the unborn at the same time. The living being appeases the ancestors through sacrifice and brings the unborn into the world with the physical labor of procreation.

Movement through these three states is marked culturally by rites of passage, such as naming ceremonies, funerals, and ancestral masking festivals. The most elaborate of the rituals suggest that the passages may themselves be a "fourth stage," as Soyinka himself suggests in his *Myth, Literature and the African World View.* In that ritual space the will to transform into another state and to keep the cosmos running smoothly is tested and proved. The transition state both connects and distinguishes the states of being; the activities that occur there ensure that the living, the unborn, and the ancestors all take their places in the order of things. It is said that the transition state is full of self-doubt, a longing for the familiar, and a distrust of the unknown. The great difficulties of negotiating this state of transition is expressed in the Yoruba proverb that asks: "When you tell the aged one approaching heaven to greet your kinsfolk over there for you, do you think the journey is willingly made?" However, a dutiful adult who has lived a fulfilled life has a responsibility to negotiate the transition successfully, assume his/her rightful ancestral status, and keep looking after the interests of those left behind. In other words, metaphysical disconnectedness of one state from the others is not desirable in the Yoruba worldview, and all thoughts and actions that threaten to bring about stasis must be combated with the exertion of will.

Under these circumstances it is imperative that the transition of the king, the spiritual and political leader of the community, be very elaborate. Traditionally, the funeral rites take a 30-day month to complete. On the last day the persons closest to the monarch while he was alive follow him to the other world and continue ministering to him so that he will have enough time to fulfill his ancestral duties to the kingdom. A misstep by the departing soul is believed to be capable of causing untold calamities for the living: crops will cease to mature, women will cease to menstruate, and semen will dry up in men.

British colonial rule in Nigeria. From 1861 to 1960 parts and then all of Nigeria were ruled by the British. Out of diverse empires, kingdoms, and ethnic groups, the British created one country stretching from the Atlantic Ocean to the savannas. They planned to govern through a system of colonial subordination that they called "indirect rule." The Oyo kingdom, the setting of Soyinka's play, was one of the most useful proving grounds for perfecting the indirect rule system, which was created by Frederick Lord Lugard, the British Governor General of Nigeria. Lugard believed that Africans were incapable of ruling themselves in a civilized manner and must therefore be trained in modern self-governance. Under Lugard's system the traditional rulers of the so-called "advanced" peoples of the colonies—meaning those, such as the Oyo, who had centralized monarchies and hierarchical political structures—would be allowed to carry out the day-to-day running of their dominions under the supervision of British officers. The kings and chiefs would be permitted, among other things, to retain their courts, levy and collect taxes, adjudicate on "native" laws and customs, oversee traditional rites and observances, and conduct other residual duties not specifically assigned to the colonial officers. In the bureaucracy set up within this theoretical framework, compliant chiefs reported to the District Officer, who reported to the provincial Resident, who reported to the regional Governor, who reported to the national Governor General, who reported to the Imperial Office in London. Lugard believed that such a regimented system would allow the Africans to follow their natural evolutionary track, nudged along by the British, gently, with measured interventions only when necessary. His assumption proved false. In practice the kings and chiefs served their own people only at the pleasure of the British authorities, who were always eager to remove so-called "difficult" persons from office.

Parallel institutions. Several parallel societies developed under indirect rule. At the upper echelon were the Europeans—mostly colonial officers, missionaries, teachers, and doctors who lived in a separate world that tried to reproduce Great Britain in the tropics. Below them were the ordinary colonial subjects whose lives were organized according to local beliefs and customs, variants of Christianity or Islam, and agriculture-driven economic activities. Sandwiched between these two groups were the African-born middle-level operators of the colonial machinery—policemen, court clerks, schoolteachers, and the like. The primary goal of the Europeans, whether they were missionaries or colonial officers, was to evangelize, "modernize," and "civilize" the African groups. These groups had to assimilate new ideas and ways of life—including Christianity, Islam (which came earlier in the century from the north), and capitalist changes in the economy. The ordinary subjects tried to make sense of the colonial reality by fitting these new ideas and ways of life to their pre-existing notions, mixing and merging the old with the new, a process known as "syncretism." A little of this syncretist impulse on the part of the ordinary folks sometimes found its way into the behavior of the middle group. Hence, the play's Sergeant Amusa practices Islam with great devotion and still remains reverent to the *egungun* cult of the ancestors. In the polytheistic world of Nigeria's colonial subjects, devotion to one deity is never a shield against blaspheming another, because various spiritual entities deserve reverence.

Commodity exchange, women, and markets. In Oyo as in other kingdoms within the Yoruba-speaking area of Nigeria, the town has a central market located close to the palace. The market is considered to be a microcosm of life itself: all people go there to seek fortune; many will find it and many others will not. The market square facilitates more than just the exchange of goods and services for humans. Spirits, goblins, and other ethereal characters are believed to come there to buy and sell, and to bless and curse humans, too.

THE YORUBA MARKET: MICROCOSM

~

Great cultural events take place in the Yoruba market, especially in the one located in front of the king's palace. Communal festivals occur there; masquerades are not uncommon even on ordinary market days; all sorts of onlookers, who have nothing to do beside people-watching, throng the square; and no market experience is complete without sighting the ubiquitous itinerant drummers and other performers who compete with the general singsong of the market atmosphere. One Yoruba saying, *aye loja oja laye* (the earth is a marketplace, the marketplace is the earth), reflects the variety of experience that the market offers.

In Yoruba culture, women control market-based exchanges. In fact, retail and wholesale trading used to be almost exclusively the prerogative of women. The traders travel far and wide to procure articles for the local market and also organize the "exportation" of local products to traders from other markets. Generally the women organize themselves into trade associations that control the flow of goods, services, and prices. The offices that were held by women in the traditional political hierarchy reflect the power they have exerted in the marketplace. Every Yoruba town has its own leader of the market—Iyaloja, in the play—who is usually a chief, the highest-ranking woman in secular matters of state. The market leader has subordinate officers who help her administer the commercial life of the community. The only other female public officials who approach the importance of the market leader are the priestesses of powerful deities.

The Play in Focus

Plot summary. The dramatic action of *Death and the King's Horseman* opens as Elesin, Master of the King's Stables, walks across a twilit market square that is closing for the day. Accompanying him is his official praise-singer.

THE PRAISE-SINGER

The praise-singer is Elesin's official herald. Like all prominent citizens of the kingdom, Elesin appoints an accomplished poet to announce his presence at social functions that involve him. A praise-singer chants the lineage poetry of his patron on these occasions. His is not a full-time occupation. In his quasi-official status as praise-singer, he entertains and reminds his sponsor of his duties to the state in the most dignified manner possible. Not an official of the state, per se, such a singer transfers his services to another patron if the one he is serving does not want or need him anymore.

Elesin's entrance at just this time prefigures the unfolding of foreboding events—twilight is a time of uncertainties, a time when every goat is black, as the Yoruba saying goes. Elesin, as the play will reveal, is in the twilight of his own life—that very night, he is to cease living and follow his dead king to the land of the ancestors, where he will continue his service to the Crown and the community. At this crucial juncture, in which the community is sending its king into the abyss of transition, his closest aide should not be seeking the pleasures of the earth by prancing into one of the most vibrant spots in the community. Elesin's first stride in the play is therefore a misstep, according to the traditions of his culture.

Elesin and his praise singer enter the emptying marketplace exchanging banter on the bravery of dying with one's master; Elesin boasts:

> My rein is loosened.
> I am master of my Fate. When the hour
>   comes

> Watch me dance along the narrowing path
> Glazed by the soles of my great precursors.
> My soul is eager. I shall not turn aside.
> (Soyinka, *Death and the King's Horseman*,
>   p. 14)

Then two adulating market women join the exchange, posing rhetorical questions that suggest some doubts. "You will not delay?" they first ask, and when Elesin affirms that he will not, they ask again: "Nothing will hold you back?" (*Death*, p. 14).

After assuring the market world that he will not shirk his duties, Elesin continues his fateful missteps by asking for the hand of a young market woman who has already been betrothed to the son of Iyaloja, the leader of the market. When the market crowd raises eyebrows over the request, Elesin rationalizes his actions, saying he wants to travel light to the other world by allowing redundant seeds (his sperm) "that will not feed the voyager at his passage [to] drop here and take root as he steps beyond this earth and us" (*Death*, p. 22). He cannot perceive, as Iyaloja does, that the fruits borne by the seed may be monstrous: "It will neither be of this world nor of the next" (*Death*, p. 22). Her observation implies that Elesin is not being mindful of his duties.

In spite of her misgivings Iyaloja allows Elesin his pleasure because she trusts the chief to be true to his office and status as an elder. Indeed Elesin chastises her, saying "The doubt is unworthy of you Iyaloja" (*Death*, p. 22). Iyaloja also agrees to give away her prospective daughter-in-law because she knows that, because of his office, Elesin cannot be denied anything he demands. Yet to the market community Elesin's acts belie his professions of readiness for communal sacrifice. He seems to be a *baseje*, a spoiler of preparations. The first act closes as Elesin and the market women consider cosmic well-being. "You wish to travel light," says Iyaloja. "Well, the earth is yours. But be sure the seed you leave in it attracts no curse" (*Death*, p. 23).

In Act 2, the scene shifts to the District Officer's quarters, where Jane and Simon Pilkings are getting ready for a colonial officers' dance. Sergeant Amusa of the local police has come to alert Simon about Elesin's pending ritual suicide and to take orders on what steps should be taken by the colonial authorities. The sergeant surprises the Pilkings as they rehearse their dance steps in an egungun cult costume.

Amusa's consternation and hysterical reaction on seeing his employer and his spouse in the egungun outfit provide the dramatic tension of

Villagers at an *egungun* festival. At such festivals, certain individuals don masks and costumes to become egungun—masqueraders who assume the personas and powers of their ancestors.

the second act. As soon as he knows that Simon and Jane Pilkings are not going to acknowledge the sacrilege they are committing in their egungun outfits, Amusa refuses to either look at or address them directly. Before clamming up he tells Simon, "Sir, I cannot talk this matter to you in that dress" (*Death*, p. 25). Bearing news of Elesin's impending death, Amusa sees an ominous significance in the Pilkings' wearing of death masks: "Sir, it is a matter of death. How can man talk against death to person in uniform of death? Is like talking against government to person in uniform of police" (*Death*, p. 25). In an uncommon act of insubordination, he will not even write down his observations about Elesin's impending suicide until the couple leaves the room. Amusa leaves the District Officer's house without waiting to take orders on what to do next. When Simon finally reads Amusa's note, he springs into action, ordering Elesin's arrest.

The third act shifts back to the market square. It opens with Sergeant Amusa and two police constables trying to reach the center of the market to arrest Elesin. The market women taunt the colonial police, and their daughters mock and assault the uniformed black men. The younger women especially pester Amusa and his men with verbal insults, chase them around, and at one point remove the cap of a policeman. The

policemen retreat as the women are about to overpower them. Why has the confrontation arisen? The market women have insisted that Elesin cannot be disturbed while he is consummating his recent marriage, and the police refuse to agree. By forcing the policemen to leave center stage, the play allows Elesin ample time to consummate both his unusual earthly marriage and his betrothal to the world of the ancestors—that is, his suicide. Elesin completes the former task promptly but is not quick enough in accomplishing the latter, as subsequent acts show.

Elesin takes the initial steps towards fulfilling his final official mission towards the end of the third act, performing "regal motions" that signify a "solemn finality" (*Death*, p. 41). The chants of encouragement sung by the Praise-Singer and the market women signify a desire for cosmic well-being that can be secured only by the kind of painful transition they want Elesin to endure. Elesin falls into a trance, suggesting his gradual move to the other realm. His incantations reinforce the "regal motions": "When the river begins to taste the salt of the ocean, we no longer know what deity to call on. . . . No arrow flies back to the string, the child does not return through the same passage that gave it birth" (*Death*, p. 44). The act closes with Elesin dancing, in a trance, towards what seems to be the abyss of transition.

The fourth act opens with Europeans, all dressed up in "a variety of fancy-dress" and other outfits appropriate for presentation to a royal presence, bowing and curtseying to the visiting English prince (*Death*, p. 45). The Pilkings' egungun costume attracts the most attention. The couple is explaining their outfit to the prince when word arrives that a riot is brewing in town, apparently over the first police attempt to stop the Elesin ritual.

EGUNGUN CULT

Egungun is a cult of the dead. All towns and cities close to the city of Oyo celebrate annual egungun festivals, which many times double as cleansing festivals. At these festivals colorful masques depict departed elders visiting the earth. Reverend Samuel Johnson, himself from Oyo, wrote in the early part of this century:

> the Egungun worship has become a national religious institution, and its anniversaries are celebrated with grand festivities. The mysteries connected with it are held sacred and inviolable, and although little boys of 5 or 6 years of age are often initiated, yet no woman may know these mysteries on the pain of death. . . . The dress of the Egungun consists of cloths of various colors or the feathers of different kinds of birds, or the skins of different animals. The whole body from head to foot is concealed from view; the Egungun seeing only from the meshes of a species of network covering the face, and speaking in a sepulchral tone of voice.
>
> (Johnson, p. 29)

To learn more about the riot, Simon leaves the ball in his egungun outfit. Waiting for him in an adjoining room is his sergeant, Amusa, who again freezes up when he sees Simon. The sergeant refuses to discuss the subject of dying with Simon while he is decked out in the egungun attire of the dead. In his usual pidgin English, the vernacular among the lower ranks of the Nigerian police, Amusa espouses his traditional Yoruba belief about the egungun: "I cannot against death to dead cult. This dress get the power of dead" (*Death*, p. 49). His boss dismisses Amusa in anger and decides to take charge of events himself.

As soon as Simon leaves the stage, Elesin's oldest son, Olunde, whom Simon had sent to England for medical training against his father's wishes, appears. Olunde has managed to quickly

book a passage home within a very short time—he arrived on the same ship that brought the English prince to Nigeria—so that he can give his father a fitting burial. Jane is shocked to see him. She is ignorant of Oyo customs and so does not realize that Olunde, on hearing of the king's death, would have anticipated that his father, Master of the King's Stables, would have to follow 30 days later. Contrary to the assumptions of his benefactors, Olunde's life in England has not erased from his cultural memory a respect for Oyo's communal processes. Unlike the Pilkings, Olunde finds no contradictions in simultaneously pursuing the most fundamental of his father's ways and the most modern medical practice.

Olunde adds to Jane's initial shock by chastising her for desecrating "an ancestral mask" and then enthusiastically informing her that he is home for his father's burial (*Death*, p. 50). The two get into an extended argument on the meaning of self-sacrifice, and the significance of Elesin's planned ritual suicide. To Olunde, self-sacrifice is "an affirmative commentary on life," whereas Jane believes that "[l]ife should never be thrown deliberately away" (*Death*, p. 51). Like her husband, Jane believes that ritual suicides are "barbaric customs" (*Death*, p. 53). Olunde, however, views such a suicide as a guarantor of communal survival. So exasperated is Jane by Olunde's philosophical calmness about his father's impending death that she exclaims: "You're just a savage like all the rest" (*Death*, p. 55). The unperturbed Olunde shakes off the accusation and repeats his endorsement of Oyo rituals when Simon returns after arresting Elesin. Simon locks Elesin in a cell that once held slaves before they were sent to the coast for transportation to the Americas. Because Olunde is well educated in European ways, he calls British policies hypocritical; reverence for monarchial tradition, he points out, is not peculiar to the native inhabitants of Oyo—the presence of the British prince in the city of Oyo that night demonstrates this very clearly.

In the final scene of the fourth act, Olunde happens upon his father being dragged into a holding cell. He turns motionless immediately and "stares above [the old man's] head into the distance" (*Death*, p. 60). His father pleads "Oh son, don't let the sight of your father turn you blind!"

Olunde replies, "I have no father, eater of leftovers," and turns his back on him (*Death*, pp. 60-61).

Their meeting, though accidental, is an abomination: tradition forbids Elesin's oldest son and heir to see his father "from the moment of the king's death" (*Death*, p. 56).

The fifth and final act takes place in the residential quarters of the colonial officers. At the center of events is Elesin, locked up in jail, who at various times engages his new bride, Simon Pilkings, Iyaloja, and the Praise-Singer in conversations. Pilkings is there as a watchman, the bride as a companion, and the others to express their outrage and disappointment at the disruption caused by Elesin's arrest. Elesin accuses Pilkings of shattering "the peace of the world for ever" (*Death*, p. 62). He asks the colonial officer, "Did you think it all out before, this plan to push our world from its course and sever the cord that links us to the great origin?" (*Death*, p. 63). Pilkings can only say that he has committed the disruption not in malice against Elesin's person but in the conduct of a lawful duty. The apparently inconsolable Elesin rejects Pilkings's rationale and turns to his bride: "You were the final gift of the living to their emissary to the land of the ancestors, and perhaps your warmth and youth brought new insights of this world to me and turned my feet leaden on this side of the abyss" (*Death*, p. 65). Elesin thus admits for the first time that his arrest by the colonial officer may actually have been a wish fulfillment for him. "For I confess to you, daughter, my weakness came not merely from the abomination of the white man who came violently into my fading presence, there was also a weight of longing on my earth-held limbs" (*Death*, p. 65).

When Iyaloja and the Praise-Singer arrive later to visit, they rain endless scorn on Elesin. Iyaloja rejects Elesin's defense that he got pulled off the path of transition to the other world against his will. Although she is not present when Elesin confesses his reticence to his bride, Iyaloja believes that Elesin harbored a sacrilegious reluctance to leave the world at the time appointed for him by the elders. Elesin admits to Iyaloja finally that he "had committed [a] blasphemy of thought," but Iyaloja is not moved by the confession; to her, Elesin has "fled his rightful cause" (*Death*, p. 69). Following Iyaloja's lead, Elesin's Praise-Singer turns on his patron, showing that his loyalty to the people overrides his feelings for Elesin. He tells Elesin that he, the Praise-Singer, has performed his duties without ever letting Elesin forget his own duties to the people. The Praise-Singer admonishes his master: "If you had raised your will to cut the thread of life at the summons of the drums, we would not say your mere shadow fell across the gateway and took its owner's place at the banquet" (*Death*, p. 75).

The Praise-Singer's words are codified announcements; as the play's final event shows, Olunde has killed himself—not to redeem his father but to save the world as the kingdom knows it. To elude suspicion, Olunde, as reported by Simon Pilkings, had assured the white man that tradition had been violated irrevocably and that he would return to England the following dawn. Iyaloja and the Praise-Singer bring Olunde's corpse wrapped in a mat to Elesin, asking him to address to it the required words he would have said to the king's favorite horse at the moment of his death. When Elesin discovers that the wrapped object is his son, he "flings one arm round his neck, once, and with the loop of the chain [holding him] strangles himself in a swift decisive pull" (*Death*, p. 75). The play closes with two dead bodies on stage. Simon Pilkings is stunned beyond belief, and Elesin's bride follows Iyaloja off stage. Iyaloja closes the play with a command: "Now forget the dead, forget even the living. Turn your mind only to the unborn" (*Death*, p. 76).

The proverbial language of the play. "Lyrical grandeur" has been one of the phrases critics have invoked to praise the use of language in *Death and the King's Horseman*. Fragments of incantatory poetry, such as "no arrow flies back to the string" and "the parent shoot withers to give sap to the younger," are some of the play's pithy expressions about the irreversible course of life and death (*Death*, pp. 44, 70). Simon Pilkings's patience is so tested by the poetic language of the Oyo people that, exasperated, he asks, "Must you people forever speak in riddles?" (*Death*, p. 71). On another occasion Pilkings himself uses a proverb to express his confusion about Elesin's willingness to die: "are these not the same people who say: the elder grimly approaches heaven and you ask him to bear your greetings yonder; do you really thinks he makes the journey willingly?" (*Death*, p. 64).

Elesin's programmed death has weighty implications for the Oyo concept of existence, the necessity of sacrifice, and other constants in human life, conveyed by the proverb-filled speeches of Elesin, Iyaloja, and the Praise-Singer. Their use of proverbs every time they speak shows them to be community elders, who weigh the implications of their thoughts before they utter them. In the language of one Yoruba proverb, "the kolanut lasts longer in the elder's mouth." Thoughts and words are like kolanuts for these elders: they chew on them. In Yoruba rhetoric, "the proverb is the horse of words; when words are lost, proverbs are used to search for them." So startling are some of the play's events that they defy words: Elesin demands a new wife on his last day on earth; a Master of the King's Stables does not die at the appropriate time as tradition requires; his oldest son sacrifices himself in place of his father; and a colonial administrator who has imagined his residence as a refuge against death ends up with two dead bodies on his premises. At critical moments, proverbs come in handy for elders who try to understand such happenings.

The first crucial proverb in the play is "The elder who licks his plate clean of every crumb will encounter silence when he calls on children to fulfill the smallest errand" (*Death,* p. 15). Privileges, this proverb reminds listeners, are not without responsibilities. Elesin is the first person to use this saying in the play, to reassure the world that he will fulfill his duties when the time comes. His subsequent actions show that he does not heed his own proverbs, in spite of Iyaloja's reminder to him after he asks for a new wife: "You are not one who eats and leaves nothing on his plate for children. Did you not say it yourself?" (*Death,* p. 20). There is an oblique reference here to two inappropriate actions on Elesin's part. First, the woman he wants to marry is already betrothed to Iyaloja's son; as an elder, he should not rake up all the pleasures of the world, especially a woman already promised to the son of another chief. More generally, Elesin should not be seeking sexual comfort at this time; all his thoughts ought to be directed at the "other world."

Two thematic proverbs are used in Iyaloja's scornful admonition of Elesin when she visits him in detention. In the first, Iyaloja asks Elesin to stop rationalizing his detention: "We said you were the hunter returning home in triumph, a slain buffalo pressing down on his neck, you said wait, I first must turn up this cricket hole with my toes" (*Death,* p. 68). As far as Iyaloja is concerned, Elesin is in jail because his will has failed him in the last and most crucial moment of his official duty. His will lapses because he is busy marrying a new bride—even though he knows he will not live long enough to care for her—when he should be preparing himself to follow his master in death when the signal is given. In the process of stopping to dig for tiny crickets with his toes—seeking earthly pleasures—the greedy hunter that is Elesin fails to carry home on time the more substantial meat. That is, he fails to complete his pact with the king by dying

at the appointed time and maintaining cosmic order, which would have provided for the larger population. A related proverb in the same conversation reiterates the moral imperatives of the previous ones: "'there's a wild beast at my heels' are not fitting words for a decorated hunter" (*Death,* p. 69). As the plot summary above indicates, Elesin is the decorated hunter; the "wild beast" colonialist Simon Pilkings is an unbecoming excuse for fleeing his responsibilities. With this proverb, Iyaloja caps the expression of her anger at Elesin, and the play directs the cause of the tragedy at him. In all the proverbs, the moral expectation is ironclad. Neither the colonialist interference that Elesin deploys at some point to defend himself, nor the idea that Elesin is a victim of colonial changes in the social ethos, can relativize Elesin's tragic unpreparedness.

The final proverb suggests that social changes are not undesirable when cardinal principles are respected. In heralding the introduction of Olunde's corpse on stage, Elesin's Praise-Singer berates his master with a series of proverbs that includes "if there is a dearth of bats, the pigeon must serve us for the offering" (*Death,* p. 75). This saying explains why Olunde's death is culturally meaningful, if not exactly desirable. Elesin, the bat, is the sacrificial object stipulated by history, which must now be replaced by Olunde, the substituted pigeon. All these Yoruba proverbs operate as verbal clues to understanding the philosophical grounds of the play's seemingly harsh and rigid indictment of Elesin.

Events in History at the Time the Play Was Written

Detecting official treason. When *Death and the King's Horseman* was published in 1975, Nigeria had been free of direct colonialism for 15 years. The city of Oyo still had its traditional offices, but the officials wielded little real political power because all matters of state were controlled by military administrators, whose egregious abuse of public office was a staple of the newspapers. A military head of state—General Yakubu Gowon—had reneged on his pledge to hand over power to an elected government, and five years earlier the country concluded a civil war (the Biafra War), during which the same military president had a lavish state wedding. As Wole Ogundele has suggested, there may be considerable historical significance in the parallels between Elesin's conduct and the behavior of some Nigerian rulers during and soon after the Nigerian civil

Death and the
King's Horseman

war. The play could, in this light, be read as dramatizing the warning signals of treason by public officials whose personal predilections might lead to the sacrifice of public good. Soyinka's other works about the Nigerian civil war are even gloomier in their representation of the conduct of the powerful. The political leaders portrayed in the play *Madmen and Specialists* and the prison autobiography *The Man Died* are even darker than those in *Death and the King's Horseman*.

Reviews. Critics are divided on how to read the importance of colonial history in the play. Is Elesin a hedonistic scoundrel, or is he a victim of a Eurocentric colonial government to whom all foreign practices are barbaric? Is the play about a clash of cultures—Elesin against Pilkings, Oyo versus England, Africa against Europe? According to historicists, the colonial circumstances are the determining factor. Elesin violates tradition only because colonialism declares all local practices backward even before they are studied. The imprisonment that prevents Elesin's suicide is therefore read as the play's main tragic event. Simon Pilkings is only acting out the classic colonial script of disregarding the ways of a colonized people. This reading, however, disregards Soyinka's warning in his "Author's Note" that the "colonial factor" is a mere catalyst to the primordial conflicts of the play.

Many other critics view the play as dramatizing beliefs that make it possible to perceive historical events in societies. Rituals, the play's main medium, are created to transcend the historical moments in which they are created, and it is against "permanent" structures like rituals that historical patterns—conformity, deviation, and acceptable changes—are recognizable as such. Elesin's irresponsibility prevents him from performing a ritual as prescribed, which, but for his son's replacement suicide, almost throws the kingdom's sense of harmonious and continuous passage of time into chaos. From this perspective, Elesin's ritual suicide is necessary, despite Pilkings's view of it as barbaric. This view, in any case, is of little consequence to Elesin's son, despite Olunde's English education. In the metaphysical logic of the play, the colonial presence is only one tick in the relentless passing of time in Oyo. Neither Elesin nor Simon Pilkings, regardless of what each feels or thinks, has the ability to stop the kingdom from making sense out of the perpetual movement of time. As the play demonstrates, such efforts can exact tragic consequences.

—Adeleke Adeeko

Wole Soyinka

For More Information

Booth, James. "Self-Sacrifice and Human Sacrifice in Soyinka's *Death and the King's Horseman.*" *Research in African Literatures* 19 (1988): 529-550.

Fage, J. D. *A History of Africa.* 3rd ed. New York: Routledge, 1995.

Gibbs, James. *Wole Soyinka.* New York: Grove Press, 1986.

Jeyifo, Biodun, *The Truthful Lie: Essays in a Sociology of African Drama.* London: New Beacon Books, 1985.

Johnson, Rev. Samuel. *The History of the Yorubas: From the Earliest Times to the Beginning of the British Protectorate.* Lagos: C. M. S. Bookshops, 1921.

Ogundele, Wole. "*Death and the King's Horseman*: A Poet's Quarrel With His Culture." *Research in African Literatures* 25, no. 1 (spring 1994): 47-60.

Ready, Richard. "Through the Intricacies of 'The Fourth Stage' to an Apprehension of *Death and the King's Horseman.*" *Black American Literature Forum* 22, no. 4 (winter 1988): 711-21.

Soyinka, Wole, *Myth, Literature and the African World.* Cambridge: Cambridge University Press, 1976.

———. *Death and the King's Horseman.* New York: Hill and Wang, 1987.

———. *Madmen and Specialists.* London: Methuen, 1971.

———. *The Man Died: Prison Notes of Wole Soyinka.* London: Rex Collings, 1972.

Dilemma of a Ghost

by

Ama Ata Aidoo

A ma Ata Aidoo (called Christina until she abandoned her Christian name in the early 1970s) was born into the Fante people of south central Ghana in 1942. Fortunately for her, her family encouraged its female members to become educated. From her father she heard the famous words of the Ghanaian educator James Emman Kwegyir Aggrey: "If you educate a man, you educate an individual. If you educate a woman, you educate a nation" (Aidoo, "To Be a Woman," p. 259). Aidoo attended the Wesley Girls High School and the University of Ghana, graduating in 1964. Since that time, she has studied and taught in the United States, Europe, and Africa. In 1982 she was named Ghana's Minister of Education by the military government of Jerry Rawlings; the next year, however, she was removed because her views were too radical for the regime. Since then, Aidoo has lived primarily in Zimbabwe and the United States. In addition to plays, her literary works include stories, poems, and books for children. Aidoo wrote her first play, *Dilemma of a Ghost,* during her days as an undergraduate, and it was performed by the Students' Theatre of the University of Ghana. In retrospect, Aidoo herself has expressed amazement at its boldness. Ten years after its creation, she stated, "I myself haven't had the courage today to confront this whole question of Africa and black America in those stark terms" (Aidoo in Vincent, p. 5).

Events in History at the Time of the Play

The Fante legacy. Aidoo's people, the Fante, are a subgroup of the Akan, a large grouping of peo-

THE LITERARY WORK

A play set in Ghana at an unspecified time; first performed in Legon, Ghana, in 1964; first published in English in 1965.

SYNOPSIS

A young Fante man returns from the United States with an African American wife, whose foreign customs and expectations alienate him from his family.

ples that makes up most of the population of southern Ghana. The Akan peoples are distinct, even though they share similar cultural practices and speak mutually intelligible dialects of the same language.

Except for the Asante, their traditional rivals, the Fante are the largest and most powerful of the Akan groups. The Asante Confederacy, which controlled the interior regions of the country from the late seventeenth century until the area's subjugation by the British, met its fiercest opposition from the coastal Fante. The Fante successfully blocked Asante expansion to the coast, and defended their own inland trading interests until the early nineteenth century. Even after losing a protracted war to the Asante, the Fante maintained their independence from their conquerors; their trade and wealth dwindled, but they remained free.

Unsurprisingly, then, the Fante were initially receptive to the British colonizers who offered a measure of protection and leverage against the Asante. The Fante entered into their initial treaties with the British in 1844. At first, the Fante saw the British as valuable trading partners and military allies; however, when the British attempted to usurp rights exercised by the people's kings and chiefs, the Fante rebelled. To protect their traders and trade interests, the British wanted to exercise control over law in the area, but the people were unwilling to relinquish this control. Although the Fante Confederacy of the 1860s failed in its attempt to oust the British, and the Gold Coast (the future Ghana) became a full-fledged British colony in 1874, this first anti-colonial protest was an important milestone. It inspired later generations of Ghanaian nationalists, reminding them that the British had not simply assumed authority where none had existed before; they had forcibly wrested it from its original owners.

Aidoo herself comes "from a long line of fighters" (James, p. 13). Her paternal grandfather was jailed and later killed for his anti-British activities. Aidoo also reports that the Fante were known for "their recalcitrance, their rudeness, their contempt for the imperial set-up, and for the white man" (Aidoo, "Male-ing Names in the Sun," p. 31).

Akan women—a mixed inheritance. In "To Be a Woman," a long, anecdotal, and passionately argued essay written in 1980, Aidoo deplores the traditional subjugation of women in Akan culture. While excepting her family, she maintains that, as a general rule

> the position of a woman in Ghana is no less ridiculous than anywhere else. . . . [O]nce you, the young man, had been bold enough to go and take her off her mother's back, you could also take it for granted that you had acquired a sexual aid;
>
> a wet nurse and nursemaid for your children;
> a cook-steward and general housekeeper;
> a listening post; an economic and general
>   consultant;
> a field-hand and, if you are that way inclined,
> a punch-ball.
>
> (Aidoo, "To Be a Woman," p. 259)

Aidoo goes on to tell story after story depicting the discrimination and degradation she has suffered as a female scholar and writer. Ghanaian culture, she asserts, still sees women as fit mainly for tending the home and bearing children. A strong woman is suspected, feared, put back in her place. The perception of this in-

equality has stoked the fires of Aidoo's feminism throughout her career. However, her claims for the totality of gender inequality among the Akan are somewhat surprising, in that certain features of Akan culture might be expected to lead to greater parity between men and women than is the case elsewhere. These factors include the method of calculating genealogy; the division of labor; and the division of authority within a household.

For most groups of the Akan, genealogy is matrilineal: people calculate their family relationships in terms of their mothers and grandmothers. This *abusua* is not simply an arrangement for organizing heredity—it has important legal and social consequences that protect women's rights and provide them a measure of autonomy even from their husbands. The authority in a clan is generally not the oldest woman, but rather her brother, so that Akan societies are, in the final analysis, male-governed. However, women play important roles in decision-making, both formally and informally. For instance, in the Asante Confederacy women were responsible for determining kings and chiefs, and the sisters of ruling men had broad powers and responsibilities, and a great deal of personal wealth. Within non-royal households, too, older women work with their brothers to apportion family duties and to determine life-paths for the family's younger members. Finally, the baroque property laws of the Akan separate men's and women's personal property (and both of these from family and clan property). Unlike most European women until recent centuries, Akan women did not surrender their personal wealth to their husbands upon marriage. Furthermore, Akan inheritance law dictates that a woman's property be willed to female family members, so that female property remains female. In spite of these powers, however, women are fundamentally measured by their success in bearing children: an infertile woman is among the most despised and pitied of creatures.

The division of labor among the Akan is similarly mixed in its effects on women. Both men and women participate in agriculture, with men responsible for clearing land and women and children for tending the fields; women are generally in charge of cooking and cleaning. Hunting and fishing, two of the most important sources of food and money for the coast-dwelling Fante, are male domains. But women dominate another, even more important segment of the economy: petty trade. In marketplaces and on street corners throughout Akan territory, women

WAYS OF THE AKAN

❧

Traditional life for all branches of the Akan people revolves around family and market. Akan religion is centered on respect for ancestors; a family's founders are celebrated throughout the year, invoked in prayer, and involved in many rituals. For instance, when a couple has a child and is given the traditional gift of a bottle of gin or wine, the first drink is poured on the earth as a libation for one's departed ancestors.

"The living have a sense of dependence on the ancestors; it is believed that they are constantly watching over the living relations and punish those who break customs" (Warren, p. 31). The Akan generally assume that early death is a punishment from these ancestors for some sin; the aged—and thus virtuous—members of a clan are accorded the utmost respect. The eldest members of an extended family are generally responsible for apportioning duties and privileges among the younger members.

Although the social and political developments of this century have led to alterations in Akan ways of life, especially in the larger cities and among the educated elite, the basic Akan social unit is still the extended family. A man pays a bride price to a woman's family, after which she enters his family unit. When the man makes his payment (in money, goods, or services), he formalizes his marriage to the woman and gains full control over her. It is still not unusual to find several generations of a family living in one large dwelling, with in-laws and various dependents. Even when modern contingencies prevent this organization, the family remains close. For instance, in *Dilemma of a Ghost,* the college graduate Ato must live in the city where his job is; however, his family not only keeps a room for him in the family compound, they actually add a wing to the house for him and his new family.

The Akan have a variety of forms of cultural expression. Music plays an important social role, especially in situations of mourning and celebration; drums are the most important musical instrument. Metalwork, terra cotta pottery, wood-carving, and especially weaving are highly developed; the Kente cloth produced in Ghana is world famous. Good storytellers are highly esteemed, and proverbs pepper everyday speech. The fundamental Akan proverb is "Wubu okwasea be a, obisa wo ase," which translates as "If you tell a fool a proverb, he will ask you its meaning" (Warren, p. 64). Proverbs pass on the common sense of the people, and express their deepest understanding of human existence.

In its slim 50 pages, *Dilemma of a Ghost* manages to include expressions of all these facts of traditional Akan life. The extended Yawson family functions almost as a single character to oppose Ato and his wife. In the foreground of the play's setting is the crossroads leading to market, farmland, and the Yawson home, symbolically uniting the major aspects of Akan life. Most tellingly, proverbs and folklore are essential to the play's content. To introduce the play, Aidoo chooses the "Bird of the Wayside," a folkloric figure symbolizing storytelling and rumor. The African characters, especially the two village women who comment on the Yawsons' troubles, use proverbs to seal arguments. Once the tribal wisdom has been produced, it seems, there is nothing left to say.

still monopolize the sale of food items and many small goods. Sociologists have estimated that 90 percent of sales of certain common items (such as clay pots, plantains, rugs, and shawls) are made by women, and over half of all women's employment is in the marketplace. Older sociologists tended to overlook the importance of trading and selling, and thus to underestimate the status of women in Ghana; more recent studies have revealed how essential such activity is, and the measure of autonomy it provides women. The spread of Western-style education has also led to more varied opportunities for girls. And, while boys have benefited more on the whole, an increasing number of parents have come to believe that education is important for all children. Aidoo herself is an early example of this growing trend.

Despite all the potential benefits which might grow from their matrilineal importance, authority within the home, and trading activity, Akan women are still second-class citizens in most ways. A United Nation's report sums up the situation:

> In all the ethnic groups in Ghana, women are not considered the equals of men, and this belief is reinforced by social practices [such as polygyny] and religious beliefs. Throughout Ghana a woman is considered in need of protection and is under the control of someone, usually male, throughout her life.
>
> (Manuh, p. 3)

Reversing the diaspora? The transatlantic slave trade of the fifteenth through nineteenth centuries decimated the population of West Africa, tearing millions of Africans from their homelands and depositing them in the Americas. These early arrivals, the African slaves and their descendents, occupied a strange, two-sided position in the western hemisphere. On the one hand, they were clearly no longer African: within a generation, they spoke the language of whatever colony had enslaved them. Meanwhile, they evolved new languages of internal communication peculiar to themselves and different from the mainstream languages of their masters—such as creole and patois in the Caribbean and the West Indies. This was a major achievement, extraordinary in the midst of calculated deprivations. Always considered second-class, inferior people fit only for forced labor, the slaves were never allowed full membership in society at large. To their colonial masters, the color of their skin, and their African origin, marked them as inferior.

It is not surprising, then, that the movement for black equality in the United States has involved profound curiosity about Africa. Historians point out that thoughts of Africa tended to rise among African Americans when racial tension in America was high. Before the abolition of slavery, a movement arose that called for the repatriation of black slaves to Africa. Supported as much by whites who wished to keep America racially "pure" as by blacks, this movement resulted in the formation of the colonies of Sierra Leone (1787) and Liberia (1822). This wish for a mass return was revived briefly in the aftermath of the Civil War, when white Southerners attempted to terrorize their former slaves back into submission. However, by this point Africa itself was being carved up into colonies by European powers in a race to extend their empires, and such wishes did not become reality.

In the early twentieth century, African American attitudes toward Africa took a different turn. Among the small educated elite grew the idea that people of color the world over had to unite to end all forms of racial oppression, be it segregation or colonialism. In America this movement was spearheaded by W. E. B. DuBois, who helped organize conferences on race that drew not only African Americans but also many members of Africa's budding nationalist movements. What DuBois was for the black American elite, Marcus Garvey was for the masses of disenchanted African Americans. While DuBois explored the intellectual underpinnings of racism, and sought out reasoned ways to combat it, Garvey stirred millions with impassioned rhetoric. He claimed that inferiority would beleaguer black people as long as they lived in a white society, and called for a return to an Africa freed of its colonial oppressors and united as one nation. Garvey's popularity indicates the depth of black disenchantment with life in the racially unequal countries of the Americas.

In the 1950s the relationship of Africans and African Americans took a new turn. In the United States the civil rights movement, which attempted to demolish the structures of racial inequality, coincided with the struggle of many African countries for independence. African Americans celebrated the liberation of Ghana in 1957, and there was an explosion of interest, on the part of African Americans, in Africa's history and cultures. (W. E. B. DuBois himself moved to Ghana in the early 1960s and became a Ghanaian citizen in 1963.) It finally seemed as if conditions were right for closer relations between Africa and diasporic Africans in the United States.

This hope was not unfounded; however, it was somewhat optimistic. From the movement that led to the formation of Liberia in the 1820s, to Garveyism in the 1920s and beyond, American blacks used the idea of Africa as a symbol of freedom and home, but gave less thought to the real differences that separated their experience in the United States from that of their kin who had not been taken. The educated elite and a handful of missionaries had actually traveled to Africa, and African American scholars had done a great deal to enrich scholarly understanding of African culture. But the average black American knew no more about Africa than did the average white American, and the picture each of them had was composed as much of movie images and postcard clichés as of actual reality. In 1960 Rayford Logan wrote, "American Negroes who grew up in the early part of this century probably first heard about Africa when a minister, priest, or missionary appealed for funds to support missions there. The missionaries frequently gave a distorted picture of the African way of life because they did not understand it" (Logan, p. 218). Other sources of "information" included adventure movies set in the African jungle and newspaper reports—hardly the most accurate portrayals of African life. When Eulalie, the young African American in *Dilemma of a Ghost*, comes to her new husband's village, she half expects to meet the simple, childlike African that she has seen on postcards and in movies; instead she finds a sophisticated culture whose ways she does not understand, and whose members she is continually offending.

So, despite their natural interest in their ancestral home, African Americans had a great deal to learn about Africa. And, as the experience of Eulalie Yawson in *Dilemma of a Ghost* indicates, the learning experience was as likely to be painful as fulfilling.

The Play in Focus

Plot summary. *Dilemma of a Ghost* covers more than a year in the life of the Yawson family, but presents the action in brief snippets spread out over time. Thus, Aidoo presents the degeneration of Ato Yawson's relationship with his family as a realistically slow progression; at the beginning of each scene, conversation between characters fills in the gap of unrepresented time. The play opens with a long speech by the Bird of the Wayside. This folkloric figure introduces the Yawsons, a family of seemingly great wealth

W. E. B. DuBois, writer, civil rights activist, and the first African American to receive a Harvard Ph.D., spearheaded the movement among the African American elite to end all forms of racial oppression, including segregation and colonialism. He moved to Ghana in the early 1960s and became a Ghanian citizen in 1963.

in the countryside outside of Accra, Ghana. Seemingly great, because the Yawsons have spent a fortune educating the firstborn son of the clan, Ato, in the United States. Now he has returned. In preparation, the Yawsons have added a wing to the clan house for him to stay in when he visits—for he must live in the city, where his job is.

The Bird of the Wayside disappears, and Ato enters onstage with his wife, Eulalie, an African American. She and Ato fell in love at school and now he has brought her to his homeland to live. In this brief introductory scene, the audience sees the young couple's anxiety and optimism. They know they are embarking on a difficult project of cultural reconciliation, but they are confident they will master the situation. For her part, Eulalie is ecstatic to be in Africa: "To belong to somewhere again . . . sure this must be bliss" (Aidoo, *Dilemma of a Ghost*, p. 9).

Act One proper begins with the two village

women, the First Neighbor Woman and Second Neighbor Woman, who will serve as chorus, commenting on the action of the play. They provide important information and reinforce the themes of family interaction in the story of the Yawsons. The first woman is childless and laments this fact; the second argues that children are as much a burden as a help. They argue this point over Esi Kom, Ato's mother. The second woman claims Esi has gone into debt to finance her son's education. But now that he is educated, the first woman points out, he can get a high-paying job to pay all her debts.

After the two women depart, the Yawsons greet Ato, who has come to the family home without Eulalie. This scene introduces the Yawsons: most significantly, his grandmother, Nana, and his spiteful, rebellious sister, Monka. The scene opens in playfulness and celebration, but closes in tears. At the midpoint of the scene, Esi Kom mentions the bride price she is assembling for Ato's wedding, anticipating that he will wed someone from their area soon. At this point, he has to admit that he is already married. The announcement creates confusion and consternation, which only increase when the Yawsons learn that their new in-law is an American. At first, they assume she is white; they soon learn that she is African American, a descendant of slaves, but this fails to placate them. In Fante society, to marry a slave is to marry a woman of no family; and not to have a family history is the worst thing that can happen to a Fante. Act One closes with Nana lamenting the fact that she has lived long enough to witness this disgrace.

Act Two consists of two brief scenes. First, the two women return and discuss the obligations of children to their parents. This discussion provides a counterpoint to a soliloquy by Eulalie, which follows immediately. In a page and a half, Eulalie recalls her life in the United States and her continual dissatisfaction with racial inequality. She again celebrates being in her spiritual homeland, where she belongs . . . but these pleasant thoughts scatter as she is frightened by the sudden beating of drums in the distance. It seems that Eulalie is not as comfortable with African culture as she would like to be. Ato enters, and the two discuss drums, witchcraft, and having children. Eulalie is reconsidering her original desire to delay starting a family. In a move that will have important repercussions, Ato insists that they keep to their original plan of waiting for children.

Act Three takes place six months later. A boy and a girl sneak into the Yawsons' house to play hide and seek. They sing the song that gives the play its title, the song of a ghost at a crossroads, who cannot decide whether he should go to Cape Coast or to Elmina. The song awakens Ato from an afternoon nap; he is upset because it gave him a bad dream. This brief scene sets the tone for the explosion that follows. Two hours later Esi Kom brings a bundle of snails to Ato and Eulalie; Eulalie, however, upon learning that they are meant as food, is repulsed and throws them away. Monka witnesses this rudeness and tells her mother. Esi Kom and Monka vent to Ato all the complaints they have been stifling since his return: he and Eulalie have been rude when the family visited them in the city; Eulalie does not respect the traditions of her husband's culture; worst of all, Ato spends all the money he makes on Western luxury items for Eulalie, while his family continues to wallow in debt. Eulalie, who does not speak Fante and so knows no more than what she can judge from their tone of voice, further irritates them by the European, unwomanly act of chain-smoking. The fight ends in an impasse, as Monka and Esi Kom storm out.

The fourth act takes place six months later. The occasion is the annual sprinkling of the stools, a ceremony that celebrates the family's ancestors. (A stool represents one's ancestors—some families keep one stool while others keep one for each of its former heads of clans. In any case, sprinkling the stool with water or wine is a way to recall the ancestors and propitiate them so that they will ensure a profitable year.) It is a time of great concentration on family, heritage, and obligations—all the things that Ato has ignored. The act begins, again, with the two village women. They repeat the rumors that Ato has not given money to his family, and that Eulalie spends all their wages on machines. Then they add news: the Yawsons believe that Eulalie is barren.

Eulalie enters, drinking whiskey. Ato futilely pleads with her to stop. His uncles enter and announce that they want to perform an Akan ritual to help Eulalie conceive. Almost all can be forgiven if Eulalie can present Nana with a great-grandchild. Ato is shocked at the proposal, and too scared to admit that the problem is not infertility but intent: he and Eulalie do not want a child yet. When he confesses the situation to Eulalie, she too is angry with him. She begins to see him as a coward who would rather let his family hate her than explain her customs to them. As Act Five begins it is the next morning, and

Eulalie is drunk. She and Ato argue. She calls his people savages; he retorts, "How much does the American negro know?" (*Dilemma*, p. 48). Finally, he slaps her, then flees as she crumbles to the floor.

Time shifts to midnight of that day. Ato wanders onstage, yelling for his mother. The two women enter as well, and discuss the evil portents surrounding this marriage. When they leave, Esi Kom opens the door to the house. Ato tells her that Eulalie has vanished, and attempts to explain the grounds of their argument. But instead of offering solace, Esi Kom castigates him. She realizes that because he has not served as an intermediary between African and African American, he has failed both sides: "Before the stranger should dip his finger / Into the thick palm nut soup, / It is a townsman / Must have told him to" (*Dilemma*, p. 52). Eulalie then wanders onstage, and Esi Kom accepts her into the house. The play ends with Ato standing, alone and disconsolate, in the courtyard. As the lights dim, the voices of children are heard, singing:

> Shall I go to Cape Coast?
> Shall I go to Elmina?
> I can't tell
> Shall I?
> I can't tell
> I can't tell
> I can't tell
> I can't tell. . . .
>   (*Dilemma*, p. 52)

The necessity of motherhood. In a soliloquy discussing Eulalie's exotic stove and refrigerator, the First Neighbor Woman says:

> Your machines, my stranger-girl,
> Cannot go on an errand
> They have no hands to dress you when you
> are dead . . .
> But you have one machine to buy now
> That which will weep for you, stranger-girl
> You need that most.
> For my world
> Which you have run to enter
> Is most unkind to the barren.
>   (*Dilemma*, p. 40)

It is significant that this speech is given to the first woman, who has, throughout the play, lamented her own failure to conceive. For her, barrenness is the worst of all curses; she would be unable to understand a deliberate effort not to conceive a child.

The First Neighbor Woman is not alone. One of the defining features of Akan society is its emphasis on fertility as the measure of a woman's success. Children are prized and coddled; the family's energy is focused on maximizing opportunities for them. But any sort of failure in the childbearing process puts a woman at risk of scorn and rejection. Barrenness is still among the most common reasons for divorce. Before the spread of modern medicine, infant mortality stood at 50 percent; all sorts of charms and rituals were designed to prevent this catastrophe. "If a new-born baby died before eight days the mother angrily whipped and mutilated the body, wrapped it in sword-grass, put it in a pot and buried it near the women's latrine; this was to discourage it from returning again" (Warren, p. 13). The burial of a child inverted the normal burial ceremony; participants wore white to insult the dead child's spirit and to prevent it from returning. Similarly, to die in childbirth was a great disgrace, and the dead woman's body was abused along with the child's. And, as witnessed in *Dilemma of a Ghost*, other rituals were designed to heighten fertility or surmount barrenness.

A SONG OF TWO CITIES

The cities alluded to in the song of the ghost, Cape Coast and Elmina, are both loaded with significance in Ghanaian history. Elmina is a fairly old city, one of the oldest of the Akan urban centers. Cape Coast, on the contrary, "is a fashionable modern city important today as an educational center" (Chew in Cox, p. 38). Cape Coast was built by the British and was used as their administrative capital until the 1870s. Elmina also has a role in Ghana's colonial past; it was there that the Portuguese built their first trading fort in Ghana, at the end of the sixteenth century. Thus, both cities evoke the encounter of Akan peoples with Europeans. The ghost's indecisiveness, which strikes such terror in Ato, seems to reflect the main character's indecisive wavering between African and Western perspectives on life. He is committed to his wife but fails to explain his own culture to her. He wants to remain on good terms with his nuclear family but fails to deal with them forthrightly. In short, he tries to have the best of both worlds by not rejecting any part of either. While at first blush he may not seem drawn to his own culture, a number of his actions indicate otherwise. At a crucial moment at the end of the play, to name one example, he slaps Eulalie and says that she knows nothing about Africa.

The immediate cultural reasons for this emphasis on childbearing can be understood simply enough. In a pre-industrial culture where the basic mode of survival is subsistence farming, a large family is more secure than a small one. Children do not drain a family of its resources; instead they become, at a relatively early age, contributors to its wealth. They help farm and harvest the crops, help their mothers in petty trade, and do housework. Furthermore, in a culture where public welfare and social services are still evolving, people cannot depend on the government for support when they grow sick or too old to work. That role must be assumed by the family. In fact, the extended family is the key social unit in Akan society. An aged person without family to take him or her in, a person who has alienated his or her family—these people are in a precarious position indeed. Thus children are not simply objects of love, not simply help around the house: they are the best investment a married couple can make in its future. The economic usefulness of children is reinforced by their religious and cultural significance. The Akan religion is founded upon family. On the one hand, a family's deceased ancestors watch over their living descendants; these ghosts or spirits are prayed to, remembered in ritual, and succored. They are imagined to have the power to help the living or to punish them for transgressions—including the failure to bear children promptly, as Esi Kom notes: "any woman who does it will die by the anger of the ghosts of her fathers—or at least, she will never get the children when she wants them" (*Dilemma,* p. 51). However, the ghosts of a family's ancestors also depend on their survivors. Without descendants to honor and remember them, these ancestral spirits are forgotten, homeless. This explains the poor treatment offered the corpses of babies who fail to survive; the family wants to drive away the spirit that cannot live, and keep it from returning to haunt them again.

Ato Yawson flouts all the responsibilities he has as a son in Akan society. He has forgotten that he was educated, not for himself but to help provide his family with a better life. The Yawsons went into debt to finance his American education, but from their point of view it was not a sacrifice but an investment. The high-paying white-collar job he gets when he returns is supposed to repay the debts and more. Instead, Ato focuses on himself and his wife, providing luxury items for their home while ignoring his mother's financial troubles. This in itself be-

speaks a neglect of his culture's traditions, but there is more. As Esi Kom comes to realize, her son has not explained his culture to his wife; he has allowed her to think of his family as ignorant, uncultured primitives. Therefore, even though it is Eulalie who eventually calls the Yawsons savages, Ato must bear the responsibility for her scorn; he has not respected his family enough to consider their traditions worth defending.

All of these flaws are focused by Ato and Eulalie's decision to postpone childbearing. For the Yawsons, this is the ultimate gesture of arrogance and selfishness. Contraception means playing god, thinking one has the right to decide when a child's spirit can enter the world. It is also selfish; choosing not to have children means assuming that a child is the sole property of husband and wife, overlooking the fact that everyone in the extended family desires to see new additions. It is, in the end, the clearest symbol of the belief that one's own life is the most important, that one has the right or even the duty to live for oneself alone. Thus, it is fitting that this, rather than machines or money or education, causes Ato and Eulalie's struggles with the Yawson family.

Sources and literary context. Aidoo's career as a writer began with short stories published in the influential West African literary journal *Black Orpheus*. However, her first popular success was as a dramatist. While still an undergraduate she became associated with Efua Theodora Sutherland's Ghana Drama Studio. Efua Sutherland was the first Ghanaian dramatist and the most prominent at the time Aidoo's play appeared; however, she was as important for her work with actors and other playwrights as for her own plays. She avidly experimented with new ways of staging plays, bringing inexpensive outdoor theaters to a country whose playhouses had largely been modeled on the expensive, indoor theaters of Europe. Sutherland's use of tropes from Greek tragedy may have spurred Aidoo to include the Greek-style chorus of the two village women. Perhaps most importantly, Sutherland provided a forum for literary-minded dramatists like Aidoo to develop their skills.

Aidoo has said that she found her subject in everyday life: she knew many married couples of mixed African and African American origins. She also points to a general Ghanaian interest in the black experience worldwide: "I come from a people for whom, for some reason, the connection with African-America or the Caribbean was a living thing, something of which we were always aware" (James, p. 20). She was also working with a tradition in West African literature of all levels: the depiction of the "been-to" (a native African who has been educated in Europe or America) returning to his people with a white wife. Aidoo ironically suggests that, in adjusting to African life, skin color does not matter: an African American will have no easier a time than any white newcomer. This ironic use of a popular type further allows Aidoo to explore the possibility of links among black peoples worldwide.

Like many of the plays of Shakespeare, *Dilemma of a Ghost* mixes poetry and prose. The language of the play varies from the emotionally charged and imagistic poetry of the two village women, to the simple marital banter of Ato and Eulalie. This variety reveals Aidoo's ambitious interest in a great number of genres, most of which she would go on to work in. After another play, *Anowa,* she began to publish volumes of poetry, short stories, and the experimental novels *Our Sister Killjoy* and *Changes.*

Aidoo has suggested that African drama should strive to maintain its own integrity by growing out of contemporary African experiences and to merge African forms of oral narrative with Western literary forms. Her *Dilemma of a Ghost* achieves both objectives—it addresses a topic of contemporary relevance in Africa, and blends African oral forms, such as the proverb, with Western dramatic forms.

Reviews. *Dilemma of a Ghost* was first performed by the Students' Theatre in Legon, Ghana, on March 12, 13, and 14, 1964. It has been revived intermittently in Ghana, other countries of West Africa, and the United States, indicating that interest in the play has survived even though Aidoo herself no longer writes drama.

Critics have seen the play as interesting, at times brilliant, but also as structurally flawed. Naana Banyiwa Horne states that "[t]he weaknesses are mostly structural, growing out of Aidoo's innovative efforts to blend African oral and Western literary elements, and, for a short play, *Dilemma* has too many acts" (Horne, p. 36). Writing for the *Journal of Commonwealth Literature,* Cosmo Pieterse agrees that the play has both strengths and weaknesses: "The play has errors rather than flaws; fair craftsmanship carries one from the poetry, whimsy and humour of the prelude to the stark climax and hopeful end"; "the chorus," he adds, "is not always structurally integrated, so that thematic coherence and depth are achieved at the cost of formal unity" (Pieterse, p. 170). Viewing the play from another angle,

Mildred Hill-Lubin charges that Aidoo's characterization of Eulalie reveals an ignorance of African American life. "Certainly many of [Aidoo's mistakes] can be attributed to the author's youth but, at the same time, they emphasize a more serious concern. They demonstrate raw lack of information, the kind of concept that many Africans possess about their brothers and sisters in the United States" (Hill-Lubin, p. 195). Karen Chapman provides a longer list of technical flaws, including the play's brevity and its tendency to leave important thematic issues hanging, but concludes, "Despite these probably youthful faults in technique, Miss Aidoo has treated human problems with an understanding unavailable to many dramatists twice her age" (Chapman, p. 30).

—Jacob Littleton

For More Information

Aidoo, Ama Ata. *Dilemma of a Ghost and Anowa.* London: Longmann, 1985.

———. "Male-ing Names in the Sun." In *Unbecoming Daughters of the Empire.* Sydney: Dangaroo Presss, 1993.

———. "To Be a Woman." In *Sisterhood is Global.* Robin Morgan, ed. Garden City, N.Y.: Doubleday, 1983.

Chapman, Karen. "Introduction to *Dilemma of a Ghost.*" In *Sturdy Black Bridges.* Eds. Roseann Bell, Bettye J. Parker, and Beverly Guy-Sheftall. Garden City, NY: Doubleday, 1979.

Cox, C. Brian. *African Writers.* Vol. 1. New York: Charles Scribner's Sons, 1997.

Hill-Lubin, Mildred. "The Relationship of Africans and African Americans: A Recurring Theme in the Work of Ama Ata Aidoo." *Presence Africaine* 124 (1982): 190-201.

Horne, Naana Banyiwa. "Ama Ata Aidoo." In *Dictionary of Literary Biography.* Vol. 117. Eds. Bernth Lindfors and Reinhard Sander. Detroit: Gale Research, 1992.

James, Adeola. *In Their Own Voices: African Women Writers Talk.* London: James Curry, 1990.

Logan, Rayford. "The American Negro's View of Africa." In *Africa as Seen by American Negro Scholars.* New York: Presence Africaine, 1963.

Manuh, Takyiwaa. *Law and the Status of Women in Ghana.* Addis Ababa: United Nations, 1984.

Pieterse, Cosmo. "Dramatic Riches." *Journal of Commonwealth Literature* 2 (1966): 168-171.

Vincent, Theo, ed. *Seventeen Black and African Writers on Literature and Life.* Lagos: Centre for Black Arts and Cultures, 1981.

Warren, Dennis. *The Akan of Ghana.* Accra: Pointer, 1986.

A Dry White Season

by

André Brink

Born in Vrede, South Africa, in 1935, André Brink was one of the first Afrikaner writers to produce anti-apartheid, politically charged literature in South Africa. (*Afrikaner*—the former term was *Boer*—refers to whites who descend mainly from the early Dutch but also from the early German and French settlers in the region.) Brink has since become a writer of international renown, publishing regularly in both Afrikaans and English. In the 1950s he earned masters of arts degrees in both English and Afrikaans literature, and then, from 1959 until 1961, engaged in postgraduate study at the Sorbonne in Paris. Brink later became part of the experimental Afrikaner "Sestiger" movement ("Writers of the Sixties"), and in 1968 planned to settle in Paris along with the exiled poet and fellow Sestiger writer, Breyten Breytenbach. However, the Parisian student revolt that year inspired Brink to return to South Africa to "accept full responsibility" for whatever he wrote (Brink in Ross, p. 55). Brink's initial novel to emerge from this new commitment, *Kennis van die aand* (1973), became the first Afrikaans book to be banned by South African censors. His own English translation of this novel, *Looking on Darkness,* was published the following year, and became successful internationally. Since then Brink has written regularly in both Afrikaans and English—often composing each novel twice to make it available in both languages. Written in the wake of the 1976 Soweto Revolt, *A Dry White Season* helped increase anti-apartheid sentiment throughout the world. With this novel, said

THE LITERARY WORK

A novel set in Johannesburg and Soweto, South Africa, in the late 1970s; published in Afrikaans (as *'n Droe wit seisoen*) in 1979, in English in 1979.

SYNOPSIS

The novel traces the last year in the life of Ben Du Toit, an Afrikaner schoolteacher who trusts fully in the state until a black friend dies in prison under suspicious circumstances.

Brink, "I have tried to accept that responsibility one owes to one's society and one's time" (Brink in Jolly, p. 18).

Events in History at the Time of the Novel

Apartheid. Like many other South African novels of the 1970s and 1980s, *A Dry White Season* is set against the backdrop of *apartheid,* or the system of legalized racial segregation enforced in South Africa from 1948 until 1990. The system rested on the Afrikaner notion that society in South Africa consisted not of one but of various nations that ought to live in their own distinct homelands or reserves; those from black homelands should, according to this system, be allowed to enter the white homeland only temporarily as workers. In fact, South Africa had a long history of segregationist and racist policies before the 1948 victory of the Nationalist Party, which would institute many of the policies of apartheid. The 1948 election was, in fact, a victory for the Afrikaner nationalists who had themselves been oppressed and condescended to by South Africa's British population. The Boer War (1899 to 1902) had essentially been an attempt on the Afrikaners' part to preserve the independence of their settler states in the face of the British desire for complete dominance in South Africa; after the Afrikaners' crushing loss in this war, a fierce and zealous nationalist movement arose that tried to maintain an Afrikaner identity and culture in the British-dominated colony.

ETHNIC POPULATION OF SOUTH AFRICA IN 1980 (IN MILLIONS)

African	20.8 (72 percent)
Coloured	2.6 (9 percent)
Indian	0.8 (3 percent)
White*	4.5 (16 percent)

* Of the white population, approximately 60 percent were Afrikaner.

(Adapted from Thompson, p. 243)

Though the two groups merged in 1910 to form the Union of South Africa, the Afrikaners always played a subordinate role to the British. While the two groups together created an entire system of power based on the oppression and exclusion of blacks (including Africans, Indians, and "Coloureds," or people of mixed racial descent), the Afrikaner nationalist movement created an entire ideology around the idea that the Afrikaners were a "chosen people" favored by God and destined to rule South Africa. Furthermore, as the country became more urbanized and industrialized and as many poor Afrikaners were forced into competition for jobs with black workers, fear of the "black peril"—the idea that Afrikaners were in danger of being overwhelmed by the black majority—added momentum to the nationalist movement already focused on ethnic separation. When the British-led government brought South Africa into World War II—Britain's war, as many Afrikaners saw it—strident Afrikaners lost pa-

tience and finally voted the fascist-influenced National Party into power in 1948.

Almost immediately after assuming power the Nationalists began constructing "an apparatus of laws, regulations and bureaucracies" that would develop into "the most elaborate racial edifice the world had ever witnessed" (Meredith, p. 54). Inter-racial marriages and sexual relationships were banned; different racial groups were compelled by law to use separate restaurants, post offices, theaters, buses, and so on, or to use separate entrances and seats in public buildings; as residential areas for each racial group were demarcated, whole communities were uprooted. Though apartheid rhetoric had spoken of separation but equality, the areas demarcated for nonwhite South Africans represented only a small percentage of the country's total land mass; as a result, many nonwhite people were left no alternative but to build makeshift shantytowns on the outskirts of white-populated cities. Such overwhelming inequality characterized apartheid legislation. Between 1948 and 1971, 151 racial laws were enacted, affecting every aspect of daily life—three times the number of racial laws enacted in the four decades preceding the National Party's reign.

South Africa in the 1970s. While the initial impetus behind apartheid was a desire to maintain Afrikaner culture and restore Afrikaner glory, by the 1970s it was clear that Afrikaners no longer had to fight for power and recognition. Once composed mainly of poor rural farmers, the now predominantly white-collar Afrikaner population had become urbanized and had taken over the economic lead formerly enjoyed by the British. And, now that the Afrikaners controlled the economy, apartheid came under critique as an impractical economic policy that left the labor force mostly unskilled. With the expansion of industry and the demand for skilled labor outweighing the supply, some Afrikaners began to see that the regulations intended to keep nonwhites powerless were preventing national economic advancement. Indeed, South Africa had become a country with a "first-world infrastructure and a third-world labour force" (Le May, p. 241).

The 1970s also saw a major philosophical shift among the black population with the advent of the militant Black Consciousness Movement (BCM), whose spokesman and founder, Steven Biko, rejected white involvement in the anti-apartheid struggle and sought to empower blacks on their own terms. In the two previous decades African revolutionaries had been defiant but muted, and had usually worked alongside white liberals and communists. But, as Biko contended,

> The biggest mistake the black world ever made was to assume that whoever opposed apartheid was an ally. For a long time the black world has been looking only at the governing party and not so much at the whole power structure as the object of their rage.
>
> (Biko in Meredith, p. 139)

Biko believed that blacks, accustomed to oppression and feelings of inferiority, could acquire strength only by distancing themselves from whites. BCM was to dominate black political activity throughout the 1970s. It found outlets in "poetry, literature, drama, music, theology and in local community projects promoting education, health and welfare" (Meredith, p. 140).

Police reaction to black dissent was harsh, once the power of the BCM was acknowledged. In March 1973 eight leaders of the movement, including Biko, were banned; the Minister of Justice, P. C. Pelser, claimed they had advocated "arson, rape and bloody revolution" (Pelser in Harsch, p. 271). Banning, for Biko, meant that he was "restricted to King William's Town, forbidden to speak in public or to write for publication or to be quoted or to be present with more than one person at a time" (Meredith, p. 141). That year more than 100 other black militants were banned or placed under house arrest. In early 1974 O. R. Tiro, another BCM leader, was killed in his home by a bomb; the Bureau of State Security was believed to be behind the murder. As a result of a crackdown during this period, the official leadership of all major BCM groups was effectively wiped out. Determined and resilient, however, other leaders continued to work behind the scenes and new leaders emerged to fill in the gaps. Such commitment was reinforced not only by widespread militant sentiment—a general unwillingness to be cowed by an oppressive system—but also by news of the gains of various liberation movements throughout Africa. The victory of FRELIMO (Front for the Liberation of Mozambique) in Mozambique, where white Portugese rule collapsed, was especially encouraging news to South African revolutionaries, and "Viva FRELIMO" rallies were held throughout the country. In South Africa, the police detained and arrested another 50 prominent BCM activists, most of whom were sentenced to five or six years in prison after an extended trial. The trial succeeded only in stimulating the BCM, whose leaders used it as a platform for revolutionary ideas, and regularly

entered the courtroom singing freedom songs and shouting *Amandla* (Zulu for "power").

This new, fierce energy on the part of black militants, as well as old resentments over low wages, police harassment, and, indeed, the entire system of racial subjugation effected by apartheid, would lead inevitably to the bloody, devastating 16 months of riots known as the Soweto Revolt.

Johannesburg and Soweto. *A Dry White Season* takes place mainly in Johannesburg, where the Afrikaner protagonist Ben du Toit lives, and Soweto, where all of the black characters live. Though it may seem surprising that du Toit could live for 50 years as a South African and have had so little direct experience with blacks that he would not be aware of the vast inequalities facing them, the fact is that nonwhite servants tended to the needs of Johannesburg whites and so entered their community, but no white people would ever visit Soweto. Soweto is an acronym for the southwestern townships (SOuth-WEstern TOwnships) of Johannesburg, where in 1984 more than 1.25 million nonwhite Africans lived. Their segregation into this area resulted, in part, from the 1950 Group Areas Act, which required nonwhites and whites to live in previously designated, racially zoned areas. Indeed, a white South African from Johannesburg may well have never even set foot in Soweto. A historian during the apartheid period noted:

> Familiar social barriers to communication between upper and lower classes are reinforced in South Africa, both by racial distinctions and by regulations which discourage the entry of Whites into Black townships. Many leading local Whites who are familiar with London, Paris and New York have never set foot in Soweto.
>
> (Mandy, p. xix)

Around the time of the novel, mine dumps and tall buildings made up the Johannesburg skyline, identifying the city as South Africa's industrial center. Both to the east and the west of the mine dumps were many industrial townships and the homes of low-income whites. North of the mine dumps were the urban center and, further to the north, the rich white suburbs where a character like Ben du Toit would have lived. To the southwest of the mine dumps sat the "drab houses of sprawling Black Soweto and the segregated areas where the Coloureds and Indians [were] required to live" (Mandy, p. xv). Though Soweto was too large to be considered a town, it was "not yet a city because it lack[ed] cohesion

White police and soldiers in Soweto attack blacks protesting a government order to use the Afrikaans language for teaching in secondary schools.

and the normal range of urban anemities" (Mandy, p. 173). It had few paved roads at the time of the novel, and no pharmacies, bakeries, modern shopping centers, or office blocks. Some 75 percent of the groceries purchased by Sowetans were bought in Johannesburg. This arrangement forced Sowetans to remain dependent on the white sections of Johannesburg.

In the early 1970s conditions in the black townships deteriorated. In an attempt to relegate more blacks to their separate homelands, the government restricted urban development, which resulted in severe housing shortages. A survey of ten cities, accounting for half of South Africa's urban black population, showed that from 1970 to 1975 the amount of housing had increased by only 15 percent when, in the same areas, the African population had grown by more than 50 percent. In 1970 an average of 13 people lived in each house; by 1975 the average rose to 17 (Meredith, p. 142). From a new system of township administration—in which local administration boards would no longer receive subsidies from, in Soweto's case, Johannesburg—came harsh consequences in Soweto. Rents rose and services for roads, garbage removal, and sewer systems all declined. A 1976 survey showed that 43 percent of Soweto households were living under the poverty line (Meredith, p. 143).

The Soweto Revolt. The spark that set off the Soweto Revolt was the government's decision to enforce an outdated and impractical 1958 law, which ruled that the Afrikaans language had to be used regularly by secondary school teachers. Despite the fact that many teachers did not even know Afrikaans—the amalgamation of Dutch and African languages used by the Afrikaners—in 1974 the government ordered that the language be used for all practical subjects and for all courses in the general sciences. Parents, teachers, school boards, and administrators protested throughout the country to no avail. In Soweto black students began boycotting classes taught in Afrikaans, which they saw as the language of the oppressor. On June 16, 1976, a large group of students marched through Soweto singing freedom songs and chanting slogans. The students gathered peacefully in front of the Orlando West junior secondary school to protest, and planned to continue the march from there.

The police arrived, and a white policeman threw a tear-gas canister into the crowd. Another white policemen opened fire into the crowd, killing a 13-year-old black boy, Hector Peterson. The students fought back with bricks and stones, and when news of Hector Peterson's death spread, students rioted, attacking government buildings and turning over and burning cars and buses. The riots lasted for days, with riot police driving through the streets of Soweto in armored convoys, firing into the crowds. "Instructions have been given to maintain law and order at all costs," said Prime Minister B. J. Vorster two days after the revolt began (Vorster in Cawthra, p. 19). According to the government, the death toll after the first ten days was 176, with 1,000 wounded; black organizations claimed the figures were much higher.

The government's July 1st withdrawal of the Afrikaans ruling was not enough, by this point, to placate those suffering under apartheid. All over the country students called for the toppling of the entire oppressive education system—or even, in some cases, for the overthrow of the government itself. Black workers and parents joined the protests, and a series of strikes, marches, and battles ensued. Hundreds of activists were arrested and detained, and many died in police custody. By September 1977 the violence had lessened; many black workers no longer participated in strikes, which they came to see as useless, and students focused their attention on school boycotts. Some 600 teachers had resigned, and 250,000 students were on strike.

Then on September 12 news came of Steven Biko's death in detention. Police claims that Biko had died from a self-imposed hunger strike were patently ridiculous. Though suspicious deaths in detention were by no means uncommon, Biko's international fame and importance drew worldwide attention to the travesties of justice in South Africa. Within the country, violence flared up once more, and this time the government responded by outlawing every black consciousness organization in the country. Though a period of relative quiet followed, the Soweto Revolt and the death of Steven Biko marked a great shift in the way that black youth were prepared to fight apartheid. Never again would the government be able to quash black political activism as thouroughly as it had managed to in the past.

The Novel in Focus

Plot summary. *A Dry White Season* opens with the unspectacular death of Ben Du Toit, a 53-year-old white Afrikaner man knocked down on the road by a hit-and-run driver—a death reported in only a few lines on the fourth page of the evening newspaper. As the narrator puts it, the report of Ben's death is "barely enough for a shake of the head" (Brink, *A Dry White Season*,

p. 9). The narrator, however, had been an old friend of Ben's from college, and had only recently encountered him again, two weeks before the accident, when, harried and suspicious, Ben had called upon him and asked him to hold on to a pile of "papers and stuff" (*Dry White Season*, p. 13). On these papers he had "written it all down," he had told the narrator; "they've taken it all from me. Nearly everything. Not much left. But they won't get that. You hear me? If they get that there would have been no sense at all" (*Dry White Season*, p. 13). The narrator, confused and slightly irritated by Ben's seemingly paranoid behavior, had agreed to this request while assuring Ben that everything was fine, that all he needed was a "good holiday" (*Dry White Season*, p. 14). Two weeks later Ben turns up dead and the narrator is left with a mess of notebooks and papers and photographs. From these materials the narrator—a middle-aged romance novelist ready to tackle a grander project—slowly, painfully reconstructs Ben's story.

Ben Du Toit is an Afrikaner schoolteacher living comfortably in Johannesburg with his wife and teenage son; he has two grown daughters as well, who live close by. Ben's life is relatively uneventful and his marriage without passion. He keeps to a steady schedule of exercise, work, and, for relaxation when he returns home in the late afternoon, carpentry. A generous man and devoted teacher, Ben inspires trust in his students and helps others when he can. He becomes especially involved in the life of Gordon Ngubene, the black man who cleans the school where Ben teaches. As a young man Gordon had showed scholarly promise, but his father's death forced him to leave school and take work as a domestic servant. Now middle-aged, Gordon hopes to nurture the promise shown by his own son, Jonathan, an intelligent child whom Ben agrees to put through school as long as the boy's grades remain high. Things go well at first, but, as he grows older, Jonathan becomes more and more sullen and angry, especially after being arrested and flogged by the police for a crime he did not commit. Once the Soweto Revolt begins, Jonathan only rarely returns home during the first month, and then one day disappears for good. Some children report that they saw Jonathan "in the crowd surrounded and stormed by the police" but the family is unable to find out any facts or specifics, neither from the police nor the hospitals (*Dry White Season*, p. 41). Gordon comes to Ben for help, and Ben hires an attorney to look into the matter, but during the subsequent investigation the authorities either deny having heard of Jonathan, or fail to respond at all. They assume this attitude despite personal accounts from a nurse and a cleaning man at the prison—the first reports seeing Jonathan in a hospital, his head swathed in bandages; the second claims to have cleaned blood from a prison cell in which Jonathan had been held. Finally the security police telephones the attorney with the news that Jonathan Ngubene died "of natural causes" the previous night (*Dry White Season,* p. 46).

Attempts to claim the body prove even more difficult, as Gordon and his wife, Emily, find themselves shuttled from one bureaucratic office to another, none of which can provide them with answers. At each dead end the couple returns to Ben, who, having utter faith in his country's government and legal system, remains confident that justice will be done and Jonathan's body properly buried. At last the attorney threatens to go public with the situation, and in this way finally elicits a response from the security police: Jonathan had never been imprisoned, but was shot during the riots, his body buried at that time. A request for the medical report elicits only a statement that the report is "unavailable" (*Dry White Season,* p. 47). For Ben the matter seems to end here; when Gordon, still determined to find out the fate of his son, appears at his door, Ben asks, "what good can it do [to keep looking], Gordon?" Gordon responds: "It can do nothing, Baas. But a man must know about his children. . . . I cannot stop before I know what happened to him and where they buried him. His body belongs to me. It's my son's body" (*Dry White Season,* p. 49).

Slowly Gordon begins to track down witnesses, many of them too frightened to sign statements. He pieces together the story of his son's detention, torture, and death. At one point, after much coaxing, an ex-prisoner who had been detained along with Jonathan agrees to sign an affidavit stating, among other things, that both of them were kept naked throughout their detention; that he heard Jonathan being beaten from the next room; that one day they were taken outside the city and forced to crawl through barbed wire fences; and that another day they were interrogated together, standing "on blocks about a yard apart, with half-bricks tied to their sexual organs" (*Dry White Season,* p. 50). Gordon persuades the nurse as well to sign a statement, and, by this point, has begun to believe that he will be able, someday, to find the body of his son and

bury it. The day after Gordon obtains the two signed affidavits, however, "he [is] taken away by the Special Branch [security police]. And with him, the affidavits [disappear] without a trace" (*Dry White Season,* p. 51).

It is at this point that Ben begins to suspect that things are not what they seem to be—or, at least, not as he has imagined them to be—in his country. Would Gordon, too, be tortured and killed in prison? Anxious to uncover the truth, however painful it might be, Ben slowly finds himself immersed in Gordon's case and spends almost the entire remainder of the novel going through the same motions, and running up against the same obstacles, as Gordon had before his own detention—and with nearly the same results. Ben visits the police, works continually with a lawyer, visits Gordon's family in Soweto, and spends a great deal of time writing letters and shuffling between various bureaucratic offices—most of this with a black cab driver named Stanley, who describes himself at one point as old-fashioned enough to believe that blacks and whites can fight for change together. Just as in Jonathan's case, the police refuse to be forthcoming, and all the while they deny, even in the face of clear evidence, that Gordon is being tortured and abused, or even that anything is amiss. The injustice of what happened to Jonathan and what is happening to Gordon begins to haunt Ben until he feels he has no choice but to pursue this case until the end. His Afrikaner friends, colleagues, and family do not agree, however, and numerous tensions begin to disrupt Ben's life. His wife, Susan, is especially intolerant of Ben's activity, even more so when this activity begins to threaten the family's safety. Police show up at the house with some regularity—to question the Du Toits, to search the house, and ultimately to threaten them. In this process the marriage dissolves.

Ben thinks of Gordon continually, and one night cannot shake the image of the broken teeth Gordon's wife has found in one of Gordon's pockets, in the clothing the police finally released to her at her request:

> [A]fter the light had been turned out he couldn't sleep, however exhausted he felt. He was remembering too much. The dirty bundle in the newspaper they'd brought him. The stained trousers. The broken teeth. It made him nauseous. He moved into another position but every time he closed his eyes the images returned. . . . Dark and soundless the night lay around him, limitless, endless; the night with

A DRY WHITE SEASON—METAPHOR FOR APARTHEID

~

The title *A Dry White Season* comes from the Mangone Wally Serote poem that is used as the book's epigraph:

it is a dry white season
dark leaves don't last, their brief lives dry out
and with a broken heart they dive down gently headed for the earth
not even bleeding.
it is a dry white season brother,
only the trees know the pain as they still stand erect
dry like steel, their branches dry like wire,
indeed, it is a dry white season
but seasons come to pass.

(*Dry White Season*, epigraph)

Like Serote's poem, Brink's book uses the image of the dry white season to refer metaphorically to apartheid and the conditions created by it. In the book the image is rooted in a specific event. When the novel's protagonist, Ben du Toit, was nine or ten years old, the Great Drought of 1933 forced his father to trek with all of the sheep from their farm to another district in the Free State, where, it was rumored, some grazing ground still remained. Ben and his father made the journey alone, but before they were able to reach their destination the drought closed in on them, forcing them to slaughter the starving lambs and sheep, and the ewes with no milk left. As Ben tells it, "in the end even the shrubs disappear . . . and day after day there's the sun burning away whatever remains" (*Dry White Season*, p. 30).

At the moment when Ben comes fully into awareness of what apartheid means for most of his country's population, and when he finds that something has changed irrevocably for him because of this awareness, he says:

The single memory that has been with me all day . . . is [of] that distant summer when Pa and I were left with the sheep. The drought that took everything from us, leaving us alone and scorched among the white skeletons.

What happened before that drought has never been particularly vivid or significant to me: that was where I first discovered myself and the world. And it seems to me I'm finding myself on the edge of yet another dry white season, perhaps worse than the one I knew as a child.

What now?

(*Dry White Season*, p. 163)

all its multitudes of rooms, some dark, some dusky, some blindingly light, with men standing astride on bricks, weights tied to their balls.

(*Dry White Season*, p. 75)

Gordon eventually dies in prison. An inquest is held, and despite all evidence to the contrary, his death is ruled to have been suicide. Throughout the course of Ben's efforts, possible witnesses are detained or deported, shots are fired into Ben's living room, the police become more and more of a hostile presence in his life, and almost everyone he knows turns against him. By the end of his life, he is able to find solace only with the black cab driver Stanley, and with Melanie, a young British South African journalist also dedicated to the plight of nonwhite South Africa. Ben and Melanie fall in love, but after Melanie visits

England she is denied entrance back into South Africa.

The last portion of the novel documents the crumbling of Ben's world. In one of the last days of his life, Ben finds that his own daughter has betrayed him by revealing the location of the papers he has kept to document the entire affair. Before handing them to the narrator, Ben moves the papers to a new location. A few days later his home is burglarized and the former hiding spot methodically ripped apart.

The novel ends with an epilogue by the narrator, who has taken it upon himself to assemble Ben's detailed but scattered notes, documents, and letters, and to tell the story. The narrator recounts again his last meeting with Ben, Ben's paranoid state, and his insistence that the narrator take his writings so that the story will not die with him. He speculates on Ben's last hours, the hours after Ben's discovery of the burglary and before the "accident" in which he is killed. And finally, having put the entire story together and presented it in the best, most truthful way he could, the narrator asks:

> why do I go ahead by writing it all down here? . . . Prodded, possibly, by some dull, guilty feeling of responsibility towards something Ben might have believed in: something man is capable of being but which he isn't very often allowed to be?
>
> I don't know.
>
> Perhaps all one can really hope for, all I am entitled to, is no more than this: to write it down. To report what I know. So that it will not be possible for any man ever to say again: I know nothing about it.
>
> (*Dry White Season*, p. 316)

Afrikaans literature and white activism in South Africa. The problem of how to contribute to the anti-apartheid struggle vexed politically committed white South Africans, especially after the rise of the Black Consciousness Movement in the 1970s, which disdained any political activity of white "do-gooders" (Biko in Ranuga, p. 93). As Ben du Toit realizes after being attacked by a group of black youths on the streets of Soweto in *A Dry White Season*:

> Whether I like it or not . . . I am white. This is the small, final, terrifying truth of my broken world. I am white. And because I'm white I am born into a state of privilege. Even if I fight the system that has reduced us to this I remain white, and favoured by the very circumstances I abhor. . . . [Yet] what can I do but what I have done? I cannot choose not to intervene: that

would be a denial and a mockery not only of everything I believe in, but of the hope that compassion may survive among men.

> (*Dry White Season*, p. 304)

Like Ben du Toit, Afrikaner activists were in especially difficult positions, often disdained on all sides of the struggle. Even as the policies of apartheid became less and less attractive for economic reasons in the 1970s, apartheid was still widely seen as aligned with the will of the Afrikaner people, and prominent anti-apartheid activists, such as Bram Fischer, were disowned by Afrikaners the way that Ben is in the novel. In the novel, Ben du Toit is eventually ostracized by every Afrikaner he knows, finding solace only among his black and his white British friends.

For Afrikaner writers the problem was just as acute. Brink, an anti-apartheid white Afrikaner writer, stands out as one of the few internationally famous South African writers who is not only Afrikaner, but who also writes regularly in Afrikaans for an obviously Afrikaner audience. Like many of Brink's other books, *A Dry White Season* was written in two languages. As Brink explains,

> I write regularly in both Afrikaans and English, usually preparing a first draft in Afrikaans, followed by a complete rewriting of the novel in English, and a final translation back into Afrikaans. I regard this laborious process as an essential part of exploring the material, using English as an aid to see more clearly and to evaluate more objectively.

> (Brink in Ross, p. 55)

Brink's habit of translating each text into English was prompted by the banning in South Africa of his first politically committed novel, *Kennis van die aand*—the first Afrikaans novel ever to be banned in the country. To write in English was necessary in order to have an audience at all. While several Afrikaner writers prefer to write only in English—J. M. Coetzee (see **Waiting for the Barbarians,** also covered in *African Literature and Its Times*) for instance, finds Afrikaans "frankly dull" (Coetzee in Gallagher, p. 48)—Brink sees Afrikaans as a language rich and full of possibility:

> [T]here is a certain virility, a certain earthy, youthful quality about Afrikaans because it is such a young language, and because, although derived from an old European language like Dutch, it has found completely new roots in Africa and become totally Africanized in the process. One writer said . . . that Afrikaans at this stage seems to resemble the English

language in the time of Shakespeare. It is not very firmly and finally organized yet. One can do almost anything with it. If you haven't got a word for something you want to express, you simply make a word or pluck a word from another language and shape it to fit yours.

(Brink in Ross, p. 104)

Afrikaans developed in the late 1800s and was first presented as a literary language in 1876, when a small Afrikaner nationalist group, the Association of True Afrikaners, turned out the newspaper *Die Afrikaanse Patriot.* In the following years many other Afrikaans texts—almost all of them fervently nationalist in sentiment—would appear, including alternative, revisionist histories told from the Afrikaner perspective. This early literature tended to glorify the Afrikaners and to commemorate the bravery and suffering of these "chosen" people, who had first settled in South Africa in the seventeenth century. In these years the existence of the Afrikaner people as a unified and distinct group was very much at risk, as the ruling power of the time, the British empire, sought to establish complete dominance over the region it had partially occupied since the late eighteenth century. When the British won the Boer War (1899-1902), after destroying about 30,000 Afrikaner farmsteads and placing thousands of Afrikaners in concentration camps, the Afrikaner people seemed "destined for decline and oblivion" (Meredith, p. 11). (Also called the South African War, the Boer War—so named by the British—erupted because the British wanted to reestablish dominance over the two independence-minded republics, the Transvaal and the Orange Free State. The two republics were joined with the Cape Colony and Natal to form the Union of South Africa in 1910.)

Resilient under British attempts to quash them, the Afrikaners rallied around the cause of ethnic unity. Their development of a unique, specifically Afrikaner language and literature coincided with the birth of Afrikaner nationalism, with much of the developing literature aligning itself fiercely with the nationalist cause. This ethnic fervor culminated in the victory of the Nationalist Party in 1948. Throughout these struggles Afrikaans literature continued to stress nationalist themes, and also began looking back nostalgically at the farm life that Afrikaners had traditionally led in South Africa; this emphasis on "the land" served to strengthen the idea that the soil of South Africa was somehow divinely connected to the Afrikaners. Where did this leave the blacks who inhabited the region before the arrival of the Afrikaners? As J. M. Coetzee points

André Brink

out, "this proprietorial attitude has made of the black man a temporary sojourner, a displaced person, not only in the white man's laws but in the white man's imaginary life" (Coetzee in Gallagher, p. 42). Playing its part in the development of this attitude, Afrikaans literature was crucial to the nationalist cause that was realized in the 42-year system of apartheid in South Africa.

Only in the 1960s did a young group of Afrikaner writers, "the Sestigers," challenge the models on which the whole of early Afrikaans literature was based. Influenced by modern European literature, writers like André Brink, Breyten Breytenbach, Jan Rabie, and others dramatically renewed Afrikaans literature by "destroying all the existing taboos pertaining to sex, ethics, religion, and politics governing [it]" (Brink in Ross, p. 54). Despite the rebelliousness and daring of these writers, however, "they could not distance themselves from the white, oppressive, bourgeois culture" (Coetzee, p. 346). Not until the next two decades, during which *A Dry White Season* was written, did a small group of Afrikaner writers break away from white burgeois culture and create, for the first time, a politically motivated and revolutionary Afrikaans literature. Many of the texts produced by these writers elicited powerful responses in their readers: seeming to have betrayed their own culture, these writers were often seen as either traitors or as revolutionaries; from another perspective they appeared to be complicit, no matter their views, with a system that granted them enormous and disparate privilege. As Brink himself points out, "through history, culture and the colour of his skin [the Afrikaner writer] is linked, like it or not, to the power Establishment" (Brink in Gallagher, p. 43). Another poet admits that "the (white) Afrikaans writers of today . . . have to live with the cultural feeling of guilt, that the language in which they write is not 'innocent of the horrors' of apartheid" (Small in Gallagher, p. 43).

Sources and literary context. *A Dry White Season* was one of many texts written in the wake of the Soweto Revolt, the unprecedented, widespread, and extremely violent rioting that shook South Africa in 1976. Writers were quick to respond to the devastation, and to the undeniable fact that the country had entered into a state of crisis. As the epigraph (from Antonio Gramsci) of Nadine Gordimer's 1978 novel, *July's People*, reads, "the crisis consists precisely in the fact that the old is dying and the new cannot be born . . ." (Gramsci in Coetzee, p. 356).

Brink's idea for the novel was more specifically triggered by "a detainee who had allegedly hung himself near King William's Town—Mohapi. The Mduli case in Durban also contributed to it, but it was mainly the Mohapi one which triggered it" (Brink in Jolly, pp. 21-22). When the famous and charismatic black leader Steven Biko died mysteriously in detention in 1977, Brink stopped working on the novel for a year, but eventually he "realised that it was also a matter of making sure the people knew about it, and were forced never to allow themselves to forget it" (Brink in Jolly, p. 23).

Reviews. *A Dry White Season* was initially banned by South African censors when it came out in 1979. By the end of that year the ban had been lifted, along with the ban on Nadine Gordimer's **Burger's Daughter** (also covered in *African Literature and Its Times*). Brink points out the apparent liberalization of the censorship sys-

tem at this time, but also criticizes the fact that "the books which were unbanned were books very obviously chosen from the works of authors with some kind of international reputation, and they were all books by white authors" (Brink in Ross, p. 56). Regardless, the novel had great international success and in 1980 won both the Martin Luther King Memorial Prize and the Prix Medicis Étranger, France's most prestigious prize for fiction in translation. In 1989 an American film version of Brink's novel was released.

—Carolyn Turgeon

For More Information

Brink, André. *A Dry White Season.* New York: William Morrow, 1980.

Cawthra, Gavin. *Policing South Africa: The SAP and the Transition from Apartheid.* London: Zed Press, 1993.

Coetzee, Ampie. "Literature and Crisis: One Hundred Years of Afrikaans Literature and Afrikaner Nationalism." In *Rendering Things Visible: Essays on South African Literary Culture.* Ed. Martin Trump. Johannesburg: Ravan Press, 1990.

Gallagher, Susan VanZanten. *A Story of South Africa: J. M. Coetzee's Fiction in Context.* Cambridge, Mass.: Harvard University Press, 1991.

Harsch, Ernest. *South Africa: White Rule, Black Revolt.* New York: Monad Press, 1980.

Jolly, Rosemary Jane. *Colonization, Violence, and Narration in White South African Writing: André Brink, Breyten Breytenbach, and J. M. Coetzee.* Athens: Ohio University Press, 1996.

Le May, G. H. L. *The Afrikaners: An Historical Interpretation.* Cambridge, Mass.: Blackwell Publishers, 1995.

Mandy, Nigel. *A City Divided: Johannesburg and Soweto.* New York: St. Martin's Press, 1984.

Meredith, Martin. *In the Name of Apartheid: South Africa in the Postwar Period.* London: Hamish Hamilton, 1988.

Ranuga, Thomas K. *The New South Africa and the Socialist Vision: Positions and Perspectives Toward a Post-Apartheid Society.* Atlantic Highlands, N.J.: Humanities Press, 1996.

Ross, Jean W. "Andre Philippus Brink." In *Contemporary Authors.* Vol. 104. Detroit: Gale Research, 1982.

Thompson, Leonard. *A History of South Africa.* New Haven, Conn.: Yale University Press, 1990.

Efuru

by

Flora Nwapa

Flora Nwapa was born on January 13, 1931, into a popular and wealthy family in Oguta, in the present Imo State of Nigeria. After a brief stint teaching at Priscilla Memorial Grammar School in Oguta, she began her university studies at the University College, Ibadan. Nwapa graduated in 1957; a year later she received a postgraduate Diploma in Education at the University of Edingurgh in Scotland. Upon returning to Nigeria, she taught briefly at a female high school in Eastern Nigeria, then joined the University of Lagos as Administrative Officer and remained there from 1962 until the outbreak of the Nigerian civil war in 1967. At this point, she, like many other members of the Igbo elite, was forced to return to the Eastern region. In 1966 she published *Efuru,* becoming not only Nigeria's first female novelist but black Africa's as well. The Tana Press, which she founded in 1976, became West Africa's first indigenous publishing house to be owned by a black African woman. Until her death on October 16, 1993, Nwapa would remain a prolific, versatile writer and a powerful influence on other black African women writers.

Events in History at the Time the Novel Takes Place

Igbo community life—an overview. Characterized by their republicanism and egalitarianism, the Igbo (Ibo) differed from most other ethnic groups in Nigeria by not having a supreme political authority, such as a monarch or a king. Instead, power was vested in the people directly or in a council of elders. A highly democratic people, the Igbo favored forums at which every male

---

THE LITERARY WORK

A novel set in rural Eastern Nigeria during the 1940s; published in English in 1966.

SYNOPSIS

An exceptional woman struggles to find her place in a traditional Igbo community.

---

member of the community had the opportunity to express his views on matters of common interest before a decision was taken. In public assemblies, a common, a poor, or a young man had as much right to be heard as an affluent, influential, or elderly man in the community.

When British colonial administrators arrived in Igboland in the middle of the nineteenth century, they discovered that enforcing colonial laws was not as simple as in the Northern and Western parts of the country. In the North, the *emir* was an influential authority through whom the masses could be reached and whose decisions and pronouncements were supreme. In the West, the *oba* exercised similar presence and authority. The neighbors of the Igbo people in the Southeast—the Efik, the Ibibio, the Kalabari—all had their paramount rulers, and hence the British penetration into these areas was relatively easier. The British attempted to get around the problem in Igboland by appointing "warrant chiefs" and establishing a system called "indirect rule," but it met with stiff resistance and generally proved unsuccessful.

The traditional Igbo lived in clusters of small, self-governing communities whose inhabitants traced their origins to a common ancestor. The community was guided by elders, who drew their inspirations from ancestral wisdom, and who settled disputes over land ownership as well as more complex matters, such as inheritance and succession. Today the Igbo occupy six states, number more than 15 million people, and, alongside the Hausa in the North and the Yoruba in the West, comprise one of the three major ethnic groups in Nigeria. Although the contemporary Igbo have assiduously taken up Western education, Christianity, and other emblems of modern civilization, traditional customs and beliefs have not been totally abandoned.

Efuru, which is set in the mid-twentieth century, describes strong, deep-rooted customs and practices. As in the novel, the two major occupations of the Igbo in the traditional society were farming and trading; for those who lived by the side of rivers and lakes—as do the people in the novel—fishing was also a major occupation.

Reorganization of trade. At the time of the novel, the British Empire controlled Northern and Southern Nigeria, formerly individual protectorates. Along with Lagos, these one-time protectorates became an amalgamated colony in 1914. The construction of roads began in the 1900s, followed by the introduction of two railroads in 1912 and 1926. The rate of industrial development was gradual, especially in rural areas. On the other hand, the imposition of colonial government was pervasive. British laws were enforced by local British commissioners and their hand-picked subordinates; the government restricted which goods could be sold and how they were to be distributed, which affected trade among the Igbo in areas like Oguta, where *Efuru* is set.

European trading companies that became active in the region took advantage of the colonial-built roads, which in many cases bypassed established Igbo market centers, thereby shifting the flow of money to new areas. This relocation of profitable trading sites upset the traditional use of Igbo marketplaces for celebrations and meeting grounds as well as centers of commerce. Many village traders had to travel to colonial outposts to engage in business with international merchants, leaving their ceremonies and customs behind. Moreover, although British colonial officers encouraged the production of farm products like yam, cassava, and palm kernel, certain items were banned or heavily taxed by the British. For example, in the novel, the colonial government bans the production of homemade gin, prompting numerous complaints from Igbo brewers,

several of whom resort to subterfuge to continue their trade. Efuru's husband, Gilbert, tells her of one brewer who concealed all her gin in her canoe, thwarting a police raid on her house. Efuru applauds the woman for defying injustice: "Why the government does not allow us to drink our homemade gin, I do not know. . . . If they must stop us from cooking gin, then the white man's gin and his schnapps should be sold cheap" (Nwapa, *Efuru,* p. 104).

Social organization and functions. Traditional Igbo society was mostly patrilineal, although a few matrilineal communities existed, especially in the Ohafia and Arochukwu areas of Igboland. In the patrilineal mainstream, kinship was traced through the father, as were inheritance and succession. The smallest social unit was the family; the largest, the clan. A family consisted of both nuclear and extended family members. Igbo culture allowed a man to marry more than one wife; the choice to do so was often dictated by economic rather than sexual circumstances. A family that needed more hands for farming was more likely to have multiple wives if the means existed. Also, a clan that needed more sons to fight wars with its neighbors was likely to encourage its menfolk to marry multiple wives. Given that the social system was mostly patrilineal, a couple aspired to have as many male children as possible, and if a couple took a long time to have children or did not have children at all, the husband was considered justified in marrying a second, third, or fourth wife as the case may be, until male children were born into the family. All members of the family lived in the same compound, over which the eldest male was the head. When a son came of age and married his own wife or wives and had children, his family was expected to live together with his father's in the same compound. The family would acquire a larger portion of land so that it could build a compound that accommodated all its members.

Gender roles were rigid. Men were the main breadwinners, supporting their families by farming, fishing, and hunting; they also contributed to public festivals, honored the ancestors, and defended their communities in times of war. By contrast, women were reared from childhood to carry out household tasks in preparation for their eventual roles as wives and mothers. The primary responsibilities of married women consisted of cooking, cleaning, raising children, and maintaining a well-run household. But women also contributed to the welfare

Igbo villagers thatching a house roof in early twentieth-century Nigeria.

of their community through their involvement in agriculture and trade. They participated in customary religious practices too, although their role in community rituals and sacrifices was usually much less significant than that played by men. In *Efuru* women participate more than usual in rituals because the novel features a lake goddess who was thought to select mostly women to be priestesses.

As a community, the Igbo supported themselves mainly by farming. Large-scale annual crops, such as yam and cassava, formed the dietary staples. Profitable cultivation of these crops required abundant land and many workers. Men and women planted on communal or family farms, with the "women's crops"—cassava, cocoyam, maize, melon, okra—maturing before yam, which was designated as the "men's crop." The harvest cycles provided the farming family with sustenance throughout the year.

The Igbo supplemented their agriculture with trade. Farmers would travel to village markets to exchange their produce for other necessities—meat, palm wine, and palm kernels. Some Igbo, like the novel's Efuru, traveled to rural areas to buy merchandise (perhaps yams or dried fish) wholesale, then sold the goods at their village markets for a profit. Village trading was first the domain of women in Igbo society; men became involved when European traders infiltrated the

market. A few women grew wealthy trading. Some even won the right to buy property and take a title (a mark of distinction in Igbo society), although these privileges were granted only in exceptional cases. In the novel Efuru learns that her late mother was such a successful businesswoman that she took several titles before her death.

Oguta is one of the few places in Igboland where a woman's personal merit and achievements can lead to her taking a title. But to be so honored, the achievement must be extraordinary and unprecedented because title taking is the preserve of men. A woman so honored can participate in community leadership. Flora Nwapa was honored by the Oguta community with a title and she explained the significance:

> In Ugwuta (Oguta) women have certain rights that women elsewhere, in other parts of the country, do not have. For instance, in Ugwuta, a woman can break the kolanut [to share it—a custom signifying goodwill and respect] where men are. If she is old, or if she has achieved much or if she has paid the bride price for a male relation and the member of the family is there she can break the kolanut. And everybody would eat the kolanut. But in certain parts of Igboland a woman is not even shown a kolanut, not to talk about breaking it.
>
> (Nwapa in Umeh, p. 668)

Marriage customs. In traditional Igbo culture, marriage had important ramifications: it brought two extended families together in an alliance that expanded economic and social opportunities. Such marriages were not exclusively love matches, though affection between potential spouses was desirable. Often a man would marry outside his village group, forging a link for himself to another village in which he could visit and trade under the protection of his wife's family. While getting married had business ramifications, having children remained the most important reason to form such a union. Children helped the family trade or farm, performed household duties, cared for elders, and carried on the name and customs of their father's lineage.

Sometimes parents betrothed their children to each other or an older man picked a young girl and waited for her to reach marriageable age (about 16 years old). In other cases, families made arrangements for a man and a woman who were of the same marriageable age. A young man could also choose a prospective bride, then seek his parents' consent to marry the girl. However the match was made, people regarded marriage as a serious matter in Igboland. Again, they considered it a union of two families rather than a private arrangement between two consenting individuals. The woman shared fully in the rights and privileges of the family, lived in the compound, and associated with everyone else there. So in the process of bringing a woman into the family through marriage, everyone was allowed a say, and the various views of the family—especially those of existing wives—were carefully taken into consideration. First and foremost, investigations were made by both families into the pedigree and ancestry of the prospective partner to ensure that he/she was socially acceptable. In some parts of Igboland a social class known as *osu* (outcast) exists, and it is taboo for a non-osu to marry an osu. Families also investigated the health of a mate's lineage—to ensure that there was no history of insanity or other abnormal disease—the relationship between the family and its neighbors, and its material circumstances. A young woman's family ensured that their prospective son-in-law had income enough to support a wife and children. A man's family made sure that their prospective daughter-in-law had a good upbringing, had not been wayward, and had generally good morals and manners. They also tried to ensure that she would be able to bear children. If all seemed promising, the bride-groom's family made a formal application by, for example, presenting a gift of palm wine to the bride's family. Often several such gifts were made before the bride price (a type of dowry paid to the woman's family) was agreed upon.

The next stage of courtship involved tests of character. The groom's family invited the prospective bride to their house, observed her housekeeping and cooking, and judged her temperament. If she passed this test, the marriage proceeded.

To formally hand the bride over to the bride-groom, her father had her publicly identify her future husband and declare openly that she chose him. Next her father handed her a cup of palm wine, first taking a sip. She then went "in search" of her fiancé, who "hid" in the crowd until she "found" him and brought him to her father, in front of whom both kneeled for a show of allegiance to each other. The girl drank a little from the cup and handed it to her fiancé, who finished off the contents. The girl's father then blessed the couple and the marriage was solemnized. The two became husband and wife, and a great feast followed.

Polygamy and divorce. At the time of the novel, polygyny—marriage to more than one wife—was standard among the Igbo. In fact, Igbo women tended to be proponents of it because their husband's heightened prestige reflected on them. Polygyny signified status and prosperity—rich men tended to have more than one wife. The additional wives gave him more opportunities to father children (preferably male) that would continue his family line. The first woman he married enjoyed the status of headwife, taking precedence over subsequent wives who joined the household. The wives lived together in the same compound, helping one another care for their children, thereby lightening the domestic load and giving themselves more time to engage in trade.

Divorce, though uncommon and generally frowned upon, was an accepted practice in traditional Igbo society. Both the man and the woman had the right to initiate it, but, regardless of who instigated the separation, the woman would be the one to leave the compound and go back to her natal home. Her children, considered their father's, remained with him, as did most of the family property, except for the possessions that the wife acquired by herself over the years. Items bought for her by her husband during the marriage might or might not be taken back, depending on the husband's disposition or the nature of the offense leading to the divorce. If circumstances proved the wife had committed adultery, the husband was justified in taking them back. In other circumstances he was considered mean-spirited if he took back such gifts. It was assumed that her years in the marriage had earned her the gifts, especially if she had borne to her husband children whom she was leaving behind. After a woman returned to her natal home, the bride price was paid back to the man to finalize the divorce. If she intended to remarry right away, the new husband usually reimbursed the old one.

Igbo religion. Traditional Igbo religious worship revolves around belief in a supreme god and a pantheon of lesser deities. The supreme god, Chukwu, is the creator of life, the elements, and all things comprising the human world and the spiritual world. Chukwu is not worshipped directly, but is thought to be the ultimate recipient of the worship given to minor deities. The people likewise share a common belief in Ala, goddess of the earth and of fertility. However, there are also local deities, such as nature gods, who vary depending on location, and these deities command a central role in the daily spiritual life of a particular community.

The goddess of Oguta Lake provides an example of such a local deity. To the Oguta people, the lake determined their farming cycles by the flooding and receding of its waters. Moreover, villagers relied on the lake for fishing, washing, and even social activities such as swimming and boating. In the novel Efuru worships the lake goddess—called Uhamiri, Uhammiri, or Ogbuide—who is the quintessence of feminine beauty and morality. In reality, as in fiction, the Oguta people's concept of the lake goddess is that of a deity personified in a beautiful, ageless woman who is herself partial to women. Uhamiri is known for her beauty, her control of entry and exit between this world and the next, her role as the goddess of crossroads, and her ability to bestow or remove prosperity. There is a discrepancy between her image in real life and in the novel, however. Uhamiri is depicted in the novel as childless; she is even blamed by some of the villagers for aggravating the childless condition of her worshippers. Efuru is the sole offspring of her late mother, who also worshipped Uhamiri, and Efuru herself loses her only daughter, Ogonim, to a childhood illness. One can speculate that Nwapa eliminated the fertility goddess aspect of Uhamiri to heighten the parallels between the deity and her heroine, to demonstrate that

being a wife and mother is not the only way for a woman to lead a rewarding life. Nwapa herself has explained this phenomenon in the novel, saying that at the time *Efuru* was written and when she was growing up, "nobody associated the Woman of the Lake with children" (Nwapa in Umeh, p. 640). So Nwapa was simply being faithful to social reality and perceptions of her time in her creative rendering.

THE MISSIONARY MOVEMENT

Although the main characters in Nwapa's novel worship the indigenous Igbo gods, they are also aware of the spread of Christianity in their region. The Anglican Church Missionary Society settled in Igboland in 1857 at Onitsha—the Igbo heartland—and spread from there to areas like Oguta, which is not far from Onitsha. In time, rivalries among different missions and denominations increased their activity. Starting in Nigeria in the 1910s and 1920s, missionary movements of various denominations established churches, schools, and health facilities. Churches were built to enhance evangelism and retain new converts. Schools were established to attract the young and promote literacy.

Christian schools disturbed Igbo community life because the schedules of students conflicted with those of their peers who stayed home. As both groups matured, the division between the schooled and unschooled widened. Those educated in mission schools secured government posts and teaching positions, while their uneducated contemporaries were left behind. Indeed, the material advantages provided by a formal education convinced parents to send their children to a Christian school, even if they did not agree with its teachings or bemoaned the loss of traditional influence in the lives of children. In the novel, Eneberi, Efuru's second husband, attended a Christian school that gave him the baptismal name of Gilbert and tried to wean him from Igbo customs: "The Church regarded it as pagan to continue dancing with your age-group when you were in school. When your parents sent you to school, you automatically became a Christian" (*Efuru*, p. 103).

The Novel in Focus

Plot summary. The novel begins after Efuru, the beautiful, rebellious daughter of one of Oguta's most respected residents, meets Adizua, a young man of limited prospects, from a much less prominent family. After a whirlwind two-week courtship, the young couple elopes because Adizua cannot afford to pay the necessary bride price. The elopement causes a great scandal in the village but Efuru's charm and determination to remain with her husband soon win over the elders and, eventually, Efuru's own father, Nwashike Ogene.

During the early days of the marriage, Adizua works on a distant farm while Efuru establishes herself as a trader and businesswoman. Motherless since childhood, she also develops close relationships with her mother-in-law, Ossai, and Ossai's outspoken sister, Ajanupu. Ossai even arranges for Efuru to undergo circumcision—euphemistically referred to as "her bath"—in hopes that it will help her daughter-in-law conceive a child. After only a month's confinement, Efuru is eager to resume her work as a trader. Meanwhile, Adizua, bored by his job, leaves the farm and joins Efuru in selling yams and crayfish in their town. They earn enough money to pay off Efuru's bride price, and their two families are reconciled at last.

A year passes without Efuru becoming pregnant, and she begins to fear that she is destined to be childless. Her sadness is compounded by malicious gossip among the other villagers. Efuru and her father consult a *dibia* (healer) who tells her to make special sacrifices to the ancestors every week. She follows his instructions and, to the joy of her family and the whole village, becomes pregnant within a year, giving birth to a baby girl, Ogonim. Thereafter, Adizua continues trading while Efuru takes care of Ogonim, but he lacks his wife's business acumen. The couple hire Ogea, a young girl whose family has fallen on hard times, to look after Ogonim so Efuru can return to work. When Efuru and Adizua visit the dibia to thank him for his help, he divines trouble in the couple's future and privately vows to counteract it. Unfortunately, he dies in his sleep before he can warn Efuru and Adizua of what lies in store for them.

Efuru resumes trading and enjoys great professional success, but her family life suffers. Adizua starts leaving home without explanation. One day Efuru hears gossip that he has gone to the village of Ndoni with another woman, who has a bad reputation as an adulteress. Worried, Efuru seeks guidance from her mother-in-law, who sadly informs her that Adizua takes after his father, a wanderer who left his family when Adizua was five years old. Ossai reveals that she remained true to her husband in his long absence

until he came home many years later to die. Despite her sufferings, Ossai advises Efuru to follow her example and remain faithful to Adizua. Efuru counters that "to suffer for a truant husband, an irresponsible husband like Adizua, is to debase suffering. My own suffering will be noble" (*Efuru*, p. 73). On the advice of her father, she decides to wait a while longer for Adizua to come home before she makes any permanent decisions.

Soon after, Efuru's daughter, Ogonim, falls seriously ill and dies. A messenger is sent to retrieve Adizua, but he fails to return and Ogonim's burial takes place without him. After mourning her child, Efuru goes in search of Adizua to discuss their marriage. Unable to locate him, she informs Adizua's family that she can no longer be his wife. Ossai and Ajanupu sadly accept her choice, remaining her friends. The rest of the community supports Efuru's decision and commends her virtue.

With Ogea, Efuru returns to her childhood home. She cares for her father, running his household and continuing to flourish as a trader until she meets Eneberi, another childhood acquaintance who is now called Gilbert, a name he received from Christian missionaries who baptized and educated him. Efuru and Gilbert fall in love and marry, Gilbert punctiliously observing all the necessary marriage customs before the wedding. At first, the newlyweds are blissfully happy and all their business enterprises prosper, but their contentment is ultimately marred by Efuru's failure to conceive, which, again, elicits considerable comment from malicious village gossips.

Around this time, Efuru consults a dibia about a recurring dream, during which she dives to the bottom of the lake and meets "an elegant woman" who escorts her to her underwater domain and showers her with riches (*Efuru*, p. 183). Efuru has discovered that every morning after she has the dream she sells all the goods she brings to the market. The dibia tells Efuru that she has been chosen to be a worshipper of Uhamiri, the goddess of the lake, who will protect and reward her with wealth and good fortune. He instructs Efuru to respect Uhamiri's laws, observe Orie as her sacred day, and make periodic sacrifices to the goddess. On hearing of the dream, Efuru's father informs her that her late mother was also a skilled businesswoman favored by Uhamiri. Awed and astonished, Efuru carries out the dibia's instructions and continues to thrive as a trader. She remains barren, however, and begins to wonder if her devotion to the childless lake goddess has something to do with her infertility. Ultimately, she reasons that "[Uhamiri] cannot give me children, because she has not got children herself" (*Efuru,* p. 208).

After four years of marriage, Gilbert grows discontented; hoping to restore his happiness, Efuru heeds the advice of his mother and suggests that he take a second wife who can bear him children. Gilbert agrees, and marries Nkoyeni Eneke, the younger sister of Gilbert's friend, an army serviceman. Nkoyeni joins the household and becomes pregnant, but the marriage is not especially successful. The situation worsens after Gilbert reveals that he has an illegitimate son from a liaison with a girl in Ndoni. Although angered by Gilbert's secrecy, Efuru rallies after the first shock; Nkoyeni, however, is outraged and refuses to let the illegitimate child stay with them. Like Adizua, Gilbert begins spending long periods away from home.

During one such absence, Efuru's father dies and is mourned by the whole community. To Efuru's rage and sorrow, Gilbert does not return for the funeral or for the birth of Nkoyeni's son. The baby is two months old when Gilbert, looking haggard and unwell, finally returns, refusing to say where he has been. Ajanupu hears a rumor that Gilbert was in jail for three months for robbery and passes the information along to Efuru, who angrily confronts her husband. Gilbert confirms the rumor, but adds, "I went to jail, but I did not steal. I was foolish that's all, and I paid for my foolishness" (*Efuru,* p. 267). Relieved that Gilbert is not a thief, Efuru stands by her husband, although other villagers, including Nkoyeni, are convinced he has done something shameful.

Hoping to alleviate the domestic strife caused by Nkoyeni's accusations, Gilbert and Efuru choose Ogea to be his next wife. But before the marriage arrangements can be finalized, Efuru falls gravely ill. One famous dibia attributes her illness to her neglect of Uhamiri and instructs her family to perform an elaborate sacrifice of white hen's eggs, palm oil, and unripened plantains to appease the goddess. Efuru still does not recover, however, and Omirima, the most vicious of the village gossips, spreads the rumor that Efuru's illness is caused by her adultery. On hearing the rumor, Gilbert exhorts Efuru to confess to this sin, lest she die. Horrified by her husband's words, Efuru sends for Ajanupu, who upbraids Gilbert for believing such gossip and reminds him of his own reprehensible behavior. Gilbert

strikes Ajanupu, who retaliates by hitting him over the head with a pestle, inflicting an injury that sends him to the hospital.

Ajanupu takes Efuru to a doctor who cures her. After her recovery, Efuru assembles the members of her age group as witnesses and proclaims herself innocent of adultery before the shrine of the goddess Utuosu. Exonerated, she returns home, packs her belongings, and leaves Gilbert, a decision that shocks the community. That night Efuru, finally at peace, dreams again of the woman in the lake. The novel concludes with a probing question about the goddess Uhamiri: she "gave women beauty and wealth but she had no child. She had never experienced the joy of motherhood. Why, then, did the women worship her?" (*Efuru,* p. 281).

The community of women. Ironically, *Efuru* is today commended for the very thing for which it was reviled upon publication: its painstaking depiction of women's lives in a traditional Igbo village. Some critics could not easily adjust to Nwapa's departure from the female image that was dominant in novels written by men and set at the same time as *Efuru.* In contrast to the image of womanhood depicted in these novels—as weak, inconsistent, promiscuous, and parasitically dependent on male partners—the female protagonist in Nwapa's novel is economically independent, resilient, adventurous, and materially successful. Critics of the time found these characteristics unconvincing largely, it seems, because they did not take into account the environment in which the novel is set. They appear to have known little of the rich tradition of Oguta, "where women paddle canoes up, down and across Ugwuta Lake transporting passengers and their wares for a nominal fee, where women are leaders in trade and commerce, where a democratic sex-gender system recognizes talent, regardless of one's sex, where confidence and perfection is nurtured in both females and males" (Umeh, p. 664).

Literary critic Florence Stratton contends that *Efuru* is not a tragedy, as some have argued, but "a novel of successful development, of a woman's successful development—a female *bildungsroman*" (Stratton, p. 86). Efuru's maturation is sometimes helped, sometimes impeded, by other women in her community. Having lost her mother as a child, she comes to value, even rely upon, the advice of her mother-in-law, Ossai, and Ossai's sister, Ajanupu. The two women provide the young bride with contrasting examples of how to cope with life's disappointments—pas-

In *Efuru,* the title character sells goods at an open-air market such as the one pictured here.

sive, long-suffering Ossai recommends patience after Efuru is abandoned by her first husband, while active, strong-willed Ajanupu understands and even predicts Efuru's decision to end the marriage.

A less direct but no less pervasive influence on Efuru's life is the atmosphere of gossip and innuendo that surrounds her every action. Nearly all the criticism directed at Efuru originates from other women in the village who seem to envy or, at the very least, disapprove of the way she challenges their most deeply ingrained beliefs. Incredulous upon learning that Efuru plans to hire a maid for her infant daughter so she herself may return to trading, a friend declares, "What is money? Can a bag of money go on an errand for you? Can a bag of money look after you in your old age? . . . A child is more valuable than money. So our fathers said" (*Efuru,* p. 40). Omirima, the most venomous of the gossips, visits Efuru's second mother-in-law to stir up trouble about Efuru's infertility. For a time, Efuru herself equates her worth as a woman with her ability to conceive a child; she feels validated after giving birth to Ogonim: "I am a woman after all" (*Efuru,* p. 32). She laments Ogonim's death just as sweepingly: "My only child has killed me" (*Efuru,* p. 89).

Ultimately Efuru finds her true calling not as

a wife and mother, but as a worshipper of the lake goddess, Uhamiri, who bestows beauty and prosperity on those she favors. Efuru continues to thrive as a worshipper of Uhamiri, becoming ever more beautiful and prosperous. She also attains a wisdom that allows her to accept with serenity the conclusion that Uhamiri, childless herself, cannot give children to her worshippers. In other words, she crosses the line between male and female and gains self-awareness in the process.

After her second marriage, like her first, fails because of her husband's infidelity and untrustworthiness, it is Efuru's worship of Uhamiri that gives purpose to her life. Once she leaves Gilbert and moves back to her late father's house, Efuru is "quite literally a free and independent woman," no longer subject to the demands of masculine authority (Stratton, p. 98). Her dream of Uhamiri, which ends the novel, seems to presage a future of wealth, beauty, and even happiness for a woman who, through her own efforts, has at last carved out a niche for herself in the community.

Efuru's metamorphosis takes place during a crucial point in Nigerian history. As Stratton observes, "Ugwuta has not as yet felt the full impact of colonial occupation, but it is on the verge of rapid social and cultural transformation"

(Stratton, p. 87). Initially the novel depicts a community in which "a childless woman is regarded as a sort of monstrosity . . . [who] has failed to fulfill her function in life," but later it acknowledges the possibility that single women can achieve professional success through its portrayal of Efuru and, to a lesser extent, of Nkoyeni, the schoolgirl who marries Gilbert (Basden, p. 213). When Gilbert complains that educating a girl destined only for marriage is a waste of money, Nkoyeni's brother lays the blame on "us men" who "should allow [girls] to finish their schooling," adding, "It does not always end in the kitchen, when the girl is allowed to finish, she can teach and thus bring in money that way" (*Efuru*, pp. 242-43). Through such deceptively casual remarks, the novel anticipates a future in which women's lives extend far beyond the kitchen and the nursery.

Sources and literary context. Igbo culture harbors a strong oral tradition of songs, folktales, proverbs, riddles, legends, and myths. Such oral traditions introduced Nwapa to the craft of storytelling during her childhood in Ugwuta and found their way into *Efuru*. At one point in the novel, for example, a traveling storyteller tells the village children the tale of a beautiful young girl who disobeys her mother's orders to stay inside the house and, as a result, is married to a malignant spirit. The girl has four sisters named for the days of the week—Eke, Orie, Afo, and Nkwo—but only Nkwo helps the girl escape her husband. This story combines a lesson in morality (obey your elders) with a lesson about kinship (help your sisters and brothers).

Efuru occupies a special place in Nigerian literature as the first novel to be written by a Nigerian woman. Published in 1966 it was also among the first novels to be written by Nigerians after independence. Chinua Achebe (who was instrumental in the publication of *Efuru*) originated a literary tradition in Nigeria with his 1958 classic, ***Things Fall Apart*** (also covered in *African Literature and Its Times*). Combining the traditional with the modern, he incorporated proverbs and other aspects of folklore into fiction, expanding the frontiers of the English-language novel to accommodate African culture. Along with male novelists such as Amos Tutuola, Cyprian Ekwensi, Wole Soyinka, and John Munonye, Flora Nwapa followed with fiction that developed this tradition. The pioneer of Nigerian female writers, Nwapa introduced a subjective female point of view and became the first to deal with issues of importance to Nigerian women, the traditional roles—wifehood and motherhood—into which they have been socialized, and the difficulties that arise from being restricted to these roles. Nwapa's detailed presentation of women's lives provided a dramatic contrast to the male-centered literary perspective of her contemporary Elechi Amadi whose novel, ***The Concubine*** (also covered in *African Litera-*

WOMEN AND LEADERSHIP

Even colonialists would learn that Igbo women could be a force with which they had to reckon. Before colonialism, Igbo women played an official role in community government. A woman chieftain (called an *omu*) was appointed to look after women's affairs and issues concerning the marketplace. The omu's influence on public life included the power to publicly punish a transgressor, much to the dismay of British authorities, who consolidated power into their own system of native leaders/agents, or warrant chiefs. When the colonialists revamped village government, the omu no longer had an official say in village proceedings. However, women still managed to exert influence by organizing groups to manage the women's affairs in their villages. Two such organizations were the Association of Daughters and the Association of Wives. Daughters had great influence in their natal homes; their opinions were valued there even after they married and moved to other compounds. The Association of Daughters disciplined erring wives and administered punishments. Although less powerful, the Association of Wives nonetheless became a forum in which women voiced their opinions. According to scholar Theodora Akachi Ezeigbo, such organizations made it possible for women across Igboland to unite during the 1929 Women's War (Ezeigbo in Umeh, pp. 655-60). This conflict took place in response to rumors that the British government planned to tax women as well as men in Igboland, even women who had no source of income because they stayed at home to tend the family. Armed with sticks, machetes, and bamboo rods, outraged women chanted war songs and rioted. At the community of Oloko, they staged a mass protest and obtained a written guarantee from the authorities that they would not be taxed. News of the triumph spread, sparking protest by women throughout the region over the women's tax and other injustices. In some areas, the outraged women burned government courts and drove off and/or looted native functionaries of the colonial power structure.

Efuru

ture and Its Times), was also published in 1966. Although *Efuru* and *The Concubine* both feature beautiful women who are mysteriously linked to water deities, Amadi's novel depicts a conventional woman passively accepting her community's rules; Nwapa's, an unconventional woman who successfully challenges those rules.

Events in History at the Time the Novel Was Written

The end of colonialism. While the colonial government is not an overwhelming presence in *Efuru,* its laws remain a source of irritation and inconvenience to the residents of Ugwuta. Disgruntled farm workers complain, "These white people have imposed so much strain on our people. The least thing you do nowadays you are put into prison" (*Efuru,* p. 7). Between the period in which the novel was set and that in which it was written, the nationalist movement grew, heralding the end of the colonial era. Although Nigerians had advocated self-government since the 1920s, the nationalists gained momentum in World War II (1939-45). Ethnic boundaries between British troops and Nigerian soldiers—such as Gilbert's friend Sunday Eneke in the novel— became less relevant than their shared military experience. Wartime ideals and the Nigerians' contribution led the British government to rethink and reevaluate Nigeria's political future. (Three battalions of the Nigerian Regiment fought for the Allies in the Ethiopian campaign, and Nigerian units served alongside British forces in Palestine, Morocco, Sicily, and Burma.)

In 1946 a new constitution was drawn up that gave more power to the regions of Nigeria while maintaining British power in central government. Later versions of the constitution (in 1951 and 1954) strengthened regional powers against those of the British government. At the beginning of the decade in which *Efuru* was written, on October 1, 1960, Nigeria was granted independence by an act of the British Parliament. The territory became a federation of three self-governing states (Western, Eastern, and Northern), and it declared itself a republic three years later.

Education. Western education was implemented in Nigeria gradually but steadily throughout the colonial period. By 1950, Nigeria had adopted a three-tiered system of education—primary, secondary, and post-secondary, with the widest participation coming from a base of students at the primary level. During the late

1950s Nigeria's remarkable educational growth led to a movement for universal primary education in the Western region. From 1947 to 1957 primary-school enrollments increased dramatically: from 66,000 to 206,000 in the North; 240,000 to 983,000 in the West; and 320,000 to 1,209,000 in the East. Meanwhile, secondary-level enrollments increased throughout the country, from 10,000 to 36,000 (Metz, p. 142).

The rising number of females in education reflects to some degree an increase in the number of women who, like Efuru, looked to avenues outside, or along with, family life for fulfillment. From 1960 to 1972 the number of female students more than doubled. Whereas in 1960 only 24 percent of girls attended school, two decades later the proportion climbed to 64 percent (Davidson, p. 190). Women had actually begun their gradual ascent in the professional world much earlier. In 1934 Nigeria called to the bar its first black woman lawyer. Longstanding efforts followed by groups like the Lagos Women's League, which before World War II had pressured the government for improvements in women's health and education. The number of women who would become political leaders was to remain scant over the next few decades, but by the time of the novel's writing, West Africa was producing a growing number of female judges, doctors, ambassadors, and businesswomen.

Reviews. Initial responses to *Efuru* were generally negative. Many critics thought that Nwapa was merely imitating Chinua Achebe's style of realism and were disappointed that the novel concentrated on women. *Efuru* suffered, too, from comparisons to Elechi Amadi's *The Concubine,* published the same year. A review in the *Times Literary Supplement* praised both Amadi's and Nwapa's novels as works of "considerable quality and promise," but Eldred Jones and Eustace Palmer—two well-known African critics—declared that the advantages were all on Amadi's side (*Times Literary Supplement,* p. 281). Other critics faulted Nwapa for elements of her style that are now thought to distinguish her, criticizing her for stating too much and dramatizing too little.

Many years later critics and academics began to recognize the merit in a writing style that embodied culture and tradition without overdramatization. Nwapa's writing has since undergone a renaissance and reevaluation. "Today," observes one scholar, "*Efuru* is seen as an early classic of African literature, since it explores a world close to its precolonial roots and women's important roles in that world" (Wilentz, p. 180). Others have called *Efuru* a literary milestone: "[W]ith the stroke of her pen, Nwapa initiated the development of African women's literature with independent-minded, savvy and successful female characters. . . . Flora Nwapa will go down in history as an illustrious woman who achieved extraordinary feats" (Umeh, p. 48).

—Pamela S. Loy and Ernest N. Emenyonu

For More Information

Afigbo, Adiele. *Ropes of Sand: Studies in Igbo History and Culture.* Nsukka: University of Nigeria Press, 1981.

Basden, G. T. *Niger Ibos.* London: Frank Cass, 1966.

Davidson, Basil. *Modern Africa.* 3rd ed. London: Longman, 1994.

Emenyonu, Ernest N. "Portrait of Flora Nwapa as a Dramatist." In *Emerging Perspectives on Flora Nwapa.* Ed. Marie Umeh. New Jersey: Africa World Press, 1998.

Green, M. M. *Igbo Village Affairs.* London: Frank Cass, 1964.

Metz, Helen Chapin, ed. *Nigeria: A Country Study.* Washington, D.C.: Federal Research Division, 1992.

Nwapa, Flora. *Efuru.* London: Heinemann, 1966.

Review of *The Concubine,* by Elechi Amadi. *Times Literary Supplement,* 7 April 1966, p. 281.

Stratton, Florence. *Contemporary African Literature and the Politics of Gender.* London: Routledge, 1994.

Umeh, Marie, ed. *Emerging Perspectives on Flora Nwapa.* New Jersey: Africa World Press, 1998.

Wilentz, Gay. "Flora Nwapa." In *Dictionary of Literary Biography.* Vol. 125. Eds. Bernth Lindfors and Reinhard Sander. Detroit: Gale Research, 1993.

An Egyptian Childhood

by

Taha Husayn

B orn in 'Izbat al-Kilu, a small village in up-per Egypt, Taha Husayn (1889-1973) moved to Cairo in 1902 at the age of 13 to study at al-Azhar University, the oldest and most prestigious center of religious learning in the Is-lamic world. Husayn (also spelled Hussein) would ultimately switch to secular studies, earning two doctorates and becoming one of the forces shap-ing the cultural domain of Egypt, doing so through his many publications and his weekly newspaper column of 1922-25. In 1926 Husayn questioned the authenticity of the classical pre-Is-lamic poetry of the Arabs and called down upon himself a storm of protest. He was dismissed from his post as dean of the Faculty of Arts at the Egypt-ian University in 1932 and was also denied any form of government employment. He survived this controversy to be reinstated in 1936, and later to serve as minister of education (1950-52). For much of the twentieth century Husayn has been revered as both an icon of Arab intellectualism and the epitome of the self-made man who sur-mounted the overwhelming odds of his rural ori-gins and his blindness to become the preeminent scholar of the Arab world. During his lifetime, he authored over 60 books, including several nov-els, but none achieved the popular success and influence of his autobiography, first published during the most controversial period of his career.

Events in History at the Time the Narrative Takes Place

European invasion. Arabs read *An Egyptian Childhood* as the autobiography of a man who was

THE LITERARY WORK

An autobiographical narrative set in Egypt, mostly from 1889-1902; published in Arabic (as *al-Ayyam*) in 1926-27, in English in 1932.

SYNOPSIS

One of the Arab world's most prominent intellectual figures recalls his days as a blind boy in a southern Egyptian village and as a young adult in Cairo.

at the forefront of social and cultural changes that occurred as a result of England's occupation of Egypt. The occupation, and the fact that Egypt was never made part of the British Common-wealth, or had any set legal status for a long pe-riod of time, is the background to Taha Husayn's life and his later prominence. Following Napoleon's invasion of Egypt in 1798, a venture that lasted three years, a young Ottoman military officer of Albanian origin named Muhammad 'Ali rose to power in Egypt and set the country on a new course. Though Egypt was nominally a province of the Ottoman Empire (based in Is-tanbul) and Muhammad 'Ali but the viceroy of the Ottoman sultan, in practice he governed as an independent ruler. Muhammad 'Ali had seen both English and French military forces in action during the French occupation and was deter-mined to modernize his own armed forces and government. He sent delegations of students and scholars to Europe, where they studied languages, military tactics, and engineering; he also invited Europeans to come to Egypt as teachers and government consultants. Under his reign new schools were established, the army was reorganized, the civil service restructured, a government printing press founded, a government newspaper published, and a multitude of agrarian reforms undertaken. Not all of these projects were completely successful or even well-advised, but Egypt's infrastructure slowly began to change.

Egyptian society at the time of the French invasion in 1798 consisted of a complex mixture of social groups and classes that included native Egyptians (both Muslim and Coptic Christian); the Ottoman Turco-Circassian upper class (including the military officer corps, major landowners, and high-ranking political figures); minority communities of Greeks, Jews, and Armenians; and a few European residents whose numbers increased dramatically over the course of the nineteenth century. The most enduring social impact of Muhammad 'Ali's reign was the "Egyptianization" of the armed forces and of many ranks of government administration; native Egyptians came to hold many positions previously reserved for Turco-Circassians. Over time, this process of "Egyptianization" emerged as a critical step toward a modern national identity for Egypt. From his death in 1849 until 1882, Muhammad 'Ali's successors at times supported these policies and at times left them to languish.

Muhammad 'Ali's grandson Isma'il, who governed from 1863 to 1879, had grandiose plans for Egypt, reflected in his adoption of a new title, khedive (from a Persian word for "ruler"), that emphasized his claim to a status more independent than that of the Ottoman sultan's other viceroys. Unfortunately, his ambitions were not matched by his financial acumen, and the debt that resulted from the disadvantageous agreement concluded for the rights to the Suez Canal and other massive projects he initiated proved to be not only Isma'il's, but also Egypt's, downfall. Already by the 1860s, when the Suez Canal (connecting the Mediterranean and the Red Sea) was being excavated, Isma'il had run up enormous debts with European lenders to finance his personal and state extravagances. This huge financial stake in Egypt's economy eventually provided the motivation for Britain's almost unwitting occupation of Egypt in 1882. In the period leading up to the occupation, the European powers forced Isma'il to accept English and French financial advisors, who were given more

and more control over Egyptian fiscal policy. When Isma'il resisted these developments, the European powers summarily deposed him in 1879, sent him into exile, and declared his son, Tawfiq, the new monarch of Egypt. Tawfiq, a young man of 27, was relatively inexperienced in government affairs and proved more malleable than his father. He was forced to accept a broad array of harsh economic measures dictated by the English and French commissioners.

Nationalist stirrings. In an attempt to prevent an outright default on the government debt to European lenders, one of the measures adopted was the forced reduction of Egypt's armed forces, a policy that was unequally carried out—the greatest hardships were visited upon the native Egyptian officers, while those of the Turko-Circassian upper class were left relatively untouched. This touched off unrest within the military. Native Egyptian officer Colonel Ahmad 'Urabi and other officers presented a set of complaints directly to the Khedive Tawfiq in early 1881. Tawfiq and his advisors lured these officers to the palace, then placed them under arrest and attempted to put them immediately on trial. No sooner had the sham trial begun, however, than Egyptian troops loyal to 'Urabi marched into the palace, released their leaders, and demanded that the minister of war be dismissed. Fearing for his life, the khedive acceded. The struggle for power between the military and the khedive continued for a full chaotic year. At the end of the year 'Urabi himself was named minister of war, though he wielded far greater power than an ordinary minister, and a parliament of sorts was convened.

The extent of the rebellion—or, as the British viewed it, the mutiny—and the degree to which nationalist feelings motivated its leaders continues to be debated among historians, but the dissatisfaction that was first sparked within the military rapidly spread throughout Egypt. The chief targets of this unrest were European residents, who represented to many Egyptians the financial powers that were bleeding the country dry to pay off Isma'il's debts. European residents in Egypt occupied a very privileged position—they were held to separate laws and could be tried only in special European-controlled courts. The rallying cry that spread rapidly throughout the land was "Egypt for the Egyptians!" Tensions between the military and the khedive continued to increase, and 'Urabi, who proved to be an inept administrator, did not move to quell them. At one point England and France orchestrated the removal of

'Urabi from power, but immediate protest from the army, religious figures, and the public forced the khedive to reinstate him. The khedive was now seen by many as acting in open collusion with England and France against Egyptian interests.

In June 1882 a riot erupted in Alexandria, and the enraged public attacked Europeans in the streets—nearly 50 were killed and many others wounded. Soon after, British warships fired on Egyptian garrisons in the port of Alexandria, and parts of the city were burned. England had stumbled into a war with Egypt. France and Italy refused to take part in a situation that the British had initiated unilaterally. Within a few weeks newly landed British troops carried out a successful surprise attack on the 'Urabi-led Egyptian army at Tall al-Kabir. Egyptian resistance crumbled. The British forces now found themselves in the position of almost inadvertently having occupied Egypt. Reactions at home in England from public and political figures alike were decidedly mixed. In a court-martial whose results had been carefully orchestrated beforehand, 'Urabi pleaded guilty to rebellion, was sentenced to death, and then immediately had his sentence transmuted to exile by the khedive. He and the other leaders of the rebellion were packed off to Ceylon (now Sri Lanka), from where he returned to Egypt only toward the end of his life in 1901.

British domination. The British forces, having ended the rebellion and reinstated the Khedive Tawfiq with his full autocratic powers, proceeded to place Egypt under temporary military occupation—or so it was thought at the time. The "temporary" occupation did not come to a final end until 1954, 72 years later. For 32 years, from 1882 to 1914, Egypt was left in a state of legal limbo that came to be referred to as the "Veiled Protectorate"; it was not incorporated into the British Empire and was officially neither colony nor dominion. Only in 1914, with the outbreak of World War I, did Britain feel the need to formalize her claim to Egypt, and at that time unilaterally declared Egypt a protectorate. This merely formalized a situation that already existed: Britain controlled Egypt's military, its foreign affairs, and its central finances, while Egypt had a nominal ruler and, at times, a parliament of sorts. Beginning in 1876 and extending, with some interruptions, until 1907, Evelyn Baring, later Lord Cromer, was placed in charge of Egypt as British high commissioner and ruled it with autocratic powers. Cromer was given the power to fire any minister of the Egyptian government

'Abbas II, the last khedive of Egypt, ruled from 1892 to 1914. Subsequent rulers would be called "king."

who disobeyed his orders or the orders of any British government official. The British military occupation and the defeat of the national rebellion came as a tremendous shock to the population of Egypt and for nearly a decade thereafter Egypt remained passive and subdued.

In 1892 the Khedive Tawfiq died and was succeeded by his 16-year-old, Austrian-educated son who ruled as 'Abbas II. The new ruler was headstrong, ambitious, and not nearly as willing as his father had been to be dictated to by the all-powerful Cromer. Indeed, since the British had no legal claim to Egypt and had only been "invited" into the country by Tawfiq to restore order during the 'Urabi rebellion, 'Abbas felt that, as the new khedive, he had the power to ask the British to depart. This proved impossible, but his ongoing struggles with Cromer caused the young 'Abbas to look ever more favorably upon the nationalist movement that, led by Mustafa Kamil, was growing among university students. The 1890s and the first decade of the twentieth century witnessed growing numbers of strikes and demonstrations protesting the English occupation and its policies.

Coupled with the nationalist anti-British movement there arose new intellectual currents calling for the reform of traditional education, the education of women, the modernization of religious teachings, and the reevaluation of the role of religious courts. Western technologies and ideas were rapidly making inroads in Egyptian society. The first telephone was hooked up in 1884, the first tramway was built in 1897, the National Bank was created in 1897, and the first calls for women's rights (such as the influential 1898 work by Qasim Amin, *On the Liberation of Women*) were published. A great debate was emerging in which Taha Husayn himself would come to play a major role: a debate involving modernity, Westernization, religion, secularism, democracy, women's rights, education, and national identity.

When Husayn arrived in Cairo from the countryside in 1902 to study at al-Azhar, that venerable institution was in the throes of a struggle for change. Though the curriculum of al-Azhar had undergone several reforms in the years just previous to his arrival, Husayn still encountered an institution and curriculum deeply rooted in medieval texts and traditions. Others were as frustrated as Husayn by this state of affairs, and in 1908, when the doors of the secular Egyptian University first opened, many shared his eagerness to attend the first lectures and courses offered there. In some sense, Husayn's transfer of his studies from al-Azhar to the new Egyptian University reflects a great debate about tradition and modernity that later encompassed all of Egypt and to some degree led to the writing of *An Egyptian Childhood,* which some have cited as the single most widely read work of modern Arabic literature in the Arab world (Malti-Douglas, p. 3).

Rural Egypt in the 1890s. At the time of Taha Husayn's childhood, the vast majority of Egypt's population still lived in rural villages and small towns, and the backbone of the Egyptian economy was agriculture. The "peasants" or *fellahin* owned very little of the land they toiled on; large estates held by a small minority—consisting of members of the Turco-Circassian upper class and, increasingly, in the late nineteenth century, of Westerners—constituted most of the arable lands. From the mid-nineteenth century onward, the central government, driven by European financial concerns, steered Egyptian agriculture towards a single cash-crop system based on cotton. When cotton prices fell on international markets, the Egyptian fellahin suffered terrible periods of poverty; when cotton prices rose, their condition improved, at least temporarily.

In many villages, only the simplest form of education could be obtained at the local Qur'an (Koran) school. This often consisted of little more than a brief introduction to the alphabet and the memorization of a handful of passages from the Qur'an. The latter is crucial in the everyday life of Muslims since there are points in the daily prayers at which one recites (usually silently or in a hushed voice) one or more passages of one's own choice from the Qur'an. In a group setting, such as in a mosque and particularly at Friday communal prayers, the selected passages might be quite lengthy and consist of an entire chapter of the Qur'an read aloud by a reciter. For most boys, once the memorization of several Qur'anic passages was complete, so was their education. Few girls were given even this rudimentary introduction to letters. Only families that were financially somewhat better off, or had a surplus of sons for the amount of land they worked, could afford to have male children spend longer periods of time on their schooling. One critical exception, which plays such an important role in Taha Husayn's story, is that blind children were often fully trained to be Qur'an-reciters, one of the few means of gainful employment open to them.

In the latter half of the nineteenth century, a new government school system was established that implemented many Western ideas about secular education. At first there were only specialized colleges in Cairo for the military sciences and engineering. Later, elementary and secondary school systems were introduced. Taha Husayn went to the traditional Qur'an school in his village in the period immediately prior to the tremendous expansion of government schooling. By 1906 there were approximately 4,500 village schools with 170,000 pupils; 500 primary and secondary schools in towns and cities reached an additional 100,000 students, of which about one-fifth, or 20,000, were girls (Vatikiotis, p. 219). Although these numbers reflect only a fraction of the school-aged children in a country whose population had topped 6 million, it was an astonishing advance accomplished in a very short period.

Although village families were often large, the high infant mortality rate and the danger of disease and epidemics frequently meant that only a few children survived to adulthood. Traditional medical practices relied as much on talismans and charms written by local religious figures as on natural cures such as herbs and other treatments. Some conditions were attributed to spirits (the *jinn* familiar to Western readers as the "genies" of the *Thousand and One Nights*). If a person was diagnosed as being "possessed" by a spirit, the family might turn to talismans and charms, to the visiting of a local saint's shrine, or even to an exorcism, complete with drummers and other musicians.

One mainstay of village life was the Sufi brotherhoods. Sufism emerged as early as the ninth century as a mystical branch of Islam that emphasized the personal experience of the love of God, ecstasy, and renunciation of the temptations of this world. Some of the greatest thinkers, poets, and leaders of medieval Islamic civilization were practicing Sufis or were strongly influenced by Sufi ideas. Over the centuries Sufism came to be organized into various brotherhoods or orders, each of which professed different views and techniques for achieving spiritual goals. Some preached strict asceticism and withdrawal from the world, while others propounded an approach much more engaged with the daily life of the masses. Many orders included special ritual prayers, sometimes to the accompaniment of music, called *dhikr* ("remembrance"), as an act of remembering God.

Over time many Sufi brotherhoods adopted more and more radical practices that demonstrated their removal from even the physical laws of this world: eating glass, piercing their bodies with metal skewers, walking on hot coals, and so forth. In some settings, Sufi figures came to be worshipped as saints who possessed supernatural powers of healing and miracle working. Islamic religious reform movements have emerged in opposition to the worship of saints, belief in magic and sorcery, and strange physical practices such as those mentioned above; these movements have directed criticism at local Sufi orders many times in recent centuries. The Islamic reformist movements of the late nineteenth century, and those of the late twentieth century, have all attacked such popular beliefs. In essence, the Sufi branch of Islam has both a classical past found in the writings of great spiritual leaders and poets of the Middle Ages, and a more recent history that has very negative associations for many educated Muslims.

The Narrative in Focus

Plot summary. *An Egyptian Childhood* begins a few years after the author's birth in 1889 and continues to 1902. It thus begins in the period in which the British had been occupying Egypt for about ten years, and extends through the period of popular demonstrations and strikes.

Though this was a time of dramatic social changes that greatly affected the protagonist's early and later life, only the faintest awareness of these upheavals is recorded in the narrative itself, most of which recounts days lived in the countryside far from the social movements that kept the great urban centers in ferment. No European appears at any point in the book.

An Egyptian Childhood opens with a series of indistinct recollections of the spaces and sounds of the central character's early childhood home. The scenes are recounted by a narrator who refers to the central character at first only by means of the third-person pronoun "he," but later as "our friend," "the boy," and "the young man." There is reason for the tentativeness of these early scenes; since Taha Husayn was himself blind, the depiction is not merely that of an adult struggling to recall his earliest memories, but also that of a blind child struggling to understand the world around him. Nevertheless, the narrative only slowly surrenders this information to the reader through oblique indications that mirror the child's own confusion as to why other people speak of so many things of which he has no direct experience. These memories are at first isolated, but then coalesce slowly into a coherent narrative.

The narrator tells us of the young boy's world, which extends only a few feet from the door of the house to a cornstalk fence: in one direction it stretches another few feet down to a small irrigation channel and in the other only as far as the neighbors' yard, which is inhabited by terrifying dogs. Surrounded by his 12 siblings and his parents, the boy is at times neglected and ignored, at times laughed at and teased, and at times cared for tenderly. But he is also surrounded by all of the various sprites and jinn of the folktales he hears told by his mother and others. He sleeps tightly bundled up in his blanket at night, certain in the knowledge that if even the smallest opening is left, the sprites will enter it and grab him while he sleeps.

In many regions of the Middle East food is handled only with the right hand. The left hand, even when thoroughly washed, is considered impure since it is reserved for personal bodily functions. One day the boy decides to grasp his food with both hands, despite what he has been taught, provoking laughter and ridicule from his siblings and the anger of his parents. The painful incident provokes a lifelong habit of eating in solitude and never in the company of others. As he further becomes aware of how food drips and stains his clothing, generating even more derision from others, he comes to refuse anything that must be eaten with a spoon.

From earliest childhood the boy loves hearing stories and songs, the recitation of the Qur'an, the chanting of the Sufi *dervishes,* the lamentations of the village women, and the epic-singing of itinerant poets. All of these he quickly learns and memorizes by repeating them to himself. The various tales and songs become woven into his daydreams and fantasies, at times indistinguishable from reality.

AN ARABIC EPIC

One of the stories that Taha Husayn mentions repeatedly is the great Arabic epic poem *Sirat Bani Hilal,* the epic of the Bani Hilal Bedouins. The epic recounts the migration of the Bani Hilal from their homeland in the Arabian peninsula and their conquest of North Africa, which they ruled until 1160. The epic's adventures and romances center on the black hero, Abu Zayd, his archrival, Diyab, and the wondrous heroine, al-Jazya. Even in the late twentieth century, singers can be found in Egypt who perform this epic in versions of up to 140 hours in length while playing the *rabab,* a two-string spike-fiddle.

The boy's parents know that in Egypt and other areas of the Islamic world, one occupation traditionally open to the blind is that of Qur'an reciter. Many Islamic rituals and celebrations of life include the public recitation of sections from the Qur'an: engagements, marriages, memorials, circumcision ceremonies, saints' festivals, Sufi services, and so forth. It is therefore with the purpose of preparing him for this occupation and providing the boy with a livelihood that his parents send him off to the village school. In perhaps the most famous sequence of the book, the narrator describes the boy's experiences in the Qur'an school. The teacher, who is also blind, is conceited and arrogant, a liar and a cheat. The boy successfully manages to memorize the entire Qur'an in a relatively short period, but after a brief celebration, he is then ignored and left to his own devices. One day his father asks him to recite a certain section of the Qur'an and it soon becomes apparent that the boy has forgotten everything he learned. When

word of this is sent to his teacher, the teacher quickly takes the boy back through the Qur'an from the beginning and then swears to the boy's father that the boy had never forgotten anything. Although it is clear that the boy did indeed forget, the father relents, satisfied that the boy now knows the Qur'an by heart. The teacher confronts the boy's father, saying:

> "so you averred that your son had forgotten the Qur'an and blamed me severely for that! Now I swore to you that he had not forgotten but was only nervous, but you contradicted me and mocked my beard. I have come to-day that you may put your son to the test in my presence, and I swear that should it appear that he has not learnt the Qur'an, I will shave off this beard of mine and become a laughing-stock among the fuqaha [religious scholars] in this town!" The sheikh replied, "Don't get excited. Wouldn't it have been better to say, 'Well, he forgot the Qur'an, so I have been through it with him again'?" Said "our master," "I swear by God three times that he did not forget it, nor have I been through it with him again. I only heard him recite the Qur'an and he recited it to me like flowing water, neither stopping nor hesitating."
>
> Our friend listened to this dispute, knowing full well that his father was right and that "our master" was lying, but he said nothing and stood waiting for the examination. . . .
>
> (Husayn, *An Egyptian Childhood* in *The Days,* Vol. 1, pp. 28-29)

The teacher makes the boy promise that he will review six sections of the Qur'an every morning, but then passes him on to the care of the teacher's assistant, the monitor. Instead of reviewing the Qur'an with the boy, the monitor similarly makes him swear to continue reviewing what he has learned. When the boy should have been practicing his reciting, he is left to play and amuse himself. Aware that the boy is once again forgetting what he has learned, the monitor extracts small gifts and bribes from the boy by threatening to report him to the teacher and his father. Worse yet, the monitor places some of the younger students under the boy's tutelage, and he, in turn, begins to demand bribes from his pupils instead of teaching them. He is caught in a vicious circle of lies and bribes.

Finally a day of reckoning arrives. The father once again asks the boy to recite for him and the boy cannot. A chain of recriminations leads to the teacher, who again swears that he has been tutoring the boy every day. The boy, in his confusion and fear, lies to his father and says that this is true. In the aftermath of this incident, the boy feels his shame and humiliation so acutely that he places his head upon the pantry chopping block and tries to deliver a blow to his neck with the cleaver, only further angering his parents. The boy is withdrawn from the school and a private tutor is eventually brought to the house to teach him the Qur'an for the third, and at last successful, time.

The boy's dreams are tied to his hopes of studying in the great al-Azhar mosque and university in Cairo, where one of his older brothers is already a student. The narrator recounts frankly that this aspiration had little to do with a thirst for knowledge, but rather with the boy's intense desire to be respected and revered as his older brother and other Azharites were. Each time his older brother comes to visit, the boy hopes desperately that he will be taken off to Cairo with him. But each time the boy is disappointed. On one visit, however, the older brother brings two books for the boy to study in preparation for al-Azhar, one on classical Arabic grammar and the other on theology. These books are beyond the ken of the village Qur'an teacher and the boy must now study with a respected religious figure, a judge in the village, who is himself a graduate of al-Azhar. The lessons with the judge mark the first step in the slow broadening of the boy's world beyond the confines of the village.

At this stage, the boy makes no distinctions between the medieval scholarly texts he is memorizing (with little to no actual comprehension of their content), the religious rituals of the local Sufi dervishes, and the sorcery and quack medicine practiced by wandering charlatans. He and a friend enthusiastically purchase cheap chapbooks that purport to contain magic spells, and experiment with trying to call forth spirits and jinn. Only slowly does he become aware of what he perceives as the fakery involved and then his attitude (which now blends almost seamlessly with that of the narrator's voice) turns toward sharp condemnation of the rural ignorance surrounding him. Various anecdotes recount the ridiculous religious rulings pronounced by villagers who have misinterpreted classical Arabic words in the Qur'an; others portray the superstitious nature and inefficacy of local healing practices. The latter become particularly poignant when the narrator informs us that this is how the boy lost his sight: his complaints (one assumes about his eyes) were at first ignored, then he was treated with a painful folk medicine that did no good, and finally the village barber was

called in and treated him in a manner that left the boy completely blind. He plainly traces his blindness to traditional medicine, referring to it as "this criminal knowledge of women and those like them" (*An Egyptian Childhood* in *The Days*, p. 71).

Another aspect of rural life that attracts the boy's critical attention is the role of the Sufi mystical orders. He comes to understand that the intense rivalry between the orders involves little more than personal feuds between powerful families. Visits by the sufis, thought by some to bestow blessings on a house, are seen as nothing more than a plague of greedy, gluttonous guests who impose severe financial hardship on families that are already struggling to survive.

THE WORLD'S OLDEST UNIVERSITY
~

The great mosque and college of al-Azhar is the world's oldest continuously operating university. It first opened in 972 and thereafter rapidly became established as one of the preeminent centers of learning in the Islamic world. Students traveled from as far off as West Africa and China to live and study there. Many students lived within the compound itself in dormitories that possessed endowments to help students from particular regions (such as the dormitory of the Moroccans), while others lived in the neighborhoods surrounding the university. Classes met at appointed times and were conducted with students seated in a circle around their teacher. Typically, the teacher would guide students through a canonical text and its various commentaries; the students often memorized the work as they studied it, even if it was in many volumes.

Eventually a government inspector who has been schooled at both al-Azhar and at the more modern College of Engineering moves into the region. The inspector begins to teach the boy *tajwid*, the full cantillation, or proper chanting, of the Qur'an, which is governed by very precise rules of pronunciation and performance, a skill far removed from the inexact, almost garbled renditions of the village Qur'an teacher. It is also at the inspector's house that the boy experiences the first glimmerings of romantic love, though he is only ten or eleven years old at the time.

At this point in his life, the boy is moving in several circles of men who are by village standards quite learned. He takes cantillation lessons with the inspector, listens to the sermons at the mosque, has sessions with the judge in the religious courts, and attends the ceremonies of the Sufi dervishes. Suddenly, however, the boy is shaken from this relatively satisfying and secure life. First, his four-year-old sister dies, an event he blames on his mother's ignorance of modern medicine. Then the family loses two grandparents in a short period. And finally, his 18-year-old brother, recently graduated from secondary school and about to travel to Cairo to study medicine, dies in a cholera epidemic. The family is nearly destroyed by this succession of tragedies. The boy, knowing that his older brother spent so much time on his studies that he had often neglected his religious obligations, takes on in secret the task of performing all of the daily prayers and the fasts twice over to save his brother's soul. He sees his brother in terrifying dreams night after night for months after his death, and continues to see him at least once a week even beyond that. It is only in this emotionally charged sequence of scenes that the author turns to the first-person pronoun and, while describing the heart-wrenching shrieks of his dying sister, suddenly speaks briefly as "I."

Then unexpectedly his time arrives. In the autumn of 1902 he is sent to Cairo to live with his older brother and to study at al-Azhar. In a scene that foreshadows much of Taha Husayn's later career as a reformer and a modernizer, the narrator records the boy's reaction to hearing his first lecture by a renowned shaykh (or sheikh): "He swore to me afterwards that from that day he despised learning" (*An Egyptian Childhood* in *The Days*, p. 83). (Something would later change this attitude, as revealed in the next volume of his autobiography.)

The final chapter of *An Egyptian Childhood* turns abruptly to the narrator/author addressing his nine-year-old daughter and explaining to her that he has tried to spare her the childhood that he survived. He closes by telling her that he knew that boy who at age 13 was sent off to Cairo, a boy who was diligent and serious, bedraggled and unkempt, but good-hearted and tenacious. And while he in some ways wishes that she too could have known him as he was then, so that she could see the difference between them, in other ways he knows that she would not be able to understand that boy, coming as she does from such a pleasant, comfortable existence:

> How has he attained the position in which he is now? How has his appearance become presentable and no longer egregious and repulsive?

How has he been able to give you and your brother the agreeable life you now enjoy? How has he aroused such envy, hatred and malice in the hearts of some and the approval, respect and encouragement in the hearts of others? If you were to ask how he has passed from that state to this, I could not tell you.

> (*An Egyptian Childhood* in *The Days*, p. 87)

The question of language. When *An Egyptian Childhood* was first published, modern Arabic literature had been experimenting for several decades with a variety of new literary forms inspired by contact with Western literatures. Classical Arabic literature possessed many forms of fictional narrative—epic poems, romances, picaresque short stories, collections of anecdotes on given themes, philosophical allegories, and so forth—but had not yet explored the potential of extended prose narrative devoid of poetry. Most medieval genres of Arabic literature combined prose, poetry, and even a third mode of composition, *saj'*, or rhymed prose. When the first "novels" or "proto-novels" were written in Arabic in the 1870s and 1880s, writers such as Salim al-Bustani regularly used poetry for the dialogue between characters or for external commentary on the situation of the characters. Similar adaptations of classical Arabic genres characterized writings such as *Hadith Isa Ibn Hisham,* Muhammad al-Muwaylihi's bitingly sarcastic social commentary on newly Westernized classes in Egyptian society, published between 1898 and 1902 and couched in a medieval genre of picaresque short stories. Throughout the nineteenth century Arab writers used European literatures as a catalyst for creative innovation in Arabic letters without fully adopting any of the Western forms.

As European nations solidified their colonial hold on Arab lands, however, the new educational systems brought not only new ideas about technology, science, and social institutions, but also literary ideas. By the turn of the century many young Arab writers were spending a great deal of their time reading and translating Western works, which soon led to their imitation in Arabic literature. While some of these works were scarcely disguised copies of European models, others developed a more indigenous mode while at the same time experimenting with Western genres. Taha Husayn's *An Egyptian Childhood* manages to be both something new in the Arabic literary tradition and yet not clearly modeled on a specific European work or genre.

In particular, the linguistic style of the work is so classical that some readers refer to it as almost Qur'anic. Although in English "Arabic" is commonly referred to in the singular, Arabic is in fact a cluster of related but distinct languages. On the one hand, all modern Arabs speak an oral, local dialect as their mother tongue and this almost never appears in written form; and on the other hand, the entire Arab world is joined by the use of a literary language—referred to as Standard Arabic, Literary Arabic, or simply Written Arabic—that students learn in school. This is similar to the situation of late medieval Europe when people spoke in Castilian, Provençal, German, or English, but used Latin for almost all written documents.

In addition to the difference between the spoken dialects and the literary language, however, the Arabic writing system allows one to read it in two different ways. The modern, easier manner is to read the words without adding the endings that are required by the rules of classical Arabic grammar; the classical manner requires the reader to pronounce case-endings on every word. The Arabic alphabet transcribes only the consonants and the long vowels of each word. Thus the sentence "Muhammad wrote a long book," which, when it appears on the page in written Arabic as "Mḥmd ktb ktāb ṭwīl" may be read two ways:

1) How one reads it in the easier, though still educated, style:
    Muḥammad katab kitāb ṭawīl
2) How one reads it in the more classical style:
    Muḥammad^{un} katab^a kitāb^{an} ṭawīl^{an}

The latter is far more difficult, since these case-endings are not actually printed on the page, but must be supplied from the reader's own knowledge of classical grammar.

One indication of the highly unusual status of *An Egyptian Childhood* as a text is that it is always published with all of the short vowel markings and case-endings displayed throughout the text—unlike any other prose work of modern Arabic literature. Indeed, only certain types of very difficult poetry and the Qur'an itself are also published in this style. This stylistic feature is as powerful and as resonant to the modern Arab reader as the style of Shakespeare or the King James Bible is to English readers. Unfortunately, since this linguistic distinction does not exist in other languages, this extremely rich dimension of the text is completely lost in translation. In the Arab world this text is as famous for its style as it is for the narrative itself. Its style reveals something about the man whose childhood is being profiled—his

lifelong esteem for and mastery of the classical Arab language.

Literary context. Before the appearance of *An Egyptian Childhood,* Arabic classical literature possessed a long history of autobiography, in the sense that authors penned accounts of their lives to be read by later generations. These texts took a variety of different forms that might (using Western labels) be termed political memoirs, intellectual histories, spiritual confessions, travel accounts, and even works of advice to children. From this tradition Taha Husayn retained the third-person voice used in many pre-twentieth-century Arabic autobiographies and coupled it with the omniscient narrator's voice common to the Western novel.

Another element that may have come from the classical Arabic tradition is the author's frank account of his childhood misbehavior. As far back as the ninth and tenth centuries Arabic autobiographies were characterized by a few revealing anecdotes about the author's childhood misdeeds. In premodern times, Arabic life-stories were often written as moral examples, for use as didactic texts or as manuals of instruction for aspiring young thinkers or spiritual seekers. The mention of childhood failings may have helped to make seemingly perfect adults approachable, and more significantly, imitable. For a respected spiritual or intellectual authority to confess his youthful wrongdoings allowed readers to hope that they too might transcend their petty failings and achieve spiritual or intellectual progress. Over several centuries, this aspect of the Arabic autobiography slowly expanded from a few scattered anecdotes to lengthy sections and even whole chapters. An autobiographical text published in 1888 by 'Ali Mubarak Pasha concerning his childhood, for example, *Al-Khitat al-tawfiqiyya al-jadida li-misr al-qahira wa-muduniha wa-biladiha al-qadima wa-l-mashhura* (A New Description Dedicated to the Khedive Tawfiq of Cairo and Egypt's other Famous and Ancient Towns and Villages), opens with page after page of childhood misadventures in which he lies, cheats, runs away from home, quits his job, and is thrown in jail (all before the age of 12!). Thus Taha Husayn's account of lying, bribery, and intimidation in the village school was not in and of itself a new development in the Arabic autobiographical tradition; however, he brought together in unique fashion elements of Western fictional narrative, stylistic features from classical Arabic literature, and an autobiographical sensibility derived from both the Arab and the Western tradition into a single text. *An Egyptian*

Childhood is not a novel in the standard sense of the term, but it is certainly something more than a standard autobiography.

An Egyptian Childhood is the first volume of a series of three books that constitute the full autobiography of Taha Husayn. This initial volume was first published serially in 1926-27 in the journal *al-Hilal* and was printed as an independent volume in 1929. Husayn's significance as an intellectual figure even at this early date is clear from the fact that in 1932, when almost no translations were being undertaken of modern Arabic writings into English, *An Egyptian Childhood* was published in English, scarcely three years after its publication in book form in Arabic. The second volume of the autobiography, *The Stream of Days,* was published in Arabic in 1940 and translated into English in 1943; the final volume, *A Passage to France,* was published serially in 1955 in the journal *Akhir Sa'a* and then separately in 1967, and was translated into English in 1976.

Events in History at the Time the Narrative Was Written

From childhood to adulthood. In 1926, when Husayn sat down to dictate *An Egyptian Childhood,* much had changed since the events of

---

PERSONAL TRAJECTORY: TAHA HUSAYN 1902-1920s

Disgruntled in real life with the restrictions of traditional learning at al-Azhar, Husayn started attending the secular Egyptian University when it opened as a private institution in 1908. He successfully wrote and defended the university's first doctoral thesis in 1914 on the blind medieval poet al-Maarri (973-1058), becoming the first to graduate from the fledgling institution. That same year he traveled briefly to Montpellier, France, returned to Egypt for three months, and then went to Paris where he studied from 1915 to 1919. In 1917 he married his wife, a French Catholic, whom he had first met in Montpellier when she applied for a job as his personal assistant. He presented his second doctorate in Paris in 1919 on the social philosophy of the late medieval historiographer Ibn Khaldun (1332-1406) and then returned to Egypt. In the 1920s Taha Husayn participated in Egypt's struggle against British colonial rule and cultural domination through his news articles and other writings.

1898-1902 that the narrative portrays. The world had undergone dramatic transformations: in 1905 a European nation, Russia, was defeated by the Asian nation Japan, an event that led to a fundamental reassessment of the apparent invincibility of European arms; in 1908 the Young Turks had brought about a constitutional revolution in Turkey; in 1911 Italy invaded and occupied Tripolitania (Libya); in 1914-18 World War I redrew the map of Europe, and U.S. President Woodrow Wilson's call for self-determination lent support to a broad range of independence movements, Egypt's included.

In Egypt a Nationalist Congress was held in 1907 out of which emerged the first political party, the *Wafd* ("the Delegation"), an organization that fought unsuccessfully for the right to represent Egypt at the Versailles treaty conference of 1919 to bring official closure to World War I. In 1914 the British had deposed Egypt's leader, the Khedive 'Abbas II, in fear of his sympathies for Turkey and the Axis powers. Prince Husayn Kamil was placed on the throne with the title of Sultan—the new title marked a break with the nominal allegiance of Egypt's ruler to the Ottoman sultan—but he died only three years later in 1917 and was succeeded by his brother Fu'ad.

When Taha Husayn returned from France in 1919, he arrived in a country wracked by anti-British demonstrations. Sa'd Zaghlul, who had served as minister of education (1906-10) and minister of justice (1910-13), had emerged as the hero of the Egyptian nationalist cause. In 1919 he was arrested and shipped to Malta by the British for his pro-independence activities. This, however, unleashed a wave of protests throughout Egypt that eventually led to both his release and permission for him to attend the Versailles conference, but there his hopes were dashed and no progress was made in ending the British occupation. He returned to Egypt but was again arrested and deported, this time to Aden and then to the Seychelles, in 1921.

Finally, in February 1922, in the face of continuous Egyptian unrest, Britain unilaterally declared Egypt an independent state. However, Britain retained ultimate control over Egypt's military, the right to intervene to protect foreign interests and minorities and to assure the security of the British Empire's communications in Egypt, and control over its relations with the Sudan. To mark the transition, Fu'ad was given the new title of King Fu'ad I. This independence, albeit incomplete, at least gave Egypt an opportunity for self-rule, ushering in a period (1922-36) described by historian ʿAfaf Lutfi Al-Sayyid Marsot as Egypt's liberal experiment. Politically, this period was marked by constant struggle between the parliamentary forces that had been created by the constitution of 1923 and the monarchy: a series of prime ministers served in rapid succession, and Parliament was elected, seated, and then dissolved by royal decree several times. Socially, the issue of women's rights again moved to the fore with the formation of the Feminist Union by Huda Shaʿrawi and her dramatic gesture of publicly removing and disavowing the veil at the Cairo train station in 1923. Taha Husayn supported women's abandoning the veil, pitching himself into the heat of this controversy. As mentioned, his involvement in this, as well as other social controversies of the period, would cost him his job and motivate him to write his three-volume autobiography.

Another significant debate in this period was sparked by the 1925 publication of *Al-Islam wausul al-hukm* (Islam and the Principles of Governance) by Shaykh ʿAli ʿAbd al-Raziq, which argued that the Prophet Muhammad had founded a religion but not a form of government. Al-Raziq advocated a separation of religion and state, along Western models. This was of course anathema to more orthodox religious thinkers, who believed that Islam offered a complete and inseparable moral system that encompassed all aspects of life and who viewed the secularization of the state as tantamount to atheism.

A literary rebel. Less than a year later, Taha Husayn unleashed a greater furor with his 1926 publication *Fi al-shir al-jahili* (On Pre-Islamic Poetry). Arab culture has throughout its history revered the corpus of poetry transmitted from the pre-Islamic era as its most beautiful—and most quintessentially Arab—artistic production. The accepted history of this corpus is that it was composed and transmitted orally in the pre-Islamic Bedouin society of the Arabian peninsula and then written down in the second and third centuries of the Islamic era (eighth and ninth centuries C.E.) in urban centers such as Kufa, Basra, and Baghdad. Taha Husayn threw doubt on the authenticity of this account and declared that many, if not all, of the individual poems were forgeries from a later period. It would have been bad enough that he was attacking one of the most highly prized elements of Arab culture, but the language of the poems was also deeply intertwined with the interpretive commentaries on the Qur'an. In the early centuries of Islam, pre-Islamic verses were often used as evidence in ar-

guments explicating difficult words and passages in the Scripture. To declare the poems to be fakes would be to throw the entire interpretive tradition into question. And there were further fears of what might result should similar methods of analysis be applied to the Qur'an itself. In the heat of the debate, Husayn was declared an apostate by several religious authorities, was forced to rescind the book (though he later revised it and published it under a slightly different title), and eventually was removed from his post at the University.

THE VEIL

In Egypt the veil was the marker of middle- and upper-class women. Lower-class women who worked in agriculture or other outdoor occupations could little afford to be encumbered by such a garment, though all women in Egypt traditionally kept their hair covered with a scarf, as do women even today throughout much of the Mediterranean. In Taha Husayn's village, for example, women certainly would not have worn face veils. Husayn himself nevertheless became a staunch supporter of women's rights and a harsh critic of the veil, an item of great controversy during his lifetime. In 1923, a few years before the release of *An Egyptian Childhood,* Huda Shaʿrawi and her companions, having just returned from an international feminist congress in Europe, exited the train that had brought them back to Cairo without their veils. They were photographed "barefaced" and the photographs were published in several daily newspapers, leading to a public uproar. Some were opposed to the very idea of upper-class women appearing publicly without veils, others were incensed that the photographs had been published, and a handful of men supported them. Despite the fracas, or perhaps because of it, the veil disappeared rapidly in Egypt, and by the early 1930s was rarely seen in Cairo or Alexandria until its resurgence in the 1990s.

It was in the thickest and bitterest period of this uproar that Husayn and his family vacationed in France. There, while under public attack on many fronts at home in Egypt, he dictated *An Egyptian Childhood.* Its immediate and enduring success stemmed from many factors: its astonishingly classical though lucid style; its endearing portrait of the young blind boy who managed to overcome all of the obstacles in his path; its trenchant critique of traditional education and religious practices; and, not least, its reflection upon the historical moment in which it was written, a moment at which Egypt was at a critical crossroads. Would Egypt (as Taha Husayn advocated in later writings) become a Western nation on the Mediterranean's eastern shore? Or would it interpret its heritage as Eastern and turn back to older models of religion, government, and education? Although many circumstances have changed in the meantime, most notably the complete independence of the Egyptian state from Britain in the wake of the Nasserite revolution of 1952, these questions remain nearly as contested and as relevant in Egypt today as they were when *An Egyptian Childhood* was first written.

Reviews. Critics paid close attention to *An Egyptian Childhood,* not only because of its author's reputation but also because it was the first contemporary Arabic literary work to be translated into English and a number of other languages. The *Times Literary Supplement* reviewed it with qualified praise:

> [I]f there are some scenes which are damningly accusatory . . . others have a fine tenderness. . . . And all the while we see the mind gradually awakening, the sense of criticism being born in a boy whose circumstances led him to lead the intense life of the imagination. The book is on all counts a very remarkable one. . . . How much some of the minor awkwardnesses are due to difficulties of translation is not possible to say. . . . These, however, are minor blemishes.
> (*Times Literary Supplement,* p. 185)

As decades passed, fascination with Taha Husayn's narrative would persist. A half century after its release, Fedwa Malti-Douglas examined the narrative in a way that, according to a reviewer of her work, brought to light features that help explain *An Egyptian Childhood*'s enduring appeal, "as not only the account of an exemplary individual but as a subtle text that forces questions about the nature of narration, society, and culture" (Beard, p. 112).

—Dwight F. Reynolds

For More Information

Beard, Michael. Review of *Blindness and Autobiography: Al-Ayyam of Taha Husayn,* by Fedwa Malti-Douglas. *International Journal of Middle East Studies* 22, no. 1 (February 1990): 112-13.

Cachia, Pierre. *Taha Husayn: His Place in the Egyptian Literary Renaissance.* London: Luzac, 1956.

Hourani, Albert. *Arabic Thought in the Liberal Age: 1798-1939.* 2nd ed. Cambridge: Cambridge University Press, 1983.

Husayn, Taha. *The Days—Taha Hussein: His Autobiography in Three Parts.* Cairo: American University Press, 1997.

Mahmoudi, Abdelrashid. *Taha Husain's Education: From the Azhar to the Sorbonne.* Surrey: Curzon, 1998.

Malti-Douglas, Fedwa. *Blindness and Autobiography: Al-Ayyam of Taha Husayn.* Princeton: Princeton University Press, 1988.

Review of *An Egyptian Childhood,* by Taha Hussein. *Times Literary Supplement,* 17 March 1932, p. 185.

Reynolds, Dwight F. *Heroic Poets, Poetic Heroes: The Ethnography of Performance in an Arabic Oral Epic Tradition.* Ithaca, N.Y.: Cornell University Press, 1995.

———. "Childhood in One Thousand Years of Arabic Autobiography." *Edebiyât: Journal of Middle Eastern Literatures,* n.s. 7 (1997): 379-92.

Rooke, Tetz. *In My Childhood: A Study of Arabic Autobiography.* Stockholm: Stockholm University, 1997.

Sayyid-Marsot, 'Afaf Lutfi. *Egypt's Liberal Experiment: 1922-1936.* Berkeley: University of California Press, 1977.

———. *A Short History of Modern Egypt.* Cambridge: Cambridge University Press, 1985.

Vatikiotis, P. J. *A History of Modern Egypt.* 4th ed. Baltimore: Johns Hopkins University Press, 1991.

The Epic of Son-Jara

as told by
Fa-Digi Sisòkò

THE LITERARY WORK

An epic set in the Manden and neighboring regions of Western Sudan in the thirteenth century C.E.; performed by bards of the Manding peoples; recorded, transcribed, and published in English in various versions from around 1960 to 1986.

SYNOPSIS

The Manding hero Sunjata founds the empire of Mali.

When told orally, an epic, as is true of a legend, a folktale, or a ballad, can have as many different versions as there are individual performances of the tale. Among the several renderings of the Sunjata epic that have been recorded and published in English are *Sundiata: An Epic of Old Mali* (1965), as told by Mamadou Kouyatè and translated by D. T. Niane; *Sunjata: Three Mandinka versions* (1974), told by Bamba Suso, Banna Kanute, and Dembo Kanute, and translated by Gordon Innes; and *The Epic of Son-Jara* (1986), as told by Fa-Digi Sisòkò and translated by John William Johnson. Although these versions vary in many particulars, they all relate the story of the founder of Mali's Manding empire, who goes by many names, but who will be herein known as "Sunjata"—his most common nomenclature. The *Epic of Son-Jara,* the version focused on here, is a linear translation of a tape-recorded and transcribed performance that occurred in 1968 in the town of Kita in the modern Republic of Mali. Since this version is a linear, or line-for-line, translation, it provides more of the feeling of an actual performance than would a "reconstructed" version. Also, as the most recently published version of the epic to date, *The Epic of Son-Jara* reflects the most current standards of scholarship regarding the Sunjata story collection.

Events in History at the Time the Epic Takes Place

The Western Sudan. *The Epic of Son-Jara* takes place in the Western Sudan, an area with roughly the same boundaries as the West African savannah, the grassy plain that separates the Sahara desert in the north from the lush tropical rainforest in the south of Africa's northwestern bulge. Unlike the Sahara, the savannah enjoys enough rainfall to support plant life, but not enough to encourage the dense vegetation characteristic of the rainforest. The Arabic name for this region is *sahel,* a word meaning "shore," and indeed both desert to the north and jungle to the south may be likened to the sea, while the towns of the sahel serve as ports, centers of travel and trade. Suitable to the transport of goods or troops, this is open country traversed by several navigable rivers that also provide irrigation for agriculture.

These factors, in addition to the region's wealth in gold and iron ore, may explain why, between the third century and the eighteenth century C.E., several great kingdoms and empires existed in the Western Sudan, not the least of which was Mali, the empire said to have been founded by the epic's hero, Sunjata.

The Empire of Ghana. Ghana was the first empire to arise in the Western Sudan. According to some accounts, it began as a small kingdom around the end of the third century C.E., swelled to a vast empire by the tenth century, and fell into obscurity by the middle of the thirteenth century. The territory of old Ghana is quite different from that of the modern nation-state of Ghana, which was named after this ancient empire. Old Ghana occupied a section of what is today the Republic of Mali, and was situated roughly between the Niger and Senegal rivers. Medieval Arab writers of North Africa described Ghana as "the land of gold," and indeed the land of old Ghana was rich in gold deposits. Perhaps even more lucrative to the empire, however, was its monopoly of the trans-saharan trade, the main article of which was salt.

It has been conjectured that Ghana overextended itself to such an extent that its diverse population was divided not only by physical distance but by ethnic, cultural, and linguistic differences as well. In 1203 Sumamuru, king of Kaniaga, one of Ghana's subject states, rebelled and conquered the empire. In 1224 Sumamuru extended his domain to include Kangaba, a small kingdom to the south of Ghana. In 1235 Sunjata, king of Kangaba, rebelled and defeated Sumamuru at the battle of Krina, annexing the territory of Kaniaga and all its subject kingdoms.

The Empire of Mali. Sunjata ruled from approximately 1234 to 1255; he established a town called Nyani as the center of his power. Later, this town came to be known as *Mali*, "the place where the king resides" (Buah, p. 15). After the defeat of Sumamuru, Sunjata expanded his domain to include many vassal kingdoms, and the Empire of Mali was born.

Accounts of Sunjata and Mali come from two kinds of sources: from medieval Arabic writers and from oral tradition, or the epic of Sunjata itself. The medieval Arabic writers downplay the greatness of Sunjata and focus much more attention on the founder's second successor, Mansa Musa, a generous benefactor and zealous proponent of Islam. In oral tradition, however, it is Sunjata who is upheld as the hero of the Manding peoples. Because he is a larger-than-life hero, accounts of Sunjata's exploits have a legendary quality and can vary greatly from bard to bard. As sources for historical fact they must, therefore, be taken with a sizable grain of salt. A basic version of Sunjata's founding of the Empire

of Mali as given in Manding oral tradition might run thus: Sunjata, the son of a Manding king, leaves his home in the Manden as a result of a conflict with his brother, Dankaran Tuma, over who shall inherit their father's kingship. Sunjata gains occult power while away from home, and his brother becomes king back in the Manden. When he learns that the supernaturally powerful Sumamuru has invaded the Manden and stolen the throne from Dankaran Tuma, Sunjata returns home. Because his occult power is stronger than that of the usurper, Sunjata defeats Sumamuru, becomes king, and expands his kingdom into an empire.

Expansion of the empire continued after Sunjata's death and reached its peak under Mansa Musa, when it encompassed more territory than the Empire of Ghana. By the end of the fifteenth century Mali, in turn, was superseded by a more powerful empire, that of Songhai. Like Ghana, Mali had grown to an unmanageable size, including diverse and far-flung populations that chafed under such distant control. This situation was exacerbated by disputes within the royal family.

The Manding. Sunjata and those who sing of him belong to a group of linguistically and culturally related peoples known as the Manding. The Manding homeland is the Manden, a region on the upper Niger river where Sunjata's hometown of Nyani lies, and from which all Manding peoples are believed to have dispersed. By the end of the twentieth century, the Manding peoples—among whom are the Mandinka (or Maninka), the Bamana (or Bambara), and the Dyula—were spread throughout a region extending from the Senegalese coast to modern Ghana's eastern edge.

Traditionally Manding society allows a man to marry more than one wife. The polygamous household consists of a circular thatched house for the male family head and similar separate houses for each of the head's wives and their respective children. A typical village includes several such household compounds, each enclosed by its own wall, in the midst of which one finds a lounging platform, a shaded place for village men to meet. Just beyond the circle of household compounds are garbage heaps, used as compost in the women's vegetable gardens that abut them. Here at the border, fetishes to protect the village are hidden under the garbage, or *nyama,* a homonym of the Manding word for occult power. Beyond the vegetable gardens are toilets, and farther on are cultivated fields where the village men work collectively, sometimes while entertained by songs of a bard. Beyond the fields lies the wilderness, a dangerous place avoided when possible; the villagers often carry protective amulets when venturing into it.

Out of the polygamous family structure come two concepts important to understanding Manding culture: *fa-denya* or "father-childness," and *ba-denya, or* "mother-childness." In a family consisting of one husband, several wives, and children of varying parentage, it is expected in Manding culture that one will have a different sort of relationship with one's half-siblings—the children of one's father but not one's mother—than the relationship one has with one's full siblings. The fa-denya or half-sibling relationship is supposed to be one of rivalry while the ba-denya relationship is supposed to be one of cooperation and affection. Fa-denya rivalry can extend to one's father—for boys must surpass their fathers in Manding culture before they can be considered important members of society—and it can also exist between rival co-wives. In the epic, the rivalry between Sunjata's mother and the mother of Sunjata's half-brother is fierce, and while the hero is opposed by his half-sibling, he is helped by his full siblings. Ba-denya and fa-denya are moreover conceived as extending beyond the family to become the forces that respectively hold society together and pull it apart, and even as the two aspects of God. While ba-denya ensures the survival and cohesion of the group it is only through fa-denya that the individual can gain power and prestige. Since society sometimes needs strong individuals, both ba-denya and fa-denya are valued in Manding culture.

Related to the concept of fa-denya is that of *nya,* or "means." The person who has much nya, which is inherited from one's forebears, has the ability to do great things, and although nya can refer to the means to do anything, it most often refers to the possession of occult-laden knowledge, tools, and power. The Manding believe the universe to be animated by a force they call *nyama,* which is present in varying degrees in all living beings and in inanimate matter. The performance of certain acts considered powerful or taboo unleashes nyama in dangerous amounts. Those who have nya are strong enough to perform these nyama-releasing acts without danger to themselves, and can even harness the resulting nyama and use it to further their own ends. Those who lack nya, however, might be destroyed by nyama if they foolishly attempted, for example, to smelt iron ore or commit murder.

Sunjata has nya; he is destined to be a hero. When Sunjata sacrifices a human baby in the epic, much nyama is released and the hero becomes more powerful. Sunjata's accomplice in murder lacks nya, however, and is soon destroyed. Nya and nyama can be viewed as fa-denya forces in that they enable the individual to gain power, often at society's expense.

Manding society has a class of people who are specifically sanctioned to perform nyama-releasing acts. These people, the *nyamakala,* are divided into at least three professions: blacksmiths, bards, and leatherworkers. It is believed that the members of these professions possess nya that enables them to perform their nyama-releasing crafts. One must be born into the professions; the nyamakala are careful to preserve their nya by practicing endogamy, or marriage within one's group. Their innate nya allows the nyamakala to be supernaturally powerful in ways that can be both helpful or harmful. Consequently, attitudes toward them are ambivalent: the nyamakala are both feared and revered.

Distinct from the nyamakala are the *hòròn,* translated as "freemen" or "nobility." The hòròn's designation as freemen relates to a time in the past when the Manding practiced slavery. In early West African society, people conquered in battle were sometimes taken as slaves by the victors, though they could eventually regain their freedom and become rightful members of the new community. Leadership in a Manding community is drawn exclusively from members of the hòròn, specifically from members believed to be the direct, patrilineal heirs of the founder or conqueror of the community. Hence lineage is very important in Manding culture, and most performances of the epic of Sunjata begin with an extensive genealogy tracing the current leader's ancestry back to the founding hero.

Apart from the nyamakala and the hòròn are the hunters. Just as hunters operate in the wilderness outside the boundaries of a village, they operate outside society's bounds in other ways too. Like the nyamakala, hunters are considered to stand apart from the hierarchy of lineages that vie for power in the Manding community, and like the nyamakala, hunters are associated with the occult. The wilderness, particularly the forest, is linked in the Manding worldview to the supernatural; both are dark and dangerous and beyond the circumference of the everyday world. Hunters engage in a dangerous activity in this supernaturally charged environment, yet they have no special nya to protect them, and so must seek

A mosque in Mali.

other means to control the dangerous nyama that threatens them. Ways to acquire occult power in Manding society include the use of fetishes, objects that are charged with much nyama and sometimes inhabited by spirits. In some versions, the epic of Sunjata begins with an episode wherein two brother hunters make a sacrifice to a fetish before hunting a supernaturally powerful buffalo. Because hunters' societies are secretive and do not share their knowledge of the occult with outsiders, they are feared, but they are also called upon to aid the people or the individual in times of need. When Sunjata joins a hunters' society on reaching manhood, it is probably to gain extra occult power that will help him to achieve political power outside the restrictions of the lineage hierarchy.

Islam in the Western Sudan. Islam is the religion based on the teachings of the Prophet Muhammad, born around 570 C.E., in the Saudi Arabian city of Mecca. After Muhammad's death in 632, Islam began to spread and within a century all of northern Africa had become Muslim (that is, practiced Islam). Soon Islam crossed the Sahara Desert with the trading caravans and took root in the "port" cities of the Western Sudan. Both the Arabic and the oral sources indicate that the royal Keita clan of Mali, to which Sunjata belonged, was Muslim, and even claimed as an ancestor one Bilali Bunama of Mecca, believed to

be Bilal ibn Rabah, an important figure in Islam who, according to Muslim teachings, was a companion to the prophet Muhammad, the second convert to Islam, and the first *muezzin,* or caller to prayer.

Although Islam had exercised a presence in the Western Sudan since the eighth century C.E., by the time of Sunjata's reign in the thirteenth century the religion had taken hold only among the merchant and ruling classes of society, and even here it was combined with traditional Manding beliefs and practices. In the epic, elements of Islam appear alongside elements of Manding religious tradition and thus, in order to understand the epic, it is important to understand some of the basic tenets of Islam. At the center of Islam is the belief, central also to Judaism and Christianity, that there exists but one supreme God, known to Muslims as *Allah.* Muhammad, Muslims believe, is the last in a series of prophets, including Moses and Jesus, who have related the word of God to humankind. As the final prophet, Muhammad relates God's final word, superseding all that came before. The main points of Muhammad's revelations, in written form known as the Qur'an, or Koran, are that God is one and that submission to God is one's primary duty. Muslims are, furthermore, required to perform five actions, which are considered the "pillars of Islam." These include regular recitation of the *shahada* ("There is no God but Allah and Muhammad is his prophet"); praying five times daily in the direction of the holy city of Mecca; giving alms to the poor; fasting for the month of Ramadan each year; and pilgrimage to Mecca (*hajj*) at least once in one's lifetime.

According to Muslim theology, human beings are affected by the presence or absence of *barakah,* divine good will or grace. The prevalance of claims of descent from Muhammad and from other important Islamic figures in West Africa may be traced to the belief that barakah is inherited from the Prophet's descendants or from his close companions. People are also affected by *jinns,* invisible spirits who inhabit the earth and are sometimes helpful, sometimes hostile to human beings. In Manding belief, jinns may inhabit fetishes. Muslim holymen, or *moris,* lead prayers and teach the Qur'an, and in the Western Sudan they also perform spells and create potions.

The Epic in Focus

Plot summary. The epic of Sunjata as told by Fa-Digi Sisòkò begins with a lengthy prologue praising the hero and establishing his genealogy as well as the genealogies of many of the major clan families that will play a part in the epic. Sunjata's ancestry is traced all the way back to Adam, the first man to be created by God according to Jewish, Christian, and Muslim theology. More directly, Sunjata (along with all the Manding peoples) is said to descend from Jòn Bilali, a Manding form for Bilal ibn Rabah, companion to the prophet Muhammad.

In a land called Du, a man referred to as "Leader-of-the-People" becomes father to a son. Following tradition, Leader sends the boy to live with his childless aunt, Leader's sister, Du Kamisa. When the boy, named Magan Jata Kòndè, grows up, he must ritually sacrifice a white spotted bull before he can succeed his father as king. Du Kamisa is for some reason excluded from this important ceremony and becomes enraged. In her fury she transforms into a ferocious wild buffalo who will henceforth slay seven men each day in the land of Du.

Many hunters try to put an end to the terrible scourge of Du, but are unsuccessful. Then, two brothers of the Taraware clan resolve to kill her. Together they journey into the deep forest, where they sacrifice groundnuts to a jinn inhabiting a fetish. In return the jinn instructs the brothers to give some rice to an old woman who lives to the west of Du. The brothers comply, and the old woman reveals to them that she is the buffalo. She gives them detailed instruction on how she must be killed when she is in buffalo form, and then commands them to swear an oath that binds the clans of Taraware and Kòndè in friendship.

The brothers follow the old woman's instructions, and when Magan Jata Kòndè learns that the buffalo has been slain, he presents the Taraware brothers with half his kingdom. The brothers refuse the gift, however, on the advice of a talking dog they meet beside a rubbish heap on the way to Magan Jata Kòndè's compound. Magan Jata Kòndè makes a second offer—this time of a maiden of their choice from among the populace of Du. Luckily, the talking dog has advised the Taraware brothers which maiden to choose; it is Sugulun Kòndè, a girl with the unappealing nickname "Sugulun-of-the-Warts." The Tarawares must choose Sugulun, the dog explains, because she will bear a son who will one day rule the Manden.

After following the dog's advice, the Tarawares begin their journey back to the Manden, with Sugulun in tow. The first night of the jour-ney, the elder Taraware brother attempts sexual intercourse with Sugulun, but she magically grows to an intimidating size while two spikes project from her breasts. "My husband's in the Manden," she tells him, and so he is. Meanwhile, in the Manden town of Nyani, Fata Magan the Handsome is accosted by a jinn who tells him that two youths will bring him an unattractive young woman whom he would be wise to accept because she will someday bear him an heir who will be a great ruler. Fata Magan follows the jinn's advice and when the Taraware brothers make the offer, he accepts Sugulun as his wife.

Some time later, Saman Berete, one of Fata Magan's wives, gives birth and sends a messenger to inform Fata Magan of the event. The old woman entrusted with the message tarries along the way, however, to accept some food that is offered to her. As the old woman eats, Sugulun also gives birth, and sends a messenger of her own to inform her husband. Sugulun's messenger is offered food but declines and announces the birth of Sugulun's son before the old woman arrives to announce the birth of Saman Beret's son, who is named Dankaran Tuma. Thus, although Sugulun's child is born second, he gains the birthright of the first-born, and is recognized as his father's heir. Sugulun's child is given the name "Son-Jara" (Sunjata), translated as "lion thief," because he was born covered with hair, like a lion, and he has stolen his brother's birthright.

Saman Berete is enraged by this turn of events and seeks the services of a mori, or Muslim holy man, to curse Sunjata so that he cannot walk. The spells are successful—for nine years Sunjata can only crawl. During this time it may be assumed that Fata Magan, who is never again mentioned in this version of the epic, dies, and his throne passes to Dankaran Tuma, who is hereafter referred to as "king."

At the end of the nine years, Sugulun is cooking couscous and goes door to door asking for some baobab leaf as a condiment, only to be turned away at every door, cruelly mocked because her "lame" son cannot get the baobab leaf for her. Sugulun returns home and tearfully berates her son for his handicap, whereupon Sunjata tells her that he will stand up, provided she bring him an iron staff forged seven times. Sugulun gets the blacksmiths to make such a staff and brings it to her son, who grasps it and attempts to rise. He gets only halfway off the ground, however, then stops, asking for another staff, twice the size. When this second staff is also ineffective, Sugulun cuts her son a staff from a custard apple tree (a tree believed to be supernaturally efficacious), and, with this staff, Sunjata is able to rise. He directs his first steps toward the biggest and best baobab tree, which he uproots and brings home to Sugulun, planting it in front of her house. Now all women wanting baobab to season their food must come to Sugulun and ask her permission.

After this triumph, Sunjata becomes a hunter, and whatever animal he kills, he gives the tail to his brother and rival, Dankaran Tuma. The tail is a prized trophy of the hunt, thought to have strong occult powers; by giving the tail to his brother, Sunjata symbolically acknowledges his brother as his better, and thus gives up his claim to the birthright of the first-born that was wrongly bestowed upon him. Nonetheless, a jinn soon warns Sunjata that Saman Berete and her son are still hostile towards him and plot against him. It is likely they fear that Sunjata became a hunter in order to gain occult power that would enable him to take the throne from his brother. In the face of open hostility from Saman Berete, Sugulun advises Sunjata to depart on a journey that will take him to several kingdoms in search of refuge.

First Sunjata goes to the blacksmith patriarch, Jobi the Seer, but the supporters of Dankaran Tuma bribe Jobi to cast him out. Next Sunjata goes to Tulumbèn, king of Kòlè. King Tulumbèn has been entrusted with the pregnant wife of another patriarch who is away making his hajj. Sunjata has a fetish that accepts only offerings of unborn babies, so Sunjata convinces Tulumbèn to help him slay the pregnant woman and make an offering of her child. When the patriarch returns from his pilgrimage and realizes the outrage, he cries out to God who, hearing his protestations, punishes Tulumbèn, who lacks the nya to protect himself against such a nyama-releasing act. While Tulumbèn is wrapped in chains and cast into a lake to drown, the nya-possessing hero Sunjata flees to the nine Queens-of-Darkness, who are feared by all.

Back in Nyani, King Dankaran Tuma now has a daughter named Caress-of-Hot-Fire. He instructs Dòka the Cat, Sunjata's bard who is in Dankaran Tuma's employ, to take this daughter to Susu Mountain Sumamuru, a mysterious king who wears clothing made of human skin and lives in a village called Dark Forest. In exchange for his life, Dankaran Tuma offers Caress to Sumamuru. Sumamuru asks Dòka to also remain with him, but the bard refuses, saying that he

cannot serve two kings, whereupon Sumamuru severs both of Dòka's Achilles tendons. Sumamuru declares war on Nyani, and soon conquers the land, ousting Dankaran Tuma, who flees. Sumamuru puts "gourds in the mouth of the poor and the powerful," meaning that he silences all criticism through force (Johnson, *Epic of Son-Jara*, lines 1905-06). Next, Sumamuru sends an offering of a bull to the nine Queens-of-Darkness, asking them to slay Sunjata so that he cannot come to claim the Manden. Seeing this, Sunjata, who is living with the nine queens, transforms himself into a lion and kills nine water buffaloes, dragging them back to the lair of the witches as a counter-sacrifice. The nine queens prefer Sunjata's sacrifice and spare his life.

Back in the Manden, Sunjata's younger sister, Sugulun Kulunkan, receives word that her brother is alive and well in Mèma (on the west bank of the Niger River). She removes the gourds from the mouths of three heroes of the Manden, and together they set forth to Mèma disguised as merchants. In the Mèma marketplace, the four offer for sale goods peculiar to the Manden. When Sunjata's mother, who is now living with Sunjata, hears of the fresh okra and eggplant leaf for sale, she realizes that these must come from home and summons the merchants selling these items so that she can hear news from the Manden. The "merchants" tell Sunjata of Sumamuru's usurpation of the Nyani throne, and urge him to return to his homeland.

To increase his power, Sunjata wishes to sacrifice shea butter to a fetish of his that will accept no other offering. There is only one shea tree in Mèma, and it bears no fruit, so Sunjata's mother recites an incantation over it and the next morning the tree is fruitful, but Sunjata's mother is dead. She had prayed to God that she might die because she knew that Sunjata must return to the Manden and she was too old and infirm to make the journey with him. Sunjata buries his mother in secret to evade grave-robbers who would seek to steal from the supernaturally powerful woman's grave any fetishes that might have been buried with her. He then chops down a tree to bury publicly in his mother's stead. He asks for a plot of land for his mother's grave, but is told he must pay for it, so Sunjata presents the Prince of Mèma with a bag containing broken shards, wild grasses, and feathers, among other things. The Prince asks his sages to interpret the meaning of such a payment, and the sages reply that if Sunjata is not given the land, he will reduce Mèma to ruins—a place of broken shards and wild grass that will serve as fodder for the birds. The land is given to Sunjata, who buries the log and then departs for the Manden.

Sunjata engages Sumamuru in battle at the village of Dark Forest, but Sumamuru repulses the attack, and Sunjata leaves in defeat to found a town that he names "Anguish." Again he attacks Sumamuru and again is defeated. This time he founds a town called "Resolve." The cycle repeats, and the result is a town called "Sharing." Sugulun Kulunkan goes to the fortress of Sumamuru and offers herself as "bed companion" to the king (*Epic of Son-Jara*, line 2690). Ignoring his mother's advice, Sumamuru accepts Sugulun Kulunkan's offer, and reveals to her that he has gained power in the Manden by making various sacrifices and burying them in the earth. He also gives her precise instructions concerning the only way he can be vanquished. After a week Sugulun Kulunkan asks to return to the Manden to get the household implements that are her dowry.

Meanwhile, despite having 100 wives of his own, Sumamuru steals his nephew Fa-Koli's only wife, who is especially desirable in that she has the ability to supernaturally increase a small amount of food into enough food to feed 100 warriors. Fa-Koli becomes enraged and joins forces with Sunjata to overthrow his uncle. Sugulun Kulunkan has told her brother all, of course, and Fa-Koli volunteers to make the counter-sacrifices necessary to deprive Sumamuru of his occult powers. When this is done, Sunjata attacks, and Sumamuru flees on horseback. Sunjata's troops give chase and repeatedly capture Sumamuru who, now that he lacks occult power, will not engage in battle, each time saying, "I am not ready!" (*Epic of Son-Jara*, line 2845). Sunjata lets him go each time, saying, "Prepare yourself!" (*Epic of Son-Jara*, line 2847). At one point during the chase Sumamuru dismounts to take a drink from a river. Just as he is about to drink, Sunjata's troops overtake him and he dries up and becomes a shriveled fetish of Kulu-Kòrò, the village where he is defeated and where he remains a fetish to this day.

Sunjata claims the Manden as his own and finds his bard, Dòka the Cat, with his Achilles tendons severed. He places Dòka upon the shoulders of Sumamuru's eldest son, who must now serve as the bard's legs. Sunjata sends a party to Dark Jòlòf to buy horses, but the king of Dark Jòlòf insults Sunjata and sends his messengers back with dogs instead. Sunjata declares war and his troops slay the king of Dark Jòlòf and several other kings as well, claiming their lands for Sunjata.

Heroes and bards: Manding epic tradition. When Sumamuru asks Dòka the Cat to remain with him and be his bard, the mysterious king threatens to steal from Sunjata more than just an entertainer. "We are vessels of speech," explains a *jali* (the Manding word for "bard"; the plural is *jeli*). "[W]e are the repositories which harbour secrets many centuries old. The art of eloquence has no secrets for us; without us the names of kings would vanish into oblivion, we are the memory of mankind" (Mamadou Kouyatè in Niane, p. 1).

Expert speakers such as bards play an important part in an oral society. In traditional Manding culture, bards are typically allied to hòròn families who provide food, clothing, and shelter in exchange for such speech-related services as praise-poetry, the maintenance of genealogies, entertainment, oral history, blessings, curses, and advice. The bard's power is indicated by the fact that he or she is a member of one of the hereditary nyamakala professions who are both feared and revered for the nyama they generate. The nyama that bards generate through their speech can be beneficial, as in the case of praise-poems that fill the recipient with positive nyama so that he or she has the power to do great things. Or it can be harmful—if, for example, the bard spews out curses or when too much nyama renders the recipient of praise-poems intoxicated or crazed. Bards perhaps wield their greatest power as oral historians, since a person's reputation in life and after death depends upon the good will

---

ORAL TRADITION—A PRACTICAL PURPOSE

A half-century after the events central to the *Epic of Son-Jara* occur, the famous tourist to the area, Ibn Battuta (see **Ibn Battuta in Black Africa,** also covered in *African Literature and Its Times*) explains a function of the bards on feast days: "They stand in front of the sultan . . . and recite their poems. Their poems exhort the king to recall the good deeds of his predecessors, and imitate them so that the memory of his good deeds will outlive him. . . . I was told that this practice is a very old custom amongst them prior to the introduction of Islam, and that they have kept it up" (Ibn Battuta in McKissack and McKissack, p. 71).

and talent of bards. Accordingly, one of the bard's most important functions in Manding society is the performance of historical epics such as that of Sunjata.

In general, epics tend to be condensed expressions of the worldview and identity of a people. In the same sense in which Homeric epic conveys what it is to be a Greek, Manding epic concerns what it is to be a Manding. On one level, the epic of Sunjata helps unite the Manding people in a sense of common origin. Although they are dispersed over the Western Sudan, the people regard the Manden, where the epic of Sunjata takes place, as their homeland, and most belong to clans that trace their ancestry back to Sunjata or one of his close companions. On another level, the epic provides a charter for Manding culture—the relations between different segments of society are explained and justified in the epic of Sunjata. The clans of Taraware and Kòndè are bound in friendship because of an oath the buffalo-woman of Du made the Taraware brothers swear. Likewise, the actions of the characters in the epic of Sunjata are sometimes offered as explanations for certain Manding customs. The Manding custom whereby a wife returns to her parents' home after the first week of marriage to obtain a dowry in "useful containers" is said to arise from a ruse employed by Sunjata's sister to leave Sumamuru's fortress.

Another common aspect of epics is that they tend to be about heroes, extraordinary individuals who upset the status quo. The Manding hero, as scholars Charles Bird and Martha Kendall suggest, is a fa-denya figure who acts outside of and sometimes against the group in order to achieve personal power. In the epic, Sunjata's life begins in competition, as his mother and the mother of his half-brother race to announce their sons' births. When Sunjata unjustly attains the status of first-born that rightfully belongs to Dankaran Tuma, he has gained a personal advantage by upsetting the cultural order. As a young man, when Sunjata becomes a hunter, he goes outside the bounds of village society and hierarchy to gain occult knowledge and power. Later, as he flees from one haven to the next, his occult power continues to increase until the day he learns that the Manden has been conquered by Sumamuru, an outsider and an unjust ruler who must be overthrown. Only then does the force of ba-denya pull Sunjata back into the group, to aid it in its time of need. The Manding have a saying: "The hero is welcome only on troubled days,"

and indeed, the Manding hero's fa-denya pursuit of personal power without regard for law or the rights of others makes him difficult to live with in more secure times.

As a hero, Sunjata is a fa-denya figure who lives outside the bounds of society's laws, even committing infanticide with impunity. He is also, in a sense, a ba-denya figure in that he brings the Manding people together and his story is regarded as the model for relationships and customs in Manding culture. He is thus simultaneously outsider and insider, and in this he is like the figure of the bard. Although they are often allied to a single family, as nyamakala, bards themselves stand outside the hòròn or noble hierarchy and are thus trusted to arbitrate disputes between clans. The sending of Dòka the Cat as emissary to Sumamuru reflects the role of bards as intermediaries between different groups, because bards are conceived to be outside any group but their own. They are, in a sense, officially recognized outsiders who are relatively free to express unpopular opinions and criticize those in power. Emblematic of their separateness, in the past dead bards were not buried alongside other Manding but rather placed in the hollow trunks of dead baobab trees, so that bardic nyama would not infect the earth. At the same time, bards are also, in a sense, the ultimate cultural insiders, since their job is to preserve, transmit, and arguably even create Manding history, values, and customs through their performance.

In the *Janjon,* a Manding epic related to the Sunjata epic, Sumamuru's nephew Fa-Koli hears Sunjata's bards singing a song of praise to Sunjata and demands that the song be sung for himself. The bards agree to sing for him but first require Fa-Koli to perform a series of brave feats, after which the song becomes his exclusively forever more. Manding heroes need bards just as bards need heroes. In performing heroic epics, Manding bards celebrate the power of fa-denya and perhaps encourage individuals in their audiences to go beyond family and village, to break with the group in order to achieve the kind of greatness remembered in song. Thus, Sumamuru's attempt to take Sunjata's bard can be understood as an attempt to take the hero's place in history. In the epic, one of Sunjata's praise-names is "Lion-Born-of-the-Cat," and one explanation offered for this sobriquet is that it refers to the hero's status as hunter, one who gains occult knowledge through observation of wild animals like the cat (*Epic of Son-Jara,* line 32). Sunjata is, however, in a sense, a lion born of another cat, his bard Dòka the Cat and bards like him, who inspire heroes to acts of greatness and preserve their memory in epic song.

Sources and literary context. Like epics from around the world, the epic of Sunjata is formulaic. In other words, performers do not memorize the epic verbatim, but recreate the story on the spot using certain stock expressions, or formulae, to describe people, places, and events. These formulae allow the epic performer to maintain poetic flow or meter while composing the epic extemporaneously. Unlike the Homeric epics of Greece, such as the *Illiad* or *Odyssey,* in which meter is rigidly defined, the epic of Sunjata gets its poetic rhythm from the interplay of the singer/reciter with his musical accompaniment.

The epic of Sunjata is perhaps the defining epic of the Manding people, but it does not stand alone. Other epics performed by Manding bards in the Western Sudan include the "Monzon" epic cycle of the Bambara, which recounts the deeds of two kings, Monzon and Da Monzon, who ruled the kingdom of Sègu in the late eighteenth and early nineteenth centuries. Epics are also performed in West Africa by non-Manding peoples (such as the Fulani) and in other parts of Africa (such as Zaire and Zambia).

Events in History at the Time the Epic Was Performed/Recorded

Change and continuity. The continued performance of any piece of oral tradition raises the question, "Why?" Why was the epic of Sunjata, a heroic poem about a medieval ruler, still being performed in West Africa in the latter half of the twentieth century? Did the epic still fascinate audiences, was it merely endured for the sake of tradition, or was it regarded uncomprehendingly as a curious artifact from a time long ago? It seems clear at least that at the time these performances were recorded, Manding epic poetry was a genuine, living tradition.

Obviously, much had changed for Manding society in the centuries since 1200 C.E. Trade with Europe, which began in the fifteenth century, led to economic and political domination of West Africa that culminated in its division into European colonies in the nineteenth century. After World War II ended in 1945, West Africans overthrew the colonial powers and formed their own nation-states. Ghana and the Republic of Mali are two such modern nations with names inspired by the past glory of ancient empires. Per-

haps behind both the reclaiming of these names and the performance of the Sunjata epic is the same sense of pride and interest in African history before European colonialism, when the Manding peoples had empires of their own.

PERFORMANCE OF A MANDING EPIC

The performance of a Manding epic is not restricted to any particular time or place, although it usually occurs outside and at night. In this culture, an epic is a lengthy poem that is sung either entirely or in part, and its performance may be drawn out over several nights or continue uninterrupted for as long as ten hours.

The bard is usually aided in his performance by musicians—who may be other bards or apprentices, singers—who take the singing parts of the epic, letting the bard concentrate on the recitation—and a *naamu-sayer*—an individual who shouts encouraging words like "yes" (*na'am* in Arabic) or "that's true" after each line of a bard's performance. Performance style varies greatly among bards, who may choose to dance, gesticulate, act out certain episodes, or simply sit still and tell the story. Most bards don special garments for the event and some hold props like a scepter or spear to help them embody the hero of the epic.

Epics are, for the most part, not restricted to any particular audience, but are attended by a large, mixed group that participates in the performance by singing, dancing, playing percussive instruments, clapping hands, and shouting remarks.

In Mali of the 1960s and 1970s, more than 90 percent of the population still lived in rural villages, less than 30 percent of children were receiving a classroom education, and patrilineal hierarchy remained an important, albeit unofficial, source of authority. Islam had grown from a religion primarily of merchants and royalty into a religion of all the people, yet elements of traditional Manding religious belief and practice remained prevalent. The Manding bard, although in general no longer fully supported by a single patron family, could still earn a living through freelance performance or sometimes through government funding. Some bards performed on radio shows or allowed themselves to be recorded while others played their instruments in dance bands. Yet despite changes in the ways in which the bard survived economically, and although the Manding had developed a literary tradition, the role of the bard in Manding culture remained intact.

The performance of epics, which is considered the bards' most important function, also remained intact. The epic of Sunjata continued to be performed because Sunjata is central to the Manding peoples' understanding of who they are. He is the hero who leaves the group on a fadenya quest for power that allows him to serve the group in its time of greatest need. He is the hero who returns and reunites the group, providing the ba-denya model for relations between individuals and exemplifying rules for behavior through his actions. In late twentieth-century Mali, the epic of Sunjata was still cited as rationale for the customs of Manding culture.

Reception. The simple fact that Manding bards continue to perform the epic of Sunjata, and that people continue to listen to them, speaks volumes for the oral tradition as a whole. Critics have reviewed all three English texts—*Sundiata: An Epic of Old Mali* by Mamadou Kouyatè, translated by D. T. Niane; *Sunjata: Three Mandinka Versions* by Bamba Suso, Banna Kanute, and Dembo Kanute, translated by Gordon Innes; and *The Epic of Son-Jara* by Fa-Digi Sisòkò, translated by John William Johnson. The reviewers have not generally critiqued the quality of the story or the eloquence of the bard who relates it. Instead, the texts have been reviewed according to three main criteria: the quality of the extensive notes and introductions, the faithfulness of the translation to actual bardic performance, and the readability of the epic.

Sundiata: An Epic of Old Mali, the earliest of the three texts, is considered to be more readable than it is faithful. First published in French in 1960, *Sundiata* is regarded as "a pioneering effort . . . undertaken before standards for faithfully reproducing oral narratives were in place" that is marked by "European-style literary phrasing" (Conrad, p. 674). Perhaps for this reason, *Sundiata* is "extremely readable and entertaining for a non-African audience" (Conrad, p. 674). The English version of *Sundiata,* although it does contain many informative notes, lacks the thoroughgoing introduction to Manding culture that marks later, more scholarly, publications.

Sunjata: Three Mandinka Versions, published in 1974, is a pioneering work in that it was the first linear, or line-for-line, translation of recorded and transcribed performances of the epic to be published in English. Translator Gordon Innes is nonetheless faulted for high-flown "expansion" of the text at times—for example, in rendering a poetic line that literally translates into "I am the child of a king" as "I am a scion of the royal line" (Bird, p. 362).

The Epic of Son-Jara is the most recently published version of the three (1986), and also the most faithfully rendered, down to the responses of the naamu-sayer given in parentheses after each line. *Son-Jara,* however, can be a challenging read for those unfamiliar with Manding culture. It too is a linear translation and also offers extensive introductory sections on the Manding and copious notes that might daunt the non-academic, yet one reviewer characterizes the text as "leaving interesting material without necessary context" (McDougall, p. 351). The version has nonetheless been singled out for praise. *The Epic of Son-Jara* has received accolades for offering a more "accurate representation of oral discourse" than its predecessors (Conrad, p. 674).

—Kimberly Ball

For More Information

Bird, Charles S. Review of *Sunjata: Three Mandinka Versions. Research in West African Literatures* 8 (1977): 353-69.

Bird, Charles S., and Martha B. Kendall. "The Mande Hero: Text and Context." In *Explorations in African Systems of Thought.* Bloomington: Indiana University Press, 1980.

Bourboune, Mourad. "L'amour, la fantasia." *Jeune Afrique Magazine,* 15 April 1985, p. 31.

Buah, F. K. *A History of West Africa from AD 1000.* London: Macmillan, 1986.

Clarke, Peter B. *West Africa and Islam: A Study of Religious Development From the 8th to the 20th Century.* London: Edward Arnold, 1982.

Conrad, David C. Review of *The Epic of Son-Jara: A West African Tradition. International Journal of African Historical Studies* 26, no. 3 (1993): 673-75.

Dieterlen, Germaine. "The Mande Creation Myth." *Africa: Journal of the International African Institute* 27, no. 2 (April 1957): 124-37.

Innes, Gordon. *Sunjata: Three Mandinka Versions.* London: University of London, 1974.

Johnson, John William, trans. *The Epic of Son-Jara: A West African Tradition.* Text by Fa-Digi Sisòkò. Bloomington: Indiana University Press, 1986.

McDougall, E. Ann. Review of *The Epic of Son-Jara: A West African Tradition. International Journal of African Historical Studies* 22, no. 2 (1989): 350-53.

McKissack, Patricia, and Frederick McKissack. *The Royal Kingdoms of Ghana, Mali, and Songhay: Life in Medieval Africa.* New York: Henry Holt, 1994.

Niane, D. T. *Sundiata: An Epic of Old Mali.* Trans. G. D. Pickett. Essex: Longman, 1965.

Equiano's Travels: The Interesting Narrative of the Life of Olaudah Equiano or Gustavus Vassa the African

by
Olaudah Equiano

Olaudah Equiano led one of the most intriguing existences in the last century of the transatlantic slave trade. Born in 1745 to the chieftain of an Igbo village in Nigeria, he was kidnapped and sold into slavery at the age of 11. By the time he was 21 he had served England's navy in its war against the French and worked on trading ships in the West Indies and the southern United States, surviving the countless dangers of sea and slavery. He acquired the slave name Gustavus Vassa, later buying his way out of bondage. Equiano managed to save enough money to purchase his freedom, after which he continued to work as a sailor, participating in an early expedition to the Arctic Ocean and visiting the eastern Mediterranean Sea. The ex-slave also aided the abolitionist cause while in London. He was appointed to a post on a project for the black poor going to Sierra Leone, a colony founded by Britain in Africa for freed slaves. He himself did not travel to Sierra Leone, though he had earlier attempted, unsuccessfully, to be ordained and sent to Africa as a missionary. In fact, Equiano left the Sierra Leone project after a conflict with white participants. He and other blacks in England went on to form the Sons of Africa, a group that would enter into public debate on issues such as slavery. His memoir was

> ## THE LITERARY WORK
>
> A memoir set primarily in Africa, England, and North America from 1745 to 1787; published in English in 1789.
>
> ## SYNOPSIS
>
> A well-traveled former slave recounts his experiences as a slave and as a free man, on trading ships and on land.

published in 1789, as the international debate over slavery reached its zenith; both his condemnations of slavery and his unflinching descriptions of slave life proved to be valuable ammunition for the abolitionist cause.

Events in History at the Time the Memoir Takes Place

The slave trade in Africa. The European slave trade, which flourished between the sixteenth and the nineteenth centuries, took an estimated 12 million Africans from their native countries to work on the plantations of the West Indies. Thousands of these captives never made it to the

Indies, dying on the transatlantic journey, while the survivors faced life in bondage on foreign shores. In many ways the slave trade devastated the cultures of West and Central Africa. It was not conducted by the Europeans alone; the active collaboration of Africans themselves was essential to the trade in slaves. In fact, Europeans rarely ventured into the continent's interior, relying on African slave-catchers to bring captives to their coastal forts.

Two aspects of African culture helped the European slave-traders. First, slavery was a significant part of most African societies before the Europeans arrived. In Africa, however, slaves occupied a very different place from that in the Americas: "It was not unknown for them to gain their freedom, marry into their captor's society and rise in economic and social status" (Shillington, p. 175). Many of the slaves in Africa were partly incorporated into their owner's family, even if they remained subordinate members. In his memoir, Equiano contrasts the treatment of slaves in his home community with that in the West Indies:

> With us they do no more work than other members of the community, even their master; their food, clothing and lodging were nearly the same as theirs, (except that they were not permitted to eat with those who were freeborn). ... Some of these slaves have even slaves under them as their own property and for their own use.
>
> (Equiano, *Equiano's Travels*, p. 10)

During the brief period when Equiano himself was a slave in Africa, he remembers being treated kindly among people who spoke his own language. Racism, the harshness of plantation work, and foreign tongues militated against similar conditions in the Americas. Nevertheless, Africans had a well-developed understanding of slavery before leaving their shores. The arrival of the Europeans profoundly altered, but did not create, African slavery.

The second aspect of African culture exploited by the Europeans was its political division into kingdoms—the primary source of slaves, both those who stayed in Africa and those who ended up in the Americas, was warfare between African peoples. The army that lost a battle was often taken captive. Before the transatlantic trade, these captives were either ransomed back to their people, or taken to serve as slaves for the victors; after the Europeans arrived, these captives were more likely to find themselves on a ship bound for the New World. In the long run, this change

debilitated western Africa: for three centuries, thousands of Africa's youngest and strongest people were bled from the continent, sapping Africa's strength and productive potential. In the short run, however, selling captives to the Europeans seemed wise. For a chieftain of, say, the kingdom of Dahomey, the difference between white slave trader and black meant nothing compared to the difference between Dahomey and its African foes. If the white foreigners offered good prices for captives, it made perfect sense to sell them, rather than keep them as personal slaves.

Thus, the coastal trade in slaves depended on wars waged in the interior of Africa. Expanding or declining kingdoms willingly sold captives as slaves; stable kingdoms frequently did not. For example, when the kingdom of Benin was growing in the late fifteenth century, it participated in the slave trade; it also traded in slaves in the eighteenth century, when it had to defend its borders against newly rising powers. In between, when it was strong and stable, Benin did not send slaves to the coast. While Western historians once believed that wars between Africans were often waged for the sole purpose of capturing slaves for the European market, modern analysts disagree. They have concluded that although raids for slaves did happen occasionally, other reasons for war—disputes over land, tribute, or economic power—remained more prevalent among the African peoples.

However, the European presence added significant new elements to African warfare. When Europeans began trading guns for slaves in the eighteenth century, war grew more vicious and more deadly. Larger kingdoms tended to profit and become more powerful at the expense of smaller powers and isolated communities, many of which disappeared altogether. Finally, the European presence created new types of jobs, most importantly the position of the African middlemen who bought slaves from the inland kingdoms and marched them to the coast, where European buyers awaited. Although Equiano is vague about details (understandably, since he was not yet a teenager at the time), it is likely that some of these middlemen bought him from his first African master and took him to the coast.

The slave ship. Few aspects of the slave trade horrify the modern imagination more than the slave ship. For the newly purchased slave, it must have been a terrifying initiation into this new life. Many, of course, had never seen or even heard of the ocean or of white people. In addition to rough treatment at the hands of Europeans, new

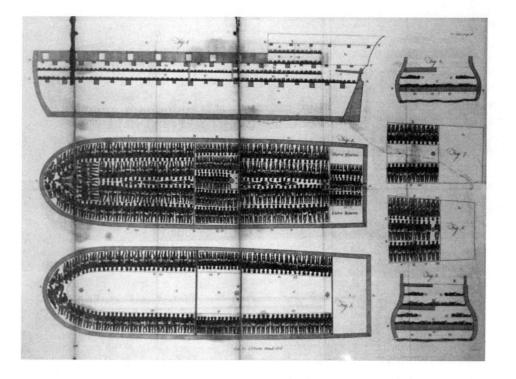

This diagram of a British slave ship shows the layout for stowing 292 slaves in the lower deck.

slaves often found themselves surrounded by many other Africans whose languages they did not understand. The experience was both mystifying and anxiety-ridden. James Penny, captain of British slave ships, reported that new slaves "frequently express fears, from an apprehension of being eaten" (Penny in Craton, Walvin, and Wright, p. 35).

Such apprehensions were nothing compared to the physical misery of life on a slave ship. It is difficult for modern historians to get a precise fix on the conditions of slaves on board: accounts from the time are highly colored by the teller's views of slavery. Undoubtedly, slavers exaggerated their accounts of treating slaves kindly, but one must also suspect that the horrifying accounts of abolitionists are less than even-handed. Slavers who paid as much as £25 for a slave were unlikely to treat their new property in a way that would kill him or her and ruin the investment. Usually, slaves were allowed to come up on deck for fresh air and allowed—or forced—to exercise. Some attention to their health and hygiene was common. However, two unchanging facts ensured a terrifying voyage for slaves on board. First, the Atlantic crossing (called the Middle Passage) was often dangerous. Hurricanes and tornadoes often threatened the safety of a ship, while prolonged periods without wind were just as dangerous, straining the ship's slender provisions of food and water. Disease ran rampant among slaves and crew: historians estimate that between a twelfth and a third of slaves died at sea, their bodies thrown overboard. Second, the traders treated the slaves not as human beings but as property, no better than a cargo of cows or horses, a philosophy that led to inhumanities. Traders often overpacked their ships to offset the inevitable mortality on the voyage. Slave captains were allowed to do whatever was necessary to quell slave mutinies. And if anything went wrong on the journey, the slaves were the first to suffer. The most infamous example of this is the *Zong* case of 1783. An epidemic was decimating the slaves aboard the *Zong* and, in order to collect insurance money, the ship's captain threw more than 130 sick slaves overboard. This combination of brutality and cold commercial calculation encapsulates the real horror of the slave ship.

Slavery and freedom for Africans. Conditions for slaves in the West Indies were atrocious. For the plantation slave, life was brutal and frequently short: at least a third of newly arrived slaves died within a year. Hours were long, work intensive, free time almost non-existent. Perhaps worse than these daily torments, colonial law made slaves' lives precarious by depriving them of almost all rights. Slaves had little recourse when mistreated; and at the end of any legitimate course of action that they could take sat a jury of white men. No black person was allowed to testify against a white person. For slaves to get any justice, they had to plead for the support of their owner, who would pursue the matter as a crime against his property, rather than against another person. Slaves mistreated by their owners had slim hope of justice.

While their legal situation was precarious, the reality of life in the West Indies was more mixed. Many slaves, Equiano among them, received or created opportunities to engage in trade, fishing, farming, and manual labor for their own profit: they had to turn over only part of the proceeds to their owners. Those few slaves who, like Equiano, worked on ships plying the West Indies could make a lucrative side-job out of selling goods themselves at the bustling port markets. The legal situation of slavery, however, made such operations unsafe. Because slaves had no legal right to property, much less to sue, they frequently had to depend on the good will of the white people with whom they traded. Equiano's narrative is spiced with complaints against whites who took his goods without payment, or who attacked him with impunity. His only recourse was to seek protection or justice from his master.

Actually the protection that a decent master provided sometimes made slavery a more attractive option than freedom. Manumission, as the legal release from slavery is called, was uncommon: free blacks rarely constituted more than 3 percent of a given area's population. In addition, manumission was most often granted to the aged and sick, to long-time personal servants, and to the children that a slave owner had fathered with female slaves. While almost all slaves must have yearned for freedom in principle, they must also have known that the freedom offered an African in the West Indies was a paltry thing. In practice, freedom hardly affected the African's legal status, except for the worse: "Manumission itself brought few practical benefits, while it deprived the ex-slaves of their master's full legal responsibility for their welfare and protection" (Craton, p. 182). Freed slaves suddenly had to find some way to make a living on their own, and they had to contend with a racist society without even the uncertain help of a master. In 1730 the island of Bermuda passed a law requiring all freed slaves to leave the island within six months of manumission; those who did not would be imprisoned and sold again. Thus, freed and enslaved Africans were more alike than not: the openly stated goal of eighteenth-century West Indian whites was to maintain and even expand white superiority—legally, socially, and economically.

Abolition. From its beginnings, the enslavement of Native Americans and Africans had troubled the moral sense of many Europeans. But the exponential development of transatlantic colonialism, and the incredible profits to be had from American plantations, had resulted in the sacrifice of such morality to economics. However, over the course of the eighteenth century, new economic and philosophical developments lent ever-increasing weight to arguments against slavery. England began the century at the forefront of all European nations in the exporting and exploiting of slaves; by 1800 the English were leading the charge to end the slave trade, and then slavery itself. England outlawed the slave trade in 1807 and sent its naval forces to the West African coast to enforce the ban; it abolished slavery in its colonies in 1834. Behind this surprising about-face were some historical developments that led the English to blend practical considerations with the philanthropic.

Technological development proved to be the key economic determinant in the decline of slavery. First, new manufacturing techniques made sugar easier to produce; the market was flooded and sugar prices plummeted, diminishing the political and economic clout of plantation owners. The crucial long-term development, however, was the Industrial Revolution—the decades-long, often cataclysmic event by which manufacturing and trade replaced agriculture as Europe's central economic business. By the end of the eighteenth century England's factories had grown enough in economic importance to challenge the power of the West Indian colonial interests. And to factory owners, slavery made much less sense than emancipation. They found paid labor more efficient and lucrative. On plantations, in exchange for a slave's labor, land owners provided the slave with food, clothing, and the like—at minimal cost, since slaves could, for instance, raise their own food. Manufacturing did not allow for such cost-saving measures. Furthermore, paying wages to workers enabled them to become buyers of the manufactured products. Factory owners required two things: raw materials for making goods and constantly expanding markets in which to sell the finished products. The West Indies would be an ideal market—but only if its inhabitants were free to earn wages they could spend on manufactured products.

Africa likewise enticed those searching for new markets. The continent also had vast stores of natural resources, but the depletion of the population through slavery interfered with the gathering of these resources for European manufacturers, thus impeding the growth of trade. All these interests became more and more difficult to overlook when manufacturing began to replace plantation agriculture as the cornerstone of British wealth.

In the late twentieth century these economic battles have largely been forgotten, except by specialists. What is remembered now is the other catalyst for emancipation: the abolitionists. The Industrial Revolution created an atmosphere in which arguments about the evils of slavery would be heard; slavery was no longer so crucial to British wealth that morality could hold no sway. Two intellectual trends of the eighteenth century further added power to the arguments of the abolitionists. The first was the Enlightenment, a movement that stressed the rationality, perfectibility, and equality of all human beings. Enlightenment thinkers rejected coercion and raw power as the basis of politics, and advanced the idea of the "noble savage," the notion that "uncivilized" people are naturally good. If earlier centuries had justified slavery by claiming that Africans were naturally inferior and barbaric, Enlightenment thinkers were more inclined to see a lack of European culture as evidence of superior morality. These philosophical ideas were bolstered by new developments in Christian religion. The rise of Evangelical denominations, particularly the Methodists, proved crucial. Evangelicals desired to do Christ's work by improving the world in practical ways. In the last decades of the eighteenth century, one of the most obvious ways to improve the world was by ending slavery. The key to Evangelicalism was conversion: the individual believer received a sudden and immediate sense of God's love. The result was absolute commitment to religion and philanthropy: "Spiritual rebirth was accompanied by a flooding love of all men and by a sense of mission" (Craton, p. 249). This intense commitment explains the vigor with which English reformers like John Wesley, William Wilberforce, and Granville Sharp pursued the cause of abolition through speeches, debates, pamphlets, letters, boycotts, and parliamentary actions.

Success came in spurts for the abolitionists. The famous Somerset Case of 1772 (described below) seemed to outlaw slavery on English soil.

Although the actual decision was more ambiguous, it was a critical victory for emancipation. The next three decades saw an unrelenting struggle to abolish the slave trade, which succeeded in 1807. Between 1807 and the late 1820s abolitionists hoped to improve conditions in the colonies to the point that slavery would wither away on its own; when this did not occur, they agitated for legal emancipation, which, as mentioned, was granted in 1834.

QUAKERS: THE VANGUARD OF ABOLITION

The Quakers, or the Society of Friends, occupy a special place in the history of religious abolitionism. The Quaker faith was not only older than the later Evangelical sects, having begun in the seventeenth century; it was also marked by extremely progressive practices, such as pacifism, the use of female preachers, and a firm belief in human equality. While some owned slaves as late as 1776, Quakers formed almost the entire vanguard of the early movement for abolition. In 1671 the Quaker George Fox pleaded with other Quakers to treat slaves humanely and to eventually free them. In 1727 the Quakers formally condemned slavery.

The Quakers were also highly influential in spreading abolitionism to members of the newly developing Evangelical sects. Two books, *Historical Account of Guinea* by the Quaker Anthony Benezet and an anonymous Quaker pamphlet called *The Case of Our Fellow Creature, the Oppressed African*, brought many non-Quakers to the cause of abolition. Of the twelve members who formed the first governing committee of the Society for the Abolition of the Slave Trade, nine were Quakers.

Equiano was lucky to have been owned by a Quaker. Although it was unusual for a Quaker to own slaves, it is clear from Equiano's narrative that this master was not deaf to the arguments of his religion. He treated his slaves kindly, allowing Equiano to improve himself by trade and education, and eventually consenting when Equiano asked to buy his own freedom.

It is important not to overlook the slaves' own contributions to ending slavery. For the most part the newly enslaved lacked the power for anything but passive or suicidal resistance. Many committed suicide, while occasional mutinies on slave ships were tantamount to organized mass suicide. Once in the colonies, however, resistance could be more effective: slave rebellions and escapes belied the slave owners' claims that Africans were happy in chains. Also, a select group of educated ex-slaves worked alongside white Europeans to agitate for abolition through speeches and writings. Most important among this small group was Olaudah Equiano.

The Memoir in Focus

Contents summary. Equiano's account of his life ends before he reaches 40, and the bulk of the book is concerned with his first 25 years. This is only to be expected. Equiano's first concern is to convey to his readers the horrors of slavery; his experiences as a free man are to him less important. But, while his book intends to persuade, it is less dogmatic and argumentative than many abolitionist tracts. Equiano's account contains passages of invective against slavery; for the most part, however, the narrative allows its author's experiences to speak for themselves.

In the first chapter, the account describes Equiano's early life in Africa. Born into the family of an Igbo chieftain, Equiano recalls in idyllic terms his boyhood in what is now eastern Nigeria. He extols the virtue and industry of African culture, and describes what he remembers of religious and social customs.

> The dress of both sexes is nearly the same. It generally consists of a long piece of calico or muslin, wrapped loosely round the body somewhat in the form of a highland plaid. This is usually dyed blue....
>
> Each master of a family has a large square piece of ground, surrounded with a moat or fence or enclosed with a wall made of red earth tempered, which when dry is as hard as brick.
>
> Agriculture is our chief employment, and everyone, even the children and women, are engaged in it. Thus we are all habituated to labour from our earliest years . . . we are unacquainted with idleness....
>
> We have fire-arms, bows and arrows, broad two-edged swords and javelins . . . even our women are warriors....
>
> The natives believe that there is one Creator of all things. . . . We practised circumcision like the Jews. . . . I have before remarked that the natives of this part of Africa are extremely cleanly. This . . . was with us a part of religion, and therefore we had many purifications and washings; indeed almost as many . . . as the Jews.
>
> (*Equiano's Travels*, pp. 4, 5, 7, 9, 10-12)

Equiano's life changes cataclysmically when, at age ten, he is kidnapped and carried down the river. After spending some time as a slave in another village, he is sold to English slavers. Equiano stresses the emotional, rather than the physical suffering that accompanies the Atlantic crossing. Africans are torn from their native lands without being told why; families are split up; and the white crew members aboard the slave ship are cruel. For a man whose life would be bound up with the sea, this is a horrible introduction to sailing.

Equiano is not sold at the ship's auction in the West Indies, so he is sent to Virginia, where he is eventually bought by an officer in the British navy, Michael Pascal. At this point, his life takes a slight turn for the better. He begins to learn English, and enjoys some amenities. Equiano describes his voyage from Virginia to England with fondness: "I had sails to lie on and plenty of good victuals to eat, and everybody on board used me very kindly, quite contrary to what I had seen of any white people before" (*Equiano's Travels*, p. 35). This kind treatment continues in England, where he remembers playing with the children of his owner's friends.

In 1757 his master resumes active naval service, and Equiano accompanies him. At 16 years of age he becomes a veteran of war at sea. With Pascal, he sails to the Mediterranean to fight the French. His brief but forceful description of an engagement with three French vessels in the pitch of night is among the most vivid passages of his memoir. His job is to carry powder from kegs to cannon: "I was a witness of the dreadful fate of many of my companions who, in the twinkling of an eye, were dashed in pieces and launched into eternity. . . . I expected therefore every minute to be my last" (*Equiano's Travels*, pp. 48-49).

After his military exploits Equiano faces trauma of a different kind. Returned to England, he and his master begin to argue. As a participant on the victors' side of a battle, Equiano believes he is entitled to a share of the spoils; since his master has never given him his share, Equiano feels he should be freed. His position is bolstered by a commonly held, but not universally enforced, belief that a slave who enters England automatically becomes free. However, regardless of issues of justice, Pascal has physical control of Equiano. Although the slave tries to arrange his escape, he is sold to another captain and carried across the Atlantic back to the West Indies.

Equiano's relationship with Captain Pascal typifies some of the paradoxes of slave-owning. On the one hand, master and slave were bound by years of mutual experience and by affection. On the other, Pascal was unwilling to lose the financial investment he had made in Equiano; when he suspects the slave might run away, Pascal sells him back to North America. Still, Pascal shows consideration despite the inhumane circumstances: the captain to whom Pascal sold him tells Equiano that his former master tried to get him the best master he could, saying that Equiano "was a very deserving boy" (*Equiano's Travels,* p. 63).

This "best" master is Robert King, a Quaker merchant. Although a slave owner, King is noted for humane treatment of his slaves; he allows Equiano to educate himself and even supports his slave's small private trading. Equiano serves as a sailor on King's merchant vessels, sailing all over the Caribbean and as far north as Virginia. In this capacity he has ample opportunity to observe and experience the cruel treatment of slaves. He devotes Chapter Seven of his book to a thorough outline of these abuses: the painful punishments for even the smallest offenses; arbitrary cruelty; lack of legal redress for mistreated slaves; whites who harass or ridicule slaves for fun; theft of a slave's meager belongings; unfair business dealings; and outright thuggery.

His own master, Mr. King, is a fair man, though. Not only does he allow Equiano to carry personal items for trade, but King even advances some goods for Equiano to sell. By selling gin, pork, glasses, and whatever else he can turn to profit, Equiano amasses enough money to buy his freedom: 40 pounds. His master, while surprised that Equiano accumulates the money so quickly, agrees to accept that sum. "Accordingly he signed the manumission that day, so that before night, I who had been a slave in the morning, trembling at the will of another, was become my own master and completely free" (*Equiano's Travels,* p. 97).

As it turns out, this state of complete freedom has much in common with the state of slavery that preceded it. Equiano stays on as a sailor on his former master's vessels, now earning 36 shillings a month. The first anecdote he relates about his new life reveals the difficulties that await freed Africans. After a fight with a slave Equiano must hide from that slave's master, who is upset at the damage done to his human property. He remains in hiding for five days, until his captain intercedes and convinces the slave owner

not to pursue the matter. A free African could be in a more dangerous position than a slave whose master was less cooperative.

Equiano longs to return to England. After a few more voyages for Mr. King—including one cut short by a harrowing shipwreck—he secures passage on a vessel bound for England: "I bade adieu to the sound of the cruel whip and all other dreadful instruments of torture; adieu to the offensive sight of the violated chastity of the sable females . . . ; adieu to oppressions (although to me less severe than most of my countrymen)" (*Equiano's Travels,* p. 121).

Arriving in England, Equiano pursues various interests, which he describes in quick succession. He apprentices himself to a hairdresser, learns to play the French horn, and sails to Turkey and around the eastern Mediterranean. He is also associated with Dr. Charles Irving, who has devised a way of removing salt from sea water. This last

"SEA HORSES" ON A FROZEN OCEAN

The Phipps expedition to the Arctic Ocean was one of the final attempts by the English to find a Northwest Passage—that is, to locate a route to India by sailing over the top of the world. This effort, which had been going on since the sixteenth century, was doomed to failure by the fact—obvious today—that the North Pole is perpetually frozen; but the English of the eighteenth century were less sure of this.

Equiano joined the voyage as a personal servant of Dr. Charles Irving, who was there to operate his water-purifying machine. Although the trip was a commercial failure, it provided Equiano with some of his book's most striking incidents. He describes the walruses (which he calls sea horses), whales, and polar bears that approached the ship; at one point, two boats of sailors were even attacked by a group of walruses. Even more strange and compelling are his descriptions of the frozen north itself: "We had generally sunshine and constant daylight, which gave cheerfulness and novelty to the whole of this striking, grand, and uncommon scene; and to heighten it still more, the reflection of the sun from the ice gave the clouds a most beautiful appearance" (*Equiano's Travels,* p. 134).

In August, as summer faded, the ships were trapped by ice. After 11 days of panic, constant struggle, and prayer, a fortuitous change in the weather freed them, and they sailed home at all possible speed, abandoning the dream of a northwest trade route to India.

tie leads Equiano all the way to the Arctic Ocean, as part of John Phipps's expedition to the north in 1773.

After the Phipps expedition, Equiano's book describes a trip with Dr. Irving to coastal South America, where Irving establishes a plantation with the help of Musquito (also spelled *Miskito*) Indians. Upon leaving this settlement Equiano is nearly kidnapped and sold into slavery again. He escapes from an unscrupulous ship's captain only by luck and his wits. The final chapter presents Equiano's concluding thoughts, including a rousing condemnation of slavery.

Air too pure—slaves in England. Throughout his memoirs Equiano expresses a burning desire to be in England. From his first visit, he is enchanted by the place. He bemoans having to leave it; and, when in the West Indies, dreams and schemes of ways to return. To some extent, this fondness is a response to the kind people he met there, and perhaps the greater opportunities for education available in England. However, there was a more specific reason for Equiano to long for England: legal tradition seemed to suggest that slavery could not exist in England and that any slave brought there was automatically free. The legal position was far from clear, however, and until total emancipation in 1834, many Africans in England were functional slaves. The fight over whether slavery could legally exist there proved to be an important battle for abolitionists.

English law, with its emphasis on caution, moderation, and the careful use of precedent, provided contradictory evidence about the legality of slavery. The first case involved not an African, but a Russian. Rushworth's *Historical Collections* states "[t]hat in the 11th [year of the reign of] of Elizabeth [1569], one Cartwright brought a slave from Russia, and would scourge him; for this he was questioned, and it was resolved, that England was too pure an air for slaves to breathe in" (Rushworth, p. 468). This ringing evocation of moral purity and equality continued to sound down to abolitionist times. Later cases, however, complicated matters. In 1677 and 1694 court rulings upheld the rights of slave owners in England; subsequent decisions in 1702 and 1706 denied slavery outright. The matter was further complicated by the issue of Christianity: since the decisions that supported slavery used the fact that Africans were heathen to justify their enslavement, some abolitionists argued that baptism freed a slave.

In short, the legal status of slavery in England was profoundly muddied. In 1729 the Law Officers of the Crown attempted to clarify matters by categorically ruling that neither being in England nor being baptized would free a slave. While this should have ended the controversy, it had quite the opposite effect. The abolitionist cause was gathering strength. Countless slaves fled from their masters, to be sheltered by sympathetic Englishmen.

The struggle to outlaw slavery in England bore its first fruits in the Jonathan Strong case of 1767. Granville Sharp encountered a young slave, Jonathan Strong, wandering the streets of London. Strong had been beaten and abandoned by his master. Sharp nursed the slave back to health, only to be sued for robbery by the original owner. Sharp threw himself into the study of English law and came to the conclusion that it did not permit slavery. He prepared a case, which he won by default, as the slave owner did not appear. A similar and more famous case decided the issue in 1772. In this later case, judge Lord Mansfield ruled in favor of the slave James Somerset, whose lawyers argued from the basis of the original 1569 decision. At issue again was whether slavery could exist in England. Somerset had claimed that the minute he set foot on English ground he was no longer enslaved and so could not be returned to the West Indies. From this case on, no English court would support the rights of slave owners to remove their alleged slaves from England.

The practical consequences of the Somerset decision were less sweeping than the rhapsodic celebrations of it by abolitionists would suggest. Lord Mansfield vacillated in later decisions on slavery; he ruled against slaves who sought wages from their owners, and repeatedly stressed the limited scope of the Somerset case. Slaves could not, for example, sue their owners for kidnapping, although the logic of the Somerset case suggested that they should be able to, for now that they were in England they were free. As far as other slaves were concerned, the Somerset victory was a moral one with little effect on their daily lives. In practical terms, most of the thousands of slaves in England continued to be subject to their masters' desires: if they tried to resist returning to the West Indies, they were simply seized and forced to comply. Most had no option but to remain in captivity. In the long run, however, the Somerset case struck a blow against the slave-owning class. It demonstrated the practical strength of the abolitionist cause and, more importantly, established that the basic philosophy of English law was opposed to slavery. If England itself could not abide slavery, why should slavery be allowed in England's colonies?

Sources and literary context. The most important context for Equiano's book is the literature of the abolitionist movement. His account belongs on a shelf alongside the countless tracts, pamphlets, polemics, and speeches published by men like Granville Sharp and John Wesley. Equiano's memoirs tend to be less argumentative than others, for good reason: Equiano had real experience with slavery, and could let his experiences speak for themselves.

Within the abolitionist canon, *Equiano's Travels* belongs to a select subgroup: the slave narrative. A very few former slaves were positioned to be effective spokespeople for abolition. Equiano is the most famous in a small group that includes such figures as Ottobah Cugoano, Ignatius Sancho, Francis Barber, and Ukawsaw Gronniosaw. Although small in number, these African writers had a profound impact on the abolitionist cause. The slave owners' claim that Africans were irredeemably barbaric met a powerful rebuke in a man like Equiano, through his personal energy and vigorous writing.

Equiano's experiences also make his memoir distant kin to another type of book, far removed from issues of slavery. The memoir takes its place alongside the literature of sea voyages and adventure that gained such popularity in the eighteenth century—an age of vigorous trade and exploration.

Events in History at the Time the Memoir Was Written

Sierra Leone. After the period of life covered by his memoirs, Equiano settled into an active routine of fighting for abolition. It was he who alerted Granville Sharp of the infamous *Zong* case (in which slaves were thrown overboard) in 1784, and he entered into close communication with the leaders of the fight against slavery. In 1786 Equiano also became briefly involved in the attempt to set up a colony in Africa to which slaves could return once they had been freed. The colony, organized by Joseph Irwin, was called Sierra Leone. By October 1786, 700 former slaves had applied for the expedition, and four ships were prepared. On the advice of Granville Sharp and General James Edward Oglethorpe (founder of the colony of Georgia in North America), Irwin appointed Equiano as Commissary for Stores

Olaudah Equiano

on the expedition to Sierra Leone, which made him responsible for acquiring and distributing provisions to the Africans.

The expedition was troubled from the start. Rumors swept through the community of former slaves that the ships were actually bound for the West Indies or Australia: hundreds backed out. Fever swept the ships, delaying the departure. As two of the ships waited in port for the arrival of another two, leaders of the voyage began quarreling. Equiano accused Irwin of corruption and dishonesty; in addition, he complained that Irwin and the ship's priest, Reverend Fraser, condescended to the Africans. In return, Irwin and Fraser complained that Equiano was insolent and insubordinate, complaints that were only strengthened when Equiano published his accusations in the letters section of various English newspapers. Before the expedition sailed, Equiano was dismissed and ordered ashore. He never returned to Africa.

Undoubtedly, both sides had some cause for grievances. Irwin, while probably not grossly dishonest, was in charge of a hastily organized venture troubled by bad luck from the start; it must have frustrated Equiano to see this important cause floundering. On the other hand, his vigorous, principled complaints struck Irwin as counterproductive, if not willfully harmful. In any case, the incident had few long-term consequences. Equiano continued to work effectively for the abolitionist cause until his death in 1797, and the Sierra Leone colony was established.

Reviews. Equiano published his memoir in 1789. Partly from the contemporary interest in slavery, and partly because Equiano traveled extensively in England to promote the book, *Equiano's Travels* became a bestseller in its day. In 1792, during an eight-month stay in Ireland, Equiano sold 1,900 copies of his book.

Reviews were almost universally favorable. The *Monthly Reviewer* said that "the Narrative wears an honest face; and we have conceived a good opinion of the man, from the artless manner in which he has detailed the variety of adventures and vicissitudes which have fallen to his lot" (Shyllon, p. 234). The *General Magazine and Impartial Reviewer* concurred: "The Narrative appears to be written with much truth and simplicity, and the reader, unless perchance he is either a West-India planter or Liverpool merchant, will find his humanity often severely wounded by the shameless barbarity practised towards the author's hapless countrymen in all our colonies" (Edwards, p. 18).

As the *Impartial Reviewer* suggests, hostility to Equiano came primarily from those devoted to maintaining slavery. Their primary weapon was libel. They attempted to cast aspersions on his character and credibility, recalling the Sierra Leone incident. Anonymous persons even spread the rumor that he had not been born in Africa at all, but was in fact a native of a Dutch colony. However, such claims were instantly discredited, and the newspapers that printed them were forced to retract them and apologize.

—Jacob Littleton

For More Information

Craton, Michael. *Sinews of Empire.* New York: Anchor, 1974.

Craton, Michael, James Walvin, and David Wright, eds. *Slavery, Abolition and Emancipation.* New York: Longman, 1976.

Edwards, Paul. *Unreconciled Strivings: Three Afro-British Authors of the Georgian Era.* Edinburgh: Edinburgh University Press, 1991.

Equiano, Olaudah. *Equiano's Travels: The Interesting Narrative of the Life of Olaudah Equiano or Gustavus Vassa the African.* Ed. Paul Edwards. London: Heinemann, 1967.

File, Nigel, and Chris Power. *Black Settlers in Britain, 1555-1958.* London: Heinemann, 1988.

Rushworth, John. *Historical Collections of Private Passages of State, Weighty Matters in Law, Remarkable Proceedings in Five Parliaments.* Vol. 2. London: John Rushworth, 1721-1722.

Shillington, Kevin. *History of Africa.* New York: St. Martin's Press, 1989.

Shyllon, Folarin. *Black People in Britain, 1555-1833.* Oxford: Oxford University Press, 1977.

Walvin, James. *England, Slaves and Freedom, 1776-1838.* London: Macmillan, 1986.

Wyndham, H. A. *The Atlantic and Emancipation.* Oxford: Oxford University Press, 1937.

The Famished Road

by
Ben Okri

Ben Okri is a Nigerian-born author known for juxtaposing incisive social critique and African mythological tradition. His Booker Prize-winning third novel, *The Famished Road,* exemplifies this duality through its narrator, Azaro, a boy with one foot in the world of modern Nigeria and one foot in the spirit world. Though Okri's novel features Yoruba characters, he is not Yoruba himself but belongs to the Urhobo, another of the more than 200 ethnic groups that make up the Nigerian populace. Born in Minna, Nigeria, in 1959, Okri moved with his family the following year to England. His father studied law there, then returned to Nigeria and served as a lawyer for the inhabitants of Ajegunle, a slum district in Lagos. Ben Okri gained an intimate knowledge there of the complaints of the poor and how they fared in Nigeria's justice system, which would profoundly affect his work. He returned to England to attend university and has lived there ever since, though focusing on Africa in his writing. In 1993 Okri followed *The Famished Road* with a sequel, *Songs of Enchantment,* in which the adventures of Azaro continue.

Events in History at the Time the Novel Takes Place

From colony to nation. Nigeria is a large nation in West Africa, extending from the Atlantic Bay of Benin northeastward into the savanna grasslands that border the Sahara Desert. Its territory contains the homelands of some 200 culturally and linguistically distinct peoples, whose only

THE LITERARY WORK

A novel set in Nigeria around 1960; published in English in 1991.

SYNOPSIS

A boy is pulled between the material world and the spirit world as he witnesses the impact of "progress" and political violence on his impoverished Yoruba community.

unity comes from being included within the arbitrary boundaries drawn by Great Britain, the power that claimed this region as a colony in the late nineteenth century. Of the 200 peoples, the Yoruba predominate in the West, the Igbo in the East, and the Hausa-Fulani in the North. In 1861 the city of Lagos and the surrounding area were officially designated a territory of the British Crown, and from there the colony spread to include all of what is now Nigeria. Officially the British adopted a policy of "indirect rule," meaning they ruled through the traditional leaders, who now owed allegiance to Britain's colonial government. This was the policy in Northern Nigeria among the Fulani people, whose own emirs or rulers still, for example, levied taxes (though they now had to distribute half the revenues to the British). Because of this policy, changes in the daily life of the Fulani were slight compared to the upheavals elsewhere in colonial Africa. But indirect rule was not uniformly applied to Nigeria's peoples. In Eastern Nigeria, the

British instituted "Native Administrations," a system of their own creation imposed on the Igbo people. In the West, among the Yoruba, the notion of controlling the populace through traditional leaders faltered because the people started to take advantage of new economic opportunities introduced by world trade, and many of them "preferred to push for European forms [of rule] which seemed more appropriate to their changing conditions" (Fage, p. 416). In the 1940s a growing African desire for independence, coupled with England's need to scale back on colonial expenditure after World War II, led to the beginnings of Nigerian self-rule. Gradually, under the Richards Constitution of 1946, Nigerians began to participate in the government of Nigeria, at first only in an advisory role. Finally, under the MacPherson Constitution of 1951, elected representatives were granted real legislative power. The country's largeness presented problems, as did the difficulty of bringing so many diverse ethnic groups under one government. The regions developed at different paces, with the West and East attaining self-government in 1957 and the North in 1959. This led to full independence in 1960, which left Nigeria with the problem of how to insure a stable, representative central government. *The Famished Road* is set during the slow, painful emergence from British colonialism and the uncertain aftermath of Nigerian independence.

Yoruba tradition and belief. The Yoruba people are composed of many culturally and linguistically related subgroups scattered over a wide area in southwestern Nigeria and the neighboring nation of Benin. They are traditionally an urban people. Before colonialism, they lived in towns and cities surrounded by farmland and separated by expanses of forested wilderness. Traditionally each town or city was ruled by a hereditary male leader, or *oba,* who operated in a hierarchy that was headed by the supreme oba of Ife, the city from which all Yoruba believe themselves to have originated.

The traditional Yoruba town was walled and at its center sat the palace of the oba. Also near the center was the marketplace, generally a large, open area with a few woven grass structures for the larger traders. Roads extended from the center to the town's periphery and then the farmland beyond. The town itself was divided into administrative units or wards, each consisting of a number of housing compounds. The individual compound, sometimes referred to as an *agbo ile,* or "flock of houses," consisted of several buildings crowded together and surrounded by a wall, or sometimes laid out in a gridlike pattern with alleys running through the compound (Eades, p. 39). It was occupied by a patrilineal kinship group whose head male might have more than one wife, each in her own separate house. After World War II such compounds mostly disappeared; the family instead inhabited one large structure, each wife in her separate quarters.

Central to traditional Yoruba belief is the relationship between earth and heaven—*Aiye* and *Orun,* respectively. *Aiye* is the domain of human beings; *Orun,* the heavenly abode of *orisa* (Yoruba gods) and ancestors (spirits of the Yoruba dead). Aiye and Orun are thought of as continuous domains, and their relationship is symbiotic: the gods and ancestors have a profound effect on living Yoruba, who seek to gain the favor of Orun's inhabitants through frequent sacrifice.

Human beings travel between the spheres of Aiye and Orun via reincarnation. The seeming contradiction between the beliefs that the ancestors reside in Orun and that they reincarnate is reconciled in the concept of the soul. According to Yoruba belief, each individual has, in addition to a physical body, two spiritual components—an *ori* and an *emi*. The emi is an individual's personality in a particular incarnation; the ori is the ultimate destiny of the soul that transcends particular incarnations. While the emi remains in Orun after a person's death, the ori travels to a new incarnation. Descendants continually appeal to their ancestors for guidance and aid, holding a special festival that honors the ancestors, the *egungun* festival. At this festival, certain individuals don masks and costumes from head to toe. They become *egungu*—masqueraders who assume the personas and powers of the ancestors. The belief is that the Yoruba can communicate in a more direct manner than usual with the ancestors via the egungun. Although one's power increases as an ancestor, the Yoruba do not see existence in Orun as preferable to existence in Aiye. In fact, spirits are thought to return to Aiye by choice to reunite with their families. Aiye is also thought to contain certain wayward spirits who do not wish to be incarnated at all and resist life by willing themselves to die in infancy. Such spirits are known as *abiku,* literally "born to die." Beliefs about the abiku child exist among other Nigerian ethnic groups as well; the Igbo, for example, call such a child *ogbanje* (see **Things Fall Apart,** also covered in *African Literature and Its Times*). The Yoruba believe that a particular abiku will be born again and again to the same mother. When a woman gives birth to a series of children who die in infancy, the parents suspect that all of them have been the same abiku child. To encourage a newborn to choose life, parents give the child names such as *Aiyedun,* "life is good," or *Durosinmi,* "stay and bury me." Sometimes they mark the infant with scarification, believing that should the same spirit return, it will be recognizable through these signs. The narrator of *The Famished Road* is an abiku child who forsakes his abiku companions in Orun, choosing instead to stay and experience life in Aiye. One of the methods the Yoruba may invoke to try to keep an abiku child in Aiye is *oogun.* Oogun, a concept that falls somewhere between medicine and magic, refers to remedies, poisons, love potions, truth serums, and invisibility charms, among other paraphernalia. Oogun is a physical substance that can be composed of plant, animal, or mineral materials, and sometimes must be combined with the recitation of a spell. Anyone may use oogun, and most Yoruba have knowledge of at least a few oogun, although some individuals have greater expertise than others. Oogun experts may sell their services, as do the herbalists in *The Famished Road,* or, like Madame Koto in the novel, use oogun for their own purposes.

Ethnic identity and nationalism. When the British Colony and Protectorate of Nigeria came into existence, its various peoples had little concept of statehood. Among most groups, power was very localized, with the village or clan serving as the main focus of individual loyalty. The clan or village was furthermore conceived of in moral terms—only as long as one abided by the norms and traditions of the community did one belong to that community. Loyalty to community was regarded as the paramount virtue. Correspondingly, those outside one's community were viewed with distrust, and any dealings beyond the village or clan were considered risky. Worldly success depended on having successful relatives or members of one's community who would come to one's aid. Those who succeeded were thought to have done so only through the help of the community, and to owe it a debt in return. Thus, the various peoples of Nigeria were much more given to local loyalty—that is, loyalty to one's clan, village, or ethnic group—than to feelings of nationalism. Nigeria's first attempts at a national government are said to have foundered because of personal self-interest and ethnic loyalties. Members of one ethnic group felt little connection with members of other ethnic groups; hence each group sought to forward its own cause with little regard for the nation as a whole.

Party politics. The Richards Constitution of 1946 divided Nigeria into three regions. Each region corresponded to one of Nigeria's three main ethnic groups: the Hausa-Fulani in the North, the Yoruba in the West, and the Igbo in the East. Because the regions had been drawn along these ethnic lines, the many groups who were not among the predominant three, who comprise almost half the Nigerian population, were rendered virtually powerless. Adding to the imbalance of power was the fact that the North was larger in territory and population than the other two regions combined. For this reason, Nigeria is sometimes conceived of as having two main divisions, North and South, the South being composed of the East and the West.

ABIKU

The poem "Abiku" by acclaimed Nigerian writer Wole Soyinka treats the figure at the heart of *The Famished Road,* the "born-to-die" abiku spirit-child. Evoked in the poem is the pain suffered by the parents:

> In vain your bangles cast
> Charmed circles at my feet
> I am Abiku, calling for the first
> And the repeated time. . . .
>
> Night, and Abiku sucks the oil
> From lamps. Mothers! I'll be the
> Suppliant snake coiled on the doorstep
> Yours the killing cry. . . .
>
> (Soyinka, pp. 28-30)

Political parties were first formed in Nigeria in the 1920s, but only in the 1950s, when elections began to be held for political offices that wielded real legislative power, did the parties gain importance. Each region had its own political party. The East had the National Council of Nigeria and the Cameroons (NCNC), a pan-ethnic party whose leaders and members were mainly Igbo but advocated national unity above ethnic affiliation. The Action Group (AG) in the Western region was conceived as the party representing Yoruba interests. However, in order to

Abubakar Tafawa Balewa was Nigeria's first prime minister, serving from 1957 to 1966.

attract support from non-Yoruba voters, the AG modified its image to espouse a progressive, liberal ideology with slogans such as "life more abundant" and "freedom for all" (Dudley, p. 47). The Northern People's Congress (NPC) restricted its membership to "people of Northern Nigerian descent." Its motto was "One North; One People, Irrespective of Religion, Rank or Tribe," but this slogan belied the fact that the NPC was primarily the party of Hausa-Fulani Muslims (Dudley, p. 49).

Unlike the situation in *The Famished Road*, in which the Party of the Poor vies against the Party of the Rich, all three Nigerian parties to greater or lesser degrees claimed to be the party of the disadvantaged and to promote social and economic change. In reality, all three parties, again to varying degrees, used politics for personal enrichment. Whichever party was in power wielded its welfare and development programs selectively, using electricity and piped water to reward communities and individuals that had supported the party in the elections. Besides the big three, many more political parties existed in Nigeria at the time of independence, but the rest were comparatively small and had to satisfy themselves with bartering their support in exchange for concessions from the major parties.

Nigerian government was modeled on the British system. It had a prime minister at its head, and a bicameral legislature, with one house representing regions based on their populations, and another with the same number of senators from each region. In such a system, the counting of the population is a matter of great consequence. The corrupt political parties attempted to grossly inflate the numbers for their respective regions in the Nigerian census of 1962. The result was a chaotic swarm of accusations and counteraccusations, and the census had to be disregarded.

Then came the 1964 elections, in which violence and corruption proliferated. As depicted in the novel, politicians campaigned only in the company of heavily armed bodyguards, and electoral officials were terrorized by political thugs who invoked criminal methods to sway the vote. The thugs intimidated, they maimed, they killed. The election results were hardly a surprise under these circumstances; those in power stayed in power. Nigerian president Dr. Nnamdi Azikiwe reappointed the incumbent prime minister, Tafawa Balewa, offending many Nigerians who felt that the elections were too tainted to be valid.

Dismayed with politics and politicians, the electorate decided in large part to stop paying taxes. On the verge of bankruptcy, the government seized more than half the profits from the one profitable Nigerian export—cocoa. Since more than half of Western Nigeria was engaged in cocoa production, widespread dissatisfaction resulted and farm workers there responded violently, setting fire to the cocoa crops. In October 1965 the West also hosted a failed regional election, in which bribery, looting, arson, murder, "and blatant inflation of election results" were the order of the day (Okafor, p. 33). Lacking the respect even of its own police force, the government was unable to stop the violence. Finally in 1966 the military stepped in and staged a coup, seizing control of the federal government. Nigeria's parliamentary democracy had lasted only five years (1960-66). From 1966 to 1991, when *The Famished Road* was published, Nigeria would experience a series of bloody military coups, with only one brief interval of civilian rule (1979-83).

Life in a changing society. Yoruba towns underwent significant changes beginning in the nineteenth century. By the time the novel takes place, some wealthier residents had built *ile petesi*, "upstairs houses" of two or more stories made of wood and concrete; other houses were still built of mud, but their thatch roofs had been replaced with aluminum or iron. An ile petesi might have electricity, running water, and toilet facilities. Occupants of mud homes, on the other hand, might have to fetch water from rivers or share a centrally located tap and to relieve themselves in bucket latrines. In a few places, such as Lagos, the excrement would be emptied nightly in the forest by "nightsoil" men. Certain Yoruba towns—such as Lagos, Ibadan, and Abeokuta—became densely populated cities. One factor attracting migration to large cities was the Nigerian government's educational program. The national government made education one of its top priorities, dedicating over 20 percent of its annual budget to this cause, while regional governments spent as much as 45 percent of their budgets on education. Most funds went toward primary schooling, however, and many who completed it found themselves unable to obtain a secondary or higher education. These primary school graduates often deemed agricultural work beneath them, yet they were insufficiently educated to qualify for government, clerical, or technical jobs. Such people flocked to the cities looking for work, which they usually did not find. The contrast between rich and poor widened. Comprising the urban majority were low-wage-earners living in slums.

Another factor contributing to urban economic disparity was a national policy encouraging private enterprise among indigenous Nigerians. Several lending institutions were provided with public funds to loan to private businesses. The institutions were controlled by government personnel and were prey to the same corruption and ethnic or clan loyalty that pervaded Nigerian politics. Thus, money was lent to individuals based on other than financial criteria and many loans went unrecovered. Moreover, the lenders exerted little control or supervision over how the money was used. Many investors put their money into substandard urban housing, intending to turn a quick profit by charging extremely high rents. This created a small class of wealthy landlords who used their political connections to obtain public funds, without contributing anything back through taxation, since Nigeria had no property tax at this time. The high cost of unregulated urban rents, combined with the expectation that city dwellers should help support their poorer relations in the countryside, made it virtually impossible for low-wage-earners to amass any savings to improve their status or that of their children. So there was little class mobility. Poor urban dwellers, such as Azaro's family in *The Famished Road,* had to struggle just to survive from day to day.

The Novel in Focus

Plot summary. *The Famished Road* begins in the "land of beginnings," a realm from which spirits are born into the world of the living, and to which spirits return after death (Okri, *The Famished Road*, p. 3). Some spirits, the abiku, make pacts with one another that they will return to their friends in the land of beginnings shortly after they are born by willing their own deaths. The narrator is an abiku who has died in infancy and been reborn many times. Although he has sworn to return to his fellow abikus at the first opportunity, at the novel's beginning he chooses to live.

THE CONDITIONS OF UNDERDEVELOPMENT

"Governments in developing countries have tended to be preoccupied with power and its material perquisites. Given the conditions of under-development, power offers the opportunity of a lifetime to rise above the general level of poverty and squalor that pervade the society. It provides a rare opportunity to acquire wealth and prestige, to be able to distribute benefits in the form of jobs, contracts, scholarships and gifts of money and so on to one's relatives and political allies. Such is the pre-occupation with power and its material benefits that political ideals as to how society can be organized and ruled to the best advantage of all hardly enter into the calculation."

(*Nigerian Constitution Drafting Committee Report,* 1976, paragraph 2.2-1)

In life, the narrator maintains a close connection to the spirit world because of his abiku nature. He can read minds, foretell the future, and understand the language of animals. His spirit companions constantly visit and entreat him to honor his pact and return to their realm. When the narrator refuses, the abikus torment him and even attempt to trick him into death. After his spirit companions lure him into some filthy water, he contracts a serious illness and does in fact die, but his will to live is so strong that, while being carried to his grave, he miraculously revives. His parents, who live in an unnamed part of Africa, call him Lazaro, a variation on Lazarus, the biblical figure whom Jesus raised from the dead. Because the association makes his neighbors uncomfortable, Lazaro is renamed Azaro.

One night when Azaro is still a child, there is a fire in the poor neighborhood where his family lives. All the buildings burn down. The landlord arrives and accuses his tenants of committing arson to avoid paying the newly increased rents, then demands they pay the damages. As the tenants begin leaving to find places to stay for the night, the police arrive and start flogging them. A riot ensues in which the family is separated. Azaro encounters a terrifying egungun masquerade and is abducted by several of its female attendants.

The women take Azaro to a small island where they treat him well, but it becomes clear that they are witches. A cat warns Azaro that he is to be a part of an unpleasant ritual and should flee. With the help of a fellow captive, he escapes and returns to the mainland. There he has disorienting visions of spirits whom most people cannot sense. When his abiku companions lure Azaro onto an expressway, he collapses and is taken to a police station. Azaro goes to live with a police officer, who offers to care for the boy until his parents are found.

The police officer and his wife provide Azaro with comforts that his poor parents could never offer. Azaro soon senses, however, a terrible presence in the house—the spirits of people whom the police officer has killed, one of whom is his own son, a boy about Azaro's age. When the officer's wife begins calling Azaro by the name of her dead son, Azaro decides to leave. He sends a psychic message to his mother, "Mum," who soon appears at the front door and takes him to the family's new home.

Azaro is reunited with his father, "Dad," who, having challenged the police during the postfire riots, was imprisoned and badly beaten. Dad takes Azaro into the forest outside their town and tells him, "sooner than you think there won't be one tree standing. There will be no forest left at all. And there will be wretched houses all over the place" (*Famished Road,* p. 34). Next Dad takes Azaro to a palm-wine bar where Dad engages another man in a game of draughts. Both men bet and drink heavily, and when Dad wins, his opponent becomes so enraged that he leaves the bar without paying his tab. The bar's proprietress, Madame Koto, follows the man into the street and tackles him to the ground, takes the money, and strips him of his trousers for good measure. A crowd of onlookers is awed by her prodigious strength.

In honor of Azaro's return, his parents throw a party for the neighborhood. Many more people attend—most of them uninvited—than Azaro's parents can afford to entertain. Dad quickly goes into debt buying drinks for the crowd, who wreck his house in a drunken frenzy. The next day Dad hunts for work, and Mum sets up shop in front of the house, where she sells "provisions." The family's creditors come to demand payment. Although the family has no money, the creditors, all of whom attended the party the night before, harass Mum, who grows ill with malaria. When Dad learns of the creditors' behavior, he insults them in the street. They nevertheless return the next day and, although Mum is still ill, encourage their children to throw things at her. With the help of Madame Koto and an herbalist, Mum survives, but the family falls further into debt in order to pay for her medication.

The one creditor who does not demand repayment is Madame Koto, who asks in lieu of money that Azaro spend time in her bar. Madame Koto believes he has "good luck" and hopes it will attract customers. Soon the bar is full, but the new clientele is mostly from the spirit world; they are drawn to the bar at least in part by a desire to take Azaro back to their realm. Like Azaro, Madame Koto can see the spirits, and their appearances are bizarre. One has eyes that are totally white, another has three fingers on each hand and a head that "was like a tuber of yam" (*Famished Road,* p. 109). They are spirits who, to participate in human reality, have borrowed bits of human beings. Two albino spirits bundle Azaro into a sack and carry him far away, but he escapes and finds his way home.

After his abduction, Azaro is reluctant to return to Madame Koto's bar, and instead tries to earn money by running errands. His father lands a job as a load carrier. One day Azaro sees his father working for a lorry garage where "if you want to vote for the party that supports the poor [as Dad does], they give you the heaviest load" (*Famished Road,* p. 81). Azaro watches as the foremen pile staggering loads onto Dad's head and shoulders, taunting him all the while. It is excruciating work that lasts from before Azaro awakens until after he lies down at night. Still, Mum and Dad can't earn enough to pay off the creditors who continue to harass the family. Dad alleviates his shame and frustration by bullying and occasionally beating Mum.

Meanwhile, the forest has been changing. "Bushes were being burnt, tall grasses cleared, tree stumps uprooted.... Houses appeared where parts of the forest had been" (Famished Road, p. 104). Azaro stumbles into a place where "the forest ... had been conquered" and observes a group of workers connecting electrical cable; for the first time he also observes a white man, giving "bad-tempered orders in an unfamiliar language," and sees the illumination of a lightbulb (Famished Road, pp. 276, 278). Soon the rainy season comes and washes away the electrical cables as well as the white man, who is drowned in the deluge.

One day a van arrives in Azaro's neighborhood, bearing politicians from the Party of the Rich, who shout campaign promises into megaphones and distribute free powdered milk to the hungry masses. The residents scoff at the campaign promises but fight for the milk. Some men rush the van. Many are hurt in the scuffle, and the politicians panic, driving off in a shower of coins they have scattered as a diversionary tactic. A photographer who ekes out a living selling pictures to the neighborhood captures it all on film. The next day everyone in the neighborhood but Azaro's family is horribly ill. Dad concludes that since everyone but his family drank the politicians' milk, it must be to blame. He strides down the streets, proclaiming that the milk, like politics, is rotten. Anger and disillusionment increase in the neighborhood.

A short while later the van of the Party of the Rich returns with more free food. This time the people hurl stones and insults at the politicians, whose thugs retaliate with whips and sticks. The people wrest the weapons from the thugs, sending them running and then gleefully burning the van. Once more the photographer takes pictures of everything, eventually publishing the pictures—one of which features Mum—in a national newspaper. The people of the neighborhood marvel that "something we did with such absence of planning ... could gain such prominence"; they begin to see themselves as heroes (Famished Road, p. 156). The photographer hides in Azaro's home to escape the political thugs, who hunt for him. When they can't find him, they terrorize the neighborhood for hiding the photographer, who finally leaves "to travel all the roads of the world" (Famished Road, p. 262).

Things continue to worsen for Azaro's family. The landlord demands that his parents vote for his party, the Party of the Rich, and when they refuse, their rent is increased. Azaro once again sees his father at work, this time as a "nightsoil" man, carrying pails of human excrement into the

forest. Azaro also sees Mum being thrown out of the marketplace, where she now rents a space to sell her wares. The men who eject her shout, "If you don't belong to our party you don't belong to this space in the market," while a bystander comments, "This Independence has brought only trouble," referring to Nigeria's independence in 1960 (Famished Road, pp. 168, 169). The neighborhood turns against Azaro's family after the Party of the Rich says they are troublemakers. They are to blame, says the Party, for all the harassment that has followed the hiding of the photographer.

Meanwhile, Madame Koto prospers when her bar becomes the favored meeting place of the Party of the Rich. As she grows richer, she also grows fatter and more arrogant. The denizens of the community marvel as her bar acquires electric lights, a phonograph, and prostitutes to serve her new clientele. At one point Azaro has a vision in which he sees that in her womb Madame Koto is carrying three abiku babies who are struggling not to be born—a trinity that echoes the three regions of Nigeria. Later, a friend of Azaro's makes the parallel clear with a statement: "Our country is an abiku country. Like the spirit-child, it keeps coming and going. One day it will decide to remain. It will become strong" (Famished Road, p. 478). Whenever Dad goes to the bar, the Party of the Rich asks him to leave and a fight ensues; Dad, refusing to be bullied, keeps returning. Madame Koto gives Azaro money for his family, requesting that he never reveal that it comes from her.

Azaro's spirit companions trick him into breaking a window in the home of a sinister old blind man in a wheelchair. The blind man comes to Mum and Dad to demand payment, which they can ill afford. When Azaro blames the spirits, his parents become angry and beat him. In a sullen rage, Azaro refuses to eat and grows weaker and weaker, gradually drifting away from the world of the living. A three-headed spirit beguiles him down a road to the spirit world with promises of a happier life; it is only with the intervention of three herbalists that Mum and Dad are able to bring Azaro back to the world of the living.

Dad trains in earnest to be a boxer. He spends all his free time shadow-boxing and practicing footwork, taking a special boxing name: Black Tyger. A dead boxer from the spirit world challenges Dad, and, after an excruciating struggle, Dad defeats him. Sometime later Dad fights seven men at once and wins. Then a huge bodyguard, "the Green Leopard," challenges Dad. Dad beats him, but is seriously injured in the fight and goes to sleep for three days, during which he struggles to stay alive. When he awakens, he speaks of "grand schemes" (*Famished Road*, p. 408). He plans to run for Head of State and goes door to door soliciting votes. Everyone, including his family, thinks him mad.

To celebrate his boxing victory, Dad throws a party. A group of beggars attend. Then, much to the chagrin of the residents, the beggars, who are crippled and deformed, come to the neighborhood to stay. Dad declares them to be his constituency and tries to put them to work beautifying the neighborhood, but his ill-conceived plans fail. The Party of the Rich and the Party of the Poor step up their campaigns, making identical promises. When Madame Koto throws a celebration for her Party of the Rich friends, Dad shows up uninvited. A fight breaks out when he rushes to the defense of the beggars, who are stealing food. Suddenly a tall, thin man in a white suit challenges him to a fight. Dad accepts. The man in white fights with seemingly supernatural strength. Dad is outmatched until he tears off the man's suit, revealing his opponent to be covered with hair "like that of a bush animal" (*Famished Road*, p. 473). Without the suit and mocked by the bystanders for his inhuman appearance, the man loses his powers and Dad wins, then collapses in exhaustion.

Once again, Dad sleeps for several days, time he spends "redreaming the world" (*Famished Road*, p. 492). In his dreams, Dad sees the world and its injustices very clearly. He argues passionately in the courts of the spirit world "for justice and balance and beauty in the world, for an end to famishment and vile wars, destruction and greed," but his arguments are futile because "other spheres of higher energies have their justice beyond our understanding" (*Famished Road*, p. 493). Meanwhile, Mum has her own aspirations, which she seeks to realize through prayer: "She prayed for food. She prayed for Dad to get well. She prayed for a good place to live. She prayed for more life and for suffering to bear lovely fruits" (*Famished Road*, p. 493). When Dad awakens from redreaming the world, he tells his family, "A single thought of ours could change the universe" (*Famished Road*, p. 497). Dad believes that struggles in the spirit world affect this world and vice versa, that harshness here is created by the limitations in people's minds. Azaro concludes that "a dream can be the highest point of a life," thus emphasizing the importance of the spirit world and its connection to this world (*Famished Road*, p. 500).

The famished road. "In the beginning there was a river. The river became a road and the road branched out to the whole world. And because the road was once a river it was always hungry" (*Famished Road*, p. 3). The contrast between river and road has important implications in African literature. Scholar Margaret Cezair-Thompson points out that roads often appear in colonial-era fiction as a symbol of "the colonizer's penetration of the African wilderness" (Cezair-Thompson, p. 33). In the forests of *The Famished Road*, roads are built under white overseers and nature is gradually destroyed. An old man complains: "Too many roads! Things are CHANGING TOO FAST!...THEY ARE DESTROYING AFRICA! They are DESTROYING the WORLD and the HOME and the SHRINES and the GODS!" (*Famished Road*, p. 382). The natural world retaliates, however, and in the rainy season "the road became what it used to be, a stream of primeval mud, a river" (*Famished Road*, p. 286).

But why is the road famished? Okri probably took his title from a line in Wole Soyinka's poem "Death in the Dawn" that reads, "May you never walk / when the road waits, famished" (Soyinka, p. 11). And why is the famished road dangerous? Soyinka wrote about the famished road after witnessing, while driving, first the death of a white bird smashed against his windshield and then the death of a motorist in a car crash. Later in the poem he speaks of "the wrathful wings of man's Progression." Like the roads in colonial-era fiction, then, Soyinka's road is linked to the destruction of nature and traditional Africa through modernization (Soyinka, p. 11). In his play entitled *The Road*, Soyinka more fully explores the hungry road as a metaphor. Okri's road has a meaning somewhat different from Soyinka's. In *The Famished Road*, Dad tells Azaro about the King of the Road, a giant with an insatiable appetite who demands sacrifice of anyone who wishes to walk the roads of the world. For a long time, people sacrifice to the King and are allowed to travel the roads in peace. Then, one day, famine strikes and people stop sacrificing to him because they have no food to spare. The King kills those who dare to venture onto the roads and he kills those who stay in their homes, so the people try to reason with him. They bring him large sacrifices, but to no avail. The King eats people anyway. Finally, the people poison the King, and the poison makes him desperately hungry so that he ends up eating everything he can, including himself. In the end all that is left is a stomach, and when the rains come, the stomach melts into the road. The King has now become a part of all the roads in the world, and his appetite can never be appeased.

The story recalls the Yoruba orisa, Ogun, who is, among other things, the Guardian of the Road. Ogun was the original ruler of Ife, the first Yoruba city. One day in a fit of anger he killed some of his human subjects and then, in remorse, killed himself. Upon his death, Ogun was absorbed into the earth. The King of the Road recalls as well "the hungry creature" in Nigerian author Amos Tutuola's 1952 novel, *The Palm-Wine Drinkard* (also covered in *African Literature and Its Times*). The hungry creature, like the King of the Road, is insatiable, as is the protagonist himself, the Palm-Wine Drinkard. Drinkard is a young man who does nothing all day but drink prodigious quantities of palm wine. In his gluttony, he neglects to sacrifice to the spirits of his ancestors, a profound oversight by Yoruba standards. In Tutuola's novel, sacrifice is the solution that restores balance to the world, but in Okri's novel, sacrifice is no solution to the problem of the King of the Road. Perhaps the old ways, the traditional ways in which sacrifice plays an important part, will no longer work, and one must take one's chances, like the photographer who bravely sets forth "to travel all the roads of the world," claiming, "I am not afraid of the King" (*Famished Road*, p. 262). To some extent, tradition is what has kept Nigeria rooted in ethnic factionalism, unable to form a nation in spirit. The photographer integrates newness into his life, exemplified in his use of modern technology, in a way that allows him to connect with the world outside his small neighborhood, publishing pictures of its struggle in a national newspaper.

Another view is offered later in the novel, when Azaro has a vision of a road being built in the spirit world. This road is very beautiful and very short. The spirits who build it can never finish the road, for "the road is their soul, the soul of their history" (*Famished Road*, p. 329). Perhaps the road is existence, which must be chosen by the abiku child in order to fulfill his destiny, and must be chosen by Nigeria, by the three regions struggling like Madame Koto's abiku triplets, in order to become a nation.

Sources and literary context. *The Famished Road* has been seen as an African example of magical realism, a literary genre generally associated with Latin American writers. African writers tend to reject the magical realist label as indicating an imitation of the work of Latin Americans. The genre has, however, been perhaps more accurately conceived as not a Latin American creation per se, but rather a form suited to postcolonial societies. Magical realism combines the supernatural elements of a traditional worldview with events in earthly history, including developments in modern technology, and thus reflects the experience of a society in transition. Postcolonial societies tend to have "encountered Western capitalism, technology and education haphazardly," so that two worlds intermingle in unique fashion, combining the old and the new ways within a single community or a single family (Cooper, p. 15). In *The Famished Road*, for example, Dad is a carrier at a city lorry garage while his father is a priest of the shrine of the roads in a village.

Okri draws upon ethnic beliefs and practices, most notably in his main character, Azaro, the abiku child. The recounting of Azaro's adventures with the spirits can be seen as a continuation of a literary tradition of supernatural adventures that began with authors D. O. Fagunwa (*The Forest of the Thousand Demons* [1939] and *The Forest of God* [1946] in Yoruba), and Amos Tutuola (*The Palm-Wine Drinkard* [1952] and *My Life in the Bush of Ghosts* [1954] in English). By merging the mythic with the mundane, the tradition evokes the nature of reality in various Nigerian societies. Building on this literary tradition, Okri's novel expands it to include political and social realities of his day, extending it into the postcolonial era in Nigeria.

Events in History at the Time the Novel Was Written

Military rule in Nigeria. Staging the coup of January 1966 in Nigeria was a group of five young army majors from the South—four Igbo and one Yoruba. Their coup was at first welcomed by the populace. The rebels conducted it as "a pan-Nigerian, trans-ethnic project whose purpose was fully articulated by its leader, Major Chukwuma Kadunza Nzeogwu: 'Our enemies are the political profiteers, swindlers, the men in high and low places that seek bribes and demand 10 per cent . . . , rotten and corrupt ministers, political parties, trade unions, and the whole apparatus of the new Federal System'" (Okafor, pp. 33-34). The coup, in other words, aimed to eliminate the two threats to beneficial nationhood that had overtaken Nigeria: ethnic- and self-promotion. The initial elation dwindled, though. People began to say that the young army majors

Ben Okri holding his novel *The Famished Road,* which won the prestigious Booker Prize in 1991.

had deceived Nigeria; they intended not to reset the nation on a stable and just course, but had engineered the coup to place the Igbos in power nationwide. Six months later army leaders from Northern Nigeria staged a countercoup, followed by mass executions of the Igbo. The Igbo fled east, then seceded and established their own republic, Biafra. The result was a bloody 30-month civil war (May 1967-January 1970), at the end of which Biafra surrendered, its patriots disenchanted. Up to 2 million people (mainly Igbo) had perished in the fighting, and to what avail? The remnant survived to see their ideals being betrayed in Biafra itself, notes one historian. Its leaders were succumbing to the same temptations that had diverted Nigeria from genuine democracy; they "transferred loyalty . . . from the

nation to the self" (Nwankwo in Okafor, p. 37). In Nigeria, the 1966 countercoup against the coup of the five young army majors had brought to power Lieutenant Colonel Yakuba Gowon, whose regime is remembered for its corruption and greed. Although federal revenues rose some 1,500 percent during Gowon's term, the condition of the average Nigerian changed very little. Gowon promised to relinquish the government to civilian rule by 1976 but later called this goal unrealistic, proposing to rule indefinitely. In 1975 he was overthrown by senior army officers, and they installed Murtala Mohammed as the new military head of state. Over the course of military rule in Nigeria, government corruption became even more pronounced than it was under civilian rule. The period saw an oil boom in

Nigeria and a concomitant decline in agriculture, the exports of which plummeted from 61.6 percent of total domestic exports under civilian rule to a mere 4.6 percent by 1975. The quality of life in the rural areas declined accordingly. Whereas agriculture had been controlled for the most part by Nigerians, the oil industry was dominated by foreign investors. Through the sale of oil rights to foreigners, the military regime grew rich, but most of the wealth did not reach the larger population. Without accountability to the public—there were no elections—corruption went unchecked.

Murtala Mohammed constituted a federal election commission during his term and in 1979 Nigeria returned briefly to civilian rule when Al-haji Shehu Shagari was elected president. Shagari was overthrown, however, in 1983 by yet another military coup that placed Major General Mohammadu Buhari in power; Buhari was in turn brought down by a coup in 1985 that brought General Ibrahim Babangida to power. Babangida promised to return Nigeria to civilian rule by 1990, but then changed the year to 1992. In 1991, when *The Famished Road* was published, the military still ruled. Ethnic factionalism had dragged the nation through a civil war and a series of bloody military coups. Nigeria had yet to achieve unified nationhood; the abiku nation had yet to choose existence.

Reviews. *The Famished Road* was widely praised in 1991, and received the Booker Prize for fiction that year. Okri was lauded for his use of the abiku child as a metaphor for the birth struggles of postcolonial Nigeria, but faulted for a tendency to "draw attention to his messages" by explaining them (Appiah, p. 147). Critic Tom Wilhelmus was initially put off by the strangeness inherent in the juxtaposition of historical Nigeria and the timeless realm of the spirits, feeling that "nothing connected, nothing was subordinated, and every experience seemed as important as every other" (Wilhelmus, p. 247). Yet the same

reviewer appreciated how the novel's structure conveyed the complex relationship between realms that is a part of the Yoruba worldview. Other critics likewise admired the novel's interweaving of events in the physical and spirit realms: "For Okri, in a curious way, the world of spirits is not metaphorical or imaginary; rather, it is more real than the world of the everyday" (Appiah, p. 147). Along these same lines, in the *London Observer,* Linda Grant wrote that "Okri's gift is to present a world view from inside a belief system" (Grant, p. 61).

—Kimberly Ball

For More Information

Appiah, K. Anthony. "Spiritual Realism." *The Nation* 255, no. 4 (August 3-10, 1992): 146-48.

Cezair-Thompson, Margaret. "Beyond the Postcolonial Novel: Ben Okri's *Famished Road* and Its 'Abiku' Traveler." *The Journal of Commonwealth Literature* 31, no. 2 (1996): 33-45.

Cooper, Brenda. *Magical Realism in West Africa: Seeing With a Third Eye.* London: Routledge, 1998.

Dudley, Billy. *An Introduction to Nigerian Government and Politics.* Bloomington: Indiana University Press, 1982.

Eades, J. S. *The Yoruba Today.* Cambridge: Cambridge University Press, 1980.

Fage, J. D. *A History of Africa.* 3rd ed. London: Routledge, 1995.

Grant, Linda. Review of *The Famished Road,* by Ben Okri. *The Observer,* 27 October 1991, p. 61.

Nigerian Constitution Drafting Committee. *Nigerian Constitution Drafting Committee Report.* Lagos: Ministry of Information, 1976.

Okafor, Dubem. *The Dance of Death: Nigerian History and Christopher Okigbo's Poetry.* Trenton, N. J.: Africa World Press, 1998.

Okri, Ben. *The Famished Road.* New York: Anchor, 1993.

Soyinka, Wole. *Idanre and Other Poems.* London: Methuen, 1967.

Wilhelmus, Tom. "Time and Distance." *The Hudson Review* 45, no. 1 (spring 1993): 247-52, 254-55.

Fantasia: An Algerian Cavalcade

by
Assia Djebar

A ssia Djebar was born Fatima-Zohra Imalayen in 1936 in Cherchell, Algeria (a small coastal town 60 miles west of Algiers), where her father was a schoolteacher. Djebar was encouraged by her father to continue her studies beyond the age at which most Algerian Muslim girls were withdrawn from school by their families. She completed secondary school in Algeria, then began her university studies in Paris, becoming the first Algerian woman to be admitted to the prestigious École Normale Supérieure de Sèvres. Djebar interrupted her studies in 1956 during the Algerian student strike that affirmed student solidarity with Algeria's independence struggle. Instead of taking her final exams, she wrote her first novel, *La Soif* (1957; *The Mischief*, 1958), which was followed by *Les Impatients* (1958). Both works deal with a young Algerian girl's coming of age in colonial Algeria. Her two subsequent novels, *Les Enfants du nouveau monde* (1962) and *Les Alouettes naives* (1967), which describe women coming to political awareness during the Algerian war, established her position as a leading Algerian novelist. *Fantasia: An Algerian Cavalcade* was the first volume to be released in a projected quartet that encompasses both historical and autobiographical themes.

Events in History at the Time the Novel Takes Place

Conquest of Algeria. Before the nineteenth-century French invasion, the Turks of the Ottoman

---

THE LITERARY WORK

A novel set in Algeria from 1830 to 1962; published in French in 1985 (as *L'amour, la fantasia*), in English in 1993.

SYNOPSIS

The novel interweaves three narratives: written accounts of the Algerian defeat of 1830 recorded by French soldiers and journalists; oral accounts of rural Algerian women who recall their participation in the independence struggle of 1954 to 1962; and autobiographical fragments of the author's own experience growing up in colonial Algeria.

Empire ruled Algeria indirectly through indigenous leaders and urban aristocratic families. A council of notables elected Algeria's *dey*, or Ottoman ruler. On April 29, 1827, the French consul in Algiers paid a visit of protocol to Hussein Dey, who reminded the consul that the king of France owed him an unpaid debt. Apparently when the French diplomat replied that the king would not lower himself to correspond with the dey, the dey struck the consul with a fly whisk. Although the dey later explained that he was angry with the diplomat and not with the French king, Charles X seized upon this pretext to send a fleet of French ships to blockade the port of Algiers. The dey retaliated by destroying two French trading posts. By 1830 the French prime minister, Prince Jules de Polignac, had succeeded in convincing the monarch that an invasion of Algeria would boost his flagging popularity. Under attack, the Algerian forces launched a counterattack led by Agha Brahim, the dey's son-in-law. The counterattack failed. On July 4, 1830, Turkish soldiers were forced to evacuate Sultan Kalassi, or Fort l'Empereur, the main fortification protecting the harbor of Algiers. They chose to destroy the remnants of their fort as they retreated rather than let it fall into enemy hands. On July 5, 1830, power was transferred from the Ottomans to the French. Any claim that the French had come to liberate the country from the Turks was meaningless in the face of the French soldiers' destruction of Algiers. The French military sacked the city as frightened Algerians fled.

PROUD HERITAGE

Djebar is a descendant of the Beni Menacer ethnic group. One of her ancestors, Mohammed Ben Aissa El Berkani, fought with the Algerian nationalist Emir Abdelkader in the 1840s. Her great-grandfather, Malek Sahraoui El Berkani, led a rebellion against the French in 1871 and was killed in battle.

Algerian resistance following the conquest.
Although the dey of Algiers surrendered, resistance against the French continued from 1830 through 1871. The population, however, was widely dispersed, and antagonisms and suspicions proliferated among various factions, which made the resistance less than unified. Yet nationalist heroes did emerge in this period. In the late 1830s, Emir Abdelkader rallied the populations of western and central Algeria, and Ahmed Bey managed to block French expansion in the east. But these two nationalist leaders clashed with each other, divided in part by personal ambitions, in part by conflicting ideology. The son of an Ottoman Turk, Ahmed Bey stood for a reformed hierarchy dominated by an aristocracy, whereas Emir Abdelkader had a more egalitarian vision. After both had been defeated, the struggle for Algeria continued in the cities, in smaller interior towns, and in distant regions: the mountains, deserts, and oases. The French military proceeded to seize the best Algerian lands for French settlers, pushing Algerians off their hold-

ings and into the less fertile interior. A major Algerian uprising in 1871 ended in defeat, which led to further expropriation of lands by French colonizers, and a period of extreme poverty and hardship for the indigenous population. With Algerian resistance crushed, the country's former Turkish elite was silenced.

At the turn of the twentieth century, however, resistance assumed a different tone, influenced by Algerian exposure to European education. Now convinced that French colonialism was there to stay, Algerian families began to enroll their children in French schools. Only 2 percent of the school-age Muslim children were in French primary schools in 1882, but the figure climbed to 5 percent by 1914. With education in the French school system came a developing political consciousness. A group called the Young Algerians emerged at the turn of the century, forming cultural clubs and founding newspapers. Its first collective action consisted of sending a delegation to Paris in 1908 to negotiate compensation for Algerians who had completed their military service and were awaiting pensions from the French government. As economic conditions worsened in the country, the budding Algerian nationalist movement grew. An Islamic reform movement developed under Shaykh Ben Badis, a leader whose early 1900s slogan, "Islam is my religion, Arabic is my language, Algeria is my nation," became Algeria's official motto decades later at independence. Ben Badis and his followers called for a revitalization of Islam in Algeria. In their search for cultural authenticity, they were critical of Algerians who had espoused French culture and values, and of the Islamic brotherhoods, who, in their view, promoted ignorance and superstition. Other leaders of the period include the most widely heard voice for assimilation, that of Ferhat Abbas. In time Abbas would shift from advocating full integration of Algeria into France to promoting a Muslim Algeria in close cooperation with France. He championed for the moment greater equality between Algeria's Muslims and its European colonists. Messali Hadj, a leader of Algerian workers in France, in 1926 formed a pro-independence political organization, the *Étoile Nord-Africaine*. Committed to independence and opposed to capitalism, Hadj's revolutionary party forged links to the French communist party. Algerian political groups remained divided and, for the most part, ineffective until World War II's Allied landing in North Africa in 1942. France was dependent upon the United States in this landing. The weakened sta-

Inspection of Algerian soldiers, circa 1957.

tus of the French nation gave nationalist movements the hope that Algerian independence would follow Allied victory in Europe.

Uprisings of Sétif and Guelma. On May 8, 1945, Ferhat Abbas's political organization, AML (*Amis du Manifeste de la Liberté*), led mostly peaceful protest marches throughout the country in the attempt to improve economic conditions. In two cities in Eastern Algeria, Guelma and Sétif, violence erupted when national flags, which had been banned by the French colonial government, suddenly appeared. Although the French government counted 1,500 Algerian lives lost in the violence, Algerian nationalists contested the figure as a gross understatement, claiming 45,000 dead. The French-controlled government promptly disbanded the AML, after which the French and Algerian communities grew further apart.

The Algerian Revolution: 1954-62. By 1954 Algerian political activists were committed to fighting for independence from France. They launched the FLN (*Front de Libération Nationale*), initiating armed rebellion throughout Algeria on November 1, 1954. The most successful operation took place in the Aurès, a mountainous region in eastern Algeria, where the rebels killed several Europeans and attacked French military installations. The French Army and French colo-

nial civilians responded by violently repressing the indigenous population.

The Battle of Algiers, a campaign waged by Algerian militants in the colonial seaport capital in 1957, began when three Algerian women successfully placed bombs in strategic locations in the European section of the city. The struggle between the French military and Algerian militants is well presented in Gillo Pontecorvo's *Battle of Algiers* (1968), a film that reveals the importance of women's participation in the liberation movement.

FROM OFF-SCREEN INFERNO TO ON-SCREEN SENSATION

Produced in 1965 in black-and-white by Gillo Pontecorvo, *The Battle of Algiers* opens in 1957. A prisoner tortured by the French informs on a member of the FLN resistance. Surrounding the member's residence, French authorities threaten to blow him and his colleagues up unless he surrenders. The film then flashes back to 1954 and the onset of the conflict. Shot at actual locations in Algeria, *The Battle of Algiers* uses local Algerians as actors. The motion picture won an Academy Award nomination for best foreign film of the year.

During the entire seven years of the conflict, war was waged simultaneously in the city and the countryside. The Algerian revolutionary organization divided the country into six wilayas (districts), which were further subdivided into zones, regions, sectors, and circles. The goal of this form of organization was to mobilize the entire Algerian population and generate guerrilla activity everywhere. Violence did indeed spread throughout the country, as evidenced, for example, by the Philippeville massacre of August 20, 1955, in which approximately 80 Algerian guerrillas attacked and killed 100 European civilians in the mining town of El-Halia. The French army responded with overwhelming violence, killing approximately 12,000 Algerians (Ruedy, pp. 162-63).

Although Algerian activists failed in military campaigns against the professionally trained French army, French public opinion turned against the war. In France, people began to question this protracted war waged at the expense of so many young French lives and reacted with outrage to reports that the French military were torturing Algerian civilians. The official French figures for casualties were 13,000 French lives lost, and 100,000 Algerian (Kraft, p. 99). At its high point, the number of French soldiers in the field is said to have reached 500,000 (Smith, p. 173). In the face of growing opposition, French president Charles de Gaulle called for a referendum to be held on January 8, 1961, asking the French if they approved of self-determination for Algeria. Although only 60 percent of the French population went to the polls, 75 percent cast affirmative votes (Ruedy, p. 179). As Algerian independence appeared inevitable, an extremist group of French colonists, the OAS (*Organisation de l'Armée Secrète*) became more and more destructive. On March 15, 1962, for example, a group of OAS militants stormed into the École des Instituteurs de Bouzaréah, a teacher training school in Algiers, and murdered the writer Mouloud Feraoun, a teacher in the school, along with several of his colleagues. (Feraoun's diary, published posthumously, records his daily struggle to maintain a life of normalcy and dignity as the war drew to a close and France was preparing to negotiate Algerian independence.) The OAS campaign of violence was a last desperate attempt to forestall what the majority in France now desired. On July 5, 1962, 132 arduous years after the French first captured Algiers from the Turkish dey, Algeria gained its independence from France.

Role of women in the Algerian War. The women who participated in the Algerian War were of different ages, social origins, and geographical regions. Most remained anonymous, although a few became well-known historical figures. Djamila Bouhired, Zohra Drif, Djamila Boupacha, and Hassiba Ben Bouali are familiar to Algerians as women who contributed to the struggle for independence.

When the war broke out in 1954, the majority of Algerian women lived in villages and most were illiterate. There were 10,949 women in the war effort, 3.1 percent of all those taking part in active combat (Amrane-Minne, "Women and Politics," p. 62). About 2,000 Algerian women joined the *maquis,* the armed national resistance. These women, half of whom were less than 20 years old, lived and worked side-by-side with male resistance fighters and, by doing so, broke the bonds that fettered women who remained subject to a traditional way of life (Amrane-Minne, "Women and Politics," p. 63). Female activists mostly cared for the needs of the freedom fighters—cooking meals; transporting water, food, medical supplies, and weapons; and tending to the wounded. Women also became advisors, informing other women in the civilian population about the political situation, and participated in the fighting. Historian Danièle Amrane-Minne cites a note, for example, from one woman's journal: "At 4PM we learned of the death of my dear sister Ghanoudja. After having killed two soldiers, she died for the country" (Amrane-Minne, *Femmes au combat,* p. 73, trans. M. Mortimer).

While most women worked in rural areas, where the majority of Algerians lived, others worked in urban areas under heavy French military control. Some were veiled, but others dressed as Europeans to infiltrate French sectors of Algerian cities. During the Battle of Algiers, the French military campaign waged in that city from January through September 1957, Algerian women became key figures in transporting weapons and supplies to guerrillas in the city and the surrounding countryside.

The Novel in Focus

Plot summary: an overview. This nonlinear novel weaves together three components: autobiography, the conquest of 1830 (as recorded in French historical archives), and the war of liberation (as told in oral narratives of Arabic-speaking Algerian women whose voices Djebar recorded and translated into French). The novel is organized into three parts:

French troops detain Algerian nationals, circa 1957.

"Part One: The Capture of the City or Love Letters" weaves chapters devoted to childhood memories with chapters that draw upon French historical documentation—military reports, journals, letters, and the memoirs of French colo-nial soldiers, officers, and journalists of the con-quest of 1830. Djebar begins to explore her re-lationship to the French language, which she calls her "step-mother tongue" (Djebar, *Fantasia: An Algerian Cavalcade,* p. 214). "Part Two: The

Cries of the Fantasia," foregrounds the destruction during the early years of French conquest. In this section, the novelist describes in graphic detail the horrible acts of *enfumade,* or fumigation, during which French colonial forces set fire to caves that served as refuge for Algerian families, asphyxiating the men, women, and children that sought shelter there.

"Part Three: Voices from the Past," weaves Djebar's autobiography with the testimony of women who participated in the Algerian war of independence. Djebar constructs this third section as a five-part symphony: First Movement: The Two Strangers; Second Movement: The Trance; Third Movement: The Ballad of Abraham; Fourth Movement: The Cry in the Dream; Fifth Movement: The Tunic of Nessus. At the end is a coda, "Air on a Nay" (an ancient flute), which is followed by a chapter entitled "Tzarl-rit," the Arabic term for ululation, the piercing sound women make to mark important events, both joyful and sorrowful. This conclusion draws upon the dual meaning of *fantasia,* a term signifying both a North African cavalry charge (with traditional battle cries and rifle shots) and a Western musical composition that allows for improvisation.

Plot summary: the story in detail. This summary follows in sequence the narrative strands of the novel to render its effect in brief:

"Part One: The Capture of the City or Love Letters." *A Little Arab Girl's First Day at School.* The novelist recalls the day her father walked her to school, linking that memory to a later souvenir when, at the age of 17, she received her first love letter; it was written in French.

Subsection 1. The next few pages describe the arrival of the French fleet on June 13, 1830, and the beginning of the French conquest.

Three Cloistered Girls. The novelist recalls a family of three sisters in her hometown who wrote secretly to male pen pals abroad.

Subsection 2. Baron Barchou, a participant, describes the Battle of Staouéli on June 19, 1830.

The French Policeman's Daughter. The novelist recalls the time the eldest daughter of a French family introduced her French fiancé to the three cloistered sisters.

Subsection 3. Fort Emperor explodes on July 4, 1830. The event is recorded by J. T. Merle, a French war correspondent at the time.

My Father Writes to My Mother. The novelist's father writes a postcard directly to his wife, thereby breaking with Algerian tradition, which would have him address the entire family, never his wife directly.

Subsection 4. These pages give a historical account of the fall of Algiers as witnessed by a Turkish religious figure, Hajj Ahmed Effendi.

"Part Two: The Cries of the Fantasia." *Captain Bosquet Leaves Oran to Take Part in a Razzia.* The French military campaign is recorded in letters received by the mother of Field Marshall Bosquet.

Subsection 1. The narrator recalls again the first love letter she received and her own letters written in French.

Women, Children, Oxen Dying in Caves. The Berber uprisings in the spring of 1845 lead to French retaliation. Under the command of French General Pélissier, French soldiers set fires to caves in which the Berbers had sought refuge.

Subsection 2. The novelist recalls a chance meeting with her brother in Algiers during the 1954 Algerian War, when he had become a militant nationalist.

The Naked Bride of Mazuna. In 1845 rivalry among indigenous factions leads to betrayal. The only daughter of Si Mohamed Ben Kadruma sets out for a wedding that ends in ambush, her capture, and the death of her father.

Subsection 3. The novelist recalls her wedding night in Paris during the Algerian War.

Sistrum. The title denotes a "jingling instrument or rattle used by ancient Egyptians" (*Fantasia,* p. 109). The one-page text constitutes poetic meditation of sound, word, and memory.

Part Three: "Voices from the Past." *First Movement: The Two Strangers.* The novelist recalls two chance encounters with strangers that marked her life. In the first, a tramway motorman's quick reflexes save her from a possibly fatal accident. In the second, a stranger's kind words reach her at a moment of emotional crisis.

Voice. Cherifa, a rural Algerian woman who participated in the Algerian War in the countryside, recalls her brother's death during the war.

Clamour. Cherifa drags her brother's body to a safe place.

Aphasia of Love. The novelist recalls her break with the girls of her generation. They were veiled at puberty and taken out of school; she was not veiled and was allowed to continue her studies.

Voice. Cherifa recounts her own imprisonment by the French when they capture her after her brother's death.

Embraces. Cherifa recounts her capture by the French.

***

Second Movement: The Trance. The novelist recalls how her grandmother's dancing would end with the old woman going into a trance.

Voice. A rural woman recalls her house being torched by French soldiers during the Algerian War.

Murmurs. An Algerian woman pounding herbs in the doorway of her home protects another woman, a rebel fugitive, during the Algerian War.

Plunder. The novelist recalls weddings she attended as a child, at which Algerian women would talk about their lives but never expose their inner hurt directly. The novelist again returns to the theme of her break with Algerian girls of her generation. At puberty, they were withdrawn from school to be married; she was allowed to continue her education because her father, a teacher, valued the French colonial school.

Voice. A widow recalls that when her house was torched by French soldiers during the Algerian War, her hair caught fire in the blaze.

Embraces. Nineteenth-century French writer Eugène Fromentin writes of the death of two Algerian dancers/prostitutes. They were killed by French soldiers pillaging the oasis town of Laghouat in 1853.

***

Third Movement: The Ballad of Abraham. The novelist explains the importance of music in religious observances she attended as a child.

Voice. A rural woman recalls sheltering Algerian rebels during the war.

Whispers. The novelist's grandmother passes down the story of the uprising of 1871 to her grandchildren.

The Quranic School. The novelist describes her dual education: French school in the village, Quranic school after the French school day ended.

A Widow's Voice. A widow recalls how she ran away and lived in the hills after her husband was caught by French soldiers and sentenced to death.

Embraces. In 1843 a pregnant Algerian woman who is part of a group of political agitators is exiled to France. She gives birth at sea, burying her stillborn child there.

***

Fourth Movement: The Cry in the Dreams. The novelist recalls a recurrent dream. At the age of six, upon learning that her grandmother has just died, the weeping child runs down the street. Her cries are stifled; she is unable to give voice to her grief.

A Widow's Voice. Having lost her husband and her three sons in the Algerian War, a widow re-calls retrieving her dead brother's body after he was killed by French soldiers.

Dialogues. Speaking with rural women about their experiences in war, the novelist asks them whether at any time they were raped.

The Onlookers. The novelist acknowledges that by writing she is able to transmit the thoughts and feelings of women she knew in her childhood, women who have rebelled in silence.

A Widow's Voice. An Algerian widow recalls the day the French soldiers torched her house, driving her family from their home.

Embraces. French paratroopers and members of the Foreign Legion torture and kill the inhabitants of the mountain village of El-Aroub in 1956.

***

Fifth Movement: The Tunic of Nessus. The novelist discusses her ambiguous relationship with the French language.

Soliloquy. The novelist acknowledges that she is using fiction to write her autobiography.

Tzarl-rit (Finale). Two English translations define tzarl-rit as a woman's cries of joy while smacking her lips with her hands, or alternatively, to shout when misfortune befalls her.

Pauline. . . In 1852 the French social activist Pauline Rolland is deported with other French radicals to Algeria. Although she is very ill, Rolland manages to record her impressions of the poverty and unjust treatment of Algerian women she encounters on her journey.

The Fantasia. In 1852 the novelist Eugène Fromentin describes the death of a dancer/prostitute. She is struck in the face by the charging horse of the French lover she has rejected.

Air on a Nay. In 1853 Fromentin describes finding the severed hand of a woman killed by French soldiers during a massacre in a Saharan oasis. The novelist seizes this hand "of mutilation and of memory" symbolically to join with the anonymous woman in writing about woman's participation in Algeria's violent history (*Fantasia,* p. 226).

From "history" to "her-story." One day Assia Djebar's father, a teacher in the French colonial educational system, accompanied his daughter, "a little Arab girl going to school for the first time, one autumn morning, walking hand in hand with her father" (*Fantasia,* p. 3). That day he set her on a journey that would transform her into a bilingual and bicultural intellectual, a woman whose experiences would differ greatly from those of other women of her generation. Her world, she noted, would be one of "the outdoors and the risk, instead of the prison of [her] peers" (*Fantasia*, p. 184). This opening scene in the novel is recalled more than 40 years after the event by a woman aware that this first school day marked her initiation into a new space and a new language. When Djebar finds herself liberated from the female enclosure that Orientalist painters such as Eugène Delacroix first depicted as the North African *harem,* she discovers that the price she pays for freedom is exile, specifically from the maternal sphere. As a child she becomes aware that her French education and freedom of movement in public space have moved her beyond the traditional world of her aunts and female cousins.

In *Fantasia* Djebar reestablishes bonds with the maternal world she left behind. She restores these bonds by assuming the multiple roles of translator, interpreter, scribe, and historian for Algerian women who had been silenced by both Algerian patriarchy and French colonialism. The small hand that grasped her father's on the way to school was given a pen, which it learned to use as both a creative instrument and a weapon in the struggle to liberate Algerian women. Djebar would express varied components of Algeria's female world.

The act of writing becomes Djebar's way of forging and maintaining links with her individual and collective past as well as opposing the silencing of women's voices throughout the Arab world today. By committing her experiences to the printed page, the writer removes the veils of privacy that some Algerians, particularly Islamic fundamentalists, consider necessary.

By including French archival documents in *Fantasia: An Algerian Cavalcade,* Djebar reconstitutes the horror of two separate incidents in which recalcitrant Algerian clans were burned to death when French officers Pélissier and Saint-Arnaud ordered their soldiers to set fire to the caves in which the clans sought refuge. More than a century later, Djebar describes the scene with emotion, refusing the role of objective historian, writing history into her novel as she deems fit: "Pélissier, speaking on behalf of fifteen hundred corpses buried beneath El-Kantara, with their flocks unceasingly bleating at death, hands me his report and I accept this palimpsest on which I now inscribe the charred passion of my ancestors" (*Fantasia*, p. 79).

The search for hidden historical events and for Djebar's individual identity converge. As French soldiers once dragged out charred corpses, Djebar now excavates the female self buried under colonial and patriarchal myths: "The date of my birth is *eighteen hundred and forty-two,* the year when General Saint-Arnaud arrives to burn down the *zaouia* of the Beni Menacer, the tribe from which I am descended" (*Fantasia*, p. 217).

In the process, Djebar is forced to come to terms with her attitude towards the French language, which has simultaneously liberated her from the harem and brought her face to face with colonial injustice. She uses French to recall her maternal world, and to inscribe the suffering and injustice inflicted upon Algerians by the colonial conquest: "This language was formerly used to entomb my people" (*Fantasia*, p. 215). She uses it today, constructively, to render history through an Algerian consciousness and to give voice to silenced women.

Djebar contrasts male French narratives of the French conquest with women's narratives of the Algerian Revolution. Combining oral narrative with colonial military and administrative reports and correspondence, she fuses narratives separated by language—French and Arabic—and by gender—colonialist male and indigenous female. More exactly, she acknowledges two languages that have informed her past—the Arabic of the town and the Berber spoken in the rural regions (Ghoussey, p. 458). Moreover, Djebar appropriates a traditionally male medium—writing—to tell women's stories.

The rural women speak of hiding in the woods, being captured, jailed, and tortured, expressing fear, pain, and triumph as they relive these memories. Djebar has noted that "the greater the woman's suffering, the more concise and almost dry manner she had in speaking about it" (Djebar in Mortimer, "Entretien," p. 202). She is struck by the women's sincerity and simplicity, and by the difference in their style from the male official discourse: men tend to construct heroic tales, women to speak of their daily lives.

Even more pronounced than the dichotomy between Algerian male and female voices is the contrast between French colonial writing and modern Algerian women's voices. The female Arabic oral narratives appear exceptionally stark, concise, and filled with understatement when juxtaposed with highly embellished nineteenth-century French prose.

Djebar uses the book's symphonic and fantasialike structure to blend her own voice with those of traditional Algerian women. Harmonizing with these female voices rather than imposing her own on them, she pays tribute to the maternal world of her past. As translator and scribe, giving written form to Algerian women's heroic deeds, the writer manages to renew her bonds with the women of her past and return to the world that she left behind that first day when, as a small child, she grasped her father's hand as he walked her to school.

Sources and literary context. As described, Djebar draws upon her own life, historical documents, and oral interviews with rural women. She embarked upon the project of recording oral narratives for her film *La nouba des femmes du Mont Chenoua* (The Music of the Women of Mont Chenoua), produced for Algerian television in 1977. The film is dedicated to a militant, Yamina Oudai, also called "Zoulikha," who lost her life in the struggle for Algerian independence. Zoulika's memory is kept alive by the women who fought alongside her in the countryside of the Mont Chenoua region. The narratives of rural women's war experiences in the book are taken from oral narratives that Djebar collected for the film and then reworked for the novel. In the mid-1970s she interviewed rural women in her native region, Cherchell, who as young girls had joined the rebels fighting in the Algerian revolution. Her fusion of their story into a novel on the war as told by an Algerian made it distinctive. Among other Algerian novels about the war—for example, Mouloud Mammeri's *L'Opium et le bâton* (1965), Mohammed Dib's *Qui se souvient de la mer* (1962), and Yamina Mechakra's *La grotte éclatée* (1986)—Djebar's is unique in combining written history with oral history and biography to create a verbal symphony.

Events in History at the Time the Novel Was Written

Status of women in Algeria in the 1980s. In the late 1970s Muslim activists conducted small offensives that manifested their desires for Algerian society. They assaulted establishments that sold alcohol and chided women who, in their view, were dressed improperly. Their activism increased in 1982, when they put forth a demand for the establishment of an Islamic government in Algeria. The government treated the activists variously—sometimes harshly, at other times respectfully, mindful of the mass support they marshaled.

The growing influence of Islamic fundamentalism was reflected in a new Family Code of 1984. Extremely conservative, the code once

again made unmarried women dependents of their family and married women the legal dependents of their husbands. According to its dictates, women could not marry non-Muslims, nor seek divorce except in limited cases, nor work outside the home without their husband's consent. The Family Code rescinded rights incorporated into the 1976 constitution. Acknowledging that women suffered disadvantages in Algerian society, the constitution had protected their right to work and prohibited discrimination on the basis of sex. In the early 1980s debates raged on television about the Family Code, shocking women because of their conservative, retrogressive nature and the reactionary comments of men. Female activists protested on their own behalf. They petitioned the National Assembly and staged demonstrations (in October, November, and December of 1981), demanding implementation of the 1976 constitution. In the end, they lost. Postponed for revisions, the Family Code was adopted with ease in June 1984.

Published in 1985, Djebar's text, which brought to the foreground women's participation in Algerian history, thus appeared at a time when women's rights were being increasingly threatened by the rising tide of fundamentalism and by the government's willingness to placate traditionalists by depriving women of their legal guarantees. Future years would see this attitude cemented with the adoption in 1989 of a new constitution, which unlike the 1976 constitution did not contain separate guarantees for women. In other words, the state chose no longer to see them as a marginalized group in need of special guarantees.

Reviews. Djebar's novel was very well received when it was published. Writing in *Jeune Afrique Magazine,* a Paris-based journal widely distributed in Africa, Algerian writer and critic Mourad Bourboune noted that, despite its fragmented composition, Djebar's text achieves a subtle unity whose richness and complexity requires more than one reading. French critic Jean Dejeux's review in the *Annuaire de l'Afrique du Nord* observed that the text is constructed like an Andalusian musical composition, a *nouba,* and is deeply rooted in Algerian culture. At the same time, Dejeux seized upon the importance of the novelist's father in her life. The text pays homage to a father's courageous act: the liberation of his daughter. Marguerite Le Clezio's review of the novel in the American journal *French Review* emphasized the poetic nature of the text while acknowledging the originality of the polyphonic voices and interweaving threads of narrative. Two more volumes of the quartet initiated by *Fantasia: An Algerian Cavalcade* have followed its publication and reception: *Ombre sultane* (1987, *A Sister to Sheherazade,* 1993) and *Vaste est la prison* (1995, Vast Is the Prison).

—Mildred Mortimer

For More Information

Amrane-Minne, Danièle Djamila. *Femmes au combat.* Algiers: Editions Rahma, 1993.

———. "Women and Politics in Algeria from the War of Independence to Our Day." *Research in African Literatures* 30, no. 3 (fall 1999): 62-77.

Dejeux, Jean. "Littérature Maghrébine d'Expression Française: Djebar (Assia), *L'Amour, la fantasia.*" *Annuaire de l'Afrique du Nord* (1985): 879-80.

Djebar, Assia. *Fantasia: An Algerian Cavalcade.* Trans. Dorothy S. Blair. Portsmouth, N.H.: Heinemann, 1993.

Ghoussey, Soheila. "'A Stepmother Tongue': Feminine Writing in Assia Djebar's *Fantasia: An Algerian Cavalcade.*" *World Literature Today* 68, no. 3 (summer 1994): 457-62.

Kraft, Joseph. *The Struggle for Algeria.* New York: Doubleday, 1961.

Lazreg, Maria. *The Eloquence of Silence: Algerian Women in Question.* New York: Routledge, 1994.

Mortimer, Mildred. *Journeys Through the French African Novel.* Portsmouth, N.H.: Heinemann, 1990: 147-64.

———. "Entretien avec Assia Djebar, écrivain algérien." *Research in African Literatures* 19, no. 2 (summer 1988): 197-205.

Ruedy, John. *Modern Algeria: The Origins and Development of a Nation.* Bloomington: Indiana University Press, 1993.

Smith, Tony. *The French Stake in Algeria, 1943-1962.* Ithaca, N.Y.: Cornell University Press, 1978.

Woodhull, Winifred. *Transfigurations of the Maghreb: Feminism, Decolonization and Literature.* Minneapolis: University of Minnesota Press, 1993.

"Farahat's Republic"

by

Yusuf Idris

Born in 1927 in Al-Bayrum, a village in Egypt's Nile Delta, Yusuf Idris moved to Cairo in 1945 to study medicine. As a student he joined the nationalist movement against British occupation, his involvement more than once leading to his arrest and jailing on political charges. When he graduated in 1951, Idris took up an internship at Qasr al-Aini hospital in downtown Cairo, and later worked in one of the most impoverished and crowded areas of the city, al-Darb al-Ahmar. He opened a clinic and served as a medical inspector, his exposure to the poor helping him portray a wide range of human experience in his literary works. Idris gained renown as a journalist, novelist, playwright, and the premier short-story writer in Arabic, leaving medicine in 1967 to devote himself to writing and to the promotion of literature in Egyptian culture. His sympathy for the average Egyptian greatly affected his writing: "I have always been moved by the character of the ordinary, simple Egyptian. He is the subject of all my stories because I admire his view of life, his heroism, timidity, and courage. I take this simple Egyptian as the model for my work, and starting from there I write whatever I like" (Idris in Kupershoek, p. 76). Idris's first collection of short stories, *Arkhas Layali* (1954, The Cheapest Nights) drew the admiration of critics. Its high quality resulted in the introduction to his second collection, *Jumhuriyat Farahat* (1956, Farahat's Republic), being written by the "Dean of Arabic Letters," Taha Husayn (see **An Egyptian Childhood**, also covered in *African Literature and Its Times*). By 1957 Idris

---

THE LITERARY WORK

A short story set in an Egyptian metropolitan police station at night, sometime between 1945 and 1952; published in Arabic (as *Jumhuriyat Farahat*) in 1956, in English in 1967.

SYNOPSIS

While manning the desk at a police station, a lowly older officer, Sergeant Farahat, describes a film scenario to an unnamed gentleman. Farahat is constantly interrupted in the telling of his story, which envisions an ideal future for the Egyptian people, by his interactions with complainants and arrested citizens.

---

had also composed several plays, the second of which, "Farahat's Republic," he adapted from his short story. Written during a pivotal period of twentieth-century Egyptian history, the short story and play articulate national aspirations for political and economic independence and prosperity.

Events in History at the Time of the Short Story

Ottoman rule to the burning of Cairo—an overview. During the era in which "Farahat's Republic" takes place, Egypt was in the midst of a profound transformation. For nearly 70 years, from the late 1800s to the 1950s, Egypt was subject to British occupation. The British had furthermore insinuated themselves in Egypt closely on the heels of three centuries (1516-1805) of foreign domination by the Ottoman Empire. In 1805 Muhammad 'Ali, a commander-in-chief for the Ottoman Army, was appointed governor of Egypt, which led to the founding of an independent dynasty that would rule Egypt until its overthrow in 1952. After the opening in 1869 of the Suez Canal, which linked the Mediterranean to the Red Sea, the strategic value of Egypt soared in the eyes of European powers, particularly in the eyes of the British. The Canal Company, comprised primarily of British and French interests, held concessions from Egypt to operate the canal for 99 years, after which control was to revert to the Egyptian government. Egypt's Ottoman ruler, the khedive, had borrowed the funds to build the canal from European sources. Mismanagement of the funds by the khedive and a downturn in the cotton market led European nations (France and Great Britain) to intervene in Egypt's affairs in 1876 to guarantee repayment of loans. This contributed to growing resentment among Egyptians against outsiders and to a drive for true independence. The result in 1881 was an uprising, led by Ahmed 'Urabi, to free Egypt from Ottoman rule. In response British forces bombed Egypt and sent in troops the following year (1882), ostensibly to restore power to the khedive. Great Britain took on an official role of "advisor" to the Egyptian Crown.

The Egyptians mounted repeated attempts to rid their country of British occupation, but it was not until 1936 that an agreement was signed restricting British military occupation to the Canal Zone. Between the two world wars, Egypt's government tried to regain some control of the economy through protective tariffs, agricultural credits, and the increasing Egyptianization of the insurance and banking industries. Worldwide depression struck in the 1930s. As elsewhere, there was an economic downturn in Egypt, which led to growing political discontent, the rise of several new political parties, conflict over the constitution, and increasing disapproval of governmental appointments by the Crown.

The 1940s saw more political turmoil with the establishment and dismissal of several governments, frequent crises in diplomatic relations with the British, and an increase in internal resentments expressed in leftist, communist, labor, and Islamic movements. Political discontent seethed on many fronts. There was mounting anti-European sentiment in Cairo, the city in which Idris's "Farahat's Republic" is set. Over the years the Egyptian government passed laws to reduce European domination of the economy. Businesses were required to use the Arabic language, to employ a set percentage of Egyptian (as opposed to European) workers, and to be controlled by an Egyptian director or partner. But such gradual Egyptianization was hardly enough to satisfy the populace. Demonstrations wracked the capital city, until finally the British started to loosen their reins. On July 14, 1946, they handed over control of the Citadel of Cairo to the Egyptians. Eight months later, on March 28, 1947, after 30 demonstrators were shot dead, the British military handed over control of the Kasr el Nil barracks and marched out of Cairo altogether. They retreated to the Suez Canal, their presence here still making them an occupying force, but for the first time in 64 years Cairo had taken charge of itself.

Public pressure continued, the goal being to eradicate the British from Egypt altogether. The next five years gave rise to demonstrations, strikes, and riots, which took place mostly on the streets of Cairo. Egypt was still a primarily agricultural country. Although manufacturing was gaining ground, industry accounted for only 8 percent of the national income in 1952 (Wheelcock, p. 139). In Cairo the growing class of laborers—a vocal group—tended to view rich businesspeople and wealthy landowners as oppressors in collusion with foreign interests. King Faruq, who in 1936 had succeeded his father, King Fu'ad as Egypt's monarch, was considered corrupt and partial to special interests in his appointments.

Meanwhile, post-World War II manipulations of the Middle East, including the partition of Palestine, and then the loss of Palestine to Israel in 1948, further aggravated the general discontent. The Egyptian army suffered major disadvantages in the Palestine War, coping with inadequate food, arms, and transportation, and with faulty ammunition. Afterward domestic unrest escalated, prompting one assassination after another, from General Selim Azki (while directing operations against student demonstrators), to Prime Minister Nokrashy Pasha, to Hasan al-Banna' (leader of the Moslem Brotherhood, which may have planned the first two assassinations). There was general unrest, too. In 1951 Egypt suffered 49 workers strikes and four peasant uprisings, all suppressed by force.

Matters climaxed on January 25-26, 1952, be-

British troops evacuate the Suez Canal Zone according to the treaty of 1954.

ginning with a violent standoff between the British military and Egyptian police in the town of Ismailiyya; in the process, 41 Egyptians but only 3 British died. The next day mobs in Cairo retaliated by torching British- and foreign-owned establishments, destroying some 700 structures and leaving 12,000 homeless. According to one historian, "Cairo looked like a ravaged war zone with gutted department stores, smouldering buildings and smashed shop fronts" (Sayyid-Marsot, p. 104). The date—January 26, 1952—went down in infamy as Black Saturday, and to the present it remains a mystery who did most of the burning, or whether it was an organized or random event. Afterward, King Faruq dismissed the government, which left a power vac-

uum that would not be satisfactorily filled in the coming months, despite several attempts by the king to forge a new coalition government.

Revolution. In 1949 Gamal Abdul Nasser (also spelled Jamal 'Abd al-Nasir) and several of his fellow officers in the Egyptian Army formed a secret association called the Free Officers, which began distributing underground political pamphlets and contemplating action. On July 23, 1952, Nasser and the Free Officers engineered a military coup d'état, ascribing the orders to General Muhammad Naguib, a respected older officer who had been brought in on the plan for less than two weeks and who, in those orders, "was deliberately mistitled as commander of the armed forces" (Beattie, p. 66). A few days later King

Faruq abdicated and went into exile. To provide transitional rule until a democratic government could be elected, the rebels formed the Revolutionary Command Council (RCC) and elected Nasser as its head.

The goals of the RCC were articulated in the Six Principles of the Revolution: to bring about the end of 1) imperialism, 2) the inequitable land system, and 3) capitalist monopolies, and to establish 4) social justice, 5) a strong military, and 6) true democratic rule. After a series of political purges by the RCC, Naguib accepted the job of interim prime minister on September 8, 1952. One day later a sweeping land reform bill was promulgated, limiting landownership to 200 fedans per individual or 300 per family (a fedan being somewhat larger than an acre). This blow to the wealthy landowners made the fledgling regime wildly popular with the peasants. In June 1953, Egypt officially terminated its monarchy and declared itself a republic, with Naguib as

IDRIS AND NASSER

Idris's own politics were socialist and nationalist. In 1951 after gaining admittance to the anti-British secret organization the Executive Committee for Armed Struggle, Idris helped collect funds and organize training camps for guerrilla fighters in the Canal Zone. Because of his political activities at the university, he was suspended from that institution and jailed twice—for two months in 1949 and three months in 1952. The early 1950s meanwhile saw him contributing to various journals and joining the authors' bureau of the communist party, Haditu. In the post-revolutionary period Idris showed even greater interest in politics; he wrote multiple articles on government, culture, and daily events in Cairo. Idris faulted Nasser for negotiating an agreement with Britain that called for gradual rather than immediate withdrawal from the Suez Canal. After Nasser took charge, he began arresting opponents, starting with the leftists. Idris's turn came in August 1954. Imprisoned for 13 months, he spent much of his jail time talking to communist prisoners, with whom he disagreed about the role of literature in the revolutionary struggle. Fiction, thought Idris, ought to be more than a tool of political events. Released from prison in the fall of 1955, he broke with Haditu, and when Nasser adopted a nationalist and socialist agenda more in line with Idris's own, the author became one of the new regime's fervent supporters.

president. Over the next year, a terrible power struggle ensued between Naguib and Nasser, amid the repression of political parties, military purges, press crackdowns, pro-democracy demonstrations, and waves of arrests. The fracas ultimately resulted in Naguib's loss of power in March 1954, though he maintained the title of president. An October 26th assassination attempt on Nasser brought about the arrest of thousands of Muslim Brothers and eventually of Naguib himself on charges of conspiracy. Nasser, as prime minister and head of the RCC, was now in charge. In the midst of these events, the RCC had negotiated a new treaty with the British, which was signed on October 19, 1954; the treaty required the phased withdrawal of the British from the Canal Zone by June 1956, while giving them rights to base themselves in that zone in the event of international warfare.

The British completed their withdrawal from the Canal Zone several days ahead of schedule in June 1956, the same month that the Egyptians elected Nasser president and ratified, by an overwhelming majority, a new constitution. A few months earlier, negotiations transpired in Washington, D.C., for the financing of the future Aswan High Dam, central to Egypt's economic plans for agricultural and industrial development. Nasser had to find some way to rescue his country, whose population was growing faster than its food supply, and reached for the dam (which would increase the farmable land area) as an answer. The Aswan Dam agreement made the United States, Great Britain, and the World Bank the lenders of the capital needed for the project. In September 1955, Nasser, badly in need of arms and unable to get them from the United States, had orchestrated a Czech arms agreement, which funneled Soviet-made weapons into Egypt. Perhaps in retaliation for Nasser's flaunting of his independence from Western powers, the United States withdrew its support for the Aswan Dam a month after Nasser's election, causing the collapse of the financial agreement. In response, Nasser nationalized the Suez Canal Company on July 26th, 1956, effectively ending the concessions of the century before, which would otherwise have expired in 1968. He gave as his reason for the early nationalization the financing of the Aswan Dam without outside aid.

The Suez Crisis. Britain and France referred their dispute with Egypt over the legality of the nationalization of the Suez Canal to the United Nations Security Council. The U.N. proposed a six-point agreement, to which Egypt gave its consent in mid-October. However, when invading Israelis struck toward the Canal on October 29th, 1956, France and Britain immediately issued a joint ultimatum to Israel and Egypt, demanding they withdraw from the Canal Zone while Anglo-French forces temporarily occupied the Zone to secure unimpeded international traffic through the canal. Israel accepted, but Nasser rejected the ultimatum, so British and French forces entered the fray. Joint pressure from the United States, the Soviet Union, and the majority of U.N. members led to a cease-fire on November 7, 1956. Egypt at this point agreed to the presence of U.N. emergency forces in the Canal Zone and Gaza Strip to guarantee the withdrawal of French, British, and Israeli forces. The British and French withdrawal was effected by the end of December 1956; Israeli withdrawal took until March 1957. The canal reopened in April 1957. Despite the military disadvantage under which Nasser had defied the three other combatants, he emerged with Egyptian sovereignty over a critical asset to his nation's development. His victory over imperial forces made the Egyptian Revolution and Nasser role models for other Arab struggles for independence.

Status of Egyptian majority. Before World War II, the Egyptian Association for Social Studies had conducted a survey of the populace. The results indicated that poor Egyptian families (90 percent of the total population) lived five to six persons to a room and got hired to work for about 7.5 weeks a year (Aldridge, p. 227). As the years passed, rural-to-urban migration increased, and living conditions improved somewhat for city dwellers. But even in cities like Cairo and Alexandria there was widespread disparity among residents. By 1952 Cairo had become the center of great contrasts.

> The beautiful new avenues and countless luxury apartment buildings built in Cairo could not solve the problem of a city composed primarily of slums. In a metropolis of over two million persons, well over one hundred thousand males were classified as unemployed; and a majority of the families existed on less than twenty dollars monthly.
>
> (Wheelock, p. 41)

How much did conditions change in the first revolutionary period, from 1952 to 1956? This was a transitional period, to be sure. In the beginning the Free Officers had no long-range plan. Their goal was simply to free Egypt from the shackles of the past. For the time being, the country was to remain a capitalist society. "Egyptians

were still being encouraged to go on investing their money in profitable enterprises. . . . Until 1956 . . . Cairo was still a capitalist city. There were still plenty of foreign cars and foreign goods from Europe, clothes still looked as if they had just arrived from London and Paris and Rome, and the usual cosmopolitan flavor in the city's sybarite tastes in food and drink and entertainment were not greatly disturbed" (Aldridge, p. 253). But at the same time Cairo became the center of an array of groups devoted to reorganizing Egypt's economy. And Nasser, advised by a team of economic experts, quickly learned that the country needed an overall plan, not only because the Aswan High Dam was a monumental scheme, but also because Egypt was in dire need of fuel, fertilizer, transportation, and other goods and services. It is in the context of these first few post-revolutionary years, an era full of promise and uncertainty, that Idris wrote his short story.

The Short Story in Focus

Plot summary. The story's unnamed gentleman narrator has been detained by the police at night

EGYPTIAN CINEMA

Very few individuals were able to amass huge fortunes in Egypt during the 1940s. Egyptian cinema featured such individuals, becoming a type of Hollywood dream factory. For the most part, films concentrated either on the privileged and their concerns about love and traditional marriage customs or on the few lower-class Egyptians who managed to make a fortune. Films allowed for dreams of wild economic success, championing the man on the street. An example is *Resolution* (1933), whose protagonist, Muhammad, is the son of a barber. Muhammad is full of the resolution suggested by the title. He is determined to better himself: he will become university educated, set up shop as a merchant, and marry Fatima, the girl next door. In other words, the film concerns itself with the attempt of the Egyptian poor to modernize themselves into something beyond a traditionalist society. Farahat's own film goes further; it concerns itself with transforming not just a class, but society as a whole. This is reflective of the era in which it was written: in 1933, Egypt was still a staunchly capitalist country; two decades later, it was beginning to reject capitalism altogether.

for interrogation the next morning in what we are led to understand is a political case. The narrator interacts with the night duty officer, Sergeant Farahat, who sits at the front desk of the sordid, stark, crowded station, processing complaints and the night's prisoners. Striking up conversation with the well-dressed narrator, whom he does not know is a detainee, Farahat complains about being the real victim in all this, since he has to process the endless crime reports. While unsympathetically taking the report of a woman who was purportedly attacked in a movie theater, Sergeant Farahat drops the remark that he once made a film.

Having piqued the narrator's interest, Farahat proceeds to relate his film's scenario, while impatiently and gruffly processing several cases

with little or no consideration for the unfortunate individuals involved. The story Farahat relates is the marvelous good-luck tale of a poor Egyptian who refused any reward for returning a valuable diamond to its Indian owner. In an attempt to repay the Egyptian's honesty, the Indian bought a winning lottery ticket, whose proceeds he then used to purchase a cargo ship. He loaded the ship with sumptuous goods, and sent it off as a gift to the honest Egyptian. The Egyptian sold the goods and reinvested his earnings by buying up a fleet of cargo ships, one by one (incidentally ridding the waters of Alexandria of all foreign-owned boats). He subsequently purchased factory after factory until he owned all the factories in Egypt. To motivate his laborers to high levels of production, he provided comfortable housing and other incentives that raised the standard of living for all. The economy was transformed and the desert reclaimed. Industry and technology appeared everywhere, while electricity, job opportunities, and education became available to all.

In the telling of his utopian film scenario, the sergeant is constantly interrupted by the cases of unfortunate victims, by the night's harvest of beggars and pickpockets, or by superior officers. He is unsympathetic to every complainant, as if he disbelieves the evidence of each case as it is presented to him. His reaction to the woman attacked at the theater is to cast aspersions on her morals and honesty. He scoffs at another woman screaming for help against a young man who had violently beaten his mother. He callously refuses to take a grocer's complaint about a broken window because the storefront is on a lane in the district of another police station, though the building itself is within Farahat's district. While he deals with the rabble and the paperwork on his desk, Farahat unburdens himself to the narrator, spinning his utopian tale, a sharp contrast to the grim realities around him. Finally, just as he is about to reach the high point, Farahat discovers by chance that the narrator himself is a detainee, and refuses to complete the tale, returning to his duties with the same withering gaze he had doled out to the supposed riffraff with whom he has been dealing all evening.

From Farahat's to Plato's Republic. In Arabic, the title, "Farahat's Republic," *Jumhuriyat Farahat,* has the same metrical structure as Plato's *Republic (Jumhuriyat Aflaton).* This allusion is reinforced by the contents of the story, which, like Plato's fourth-century B.C.E. treatise, envisions an ideal society—significantly more just than the society

---

LOCALISMS IN "FARAHAT'S REPUBLIC"—A GLOSSARY

Afreet: A devil, demon, or imp.

From Manzala to Uneiba, from Arish to Mersa Matrouh: Place names that trace the extent of Egypt on north-south and east-west axes. Manzala is a major lake by Port Said on the Mediterranean and Red Seas; Uneiba is a town on the Nile River near the Sudan border; Arish is a Mediterranean coastal region near the Gaza Strip; Mersa Matrough is a Mediterranean coastal resort about halfway to the Libyan border from Alexandria.

Galabia: Traditional male garb—a long-sleeved, full-length gown.

Mitwalli Gate: A huge gate of medieval Islamic Cairo, in a modern-day neighborhood characterized by genteel poverty and strong social tradition.

Mycerinus: Egyptian king of the twenty-sixth century B.C.E., also known as Menkaure.

Nagib al-Rihani: Well-loved Egyptian movie actor of the 1930s and '40s; he played comic roles of the poor, ingenuous, good-hearted man on whom fortune either smiled or frowned.

Ramdan: Islamic holy month of fasting from food, drink, and all pleasures from sunrise to sunset.

Ramses: Egyptian pharaoh of the thirteenth century B.C.E.

Shubra: Large, densely populated neighborhood of contemporary Cairo, famous for ethnic and socioeconomic diversity.

Upper Egyptian (Sa'idi): In Cairo, Upper (southern) Egyptians have been the butt of jokes about naiveté, country bumpkins, and stubbornness. Their dialect of Arabic differs from that of Cairo.

being portrayed in Farahat's police station. The play on philosophical discourse is certainly not coincidental; in 1953 Nasser released his *Philosophy of the Revolution,* in which he articulated his hopes for the revolution he had helped instigate in 1952, and to which Farahat's dream relates. Some scholars say that Idris changed the name of the story and of the main character from the original "Abd al-Baqi's Republic"; if this rumored change indeed occurred, the original title was a morphological echo of Abd al-Nasir (Nasser), and the change was a move away from it. Nasser may resemble more the unnamed Egyptian in Farahat's film scenario than Farahat himself.

The details of the physical layout of the police station are timelessly accurate: filthy, poorly lit, littered with seemingly discarded furnishings—a description valid for countless government offices in Cairo. This grounds the setting in the poverty of the state, as well as the poverty of individuals in the police station, conveyed by details such as the faded gray overdress, worn kerchief, and unkempt hair of the first woman complainant. The facts of poverty are underscored by Farahat's account of little details of his police work: the unidentified body found on a rubbish heap, and "men who murder for a stick of sugar-cane, burn down a barn for a corncob" (Idris, "Farahat's Republic," p. 7). Between the horrors coming in off the street to his desk and the rigid appearance of efficiency he musters for his superior, the Assistant Superintendent, Farahat spills his frustrations and utopian film scenario to the narrator.

This irony of the short story relates to the problems, policy issues, and developing ideology of post-revolutionary Egypt. In the film's plot, the integrity of the Egyptian protagonist contrasts sharply with Farahat's attitude that every complaint is a lie and with the joking attitude of the police (except in front of their commanding officers). The windfall of the lottery ticket contrasts with the depressed economic conditions in the police station and in the real world of Egypt. The reinvestment of the windfall in purchasing more goods and ships and ultimately factories in Egypt is related to the program of state-guided capitalism that the nascent regime wished to encourage. The lands purchased and developed by the fictional Egyptian for his industrial complexes are, in retrospect, a remarkable prediction of the outlying industrial cities that would later be built around Cairo under President Anwar al-Sadat. The emphasis on providing for the social needs and satisfactions of the labor force anticipates the

shift to the discourse of scientific socialism that increasingly characterized Nasser's regime after the Suez Crisis. In the story, socialist, anticapitalist discourse is wedded to ancient and modern Egyptian identity:

> He didn't make a profit at all from the workers' sweat. The man who did work worth five piastres got five piastres, the one who did work for ten got ten. Forgive me for saying so, a worker will put his heart and soul into his job if he's properly paid. We're a people who've had an inheritance of hard work handed down to us from father to son ever since the time of the Pharaohs. Instead of making a metre of cloth he'd make two; instead of just one shoe he'd make a pair. That's how it was—give and take, give me my right and take yours.
>
> ("Farahat's Republic," p. 15)

In this utopia, the need for the police practically disappears. The new workers are well dressed, and enjoy all kinds of wholesome pleasures. There is no strife or victimization. Everything is electric, an allusion perhaps to the hopes surrounding the planned Aswan High Dam ("Farahat's Republic," p. 17). The vision spins off in a dream of industrial, agricultural, and technological development for all of Egypt, eclectically weaving together snippets of various ideologies that were present in Egyptian society at the time (socialist, communist, labor, Muslim Brotherhood, democratic, and capitalist ideologies). These snippets are bound to one another in the dream of economic independence and social justice.

Although the story avoids any direct mention of the Suez Canal, the canal-related implications are quite clear: the ship coming from the rich Indian gentleman had to have arrived by means of the Canal. The miraculously rich Egyptian in Farahat's vision expresses and achieves a common Egyptian aspiration to own or control canal trade.

> The man was extremely fed up with all the European ships, but in the space of a year God was good to him and he expanded a lot. Bit by bit he began buying up all the ships of Alexandria so that there wasn't a single one, English, Italian or what you will—all were flying the green flag.
>
> ("Farahat's Republic," p. 14)

The generous Egyptian in Farahat's tale builds his capitalist monopoly to the benefit of all Egyptians. It is ironic that the Egyptian capitalists and industrialists who were in a position to help Nasser achieve his vision for Egypt were also

Gamal Abdul Nasser, Egypt's popular premier, waves to cheering women in 1956.

badly stung by some of his policies. For example, the Egyptian industrialist Muhammad Ahmad 'Abbud patriotically lent his fleet of ships for use in delivering the weaponry purchased through the Czechs in 1955. Once the arms were delivered, the ships were confiscated by Nasser's

POLITICAL PRISONERS

Under the monarchy in the period surrounding World War II, political detainees, dissidents, or suspected spies may have included foreigners, members of the intelligentsia, and even government ministers. Called "special prisoners," such detainees were kept apart from the general prison population. They were fed special meals and received privileges that criminal prisoners did not enjoy. However, as Nasser's regime turned into a military dictatorship, the fate of political prisoners worsened considerably. Leftist, communist, and Islamic extremists suffered arrest and detention without due process, particularly communists, some of whom would remain in detention for decades.

regime. In 1956 the government started a round of nationalizations and confiscations that frightened off both foreign and domestic investors, derailing the guided capitalism and the investment strategies that sow prosperity in Farahat's imaginary republic.

Another parallel lies in the unrevealed ending of Farahat's utopian film plot. The fortunate and beneficent Egyptian who has transformed society becomes bored with running the world for everyone and decides to give it all up. He is about to announce his decision on the radio, which he had established (just as Voice of the Arabs radio programming was initiated shortly after the Revolution), when Farahat refuses to reveal the rest of the tale. We never hear if or when and why the benevolent Egyptian peasant-turned-patriarch would leave utopia-building to someone else. This perhaps reflects the political uncertainty that gripped Egypt at the time.

Indeed there were very long and complicated discussions in the RCC concerning the nature and length of the transitional period to stated goals of democracy. Nasser had convinced everyone of his desires for democracy in Egypt. In view of needed reforms and the desire for independence from foreign influence and economic development, his regime resorted to centralized authoritarian control as a means of achieving these ends quickly while preparing for more democratic institutions. But the length of the transitional period kept growing—from months to three years to six years to finally a designated 30-year authoritarian rule, after which Nasser said he would turn Egypt into a true democracy. This debate was at its height in the days preceding the Suez Crisis, and "Farahat's Republic" seems to beg the question: when would Nasser step down or allow more democratic representation? The story deliberately leaves the question unanswered.

Once Farahat discovers that the narrator is among those brought in for interrogation on political charges, his camaraderie disappears, and he turns back to his duties with renewed fierceness. Yusuf Idris served time in jail under the British and Nasser's regime; there is little doubt that the narrator of the short story represents Idris's persona to a great extent. By ending in this fashion, the story questions the means by which authoritarian control achieves its ends, whether the power broker is the British or the new regime, which had begun to repress critics and competing ideologies.

Sources and literary context. The twentieth century has seen a tremendous blossoming of Arabic prose fiction, especially in Egypt. Some of the earliest novel-like experiments expressed outrage at the British presence in Egypt, such as Mahmud Tahir's 1906 novelette, *The Maiden of Dinshaway,* a fictionalized account of actual events surrounding the death of a British officer in the Nile Delta village of Dinshaway.

Yusuf Idris's fiction covers a wide range of human issues, and is perhaps better known in Arabic reading circles for its wrenching explorations of moral and social issues (as in his 1971 "House of Flesh"), but he never shied from political commentary. In 1955 critics in Egypt called for writers to commit their literature to social betterment. In a collection of essays called *Fi-th-Thaqafa al-Misriyya* (On Egyptian Culture), two critics, Muhammad Amin al-'Alim and 'Abd al-'Azim Anims, complained that Egyptian prose and poetry still traveled in a very narrow social milieu, the middle class, whose problems were portrayed in a style grown stale. Calling their movement the "New School," the critics argued that literature should bring about and emanate from social and political change. There were certain similarities between them and Idris, who himself is considered the founder of a new school of short stories in Egypt.

In the film scenario in "Farahat's Republic," the poor-Egyptian-turned-rich-industrialist in some ways resembles an actual historical figure, the previously mentioned Muhammad Ahmad 'Abbud, who started building a huge business empire in Egypt in the mid-1920s. 'Abbud entered sector after sector of economic development until his family was forced to flee Egypt on the heels of confiscations and nationalizations in 1955 and 1963. But 'Abbud resembles the do-good Egyptian in the short story, with one remarkable exception. The story envisions an Egypt for Egyptians without foreign influence or control. 'Abbud, however, was viewed as a collaborator with the British and foreign-supported monarchy. If one identifies 'Abbud with the Egyptian industrialist, the short story can be read as a tale that addresses Egypt's economic elite, who gained huge fortunes in the 1930s and '40s, calling for the Egyptianization of their interests to the benefit of the nation.

Reviews. The foremost literary figure and critic of the day, Taha Husayn, wrote an introduction to *Farahat's Republic,* in which he both praised Idris and launched a critique of his work that would dog Idris for much of his career.

I read and find in [this book] enjoyment, power, acute sensitivity, refined taste, veracity of observation, and skillful rendering . . . with a profundity in accord with life's details, and a harshly accurate documentation of momentous and prodigious events which occur in it without hesitation or constraint.

(Husayn in Idris, *Jumhuriyat Farahat,* p. 4; trans. C. Burt)

Husayn goes on to say that Idris seems to be a born story writer, with great abilities to portray not only individuals in brilliant cameos, but also the characteristics of social groups. Husayn

COLLOQUIAL VERSUS STANDARD LITERARY ARABIC

Idris was accused of writing in substandard Arabic, of violating the literary values that uphold classical Arabic as the standard for literary composition. The linguistic critique launched at his work reflects an important debate in twentieth-century Egyptian society over the use of dialectical Arabic in written, literary communication. In the contemporary Arab world there are two linguistic codes assigned to specific functions in society: colloquial Arabic and standard literary Arabic. Colloquial (or spoken) Arabic differs widely from country to country, even to the point of mutual unintelligibility. In Egypt itself, there are very significant dialectical variations. These colloquial Arabic dialects are primarily unwritten, while education and writing have historically been the almost exclusive provinces of standard literary Arabic, regarded as the modern continuation of the Arabic of the Qur'an and classical Arabic literature.

With the blossoming of the Arab press in the late nineteenth century, the push toward mass education, and the growth of nationalism, language reform was debated in Egypt in order to make the written word more accessible and less stultified by archaic stylistic conventions and paralyzing grammatical rules. None of the reform schemes reached fruition. The historical advantage of Fusha, the language of the Qur'an, and its unifying power as a cultural standard among Arabs made it unassailable on the level of official usage. The twentieth century, however, has witnessed a steady seeping of colloquial expression into literary media in Egypt. Over the years, with the exception of drama, where colloquial has won the floor, colloquial Arabic literature has been marginalized, labeled as folk poetry, and denied publication. The impulse to write in colloquial Arabic seems to survive, however, resurfacing with every generation.

dampens this praise, however, with withering criticism of Idris's use of colloquial Arabic in dialogue and elsewhere, as opposed to the standard literary Arabic of the body of the story's text: "How greatly our young writers err when they think depicting reality from life requires them to have people in books utter what is current on tongues in the streets and clubs" (Husayn in Idris, *Jumhuriyat Farahat,* pp. 6-7; trans. C. Burt). This critique was followed by others like it, although more recent Egyptian and foreign critics have celebrated this aspect of Idris's style, applauding his works for documenting the variety and specificity of Egyptian characters, even on the level of the dialect that they speak.

Critics have observed that "Farahat's Republic" is a prism through which one can refract history: "When we observe that the title of the story refers to the police station as a 'republic,' it becomes clear that we are dealing with a portrayal of a microcosm of the larger reality of Egypt and perhaps a not entirely complimentary portrait of its leader" (Allen, p. 44). Some scholars view the story as the height of Idris's optimism and hope for the future of the Revolution. Others feel that the juxtaposition of the utopian film scenario and sordid police station makes even Farahat's name (which means "joy" in Arabic) farcical (see Mikhail, pp. 42-43).

—Clarissa Burt and Joyce Moss

For More Information

'Abd al-Nasir, Jamal (Gamal Abdul Nasser), *The Philosophy of the Revolution.* Cairo: State Information Service, 1953.

Aldridge, James. *Cairo.* Boston: Little, Brown, 1969.

Allen, Roger. "The Artistry of Yusuf Idris." *World Literature Today* 55 (1981): 43-47.

Armbrust, Walter. *Mass Culture and Modernism in Egypt.* Cambridge: Cambridge University Press, 1996.

Beattie, Kirk J. *Egypt During the Nasser Years: Ideology, Politics and Civil Society.* Boulder, Colo.: Westview, 1994.

Fawzi, Mahoud. *Suez 1956: An Egyptian Perspective.* London: Shorouk International, 1987.

Idris, Yusuf. "Farahat's Republic." In *Modern Arabic Short Stories.* Trans. Denys Johnson-Davies. London: Oxford University Press, 1967.

Kupershoek, P. J. *The Short Stories of Yusuf Idris: A Modern Egyptian Author.* Leiden: E. J. Brill, 1981.

Mikhail, Mona. *Studies in the Short Fiction of Mahfouz and Idris.* New York: New York University Press, 1992.

Sayyid-Marsot, 'Afaf Lutfi. *A Short History of Modern Egypt.* Cambridge: Cambridge University Press, 1985.

Stagh, Martina. *The Limits of Freedom of Speech: Prose Literature and Prose Writers in Egypt under Nasser and Sadat.* Stockholm: Almquist and Wiksell, 1993.

Wheelcock, Keith. *Nasser's New Egypt: A Critical Analysis.* New York: Frederick A. Praeger, 1960.

God's Bits of Wood

by

Ousmane Sembène

~

Ousmane Sembène was born in 1923 in Ziguinchor, Senegal. The son of a fisherman, Sembène received virtually no formal Western education; he worked as a fisherman, plumber, bricklayer, and apprentice mechanic. Serving in the French colonial army during World War II, Sembène came into contact with ideas and events that would influence his creative endeavors for years to come. He was a manual laborer in Dakar, Senegal, after the war, then left to become a dockworker in Marseilles, France. Though Sembène did not participate directly in the 1947-48 Dakar-Niger Railway strike, he kept in contact with the strikers through their weekly reports to the Confédération Générale du Travail (CGT) in France. After being exposed to the radical ideology of the French Left, Sembène joined the French Communist Party and served as a trade union leader. In the twilight years of French colonial rule in Africa, he completed three novels: *Le Docker Noir* (1956; The Black Dockworker), *Ô pays, mon beau peuple* (1957; Oh, Country, My Beautiful People), and *Les bouts de bois de Dieu* (1960; God's Bits of Wood). Arguably his most famous novel, *God's Bits of Wood* has been praised for its vivid depiction of African workers struggling against colonial oppression and exploitation.

Events in History at the Time the Novel Takes Place

Economic protests in postwar French West Africa. In *God's Bits of Wood*, the Dakar-Niger

---

THE LITERARY WORK

A novel set in Senegal and the French Sudan (now Mali), in colonial French West Africa, from October 1947 to March 1948; published in French in 1960 (as *Les bouts de bois de Dieu*), in English in 1962.

SYNOPSIS

African railway workers on the French-owned Dakar-Niger Railway stage a five-month strike for wage and benefits improvements, developing, in the process, a sophisticated view of workers' rights and industrial relations.

Railway strike and its effect dominate the lives of Sembène's characters. The protest itself grew out of economic and social changes that took place in the years during and after World War II. Various factors contributed to the creation in the 1940s of a class of urban African wage earners, who became militant in the postwar era. The expanding wartime economy allowed more Africans to work in the transportation, commercial, and public works sectors. After the war high-priced imports and the failure of wages to keep pace with inflation helped galvanize African activism. Urban Africans demanded a more complete education because they "had high expectations that their lives would continue to improve once the war was over" (Keller, p. 159).

From 1945 to 1948 workers opposed to discriminatory treatment from their employers

Ousmane Sembène

generated a wave of general strikes. By 1945 African wage earners in a variety of vocations had begun to formulate common demands of their employers. Specifically, African workers wanted to end the two-tiered system of benefits that favored expatriate French employees, giving them but not the Africans work breaks, management bonuses, and the like. Seeking to eliminate pervasive workplace discrimination, the participants in the Dakar general strike of 1945—which lasted about a week in December 1945—called for the creation of a *cadre unique* (single-staff system). Assuming the same goal a month later were the civil servants and industrial workers who took part in the Dakar general strike of January 1946, which lasted 12 days. Sembène, having just been discharged from the army, had joined the Construction Workers' Union by this time and, although still unemployed, attended all union meetings during the general strike. The plan was for the cadre unique to grant African workers all of the benefits—except hardship pay—that European employees already enjoyed. An equally significant demand in 1946 was for the permanent integration of temporary employees into the single staff system. Both strikes met with mixed results—higher wages were granted, but the demands for the *cadre unique* remained unanswered.

Although the Dakar-Niger Railway strike of 1947-48 was limited to the railroad company itself, it advanced the same agenda as the earlier general strikes: higher wages, a single-staff system, and family benefits for African as well as French employees. In terms of intensity and duration, however, the rail strike might be said to represent the culmination of the protests that had preceded it. In the novel, the shadow of earlier, less successful strikes haunts the memories of those old enough to have experienced the years before World War II. Niakoro, mother of labor activist Ibrahim Bakayoko, recalls "a terrible strike, a savage memory for those who had lived through it, just one season of rains before the war. It had taken a husband and a son from her, but now no one even came to seek her advice" (Sembène, *God's Bits of Wood*, p. 2). And Mamadou Keïta, the oldest union member, cautions his fellow workers to think long and carefully before committing themselves to a strike, reminding them: "Years ago the men of Thiès went out on strike, and that was only settled by deaths, by deaths on our side. And now it begins again" (*God's Bits of Wood*, p. 8). In fact, a 1938 railway walkout in Thiès, a railway center and maintenance depot inland from Dakar, had led to tragic consequences as colonial soldiers faced down 200 to 300 strikers: "Stone throwing by strikers . . . led the inexperienced soldiers . . . to fire. Six strikers died" (Cooper, p. 106).

The Dakar-Niger Railway strike of 1947-48. The rise of African trade unions played a significant role in the strikes of the 1940s. Although Africans had been eligible to join trade unions since the 1920s, their participation in these organizations did not become significant until the late 1930s. By then a number of African trade unions had developed into affiliates of the radical metropolitan French Confédération Générale du Travail (CGT). Among trade unionists, railway workers often made the most effective activists. The majority of the African employees of the Dakar-Niger Railway refused to work from October 10, 1947, to March 19, 1948, the longest strike in the history of French West Africa (*l'Afrique Occidentale Française*, or AOF). Of four railway lines in the region, the Dakar-Niger Railway was the most powerful. Like the civil servants in the general strike of 1946, its railroad workers called for a single-staff system and job security for the so-called temporary workers. Known as auxiliaries, these workers objected to their temporary status, since some of them had worked for the company for years and they did the same labor as the permanent staff, without receiving the same benefits—for example, paid housing. The auxiliaries greatly outnumbered the permanent workers. In 1946 the Dakar-Niger Railway counted 478 European permanent workers, 1,729 African permanent workers, and 15,726 auxiliaries (Cooper, p. 243).

For a time the AOF government seemed willing to consider proposals for a single-staff system. Late in 1946 colonial officials formed a parity commission, consisting of administrative representatives and an equal number of Africans and Europeans, to address this issue. The commission's work was shelved, however, because of an important administrative change. Through a ministerial decree of July 17, 1946, the French Republic shifted control of transportation from the government's Department of Railways and Transport to the Railway Administration of West Africa (a commercial enterprise). This was done because the metropolitan government in France wanted to rid itself of the costs and responsibilities of running such operations. The decree led to the raising of freight rates and the firing of a substantial number of railroad workers. After the transfer took place in January 1947, the Railway Administration's board of directors altered this policy to the benefit only of the commercial community: it halted increases to freight rates, obtaining additional funds solely from the termination of 3,000 African railroad personnel. Incensed by the call of many European trade union members to abandon efforts in support of the cadre unique, African members left the parity commission in protest. They called a work stoppage for April 1947, which was halted one day later when the AOF government agreed to the single-staff system. Railroad union leaders soon realized, however, that the government was not negotiating in good faith. The union motion of September 8, 1947, affirmed that a strike would commence at midnight on October 10, unless management satisfied several union demands: cost of living increases, family allowances (money alloted for each child in a family), management bonuses for some of the African staff, the enactment of the cadre unique, and the cessation of skills testing for promotions, which was required only of African personnel. The timing was strategic—the strike coincided with the visit to Senegal of colonial dignitaries.

The unusually high levels of participation by union members in the strike were evident from the start. Out of a combined total of almost 20,000 rail, wharf, and shipyard workers (of which 17,300 worked for the railroads), only 38 African and 487 expatriate French employees were on the job on November 1, 1947. By December 31, all but 838 permanent workers were still on strike (Suret-Canale, pp. 137-38). Several factors were responsible for the vitality of the railroad strike. First, union members supported the nonviolent stratagems decided upon by their leadership. In a circular of October 8, strike committee members rejected picketing, plant takeovers, or any other tactics that would give the impression of sabotage and lawlessness. Second, there was a very high level of internal union communication. General assemblies were held, wherever the numbers of strikers warranted them, on a daily basis. During such meetings, the leadership informed the rank-and-file of the latest news and imparted instructions and encouragement. Finally, union members were sustained materially from a variety of sources: loans from retail merchants, food and other donations from relatives, and money from traditional African leaders and CGT chapters in France and Africa. (While the union maintained close ties with the CGT, it was not one of its official affiliates.) Nonetheless, strikers had a difficult time providing for their families. In the novel, the strikers' wives forage, set animal traps, sell their belongings, and even resort to theft to feed their hungry children. In fact, women played a vital role in marshaling resources, "although there is no evidence that the women's march which climaxes Sembène's novel ever happened"; such a march probably never took place (Cooper, p. 244).

After an initial failure with mediation, the matter was turned over to a judge in Dakar, who ruled for the government. Emboldened by the verdict, the government took a more hardline stance: the strike was declared illegal and any workers who did not return immediately to their jobs would be considered to have resigned. Although management did not create a rival union, it did use several other tactics to undermine the strike: the publication in December 1947 of notices ordering the strikers to go back to work, the recruitment of workers from France, and the employment of undesirables (criminals and the ill) to man the railroads. However, the strike did not end until Paul Béchard, who was sympathetic to African goals, was appointed Governor-General of French West Africa.

The final outcome of the strike was a partial victory for the union. By calling most of its employees back to work, the administration was forced to renounce its earlier claim that the strikers would be terminated from their jobs. The railroad union members also won a 20 percent increase in wages and benefits. Otherwise, however, the railroad management prevailed. African workers were still denied such benefits as employee housing, work breaks, and management bonuses. Moreover, only the more skilled temporary workers were given permanent contracts, a development that resulted in layoffs for unskilled workers. By 1950 the union strikers gained leverage; over 30 percent of the railway workers were in the regular staff system, in contrast to only 12 percent at the time of the strike (Cooper, p. 247). Sembène's novel, however, ends before these compromises take place, concluding instead with the guarded optimism of the workers and the astonished anger of the French expatriates who sense that their influence in Africa is on the wane. In retrospect, the strike was a competition for power within an accepted labor system. Both parties gained. The Africans succeeded in asserting themselves—they would have a voice in worker policies; French management succeeded in placing limits on that voice. Whether the strike had any larger significance beyond labor relations is debatable. *God's Bits of Wood* "portrays the strike as a giant step in a wider popular struggle against colonialism," an impression not universally shared by historians: the strike, argues one, was indeed "an epic event," but the labor struggle and decolonization, though related, were not one and the same, and "the tension between the two should be preserved" (Cooper, p. 241).

French colonialism and social change. France and Great Britain competed for control over West Africa throughout most of the nineteenth century. By 1895 Senegal was officially recognized as a French colony and, during the early decades of the twentieth century, France strengthened its hold over the region by founding schools, constructing railroads, and promoting such money-making crops as peanuts and maize. France also adopted a doctrine of assimilation among the Senegalese, granting French citizenship rights to Africans born in certain regions—namely, the "Four Communes" of Dakar, Gorée, Rufisque, and Saint Louis. African men from these cities could vote, hold political office, and, as "citizens" rather than "subjects" of France, aspire to professional positions in the social hierarchy. Many Africans embraced the doctrine, demanding more assimilation than France was willing to grant. Comprising only 5 percent of its population, Senegal's African "elite" hoped to achieve equality with the French. Such a dream, however, was seldom easy to realize.

Despite France's policies of assimilation, French expatriates tended to regard Africans, however well educated, as their "inferiors." The French founded schools that trained Africans as farmers, teachers, clerks, and interpreters who would assist the French in running the colony; self-government by Africans, at the time of Sembène's novel, was not a fully realized goal. Moreover, French-run schools and the media painted a picture of France and Europe as civilized and "superior," while condemning all things African as savage, ignorant, and primitive. Exposure to these cultural biases left in some African children the desire to become part of the "winning"—French—side.

In *God's Bits of Wood*, African attitudes towards the French range from the slavishly imitative to the downright hostile. N'Deye Touti, a young student undergoing training as a teacher, is an ardent Francophile, addicted to books and movies with European themes and disdainful of her own culture. By contrast, older members of African communities shun all European influences; Niakoro, the elderly mother of Ibrahim Bakayoko, threatens to whip Ad'jibid'ji, her precocious granddaughter, after the child speaks a French phrase. French feelings towards local Africans are similarly troubled. French employee Isnard and his wife, Beatrice, belittle the African workers as "children who want to learn to walk by themselves" (*God's Bits of Wood,* p. 168). Another expatriate, Leblanc, turns to drink after failing to "establish some sort of friendly relationships with the Africans. . . . He had become a narrow, bitter person, laughed at by the blacks and mistrusted by the whites" (*God's Bits of Wood,* p. 166).

The Novel in Focus

Plot summary. *God's Bits of Wood* begins in Bamako, French Sudan, in October 1947, as railroad union leaders and members meet to discuss whether or not to strike. The whole community finds itself preoccupied by the possible ramifications of such a decision, including the family of Ibrahim Bakayoko, an influential African labor activist traveling throughout nearby Senegal to muster support for the strike. Niakoro, Bakayoko's elderly mother, is particularly disturbed to learn of her son's involvement in the impending imbroglio because an earlier strike claimed the lives of her husband and older son.

Meanwhile, Ad'jibid'ji, Bakayoko's precocious stepdaughter, visits the railroad union's headquarters and overhears much of the ongoing debate. The union's oldest member, Mamadou "Fa" Keïta (also called the Old One) agrees on the validity of his compatriots' grievances but urges them to weigh the costs before undertaking a strike. Tiémoko, a budding labor activist, interrupts Fa Keïta and persuades the members to vote for a strike, which will begin at dawn the following morning. An uneasy Fa Keïta fears the consequences of the members' decision and privately hopes the strike will not last beyond a few days.

The scene shifts westward to Thiès, Senegal, a vital link in the upcoming strike: "The maintenance and repair shops were located here, as well as the headquarters of both the railroad company and the union. Every inhabitant of Thiès, no matter who he was, depended on the railroad, and on the traffic between Koulikoro [in the French Sudan] and Dakar [in Senegal]" (*God's Bits of Wood*, p. 13). As dawn approaches, the tense railroad workers argue among themselves about the merits of the strike, some accusing others of cowardice and collaboration with the French-owned railroad company. Quarrels are cut short, however, when a troop of soldiers arrives and attacks the assembled strikers. A riot ensues, in which eight are killed and many more injured.

After the riot the survivors tend to the injured, and the union directors, Doudou and Lahbib, tally the dead and ponder their next move. Meanwhile, Dejean, the French regional director of the railroad company, summons Victor, his lead assistant; Isnard, the director of the repair shop; and Leblanc, the sole French critic of his countrymen's oppression of Africans, to his office for a meeting on how to end the strike. In addition to promoting the creation of a rival union, Dejean decides to starve the striking families into submission by prohibiting shopkeepers from selling to them.

The psychological hardships of the strike transform not only the union members but also their families. Unable to buy food from the shops, the women must find ingenious ways of providing nourishment for their children. In Dakar, Ramatoulaye, mistress of the N'Diayène compound that houses 20 people, tries to bargain first with a shopkeeper, then with her brother Mabigué (the district chief and a French sympathizer) for rice to feed her hungry family. Although Ramatoulaye's attempts are unsuccessful, though

other members of her household manage to obtain food and water from other sources. The family's happiness is short-lived, however, when Mabigué's prized ram, Vendredi, breaks into Ramatoulaye's compound and eats the rice meant for the children. Enraged, Ramatoulaye tackles and kills the ram, which is then served up for the evening meal. The police attempt to collect what is left of Vendredi and to arrest Ramatoulaye, but the women of the community, armed with clubs and flatirons, rush to her defense. A fight between the women and the police breaks out, reaching its peak when a fire, designed to frighten mounted patrols, accidentally engulfs several dwellings, including Mabigué's. Conceding that the conflict has gotten out of control, Ramatoulaye goes to the police station. During her interrogation, the chief of police orders firemen to hose down her supporters outside the station, which results in the death of Houdia M'Baye, a widowed mother of nine. The local Imam (a Muslim cleric) tries to shame the surviving women into abandoning their support for the strikers and demands that Ramatoulaye beg Mabigué's pardon for killing Vendredi, but she refuses. Houdia M'Baye's death, however, devastates Ramatoulaye, who exhorts the strikers to find some way to resolve the situation: "If you won't put a stop to it for your own sake, then do it for us. We can do no more, and there are too many dead" (*God's Bits of Wood*, p. 126).

Meanwhile, in Bamako, railroad union members try to determine how to discipline Diara, a ticket collector and strikebreaking union member. Tiémoko, the official record keeper for the local strike committee, tries to introduce to the community the idea of a trial for Diara's various offenses. Tiémoko also seeks to combine this innovation with the nearly forgotten Bambara charge of *dynfa* (treason against one's people). Although a variety of options are considered, Fa Keïta convinces the union that being shamed before one's community is the most effective way to punish a man. The truth of his words is borne out by Diara's chastened demeanor in the aftermath of his trial. Ironically, the peace-loving Fa Keïta becomes the next person to suffer from the effects of the strike, when militiamen break into his bedroom—where he is undergoing a spiritual retreat—and without apparent cause drag him off to prison. Trying to come to the Old One's defense, Ad'jibid'ji and Niakoro are injured by the police, the latter fatally.

In Thiès, the atmosphere is similarly tense. The women have sold everything of value to buy food, and are supplementing their meagre rations with whatever they can forage. Lahbib enlists the aid of Penda—an unmarried woman, more liberal than many others in her community. He seeks her help with the distribution of rations to the women and with other union-related matters. Penda proves to be a strong leader, keeping the women in line and earning the respect of the men. Anxiety and hunger take their toll on the strikers, but they receive an unexpected boost of confidence after Isnard offers Doudou, the secretary-general of the union, promotion and three million francs to return to work. Realizing that management is also feeling the effects of the strike, Doudou rejects Isnard's offer, to the delight of his compatriots, who now feel they might succeed in having their demands met.

Elsewhere in Thiès, a bored group of African railroad apprentices amuse themselves by shooting lizards and birds with their slingshots. Growing bolder, the apprentices stage raids on chicken coops, steal provisions from the local shops, and

THE RULES OF POLYGAMY

According to the precepts of Islam—a faith practiced by more than 80 percent of the Senegalese population—polygamy is permitted, provided that the number of wives does not exceed four and that the husband treats all of his wives equally and does not favor one above the others. Usually co-wives in a village have living quarters of their own. The husband keeps his belongings in his principal wife's abode but otherwise ought to treat his wives impartially, an ideal to which reality often fails to measure up. A man's wealth limits the number of wives he takes, since for each he pays a brideprice, and then contributes to the upkeep of the family produced. Mid-1950s statistics on Wolof men in Thiès with one to three wives testify to a monogomous majority: close to half the laborers were married, most to a single spouse. Only about a fifth had two wives and less than a tenth had three. In the novel, the women of Thiès are incensed when the French management denies family benefits to African workers by labeling the women in polygamous marriages as concubines instead of wives. The women's outrage over this designation fuels their decision to march to Dakar to show their support for the strikers' demands: "Yes—we will go together to Dakar to hear what these toubabs have to say and to let them see if we are concubines!" (*God's Bits of Wood*, p. 185).

even sneak into the European quarter to vandalize French-owned property. Tragedy strikes one evening, however, when one apprentice, aiming for a lizard with his slingshot, hits the car in which Isnard is riding. In a panic, Isnard opens fire on the apprentices, killing two of them instantly.

The African community's outrage over the shootings catalyzes the railroad managers into realizing that their only option is to negotiate with union leaders. Three days later both sides meet to discuss their differences; Ibrahim Bakayoko, the mastermind of the strike, returns especially for the occasion. Unfortunately, negotiations quickly deteriorate after the French and Africans reach a stalemate over the issue of polygamy and family benefits. An enraged Dejean goes so far as to hit Bakayoko, who retaliates by half-throttling the railroad director; the two men must be forcibly separated by their colleagues.

On learning of this latest deadlock, the women of Thiès decide to show their support for family allowances by marching to Dakar, a plan that Bakayoko heartily endorses. Led by Penda, the women make their way across the rugged, drought-parched countryside; villages between Thiès and Dakar turn out to support the women on their march, providing them with food, water, and shelter when they stop to rest. Attempting to prevent the women from reaching their destination, soldiers fire upon the crowd; two people, including Penda, are killed. But the marchers ultimately prove too numerous, and the women successfully enter Dakar, carrying banners expressing their support of the workers' demands.

The government of French West Africa convenes an assembly of workers at the local race track, urging them to avoid a general strike. But most of the assembled workers cannot understand the government speakers, who communicate in French. Towards the end of the meeting, Bakayoko seizes his own chance to address the crowd. Speaking in Bambara and French, Bakayoko summarizes African grievances under colonialism; he concludes by advocating a general strike, an appeal that is taken up by the workers in attendance. A ten-day general strike promptly ensues, after which both sides return to the bargaining table. Meanwhile, Bakayoko, having heard of his mother's death, returns to Bamako to visit his family.

Shortly after, the union members in Bamako receive a telegram from Thiès stating that the workers' conditions have been met and that the strike is officially over. The militia then releases those jailed during the strike, including Fa Keïta. Reunited with the Bakayoko family, Fa Keïta speaks to an audience of friends and fellow prisoners about the effect that his imprisonment has had upon his thoughts and beliefs. He enjoins all those assembled, especially Bakayoko, to do battle without hatred.

The following morning the trainmen of Thiès report to work but refuse to engage in any active labor until Isnard is removed from his position. Dejean has already left for Dakar, but Isnard attempts to prevent his own dismissal by contacting all his influential friends and asking for their support. No help is forthcoming, however, and Isnard's colleagues urge him to leave while he still can. Enraged at their abandonment by the railroad company, Isnard and his wife, Beatrice, deplore the rise to power of Africans "who don't even know what's good for them" (*God's Bits of Wood,* pp. 243-44). Observing a group of African women chanting outside their house, a maddened Beatrice seizes a gun and fires wildly upon them; she is immediately cut down by a hail of bullets. Her death heralds the true end of the strike and the waning of French dominance in Senegal.

Women's involvement in the strike. Sembène's depiction of women as a vital force in the strike is considered one of the novel's finest achievements. Literary critic Dorothy S. Blair observes that "Sembène shows his understanding of female characters of all ages and types. In fact, the lives of the African women—the heroines of the strike—form the central core of the novel, raising it from a political statement to a moving human drama" (Blair, p. 82).

In *God's Bits of Wood,* African women are exposed to new ideas through the experiences of their male relatives, which results in their discovery of new options for themselves. Some female characters, ever distrustful of innovation, are content with their roles in traditional African culture. For other women, learning about the wider world encourages them to combat colonial oppression in their own way.

Niakoro, Bakayoko's mother and Ad'jibid'ji's grandmother, provides perhaps the definitive example of a traditional African woman. Distressed by the apparent erosion of traditional relations between adults and youths, and disturbed by her own memories of an unsuccessful strike, Niakoro believes union members should not strike without first consulting the elders in the community. Unlike her contemporary, the more flexible Fa Keïta, Niakoro maintains to the bitter end that knowledge can only be passed from adults to children. By contrast, other women, subjected to the same strike-related deprivations as the men, undergo a psychological metamorphosis, abandoning traditional roles and customs as they strive to provide for their families. In Dakar, Ramatoulaye, a Senegalese matriarch, defies the authority of the police and her own brother, the district chief, by killing a prized ram to feed her 20 relatives. She receives the unwavering support of other women in the community, who come to her defense armed with iron bars, clubs, and sand-filled glass bottles. Meanwhile, the women of Thiès abandon long-held prejudices to rally behind the leadership of Penda, who proposes that they march to Dakar to express solidarity with the strikers' demand for family benefits. The marching women brandish pro-labor banners in full view of colonial officials in Dakar, revealing a more sophisticated understanding of the struggle than they may have previously possessed.

Besides battling with police and marching for their cause, the women in the novel also serve as political commentators, using their songs and chants to record the history of the strike. Gathering outside Dejean's office on the morning of a negotiation session, the women activists improvise lyrics to one of their traditional chants to boost the strikers' morale:

> On the 10th of October, fateful day,
> We swore before the world
> To support you to the end.
> You have lit the torch of hope,
> And victory is near.
> The morning light is in the east;
> It is daybreak of a day in history.
> (*God's Bits of Wood,* p. 172)

Although the French expatriates dismiss the women's song as mere "shouting and yelling as usual," the chant accomplishes its purpose, encouraging the union members to continue fighting for their rights after negotiations break down (*God's Bits of Wood,* p. 179). Finally, it is the women who have the last word in the novel, after the death of Beatrice signals the true end of hostilities:

> From one sun to another,
> The combat lasted,
> And fighting together, blood-covered
> They transfixed their enemies,
> But happy is the man who does battle
> without hatred.
> (*God's Bits of Wood,* p. 245)

The message of war has been replaced with a message of peace and tolerance.

While noting that the women's march in Sembène's novel has no apparent basis in fact, historian Frederick Cooper nonetheless acknowledges that "women played a crucial role in pulling together such resources [as agricultural products and fish]" during the strike (Cooper, p. 244). Certainly Sembène's novel anticipates a future in which men and women, freed from gender-related prejudices, band together against a common oppressor: "And the men began to understand that if the times were bringing forth a new breed of men, they were also bringing forth a new breed of women" (*God's Bits of Wood*, p. 34). Sembène's vision was gradually to become a reality in the postcolonial era, during which more Senegalese women received formal schooling, gained the right to vote (denied them entirely until 1946), and became actively involved in politics.

BEHIND THE TITLE—A CULTURAL REVOLUTION

Sembène draws the title of his novel from Wolof culture. There is a Wolof belief that counting human beings can bring bad luck, possibly even death. Thus, instead of saying that there are ten people in a room, the Wolof would say there are ten "god's bits of wood" in the room. This deference to traditional beliefs in the novel's title reflects a belief of its author. His novel deals with popular revolution, a revolution of the masses. A necessary part of this revolution, in Sembène's view, is the revival of their culture, which has been displaced by colonial occupation.

Sources and literary context. When Sembène began his literary output in the 1950s, the changing connection between Africa and Europe shaped the creativity of African writers. Freed from wartime censorship, authors from West and Equatorial Africa engaged in vigorous attacks on French colonial rule. Such a phenomenon had its origins in *négritude*, an artistic movement of the 1930s through the 1950s in which Léopold Senghor, Aimé Césaire, Leon Damas, and others condemned foreign dominance. In a 1956 speech in Paris, Senghor summarized the concern that African writers of the 1950s felt for all aspects of

their societies when he noted that "African literature is a committed literature" (Senghor in Blair, p. 204).

It was not until the arrival of independence in 1960 that Africans were free to express support for Marxist ideas. The influence of radicalism upon Sembène is evident in *God's Bits of Wood*. The author is not concerned here with advancing Marxist ideology, but he does use some of its terminology to show the mental transformation of the African railway workers. During the second meeting between management and union leaders, for example, Dejean accuses the railroad workers of conspiring with communists to destroy French civilization. The response of Lahbib, one of the union activists, is more profound: "*Monsieur le directeur* . . . you do not represent a nation or a people here, but simply a class. We represent another class, whose interests are not the same as yours" (*God's Bits of Wood*, p. 184). But Sembène himself denied the presence of any overt socialist or Marxist agenda in his work, declaring: "What I want to represent is a social realism. I have no intention of creating great heroes, on the contrary, I am concerned with everyday reality: the woman who struggles for life and toils to nourish her child, her sorrows, her hopes. I work with the material of everyday life of ordinary people" (Sembène in Schipper, pp. 139-40).

Events in History at the Time the Novel Was Written

The evolution of industrial relations in Senegal. Although the Senegalese government enacted its own labor law, France imposed most of the changes affecting African workers in the waning years of colonial rule. Enforcement of the Labor Code, which was passed by the government of the French Republic in December 1952, granted African workers a reduction of work time to 40 hours per week (48 for farmers), the observance in West Africa of paid French holidays, and overtime wages if work duties were performed on Sundays and holidays. Women and children were prevented by law from working at night, and the employment of persons under age 14 was prohibited.

By 1955 a comprehensive system of family benefits—one of the primary demands of the 1947-48 strike—had been established. These benefits included a stipend for prenatal care, one year of maternity leave, and a "family allowance" for each child from the first birthday until age

14 in most cases, or until 18 or 21 years of age if an apprentice or a student, respectively (Bloch, pp. 19-20). By June 1961 Senegal, like the other newly independent states of French West Africa, had adopted—almost entirely—the 1952 Labor Code. The Senegalese government, however, did pass a few new laws regarding trade unions. Senegal's Labor Code mandated that unions be free from control by the government as well as from sanctions by employers. Furthermore, union membership was voluntary (Bloch, p. 12). Disputing parties, labor and management, had to submit their conflict to mandatory arbitration. Strikes were to be legal, but permission for a work stoppage was to be granted by the Ministry of Labor, which allowed a strike only if it did not violate the interests or order of the general society (Bloch, p. 26). There was still marked inequity, though. The Senegal work force in 1957 included Frenchmen who, on the average, earned 4.2 times the pay of the black Senegalese worker (Cooper, p. 460).

Senegalese independence. Appropriately, the publication of Sembène's novel in 1960 coincided with France's decision that same year to grant independence to all of her territories on the mainland of sub-Saharan Africa. Progress towards Senegalese independence had accelerated during the preceding decade. In 1946 the entire population of French West Africa was granted citizenship rights and Senegal itself became an overseas territory, receiving representation in the French parliament and a territorial assembly of its own. Léopold Sédar Senghor and Lamine Guèye, two Senegalese deputies, were elected to the French parliament and played major roles in shaping Senegal's political future. The *loi-cadre* (or "enabling act") reforms of 1956 conferred universal suffrage upon all Senegalese and expanded the territorial assemblies' powers. More and more African countries voiced their desire for independence, leading to the disintegration of the federation of French West Africa. Léopold Senghor and Modibo Keita of the Sudan created the Mali Federation—formed by Senegal and French Sudan in 1958—which obtained independence from France on June 20, 1960. Senegal seceded from the Mali Federation 2 months later, becoming a separate country on August 25. Senghor was unanimously elected the first president of Senegal, holding the office until his retirement in 1980. Like the other former French territories of West Africa, when Senegal gained independence, it retained the Labor Code of 1952.

Léopold Sédar Senghor remained president of the Republic of Senegal for 20 years following its independence from France in 1960.

Reviews. The translation of *Les bouts de bois de Dieu* into English, Italian, Dutch, Japanese, and other languages reaffirms its position as one of the most significant of the African protest novels of the twentieth century. Upon its appearance in English in 1962, *God's Bits of Wood* earned generally favorable reviews. The *Springfield Republican* observed that Sembène "shows how the native African people were affected by the impact of European technological developments, and the stresses and strains which resulted" (*Springfield Republican* in Davison, p. 909). Milton Bracer argued that the strength of Sembène's novel comes from "the fact that at least half a dozen of his people are swiftly identifiable, unforgettable, even amid a welter of different names" (Bracer in Davison, p. 909).

Reviewers have continued to take note of the novel well into the era of African independence. Some evaluations reflect the rise in recent years of feminism, multiculturalism, and grass-roots activism in public discourse about literature. Meredith Tax notes that the crowds of angry women "become not just background or local color, but part of that collective hero, the people" (Tax in Matuz, pp. 346-47). Another reviewer maintains that the novel's "insistence on diversity," in terms of both ethnicity and gender, shows that trade unions were able to triumph by transcending ethnic ambition and traditional social conventions (*Times Literary Supplement* in Matuz, p. 333).

Since its publication nearly four decades ago, *God's Bits of Wood* has been the subject of numerous scholarly studies. Dorothy Blair compares *God's Bits of Wood* with André Malraux's *Les Conquérants*; during an era in which very few African writers dealt with industrial relations, both Sembène and the French writer Malraux center their novels on strikes (Blair, pp. 204, 235). A. C. Brench lines up Sembène's novel with *L'aventure ambiguë* by Hamidou Kane. Kane and Sembène, Brench argues, are not interested in colonial domination per se, but in depicting "confrontation between two different ways of life. Each has something to offer the other" (Brench, p. 12). Mildred Mortimer compares *God's Bits of Wood* to Kateb Yacine's **Nedjma** (also covered in *African Literature and Its Times*); both, she says, "stress the importance of historical events that promote a new sense of communal identity," replacing ethnic factionalism with nationalism (Mortimer, p. 70).

—Brian P. Thompson and Pamela S. Loy

For More Information

Blair, Dorothy. *African Literature in French.* Cambridge: Cambridge University Press, 1976.

Bloch, Peter C. *Labor Relations in Senegal History, Institutions and Perspectives.* Ann Arbor: Center for Research on Economic Development, University of Michigan, 1978.

Brench, Anthony Cecil. *The Novelists' Inheritance in French Africa: Writers from Senegal to Cameroon.* London: Oxford University Press, 1967.

Cooper, Frederick. *Decolonization and African Society: The Labor Question in French and British Africa.* New York: Cambridge University Press, 1996.

Davison, Dorothy P., ed. *Book Review Digest 1962.* New York: H. W. Wilson, 1963.

Freund, Bill. *The African Worker.* Cambridge: Cambridge University Press, 1988.

Keller, Edmond J. "Decolonization, Independence, and the Failure of Politics." In *Africa.* 3rd ed. Eds. Phyllis Martin and Patrick O'Meara. Bloomington: Indiana University Press, 1995.

Matuz, Roger, et al., eds. *Contemporary Literary Criticism.* Vol. 66. Detroit: Gale Research, 1991.

Mortimer, Mildred. *Journeys through the French African Novel.* Portsmouth, N. H.: Heinemann, 1990.

Schipper, Mineke. *Beyond the Boundaries: African Literature and Literary Theory.* London: Allison and Busby, 1989.

Stride, G. T. and C. Ifeka. *Peoples and Empires of West Africa.* Walton-on-Thames: Thomas Nelson and Sons, 1971.

Suret-Canale, Jean. "The French West African Railway Workers' Strike, 1947-1948." In *African Labor History.* Beverly Hills, Calif.: Sage, 1978.

Houseboy

by

Ferdinand Oyono

Ferdinand Oyono was born in 1929 in the village of N'Goulemakong, Cameroon, and educated in the town of Yaoundé. After secondary school he studied law and political economy at the Sorbonne and the École Nationale d'Administration in Paris. He pursued a theatrical career in Paris as well, acting in his spare time. His mind on Cameroon, in 1956 Oyono wrote and published his first two novels *Une Vie de Boy (Houseboy)* and *Le Vieux Nègre et la médaille (The Old Man and the Medal)*—both set in his homeland. In anticipation of Cameroon's gaining independence in 1960, Oyono returned home in 1959 to join the diplomatic service. He would be posted as ambassador to France, Liberia, and the United States. Meanwhile, this final decade of colonial rule saw a new body of literature emerge in French West Africa. Shaping this literature were Africans such as Oyono, Camara Laye, Ousmane Sembène, and Mongo Beti, whose works expressed a range of indigenous sentiments (see **Dark Child, God's Bits of Wood,** and **Mission to Kala**, also covered in *African Literature and Its Times*). Riddled with satire, *Houseboy* exposes the hypocrisies and injustices of the French colonial system from the perspective of a disenchanted Cameroonian.

Events in History at the Time of the Novel

Cameroon after World War II. *Houseboy* takes place after World War II, during the final phase of French rule, shortly before today's Cameroon won independence on January 1, 1960. During the nineteenth century, Britain and France had competed for control over most of West Africa.

THE LITERARY WORK

A novel set in French Cameroon in the 1950s; published in French (as *Une Vie de boy*) in 1956, in English in 1966.

SYNOPSIS

The diary of a Cameroonian young man details his experience as a domestic servant in French colonial Cameroon.

Germany, eager to establish itself as a colonial power too, staked out Cameroonian territory. In 1844, after signing treaties with local rulers, the Germans claimed an area as the colony of Kamerun. Germany's control would persist into the twentieth century until, defeated in World War I, it lost the African colony. In 1918 Kamerun became a mandate, a territory designated by the League of Nations to be administered, in this case, by France and Britain. Britain received one-sixth of Kamerun—in two small, discontinuous pieces bordering Nigeria, called Northern Cameroons and Southern Cameroons. France received five-sixths of Kamerun, renaming its share "Cameroun."

In 1946, after World War II, Cameroon officially became a trusteeship of the United Nations, successor to the League of Nations. Theoretically, in the event of a complaint against France, Cameroonians could appeal to U.N. authorities. But practically, there was little change in daily life. France continued to govern Cameroon as a colony; in fact, the projected long-term goals of trusteeship—independence and self-government—were at odds with the policy of assimilation, by which France governed its colonies from Paris and aimed to make French citizens of its colonial subjects. Historians, however, suggest that the practice fell far short of policy: the attempt to assimilate West Africans was rather feeble.

World War II had an unforeseen psychological impact on France's colonial subjects in Cameroon. Before emerging victorious with the Allies, France had suffered defeat at the hands of the Germans. Now, after the war, France's hold over Cameroon continued undisputed, but, in the eyes of Africans, the colonizer's supremacy was somehow tarnished by its wartime defeat: "French political control over Cameroon had until now been unquestioned and a generation of young Africans had been taught that Paris was the pinnacle of civilization ... [yet] it had fallen to the Nazis. . . . France would never again control Cameroon in the way it had before the war" (Quinn, p. 171). In *Houseboy* the gradual waning of French influence over the Africans is portrayed through the often irreverent reactions of servants to the behavior of their white masters. Although the houseboy, Toundi, remains in awe of the French for much of the novel, fellow servants at Commandant Decazy's "Residence" surreptitiously mock the colonizers. On learning that condoms were found under Madame Decazy's bed, the laundryman and the cook laugh uproariously over "[t]hose whites with their craze for putting clothes on everything" (Oyono, *Houseboy*, p. 88). Another servant, Ondoua, hired by the agricultural engineer to sound out the hours on his drum, encodes irreverent messages about his French employer in his drumbeats but

---

BRINGING "CIVILIZATION" TO THE CAMEROONIANS

Houseboy turns mid-1900s perceptions inside out, casting European civilization as confused and seemingly senseless. The novel achieves this through subtle irony, as in the following revelation about a chief, whose family fell under the control of first the Germans, then the French. His family is dragged through two world wars by so-called civilized European nations, which, from the African point of view evinced by the narrative, appear to be something less than civilized: "When the Germans made the first war on the French his younger brother was killed fighting the French. When the Germans made the second war on the French his two sons were killed fighting the Germans" (Oyono, *Houseboy*, p. 36).

---

avoids punishment because in his enlightened view "[i]t's easy enough to lie to a white man" (*Houseboy*, p. 30). By the end, Toundi himself, disenchanted by the immorality of his so-called superiors, shows irreverence. Asked if the water he brings has been boiled and purified, Toundi replies "yes." Unconvinced, the Commandant has Toundi bring a fresh glass, into which the no-longer-naive houseboy surreptitiously spits.

Missionaries in Cameroon. Preceded by Presbyterian and Baptist missions, the first Catholic mission to be established in Cameroon appeared in Marienberg in 1889 under the auspices of German missionaries, the Pallotin Fathers. By 1913 the Pallotiner Mission counted 19 European missionaries and over 12,000 students in its schools. Unlike the Muslims of northern Cameroon, who wielded no state power in the colonial period, Christian missionaries worked closely with the colonial authorities. Representatives of the Catholic Church focused on "issues of morality and on the sacraments, insisting that Africans become monogamous and eliminate superstitions before they could be accepted into the church" (Manning, p. 96). This insistence upon the moral dictates of Catholicism manifests itself in *Houseboy*, when the Commandant questions Toundi about Heaven and Hell while interviewing him for his position.

> "What is it like, hell?"
> "Well, Sir, it is flames and snakes and the Devil with horns. . . ."
> ". . . if you steal, I shan't wait till you go to hell. . . . If you steal from me, I shall skin you alive."
> (*Houseboy*, pp. 21-22)

Peoples of southern Cameroon, such as the Ndjem, Maka, and Ewondo, were deeply affected by Christian missionary activity. It was not the religious beliefs per se that made an impact, however. At one point in *Houseboy*, Madame Decazy asks Toundi if he is a Christian. He replies that he is, more or less. What does he mean, she wonders, more or less? "Not very Christian, Madam. Christian because the priest poured water on my head and gave me a European name" (*Houseboy*, p. 56). Clearly, from the African point of view, conversion had little to do with religious faith:

> It cannot be stressed too often that the mission schools flourished in the Cameroons and elsewhere in West Africa because they were . . . means to the ends sought by . . . many Cameroonians. Until the secular authorities began providing acceptable substitutes for mission education, the mission schools continued to be highly sought after as places

where the African might learn the white man's skills, and, with them, find work that would provide economic rewards and a measure of deference from both the Africans and Europeans. Thus, in many instances, the mission schools produced Africans with literacy and manual skills, but with only a thin veneer of Christianity.

(Le Vine, p. 70)

Oyono's novel presents an ambiguous portrait of the missionary movement itself: the actual practices and beliefs of the missionaries are depicted as diverging sharply from what one would regard as the humanist underpinnings of Christianity. Toundi's accounts of the Europeans' conversations and behavior illustrate the discrepancy between the methods and practices of the French institutions and personnel in Cameroon and the assimilationist ideals they claimed to advocate. There is, moreover, an undercurrent of irony to the revelation: while the European colonists and missionaries refer to their Cameroonian underlings as inherently dishonest and violent, Toundi observes Europeans deceiving each other and channeling their own insecurities or anger into irrational or sadistic violence. The portrayal amounts to a stringent critique of the assumption of African cultural inferiority by Europeans and even by the Africans themselves. The novel's criticism of Church and state are necessarily intertwined, since French authorities relied on the missions and their schools more heavily in Cameroon than in any of their other colonies. During World War I French army chaplains even oversaw schools in the areas they occupied.

Indigènes vs. évolués. In mission schools and elsewhere, Cameroon was exposed to French assimilationist policies. As historians Tambi Eyongetah Mgbuagbaw, Robert Brain, and Robin Palmer observe, "Although the aim of French colonial policy was the assimilation of Africans to French language and culture—that is, their conversion into black Frenchmen (évolués)—in fact assimilation was never widely applied" (Eyongetah, Brain, and Palmer, p. 116). For all the political equality the French promised the colonized, they extended it only to an elite group of the population. These évolués ("civilized" or "cultured"), as they were called, were not subject to the same laws as the rest of the indigenous population, called the indigènes. To be classed as a French citizen, the évolué had to exhibit fluency in French, reject the practice of polygamy, be willing to serve in the French armed forces, and possess a skill or profession, usually compatible with Western technology. Those who qualified

were considered to be under the jurisdiction of courts modeled on those in metropolitan France.

Unlike évolués, indigènes were denied the rights of the French legal system and were subject to a separate legal regime, the *indigénat*. Under the strictures of the indigénat, the colonized were punished—by imprisonment of up to 15 days or fines of up to 100 francs—without trial for a wide variety of acts, from failure to pay taxes, to gambling, to vagrancy.

ETHNIC GROUPINGS

While *Houseboy* does not overtly reveal in which part of Cameroon it takes place, the novel provides details that situate it in a specific region. Toundi, the dying man whose diary drives the novel, identifies himself as "Maka by my mother and Ndjem by my father" (*Houseboy*, p. 9). The Maka and the Ndjem are in fact peoples of Cameroon, who populate one of the densest regions in the South. Toundi mentions the ability of a missionary to speak a few words in Ndjem, which suggests that the boy lives among his father's people; however, he calls himself Maka, identifying with his mother's people. About the time of the novel, the Maka numbered 64,000; the Ndjem, who lived slightly south of the Maka, numbered 41,000 (Le Vine, p. 12). The vernacular of both belongs to the Bantu family of languages, which also includes Ewondo, from a much larger neighboring group. It is in Ewondo that Toundi writes his diary.

The indigénat system led to flagrant abuses of power: "The obvious defect of the system lay in its arbitrariness; any colonial administrator might inflict summary, extrajudicial punishment for a list of offenses, vaguely defined and poorly differentiated" (Le Vine, p. 101). While the indigénat was abolished in decrees of December 1945 and February 1946, it had for 22 years sanctioned discretionary behavior from the Europeans toward the Africans. The habits it promoted were not so easily broken, and would continue into the next decade, as shown in *Houseboy*. Toundi works for the Commandant until midnight, then sleeps at his sister's house in the African quarter, whose residents are vulnerable to midnight raids and arbitrary arrests by the French colonial police.

Despite the lip service paid to assimilation, in Cameroon, as elsewhere, European colonial practice was largely determined by a desire to exploit the resources of a colony. In fact, the people were themselves regarded as a resource to exploit. That this was not the universal view is, however, acknowledged in *Houseboy*. One of its Frenchman, the schoolmaster, attempts to persuade his compatriots that young Africans are just as intelligent as young Europeans. He tries explaining African behavior to the small clique of European colonizers in which he finds himself, but everyone tells "his own little African story to refute him and demonstrate that the African is a child or a fool" (*Houseboy*, p. 52).

FROM THE *INDIGÉNAT*, ADOPTED IN 1924

"The special infractions restrained by disciplinary methods are the following:

1. Acts of disorder.
2. The organizing of games of chance.
3. Circulating rumors of a nature to disturb the public peace. Seditious utterances, acts showing disrespect to a duly authorized officer. . . .
15. Reluctance in paying rates, contributions, and taxes of all sorts. . . .
18. Attempting to simulate or aggravate natural ills or wounds. . . .
34. The practice of medicine or the use of medicines outside the control of the Administration."

(*Indigénat* in Le Vine, pp. 252-53)

The confusion that beset Africans forced to confront the injustices of French policy reverberate throughout Oyono's novel. At the beginning, a dying Toundi asks the narrator, "Brother, what are we? What are we blackmen who are called French?" (*Houseboy*, p. 4). Toundi has fled down the path of assimilation, leaving his village for missionary school, then working for the Commandant, becoming the chief European's houseboy. His dying question shows that his departure from the village precipitated an identity crisis. As a black man who has aspired to be French, recognizes the dying Toundi, he is now neither fully accepted as French, nor is he fully African anymore. He fled home just before he was to be initiated as a man into his own ethnic group, only, ironically, to receive a brutal initiation into colonial life instead. In the course of

his education and employment, Toundi, still a young man, has been initiated into the ways in which local authorities manipulate French colonial and Christian ideals to rationalize attitudes and behaviors that dehumanize and ultimately destroy him.

The Novel in Focus

Plot summary. The novel opens with a preface in which a narrator describes his last night of a holiday in Spanish Guinea before he is to return to his home in Cameroon. After the customary meal of fish and cassava, he settles in for an evening of storytelling and music with his host. Suddenly they hear drums in the distance, announcing the impending death of a "Frenchman" (their term for the French-speaking Gabonese and Cameroonians) in the neighboring village. The narrator, compelled by pity, decides to go keep the dying man company. Entering the thatched house where the man is lying, the narrator is shocked to discover that the Frenchman is quite young and badly injured, his shirt "covered with blood" (*Houseboy*, p. 3). The dying man revives slightly after seeing a fellow Cameroonian and begins a brief conversation with him, remarking, "I'd have made old bones if I'd been good and stayed at home in the village" (*Houseboy*, p. 4). Despite this brief interval of lucidity, the man soon goes into convulsions and dies; his body, already gangrenous, is hastily buried and his belongings given to the narrator, who discovers that the dead man—whose name was Toundi Ondoua—had kept a diary consisting of two notebooks. The narrator decides to translate the diary from Ewondo into French, so that Toundi's story will not be lost.

Toundi begins his diary with an account of his childhood in a small rural village, where he first met the Catholic missionary Father Gilbert. On the day before his initiation, Toundi has a fight with another boy over the lumps of sugar that Father Gilbert threw out to them. Toundi's father, enraged by his son's behavior, threatens to beat him, prompting Toundi to run away from home to Father Gilbert, who offers him a meal and a bed for the night. Suggesting that their family life is less than ideal, his mother concurs with Toundi's decision to leave home—in her estimation her husband does not love Toundi the way a father ought to love a son.

Toundi quickly attaches himself to Father Gilbert, explaining in sign language that he wishes to remain with the missionary. Pleased to have recruited another Cameroonian, Father Gilbert agrees. After a tearful goodbye to his mother, Toundi leaves with Father Gilbert for St. Peter's Catholic Mission in the city of Dangan. While riding on Father Gilbert's motorcycle, the youth experiences conflicting emotions about this new phase of his life: "I was happy.... I was going to learn about the city and white men and live like them. I caught myself thinking I was like one of the wild parrots we used to attract to the village with grains of maize" (*Houseboy*, p. 13).

In Dangan Toundi begins his conversion to the Catholic faith, eventually being baptized and receiving the Christian name Joseph. Father Gilbert treats the boy as a pet, enjoying his amazement at everything and showing him off to white visitors as his crowning achievement, the exemplar of a successful conversion. Toundi, in turn, is very grateful to the missionary: "Everything I am I owe to Father Gilbert. He is my benefactor and I am very fond of him.... I am his boy, a boy who can read and write, serve Mass, lay a table, sweep out his room, and make his bed" (*Houseboy*, pp. 14-15). He is repelled, however, by Father Vandermayer, the censor of the parish, who seems to take excessive pleasure in interrogating, undressing, and beating possible malefactors: "He has never managed to catch me out. I could never stand what he does to people who have misbehaved" (*Houseboy*, p. 15).

One day, Father Gilbert is killed in a motorcycle accident, crushed by the fallen branch of a giant cotton tree. A devastated Toundi wonders about his own fate; shortly after the funeral, he learns that he is to be interviewed for a position as houseboy to the new commandant (district officer). Relieved to be escaping Father Vandermayer, who has succeeded Father Gilbert at the Mission, Toundi thinks: "I shall be the Chief European's boy. The dog of the King is the King of the dogs" (*Houseboy*, p. 20). The next day he leaves the Mission for the African district—where his sister and brother-in-law already live. From 6:00 a.m. to midnight, he is to work at the Commandant's Residence. The few hours in between he will sleep at his sister's house in the African district.

In his new position as the Commandant's houseboy, Toundi quickly learns that remaining passive and invisible are essential survival techniques for a domestic servant. Decazy is sometimes verbally abusive and prone to inexplicable outbursts of sadistic violence, kicking and striking his servants without provocation. Nonetheless, Toundi diligently fulfills his duties and re-

gards his new employer with awe, until one day he sees him in the shower and notices that, unlike African men, he is uncircumcised. Toundi's reverence for the Commandant begins at this point to evaporate: "His eyes had once struck panic into me. Now I stood unconcerned under their gaze" (*Houseboy*, p. 28)

CITY LAYOUTS IN FRENCH WEST AFRICA

In most towns in French West Africa, the Europeans lived in their own quarter, with running water, electricity, and spacious homes located near the government offices. The blacks who served them lived in an African quarter, in small, densely built homes without running water. Their restriction to an identifiable zone enabled the police and colonial administrators to keep the African population under surveillance. In the novel, Toundi's diary gives this scenario a telling twist: "In Dangan the European quarter and the African quarter are quite separate. But what goes on underneath those corrugate-iron roofs [of the European homes] is known down to the smallest detail inside the mud-walled huts" (*Houseboy*, p. 71). Again the novel turns perceptions of the mid-1900s inside out, raising the question of which group—the Africans or the Europeans—was truly "under surveillance."

Toundi accompanies the Commandant on official visits and to social functions, observing French colonial society up close. Details of visits to the Government School, the prison, and even St. Peter's Mission find their way into Toundi's diary. Describing a Mass conducted by Father Vandermayer, Toundi observes the mix of piety, intimidation, and racism that governs Dangan's colonial and (Christian) religious institutions: "The [African] faithful are supervised by catechists ready to pounce at the least sign of inattention. These servants of God march up and down the central aisle that divides the men from the women, carrying sticks" (*Houseboy*, p. 34).

Toundi learns even more about racism and sexual politics when he accompanies the Commandant on tour. They are joined by Monsieur Magnol, a French agricultural engineer, and his African mistress, Sophie. The engineer publicly snubs Sophie, making her ride in the back of the truck, eat separately from the whites, and share

Youngsters push a watercart along a street near the main highway between Yaoundé and Douala, two of Cameroon's principal towns.

sleeping quarters with Toundi when the quartet stops at an African village for the night. Meanwhile, Magnol flatters his mistress in private and crudely warns Toundi against having sexual relations with Sophie. Offended by her lover's hypocrisy, Sophie confides in Toundi; miserable, she covets the luxuries and treatment enjoyed by white women.

After the tour Toundi meets the Commandant's wife, who has arrived from France. Impressed with "Madame's" beauty and elegance, he rhapsodizes about her in his diary: "My hand belongs to my queen whose hair is the colour of ebony, with eyes that are like the antelope's, whose skin is as pink and white as ivory" (*Houseboy*, p. 47). Observing Madame during a dinner party, the infatuated Toundi decides that she is superior in looks and breeding to all the European women of Dangan. He is eager to please her and disappointed when she pays him no heed. Thus, Toundi is shocked to learn from other servants at the Residence that Madame has begun a love affair with Moreau, the prison director. The houseboy's sympathies shift to the cuckolded Commandant, who returns home from his latest tour suspecting nothing.

The second volume of Toundi's diary begins with the houseboy's uneasiness about the esca-

lating affair between Moreau and Madame. Toundi involuntarily becomes involved in the affair, serving as a go-between for the adulterers. The prison director hands the houseboy a five-franc note, payment for his complicity; in transit, revolted by the affair and his role in it, Toundi tears the note to pieces. Sensing that the servants are aware of her infidelity, a guilt-ridden Madame lashes out, screaming at her staff for imagined offenses and docking their pay at the least excuse. Despite Toundi's attempts to cultivate an impassive, invisible demeanor, Madame singles him out for threats and verbal abuse, even as she demands that he carry letters to her lover. On one such errand, a horrified Toundi observes Moreau interrogating and torturing two African prisoners, who are nearly beaten to death before his eyes: "There are some things it is better never to see," thinks Toundi. "Once you have seen them, you can never stop living through them over and over again" (*Houseboy*, p. 77). The incident foreshadows his own fate.

Back at the Residence, Madame accuses Toundi of insolence towards her, while the other servants warn him of the danger of appearing too confident and knowledgable before the whites. Toundi soon learns that Madame wants him fired, but the Commandant insists on retaining him. When the doctor's wife tells Madame that the servants are gossiping about her affair, Madame's hostility towards Toundi escalates. "At the Residence," a servant tells him, "you are . . . something like the representative of the rest of us" (*Houseboy,* p. 100). After Toundi accidentally sweeps two "little rubber bags" from under the bed, Madame completely loses her temper. "Contraceptives: contraceptives," she screams. "Go on, tell everybody. . . . Get out" (*Houseboy,* p. 86). The cook explains to the bewildered Toundi that he has become too visible a reminder of Madame's guilt and shame: "Your broom reached a bit too far" (*Houseboy,* p. 89).

The situation comes to a head when the Commandant returns unexpectedly from a tour. Alarming Madame with his moodiness, he throws Moreau's cigarette lighter at his wife and reveals that he knows about her affair, apparently not the first in their marriage. An ugly quarrel ensues, which Toundi witnesses. After the Commandant accuses Toundi himself of complicity, the houseboy hastily leaves the room. Alarmed, Madame's new African maid, Kalisia, urges Toundi to flee the Residence before his employers make a scapegoat of him: "I'd go now before the river has swallowed me up altogether. . . . While you are still about the Commandant won't be able to forget" (*Houseboy,* p. 100). Despite her warning, Toundi stays.

Kalisia's words prove prophetic: within several days, the Decazys have reconciled, and turned their hostility upon Toundi. They begin to taunt him, and the Commandant resumes his abusive behavior toward the houseboy. A short time later Toundi is arrested. Sophie, the engineer's African lover, has vanished with his cashbox and clothing, and Toundi is accused of being involved in her defection. The police torture the houseboy until he blacks out, then continue with the interrogation after he regains consciousness. Toundi is taken to his sister's home, which is searched, then returned to the police camp, where, along with other Africans "in trouble," he must carry water to all the whites' houses in Dangan (*Houseboy,* p. 115). Struck in the chest with a rifle butt, he grows too ill to continue the forced labor. Toundi is sent to the hospital, where he suffers hallucinations and delirium. Moreau visits the hospital and informs the doctor that he will "set to work" on the houseboy the next day and "make him talk" (*Houseboy,* p. 121). An African orderly warns Toundi, "No one will believe you when there's only you to tell the truth. . . . You're only good for Spanish Guinea . . . or the prison cemetery" (*Houseboy,* p. 122). As the diary ends, Toundi resolves to escape the hospital in the middle of the night and flee to Spanish Guinea.

Two faces of "savagery." Literary scholar Chris Dunton describes Oyono's African protagonists as "wrapped in a dream of assimilation" and "driven by the desire to become a 'somebody' under the colonial regime" (Dunton in Cox, p. 643). In Toundi's case, the dream of assimilation becomes a nightmare, which ends only with his death. The novel exposes the hypocrisy of the French colonizers as well as the gullibility of the Africans foolish enough to buy into the assimilationist myth. Literary scholar Leonard Kibera contends that "Oyono does not intend Toundi to be the child of two worlds who comes back to his people, for better or worse, after his experiences in the white world. What is intended is a study of the extent to which the African *could* sign himself into bondage under colonialism" (Kibera in Jones, p. 79).

Significantly, the novel does not idealize its protagonist's home life in the African village. Toundi himself mentions disparagingly an uncle with scabies who smells of bad fish and describes his father as a domestic tyrant who frequently beats his wife and son with a stick: "Whenever he went for either my mother or me, it always took us a week to recover" (*Houseboy,* p. 10). Likewise, the novel does not paint every white colonizer as exploitative or insensitive, including in the small clique of Europeans in Dangan the French schoolmaster who champions the Africans' cause.

Toundi himself is complex. As a youth, he is excited by the prospect of living like a white man and takes prides in his new position as Father Gilbert's "boy" at the Catholic mission. His experiences there and later at the Commandant's Residence soon teach him how hollow the promise of assimilation is. Perhaps most alarming is Toundi's discovery that the French are just as capable of violence as his own father. Indeed Toundi's diary begins with the remembrance of Father Gilbert's kicking him. Father Vandermayer seems to take pleasure in beating converted Africans, and the Commandant often assaults Toundi. In his first days at the Residence, his master gives Toundi "a kick to [his] shins that sent [him] sprawling under the table. The Commandant's kick was even more painful than that of the late Father Gilbert. He seemed pleased with his effort" (*Houseboy,* p. 23). Moreau, the prison director, projects an altogether different image of his brutal handling of African inmates that a horrified Toundi would soon witness himself: "From the way he talked, you would have gathered that Dangan prison was a kind of African paradise and that those who came out feet first had died of sheer delight" (*Houseboy*, p. 72).

The more Toundi learns of his employers' imperfections, the more he himself becomes a target of their violence. Kalisia warns him that "because you know about all their business, while you are still here, they can never forget about it altogether. And they will never forgive you for that" (*Houseboy*, p. 100). With almost cynical detachment, Toundi notes in his diary that Commandant Decazy has resumed his physical abuse: "Nothing today, except steadily mounting hostility from the Commandant. He is becoming completely wild. Kicks and insults have started again. He thinks this humiliates me and he can't find any other way. He forgets that it is all part of my job as a houseboy" (*Houseboy*, pp. 101-102). Toundi's scornful description of the lead-

ing European brings to mind condescending remarks made by Europeans about African "savagery": "The Commandant trod on my left hand. . . . He has no memory and no imagination. He forgets he has already tried this on me and it did not make me cry out" (*Houseboy*, p. 102). In the end his presence becomes intolerable not only because he reminds the Decazys of their own imperfections but also because he seems not to accept their limitations on him, and by extension, on all Africans. "You give the impression," says Madame Decazy, "that you are doing a houseboy's job while waiting for something else to come along" (*Houseboy*, p. 55).

To the end, Toundi defies the European image of the African as a child or a fool of limited ability. The houseboy manifests dignity even in his own decline. Arrested on trumped-up charges and thrown into a police camp, he fights back first by refusing to cry out during his interrogation, then by planning his ill-fated escape to Spanish Guinea. Toundi's life comes full circle with this escape from further torture, which parallels his adolescent flight from the beatings inflicted upon him by his father. These two escapes frame the story, giving the lie to the dichotomy between the "civilized" colonizer and "uncivilized" colonized.

Sources and literary context. Oyono writes from personal experience. He belongs to the Beti, a large family of Bantu-speaking peoples who neighbor the Maka and Ndjem of the novel. His mother was Catholic. Refusing to live with a husband who practiced polygamy, she left the marriage and became a seamstress to support her children. Young Oyono went to work as a "boy" for the local missionaries, experience that no doubt served him well in writing *Houseboy*.

Ironically, at the same time the colonial authorities were attempting to divide and rule, their educational system allowed new bonds to form across ethnic and national lines. The bursary system, by means of which a select group of young Africans traveled to France to pursue their studies, brought African and Caribbean writers into contact with one another. Their discussions led to collaborations on literary and political fronts. Moving to Paris, Oyono and Mongo Beti, the two most famous Cameroonian novelists, wrote stories that reflected similar concerns: the development of individual and collective identity given the cultural and political repercussions of colonialism, and the desire for personal freedom.

Oyono's and Beti's fictions suggest that Africans internalized colonial assumptions about

---

FROM ISOLATED TO ORGANIZED RESISTANCE

None of the characters in the novel participate in organized resistance movements. However, Toundi's gradual disillusionment with his French "superiors" coincides with a real-life rise in Cameroonian anticolonial activity. Among the most influential of the political parties to emerge was the *Union des Populations du Cameroun* (UPC), founded in 1948 by trade-union organizer Ruben Um Nyobé. A radical movement, the UPC demanded reunification with the British Cameroons and full independence. Its activities eventually led to the party's being banned by French colonial authorities, which prompted a guerrilla war led by Nyobé himself. After Nyobé was killed in 1958, the French managed to defeat the guerrillas. The UPC splintered into several different groups and lost much of its support to the nonmilitant *Union Camerounaise* (UC), which demanded a fixed date of independence for Cameroon. Ultimately, the French granted Cameroon full internal autonomy January 1, 1959, and independence one year later on January 1, 1960. Ten months after that, on October 10, 1961, the British-controlled Northern Cameroons voted to become a province of Nigeria; the Southern Cameroons voted to merge with the former French region, becoming part of today's Republic of Cameroon.

themselves to devastating effect. Oyono's work offers a distinctive twist through its presentation of components familiar to readers of the *roman colonial,* or French colonial novels of the early part of the twentieth century. One scholar describes early francophone African writing as "essentially assimilationist," citing such examples as Félix Couchoro's *L'Esclave* (1929, The Slave) and Bakary Diallo's *Force-Bonté* (1926, Benevolent Power); both of these works assert the overall benevolence of the colonial regime and praise the "great goodness" to be found in white people (Dunton in Cox, p. 641). Oyono's novel presents a darker, far more cynical picture of the relationship between colonizer and subject. Toundi, the naive houseboy, is exposed to French colonial society but the results are fatal for him. Another scholar points to the lack of interest shown by the novel's European colonizers for the well-being of the African. "Even in the hospital the racial considerations of the white doctor exclude the African from getting good medical attention"; the preponderance, continues this scholar, of the whites' cruelty and inhumanity toward Africans renders *Houseboy* a "striking 'roman-anticolonialiste'" (John, p. 16).

Oyono's novel also counteracts another trend, found in works by such noted French writers as André Gide (in *The Immoralist,* for example) that explore the exoticized atmosphere and culture, opulent lifestyle, and extramarital affairs and sexual decadence found in a colonial environment. While the reader of Gide's writings might be led to expect a similarly exoticist or confessional adventure tale from *Houseboy,* it continually undercuts any exoticist reading. Toundi's initial worship of Madame Decazy, for example, remains chaste, never progressing beyond adolescent infatuation, and it peters out when he is confronted with her infidelity to her husband.

Finally, *Houseboy* constitutes a new genre in African literature—the diary novel, which "allows [writers] to hold back information from narrator and reader, although they themselves know what they want their narrator/main character to become, in the course of their story" (Schipper, p. 116). Oyono displaces the reader twice: first by shifting the perspective of the typical *roman colonial,* and second by tailoring the tradition of the novel-memoir to his own society. The latter is achieved first by having Toundi write his history—an act of defiance against the colonists' attempts to silence him physically and to sanitize their past—and then by having another African narrator transcribe it, as a story within a story.

Reviews. Oyono's work has received widespread acclaim, both in Africa and Europe. His first two novels, *Houseboy* and *The Old Man and the Medal,* received considerable attention in French journals. Reactions were mixed: "Some papers greeted [the novels'] anticolonial critique with virulent hostility, but most had only praise for their brilliant construction and for the density and sharpness of their attack" (Dunton in Cox, p. 642).

The English translation of *Houseboy* was also well received. An anonymous review in London's *Times Literary Supplement* called the novel "a superb demonstration of how to write devastatingly about a political system without using or invoking situations at all political" but took exception to the novel's critique of colonialism: "Of course, M. Oyono is unfair to French colons [settlers], and at moments his ribaldry is ... outrageous artistically (*Times Literary Supplement,* p. 281). Irving Wardle, writing for the *Observer Weekend Review,* espoused a somewhat different position: "It is a modest, unassertive book, alert to the false values and self-deceptive tricks arising from the colonial situation" (Wardle, p. 27). His description reflects the moderate praise initially received by the novel. A half century later *Houseboy* would be ranked as a classic of contemporary African literature.

—Victorian Sams and Pamela S. Loy

For More Information

Cox, D. Brian, ed. *African Writers.* Vol. 2. New York: Charles Scribner's Sons, 1997.

Eyongetah Mgbuagbaw, Tambi, Robert Brain, and Robin Palmer. *A History of the Cameroon.* Essex: Longman Group, 1974.

John, Elerius Edet. *The Rise of the Camerounian Novel in French.* Topics in African Literature. Vol. 2. Lagos: Paico, 1986.

Jones, Eldred Durosimi, ed. *African Literature Today.* Vol. 13. London: Heinemann, 1983.

Le Vine, Victor T. *The Cameroons from Mandate to Independence.* Westport, Conn.: Greenwood Press, 1964.

Manning, Patrick. *Francophone Sub-Saharan Africa 1880-1985.* Cambridge: Cambridge University Press, 1988.

Nelson, Harold B. *Area Handbook for the United Republic of Cameron.* Washington, D.C.: Foreign Area Studies, 1974.

Oyono, Ferdinand. *Houseboy.* 1966, Reprint, Oxford: Heinemann, 1990.

Quinn, Eugene Frederick. "Changes in Beti-Society—1887-1960." Ph.D. diss., University of California at Los Angeles, 1970.

Review of *Houseboy. Times Literary Supplement,* 7 April 1966, p. 281.

Schipper, Mineke. *Beyond the Boundaries: African Literature and Literary Theory.* London: Allison & Busby, 1989.

Wardle, Irving. Review of *Houseboy,* by Ferdinand Oyono. *The Observer Weekend Review,* 20 February 1966, p. 27.

Ibn Battuta in
Black Africa

by
Abu Abdalla ibn Battuta

~

Born in Tangier, Morocco, in 1304, Abdalla ibn Battuta is often regarded as the foremost traveler of medieval times. In three decades of nearly constant wandering, he set foot in the territories of more than 50 modern nations. His journeys took him from northern Africa to the Arabian Peninsula, then on through southwest and central Asia, India, Southeast Asia and China, and back across North Africa to Spain. He distinguished himself especially by recording his two trips into black Africa. While there are some other medieval accounts of cities like Mogadishu and empires such as Mali, many were written by sedentary scholars who transcribed the tales of merchants and travelers. Ibn Battuta actually visited Africa and came home to write an eyewitness report of what he saw. After returning to Morocco in the 1350s, he dictated an account of his many journeys at the request of the reigning Marinid Sultan there. His *Rihla* (*Book of Travels*), of which *Ibn Battuta in Black Africa* is an excerpt, remains one of the most important documents of a great age of travel, commerce, and exploration.

Events in History at the Time the Account Takes Place

The Dar al-Islam. Amazingly, the journeys that took Ibn Battuta from the western edge of Europe to the eastern edge of China very rarely carried him out of Muslim territory. The *Dar al-Islam,* or "house of Islam," consisted of the lands where Muslim populations predominated or at

THE LITERARY WORK

A travel narrative set in East Africa from 1329 to 1331 and in West Africa from 1352 to 1354; part of a larger work written in Arabic (as *Rihla*) in 1355, republished as *Voyages d'Ibn Batoutah* in 1893-95, excerpted and translated into English in 1975.

SYNOPSIS

Ibn Battuta recounts his voyage to the East African coast, and a journey over 30 years later from Morocco across the Sahara Desert to the empire of Mali.

least where Muslim communities ruled. Islam was arguably the first worldwide religion. From 632 C.E. Arab armies began to move out from the Arabian Peninsula and within a century they had expanded the amount of territory under Muslim rule to include a swath of lands extending from the Straits of Gibraltar to the borders of China. Over the following centuries, the population in those territories gradually achieved Muslim majority status, and a recognizable Muslim civilization developed based on cultural patterns strongly influenced by Islam. By Ibn Battuta's day this expansive zone of influence, which gave rise to a comparatively cosmopolitan culture of traveling, had broadened to include much of central Asia, from the Caucasus to Mongolia, to an urbanizing region of West Africa, and to parts of India and the lands that rim the Indian

Ocean (including East Africa). In many of these regions, Islam was not yet the faith of the majority, but Arabic was the lingua franca for trade and scholarship, and Islamic customs were as familiar as the Muslim traders, scholars, spiritual leaders, and others who had settled in or regularly visited towns along the maritime and overland trade routes. Even more amazing than the size of the Dar al-Islam was the mobility of its inhabitants and the variety of cultural interactions that took place within and even beyond its far-flung borders. Such mobility was a function of two factors. The first was geography: the land masses and bodies of water in the Dar al-Islam were linked in such a way that they facilitated rather than hindered intercommunication. Secondly, the combination of a rapidly spreading faith with unifying features and the religious tolerance embodied in Islamic law helped extend Muslim cultural and political influence. "Islam encompassed both a faith and a sociopolitical system" (Esposito, p. 38). By Ibn Battuta's time, the Muslim state had long since broken up into a fragmented commonwealth of semiautonomous principalities, emirates, and sultanates governed by military commanders and local rulers. In the mid-thirteenth century, the Mongol army had captured the capital Baghdad Abbasid and destroyed the city that symbolized Muslim political unity and cultural splendor. By the fourteenth century, however, the vanished political unity had been supplanted by a remarkable degree of cultural cohesiveness. Historian Richard Bulliet contrasts a view of Islamic history from the political "center" with the view from the "edge" in order to explain the cultural unity of Islamic society in later centuries:

> Where the view from the center starts with a political institution, watches it expand mightily, and then observes its dissolution, the view from the edge does the opposite. It starts with individuals and small communities scattered over a vast and poorly integrated realm, speaking over a dozen languages, and steeped in religious and cultural traditions of great diversity. From this unpromising start, an impressive measure of social, institutional, and doctrinal cohesion slowly emerges, the product of immense human effort. . . .
>
> (Bulliet, p. 8)

Bulliet places Muslim scholars, or *'ulama*—of whom Ibn Battuta was one—at the center of this social and religious process. It is not only through the extension of Muslim rule that an intercommunicating zone broadly influenced by Islam developed. The growth of cities and trade,

the spread of literacy and the dissemination of ideas, the migration of diverse groups, and the establishment of Muslim institutions also fostered the development of this intercommunicating zone. In short, Ibn Battuta lived in a fundamentally Muslim cultural milieu, a milieu that was the result of over six centuries of Muslim political, economic, religious, and cultural development, and it was this fact that made it so easy for him to travel across the face of the earth. In the Dar al-Islam, peaceful trade was encouraged; piracy and thievery were punished. The lanes of trade ran openly from the Straits of Malacca to the Straits of Gibraltar by sea, and from Xian, China, to Timbuktu, Mali, over land. While never easy, even crossing the Sahara Desert was relatively safe; centuries of trade had led to methods of assuring the safety of caravans. Everywhere Ibn Battuta went, he could count on finding a *masjid* (mosque), the Arabic language, and people who would respect, house, and sometimes even employ a man learned in the study of the Qur'an and Islamic law.

Ibn Battuta—the world traveler. Ibn Battuta belonged to an esteemed family of judges and legal scholars who worked in Morocco and in Andalusia, or Muslim Spain. Ethnically, he was descended from the Berbers who inhabited rural Morocco, but his family lived in the city, spoke Arabic, and identified with urban, Arab, and Muslim culture. He attended mosque schools from a young age, going on to obtain a religious and legal education that included studies in basic skills such as grammar, rhetoric, and logic. An important part of such an education was acquisition of cultivated attributes associated with *adab,* or refined manners—restrained and devout conduct, proper grooming, and the ability to engage in witty and intelligent conversation. "From his accounts . . . it is evident that even though he may have had no profound intellectual gifts, he was, to use the modern phrase, a 'class act'" (Dunn in Ibn Battuta, p. xv).

Ibn Battuta belonged to the class of 'ulama, trained in law and theology. He was not exceptionally talented or ambitious except in one area typical of the 'alim's life—traveling. Born on the western edge of the Dar al-Islam, his journey began with his wish to carry out the fifth pillar of Islam, the *hajj,* or the obligatory pilgrimage a Muslim must make to Mecca (or "Makkah"), while he was in his early twenties. The hajj journey was the start of over three decades of uninterrupted roving, conversing, and observing. While he occasionally served as a diplomat, or

THE 'ULAMA: SCHOLARS FOR HIRE

~

Islam was, from the beginning, both a popular religion and a learned one. Its basic beliefs and practices are simple and succinct, but the Islamic scholarly tradition that developed from study of the *Qur'an* (its holy book) and the *Sunnah* (examples based on the life, words, and deeds of the Prophet Muhammad) quickly attained great depth and breadth. Branches of Islamic religious scholarship ranged from scriptural exegesis and law to linguistics, history, and philosophy, and they were enriched by the encounter with scientific and literary traditions from the Greek, Persian, Indian, and Roman civilizations. Because Islam is both a religion and a way of conducting daily affairs, including principles for organizing civic, economic, and social life, interpretation of the Qur'an and Sunnah can have far-reaching political consequences. Therefore, Muslim rulers acquired the services of Muslim scholars of law and the religious sciences known collectively as the *'ulama*. The very legitimacy and prestige of rulers have, in fact, been associated with the degree of respect and hospitality they showed toward scholars. Patronage of scientists such as geographers, astronomers, mathematicians, and physicians, whose expertise was also grounded in a thorough religious education, offered a paramount way of embellishing a ruler's reputation. One sure sign of a wealthy and influential state was its intellectual apparatus: grand courts of law, extensive libraries, and famed universities. Even outlying areas sought out the best they could find in scholarship; scholars, no less than traders, were agents for transmitting culture from one area to another. Muslim rulers in territories that had only recently begun to Islamize, such as parts of India, Africa, and Southeast Asia, were particularly keen to enhance their images by attracting 'ulama to their courts. A member of the 'ulama—an *'alim*—was likely to be much in demand. In other words, the 'ulama had reason to travel. In an age when reading a syllabus of works often meant traveling to the libraries where they were housed, or perhaps reading the work at the feet of its author, an 'alim might decide on his own to journey to Baghdad, Damascus, Cordoba, or Cairo to peruse a certain book or to converse with a famous scholar of the law or science. Scholars also corresponded regularly, and sent agents to seek out important works in the book markets of major cities. The 'ulama were, in fact, "the best-traveled and most cosmopolitan intellectual class in world history up to that time" (Dunn in Ibn Battuta, p. xii).

studied in a particular place, he seems to have been much more excited by the mere fact of travel. He tells the reader in the *Rihlah* that he resolved never to travel by the same road twice. Contemporary historians have determined that he probably did retrace his steps on occasion, but this self-prescribed condition did result in his covering new ground most of the time. Rather than anything he might have committed to paper as a second-rate scholar of the law, the contribution Ibn Battuta made by recording his observations of places and people has been best appreciated. The *Rihlah* is a gold mine for historians, and a testament to the cosmopolitan character of Muslim society at the time.

Today's scholars have noted that as a writer Ibn Battuta "has his pettinesses," such as name-dropping (Hamdun and King in Ibn Battuta, p. 4). There is reason for this, though, in that his connections to prominent holy men and scholars of his day provided him with funds from donors for his travels, and the record of how all these rulers received Ibn Battuta at their courts gave weight to his claims of veracity and embellished the *Rihlah* in the eyes of his audience. Thus, there was more at stake than a mere recording of his observations. They were a means to winning future financial support and luxuries. Although he certainly showed himself able to endure hardships with equanimity, Ibn Battuta showed a fondness for luxury that donations and gifts from Muslim rulers helped him indulge. Yet he also demonstrated compassion for the less fortunate—the slave, for example, in the desert, even if he himself traveled with the aid of slaves, whom he received as presents. He likewise demonstrated daring and perseverance in overcoming the hazards and hardships of various means of transport in all sorts of weather.

East Africa—from Mogadishu to Kilwa. The East African coastline varies from an arid landscape of dunes and marginal grazing land around the Horn of Africa to rich grazing and cropland and forested regions beyond the equator. Numerous ports harbored coastal trading and fishing craft as well as ocean-going dhows typical of the international trade around the Indian Ocean rim. From Greeks and Persians to Arabs and Indians, East Africa welcomed visitors from all the great seafaring nations. These traders came in search of products unique to Africa: gold, ivory, turtle-shell, coconut oil, and spices, as well as fabrics manufactured there. From foreign ports, they brought to the coast of East Africa textiles, metal tools, glassware, wine, and wheat.

There is evidence of Islamic influence along East Africa's coast as early as the eighth century—almost directly after the initial spread of the faith. The rise of Islam brought an increase in trade

and migration to and from East Africa. Arab merchants settled and intermarried with indigenous royal families, and helped populate prosperous trading towns. "Kiswahili" refers to the blended culture that sprang up in towns and cities such as Kilwa, Mogadishu, Mombasa, and Zanzibar. These communities were poised on the coast (on islands, if possible) to take advantage of trade from both sides—the interior and the foreign ports. In Ibn Battuta's time, the townspeople were predominantly Muslim, of mixed African and Arab heritage. Ibn Battuta took note of the fabrics manufactured at Mogadishu, which were named after the city (Gibb, p. 374). The rich suit of clothes he was given by the ruler of the city attests to the far-flung trade links in which East African towns were involved:

> These robes of theirs consist of a silk wrapper which one ties around the waist in place of drawers (for they have no acquaintance with these), a tunic of Egyptian linen with an embroidered border, a furred mantle of Jerusalem stuff, and an Egyptian turban with an embroidered edge. . . . He brought also a jug of rose-water of Damascus, which he poured over me and over the qadi.
>
> (Gibb, pp. 376-77)

Relatively few reports have come down to us describing the day-to-day lives of the cities of the East African coast south of the Horn. This land, called "Zanj" by Arab geographers, encompassed the coast south of the Horn of Africa to Kilwa. There is a wealth of stories about how Arabs came to settle this coast, but modern historians doubt their accuracy. Those written down in the early eighteenth century suggest the region was first introduced to Islam in the seventh or eighth century by the Omani Julanda family; however, it seems more likely that the African people called the Zanj mingled with the Arabs through trade and settlement. Intermixing and migration continued over several centuries, and was still in process during Ibn Battuta's visit.

Kilwa is the southernmost of the large trading cities of the Zanj region, and also the one about which the most is known now, owing to the excellent archeological record there. Before the twelfth century, Kilwa served mainly as an outpost directing trade to and from Mogadishu. All this changed when the Mahdali dynasty took power in the late twelfth century. Through means still unknown, the Mahdali made Kilwa a great center for traders in gold mined in the area known today as Zimbabwe. Through the early fifteenth century, Kilwa boomed. Mahdali sultans

THE DHOW: VEHICLE OF INDIAN OCEAN COMMERCE

While enormous Chinese merchant vessels called *junks* plied eastern waters, the typical vessel in the western regions of the Indian Ocean trade was the dhow, a relatively small vessel made of planks lashed together with coconut-fiber rope, called coir. In contrast to iron nails, which had to be replaced about every 10 years, the lacing might last as long as 60 years. The hull was carvel-built, meaning that the planks were laid side-by-side rather than overlapping. Unlike the square sails used in the Mediterranean and the Atlantic for over a thousand years, the large triangular lateen sail was an innovation that allowed ships to tack against the wind. A lateen-rigged dhow, often with two masts, allowed a pilot to run with the wind in any direction except directly into it. Introduced into shipping in the Mediterranean Sea following the Arab conquests, the lateen sail became an important technical innovation in medieval shipping, one that made possible the transoceanic voyages that ushered in the Age of Exploration.

Remains of an adobe structure in Timbuktu from the Empire of Mali.

issued their own coinage and erected grand stone buildings, many of which have since been excavated, giving modern archeologists a clear picture of Kilwa's splendor.

There were three main social groups in Kilwa. The ruling class were of mixed Arab, Persian, Indian, and African ancestry, and controlled both government and commerce. Recently arrived traders who came to seek a fortune formed, along with the artisan classes, a middle group. Below them were servants and slaves who performed menial and agricultural tasks and were probably brought to Kilwa as a result of raids into the interior. Relations between coastal peoples and those of the interior hinged on trade and raiding. Cities existed because of the trade in African products like ivory or gold, but the coastal groups did not attempt to rule those of the interior.

Kilwa, like its neighbors, swung on the fortunes of trade. It expanded as trade burgeoned, and shrank when ships went elsewhere. Not surprisingly, then, excavations have shown that towns in the area grew up rather haphazardly. Streets were no more than the empty space between buildings. Public structures like the mosque and the shaykh's (ruler's) palace were mixed among private dwellings. Poorer people built their homes of mud, with palm-frond roofs; the wealthier built houses of stone. Ibn Battuta related that "The city of Kulwa is one of the finest and most substantially built towns; all the buildings are of wood, and the houses are roofed with dis reeds. The rains there are frequent" (Gibb, p.

380). His claim that the buildings were wooden has puzzled archeologists, since the remains that have been excavated are clearly of stone. Students of the *Rihlah* assume that his memory was faulty.

This, then, was the physical nature of the towns Battuta visited along Africa's east coast. They were far from the central lands of the Dar al-Islam, yet they were home to devout and often learned scholars and rulers. These centers bustled with energy and reflected the heritage of African culture alongside Muslim ways of life.

Mali, 1352. Mali was one in a line of powerful West African empires just south of the Sahara Desert. Like the Kingdom of Ghana before it, the basis of its wealth was the inland delta of the Niger River, a region that hosted agriculture, herding, and fishing. Muslim Berber traders who crossed the Sahara Desert from the north brought copper and salt from mines in the Sahara, as well as luxury products from the North African coast. Coming in the opposite direction were traders with gold, who traveled northward along the Niger to exchange gold for these goods.

Mali arose from the ruins of the declining empire of Ghana. Most people in Ghana had lived by farming and tending livestock, but the ruling class grew wealthy by the trade in gold and other commodities. Ghana did not produce gold, but did control its points of exchange. The gold trade was taxed, and the king of Ghana kept all gold nuggets for himself, restricting the trade to gold dust. Ghana declined after 1200, in part because the discovery of new gold fields prompted its southern regions to assert independence. Civil war toppled the empire, after which a man named Sunjata emerged to found the Mali empire, which lasted into the seventeenth century (see **Epic of Son-Jara**, also covered in *African Literature and Its Times*). The dominance of Mali brought a number of developments to West Africa. First, Mali's kings were mostly Muslim, although they tolerated traditional religious and social practices alongside those of Islam. The matrilineal family and inheritance structure common in West Africa was retained even after the spread of Islam, influencing political, economic, and intellectual life. Malian merchants pushed farther south to open up new trade routes and sources of gold. By the time of Ibn Battuta's journey, Mali's fame had begun to spread beyond North Africa to medieval Europe, which received as much as two-thirds of its gold from West Africa by way of North African ports. Though Mali survived in various forms until the seventeenth century, its heyday was over by the end of the 1400s.

At the height of Malian power, in 1324, a few decades before Ibn Battuta's trip to West Africa, the ruler Mansa Musa made a famous pilgrimage to Mecca, which became legendary in Muslim history as well. "His caravan was said to have been preceded by 500 servants carrying staffs of solid gold, and the Arabs were astounded by the prodigality with which he gave alms" (Adloff, p. 112). One of Mansa Musa's contributions following his pilgrimage was to strengthen Mali's links with the great urban centers of Muslim culture. He encouraged Muslim scholars to visit his realm, brought back books as treasures, and commissioned a North African architect to construct a grand Friday mosque in Timbuktu, as well as several palaces. But Islam gained adherents mostly in Mali's towns; in the countryside, there were fewer adherents.

There were distinctions between town and country in other regards too. Though trade was the most lucrative aspect of the economy, and the basis of Mali's claim to fame in the world across the Sahara, the vast majority of the population were engaged in farming, herding, and fishing, especially during the Niger delta's seasonal floods. Agriculture was well developed, the chief crops being sorghum and millet. There was a more varied economy in the major trading centers, which also saw the emergence of an Arabic and Islamic scholarly tradition alongside the rich West African oral tradition. As he settled into his house in the quarter of Timbuktu where Moroccan merchants and scholars lived, Ibn Battuta was introduced to Dugha the *griot*. (A griot is a traditional figure in West African society; the griot served as an advisor and confidant to rulers, as well as a keeper of the oral traditions.)

When Ibn Battuta visited the court of Mansa Suleyman (Mansa Musa's brother), he witnessed ceremonies that seemed designed to reinforce the Mansa's authority. For example, he described how the Mansa's subjects threw dirt on themselves when in the presence of the sovereign to demonstrate their humility in the presence of his power. In reality, the Mansa's hold on power was more limited and tenuous. The sovereign's prime function was to dispense justice. Cases that others had failed to resolve were referred to him, and his was the last word. In other matters, his power was less than absolute. Scholars have noted that the Niger delta towns, which preceded and outlasted the reign of the larger states, enjoyed both prestige and a measure of self-rule based on their wealth and the power of their ruling families (Saad, p. 11) .

The Account in Focus

The *Rihlah*—an overview. Striving to write a factual, though elegant, literary account of his journeys, Ibn Battuta did not merely set out to tell a good story. Upon Ibn Battuta's return to Morocco, the Marinid Sultan Abu 'Inan commissioned Ibn Juzayy, a young Andalusian scholar, to help set down an account of what Ibn Battuta had seen and done. His account makes fascinating reading, especially since he is the only eyewitness to have described some of the places and things he saw. The style of the *Rihlah* follows a long tradition of pilgrimage accounts, travel narratives, and geographic surveys by Muslim scholars. There are implicit as well as explicit references, for example, to the twelfth-century *Rihlah* of Ibn Jubayr, or to well-known geographers like al-Yaqut, al-Masudi, or al-Bakri, who also wrote about some of the regions visited by Ibn Battuta. Such works would have been familiar to a well-read Muslim scholar. Ibn Battuta's *Rihlah* describes what would have interested a fourteenth-century educated Muslim reader—religious institutions and scholars, mosques, Sufi lodges and their spiritual leaders, as well as the rulers in each locality, their courts, and customs. The account also relates various adventures, close calls, and hardships, which Ibn Battuta survived with regularity. He describes a variety of landscapes and forms of transport, though not always with the detail that modern historians might wish for. The same can be said of the economic, social, and political conditions he encountered, though the *Rihlah* is a rich source in the aggregate. His purpose in writing, unlike some Muslim geographers and travelers, was not as much scientific as literary and biographical. Ibn Battuta's fellowship with various traveling companions, jurists, holy men, and various women (always within the limits of Muslim propriety) was woven into the account along with the pleasures of food, excellent lodging, pleasant conversation, and fine clothing, which was heaped upon him as a traditional sign of honor by most of the rulers whose courts he visited. Political commentary tends toward the judgmental, being more dispassionately descriptive than analytical, with the exception of his commentary on the Muhammad Tughluq, the Delhi Sultan in whose employ he spent some time.

The *Rihlah* of Ibn Battuta, while not widely known in Muslim literary circles until the twentieth century, circulated among learned folk in North Africa, West Africa, and in Egypt, where it was copied and preserved in numerous libraries. Until the early nineteenth century, when two German scholars translated parts of it, the *Rihlah* remained unknown to Western readers. John Burckhardt, the famous nineteenth-century Swiss traveler, acquired an Arabic copy in Egypt, and in 1829 British orientalist Samuel Lee published an abridged English translation. Several additional manuscripts came to light in the mid-1800s, from which a printed edition of the Arabic text and a French translation were prepared. Using that authoritative Arabic text, later translations have since been made, the best known of which is perhaps Sir Hamilton Gibb's 1929 abridged version, and a complete translation in several volumes for the Hakluyt Society. In spite of Ibn Battuta's somewhat dubious scholarly status as a "geographer in spite of himself," the *Rihlah* has become a standard source for studying the period (Gibb in Dunn, p. 5). Over the past two centuries, an extensive body of articles, commentaries, and historical pieces, as well as translations in many languages, have accumulated in connection with the work (Dunn, p. 5).

Account summary. Ibn Battuta's early trip to East Africa was shorter and simpler than his later visit to West Africa, both of which are covered in *Ibn Battuta in Black Africa*. Beginning with an adventure-laden Red Sea crossing, Ibn Battuta's journey to East Africa started at Aden, on the southwestern tip of the Arabian Peninsula. He sailed to Zaila, on the coast of what is now Ethiopia in East Africa, where, as he describes it, the stench of fish and slaughtered camels and the oppressive heat led him to stay on board ship even in rough waters. He describes this city as "one of the dirtiest towns in existence, vile and evil-smelling" (Ibn Battuta, *Ibn Battuta in Black Africa,* p. 15). The next day his party set sail for Mogadishu, arriving there two weeks later. Ibn Battuta describes the inhabitants' custom of rowing out to meet the ships with trays of food, each laying claim to a merchant on the vessel and obligating the traveler to let the resident act as his agent in commercial transactions. From then on, the visiting merchant was his host's responsibility and all business was conducted in the host's presence. As a jurist, Ibn Battuta became the responsibility of the local shaykh, or administrator. Not only did the Shaykh of Mogadishu lodge Ibn Battuta, but he also honored the jurist with ceremonies and gifts. Ibn Battuta provides a long description of the shaykh's administrative duties, which included arbitrating civil disputes and judging points of law. He describes the food served to him at length, a menu of fresh tropical fruits and vegetables exotically preserved and spiced:

> Their food is rice cooked with ghee placed on a large wooden dish. They put on top dishes of kushan—this is the relish, of chicken and meat and fish and vegetables. They cook banana before it is ripe in fresh milk . . . and they put sour milk in a dish with pickled lemon on it and bunches of pickled chillies, vinegared and salted, and green ginger and mangoes.
>
> (*Ibn Battuta in Black Africa*, p. 13)

PERILOUS PASSAGE: CARAVANS

Crossing the Sahara Desert successfully depended on precise navigation to reach the string of oases at which a caravan could water horses or oxen, eat, and rest. Not surprisingly, the trans-Saharan trade was controlled by experts, the nomadic Berbers who made their home in the desert. By Ibn Battuta's time, the nomadic way of life was giving way to more settled patterns as the stability and prosperity of the trade routes provided opportunities to establish rule in certain areas. Also by this time camels had become the preferred beasts of burden. In fact, it was the camel, introduced to North Africa around the time of Christ, that made possible regular trade across the Sahara (Bovill, p. 15). The camel could travel more than twice as far as horses or oxen before needing food and water. Without this "ship of the desert," Mali would not have been as significant to regions north of the Sahara, nor would Islam likely have spread to Mali as early as it did. Camels formed part of the caravan in Ibn Battuta's time, which resembled a miniature and mobile state. Its leader was called a *khabir* (Arabic for "one having experience"); like the captain of a ship, he was responsible for following the proper route and ensuring the safety of the caravan. There were also *muezzins* and *imams*: those who called and led the prayers for the Muslim community. Finally, a scribe or notary was usually employed to formalize fiscal transactions and legal documents. Mostly the caravan consisted of traders, but it might also include pilgrims, members of the 'ulama, and curious travelers like Ibn Battuta. Often it made progress to the beat of kettle drums, of chanting, or of singing; the Qur'an was frequently recited, as Ibn Battuta reported doing on his return trip from Mali. When the caravan arrived at an oasis or at its final destination, the people waiting there rejoiced in celebration, for its safe arrival signified an opportunity to gain wealth, and thus constituted an occasion for revelry.

From Mogadishu, Ibn Battuta sailed south to Mombasa, and thence to Kilwa. Here he met the Sultan Abu al-Muzaffar Hasan, called "Abu al-Mawahib." His nickname means "father of gifts," a tribute to this sultan's generosity. In his account, Ibn Battuta notes that the people of Kilwa engage in regular raiding of the neighboring non-Muslim Zanj, but also showers praise on the sultan for his piety and his reputation for generosity. Ibn Battuta recounts a time when the sultan literally gave a beggar the clothes off his back. Leaving Kilwa, Ibn Battuta sails back to Arabia. His next journey to black Africa will not take place until his visit to Mali two decades later.

In 1352 Ibn Battuta set out with a caravan of merchants from Tangier on the route that led toward Fez and the town of Sijilmasa across the Atlas Mountains. After 25 days, they arrived in the desert outpost of Taghaza, "a town with no good in it" (*Black Africa*, p. 30). Taghaza was populated only by slaves who worked the salt mines there, living in houses built of salt slabs for lack of lumber, drinking brackish water, and eating only camel meat and dates brought in by the caravans. Ibn Battuta bemoans the bitter water and plagues of flies; his party stayed in Taghaza ten days, then moved on toward Tasarahlha. From there, the next caravan stop was Iwalatan, ten days' march across the open desert. The *takshif*, a scout, was hired to go ahead to the city and alert friends of the merchants that the caravan was approaching. Devils, Battuta warns, attempted to mislead the takshif, and if he became lost, the caravan would have almost certainly perished before reaching the safety of the town.

Ibn Battuta remained in Iwalatan, the northernmost outpost of Mali, for 50 days. Upon his arrival, he was given a symbolic meal—a sparse mixture of grain with honey and milk. Overlooking the symbolism, Ibn Battuta mistook this meager offering as a sign that he should expect "no good" from the blacks (*Ibn Battuta in Black Africa*, p. 37). However, he decided to stay, and was eventually won over by their hospitality. Ibn Battuta expresses shock at the lack of modesty displayed by women in Mali, at the freedom with which they mingled with men, and at the women's manner of dressing, which was much scantier than in other Muslim societies, where women were never seen in public with bare breasts.

From Itawalan, Ibn Battuta engaged a guide to take him to the capital city of Mali. En route he encountered the Niger River, which, like many travelers before and after him, he mistakenly assumed to be a western branch of the Nile

River. He speaks of the massive baobob tree, and relates an incident about crocodiles that is typical of the relaxed manner in which he sometimes recalls life-threatening incidents:

> One day I went down to the Nile to answer a need [i.e., to relieve himself] and one of the blacks came and stood between me and the river. I was astonished at his bad manners and the paucity of his shame. I mentioned that to someone. He answered, "He only did that for fear on your behalf of danger from the crocodile. . . . He made a barrier between you and it."
>
> (*Ibn Battuta in Black Africa,* p. 43)

He also describes the strange foods of the land—for example, *gharti* (a plum-like fruit); *fonio* (mustard); and *nabaq* (lotus). At first, Ibn Battuta was less than impressed with Mansa Suleiman, the Emperor of Mali. To his chagrin, the Mansa did not shower him with gifts, at least not until Ibn Battuta pointed out to the ruler that he might be unfavorably compared to others who had been more generous hosts, including his brother, the great Mansa Musa: "I have indeed traveled in the lands of the world. I have met their Kings. I have been in your country four months and you have given me no hospitality and have not given me anything. What shall I say about you before the Sultans?" (*Ibn Battuta in Black Africa,* p. 46). Ibn Battuta comments on certain Mali customs that strike him as being inconsistent with Islamic practice. One such custom required those subjects who approached the Mansa to strip the clothing off their backs and cover themselves with dirt. Ibn Battuta finds this debasing. He is also disapprovingly amused by a poetic recitation in which the poets dressed as birds. Worst of all, from his point of view, is the aforementioned lack of modesty among women.

In spite of these shortcomings, Ibn Battuta finds much to his liking in Malian culture. He lauds the people's piety, sense of order, and intolerance of injustice, even stating that "of all people they are the furthest from [injustice]" (*Black Africa,* p. 58). As proof of their religious devotion, he notes that some parents were so dedicated to the importance of learning to recite the Qur'an by heart that they confined those offspring who showed insufficient devotion to this mastery until they demonstrated improvement.

Leaving Mali after eight months' residence, Ibn Battuta set out on the Mima road. It carried him home by a more easterly route than the one by which he came. He notes the presence of hippopotami in the river, and also the great heaps

A minaret made of mud bricks in Timbuktu, Mali. From this tower the muezzin would summons the people to prayer.

of their bones left by river-dwellers after slaughtering and eating them. After a long journey from Walata, Ibn Battuta arrived at Timbuktu, where he encountered the hospitality of one Farba Suleiman, who gave him a quantity of millet and a slave boy. "The boy he gave me," reports Ibn Battuta, "is still with me up till now" (*Ibn Battuta in Black Africa,* p. 66). He moved further along the Niger River toward the city of Goa, from whence he finally struck out into the desert. At Takadda he received the command of the Sultan Abu 'Inan to return home. He traveled through the land of the Berber Hakkar, another of the few groups he judges to have "no good in them"; their occupation of robbing passing caravans probably made him feel threatened (*Ibn Battuta in Black Africa,* p. 74). Finally he arrived at Fez, and his long journey ended. It was the last significant trip in a remarkable career. Almost 50, Ibn Battuta had spent the majority of his adult life away from his native Morocco. After completing his collaboration with Ibn Juzayy to compose the *Rihlah,* and after retiring to what was probably a comfortable existence, he died in 1368.

Whom can you trust? Ibn Battuta conducted his travels in a world very different from our own, one in which the great majority of people were born, lived, and died within narrow geographic confines. The vast region of Afro-Eurasia where Islam was the majority faith and cultural influence, however, was one in which people from all walks of life managed to travel a great deal.

All through the literary sources from the medieval Islamic world are found accounts that suggest an almost incomprehensible amount of coming and going across huge stretches of land and water. . . . Muslims from every region and of every station left home and roamed to and fro over the continents, taking with them knowledge of the farming techniques, plant life and cookery of their homelands and seeing on their way the agricultural practices, plants and foods of new lands.

(Watson, p. 93)

FROM LEO AFRICANUS TO IBN BATTUTA

Although Ibn Battuta's *Rihlah* was not known in Europe until the nineteenth century, a description of Mali produced for Pope Leo X in the sixteenth century sparked European curiosity and fired the imagination of explorers for centuries to come. This famous account of the mysterious land of gold beyond the Sahara was the work of Leo Africanus. Leo, whose Arabic name was al-Hassan al-Fasi, was an Andalusian Arab born in Granada, Spain, around 1494, just after the city was taken over by Christian rulers Ferdinand and Isabella. Al-Hassan's family was either exiled or fled to Fez, Morocco, a city known for learning and culture. His occupation as a notary and a judge in rural Morocco took him into the lands bordering the Sahara, including a trip with a merchant caravan across the Sahara to Mali, Bornu, and the Lake Chad region.

Returning from a journey to Constantinople around 1520, Leo was captured by Venetian pirates. Taking note of the value of an educated captive, the pirates carried their prize to Rome and presented him to Pope Leo X. The Pope had him baptized as Leo Giovanni, but he may have secretly remained Muslim. Learning that Leo possessed coveted knowledge of Africa, the Pope encouraged him to write a book on his travels, which Leo composed in Arabic and translated into Italian. After the Pope passed away, Leo returned to Africa, where he died in 1552.

Leo Africanus's *Description of Africa* was printed in Latin and Italian. By 1600, translations into English and other languages were in print. The description, which proved accurate, had become one of very few firsthand sources of knowledge about sub-Saharan Africa. For three centuries this work was the standard guide on sub-Saharan Africa.

The *Rihlah* of Ibn Battuta, like the long list of travel narratives before it, attests to the continuation of this general state of affairs. Ibn Battuta is a symbol of the cosmopolitan atmosphere that prevailed in the eastern hemisphere during his time, which facilitated his travel not only in the sense that transportation and facilities for the comfort of travelers were available, but also in the cultural sense. Ibn Battuta's account shows that a reasonably educated, though not prominent, individual could easily find lodgings, make a living along the way, be received graciously by the great and the humble alike and—most important for a pious person—carry out his Islamic duties without interruption, wherever he traveled along the network of trade routes, cities, and principalities under Muslim rule or influence. While Ibn Battuta certainly faced the perils of his era—such as illness, rough terrain, warfare, and harsh weather—his proven ability to reach safe haven among people who could speak some Arabic, offer him hospitality, and share his Muslim sensibilities demonstrates how well-woven was the cultural fabric of his era.

Even in a cultural milieu where travel was not unusual, Ibn Battuta stood out as extraordinary. It was to be expected that the tale of his extensive travels might be greeted with some skepticism. Fanciful travel accounts and fantastic tales and legends were also a part of Muslim literary culture. One need only think of the tales of the voyages of Sindbad, which were transmitted as much by oral storytellers as in written form. Thus, it is not surprising that Ibn Marzuq, a North African scholar of Tlemcen who was present as the *Rihlah* was being composed, wrote that some in the court of Sultan Abu 'Inan suspected that Ibn Battuta was telling lies. Ibn Marzuq stated his conviction, however, that Ibn Battuta was innocent.

Literary context. Ibn Battuta is among the best-traveled of medieval writers, but he is not the most famous to Western readers. That honor goes to Marco Polo, the Venetian whose voyages to India and China stimulated the European imagination from the fourteenth century on. In the Muslim world, Ibn Battuta's name must be mentioned alongside those of al-Muqadassi, Yaqut, Ibn Jubayr, al-Masudi, and Ibn Fadlan, among many other geographers, scientists, and literary figures. Al-Muqadassi lived in the tenth century, and spent twenty years traveling in Muslim lands, of which his books give detailed material accounts. Unlike Ibn Battuta, however, he did not travel to or describe non-Muslim lands, although al-Masudi and the historian al-Tabari did do so. Yaqut, slightly earlier than Ibn Battuta, was a Greek by birth, who was enslaved and taken to Baghdad, where with the support of his merchant owner, he traveled widely and eventually wrote an influential work of geography. Ibn Jubayr was far less widely traveled than the others; his book describes only his two-year pilgrimage to Mecca and the eastern Mediterranean as far as Iraq. Nevertheless, he gives a minute and evocative account of Muslim life during the Crusades. Still, Ibn Battuta remains "the only eyewitness account we have of both the East African city-states and the Mali empire in the fourteenth century" (Dunn in Ibn Battuta, p. xix).

Latter-day reception. The *Rihlah* has held up very well under the scrutiny of modern critics and historians, who have generally judged Ibn Battuta to be honest and accurate to a remarkable degree. Attempts to trace the exact itineraries and time of the various legs of his journey have certainly pointed out problems in the sequence and exact location of his exploits. Multiple travels in an area may have been consolidated as the account was written. What has emerged from these efforts, however, is a testimony to his remarkable memory, especially considering the fact that he apparently possessed no extensive record of notes that he could consult. On the other hand, there were undoubtedly many works that he and his ghost-writer Ibn Juzayy could consult in constructing a reasonable account. These would have served both to jog his memory and to fill in where detail was lacking—for example, in the descriptions of Baghdad and some other cities that closely "resemble" passages of Ibn Jubayr's own, and earlier, *Rihlah*. Such plagiarism, if it could be called that in an age that accepted and even expected the citation of earlier, well respected works, was normal literary practice. There is also the possibility that Ibn Juzayy included such citations more liberally than Ibn Battuta might have done on his own, and later copyists might have further "enhanced" the manuscript with such additions. Clearly, at certain points, Ibn Battuta succumbed to faulty memory; for instance, he reports having traveled a distance of over a thousand miles in less than a week. Occasionally too he lapsed into excessive credulity or hearsay, but, to be fair, part of his method seems to be deliberate objectivity. Following a well-established tradition of scholarly responsibility, Ibn Battuta makes clear distinctions in his account between what he has seen for himself and what he has been told, leaving it to the reader to judge the credibility of the account.

On the whole, Ibn Battuta's narrative is marked by temperance and sobriety, even while it reflects the traveler's wide-ranging fascination and appreciation for the varied world that unrolls itself before him. Among the best passages of the *Rihlah* are those that report on the everyday: the foods and simple practices of the people he visits. Other times he reveals tantalizing glimpses of his own personality, although the account is very restrained in this regard, except when he waxes judgmental upon seeing something of which he disapproves. Overall it is a testament to his observational abilities, and to the wonderful variety of the medieval African world, that his simple narrative still captivates both scholarly and more casual readers after so many centuries, and that extensive examination of historical and literary evidence has verified much of his account to the best of our current knowledge.

—Susan Douglass and Jacob Littleton

For More Information

Adloff, Richard. *West Africa: Yesterday and Today.* New York: Holt, Rinehart and Winston, 1964.

Bovill, W. *Caravans of the Old Sahara.* Oxford: Oxford University Press, 1933.

Bulliet, Richard. *Islam: The View from the Edge.* New York: Columbia University Press, 1994.

Dunn, Ross E., *The Adventures of Ibn Battuta.* Los Angeles: University of California Press, 1986.

Esposito, John. *Islam: the Straight Path.* Oxford: Oxford University Press, 1988.

Freeman-Grenville, G. S. P. *The East African Coast.* Oxford: Clarendon Press, 1962.

Hourani, George. *Arab Seafaring.* Princeton, N.J.: Princeton University Press, 1951.

Ibn Battuta, Abu Abdullah. *Ibn Battuta in Black Africa.* Trans. Said Hamdun and Noel King. Princeton, N.J.: Markus Wiener, 1994.

Gibb, H. A. R., trans. *The Travels of Ibn Battuta A.D. 1325-1354, Translated with Revisions and Notes from the Arabic Text Edited by C. Defrémery and B. R. Sanguinetti.* Vol. 1. Cambridge: Cambridge University Press for the Hakluyt Society, 1958.

Pory, John, trans. *The History and Description of Africa, and of the Notable Things Therein Contained, Written by al-Hassan ibn-Mohammed al-Wezaz al-Fasi, a Moor, Baptised as Giovanni Leone, but better known as Leo Africanus, Done into English in the Year 1600.* London: Hakluyt Society, 1896.

Saad, Elias N. *Social History of Timbuktu, 1400-1900: the Role of Muslim Scholars and Notables.* Cambridge: Cambridge University Press, 1983.

Watson, Andrew M. *Agricultural Innovation in the Early Islamic World.* Cambridge: Cambridge University Press, 1983.

Jagua Nana

by

Cyprian Ekwensi

L ike many of the characters he wrote about, Cyprian Ekwensi grew up outside his Igbo (Ibo) homeland in eastern Nigeria. Born in Minna, northern Nigeria, in 1921, Ekwensi was educated at Government College, Ibadan; Achimota College in what was then the Gold Coast (now Ghana); and finally at the Chelsea School of Pharmacy at the University of London. Also like many of his characters, Ekwensi tried his hand at several professions. Trained as a pharmacist, he taught biology and chemistry before joining the Nigerian Broadcasting Corporation, where he became head of the features department. He also practiced journalism, for which he had a certain flair, and began writing fiction. Ekwensi's first published work, *When Love Whispers,* appeared in the market town of Onitsha in 1947. By all accounts (including the author's) this novella was of a piece with the other "market literature" coming out of Onitsha in the fast-changing years between the end of World War II and the Nigerian civil war (1967-70). It is urban, erotic, picaresque, written in a popular idiom, and devoted to the dilemmas of romantic love, a subject that university-educated Nigerian writers avoided, at least at that time. Ekwensi became ever more proficient at refining his pulp fiction. In the U.S. edition of *Jagua Nana,* he lists his complete works: seven novellas, four works of "folklore," two collections of short stories, and six full-length novels. Of these, *Jagua Nana* is his widely acknowledged masterpiece. It captures the heady spirit of an era in which everything seemed possible, even the improbable good for-

THE LITERARY WORK

A novel set in Lagos, the capital city of Nigeria, and in the eastern Nigerian village of Ogabu in the 1950s; published in English in 1961.

SYNOPSIS

Jagua Nana details the affairs and adventures of an aging prostitute in the "wicked" city of Lagos, and in her idyllic home village of Ogabu, during the turbulent years preceding Nigerian independence in 1960.

tune of a sexy middle-aged prostitute who somehow always lands on her feet.

Events in History at the Time of the Novel

Pre-independence Nigeria. From the mid to late nineteenth century, Great Britain exercised authority over parts and then all of Nigeria. Forming a colony with little regard for the cultural mix, the British created a restless amalgamation of ethnic groups. Over the decades power in the colony shifted from British to Nigerian authorities, who belonged to the various ethnic groups. By the time of the novel, most local rule had in fact devolved into Nigerian hands with the promise of complete independence in the offing. Ekwenski sets *Jagua Nana* in the city of Lagos and the town of Ogabu during this era of promise, the decade preceding Nigerian independence in 1960. It was a decade of extreme turbulence, as Nigeria's various ethnic groups vied with one another to take over the senior service positions being abandoned by departing English colonialists, and to grab as much of the "national cake" as skill, muscle, and bribery would permit. The three largest ethnic groups in Nigeria—Igbo, Hausa, and Yoruba—were also the three largest in Africa, and each had a political party dedicated primarily to its welfare. The northern Hausa were ruled by the Northern People's Congress (NPC), the western Yoruba by the Action Group (AG), and the eastern Igbo by the National Council of Nigerian Citizens (NCNC).

Of these, the Hausa were the most numerous and the most conservative; they were ruled through emirates established by the marauding Fulani in the early nineteenth century. Fiercely religious, the Hausa-Fulani rulers had kept Christian missionaries—and their schools—out of the northern emirates. The North was therefore at a comparative disadvantage in relation to the South, where the Igbo and Yoruba had accepted missionary schools and therefore had many more Western-educated professionals prepared to take over government administration. For this reason the North purposely delayed the date of independence, which Nigeria might otherwise have been granted several years earlier, until a sufficient number of northerners had achieved higher education.

Since the foundation of the colony in the nineteenth century, the steamy Yoruba port city of Lagos, in the southwest corner of the country, had been its designated capital. As the colony grew, so did the city, becoming the country's commercial as well as political center. There were positions to be had in government ministries, schools, businesses (especially those with government contracts), import/export trade, and all the services these jobs required: petty traders, taxi drivers, musicians, prostitutes, and hustlers of every variety. Changing the ethnic composition of the city, migrants from all over Nigeria—mostly Igbo, but also people from smaller tribes—flooded into Lagos in quest of those jobs. Lagos was transformed into one of the most cosmopolitan cities in Africa.

The greatest number of these migrants came from the east, the overcrowded homeland of the Igbo people who looked to Lagos as if it were a foreign country where men and women could make their fortunes, as long as they did not forget who they were and why they had come to this place. Diaspora Igbos gathered together in urban ghettos, and joined "Progressive Unions" and "Town Societies" that reaffirmed ethnic loyalties and provided mutual support.

The Nigerian economy grew very quickly in the 1950s, based primarily on agricultural exports (cocoa, palm products, peanuts), and increasingly on oil, which had been discovered in the eastern delta region. Nigeria would soon become one of the main oil exporters in the world, increasing the national income. In short, there was a great deal of money in the city, but a lot more people who were in pursuit of it.

Ethnic background. The first independent Nigerian government was an alliance of the NPC and NCNC, with a Hausa prime minister (Tafawa Balewa) and an Igbo governor general (Nnamdi Azikiwe). The Yoruba AG was in opposition. By 1965 this uneasy coalition fell apart and the rivalry among the main ethnic groups increased greatly. In January 1966 a bloody coup d'état was staged by five young majors, four of them of Igbo ethnic origin and the fifth a Yoruba. The coup faltered and was downgraded to a mutiny, a failure engineered by the mass of loyal government soldiers and the Igbo general who was the British-appointed head of the Nigerian army of independence. There was, in effect, a coup within the coup. The loyal military stepped in and took control of the government. Within six months, however, there was a genuine coup d'état, beginning a series of military regimes that took control of the country thereafter. Civil war followed in 1967, in the wake of pogroms that decimated the Igbo communities in Lagos and elsewhere in the Federation of Nigeria. Within a decade of *Jagua Nana*'s publication, then, the society described by the novel had already disappeared.

As with most countries in modern Africa, the borders of Nigeria were artificially constructed by European imperialists. It was Britain, at the end of the nineteenth century, that cobbled together a nation out of the three largest ethnic groups in Africa: the Hausa in their emirates north of the Niger River, the Yoruba in forest kingdoms west of the Niger, and the Igbo in village clusters mostly east of the Niger. Of these three groups, the Igbo were the least cosmopolitan at the time of conquest. Political allegiances rarely transcended villages, which were usually ruled by councils of elders, together with people (usually men) who had achieved status through prowess and entrepreneurship. This period of Igbo history is captured by Chinua Achebe in

Things Fall Apart (also covered in *African Literature and Its Times*).

Igbo diaspora. British rule caused the Igbo to question many of their traditional measures of success, which stressed defiance over negotiation, and prowess over pliancy. Why, they asked, had the British succeeded in conquering them? At first it seemed their old adamant gods may have been deficient, and so Igboland experienced one of the most rapid and thorough conversions to Christianity in all of Africa. But the Bible did not bring power, so the Igbo turned to Western education. Villages taxed themselves to send favored sons overseas to school, and to build so many high schools that teachers could not be found to staff them.

Many of the semieducated, who left school before graduation, became disenchanted with village life and so struck out for the rapidly growing cities in search of new lives. By midcentury these malcontents constituted a new urban class known simply as "school leavers." This is the class from which Ekwensi drew both his characters and his readership for *Jagua Nana*. Jagua and her erstwhile boyfriend, Freddie, are living, like hundreds of thousands of other Igbo, in the Yoruba city of Lagos. Every important Nigerian city had a similar diaspora community. Because jobs were always scarce, there were constant tensions between the original inhabitants and the newcomers. Frequently willing to take any job without regard to its prestige, and to work tirelessly to achieve commercial success, the Igbo often proved more financially successful than other groups in these new urban environments. Because of their entrepreneurship—and their valorization of education—the Igbo were taunted as "the Jews of West Africa," an epithet they seemed to enjoy. Many joked that perhaps they really were the lost tribe of Israel, and should be known as the "Heboos."

The Novel in Focus

Plot summary. Jagua is a 45-year-old "good time girl" who earns her income from sexual liaisons made at the Tropicana, a bar frequented by businessmen, politicians, and the assorted low-lifes who dominate Lagos, the fetid but alluring capital city of Nigeria. Afraid of losing her beauty, Jagua (whose assumed name is meant to evoke the glamour of the Jaguar automobile) clings to Freddie, a young, impoverished law student whom she hopes to marry after he completes his studies. However, taking a cue from his promis-

cuous mistress, Freddie proves unfaithful, leaving Jagua to descend ever deeper into the moral swamps of Lagos society.

The first two-thirds of the novel detail Jagua's picaresque adventures as she jousts with friends, rivals, and lovers, each competitor locked into a brutal and hopeless search for money. Uncle Taiwo, Jagua's sometimes boyfriend and the most charismatic politician in Lagos, represents a political system so meaningless that his party is merely identified as OP2 (Opposition Party # 2). With his Pontiac car, his bagful of ten shilling notes, and his Falstaffian laughter, Uncle Taiwo seems immune from the race for money, since the corrupt nature of Lagos politics keeps his pockets well-lined with cash. Nonetheless, as Taiwo contemplates the specter of a lost election, Jagua tartly observes, "Uncle, you look like you pissin in your trouser" (*Jagua Nana*, p. 105). Even Freddie Namme, Jagua's other boyfriend and Uncle Taiwo's nemesis, tells Jagua that he has settled on legal studies because "I wan money quick-quick and politics is de only hope" (*Jagua Nana*, p. 103). At the novel's outset, Jagua is arranging to send Freddie to England to study law. She is motivated by a clear-eyed realization that old age is approaching and that she needs a

---

PIDGIN ENGLISH

Among themselves the diaspora Igbo spoke various dialects of Igbo. But in the town they adopted Pidgin English as the lingua franca. Pidgin is a hybrid language, derived from several European and African languages. Its grammar and intonation closely resemble the coastal languages of West Africa. In a country as ethnically diverse and commercially active as Nigeria, Pidgin is one of the few elements of national unity.

Ekwensi has explained that, like other African writers, he tried to recreate the Pidgin idiom in his novel: "African writers in English consciously or unconsciously try to Africanise the English language by colouring it with African idioms or pidgin English or in any other way retaining the speech rhythms of the African language" (Ekwensi in Larson, p. 24). But Ekwensi is also sensitive to the reading abilities of his non-Nigerian audience, so the dialogue of his characters often drifts from one register to another, Pidgin to "broken" (or substandard) to standard Nigerian-English dialects, sometimes within the same paragraph.

proper husband to take care of her. As she tells Freddie:

> But as you is only a poor school teacher you no reach yet for marry Jagua woman. You mus' go train yousself to be a proper man. . . . Den I kin born chil' for you. An you can look after me, in me old age.
>
> (*Jagua Nana*, p. 20)

Jagua sets to the task of getting Freddie to England with the same acumen and drive that she displays in all her affairs. She bribes just the right people to get a passport Freddie cannot get for himself. She makes all the arrangements for his room and board in England. Clearly, Jagua has not spent her time merely drifting in Lagos—she has mastered the wiles of the city.

ALL THAT GLITTERS . . .

~

Ekwensi's portrait of Lagos as both corrupt and alluring was already a cliché in the market literature tradition of Onitsha (see "Sources and literary context"). The source of the corruption and the allure is the same: money, which arbitrates everything in this wicked city. It decides all matters of life and love among Jagua and her friends. The relentless pursuit of money brings Jagua and the other hotel girls to the Tropicana club to solicit, motivates the politicians to murder each other with hired thugs, and gives everyone a market value. "They and many others were practically strangers in a town where all came to make fast money by faster means, and greedily to seek positions that yielded even more money" (Ekwensi, *Jagua Nana*, p. 24).

During Freddie's 18-month absence, Jagua throws herself into Uncle Taiwo's arms—and into his political campaigns. She addresses the Lagosian market women so powerfully that Uncle Taiwo asks in disbelief, "Jagua, who teach you politics?" (*Jagua Nana*, p. 111). She further demonstrates her political skills by visiting Freddie's home town of Bagana. There she manages to end a chieftaincy dispute with a neighboring village that had been threatening to flare into war for years. Between these delicate political maneuvers, she also manages to slip in a brief but torrid affair with Bagana town chief Ofubara.

The only dark side to this quick trip back east is Jagua's discovery that she does not have sufficient capital to establish herself as an Onitsha

cloth merchant. For her, the cloth trade has always represented the best alternative to prostitution at the Tropicana. Her brother, Fonso, a merchant prince, explicates the attractiveness of trading for a certain kind of Igbo woman:

> The merchant princesses, he boasted, were independent women, and he knew that his sister loved independence. And they were free. They turned their minds to business, not frivolities. They were grown-up women.
>
> (*Jagua Nana*, p. 18)

Before the period described in the novel, Jagua had toured the west coast of Africa, collecting cloth to sell. With her hoard she then settled in Lagos and became the talk of the town. Her fashions were sought by all the smart set. Despite her entanglements in the affairs of Lagos, Jagua keeps reiterating her desire to return to the cloth trade, even singing the praises of her home market to a group of Lagos women merchants: "Go to Onitsha and see what a market should be like" (*Jagua Nana*, p. 110). But, we are told, three years have elapsed since Jagua has collected any new stock. She is prevented from such a trip by the (realistic) fear that younger women might replace her as Queen of the Tropicana should she leave Lagos for any length of time. And now, in a brief visit back home, she discovers that she will need more than Tropicana payoffs to begin the life of a merchant princess.

Unlike all of her peers, Jagua is conscious of the vicious nature of Lagos and of her precarious position in the city's society. She has lived beyond the dewy age of most fictional prostitutes largely because of her clear vision of Lagos's traps:

> She knew that if a girl went to the Tropicana every day, that girl was a pawn; a pawn in the hands of criminals, Senior Service men, contractors, thieves, detectives, liars, cheats, the rabble, the scum of the country's grasping hordes and headlong rush to "civilisation," "sophistication," and all the falsehood it implied.
>
> (*Jagua Nana*, p. 96)

After her return from trips to Bagana and Onitsha, Jagua throws herself into Lagosian affairs with undiminished energy. She resumes her relationship with Uncle Taiwo, and becomes one of his chief campaign assets. By this time Freddie has returned from England and, with galling ingratitude, marries a younger woman and becomes Uncle Taiwo's chief opponent for a seat on the Lagos City Council. Poor Freddie has not taken proper measure of his opponents. Taiwo sends out his goons to rough him up, and he dies from their blows. There is an uproar over this assassination and Uncle Taiwo loses the election.

Following the election fiasco, an apocalypse engulfs Jagua's Lagosian friends and lovers. Uncle Taiwo is murdered, as is his chief henchman, Dennis Odoma (with whom Jagua also has had a little fling). Even Odoma's girlfriend, Sabrina, is killed, along with an assortment of lesser hangers-on, in what Ekwensi surely means us to see as a judgment on their way of life. It is only the arrival of her brother, Fonso, who appears like "the day of Judgment," with the news that their father is dying, that saves Jagua from this general doom. Accepting the traditional call back home to attend a parent's funeral, Jagua escapes Lagos to begin life anew.

Although Jagua had deserted her father and her village ten years before the start of the novel, she knows she can return and be welcomed as the prodigal daughter. In fact, it is only when this nearly 50-year-old woman returns to her roots that she is able to conceive a child—by an anonymous lover, during a tryst near the river shrine of the traditional Igbo deity of fertility. The death of that infant a few days after its birth seems like the penitential price Jagua must pay for all her decadent years in Lagos. She is discovered by her mother near the river, holding the infant, "silent and stiff as an effigy before the oracle" (*Jagua Nana*, p. 144).

But the gods have one more trick left to play. Jagua has returned to Ogabu with Uncle Taiwo's briefcase, which he had entrusted to her the night he lost the election. She believed the case was full of party documents, but when she opens it some months later, she finds that it is filled with money, thousands of pounds stolen from the party treasury, which will now finance Jagua's dreams of becoming a merchant princess. So, full of her incorrigible optimism, Jagua muses at novel's end, "I goin' to Onitsha. I wan' to become proper merchant princess. I goin' to buy me shop, and lorry, and employ me own driver. I goin' to face dis business serious. I sure dat God above goin' to bless me" (*Jagua Nana*, p. 144).

Flight east. In contrast to the greed and corruption of Lagos, Ekwensi describes Ogabu as a paradise, not lost to our heroine, but temporarily set aside:

> In Ogabu the people tilled the soil and drank the river water and ate yams and went to

church, but came home to worship their family oracles. They believed that in a village where every man had his own yam plots, there is much happiness … but where it is only one man who has the yam plots there is nothing but anger and envy.
>
> (*Jagua Nana*, p. 52)

This lack of artifice accentuates the artificiality of Lagos, and the disharmony of those who live the high life there. The village children wonder if Jagua is bleeding when they see her red lips, and a village woman comments that "she walks as if her bottom will drop off" (*Jagua Nana*, p. 53). But regeneration comes to Jagua when she resumes the natural rhythm of Ogabu life. While bathing nude in the village stream, she comes to the realization that this freedom to live naturally is denied to all those who escape to the city to find "freedom."

A FEMALE-DOMINATED TRADE—FROM LAGOS TO ONITSHA

Most of the cloth traders in Lagos were Yoruba rather than Igbo women. There were sizable cloth shops in Lagos, some with stock worth £5,000 or more in the 1950s. Most of the Igbo women who engaged in trade in Lagos concentrated instead on foodstuffs. In the novel, Jagua Nana logically plans on centering her cloth trade in Onitsha, one of Igboland's two main trading centers, the other being Aba.

Jagua's return to the East marks her transformation from harlot to heroine, from call girl to merchant princess. In an odd sort of way, her shameless story becomes the archetypal quest narrative for the Igbo in diaspora. For a while, a woman of unparalleled beauty and great natural skills forsakes her village, her family, and the traditional path of duty. But in the end she returns to Igboland, ready to commence the trade that will make her rich and happy. Jagua Nana's ordeals and her return home blaze a fictional trail that became, in fact, a bloody highway for hundreds of thousands of Igbos who fled from Lagos (and other cities) back to their eastern villages after the pogroms of the 1960s.

Between the years of the novel's publication in England (1961) and the United States (1969), resentments towards the Igbo grew. Communal attacks against them marked periods of political

View of an old district in Lagos, the capital of Nigeria and center of commercial and
political activity.

tension throughout the 1950s and 1960s. Following the overthrow of the First Nigerian Republic in 1966, thousands of Igbo were killed in
riots, and hundreds of thousands more fled back
to the East. In 1967 eastern Nigeria declared its
independence as the Republic of Biafra, and a
bloody civil war followed. Unsuccessful in their
attempt to secede from the rest of the country,
the Igbo would be reintegrated back into the federation of Nigeria in 1970.

Much of the plot of *Jagua Nana* is shadowed
by this history: the social life of the Igbo diaspora community in Lagos; the competition for
jobs and scholarships; and the haunting desire
of many Igbo to flee back to the safety of their
natal villages. In her own return to Ogabu, the

fictional Jagua precedes by a decade the mass exodus of her fellow Igbos from Lagos at the start
of the Biafra War.

Sources and literary context. Urbanization and
the spread of education created a new social class
in Nigeria. Originally from overcrowded rural
areas, members of this class came to the city
looking for further education and a chance to
make money. A natural center for this migration
was Onitsha, a city that has always had the
largest number of secondary and commercial
schools in the country. The students, petty
traders, artisans, and school leavers who constituted this new class developed a taste for reading through their limited education, but did not
have the background reading ability to appreci-

ate most conventional forms of literature. For a time, "penny dreadfuls" and "shilling shockers" from England and extravagant romances from India satisfied the popular reading taste. But following World War II an indigenous body of "market literature"—produced by local publishers who set up their presses in the marketplace—arose in Onitsha to eclipse these foreign rivals. *Jagua Nana* is the best realized novel to come out of this tradition.

Perhaps the most popular Onitsha titles were pamphlets of the "How To" variety: *How to Write Good English*; *How to Conduct Meetings*; *How to Know Hausa, Ibo, Yoruba, and English Languages*. Another popular form of the didactic pamphlet offered advice on the ways of the city, the pursuit of money, and success in the "game of love." A bestseller in this variety, J. Nnadozie's *Beware of Harlots and Many Friends: The World Is Hard*, levels 24 charges against hotel girls, all of whom resemble Jagua.

Although the majority of market literature is didactic, the most vigorous writing was fictional, and the bestsellers were novellas or plays. Their themes were similar to those of the didactic tracts: the treacherous glamour of "true love" versus the mores of traditional marriage; the pleasures of the "high life" versus the respectable duties of achieving success in the world. Although the Onitsha novelists occasionally chose a schoolboy as hero in their romances, the most frequent protagonists were "Highlife" queens: women of dubious virtue and immense desirability.

Highlife queens seemed to share the same life story: all were born beauties and were pampered by doting parents. Though intelligent, they lost interest in school when they discovered the game of love. Marriage was a disaster: the husband was either too poor, too old-fashioned, or a thief. Eventually they became harlots, a profession that their love of Highlife, fashion, and money made inevitable. Repentance came too late for most, as the heartbroken heroine died "a miserable, lonely and lamentable death" (Maxwell, p. 1). Within the limits of the stereotype each author brought his peculiar imaginative and linguistic skills to the portrait. While an individual author might repeat a successful characterization in a later novella, no two authors created the same heroine, and thus the composite of the Highlife queen gained fresh nuances from each publication.

In the pursuit of love, the Onitsha heroine was most resourceful. She could be charmingly coquettish, or as direct as the heroine who would write a letter to her boyfriend demanding to know his intentions regarding carnal love, and then throw the poor lad into a frenzy by enclosing "a partially nude picture of mine which I took specially for you to show you that I mean all I say in this letter" (Iguh, p. 13). Although the strategies of love were fully explored, the brass

THE WORLD OF "HIGHLIFE"

A few years after the publication of *Jagua Nana*, many Nigerian radio stations and outdoor record shops were playing the Highlife tune, "Baby One Pound, No Balance," by Stephen Osadebe and his Nigerian Sound Makers. The lyric (transcribed and translated by D. Cosentino from the original 45 rpm disk) sings of a young man chastising his girlfriend for her harlot ways:

> Baby, wat thing yu dey fine?
> One pound, no balance . . .
> All men yu go sabi, because of money-o,
> When I give yu my love, yu no go tek.
> Sisi, I say wat ting yu dey fine,
> Yu say na money-o.
> When I give yu money, wat ting you go do-o?
> Yu go drink, yu go smoke
> Yu tire, I dey go. . . .
>
> Baby, What turns you on?
> [You answer] 'Big bucks, no small change' . . .
> You go for every guy, because of money,
> When I give you my love, you won't take it.
> Babe, I ask, What turns you on?
> You say it's money.
> But when I give you money, what things do you do?
> You drink, you smoke,
> get bummed, and I scram.

Osadebe's lyrics describe a world of harlots, sexually frustrated boys, cigarettes, beer drinking, lipstick and pancake makeup, sleazy bars, and rent-by-the-hour hotel rooms. These are the elements of the social world created by and for the school leavers who made a new world for themselves in the post-World War II cities of Nigeria. Although the particular elements of this glitzy world were more often fantasized about than lived out, nearly every school leaver could dance the "Highlife," a highly syncopated, percussive, and brassy blend of traditional and imported African sounds, which was the music of Jagua Nana's world. They could also speak in and about that world in the idiom of Pidgin, the universal language of Highlife.

JAGUA NANA AS POP CULTURE ICON

Although several of Ekwensi's *Jagua Nana* characters are distinctly drawn, they are hardly originals. He had created similar urban tough guys and fallen women in his earlier fiction, especially in *People of the City,* which is a kind of prequel to this novel. Their analogues can also be found in the tough guys, hotel girls, and "been-tos" (been to foreign lands) of Onitsha literature, and in the melodramatic actors and actresses who starred in the grade-B American and Indian movies popular during the 1950s in Nigeria.

In *Jagua Nana,* it was Ekwensi's inspiration to take the common figure of the prostitute with a heart of gold and transform her into an aging but highly determined cover-girl-like character. Jagua Nana is the composite perfection of pop culture fantasies: her superb breasts are "God's own milk to humanity"; three times in the novel they "swell in sensuous arcs" (pp. 5, 26, 84). Her "olive-orange skin" makes her look like "an Indian beauty"—an aesthetic quality much appreciated from the romantic novels that were flooding into Nigeria from India.

What descriptions of Jagua and her attire most resemble, however, is advertising copy from the popular press, especially from *Drum,* the first and most popular pan-African "fanzine." Through the following sort of language, clearly derived from marketing, Jagua becomes a model for what sociologists term "the Revolution of Rising Expectations"—the way in which advertising language creates a desire for and expectation of commodity acquisition:

> She had chosen the brightest lipstick in her bag, her blouse was sleeveless and cut so low that only the tips of her breasts were covered. The skirt was so tight she could not take a stride of more than six inches at a time. It was a grey skirt with three big buttons down the front and a big slit down the back. Her olive-skinned calves were fully on show and her feet were barely kissed by open-worked wedge-heeled shoes. . . .

(*Jagua Nana,* p. 67)

Ekwensi's easy use of *Drum*'s visual language gives a tactile quality to his characters that sometimes seems cinematic. Perhaps for this reason an Italian film company proposed making *Jagua Nana* into a movie, the first "Spaghetti" African romance. Ekwensi carried that same language into the sequel, *Jagua Nana's Daughter,* which may partly explain why that novel caused a cultural mania during the last years of the Nigerian oil boom in the 1980s.

tacks of lovemaking were usually avoided. Authors tended to draw a discreet veil around the lovers' beds. It may be that pornography is a culturally developed taste, or that traditional Igbo mores inhibited detailed literary discussions of the acts of love (inhibitions certainly not on display in the graphically satiric *mbari* art tradition). In any case, Onitsha writers did not have to undress their heroines in order to inflame the imagination of their readers.

Where did she come from, this Onitsha heroine? The authors who created her were first and foremost good observers of their own society. The same forces that brought these men and their readers to the city also helped create a new urban woman, one less bound by traditional expectations. For the first time this new Igbo woman could play an independent role in society. The wealthy and independent merchant princess of Onitsha, whose flamboyant entrepreneurship inspires Jagua, is one example of this new woman; the hotel harlot described by the market literature authors is another. Most urban Igbo women conform to neither stereotype, yet as a new class these women have inspired a whole genre of literature devoted to examining their independence and the dangers that men feel arise from it.

Like the servant girl in Victorian literature, or the cowboy in American movies, the Onitsha heroine became a symbol of her age and society. She summed up a time of transition between a rural and at least a partially urbanized Nigeria. Often condemned as a harlot, she must have been secretly admired by writers who wrote obsessively of her adventures, and by readers who spent precious shillings to buy the works.

There were approximately 250 titles of Onitsha market literature extant in 1963, though this was only a fraction of the total number published. No effort had been made to preserve all the titles, and no adequate bibliography exists. A few years after the publication of *Jagua Nana,* the Onitsha market was badly damaged in the Nigeria civil war (1967-70). The presses that printed the novellas were not repaired or replaced following the war, and a tradition ended.

Reviews. The first critical responses to *Jagua Nana* were in the English press, and they were positive. An unsigned review in the *Times Literary Supplement* stated:

> *Jagua Nana* in its own right is a very good novel indeed, and one of the first to give us a truly authoritative picture of a little-known side of the New Africa, of the "High-life" of the towns and their night-clubs and bars and political intrigues. . . . [Ekwensi] has dealt with themes of great importance, and though he has not solved them—is that the novelist's business?— he has depicted them eloquently and with compassion.
>
> (*Times Literary Supplement* p. 197)

Bernard Bergonzi, writing in *The Spectator,* succinctly concluded, "Mr. Ekwensi tells [Jagua Nana's] story in a smooth but colorful prose; if this book is anything to judge by, the West African novel is growing up fast" (Bergonzi, p. 416).

African responses to the novel were more mixed. Embarrassed by the subject, and perhaps annoyed by the author's commercial success (especially when an Italian film company explored the possibilities of turning *Jagua Nana* into a movie), academic critics either shunned the novel or attacked it as unseemly. Sierra Leonean critic Eustace Palmer led the charge:

> Ekwensi hardly manifests a consistent moral attitude, his main preoccupation being the sensationalism created by vice. All these weak-

nesses are clearly present in his most successful novel *Jagua Nana.* . . . [She] is a nymphomaniac with a crazy passion for sex and the bright lights of Lagos. . . . One would expect a serious novelist to show some signs of disapproval of Jagua's conduct, but instead Ekwensi seems to try to persuade the reader to share his captivation with her: there is very little criticism, either of her or of the threat which the dangerous Lagos underworld presents to civilized standards. . . . *Jagua Nana* represents Ekwensi at his best, and yet by any standards it is a failure.

> (Palmer in Chinweizu, p. 137)

Igbo critics Chinweizu, Onwuchekwa Jemie, and Ihechukwu Madubuike attacked Palmer for prissy Victorian definitions of morality and invoked Shakespeare's refusal to take a moral stand towards his villains as precedent enough for Ekwensi's objective portrayal of Nigerian corruption (Chinweizu, pp. 98-146).

Jagua's final return to Ogabu was also the subject of critical debate. Robert July, accepting the novel as a comment on the urbanized African, found Jagua's return unconvincing: "In the end, Jagua goes home to her village to live, but this is the weakest part of the book and remains unconvincing" (July, p. 223). July described Jagua's return as a triumph of "outdated customs and superstitions" over the "meaningful emancipation" and freedom that Lagos offers. Austin Shelton, however, found the opposite meaning in Jagua's return, discerning in it an archetypal reintegration of the African into natal society, a rejection of acculturation through what he called an "ontological recoil" from the Westernized city to the village in the forest (Shelton, p. xx).

There has been no controversy in the popular reception of the novel. The novel's popularity has proved so enduring that Ekwensi wrote a sequel, *Jagua Nana's Daughter,* in 1986, which inspired a popular Nigerian bumper sticker: "I Love Jagua Nana and her Daughter too." No other fictional character has ever come close to capturing a similar hold on the Nigerian imagination.

—Donald Cosentino

For More Information

Bergonzi, Bernard. "Despite His Cleverness." *The Spectator,* 24 March 1961, p. 416.

Chinweizu, Onwuchekwa Jemie, and Ihechukwu Madubuike. *Toward the Decolonization of African Literature.* Howard University Press, 1983.

Cosentino, Donald. "The Onitsha Heroine." *Ba Shiru* 2 (fall 1970-spring 1971): 52-59.

———. "Jagua Nana: Culture Heroine." *Ba Shiru.* 8, no. 1 (1977): 11-17.

Ekwensi, Cyprian. *Jagua Nana*. Panther: London, 1963.

Iguh, Thomas. *The Sorrows of Love*. Onitsha, n.d.

July, Robert. "The African Personality in the African Novel." In *Introduction to African Literature*. Evanston: Northwestern University Press, 1967.

Larson, Charles. *The Emergence of African Fiction*. Bloomington: Indiana University Press, 1971.

Maxwell, Highbred. *Our Modern Ladies Characters [sic] Towards Boys*. Onitsha, n.d.

"A New Regionalism." *The Times Literary Supplement,* 31 March 1961, p. 197.

Obiechina, E. N. *Onitsha Market Literature*. London: Heinemann, 1972.

Shelton, Austin. "Le Retour a la Brousse ou le Recul Ontologique." *Presence Africaine* 46 (1963): xxx.

The Joys of Motherhood

by

Buchi Emecheta

Florence Onyebuchi ("Buchi") Emecheta was born in Lagos, Nigeria, in 1944. Her childhood was divided between the large city of Lagos in southwestern Nigeria and the town of Ibuza in south-central Nigeria. She attended Christian schools, including the Methodist Girls' High School in Lagos, and after marrying Sylvester Onwordi in 1960 she worked briefly at the U.S. Embassy there. Two years later she moved to London with her two children to join her husband who had emigrated there to pursue his studies. After separating from her husband in 1966, Emecheta struggled to support herself and her now five children while continuing her college education and fiction writing. In 1972 she published an autobiographical novel, *In the Ditch,* and two years later received a bachelor's degree in sociology from the University of London. Emecheta wrote three more novels and two teleplays before she published what is usually regarded as her finest fiction—*The Joys of Motherhood.*

Events in History at the Time the Novel Takes Place

Colonial reorganization. *The Joys of Motherhood* ends as Nigeria is on the brink of becoming an independent republic. (Independence was achieved in 1960.) Its colonizers, the British, had been active in trading and missionary activities in the Niger River delta and along the rest of the West African coast since the seventeenth century, but formal rule over parts of present-day Nige-

> ### THE LITERARY WORK
>
> A novel set in southern Nigeria from 1909 to the late 1950s; published in English in 1979.
>
> ### SYNOPSIS
>
> The novel chronicles the life of an Igbo woman from her adolescence in the village of Ibuza in western Igboland, through her adult married life in Lagos, to her lonely death back in Ibuza.

ria dates only from the establishment of Lagos Colony in 1861. Over the course of the following five decades, a British sphere of influence to the north and east of Lagos was carved out by treaty and by conquest. Major British military actions against the kingdom of Benin in the late 1890s and against the powerful Aro people (a subset of the Igbo people, spelled "Ibo" in the novel) in 1902 were accompanied by numerous smaller-scale actions. Between 1904 and 1909, the British took control of approximately 16,000 square miles in southern Nigeria. It is in southern Nigeria that Ibuza (sometimes spelled Ibusa)—the hometown not only of Emecheta but also of her protagonist in *The Joys of Motherhood*—is located. By 1914, five years after the novel's chronological starting point, the large and populous colony of Nigeria had been formed by the amalgamation of the Protectorate of Southern Nigeria with the colony of Lagos and the Protectorate of Northern Nigeria. In addition to dividing the area into districts overseen by European District Officers (also called Residents), the British designed "native courts" to be headed by "warrant chiefs" selected from local political leaders, including kings and chiefs.

Though the newly created "warrant chief" was expected to rule fairly on criminal and civil cases in accord with his people's ethical and legal systems, many complained that he instead extorted money and unjustly deprived villagers of their possessions and rights. "Indirect rule" in Igboland resulted in a concentration of power in the hands of one individual that ran counter to the more egalitarian method of rule that had existed before colonialism. Before the coming of the British,

> the heads of the lineage groups, known as elders, met informally and infrequently to interpret the 'laws' and sanctions handed down from the supernatural world through the ancestors. The communities did not recognise the elders as chiefs but merely as intermediaries between the dead ancestors and the living. Individually, each elder exercised within his own lineage an informal kind of domestic authority. The work of government in the Ibo . . . communities [thus] was not formalised or institutionalised."
>
> (Anene, p. 258)

British rule had a significant impact on religious and cultural practices, family and household structures, employment patterns, and governance among the Igbo and other Nigerian peoples. For example, the British introduced many European consumer goods into Nigerian society and put taxes on property. These economic changes, combined with the rise of Christianity and Western-style education, caused many social changes as the earning power and needs of the individual came to matter more than the collective prosperity of the family household and the larger ethnic community. The British opposition to domestic slavery also changed village and family life considerably. From early on in their contact with the peoples of the Niger delta region, the British had strongly discouraged slavery and they outlawed the domestic slave trade in three separate proclamations in Lagos Colony and the Northern and Southern Protectorates in 1901.

The clash between the British and Africans over slavery is presented in *The Joys of Motherhood* through a local chief's ambivalent attitude toward his slaves. Nwokocha Agbadi knows how

important slaves are to his village household, but he also wishes to please the British. Eventually, he "stop[s] dealing in slaves" and "offer[s] freedom to the ones in his household. He even join[s] a group of leaders who encouraged slaves to return to their places of origin. . . . All those in his own compound who refused to go were adopted as his children" (Emecheta, *The Joys of Motherhood*, p. 35).

Traditional beliefs and the introduction of Christianity. The traditional spiritual beliefs and religious practices of the various ethnic groups in southern Nigeria have much in common. Many of these traditional religions stress the importance of a supreme god and use the sky as a representative figure for that god. The Igbo view the earth as a sacred female entity and believe that other natural phenomena, such as the sun and rivers, are manifestations of the spirit world. Moreover, each Igbo has a personal god, called a *chi,* and is expected to offer prayers and sacrifices to that god.

A belief in witchcraft was also a part of many traditional Nigerian religions. Because witches were thought to cast spells on people to make them ill and die, epidemics that occurred in the colonial period frequently led to large-scale witch-hunts as people tried to discover the living source of the illness. Indigenous spiritual leaders/healers, called "medicine men" or *dibia* in the novel, not only offered curative herbs and charms but also sought to clear the community of evil by subjecting certain people to ordeals meant to discover which villagers were witches.

Beginning in the 1840s, Christian missionary work was conducted in many parts of southern Nigeria. In the early stages, much of the evangelization was undertaken by Africans who had been converted to Christianity and educated in England. The most important of these Nigerian-born Christians in the nineteenth century was Samuel Ajayi Crowther, a Yoruba who had been sold as a slave but was set free when the British intercepted the slave ship in which he was being transported across the Atlantic Ocean. Educated first at a Church Missionary Society school in Sierra Leone and then at a school in London, Crowther became the first Anglican Bishop of the Niger region in 1864. Despite the presence of some other native-born Christian evangelists like Crowther, the majority of Christian missionaries were Europeans or North Americans. Catholic priests came from France while Methodist, Baptist, and other Protestant missionaries arrived from Britain and the United States. Because the missionaries focused on converting individual Africans rather than on convincing indigenous leaders to forfeit their old beliefs and adopt new ones, conversion rates remained low. Individual converts were often shunned by their communities because their new faith made necessary a rejection of most of the social and cultural aspects of indigenous life. An Igbo or other Nigerian who became a Christian would have to give up not only the many religious rituals and festivals that punctuated daily life but also the polygamous marriage structure that underpinned social organization.

Resistance to Christian evangelization and to British rule more generally was very strong in western Igboland (west of the Niger River, across from the important trading town of Onitsha). Rebellion blazed up most spectacularly at the turn of the century in the form of a secret society called the *Ekumeku*, whose members burned many mission stations and local court buildings and terrorized local chiefs known to be sympathetic to missionaries and the colonial government. "The most formidable opposition to the spread of missionary work was centred on Ibusa," the town in which the novel takes place (Anene, p. 240). This opposition to European incursion is mentioned by the novel's narrator: "In places like Asaba and Ibuza, Igbo towns in Western Nigeria, the inhabitants were very hostile to the arrival of Europeans, so that the few white people who came fled for their lives. The graves of many missionaries and explorers tucked inside the forest bushes tell this tale" (*Joys of Motherhood*, p. 142). In hopes of stamping out the Ekumeku, the British used local and foreign troops to attack villages controlled by the secret society, killing scores of people in the process and forcing large numbers of people from their homes.

Education. Western-style education was an important component of missionary activity in southern Nigeria. At the beginning of the twentieth century primary school education became widely available but secondary schools were located mostly in large cities like Lagos. Competition for entrance to these secondary schools was intense. In 1934 the country's first university-level institution opened, the Yaba Higher College, but it offered only diplomas rather than degrees. Within secondary education, a focus on individual rights and the equality of all human beings contributed to the growth of the Nigerian independence movement, which strengthened from the early 1940s through the late 1950s.

Some people chose to gain advanced degrees abroad, but the cost of doing so was prohibitive to the vast majority of the population. Because of the heavy emphasis in schools on Christianity, the upward mobility offered by higher education sometimes entailed a rupture between the educated person and traditional life in Nigeria. In *The Joys of Motherhood*, the protagonist's two eldest sons both receive an excellent education that requires much economic sacrifice on the part of their parents. However, this education alienates them from traditional Igbo religion and social customs, and both boys ultimately move to North America.

THE IMPORTANCE OF THE *CHI*

"In many Nigerian traditional religions," writes historian Elizabeth Isichei, "the individual worships an individual manifestation or emanation from the Supreme God, a kind of personalized providence. In Igbo, this is *chi* and Chukwu (Supreme God) is often explained as *chi ukwu* (great chi)" (Isichei, *History of Nigeria*, p. 284). The Western Igbo often visualize the chi not as solely a spiritual force but also as a person, perhaps an ancestor or other village inhabitant, who has been reincarnated in an individual at birth. The chi is thought to influence one's life either for good or evil, depending on the amount and quality of the sacrifices and prayers offered to it. Therefore, it is imperative that one keep one's chi happy and satisfied. In *The Joys of Motherhood*, Nnu Ego tries hard to lessen the difficulties in her life by remembering her chi, but her co-wife Adaku abandons the family household and indicates her liberation from traditional ways of life by abandoning her own chi altogether. She shouts to Nnu Ego, "My *chi* be damned! I am going to be a prostitute. Damn my *chi*!" (*Joys of Motherhood*, p. 168).

Colonial-era Lagos. Over the course of the colonial era, Lagos gradually became the most populous and most important of Nigeria's metropolitan cities. Located in the western part of Nigeria's southern coastal region, Lagos played an important role in the West African slave trade of the early nineteenth century. After Britain declared the exporting of slaves to be illegal in 1807, Lagos became attractive to illicit slave traders anxious to use a harbor removed from the Niger delta ports on which the antislavery blockade concentrated most of its efforts. Other kinds of trade were also conducted through Lagos, and in 1861 the town was annexed by Great Britain. Britain appointed a governor to administer the new colony, and from this foothold on the coast British colonial officials pushed into the interior through a combination of trading, missionary activities, and military actions. By the early twentieth century Lagos had also become home to a large percentage of the Western-educated black elite who would later be instrumental in Nigeria's transition from colony to independent republic. Mostly Christians, members of this African elite filled positions in business, entered professions such as the law, or held jobs in the lower levels of the civil service.

Like other Nigerian cities such as Kano, Ibadan, and Port Harcourt, Lagos witnessed much migration from rural areas during the first half of the twentieth century. In addition to its original inhabitants, Lagos came to include Igbo, Hausa, Fulani, and members of many other ethnic groups. For instance, the number of Igbo living in Lagos grew from only 291 in 1911 to 31,887 in 1951. By that year, the Igbo represented nearly 45 percent of the non-Yoruba inhabitants of Lagos (Isichei, *A History of the Igbo People*, p. 214). Sometimes the groups coexisted peacefully, but at other times tensions flared up. These tensions were aggravated, if not created, by the differing treatment the British accorded to the various groups. The British viewed the Igbo as good domestic workers, as reflected in *The Joys of Motherhood* by the protagonist's husband, who launders clothes for a white couple. The Hausa, in contrast, impressed the British as good soldiers, and consequently found employment as army troops and policemen. Their role as enforcers of British rule made the Hausa feared and hated by many other ethnic groups. Similarly, the Yoruba, the dominant group in the region of Lagos, came to hold a prominent position in Nigerian politics after independence and therefore often seemed to aid the colonial government in the suppression of other Nigerian peoples. Branches of the region-wide ethnic improvement unions existed in Lagos to help migrants maintain a sense of ethnic community. Unions such as the Egbado Union, the Ibo State Union, and the Uratta Improvement Union provided opportunities for social interaction as well as legal aid and scholarships. They also offered a level of political organization that eventually helped apply pressure to end the colonial system in Nigeria.

Status of Igbo women. In traditional Igbo society, women had various responsibilities in relation to their families and their communities. Generally, a girl would help her mother until adolescence. The girl usually married in her teenage years, at which point she moved to the household, or compound, of her husband's family, where she prepared meals and performed other domestic tasks. Virtually everywhere in Igboland, women would work at planting and harvesting yams as well. Many Igbo women became heavily involved in trading activities. Polygamous households were the norm, with each of the wives possessing her own house and a small garden. Her ability to bear children was crucial to her standing in the community, partly because large families were so important in the subsistence economy. A woman who did not bear a child after marriage sometimes returned to her father's household, as young Nnu Ego does during her first marriage in *The Joys of Motherhood*.

Though they exerted little influence in the political decision-making process, Igbo women did hold some public sway through their own social organizations. Most important were the *inyemedi* (wives of a lineage) and *umuada* (daughters of a lineage) associations. The women held meetings—called *mikiri*—in which they discussed trading, cultivation, social and religious rituals, and offenses against the moral code of the society. In the towns of Asaba and Onitsha, both located near Ibuza, women took part in religious activities; in many other sections of Igboland, however, women were not allowed to visit shrines or possess certain religious objects. A few women managed to gain titles that were similar to those granted to men. The most coveted title was the *omu*, who served as head of the women's omu society, which controlled the marketplace and local trading, and also acted as a pressure group on the council of chiefs. It was mandatory for leaders of the omu society to attend meetings of the councils of chiefs and elders. An omu's exact role, however, depended on the particular Igbo community; in communities that had a head chief, she was his equivalent. However, her political power was not equal to that of a chief, and "her councillors did not possess most of the powers and privileges of the chiefs" (Mba, p. 24).

Colonization lessened women's already minimal formal public roles. Until 1929 no woman was appointed a warrant chief, and no woman held the position of court clerk, interpreter, or messenger. Women did not participate in the army or the police force. They occasionally took direct action, however, against aspects of the colonial regime that they perceived as oppressive. One especially important rebellion was the so-called "Women's War" of 1929. In several eastern provinces, the women of various ethnic groups (especially the Igbo) came to believe, erroneously as it turned out, that women would be taxed for the first time. Angered by this information, thousands of women participated in demonstrations, lootings, and torchings of native courts and factories. Fifty-five women were killed in the disturbances. The participants called their actions a "women's war"—*ogu umunwanyi*—but the colonial administration dubbed them the "Aba Women's Riots." The women sought some voice in the selection of the warrant chiefs, and achieved a modicum of success—the selection process was changed and a few women were hired to work in the native courts. Women continued to be involved in protests throughout Nigeria through the end of the colonial era.

In urban settings during the colonial era, polygyny, or marriage to more than one wife, became burdensome to women in ways that it had not been in the villages. Whereas in a village each wife had a separate house where she and her children lived, in big cities like Lagos the co-wives and all the children often were forced, for economic reasons, to share one house or apartment. The cooperation and friendship that had often existed between co-wives in the large village compounds disappeared in tight living spaces. In *The Joys of Motherhood,* the problems of urban polygyny become clear in the failure of joint action between the first and second wives of Nnaife Owulum. In Igbo villages, co-wives sometimes banded together to protest unfair treatment by their shared husband, but Nnaife's wives, Nnu Ego and Adaku, fail in their one attempt at joint action—a cooking strike intended to awaken Nnaife to the negative consequences of his unwise spending habits.

The impact of World War II. World War II (1939-45) was significant in the transition of Nigeria from colony to independent nation. With Europe only a distant entity for most Nigerians, all but the highly educated elite found it difficult to understand precisely which countries or peoples were at war and why. Frequently paired with that lack of knowledge was anger that the Africans had to fight for and in these unknown countries. As one character in Emecheta's novel says, "Why can't they fight their own wars? Why drag us innocent Africans into it?" (*Joys of Motherhood,* p. 148). Many black Nigerian national-

ists supported the British because of Britain's opposition to German racial theories and because of the belief that British democracy was preferable to fascism. Promised good pay while in the armed forces and guaranteed employment after the war ended, many Nigerian men enlisted; by 1941, 418 Europeans and 16,000 Nigerians had entered the Nigerian armed forces (Olusanya, p. 46). Upon returning from service—mostly performed in other British colonies, such as Burma—many enlistees failed to find adequate jobs and faulted the British for reneging on their promises. The high unemployment and inflation that followed the war contributed to the dissatisfaction with colonial rule that had been on the rise for decades.

World War II also contributed to the nationalist movement by affording many Nigerian men the chance to come into contact with a range of classes of white people. Whereas previously they had known only the relatively wealthy and well-educated colonial class in Nigeria, now they met Europeans "who were farmers and private soldiers, traders and shopkeepers, bootblacks and servants like themselves" (Crowder, p. 270). Contact with "average" British people convinced many Nigerians, previously daunted by the rich and powerful British colonialists, that they could successfully lobby for independence. Nnaife, husband of the novel's main character, Nnu Ego, gets to see a different side of the British when he works for a time on a British ship plying the African coast during the early years of the war. Returning home, he enlightens Nnu Ego and his neighbors as to the drinking habits of the British. He says he has seen the "white men" on board the ship drinking "Scotch Whisky." When Nnu Ego expresses astonishment, "Nnaife laugh[s], the bitter laugh of a man who ha[s] become very cynical, who now realise[s] that in this world there is no pure person. A man who in those last months had discovered that he had been revering a false image and that under white skins, just as under black ones, all humans are the same" (*Joys of Motherhood,* p. 111).

During and immediately following the war many nationalist groups pushed for independence. Nigerians had become aware of the hypocrisy behind the British claim that World War II had been fought for democracy and freedom even as the United Kingdom maintained an iron grip on its colonies around the world. Partly in response to political agitation by such groups as the Nigerian Union of Students, the government devised new constitutions in 1945 and—

this time with input from Nigerians—in 1950-51. This last constitution created a federal system that ultimately made ethnic divisions more pronounced toward the end of the time period covered by the novel. In 1960 Britain relinquished its colonial control over the country and Nigeria became an independent republic. The novel looks ahead to both the potential and the difficulties that characterized post-independence Nigeria. The following conversation takes place between Nnu Ego and two Igbo men in mid-1950s Lagos. One of these men, Ubani, observes, "Things are changing fast. . . . They say that in the not-too-distant future we shall be ruling ourselves, making our own laws."

In response Nnu Ego asks, excitedly, "Do you mean we'll have a black District Officer in a place like Ibuza? And a Nigerian Reverend Father, and all our doctors Nigerian?"

Nnu Ego's son answers in the affirmative, but a man named Nwakusor expresses significant reservations about the success of the coming changes in making the average person's life better. He wonders, "[T]hese new Nigerians, will they do the job well?" (*Joys of Motherhood*, p. 199).

The Novel in Focus

Plot summary. Centering on a fictional Igbo woman's life in colonial Nigeria, the novel opens in 1934 in Lagos, a city in southwestern Nigeria. The first chapter focuses on the actions and thoughts of a young woman named Nnu Ego as she runs with desperation toward a bridge from which she plans to throw herself. The novel then shifts in time and location, taking the reader back 25 years to 1909, and eastward from Lagos to the Igbo town of Ibuza. The reader learns about Nnu Ego's parents, the circumstances of her birth, and her life up to the alarming moment in 1934 with which the novel begins.

Nnu Ego's mother, Ona, was a strong and beautiful woman from an influential family, who refused to marry her lover, a local chief named Nwokocha Agbadi (who himself had seven wives and another mistress), because she was expected to provide a male heir for her aging father who had no sons. If she were to marry, any male child of the union would become part of the husband's family. Upon becoming pregnant by Agbadi, Ona promises that if the child is a girl she will give her to Agbadi to rear. She does indeed give birth to a girl, whom Agbadi names Nnu Ego—literally "a thousand cowries"—because of her remarkable beauty. Boding ill for the beautiful

baby's future, however, is the determination made by the dibia, or medicine man, that the baby's chi, or personal god, is a slave woman violently killed just a few days before Ona conceived Nnu Ego. He determines the identity of the chi by linking a large lump found on baby Nnu Ego's head with a lump that appeared on the slave woman's head as she was being beaten.

At age 17 Nnu Ego is married to a handsome man named Amatokwu, but she becomes depressed when she fails to become pregnant and Amatokwu takes a second wife who gives birth to a son very soon after her introduction to the household. Though jealous of the second wife, Nnu Ego is close to the child, even breast-feeding him during the second wife's absence. When Amatokwu beats Nnu Ego after seeing this tenderness between her and the child, Nnu Ego's father comes to the compound and takes Nnu Ego home with him. Her father then arranges for her to marry Nnaife Owulum, an overweight, homely man who lives in Lagos and launders clothes for a white couple named Meers. Though disappointed in her husband and feeling lonely in this rapidly growing city of seemingly countless ethnic groups and languages, Nnu Ego rejoices when she finally has a child, a boy whom they name Ngozi. The boy dies within a few weeks, however, and it is at this point that the novel returns to the scene depicted on its opening page: Nnu Ego running through the streets, preparing to commit suicide in shock that her only child has died. An Ibuza man who happens to see her on the bridge prevents her from fulfilling this death wish and Nnu Ego resumes her difficult life with her husband. She soon gives birth to another boy, Oshiaju, but just as her life seems to be settling into a pleasant routine, Nnaife is left without a job when his employers, the Meerses, return to England at the start of World War II. Eventually Nnaife gets work on a ship that travels to Fernando Póo, an island off the West African coast. During his absence, Nnu Ego bears another son, Adimabua, then has to move with her children from the small rooms they had occupied on the Meerses' estate to an apartment owned by a Yoruba man. When Nnaife returns from the ship, he hears of his elder brother's death and rushes to Ibuza to assume his responsibilities for the brother's household. Nnu Ego must contend with the introduction of other people into her own household when Nnaife returns from Ibuza with the brother's youngest wife, Adaku, and her young daughter in tow. Soon, both Nnu Ego and Adaku are pregnant, and Nnu Ego gives birth nine months later to twin girls, Taiwo and Kehinde. Nnaife is happy now that he has daughters whose bride prices he expects will pay for the older boys' higher education. Adaku gives birth to a boy who soon becomes ill and dies. More trouble lurks ahead.

Great personal and financial problems beset Nnu Ego after Nnaife is practically forced into the army and shipped off to Burma to fight for the British Empire in a war that he does not fully understand. During Nnaife's absence, Nnu Ego returns to Ibuza, where she witnesses the death of her ailing father and gives birth to a boy who is given the name *Nnamdio*—meaning "my father lives on"—because of his striking resemblance to Nnu Ego's father, Nwokocha Agbadi. Upon her return to Lagos eight months after her departure, she finds life increasingly difficult, primarily because her own poverty contrasts so sharply with the prosperity Adaku has been able to gain through trading during Nnu Ego's long sojourn in the village of her birth. After an argument between the two women, Adaku is censured by her male Igbo relatives in Lagos for failing to produce sons, so she decides to leave the apartment in the hopes of becoming rich and giving her girls a good education through work as a prostitute and market vendor.

Adaku's departure decreases Nnu Ego's mental anguish but not her economic problems. With the promised money from Nnaife nowhere in sight and with her own stock of money nearly depleted, she must do backbreaking labor—gathering, cutting, and selling firewood—to pay the rent, feed the children, and send the boys to school. Just after she makes the difficult decision to remove the boys from school because she can no longer afford the school fees, Nnu Ego receives a windfall in the form of £60 from Nnaife that had been sitting, undelivered, at army headquarters. This large sum of money enables her to continue the boys' education, rent a large market stall, and create a considerable savings account. Nnaife then returns from the war and decides to get another wife in Ibuza. He brings back a kind and jolly 16-year-old girl named Okpo, with whom Nnu Ego gets along relatively well. He decides to send the eldest son, Oshiaju, to a prestigious and expensive boarding school in the city of Warri. Over the next few years, Nnu Ego becomes pregnant twice more. She has another set of twin girls, Obiageli and Malachi, and later gives birth, alone and depressed, to a stillborn baby during a period of intense dissatisfaction with her life. Not only has she and the rest of the

family had to move to a mud house in an area of Lagos without running water, but she has slowly come to realize that her two eldest sons are becoming alienated from her due to their Western-style education.

From this point onward, the novel focuses on the mostly negative impact the children's actions and thoughts have on their parents. In the traditional way of life, parents cared for their male children and made sacrifices on their behalf with the expectation that those children would take care of them in their old age. They took care of their female children's basic needs and sought proper matches for them with the understanding that the bride prices they drew would offer financial compensation for those years of rearing. Unfortunately for Nnu Ego and Nnaife, Oshiaju does not see the importance of this reciprocal relationship, and decides that he will take a scholarship to study science in the United States rather than work at a relatively well-paid government job in Nigeria. Similarly, Adimabua goes away to a boarding school and ultimately emigrates to Canada. The parents are accorded

---

THE SIGNIFICANCE OF NAMES IN IGBO CULTURE

Children in Igbo society receive multiple names, often including names that reflect the position of the parents at the time of the child's birth or their hopes for the child's future. The name of Nnu Ego's first child, *Ngozi,* meaning "blessing," reflects in part Nnu Ego's appreciation of her good fortune at having escaped the infertility that plagued her in her first marriage. Other popular Igbo names include the days of the week. Thus, a *nwa* (child) born on *Afo* market day may be called "Nwafo," or "child of Afo." Nnu Ego's last two children, female twins, are given names that capture the potential for triumph and disaster in postcolonial Nigeria. One is named *Obiageli,* meaning "she who has come to enjoy wealth," and the other is called *Malachi,* meaning "you do not know what tomorrow will bring" (*Joys of Motherhood,* p. 187). Still other names acknowledge the power of the supreme god in relation to the birth of the child: examples include *Chienyekwa,* "God has given"; *Chikwe,* "God agrees"; and *Chinaelo,* "God reckons" (Njoku, p. 188). Finally colonialism and Christianity introduced European saints' names into the mix, which led to many parents in the twentieth century giving their children European Christian first names or middle names.

great respect because of the scholarly achievements of their sons—"Everybody referred to Nnu Ego, as she proudly carried her back-breaking firewood up from the waterside, as the mother of very clever children." But the respect offers them little solace, in view of the fact that they have lost touch with their eldest children and will remain poor (*Joys of Motherhood,* p. 197). The female children also cause great mental anguish. Though Taiwo pleases Nnaife by marrying a husband he has chosen for her, Kehinde goes against the wishes of her father by running away from home to marry a Muslim Yoruba man, the son of a butcher.

Kehinde's action has serious consequences for the unity of the family, since Nnaife is ultimately given a five-year prison sentence after attacking the Yoruba man's family with a cutlass. This sentence is quietly commuted to a few months in prison upon the condition that Nnaife leave Lagos. He ultimately returns to Ibuza. Leaving one of the younger set of twins with Taiwo and her new husband, Nnu Ego also leaves Lagos and goes to Ibuza with her youngest son and daughter. Rejected by her husband's family because of the pain her children have caused him, she must live apart from him and Okpo (his third wife), and she dies several years later "with no child to hold her hand and no friend to talk to her. She had never really made many friends, so busy had she been building up her joys as a mother" (*Joys of Motherhood,* p. 224). Her geographically scattered children return to the village to honor her memory. They build a shrine "so that her grandchildren could appeal to her should they be barren" (*Joys of Motherhood,* p. 224). Even after her death, however, the community considers her a "wicked woman" because "however many people appealed to her to make women fertile, she never did" (*Joys of Motherhood,* p. 224).

Ownership in male-female and in colonial relations. At one point during the testimony she gives at her husband's trial, Nnu Ego says, "Nnaife is the head of our family. He owns me, just like God in the sky owns us" (*Joys of Motherhood,* p. 217). Here, Nnu Ego compares married women in traditional Nigerian society to possessions and links a husband's power to the authority that God appears to have over human beings. Nnaife confirms a sense of ownership over his wives when he says to Nnu Ego: "Did I not pay your bride price? Am I not your owner?" (*Joys of Motherhood,* p. 98). In some villages, when a man died, any wife that survived him be-

came the responsibility or property of that man's brother or other male relative. According to tradition, a married woman's children belonged to her husband, as did any money she might earn. Nnu Ego perceives herself as a slave not only to her husband's will but also to that of her children. Though she never directly challenges either form of slavery, she does pray for release from the familial obligations that limit her personal freedom:

> "God, when will you create a woman who will be fulfilled in herself, a full human being, not anybody's appendage?" she prayed desperately. . . . "Yes, I have many children, but what do I have to feed them on? On my life. I have to work myself to the bone to look after them, I have to give them my all. And if I am lucky enough to die in peace, I even have to give them my soul. They will worship my dead spirit to provide for them: it will be hailed as a good spirit so long as there are plenty of yams and children in the family, but if anything should go wrong, if a young wife does not conceive or there is a famine, my dead spirit will be blamed. When will I be free?"
> (*Joys of Motherhood,* pp. 186-87)

A casualty of "progress," Nnu Ego dies alone, caught in a changing time that brought more independence for children.

Unlike Nnu Ego, who never vocally expresses her dissatisfaction with her position, Nnaife's second wife, Adaku, whose name means "daughter of wealth," rebels against her society's strictures. Anxious to provide a good life for her two daughters and to enjoy more personal freedom, Adaku leaves Nnaife's Lagos household. After working as a prostitute for a short time, she rents a large market stall and soon makes enough money to have fine clothes and to send both girls to excellent schools. Late in the novel, she gently reminds Nnu Ego that the old ways of Igbo society, including male ownership of females, no longer have the force they once had. "Nnaife does not own anybody, not in the new Nigeria" (*Joys of Motherhood,* p. 218). One wife holds tenaciously to old prescriptions for her behavior while the other breaks new ground.

The Joys of Motherhood draws a parallel between traditional and colonial societies, presenting colonialism as a case of unfair and illegal ownership of one group of human beings by another. In a discussion of the Nigerian political situation at the outbreak of World War II, one character says, "I think we are on the side of the

British. They own Nigeria, you know" (*Joys of Motherhood*, p. 98). An incredulous Nnu Ego wonders if the British also own the town of Ibuza. Through this depiction of colonialism as ownership, the novel presents men in a slavelike position similar to that of Nigerian women. Soon after her arrival in Lagos, Nnu Ego remarks that low-status work done for the English inhabitants of Lagos has turned Nigerian men into slaves: "[M]y father released his slaves because the white man says it is illegal. Yet these our husbands are like slaves, don't you think?" (*Joys of Motherhood*, p. 51).

Sources and literary context. In her 1986 autobiography, *Head Above Water,* Buchi Emecheta describes a clash with her eldest daughter, Chiedu, that played a crucial role in her depiction of the lonely and forgotten mother in *The Joys of Motherhood.* In December 1976, Chiedu, then 15, asked her mother to transfer her to an expensive private school. When Emecheta refused to do so because of the tightness of the family budget, Chiedu left the apartment and went to live for a time with her father, from whom Emecheta had been separated in the mid-1960s. Astonished at this betrayal, Emecheta "banged away [on the typewriter] the whole of Christmas, the whole of January 1977, and by the end of that month, almost six weeks after Chiedu left, *The Joys of Motherhood* was finished" (Emecheta, *Head Above Water,* p. 224). Another part of the novel probably inspired by the author's personal experience is Nnaife's service in the British army during World War II. While growing up, Emecheta was sometimes referred to as "the daughter of the one who went and fought and killed a bad man called Hitler" (Emecheta, *Head Above Water,* p. 12). Though he had not, of course, killed Hitler, Emecheta's father did fight in Burma, just as Nnaife does in the novel.

The Joys of Motherhood differs from male-authored African literature of the 1960s and '70s. Male novelists offered two extremes in their depiction of women—the saintly mother, portrayed as the highest feminine ideal, or the debased prostitute (see **Jagua Nana,** for example, also covered in *African Literature and Its Times*). *The Joys of Motherhood* provides a strong corrective to novels authored by males because it realistically portrays the suffering experienced by women who try to fulfill the role of perfect mother and wife. Like **Efuru** by Flora Nwapa (also covered in *African Literature and Its Times*), Emecheta's novel focuses on everyday women's lives, portraying both positive and negative aspects of women's experiences. Whereas *Efuru* features a relatively unconventional protagonist, *The Joys of Motherhood* portrays the suffering experienced by women who try to fulfill the traditionally sanctioned role of perfect mother and wife.

> Critics generally view Emecheta's novels as providing an authentic representation of African women . . . [through] her portrayal of . . . social and historical context. In *The Joys of Motherhood,* this contextualization . . . constitutes Emecheta's strongest statement in response to male idealizations of motherhood.
>
> (Stratton, p. 113)

Emecheta started her writing career with two autobiographical accounts of a Nigerian woman in London—*In the Ditch* (1972) and *Second-Class Citizen* (1974). She then turned to earlier times—colonial Nigeria in the 1940s and 1950s (*The Bride Price,* 1976) and early twentieth-century Igbo life (*The Slave Girl,* 1977, which was based partly on the life experiences of Emecheta's mother, Alice Obanje Ojebeta Emecheta). Addressing Nigerian culture from the 1910s through the 1950s, *The Joys of Motherhood* encompasses a larger swath of Nigerian colonial history, synthesizing Emecheta's historical and social concerns into one literary work.

Events in History at the Time the Novel Was Written

Political instability. The 1960s and 1970s saw considerable economic and political turmoil in Nigeria. A parliamentary democracy existed from the time of independence in 1960 to January 1966, when a coup led mostly by Igbo army officers took place. Another coup occurred in July and led to the massacre of the Igbo living in northern Nigeria. In response to this decimation and to the discovery of oil in Southeast and South Central Nigeria, most of Igboland attempted to secede from Nigeria in 1967 and form an independent country, the Republic of Biafra. The civil war that ensued lasted more than 30 months before the secessionists were defeated. The next 10 years (1970-80) were marked by more coups and unfulfilled promises of a return to democracy. However, when Emecheta wrote *The Joys of Motherhood* concrete steps were being taken to reintroduce civilian rule. In 1977 and 1978 a new constitution was drafted, a voter list

A soldier involved in the Nigerian civil war, which erupted in 1967, after the eastern region attempted to secede.

was created, and a ban on forming political parties was lifted. Elections were held in 1979, the same year in which the novel was published, and on October 1st of that year Nigeria returned to civilian rule.

Status of women in 1970s Nigeria. After independence, the number of educated women expanded greatly, and most educated married women worked outside the home. The increase in educational and professional opportunities for women was not accompanied, however, by a lessening of their overall burden. A lack of conveniences such as supermarkets, prepared foods, and mechanized appliances, combined with the refusal of many Nigerian men to participate in domestic duties, meant that Nigerian women continued to spend large periods of the day taking care of domestic matters.

A symposium initiated in 1974 by the Nigerian Association of University Women exposed some concerns of Nigeria's female population during the decade. Whereas the continued practice of polygyny created resentment among some middle-class women, women in trade showed little anxiety over the issue. In fact, a number expressed a desire for the household help of co-wives, a "convenience" that made it more possible to engage in trade. On the other hand, they objected to the breakdown of certain aspects of the traditional polygynous marriage. Once, the first wife had exercised authority over later wives, but in the 1970s she was sometimes "relegated to the background by an uncaring husband" and the younger wife did not necessarily "keep her lower and deferent place within the polygynous family" (*Women in Nigeria Today,* p. 123).

On the positive side, 1970s society allowed women more chance to acquire an education and participate in public life. This, however, reduced the ability of a woman to rely on sisters, daughters, and other women as helpmates, and so did not have an altogether positive effect. Likewise changes in the economy sometimes detracted from a husband's ability to meet much of the financial burden of supporting a wife and children, placing it more fully on her shoulders than it had been in the past.

Reviews. *The Joys of Motherhood* met with a generally favorable reception, and was frequently praised as a technically more refined and more complex treatment of the issues of women's oppression, race relations, and colonialism/post-colonialism than had already appeared in Buchi Emecheta's four earlier novels. Though generally applauding the quality of her style, critics could not agree on how best to interpret Emecheta's presentation of women's struggles—indeed, one critic classified *The Joys of Motherhood* as Emecheta's "most controversial" novel (Fishburn, p. 104). Noting both the failure of the heroine, Nnu Ego, to escape her oppressive situation in Lagos and the sympathetic portrayal of traditional Igbo life, a few female critics questioned Emecheta's commitment to feminism, a commitment that had seemed so central to her earlier work. At the same time, at least one male critic took issue with the novel's portrayal of men, claiming that they were essentially exaggerated, one-dimensional strawmen.

Scholarly assessments continue to focus mostly on the feminist implications of the experiences that the women in the novel have. Lately, their range of analysis has expanded to include the novel's incorporation of Igbo storytelling practices. Highlighting Emecheta's frequent use of dialogue, proverbs, and songs, Susan Arndt compares Emecheta's narrative techniques to those employed by female storytellers in Igbo villages.

—Laura Franey

For More Information

Anene, J. C. *Southern Nigeria in Transition, 1885-1906.* Cambridge: Cambridge University Press, 1966.

Arndt, Susan. "Buchi Emecheta and the Tradition of Ifo: Continuation and Writing Back." In *Emerging Perspectives on Buchi Emecheta.* Ed. Marie Umeh. Trenton, N.J.: Africa World Press, 1996.

Crowder, Michael. *A Short History of Nigeria.* New York: Praeger, 1966.

Emecheta, Buchi. *Head Above Water.* Oxford: Heinemann, 1994.

———. *The Joys of Motherhood.* New York: George Braziller, 1979.

Fishburn, Katherine. *Reading Buchi Emecheta: Cross-Cultural Conversations.* Westport, Conn.: Greenwood, 1995.

Isichei, Elizabeth. *A History of the Igbo People.* London: Macmillan, 1976.

———. *A History of Nigeria.* London: Longman, 1983.

Mba, Nina Emma. *Nigerian Women Mobilized: Women's Political Activity in Southern Nigeria, 1900-1965.* Berkeley, Calif.: Institute of International Studies, 1982.

Njoku, John E. Eberegbulam. *The Igbos of Nigeria: Ancient Rites, Changes and Survival.* Lewiston, N.Y.: Edwin Mellen, 1990.

Olusanya, G. O. *The Second World War and Politics in Nigeria, 1939-1953.* London: Evans Brothers, 1973.

Stratton, Florence. *Contemporary African Literature and the Politics of Gender.* London: Routledge, 1994.

Women In Nigeria Today. London: Zed, 1985.

The Last Duty

by

Isidore Okpewho

Isidore Okpewho was born November 9, 1941, at Agbor in the Midwest region of Nigeria, now Delta State and Edo State. Delta is predominantly Igbo (Ibo) speaking, while Edo is predominantly Urhobo speaking. Okpewho, who has an Igbo-speaking mother and an Urhobo-speaking father, graduated from University College in Ibadan in 1964, then worked for the Federal Ministry of Education, the Ministry of External Affairs, and Longman publishers. He spent eight years at Longman as an editor at its Nigeria office. During this time, before emigrating to pursue a doctorate in English in the United States, Okpewho published his first novel, *The Victims* (1970), and completed the first draft of his second novel, *The Last Duty*. He began the latter novel toward the end of 1969 (when the Nigerian civil war was drawing to a close), completing it the following year. *The Last Duty* has gained renown as one of the finest fictional accounts of the psychological damage done to ordinary citizens by the three-year Nigerian civil war.

Events in History at the Time of the Novel

Colonial legacies. *The Last Duty* is set at a time when the Nigerian nation was at the brink of disintegration. In precolonial times, the people living in what was to be Nigeria were culturally and linguistically unrelated communities inhabiting a vast area from the Atlantic Ocean in the South to the Sahara Desert in the North. In the second half of the nineteenth century, Great Britain be-

> ## THE LITERARY WORK
>
> A novel set in midwestern Nigeria during the Nigerian civil war (July 1967 to January 1970); published in English in 1976.
>
> ## SYNOPSIS
>
> A husband and wife from opposing ethnic groups and their small son confront pressures in a Nigerian border town during the civil war.

gan to annex portions of this area as part of its colonial empire. By the early twentieth century, British colonies had been established in both the South and the North and were designated as protectorates. By what seems like an arbitrary action known in Nigerian history as "The Amalgamation," Britain brought the southern and northern protectorates under one broad colonial administration, collecting all the peoples in these diverse areas into one country, their cultural and linguistic pluralism notwithstanding. Britain proceeded to send over colonial officers to administer the provinces and districts into which the peoples had been grouped. Nigeria would remain a British colony until it attained independence on October 1, 1960. In the colonial era, Britain made no serious effort to address the cultural, linguistic, and ethnic differences in the country; after independence, these differences would pose the most dire threat to the survival of Nigeria as a sovereign nation. Its peoples continued to relate to one another on the strength of ethnic and linguistic affiliations rather than with any sense of common nationality. Ethnic prejudice, a legacy of the haphazard amalgamation of peoples under colonial rule, has remained a root cause of political instability in Nigeria ever since, breeding rivalries that climaxed in the civil war whose effects pervade *The Last Duty*.

Postindependence geopolitics. Africa's most populous country, Nigeria currently contains about 120 million people, who belong to 250 ethnic groups and speak 394 different languages. Random clashes between different ethnic groups have been a fact of life since independence. There have been various attempts to accommodate diverse ethnic interests in government and to achieve equity in power sharing and the distribution of amenities, but ethnic jealousies, rivalries, suspicions, and mistrust still abound.

In addition to ethnic prejudice, corruption has militated against progress since independence. Government officials have at one time or another

FROM FICTION TO FACT

Chinua Achebe's novel *A Man of the People* (written 1964), captures the temper of the times, showing how corruption was so overwhelming that Nigerians not only resigned themselves to it but even rationalized it:

> Let them eat, was the people's opinion, after all, when the white-man used to do all the eating, did we commit suicide? Of course not. And where is the all-powerful white-man today? He came, he ate and he went. But we are still around. . . . Besides, if you survive, who knows? It may be your turn to eat tomorrow. Your son may bring home your share.
>
> (Achebe, p. 145)

A Man of the People ends with the army sacking the civilian government through a coup d'état, and hints at a later mutiny in the army and a countercoup. Although written in 1964, the novel was published the first week of January 1966. On January 15, 1966, Nigeria actually experienced a coup; soldiers assumed control of the government, abolished all democratic institutions, suspended the constitution, and ruled by decree. And, as predicted in *A Man of the People,* another coup took place a few months later, which gave rise to military dictatorship in Nigeria. Events degenerated so badly that by July 1967 Nigeria had become deeply embroiled in the ethnic civil war that inspired *The Last Duty*.

been accused of an assortment of corrupt practices—kickbacks, massive fraud, brazen inflation of contract figures. Aside from stymying national economic growth, this corruption has created mass disillusionment about independence. Within a few years of independence, the country was sliding into misrule, materialism, a betrayal of societal values, and the ruthless silencing of divergent viewpoints. By 1964-65 political violence was rife, especially in the southwest, where private armies were terrorizing citizens and the civilian government seemed powerless to prevent the anarchy.

Military rule and civil war. Army rule in Nigeria actually began with the bloody coup d'état of January 15, 1966, which included the assassinations of Prime Minister Alhaji Tafawa Balewa, members of his cabinet, and some prominent politicians—including the cultural and political leader of the North, the Sarduana of Sokoto; the premier of the western region, Chief Lagoke Akintola; and a flamboyant politician from the Midwest, Chief Festus Okotie, the Federal Minister of Finance. Two governors survived the coup, Chief Michael Okpara and Chief Dennis Osadebe, of the East and Midwest regions, respectively; they happened to be of the Igbo ethnic group. After the coup Nigeria's highest ranking military officer, Major General Aguiyi Ironsi, assumed leadership of the country. Ironsi had not participated in the coup, which was the handiwork of young army officers, mostly majors. He in fact ordered their arrest.

Initially the people did not ascribe any ethnic motives to the coup. They welcomed the army's seizure of the corrupt government. People celebrated in the streets, accepting warmly the new military dispensation. But six months later new interpretations set in and reactions changed. The once-popular coup was tarnished by propaganda and redefined as an ethnically motivated plot to enthrone Igbo leadership in the federal government. In various parts of the country, especially in the Muslim North, the Igbos became victims of violent harassment. A mutiny in the army and a countercoup in July 1966 resulted in Ironsi and several Igbo army officers being assassinated.

The once highly respected national army would never be the same. In a matter of months thousands of Igbos in the northern region of Nigeria were murdered by military officers. There was a mass exodus of the Igbo to the eastern region, their place of origin. Other ethnic groups from the East had members in the North too, and they were forced home as well, although it re-

The victors parade through the streets following the cease-fire announcement ending Nigeria's 30-month civil war.

mains debatable whether their lives were in as grave danger as those of their Igbo counterparts.

The new head of the military government was a young lieutenant colonel from the North, Yakubu Gowon, the most senior officer after the assassinated Ironsi. Gowon's ascension brought about serious conflicts. The military governor of the East, Colonel Odumegwu Ojukwu, refused to recognize Gowon's leadership or take orders from him. A serious rift broke out within the army, only worsening the situation in a country already riven by ethnic feuding.

Ojukwu advised easterners residing elsewhere in the country to make their way back to their home region, as there was no guarantee of their safety elsewhere. Within months the East was teeming with millions of refugees. The massacre continued, raising cries of genocide throughout eastern Nigeria. Attempts at a political solution yielded no positive results. The most far-reaching attempt was made in Ghana at a location called Aburi. At the end of the negotiations, an accord (the so-called "Aburi agreement") was reached between Ojukwu and Gowon, which enshrined the decision to adopt a system of confederation that made the regions semiautonomous. However, after closer examination of the implications of such a confederation, Gowon refused to abide by the Aburi agreement;

Ojukwu demanded full compliance with it. Oil, a major foreign exchange earner for the country (accounting for more than 70 percent of Nigeria's annual revenue), was found primarily in the East. Prompted by a strong feeling of self-sufficiency, the eastern region, with encouragement from Ojukwu, clamored for the confederation—or for secession. On May 30, 1967, Ojukwu declared the eastern region to be a separate country from Nigeria and named the new nation the Republic of Biafra. Four African nations—Zambia, Tanzania, Gabon, and Ivory Coast—and one outside the continent—Haiti—recognized Biafra. Many Haitians trace their African origins to the Igbos, a heritage exploited by Biafran propagandists, although they apparently neglected to exploit the fact that Olaudah Equiano (see ***Equiano's Travels,*** also covered in *African Literature and Its Times*) was an Igbo who established roots in Barbados.

On July 30, 1967, Nigeria declared war on Biafra under the slogan: "To keep Nigeria one is a task, which must be done." (In *The Last Duty,* this political slogan is echoed in "to keep Zonda one is a task, which must be done," Zonda being a fictional name for Nigeria.) Thus began the Nigerian civil war, a conflict that would drag on for 30 months. One dilemma on both sides was how to treat families with heritages in both Nigeria and Biafra—for example, a family with spouses who came from different sides. This problem was felt most acutely in border towns where people of different ethnic groups had intermarried and intermingled for decades. Generally families with members of different ethnic groups on different sides of the war had a hard time establishing their unquestionable loyalty, and in the end many of them split up and returned to their individual places of origin rather than live under daily suspicion of their loyalty to a particular side. Some families chose to remain together and show by their deeds that they had no divided loyalties, but such families might be kept under close surveillance. This type of family is at the root of the crisis in *The Last Duty*.

The novel opens when the civil war has begun and people not born in the territories in which they find themselves are at the mercy of their neighbors, who may trump up allegations of sabotage and collaboration with the enemy. Many innocent lives were in fact lost to such charges, the means, as evident in the novel, by which some malicious people settled old scores.

The Novel in Focus

Plot summary. An interethnic family finds itself caught in the crossfire of the Nigerian civil war. At the center are Mukoro Oshevire, an innocent man detained in prison for allegedly collaborating with the rebel troops during their occupation of a small border town, Urukpe; his wife, Aku, who has migrated from Simba and married into Urukpe; and their four-year-old son, Oghenovo. The family struggles for survival amid the malice of the community, the treachery of the town chief, Toje Onovwakpo, and the idealism of the commander of the federal troops, Major Ali S. Idris. When the novel opens, Oshevire has been in detention for almost three years. From this fact, it can be surmised that the plot takes place in the last quarter of 1969, in the final weeks of the war, which ended in January 1970. The characters take turns narrating the events from their separate perspectives.

Urukpe is at the border between Igabo (in Nigeria) and Simba (fictional name for Biafra). Before the war the neighboring communities of Urukpe and Simba had the best of relationships; they shared common interests, intermarried, and felt at home in each other's territory. When the war began, the Simbian troops were the first to occupy Urukpe. Later in the war the federal troops retook the town, and confusion de-

scended. Overnight, families found themselves in disarray. Wives born in Simba fled there with their children, leaving husbands among their own kin in Urukpe. Oshevire's wife, Aku, however, puts her family ahead of everything else, remaining in Urukpe with her husband and their only child, Oghenovo. Her decision does not sit well with the community, as the federal government encourages Urukpe's citizens to sever all cordial relationships with the Simbians, who are considered agents of rebellion and disunity. This attitude makes any Simbian a target for molestation and murder. Still, Aku refuses to leave Urukpe. While the people of Urukpe resent Aku's dogged determination to remain, the local chief, Toje Onovwakpo, a prosperous rubber merchant in less fractious times, see in the delicate predicament of the Oshevire household an opportunity for personal gain. Oshevire had joined the rubber business at a time when Toje virtually had a monopoly on it. Oshevire, however, soon outstripped Toje in the business and so earned his hatred. Toje saw himself as the town's foremost citizen, "one of those few names that mean anything here in Urukpe. Everybody knows that— or should" (Okpewho, *The Last Duty,* p. 5). To stamp out this rival in the rubber business, Toje alleged that Oshevire had collaborated with enemy soldiers. Because of the gravity of the crime, he was imprisoned without trial at Iddu, the state capital, for about three years.

With Oshevire behind bars, Toje's business worries seem over, but his vicious schemes are not. His next target is Oshevire's beautiful wife, Aku, whom he decides to seduce. If nothing else, the seduction, he thinks, will restore his virility; Toje had suddenly become impotent as a result of his indiscretion with prostitutes. "I have not hesitated," says Toje, "to seek carnal pleasure with [Oshevire's] forlorn wife now that I feel my manhood flawed, my potency questioned. . . . And what town is there that can survive if it becomes known that one of its most pre-eminent citizens has no claims to manhood?" (*The Last Duty,* p. 5).

Tojo times his treachery at Aku's most vulnerable moment. She is alone with her son without a protective husband to help her face the cruelty and hostility of an entire community. She has been ostracized by Urukpe's people, who have barred her from buying or selling in their markets, and needs some solace if she and her son are to survive in her resolute determination to safeguard her husband's house and maintain his honor while he is in detention.

Toje aims not only to put Oshevire out of business but to destroy his family life entirely. To camouflage his plot, Toje uses his nephew, Odibo, a cripple born without one hand who depends on his rich uncle for survival, as a go-between with Aku. Toje showers Aku with gifts of food, clothes, and money—vital items for a woman whose isolation from the community gives her no access to necessities. To shield the affair from his wives and family, and the open eyes of the town, Toje uses his helpless nephew's residence for his liaisons with Aku. He sends Odibo to Aku's house to fetch her, then has Odibo stay behind to keep her young son company. Sometimes Odibo spends the night at Aku's house when her late return makes it impossible for him to venture home. Although Toje succeeds in his advances to Aku and on occasion arouses her physically, his impotence interferes, making it impossible for him to achieve consummation or to satisfy her sexual desires.

Eventually Aku succumbs not to Chief Toje, but to his humiliated, derided nephew, Odibo (*Odibo* means "a lowly servant"). Aku ascribes her behavior to emotions beyond her control: "Frustration had driven me to the point where I would rather live the fact than the fiction of sin" (*The Last Duty,* p. 184). In time Chief Toje discovers the love affair between Odibo and Aku and, like a wounded lion, unleashes his fury on Aku. Odibo intervenes to divert Toje's violence to himself. In the ensuing fight, venting longstanding contempt for each other, the two men exchange deadly machete wounds.

While his family is being torn to shreds at home, Oshevire finally gets his day in court. After about three years, his case comes up for hearing before a military tribunal. Toje thinks he has concocted a foolproof case against Oshevire and that Oshevire is destined for execution:

> Yes, I exploited the situation and secretly reported Oshevire to Major Bello, and thereafter Oshevire was whisked off into detention at Iddu. And yes, I later got together a number of trumped up charges, and proceeded to suborn the son of Oshevire's old enemy to appear in evidence against the man who put the shame on his father only a few years back. Yes, I did all these things . . . and who is there that can challenge my civic responsibility. . . ?
>
> (*The Last Duty,* pp. 120-21)

The falsity of the trumped-up charges, however, is shown by inconsistent witnesses. Oshevire is acquitted and discharged, but too late to salvage his shattered family life. Aku's betrayal is

yet unknown to him; he thinks of her as a "very jewel of a wife. A matchless queen, whose courage and nobility demand only equal demonstration of fortitude from me now as always" (*The Last Duty,* p. 209). It is this belief in her unflinching virtue that will make her betrayal his greatest blow. His confidence in her is wholehearted:

> I know what women are, but I also know my woman. My only worry as far as that is concerned, is that if anyone sought to visit any dishonour upon her, she might try to do a desperate thing, perhaps not even short of taking her own life. Every Simba woman that I knew of in Urukpe deserted her family and escaped to save her life at the liberation of our town by federal troops. Now would a woman who stood through all the horrors of that moment, when devil-driven citizens of the town took the law into their hands and tormented the lives of innocent people—would such a woman, who stood through it all just so she would stand beside her man, submit her honour to base desire when things were relatively calm?
>
> (*The Last Duty,* p. 156)

Before Oshevire can rejoin his family, however, Aku and Oghenovo are taken into protective custody at the army barracks because of the bloody fight between Toje and Odibo. Oshevire grows distraught and apprehensive when he arrives home to find not his wife and son, but a soldier on guard.

Later at the army barracks, his guilt-ridden wife, instead of welcoming him, breaks down in tears, and Oshevire grows more apprehensive, fearing an impending calamity. The Brigade Commander, Major Ali, breaks the news to him as subtly as possible: "I gave him as much information as either decency or concern for his feelings would allow. An infant would have been able to tell that what brought two men to fight with a machete over a woman was not a decent affair" (*The Last Duty,* pp. 234-35). Oshevire finds it difficult to believe that his wife has betrayed him. He suspects that she may be pregnant with another man's child, an eternal disgrace for a man of his strength of character and reputation. "And what man would choose to be alive to face everyday the ill-conceived fruit of shame?" (*The Last Duty,* p. 238). The humiliation is too much for him to even want to hear her side of the story. He treats her with absolute scorn and silence. At night Oshevire leads his wife and son outside the house and sets it on fire, then flees Urukpe with them. As they make their way through the bush, Oshevire is shot dead by a soldier on guard. His wife ends up on her knees; his son ends up bewildered about the goings-on of the adults in the world around him.

Casualties of war—from Oshevire's idealism to Aku's virtue. Two critical actions define Oshevire and Aku in the novel, and help us understand historical realities of the period. The immediate conflict between Oshevire and his community, which charges him with collaborating with the enemy, is prompted by his intervention to rescue a 13-year-old boy from being lynched by people of Urukpe simply because he is Simbian. Blinded by ethnic malice, driven to betray their own ancestral traditions, the adult community no longer cherishes the innocence of childhood, nor does it heed an age-old custom that requires an adult to protect a child fleeing danger. The lynchers perceive the boy they set out to murder not as a human being but as the symbol of a deadly foe. Determined to protect innocence, Oshevire stands alone against the mob, prepared even to lose his life if need be:

> I saw that boy as a human being, and that was my only concern. It still *is* my only concern. I felt deeply moved to see human life in danger. Though that boy's face had been slightly disfigured I could clearly see that he was too young and I could not bear to watch him fall into the hands of a merciless mob that could have taken his life right there before me. I felt concerned then at the total loss of reason among many people in our town—how several helpless people who could not possibly have been soldiers were hunted down and pitilessly brutalised for no just cause. . . . I am not ashamed or afraid to have done what I did. I am willing to stand by my action, even if I should die for it.
>
> (*The Last Duty*, p. 194)

Oshevire's actions represent a concern for human decency and justice in a world beleaguered by anarchy and hate. Amidst ethnic antagonisms and personal agendas, his is a voice of idealism whose presence the novel acknowledges alongside the negative factors in the devastating civil crisis in Nigeria.

Aku's emotional crisis climaxes when she drops her defenses against the lecherous Toje, and later amorously submits to a surprised but appreciative Odibo. In the case of Toje, she throws her hesitation and reluctance to the winds, ruminating on the possible consequences: "What would I lose if I did? What wouldn't I lose if I didn't?" she asks, realizing she must do everything possible to ensure physical survival for herself and her child (*The Last Duty*, p. 68). In the case of Odibo, whom she literally seduces, she blames her behavior on loneliness and frustration; her excuses expose the agonies of separation endured by spouses forcibly distanced by the war. During the war, families were separated and scattered; it was not uncommon to find a husband or wife left to fend for himself or herself and their children. Scarcity of food and other necessities often forced women to compromise their virtue to ensure survival. They might attach

---

COLLECTIVE EVIDENCE
~

One of the most distinctive qualities of *The Last Duty* is its method of narration. Instead of one narrator, multiple narrators together comprise what Okpewho describes as "the collective evidence technique." The technique conveys an amalgamation of views and representative personalities perceived by the author to be characteristic of a situation—in this case, events in a border town during the Nigerian civil war.

> The story could be said to be told in the first person where every character refers to himself or herself as 'I' as soon as the reader's focus is on him. . . . Each of the major characters is involved unconsciously though, in the story-telling. . . . The whole story thus becomes the recording of the experiences and utterances of certain important characters in a community who are bound together by the plot. As each character goes over moments of the war in his or her life the reader shares his or her thoughts and becomes a kind of witness to the secrets in the mind of the character. The characters are reliable and judgement is left to the reader.
>
> (Okpewho in Emenyonu and Oguzie, p. 186)

Each character's speech reflects his or her age and status. Oghenovo's young mind and age are distinguished from the other characters by putting his speech in lower case with irregular punctuation: "*i do not like my father because he will not let me sleep and my mother is crying and my father has set fire to our house*" (*The Last Duty*, p. 241). We are likewise made aware of Odibo's physical disability, low self-esteem, and slavish dependence on Toje from his plaintive, timid speech: "*I know I am nothing. I know I have nothing. . . . But why does he keep making me feel so bad?*" (*The Last Duty*, p. 6). But later, after a sexual affair with the highly coveted Aku, he speaks with new confidence: "For too long I have felt my body encaged in fear. . . . Now all that is gone. *Gone!* (*The Last Duty*, p. 179).

themselves to soldiers who could afford to support them or perhaps they resorted to covert prostitution. Many marriages were sacrificed at the end of the war when couples could not come to terms with the consequences of their actions. Many of the women caught in such moral quagmires were victims of circumstance, as Aku illustrates through her musings at a critical point in the story:

> Loyalty and devotion had been strained beyond all possible endurance, and neither the mind nor the body could any longer fight the overwhelming presence of temptation. The passive resistance of the body could no longer be supported by the will of the mind, until the entire defence came tumbling down, like an unsheltered mud wall under the relentless downsurge of rain.
>
> (*The Last Duty,* p. 184)

Sources. In a 1999 telephone interview, Okpewho revealed the actual event that inspired him to write the novel. He was away from the fighting during the civil war, working in western Nigeria in Ibadan as an editor at Longman Publishers. His family, however, was in the Midwest, a fierce theater of war. After federal troops recaptured the region from Biafran troops late in 1967 he anxiously traveled there to check on the whereabouts of his family. He traveled with a Brigade Major to Asaba, his mother's natal home, then occupied by the federal soldiers. Although he did not see his uncle, whom he had hoped to find at the family home, he did meet people he knew—but when they saw him in the company of the Brigade Major (a federal soldier) they ran away. Even the priest at the Catholic Mission was reluctant to talk, let alone tell him where his uncle was. While he was in the company of the Brigade Major, people were afraid to identify with him—and yet this was a "liberated' town. The sense of fear and insecurity in the people Okpewho met made the experience totally devastating. Later the priest revealed to Okpewho his uncle's whereabouts and the Brigade Major arranged protection for the family. Okpewho learned that some of his relatives had been killed and others had crossed the border and fled to the East, to the Biafran homeland.

Okpewho continued to tour villages, looking for people he knew, this time accompanied by a close friend, not the Brigade Major. He was stunned by the estrangement that greeted him when he met these people who had been his friends but happened now to be in the so-called federal territories. It was shocking to discover how merely residing on different sides of the war zone could change people's attitudes, even to their friends. As he observed the people he met and perceived their internal conflicts even in the absence of bombs, guns, and battle, he realized that beyond the physical devastation, the war had done psychological damage. This is what Okpewho refers to when he explains that *The Last Duty* "is essentially the tragedy of any civil war: lofty political speeches, declarations, etc., take little notice of the lives of the small people involved in the war, yet have far-reaching effects on their fortunes" (Okpewho in Povey, p. 14).

Literary context. The end of the Nigerian civil war gave rise to a multitude of civil war literary works, ranging from opportunistic writings to factual and fictional accounts of the war. Some of the writings approach the level of invaluable historical documents; others reflect conscious or unconscious distortions of reality. To date, many of these writings have been by members of the defunct Republic of Biafra, in particular by members of Igbo origin.

More than any other group, novelists have been the most prolific producers of literary works on the civil war. While it is impractical to identify them all, they include Eddie Iroh, Chukwuemeka Ike, John Munonye, I. N. C. Aniebo, Flora Nwapa, Buchi Emecheta, Elechi Amadi, Okechukwu Mezu, Phanuel Egejuru, Cyprian Ekwensi, Ossie Onuora Enekwe, Kalu Okpi, Kole Omotosho, Kalu Uka, and Ken Saro Wiwa. Of the novels published within ten years of the war, others that achieved an impact on par with Okpewho's *The Last Duty* are Chukwuemeka Ike's *Sunset at Dawn* (1976) and Eddie Iroh's *Toads of War* (1979). Ike's *Sunset at Dawn* explores various dimensions of the war to reinforce the notion that such conflicts are created by the elite whose power plays turn others into innocent victims. Iroh's *Toads of War* focuses on the moral decay inside Biafra brought about by greedy millionaires, self-proclaimed messiahs, and prodigals who looted the country. Common to these and other such novels is a focus on the political dimensions of the war and an almost exclusive concern for how and why the Biafran dream failed to materialize. In contrast, *The Last Duty* explores the psychological damage that any war does to the minds of people, high and low.

> Okpewho tries in the novel, to show his readers other aspects of the war rather than the shooting. In the face of fear, violence and corruption, there were individuals who still maintained their self respect and conducted

themselves according to the dictates of their conscience by doing what honour and fair play demanded.

(Emenyonu and Oguzie, p. 183)

Physical devastation of life and property are the domains of most of the novels set at the same time and place as *The Last Duty*. What gives *The Last Duty* its distinct place is its profound exploration of "the internal conflicts within and among the characters which supply an even greater tension" (Obiechina, p. 270). Aside from the differences in content, there is a difference in setting. While most Nigerian war novels concern the war inside Biafra, *The Last Duty* focuses on "liberated" areas, where there is no war in the conventional sense and people are supposed to be free and secure—but in fact are not.

Reviews. In 1972, when *The Last Duty* was published in manuscript form, it won the U.C.L.A. African Arts Prize for Literature. "*The Last Duty* handled this potentially dangerous subject [the Nigerian civil war] with compassion and skill.... The structure of the novel is unusual and highly calculated" (Povey, pp. 8, 14). A review in *British Book News* described the structure as sometimes leading to "self-consciousness" but nonetheless deemed the novel to be "a highly sophisticated and successfully achieved piece of work.... In its deep moral concern, and in its technical accomplishment, *The Last Duty* ... has earned an honourable place in the development of African Literature" (Pullin, p. 334). Reviewing the novel for the *Times Literary Supplement*, Adolf Wood complimented the novel's "collective evidence technique":

> Mr. Okpewho has constructed his story by intercutting his characters' evocations of what is happening to them. This makes for slow narration because of the constantly alternating viewpoints, but it serves to convey the characters' lives quite effectively.
>
> (Wood, p. 122)

In Africa, one reviewer complimented the realism achieved by the work: "The reader leaves the novel, *The Last Duty* with the conviction that he has been to Urukpe, and met its people" (*West Africa*, p. 1669). Between 1978 and 1983 the novel was reviewed three times in *African Literature Today*, the leading journal of African literature.

The popularity of the novel in Nigeria was evident by the rapidity with which it was adopted as a reading text in high schools, colleges, and universities. Newspapers in the country carried several reviews of the novel, all positive. In the leading Nigerian newspaper, *The Guardian*, Bayo Ogunjimi declared that "Okpewho feels the pulses of his age, and prepares [his people's] souls . . . for a humane futuristic socioculture" (Ogunjimi, p. 531).

—Ernest N. Emenyonu

BEYOND THE NOVEL—LITERARY WORKS ON NIGERIA'S CIVIL WAR FROM OTHER GENRES

Poetry

Beware Soul Brother (1972), by Chinua Achebe

Don't Let Him Die: An Anthology of Memorial Poems for Christopher Okigbo (1978), by Chinua Achebe and Dubem Okafor

Casualties (1970), by J. P. Clark

Songs in a Time of War (1985), by Ken Saro Wiwa

Short Stories

The Insider: Stories of War and Peace from Nigeria (1971), by Chinua Achebe and others.

Girls at War and Other Stories (1972), by Chinua Achebe

Plays

No Heaven for the Priest (1971), by Ogali Ogali

The Last Days of Biafra (1973), by Orlando Thomas Iguh

Enough is Enough (1976), by Ene Henshaw

Peppersoup and the Road to Ibadan (1977), by Elechi Amadi

The Prisoners (1985), by Chris Nwamuo

Memoirs

My Command (1980), by Olusegun Obasanjo

The Nigerian Revolution and the Biafran War (1980), by Alexander Madiebo

Why We Struck (1981), by Adewale Ademoyega

No Place to Hide: Crises and Conflicts Inside Biafra (1985), by Bernard Chukwuemeka Odogwu

---

For More Information

Achebe, Chinua. *A Man of the People.* London: Heinemann, 1966.

Emenyonu, Ernest. *Studies on the Nigerian Novel.* Ibadan: Heinemann, 1991.

Emenyonu, Ernest, and Benaiah E. C. Oguzie. *African Literature for Schools and Colleges.* Ibadan, Nigeria: University Press, 1989.

Obiechina, Emmanuel. "Isidore Okpewho." In *Dictionary of Literary Biography.* Vol. 157. *Twentieth-Century Caribbean and Black African Writers.* Detroit: Gale Research, 1996.

Ogunjimi, Bayo. Review of *The Last Duty. The Guardian* (Lagos), 24 October 1992, p. 531.

Okpewho, Isidore. *A Portrait of the Artist as a Scholar.* Ibadan: Longman Nigeria, 1990.

————. *The Last Duty.* London: Longman, 1976.

Povey, John F., ed. *African Arts* (winter 1973): 8-12, 14-15, 70-77.

Pullin, Faith. Review of *The Last Duty,* by Isidore Okpewho. *British Book News* (April 1977): 334.

Review of *The Last* Duty. West *Africa* (London), 8 November 1976, p. 1669.

Wood, Adolph. Review of *The Last Duty,* by Isidore Okpewho. *The Times Literary Supplement,* 1 October 1976, p. 1229.

The Maze of Justice

by

Tawfiq al-Hakim

THE LITERARY WORK

A novel set in Egypt in the early 1930s; published in Arabic (as *Yawmiyyat Na'ib fil-Aryaf*) in 1937, in English in 1947.

SYNOPSIS

A prosecutor assigned to a village in the provinces investigates a local murder.

Born in Alexandria in 1902 to an Egyptian father and a Turkish mother, Tawfiq al-Hakim completed his secondary education in Cairo, where he was able to indulge his passion for novels and the theater. He obtained his law degree in 1925 and then traveled to Paris to study for a doctorate. In 1927 he returned to Egypt, became a civil servant in the office of the Public Prosecutor in Alexandria, and was posted to numerous villages in the provinces. Literature was al-Hakim's true vocation, however. Upon his return to Egypt he embarked on a parallel, prolific career as a playwright, novelist, and essayist. Al-Hakim is internationally acclaimed as the founder of modern Arabic drama. Among his novels, *The Return of the Spirit* (1933) is considered a literary masterpiece and influenced a whole generation of nationalist intellectuals, including the leader of the 1952 revolution, Gamal Abdul Nasser (also spelled Jamal 'Abd al-Nasir). Al-Hakim's death in 1987 marked the end of a golden era in Arabic letters. *The Maze of Justice,* which provides a scathing critique of the justice system in early twentieth-century Egypt, is considered by contemporary critics to be one of his finest and most original works.

Events in History at the Time of the Novel

Political background. Between 1516 and 1805, Egypt was ruled from Istanbul as a province of the Ottoman Empire. In 1805 Muhammad 'Ali, commander in chief of the Albanian forces of the Ottoman Army, was appointed governor of Egypt, which led to the founding of the independent dynasty that would rule Egypt until its overthrow in 1952. By 1876 Muhammad 'Ali's grandson, Isma'il had, because of his extravagant expenditure of public funds, plunged the country into a major financial crisis. Both the British and the French had long been eyeing Egypt. Already they owned controlling stakes in the newly built Suez Canal, which linked the Mediterranean and Red Seas. They proceeded at this point to take over the country's crumbling finances and began to interfere in its domestic affairs. Using the excuse of an Egyptian army-instigated nationalist rebellion, the British occupied Egypt militarily in 1882 and became "advisors" to the king.

From the 1920s until 1952, when a military coup put an end to both the monarchy and seven decades of British occupation, Egypt was ruled by a triangle of competing but unequal institutions: the British High Commissioner's Office, the Egyptian royal palace, and a fractious parliament.

In 1922 a limited constitution was drawn up, and in 1924 a popular opposition parliament, supported by the urban nationalist intelligentsia as well as the Egyptian peasantry, was elected. In what was to become a recurrent pattern, the scandalous political assassination nine months later of Sir Lee Stack, the British commander in chief of the Egyptian army, prompted the Egyptian king, in complicity with the British, to dissolve parliament. A series of fractious and short-lived coalition governments followed, and in 1930, when a Wafd prime minister injudiciously resigned, the king seized the opportunity to appoint a cabinet headed by Isma'il Sidqi Pasha, who suspended parliament, amended the constitution to diminish suffrage, and ruled with an iron fist until 1933. "His government," says one historian, "was to become a byword for corruption and the abuse of power" (Sayyid-Marsot, p. 88). Sidqi's government, though allied with both the King and the British, did not go unchallenged by the larger Egyptian population, particularly the peasantry. During the early 1930s nationwide student strikes and demonstrations spread throughout the provincial towns and villages and found much support amongst the radicalized and rebellious peasantry.

THE WAFD PARTY AND THE 1919 REVOLUTION

The party Wafd took its name from the delegation of Egyptian politicians formed in 1918 with the express purpose of lodging Egypt's demand for independence at the Paris Peace Conference that ended World War I. Sa'd Zaghlul, the party's charismatic leader, appealed directly to the patriotism of the oppressed Egyptian masses, particularly the peasantry to which he himself claimed to belong. Under his leadership, the Wafd enjoyed massive support; in 1919 the British authorities had Zaghlul arrested and sent into exile, whereupon revolutionary insurrection broke out throughout the entire country, in cities and villages alike. In fact, the revolution of 1919 helped bring about the radicalization of the Egyptian peasantry, ushering in an era of periodic rural revolt that would last until the revolution of 1952.

The land and the peasantry. Egypt has always been primarily an agricultural country, with most of its population concentrated in the extremely fertile land of the Nile Delta and along the nar-

row strip of the Nile Valley. Given the scarcity of rainfall, irrigation has, from antiquity to the present, relied on the waters of the Nile and an elaborate network of canals and drainage systems. This type of hydraulic engineering has been highly labor-intensive and costly to construct and maintain. Some historians argue that this alone has been responsible for the development and continued existence of a strong, authoritarian central state in Egypt. While the effect on government is debatable, more certain is the fact that the Egyptian peasant has been forced to deal with the tyrannical interventions of exploitative authorities from such a state. The peasant has had to contend with heavy taxation, forced labor, military conscription, and often brutal social and economic conditions, not to mention the unceasing contempt of the educated and urbanized elites.

Historically, all agricultural land in Egypt was owned by the state. It oversaw a semi-feudal arrangement of lifelong land tenure, in which vast properties were parceled out to individuals who collected taxes for the state. Gradually, the system gave way to outright individual legal ownership of the land, which by the mid-nineteenth century led to the formation of a landed oligarchy of Turco-Circassian elites, aligned for the most part with the royal family.

By the turn of the twentieth century, Lord Cromer, the notorious British High Commissioner, had successfully transformed Egypt's agricultural economy into an export-based monoculture based on cotton. Cotton, destined exclusively for England's textile mills, became the country's primary crop. This focus resulted in the gradual destruction of traditional subsistence farming; the concentration of lands into ever larger, privately owned estates; spiraling stock-market speculation that further enriched the landowning elites; and growing landlessness among the peasantry, who formed 82 percent of the Egyptian population. By 1926 half of Egypt's arable land was controlled by 2 percent of the population (Sayyid-Marsot, pp. 86-87). The worldwide Great Depression of the 1930s, which hit Egypt extremely hard (due to its connection with the British economy), accelerated rural patterns of land dispossession, unemployment, violent crime, and government repression.

Prime Minister Sidqi's government, made up mostly of wealthy landowners, was avowedly antilabor; it repeatedly blocked legislation that would have created peasant labor unions and minimum wages for landless agricultural work-

Workers harvest a sugar-cane field on the banks of the Nile River in Egypt.

ers. By 1933 wages had fallen to pre-World War I levels and inflation had skyrocketed. Outrageously high taxes, spiraling rents, periodic land confiscations, and forced labor all provoked the peasants (or *fellahin*) to violent rebellion, which broke out in various locations throughout the 1930s.

Illiteracy, disease and poverty were endemic. Some 65 percent of the peasantry suffered from chronic bilharzia (a potentially fatal kidney disease peculiar to Egypt) and 75 percent from degenerative eye disease, while most were severely malnourished. Modern healthcare and basic hygiene were virtually nonexistent in peripheral rural areas. Tawfiq al-Hakim's generation of Westernized, urban intellectual reformers decried these conditions and questioned Egypt's ability to modernize and achieve true independence while more than two-thirds of its population still lived in such misery and squalor.

The legal system. In the 1930s the Egyptian judicial system was comprised of three main institutions: the Muslim Shari'a Courts, the Mixed Courts, and the Native Courts. It is the latter that figures most prominently in *The Maze of Justice*. The Shari'a Courts predated European influence. They administered the traditional Islamic law of one of four major schools of jurisprudence through a *qadi*—a Muslim legal scholar usually

trained at al-Azhar in Cairo, the oldest and most venerated university in the Islamic world. The jurisdiction of these traditional courts was increasingly restricted throughout the nineteenth century due to the rapid social and economic

THE CORVEE

Forced, unpaid labor (known as corvee) had deep historical roots in the Egyptian countryside. The annual flooding of the Nile basin required a massive labor effort (roads, dikes, and canals throughout the country had to be strengthened and repaired on a regular basis). By the nineteenth century, the corvee system of forced labor had developed into a well organized and particularly brutal state enterprise. The Suez Canal was actually constructed with corvee labor; 100,000 Egyptian peasants died digging the Canal with their bare hands since the Canal Company "refused to provide them with either tools, food or shelter" (Sayyid-Marsot, p. 66). Though corvee was officially abolished late in the century, both the state and wealthy private landowners continued to make use of massive rural work gangs, who received poor payment, if any, and labored under miserable working conditions.

transformations taking place in Egypt. A haphazard secular court system based on French law—the Code Napoleon—was to increasingly replace Shari'a jurisdiction. By the turn of the twentieth century, Shari'a Courts were permitted to hear cases only on personal status issues: marriage, divorce, and inheritance.

CROMER AND DINSHAWAY

Sir Evelyn Baring, later Lord Cromer, came to Egypt as "Her Britannic Majesty's Consul-General and Agent" after service in India. He established "the Granville Doctrine," which installed British advisors in key ministries, institutionalized British control over them, and inaugurated the "veiled protectorate," Britain's thinly disguised military and administrative occupation of Egypt. A ruthless conservative, he made no attempt to hide his contempt for Egyptians and the growing nationalist movement, nor to conceal the fact that he was the real power behind Egypt's throne. In 1906 a violent fight broke out between a group of British officers who were pigeon hunting in the village of Dinshaway and the local peasants to whom the pigeons belonged. One of the officers was injured and subsequently died of sunstroke. The villagers were arrested and subjected to a court martial, which ended in shockingly severe sentences (presumably for the murder of the officer): four men were hanged, two sentenced to penal servitude for life, six faced seven years' imprisonment, and the rest received public floggings. Egyptians everywhere were outraged. In London, a newly elected liberal government forced Cromer to resign; he returned to England amid the jubilation of the Egyptian masses. Meanwhile, the peasant came to symbolize nationalist resistance to the British occupation.

The Mixed Courts, established in 1875, were an attempt to soften the judicial inequities of the European Capitulations, a provision worked out with the Ottoman Empire that allowed foreign nationals in Egypt to be tried before their own consular court administering its own system of national law. This extra-judicial system guaranteed that foreign communities enjoyed total freedom from native authority. The Mixed Courts operated under a tribunal of European and Egyptian judges (with Europeans in the majority), administered French law, and exercised jurisdiction over commercial and civil cases involving either foreigners or a foreigner and an Egyptian. Though these courts set out to mitigate bias, in practice they were used by European powers to prosecute any important case in which Europeans felt they had a strategic interest, even if it involved only Egyptian nationals.

The Native Courts were reformed and institutionalized in the 1880s. They too administered an exact replica of France's Code Napoleon, which was based on the political and economic principles of modern French society—the sanctity of private property and the liberty and equality of citizens. Egypt's Native Courts were responsible for trying civil and criminal cases involving only Egyptians. By the 1930s these courts were staffed by Egyptian judges trained at the still-young Cairo University Faculty of Law (or like al-Hakim himself, at the Sorbonne in Paris), and included three main levels of tribunals: central tribunals in the governorates, Markaz (district capital) tribunals in the provinces, and summary tribunals in the outlying rural areas. It is this third tier of courts that is lampooned in al-Hakim's novel.

Were these courts successful in controlling the rising rural crime rate and in ensuring easy access to justice for the peasantry? According to observers (including al-Hakim), the answer is "no." Even with the establishment of the summary tribunals, peasants still had to travel a long way to use the courts. "Most did not have the leisure time or money, for court procedure was expensive and slow [and] the courts were always in arrears in their cases" (Tignor, p. 139). Echoing al-Hakim's indictment of the Code Napoleon almost 30 years earlier, historian Robert Tignor comments that "French law was not well-suited to Egypt. Much of it was completely incomprehensible to the Egyptian populace"—especially in the countryside, where illiteracy, traditional forms of piety, and a much older kind of communal, customary law still held sway (Tignor, p. 140). Moreover, Tignor notes that the administrative structure of the French system often resulted in serious friction between the judicial authorities and the police—a subject dramatized in *The Maze of Justice*. The former were responsible for collecting evidence and preparing the case for prosecution while the latter were merely supposed to render any assistance necessary to this end. Disputes over respective spheres of authority arose often, further complicating and slowing the administration of justice.

As always, the capital exercised undue influence over the provincial court system, since all

Al-Azhar Square, the heart of the old city of Cairo, is outside al-Azhar Mosque (on the left), which was the congregational mosque of the old city and is still the seat of Egypt's oldest university.

members of the judicial and police administration were appointed from Cairo, which gave rise to party politics, cronyism, and corruption. There was, moreover, a massive Cairo-centered legal bureaucracy, and it demanded adherence to the letter of the law and proper procedure through a highly centralized system of endless and complex paperwork, making justice for the peasant a secondary priority. Cairo-appointed officials were frequently less than enthusiastic about their rural postings, which they often viewed as a kind of political exile. Their main concerns tended to be making their lives as comfortable as possible in such adverse circumstances and continually plotting to get a much-coveted post in Cairo.

Intellectuals and reformers. Al-Hakim's generation was a product of the *Nahdah*—the great cultural renaissance that swept the urban centers of the Arab world in the late nineteenth and early twentieth century. The Nahdah was essentially an ambitious and inspired movement for reform of all aspects of the social, political, and cultural life of Arabs, who were perceived as inadequately prepared to meet the demands of an increasingly global modernity. In Egypt, as elsewhere in the region, the dominant model for this new modernity was identified as the secular, sovereign, lib-

eral nation-state as exemplified by the European powers (England and France) and the United States. By the revolution of 1919 Egypt was no longer content to be ruled as a province of a distant empire. Self-determination and independent nationhood were the ideals that motivated millions of Egyptians to take to the streets in the early 1900s. On the cultural level, a concerted attempt was made to reform and modernize the Arabic language and its literature, and the great medieval Islamic traditions were subjected to renewed scrutiny and reformulation in light of the demands of an increasingly secular, scientific climate. The Egyptian University (later renamed Cairo University) was established during this period; its scholars championed modern educational methods and curricula as the means by which the new Egyptian citizen of a proud, healthy, democratic nation would be formed.

How rosy could the immediate future be, though? More than 70 percent of the population remained illiterate, living at subsistence level without much awareness of the great changes sweeping the cities. Control of the country lay in the hands of a coterie of native and foreign elite—the British colonial authorities, Egypt's royal family, European financial and commercial interests, and the native landed oligarchy. Egypt's urban reformist intellectuals, including al-Hakim, tended to belong to this last, self-interested class. Under such conditions, true reform often remained hostage to the tension between imported ideals and grassroots realities, between progressive social theories, and veiled economic and political interests. In fact, many of the great politicians and reformers who glorified, romanticized, and championed the cause of the Egyptian peasantry in public, harbored a powerfully ingrained contempt for the illiterate, impoverished peasants; al-Hakim's novel itself likens them to cattle, flies, worms, and monkeys at the zoo. It is this crucial, quixotic tension that forms the thematic background to *The Maze of Justice*.

The Novel in Focus

Plot summary. Al-Hakim's novel takes the form of a journal that spans 11 entries from October 11 to October 22. The exact year in which the events take place is not identified, but we can assume that it is in the early 1930s—the time of the author's judicial posting in the Egyptian countryside. Like the author himself, the narrator is a young district prosecutor assigned to a small village in the Delta. The plot is loosely

structured around a murder mystery but generally the novel is a scathing social and political indictment of the provincial judiciary and bureaucracy in Egypt.

October 11. The novel opens with an obscure summons in the dead of night to investigate a murder that has occurred in a neighboring village:

> Tonight at 8 pm, while Kamar al-Dawla Alwan was walking on the river-side, near our village, a shot was fired at him from a sugar-plantation by a person or persons unknown. On being interrogated the victim was unable to divulge anything. His condition is grave. For your information—The Umdah.
> (al-Hakim, *The Maze of Justice*, p. 15)

After hastily gathering the official team of investigators—his legal assistant, the Ma'mur, the inspector and a few policemen—the prosecutor sets out on the long journey (by car, ferry, and mule) to the village in question. On the way, they pick up a local Sufi shaykh (also spelled *sheik*) by the name of Asfur who figures prominently in the unfolding mystery.

Shaykh Asfur is known to the authorities as a vagrant quack who speaks only in riddles and rhymes but nonetheless serves as a local guide and informant from time to time. Upon arrival at the scene of the crime, the team examines the unconscious victim and proceeds to question one villager after another, to no avail. As the prosecutor had expected, the locals are either unable or unwilling to assist the investigation. Even the Umdah has no information to offer. Shaykh Asfur is consulted as a last resort and he replies with yet another of his riddle-like couplets:

> Watch out for women; they're the mark
> Of ruin to men's pride;
> My loved one's eyelash, long and dark,
> Would span an acre wide!
> (*Maze of Justice*, p. 26)

The prosecutor is intrigued by this reference to a female suspect. He suddenly remembers that the victim, whose wife had died some years previously and who lived a solitary life with his aging mother, had a baby daughter. Upon further inquiry he discovers that this child has been in the care of the dead wife's 16-year-old sister. This mysterious sister, Rim, is summoned and all present, including Shaykh Asfur, are stunned by her beauty and innocence. When questioned, she tells the prosecutor that her brother-in-law, who was also her legal guardian, had repeatedly refused to accept offers of marriage on her behalf. The last such rejection was directed against a

---

THE VILLAGE HIERARCHY

In a typical Delta village, the *Umdah* or "mayor" was recruited from one of the wealthy local landowning families. Appointed from Cairo, he became responsible for resolving local disputes, maintaining order and public safety, and overseeing the collection of taxes. He personally commanded a body of *ghafirs*, or armed guards, also recruited locally, to help him fulfill his duties. The *Ma'mur*, or Chief of Police, and the District Prosecutor were also appointed from Cairo, but they usually came from the ranks of the Westernized, urban, middle classes, and their jurisdiction encompassed the cluster of villages that belonged to the larger District, or *Markaz*. The local Umdah was subordinate to the Ma'mur and ceded jurisdiction to him in felony cases. In practice, while Umdahs often exercised absolute power in their home villages, they were mere underlings of the Ma'mur. Unlike the Umdah and the Ma'mur, who were both employees of the Ministry of the Interior, the District Prosecutor was appointed by the Ministry of Justice and hence maintained a degree of administrative and political independence within the rural hierarchy.

young man whom she, Rim, had taken a liking to. When she hears the news of the attempted murder, she faints and the investigation is postponed until the afternoon.

October 12. Meanwhile, the prosecutor rushes back to his village in order to attend the morning session in court. This gives the narrating prosecutor the opportunity to describe, at humorous length, the vagaries of the provincial court bureaucracy, the indifference and corruption of the judges who administer it, and the ignorance of the unfortunate villagers, who find themselves at the mercy of an incomprehensible and inadequate legal code. There are two judges who sit on alternate days: one, the Conscientious Judge, is the prototype of a by-the-book bureaucrat who resides in the village and, out of sheer boredom, conducts interminably long sessions. The other—the Brisk Judge—is a commuter from Cairo who is always rushing to catch the 11:00 train back and whose primary concern is acquiring fresh village meat and produce before returning to the capital. The former judge has a reputation for imposing cheaper fines, and so his courtroom is always full. The latter makes a point of imposing maximum fines in order to guarantee a minimum crowd and hence a speedy departure. In the midst of all this dogmatism and self-interest, the human negotiation of justice becomes irrelevant and the illiterate villagers are condemned to sentences they cannot comprehend.

October 13. Back at his office, the exhausted prosecutor has no choice but to postpone the investigation until the following day. It is decided that Rim will spend the night at the Ma'mur's house. The prosecutor returns home to sleep but wakes at midnight anxious about Rim's safety at the lecherous Ma'mur's house. Luckily, he receives a telegram regarding a minor incident in the next village. Seizing on this excuse, the prosecutor summons the furious Ma'mur and the rest of the team and sets off to investigate. After this pointless investigation, during which the Ma'mur manages to extort a huge homemade feast from the reluctant Umdah, they return to learn that the victim, Kamar al-Dawla, has regained consciousness. They rush to the filthy local hospital. Upon repeated questioning as to who shot him, a barely conscious Kamar al-Dawla pronounces the single word, "Rim."

October 14. The stunned prosecutor returns to his office and meets with his young assistant—also an exile from the capital. They discuss the boredom of provincial life. A few cases are brought before them. The first is that of an old,

destitute man who is accused of stealing a jar of maize. Far from denying the charge, he freely admits that he stole out of hunger. Since he cannot pay bail ("if I had the money, I'd use it to get some food," the man pathetically declares), he is taken into "preventative custody for four days with the option of renewal" (*Maze of Justice,* p. 57). The second case involves a lost cargo of clothes. In the middle of the night, a truck passing the village hits a pothole, which dislodges a bag of new clothes headed for a Cairo warehouse. The crate ends up in the canal and the next morning the impoverished villagers make off with the providential gifts. The villagers are brought before the prosecutor and charged with theft. They cannot understand the logic of this law but are led away in chains nonetheless. Suddenly, the Ma'mur turns up and informs the prosecutor that Rim has disappeared with Shaykh Asfur.

October 15. Later that day, the prosecutor goes off in search of the Ma'mur, who also seems to have disappeared. His search takes him to "the Club," a ramshackle room above the only café in

VILLAGE SUFIS

Sufism, or Islamic mysticism, emerged in the ninth century and emphasized the personal, individual experience of divine love and ecstatic ritual practice over the literal formalism of orthodox Islam. Sufis formed orders or brotherhoods, which were usually organized hierarchically around a series of masters and disciples and were associated with a local saint's shrine. A number of these Sufi orders became entrenched in the Egyptian countryside from the Middle Ages onwards and contributed to the formation of a popular rural Islam. Disciples commonly wandered through the countryside, at times establishing temporary residence in some village or other, dispensing blessings and spells and charms against various ailments, from infertility to impotence. To the urban reformist intellectuals of the Nahdah, these shaykhs were nothing more than charlatans who made a living by exploiting credulous villagers. In *The Maze of Justice,* Shaykh Asfur's rhymed riddles and demeanor of the divine fool are used to mask the shrewd cunning and opportunism regarded as typical of the vagrant village Sufi. At the same time he is associated throughout the novel with the famous and mysterious popular saint al-Khidr, through the emblematic green staff he always carries and through his clever folksy rhymes.

town that serves as a meeting place, gaming room, and watering hole for the small group of inexorably bored local bureaucrats and professionals. At the club, the prosecutor hears the latest gossip and learns that the Ma'mur is a rapacious gambler. He leaves the club, lost in thought about the mysterious triangle that connects the beautiful Rim, the lunatic Shaykh Asfur, and the dying Kamar al-Dawla. Suddenly he spots Rim and the Shaykh sitting outside the hospital. He rushes back to the police station and finds the Ma'mur, who has been out all day searching for the pair. They send a police detail to pick them up, but it is too late: Rim has once again disappeared, and a handcuffed Shaykh Asfur refuses to provide any information on her whereabouts, taking refuge once more in his rhymes. The prosecutor begins to wonder whether he only imagined seeing Rim earlier.

October 16. The prosecutor releases Asfur. The next morning the prosecutor attends yet another court session, this time with the Brisk Judge, who sentences all the misdemeanors in absentia (regardless of whether the accused are present or not) in order to save time. The felonies are dealt with in an equally summary manner, and sentences handed down without recourse to witnesses or legal arguments. One such case involves a man who is charged with having eaten his own crop of wheat, which had been "reserved" by the government in lieu of unpaid taxes. The hungry man cannot comprehend why it should be a crime to eat one's own food. He is sentenced to one month's imprisonment with hard labor.

Back at the office the prosecutor discovers that the Ma'mur has arrested Shaykh Asfur on vagrancy charges. He then receives an anonymous letter implicating Rim and Kamar al-Dawla in Kamar's wife's death: another potential piece in the jigsaw-puzzle investigation. He makes preparations to exhume the wife's body in order to confirm the accusation of death by strangulation. The expectation of new elections forces the prosecutor to conduct a sham "surprise" prison inspection in which everything has been prepared beforehand. When he is finally free to proceed with the exhumation, he confirms that death occurred by strangulation. On the way back to his village, the prosecutor sees more evidence of the ruckus caused by the new government: a new Umdah has been appointed and the old Umdah is forced to cede the official telephone in an ignominious ritual of political and social rivalry.

October 18. Further questioning of Shaykh Asfur and the village barber who signed the mur-

dered wife's death certificate yields nothing new. The prosecutor muses on the appalling health system in Egypt and remembers a case described to him by the local doctor, in which a midwife stuffed a pregnant woman's uterus with straw in the belief that this would assist in the delivery. Both the woman and the baby were dead by the time the doctor arrived two days later. The prosecutor concludes that "human life has no value in Egypt" (*Maze of Justice,* p. 89).

Believing that the anonymous letter may have been written by an Azhari-trained court clerk, the prosecutor pays a visit to the qadi of the Shari'a Court to consult him on its handwriting. There follows a highly amusing portrait of this qadi, an avaricious, ignorant, and hypocritical opportunist; consultation with him yields nothing. The prosecutor heads for the police station only to discover that the entire staff is too busy with electioneering business to assist the investigation any further. The Ma'mur himself is giving an assembly of local Umdahs an earnest lesson in election-rigging. Returning to his office, the prosecutor attempts to question one of Rim's neighbors on the identity of Rim's mystery suitor, but the garrulous, senile old woman's testimony proves fruitless. This gives the prosecutor the opportunity to muse on the general physical, mental, and moral deficiencies of the Egyptian peasantry.

October 20. The next morning the Conscientious Judge pays the prosecutor a visit at his office in reference to a political intrigue instigated against him by the Ma'mur. The judge, who is a client of the outgoing national ministry, is afraid that the Ma'mur will use his opportunistically acquired position with the new ministry to have the judge transferred to an even more remote corner of the country. The prosecutor promises to intervene and goes to see the Ma'mur. Outside the police station, he spots Shaykh Asfur getting into the back of a truck with a group of policemen. Upon inquiry, he discovers that the shaykh has been recruited to help keep order during the upcoming voting.

October 21. The prosecutor receives news of Kamar al-Dawla's death. He sends his assistant to attend the postmortem. He is then summoned to investigate a poisoning case. The woman in question is practically unconscious and "drowning in the contents of [her] own stomach," but is nonetheless expected to respond to a variety of precise, detailed questions that are issued as part of the standard government form for such cases (*Maze of Justice,* p. 116). This provides the prosecutor another opportunity to denounce the irrelevancy of the national legal bureaucracy. Back at his office, he hears the sudden news of Rim's death—her body was discovered in the village canal. The prosecutor is stunned and saddened, "not because ... Rim was one of the keys to the case. It was because she had been such a dazzling spectacle and had moved us all deeply—the mad and the sane amongst us alike" (*Maze of Justice*, p. 122). A delirious Shaykh Asfur is sighted in the street, running amok, mad with grief. He recites a rhyme that implies that Rim was murdered, but after some deliberation, the prosecutor refuses to order a postmortem in deference to Rim's beauty and decides to close the whole bizarre investigation, which is filed away as just another insignificant and unsolved rural crime.

October 22. On the last day of his journal entries, we find the prosecutor up to his ears in end-of-year reports and trivial complaints. In search of help, an overburdened colleague drops by to unload two suitcases of his own reports and complaints onto the conscientious prosecutor, who grudgingly agrees to lend a hand. The two friends commiserate about their professional exile in the provinces and discuss the corruption of the legal bureaucracy. The prosecutor is left alone with his endless files and papers to reflect on the abysmal political, legal, and social condition of contemporary Egypt.

Parliament and the national hierarchy of power. *The Maze of Justice* uses the corruption of the political system in Egypt as a metaphor for the general hypocrisy, inefficiency, and chaos of national life in the early 1930s. Towards the end of the novel, the description of the new parliamentary elections—possibly those called by Sidqi in 1931—reflects the way that corruption and cronyism filtered down into the lowest levels of society.

In the novel, al-Hakim presents the rivalry between two unnamed national parties. Power and influence are traded back and forth between these parties in a tragicomic game of opportunism and patronage that reflects the clan-oriented political rivalries of village life. No one is free of this intrigue, from the Ma'mur, who hastens to declare allegiance to the new cabinet and who is responsible for rigging the village elections for their benefit—"I let the people vote as they like ... then I simply take the ballot-box and throw it in the river and calmly replace it with the box which we prepare ourselves"—to the local Umdahs, who are appointed and dis-

missed according to the whims and machinations of those newly in power (*Maze of Justice*, p. 112). The hilarious scene in which the narrator describes the procession accompanying the transfer of the village telephone—symbol of the Umdah's authority—from the home of the old Umdah to that of the new one captures the essence of this farcical game of power and the absurdity of both its winners and losers.

THE ELECTIONS OF 1931

The two major parties of the day—the Wafd and the Liberal Constitutionalists—were banned by Sidqi from political organizing prior to the elections of April 1931. They nonetheless issued a manifesto proclaiming loyalty to the abrogated constitution of 1922 and repudiating Sidqi's elections. The manifesto also declared that no acts of the current government were binding on the nation. Sidqi responded by calling in the army to "supervise" the elections, which were held despite widespread accusations of fraud. Meanwhile, the police terrorized the provinces. Political demonstrations were met with violence by provincial authorities: indiscriminate mass arrests and torture were common.

Even the Conscientious Judge is a potential victim of the system. Since he is a known supporter of the outgoing government and since he and the Ma'mur have an ongoing personal rivalry, he justifiably fears that the Ma'mur will use his influence with the incoming government to have him transferred to an even more distant provincial post. In the middle of all this political jockeying, justice is sacrificed: the judge cannot force the newly appointed Umdah to comply with a civil judgment. The Umdah can simply ignore the judgment because he is protected by those in power. The police will do nothing because their chief, the Ma'mur, is a client of the same new government—a government that has come to power through blatant fraud. Outside the novel, in 1930s Egypt, the consequence of such political jockeying was real-life injustice, which resulted in widespread disillusionment among the masses and intellectuals alike.

Sources and literary context. When al-Hakim wrote *The Maze of Justice*, the Egyptian countryside and the peasant were already the subject of debate among intellectuals and politicians, and there existed a well-established body of literature dealing with these issues. The 1906 Dinshaway incident was responsible for pushing the cause of the oppressed peasantry to the fore of national consciousness. Urban elites who had traditionally despised and shunned this marginalized sector of the population suddenly came to see it as the very heart of the authentic, resistant Egyptian nation. Immediately following Dinshaway, Muhammad Tahir Haqqi, a journalist, published a novel based on the incident (*The Maiden of Dinshaway*), in which the heroine is a beautiful young peasant girl whose father leads the rebellion against the British. This was the first time that the peasantry had been endowed with central heroic status in Egyptian literature. The novel became an immediate bestseller and went into multiple editions. In 1913 Muhammad Husayn Haykal, the Paris-educated son of a wealthy landowner published his first novel, *Zaynab*, which told the tragic story of another lovely young peasant girl and described in great detail the serene beauty of the Egyptian countryside as well as its manners and customs. Haykal, like many young men of his generation, was much influenced by French romanticism and in *Zaynab* he gave his readers a highly romanticized, pastoral image of the noble Egyptian peasant and his millennia-old way of life. Other writers of the period, like Taha Husayn and Ibrahim al-Mazini, wrote about the countryside, and in an earlier novel (*The Return of the Spirit*, 1927) Tawfiq al-Hakim himself paid tribute to the noble, self-sacrificing Egyptian peasant, whose way of life and dedication to the service of his masters had not changed since the days of the pharaohs.

In 1937, the same year in which *The Maze of Justice* was published, Henri Ayrout, a French Jesuit missionary, published a highly influential book of nonfiction about the Egyptian peasant. At the American University in Cairo, a respected female essayist and novelist, Bint al-Shati', lectured on the reform of the peasant's wretched condition. Also it became immensely popular to pay lip service to the authenticity and nobility of the Egyptian peasant during this period. A popular weekly magazine described him as "a pearl in its shell, a moon hidden by clouds" (Berque, p. 490). Politicians, who inevitably had votes and mass popularity in mind, hastened to claim lineage from these long-toiling sons of the soil. The Wafd Party's Sa'd Zaghlul, the millionaire parliamentarian Muhammad Badrawi, and King Faruq himself were all self-described peasant Egyptians!

Al-Hakim's *Maze of Justice* is thus a highly political intervention into the dominant romantic reformist discourse on the *fellah*. It is an exposé of sorts that seeks to demonstrate the essential incompatibility between myth and reality, between the grand prototype of the nation that was being developed by urban elites and the squalid condition of the people who were supposed to exemplify the living heart of this nation. On a deeper level, it is an indictment of the very hypocrisy of the reformist project itself.

Reviews. In the midst of all this highly charged rhetoric, *The Maze of Justice* was received by contemporaries like a breath of fresh air. Critics were duly impressed by its candor, humor, and most of all, by the uncompromising realism of its style. Writing in the weekly *al-Risalah,* Mahmud al-Khafif praised the novel's original use of "the element of suspense" in the form of a murder mystery, and the realistic portrayal of a cast of characters heretofore completely unknown (and perhaps unbelievable) to complacent urban audiences (Al-Khafif, p. 1719; trans. S. Selim). The reviewer for *al-Hilal,* Egypt's most popular cultural monthly, praised the author's "sensitivity" and "gentle sense of humor" in dealing with the squalor and criminality of the countryside. He went on to call the novel "a new type of reformist literature" that imaginatively combines social consciousness, entertainment and instruction (*al-Hilal,* p. 234; trans. S. Selim).

However, the novel was quickly forgotten in favor of al-Hakim's next novel, *Bird of the East* (1938), which attracted much more attention and critical commentary than *The Maze of Justice*. Because of its uncompromisingly satiric and realist style, *The Maze of Justice* can be seen as something of an anomaly in al-Hakim's larger oeuvre. The author continued to be identified with his grander, philosophical plays and nationalist novels (like *Shahrazad* and *The Return of Consciousness*) until the 1950s, when social realism became the dominant literary school of the day and *The Maze of Justice* was once again revived as an example of the corruption of the old regime in Egypt.

—Samah Selim

For More Information

Allen, Roger. *The Arabic Novel: An Historical and Critical Introduction.* Syracuse, N.Y.: Syracuse University Press, 1982.

Berque, Jacques. *Egypt: Imperialism and Revolution.* New York: Praeger, 1972.

Cachia, Pierre. *An Overview of Modern Arabic Literature.* Edinburgh: Edinburgh University Press, 1990.

Gershoni, I., and J. P. Jankowski. *Redefining the Egyptian Nation, 1930-1945.* Cambridge: Cambridge University Press, 1995.

al-Hakim, Tawfiq. *The Maze of Justice.* Trans. Abba Eban. Austin: University of Texas Press, 1989.

al-Khafif, Mahmud. Review of *The Maze of Justice,* by Tawfiq al-Hakim. *Al-Risalah,* 18 October 1937, p. 1719.

Hourani, Albert. *Arabic Thought in the Liberal Age, 1789-1939.* Cambridge: Cambridge University Press, 1970.

Review of *The Maze of Justice,* by Tawfiq al-Hakim. *Al-Hilal,* December 1937, p. 234.

Sayyid-Marsot, Afaf Lutfi. *A Short History of Modern Egypt.* Cambridge: Cambridge University Press, 1992.

Starkey, Paul. *From the Ivory Tower: A Critical Study of Tawfiq al-Hakim.* St. Anthony's Middle East Monographs, no. 19. London: Ithaca Press, 1987.

Tignor, Robert. *Modernization and British Colonial Rule in Egypt, 1882-1914.* Princeton, N.J.: Princeton University Press, 1966.

Wendell, Charles. *The Evolution of the Egyptian National Image from its Origins to Ahmad Lutfi al-Sayyid.* Los Angeles: UCLA Press, 1972.

Midaqq Alley

by

Najib Mahfuz

~

Najib Mahfuz (also spelled Naguib Mahfouz), winner of the 1988 Nobel Prize for Literature, was born December 11, 1911, in the Jamaliyya quarter of Cairo, a part of the city that dates back to the tenth century. The quarter is situated near the area in which the events he recounts in *Midaqq Alley* are set. Mahfuz grew up as the son of a minor civil servant, eventually following in his father's footsteps. He began his civil service career in 1939, also publishing his first novel that year. Mahfuz would go on to publish more than 50 novels, short stories, and plays. His sixth novel, *Midaqq Alley* is set during the waning days of World War II, a period of social malaise and rising political tension in Egypt. The novel, both a thriller and a carefully crafted literary meditation, is generally regarded as the rehearsal for his three-volume masterpiece, *Trilogy*, which evokes on a grand scale the panorama of Cairene society between 1917 and 1945.

Events in History at the Time of the Novel

A question of fictional timing. There has been controversy over the exact time period in which *Midaqq Alley* is set. Although it is clearly situated during World War II, early critics placed it during the winter of 1941-42 or 1943-44, while more recently scholars have concluded that it transpires in the winter and spring of 1944-45. The textual evidence for this latter view seems convincing: in the novel's first pages one char-

THE LITERARY WORK

A novel set in the Islamic quarter of Cairo at the end of World War II; published in Arabic (as *Zuqaq al-Midaqq*) in 1947, in English in 1966 (corrected translation published in 1975).

SYNOPSIS

Modernization affects the traditional ways of life on a secluded street near the heart of the old city of Cairo.

acter mentions that "we've been suffering terrors of blackouts and air-raids for five years," suggesting that the war (1939-45) is drawing to a close (Mahfuz, *Midaqq Alley*, p. 2).

The distinction is important because in 1942 German general Erwin Rommel's Afrika Corps was still menacing the major cities of Egypt, and the British presence on Egyptian soil had some legitimacy, while by 1945 nearly everyone, including many of the British soldiers themselves, wished the British army well out of the country. Further, if the novel was composed late in the war, the social world evoked in *Midaqq Alley* can more justifiably be seen as reproducing the backdrop for probably the most significant change in Egypt during the twentieth century, the 1952 revolution that brought Gamal Abdul Nasser (also spelled Jamal 'Abd al-Nasir) to power. It is only by understanding the national sense of discontent, of frustration with the stalemate into which democratic parliamentary life had degenerated by the close of the war years, that one can appreciate why Egyptians were willing in the 1950s to surrender some of their hard-won freedoms in the name of social progress under Nasser.

Seeds of discontent. Although most of the events in *Midaqq Alley* take place in or near the alley itself and the British as a colonial force are rarely allowed to intrude upon the action, the few references in the novel to their existence would have been sufficient to remind Egyptian readers of the chronically distorting effect that colonial policy had been exerting on life in their country, even in places like Midaqq, which appeared outwardly untouched by its influence.

The political relationships operative in 1944-45 were set in motion more than 60 years earlier, in 1882, when Britain invaded Egypt to put down a rebellion against the financial exactions ordered by the French and British Controllers who oversaw all aspects of public expenditure by the Egyptian government. Egypt was at that time more than £E90,000,000 in debt to various European creditors, and the Controllers were there to ensure that the debts were paid. Shortly after being appointed in the late 1870s, the Controllers divided the projected revenues of the country (approximately £E9,000,000 per year) in two, with half going directly to pay off the foreign creditors and half to the expenses of administering Egypt. But it was quickly found that the actual encumbrances placed on the revenues were well in excess of the estimated £E4,500,000 earmarked for servicing debts. This was followed by the discovery that the government revenue had been overestimated by approximately a million Egyptian pounds, so in the end only about £E2,000,000 was left to run the country. Since the Controllers were unwilling to offend Egypt's foreign creditors by reducing payments on debts, this meant draconian cuts had to be enacted in expenditures in the country itself on education, the army, government departments, and public works. At one point, taxes were being collected as much as 6 months in advance while government salaries were as much as 18 months in arrears. The situation bred popular discontent, especially in the army.

The 'Urabi revolt. In 1879 the ruling khedive, Isma'il, was deposed by the British and French because of his attempts to exert more control over how the meager government revenues were being spent. He was replaced by his son, Taw-

fiq, who was at first welcomed by reformist elements within the country; they believed he would summon a *shura* (a consultative body similar to a parliament) and would rule as a constitutional monarch. Their hopes were dashed when Tawfiq discovered that he would continue to receive British and French support only as long as he made sure the debt payments were on time. Armed with this knowledge, he decided to rule as an autocrat without a popular mandate. This eventually led to a confrontation with Colonel Ahmad 'Urabi, leader of the nationalist, constitutionalist elements in the army.

'Urabi was a native Egyptian, from the peasant class of farmers (the vast majority of Egypt's population at the time) known as *fellahin*. The army officer corps had long been recruited not from the peasants but from the descendants of the Turco-Circassians who had arrived in Egypt with the Ottoman conquest in 1516. The khedive Isma'il, however, had continued his predecessor's initiative of allowing some native Egyptians to enter the officers' ranks. Since these officers tended to depend solely on their pay for living expenses, they felt great discontent at the government's budget cuts. In September 1881 'Urabi, champion of the Egyptian officers, presented their requests for reforms to the new khedive, Tawfiq, who was reputed to have replied: "I am the Khedive of the country and shall do as I please" (Ahmed, p. 25). The next year people rioted in Alexandria, and this led to battle between the British and 'Urabi, who by this time had become a hero linked to the notion of "Egypt for the Egyptians." In the end, 'Urabi was defeated by the British and exiled.

The British occupation. The bloody suppression of 'Urabi's defiance in 1882 began a long military occupation of Egypt by British troops that would be decisively ended only by the Suez War in 1956. This was long after the debts Isma'il had contracted were paid; Britain remained in Egypt as much because of emerging strategic interests as purely financial ones. In 1869 the Suez Canal opened. Linking the Mediterranean Sea to the Red Sea across Egypt's Isthmus of Suez, it shortened the journey between England and its overseas possessions in the East—primarily India—by more than 6,000 miles. By the 1880s as much as 80 percent of the traffic through the Canal was British, and keeping this vital transportation artery open had become a prime factor in England's foreign policy. This resolve would only increase with the discovery of oil in Iran (and later Iraq). Fuel transported through the Suez Canal became the mainstay of Britain's military forces, especially its powerful navy.

So, although the British government had initially declared that it was occupying Egypt only temporarily and would leave as soon as Egypt could govern itself, that day never seemed to arrive.

World War I. The 'Urabi Revolt inaugurated the fundamental pattern followed in Egypt's political life until the 1952 revolution: a three-cornered power game involving the British, the khedive (later "king"), and various coalitions of nationalist politicians seeking independence and a democratic (or at least a representative) government. The relations between these three centers of power were constantly shifting; on one occasion or another, any of the three groups might join with one of its opponents to deprive the third of a share in political power. Since no one group was strong enough to completely overwhelm the other two, the situation resembled nothing more closely than an endless game of musical chairs. Sometimes, however, the internal political battles in the upper echelons of power took on a more epic note that involved the entire Egyptian nation. One of the most important of these instances occurred in late 1918 as the carnage that was World War I stumbled to an exhausted close.

Egypt had been dragged into the war in ways that profoundly changed the life of the country. First, the British formalized their control over Egypt by declaring it a Protectorate at the start of the war, when Egypt's nominal suzerain, the Ottoman Empire, allied itself with Germany, England's enemy in the conflict. This unilateral act, followed by a declaration of martial law, made many Egyptians acutely conscious that their last shreds of independence were being stripped from them. Second, although much of Egypt's governmental revenue was already used to pay for the costs of the military occupation of their country (as well as for the salaries of the foreign—mostly English—employees who made up approximately 70 percent of the higher posts in the civil service), at the start of the war additional imposts to support the military effort were levied on the people. Meanwhile, inflation, which had roughly doubled prices between 1914 and 1917, sapped the buying power of those on fixed incomes. Finally, the British recruited the fellahin into a Labor Corps that was made to dig entrenchments and construct roads and railways in the Sinai Desert for the British who fought the Turks in the Levant. By 1918 nearly 100,000 Egyptians were serving in this Labor Corps,

which not infrequently was exposed to enemy fire even though its members were not armed. Animals, foodstuffs, and machinery were also requisitioned from the peasants. Toward the end of the war, conscription was introduced, since the fellahin could not be persuaded to voluntarily remain away from their families and their crops for long periods, despite the relatively high salaries the British offered (paid for by the Egyptian government, of course). Late in 1918 Britain's General Allenby envisioned that all these practices—martial law, extra taxation, conscription into the Labor Corps, and widespread requisitioning of equipment and supplies—would have to be extended well past the end of the war itself.

The revolution of 1919. The Versailles Peace Conference marked the close of World War I. News reached Egypt of U.S. President Woodrow Wilson's proposal to adopt as the basis for negotiations at the peace conference his "Fourteen Points"—one of which promised the chance to develop self-government for nationalities formerly under Turkish rule. Many Egyptians responded enthusiastically. In their minds, this was Egypt's opportunity to finally regain its independence and negotiate for British withdrawal from its territory. Two days after the Armistice (November 13, 1918) ending World War I, a delegation of Egyptian politicians, with Sa'd Zaghlul at their head, called upon the chief representative of the British in Egypt, the Resident, asking for leave to attend the peace conference and put their case to the assembled delegates. They were summarily turned down by the current Resident, Sir Reginald Wingate, and on March 9, 1919, were arrested and then deported to Malta. Egypt rose the next day in a massive rebellion against British rule, which was quashed only with great loss of life.

In interviews Najib Mahfuz has often spoken of watching with his mother behind the latticed window of their old-fashioned house as British soldiers paraded through Cairo and set up their emplacements on street corners (he was just short of his eighth birthday at the time). Nothing seems to have made a stronger impression on young men and women who would come to maturity in the 1930s and 1940s than the spectacle of their parents and older brothers and sisters marching in huge demonstrations, at the risk of being shot by British soldiers, to press for freedom of expression and the right to democratic representation. Mahfuz himself has spoken of the movement's leader, Sa'd Zaghlul, in almost wor-

Encouraged by Woodrow Wilson's "Fourteen Points" presented at the Versailles Peace Conference in 1919, an Egyptian delegation requested leave from Sir Reginald Wingate, the current British representative, to go to Versailles to peacefully negotiate independence from British rule. The request was denied and by March of the same year Egypt rose in armed rebellion.

shipful terms, calling him "a national hero" and "spiritual father of the Egyptians." (Mahfuz in Naqqash, trans. T. DeYoung, p. 209.)

The revolution of 1919 in *Midaqq Alley*. The great idealism that Mahfuz evinces when speaking about the revolution of 1919 contrasts jarringly with the way in which the event is presented through the lens of the characters in *Midaqq Alley*. Chapter 19, in particular, because it deals with a political rally being staged in Midaqq for the local parliamentary candidate, Ibrahim Farhat, has a number of pointed references to 1919, none of which give favorable impressions. The chapter starts with the ruminations of Uncle Kamil, one of the book's more sympathetic characters. He discovers that all the bustle and activity of setting up a big pavilion in a vacant lot across from the alley heralds an election rally, whereupon he thinks, "Saad and Adly again" (*Midaqq Alley*, p. 127). This is an allusion to the first major split in the Wafd Party, as the nationalist coalition under Zaghlul's leadership came to call itself. It was an event that did not reflect well on the character of Zaghlul. In 1921 Zaghlul withdrew his support for a colleague, 'Adli Yakan Pasha, a former minister like him-

self, who had been put forward by other Wafdists as an alternate negotiator with the British when Zaghlul's own negotiations came to naught. In withdrawing his support, he split the ranks of the new party at a time when unity would have been much more to the country's advantage. The subsequent failure of the British-Egyptian negotiations led to a unilateral declaration by the British government of Egyptian independence on March 1, 1922, but on terms very detrimental to Egypt. Everyone considered independence a façade—in reality, Egypt was still a colony. This was the first in a two-decade series of quarrels within party ranks that would eventually splinter the party and make it vastly easier for the British and the king to manipulate to their own advantage the resulting offshoot parties.

For Mahfuz, as for many others, the event that would destroy his last shred of confidence that the Wafd party leadership stood for any lofty principle occurred on February 4, 1942. That evening Sir Miles Lampson, the British Resident, or High Commissioner, supported by lightly armored vehicles and tanks, forced King Faruq to name as his new prime minister Mustafa Nahhas, then at the helm of the Wafd (Zaghlul had died in 1927). The British had decided that the Wafd should be allowed to accede to power if it pledged unconditional support to the Allies in World War II. For many Egyptians, it was a matter of disgust to see where Nahhas had taken the idealistic principles of the party. In their minds, he was toadying to the hated British in order to achieve a precarious toehold on power (Sayyid-Marsot, pp. 100-101). Their disgust was soon exacerbated by the tawdry spectacle of Makram 'Ubayd, once Nahhas's most loyal lieutenant, being driven from the party on the apparently trivial grounds of questioning some of Nahhas's ministerial choices. 'Ubayd retaliated for his dismissal by publishing a tract he called his *Black Book*, which detailed a raft of corrupt practices within the highest echelons of the Wafd. This seemingly unending string of revelations about chicanery in the ranks of the political party that was most revered and trusted by Egyptians began to undermine their confidence in parliamentary rule. Understanding this decline of faith lends a richly nuanced irony to Uncle Kamil's seemingly random ruminations in *Midaqq Alley* on Wafd politicians whose portraits happen to hang on the walls of various businesses in and around the area.

The last portrait of which Uncle Kamil thinks is that of the Khedive 'Abbas, which hangs in Kirsha's coffeehouse. Kirsha, in contrast to Uncle Kamil, is probably the least sympathetic character in the alley. An unscrupulous bully and a tyrant to his family, he also proves to be a man of uncontrollable sexual appetites whose favorite target is young and vulnerable boys, whom he seduces, exploits, and abandons. It seems quite natural to discover that his hero is the Germanophile authoritarian 'Abbas II, who was replaced by the British as khedive at the beginning of World War I for plotting to take Egypt into that war on the German side. Also disclosed in the novel is a sinister secret about Kirsha's own political past:

> In his youth he had distinguished himself in the field of politics. He had taken an active part in the rebellion of 1919 and was reputed to have planned the great fire which destroyed the Jewish Cigarette Trading Co. in Hussain Square. He was one of the heroes in the fierce fighting between the revolutionaries on one side and the Armenians and Jews on the other. When the bloody revolt subsided he had found a new, though restricted outlet for his energies in the subsequent election battles. In the elections of 1924 and 1925 his work was much appreciated even though it was rumored that he accepted bribes from the government candidate while supporting the Wafd party.
> (Mahfuz, *Midaqq Alley*, pp. 129-30)

Here we see the revolution from a very different perspective from the official one. One of the axioms of Wafdist mythology holds that this was the era when Egyptians of all religions and origins were united, when they spoke with a single voice, demanding their independence from the hated British. Certainly the assortment of prominent and activist Wafd members included a number from religious minorities, Jews as well as Christians. But clearly Kirsha does not view the (Christian) Armenians and the Jews whom he attacks as part of some overarching Egyptian polity. On the other hand, nothing about him suggests that he views them as collaborators with the enemy either. Rather politics seems to serve as a cover here for the type of internal, target violence associated with old-fashioned protection rackets and organized crime. More ominous is the last sentence in the passage, which associates

---

THE EGYPTIAN JEWISH COMMUNITY

One noticeable element in the social picture Mahfuz paints of the alley is the references his characters make to Jews, who in the 1940s numbered about 65,000, living mainly in Cairo and Alexandria (Krämer, p. 10). These numbers are not inconsequential when one considers that at the time the total population of Cairo was only around 2 million and that of Alexandria less than 1 million. In the novel Hamida makes a reference to factory girls who "worked in public places just like the Jewish women" (*Midaqq Alley*, p. 35). She seems to be referring not to the Europeanized Jews at the highest levels of society but to the Karaites, a sect living in Egypt since the Middle Ages that rejected the practices of Rabbinical Judaism as codified in the books of Jewish oral law (the Talmud). Instead, they stressed a return to the direct interpretation of scripture. In this, and in certain other respects, their practices resembled Islamic practices. On the other hand, an area in which they differed noticeably from their Muslim neighbors was in the greater social freedom accorded their women, who, "rather than veiling themselves, seem to have displayed their beauty quite openly, at least within their quarter" (Krämer, p. 25). That the Karaites, in particular, were known for this tolerance helps explain Hamida's attitude of mixed envy and admiration for the Jewish women she knows.

the Wafd with corrupt practices at a much earlier time than is usually acknowledged as the starting point for such machinations.

Rising violence. Kirsha's reminiscences about his past as a Wafd enforcer would evoke for Mahfuz's Egyptian readers another feature of political life in the waning days of World War II: a disquieting return to violence to solve political problems. Early in its struggle for independence certain elements in the Wafd (the inner circle around Zaghlul seems to have been ignorant of these happenings) had on occasion resorted to assassination to punish party disloyalty and to terrorize British officials who opposed the party's goals. The most spectacular incident was the assassination in November 1924 of Sir Lee Stack, commander in chief of the Egyptian army and a close confidant of General Allenby—British Resident in Egypt at the time. The assassins later confessed to being Wafdist agents, though the Wafd denied complicity. In any case, the deed backfired, since Allenby exacted heavy indemnities on the Egyptian government as vengeance for his friend's death, which placed the British in a stronger position than they had been in before. From that time on, at least in public, the Wafd scrupulously dissociated itself from political violence.

In 1945, however, the specter of assassination returned to Egyptian politics. In October 1944 the success of Mustafa Nahhas's initiatives in drafting a treaty of cooperation among the Arab states (which would eventually lead to the founding of the Arab League) encouraged him to consolidate his position vis-à-vis the young King Faruq by tendering his resignation. His resignation would have forced the king to call new elections, with the Wafd standing a good chance of increasing its margin in parliament. To forestall this, Faruq summarily dismissed Nahhas and his cabinet before they could resign, which allowed Faruq to appoint a new prime minister of his own without having to call for elections. Faruq chose Ahmad Mahir, who was acceptable to the British. Mahir had been an original member of the Wafd leadership but split with Nahhas in the late 1930s and formed a new party that he and his supporters called the Sa'dist Party, an allusion to their slogan that they were returning to the original principles of the early leader Sa'd (Zaghlul). After forming a new cabinet, in February 1945 Mahir called elections, whose outcome he controlled (they were boycotted by the Wafd). It is likely that Mahfuz means us to associate these elections with those portrayed in Chapter 19 of *Midaqq Alley*.

At the end of February 1945, Mahir, pressured by British prime minister Winston Churchill, agreed to have Egypt officially declare war on Germany. Mahir duly shepherded the declaration of war through both houses of the Egyptian Parliament, but as he left the Chamber of Deputies on February 24, 1945, he was shot dead by a Nazi sympathizer, a young Egyptian lawyer. A few months earlier, on November 6, 1944, while on his way to dinner, Lord Moyne, British Minister of State in Cairo, had been killed by members of the Zionist underground terrorist organization, the Stern Gang. However the Egyptians may have felt about the political murder of a high British official, the death of Lord Moyne brought to mind the heavy indemnities exacted by Allenby in the wake of the earlier assassination of Sir Lee Stack and aroused fears that they might be repeated. The execution of the Moyne assassins in March 1945, coming closely on the heels of Ahmad Mahir's killing, only heightened the sense of tension. Although no explicit mention of these events occurs in *Midaqq Alley* the atmosphere of violence and disorder they engendered forms the perfect backdrop to the deteriorating situation in the alley, which culminates in the death of a main character, the generally gentle and sensitive 'Abbas, at the hands of British soldiers, after he has disfigured his fiancée, Hamida, for life because of her decision to take up prostitution to service these same British soldiers. The sense that the world portrayed in *Midaqq Alley* is on the verge of breakdown, waiting for some cataclysmic change to stem the tide of violence, increases when one considers the fact that between the time that the events in the novel take place (probably in 1944-45) and the time of the novel's publication (in late 1947), a wave of civil protests, bloodily suppressed by British and government troops, swept through Egypt, resulting in the deaths of many ordinary people. Uthman Pasha, a harmless but pro-British finance minister, was assassinated early in 1946. And, in 1948 (shortly after *Midaqq Alley* appeared in the bookstores) Prime Minister Mahmud Fahmi Nuqrashi Pasha was killed by members of the Muslim Brotherhood in retaliation for outlawing their organization. In view of these events, the political disillusionment permeating Mahfuz's novel presents a disturbingly prescient picture of life in postwar Egypt.

The Novel in Focus

Plot summary. *Midaqq Alley* has sometimes been labeled a novel "without a central plot," but actually there is a great deal of plot in the novel (El-Enany, p. 54). Every character seems to participate in his or her own independent story while contributing to the greater whole—the texture of daily life in the alley. Aside from these branchings, the central plot consists of relatively straightforward action that recalls the conventional plots of pulp melodrama, in which vice is punished and virtue rewarded, but not without a few sacrifices along the way.

The story involves the fortunes of three of the alley's young people on the verge of adulthood and the formation of their independent identities: Husayn Kirsha, son of the alley's coffeeshop owner; Hamida (significantly without a family name), adopted daughter of the alley's resident professional matchmaker, Umm Hamida; and 'Abbas Hilu, the local barber. Husayn and Hamida are by Islamic tradition considered foster brother and sister because both were suckled by the same wet-nurse, and this means they are seen as having certain family obligations toward each other that go beyond their association as playmates. 'Abbas, who grew up in the alley, has an even more nebulous family background than Hamida and appears by contrast to the other characters to be an outsider. He has, nevertheless, forged strong ties with people in the alley. He has become close friends with Husayn and his neighbor, Uncle Kamil, owner of the candy store. During the course of the novel's action, he will fall in love with Hamida and seek to marry her.

Hamida, however, has ambitions to gain wealth and social position and is hesitant to accept the poor but loving 'Abbas, even though he has gone to work with Husayn in the British military camp at Tell el-Kebir and is earning lots of money. She has another suitor: the rich merchant Salim 'Alwan, who operates a perfume shop in the alley and wants a second wife to help service his sexual needs, which he feeds quite literally with a daily dose of aphrodisiac at lunch. Just as something is about to come of this relationship, however, Salim 'Alwan has a heart attack and Hamida is thrown back on her own resources. She is soon "rescued" at a political rally, where she is spotted by Ibrahim Faraj, a pimp who trains prostitutes for the Allied soldiers. He follows her from the rally, strikes up a conversation, and eventually persuades her to leave Midaqq behind and become his newest recruit. As Hamida is being educated for her new profession at Ibrahim Faraj's "Academy for Whores," Husayn Kirsha reappears in the alley, having lost

his job but gained a pregnant wife. 'Abbas returns at the same time but only for a brief visit, since he is still working for the British. As luck would have it, he runs into Hamida, at work in her new trade as a prostitute, on the way back to camp. In order to shift blame from herself, Hamida identifies Ibrahim as the criminal, her seducer. 'Abbas makes her promise to bring Ibrahim to a nearby bar the next week so that 'Abbas can avenge her honor. When the day comes, on impulse 'Abbas recruits his old friend Husayn Kirsha to come with him to the bar to help, but when they arrive, Ibrahim is not there. They see only Hamida, laughing and flirting with a group of soldiers. 'Abbas loses control and cuts Hamida's face with a broken bottle. The soldiers beat him to death as Husayn watches, unable to move.

In the final chapter, a guilt-ridden Husayn returns to the alley to tell the assembled inhabitants of 'Abbas's demise. Uncle Kamil and Salim Alwan (now recovered from his heart attack) are at first deeply affected by 'Abbas's fate. But eventually the alley's denizens return to their old routine. Among them is Sheikh (or Shaykh) Darwish, a half-mad retired government employee who wanders the alley making oracular pronouncements, "a fine and holy man of God, to whom revelation came in two languages, Arabic and English"; one day Sheikh Darwish spots Uncle Kamil laughing and joking with his friends as though 'Abbas had never existed and pronounces the story to be at an "E-N-D" (*Midaqq Alley*, p. 13).

The critique of Arab nationalism. In Egyptian history, one of the few positive initiatives to emerge from the Wafdist government during World War II was a treaty that set up the framework for an international body, the Arab League, that would give Arabic-speaking countries a forum for cooperation and institution-building in the postwar world. The favorable climate for such a body was in large part due to the success of the Arab nationalist movement in nurturing the notion that there was such a thing as an "Arab" identity and that the people holding allegiance to this identity shared certain concerns that could best be addressed by some kind of concerted action. Thus, the question of Arabness was very much "in the air" during the writing of *Midaqq Alley*.

What exactly this "Arab" identity entailed, however, involved a certain elasticity, since it had to appeal to an ever-widening audience during the 1940s. Most intellectuals agreed that it involved at least three basic elements. The first two were easy enough to formulate. To consider oneself Arab, one had to be a speaker of the Arabic language and, more importantly, had to prefer the standard variety of Arabic in common use across the Arab world over the local dialects as a vehicle for communication. Secondly, one had to identify with the history of Arab achievement in the public and cultural spheres as a noble heritage worthy of emulation. Defining the third element of Arab identity was more difficult. One had to accept certain values found in the Islamic religion, such as tolerance and egalitarianism, as having a moral and ethical effect beneficial to society, even if one were not a practicing Muslim. In other words, one could be a Christian or a Jew, or even potentially an agnostic or an atheist, and still call oneself an "Arab," as long as one saw the rise of Islam as having exercised a benevolent rather than detrimental influence on the societies in the region. At various points in *Midaqq Alley* (which appeared around the time of the founding of the Arab League), these three cardinal points of Arab identity—as well as subsidiary ones deriving from them—come under close scrutiny. The novel implicitly questions just how applicable each of these ideas is to the complex reality of Egyptian society in the period of British occupation.

The first formulation to be placed under the microscope is that the glorious past of the Arabs is directly relevant to the world of Mahfuz's characters. Since so much of old Cairo contains historical monuments—mainly because it was spared the wars and sieges that regularly swept over many other Arab cities—it is particularly susceptible to the sleight-of-hand that might transform it into a living memorial of the Arabs' historical experience. But there is irony in such statements as "[m]any things combine to show that *Midaqq Alley* is one of the gems of times gone by and that it once shone forth like a flashing star in the history of Cairo" (*Midaqq Alley*, p. 1). The irony is revealed both by the subsequent uncertainty of the narrator about the nature of this glory, and by the general obliviousness of the characters to this element of their surroundings.

This opening is followed by a scene that evokes and then reveals the contradictions in some of the commonplaces found in the nationalist representations of society in the 1940s. We have moved inside Kirsha's coffeeshop, the social center of the alley. It is evening and an old blind man enters the café, takes up his accustomed seat, and begins to tune a long-necked

stringed instrument called a *rebaba,* which he has brought with him. He starts to sing, or rather chant, the conventional introduction to a poem: "We are going to begin today by saying a prayer for the Prophet. An Arab Prophet, the chosen son of the people of Adnan. Abu Saada, the Zanaty, says . . . "; before he can proceed, however, he is driven off the premises by Kirsha, who tells him: "We all know the stories you tell by heart and we don't need to run through them again. People today don't want a poet. They keep asking me for a radio and there's one over there being installed now. So go away and leave us alone and may God provide for you" (*Midaqq Alley,* p. 5). The man being replaced by the radio is a traditional storyteller of popular epic tales, a neighborhood fixture everywhere in the Arab world before the middle of the twentieth century. These storytellers had a number of epic cycles in their repertoires, the favorite and most elaborate being the story of the adventures of the Bani Hilal people as they accompanied the first Muslim Arab armies of conquest sweeping across the Levant and then North Africa in the seventh and eighth centuries C.E. Such tales present analogues to the pictures of daring and chivalry found in European accounts of knightly deeds and could equally be said to form the basis for the idealized value system found in modern master narratives of Arab identity. Yet here, in *Midaqq Alley,* that "hallowed tradition" is being displaced by the radio, purveyor of modern news and sports broadcasts and—in this time period—of the highly problematic "truths" of both Axis and Allied propaganda. The incident points yet again to the delusive nature of an unadulterated shared sense of history and cultural values among any "people," not to speak of a group as large and with such diverse experiences as the Arabs.

The choice of the oral epic as the "hallowed tradition" to be supplanted raises issues about language as well. Arabic has always existed in two varieties, a standard version used mostly in writing, intelligible throughout the Arab world, and colloquial versions that are regionally based, used for day-to-day oral communication, which can be mutually unintelligible. *Midaqq Alley,* as a written literary work, uses standard Arabic. The oral epic is always delivered in the colloquial language of the area where the poet lives. The banishment of Midaqq Alley's poet, then, highlights a tension inherent within an element of Arab nationalist ideology. The victory of the unified language (in the novel and on the radio) in this case entails the suppression of the oral epic, which, though conveyed in various colloquial dialects, was used to express shared, uniquely Arabic cultural values.

The fact that standard Arabic is not a transparent and universally valid medium of communication for all Arabs is highlighted later in the novel. Hamida returns to the alley to find Ibrahim Farhat's election rally in full swing and is delighted with the entertainment provided, especially as "she had thought it would be merely a political rally with long speeches delivered in almost incomprehensible classical Arabic" (*Midaqq Alley,* p. 134). Barely educated, Hamida has likely never had the opportunity to study the standard language; for her, standard Arabic means little. The jokes, monologues, and skits of Ibrahim Farhat's innovative program delivered in the local colloquial, on the other hand, appeal greatly to Hamida and to the other inhabitants of the alley as well.

Continually, then, *Midaqq Alley* questions Arab nationalist ideas that were prominent in Egyptian public discourse at the time. It does not follow, however, that the novel rejects the task of national identity formation. Rather the novel suggests that even the most attractive allegiances need to be subjected to constant scrutiny; otherwise they lose their capacity to grow and change with the times, becoming sterile and meaningless slogans.

Sources and literary context. *Midaqq Alley* was recognized from the time of its publication for its innovations in realism and for the class of people it chose to deal with. The fact that it did not sentimentalize its subject matter was especially striking in the decade that followed its publication, the 1950s, when socialist realism took hold more strongly and virtually dictated that the working class be treated in heroic fashion. *Midaqq Alley* is frequently compared to Tawfiq al-Hakim's novel *Return of the Spirit* as heralding a shift in literary sensibility. At the same time the contrast between the two novels has been called to people's attention. While *Return of the Spirit* achieved near-mythic status in the 1950s as the favorite novel of Gamal Abdul Nasser, quintessential hero of modern Arab nationalism, *Midaqq Alley* was seen by contemporaries as a far more realistic picture of Egyptian life. This perception of greater realism may in large part reflect the novel's skeptical attitude toward the simplistic formulas espoused by some proponents of Egyptianism and Arabism.

Equally important for fixing the place of *Midaqq Alley* in contemporary Arabic literature are the thematic parallels between it and Nawal Sa'dawi's famous novel of the 1970s, **Woman at Point Zero** (also covered in *African Literature and Its Times*). Both novels include a female prostitute as their central character; the portrayal of Sa'dawi's prostitute, Firdaus, a few decades after Mahfuz's can be interpreted as a feminist challenge to some of the assumptions underlying his portrayal of Hamida.

WOMEN AND THE LAND IN ARABIC LITERATURE

As Mahfuz himself has noted, Hamida and to a lesser extent the other female characters in *Midaqq Alley* can be seen as having an important symbolic dimension (Mahfuz in Naqqash, p. 56). On some level, Hamida represents the land—Egypt—whose possession is sought by both the British and indigenous males. Such an equation is very old in Arabic literature, going back to pre-Islamic times. How much this trope is used in portraying her can be seen most profitably by comparing her with Saniyya, the hero of Tawfiq al-Hakim's *Return of the Spirit,* who is much more overtly linked to the land and Egypt. Saniyya, too, is sought by all the male characters. Her idealized beauty and goodness works a magical transformation on characters, moving them from sordid selfishness to noble generosity and self-sacrifice for their fellow Egyptians. By contrast, it goes hand in hand with Mahfuz's deflation of the pretensions of nationalism that Hamida is introduced by a scene in which her stepmother combs lice out of her beautiful long dark hair (so similar to Saniyya's). Likewise Hamida's temperament is rough and harsh, in contrast to Saniyya's sweetness and gentleness. In making Hamida's character the inversion of all the idealized female's traits, *Midaqq Alley* risks dehumanizing her. When compared with these earlier examples, *Woman at Point Zero*'s heroine, Firdaus, may be seen as a critique of a past penchant for turning female characters into simple automatons of symbolism, rather than fully rounded characters in the tradition of the realistic novel.

Reviews. Although Mahfuz was still in the early stages of his career as a novelist when *Midaqq Alley* appeared, the generally laudatory and respectful Arabic reviews of the novel make it clear that he had already established a considerable reputation as an innovator and stylistic craftsman. This approbation has not, however, been unequivocally shared by Western commentators.

Michael Beard, among others, expressed a certain hesitancy:

"The non-western novel, with its occasional deviation from patterns western readers anticipate, . . . often strikes western readers as unworthy of their attention. . . ." I had Mahfouz in mind when I wrote those lines, specifically the Mahfouz of Midaqq Alley. . . . I could spend time on an apology here, explaining away my insensitivity by citing . . . the fact that I suspect I am describing the experience of a lot of Western readers. But in any case, the strangeness of Mahfouz is, for us, the irreducible fact with which we have to come to terms.

(Beard, p. 96)

In contrast, the Arabic reviewer Tharwat Abazah, writing in the influential periodical *Al-Risalah,* praised Mahfuz's creativity and originality, calling the novel "the first story of its kind in Arabic" (Abazah, p. 125; trans. T. DeYoung). Sayyid Qutb wrote a review for the journal *Al-Fikr al-Jadid* in which he too heralded the novel's originality, especially in its presentation of character. He then went on to call the work "a novel of presentation (*'ard*) or panorama (*isti'rad*) in that it follows a group of individuals, upon [all] of whom the spotlight shines the entire time, and in this respect no one of them is the focus and no one of them is given greater importance than the others" (Qutb, trans. T. DeYoung, p. 201). Chances that Western readers can share such appreciation are bolstered by recent trends in literary criticism, which highlight increased sensitivity to the concerns that drive non-European works and circumstances under which they are written.

—Terri DeYoung

For More Information

Abazah, Tharwat. "Zuqaq al-Midaqq." *Al-Risalah,* 26 January 1948, pp. 124-25.

Ahmed, Jamal. *The Intellectual Origins of Egyptian Nationalism.* London: Oxford University Press, 1960.

Badrawi, Malak. *Isma'il Sidqi (1875-1950): Pragmatism and Vision in Twentieth Century Egypt.* London: Curzon, 1996.

Beard, Michael. "The Mahfouzian Sublime." In *Naguib Mahfouz: From Regional Fame to Global Recognition.* Eds. Michael Beard and Adnan Haydar. Syracuse, N.Y.: Syracuse University Press, 1993.

El-Enany, Rasheed (Anani, Rashid). *Naguib Mahfouz: The Pursuit of Meaning.* London: Routledge, 1993.

Gershoni, Israel, and James P. Jankowski. *Redefining the Egyptian Nation, 1930-1945.* Cambridge: Cambridge University Press, 1995.

Hakim, Tawfiq. *Return of the Spirit.* Trans. William Hutchins. Washington, D.C.: Three Continents Press, 1990.

Krämer, Gudrun. *The Jews in Modern Egypt: 1914-1952.* Seattle: University of Washington Press, 1989.

Mahfouz, Naguib (Mahfuz, Najib). *Midaqq Alley.* Trans. Trevor Le Gassick. Washington, D.C.: Three Continents Press, 1975.

Naqqash, Raja. *Najib Mahfuz: Safahat min Mudhakkiratihi wa-Adwa Jadida ala Adabihi wa-Hayatihi.* Cairo: Markaz al-Ahram li-al-Tarjama wa-al-Nashr, 1998.

Qutb, Sayyid. "Zuqaq al-Midaqq." In *Masadir Naqd al-Riwaya fi al-Adab al-Arabi al-Hadith fi Misr,* by Ahmad Ibrahim al-Hawwari. Cairo: Dar al-Maarif, 1979.

Sa'dawi, Nawal. *Woman at Point Zero.* Trans. Sherif Hetata. London: Zed Books, 1983.

Sayyid-Marsot, Afaf Lutfi. *Egypt's Liberal Experiment: 1922-1936.* Berkeley: University of California Press, 1977.

Mine Boy

by

Peter Abrahams

Born in Vrededorp—a suburban slum of Jo-hannesburg—in 1919, Peter Abrahams was the son of James Henry Abrahams, an immigrant descended from the Ethiopian imperial dynasty, and Angelina DuPlessis, a "Cape Coloured" widow (of mixed descent). They could not afford to send their son to school until he was 11. Abrahams worked his way through school, taking jobs as a porter, a clerk, and a dishwasher. In his adolescence, he studied at two elite secondary schools for blacks, the Diocesan Training College at Grace Dieu and St. Peter's Rosettenville in Johannesburg. While at Diocesan, he published poetry in *Bantu World,* a white-owned newspaper catering to black readers; later during his time at St. Peter's, he became involved in left-wing politics. He left South Africa to become a crew member on a freighter during World War II. After two years at sea, Abrahams settled in England, joining the staff of the Communist newspaper, *The Daily Worker,* and continuing his career as a writer. Abrahams's first literary work was a collection of short stories, *Dark Testament* (1942), followed by the novels *Song of the City* (1945) and *Mine Boy* (1946). *Mine Boy* distinguished itself as a work that depicted, for the first time in South African literature, the black perspective on urban life, and challenged white stereotypes of African workers.

Events in History at the Time of the Novel

The South African mining industry. Although diamond mining was a thriving industry in the

---

THE LITERARY WORK

A novel set in Johannesburg, South Africa, during the 1940s; published in English in 1946.

SYNOPSIS

A young black man, fresh from the country, becomes a mine worker in Johannesburg, adjusts to his harsh new environment, and learns to combat racial injustice.

---

nineteenth century, gold mining soon out-stripped it in importance. After the 1886 discovery of huge deposits of gold in Witwatersrand (commonly known as "the Rand"), a feverish rush for gold descended on the region. The rush gave rise to a settlement of crude shacks and canvas tents—called "Johannesburg" in honor of the president of the Transvaal and the director of mines, both named Johannes. The settlement seemed to spring up overnight around these early mining operations. Ten years later, Johannesburg had grown into a bustling city, complete with gardens, parks, clubs, and even a stock exchange. At the time of the novel, Johannesburg is a sprawling metropolis, characterized by extremes of great affluence and grinding poverty. Shantytowns and slums, like the novel's Malay Camp, existed on the outskirts of the city.

During the 1930s and 1940s, the gold-mining industry was the backbone of the South African economy. In 1939 the mines employed

South African laborers at work in the Sallies Mine on the East Rand near Johannesburg.

364,000 workers: 43,000 whites and 321,000 blacks; the proportion of white to black workers in the mines was approximately 1 to 7.5 (Thompson, p. 168). Skilled labor positions—and the higher salaries such positions merited—had been legally reserved for whites since the Mines and Works Act (1911), which formalized what had long been customary practice. Around 1920 white miners were earning at least 11 times more than blacks. By 1939 they were also receiving paid leave and pensions, privileges denied to black miners.

The mines themselves were organized along military lines; women were not permitted in the mines or in the housing compounds where the laborers lived. "The officers—the shift bosses and compound managers—were white; the non-commissioned officers—the underground 'boss-boys' and compound 'indunas' (mine police-men)—as well as the mass of laborers, were black" (Thompson, p. 168). Even the living arrangements recalled a military barracks: most black miners were housed in compounds that averaged between 3,000 and 6,000 inhabitants. Beds were not provided; African workers had to sleep on short concrete bunks or make or buy wooden beds of their own. Only one percent of black mine workers were deemed legally eligible for family housing. In the novel, Johannes and Xuma are considered fortunate because they land positions as "boss-boys" and do not have to live in the compounds.

Working conditions in the mines were dangerous and exhausting; workers labored in extreme heat and spent most of their time crouching. In the novel, Xuma, the protagonist, is overwhelmed by the apparent lack of progress that he and his fellow miners have made on his first day at the job: "And for all their sweating and hard breathing and for the redness of their eyes and the emptiness of their stare there would be nothing to show. In the morning the pile had been so big. Now it was the same. And the mine-dump did not seem to grow either" (Abrahams, *Mine Boy*, p. 42). Accidents and illness also took their toll on black miners. From 1933 to 1966, 19,000 gold miners, most of them Africans, died in mining accidents. In 1931 the Miners' Pthisis Medical Bureau documented 1,370 African miners as "suffering from tuberculosis or lung diseases, or both, caused by mining" (Thompson, p. 168). Both tragedies are chillingly depicted in *Mine Boy*: one of the miners on Xuma's crew contracts a lung malady and is sent home to die, and, towards the end of the novel, Xuma's friend, Johannes, is killed when a mine tunnel collapses.

Slums and shantytowns. Close on the heels of the 1910 formation of the Union of South Africa came legislation restricting the rights of black South Africans. The Natives Land Act (1913) set aside small portions of land exclusively for Africans and prohibited them from purchasing land outside these colonial reserves. During the 1930s and 1940s the increasing difficulty of making a living through subsistence farming on reserve lands damaged by drought and soil erosion drove many Africans to seek employment in large cities such as Johannesburg and Cape Town. This mass migration to the cities prompted a large-scale housing crisis. While Africans were permitted to settle in black suburbs, like Sophiatown, Alexandra, and Pimville near Johannesburg, those who could not find rooms or afford houses were forced to build squatters' camps and shantytowns. Black migrant workers constructed crude shacks of corrugated tin, cardboard boxes, newspaper, and wood. During the latter half of the 1940s, between 60,000 and 90,000 Africans inhabited such dwellings just outside Johannesburg: from 1944 on, large squatter camps sprang up on the outskirts of Johannesburg, and, to a lesser degree, outside other major cities. Despite the attempts of local authorities to do away with them, these camps, "well organized and ably led, persisted until the 1950s when their inhabitants received municipal housing and eventually housing by the central government" (Cameron, p. 265).

Living conditions in camps and shantytowns were frequently abysmal and unsanitary; municipal officials often argued that such environments produced criminals. Some settlements, however, were well-maintained and experienced no more crime than in non-squatter areas. It was not unusual for inhabitants of camps and shantytowns to establish their own form of government, in an

THE AFRICAN MINE WORKERS' UNION

During World War II black miners became more outspoken about the low pay and dangerous working conditions in the mines. In 1941 two important organizations were formed—the Council of Non-European Trade Unions (CNETU) and the African Mine Workers' Union (AMWU), the latter of which was led by Gaur Radebe, Secretary for Mines in the Transvaal African Congress and a member of the Communist Party. By 1946, the year in which *Mine Boy* was written, CNETU claimed 158,000 members organized in 119 unions. Meanwhile, AMWU, which claimed a membership of 25,000 by 1944, persuaded the government to establish the Lansdown Commission to investigate conditions in the mines. The commission's 1944 report acknowledged that the reserves no longer supplemented the wages of landless miners (white mine owners had argued that black workers needed less income because they had family farms in the reserves to meet some of their needs). Among the reforms recommended by the report were higher wages for Africans. The AMWU found the recommendations inadequate but refrained from striking. After the war, however, the AMWU demanded a wage of 10 shillings per day, family housing, paid leave, gratuities, and repeal of War Measure 145, which made strikes by Africans illegal. These demands led to a major strike in 1946, during which 73,000 mine workers—most of them black—stopped work for four days, shutting down production completely in ten mines. Police intervention brought the strike to a rapid end, leaving 12 dead and more than 1,200 injured. The AMWU was seriously crippled by the debacle—none of its aims were achieved—but the strike had nonetheless "demonstrated the potential strength of organized black workers in challenging the cheap labor system" (Byrnes, p. 53). In the novel, Xuma rallies his fellow mine boys to protest the hazardous working conditions in the mine, which have just claimed two lives. The white engineers panic, summoning the police to try to quash what they perceive as an incipient strike.

South African women of the 1950s protest the government's decision to do away with their township and replace it with an area designated for whites.

attempt to create a sense of order and community. Outside Johannesburg, one well-known camp leader, James Mpanza, declared himself king of his Orlando squatter encampment, setting up his own system of local government and taxation. In the novel, Malay Camp—a "slum area of Johannesburg once populated by Africans, Coloureds and Indians"—has its share of leaders, including the saloon-owner, Leah (Wade, *Peter Abrahams,* p. 27). ("African" refers to black South Africans; "coloured" to descendants of mixed unions; and "Indians" to immigrants from India). Tall and powerfully built, Leah can physically defeat an armed man, break up a brawl between two drunken women, and subdue an unruly crowd with her forceful presence alone. The residents of Malay Camp both respect and fear her.

Shebeens and liquor peddling. The liquor trade in the Transvaal—the South African province in which Johannesburg is located—can be traced back to "a distillery called Volkshoop ('People's Hope') that opened in 1883 on a charter granting it a monopoly within the borders of the Boer republic" (Lelyveld, p. 267). The Boers (early white settlers, primarily of Dutch descent), or, as they are presently called, Afrikaners, found a

profitable way to use their surplus grain and fruit when they entered the liquor trade. Bars and distilleries soon found a steady clientele among black migrant workers, many of whom had come to labor in the new gold mines.

> Up to a point black drunkenness served the interests of the mine owners, who calculated that blacks returned to their tribal areas once they had accumulated a little cash. The more they spent on drink, the longer they stayed, limiting the turnover in the work force. But by 1895 at least 15 percent and possibly 25 percent of the black work force was disabled by drink on any given day. The mine-owners then became converted to the righteous cause of total prohibition—for blacks only.
>
> (Lelyveld, p. 268)

Thus from 1912 to 1962, it was a criminal offense in South Africa for Europeans to sell alcoholic beverages to Africans, who were prohibited entirely from selling or purchasing alcohol. "As a result, the practice of illicit liquor selling flourished, especially in the towns, where it became institutionalized in various forms" (Wade, p. 28). One such form was the *shebeen,* an unlicensed saloon bar. In the novel, Leah runs a thriving shebeen, frequented by many residents of Malay

Camp. Because of the laws forbidding Africans to sell or buy liquor, however, Leah must be constantly on guard against visits from police hoping to catch her in the act. Leah eludes arrest for a long time by bribing a policeman to inform her when raids on the camp are expected, but she is ultimately caught and sentenced to nine months in prison when her informant inadvertently passes along the wrong information.

Pass laws. As more black Africans traveled to the cities in search of work, the government tried to limit the urban population of black migrant workers by implementing pass laws. The origin of such laws dates from the eighteenth century, when slaves were required to carry documents signed by their masters when they were absent from their masters' property. Some modern pass laws were designed to ensure that white farmers would not lose their black laborers, while other pass laws were intended to prevent blacks from living in towns, except as laborers for whites. In the Transvaal during the 1930s, a black person entering a proclaimed urban area had to report to an official within 24 hours and obtain a permit to seek work. The official would issue a permit—valid for six days—but only if the black person's other passes were in order. These government-issued permits, which stated the bearer's identity, racial classification, and the reasons for his or her presence in the city or town, had to be produced on demand. Africans who failed to show their passes when questioned by an official could be jailed or expelled from the town. Attempts to enforce pass laws created a vast number of rebellious lawbreakers—in 1930, 42,000 Africans were convicted of violating their pass laws in the Transvaal. Despite the increasing stringency of pass laws, however, African populations in the cities continued to grow. In 1944 an anti-pass campaign, boasting 20,000 supporters, began in Johannesburg but failed to achieve the goal of a million signatures on a petition against the pass laws. In the novel, pass laws are part of the daily routine for Xuma and other Africans. Before Xuma begins his new job at the mine, he is inspected by a mine official and issued a pass stating his name, race, and occupation. Although Xuma becomes a "boss boy" who can afford his own room in Malay Camp, policemen still stop him on the streets and demand to see his pass. Even the miner who contracts lung sickness and is sent home to die has to receive "a pass to show that he was not escaping from the mines" (*Mine Boy*, p. 109).

The Novel in Focus

Plot summary. Xuma, a young black man from the country, arrives early one morning in Malay Camp, hoping to find lodging. One of the camp residents, a woman named Leah, inspects him carefully, decides he poses no threat, and agrees to let him stay in her house. Once inside, Xuma meets the other inhabitants: an old woman, Ma Plank; a drunken old man known as Daddy; and two younger men, named Joseph and Dladla. Dladla and Xuma size each other up, but Leah averts a brawl between them by taking away Dladla's knife. Once they are alone, Leah explains to Xuma that Joseph is the brother of her own man, who is in prison for killing someone who tried to kiss her. Meanwhile, Leah is sleeping with the bad-tempered Dladla out of loneliness. Xuma, in turn, explains that he has come to the city to look for work in the mines. Leah, who disapproves of this plan because so many men sicken and die after working in the mines, offers to make Xuma her "head-man" instead. She reveals that she sells liquor illegally in a shebeen—a kind of saloon—and needs someone to help her run her business. Xuma remains determined to work in the mines; reluctantly Leah accepts his decision and shows him to a small bedroom where he can sleep.

Xuma awakens much later in the day and finds the residents of Malay Camp watching a brawl between two women, which Leah quickly breaks up. When Joseph arrives at the house, Leah tells him to take Xuma into town. It is Saturday, and therefore a half-holiday for the black people of Johannesburg. Xuma sees various people, dressed in their brightest clothes, shopping, talking, and flirting. In another area, men are playing dice and, some distance up the road, two men are in the middle of yet another brawl. Xuma and Joseph are watching all the goings-on when a van suddenly swerves around the corner. The people scatter as policemen emerge from the van. Joseph tells Xuma to run but the young man refuses, saying he has done nothing. A policeman strikes the astonished Xuma with his stick; Xuma knocks his adversary unconscious, then runs. He receives some help from a coloured man who hides him in his own house until the search dies down.

Later, Xuma returns to Malay Camp. Joseph and Leah greet him with relief, cautioning him to avoid the police whenever possible. Xuma sees Leah give a hefty bribe to a black policeman in exchange for a warning about when the cops will raid her place for liquor. Leah takes Xuma back to the house and introduces him to Eliza, a young teacher, who feeds him and tends to his bruises from the police attack. Struck by Eliza's beauty, Xuma is surprised to learn that the soft-spoken girl is the forceful Leah's niece. Later, Xuma and Eliza go for a walk and she takes him to a grassy area where they can see the city from the east and the tall mine dumps from the west. Eliza explains, "They are made of the sand that's dug out of the earth when the miners seek for gold. . . . It took many years to make them all. And more are being made every day" (*Mine Boy*, p. 26). As they sit together, Xuma senses Eliza is attracted to him and tries to kiss her, but she rebuffs him, leaving him confused and angry.

Back at Malay Camp, Dladla and two henchmen attack Xuma, supposedly for stealing Dladla's woman, Leah. Xuma overcomes one henchman; the other is subdued by another camp resident, Johannes. Leah, meanwhile, tackles and defeats Dladla herself. After the brawl, Xuma, his bleeding face stitched up by a doctor, meets Johannes, a mine-worker who offers to help Xuma find employment like his own.

The next morning the two men walk to the mine. Xuma asks what it is like in the mines; Johannes is evasive, saying only that the work is "not hard to learn" (*Mine Boy*, p. 33). Pointing out a line of approaching workers, Johannes explains that most mine workers live in compounds, but he, as a boss boy for one of the white men, does not have to abide by this rule. After introducing Xuma to his white boss, Chris, Johannes suggests Xuma for the position of boss boy for another white man, known as the Red One because of his red hair. The Red One has not yet arrived at the mine, however, so Xuma is assigned to another boss, a hostile white man who takes an instant dislike to him. The boss demands that Xuma push a truck full of sand, a job for two men, and gloatingly watches as he struggles with his task. But Xuma exerts himself and manages to move the truck into position, despite cutting his leg in the process. The other men, white and black, are impressed, including the Red One, who has now arrived and who reprimands the boss for his mistreatment of Xuma.

Work resumes and Xuma grows discouraged at the grueling labor, hectic pace, and apparent lack of progress, as the mine dumps appear not to grow any taller. A co-worker reassures him that he will soon grow accustomed to all these things. After work Johannes takes Xuma to be examined by the mine doctor and to meet the Red One—an Irishman named Paddy O'Shea.

The doctor gives Xuma a clean bill of health, while Paddy tells Xuma he must be a hard worker and a strong leader to work for him. Xuma decides the Red One is tough but fair and agrees.

Back at Malay Camp, Xuma learns that several women have been arrested for bootlegging and becomes upset with Leah for not having warned them. Leah reminds him that life in the city is a daily struggle and one must look out for oneself. She introduces Xuma to more people in the camp, including Maisy, a lively young black woman who takes an instant fancy to him. Maisy entices Xuma out of the house for dancing in the streets. Despite himself, Xuma has a good time but his happy mood is spoiled when he returns to Leah's house and finds Eliza there with another man, a sickly-looking teacher in a fine suit. For her part, Eliza is not happy to see Xuma with Maisy. Later, Eliza visits Xuma alone in his room. They kiss, but Eliza again rejects Xuma, tearfully explaining, "I want to be like the white people and go where they go and do the things that they do and I am black. I cannot help it. Inside I am not black and I do not want to be a black person. . . . And it is that that makes me hurt you" (*Mine Boy*, p. 60). More hurt and confused than ever, Xuma does not understand.

Winter arrives—Xuma has been in the city for three months and now has a room of his own in Malay Camp. While walking around Johannesburg one Saturday night, he meets Paddy O'Shea and Paddy's girlfriend, Di, who invite him back to their place for dinner. Xuma, who, because of their racial difference, has in the past deflected friendly overtures from Paddy, reluctantly accepts. The comfort and fine possessions he sees in Paddy's apartment amaze him; in an unguarded moment, he confides in Di about Eliza. Di tries to explain how she and Eliza, despite their different skin colors, are alike because they want the same things, but Xuma refuses to recognize a resemblance. After Xuma leaves, Paddy tells Di that he believes the young man will grow into a strong leader who will fight back against racial oppression. Di, however, disagrees, arguing, "A man's a man to the extent that he asserts himself. There's no assertion in your mine boy. There is confusion and bewilderment and acceptance. Nothing more" (*Mine Boy*, p. 68). Unconvinced, Paddy argues that Xuma will eventually wake up and realize his potential as a leader.

Xuma continues to wander around the city, then finds his way towards Leah's place, where he makes love with Eliza. Xuma is ecstatic, believing that love will solve all their problems, but his hopes are dashed the next morning when Eliza tells him the previous night was a mistake. Hurt, Xuma turns to Maisy for comfort, accompanying her to Hoopvlei, a township on the outskirts of Johannesburg. They enjoy a pleasant Sunday excursion, visiting Maisy's friends and returning late at night after dancing and drinks. Maisy takes a tipsy Xuma to her rooms in the city—where she works as a maid for a white family—and lets him sleep it off alone in her bed. Touched by her kindness, Xuma wishes it were Maisy, not Eliza, whom he loved.

Xuma's next day at work is eventful. First, Johannes tells him that Dladla, Leah's knife-wielding former lover, may be the police informant who snitches on residents like the liquor-peddling Leah. Then Paddy notifies him that their crew will be working the night shift for the next month. Next, during a backbreaking stint underground, Xuma and Paddy notice a weakness in the supports holding up the tunnels. One of the engineers gives the spot a cursory inspection, then tells the crew it is safe to resume working. Meanwhile, Xuma gets a firsthand look at the hazards of mining when it becomes clear that one of his men has lung sickness. The dying man explains that he was in debt to a white man and feared that he would lose the family farm unless he kept working. Horrified by the worker's cadaverous appearance, Paddy arranges for him to receive severance pay—enough to settle the debt—and free passage home to spend his last days with his family.

After work Xuma and Maisy go to tell Leah about Dladla. At the camp, Xuma again encounters Eliza, but this time she confesses her love for him: "I am your woman. If I want it or not it is so. I cannot help it" (*Mine Boy*, p. 119). A delighted Xuma agrees to give their relationship a chance; the young couple breaks the happy news to the Malay Camp residents, including the lovelorn Maisy, who congratulate them.

Eliza moves into Xuma's rooms and they establish a comfortable domestic routine, but their happiness is soon threatened by outside events. First, Dladla, the suspected informant, is found dead. Next, the old man, Daddy, suffers fatal injuries after being struck by a car. His death breaks Eliza's resolve; the night after Daddy's wake, she leaves Xuma for good. Leah tries to explain to the bewildered young man, "She has gone because she is sick of this place, sick of us, and because she wants things that we cannot give her. Things that she cannot get here" (*Mine Boy*, p. 154). Xuma suffers another blow when Leah, on

whose strength he has often leaned, is arrested for selling liquor illegally and sentenced to nine months in prison.

Reeling from these losses, Xuma sinks into a deep depression. Sensing the young man's distress, Paddy reaches out to him but an angry Xuma demands: "How can you understand, white man! . . . How can I be your friend when your people do this to me and my people?" (*Mine Boy*, p. 172). Paddy tries to explain that unhappiness can be felt by both whites and blacks and that race should matter less than shared feelings: "[I]t is not good to think only as a black man or only as a white man. The white people in this country think only as white people and that is why they do this harm to your people" (*Mine Boy*, pp. 172-173). Alone, Xuma begins to imagine what a society without color might be like and, despite himself, he finds the idea very appealing: "Picture after picture slipped through his mind. He felt light and free and gay. People were people. Not white and black people. Just people" (*Mine Boy*, p. 174).

Xuma reports for work at the mine, only to learn that disaster has struck again. The weakened tunnel that Xuma and Paddy had noticed several days before has collapsed. Chris and Johannes held the roof up while their men escaped and now both are trapped. Xuma and Paddy go underground, returning with the dead bodies of their friends. When the manager of the mine and the engineers try to attribute the deaths to unnecessary panic and order the miners to go back underground, an outraged Xuma demands that repairs be made first. The other black mine boys side with him, and so does Paddy, recognizing that his own principles are being put to the test. The manager screams that this is a strike and the police immediately swarm to subdue and arrest the recalcitrant miners. Xuma's first impulse is to flee, but after he calms down, he decides to stand up for his beliefs and turn himself in, even if it means going to jail. He pays a quick visit to Maisy to tell her what has happened and what he plans to do, explaining, "It is good that a black man should tell the white people how we feel. And also, a black man must tell the black people how they feel and what they want. These things I must do, then I will feel like a man" (*Mine Boy*, p. 183). Xuma also tells Maisy that he loves her and wants to make a life with her someday. Maisy promises to wait for him, then accompanies him to the police station.

A world without color. The African scholar Kolawole Ogungbesan writes, "Abrahams' vision is, as he puts it in *Mine Boy*, of 'man without colour,' a world in which every man will be judged as an individual and where colour will be irrelevant" (Ogungbesan, p. 2). In order for such a vision to be realized, however, blacks must have the courage to defy white expectations, especially regarding Africans in urban settings. The expectations of the time were that blacks flooded into cities because they practiced rudimentary, unproductive farming techniques.

> Once in the towns the blacks are [believed to be] feckless, lazy, irresponsible, and unable to improve their miserable material conditions; this situation is largely because of their innate disabilities. . . . [It is thought that] the best way to deal with this self-generated problem is probably to encourage as many blacks as possible to return to the countryside and try to learn better farming techniques.
> (Wade, "Peter Abrahams," p. 6)

Mine Boy, Wade contends, challenges those very assumptions through its depiction of how one black man, Xuma, manages to adapt to city life without compromising his integrity or succumbing to criminal temptation. Xuma emerges from his urban experience stronger and more resolute than he initially was.

The process of Xuma's maturation is set in motion early in the novel, when the naive young man receives a lecture from Leah on his first morning in Malay Camp. Although Xuma hails from the north and Leah from the south, she reminds him that such distinctions no longer matter in the city: "I come from my people, but I am no longer of my people. It is so in the city and I have been here many years. And the city makes you strange to the ways of your people" (*Mine Boy,* p. 10). All Africans, she implies, are bound together by the fight to survive in the urban jungle. Xuma takes the lesson to heart and determines to adapt to his new environment, soon landing the coveted position of "boss boy"—or gang leader—at the mine. He begins a gradual ascent up the social ladder, earning the respect of his white foreman, Paddy O'Shea, who is impressed by his strength and leadership. Paddy, a liberal thinker, believes that Xuma represents the future black South African: strong, dignified, and capable of great achievements in the modern world.

Xuma's varied experiences in the city further shape his destiny—he experiences racial discrimination in the form of daily pass inspections, sees new friends killed or defeated by the law, and copes with abandonment by his first love, Eliza, who longs to live as white people do. At the novel's climax, an embittered Xuma engages in a heated debate with Paddy over whether whites and blacks can ever reach a common understanding. Paddy contends, "You must be a man first and then a black man. And if it is so you will understand as a black man and as a white man. . . . When you understand that you will be a man with freedom inside your breast" (*Mine Boy,* p. 173). Initially incredulous, Xuma ultimately embraces those ideas when an accident at the mine claims two lives (one black, one white), prompting him to protest against the hazardous working conditions. He achieves his apotheosis not by retreating to the country to lick his wounds, but by making a place for himself in the white man's world and by standing up for the rights of his fellow workers, black and white.

Ironically, Xuma's transformation takes place at a time in history when South African policies of racial segregation were on the ascent. After World War II, the National Party, comprised of Afrikaners, increased in popularity. The British-influenced United Party's decision to enter the war on the Allied side had antagonized Afrikaners, many of whom sympathized with Nazi ideas about a white master race. In the 1948 general election, the National Party united rural and urban Afrikaners by appealing to their racial attitudes as well as their economic interests, and won. The new government, led by prime minister D. F. Malan, swiftly introduced *apartheid* (derived from the Afrikaner word for "apartness"), a policy that separated the races into distinct "homelands." Whites and nonwhites were considered to have separate destinies, which could be fulfilled only by isolating the races. For many years, Abrahams's ideal of "a world without colour" would remain an unattainable dream.

Sources and literary context. While the events and characters in *Mine Boy* are Abrahams's own invention, the author nonetheless drew upon his experiences as a child of the slums when creating the atmosphere of Malay Camp. The daily routines of migrant workers, shebeen keepers, and prostitutes are meticulously rendered, as is the sense of community that manages to evolve in these settlements, despite adverse living conditions.

Abrahams's *Mine Boy,* along with his other writings, occupies a significant position in South African literature. Scholar Martin Tucker describes South African novels as falling into three main categories: novels of geographic and racial isolation; novels of violence that deal with the explosion of racial and political tensions; and novels of forgiveness that advocate understanding and acceptance between black and white races (Tucker, p. 160). Along with Abrahams's works, writings by Alan Paton and Nadine Gordimer (see *Cry, the Beloved Country* and *Burger's Daughter,* also covered in *African Literature and Its Times*) belong in this third category. Tucker observes that these authors often depict "the problem of adjustment" by showing how a black person copes with the trials and temptations of life in the city "before he comes to that superior measure of understanding which obliterates his hate, resentment, and envy," a description that sums up the gist of *Mine Boy*'s plot (Tucker, p. 218). Michael Wade contends that *Mine Boy* distinguishes itself, presenting "for the first time in a South African novel, a convincing account of the state of mind of urban blacks" and calls Abrahams's novel "the first Marxist bildungsroman ['novel of growth'] in South African literature" (Wade, "Peter Abrahams," p. 6).

Reviews. *Mine Boy* was first published in England in 1946 but received little attention at the time. An anonymous review in the *Times Literary Supplement* merely noted that *Mine Boy* "marks an improvement" over Abrahams' first novel, *Song of the City,* but observed that both works depicted "the same limited society" (*Times Literary Supplement,* p. 477). Otherwise, critics ignored *Mine Boy* until it was reprinted by Knopf in 1955. Overall, reviews tended to be mixed.

Some critics found the novel's loose structure problematic. L. O. Coxe of *The Yale Review* complained: "Mr. Abrahams has not focused his lens. He does not decide, at any point, whether he is writing a picaresque novel, a tract, a love story, or a kind of *bildungsroman*" (Coxe in James and Brown, p. 2). John Hughes, writing for the *Christian Science Monitor,* also had reservations, feeling that "Mr. Abrahams has oversimplified the picture of South Africa which is not as clear-cut as he would have us believe" (Hughes in James and Brown, p. 2). Hughes recommended that the novel "should be taken for what it is—a good story of what happened to one African country boy who sought the City of Gold" (Hughes in James and Brown, p. 2).

Others found the novel's simplicity effective. Sylvia Stallings, writing for the *New York Herald Tribune Book Review,* commended Abrahams for "not sacrific[ing] poetry to propaganda. His simple story, dealing with simple people, is dignified and moving" (Stallings in James and Brown, p. 2). Hollis Alport, writing for *The Saturday Review,* praised the author's use of local color, so to speak, which he considered to be one of *Mine Boy*'s strongest attractions: "[W]hen Mr. Abrahams tells us about Xuma, a 'Skokiaan Queen' called Leah, a pretty 'coloured' schoolteacher called Eliza, and some of the other inhabitants of Malay Camp, the reader is both fascinated and moved" (Alport in James and Brown, p. 2).

—Pamela S. Loy

For More Information

Abrahams, Peter. *Mine Boy.* Portsmouth, N.H.: Heinemann Educational Books, 1989.

Byrnes, Rita M., ed. *South Africa: A Country Study.* Washington, D.C.: Federal Research Division, 1997.

Cameron, Trewella, ed. *A New Illustrated History of South Africa.* Johannesburg: Southern Book Publishers, 1986.

Huddleston, Trevor. *Naught for Your Comfort.* New York: Doubleday, 1956.

James, Mertrice M., and Dorothy Brown, eds. *Book Review Digest 1955.* New York: H. W. Wilson, 1956.

Lelyveld, Joseph. *Move Your Shadow: South Africa, Black and White.* New York: Times Books, 1985.

Ogungbesan, Kolawole. *The Writing of Peter Abrahams.* London: Hodder and Stoughton, 1979.

Thompson, Leonard. *A History of South Africa.* New Haven, Conn.: Yale University Press, 1990.

Review of *Mine Boy,* by Peter Abrahams. *Times Literary Supplement,* 5 October 1946, p. 477.

Tucker, Martin. *Africa in Modern Literature.* New York: Frederick Ungar, 1967.

Wade, Michael. *Peter Abrahams.* London: Evans Brothers, 1972.

———. "Peter Abrahams." In *Dictionary of Literary Biography.* Vol. 117. Eds. Bernth Lindfors and Reinhard Sander. Detroit: Gale Research, 1992.

Mission
to Kala

by
Mongo Beti

One of the most important figures in modern African letters, Mongo Beti has been called "francophone Africa's most effective gadfly in literature and social commentary" (Arnold, p. 1). He was born Alexandre Biyidi in 1932, son of a man known for resisting the power of colonial authorities. As a child Beti was expelled from Catholic school for questioning religious doctrine. Thenceforth, he was educated in public schools, eventually earning a university degree in France. A prominent Marxist, Beti has been as prolific in producing essays, criticism, and journalism as in writing novels. His career began in the early 1950s, when most of Cameroon was still under French rule, with a series of four satiric novels that questioned the right of Europeans to colonize Africa. Beti left Cameroon shortly after independence, and has lived in France ever since, teaching classical literature. However, he has continued to comment on the political situation in Cameroon; his book critiquing his country's post-independence relationship with France was banned in both countries in 1972. Beti stopped writing novels in the 1960s and '70s, devoting his attention to criticism and theory. In the late 1970s he returned to fiction, producing a series of novels that address problems of neocolonialism that Cameroon encountered after independence. These later novels, however, are generally regarded as less important and less successful than the quartet produced in the 1950s, which tackle serious political and social themes with an irony and lightness that reveal a profound comic understanding of human nature.

THE LITERARY WORK

A novel set in the Cameroon Republic in the late 1950s, before it gained independence; published in French (as *Mission terminée*) in 1957; in English in 1958.

SYNOPSIS

A young student is sent to a rural village to persuade a wayward wife to return to her husband.

Events in History at the Time of the Novel

Colonial background. *Mission to Kala* is unusual for a novel concerned with the impact of colonialism on Africans: not a single European appears as a major character. Indeed, the only European in the book is a surly Greek bus driver who appears for less than a page. Nevertheless, the novel is deeply concerned with the colonial presence, and its plot cannot be understood without some awareness of Cameroon's colonial history.

Cameroon's encounters with Europe follow a pattern similar to those of most of the West African coast. In the fifteenth and sixteenth centuries, European explorers established trading contacts with coastal peoples; by the end of the sixteenth century, the traders trafficked mostly in slaves: Cameroon, like Nigeria and Ghana to the north, lost thousands of people to the plan-

Germans taking possession of Cameroon in the 1880s.

tations of the West Indies. However, while its northern neighbors were allied almost exclusively with the British, Cameroon had ties to Germany as well as Great Britain. Britain, always the dominant colonial power in West Africa, had its hands busy with other areas of West Africa—specifically, the Gold Coast and Nigeria. The lands that would become Cameroon were nearly always the last in the area to receive British attention.

This situation changed in the so-called "scramble" for Africa that transpired in the nineteenth century. In competition with one another, European powers rushed to increase their prestige and wealth by seizing colonies in Africa. Germany had been growing as a military power throughout the nineteenth century; it longed to demonstrate its might to the world by becoming a colonizer, and Cameroon was an ideal place for it to create a colony. In 1884 some local chiefs of Cameroon signed treaties ceding their sovereignty to the German government. The Germans resorted to bribery and subtle shows of force to negotiate these treaties; still they faced resistance, to greater and lesser degrees, from nearly every cultural group they encountered.

The British were happy to play on this hostility. British traders and missionaries encouraged local peoples to rise up against the Germans; these minor rebellions were put down with relative ease. A decade of legal wrangling and occasional confrontation followed. Only in 1895 were the precise claims of German, British, and also French traders and missionaries firmly set—in a way that would create great problems in later decades. As elsewhere, in Africa the Europeans set colonial boundaries with absolutely no regard for African realities. Some of Cameroon's native ethnic groups were split right down the middle, while others were yoked to traditional rivals or enemies.

Over the next 30 years Germany extended its influence from the coast to the interior regions of Cameroon. The Germans established or built up mission schools that provided a basic education for a minority of the native population; they created a colonial trusteeship, in cooperation with local chiefs; and they instituted a plantation system that depended on forced labor. In sum, Germany developed the region into a fairly stable and fairly prosperous, if at times brutal, colony, only to have it taken away at the end of World War I (1914-18). In 1916 the victors Britain and France divided the former German colony between themselves, a division later sanctioned by the League of Nations. France got the lion's share of Cameroon, while Britain got only two discontinuous sections that bordered Nigeria. The French section would be called La Republique du Cameroun; the two far smaller British sections, Northern Cameroons and Southern Cameroons. From 1918 to independence in 1960, Cameroon would be ruled mainly by the French.

French rule in Cameroon differed profoundly from the old German regime. First, the French doctrine of assimilation mandated a very different philosophy towards colonial subjects than that of the Germans. In theory, the French conceived of their African subjects not simply as colonized people, but as potential French citizens; the goal was to turn their Cameroonian subjects into citizens with rights, responsibilities, and status equal to anyone born in Paris. This willingness to regard Africans as potentially equal to Frenchmen must not be misunderstood to mean that France saw Africans as *already* equal to the French. On the contrary, the whole rationale of colonialism was to create *évolués* [which means "the civilized"]—a condescending concept denoting Africans who had been improved by contact with the French to the point at which equality of a sort was possible.

To this end, the French adopted a very different approach to colonial management than did the British or Germans. Instead of indirect rule, by which colonial powers ruled in partnership with traditional chiefs, the French appointed native leaders who had no other authority than that which the French granted. In addition, the French created a two-tiered justice system to reward assimilation. The upper level was used for French citizens and native Cameroonians judged to have achieved sufficient proficiency in French culture and language. The lower level, called the *indigénat,* was used for the majority of Africans without French education or social habits. Of course, those people subject to the indigénat were judged less fairly and more harshly than their Europeanized counterparts.

It is generally agreed that colonized Africans who did assimilate into French culture remained more loyal to France than their counterparts did to England. However, apart from this, little practical difference can be discerned as a result of the French theory of assimilation. Cameroonians were no less eager than Ghanaians or Kenyans (ruled by the British) to acquire their liberty; and French colonial administration, while generally less inclined to use overwhelming force against uncooperative Africans than its German predecessor, was not fundamentally more benign or sensitive to the needs of Africans.

Independence came to the Cameroons in a fairly undramatic fashion. Although France was victorious in World War II, that long conflict drained its strength and crippled its ability to maintain recalcitrant foreign holdings. Through the 1950s Cameroonian political parties worked for independence through a mixture of political activity, including delegations to France, and occasional small-scale violence. By the period covered in *Mission to Kala,* their efforts were gaining momentum—independence would be achieved directly after this period, on January 1, 1960.

However, the struggle for independence is not Beti's main concern in this novel. The residents of Kala, and the novel's protagonist, all seem to accept French rule as an inescapable fact: the villagers' reverence for things French is treated sardonically in the novel. However, Beti is deeply concerned with the impact of French culture on his homeland, and this is nowhere more obvious than in one of the novel's main concerns: education.

Schooling the French way. When the Germans annexed Cameroon in 1885, they found a European-style educational system already existing to an embryonic degree. Elementary education had been provided by Christian missionaries from various European countries. The Germans kept the basic framework of mission education but made some attempts to broaden the curriculum and to educate greater numbers of young Cameroonians. They were especially interested in promoting German as the official language of the country and in preparing Cameroonians for the practical business of running a colony: agricultural colleges had been founded by the first decade of the twentieth century.

Mission to Kala

CAMEROONIAN COLONIAL HISTORY: AN OVERVIEW

1884: After signing several treaties with local rulers, Germany raises its flag in the area that it designates as Kamerun; Kamerun becomes a German protectorate/colony.

1916: Germany suffers defeat in World War I, loses control of Kamerun; it becomes a mandate, an area authorized by the League of Nations to be administered by France and Britain. France gets 5/6ths of the area and calls it Cameroun. Britain gets 1/6th along Nigeria's border, divided into two parts—Southern Cameroons and Northern Cameroons. (A 45-mile, or 72-kilometer, gap subdivides the British Cameroons into discontiguous parts.)

1946: United Nations (U.N.) assumes authority that League of Nations formerly held over the area; Cameroun becomes a U.N. trusteeship. Though it is governed like a French colony, this status gives Camerounians recourse to a higher authority and supports drive for independence.

1960: Cameroun achieves independence from France; becomes the Republic of Cameroon.

1961: British-controlled Northern Cameroons votes to merge into Nigeria; Southern Cameroons joins Republic of Cameroon

When the French took over the colony after World War I, they allowed the mission school structure of the Germans to continue. But, in line with their ideas about assimilation, they also established a system of schools run by the government, which closely followed the structure of schooling in France. Primary school lasted six years; at the end of primary school, a comprehensive examination determined whether students would continue to secondary school. These examinations were extremely competitive, since applicants always outnumbered the spaces available. In addition, the French government used education as the primary tool of assimilation: Africans with an advanced education might be sent to France, and were certainly in a good position to find bureaucratic jobs in Cameroon. There were several types of secondary schools in the colony. The most comprehensive, and the most prestigious, were the *lycées*; these offered a standard academic education and some types of technical education. *Lycées polyvalent* offered more thorough technical and vocational training. There were also a larger number of private schools, both religious and secular, which varied widely in prestige and curricula. For a lycée student like Beti's protagonist, Jean Medza, secondary education ended, after seven years, with the baccalaureat exam. This exam—which Medza fails—was critical in determining a student's career path: college, a career, or disgrace.

Native Cameroonians quite rightly viewed a European-style education as the key to success in colonial society; however, this education was never available to more than a fraction of African children. Around the time of the novel, the average Cameroonian got, at most, a year or two of primary education and of those who went on, only one-tenth of a percent finished secondary school (Le Vine, p. 76). In rural areas such as the village of Kala, few children received any formal schooling at all. Thus, when Medza visits Kala, he encounters people whom he finds exotic, but to whom he is equally exotic: they are, almost literally, from different worlds, even though many of them are blood relatives.

The village. Surveys identified about 200 ethnic groups in all of Cameroon at the time of the novel (Le Vine, p. 6). The residents of Kala appear to be Bantu, a family of loosely affiliated ethnic groups that dominate the lowlands of central and southern Africa. It is generally agreed that the Bantu peoples, now spread from the Atlantic to the Indian Oceans and from Cameroon to South Africa, originated in the forests of Cameroon, from which they began to move more than 2,000 years ago. At the time of the novel, a large concentration of Bantu peoples lived in Cameroon's equatorial forests, the most numerous of these being the Beti-Pahouin people (around 655,000, all in the French-controlled region [Le Vine, p. 12]). Northward in the central highlands lived other ethnic groups such as the Bamiléké, and north of them lived another collection of Bantu peoples, the largest of these being the Douala (around 47,000, most in the French region, a fraction in the British [Le Vine, p. 12]). The blanket term "Bantu" is both misleading and accurate. On one hand, Cameroon has various distinct Bantu peoples; on the other, these peoples share many common cultural, social, and economic practices. The most numerous Bantu people in Cameroon, the Beti-Pahouin, is the one to which Mongo Beti himself belongs. This group actually includes subgroups—the Ewondo, Bulu, and Fang.

When Medza travels from his fairly large hometown into the forest where Kala sits, he has the impression of travelling backwards in time. This impression is not unjustified. Although centuries of the slave trade and a half-century of incursions by the Germans and the French certainly had a profound impact on Cameroonian life, in many important respects life for the average Bantu villager was fundamentally similar to the life of his or her ancestors hundreds of years before. The Germans created, and the French maintained, a system of plantations that drew its workers from the native populations. However, many ethnic groups and villages, including Kala, were not touched by the plantation system; this was especially true of those, like Kala, tucked into the forested highlands of central Cameroon.

In these regions, traditional culture thrived in a way it did not in the larger cities. Polygamy was still practiced; kinship and age-group were still the predominant determiners of one's friends, peers, and social status. Traditional methods of carpentry and architecture flourished. The popular arts of the regions—pottery, weaving, and music—continued to be practiced. Even the chief, though he now derived his power from the French, largely retained the habits and way of life inherited from his precolonial predecessors. At any rate, chiefs held less power in the forest villages, where social life tended to be more democratic, than among the ethnic groups of the grasslands. And, of course, that way of life was determined by farming and livestock: even today, 80 percent of Cameroonians earn their living as farmers. In addition to raising subsistence crops and tending small animals such as goats and chickens, mid-twentieth-century villagers grew cash crops—cocoa, coffee, and groundnuts being the most important. Produced to be sold to larger cities and even abroad, these crops were generally grown in large, communal plots at a distance from the village. Each family, nuclear or extended, had its own strip of land in this communally cleared plot; families and kinship groups labored together to plant, tend, and harvest the crops. Women worked at least as hard as the men at these tasks. Although the exact proportions of work varied from group to group, in general men took responsibility for clearing the forest land that was to be tilled, while women and children tended and harvested the crops.

Land ownership was loosely defined before the arrival of the Europeans; there was plenty to go around, and tasks that required village-wide cooperation were, quite simply, performed by the whole village. These patterns were disrupted by colonization only in specific places and for specific reasons; the establishment of a plantation could disrupt a village's social fabric considerably, and large public works projects like railroads or highways often sent the French scouring the countryside for laborers, whom colonial laws compelled to provide services for the French on demand. The French laws governing indigénat people allowed French-backed chiefs broad and sometimes coercive powers of control. But in many areas, life continued without much change.

The Novel in Focus

Plot summary. *Mission to Kala* is a comic novel that draws on several classic traditions: the coming-of-age story, the fish-out-of-water story, and the story of mistaken identities. Its hero, Jean Medza, is at the center of all these elements—at times, "victim" seems to be a better word than "center." Written in the first person, the novel creates a voice of subtle, slightly self-mocking irony for its protagonist. But underneath the humor and gentle satire, Beti shapes a compelling critique of the harm that Western education can do to an African mind, and the novel ends pessimistically, as Medza exiles himself from his family and the culture that is so attractive, but so alien, to him.

The novel opens as Medza returns to his hometown. School has just finished for the year, and Medza has just failed the all-important baccalaureate examination. He is confused, uncertain about his future, and—perhaps most of all—terrified: he expects his demanding father to be furious. However, when he arrives in the town of Vimili, near his home village, he meets his Aunt Amou, who gives him news of a development that will allow him to avoid meeting his father.

Amou tells him of a man named Niam, who is in fact his cousin. Niam married a woman from another clan and then began treating her badly: he forced her to work too hard, while doing nothing himself, and insulted her because she did not bear him any children. Niam's wife began an adulterous affair. In itself, the novel notes, this did not attract disapproval: adultery was common, and people did not take it very seriously. However, Niam's wife made the unpardonable error of choosing as her lover a man from a clan that is not her husband's: "For a woman to grant her favours to a man from a neighbouring tribe is bad enough; if she goes with some rootless stranger she is, in all intents and purposes, deliberately giving the most deadly insult possible to her own kin" (*Mission to Kala,* p. 8). Finally, Niam's wife flees, and returns to the forest village in which she was born.

BANTU AGRICULTURE

Jean Medza and his friends, while wandering through the forest, come across Kala's agricultural clearing:

> The women were bent over the furrows, delicately hoeing up the last of the ground-nut plants, while young boys and girls gathered them and stripped off the ripe nuts. . . . There was a mingled scent of freshly-turned earth, ripe crops, and sprouting vegetables, while all around the jungle stood austerely on guard in the glory of its sombre greenery.

(Beti, *Mission to Kala,* p. 119)

Forest dwellers such as the residents of Kala cleared some of the ground around them for crops by slashing and burning: cutting away the trees and ground-growth in an area, and then burning the cuttings. At the end of the season, they restored the tilled area to nature, only to pick a new spot the next year. This process has been going on so long that it has actually changed the geography of the country. After a farming plot is left to regenerate itself in nature, it does not grow back as forest; instead, it becomes a clearing dominated by grass. Over the centuries, as farming continued and new plots abutted old plots, vast tracts of forest have been turned into this new terrain, called "derived savannah." No wonder, then, given this ancient relationship with their land, that common Africans had difficulty understanding that it had been "annexed" by outsiders.

It makes little difference that Niam does not like his wife, or even that she does not want to be with him. She must be brought back: his honor and the honor of his kinsfolk demand it. However, all their attempts at negotiation have failed, and now, desperate, they see Medza's arrival as the perfect solution. Almost at once, they request that he travel to Kala to secure the return of Niam's wife. Medza is confused: he does not understand how he, a teenaged boy, can succeed where others have failed. He debates this point with Niam and the other villagers. Finally, an elder named Bikokolo tells him the truth:

> Shall I tell you what your special thunder is? Your certificates, your learning. . . . Have you any idea what these upcountry bushmen will seriously believe about you? That you only have to write a letter in French, or speak French to the nearest District Officer, to have anyone you like imprisoned, or get any personal favour you like.
>
> (*Mission to Kala*, p. 15)

Convinced, and more than willing to avoid having to tell his father of his failure, Medza sets out on bicycle to Kala. When he arrives, the villagers are engaged in a game against the neighboring village. This game, a particularly vicious version of dodgeball, highlights the prowess of a tall, muscular Kalan named Zambo—Medza's cousin, and the son of Mama, the uncle with whom Medza is supposed to stay. After the game Zambo recognizes him and they greet each other warmly. Zambo is prepared to see in his citified cousin the embodiment of sophistication, and Medza is quite willing to take this view of himself. However, as soon as they arrive at Mama's house, a meeting imposes a different pattern on their relationship. Zambo introduces Medza to his mistress, who lives with him quite openly in the house of his father. Medza is shocked, even scandalized. He knew that the sexual mores of his people were more permissive than those of the French colonizers; but he was not prepared for the actual experience of this looseness. He hides his surprise, but the central irony of the novel is established. The people of Kala are fascinated by Medza, seeing him as a sophisticated, French-educated cosmopolite. So dazzled are they by his scholastic accomplishments that they cannot see his perpetual amazement at *their* subtlety, manners, and firm grasp of life. He struggles to project an air of unsurprised acceptance, while attempting also to comprehend their ways.

Medza's stay in Kala falls into a pattern that has very little to do with his mission. On the second day he and his uncle—a taciturn carpenter—visit the father of Niam's wife in a fruitless attempt at negotiation. After this solitary attempt, Medza proceeds to party. During the day he spends time with Zambo and his village friends, a jocular crew that appears to have no particular ambition and no work—at least not work that they care to perform. At night Mama parades his nephew around the various houses of the village. Everyone is eager to host a dinner for the newcomer, and Mama, for reasons of his own, is equally eager to oblige them. These dinners are attended not just by the host and Medza, but also by all the villagers who can squeeze in—and almost everyone can. After the food is eaten, the dinners turn into extended interrogation sessions. Medza is placed in the center of the room and forced to answer rapid-fire questions about his future, the white man's knowledge, the country's future—anything that comes into anyone's mind.

These sessions leave Medza drained and weak, but they have their benefits. The morning after each visit the host sends a gift to his visitor, generally in the shape of a goat or chicken. By the time Medza has been in Kala a week or two, his uncle is obliged to build a corral and a pen for Medza's growing wealth in livestock. However, Mama does not mind: he has been orchestrating Medza's visits for maximum impact, accepting invitations only from the richer and more generous visitors. One day he calls Medza into his workshop and gives him a long and circuitous lecture on the twin virtues of gratitude and respect for blood. Medza is slow to grasp the point, but when he does, he is more than willing to grant what Mama has hinted at: he offers his uncle half of all the hooved or beaked gifts he has received. And the visits continue.

At the same time Zambo is attempting to orchestrate a gift of his own for Medza: he is trying to find Medza a woman. Zambo is convinced that if a country boy like him is sexually experienced, a city boy like his cousin must be unbelievably sophisticated. Little does he realize that Medza is not only a virgin but also terrified at the prospect of sex. More precisely, he is tantalized, but at the same time terrified that the woman will be disappointed. He suspects (probably with some justification) that she will not keep her disappointment to herself. In short, if he fails, his façade of sophistication will crumble. It does not help that Zambo's first choice for him is a girl from the city who has spurned every other man in Kala, or that one morning Medza awakens from uneasy, drunken slumber to find Zambo and this girl sitting on his bed. Zambo leaves, smiling, but Medza ignores the girl's obvious advances, and she leaves, baffled. Medza explains to Zambo that he suspected the girl had venereal disease, and Zambo is satisfied. But he does not give up the chase. Instead, he turns his attention to the daughter of the village chief. Late one night he awakens Medza and leads him through the dark to a house where this girl, Edima, is waiting. Medza and the girl fumble at each other in the dark, but she leaves before consummation. Nevertheless, Medza is lovestruck. From this point on, he devotes all his attention to spending time with Edima, who, for her part, is more than willing to be chased.

Medza's life in the village settles into a customary pattern; he spends time with young people during the day, and is feasted by the older people of the village at night. The affair with Edima is consummated, ironically, during the wedding feast of her father, who has just married his seventh wife. During these gaudy festivities, no one is paying attention to Edima or Medza. The two take advantage of the opportunity to sneak away to Mama's house.

Their idyll is interrupted by the unwelcome arrival of Edima's mother. She bursts into Medza's room, screaming, and drags her daughter out of the house naked, hitting and scolding her violently. Medza is terrified; he assumes he must face dire consequences and cannot imagine what will happen to his young lover. But when Edima has been dragged off, Zambo bursts out laughing. He explains, "That old bag simply wanted to be able to tell the whole village that it was *her* daughter you'd honoured with your—h'm—attention.... Did you see *how* she was beating the kid? Pulling her punches like mad, and trying to make each smack sound as loud as possible at the same time?" (*Mission to Kala,* p. 140).

At this dramatic point, when she has been all but forgotten, Niam's wife reappears. It turns out that she has been living with a man of ill repute in a house outside her village; her open return with him creates a scandal. Though adultery is tolerated, shamelessness is not. Medza is convinced that he should leave Niam's wife to her own abandonment, but Mama and Zambo convince him otherwise. The wife may be an immoral slut, but she is, nevertheless, a wife: she is necessary to Niam as a cook, field worker, and (potentially) mother of his children. Besides, colonial French law dictates that either she return to the marriage or the wronged family benefit from the situation. According to the formalized French precepts about divorce, Niam's wife has a choice: she can leave her husband, but if she does, she must return his dowry. Thus, if Medza complains to the chief, he will win back either the woman or a sizeable dowry.

Accordingly, the family goes to the chief, and the matter is quickly decided: Niam's wife cannot afford to repay the dowry, so she will return to her husband. After settling the affair, the chief invites Medza, Mama, and Zambo to his house for dinner; they decline, but the chief insists. As they eat, they are entertained by dancers, drummers, and processions that grow steadily more elaborate, reminding Medza of the chief's wedding celebration. At this point, Edima paces in, accompanied by handmaids and dressed as a bride. To his shock (although he certainly does not object) he has been tricked into a wedding. The chief marries the young couple.

Now Medza has done about all he can do in Kala, and he has little choice but to leave. He knows his father will be unspeakably furious now. Failing the examination was terrible enough, but to return home married, without getting the consent or even the advice of one's own father, is to have gone beyond the pale. But Medza has no choice. He sets out alone. Edima, Niam's wife, Mama, and Zambo will follow in a week or two, along with Medza's ever-increasing herd of goats.

At home, Medza finds his father in a mood of indifference. The father utterly ignores the boy. Medza attempts to provoke a confrontation by whistling and being insolent, but his father is imperturbably icy. Only when Edima arrives is there a confrontation. His father attempts to beat Medza, who alternately fights back and runs away. Zambo comes to his cousin's aid, tackling a man who tries to capture Medza. This prompts Mama to begin chasing Zambo, with the whole town watching. Finally, Medza's father gives up and goes huffing into the house. Medza watches him for a moment, feeling genuine pity, but then he decides the only recourse left is to leave. He walks along the dusty path out of town, followed by Zambo.

A brief epilogue informs the reader that neither boy ever returned to Kala or to Medza's village. Edima eventually married Medza's older brother. Medza and Zambo wandered together, adventuring in unspecified ways. But the tone is as much elegiac as humorous; at the end, Medza informs the reader that he is haunted by "his first, perhaps his only love: the absurdity of life"

(*Mission to Kala*, p. 183). Taking on a sober tone, the novel allows the veneer of light irony to melt away. Revealed is the irresolvable dilemma of the African too educated to live comfortably among his people, but still too African to attempt to live as a white man. Like Medza, he must simply wander.

The colonized mind. On the first of the many feasts held in his honor—feasts that invariably turn into interrogation sessions—Medza realizes how wide a gap separates him from his people's ways of living and thinking. As he struggles to find the words that will explain abstract, Western modes of knowledge such as geography and economics, he comes to question whether or not his education has prepared him for life any more appropriately than growing up in the old way would have. He watches the easy interaction of Zambo and his friends with appreciation, but also with something like envy. Although they incorporate him into their community with great ease, he always feels like an outsider. He is perhaps most envious of the absolute certainty with which the villagers of Kala assume that their own worldview is adequate. Toward the end, he comments on the placidity with which Zambo accepts the treachery of Niam's wife, a placidity that makes Zambo seem much older than his 20 years: "This unshakeable stoicism in the face of all life's accidents and vicissitudes is probably the townsman's greatest loss, when he abandons village, tribes, and local culture. We who choose the city have lost this ancient wisdom: irritable, ambitious, hot-headed, fed on illusion, we have become the world's eternal dupes" (*Mission to Kala*, p. 145).

Perhaps the most amusing example of Medza's confusion occurs when his uncle asks him if he knows what "blood" is. Medza replies, "Blood is a red liquid circulating through our veins and—." Of course, Mama means blood *relations* (*Mission to Kala,* p. 87). However, a serious tragedy lurks beneath this humorous misunderstanding. As soon as Medza realizes that his uncle is lecturing him only in an attempt to get some of his gifts, he stops paying attention. All he gets from the lecture is a lesson in the earthbound avarice of village life. Prepared by his French education to be idealistic, to expect noble motivations from people, he does not understand that greed is only one part of Mama's lecture. For Mama and Zambo, kinship is the controlling factor of life: people are saved by their families, for children and parents provide each other with a reason for living and working. Thus,

Mama's loving relations with Zambo are contrasted with Medza's strife with his father. Even more seriously, Medza is an idealist. That is, he has a sense of how things should be (in contrast to the villagers, who accept what comes). Because of this idealism, he finds some actions distasteful. He does not like his father so he simply leaves in order not to face the reality of how his father is. Ultimately his unwillingness to face his obligations to his father and his flight from home lead to his most treacherous move, his abandonment of Edima. As one critic notes, this abandonment is the most telling indication of the deficiencies in Medza's education. He has not been prepared, by centuries of tradition, to understand the obligations that marriage brings: "he has no conception of consequences, no long-term commitment to the group, no concern for the perpetuation of the tribe" (Mickelson, p. 76). Rejecting his father seems like an act of self-liberation; but the fact that it also forces him to abandon the wife he loves, and who depends on him, should hint to the reader that Medza's flight is not an unmixed triumph. The melancholy tone of the last two chapters provides more evidence. The pleasant humor of the chapters in Kala gives way to a flat reportage of a life spent roaming and unsatisfied. Medza's final comment sums up the plight of the "colonized African," who has been separated from the ancestral wisdom of his people but not given a new way of understanding life: "The tragedy which our nation is now suffering is that of a man left to his own devices in a world which does not belong to him, which he has not made and does not understand" (*Mission to Kala,* p. 181).

Thus, even though Beti's novel contains only one minor European character, and completely ignores the political struggle for independence occupying Cameroon at the time that it takes place, it is nevertheless concerned with the effects of colonization at a level far deeper than that of land laws and the aftermath of wars. The novel explores the effects of colonization on the mind.

Beti himself seems to have been somewhat unimpressed with the way in which Cameroon achieved independence. He left the country in 1958, and did not return even for a visit until 1990. His novels published in the 1970s and '80s severely critique the repressive political regime that ruled Cameroon after independence. More importantly, he joined the continent-wide critique of neocolonialism: political independence means nothing if African countries con-

PARADOXICAL EXILE: THE LANGUAGE ISSUE

~

From the beginning, Beti's journalism has involved him in the most controversial aspects of African intellectual life. Few have been more contentious than he in his espousal of a literature written in African languages. While this plea for a rejection of European languages is hardly unique to Beti, Beti's odd position has drawn a great deal of acrimony. For Beti to praise and promote African culture is all well and good; but then, why has he lived in France, the land of the colonizer, for three decades? If he calls for books to be written in African languages, why does he write them in French? He has been seen, according to one critic, as "one of those gallicized Africans who, while basking contentedly in Parisian elegance and splendour, feel periodically called upon to pay lip service to the superiority of African values" (Palmer, p. 95).

This rejection vastly oversimplifies both Beti's position and his aims. For Beti, it seems, exile is acceptable precisely because of neocolonialism: independent Cameroon's continued dependence on France made its freedoms paltry and essentially meaningless. His later, more political, novels were banned in Cameroon, and Beti could not find a publisher there even for acceptable books. Thus, to live in Paris made perfect sense; he could be close to his publisher, and write journalism that attacked Cameroonian injustices without fear of political reprisal. Language is a slightly more complicated problem. The continued presence of the colonizer's language is one of the chief problems facing postcolonial writers; many ways have been found to surmount this problem. Beti has praised countries in which English is the dominant colonial language that have successfully Africanized their English, changing it enough so that it reflects native realities. An example of this would be the Africanized English deployed in the novels of Nigerian writer Chinua Achebe. Beti would presumably also praise the efforts of writers like Kenya's Ngugi wa Thiong'o who have returned to their native tongues in writing literature. However, Beti is not in a position to follow either example. Unlike English in Nigeria, French never spread widely enough in Cameroon to allow authors to speak to the whole nation in it: French remained almost exclusively the language of the elite. And, unlike Ngugi's Kikuyu, Beti's native tongue is spoken in a country that, even by African standards, contains a dizzying variety of peoples and languages. In short, French has continued to serve as Beti's vehicle of literary expression, and exile as his mode of life, for practical as well as other reasons. While neither he nor perhaps anyone else would call his situation ideal, it is the best available to him at the present time. Actually, it reaffirms one of Beti's most famous statements on colonialism: once broken, a mirror cannot be put back together.

tinue to be intellectually dependent on their former colonizers. To combat the pernicious effects of neocolonialism, he has published a steady stream of articles and reviews calling for a return to African wisdom, for a literature written in African languages, and for an end to a debilitating inferiority complex in which the success of his country is measured by the extent to which it can mimic the outward signs of European civilization.

Sources and literary context. Like almost all African writers of his generation, Beti has had to reconcile his inherited African culture and his European education. Critics have attempted to divide what is African in his novels from what is derived from European traditions, not always understanding that Beti is a unique hybrid of the two. His years as a professor of Latin and Greek literature undoubtedly leave their mark on his style; just as certainly, he is energized by such aspects of African culture as folklore, proverbs, and tribal life. Parallels have been drawn between Niam's wife in the novel and Helen of Troy, whom the Greeks seek to rescue much as Medza, more comically, sets out to retrieve the missing bride.

More specifically, *Mission to Kala* belongs to a European tradition of *bildungsroman,* the novel of a young person's education in the ways of life. However, Beti's treatment of the bildungsroman is heavily inflected by the specifics of the colonial experience: specifically, the tension between Western and African forms of education. In this regard, it is part of a developing genre of African novels that includes Cheikh Hamidou Kane's *Ambiguous Adventure* and Chinua Achebe's *No Longer at Ease* and *A Man of the People.*

In addition, *Mission to Kala* can be placed alongside all the novels produced by Africans under colonization. These works, few and often rudimentary, nevertheless helped immensely in defining the African voice as it screamed for liberty. Beti was among the loudest Cameroonian voices for independence; in fact, after independence he fell silent as a novelist for a decade and a half. As a result of his early success and his later journalistic radicalism, Beti has remained a voice of liberty and an eminent Cameroon literary figure despite his long exile.

Reviews. *Mission to Kala* was almost universally praised. It forms part of an informal tetralogy—the group of four novels that Beti produced from the mid- to late 1950s: *Ville cruelle* (Cruel City), *Le pauvre Christ de Bomba* (The Poor Christ of Bomba), *Mission terminée* (Mission to Kala), and *Le roi miraculé* (King Lazarus). This group is unified by humor, balance, and an ironic way of criticizing the French presence in Cameroon. Critics have generally considered these four novels as superior to the novels Beti produced in the 1970s and after, which are more explicitly political and less humorous.

Within this early group, *Mission to Kala* is considered second to *The Poor Christ of Bomba* in terms of artistic success. Critics praise the wit and vigor of Medza's voice; politically like-minded critics have appreciated the loving portrait of vil-

lage life. More recently, critics like David Mickelson have persuasively argued for the complexity of Medza's voice. Whereas early reviewers assumed that Medza was simply Beti's fictional alter ego, Mickelson notes the complex mix of good and bad in Medza and suggests that Beti wants the reader to distance him or herself from the novel's hero. What remains undeniable is that the novel has been seminal in the development of Cameroonian fiction. Beti is a figure almost revered, and *Mission to Kala* is one of the major foundations of his reputation.

—Jacob Littleton

For More Information

Arnold, Stephen. "The New Mongo Beti." In *Critical Perspectives on Mongo Beti.* Ed. Stephen Arnold. London: Lynne Rennier, 1997.

Beti, Mongo. *Mission to Kala.* Trans. Peter Green. London: Heinemann, 1958.

Cassirer, Thomas. "The Dilemma of Leadership as Tragicomedy in the Novels of Mongo Beti." In *Critical Perspectives on Mongo Beti.* Ed. Stephen Arnold. London: Lynne Rennier, 1997.

Eyongetah Mbuagbaw, Tambi, Robert Brian, and Robin Palmer. *A History of the Cameroon.* London: Longman, 1987.

Fowler, Ian, ed. *African Crossroads.* Providence: Berghan, 1996.

Koenig, Barbara. *Sex, Work and Social Class in Cameroon.* Ph.D. diss., Northwestern University, 1977.

Le Vine, Victor T. *The Cameroons: From Mandate to Independence.* Westport, Conn.: Greenwood Press, 1977.

Mickelson, David. "The *Bildungsroman* in Africa." In *Critical Perspectives on Mongo Beti.* Ed. Stephen Arnold. London: Lynne Rennier, 1997.

Ngwa, J. A. *A New Geography of Cameroon.* London: Longman, 1978.

Palmer, Eustace. "An Interpretation: Mongo Beti's *Mission to Kala.*" In *Critical Perspectives on Mongo Beti.* Ed. Stephen Arnold. London: Lynne Rennier, 1997.

Tchoungui, Pierre. "Ethnic Survivals and the Modern Shift: Literary Imagology and Ethno-psychology in Cameroon as Reflected by its Writers." *Diogenes* 80 (1972): 95-110.

Nedjma

by

Kateb Yacine

THE LITERARY WORK

A novel set in Algeria in the late 1940s; published in French in 1956, in English in 1961.

SYNOPSIS

Against the background of economic dislocation caused by more than a century of French colonialism and World War II, four young Algerian men are obsessed with Nedjma, a young woman of uncertain origin.

Kateb Yacine was born in 1929 in the eastern Algerian city of Constantine. Kateb, his family name, means "writer" in Arabic, indicating that he was part of the literary branch of his clan. His father chose to have him educated at a French *lycée* (roughly the equivalent of a high school) in Constantine, rather than sending him to a Koranic school. Kateb would later call this being "cast into the jaws of the wolf" (Arnaud, p. 114; trans. R. Serrano). On May 8, 1945 (V-E Day, marking the end of World War II in Europe), Kateb participated in demonstrations in the city of Sétif against French colonial rule, resulting in brief imprisonment and interrogation. In 1950 he moved to France, though his active support of the Algerian Revolution forced him to leave in 1955, shortly after *Nedjma* was accepted by a major French publishing house. He lived in Tunisia, Germany, Italy, Belgium, Vietnam, and the Soviet Union, before returning definitively to Algeria in 1970 to form a theatrical company. In the 1950s and '60s he wrote another novel, *Le Polygone étoilé* (The Starred Polygon), and plays inhabited by the same characters as *Nedjma*, in addition to a play about Ho Chi Minh, *L'Homme aux sandales en caoutchouc* (The Man in Rubber Sandals). In the 1970s and '80s he continued to write plays performed in colloquial Arabic. He died in 1989. Despite his 40 years of literary production, he is best remembered for *Nedjma*, which introduced radical innovations in style and content to North African literature in French.

Events in History at the Time the Novel Takes Place

Algeria in the 1940s. On May 8, 1945, nationalists throughout Algeria organized marches and demonstrations to mark the liberation of Europe from the World War II Axis powers (Germany, Italy, and Japan) and, seizing on the political symbolism, to call as well for Algeria's liberation from 115 years of French colonial rule. In Sétif, a city about 75 miles from Constantine in eastern Algeria, marchers insisted on hoisting nationalist flags and placards, despite orders from local French authorities not to do so. The result was an armed clash between police and Muslim Algerians. News of the violence spread to the countryside, leading to general insurrection, which was eventually put down by 10,000 French troops, planes attacking Algerian villages, and bombardment from a cruiser offshore. About 100 Europeans had been killed by the time the violence ended a few days later. As for the Algerians, "French government estimates spoke of 1,500 dead, the [French] army of 6,000 to 8,000, American sources of from 7,000 to 40,000, and some Algerian nationalists of 45,000" (Ruedy, p. 149). In the ensuing weeks nearly 6,000 Algerian men were imprisoned, including Kateb

Men of the nationalist Algerian army prepare for rebellion against French rule.

Yacine. Of these, 99 were sentenced to death. European retaliation against Muslim Algerians was indiscriminate and out of all proportion to the violence they had committed. This would continue to be the case throughout the Algerian Revolution.

The distortions of more than a century of French colonialism and the dislocations of World War II had created a situation in Algeria in which, in retrospect, violence appears to have been inevitable. Nearly half the Algerian men of working age were unemployed, hundreds of thousands having abandoned their ancestral villages to migrate to the cities in search of work. The best lands had been expropriated or purchased primarily for viticulture by French *colons,* the great landlords who comprised about 0.5 percent of the entire population of Algeria but controlled over 80 percent of its European-held lands (Alleg, p. I.103). By the late 1930s Algeria was the third-largest wine-producing country in the world, after France and Italy. Muslim Algerians labored in vast numbers on extensive tracts of land removed from the production of staple foods, in short supply, in order to produce a beverage that their religion prohibited them from drinking.

Since the French kept Algeria primarily as a producer of raw materials, there was a severe shortage of manufactured goods during World War II. An economy already out of balance from the demands of colonial exploitation could hardly withstand the shock of a two-thirds reduction in the grain harvest due to poor rains in 1945. Muslim Algerian soldiers who had served in the Free French forces (under the exiled Charles de Gaulle) in the liberation of France also swelled the ranks of the unemployed upon demobilization, although many would go on to fight in the colonialist war in French Indochina. As in the case of the hundreds of thousands of West Africans who fought for the French, Muslim Algerian soldiers were embittered by the French refusal to allow them to participate in the liberation of Paris from the Germans and by the cavalier treatment they received after the war. As the Allies approached Paris, nonwhite soldiers were sent southward, where they were repatriated hastily and often without the documentation they would later need to secure their pensions. There has since been a systematic refusal to recognize the contributions of colonized peoples in the defense and liberation of France in both world wars. In addition to hunger, unemployment, and material want, Algerians were frustrated with a political system that left them essentially disenfranchised. The European minority in Algeria managed to block nearly all reforms proposed in Paris.

In the late 1940s Algeria was not legally a distinct political entity. Northern Algeria was divided into three *départements* (or provinces) integrated into metropolitan France. Algeria south of the Atlas Mountains, the Sahara region, was a military territory. It was often pointed out in the 1950s that the Algerian départements had been part of France longer than some regions in metropolitan France (Nice and Savoy, for example). Proponents of French Algeria claimed that the Mediterranean Sea flowed through France the way the Seine flowed through Paris. The integration of Northern Algeria into France did not, however, mean that all its inhabitants were French, with rights and privileges equal to those of Parisians. European settlers in Algeria and their descendants (*pieds noirs*, or black feet), who numbered nearly one million on the eve of the revolution in 1954, were recognized as French citizens, although those of French descent never made up more than 40 percent of this group, the rest being Spanish, Italian, Maltese, or Greek settlers or their descendants. Muslim Algerians became French only upon demonstrating a certain level of education and renouncing Islam. Reforms after World War II created an Algerian parliament with limited powers, divided into two chambers, one European and one Muslim (Droz, p. 33). This provided Muslim Algerians with representation on par with Europeans in Algeria, but since they outnumbered Europeans by about eight to one, this solution was far from democratic.

Mission civilisatrice. The primary philosophical justification for such an unfair system was the French mission civilisatrice, or civilizing mission. Most French believed (and many still do) that the ideals of French civilization marked the pinnacle of human achievement. Therefore, French culture was not merely a national accomplishment, but was the great gift of the French people to the world. Perhaps the greatest achievement of French culture was the codification in 1789 of the Rights of Man; unfortunately, imposing the wonders of French culture on Africans and Asians nearly always resulted in the abrogation of some of these rights.

The stated aim of the French was to impart their culture to the native inhabitants of their colonies. Any inhabitant, whether of Algeria, Madagascar, or Vietnam, who successfully learned to read, speak, and think like a French person was termed an *évolué*. Becoming an évolué was no simple task, since even on the eve of the revolution, 86 percent of Algerian men and 95 percent of Algerian women were illiterate. These statistics are even more shocking when we consider that in 1830 when the French first invaded, Algeria's literacy rate for men was actually higher than that in France (Ruedy, p. 103).

WHY DID FRANCE INVADE ALGERIA?

In the final decade of the eighteenth century, the Dey of Algiers had exported large amounts of grain to the south of France and to the French Republican armies of Napoleon in Italy and Egypt. France and Algeria broke off relations before all the shipments had been paid for. Two Jewish merchant houses, Bushnaq and Bakri, which were responsible for the deal, still owed a large sum to the Dey three decades later, but the restored monarchy of France was reluctant to recognize the debts of Republican France. When the French consul to Algiers, Pierre Deval, went to pay his respects to the Dey on April 29, 1827, at the end of Ramadan, the annual month-long period of fasting observed by Muslims, he was asked why Charles X had not responded to his written queries about the debt. "Deval allegedly responded," none too respectfully, "that His Most Christian Majesty could not lower himself to correspond with the Dey. Losing his customary self-control, Hussein [the Dey] struck the consul three times on the arm with the handle of a peacock-feather fly whisk and ordered him to get out" (Ruedy, p. 46).

Despite the orientalist charm of this famous *coup d'éventail*, it is unlikely that 130 years of colonial rule resulted from French umbrage at a fit of pique by a representative of Ottoman Turkey who nominally ruled over Algeria. Less than two decades earlier, France had lost most of its international possessions with the collapse of Napoleon's empire. With British supremacy at sea a foregone conclusion, a colonial venture closer to home, just across the Mediterranean, made sense. Charles X was not a universally beloved king and his advisers felt that a successful overseas adventure would strengthen the restored Bourbon monarchy. Ironically, while Algiers surrendered to the French on July 5, 1830, before the end of the month Charles X was himself sent into exile and replaced by Louis-Philippe of the house of Orléans, who decided to pursue the conquest of the hinterland beyond Algiers. Thereafter no French ruler until Charles de Gaulle in the early 1960s was willing to preside over a French departure from Algeria. This 132-year rupture in the history of Algeria is reflected in the discontinuities and uncertainties central to *Nedjma*.

By any standard, the mission civilisatrice was not only a failure, but little more than an excuse for the exploitation of non-European peoples. The war in Algeria, which lasted from 1954 to 1962, was the longest, bloodiest, and most expensive France would fight to retain its empire.

Algerian women. In the 1940s and '50s the vast majority of Muslim Algerian women were still peasants working in the fields, although village life was carefully organized to keep men and women separated, even outdoors. The women of the rich or of religious leaders were kept indoors and probably enjoyed even less freedom than their poorer sisters did. The relatively affluent situation of Nedjma's family accounts for her near-total seclusion. Education of females was severely restricted: in 1954 only 10.7 percent of Algerian girls 6-13 years old attended school and there were only 22 Algerian women studying at the university (Amrane, p. 27). Throughout the nineteenth and early twentieth centuries, the near absence of Muslim Algerian women from the public sphere tantalized the French colonial imagination, which seldom failed to eroticize the veiled and sequestered women.

Although Westerners remain obsessed with the Islamic issue of the veil, in reality the status of Algerian women in the 1940s was due less to the strictures of Islam than to the Mediterranean culture of which Algeria is part. In this culture "masculine honor is protected by the seclusion of women" (Gordon, p. 8). We should keep in mind that as late as 1966 a French woman could not open a checking account without her husband's permission (Gordon, p. 20). There were also many European women in Algeria in the 1940s and early '50s, but they were either from relatively conservative southern European cultures and therefore not much more liberated than their Algerian counterparts or, if more independent and visible, were viewed as a negative example for Muslim women.

Small numbers of Muslim women were nonetheless radicalized by the massacres at Sétif in 1945 and by the increasing weight of French rule as the Algerian Revolution continued. Young women worked as nurses and cooks in the *maquis* (Algerian underground forces) in the countryside. Several young women also played a key role in the urban terrorism depicted so unforgettably in Gillo Pontecorvo's film *Battle of Algiers* (1966). Dressed as young Frenchwomen, three Algerian Muslim women placed bombs in cafés frequented by young pieds noirs, killing four and injuring 52 (Droz, p. 129). Although it is diffi-

cult to imagine the Nedjma of the novel walking across Algiers, let alone planting bombs, in Kateb's 1959 cycle of plays, *Le Cercle des représailles* (The Circle of Reprisals), Nedjma marries Mustapha and becomes a member of the maquis. The Algerian Revolution enables her to shake off her passivity, to break her silence, and to participate in the public life of her country.

The Novel in Focus

Plot summary. Any description of the plot of *Nedjma* risks being insufficient and misleading, because Kateb created a structure for the novel that runs counter to the chronological order of events. The events of *Nedjma* can be traced from mid-1945 to 1952, with flashbacks to the 1920s, but the novel ends at nearly the same moment at which it began: sometime in 1946 or 1947, just before four young men go their separate ways. Despite this chronological ambiguity, it is clear, however, that the novel is, in part, about an attempted return to origins: the origins of the Algerian people, the origins of the violence that surfaces at key moments, and the origins of Nedjma herself.

Lakhdar, Mourad, Mustapha, and Rachid are comrades in the eastern Algerian city of Bône (today's Annaba) who have found temporary work at a construction site. Each follows a different path in his obsession with the young married woman, Nedjma (Arabic for "star"). Although we learn a great deal about her possible origins—her mother was French and her father could have been one of two men among the mother's many lovers—Nedjma remains an unknown and ultimately unknowable quantity throughout the novel. The reader has access to the thoughts of the four young men, sometimes even to their writings, but only to enigmatic fragments of what Nedjma herself thinks.

These four young men literally take different paths in the first part of the novel. Lakhdar strikes their foreman, M. Ernest, during an argument on their first day of work in an unnamed village. He is arrested but later escapes, which causes him to reflect on his earlier arrest in connection with the demonstrations in Sétif in 1945. Sometime later, Mourad kills the wealthy, aged, and infirm French colon M. Ricard, for whipping his Muslim Algerian maid in a drunken fit shortly before he is to consummate his marriage to the foreman's daughter. Mourad is imprisoned and the three others take to the road and part ways. Although it is not immediately obvious, most of the events of the novel take place *before* this parting of ways. We come to see the violence just described not as the source but the culmination of events.

Rachid's obsession with Nedjma is described in most detail. In conversation with an old man who was once a noted seducer, Si Mokhtar, Rachid discovers that Nedjma is the daughter of a Frenchwoman who had four different lovers, including Rachid's father. Nedjma was conceived on a night that Si Mokhtar and Rachid's father spent in a cave with the Frenchwoman. The body of Rachid's father was found the next day. Neither Rachid nor the reader are ever certain whether Rachid's father is Nedjma's father as well, making them half-siblings, or whether Si Mokhtar murdered Rachid's father.

Thereafter, Rachid follows Si Mokhtar everywhere, refraining from taking revenge on the man he believes murdered his father, in order to find out just who Nedjma is. After a would-be pilgrimage to Mecca that gets the two no closer than the port of Jedda on the Red Sea, Si Mokhtar reveals to Rachid that he is actually the father of Nedjma's husband, Kamel. Rachid and Si Mokhtar decide to kidnap Nedjma from her possibly incestuous marriage and spirit her off to Nadhor, a nearly inaccessible mountain where the last descendants of the legendary Keblout people still live. A mysterious black man, in turn, steals Nedjma away from them before they have accomplished what they believe to be her destiny in returning to her origins.

The novel itself then returns to its own origins, with an account of Lakhdar's escape from prison. We are reminded that Mourad remains in prison for having killed M. Ricard and the three remaining friends go their separate ways. It is as if the characters are imprisoned in a historical moment that will be resolved only with the Algerian Revolution that begins just beyond the limits of the novel's narrative.

Origins of Algerian identity. Although Si Mokhtar is one of the most vivid figures of the novel, Kateb Yacine presents him so obliquely that we might wonder if he exists at all. Practically all we know about Si Mokhtar is what he says himself, although we know him to be a liar and a fraud. As if this were not enough to raise doubts about his true role in Nedjma's mysterious origin, the only account of Si Mokhtar is made by Rachid during a malarial fever. Even Rachid himself "seemed to consider everything he had told" Mourad during the attack of malaria "a delirium" (Kateb, *Nedjma*, p. 137). Mourad re-

constitutes the disjointed story recounted by a delirious person, repeating what may be only the lies of a dying old man. Through these narrative strategies of distancing the reader from the events recounted, Yacine insists on the impossibility of knowing the truth about the origins of Nedjma or Algeria.

Rachid cannot remember when he first met Si Mokhtar. He believes that he has always been aware of him, since his earliest childhood:

> He had always belonged to the ideal city that's been lying like a deposit in my memory since the blurred age of circumcision, of escapes from the house, of the first weeks when Madame Clément had given me a slate—for me he was one of the tutelary spirits of Constantine, and I never saw him age, any more than there is an age or one particular countenance for the historical Barbarossa, the legendary Jupiter; I had always lived in Constantine with ogres and sultanas, with the locomotives of the inaccessible station, and the specter of Si Mokhtar.
>
> (*Nedjma*, p. 142)

Si Mokhtar is Rachid's link to the past, at once historical and legendary, unavoidably real and suspiciously ideal. His existence predates Rachid's earliest memories, yet stretches off into the future. In a land cut off from its past by over a century of French rule, this connection to the past, however tenuous and potentially deceptive, is vital.

Si Mokhtar inspires Rachid's two attempts to return to possible origins of Algerian culture: the pilgrimage to Mecca and the journey to Nadhor, each indicating a different facet of Algerian identity. Rachid first meets Si Mokhtar while a deserter from the French army during World War II, still wearing his uniform. When he discovers that Si Mokhtar intends to make the pilgrimage to Mecca, Rachid obtains false papers and a new identity as a sailor. Once they reach Jeddah, the Arabian port on the Red Sea that serves as point of entry to Mecca, Si Mokhtar decides not to continue to Mecca, claiming that he does not have enough money and is too sick to make the voyage. Rachid wonders why Si Mokhtar had wanted to make the pilgrimage in the first place, since he had already satisfied the demands of Islam by traveling to Mecca 25 years earlier.

Although it is possible to consider the profane Si Mokhtar as embodying a stinging rebuke to Islam, Kateb Yacine was more likely criticizing not the religion itself but the corruption and hypocrisy of a certain class of Muslim Algerians who professed Islam yet collaborated with and profited from French rule. Rachid's inability to complete the pilgrimage to Mecca after his escape from French military service reminds us how Algeria has been cut off from its Muslim traditions by French colonization and the Europeanization of its young men. Just as Rachid questions Si Mokhtar's motives, we must question Rachid's—nothing in his behavior to this point suggests that he is a practicing Muslim. We can only guess that his fascination with Si Mokhtar's claim to be the key to understanding Nedjma's past (as well as Rachid's own) inspires the impetuous decision to visit Mecca and the equally impetuous decision to return to Algeria without having actually seen Mecca. Going to Mecca accomplishes nothing because Rachid does not know why he goes; he can never arrive. Claiming Islam as part of an Algerian identity requires an intellectual commitment to understanding the place of Islam in Algerian history and should be taken more seriously than changing from a French uniform to a sailor's.

It may be that aborting the pilgrimage to Mecca is meant to dispute a solely Arabo-Islamic identity for Algerians, since the city is not only the religious center of Islam but also the homeland of the Arab people who invaded North Africa in the tenth century. Since his turn to an Arab or Islamic identity fails, Rachid veers toward the other axis of Algerian identity: the *ferqa* or group "descended from a partly mythical ancestor" (Gordon, p. 7). The Keblout, to which Rachid and Si Mokhtar intend to "return" Nedjma, are said to be descended from the Beni Hilal, the Arab people who participated in the conquest of Spain (Arnaud, p. 39). Even if we accept the Keblout account of their origins—nearly all Arab and Berber groups in North Africa claim descendance from the Prophet Mohammad or the Beni Hilal—their many centuries in Algeria imply a great deal of intermarriage with the non-Arab inhabitants. Kateb himself recognized that he was Berber and became sympathetic to the Berber movement that later appeared but did not yet exist in the 1940s. Although not explicitly described as Berber, the mysterious Keblout suggest the complexity and ambiguity of the origins of Algerians.

Forcing a specific ethnic identity on Nedjma, whose mother was a French Jew and whose father's identity, let alone origin, is a mystery, is as unsuccessful as the aborted pilgrimage to Mecca. The voyage itself reveals little about the Keblout. Where a typical French colonial novel or travel account about Algeria would provide numerous details about exotic or "primitive" peoples, Kateb Yacine has nearly nothing to say about the Keblout, except they are inaccessible and intend to take Nedjma from Rachid and Si Mokhtar. The conflict is resolved only by yet another man's kidnapping of Nedjma. Since he is a black African of near-complete anonymity, he seems to be little more than a figure in Rachid's feverish nightmare, although he may represent yet another facet of Algerian identity as part of Africa.

Sources and literary context. Kateb Yacine was part of the first generation of Algerians writing in French, including Mouloud Feraoun, Mouloud Mammeri, and Mohammed Dib. Unlike these other writers, who wrote realistic novels in the style of Honoré de Balzac, Emile Zola, and other nineteenth-century French writers, Kateb wrote in an unconventional form. Events are not related in chronological order, nor are they related from a single perspective, whether that of an omniscient narrator or a single character. Kateb was an enthusiastic reader of William Faulkner, especially *The Sound and the Fury,* whose influence is obvious, if limited.

No Francophone Algerian writer following Kateb Yacine has been free of his influence. Even the novelist Rachid Boudjedra, one of Kateb's harshest critics, has felt compelled to respond to *Nedjma.* His second novel, *L'Insolation* (The Sunstroke), is in part a parody of the mythology of Kateb's novel, including a rather corrupt and aggressive version of Nedjma herself. The mysterious female character and forays into fantasy of Mohammed Dib's *Qui se souvient de la mer?* (Who Remembers the Ocean?) owe a great deal to *Nedjma* as well.

Events in History at the Time the Novel Was Written

Collapse of French rule. Kateb Yacine completed *Nedjma* shortly after the Algerian Revolution began in 1954. Indeed, as Kateb himself pointed out, it was probably the outbreak of fighting that made the publication of *Nedjma* a viable enterprise, since prior to this the French had little interest in reading about contemporary Algeria, except perhaps as a land of "beautiful sheep" (Aresu in Kateb, p. xxxi). Oddly enough for a book written as France was about to plunge into its bloodiest and costliest colonial war, and despite the violence both threatened and realized in the novel, there is little sense in *Nedjma* that

WHO ARE THE ALGERIANS?

Although at independence Algeria was declared to be an Arab nation, Algeria is actually a multiethnic and multicultural country. French invaders in 1830 found not only Arabs, but Moors (Spanish Muslim refugees from fifteenth-century Spain), Turks (as part of the ruling military regime), *Koulouglis* (a mixture of Turk and Arab), Berbers, and Jews (Prochaska, p. 49). Today the Turks, Moors, and Koulouglis have disappeared as recognizably different groups. Although most Berbers, whether in Algeria or in exile in France or elsewhere, now identify themselves as such, there was no sense of Berber ethnic identity in North Africa until the French colonialists decided to divide the local population into three groups: Arabs, Berbers, and Jews. In 1870 the Jews were declared to be French and nearly all immigrated to France by the end of the Algerian Revolution.

Most historians believe that there is little ethnic difference between Arabs and Berbers in contemporary Algeria, since the number of Arabs who participated in the eighth-century invasions of North Africa was quite small. Nearly all Algerians are then ethnically Berber. Nonetheless, centuries of arabization and islamization have divided Algerians into those who speak an Arabic language and those who speak one of several Berber languages. Despite the essential ethnic homogeneity of Algerians, this century has seen the rise of Berber (or "Amazight," as one group, the Kabyles, prefer to call themselves) studies, the institution of Berber literature, and the production of Berber films and recorded music, all as distinct from Arab culture.

In the nineteenth century the French saw the Berbers as lapsed Christians who may have been related to the French, either as leftover Romans, distant cousins to the Basques, or the descendants of seafaring Celts. Because they were perceived as natural allies of the colonizing French, Berbers were much more likely to benefit from French education and missions. As a result, disproportionate numbers of Algerian immigrants to France, leaders of the Algerian Revolution, and Francophone literary figures, including Kateb Yacine, have been Berber.

In *Nedjma*, Kateb explores the contradictions behind attempts to forge an Algerian identity. Every attempt to determine the origins of Nedjma and, by extension, Algeria, fails. Rachid's pilgrimage to Mecca "becomes a burlesque epic, and a failed one at that," revealing the limits of a merely Islamic or Arab identity (Bonn, *African Writers*, p. 393). The trip to Nadhor fails as well, revealing the limits of a more narrowly ethnic identity. Although Kateb himself was of Berber origin, he never specifies in *Nedjma* that the Keblout are Berber, although the very remoteness of their origins would imply that they are. *Nedjma* remains a cry for tolerance of multiple and shifting identities, for the necessity of tolerating the taking of different paths.

Algeria was about to be engulfed in a war that would eventually result in her independence. Nonetheless, although the Revolution has not yet come to pass at any point in the novel's constantly shifting chronology, *Nedjma* always seems to be about this unspoken event. The Algerian Revolution is the epic upheaval that will correct the apparent aimlessness portrayed in Kateb's novel. None of the characters nor Algeria itself can move forward; they can only languish in prison or go round and round in narrative circles, until the violence depicted in the novel is redirected toward liberation.

That the Algerian Revolution began on November 1, 1954, is evident only in retrospect. Although the Algerian nationalist group, the

FLN (*Front de Libération Nationale,* or National Liberation Front) coordinated 70 attacks of varying degrees of effectiveness across the three départements of Algeria, French authorities did not at first recognize the threat it posed. Nor did the entire Muslim Algerian population suddenly rise in support of the FLN. Unlike in neighboring Morocco and Tunisia, where a cohesive and activist middle class led the nationalist movements, Muslim Algerians splintered into groups of wildly different sympathies. Many in the Algerian middle class had benefited enormously from French colonization, had sent their children to French schools (or even to France), and had little sympathy for the socialist and communist factions within the nationalist movement. Others, such as the writer Mouloud Feraoun, who would be assassinated by the OAS (*Organisation armée secrète,* or Secret Army Organization—a radical group of pieds noirs) in 1962, condemned the violence of both the nationalist guerrillas and the tactics (including torture) employed by the French army. Kateb Yacine was squarely on the side of an independent Algeria, although he did not fight in the war.

It should be noted that the French military successfully defeated every military campaign and strategy of the FLN. Each stage of the war brought increasingly repressive measures against the Muslim Algerian population, so that every French military success resulted in increased Muslim Algerian support for the FLN. The Algerian Revolution owes its success to weariness in France with the high costs of the war, international criticism of the French position, the deepening gulf between the European and Muslim communities in Algeria, and the realization that the needs of the French colonial community and France were in fundamental conflict. The tensions that would bring about the collapse of French rule in Algeria are evident in Kateb's depiction of pied noir and Muslim Algerian interaction in *Nedjma*.

Reviews. Although *Nedjma* was quickly recognized as a masterpiece by French critics in the mid-1950s, its place as the founding work of modern Algerian literature has not gone uncontested. After the successful close of the Algerian Revolution in 1962, the new government instituted a policy of "Arabization" to replace French with classical Arabic in education and administration. Although this policy has never been entirely successful, at least in the manner intended, it has made novelists writing in French increas-

ingly ideologically suspect. Kateb turned to writing plays performed in colloquial Arabic in the 1970s and '80s, and *Nedjma* was published in Arabic in 1984 (in Tunisia), but some Arab nationalists and Arabophone writers have refused to accept Kateb as "an authentically Algerian writer" (Déjeux, p. 8). Some have even gone so far as to call him "impious" (Stone, p. 153).

Despite such criticism, Kateb Yacine remains a towering figure in the history of Algerian literature. Charles Bonn praises *Nedjma* for being "above all a colossal dismantling of the model inherited from the nineteenth-century French novel" (Bonn, *Research in African Literatures,* p. 65). Kateb Yacine recognized that the traditional forms of French literature could not embody the historical moment of Algeria on the verge of revolution. In creating a new form of novel that seems to owe little to either French literature or traditional North African literary forms, Kateb Yacine wrote the founding text of Algerian literature. *Nedjma* continues to this day to be the touchstone of all Algerian writers in French.

—Richard Serrano

For More Information

Alleg, Henri. "De l'Algérie des origines ... l'insurrection." In *La Guerre d'Algérie.* Ed. Henri Alleg. Paris: Temps Actuels, 1981.

Amrane, Djamila. *Les Femmes algériennes dans la guerre.* Paris: Plon, 1991.

Arnaud, Jacqueline. *La Littérature maghrébine de langue française.* Paris: Publisud, 1986.

Bonn, Charles. "Kateb Yacine." *Research in African Literatures* 23:2 (summer 1992), 61-70.

———. "Kateb Yacine." *African Writers.* Vol I. Ed. C. Brian Cox. New York: Scribners, 1997.

Déjeux, Jean. "Francophone Literature in the Maghreb: The Problem and the Possibility." *Research in African Literatures* 23:2 (summer 1992), 5-19.

Droz, Bernard. *Histoire de la guerre d'Algérie.* Paris: Editions du Seuil, 1982.

Gordon, David. *Women of Algeria: An Essay on Change.* Cambridge, Mass.: Harvard University Press, 1968.

Kateb, Yacine. *Nedjma.* Trans. Richard Howard. Charlottesville: University Press of Virginia, 1991.

Prochaska, David. *Making Algeria French: Colonialism in Bône, 1870-1920.* Cambridge: Cambridge University Press, 1990.

Ruedy, John. *Modern Algeria: The Origins and Development of a Nation.* Bloomington: Indiana University Press, 1992.

Stone, Martin. *The Agony of Algeria.* New York: Columbia University Press, 1997.

Nervous Conditions

by

Tsitsi Dangarembga

~

Born on February 14, 1959, in Mutoko, Rhodesia, Tsitsi Dangarembga spent her early childhood in England, where her parents pursued their academic education. She and her brother completely forgot their native language, but in 1965 she returned with her family to Rhodesia and relearned Shona. As an adult Dangarembga attended Marymount Mission School in Mutare (formerly Umtali), and later completed her education at an American convent school in Salisbury (now Harare). She taught for a while in Rhodesia, then moved to England again to study at Cambridge University. But homesickness and the racism she confronted in England drove her back to her own country just a few months before it was transformed as the result of a bitter civil war. White-dominated Southern Rhodesia became the politically black-dominated republic of Zimbabwe. Dangarembga enrolled in the psychology department at the University of Zimbabwe; the university Drama Group produced three of her plays—*She No Longer Weeps, The Lost of the Soil,* and *The Third One.* But it was her debut novel, *Nervous Conditions,* that won her international acclaim. She finished the novel three years before its release, but was unable to publish it sooner in Zimbabwe because of the antagonistic reception of male reviewers. Demanding a full indictment of colonialism from literature, they objected to the novel's focus on gender issues in African society.

THE LITERARY WORK

A novel set mainly on an impoverished homestead and at the Umtali mission in Rhodesia (now Zimbabwe) in the 1960s and early 1970s; published in English in 1988.

SYNOPSIS

A young Shona woman recounts her struggles to receive an education in colonial Rhodesia, and the experiences of four women she loves.

Events in History at the Time the Novel Takes Place

Shifting status of Shona women. Zimbabwe (formerly Rhodesia) has an overwhelmingly indigenous African population—some 79 percent are Shona, and the remainder are mostly Ndebele. The Shona cultivate crops such as maize, millet, yams, beans, and pumpkins, often on communal lands, as Tambudzai's (or Tambu's) nuclear family does in the novel. Most Shona have adopted Christianity but continue to subscribe to their native faith, centered on a high god and hierarchy of spirits with whom humans communicate through a medium. There is still among the Shona a very widespread belief in witches, who are blamed for illness, death, and other misfortune.

The most important unit in society is the patrilineage, or family line descending from a common male ancestor. At the time of the novel, adult males and their wives and unmarried children often lived in the same homestead or cluster of homesteads. The extended family was a tightly knit unit; in the novel Tambu's uncle and aunt call her "daughter" and plainly regard her as such. Her uncle, Babamukuru, patriarch of the extended family, and also a school headmaster, exerts a godlike authority over his relatives. In Tambu's nuclear family, her mother, siblings, and any property they have belong to her father, a shiftless man who fawns over Babamukuru for the handouts he gets from his more successful brother. Yet Tambu's father wields authority in his own nuclear household.

According to Shona tradition, at marriage a man gives to his prospective wife's family a *roora,* or bride-wealth, usually a mix of cash and cattle. The roora legitimizes the husband's right to his wife's labor and to sexual access to her body. He also gains authority over her reproductive powers—the right to possess all children born to her.

In the past, the wife's subordinate status manifested itself in daily customs. At the center of the traditional homestead was the hearth, three stones that supported cooking pots, above which sat a horizontal bar on which fish, meat, and maize cobs were dried. If there was a gathering there, the women would sit on the ground, perhaps on reed mats, while men sat above them on a mud ledge. These customs had begun to change by time of the novel, as reflected in the chairs and couches with which Babamukuru's home is furnished. And despite the sexist customs, women appeared to have exerted some leverage even in the traditional household. "Despite their subordinate status," notes one historian, "many observers [have] concurred that any given Shona woman was not, as one colonial official phrased it, 'the downtrodden timid individual she is often supposed to be'" (Schmidt, p. 19). In keeping with this perception, various female characters in *Nervous Conditions* stand up for themselves, making their suffering and opinions known.

The status of Shona women deteriorated under colonial rule. Before the colonial period, women served as mediums, mediators in local disputes, and even heads of communities. However, by the late 1930s very few headwomen remained in power, and the division of labor in agriculture had begun to change. Suddenly women took on tasks formerly reserved for men—threshing, for example, in addition to the planting, hoeing, weeding, and harvesting.

Meanwhile, colonial railways took the men away from the homesteads to copper mines and farming enterprises to make money for the Europeans, leaving the women behind to raise the crops that would feed the family. Men's status, given the wages they earned as migrant laborers, increased, while the role of women deteriorated as their workload mounted. By 1944, 80 percent of Rhodesia's subsistence agriculture was conducted by women (Schmidt, p. 83).

A typical day began before sunrise; women and girls started the fire, fetched water from a well, swept, and prepared the morning meal of *sadza* and relish. (The dietary staple, sadza is a stiff porridge, often made of maize and almost always accompanied by relish—a paste of stamped groundnuts mixed with greens.) By 7:00 A.M. mothers would leave to labor in the fields, perhaps returning to prepare lunch for their children, or if the fields were too far, arriving home only between 4:00 and 6:00 P.M. After school children helped by tending the garden or caring for younger family members. Boys were supposed to herd cattle and help plow while girls busied themselves with domestic work, but if sons were not around, as happens in the novel, daughters took on their work.

Women who sought escape from these conditions had few options. They could flee to a Christian mission, in which case they would be exchanging the patriarchal control at home for that of the missionaries. Or they could escape to a town, where they would have to find a male patron, whose domestic and/or sexual needs they could satisfy in exchange for shelter. Or they might find work as a servant, teacher, or nurse, as a very few managed to do. In the novel, Tambu's independent aunt, Lucia, consorts with two men and relies on a third, Babamukuru, to find her a job. Tambu's other aunt, Maiguru, in a show of defiance, runs away from her husband's home for a brief interval—but only to her brother's house, substituting one male authority for another.

Education. Under colonial rule, the Shona showed an almost passionate interest in education. Determined to attain it, whole families would strive to send at least one of their offspring to school, convinced that education led to money and the betterment of the family. Even children in their spare time would go around townships trying to sell items sewn by their mothers or vegetables raised in the family garden to pay their school fees, which is why Tambu attempts to raise and sell her own maize in the novel.

Education in Rhodesia was patently unequal. Until 1979 the country operated two school systems, one for the Africans, and a second, infinitely better financed one for the non-Africans. The Compulsory Education Act of 1939 required all whites aged 7 to 15 to attend school, for free if they so chose; in contrast, there was no such requirement for Africans, and those who did attend often paid their own fees. Missions and other private groups ran 83 percent of the schools that catered to the African majority. By the early 1970s, during the time of the novel, half the primary-school-age African population was enrolled. Far fewer, only 4 percent, proceeded to a secondary school for Africans, as Tambu does in the novel, and just a tiny fraction completed the full six years required here before becoming eligible for university study. Again only a minority of these schools were government-run, but the government went so far as to introduce an abbreviated option at this level, the junior secondary school, a Grades 8-9 program only, in which at least one third of the time was to be spent on vocational training. In fact, there was disagreement between white officials and businessmen on the one hand and missionaries on the other hand over the best kind of secondary education for Africans. Whereas the officials and businessmen focused on vocational education, the missionaries stressed academic education, although not to the exclusion of vocational subjects. It is this latter, missionary viewpoint that directs the schooling of the protagonist in *Nervous Conditions.*

The education of boys took precedence over that of girls, for economic as well as other reasons. Given the custom whereby a woman joined her husband's family after marriage, the better economic investment was to educate a son, since the money he earned would stay in the family. "Have you ever heard," rants Tambu's father when considering sending his daughter to school, "of a woman who remains in her father's house? . . . She will meet a young man and I will have lost everything" (Dangarembga, *Nervous Conditions,* p. 30). He dismisses her intellectual aptitude as of little use to him. Undaunted, Tambu resolves to be educated and learns later that her Aunt Maiguru had shown the same resolve: "I . . . studied for that [Master's] degree and got it in spite of all of them—your uncle, your grandparents, and the rest of your family"(*Nervous Conditions,* p. 101). Returning to Rhodesia with her degree, Maiguru pursues teaching, almost the only profession open to African women outside domestic service. Men too had a very limited range of options:

> To sum up the situation of the African people by mid-century . . . they were excluded from nearly every possible route to advancement . . . from the lands beyond the [overcrowded, soil depleted] reserve and from skilled jobs in government, mining, and business.
> (Beach, pp. 178-80)

Girls who attended school in Rhodesia studied reading, writing, and arithmetic, but the curriculum was largely directed toward training them to become good Christian wives of African men. They received daily lessons in hygiene and Bible study. At the secondary level, needlework and cookery appeared alongside other subjects. This type of gender conditioning was not limited to Rhodesia or, for that matter, to Africa. During the 1960s such conditioning occurred outside the continent, in countries like England too.

England in the 1960s. Tambu's uncle spends five years (1960-65) with his nuclear family in England. His daughter, Nyasha, returns to Rhodesia transformed, as does her brother, Chido. What type of events had characterized England during the family's stay?

The 1960s were a volatile decade in England. Teenagers had just become an identifiable market for the fashion industry and for popular music. Groups like the Beatles were achieving success with lyrics that reflected a search for new values, a drive to reject the past and reshape the world into a finer place. It was a time of optimism, of hope that life could be improved. England was replete with pop-music festivals, psychedelic drugs, protest movements, and the stirrings of a women's rights movement. "The social and cultural tone of the period, at least among some groups of the young and the well educated and particularly among the cultural avant-garde, was unconventional, anti-authority and experimental" (Williamson, p. 157). In this light, Nyasha's rebellious unconventionality in the novel becomes almost ordinary for her times and for her partly English upbringing.

In 1966 England saw the publication of *The Captive Wife,* a book by Hannah Gavron that spoke of the feeling of entrapment shared by young married women in England. "Is your wife just a bird in a plastic cage?" asked a newspaper that spoke of the book (Williamson, p. 154). Yet in England too public opinion "was still dominated . . . by the assumption that the appropriate role for women was in the home. . . . There

Cutting British ties, Ian Smith signs the Unilateral Declaration of Independence in Salisbury, Rhodesia, 1965.

may have been voices of dissent, but what [these discontented women] were dissenting about was a problem they couldn't [yet] name, ... 'a strange stirring, a sense of dissatisfaction, a yearning'; guilt, anger, loneliness, frustration, the dehumanization of women, their forfeited selves"—a description that applies as well to Tambu and her female kin in faraway Rhodesia (Oakley in Williamson, p. 185).

Second Chimurenga. Southern Rhodesia's colonial history and the dispossession of the Shona people by Europeans provide the background for the events in *Nervous Conditions*. For nine decades (1890s-1979) the Europeans remained in control of what is now Zimbabwe. Their rule began visibly to unravel during the 1960s, the first decade in which *Nervous Conditions* takes place. The War of Liberation, or the Second Chimurenga, is raging in Rhodesia at the time. Dangarembga keeps the Second Chimurenga in the background of her narrative, referring to the war vaguely only twice.

In the early 1960s the British empire began to abandon its colonial possessions in Africa, turning over power to the local African peoples. However, in Southern Rhodesia, the transfer of power did not go smoothly; white settler rule had become entrenched through decades of self-gov-

ernment. Under pressure from the global decolonization movement, a white backlash formed their own block, the Rhodesian Front (RF), and won the 1962 elections overwhelmingly, intending to prevent the transfer of power. In 1964 Ian Smith came to power as the RF's second prime minister. An ardent advocate of Rhodesia's independence under minority white rule, Smith's first official act was to consolidate white political power by detaining and banishing four black African nationalists. Riots erupted everywhere, but the police managed to suppress them, and Smith refused to discuss a new constitution that would lead to eventual black-majority rule. On November 11, 1965, Smith cut the umbilical cord to Britain, proclaiming the Unilateral Declaration of Independence (popularly known as the UDI). Although guerrilla warfare flared in 1965, it was the 1966 Battle of Sinoia (or Chinoyi) that marked the beginning of the Second Chimurenga.

Combat for the first few years amounted to little more than raids of several days. Finally, in 1972 African fighters based in Zambia and Mozambique started waging a sustained guerilla war against white Rhodesia's forces in the far north. It was not until 1976 that the war spread to other areas. So, despite the fact that it went on for more than a decade, for most of the country the war raged for only four years, in the latter half of the 1970s, just after the novel takes place. And even then, people went about their daily lives: "Historians of wars, and not just those of the ... 1960s-1980s here in Zimbabwe, sometimes underplay the point that the great majority of the population were trying to carry on the unheroic and mundane but essential task of making a living" (Beach, pp. 179-80). This task was anything but easy under the control of the whites, given laws such as the Land Apportionment Act of 1930, which had divided the territory between whites and blacks, with the latter receiving the "grey, sand soil" that was "so stony and barren that the wizards would not use it" (*Nervous Conditions*, p. 18). And the Land Apportionment Act made no provision for blacks who chose an urban life; towns were designated as white areas. Hence, blacks lived in rented homes in townships located some miles from the prosperous white cities.

The Novel in Focus

Plot summary. In *Nervous Conditions* the narrator, Tambu, tells not only her own story but also "the story of four women whom I loved, and our men" (*Nervous Conditions*, p. 204). Tambu's struggles to receive an education serve as the main plot, which unfolds in a variety of settings, separated here into three major parts, which trace Tambu's development in different locations—the rural Siguake homestead, the Umtali mission, and the Young Ladies College of the Sacred Heart.

The rural Siguake homestead. As the novel opens, Tambu describes how she got her chance to pursue her education at the Umtali mission school, where her uncle Babamukuru, the head of the Siguake family, was headmaster and Academic Director of the Church's Manicaland Region. This happened in 1968 after the death of her brother, Nhamo, who had first joined the uncle and his family to study at the mission. Following his 1965 return with his wife and two children from England, Babamukuru visited the homestead and convinced his brother, Jeremiah, to send Nhamo to the mission. Nhamo had been at the top of the class in his first two years of primary school, which excited the uncle very much. At the mission his habits and attitudes towards his nuclear family and their ancestral homestead changed drastically: he would return to his rural home only when he was forced to help with the harvest. When he did come, Nhamo bullied his sisters, Tambu and Netsai. If Netsai did not heed him, Nhamo would take a stick to her. Tambu states flatly, "I was not sorry when my brother died," but fears she is too harsh in her judgment of him (*Nervous Conditions*, p. 1). She ponders whether he was a victim of sexist ideology, which did not consider "the needs and sensibilities of the women in my family . . . a priority, or even legitimate" (*Nervous Conditions*, p. 12).

Next Tambu recalls the time before her uncle's return from England, and relates how her relationship with her brother deteriorated when he tried to stop her from attending the local school. Tambu's family wanted to send Nhamo and Tambu to school; however, the family was poor and could not afford tuition fees for both children. When Tambu complains that she loves school, her father assures her that since a woman can not cook books and feed them to her husband, she is much better off staying home and learning to cook and clean. Undaunted, Tambu decides to earn the fees herself by growing maize for sale. Her crop is nearly ripe when it begins mysteriously to disappear. When she learns that Nhamo is the guilty party, she gives him his just desserts: "I sat on top of him, banged his head

into the ground, screamed and spat and cursed" (*Nervous Conditions*, pp. 22-23). Mr. Matimba, the local teacher, breaks up the fight, and helps Tambu sell her crop in the city, where—out of pity and indignation at what she thinks of as "child labor" and "slavery"—a white woman contributes ten pounds for Tambu's school fees.

The narrative next describes Babamukuru's homecoming with his wife and children from England, and the extended family's reception of them at the ancestral Siguake homestead. Tambu captures not only the excitement of the family at the arrival of their head, but also her disappointment with her cousins, Nyasha and Chido, who speak only English and have forgotten the Shona language. Babamukuru, together with the rest of the Siguake patriarchy, decides to send Nhamo to the mission school, to help improve the miserable economic conditions on the homestead. Tambu is jealous, but concludes that Babamukuru knows better; his decision must be wise and justifiable. She recounts more of her brother's behavior changes during his three-year residence at the mission; to the pain of his mother but the delight of his father, he forgets the Shona language and becomes estranged from his nuclear family.

In November 1968 the family expects Nhamo at the homestead, but he never appears. Late that

COLONIAL EDUCATION AND ALIENATION

The way in which colonial education estranged African children from their own families and cultures has been discussed by Kenyan writer Ngugi wa Thiong'o in *Decolonizing the Mind*. Ngugi explains that imposing English as *the* language of communication caused African children to suppress their authentic selves and assimilate into a colonial identity. "Language and literature were taking us further and further from our selves to other selves, from our worlds to other worlds" (Ngugi wa Thiong'o, p. 28). Colonial education began "with a deliberate disassociation of the language of conceptualization, of thinking, of formal education, of mental development, from the language of daily interaction in the home and in the community. It is like separating the mind from the body so that they are occupying two unrelated linguistic spheres in the same person. On a large social scale it is like producing a society of bodiless heads and headless bodies" (Ngugi wa Thiong'o, p. 28).

evening Babamukuru drives up and announces that Nhamo has died after catching the mumps. Babamukuru laments the fact that there is no other male child in the family to assume Nhamo's duty, but suggests that Tambu, now 13, "be given the opportunity to do what she can for the family before she goes into her husband's home" (*Nervous Conditions*, p. 56). After some resistance from her mother, Mainini, Tambu is allowed to attend school at the mission and live in Babamukuru's modern home with her cousin Nyasha.

The Umtali mission. The second part of the novel intertwines Tambu's story with events in the lives of other characters, especially her cousin, Nyasha, her uncle's wife, Maiguru, and her Aunt Lucia. After her brother's death, Tambu

moves into her uncle's house near Umtali to attend the protestant mission school for Africans. Tambu describes her relocation in a spiritual vocabulary, describing it as an experience of reincarnation. "Babamukuru was God, therefore I had arrived in Heaven. I was in danger of becoming an angel, or at the very least a saint, and forgetting how ordinary humans existed—from minute to minute and from hand to mouth" (*Nervous Conditions*, p. 70). Trusting in Babamukuru's wisdom and thirsting for education, Tambu feels her transfer to this new place is the right step in her development. Nyasha is excited to see her cousin. Tambu, on the other hand, frowns on Nyasha's disrespectful attitude to her mother, Maiguru, whom Tambu considers "the embodiment of courtesy and good breeding" (*Nervous Conditions*, p. 74). When she knows that she will share a room with Nyasha, Tambu expresses mixed feelings. In the end, however, she comes to love Nyasha deeply.

Tambu experiences success in academics, social relations, and English language skills. But at her new home the atmosphere is less than peaceful. Tambu recounts the first crisis in the relationship between her uncle and Nyasha: Nyasha's parents object to her reading D. H. Lawrence's "indecent" novel *Lady Chatterley's Lover*, which she brings to the dining room.

A friendly, loving relationship develops between Tambu and Nyasha, who begins to disillusion Tambu about the power structures of their society and to shake Tambu's naive convictions about right and wrong. Nyasha points out the complexities of Babamukuru and Maiguru's behavior as well as those events shaping the history of Rhodesia and the world. Tambu feels sorry for Maiguru, who has made sacrifices in her academic career (she has a master's degree) to attend to her duties as a mother and wife, and who has no control over the money she earns from teaching.

The crisis between Nyasha and her father escalates, reaching a climax after the school Christmas party. On the teenagers' way home from the party, Nyasha lags behind with her brother's friend, Andy Baker, who wants to teach her a new dance. Demanding to know why his daughter is late, Babamukuru spies on her and then questions her about her tardiness, growing infuriated because she talks back to him. When he calls his daughter a "whore" and slaps her, she punches him back, at which point her father threatens to kill her, because there cannot be "two men in this house" (*Nervous Conditions*, p.

LADY CHATTERLEY'S LOVER

~

Disenchanted with much of the fiction in her day, the adolescent Nyasha in *Nervous Conditions* finds D. H. Lawrence's *Lady Chatterley's Lover* compelling, as did many young people in England around this time. When Nyasha's family is said to have arrived there in 1960, the novel—about to be released in England in its final, unexpurgated version—was the subject of a controversial obscenity trial (*Regina* v. *Penguin Books Limited*). Lady Chatterley is an Englishwoman whose husband returns from World War I paralyzed from the waist down. The sexually explicit novel describes how Lady Chatterley satisfies her desires with a gamekeeper on her husband's estate. Adults hotly disputed the propriety of the novel in the 1960s; the author's own nephew, Ernest Lawrence, pronounced it unsuitable for teenagers. Others, however, found redeeming value in the novel. At the trial Jack Walter Lambert, an editor of London's *Sunday Times,* was asked about the quality of the book—did it make him realize anything new?

Yes, naturally. One thing which it made me realise was that this [lovemaking] was a mutual process in which, shall we say, the woman had as much right to consideration as the man, that the thing was not in fact simply two people doing a certain thing as separate entities but a mutual process. He makes this very clear in the book and I do remember that this struck me very strongly at the time.

(Lambert in *The Lady Chatterley's Lover Trial*, p. 218)

Lasting for six days, the obscenity trial ended with a "not guilty" verdict, allowing Penguin Books to proceed with its release of the novel to the general public.

115). Tambu realizes then just how universal gender oppression is:

> The victimisation, I saw, was universal. It didn't depend on poverty, on lack of education or on tradition.... Men took it everywhere with them. ... You couldn't ignore the fact that [Nyasha] had no respect for Babamukuru when she ought to have had lots of it. But what I didn't like was the way all the conflicts came back to this question of femaleness. Femaleness as opposed and inferior to maleness.
>
> (*Nervous Conditions*, pp. 115-16)

After this incident, Nyasha grows isolated and detached, retreating into a private world that nobody else can reach.

Babamukuru, his family, and Tambu return to the ancestral homestead for the Christmas holiday in 1969. All the members of the extended family gather for an annual reunion, during which they hold a *dare,* a patriarchal convention about family business. This year the Siguake patriarchy has to discuss the relationship between Lucia, Tambu's maternal aunt, and Takesure, a cousin whom Babamukuru had employed to help with the farm work so that Takesure could earn the money to pay the bride-wealth for his second wife. Takesure, however, has impregnated Lucia, who shrewdly credits the baby to Jeremiah, judging him to be the better man of the two. In fact, she later got involved with him. Indignant at his brother's sinful behavior, Babamukuru ordered Takesure to leave with Lucia, but the two of them have stayed. Initially kept out of the trial-like convention with the other women and children, Lucia rushes in to confront Takesure and his lies, and to make it clear that her interest in staying was to help her sister Mainini out of the misery of her life with Jeremiah. Babamukuru settles the matter. Deciding that all this misfortune is because Jeremiah and Mainini did not have a Christian wedding, he directs them to be remarried "in church before God" (*Nervous Conditions*, p. 147).

Tambu feels that her uncle is making a mockery out of her parents' union and her own existence. She refuses to take part in the comedy of her parents' church wedding. On the morning of the wedding, her emotions leave her weak and unable to get out of bed. She risks losing everything by refusing to attend the wedding. Later, her uncle punishes her with 15 lashes and orders her to do all the housework for two weeks, during which Lucia and Maiguru give Babamukuru a piece of their own minds about family matters. Disposing of her submissive, compliant image, Maiguru explodes: "When it comes to taking my money so that you can . . . waste it on ridiculous weddings, that's when they are my relatives too. . . . I am tired of my house being a hotel for your family. I am tired of being a housekeeper for them. I am tired of being nothing in a home I am working myself sick to support" (*Nervous Conditions*, p. 172). To show Babamukuru that she is serious about what she is saying, Maiguru walks out the door. She takes refuge at her brother's house, until Babamukuru brings her home; she is now less submissive and more genuinely happy than before the emotional outburst.

The action of the novel advances quickly. Tambu is offered a scholarship to the multiracial Young Ladies College of the Sacred Heart, "a prestigious private school that manufactured guaranteed young ladies" (*Nervous Conditions*, p. 178). Believing that such schools are meant to assimilate Africans into white European culture, Nyasha is disappointed to see her cousin so thrilled about this opportunity. Babamukuru also expresses his reluctance to let Tambu go, since "it is not a good thing for a young girl to associate too much with these white people" (*Nervous Conditions*, p. 180). But Maiguru stands by Tambu's right to pursue her education, and Babamukuru relents. After some persuasion, Tambu's parents agree.

The Young Ladies College of the Sacred Heart. Babamukuru and his family drive Tambu to the multiracial convent in Salisbury (now Harare), where she is to sleep in a segregated African section. After they leave, Tambu becomes so overwhelmed with her academic studies that she does not have time to miss Nyasha and the rest of her family. Nyasha writes, complaining that she has become isolated from the girls at school, who consider her a snob and an unauthentic Shona. She feels that she needs Tambu badly: "In many ways you are very essential to me in bridging some of the gaps in my life" (*Nervous Conditions*, p. 196).

By the time they meet again, Nyasha has grown overly thin, the result of a problem that began before Tambu left for the convent. When Nyasha's father forced her to finish her food, she complied, then went into the bathroom and made herself throw up. Three months later, when Tambu comes home on another visit, Nyasha is looking skeletal. She grows weaker by the day, losing weight steadily, and studying herself into a frenzy. Her health deteriorates until she has a nervous breakdown. The next morning, the family takes her to Salisbury to see a white psychiatrist, who refuses to diagnose Nyasha as anorexic, insisting that Africans do not have such problems. A black psychiatrist, however, recognizes her suffering and puts her into a clinic. Forced to leave her cousin to improve on her own, Tambu visits her family before returning to school. There her mother attributes Nyasha's problems to "Englishness"; the ancestors, she thinks, could not "be expected to swallow so much Englishness" (*Nervous Conditions*, p. 203). The novel ends with Tambu reassuring herself and her readers that she refuses to be brainwashed and that she can no longer "accept Sacred Heart and what it represented as a sunrise on [her] horizon" (*Nervous Conditions*, p. 203).

ANOREXIA NERVOSA

In *Nervous Conditions*, Nyasha suffers from a condition that was on the rise globally among teenagers in the 1960s and 1970s. A dangerous disease that afflicts primarily adolescent females, anorexia nervosa causes people to starve themselves, even to the point of death. The affliction surfaced with increasing frequency in England, among other places, and it showed "a substantial prevalence among the Caucasian population in South Africa," Rhodesia's African neighbor (Gordon, p. 36). Books like Hilde Bruch's *Eating Disorders* (1973) called attention to the psychological and political dimensions of the disease. The female victim was asserting the right to control her own body—while conforming to cultural standards of beauty. In Nyasha's case, these standards were those that prevailed in England during and after her stay. In 1966 the female model Twiggy, with her sticklike figure, became all the rage in England; within a decade, anorexia was afflicting about 1 in 100 girls in English secondary schools (Gordon, p. 38). It is during this decade that the fictional Nyasha succumbs to anorexia, struggling to exercise control over her own life in a society that demands conformity to ways that she literally cannot stomach. The disease is characterized, writes Bruch, by "an all-pervasive sense of ineffectiveness, a feeling that one's actions, thoughts, and feelings do not actively originate within the self but rather are passive reflections of external expectations and demands" (Bruch in Gordon, p. 15). Its victims feel trapped, like they are not in control of their destiny, a nervous condition that troubles Nyasha in the novel.

Nationalism and feminism. In *Nervous Conditions*, Tambu's mother, Mainini, acknowledges that "[t]his business of womanhood is a heavy burden" (*Nervous Conditions*, p. 16). Certainly Mainini is a victim of Shona beliefs and sexist practices. Less obvious but also embedded in the novel is the idea that African tradition and European colonialism were complicit in the subordination of women. When Tambu takes her qualifying exam for Sacred Heart College, the nuns test her on Louisa May Alcott's *Little Women*. Set across the globe in New England a hundred years earlier, this novel follows four daughters and their prospects for marriages that will lift them out of poverty. The emphasis, endorsed by the colonial test givers, is on the young woman as prospective wife. Actually one of the four daughters, Jo, chafes under the limitations placed on women in her society and longs for the freedom enjoyed by men, but this does not keep her marriage too from being featured in Alcott's novel. Directly and indirectly, *Nervous Conditions* brings the joint sexism of traditional and colonial attitudes to the forefront .

Other African coming-of-age novels (or *bildungsromans*) focus on the colonial education of the heroes and heroines and the ethical choices they make growing up in changing societies. In a number of these novels, the protagonists struggle with the alienation they experience from their cultures because of colonial education. (See Mongo Beti's **Mission to Kala,** also covered in *African Literature and Its Times*). Such novels, points out one scholar, concern more than the individual experience; they are often about "the postcolonial culture affirming its own identity as well as about individuals achieving independence and a sense of self" (Fister, p. 37). *Nervous Conditions*, however, is not a conventional postcolonial novel; the novel is better seen as a revisionist bildungsroman. Although it shows how colonial education pulled African children away from their roots and cultures, it also depicts how local patriarchal society worked hand-in-hand with colonialism to repress Shona women. In other words, the novel refuses to celebrate native culture as long as it subordinates or sanctions the colonial subordination of women.

In Africa, especially in the period of decolonization and independence, writers—including feminist writers—were encouraged to write about the liberation of African societies from colonial rule. A popular belief was that feminists ought to pledge their primary allegiance to the nation and its traditions. Affirming the potency of African cultures and negating the colonial stereotypes about Africans were deemed more important than posing difficult questions about gender relations. Feminist writers thus found themselves faced with a difficult dilemma: how could they praise African traditions and nationalist groups that made women second-class citizens? Along with other writers, Dangarembga responded through fiction that refused to condemn colonial exploitation alone for women's miserable lot or to celebrate the national struggle as a step forward in the emancipation of the whole society.

Sources and literary context. After the publication in 1966 of Flora Nwapa's *Efuru* (also covered in *African Literature and Its Times*), the bildungsroman, or novel of development, became a popular genre among female African writers, whose works began to enjoy widespread acceptance only in the 1970s. Many novels were written about the dawning self-awareness and personal growth of African women at various ages, the mature Efuru and the adolescent Tambu being two examples.

The very existence of the genre in African letters was revolutionary in that it introduced women as active, dynamic agents of their own lives rather than as passive background characters or companions to male protagonists. How much such novels reflect reality and how much they are meant to affect reality by the ideas they convey remains an open question:

> Many [women] . . . have confessed that they are motivated to write by the impulse to change the status quo. . . . This is closely related to the desire to liberate African women, change their consciousness and recreate a positive self-perception. . . . Consequently, many have recreated women in their literature as agencies . . . of active socio-political change.
>
> (Kolawole, p. 153)

Nervous Conditions is credited with helping to restructure the nature of African heroines by presenting women who face down tradition and force change in society. Tambu defies her father by acquiring an education and her uncle by refusing to attend her parents' Christian wedding; her cousin Nyasha goes so far as to hit her father; and the girls' mothers, Mainini and Maiguru, though entrapped, voice their suffering and opinions.

Events in History at the Time the Novel Was Written

Women's rights in Zimbabwe. After the initiation of black majority rule in 1980, the Zimbab-

wean government recognized the vital contribution that women had made in the national liberation war and promised to support their emancipation.

Nervous Conditions

FRANTZ FANON

The title and epigraph of *Nervous Conditions* are drawn from Frantz Fanon's ***The Wretched of the Earth*** (also covered in *African Literature and Its Times*). "The status of the 'native'," says Jean-Paul Sartre in his preface to this set of essays, "is a nervous condition introduced and maintained by the settler among colonized people *with their consent*" (Sartre in Fanon, p. 20). The colonized, who envy colonial privilege, dream of substituting themselves for the colonizer and adopting his system of values, in the process adopting a conception of themselves as inferior, which creates a permanent tension, a nervous condition. Fanon himself explains that afraid of being punished by colonial authorities for unintentionally trespassing rules, the colonized are fearful, always on the alert. This fear, combined with Babamukuru's share of Shona authoritarianism, helps explain his fierce reactions to his daughter's unconventional behavior in the novel.

Zimbabwe proceeded to pass new laws on behalf of the female population. In 1982 the Legal Age of Majority Act gave women the status of legal major instead of legal minor, their classification under customary laws written down in the colonial period. The government instituted free primary education for everyone, regardless of gender or race. By 1984 girls alone comprised almost half the total primary school enrollment and about a third of the secondary level enrollment (*Tabex Encyclopedia Zimbabwe*, p. 409). In the work force, the Labour Relations Act (1984) prohibited gender discrimination and guaranteed new mothers three months maternity leave. Within the family, the Matrimonial Causes Act of 1985 made women beneficiaries of property that was accumulated during marriage, and children no longer automatically were awarded to the father in case of a divorce. Still, society regarded men as the main breadwinners, and a man's need for a job took priority over a woman's, even though women now comprised 51 percent of the country's population. Passing new laws was one hurdle; implementing them was another, and the persistence of old attitudes

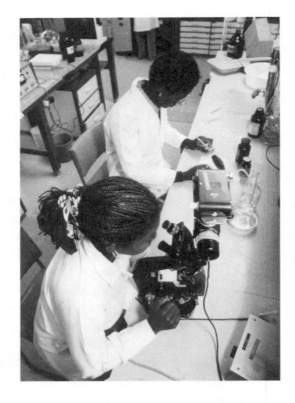

Educational opportunities for women increased after the Second Chimurenga, or War of Liberation.

militated against rapid implementation, as did the daily struggle for survival. In the end, like the women (and men) in *Nervous Conditions,* much of late 1980s society would continue to live off employed relatives.

> Harare offers the most dramatic illustration of change in [the twentieth] century: within 30 km are . . . [Shona] villages with what look like traditional homesteads, whose owners still sometimes practise polygamy . . . while at the centre are shopping malls, computerized banks and traffic jams. Yet, alongside all the urban glitter are thousands of unemployed living off their employed relatives. . . .
>
> (Beach, p. 189)

Reviews. Tsitsi Dangarembga's *Nervous Conditions,* written when she was 25, received international acclaim and won the African section of the Commonwealth Writers Prize in August 1989. The African American novelist Alice Walker commended the novel as having a new voice that spoke with such self-assurance that at times it sounded very old. Stella Dadzie called *Nervous Conditions* "compelling and unpretentious," identifying its strength as "Dangarembga's sensitivity to the lived reality of her people, providing her with a finely tuned gauge with which to measure their relative strengths and weaknesses" (Dadzie, pp. 374-75). Charlotte Bruner, reviewing the novel for *World Literature Today,* wrote that Dangarembga's "excellent style and power of characterization make the book outstanding" (Bruner, p. 354). More than a decade after its publication, *Nervous Conditions* continues to generate vigorous discussion about the female condition, colonialism, nationalism, and feminism in contemporary Africa.

—Jamil Khader

THE CONTRIBUTION OF ZIMBABWEAN WOMEN TO LIBERATION

~

Women played a major role in the national struggle for liberation, or Second Chimurenga, which altogether claimed an estimated 30,000 lives (Beach, p. 182). The young and the childless were recruited as combatants and freedom fighters. Dressed in fatigues, they were nearly indistinguishable from their male comrades. They provided traditional services too, like preparing the food and clothing that the freedom fighters needed for survival. Like other war heroes, these female combatants were honored by public memorials that pay tribute to their patriotism, courage, and love of freedom. However, the national monuments portrayed the male freedom fighters in trousers but the women wearing skirts, an indication perhaps that the struggle for women's rights after independence would, to some degree, be an uphill battle.

For More Information

Beach, David. *The Shona and Their Neighbours.* Oxford: Blackwell, 1994.

Bruner, Charlotte H. Review of *Nervous Conditions,* by Tsitsi Dangarembga. *World Literature Today* 64, no. 2 (spring 1990): 353-54.

Dadzie, Stella. Review of *Nervous Conditions,* by Tsitsi Dangarembga. *Journal of Southern African Studies* 16, no. 2 (June 1990): 374-76.

Dangarembga, Tsitsi. *Nervous Conditions.* London: The Women's Press, 1988.

Fanon, Frantz. *The Wretched of the Earth.* New York: Grove, 1968.

Fister, Barbara. *Third World Women's Literatures: A Dictionary and Guide to Materials.* Westport, Conn.: Greenwood Press, 1995.

Gordon, Richard A. *Anorexia and Bulima: Anatomy of a Social Epidemic.* Oxford: Blackwell, 1990.

Kolawole, Mary E. Modupe. *Womanism and African Consciousness.* Trenton, N.J.: Africa World Press, 1997.

The Lady Chatterley's Lover Trial. London: The Bodley Head, 1990.

Ngugi wa Thiong'o. *Decolonizing the Mind: The Politics of Language in African Literature.* London: James Curry, 1986.

Schmidt, Elizabeth. *Peasants, Traders, and Wives: Shona Women in the History of Zimbabwe, 1870-1939.* Portsmouth, N.H.: Heinemann, 1992.

Tabex Encyclopedia Zimbabwe. Harare: Quest, 1987.

Williamson, Bill. *The Temper of the Times: British Society Since World War II.* Oxford: Basil Blackwell, 1990.

The Oil Man
of Obange

by

John Munonye

⌁

John Munonye was born in 1929 in Akokwa, Imo State, Nigeria. Like most young boys in the region, he was raised as the son of a farmer. But unlike his father, Munonye attended Christian schools and received a Western education. The experience of negotiating the cultural, psychological, and ideological differences between the Western and traditional Igbo worlds forms the backdrop of four of his novels: *The Only Son* (1966), *Obi* (1969), *The Oil Man of Obange* (1971), and *Bridge to a Wedding* (1978). In his own life, Munonye confronted the ideological conflict inherent in attempting to follow traditional beliefs while receiving a Western education. Educated first at Christ the King College in Onitsha and the University of Ibadan, Munonye later earned a Masters in Education at the University of London's Institute of Education. He spent much of his professional career in the service of Nigerian education, as a teacher (1954-57), an administrator and school inspector (1958-70), and in the Ministry of Education of Eastern Nigeria as principal of the Advanced Teachers College (1970-73). In keeping with his professional posts, he wrote firmly in support of Western education. In *The Oil Man of Obange*, Munonye tells the story a palm-oil seller who literally works himself to death to earn enough to pay the school fees for his six children.

Events in History at the Time the Novel Takes Place

The Igbo family. The Igbo occupy the south-eastern region of Nigeria in a territory bisected

THE LITERARY WORK

A novel set in Igboland, eastern Nigeria, circa 1945; published in English in 1971.

SYNOPSIS

A palm-oil seller sacrifices everything so his children can receive Western education.

by the Niger River, a major artery of trade in pre-colonial times. One of the most densely populated regions of Nigeria, Igboland is characterized by thousands of small villages, interconnected by familial and political alliances. The absence of a centralized authority during the colonial era gave rise to competition among villages, particularly in the realm of education. Outsiders describe the Igbo as highly democratic and adaptive to Western ways, while the average Nigerian speaks of them as hardworking and acquisitive. Indeed, say Igbo scholars, their society places high value on hard work, wealth, and success—accomplished through legitimate means.

The family remains the most important unit of socialization in Igboland. Its significance cannot be overstated. "Family" in this context refers to the extended family, including cousins, aunts, uncles, co-wives, and siblings. Polygyny, the practice of marrying more than one wife, is common in Igboland, as is the large family. Part of the "big compound" ideal, the large family has traditionally been a sign of prosperity and status; it has, however, gone through considerable permutations as a result of Christian influence. As more and more Igbo families have aligned their beliefs with Christianity and its attendant principle of monogamy, the "big compound" ideal has changed. In addition to choosing monogamy, many newly Christian couples are electing to have fewer children.

In Igbo culture marriage is viewed as a joining of two families, and it is expected that the union will produce offspring. Parenthood is revered and ushers an adult into a new status in Igbo society, since parents contribute heirs to the lineage. Children are the bridge to the future; their existence insures the survival of the family line and the future security of the parents. In Igboland, as in other parts of Nigeria, parents are expected to do their best for their children. By the same token, children are expected to take care of their parents when the parents grow elderly.

Land tenure in precolonial Igboland. Land was an extremely valuable asset in precolonial Igboland. A degree of private ownership existed among the traditional Igbo, but in most cases, territory was held communally, with the lineage owning a stretch of land. Technically no member of the lineage was without land; in reality, who had the right to control the land was often a basis for dispute. Munonye dramatizes this point by beginning his novel with a land dispute. After a vicious battle for the land, his protagonist renounces his claim to the ancestral holding, allowing other family members to keep it.

Land held such high importance largely because it was the basis for wealth. In precolonial times most Igbo were subsistence farmers, which meant that land was a source of security. The belief was that a people could not have too much of it. Yams were the staple crop, and although the farmers engaged in trade, most concentrated first on producing enough to feed their families. Before the discovery of petroleum in Nigeria in 1956, agricultural products were also the main source of national revenue. Trading in agricultural products, such as palm oil, could therefore be lucrative—albeit uncertain, because of factors such as price fluctuations, unpredictable soil fertility, and changes in the weather.

British colonial rule. Formal colonization of present-day Nigeria by the British occurred in the last quarter of the nineteenth century. In 1914 the British extended their control over all of Nigeria, amalgamating the southern and the northern territories into one protectorate. But "it was not until 1928, when Igbo men were made to pay

tax for the first time in their history, that it became clear to them that they were a subject people" (Uchendu, p. 4).

With the amalgamation of Nigeria, the protectorate's governor, Sir Frederick Lugard, instituted in southeastern Nigeria the policy of "indirect rule," by which the colonial officials would govern through local African authorities. However, because of the democratic tradition of governance in much of Igboland, there was no established tradition of chiefs or kings with supreme power over their subjects. Instead, the local ruling structures varied from place to place. Some Igbo villages were ruled by village councils, while others had chiefs. But even those who were regarded as chiefs did not have absolute authority. Underlying the various arrangements was a basic egalitarian ideal that anyone could rise to the top.

Because of these varied and less than hierarchical political structures, British colonial officials had difficulty figuring out how to rule Igboland indirectly. In fact, indirect rule worked best outside Igboland, in Northern Nigeria, where a hierarchical system of control was already in place. Colonial authorities in Igboland went through a great deal of effort to set up a system of warrant chiefs, creating the institution of chieftaincy in areas that did not have this tradition. However, because they did not understand traditional Igbo governing structures, they often vested authority in people who had no standing in the community.

The colonial economy. Extensive trading networks existed among the Igbo before contact with Europeans, particularly in the Niger Delta, which was a major crossroads of trade. Nigeria experienced several stages of forcible integration into the world economy, first because of the slave trade. Nigeria's manpower was undermined by its participation in this trade, even if some groups, like the Aro (an Igbo people), profited in the short run. Despite the slave trade, the bulk of the goods exchanged at the time were raw materials, and most people were subsistence farmers.

The implementation of colonial rule forced a change in tune with British needs. British colonialism aimed to create new markets for manufactured goods and to ensure monopoly control of the raw materials coming from its colonies. At least two types of economy developed in Nigeria—one in which people continued to concentrate on subsistence agriculture, and another in which people produced or traded goods for the international markets. In this second economy, existing trade networks expanded and European currencies grew in importance. Western education became a valued commodity too, since there was a demand for Western-educated Nigerians to work as civil servants and clerks in British firms. Among Nigeria's commodities for international trade were petroleum and palm oil. Discovered in 1956—primarily in the eastern region, where the majority of Igbos live—petroleum would surpass agriculture as the main source of revenue in the economy by the early 1970s. At the time of the novel, though, agriculture still dominated.

The trade in palm oil. Palm trees were common in eastern and western Nigeria. Harvesters would cut the palm fruits from under the leaves, then press the fruits to release the oil and the kernels. The kernels were themselves later crushed to release further oil, although much was lost using this method. Several parts of the palm plant became trade items. The leaves could be used to make mats, baskets, and other woven items. Tapped from the palm tree, palm wine was a common beverage in Nigeria, and its people used palm oil to cook soups and stews. In Europe, palm oil was in demand to make soaps, candles, and lubricants for industrial machinery.

Much of the trade for the international market was conducted by Nigerian middlemen at the coast, who purchased oil from smaller-scale traders further inland. Small traders, such as Munonye's "oil man," would buy the oil from its source or from another trader and then transport it to larger markets to sell to the middlemen. In Munyone's novel, Jeri brings his oil to the market in tins attached to his bicycle. In the big towns and cities where he trades, the middlemen buy his oil, then store it in large barrels.

To protect producers from the fluctuation of prices on the world market, the colonial government created marketing boards that were supposed to buy the products from the producer at a fixed rate and invest the proceeds, thus protecting the economy in the event of a downturn in world prices. But the boards proved only moderately successful, leaving producers vulnerable to price fluctuations.

The development of Western education. Western education came to Nigeria by way of Christian missionaries in the nineteenth century. Initially the response to missionary activity was lukewarm; people regarded it with suspicion, many of them failing to see much value in West-

Market vendors sell palm oil in Nigeria.

ern education at first. In general, the missionaries posted to Nigeria concentrated their efforts almost exclusively on convincing the local chiefs and rulers to send their children to school. They hoped that others would become interested in Western education because they wanted to follow the lead of the rulers. In Igboland the missionaries were forced to adopt a somewhat dif-

---

PALM-OIL PRODUCTION

The production of palm oil was a tedious, time-consuming process. There were two methods to process palm oil, the soft-oil press and the hard-oil press. In the soft-oil press, kernels were boiled in water until tender. Next, men pounded the kernels in a mortar, after which women and children separated the nuts from the fibers. The fibers were then pressed over heated pieces of stone to stimulate the flow of oil. In the hard-oil method, people pounded the nut without boiling it. Next they poured water over the pulp and skimmed off the resultant oil. Workers recovered about 50 percent of the oil using the soft-press method, and 55 to 60 percent using the hard-press method. Even though less oil was produced by the soft-press method, people generally preferred it because this method yielded better cooking oil.

ferent strategy; since many areas did not have an established institution of chieftancy, they could not endeavor to simply convert the chiefs. Their first successes here were with the poor and with people considered to be social outcasts. As in other areas, gradually the Igbo became more receptive as they began to realize that reading, writing, and speaking English gave them more opportunities in the expanding economy.

WORLD WAR II AND THE PALM-OIL TRADE

The Oil Man of Obange takes place during the final year of World War II, which affected colonial subjects in different ways. On the one hand, taxes were increased in order to help Britain pay for the war effort. On the other hand, producers of palm products benefited from wartime boosts in the demand for their oil. The following song from the novel was composed by young Nigerian men operating a palm-oil press:

> Thanks be to Hitler
> Thanks to him
> He caused the great war
> Thanks to him
> Since that very great war
> Oil's been selling well
> Thanks to him
> Thanks be to him
> But may his type never
> Thanks to him
> Step into our land
> Thanks to him

(*Oil Man of Obange*, p. 113)

The first Protestant missions appeared in Igboland in the mid-to-late 1800s, followed by the Roman Catholic missions. Encouraging the spread of Western education was a source of rivalry between the Catholic and Protestant missions, both of which sought the most converts. Another rivalry encouraging education was the competition between villages. Coupled with the high value Igbo parents placed on children, these rivalries resulted in an early-twentieth-century explosion of Igbo interest in education.

With the expansion of Western multinational corporations into Nigeria and increased migration to cities, more people began to desire Western education to gain access to jobs. As people gained education, expectations rose for commensurate employment opportunities and salaries. Igbos who migrated to cities realized that they were at a disadvantage when competing with Yoruba job seekers (the Yoruba being another Nigerian people), who had received Western education sooner than the Igbo and thus received the best job offers. Whatever the ethnic group, colonial officers discriminated against blacks: educated Nigerians did not receive the same opportunity for advancement or the same salary and living conditions as their British counterparts, who often had less education and experience. Resentment festered among the educated black elite, who would become the vanguard in the struggle for national independence (achieved in 1960).

The introduction of Western education into eastern Nigeria ushered in new ways of understanding the world. Since education was initially tied to Christian conversion, becoming Western-educated meant renouncing (at least superficially) the traditional religion. Many missionaries believed that a society's path to conversion was through its children, which meant that an entire generation of Igbos was being raised with an ideological outlook that differed from that of their parents. It is hardly surprising, then, that not everyone in a village gladly accepted the prospect of Western education for their children. Others, however, became pioneers, doing everything that they could so that their children might receive a Western education. The protagonist of *The Oil Man of Obange* is one such pioneer.

The Novel in Focus

Plot summary. *The Oil Man of Obange* begins at the deathbed of Ogazi Oko. A land dispute involving one branch of Oko's family has resulted in both branches resorting to witchcraft, poisons, and trickery. Gradually every man in his family is killed in the feud, except for Ogazi Oko, who is wasting away because of some incurable disease. His salvation comes in the form of a priest who baptizes him, changes his name to Jeremiah, and gives him something to drink that cures his illness. Upon recovery, Jeri decides to end the dispute. He gives up the family land, buries the family idols, converts to Christianity, and moves to another area. His only surviving sister, Onugo, is convinced he has gone mad. After several attempts to harvest yams on his new land, Jeri decides that instead of farming, he will earn his living selling palm oil. He sells off his remaining yam harvest and with the proceeds buys a bicycle and oil tins. These actions shock his extended family and neighbors. Why would a man want to sell palm oil when farming is his way of life?

Jeri approaches his new occupation, the oil trade, with determination. Each morning he rises before dawn, dons a tattered shirt and threadbare shorts, and mounts his creaking bicycle in search of palm oil. After filling his tins with oil, he rides several miles to sell the oil to the middlemen stationed in the larger towns. Despite extreme hardship and poverty, he insists that each of his six children, including his daughter, will be educated in Western schools. His entire purpose in life is to earn enough money to subsist and to pay for his children's school fees. In contrast to other parts of Igboland, whose inhabitants have begun to see the need for their children to be educated, Jeri's neighbors cannot understand why he works so hard to educate all of his children. His decision to educate his daughter causes particular consternation.

Still, the neighbors and family are impressed with how intelligent Jeri's children are. Jeri envisions the future prestige of his children, believing that they will grow up "wise in the new way of life—the way of educated men, prosperous, well-known, highly regarded" (Munonye, *The Oil Man of Obange*, p. 119). This vision drives him.

Despite poverty and the difficult circumstances that come with being pioneers, his family is happy. His wife, Marcellina, supports the family's endeavors, caring for the children and encouraging her husband. It is a strong marriage—they "behaved towards each other like brother and sister—one heart, one mind and one will in nearly everything" (*Oil Man*, p. 21). Jeri needs her support since there are many things he has no time to do for his family, a fact made apparent by the decaying compound walls and the rotted door of their home, already half-eaten by termites.

Repeatedly Jeri must defend his decisions to his extended family. The voice of tradition emanates loudly from his sister, Onugo. On each visit to the family home, she implores her brother to return to the farming life and is most disturbed when she realizes Jeri's determination to keep his daughter in school. "She had warned them many times now to stop sending the girl to school. One could perhaps overlook the case of the boys, but not a girl, who had to be watched from her earliest years, and should spend most of her time assisting her mother and in turn getting used to family chores and routine" (*Oil Man*, p. 28). Onugo believes that Jeri and his wife are mad for continuing on this course.

These criticisms are minor irritations for Jeri, who is determined to achieve success for the sake of his children. Hard work and stubborn resolve take him only so far, however. Selling palm oil is a career marked with calamities. He is injured in several falls and is often forced to travel through Ukeleke, "the land of strange people and strange happenings!" (*Oil Man*, p. 9). Jeri always approaches Ukeleke with a sense of foreboding. Ukeleke is unpredictable. It poses the threats of armed robbery and of people who are not to be trusted. Obange is a small village compared to Ukeleke, a fictional place that dramatizes how Jeri's trading efforts take him through treacherous terrain.

Each fall from his bicycle highlights Jeri's vulnerability to circumstances beyond his control. An unexpected rut in the road is all that it takes to pitch him from his bicycle and spill his oil for the day. One fall leaves him with a fractured arm and unable to trade for a while. Because of the dangers of potential injury or theft, Jeri takes extreme care when he sets out to trade. Unpredictable income will not do for a man who must have enough money to pay school fees for all his children.

The tragic death of Marcellina initiates the downward spiral of the family. Marcellina dies of tetanus after cutting her leg with a machete, and a local healer cannot save her. Both the treatment and the costs associated with the funeral are borne by the family. After a brief period of mourning, Jeri must continue the trade. His daughter, Celia, leaves school in order to care for the family.

Shortly after resuming work, Jeri is injured in an accident that damages his bicycle. Because of the cost of the funeral expenses and the continued cost of school fees, Jeri does not have enough money to pay Ogonabo, the greedy and dishonest bicycle repairer, for fixing his bicycle. In lieu of payment, Jeri allows Ogonabo to farm on his only remaining parcel of land for one season, until Jeri can pay for the repairs.

A short time later, Jeri is seriously injured in another accident, which this time destroys the bicycle. His leg is broken and, when a local healer is unable to alleviate his pain, he turns to a Western-trained medical doctor. He has a lengthy stay in a Western hospital, suffering terrible pain and depression. He gains the strength to go on only when he learns that his children are hungry. His children are forced to begin working after school: one son sells palm kernels; another son goes to live with a teacher to serve as his houseboy. At each juncture of failure and frustration, Jeri's sister appears to beg, cajole, and threaten him in her attempts to get him to return to the family land.

The children are saved by the intervention of Onugo, who brings them yams and looks after them. After Jeri's return from the hospital, she again encourages him to return to farming, and to fight the other relatives for the family land, something he still refuses to do. He ransoms his remaining land to Ogonabo to borrow a new bicycle from him.

In all of his tribulations, Jeri's honesty, dignity, and determination remain paramount. Even when he is clearly cheated by men he considers to be friends, Jeri makes no effort to avenge the injustice. He remains unflagging in his determination that his children will have a different life.

When it is time for the two youngest children to go to school, Jeri still does whatever he can to send them there. He is rewarded by his children's academic performance. His son Mica is one of only three students to pass his examinations with distinction and has an opportunity to enter the prestigious College of the Blessed Trinity (C.B.T.), a place where the "boys moved with an arrogant confidence . . . their handkerchiefs stuck out from their trouser pockets; and they spoke English all the time" (*Oil Man*, p. 187). Mica, who has inherited his father's determination, studies doggedly for an arduous examination and is accepted to C.B.T. News of his success spreads throughout the town, filling others with admiration and Jeri with great pride.

Unfortunately, the school fees and related expenses are exorbitant. It is clear that this school is a ticket to the boy's future success, beyond even the wildest dreams of his father. The sacrifice that must be made in order to pay the fees, however, is great. At first, Jeri decides not to send the boy to the secondary school. With a primary school degree, Mica could become a teacher and earn a satisfactory salary. But Mica grows despondent at the news that he will not be able to attend the school. Witnessing his son's despair, Jeri agrees to try to raise the money. He redoubles his efforts to trade. Fortunately the palm-oil trade is beginning to experience a great boom. Things are finally improving for him, and his only fear is that political unrest will cause the District Officer to close down the trade. While

riding to different towns to trade his oil, he hears talk by agitators who argue that the District Officer has not benefited the people. But Jeri has his own concerns and shows little interest in politics as long as it does not affect the trade.

On the return from one of his most lucrative trading trips, Jeri is tricked by thieves and robbed of all of his money and his borrowed bicycle. The ransomed land is gone forever, as are the school fees for his children. The indignity is devastating. So distraught is Jeri that he considers suicide. By the time he returns to his village, he has gone completely mad. Shortly thereafter, he dies in his sister's arms. The story ends with neighbors and family members talking about what really killed Jeremiah Ogazi Oko. Was it love for his children? Did he do too much for them? Is the love of the Igbo parent too self-sacrificing?

> But should this not be a lesson for the living and sane? Was it fair that a man should practically destroy himself in the interest of his offspring? In his efforts to bring up his children? Must child-rearing mean self-effacement?
>
> (*Oil Man*, p. 238)

The struggle to educate girls. Jeri has only one daughter, Celia, whose story illuminates prevalent attitudes at the time towards the education of girls. The narrator makes much of the fact that Celia is a very smart girl—in many ways, smarter than her brothers. Her parents recognize this fact, and it enables them to ignore Jeri's sister, Onugo, when she complains about their sending their daughter to school.

One incident, however, highlights the circumstances under which many Igbo girls ended up dropping out of school. Realizing that they may not have enough money to pay for school fees and books, Jeri and Marcellina decide that Celia should be the one to stop attending. Despite the fact that girls did not have to pay fees at this time because there were so few of them in school, Jeri still reasons that he will save money by not having to buy her books and clothes. When Celia is told of his decision to take her out of school, she becomes extremely distraught:

> Celia wept aloud and openly. The day was Saturday. They thought her sorrow would be spent before the sun would begin to set. But the following day she continued to weep. She wept on her way to church and on her way back. And when she went to bed at night she resumed weeping.
>
> (*Oil Man*, p. 42)

Celia's despair quickly touches her father and after three days, he relents, telling her, "Don't cry yourself to death, my daughter. I will do my best to see that you—all of you—continue at school" (*Oil Man*, p. 43).

Jeri's attitude towards educating his daughter was not common in Igboland during the time when the novel takes place. In fact, many parents were adamantly opposed to sending girls to school. Because of this, girls lagged behind boys in Nigerian education. In the early 1950s girls made up only 21 percent of the primary school population (UNESCO, p. 18). Between 1960 and 1972 their numbers increased but still remained less than 40 percent of the total primary school enrollment (*Women in Nigeria Today*, p. 150). There were societal reasons for the lag. While parents might view the education of a male child as an investment, they did not always see the value in educating a girl. It was expected that a girl would eventually marry and leave the household; as for the present, she was often needed around the home to perform domestic duties. Also, many parents desired to keep a close watch on their daughters for the sake of their chastity. They feared that going to school would expose the girls to unscrupulous men and that the girls would run the risk of becoming pregnant.

Jeri, then, is a pioneer in deciding that his daughter will receive Western education and agreeing to see to it that she can continue to attend. Even with such a progressive father, Celia is the first to be taken out of school in a crisis. After Marcellina dies, Celia effectively becomes the mother of the house. In spite of her previous resistance to leaving school, she voluntarily remains home to care for her youngest siblings, who are not yet ready to be left alone.

Sources and literary context. *The Oil Man of Obange* dramatizes the struggle of the common man to achieve success in colonial Nigera. Although Obange is a fictional location, Munonye makes it clear that Jeri is a typical character, modeled after many hardworking individuals in Igboland. In a 1973 interview Munonye stated, "There are plenty of men like him who have sacrificed themselves to bring us up, though not all have had stories as sad as his. He is a typical man, a common man in our society." (Munonye in Lindfors, p. 37) What is common about Jeri in Igbo society is his determination to succeed in the face of seemingly insurmountable odds.

In the 1950s Munonye began a lifelong career in the service of Nigerian education, serving first as a teacher, then later as an administrator and

In the twentieth century the Igbo made education a priority. By 1971 primary education had become partly free in their homeland in eastern Nigeria.

principal. He began to write while working for the Ministry of Education because he "didn't feel that the civil service set-up provided enough scope for self-realization" (Munonye in Lindfors, p. 35). He was a close friend of Chinua Achebe (see **Things Fall Apart,** also covered in *African Literature and Its Times*), and Achebe's success encouraged him as a writer. Along with Achebe, Wole Soyinka (see **Death and the King's Horseman,** also covered in *African Literature and Its Times*), and Chukwuemeka Ike, Munonye is part of the "first generation" of Nigerian writers to publish their initial literary works after Nigeria gained independence in 1960. In the 1970s Munonye retired from his career in education to concentrate on his writing. Munonye's final post was as writer-in-residence at Alvan Ikoku College of Education in Owerri, Eastern Nigeria. He died in 1999.

Events in History at the Time the Novel Was Written

Nigeria in the 1970s. *The Oil Man of Obange* was published in 1971. By this time, the resistance to education expressed by many of Jeri's neighbors in the novel had been eradicated. Changes in the Nigerian economy had shown the Igbo the importance of Western education in gaining a competitive edge in Nigerian society. As a result more Igbo parents were sending their children to school.

In the 1950s both the eastern and western regions of Nigeria embarked on massive educational expansion programs with the goal of providing free primary education. "By 1960 each region was devoting over 40 percent of its annual recurrent expenditure to education" (Abernethy, p. 19). By 1971 primary education had become free in the city of Lagos, and in the midwestern and western states; it had become partly free in the eastern states (*Nigeria Year Book*, p. 153). The North, however, lagged behind these regions.

Although petroleum surpassed palm oil as Nigeria's largest export, palm-oil production remained important. In 1971 Nigeria provided 50 percent of the world's trade in palm kernels and over 50 percent in palm oil, its eastern states providing the bulk of the palm oil (*Nigeria Year Book*, p. 127). Nigeria would remain the world's dominant producer of palm oil until it was surpassed by Malaysia in 1977. However, by the early 1970s, when the novel appeared, the focus on agricultural products as a source of wealth among the Igbo had changed. Migration to cities meant that many Igbo no longer relied on farming for their livelihood, preferring wage labor instead. There was still a strong commitment to village life, though. In 1971 many parents continued to believe that the village was the best place for their children to be raised.

Reviews. *The Oil Man of Obange* was described by one critic as a novel "in a class by itself" and a book with the makings of a classic; this same reviewer lamented that Munonye has not received more critical acclaim, declaring that the "critics are determined to ignore him" (Nnolim, p. 164). According to another reviewer, Munonye has been favorably compared to, but most likely overshadowed by, his friend and countryman Chinua Achebe (Carter in Nnolim,

p. 164). His protagonist, Jeri Oko, is described as

An enduring Igbo cultural/mythic hero who is both an antithesis to, and a complement of, Chinua Achebe's Okonkwo [the protagonist of *Things Fall Apart*]. Achebe's hero is a symbol of initial Igbo resistance—to colonial change by uncompromising defenders of the integrity of the indigenous society and its values. Munonye's hero is a symbol of later Igbo adjustment to that change.

(Iloeje, pp. 95-96)
—Mary Dillard

For More Information

Abernethy, David B. *The Political Dilemma of Popular Education: An African Case*. Palo Alto, Calif.: Stanford University Press, 1969.

Acholonu, Rose. *Family Love in Nigerian Fiction: Feminist Perspectives*. Owerri: Achisons, 1995.

Iloeje, Azubike. "Defection, Martyrdom and the Vindicated Hero in John Munonye's *The Oil Man of Obange*." *The Literary Half-Yearly* 34, no. 1 (January 1993): 83-97.

Lindfors, Bernth. *Dem-Say: Interviews with Eight Nigerian Authors*. Austin, Texas: African and Afro-American Studies and Research Center, 1974.

Munonye, John. *The Oil Man of Obange*. London: Heinemann, 1971.

Nigeria Year Book. Apapa: Daily Times of Nigeria, 1971.

Njoku, John E. Eberegbulam. *The Igbos of Nigeria: Ancient Rites, Changes and Survival*. Lewiston, N.Y.: Edwin Mellen, 1990.

Nnolim, Charles E. "Structure and Theme in Munonye's *The Oil Man of Obange*." *African Literature Today* 12 (1982): 163-73.

Okigbo, P.N.C. *Towards a Reconstruction of the Political Economy of Igbo Civilization*. Ahiajoku Lectures. Owerri, Nigeria: Ministry of Information, 1986.

Uchendu, Victor. *The Igbo of Southeast Nigeria*. Orlando: Holt, Rinehart, and Winston, 1965.

UNESCO. *Basic Facts and Figures*. Paris: United Nations Educational, Scientific and Cultural Organization, 1952.

Women in Nigeria Today. London: Zed, 1985.

Out of Africa

by
Isak Dinesen

In 1913 Karen Dinesen left her home in Denmark and boarded a steamer to East Africa, where she would marry her second cousin, Bror Blixen, and embark on a new life. She and Bror settled among the European aristocracy in the Protectorate of British East Africa and ran a coffee plantation while exploring the vast wilderness around them. Soon after establishing this life, however, Karen found her new land embroiled in World War I, her coffee business struggling, and her marriage to Bror a failure (they divorced in 1922). When at last she was forced to sell the farm and leave Africa in 1931, she brought with her the memories of her time there—of the Somalis, Indians, and Gikuyu (also known as Kikuyu) with whom she lived and worked; of her Maasai neighbors; of the dignitaries and aristocratic settlers she rubbed shoulders with; and of the natural world she found so beautiful. Back in Denmark, she took the pen name Isak Dinesen, and began writing a collection of anecdotes, sketches, and stories about her time in Africa. In 1937 this collection was published as *Out of Africa*.

Events in History at the Time of the Memoir

Into Africa. In the second half of the nineteenth century, Britain and other European nations became increasingly interested in East Africa. Explorers, missionaries, hunters, traders, and scientists roamed the land and interacted with its people, and their reports home stirred up an in-

THE LITERARY WORK

A memoir set in Kenya from 1914 to 1931; published in English in 1937.

SYNOPSIS

A Danish settler reflects on her life, her native and European neighbors, and her surroundings as she struggles to maintain a coffee plantation in colonial East Africa.

terest in "civilizing" this "savage" territory. Meanwhile, European governments evaluated the political and economic benefits of further involvement with the region. East Africa was not teeming with natural resources, but it did contain seemingly fertile land and the important port of Mombasa, which attracted the attention of import/export companies. By the 1880s, however, concerns about the profitability of investment in East Africa had been superceded by fear that other European nations would get there first. Britain, France, Belgium, Portugal, and Germany scrambled to appropriate as much African land as possible in an attempt to limit the imperial reach of their rivals. By 1886 Germany had already taken possession of a sizable portion of East Africa, so Britain felt compelled to stake its claim on present-day Kenya, the region it named British East Africa. In 1888 the British government entrusted its new land to the Imperial British East Africa Company, which was charged with developing it for trade. Poorly staffed and ignorant of African culture, however, this company succeeded only in alienating indigenous peoples who got in the way of its disorganized trade route; it was not until British East Africa became a "protectorate" in 1895 that colonization truly began.

AFRICA THROUGH IMPERIALIST EYES

~

An 1873 London *Times* article reflects the imperialist views of the day, describing in glowing terms the beauty and potential waiting to be "cultivated" in East Africa (referred to here as Central Africa because of its position between northern and southern Africa):

It is not long since Central Africa was regarded as nothing better than a region of torrid deserts or pestiferous swamps, and its people as a race hopelessly sunk in the lowest degradation. The lid has since been lifted sufficiently to give us glimpses of elevated temperate plains, magnificent lakes, and beautiful scenery and people who, however miserable, seem not incapable of some cultivation. There seems no reason to believe that one of the finest parts of the world's surface is lying waste under the shroud of malaria which surrounds it, and under the barbarous anarchy with which it is cursed. The idea dawns upon some of us that some better destiny is yet in store for a region so blessed by nature, and the development of Africa is a step yet to come in the development of the world.

(*Times* in Ochieng', p. 82)

With its new protectorate status, British East Africa was a territory protected and partially controlled by Britain. It would not officially become a colony until 1920. Nonetheless, the British government began to assert its presence immediately, organizing a series of military expeditions between 1895 and 1914 against any group that resisted its rule, and constructing a railroad from Mombasa to Lake Victoria to connect the country and more easily establish full political control. This railroad, completed in 1901, cost British taxpayers almost 6 million pounds. In an attempt to offset some of the expense, the governor of the Protectorate, Charles Eliot, decided to recruit Europeans as settlers. He reasoned that only white settlers could develop the Kenyan economy effectively enough to make the railroad viable. To begin the recruitment process, the British Foreign Office gave hundreds of thousands of acres to men of "position and means"—including Blixen's acquaintances Lord Delamere (Hugh Cholmondeley), and Berkeley and Galbraith Cole—hoping to entice further settlers to join them. This approach, combined with the low prices for seemingly fertile land, brought in a wave of enthusiastic settlers who by 1914 had taken over half of the arable land in Kenya. Among these settlers was Karen Blixen.

European settlers and Gikuyu "squatters." Karen Blixen's farm at the foot of the Ngong Hills was in the southern part of East Africa's Gikuyuland. Members of the Gikuyu people had lived there since the 1880s as farmers, raising livestock, bananas, yams, corn, and beans for food and trade. With the influx of European settlers in the early 1900s, however, these southern Gikuyu found their land supply depleted and their way of life changed. The British government maintained that most of Kenya's Africans technically owned only their crops and homes, not their land; therefore, the British felt entitled to seize this land and sell it to eager European settlers. Seeking a labor force to work the land, the settlers and the colonial government then devised a number of methods to employ the very farmers they had uprooted. Many Gikuyu simply remained on the land as squatters, working a portion of the year for a European landowner in exchange for permission to stay on the land and perhaps a small wage. Others lived in government-designated reserves and were paid to plant and harvest a settler's crops. Wary of these unfamiliar practices or preferring to work on the remaining Gikuyu-held land, many Gikuyu refused to labor for the settlers, prompting government officials to in 1902 impose a "hut tax," or tax per house, on the Africans, which could be paid only in currency. Unless they chose to sell their livestock, the Gikuyu were thus compelled to sell their labor to raise the necessary funds. By the time Blixen arrived in 1914, the Gikuyu had become a reluctant but large labor pool for European settlers, while the few remaining Gikuyu landholders were left with a labor shortage of their own. Needless to say, though Blixen paints a rosy picture of her own relations with the Gikuyu, with both land and labor in such high demand, tensions between Africans and Europeans remained high throughout her time in Kenya.

New politics in Gikuyuland. At the time *Out of Africa* takes place, the political landscape in Gikuyuland began to change. Before Britain established its protectorate government at the turn

A group of Gikuyu women.

of the century, Gikuyu society had been organized into lineages, or family groups, that lived and farmed together. No kings or chiefs existed, and political decisions were usually made collectively, with the guidance of a few elders. Members of different lineages might come together to fight a common enemy, but such alliances were generally short-lived. In the 1890s British officials began trading with the Gikuyu and offered military aid to certain lineages in their struggles against other lineages. In this way, the British took advantage of the fragmented nature of Gikuyu society, building alliances that gradually strengthened their control of central Kenya. By the early 1900s the Protectorate government was firmly established throughout British East Africa. It consisted of a governor, provincial commissioners (PCs), district commissioners (DCs), and district officers—all of whom were British—and of indigenous chiefs, who answered to the local DC.

The most powerful chief of Gikuyuland was Kinyanjui wa Gathirimu (spelled "Kinanjui" in *Out of Africa*), a successful trader who had gotten his start as a porter for a British company. Kinyanjui was loyal to the British government and performed his official duties diligently, often eliciting the fear and ire of his own people in the process. For example, in his early years

as a chief he collected hut taxes by seizing goats with the help of a spear-toting army. Like many other Kenyan chiefs, Kinyanjui took full advantage of the power granted to him, amassing a great fortune in transactions that were probably not all legitimate. He was viewed as a collaborator and an opportunist by a number of Gikuyu, though his influence with the colonial government eventually gained him the respect of many

---

SQUATTER ECONOMICS

Isak Dinesen describes the economic concerns of the squatters on her land in the following passage:

The squatters knew that in order to stay on the land they had got to work for me one hundred and eighty days out of each year, for which they were paid twelve shillings for every thirty days; these accounts were kept at the office of the farm. They also knew that they must pay the hut-tax to the Government, of twelve shillings to a hut, a heavy burden on a man, who with very little else in the world would own two or three grass-huts,—according to the number of his wives, for a Kikuyu husband must give each of the wives her own hut.

(Dinesen, *Out of Africa*, p. 358)

of his own people—when they wanted something from the DC, Kinyanjui could often deliver it.

By appointing chiefs like Kinyanjui, the British were able to maintain control over the Gikuyu population and the rest of native Kenya, for there were no large-scale political organizations that could compete with the chiefs' power. However, with the coming of World War I this situation was to change.

World War I in Africa. In August 1914, after a long period of political tension in Europe, Great Britain declared war on Germany. The consequences of this act were felt immediately in Africa; in fact, the first shots of the war were fired in western Africa, just a few days after the declaration, when French and British forces invaded German Togo. Throughout Africa, British colonial officers were under orders from the Foreign Office to capture as many German colonies as possible, so that they could be used "as pawns when negotiating peace terms" (Reader, p. 604). Like Britain, Germany also had territorial ambitions in Africa but, after a series of early defeats in the western and southern parts of the continent, focused its efforts on keeping the British East African forces busy for the remainder of the war.

Like almost all of the inhabitants of British East Africa, which bordered German East Africa, Karen Blixen was affected by the war. Initially, her husband joined the British forces, working as an intelligence officer for Lord Delamere's border patrol, and Karen led a series of expeditions delivering supplies to the front. Despite these acts of loyalty to Britain, however, Karen's friendship with German General Paul von Lettow-Vorbeck led many British settlers to suspect her of spying for the Germans.

While a number of European settlers continued to fight as the war progressed, the great majority of soldiers and military personnel fighting for the British in East Africa were Africans, who knew nothing of the European entanglements and disagreements that had led to the war. In Kenya, African soldiers and porters were first recruited by chiefs, but in 1915, an ordinance decreed that all males between the ages of 18 and 45 could be forced into some sort of military service. By the war's end, 10,000 African soldiers and 195,000 African porters (the "Carrier Corps" referred to in *Out of Africa*) had served the British forces. The consequences of this service were devastating to the black population. Thousands were killed or wounded in the fighting, and tens of thousands died of disease on the front as a result of poor food and medical facilities. Furthermore, because so few able-bodied farmers were left to plant and harvest crops, a famine swept across East Africa, killing even more of Kenya's Africans.

Clearly, the African population sacrificed a great deal to achieve a British victory in East Africa, but the government of the Protectorate did little to reward these sacrifices. In *Out of Africa*, Dinesen describes a ceremony on her farm in which medals were distributed to Maasai chiefs who had recruited scouts for the British. She claims the ceremony "was an event of great dimensions and weight," but it had no dimension or weight for those who had actually risked their lives for the British—the African soldiers and porters themselves (*Out of Africa*, p. 213). In fact, when these indigenous people returned home from the front—many with their wages still unpaid—they found that their house taxes had been increased and they were now required to wear a metal box around their necks containing a record of their labor history. Some who had managed to hold on to their land before the war years returned to find that it had since been seized and given to British veterans as part of the 1919 Ex-Soldiers Settlement Scheme. Furthermore, in 1921 the government adopted a new currency and invalidated the previous currency, in which African soldiers and military porters had recently been paid. These abuses prompted a number of Africans in Kenya to political action; founded at this time were organizations—including the influential Young Gikuyu Association—that planted the seeds for the Kenyan nationalist movement (which would achieve independence for Kenya in 1963).

Maasai, Somalis, and Indians. When Karen Blixen arrived in Kenya (then British East Africa), the indigenous population was about 3 million and consisted of numerous different ethnic groups. One of the three largest was the Gikuyu, with whom Blixen had the most contact. Her neighbors to the southeast, however, were members of the Maasai (also spelled "Masai"), a formerly nomadic, cattle-raising people known for their skill as warriors. They are described in *Out of Africa* as native Kenya's "nobility" because of their "rigid, passive, and insolent bearing" and their inability to survive imprisonment or slavery (*Out of Africa*, p. 130). In the early 1890s the Maasai, who had sought and won British support in a dispute with the Gikuyu, became British allies in a series of battles against other native

Kenyan peoples. This service did not insulate them from the land seizures of the early 1900s, however. Confined to reserves in 1904, they were forced to end their cattle raids and battles for new land, and found it difficult to adjust to life in such a limited area.

The Somali also had a proud past as herdsmen and warriors. They had crossed into the desert region of northeastern Kenya from Somalia and carried their strict Muslim faith with them. Although they tended to look down on non-Muslim groups, the Somali did sometimes work for Christian Europeans. Farah in *Out of Africa* is Blixen's Somali servant, right-hand-man, and confidant from the time she arrives in Africa to the time she leaves. Although Blixen describes her relationship with him as a "creative unity" in which "he knew of all that I did or thought," most Somali servants did not become so close to their European employers (Blixen in Thurman, p. 115). In fact, one historian claims that they "maintained an aloofness the whites distrusted and considered impudent" (Thurman, p. 120).

Indian immigrants in Kenya made up a sizable portion of the population in the early twentieth century. Because Britain controlled both India and Kenya and because the two regions were linked by the Indian Ocean, many Indians moved to Kenya to try their luck in a new land. Indian merchants dominated trade on the Kenyan coast, and some 32,000 indentured Indian laborers helped to construct the railroad, which drew clerks, shopkeepers, and skilled artisans—such as Blixen's blacksmith and carpenter, Pooran Singh—into inland Kenya. In fact, in the early 1900s Indians seeking to turn Kenya into the "America of the Hindu" had lobbied the British government to make it part of the Indian Empire, ruled by an Indian Viceroy (Ochieng', p. 105). This proposal was rejected, however, and white settlers became the favored, though smaller, immigrant group. Indians were forbidden from buying land in the "White Highlands" where Blixen lived, though many managed to establish flourishing shops and small businesses, opening soda and soap factories, oil and saw mills, and even a cotton ginnery. Though Kenyan Indians founded political organizations early on and fought actively for their rights, throughout the first three decades of the twentieth century they were treated as second-class citizens.

The coffee business. When Karen Dinesen and her fiancé Bror Blixen began planning their East African adventure in 1913, they decided to operate a small dairy farm and raise cattle, two enterprises that Bror was familiar with through a family business. However, soon after arriving in Africa, Bror sold the dairy farm he had purchased and bought a much larger plot of land near Nairobi, where he was determined to grow coffee. "Coffee growing was the only thing that had any future," he wrote later in a memoir. "The world was crying out for coffee from Kenya" (Blixen in Thurman, p. 107). Since 1910 there had been a worldwide increase in demand for coffee, and many coffee growers in Kenya had been successful because of this demand; the Blixens, however, were not to share in this success.

GRASSHOPPER STORM

~

A grasshopper invasion is described in the following excerpt from *Out of Africa*:

At times a small swarm would come along, a free-corps which had detached itself from the main force, and would just pass in a rush. But at other times the grasshoppers came in big flights, which took days to pass over the farm, twelve hours' incessant hurling advance in the air. When the flight was at its highest it was like a blizzard at home, whistling and shrieking like a strong wind, little hard furious wings to all sides of you and over your head, shining like thin blades of steel in the sun, but themselves darkening the sun. The grasshoppers keep in a belt, from the ground up to the top of the trees, beyond that the air is clear. They whir against your face, they get into your collar and your sleeves and shoes. The rush round you makes you giddy and fills you with a particular sickening rage and despair, the horror of the mass.

(*Out of Africa*, pp. 314-15)

The nature of the farmland itself was their main source of difficulty. Their land was too high, the soil too acidic, and rainfall too infrequent for coffee to thrive; in fact, dairy farming would have been a much more successful enterprise in this location. Despite these obstacles, Karen Blixen did manage to maintain her farm until its eventual failure in 1931. Many of the settlers on smaller farms, however, experienced failures even before the start of World War I. Most had not tested how conducive conditions were to raising crops and had little or no experience growing them. This was certainly the case with the Blixens, although Karen learned quickly what she needed to know about coffee produc-

British East Africa's abundance of natural resources lured adventure seekers, including U.S. President Theodore Roosevelt, to go on safari during the late nineteenth and early twentieth centuries.

tion. She and Kenya's other coffee farmers also benefited from government subsidies and helpful economic policies, such as a law that forbade Africans to maintain coffee farms. This assistance, however, was not enough to combat the drop in coffee prices that resulted first from Britain's postwar economic slump and then from the worldwide Great Depression that began in late 1929. Nor could the assistance save Blixen's farm from the swarms of grasshoppers that invaded Kenya between 1927 and 1931. In 1931 Blixen was forced to sell her farm and leave Africa.

Denys Finch Hatton and the safari lifestyle.
One of the earliest sources of foreign interest in East Africa was its seemingly endless supply of wild game. Once the railroad was completed and

a hotel built in Nairobi, a stream of wealthy hunters—including United States president Theodore Roosevelt—came to test their skill and bravery on safaris. Safaris brought a great deal of money into the region: not only did visiting hunters hire white guides, but they also required at least 30 African porters each to transport their food and equipment, as well as cooks, gun-bearers, and assorted other servants, sometimes including a safari jester charged with entertaining the group. Trips occasionally lasted as long as four months; their success was dependent on the skills of the guide. He had to speak Swahili, know the terrain perfectly, interact skillfully with various African peoples, be aware of the habits of the game, deal tactfully with his clients, and display proper manners all the while. Young aristocratic sportsmen, such as Denys Finch Hatton, who was Blixen's lover, proved ideal for the job.

Finch Hatton, an English earl's son and a graduate of Eton and Oxford, moved to British East Africa in 1912, bored with conventional life in England. He bought a farm and a mansion, established a lucrative trading business, and eventually took up hunting. By the 1920s he had begun to lead safaris professionally, and he soon built up a worldwide reputation among the adventuring elite of Europe and America. Guides like Finch Hatton were able to give their clients a taste of romanticized Africa and a new type of thrill, without the hard work of carrying gear, cleaning guns, and skinning game. As one historian puts it, safaris offered "the appeal of the simple life on a short term basis" (Trzebinski, p. 136).

This life evidently appealed to Blixen as well, for she accompanied both her husband and Finch Hatton on a few safaris of her own, and the romanticized version of some of these trips can be found in the pages of *Out of Africa*. During one such adventure, she and Finch Hatton come across a lion gnawing on a giraffe carcass only minutes after Finch Hatton shot another lion in the same place. "The lion," she writes, "stood straight up over it, dark, and behind him the sky was now all aflame.... A bit of his mane was lifted by the wind.... As I shot it seemed to me that the lion jumped straight up in the air, and came down with his legs gathered under him. I stood, panting, in the grass ..." (*Out of Africa*, p. 222).

The Memoir in Focus

Contents summary. *Out of Africa* is the largely autobiographical but partly fictionalized account of Karen Blixen's life in the Ngong Hills of Kenya. She begins it with a nostalgic, almost dreamlike description of her farm and the surrounding land, people, and animals. Then, in a series of short stories, vignettes, and less structured recollections, she tells of her struggle to maintain an unprofitable coffee business; of adventures on and off the farm; and of her relationships with squatters, employees, European and Maasai neighbors, visiting dignitaries, and even a baby gazelle whom she adopts as a pet.

The first relationship she recounts is with a sick young Gikuyu boy, Kamante, the son of a squatter on Blixen's farm. She comes across Kamante one day while riding around the farm and notices that his small, bony body is covered with running sores and his eyes are "dim like the eyes of a dead person" (*Out of Africa*, pp. 21-22). Taking pity on Kamante, Blixen asks him to come to her house the next day for treatment, then begins administering a series of dressings for his wounds. As she comes to know Kamante, she is struck by his aloofness, but he gradually comes to trust and open up to her. After judging her own treatments ineffective, she sends Kamante to a Scotch Mission hospital, where he is cured and converted to Christianity; he returns grateful for her help. Blixen eventually hires Kamante as her medical assistant and, later, her cook. His personality, now spirited and eccentric, makes him a constant source of entertainment to Blixen in the rest of her years on the farm.

Later in the memoir, Blixen tells of her early friendship with Denys Finch Hatton, the aristocratic English adventurer who becomes her lover, and with Berkeley Cole, one of the original English immigrants recruited to British East Africa by Charles Eliot. In recounting the men's frequent visits to her farm, bearing wine, tobacco, and other luxuries, she describes Berkeley as a "noble pioneer" better suited to an earlier, more aristocratic era (*Out of Africa*, p. 205). His behavior certainly supports her description. For example, Cole habitually has champagne brought to him in the forest in the late morning whenever he stays on her farm, and he once complains to Blixen that her servants have not delivered it with her finest glasses. She replies that she has few good glasses left and is afraid the servants will break them on the long trip to the woods, but his charm wins her over, and from then on her good glasses are always at his disposal.

In addition to her long-term relationships with servants and European friends, Blixen describes a number of brief encounters with dignitaries passing through Kenya. One of her most unusual encounters is with a Muslim high priest from India, invited to her farm by a local Indian merchant and friend of Blixen's servant Farah. With no languages in common, Blixen and the priest must communicate through sign language, but she is very taken by his calm, dignified presence, and he is taken by her grey deerhounds. Three months later, she receives a letter from an Indian prince, an acquaintance of the priest, asking to buy one of these dogs.

Character sketches and dinner table anecdotes like these comprise a great deal of *Out of Africa*, but Blixen also includes in her memoir a number of real adventures and challenges. The first major challenge occurs after a shooting accident on the farm in which one young boy is killed and another wounded. Blixen is asked to sit on the Gikuyu panel that will determine the appropriate response to this tragedy; in making her determination, she must adjust to the Gikuyu justice system. Rather than issuing a verdict and a sentence for the boy responsible for the deaths, Blixen must help to decide how many cows the father of the responsible boy owes the fathers of the dead and wounded boys. Because the first boy's death has left his family with one fewer body on their team of farmhands and the other, wounded boy's disfigurement has made him less attractive to potential wives, the Gikuyu system requires that reparations be made to the fathers of these children. Blixen describes the difficulty of calculating the appropriate number of cows and of dealing with the ill will engendered among the families involved. The grandmother of the injured boy is suspected of bewitching the cows belonging to the responsible child's father. Eventually Blixen throws up her hands and turns to Chief Kinyanjui, who comes to the farm to resolve the issue.

Later in the memoir, Blixen recounts one of her adventures off the farm. She tells of the months early in World War I when she leads a supply caravan to British soldiers on the border with German East Africa. She has left the farm to oversee a military messenger service at a nearby train station and soon begins to receive urgent messages that the soldiers on the front need supplies and ammunition. Blixen hires a man to lead a wagon train of supplies, but he is arrested at the last minute, and she is left to lead the caravan herself. This is Blixen's first trip "alone with the Africans," and it is a long trip; for three months she and her servants steer wagons through muddy roads and fight off lions interested in their oxen (*Out of Africa*, p. 257). However, on this "war-time safari," as Blixen calls it, she is still entitled to special treatment (*Out of Africa*, p. 255). Her servants carry bath water for her across long distances and set up a canopy to protect her from the sun. Still, despite their protective treatment of her, Blixen concludes that she is perceived as "a kind of Guardian Angel" to all those on the expedition (*Out of Africa*, p. 260).

Back on the farm, Blixen experiences other exploits, often with Denys Finch Hatton, who comes to live with her off and on after her divorce. She shares with Finch Hatton a love of European literature and a taste for adventure; she

tells him stories, they discuss Shakespeare, he takes her flying in his airplane, and together one night they shoot a lion by flashlight.

As her memoir draws to a close, Blixen begins to tie up the loose ends of her life in Africa. Faced with the failure of the farm, she must sell it and her belongings, find a new home for the squatters on her land—which she does after petitioning the colonial government for help—and say goodbye to her friends. Further compounding the sorrow of her departure, Finch Hatton dies in a plane crash shortly before she is scheduled to return to Denmark. When she finally has boarded the train that will take her to Mombasa, Blixen looks back to her home but can barely distinguish the Ngong Hills, which she is never to see again.

Africans in Kenya through Blixen's eyes. In a letter to her Danish aunt a few months after arriving in Kenya, Karen Blixen writes:

> The natives . . . are my greatest interest out here; but I think that I,—and Bror,—are about the only people here who really do have this interest. Where the natives are concerned the English are remarkably narrow-minded; it never occurs to them to regard them as human beings, and when I talk to English ladies on racial differences and such matters, they laugh patronizingly, touched by my eccentricity.
> (Dinesen, *Letters from Africa*, p. 4)

Years later, in the final pages of *Out of Africa*, she writes "In some respects . . . the white men fill in the mind of the Natives the place that is, in the mind of the white men, filled by the idea of God"(*Out of Africa*, p. 358). These two quotes seem to come from two different people, one a young idealist who considers her views progressive, the other a middle-aged writer who views her past power nostalgically and her past employees paternalistically. What is remarkable about *Out of Africa* is that it merges both of these personalities into one. The voice in this memoir belongs to a woman whose wealthy European background has given her access to a world of privileges at the expense of the Africans who surround her. And though she praises their nobility and morality, she portrays herself as the benevolent mother of them all.

Blixen often speaks respectfully in her memoir of the Africans she encounters, usually generalizing by ethnic group. She praises the Gikuyu for their courage and patience. She describes the beauty of Maasai and the nobility of their demeanor and claims they should be ranked "with the immigrant aristocracy" because of their inability to survive imprisonment or slavery (*Out of Africa*, p. 143). For the Somali she reserves her greatest accolades, perhaps because she considers them the least "native" of Kenya's African peoples. She refers to them as immigrants because of their origins in Somalia and seems to endorse their condescending treatment of the Gikuyu, explaining that they had been slaveholders and "their relation to the Natives was nearly exactly that of the sheepdog to the sheep" (*Out of Africa*, p. 143). With a tone of nostalgia for the aristocratic structure of old Europe, she also describes the social hierarchy of the Somali and the "exquisite dignity and demureness" of Farah's sisters-in-law, whom she compares to the Danish ladies of her grandfather's day (*Out of Africa*, p. 172). While Dinesen appreciates the culture of each of these Kenyan groups, it seems that her greatest respect is reserved for the group she can connect most clearly to her own.

It is one thing for Blixen to write respectfully of the Africans she encounters but quite another for her to earn their respect. Her anecdotes in *Out of Africa* suggest, however, that the nearby Africans did pay deference to Blixen and appealed to her for aid. She is asked to nurse the injured Gikuyu on her land and to shoot the lions that prey on the neighboring Maasai's cattle. And even after she has sold the farm, the squatters who live there appeal to her for help finding new land. She follows through enthusiastically on each of these requests, and from her descriptions seems to have friendly relations with her employees, especially Farah. Still, it is difficult to perceive her as having being able to break through the boundaries between the Africans and Europeans. She was, after all, a member of the conquering group, and her authority stemmed from her European heritage. It is likely that the Africans asked Blixen for favors precisely because she was a European who had the medical equipment or guns or government connections to grant them.

In any case, Blixen's views toward the Africans were more enlightened than those of many European setters in Kenya. Even so, her reluctance to discuss critically the injustices dealt to them by the British government reveals a refusal to face the unpleasant reality of their circumstances. In a short section of *Out of Africa* entitled "Kitosch's Story," Blixen tells of the case of a young Kenyan who is flogged, tied up, and left to die by his employer, a European settler. The case is brought before a colonial court. There are witnesses to the murder, both native-born Kenyan and Euro-

pean, and a European doctor testifies that the wounds from the flogging killed Kitosch, yet the jury finds the settler guilty only of "grievous hurt," not first- or second-degree murder (*Out of Africa*, p. 271). The reason for this judgment is that two doctors for the defense have argued Kitosch willed himself to die, a uniquely African skill. Rather than condemning the judgement, Blixen interprets it as a declaration of African freedom. "The figure of Kitosch," she writes, "stands out with a beauty of its own. In it is embodied the fugitiveness of the wild things who are, in the hour of need, conscious of a refuge somewhere in existence; who go when they like; of whom we can never get hold" (*Out of Africa*, pp. 271-72). This naive romanticization of a tragic injustice is typical of Blixen's approach to portraying the plight of Kenya's Africans. For all her words of respect and praise, in the end some Africans are conceived by her as only beautiful symbols, wild beings to whom true European justice does not apply.

Blixen's portrayal of the Africans in *Out of Africa* is complex, and her behavior toward them is as well. On the one hand, she shows an interest in the different peoples and writes admiringly of their traits. She also helps the neighboring Maasai and the squatters on her land, even to the point of lobbying the colonial government successfully for new land. On the other hand, she barely mentions the unrewarded sacrifices made by Gikuyu soldiers during World War I, and she requires the squatters on her land to work half the year for her, knowing full well that the land was theirs until it was seized by the British. She speaks of Kenya's Africans lovingly, but in the tone of a detached poet—using men like Kitosch as symbols—or of a benevolent parent, calling the squatters "a flock of sheep" to her "herd-boy" (*Out of Africa*, p. 319). Perhaps the best way to explain Blixen's treatment of Africans in her memoir is that she chose her facts carefully; she set out to create an idealized vision of Africa and an idealized account of her own life there. Though this account contains the personal tragedies found in any good romance—the failure of the farm, the death of Finch Hatton—it could not acknowledge the larger tragedy of colonization, for in the process of colonization Blixen was not a victim or a heroine, but a willing, though humane, participant.

Sources and literary context. *Out of Africa* is not the only book to recount the adventures of a European in Kenya. In fact, two of Blixen's contemporaries, her ex-husband Bror Blixen and fellow settler Elspeth Huxley, wrote memoirs of their own: *The African Hunter* and *Flame Trees of Thika,* respectively. Still, Blixen's memoir is one of the best known of its class. It was inspired by a wide variety of sources, the earliest of which may have been *Letters from the Hunt,* a book of anecdotes and images composed by Karen Dinesen's own father after his retirement from the military. In her teen years, Dinesen read **The Story of an African Farm** (also covered in *African Literature and Its Times*), Olive Schreiner's novel about a European settler in Africa, and she would think of it often on her own farm in Kenya.

If the books mentioned above gave Karen a taste for adventure that would eventually lead her to Africa, it was her return to Denmark that actually prompted her to write *Out of Africa.* Back on the estate where she had grown up, feeling confined and frustrated and searching for meaning in her life, she completed *Seven Gothic Tales,* an unrelated story collection, and then felt ready to face the past she had left in Africa. After some prompting from her publisher, she began to transform the sketches and notes she had collected in Kenya into a story. As the story took shape, one biographer suggests, her identity did as well. "For within the whole universe," she would write later, "the story only has the authority to answer that one cry of the heart . . . 'Who am I?'" (Dinesen in Thurman, p. 285).

Reviews. *Out of Africa* was the second major work published by Isak Dinesen (Blixen's pen name) after her return to Denmark from Africa. In 1934 she had published *Seven Gothic Tales,* a huge critical and commercial success in the United States but a flop in Denmark, where it was criticized for its "decadent, fantastic, cynical and perverse quality" (Langbaum in Thurman, p. 287). *Out of Africa,* which she wrote first in English and later in Danish, was well received in both countries. In the United States it became a Book-of-the-Month Club selection and was lauded by the critics. Critics who had rejected her story collection were pleased to see that "Isak Dinesen had, after all, a regard for and knowledge of reality and humanity" (Langbaum in Thurman, p. 287). In England Dinesen's publisher reported that the book was popular in "intellectual circles" but disliked by the "great gov-

erning class" who "think that there is a lion in the streets" (Huntington in Thurman, p. 287). It is not clear precisely what perceived danger Dinesen's publisher is referring to here; perhaps her close relationships with her African employees and her relatively progressive notions about African humanity were too radical to be reconciled with traditional British notions of race. In any case, *Out of Africa* established Blixen—or, more properly, the persona of Isak Dinesen—as an international star. In a time when the Great Depression had crippled hopes and another world war was on the horizon, her memoir told its own story of failed idealism, but with an air of romance and adventure that captivated the reading public and made her a beloved romantic heroine.

—Allison Weisz

For More Information

Clough, Marshall S. *Fighting Two Sides: Kenyan Chiefs and Politicians, 1918-1940.* Niwot: University Press of Colorado, 1990.

Dinesen, Isak. *Letters from Africa, 1914-1931.* Trans. Anne Born. Ed. Frans Lasson. Chicago: University of Chicago Press, 1981.

———. *Out of Africa and Shadows on the Grass.* New York: Vintage International, 1989.

Donelson, Linda. *Out of Isak Dinesen: Karen Blixen's Untold Story.* Iowa City, Iowa: Coulsong, 1998.

Henricksen, Aage. *Isak Dinesen/Karen Blixen: The Work and the Life.* Trans. William Mishler. New York: St. Martin's Press, 1988.

Kennedy, Dane. *Islands of White: Settler Society and Culture in Kenya and Southern Rhodesia, 1890-1939.* Durham, N.C.:Duke University Press, 1987.

Knappert, Jan. *East Africa: Kenya, Tanzania & Uganda.* New Delhi: Vikas, 1987.

Ochieng', William R. *A History of Kenya.* London: Macmillan, 1985.

Oliver, Roland, and J. D. Fage. *A Short History of Africa,* Sixth Edition. New York: Facts on File, 1989.

Reader, John. *Africa: A Biography of a Continent.* New York: Alfred A. Knopf, 1998.

Thurman, Judith. *Isak Dinesen: The Life of a Storyteller.* New York: St. Martin's Press, 1982.

Trzebinski, Errol. *The Kenya Pioneers.* London: Heinemann, 1985.

The Palm-Wine Drinkard and His Dead Palm-Wine Tapster in the Deads' Town

by

Amos Tutuola

Born in 1929 in western Nigeria, Amos Tutuola achieved only a sixth-grade education due to financial constraints following his father's death. He later tried his hand at farming, without success, then pursued the blacksmith trade. He served as a coppersmith in the West African Air Corps of the British military in World War II. After the war Tutuola had to take a job as a messenger, and it gave him time, between errands, to write down stories he had heard. His first novel, *The Palm-Wine Drinkard and His Dead Palm-Wine Tapster in the Deads' Town*, became the subject of much controversy because of its frequently ungrammatical, though stylish and vivid, writing. A landmark work, it was the first novel to be published by a Nigerian author, and also the first novel by a black African to be written in English. The work is classified as a novel, but there has been some debate about whether this designation is accurate, since *The Palm-Wine Drinkard* incorporates so much oral tradition. Indeed, this novel has provided many with their first glimpse into Yoruba folklore. *The Palm-Wine Drinkard* draws heavily on traditional folktales, which has been another source of controversy, prompting some to claim that the work plagiarizes the intellectual property of the Yoruba people. In fact, Tutuola, who was Yoruba himself, acknowledged his debt, in particular to an old man who told him tales on Sundays over tumblers of palm wine. Although

---

THE LITERARY WORK

A novel set in Nigeria in the timeless folkloric past; published in English in 1952.

SYNOPSIS

Drinkard, the protaganist and narrator of the novel, goes in search of his deceased palm-wine tapster in Deads' Town. On the way he meets with a series of adventures, in the process gaining a wife and wisdom.

The Palm-Wine Drinkard brought him international acclaim, Tutuola afterward remained a literary outsider, preferring to spend his time with blacksmiths and other working-class men rather than with writers and intellectuals. He continued his literary career, completing five more novels before his death in 1997, but none of them received the international notoriety gained by his first published work.

Events in History at the Time of the Novel

An unspecified era. *The Palm-Wine Drinkard*, like the folktales on which it is based, takes place in mythic time, in an indefinite past when, according to the novel's protagonist (nameless in

A group of Yorubas posing with a masked dancer.

the novel but herein referred to as "Drinkard"), the people "did not know other money except COWRIES"—the currency of traditional precolonial Yoruba society (Tutuola, *The Palm-Wine Drinkard,* p. 7). Aspects of colonialism creep in, however—for example, Drinkard sells his death for the sum of "£70: 18: 6d" in British pounds sterling—but for the most part the novel is literally timeless (*Palm-Wine Drinkard,* p. 67). This entry therefore focuses on the elements of traditional Yoruba culture that have persisted through time, as well as on the history of change in Yorubaland that led to the writing of *The Palm-Wine Drinkard* in the English language.

The Yoruba people. In Yoruba lore, the god Obatala descended on a golden chain from the heavens—ruled by Olodumare, the supreme deity—to an earth that was covered with water. Obatala scattered grains of sand on the water that formed solid earth, and he named this first place Ife, which became the original Yoruba city. In the new ground he planted a palm nut that brought forth palm trees, the first vegetation. Orunmila then formed human beings out of clay. While working, he drank palm wine—an alcoholic beverage fermented from the sap of palm trees—so a few of these beings came out misshapen, with crooked backs, crippled limbs, and other deformities. The new humans were the Yoruba people, and Ife became their cultural center.

The Yoruba homeland, or Yorubaland, spread from Ife, also known as Ile-Ife (literally, "the household that spread"), to cover an area about the size of England lying in the southwestern portion of modern Nigeria and the neighboring state of Benin. Yorubaland extends from the Atlantic coast, where navigable rivers crisscross swamps and marshy forests, to more temperate forests of the inland regions that gradually give way to savanna grasslands speckled with trees. It is not clear whether the various subgroups living in this region and identified as "Yoruba" are ethnically related, but they are certainly related culturally and linguistically, and all regard Ife as their place of origin.

The Yoruba have always been an urban people. In the precolonial era, they lived in well-ordered towns and cities separated by expanses of wild countryside referred to as "bush." Despite this urbanity, agriculture was the main occupation of the Yoruba, who would commute from their homes within a town to surrounding farms via roads that extended outward from the center of each Yoruba town. These roads stretched past the farms, into the bush, until they merged with roads leading into the centers of other towns. In the middle of a town, where all the roads converged, sat the palace of the ruler, or *oba*. Each of the towns was ruled by an *oba*, who might owe allegiance to the *oba* of a mightier town or command the allegiance of subordinate obas. All obas ultimately deferred to the Oni of Ife, who was considered the paramount oba.

Yoruba belief. Olodumare, the supreme Yoruba deity, is served by many lesser deities known collectively and singularly as *orisa.* The orisa are numerous; estimations of their number range from 400 to 1,700. Some orisa, like Faithful-Mother in *The Palm-Wine Drinkard,* are connected to specific sites—certain rivers, trees, or hills—and are worshipped only by the inhabitants of a single town. Others are more widely worshipped, like Ogun, the orisa of iron and war, or Sango, the orisa of thunder and rain. The orisa both punish and reward human beings and are amenable to sacrifice. Like the gods of Greece and Rome, the orisa are flawed and sometimes fail, the way the drunken crafter of some of the Yoruba people did, to perform their duty. It is up to the Yoruba, therefore, to persuade the orisa through sacrifice to do what is best for human beings.

The Yoruba universe is divided into two major realms: *Orun* (heaven), and *Aiye* (earth). Olodumare and the orisa reside in Orun, which is also home to the ancestors—the spirits of the Yoruba dead—while Aiye is the world of living human beings. The ancestors are actively concerned with the welfare and behavior of their descendants, whom they may protect or punish, and from whom they require sacrifice in order to be admitted into the realm of Orun. The divination system called *Ifa* allows communication through priests between the living and the ancestors, and also between the living and the orisa. The ancestors and the orisa proffer their advice and predict future events through their influence on the throwing of palm nuts by an Ifa priest; the patterns into which the palm nuts fall are related to certain prophetic verses that the Ifa priest will recite. Yoruba consult Ifa regularly once each year and on any important occasion, such as birth, death, illness, marriage, or the undertaking of a business venture. Thus the relationship between Orun and Aiye—between gods and mortals, and between the living and the dead—is very important in the Yoruba worldview.

The responsibility for maintaining balance and harmony between heaven and earth belongs to living Yoruba who, through sacrifice, both appease the inhabitants of Orun and replenish their power. The two domains engage in a constant exchange of energy as the living Yoruba of Aiye offer sacrifices to Orun and receive in return all the good things in life via the ancestors and the orisa.

Human beings travel back and forth between Orun and Aiye through reincarnation. Ancestors are believed to reincarnate through their descendants, and the names *Babatunde* ("father returns") and *Yetunde* ("mother returns") are frequently given to children whose grandparents are deceased. The only way for a spirit to reincarnate is through its own progeny; thus the bearing and raising of children is extremely important to the Yoruba, and one is not considered a full-fledged adult in Yoruba society until one has married and become a parent. Because of their belief in reincarnation and the exalted status of ancestors, the Yoruba celebrate the deaths of old people, for through death the individual moves on to the next stage of existence. Sudden deaths of young people, however, are considered tragedies, especially if the deceased did not have a chance to marry and procreate before he or she died.

In *The Palm-Wine Drinkard,* the protagonist has frequent recourse to magic or what the author describes as *juju* The Yoruba concept that comes closest to magic is *oògùn,* which refers to medicines, poisons, love potions, truth serums, invisibility charms, and the like. The Yoruba word *egbōgi* is considered a synonym for oògùn, and means literally "root of trees," indicating the primarily botanical nature of the powerful substances both words describe, though oògùn or egbōgi can also be composed of animal or mineral elements. Sometimes oògùn is accompanied by a spell that must be recited by the user, and sometimes oògùn is effective on its own; in either case, the operation of oògùn is automatic—no special skill or concentration is required on the part of the user. The use of oògùn is moreover not restricted to any special class of individuals; anyone may use oògùn, and most Yoruba have knowledge of at least a few oògùn. Yoruba men, like the narrator of *The Palm-Wine Drinkard,* typically have knowledge of some oògùn of the occult variety.

Historical overview. In the fourteenth century C.E., the Yoruba city-state of Oyo rose to power and extended its authority over much of Yorubaland, uniting what had been several independent kingdoms into an empire with a common language. In the late eighteenth century, the powerful kingdom of Oyo began to decline. Subject kingdoms revolted against Oyo domination, and in 1837 the city of Oyo fell to Fulani invaders from the north. A series of wars fought between the various Yoruba city-states followed hard upon the dissolution of centralized power at Oyo.

The victors in these conflicts sold captured prisoners of war to European merchants who were by this time conducting a profitable trade in African slaves. Yoruba captives filled the cargo holds of slave ships headed across the Atlantic Ocean to the New World, carrying Yoruba culture to such far-flung places as Cuba and Brazil. Combined with the internecine warfare, the sale of the defeated into slavery decimated the Yoruba population, and this decline set the stage for the ascendancy of the British in Yorubaland.

In the mid-nineteenth century, Yorubaland became the focus of British interest. At this time British missionaries arrived to convert the Yoruba to Christianity, and British merchants noticed that Yorubaland was rich in trees yielding palm oil, an important product for European industry. In 1851 the British military conquered the city of Lagos with the twin goals of dominating the palm-oil trade in the area and putting an end to the slave trade. In 1861 Lagos and the surrounding area were officially designated a colony of the British Crown. Some of the Yoruba kingdoms offered their submission to the British in hopes of ending the long years of internecine warfare and the depredations of slavery. By the turn of the century the British had expanded their colony to include all of Yorubaland. The city of Lagos became the administrative capital of the new British colony of Nigeria.

The British maintained a policy of "indirect rule" in Nigeria, meaning that Britain ruled through the traditional system of obas, who now owed allegiance to the new colonial government. (Of course, there were some changes in the selection of these obas to insure the presence of ones friendly to the colonial authorities.) British missionaries opened schools, and the colonial government, through taxation of the Nigerian populace, partially funded primary and secondary education for Nigerian children, in English. In the 1930s, however, when author Amos Tutuola attended primary school, students still had to pay a cash tuition, which was often hard to come by, forcing many to drop out of school early or go without an education altogether. Those Yoruba who did manage to get an education often sought positions within the civil service, which would allow them to earn a salary and escape the backbreaking labor of agriculture. A few even obtained a higher education. Finding no place for themselves in the upper echelons of the colonial government, where the British blocked African participation, these university-educated Nigerians began to foment a nationalist movement that would eventually lead to Nigerian independence.

Another factor contributing to Nigerian independence was World War II. Because the war drained British resources, the British government wished to scale back its expenditures overseas, and the notion of self-rule for British colonies gained popularity. The development of a new constitution and government for an independent Nigeria progressed slowly, however. The colonial government, uncertain how to balance the rights and privileges of the diverse ethnic groups that comprised Nigeria, made a series of constitutional changes that gradually moved the colony toward self-rule. As a result of these constitutional changes, educational and economic opportunities increased for Nigerians, and nationalist fervor, born of outrage and desperation, waned, further slowing the movement toward self-rule. Thus, Nigeria would wait until 1960 for independence.

Nigerians like Amos Tutuola had meanwhile served and fought in the British military during World War II. Ironically, one group that did not benefit in postwar Nigeria was that of the ex-servicemen. Many of these men had seen the world and returned to Nigeria ever more aware of the disparity between colonized and colonizer in their own land. A great number of them spent years searching for adequate work after their return. In 1949 *The West African Pilot* questioned, "Are not thousands of these heroes still roaming about Lagos and the Provinces in search of the wherewithals of life?" (Olusanya, p. 98). Government promises to secure employment for these men, or to loan them money for starting new businesses, did not materialize. The Nigerian author and ex-serviceman Mokwugo Okoye would later write, "The brave new world that they had fought for had very easily faded into a rotten world of unemployment and frustration" (Okoye in Olusanya, p. 99). Amos Tutuola joined the ranks of the unemployed ex-soldiers for a year before landing a messenger job, the only position he could get. As a messenger Tutuola had to spend a great deal of time waiting for errands. Rather than sit idly, he began writing down the stories he had heard throughout his life, stories that would merge in his first novel, *The Palm-Wine Drinkard.*

Oral tradition. Pre-colonial Yoruba culture had a written counting system devised for use in the Ifa divination ritual, but the primary means of communication was oral. Despite the spread of literacy through missionary-run programs, by the mid-twentieth century Yoruba culture was still highly oral, and in an oral culture, storytelling is an important art form. When Amos Tutuola wrote *The Palm-Wine Drinkard,* he worked from a firm grounding in Yoruba oral tradition, revising tales he had heard from others to create something new. In so doing he followed the tradition of the storyteller who recycles, revises, and renews traditional stories to adapt them to the present.

The most common type of tale in Yoruba culture, told by almost everyone, is the *alo* story or song-story—so-called because a song, or alo, integrated into the plot of the tale is an essential part of its performance. When asked to define an alo story, Yoruba informants responded "Alo is a lie!" (LaPin, p. 95). Alo stories are indeed fictional, and are "lies" in this sense, but the Yoruba concept of falsehood or *iro* includes not only fictional statements but also "divergence from what ought to be," and indeed, alo stories invariably present a lamentable state of affairs (LaPin, p. 95). Although alo stories usually have happy endings, the body of the tale deals with the negative consequences of antisocial or simply socially unacceptable behavior (for example, vicious jealousy between rival co-wives). Although alo stories are the most common form of Yoruba tale, they are a guilty pleasure. The telling of alo stories is strictly proscribed during daylight when responsible individuals ought to be working, and men often dismiss alo stories as being "for women and children" (LaPin, p. 78). The justification most often given for the telling of alo tales is the instruction of youth through negative example, and the most common plot, which is conflict between the individual and society, invariably resolves in society's favor.

The Palm-Wine Drinkard can be likened to an alo tale in several respects: The initial situation of the novel, in which the protagonist, Drinkard, does nothing but drink palm wine in prodigious quantities, can certainly be described as a "divergence from what ought to be." Drinkard's behavior—failing to work, to honor his dead father with sacrifice, to marry, or to procreate—is antisocial, and things go badly for Drinkard through much of the novel. The ending of *The Palm-Wine Drinkard* is, however, happy. Drinkard at first presents an example of how not to live, then advises the people how to rectify their plight by acknowledging the superiority of heaven. His final advice results in a boon to society—the end of drought and famine.

Another type of tale to which *The Palm-Wine Drinkard* can be compared is the long tale or ro-mance. Like alo tales, romances are told in the evening, but unlike alo tales, romances are told only by accomplished male storytellers and deal with a series of heroic adventures undergone by a single character in the bush. Although romances are not necessarily believed to be true stories by teller or audience, these tales at least have the ring of plausibility to them—such things, even magical things, *could* have happened, even if they in fact didn't. Romances have to do with the protagonist's journey from a sub-human or socially unacceptable condition to a state of social acceptability—a transformation achieved during a quest of a more tangible nature that takes the hero or heroine away from society and into the bush. The protagonist, while suffering an inhuman condition, must also suffer an inhuman world (the wilderness); his return to society coincides with a return of his own humanity.

According to scholar Deirdre LaPin, "The triumph of good character over selfish motives is a theme repeated in many [Yoruba] romances" (LaPin, p. 56). This theme is certainly evident in *The Palm-Wine Drinkard,* which also follows the romance pattern of a quest leading from society into the bush and back again. Drinkard, upon returning to his village, returns to social acceptability. He has gained a wife, wealth, and an appreciation for things other than palm wine.

The Novel in Focus

Plot summary. *The Palm-Wine Drinkard* opens with the narrator, Drinkard, explaining his name: "I was a palm-wine drinkard since I was a boy of ten years of age. I had no other work more than to drink palm-wine in my life" (*Palm-Wine Drinkard,* p. 7). Although the rest of his siblings worked, Drinkard spent all his time day and night drinking palm wine until "I could not drink ordinary water at all except palm-wine. But when my father noticed that I could not do any work more than to drink, he engaged an expert palm-wine tapster for me" (*Palm-Wine Drinkard,* p. 7). The tapster kept Drinkard supplied with wine, as well as Drinkard's many friends, who joined him every day.

Fifteen years later, however, Drinkard's father dies, and six months after that the tapster falls to his death while tapping a palm tree. No other tapster is skilled enough to replace the dead one. Without palm wine, Drinkard loses his happiness and his friends, but then realizes that he has a chance to get his tapster back:

Old people were saying that the whole people who had died in this world, did not go to heaven directly, but they were living in one place somewhere in this world. So that I said I would find out where my palm-wine tapster who had died was.

(*Palm-Wine Drinkard,* p. 9)

Drinkard embarks on a journey fraught with danger and adventure, a journey into the bush in search of his dead tapster. Luckily, he possesses a certain amount of magical power, or juju, with which he transforms himself and defeats, or escapes from, adversary after adversary.

Drinkard meets an old man who claims to know the location of the dead tapster, but to learn the secret he must pass the man's test: he must capture Death himself. Although the old man thinks this task will end only in Drinkard's demise, Drinkard succeeds. He finds Death living on an isolated farm, and Death invites Drinkard to stay the night. Drinkard accepts and, after avoiding Death's attempt to murder him in his sleep, manages to fool and snare Death. When Drinkard returns to the old man with Death in tow, the old man flees in terror without revealing the location of the dead tapster.

Months later the head of a village promises to tell Drinkard the whereabouts of the tapster but only if Drinkard will rescue the headman's daughter. She has fallen into the clutches of a "curious creature," whom she met at the marketplace (*Palm-Wine Drinkard,* p. 17). He appeared to be a handsome young man, a "complete gentleman," but when she left the market and went with him into the forest, he began to return first his fine clothes and then his body parts to those from whom he had borrowed them, until all that was left of the "complete gentleman" was a bare skull (*Palm-Wine Drinkard,* p. 17). By the time she realized her mistake, the girl was already the skull's prisoner, and he took her back to his underground home to live with his skull family. Drinkard uses his magic to locate and rescue the woman. Soon they marry and live in her father's village, but the father refuses to reveal the secret location of the dead tapster because he does not want his daughter to depart with Drinkard.

Three-and-a-half years later the thumb of Drinkard's wife swells, and a child bursts forth, already able to speak like a ten-year-old. The child grows in hours to a height of three feet, and declares his name to be "'ZURRJIR' which means a son who would change himself into another thing very soon" (*Palm-Wine Drinkard,* p.

17). The child drinks palm wine and eats food in prodigious amounts. He also possesses great strength and ferocity, which he uses to attack people and burn their homes. Seeing the child's bad character, Drinkard sets his house on fire while the child sleeps within.

His father-in-law finally informs Drinkard of the tapster's whereabouts. Before Drinkard and his wife leave for good, however, a "half-bodied baby"—their son disfigured by the fire—rises from the ashes of the burnt home, and commands his parents to carry him on their journey (*Palm-Wine Drinkard,* p. 35). The baby dominates the couple, eats all their food, and refuses to let them rest or sleep.

They finally escape his clutches when they encounter three spirits—Dance, Song, and Drum—with whom they are compelled to dance for five days. They reach the spirits' home, which the monster baby enters with the spirits, and without his parents, who are released at once from the spirits' dance and from the clutches of their son. Soon Drinkard and his wife reach the place to which the dead tapster first went, only to find he left two years earlier for Deads' Town, the abode of all the "deads."

The couple's adventures continue as they escape from a king who lives in a palace made of refuse. They then come to live among the beautiful and friendly creatures of Wraith-Island. Here, Drinkard works successfully as a farmer and gains some magic seeds once he makes a sacrifice to the creature-owner of the land that he farms. Eighteen months later the couple decide to continue their journey: "While we had enjoyed everything in that 'Wraith-Island,' to our satisfaction, there were still many great tasks ahead. Then we started our journey in another bush, but remember that there was no road on which to travel in those bushes at all" (*Palm-Wine Drinkard,* p. 51).

They next escape from a fantastic monster called "Spirit of Prey," but they then fall into the grasp of the cruel creatures of Unreturnable-Heaven's town, who do everything incorrectly; they dress their animals in fine clothes and wear only leaves themselves. The couple is physically tortured, but they finally escape.

Exhausted, they rest for five months in a house they build in the bush, and then discuss returning home, though they do not know its direction anymore: "To go back was harder and to go further was the hardest, so at last we made up our mind and started to go forward" (*Palm-Wine Drinkard,* p. 64). In the bush the pair encounter a talking tree with hands that beckon them to come inside. Within the tree is the palatial home of the spirit Faithful-Mother. Before entering they deposit a couple of potential handicaps:

> We had "sold our death" to somebody at the door for the sum of £70: 18: 6d and "lent our fear" to somebody at the door as well on interest of £3: 10: 0d per month, so we did not care about death and we did not fear again.
> (*Palm-Wine Drinkard*, p. 67)

In the lavish interior of the tree they recover their strength and enjoy food and drink. The Faithful-Mother's home resembles a twentieth-century nightclub with dancing, feasting, and gambling, rather than anything from Yoruba tradition. After a year, however, the Faithful-Mother instructs them to return to their journey. Drinkard does not want to resume the arduous odyssey, but Mother will not let them tarry any longer, nor will she join them. As they leave her home, they collect their "fear" and interest payments, but the buyer of their "death" refuses to return it.

Back in the bush they meet a "Red-lady" who leads them to a territory where everything—the trees, ground, and living creatures, including Drinkard and his wife—are deep red in hue. They come to the Red-king who wants to sacrifice one of the couple. Since he has already sold his "death," Drinkard volunteers for the sacrifice. He battles, and unexpectedly kills with a gun, the red-fish and red-bird that had been responsible for all the red color.

> [I]ts head was just like a tortoise's head, but it was as big as an elephant's head and it had over 30 horns and large eyes which surrounded the head. All these horns were spread out as an umbrella. It could not walk but was only gliding on the ground like a snake and its body was just like a bat's body and covered with long red hair like strings. It could only fly to a short distance, and if it shouted a person who was four miles away would hear. All the eyes which surrounded its head were closing and opening at the same time as if a man was pressing a switch on and off.
> (*Palm-Wine Drinkard*, p. 79-80)

The Red-king fears Drinkard's power, so when Drinkard returns, the red-people burn down their town and leave the area in the form of two walking trees, taking with them Drinkard's wife. Drinkard finds her in the new town of the red-people, who are no longer red, and with whom he becomes reconciled. The couple lives there for

a year while Drinkard farms with the magic seeds from Wraith Island and becomes quite wealthy.

A man called "GIVE AND TAKE," who has never known poverty, asks to work for Drinkard. The laborer is actually the head of all the bush creatures, and after a while he steals all the crops of the red-people. They blame Drinkard, but "GIVE AND TAKE" protects him from their wrath by killing them all.

Drinkard and his wife continue their journey to Deads' Town and before long meet a man in the bush carrying a bundle. In exchange for their carrying his burden, he promises to lead the pair to Deads' Town immediately. Unbeknownst to Drinkard and his wife, the bundle contains the body of a dead prince, and the next town is not Deads' Town but that of the dead prince's father. The stranger informs the king that the couple has murdered his son and that the sack they carry contains the corpse. The king captures the pair but decides to give them a week of enjoyment before they are executed. The real killer is confused when he sees the king treat the couple so well and, out of desire to enjoy such luxuries himself, confesses to the murder. Soon the festivities end, and the killer is executed.

The couple finally reaches Deads' Town where the "deads" do everything opposite from the "alives," such as walking backwards. The deads forbid alives to enter the town, and before they can meet the tapster, the couple is dragged from Deads' Town. The tapster meets them outside the town's gates, and recounts his story of the ten years since his death. For the first two years he trained in a place for the recently dead before qualifying as a fully dead man and resident of Deads' Town, where he has "lived" since. Drinkard and his wife cannot remain among the dead, "Because everything that they were doing there was incorrect to alives and everything that all alives were doing was incorrect to deads too" (*Palm-Wine Drinkard*, p. 100). The tapster gives Drinkard a magic egg as a present but will not return to the land of the living.

On their journey home the couple continue their adventures in the bush. They escape from 400 malicious dead babies, from a monstrous creature that traps them in a bag, and then from the stomach of a "hungry creature" that swallows them. They arrive in "mixed town," a place of mixed people—exactly what they are a mixture of is never explained. Drinkard's wife is ill, and while she recovers, Drinkard attends the local court and is asked to judge two different cases.

Unable to determine a fair outcome, he asks for an adjournment of a year before deciding.

The couple resumes their homeward journey, but dancing mountain-creatures trap Drinkard's wife and force her into a perpetual dance with them. Drinkard saves her by temporarily turning her into a wooden doll, and then with her in his pocket he turns himself into a pebble, which he manages to throw across a river and into his own town.

The town has fallen victim to a terrible famine due to a dispute between Land and Heaven over which has seniority and therefore claim over a mouse they caught together, which is too small to divide. Heaven has stopped the rain to show its anger, and the drought has caused the famine.

The magic egg that the Drinkard received from the tapster produces copious amounts of food and drink. Drinkard uses it to feed the people, who flock to his house from all over. After eating and drinking their fill they start to wrestle and accidentally break the egg. Without more food and drink the people leave. In order to teach them a lesson Drinkard puts the egg back together and has it make whips that attack all the lazy people. He then tells everyone how to end the famine—by sending a sacrifice to Heaven to acknowledge Heaven's superiority. The sacrifice is sent, Heaven relents, the rains return, and the famine ends.

Harmony between the domains. Because of the sacrifice that Drinkard has advised the people to make to Heaven, Heaven and Land are reconciled, and harmony is reestablished between the two domains. In this episode from *The Palm-Wine Drinkard,* Amos Tutuola is retelling a Yoruba myth about the confrontation between Olodumare—supreme deity and representative of heaven—and Oduduwa—orisa of the earth. In the myth, as in the novel, humans send the disputed animal as a sacrifice to Olodumare in acknowledgement of his superiority, thus settling the argument and ending the drought. Both the myth and *The Palm-Wine Drinkard* reflect the high value that the Yoruba place on maintaining a harmonious relationship between the domains of Aiye (earth) and Orun (heaven), with which the plot of *The Palm-Wine Drinkard* has much to do.

An important part of the relationship between Orun and Aiye is the relationship between the living and the dead. The Yoruba who dwell on Aiye consult as well as make sacrifices to the ancestors in Orun and to the orisa who dwell there and exert control over life on earth. Yet at the beginning of the novel, Drinkard hardly notices when his own father suddenly dies. In a culture in which great importance is placed upon the proper burial of and sacrifice to one's deceased parents, Drinkard's behavior is particularly shocking. This is not the proper relationship, as conceived by the Yoruba, between the living and the dead. It is only when Drinkard's tapster dies, and the supply of palm wine is cut off, that Drinkard takes notice of death. His response—to seek his tapster in order to bring him back from the land of the dead—is also improper, as Drinkard will eventually learn when he reaches Deads' Town. The dead do not belong in the same domain as the living; their ways are different. Tapster cannot leave the Deads' Town and Drinkard cannot remain. As a result of Drinkard's contacting Tapster, however, good things result: Drinkard receives from Tapster the food-providing egg. In the Yoruba worldview the living should look to the dead for help and advice.

Scholar David West has likened the palm wine in *The Palm-Wine Drinkard* to *Nommo,* "the expression of the life-force which forms one's personality, and which remains even in the deads after they have become non-living" (West in Lindfors, p. 84). This life-force flows from Orun to Aiye, from the orisa and the ancestors to the

EXCERPT FROM FAGUNWA'S *THE FOREST OF GOD*

My friend, it was in the twenty-fifth year of my father's life, that he got himself ready [to go]. One day, early in the morning, he headed towards a strange forest near our hometown to hunt; our town's people knew the forest as the Forest of God, for it was a very dreadful forest indeed. Even the hunters dreaded the Forest of God more than the Forest of Four Thousand Demons; and it was a law in our town that any hunter who had not hunted elephant must not go there to hunt, for it was the abode of wonders; it was where the birds talked like human beings, and animals bought and sold from and to one another; where many trees did not have roots, but looked fresh with evergreen leaves. Mice were bigger than pouched rats, and snails were bigger than tortoise in the Forest of God. The gnome and hoodlumish spirits were friends; it was there that the strong headed snakes terrify the hunters, for the abode of the head of the entire snakes in the world was there.

(Fagunwa in Ajadi, p. 13)

living, but in return Orun requires a sacrifice of a portion of that life-force. Perhaps Drinkard is without palm wine for the same reason that the land is without rain: failure to sacrifice—in Drinkard's case, to his father. One must not be greedy, in the Yoruba worldview, and begrudge Orun its fair share. When Drinkard is cut off from palm wine, from the life-force, he must reestablish a connection with the world of the dead that he has neglected, which he does by going in quest of his dead tapster. In Yoruba cosmology it is largely through the ancestors that good things come to the living—the dead in a sense serve as tapsters of the life-force that the living need to drink.

As a prodigious drinker of palm wine, Drinkard is like the original crafter of Yorubaland and the Yoruba people: the orisa Orunmila. Orunmila is also known as the orisa of Ifa, the divination system whereby living Yoruba communicate with the ancestors and the orisa. His knowledge of divination gives him authority to communicate to humans on behalf of the supreme deity, Olodumare. Orunmila is a link between Orun and Aiye, between gods and men, between the dead and the living: he is the means by which earth, created by Olodumare in heaven, becomes habitable by human beings; and he is the means through which the ancestors in heaven communicate with their descendants on earth. In the novel, Drinkard likewise serves as a link between Orun and Aiye when he instructs the people to sacrifice so that harmony between the domains may be regained. Those who make sacrifices, according to Yoruba beliefs, enlist the aid of another orisa, Esu. Master of languages and the orisa of unpredictability, Esu carries messages and sacrifices from earth to heaven, or from the descendants to the ancestors and gods.

Sources and literary context. Both the content and style of Tutuola's *The Palm-Wine Drinkard* owe a debt to Yoruba oral tradition. Throughout his life Tutuola enjoyed hearing and telling folktales, and he used them freely in his work. Tutuola once commented, "I wrote Drinkard for the people of the other countries to read the Yoruba folktales" (Tutuola in Lindfors, p. 280). And in fact his novel has brought Yoruba stories to many who would otherwise never know them.

One example of Tutuola's borrowing from folktales is the incident of the "complete gentleman" who is actually a skull that abducts the woman who would later become Drinkard's wife. There is a traditional tale about a disobedient daughter who defies her parents and insists on the mate of her choice, a man of beauty, actually a skull garbed in borrowed body parts. It whisks her back to the land whence it came, returning the body parts on the way. Before the woman is rescued she promises ever after to obey her parents. Among other characters and items common to Yoruba folklore that surface in *The Palm-Wine Drinkard* are the monstrous child, the magic egg, and various monsters in the bush.

Another Yoruba author who wove folklore into his writings is D. O. Fagunwa, whose Yoruba-language adventure novels preceded and served as a model for Tutuola's *Palm-Wine Drinkard.* Fagunwa's novels *The Forest of the Thousand Demons* (1939) and *The Forest of God* (1946), the first long works of fiction written in Yoruba, were extremely popular. The similarities between these works—which concern adventures in the bush—and the works of Tutuola are so striking that Tutuola received criticism from Yoruba reviewers for being too derivative. While Tutuola did not plagiarize Fagunwa, the major difference between the two is that Tutuola chose to write in English. This brought his work into the purview of an international audience.

Tutuola was considered an honorary member of the Mbari Club, a group of artists and writers based in the Nigerian city of Ibadan in the 1960s. Their work marries traditional African culture

---

TUTUOLA HEARS THE STORY OF THE PALM-WINE DRINKARD

Tutuola has described hearing the story of Drinkard told by an old man on a Yoruba palm plantation:

"He started to serve the wine with bamboo tumbler. This bamboo tumbler was as deep as a glass tumbler, but it could contain the palm-wine which could reach half a bottle. Having taken about four, my body was not at rest at all, it was intoxicating me as if I was dreaming. But when he noticed how I was doing, he told me to let us go and sit down on the bank of a big river which is near the farm for fresh breeze which was blowing here and there with strong power. Immediately we reached there and sat under the shade of some palm trees . . . I fall asleept [sic]. After an hour, he woke me up, and I came to normal condition at that time.

"When he believed that I could enjoy what he wanted to tell me, then he told me the story of the Palm-Wine Drinkard."

(Tutuola in Lindfors, p. 279)

with modern techniques, styles, and forms. Members of the club have included the writers John Pepper Clark, Christopher Okigbo, and Wole Soyinka (see **Death and the King's Horseman,** also covered in *African Literature and Its Times*). Tutuola is associated too with the Oshogbo artists movement—a group of artists who came together in the late 1950s to renovate a shrine of the traditional religion in the Nigerian city of Oshogbo and whose art, like Tutuola's writing, often contains imagery of the sacred and the supernatural. Oshogbo painter Twins Seven-Seven created several works based on episodes from Tutuola's novels.

Reviews. In the early 1950s Western and African critics greeted *The Palm-Wine Drinkard* quite differently. Western reviewers reacted positively to the novel's distinct language and departure from the conventional novel. The Welsh author Dylan Thomas wrote a glowing review in which he called the book a "brief, thronged, grisly and bewitching story, or series of stories" (Thomas in Lindfors, p. 7). Arthur Calden-Marshall praised "this strange, poetic, nightmare volume" (Calden-Marshall in Lindfors, p. 10). Others remarked on its use of folklore; Anthony West praised Tutuola for combining the folktale's "freedom of embroidery" with the novel's "freedom of invention" (West, p. 17).

However, the same qualities that were praised by English and American reviewers drew disapproval and even disgust from Nigerian critics. They regarded the language as a poor relative to standard English. Babasola Johnson wrote that the novel "should not have been published at all. . . . It is bad enough to attempt an African narrative in 'good English,' it is worse to attempt it in Mr. Tutuola's strange lingo" (Johnson in Lindfors, p. 31). I. Adergbo Akinjogbin censured Tutuola's use of folktales since it perpetuated Eu-

ropean misconceptions of African as primitives, and wrote that the novel had "no literary merit" (Akinjogbin in Lindfors, p. 41). These Yoruba reviewers also criticized Tutuola's use of folktales as derivative from the very popular work of Fagunwa, and as receiving undeserved praise from foreign critics. Later African critics reversed such assessments of Tutuola and recognized *The Palm-Wine Drinkard* and his subsequent novels as vital works of fiction that reflect African concerns and traditions. Western critics, on the other hand, neglected Tutuola's later works when the novelty of *The Palm-Wine Drinkard* had run its course.

—Kimberly Ball and John Roleke

For More Information

Ajadi, Gabriel Ajiboye. "A Critical Introduction for and an Annotated Translation of D. O. Fagunwa's *Igbo Olodumare (The Forest of God)*." Ph.D. diss., Ball State University, 1984.

Atanda, J. Adebowale. "The Yoruba People: Their Origin, Culture, and Civilization." In *The Yoruba History, Culture, and Language*. Lagos: Ibadan University Press, 1996.

Courlander, Harold. *Tales of Yoruba Gods and Heroes*. Greenwich, Conn.: Fawcett, 1973.

LaPin, Deirdre Ann. *Story, Medium and Masque: The Idea and Art of Yoruba Storytelling*. Madison: University of Wisconsin Press, 1977.

Lindfors, Bernth, ed. *Critical Perspectives on Amos Tutuola*. Washington D.C.: Three Continents Press, 1975.

Olusanya, G. O. *The Second World War and Politics in Nigeria 1939-1953*. London: Evan Brothers, 1973.

Tutuola, Amos. *The Palm-Wine Drinkard*. London: Faber and Faber, 1969.

West, David S. "The Palm-Wine Drinkard and African Philosophy." *The Literary Half-Yearly* 19, no. 2 (July 1978): 83-96.

The Pillar of Salt

by

Albert Memmi

∽

orn in 1920, Albert Memmi grew up in a religiously conservative Jewish family of humble origins in the old city of Tunis. His father was a saddler who barely earned enough to feed his wife and eight children; his mother was illiterate and spoke only the Judeo-Arabic dialect of Tunisian Jews. In his boyhood Memmi attended a traditional religious school to learn Torah and Hebrew, then a private school, Alliance Israélite Universelle, for a secular education. In 1932 he was chosen as a scholarship student at the Lycée Carnot, which educated mainly French or European boys. By the eve of World War II he had gained a post at his school and was pursuing university studies. During the 1942-43 German occupation of Tunisia, Memmi and other Jews were rounded up and sent to harsh labor camps in the countryside. Escaping the Nazis, he signed up to fight them with the Free French. After the war, at age 26, he left Tunisia for France, where he began to write his first novel, *The Pillar of Salt*. Based on his own experience, the novel was first published in a Paris revue, *Les Temps Modernes,* directed at the time by Jean-Paul Sartre. Appearing in four installments, then a single volume, the novel concerns the life of a mid-twentieth-century Tunisian Jew.

Events in History at the Time the Novel Takes Place

Education under the French Protectorate (1881-1956). Invaded by the French army in

---

THE LITERARY WORK

An autobiographical novel set in colonial Tunisia from 1920 to 1943; published in French as (*La Statue de Sel*) in 1953, in English in 1955.

SYNOPSIS

A young Arab Jew in French-ruled Tunisia struggles with multiple identities related to religion, his family's poverty and illiteracy, and his success in French colonial schools. In the World War II era, he confronts anti-Semitism and the Nazi occupation of Tunisia.

1881, the North African country of Tunisia became part of France's African empire. French imperialism assumed a different form in Tunisia, however, than in neighboring Algeria, which was folded into France proper. In contrast, Tunisia became a Protectorate; its sovereignty appeared to remain intact and the local ruling family continued to occupy the throne. In fact, however, the French resident general actually wielded the most power in the country. France controlled Tunisia's finances, public works, education, armed forces and security, and agriculture. The legal system and courts were, for the most part, also under French supervision.

Probably the most important change brought by France to Tunisia was modern education. While institutions offering European educational curricula had existed prior to the Protectorate, these were usually private, religious schools maintained either by Protestant or Catholic missionaries. In 1883 colonial authorities created the Directorate of Public Education, which established a more or less unified school system for French and other European nationals residing in the country, and for native Tunisians of the elite class. Known as Franco-Arab schools, these institutions used French as their language of instruction and otherwise patterned themselves after schools in metropolitan France. Successful completion of studies at a *lycée,* such as the Lycée Carnot in Tunis, could later lead to advanced studies either in French Algeria or in France itself. Only rarely were children of the indigenous Arab Jewish population admitted to these schools before World War II, particularly if they came from poor families.

The creation of private, largely secular primary schools by the Parisian organization Alliance Israélite Universelle in Tunisia and other North African countries during the 1860s brought modern French ideas in social, political, and cultural life into Jewish education. European teachers, modern textbooks, and Western curricula provided by the Alliance Israélite constituted a revolutionary break with the past for North African Jews.

> Although the Alliance leaders were committed to the congruence of Western culture and a modern understanding of Judaism, Jewish learning was not at the center of their educational vision. Following the French primary system, the Alliance schools devoted their curriculum to French language and reading, arithmetic, natural science, geography, and local history.
>
> (Hyman, p. 84)

Jews in North Africa. North Africa has long been home to different communities of Jews. They have inhabited the region at least since the Jewish Diaspora in 70 C.E., after the Roman emperor Titus destroyed the Temple and the city of Jerusalem. Some North African Jews even trace their roots to the Punic or Carthaginian period (circa 814 B.C.E.-146 C.E.). Under Roman, Byzantine, Vandal, and subsequent Arab Islamic rule (i.e., from late seventh century C.E. on), the Jews of North Africa resided both in the countryside and particularly in the cities and towns. Over the centuries, many became Arabized, while retaining their Jewish faith and cultural heritage; a smaller number were Berber-speakers (a family of Afro-Asiatic languages), residing mainly in the mountains or in remote oases on the edge of the Sahara Desert. By the late medieval or early modern period (1300-1500 C.E.), Arab and Berber Jews regarded themselves as native North Africans, although they developed their own vernacular language in an act of deliberate self-segregation from the majority Arab Muslim or Berber Muslim populations. The synagogue was the center of community life and children were sent to rabbinic schools for primary education; advanced studies were available at an institution of learning (or *yeshiva*) that trained the rabbinical elite. But, otherwise, the customs, attitudes, and lifestyles of North African Jewry hardly differed from those of their Muslim neighbors. Superstitions, such as the evil eye, were observed both by Jews and Muslims. The veneration of holy persons and organized collective pilgrimages to honor the "very special dead" were also prominent features of North African Jewish and Muslim cultures alike. Cults to venerate especially pious rabbis or Jewish sages constituted an important expression of North African Judaism. Often the tomb or burial place of the holy man attracted a following that evolved into a system of rituals as well as shared beliefs in his miracle-working abilities. According to one study, Morocco alone boasted some 600 Jewish holy persons, whose shrines became the focal points of local or regional pilgrimages (Weingrod, pp. 221-22).

Augmenting the contingent of Jews in Tunisia was a second group from Spain. These Spanish Jews (called Sephardim) arrived in waves between the fifteenth and seventeenth centuries as refugees during the Reconquista of Spain and Portugal, the campaigns by Christians to recover territory that had been taken over by Muslims. Later, during the eighteenth and nineteenth centuries, Jews from Italy—mainly from the region of Livorno—moved to Tunisia, making a place for themselves here as commercial and financial middlemen between Europe and the ruling elite of Tunisia.

Italian vs. Tunisian Jews. The Italian Jews generally thought of themselves as superior to Tunisian Jews, an idea encouraged by basic legal and social distinctions. Speaking European languages, the Italian Jews frequently enjoyed the protection of a power like Italy, France, or Great Britain that had interests in Tunisia. In general, non-Tunisian Jews were not governed by the laws of the Arab Muslim Tunisian state but rather by the laws of whichever European nation had extended diplomatic protection to them.

On the other hand, Tunisian Jews were subjects of the *beys* (princes or regents ruling in the name of the Ottoman sultan) or of native-born rulers who governed in accordance with Islamic law and custom. These Jews held a socio-legal status inferior to that of Muslims and suffered both informal and official discrimination—for example, they had to pay special taxes and observe sumptuary laws governing the wearing of certain types of clothing. Their situation improved after 1857, when some of these restrictions were lifted.

Other differences encouraged the distinction between North African and European Jews. While the Italian Jews were more or less secularized by the mid-nineteenth century, the Tunisian Jews remained deeply religious. Intermarriage between the two groups was rare, though not completely unknown. In the socioeconomic realm, European Jews tended to occupy a higher status than Tunisian Jews due to trade connections with Europe. While some *Tswana,* or Tunisian Jews, achieved middle-class status, the group generally belonged to the least privileged stratum of society. Like most of the European Jews, the few prominent Tunisian Jews resided in or near Tunis. Meanwhile, micro-communities of poorer indigenous Jews were scattered around the country: in the deep south; on the island of Djerba; in towns along the Mediterranean coast; and in the ghettolike *hara* in Tunis.

By the time Memmi's novel opens in the 1920s, uneven modernization had turned the capital into a divided city. Resembling urban areas in France, the recently built European zone was organized in a regular gridlike pattern with wide boulevards, cafes, theaters, and restaurants. The few wealthy European Jews, or even those of middling means who had acquired European citizenship, lived in the modern neighborhoods of the *ville nouvelle* ("new city"). Secular education, Western dress, and facility in the French language continued to set them apart from other Jews.

Modern Tunis contrasted starkly with the ancient *medina* (the old or traditional city), which was characterized by narrow winding streets, covered bazaars, and crumbling ramparts; by 1920, the medina had come to symbolize blind tradition, backwardness, and abject poverty. When Memmi was growing up, poor Tunisian Jews like his family still resided in or near the hara in the old city. The hara was not exactly synonymous with European-type ghettos because Tunisian Jews (only 2.7 percent of

Tunisia's population at the time) were not obliged by law to reside there (Abitbol, p. 1520). Even a few non-Jewish families lived in the hara. In any case, the Jewish population there as elsewhere rose over time. The total Jewish population, both Arab and Iberian-Italian, expanded during the twentieth century, peaking in the World War II era at between 71,000 and 85,000 (Audet, pp. 4-7; Abitbol, p. 1520).

Anti-Semitism and the rise of fascism in Tunisia. The worldwide economic depression of the 1930s brought misery to many in Tunisia's countryside and cities. Meanwhile, the decade saw the rise of an increasingly assertive Tunisian nationalist movement, which became linked with organized labor and trade unions and resorted to tactics such as strikes and demonstrations against the French colonial regime. These tactics led to violence and loss of life, in part because the French government in Paris felt little inclined to negotiate with Tunisian nationalists, given the menacing political situation in Europe after 1936. The rise of fascism and Nazism portended yet another major global conflict on the horizon. Complicating matters was the fact that the single largest European settler group living in Tunisia was comprised of Italian nationals, including 5,000 Jewish Italian nationals (Abitbol, p. 1522). For the most part, these Italian nationals were politically and culturally associated with fascist Italy. Italian leader Benito Mussolini's rise to power and his public renunciation of the terms of the French Protectorate over Tunisia caused French officials to become increasingly harsh in their treatment of the colonized, partic-

> ### PROCLAMATION ISSUED BY GENERAL VON ARNIM REGARDING A FINE LEVIED UPON ALL JEWS
>
> ~
>
> "To the victims of the Anglo-American bombardments: The war has been desired and prepared by international Jewry. The population of Tunisia, French, Italian, and Muslim, has suffered cruelly from the war due to the bombings of these past days. This is why I have decided to levy a fine upon the Jews of Tunisia amounting to twenty million francs. This sum will be used to provide assistance and succor to the civilian victims of the bombings."
>
> Signed: Tunis, 23 December 1942
>
> The Commanding General of the Axis Forces
>
> (Attal and Sitbon, pp. 186-187; trans. J. Clancy-Smith)

British troops, supported by American tanks, advance on the Tunisian front in 1943.

ularly of the Tunisian Muslims and Jews who were involved in the nationalist movement. French colonial authorities feared that Tunisian nationalists would throw in their lot with Italy against France.

Once France fell to Germany in 1940 and the puppet Vichy regime was installed as the French government, anti-Semitic laws and policies were enacted in both France and Italy. These policies "did not apply automatically to their overseas colonies but they went through great pains to have similar legislation adopted in those territories, especially in North Africa where there were important Jewish communities" (Audet, p. 39).

In Tunisia efforts were made both by local French colonial officials, particularly by the Resident General, Admiral Jean-Pierre Estéva, and by the Tunisian ruler, Sidi Muhammad Munsif Bey, to limit the application of anti-Semitic laws to Jews, whether native Tunisian or European. Until March 1942, both Estéva and the Bey were able to block the implementation of major anti-Jewish decrees, such as laws authorizing the seizure of Jewish properties. New laws in the spring of 1942 severely curtailed the professional and economic activities of all Jews in Tunisia, but these measures too were not immediately implemented.

This changed abruptly in December of 1942 when Tunisia was occupied by German and Italian troops. Allied armies began advancing upon Axis-occupied Tunisia and fighting broke out during the winter of 1942-43. The German occupation of Tunisia posed great dangers not only to Tunisian Jews but to all Jews of whatever nationality residing in the country. The Germans set up headquarters in Tunis as well as along the Mediterranean coast in the region of Nabeul. In the capital they immediately began to round up Tunisian Jews from the hara and from the central synagogue not far from Memmi's home. The Alliance Israélite schools were also targeted. Under the auspices of the Jewish Community Board, headed by Moïse Borgel, members of the Jewish community in Tunis agreed to provide labor for the German army from the ranks of their young men, if Jewish women, children, and the elderly or infirm were spared. The Gestapo seized private and communal property, imposed collective fines, and took Jewish hostages as "security" against this pledge to form a labor force.

Despite German promises, some Tunisian Jews suffered rape, beatings, and/or summary executions. In contrast to their harsh treatment, as Daniel Carpi has pointed out, "the small community of Jews holding Italian citizenship had enjoyed preferential treatment throughout the entire period—in practice, if not in principle—

thanks to the protection granted them by the Italian authorities" (Carpi, p. 239). Finally, on May 7, 1943, the British Seventh Division entered Tunis and the American Ninth Division took the port of Bizerte. By May 13, Tunisia was completely liberated, whereupon all anti-Jewish legislation was abolished.

The Novel in Focus

Plot summary. Told in the first person, *The Pillar of Salt* is divided into three main parts. Arranged chronologically, they reflect the author's life in Tunis from birth in 1920, through childhood and early manhood, to the Nazi occupation in 1942 and 1943. Each part concerns a different identity imposed upon, developed by, or assumed by Alexandre Mordekhai Benillouche. Alexandre struggles unsuccessfully to reconcile his African, Jewish, and Arab-Berber identities with a fourth overlay of French knowledge and culture.

In the prologue that opens the novel, the narrator is Alexandre as a young man in the 1940s. Having managed to survive the war and continue his studies, he sits for entrance examinations to the University of Algiers, which may lead to a life in France. The exam represents a long-coveted academic future. By successfully answering the exam's question in philosophy, Alexandre can finally achieve his goal—to become something he is not. Instead, he rebels and spends seven hours in the examination hall writing the story of his life in retrospect. "At the close of this exhausting session, I had some fifty pages to carry away with me. Perhaps, as I now straighten out this narrative, I can manage to see more clearly into my own darkness and to find a way out" (Memmi, *The Pillar of Salt*, p. x).

Part One: The Blind Alley. Part One, set in the Impasse Tarfoune in the old city of Tunis, is mainly concerned with Alexandre's early childhood, family relations, and participation in Jewish communal activities. Though told in first-person narration, the part employs several voices. Time is fractured. We hear the voice of the young boy but also that of the man and writer he will become. Privy to his daily life and routine, the reader follows the boy from the safety of his family's humble dwelling, to the streets, to school and summer camp, through his ritual coming-of-age ceremony, or bar mitzvah, to the threshold of another existence.

Alexandre's neighborhood is one of the most densely populated quarters of the old city; its denizens eke out a meager living as artisans, butchers, or peddlers. While traditionally the artisan class, whether Jewish or Muslim, had earned a decent wage and thus had been respected in Tunisian society, modernization and the inroads of the world economy had undermined artisans and handicraft workers, so that by the interwar period their social rank had fallen. Most scrambled to earn a wholly inadequate income. Because they are poor, Alexandre's family shares part of a ground-level apartment with another equally impoverished Jewish family; cooking and bathroom facilities are common areas. Since the memory of attacks upon Jews is still fresh in the family's mind, they bar the windows and door at night.

Alexandre's ailing father is an artisan, a saddle-maker who barely earns enough income to feed and house his family. The narrator's mother is an illiterate Berber Jew from the countryside (likewise many Jews living in the old Jewish quarter in Tunis were illiterate, though most boys and a few girls learned a bit of Hebrew from the rabbi). "She was a primitive and unsophisticated woman who had never learned to count or to speak a word that was foreign to her native dialect" (*Pillar of Salt*, p. 27). His father's family had emigrated from Italy to Tunisia several generations back. "I was not born in the ghetto. Our alley was at the frontier of the Jewish quarter of Tunis, but this was enough to satisfy my father's pride" (*Pillar of Salt*, p. 20). Here the narrator refers to the fact that only the poorest Jews live in the Jewish quarter; residing just outside it gives his family a slightly higher social status. Also his father takes great pride in being an artisan with his own shop, though clients for handmade saddles are growing ever scarcer.

A defining moment in the first part occurs when Alexandre learns the meaning of class differences. Oblivious to his own poverty, he taunts an even poorer Jewish boy for wearing secondhand clothes. Furious, his mother reprimands him; all his clothing, she points out, is cast-off, hand-me-downs from more affluent relatives. In due time, at the Alliance school, Alexandre mingles with more prosperous Jewish boys who come to class in new clothes, with plenty of money to buy chocolates that they throw away without eating: "Up till then, I had never experienced the revelation of jealousy and envy. I had envied Saul his fine clothes and his pocket money, but it had been without any true bitterness or animosity. Later, I began to hate the Sauls of life, but the power of the rich, at that time still inspired in me some respect" (*Pillar of Salt,* pp. 39-40).

Also in Part One, Alexandre's education and growing involvement in the world beyond the Jewish quarter erodes his respect for his parents. "I must have been about ten years old and already in the fourth grade when I suddenly ceased to believe in my father" (*Pillar of Salt,* p. 43). The first inkling of his parents' inferior social status, their lack of refinement, their powerlessness, comes when Alexandre's school decides to send the poorest boys away to a free summer camp in the mountains of Tunisia. While the prospect of camp seems like a great adventure to the young boy, to his parents it means that he will live for weeks among non-Jews and, worse, that it will cost them money they can ill afford: "I was expected to take with me a number of things we didn't own, a toothbrush, tooth paste, pajamas, and other items of which we had only a single sample for the whole family: a comb, a towel, a shoeshine kit" (*Pillar of Salt,* p. 45). As Alexandre and his parents wait in modern Tunis for the truck to transport the boys to camp, he compares his mother and father with the assembled crowd of European families also bidding farewell to their sons bound for the same camp:

> We were alone in a crowd of Europeans who were waiting in the shade of the trees and joyously shouting remarks from group to group. The loneliness of my parents, silent and scared, moved me even more than my own. I was seeing them, for the first time, uneasy and ashamed, with all their prestige left behind them in our blind alley. They spoke in muffled tones, probably ashamed of their dialect which, to me, now seemed vulgar and out of place.
> (*Pillar of Salt,* p. 45)

Alexandre begins to fully comprehend the colonial order of things, which automatically places Europeans of whatever social background in a higher social category than Tunisians. Living among Muslim and Christian boys at the camp, which is run by the French army, Alexandre also comes into contact for the first time with anti-Semitism and the "device of explaining a defect or a fault in an individual by referring it back to his Jewish faith" (*Pillar of Salt,* p. 48).

The last two chapters in the first part bring childhood to a close and suggest momentous changes ahead. Since Alexandre has excelled in his studies, he is nominated for a scholarship that will permit him to continue his education in the French school. Upon the recommendation of the Alliance Israélite Universelle, the Jewish community of Tunis is prepared not only to underwrite his high-school studies but also his university career as well. The opportunity threatens to deprive his parents of the income he would have earned at a menial job. Reluctantly they agree to the scholarship, unable to foresee the intense ruptures that a French education will bring to family life and relationships.

> Our alley and the Alliance School belonged to one society, but the European sections of town and the high school to another. Above all, I was setting forth on the adventure that leads to knowledge.... Knowledge was the very origin, perhaps, of all the rifts and frustrations that have become apparent in my life. I might have been happier as a Jew of the ghetto....
> (*Pillar of Salt,* p. 82)

Part Two: Alexandre Mordekhai Benillouche. In Part Two the narrative style assumes the quality of a confession as Alexandre tries to rid himself of "obsession" (Roumani, p. 19). Alexandre consciously contends with his own "inferior" identities—African, Jew, Oriental, and poor—as revealed to him by the racism of the French high school. Even the sound of his name elicits snickers from his classmates; he begins a vain attempt to discard his heritage, to deny his family origins, and to stop using the name Mordekhai. His efforts to master the French language provoke mirth from wealthy classmates, since his pronunciation of French words are deformed by the "nasal ghetto accent" (*Pillar of Salt,* p. 104). Excluded from the social company of his peer group, he throws himself violently into learning as revenge for ceaseless humiliations. As he embarks upon a form of "hand-to-hand struggle" with the French language, he experiences the terrible yet marvelous joy of writing, the power of words, of committing thoughts to paper (*Pillar of Salt,* p. 108). It is in this period that he believes he can abandon the East for the West by embracing European learning, culture, and civilization as enunciated, above all, by French philosophers.

However, his steady scholarly triumphs at school estrange him from his immediate and extended family: "I could see their increasing bitterness and disapproval of the turn my life was taking" (*Pillar of Salt,* p. 114). As Alexandre immerses himself in modern science, the daily and weekly Jewish rituals and observances become increasingly irritating to him, and eventually they appear totally irrational. When electricity is introduced to his neighborhood, the faithful consult local rabbis regarding its lawfulness, anxiously demanding whether Jews can legally turn off a light switch during Sabbath, or whether this constitutes "work," from which they are obligated to abstain. The protagonist, who keeps long nightly vigils studying, loses patience one Sabbath and turns off the electric lamp himself—much to the horror of those around him. Finally, things come to a boil at home and a family member hurls the gravest of charges at Alexandre: "It's all the same to him, he's not a Jew!" (*Pillar of Salt,* p. 146).

Rejected by his own kin, Alexandre is likewise not accepted by European or French society; from that moment on, he straddles two social worlds, two cultural universes, belonging to neither. "In my effort to break the mythical ties that I feared while believing that I merely despised them, I used to experience transitory moments of happiness as well as sudden defeats" (*Pillar of Salt,* p. 166). Disappointed in love as well, his only solace at this stage is books and learning, particularly philosophy. His sole friendships with Europeans are intellectual ties with some of his professors; one French man named Poinsot, who befriends him and impresses the boy with his knowledge, will ultimately betray his prize pupil's trust during the German occupation.

Part Three: The World. The politics of fascism, Nazism, and anti-Semitism intrude ever more violently into Alexandre's world in Part Three. A pogrom breaks out in the ghetto of Tunis, bringing death to one of the narrator's boyhood friends. Whether the novel is referring to the actual anti-Jewish attacks of 1938 is uncertain; historically accurate in any case is the suggestion that the rise of European anti-Semitism had an impact on French-controlled Tunisia. As the Jewish community emerges from their hiding places behind locked doors and in barricaded homes, they search for explanations for this outbreak of hatred. Uncertainty as to the identity of the perpetrators or their motivations only adds to the pervasive sense of fear. The rumors that abound reflect the deteriorating political situation of the period. Some say that Arab Muslim troops, called up to fight in Europe, descended upon the hara to pillage, kill, and rape before being shipped off to an uncertain fate across the Mediterranean. Others argue that the French colonial government in Tunisia fomented the pogrom to deflect public attention from its own shortcomings. In either case, Alexandre's position in the French school becomes more and more difficult: "It was in high school that I discovered how painful it is to be a Jew" (*Pillar of Salt,* p. 255). Growing anti-Semitism in Europe at the time is reflected in the be-

havior of the schoolboys from various European countries. Papachino, a classmate of Italian origins whose family has only recently become naturalized French citizens, accuses the Jews of "ruining France" (*Pillar of Salt,* p. 257). Nor are the professors immune—one of the history instructors expounds in his lectures on the scientific basis for racial prejudice and anti-Semitism; later this particular teacher will actively collaborate with the Axis occupiers of the country. The mathematics teacher, originally from Alsace in eastern France, constantly denigrates not only the Tunisian Jews but also the Tunisian Muslims in his class. Still Alexandre obstinately clings to his belief in the superiority of France and French civilization, thinking that his salvation and that of other culturally assimilated Jews rests with Europe.

However, military events elsewhere in North Africa and in war-torn Europe soon overwhelm Alexandre, the Jewish community, and all Tunisians. Unable to achieve a decisive victory over the Axis powers in Europe, the British and American Allies decide to land troops in Morocco and Algeria and to use North Africa as a base against Italy and Germany. In November 1942, British and American troops land in Casablanca, Oran, and Algiers, in what is called "Operation Torch." In response, Germany occupies Tunisia; Italian troops also pour into Tunisia from adjacent Libya.

"And then, all of a sudden, one day we found ourselves right in the middle of the tragedy" (*Pillar of Salt,* p. 271). German war planes land in Tunis and the *Kommandatur* (German military high command) passes its first anti-Jewish measures. Hostages are taken; then come murders, deportations, requisitions of supplies and animals, and rapes. In Tunis, the Arab Jews, being the weakest of the Jewish communities, are targeted. The leaders of the Tunisian Jews are ordered to assemble all men between the ages of 18 and 40. Italian or European Jews are left alone for the most part. Erroneously believing that France as the colonial power in Tunisia will protect them, Tunisian Jewish leaders send a delegation to the French resident general begging for protection. The most potent man in the French colonial edifice in Tunisia replies that he is powerless to help; German orders must be obeyed. Even Alexandre's former teacher and friend, the Frenchman Poinsot, whom Alexandre so admires, proves unwilling and unable to lend a helping hand. Alexandre begins to dimly comprehend that the high-minded philosophical principles that he has learned are hollow.

Although he could have escaped the work camps because of his fragile health, Alexandre enrolls voluntarily and is transported to the countryside. There, amid horrific human suffering, he begins to find peace within himself; he who had rejected Judaism in all its manifestations even organizes a Sabbath prayer service. As the German army starts to lose ground to the advancing Allied armies, the labor camps are continually moved about; soon it becomes clear that the Jewish workers will either be deported to Germany or massacred by their captors. Alexandre organizes some of his comrades and they make a daring escape back to Tunis, during which they are nearly caught in the crossfire between the Anglo-American military and the retreating Axis soldiers.

Back in liberated Tunis, Alexandre begins to pick up the pieces of his shattered life and even begins "to doubt the treason of France" (*Pillar of Salt*, p. 315). He tries to forget that French officials, as well as close friends, refused to help the Tunisian Jews during the Nazi occupation. This leads him to the recruiting office of the French army, which has been exhorting all Tunisian males to enroll with the Free French forces to continue the battle against the Axis powers in Europe. Here, at last, Alexandre is forced to face the full extent and meaning of his own betrayal by his beloved France. As the recruiting officer asks the narrator to sign his name to the register, Alexandre lets slip that he is an African Jew. The officer, embarrassed, makes it clear that in order for him to enlist, he must hide his Jewish identity; it is even suggested that he could assume a Muslim name and thereby be accepted into the army. Alexandre walks out of the recruiting center:

> I would never be a Westerner. I rejected the West. Still, my ideas were too confused and my heart too passionately involved in all that happened, so that I could not fully realize my position or draw practical conclusions from it. I had rejected the East and had been rejected by the West. What would I ever become?
>
> (*Pillar of Salt*, p. 321)

Alexandre begins to confront this agonizing question only when the novel comes full circle. In its second to last chapter, he takes the train to Algeria in order to sit for the university entrance examinations in Algiers. In a tense moment, he deliberately chooses to fail them by writing his life story instead of expounding on a pre-selected topic—the influence of Condillac on the British philosopher John Stuart Mill, an ar-

guably absurd question, since the eighteenth-century French sensualist philosopher Condillac probably exerted little, if any, influence on the British economist Mill. On the long train ride home, he decides to leave Tunis with his best friend, Henry, who longs to go to Argentina. Before setting off, Alexandre Mordekhai Benillouche destroys the eight big notebooks making up his diary.

Labor camp experience. Like Alexandre, young men were interned in brutal labor camps in Tunisia for months. It is estimated that about 5,000 Jews, mainly Tunisian, were forced into over 30 labor camps scattered around the country and mainly located along the shifting military front lines created by the Allied armies' advance from eastern Algeria into Tunisia. While the board attempted to select Tunisian Arab Jews from all socioeconomic classes to serve in these camps, it became increasingly apparent that young men from the poorest classes, above all from the Tunis ghetto, were being recruited in the largest numbers. By far the largest and the worst camp was that in the city of Bizerte on the Mediterranean Sea. As many as 500 Jews, under the surveillance of the German army, were subjected to arduous work assignments for up to 14 hours per day. As the Allies advanced across western Tunisia, disorder broke out in the sectors controlled by the Italian, German, and Vichy French military forces. The mayhem allowed many Jewish labor conscripts and prisoners to flee the labor camps. This helps explain why by early May 1943, when Axis control of Tunisia collapsed, only about 1,600 of the total 5,000 Jewish forced laborers remained in the camps (Abitbol, pp. 1522-23). Around 20 additional Tunisian Jews had by then been deported from Tunisia and sent to their deaths in extermination centers in Europe (Abitbol, p. 1523).

Sources and literary context. In the 1965 preface to the American edition of *The Colonizer and the Colonized*, Memmi refers back to his first book, *The Pillar of Salt*, noting that it was a "life story which was in a sense a trial balloon to help me find the direction of my own life" (Memmi, *The Colonizer and the Colonized*, p. vii). The autobiographical novel as "life compass" is a genre that has attracted other writers from North Africa. When Memmi was composing his work during the 1950s, his friend and literary companion, Albert Camus, was also struggling to come to grips with similar issues of identity and origins. Born in Algeria in 1913, Camus, like Memmi, was from a poor working-class family, although the fact that his father was French meant that Camus's social position was slightly superior to Memmi's. Known for his philosophical works and his pivotal role in the French existentialist movement, Camus was in the midst of writing a piece of autobiographical fiction when he was killed in a car accident in France in 1960. Posthumously published only in 1994 as *Le Premier Homme* (The First Man), this unfinished work relates the story of Jacques Cormery, a child who leads a life very similar to that of its author. Taken together, Albert Memmi's *The Pillar of Salt* and Albert Camus's *Premier Homme* offer readers intensely personal and evocative portraits of the complexities of the French civilizing mission on the African shores of the Mediterranean. At the same time, they pose universal and timeless questions about memory and identity, about the truths and deceptions of childhood, and about moral courage and cowardice.

Many details in *The Pillar of Salt* correspond with Memmi's own life. His family home was adjacent to but not located in the Jewish quarter, where indigent Jews resided in misery and squalor. Memmi, like his protaganist, was selected to become a scholarship student and he too developed a passion for philosophy. Memmi, however, completed his education, taking a teaching post in Tunisia in 1951, in his former school, the Lycée Carnot. In addition, he directed a center for psychology and served as editor for the literary section of the Tunisian French-language weekly *L'Action*.

As Judith Roumani has pointed out, *The Pillar of Salt*'s short chapters are "similar to the traditional Middle Eastern way of teaching a moral lesson based on practical wisdom through stories" (Roumani, p. 8). The novel's structural arrangement can be viewed as drawing upon this old narrative and literary tradition. Moral lessons were often orally transmitted by Tunisian storytellers, and many of the short chapters in the novel end with some moral insight. For example, in one chapter Alexandre recounts his first disappointment in love to his friend Henry, who fails to comfort the lovelorn narrator. Alexandre concludes the chapter with a moral-like observation: "I decided that great joys, like great losses, can never be shared" (*Pillar of Salt,* p. 191).

Events in History at the Time the Novel Was Written

Muslim-Jewish alliance. France relinquished colonial control over Tunisia only in 1956, after decades of nationalist protest. In the early years of the nationalist movement, educated Tunisian Jews agitated alongside Muslims for more political freedoms and better representation under France's Protectorate. One early Tunisian nationalist was a Jewish woman named Gladys Adda, who was born in 1921 in Gabes on the southern Mediterranean coast of Tunisia. Adda recounts in her memoirs that a pogrom fomented by Italian fascists broke out in Gabes in 1938, during which several Jews were killed. During the pogrom, many of their Muslim neighbors attempted to shield the Jews from harm. Pogroms, or organized attacks upon Jews and upon Jewish property, were relatively rare in Tunisia during this period, although in 1917-18, during and just after World War I, there had been pogroms in several cities. In Tunis, the capital, Tunisian Jews and Muslims, joined by some sympathetic Europeans in the Socialist or Communist parties, demanded complete independence from France during the inter-war period and particularly in the years just after World War II. In the 1920s Jewish and Muslim intellectuals in Tunis established the *Alliance Judéo-Musulmane* (Jewish-Muslim Alliance) as part of their cooperative nationalist project.

FROM THE BIBLE TO MEMMI'S NOVEL

The novel's title is taken from the Book of Genesis in the Old Testament of the Bible, which relates the story of Lot and the destruction of the cities of Sodom and Gomorrah. After Lot and his family flee from the wickedness of Sodom, these cities are visited by divine retribution. Lot's wife disregards God's command to not look back as the family leaves: "But his wife looked back from behind him, and she became a pillar of salt" (Genesis 19:26). Various interpretations can be ascribed to Memmi's choice of this biblical passage for the title. One interpretation connects the passage to the unresolved question of the protagonist's cultural identity. Through his French education, Alexandre Mordekhai Benillouche seeks to escape his family's poverty and their doubly marginalized status as Jews and as Arabs colonized by France. By not "looking back" to his humble origins, he hopes to become French—an impossible quest. When he looks back, he sees his multiethnic origins and is forced to acknowledge the impossibility of the quest.

However, the rise of political Zionism and events in Palestine as well as the Holocaust caused a major split between Tunisian Jewish nationalists and their Arab Muslim counterparts in the independence movement. Until the Holocaust many Tunisian and North African Arab Jews were hesitant to embrace Zionism, with its objective of creating a Jewish state in Palestine. However, once they learned of Nazi atrocities, many North African Jews became convinced that only a Jewish state could bring them real security and freedom from persecution. By embracing Zionism these Jews alienated their Muslim counterparts in the nationalist movements, since the creation of a Jewish state in Palestine meant the forced exile of the Arab Palestinians.

With the establishment of the state of Israel in 1948, the position of both native and European Jews in North Africa became precarious; sporadic attacks against Jews occurred in Morocco, forcing many to emigrate from there. Tunisia's independence from France in 1956 and uncertainties surrounding the status of Jews in a Muslim state caused many Tunisian Jews, especially the French acculturated elite, to emigrate as well. Tunisia's Jews often opted to move to France, as Memmi did at this time. "Jews began leaving Tunisia in large numbers in 1961, with twenty-five thousand emigrating in the course of two years" (Hyman, p. 194). Between 1948 and 1970 about 40,000 Tunisian Jews immigrated to Israel; a few hundred moved to the Americas, particularly to Canada. Tunisia's ancient Jewish community was nearly erased by the intersecting forces of colonialism, anti-Semitism, and nationalism. After World War II nationalist leaders defined Tunisian political identity more narrowly, basing it on being Muslim as well as Arab, which left little room for indigenous Tunisian Jews in the country's future. Today there are fewer than one thousand Jews, mainly elderly, living in Tunisia.

Reviews. *The Pillar of Salt* was received with acclaim by North African Francophone writers and by the Parisian literary establishment. Albert Camus, a contemporary of Memmi, characterized it as a beautiful book and wrote the preface to one of the French editions. The philosopher and writer Jean-Paul Sartre was equally enthusiastic in his praise. In 1957 he wrote an essay in *Les Temps Modernes* extolling Memmi's works for their authentic voice, attributed to the writer's triple identity as a colonized African Arab Jew who had experienced the contradictions and racist dimensions of colonialism (Sartre, p. 289). According to a London review, *The Pillar of Salt* is one of a growing number of North African novels to receive critical applause in France. The novel, says the review, deserves praise for its description of the hero's reactions, which "are conveyed with complete conviction and an intelligent lack of self-pity"; the novel is not faultless but "this is one of those books . . . that are in a sense beyond criticism due to the painful subject and the honesty with which it is exposed" (*London Magazine,* p. 62).

—Julia Clancy-Smith

For More Information

Abitbol, Michel. "Tunisia." In *Encyclopedia of the Holocaust.* Vol. 4. New York: Macmillan, 1990.

Attal, Robert, and Claude Sitbon, eds. *Regards sur les Juifs de Tunisie.* Paris: Albin Michel, 1979.

Audet, Caroline. "French and Italian Policies Toward Tunisian Jewry During W.W.II." Master's thesis, University of Durham, U.K., 1997.

Carpi, Daniel. *Between Mussolini and Hitler: The Jews and the Italian Authorities in France and Tunisia.* Hanover, Mass.: Brandeis University Press, 1994.

Hyman, Paula E. *The Jews of Modern France.* Berkeley: The University of California Press, 1998.

Laskier, Michael M. *North African Jewry in the Twentieth Century: The Jews of Morocco, Tunisia, and Algeria.* New York: New York University Press, 1994.

Memmi, Albert. *The Colonizer and the Colonized.* Trans. Howard Greenfeld. New York: Orion Press, 1965.

———. *The Pillar of Salt.* Trans. Edouard Roditi. 1955. Boston: Beacon Press, 1992.

Perkins, Kenneth J. *Tunisia: Crossroads of the Islamic and European Worlds.* Boulder, Colo.: Westview Press, 1986.

Roumani, Judith. *Albert Memmi.* Philadelphia: Celfan Edition Monographs, 1987.

Sartre, Jean-Paul. "Les Livres." *Les Temps Modernes,* nos. 137-138 (1957): 289-292.

Review of *The Pillar of Salt,* by Albert Memmi. *The London Magazine* 3, no. 10 (Oct. 1956): 62.

Weingrod, Alex. "Saints and Shrines, Politics, and Culture: A Morocco-Israel Comparison." In *Muslim Travellers: Pilgrimage, Migration, and the Religious Imagination.* Eds. Dale F. Eickelman and James Piscatori. London: Routledge, 1990.

"The Rivonia Trial Speech"

by

Nelson Mandela

~

Born in the small village of Mvezo in South Africa's Transkei region in 1918, Nelson Mandela grew up listening to the stories of his village elders, who spoke of the time before the white man arrived. Mandela's father was a trusted adviser and a cousin to the paramount chief of Tembuland. According to Mandela himself, it was this strong sense of heritage that set him on the path of activism and revolution: "I hoped then [when listening to these stories] that life might offer me the opportunity to serve my people and make my own humble contribution to their freedom struggle" (Mandela, "Rivonia Trial Speech," p. 163). Mandela attended law school at the Cape Province's Fort Hare University College, where he was active in student politics. In 1944 Mandela joined the African National Congress's Youth League, and in the next decade would emerge as a central figure of African nationalism in South Africa: he developed plans for ANC's underground movement and eluded authorities during his own years underground. He was a key member of the ANC military wing *Umkhonto we Sizwe* and headed its early 1960s campaign of sabotage. The 1963 police raid on the group's headquarters led to the Rivonia Trial, in which Mandela and eight other men were accused of a variety of offenses, and all but one were sentenced to life in prison. Despite warnings from his lawyers that he would weaken his own case, Mandela chose to open the defense with an oration from the docks, popularly known as "The Rivonia Trial Speech." He preferred this public platform so that he could

---

THE LITERARY WORK

A speech given by Nelson Mandela in his own defense on April 20, 1964, in Pretoria, South Africa.

SYNOPSIS

Mandela defends the actions of the paramilitary group *Umkhonto we Sizwe* by describing African life under apartheid.

---

present, without interruption from the prosecution, the beliefs of the African nationalist movement.

Events in History at the Time of the Speech

Africans in South Africa. By the turn of the twentieth century, South Africa had become home to four large racial groups: whites (the British, who had ruled the Cape colony since 1806, and the Afrikaners—descendants mainly of seventeenth-century Dutch settlers); Africans (Bantu-speaking peoples such as the Xhosa, Tswana, Pedi, and Zulu); coloureds (racially mixed South Africans), and Asians (mostly from India). Throughout the nineteenth century the Afrikaners and British had waged "wars of dispossession" on the African peoples and had done so with increasing efficiency and technology, especially after the discoveries of diamonds in the

A segregated public restroom in Johannesburg.

Kimberley and gold in the Witswatersrand areas prompted a "massive influx of machinery and capital goods" into the country (McKinley, p. 2). Large numbers of Africans became wage workers for the newly formed mining companies, which led to the development of an increasingly rich white settler class and a dependent African labor class. Some African peoples, like the Pedi, quickly accommodated themselves to the new industries, and became very skillful at certain occupations at the mines. These people were soon joined by others, such as the Zulu and Sotho. Despite strong resistance, by the early twentieth century all the African societies had lost their political independence and were forced to live under white rule.

The Afrikaners and British were hardly friendly allies in the amassing of wealth and subjugation of Africans, however. Not only was a great deal of wealth at stake, but the Afrikaners were a fiercely independent and nationalistic group, deeply resentful of British domination. The South African War (Boer War) of 1899-1902, an eruption of this ill will, was essentially an attempt by the Afrikaners to preserve the independence of their settler states in the face of the British desire for complete dominance in South Africa. The British were victorious, and in 1910 the two groups joined to form the Union of South Africa. Although the Afrikaners were still subordinate to the British, together the two groups created a system of rule based on the oppression and segregation of Africans, Indians, and coloureds. Meanwhile, the Afrikaner nationalist movement grew, creating an entire ideology around the idea that the Afrikaners were a "chosen people" and that their destiny was to rule South Africa. This single-mindedness would eventually lead to the Afrikaner electoral victory in 1948, when South Africans voted the Nationalist Party into power under the campaign slogan *apartheid*—the system of racial segregation that legalized, in an increasingly intricate fashion, white supremacy.

The African National Congress. The African National Congress (ANC) was the first of several twentieth-century African organizations to address the dire situation of blacks in South Africa. After the Union of South Africa was formed, Africans were subjected to a barrage of repressive laws "designed to relegate [them] to a strictly subordinate role and to exploit [their] labour potential" (Meredith, *In the Name of Apartheid*, p. 35). The most severe of these laws were the 1913 Natives Land Act and the 1936 Native Trust and Land Act, which forced territorial segregation by race, and allotted only about 13 percent of the country to the Africans, who made up 70 percent of South Africa's total population. Founded in 1912, the early ANC was conservative in nature, composed primarily of prominent, westernized Christian African men. The group's first efforts focused on making pleas to both the South African and British governments for equal civil and political rights, but by the end of the decade, when it was clear that nothing was to come of these pleas, the ANC began to lose its momentum:

> [T]he support of the chiefs ebbed away, membership stagnated and later declined, and Congress began a long struggle through a quarter of a century of political frustration and organizational weakness that at times all but overwhelmed it.
>
> (Walshe in McKinley, p. 7)

During the following years, black political struggle seemed centered on the newly formed African worker's unions that accompanied the rapid growth of South African industry after World War I. These workers staged strikes and protests with little support from the ANC, which distanced itself from the masses.

By the mid-1930s the ANC was extremely weak. Government legislation increasingly limited African rights over the years. Since the ANC posed relatively little threat to the government, its repressive measures were aimed mostly at the black labor movement, which became even more active before, during, and after World War II. As Mandela explains, "For thirty-seven years—that is, until 1949—[the ANC] adhered strictly to a constitutional struggle.... White government remained unmoved, and the rights of Africans became less instead of greater" ("Rivonia Trial Speech," p. 165).

The 1940s saw an increase in militancy, however, in the African population at large. Increasing urbanization and industrialization led to greater overcrowding and poverty, and the housing shortage was acute. In 1943 a group of distinguished African leaders drew up a document called "African Claims," demanding "freedom of the African people from all discriminatory laws whatsoever," and presented it to the government (Meredith, *In the Name of Apartheid*, pp. 41-42). Two years later the document became formal ANC policy. Inspired by this shift in mood, the Congress Youth League (CYL) was created within the ANC in 1944 and became a group committed to a more militant type of nationalism. Members of this group, such as Oliver Tambo, Walter Sisulu, Robert Sobukwe, and Nelson Mandela, would make a lasting impact on South African life.

When the white National government came to power in 1948, the new era of apartheid began. The white Nationalists turned their full attention to securing white dominance by constructing "an apparatus of laws, regulations and bureaucracies" that would develop into "the most elaborate racial edifice the world had ever witnessed" (Meredith, *In the Name of Apartheid*, p. 54). Interracial marriages, as well as sexual acts between the races, were banned. Different racial groups were compelled by law to use separate restaurants, post offices, theaters, buses, and so on, or to use separate entrances and seats in public buildings. As residential areas for each racial group were demarcated, whole communities were uprooted to effect widespread racial separation. In the 1950s, when racist legislation was intensified by the new Minister of Native Affairs, the ANC became more strident. It was in this decade that "the young lions" like Mandela, Sisulu, Tambo, and Sobukwe came to the fore— all "educated men who were unwilling to wait, as their elders had done, for some indefinite future when white men should have experienced a change of heart" (Le May, p. 215).

At Mandela's behest, the rejuvenated ANC shifted its policy, deciding to demonstrate peacefully, but unlawfully, against specific legislation, rather than protesting only through constitutional means. The "Defiance Campaign" was launched. Based on the principle of active resistance, plans for the campaign focused on illegal but nonviolent acts such as using facilities marked "for Europeans only," or failing to carry the obligatory pass books that dictated where one was and was not allowed to travel. The protestors were instructed by the ANC to comply with the authorities, and so allowed themselves to be arrested without struggle. If the prisons became overrun with minor offenders, it was thought, the system would break down and be forced to change.

The campaign began on June 26, 1952, when a group wearing ANC armbands and shouting "Mayibuye Afrika," or "Let Africa Return," marched through an entrance into a train station that was designated for "Europeans only." They were immediately arrested. Many similar acts followed, and in the process the ANC gained mass support. Members were optimistic about what the campaign could achieve, but the government responded only with police raids, the lifelong banning of 50 prominent antiapartheid leaders, and multiple arrests. Among those arrested, Mandela and Sisulu were found guilty of promoting communism but received suspended sentences. The government proceeded to increase security measures and its own power. The Public Safety Act of 1953 allowed the government to declare states of emergency whenever public order could not be maintained. As a result of these measures, the Defiance Campaign lost much of its momentum.

BANNED IN SOUTH AFRICA

The word *ban* had very specific meanings in South Africa, depending on whether the object of the banning was a person or a group. People who were banned could no longer publish, give speeches, or talk or meet with more than one person at a time. Sometimes they had to move to isolated, largely Afrikaner villages in the middle of the rural Orange Free State or elsewhere. Their mail was opened; their phones were tapped; they were constantly watched and harassed. They had to report to the police daily. Also their passports were confiscated and they could not travel anywhere without government permission. When an organization was banned, it lost its right to publish literature, stage a demonstration, have an office, or operate in any normal way. Mandela was banned, as was the African National Congress. This explains why there is a huge gap in photographs of Mandela; between the time he went into prison in 1964 and came out in 1990, it was illegal in South Africa to publish photographs of him. Likewise, it was illegal to publish information on the African National Congress.

Hoping to maintain the mass political fervor roused by the Defiance Campaign, the ANC began to work more closely with other antiapartheid groups. The ANC's president, Chief Albert Lutuli, strongly supported turning the ANC into a multiracial movement, believing that help from nonwhites and liberals would hasten the demolishing of apartheid. The ANC's goal, he later wrote, "is not that Congress shall rule South Africa, but that all Africans shall fully participate in ownership and government" (Lutuli in Meredith, *In the Name of Apartheid*, p. 66). In 1955 what came to be known as the Congress Alliance was therefore formed among different antiapartheid groups: primarily, the ANC, the South African Indian Conference, the National Union of the Organization of Coloured People, and the Congress of Democrats—a white organization with communist connections. The alliance produced a document titled the Freedom Charter, which called for the abolition of apartheid, universal suffrage, land redistribution, and other rights denied to blacks in South Africa. Once again, however, the government responded with a series of police raids and, a year later, accused 156 revolutionaries, including Mandela, of high treason. The defendants were released on bail, and in 1956 the long Treason Trial began; by 1959 only 30 of the accused, including Mandela, remained on trial. In 1961 all were acquitted.

Sharpeville. In 1959 part of the ANC broke away, and founded the Pan Africanist Congress (PAC). The argument between the two groups centered mainly on the role of non-Africans in the ANC, as well as the widespread influence of communism within the Congress Alliance; unlike the ANC, with its goal of a nonracial, democratic society, the PAC "aimed at the complete replacement of White minority rule with African rule" (Ranuga, p. 5). In December 1959 PAC's president, Robert Sobukwe, announced plans for a nonviolent protest to be held the following year, targeting the pass laws. On a set day Africans would leave their pass books at home, skip work, and arrive at police stations demanding to be arrested; the resulting prison overcrowding and shortage of workers, Sobukwe reasoned, would disrupt the economy while provoking more widespread protest. The protest was scheduled for March 21, a day that would, as it turned out, leave "an indelible stain on South Africa" (Meredith, *In the Name of Apartheid,* p. 80).

As planned, protestors gathered in front of police stations in Johannesburg, Evaton, and Vanderbijlpark, among other places. Sharpeville, a township 50 miles south of Johannesburg, had been until this point fairly immune from the disorder and unrest marking other African towns in the 1950s. On the morning of the protest PAC members walked the streets and actively implored workers to gather at the police station rather than go to work. By mid-morning several thousand Africans were participating in the protest in front of the police station at Sharpeville. By most accounts the mood of the crowd was relaxed. Police reinforcements were called, and by early afternoon 300 police stood facing a crowd of roughly 5,000 protestors. A small fight broke out near the police station gates. A policeman was knocked over in the scuffle and the crowd pressed forward to see. Though accounts differ, it seems that at this point, without warning and without acting on direct orders, the police opened fire on the crowd. They kept shooting, even as the protestors turned and fled. All in all, 69 Africans were killed, and another 186 wounded. Most had been shot in the back.

The events of March 21, 1960, later known as the Sharpeville Massacre, were followed by an enormous amount of protest both from Africans and from people abroad. Thousands of Africans demonstrated, which led to pass-book burnings and violence throughout the country. To many it seemed that a crucial turning point had been reached, that Africans had run out of patience and were now on the verge of liberation.

As G. H. L. Le May puts it, however, "Sharpeville was the turning point where nobody turned" (Le May, p. 221). On March 30 the government declared a state of emergency, essentially giving the police license to arrest and/or detain whomever they wished. Police began staging huge raids, and, in an increasingly brutal fashion, rounded up hundreds of African dissidents; by May more than 18,000 people had been arrested (Meredith, *In the Name of Apartheid,* p. 83). And on April 8 both the ANC and PAC were outlawed and forced to go underground.

Umkhonto we Sizwe. The government crackdown in response to Sharpeville stunned ANC members. After decades of nonviolent resistance, it was clear that conventional methods of protest were no longer effective—and apparently never had been. Mandela proposed the use of violence and sabotage to promote change, arguing that if the ANC did not act aggressively, more devastating violence would occur, given the Africans' growing hatred of apartheid leaders. At a June 1961 secret ANC meeting, members agreed with Mandela's strategy, and a separate military wing of the ANC called *Umkhonto we Sizwe,* or "The Spear of the Nation," was formed. The ANC itself would remain dedicated to a policy of nonviolence, while Umkhonto was to be an elite paramilitary group, formally separate from the rest of the congress.

In December 1961 Umkhonto members set off a series of bombs near pass offices, courts, and other government buildings in cities like Johannesburg and Durban. An Umkhonto leaflet claimed responsibility for the bombings and clearly stated its goal of pressuring the government into shifting its policy:

> We hope that we will bring the Government and its supporters to their senses before it is too late ... so that both Government and its policies can be changed before matters reach the desperate stage of civil war.
>
> (Umkhonto leaflet in Harsch, p. 250)

Between December 1961 and July 1963, almost 200 separate sabotage operations took place all over South Africa. In response, the government passed the 1962 Sabotage Act, giving the minister of justice the power to ban all potential terrorists. The government's most effective tool, however, was its massive intelligence operation, which easily infiltrated the loose membership of the ANC.

Still, it took police 19 months to bring down the Umkhonto we Sizwe, though the organization's flaws were, in retrospect, numerous: "lack of bases, inadequate organization and discipline, logistical difficulties, insufficient international support, poor political motivation, [and] shortage of funds" (Davis, p. 19). Umkhonto headquarters was a farmhouse situated on 28 acres in Rivonia, an area north of Johannesburg. When police raided the Rivonia farm in July 1963, they not only arrested Walter Sisulu and eight other men at the house but also were able to gather a significant amount of intelligence information. Nelson Mandela, already serving a five-year term for a 1962 arrest, remained in prison until October, when he was returned to court to stand trial with his Umkhonto colleagues. The accused were charged under the Sabotage Act (which carried the death penalty) and the Suppression of Communism Act "with complicity in more than 200 acts of sabotage aimed at aiding guerrilla warfare and facilitating violent revolution and armed invasion of the country" (Meredith, *Nelson Mandela,* p. 253). Eight of the nine men, including Mandela, were given life sentences; the only man to be found innocent, Rusty Bernstein, was immediately surrounded by security police, taken back to jail, and charged with new offenses.

The Speech in Focus

Contents summary. After the state presented its case, Mandela opened the defense with a statement from the dock. Mandela's speech lasted over four hours and had a powerful effect on the courtroom audience: "Standing in the dock, Mandela began reading his statement slowly and with calm deliberation, his voice carrying clearly across the courtroom. Gradually, as he spoke, the silence in the courtroom became more profound" (Meredith, *Nelson Mandela,* p. 264). His tone was self-controlled and analytic.

The speech is, in essence, a persuasive justification for the revolutionary actions of the Umkhonto we Sizwe in light of the long oppression of African peoples in South Africa. In the text of the speech, Mandela presents Umkhonto's violent actions not as savage or undisciplined, but as a reasoned response to the decidedly unreasonable situation in which Africans find themselves in South Africa. The formation of Umkhonto by the ANC and its decision to use violence was, Mandela argues, a logical response—in fact, the only response—for a people suffering under the tyranny of white supremacy. Mandela explains his intention:

> I did not plan [sabotage] in the spirit of recklessness, nor because I have any love of violence. I planned it as a result of a calm and sober assessment of the political situation that had arisen after many years of tyranny, exploitation, and oppression of my people by the Whites.
>
> ("Rivonia Trial Speech," p. 163)

In his speech, Mandela acknowledges his central role in the ANC, as well as in forming Umkhonto and deciding upon its program of sabotage. He took this role, he says, because of his "own proudly felt African background" ("Rivonia Trial Speech," p. 163). Having claimed responsibility, he turns to the specific and unavoidable reasons Umkhonto had to be formed: first, because violence against Africans has led them to a state of hostility that threatens uncontrolled civil war; and second, because counterviolence was the only legitimate response left for Africans after "all lawful modes of expressing opposition . . . had been closed by legislation" ("Rivonia Trial Speech," p. 164). With no acceptable choice but to take violent action, he and the other members of Umkhonto decided against terrorism, having come from the long ANC tradition of nonviolence and negotiation. Mandela then puts forth the ANC's vision of a nonracial, equal, and democratic society, and gives a brief history of the ANC's continually thwarted and ultimately ineffective campaigns of nonviolence against apartheid. When, 50 years after the formation of the ANC, the situation of Africans in South Africa is much more dire and restrictive—when something like the massacre at Sharpeville can happen—there is little choice but to turn to that which has been avoided for so long. It was, therefore, "only when all else had failed, when all the channels of peaceful protest had been barred to us, that the decision was made to embark on violent forms of political struggle, and to form Umkhonto we Sizwe" ("Rivonia Trial Speech," p. 169).

Four possible forms of violence were considered, Mandela explains: sabotage, guerrilla warfare, terrorism, and open revolution. The group immediately chose to embark on a campaign of sabotage, this being the least violent and most hopeful course of action. Mandela describes the planning behind the campaign, as well as the group's decision to plan for guerrilla warfare and subsequent military training should they become necessary. He explains how all whites in South Africa undergo compulsory military training, and that if war were inevitable—given the government's own violence and unwillingness to acknowledge the rights of Africans—then it would be necessary for Africans to prepare themselves for this worst-case scenario.

Throughout the speech, Mandela makes clear that the actions and decisions of Umkhonto we Sizwe were all made after the most careful and rational reasoning—and that any form of violence or militarism was considered only in times of absolute necessity: "But it was precisely because the soil of South Africa is already drenched in the blood of innocent Africans that we felt it our duty to make preparations as a long-term undertaking to use force in order to defend ourselves against force" ("Rivonia Trial Speech," p. 173).

Mandela also takes care to explain the differences between the ANC and Umkhonto (as the two were formally distinct), and to deny various acts that had been linked to Umkhonto. He then addresses charges that the aims of the ANC and the Communist Party are the same, explaining that the ideology of the ANC centers, and has always centered, on the creed of African nationalism rather than a desire for socialism: "Its chief goal was, and is, for the African people to win unity and full political rights" ("Rivonia Trial Speech," p. 179). If the ANC and the Communist Party have worked together, he explains, it is because of a shared goal—the abolition of white supremacy—rather than a shared philosophy. In Mandela's words, "theoretical differences amongst those fighting against oppression is a luxury we cannot afford at this stage"—something white South Africans may have a difficult time understanding ("Rivonia Trial Speech," p. 181). Mandela ends his speech with a long and powerful indictment against white South Africa:

> The Whites [in South Africa] enjoy what may well be the highest standard of living in the world, whilst Africans live in poverty and misery. Forty per cent of the Africans live in hopelessly overcrowded and, in some cases, drought-stricken Reserves, where soil erosion and the overworking of the soil make it

impossible for them to live properly off the land. Thirty per cent are labourers, labour tenants, and squatters on White farms and work and live under conditions similar to those of the serfs of the Middle Ages. The other 30 per cent live in towns where they have developed economic and social habits which bring them closer in many respects to White standards. Yet most Africans, even in this group, are impoverished by low incomes and high cost of living.

("Rivonia Trial Speech," pp. 184-85)

He states his case bluntly: "The lack of human dignity experienced by Africans is the direct result of the policy of White supremacy. White supremacy implies Black inferiority" ("Rivonia Trial Speech," p. 187). Africans, he says, want "to be paid a living wage. Africans want to perform work which they are capable of doing, and not work which the government declares them to be capable of" ("Rivonia Trial Speech," p. 188). Africans want to be part of the general population, and not be relegated to ghettoes. African families want to live together, and not be separated because a man or woman cannot work where they live. Above all, Mandela says, "we want equal political rights, because without them our disabilities will be permanent" ("Rivonia Trial Speech," p. 188). Mandela finished his speech without notes, facing the judge, his voice low:

During my lifetime I have dedicated myself to the struggle of the African people. I have fought against white domination, and I have fought against black domination. I have cherished the ideal of a democratic and free society in which all persons live together in harmony and with equal opportunities. It is an ideal which I hope to live for and to achieve. But if needs be, it is an ideal for which I am prepared to die.

("Rivonia Trial Speech," p. 189)

Violence and the antiapartheid movement in South Africa. Throughout his speech Mandela emphasizes the ANC's hesitation to adopt violence as a strategy with which to battle apartheid. The organization had been built on the policy of nonviolence, and for this reason would not undertake violence; at the same time, in the wake of Sharpeville it had become increasingly clear that passive resistance and protest through constitutional means were ineffective. Faced with the fact that a shift in strategy was necessary, the ANC compromised. While the ANC itself would retain its policy of nonviolence, it would neither condemn nor discipline members who chose to join Umkhonto and engage in "properly controlled violence," which Mandela explains in this

way: "I say 'properly controlled violence' because I made it clear that if I formed the organization I would at all times subject it to the political guidance of the ANC and would not undertake any different form of activity from that contemplated without the consent of the ANC" ("Rivonia Trial Speech," p. 170). Thus, the Umkhonto, composed of ANC members and more or less approved by the ANC itself, remained officially separate from the ANC. As Mandela further explains:

The ANC remained a mass political body of Africans only carrying on the type of political work they had conducted prior to 1961. Umkhonto remained a small organization recruiting its members from different races and organizations and trying to achieve its own particular object. The fact that members of Umkhonto were recruited from the ANC ... did not, in our view, change the nature of the ANC or give it a policy of violence.

("Rivonia Trial Speech," p. 176)

Days before the first Umkhonto bombing, the ANC's president, Albert Lutuli, was awarded the Nobel Peace Prize in recognition of the ANC's attempts to effect change through nonviolent protest. The fact that the ANC seemed to resist and abhor violence to such an extent, and yet felt driven to tacitly support it suggests a dichotomy reflected within the antiapartheid movement itself. Given the extremely difficult position of antiapartheid groups in a highly restrictive society like South Africa, such internal conflicts were not uncommon. The question of how to most effectively oppose such a monolithic system of oppression plagued many freedom fighters in South Africa, and the issue of violence became more and more central to the debate, and to the programs of the leading antiapartheid groups. The ANC's apparently contradictory views toward violence, as well as the Umkhonto's paradoxical idea of a "properly controlled" or "rational" violence in which no one would be harmed, are indicative of the movement's almost impossible position.

The PAC and its own offshoot group, Poqo, took a different approach toward the problem. Poqo was somewhat equivalent to Umkhonto, but far more open to the use of extreme violence, as made clear by a December 1961 leaflet: "The white people shall suffer, the black people will rule. Freedom comes after bloodshed. Poqo has started" (Meredith, *In the Name of Apartheid,* p. 102). Its operations were arbitrary and undisciplined; its supporters killed African policeman and informers, as well as random whites. In 1963 the group's plans for a large-scale African uprising and massacre of whites were thwarted when the leader of PAC, Potlake Leballo, announced these plans at a press conference; police raided PAC headquarters and began rounding up hundreds of PAC supporters. By mid-1963 Poqo had been crushed.

Another group, the African Resistance Movement, made up of radical whites, began its own campaign of sabotage, bombing railway stations and telephone kiosks in an attempt to "inconvenience and confuse, disrupt and destroy" (Meredith, *In the Name of Apartheid*, p. 102). By 1964 both this movement and the country's other radical, predominantly white group, the Communist Party of South Africa, were wiped out. In each case the move to violence—a last resort for many

groups—resulted in a heightening of government violence that left the revolutionaries brutally defeated. It would be another decade before the antiapartheid movement, in its various forms, would again gain prominence in South Africa.

Sources and literary context. Though realizing he would weaken his own case substantially, Nelson Mandela chose to deliver a speech from the docks rather than testify and face cross-examination in the witness box. Testimony could only be given in response to specific questions posed by attorneys, and Mandela did not want his defense limited to that format:

> Our attorneys warned me that it would put me in a more precarious legal situation; anything I said in my statement regarding my own innocence would be discounted by the judge. But that was not our highest priority. We believed it was important to open the defense with a statement of our politics and ideals, which would establish the context for all that followed. I wanted very much to cross swords with [the prosecutor], but it was more important that I use the form to highlight our grievances.
>
> (Mandela, *Long Walk to Freedom*, p. 315)

Mandela spent two weeks drafting his speech. A man who had been continually banned and/or imprisoned and unable to speak freely to the public, Mandela was now presented with a platform in which he could say whatever was necessary to rouse public sentiment against the state. Like others in South African history, Mandela was forced to use this forum if he wanted to speak out against injustice and be heard:

> It is a procedure of utilizing the public record as autobiographical witness that has continued to be necessary in a country where opponents of the state have been "silenced" (that is, forbidden to be quoted) in any other form than in their own trial proceedings in an open court.
>
> (Chapman, p. 92)

Impact. Although Mandela's speech would not prevent him from being sentenced to life in prison in South Africa, his testimony had a huge impact internationally, sparking demonstrations in both Europe and the United States. Two days before the judge was to give his decision, the United Nations Security Council urged the South African government to grant amnesty "to the defendants and to all others who had been restricted or imprisoned for opposing apartheid" (Meredith, *Nelson Mandela*, p. 271). An all-night vigil was held at St. Paul's Cathedral in London.

MANDELA'S ACTIVISM UP TO THE RIVONIA TRIAL

1937: At age 19, Mandela begins college at Healdtown.

1940: Mandela begins college at Fore Hare; organizes protest and is suspended from school.

1942: Mandela completes college B.A. degree.

1944: Mandela joins ANC's Youth League.

1948: Mandela qualifies as an attorney; becomes the national secretary of the Congress Youth League.

1952: Mandela becomes national volunteer-in-chief of the Defiance Campaign; gets arrested and receives a suspended sentence; is elected president of ANC's Transvaal's Branch; gets banned.

1953: Mandela's ban expires; Mandela is later put under a two-year banning order.

1956: Mandela and 155 other activists are arrested for treason.

1960: Violence erupts at Sharpeville; ANC and PAC are banned.

1961: Treason Trial ends; Mandela goes underground, forms Umkhonto we Sizwe; sabotage campaign begins.

1962: Mandela begins five-year prison sentence for incitement to strike and for leaving South Africa without a valid permit.

1963: Rivonia farmhouse is raided; Mandela is taken from his cell to join those facing trial for sabotage and conspiracy to overthrow South African government; Rivonia Trial begins.

1964: Mandela and seven others are sentenced to life in prison.

(Juckes, pp. 174-79)

Despite such pressure, it took Judge de Wet only three minutes to arrive at a guilty verdict for all the accused men but one.

The guilty verdicts and life sentences had little effect on white South Africa's public opinion, but reaction abroad was impassioned: the London *Times* proclaimed that "the verdict of history will be that the ultimate guilty party is the government in power—and that already is the verdict of world opinion"; the *New York Times* wrote of how "to most of the world, these men are heroes and freedom fighters. The George Washingtons and Ben Franklins of South Africa" (Meredith, *Nelson Mandela,* p. 275).

Nelson Mandela spent 27 years in prison. In the mid-1980s the National Party began dismantling apartheid, which had become unworkable in the face of black opposition. All seven men found guilty at the Rivonia Trial were ultimately released from prison. Mandela, freed in 1990, was the last to be released. Three years later, he became a winner of the Nobel Peace Prize, and in 1994, after South Africa's first multiracial election, was sworn in as the first president of a postapartheid South Africa.

—Carolyn Turgeon

Nelson Mandela

For More Information

Chapman, Michael. *Southern African Literatures.* London: Longman, 1996.

Davis, Stephen M. *Apartheid's Rebels: Inside South Africa's Hidden War.* New Haven, Conn.: Yale University Press, 1987.

Harsch, Ernest. *South Africa: White Rule, Black Revolt.* New York: Monad Press, 1980.

Juckes, Tim J. *Opposition in South Africa: The Leadership of Z. K. Matthews, Nelson Mandela, and Stephen Biko.* Westport, Conn.: Praeger, 1995.

Lazerson, Joshua L. *Against the Tide: Whites in the Struggle Against Apartheid.* Boulder, Colo.: Westview Press, 1994.

Le May, G. H. L. *The Afrikaners: An Historical Interpretation.* Cambridge, Mass.: Blackwell Publishers, 1995.

Mandela, Nelson. "The Rivonia Trial Speech." In *No Easy Walk to Freedom: Articles, Speeches, and Trial Addresses of Nelson Mandela.* London: Heinemann, 1965.

———. *Long Walk to Freedom.* New York: Little, Brown and Company, 1994.

McKinley, Dale T. *The ANC and the Liberation Struggle.* London: Pluto Press, 1997.

Meredith, Martin. *In the Name of Apartheid: South Africa in the Postwar Period.* London: Hamish Hamilton, 1988.

———. *Nelson Mandela: A Biography.* New York: St. Martin's Press, 1998.

Ranuga, Thomas K. *The New South Africa and the Socialist Vision: Positions and Perspectives Toward a Post-Apartheid Society.* Atlantic Highlands, N. J.: Humanities Press, 1996.

The Sand Child

by

Tahar Ben Jelloun

THE LITERARY WORK

A novel set in Morocco from before 1956 to the early 1980s; published in French (as *L'Enfant de sable*) in 1985, in English in 1987.

SYNOPSIS

A girl raised as a boy by her Moroccan family searches for her female identity through a series of physical, psychological, and erotic adventures.

Born in Fez in 1944, Tahar Ben Jelloun attended the French lycée in Tangier, where he moved with his family at the age of 18. He went on to study at the University of Morocco in Rabat and participated in the publication of the radical political review *Souffles*. After graduating, Ben Jelloun taught philosophy in Tetouan and then in Casablanca. During this time he published his first poems and a novel, *Harrouda* (1973). Afterwards he studied social psychiatry in France, writing his doctoral dissertation on case histories of North African immigrant workers. He worked with North African immigrant patients for three years at the Dejerine Center for Psychosomatic Medicine, basing his second novel, *Solitary Confinement* (1976), on this work. A poet, novelist, essayist, journalist, and playwright, Tahar Ben Jelloun frequently speaks out against injustice, racism, and discrimination against North Africans and Palestinians. In *The Sand Child,* his sixth novel, he focuses, among other issues, on gender relations and the plight of females in Moroccan society.

Events in History at the Time of the Novel

Locating *The Sand Child* in history. From the novel's allusions to certain social and political events, such as the presence of French police, we can date the beginning of the action at a time prior to 1956, the year France relinquished its claim on Morocco. The Blind Troubadour, one of the storytellers in *The Sand Child,* mentions 1957 as the year in which he gathers with others in a Marrakech square to speak of the destiny of the protagonist, Ahmed/Zahra (Ben Jelloun, *The Sand Child,* p. 136). From their discussion one can surmise that she was born in the late 1930s. Later, the Troubadour gives 1961 as the year in which he met a mysterious Arab woman (probably Ahmed/Zahra) in his library in Buenos Aires (the English translation erroneously gives the date as 1951). Near the end of the novel, another storyteller speaks of meeting in a vision Ahmed/Zahra's dead parents and wife, Fatima, who tell him of the people being cruelly oppressed, rising up, and being massacred by "the army" (*Sand Child,* pp. 162-63). One can surmise that the violence occurs, and the novel concludes, in the late 1970s or early 1980s under the repressive neocolonial regime of Hassan II.

The novel alludes, usually indirectly, to several social and political issues: the questions of colonial rule and the imposition of French cul-

An outdoor market in Marrakech.

ture on Morocco; the Moroccan writer's use of the colonial French language; the various authoritarian power structures during and after French rule; and relations between North Africans and metropolitan France (in particular regarding immigration). The novel's allusions also reflect the customs and mores of contemporary Moroccan society, as well as a preoccupation with the Islamic holy book, the Qur'an (or Koran). Of particular importance are the issues of gender identity and women's sexuality under Morocco's application of Islam.

Historical background. A brief historical summary establishes the longstanding presence of Islam in Morocco, and the rivalries that led up to the European colonial and postindependence periods.

680s: Following the advent of Islam in 620, the Arab conquest sweeps across North Africa, reaching Morocco.

788: Morocco becomes an independent state but later breaks up into competing ethnic states.

1056: The Almoravids establish a kingdom in Morocco. With successive rulers come continuing conflict and disunity.

1660: The present ruling dynasty, the Alaouites, assumes power.

1700-1800s: Along with other North African countries, Morocco serves as a base for pirates preying upon Mediterranean trade. European powers begin to encroach upon North Africa, laying the foundation for colonization.

1830s: France occupies neighboring Algeria.

1840s: Advancing from the south, France defeats the Moroccan sultan 'Abd-ar-Rahman.

1904: Rivalries among European powers vying for control over Morocco lead to a secret treaty between Spain and France wherein the two European nations partition Morocco between them.

1905: In the face of German objections, France demands protectorate status over Morocco from its sultan.

1906: The Algeciras Conference results in Morocco becoming a *de facto* protectorate under France and Spain.

1912: The sultan agrees to an official French protectorate, whereupon the French and Spanish divide Morocco into three zones: the northern and far southern peripheral areas administered by Spain and the considerably larger midregion administered by France. The French government appoints Louis-Herbert Lyautey as governor, which he remains until 1925.

1940-42: France falls to Germany in World War II; France's Vichy government controls Morocco; Allied invasion ends Vichy control.

1945: France resumes its prewar control of Morocco; Sultan Sidi Mohammed supports Istiqlal, a powerful nationalist independence movement.

1953: The French ban Istiqlal and depose the sultan.

1955: Following insurrection in Algeria and disturbances in Morocco, the French restore Sidi Mohammed.

1956: France relinquishes its rights to Morocco, Spain surrenders its protectorate, and Morocco achieves independence.

Immigration. Alluded to in *The Sand Child* is the migration of North Africans, especially males, to France in search of work. The issue of migration and immigration have, particularly in the past three decades in France, stirred enormous controversy. On one side are Jean-Marie Le Pen and the National Front, which grew out of the ultraviolent "New Order" movement in 1972. With its slogan "France for the French," the National Front has fought fiercely against immigration and has supported anti-Semitism. On the other side, writers of Semitic origin, like Tahar Ben Jelloun, champion immigration, pointing out that it enriches French society by promoting cultural diversity.

The novel alludes to the harshness of immigration when Fatuma, one of the narrators, speaks of the emptying of her country: "[M]en and history, plains and mountains, meadows and even the sky are disappearing. Only the women and kids remain. It looks as if they were staying to guard the country, but there's nothing to guard" (*Sand Child*, p. 131). Here she refers to the problem in North African coastal societies of widespread emigration of the adult male population to Europe, and the consequent social decline at home. A survey of the southwest Moroccan region of Wedinson has shown, for example, that in 1978, 227 of 297 households included members who migrated to Europe for work. About 60 percent of these migrants went to France; the remainder migrated mainly to the Netherlands, Belgium and Scandinavia (Najib, pp. 102-104).

In *The Sand Child,* after the narrator Fatuma speaks of the departure of men seeking work in France, she goes on to describe the poverty and plight of those left behind:

Those who have been driven out of the countryside by drought and irrigation projects roam the cities. They beg. They are rejected, humiliated; they go on begging, snatching what they can. Children . . . [m]any of them die, far too many, so more are produced, more and still more. To be born a boy is the lesser of two evils.

To be born a girl is a calamity, a misfortune that is left at the roadside where death passes by at the end of the day.

(*Sand Child,* p. 131)

While poverty and insufficient social and educational programs have plagued Morocco since independence in 1956, mass migration of the male population has exacerbated the situation. Left to suffer the intensified problems, as indicated in the novel, are women and children.

The law of inheritance in the Qur'an and in *The Sand Child*. *The Sand Child* turns on the Islamic law of inheritance as dictated by the Qur'an. This law of inheritance appears differently in the novel than in the Qur'an. As decreed in the Qur'an, the law of inheritance states:

Allah (thus) directs you as regards your children's (inheritance): to the male, a portion equal to that of two females: if only daughters, two or more, their share is two-thirds of the inheritance; if only one, her share is half.

(*The Holy Qur'an,* 4:11; trans. 'Abdallah Yusuf Ali)

The law, which accords the male child twice as much as the female, must be viewed within its social and legal framework. As explained by Haifaa A. Jawad in *The Rights of Women in Islam,*

[T]he wife [in Islam] is to be cared for by her husband, even if she is wealthy enough to maintain herself. By law she is entitled to claim maintenance from her husband. At the same time she is not obligated to spend any of her wealth on the household. In addition a Muslim woman receives at the time of her marriage a considerable sum of money. This money, which the husband is obliged to pay, constitutes her dowry, or *mahr,* which belongs to her alone. She is free to use, spend or invest it in any way she likes. Therefore, as a wife she adds to whatever she receives through inheritance in her capacity as daughter and that, too, without any legal commitment to support either herself or her children.

(Jawad, p. 66)

According to Islam, it is the male's responsibility to earn money in order to support his wife and children. Furthermore, it is the male's responsibility to give his wife a mahr or dowry upon marriage. As Jawad makes clear, women are entitled to claim maintenance from their husband and are not obligated to spend any of their own wealth on the household. Since the male bears the financial burden in society, the Qur'anic law of inheritance grants him twice as much as the female in order to balance the flow of wealth by ensuring that the male can adequately provide for his family and that the female can provide for herself.

The following example further elucidates the situation:

> [I]f you [a male] were to inherit from your father one thousand dirhams, and your sister 500 dirhams, at her marriage she will take another 500 dirhams as dowry, making her share one thousand; whereas when you marry you will give 500 dirhams as dowry that shall leave you with half of what your sister has received. In this manner, the Divine Law would produce the result [it] desire[s] and hint[s] at.
>
> (Engineer in Jawad, pp. 66-67)

Thus, a strict application of the Islamic law of inheritance is not as unfair as it might at first seem to Western readers.

The law of inheritance as presented in *The Sand Child* differs somewhat from the Qur'anic text: a man's son shall inherit two-thirds of the family wealth upon the death of the father. The son, furthermore, becomes the central authority figure who rules over all females in the family, including younger and elder sisters as well as the mother. Should the family lack a male heir the daughters inherit one-third of the family wealth and the father's brothers inherit the other two-thirds. In Ben Jelloun's novel, there is no male heir so the father, in order to keep his brothers from inheriting his wealth, raises his eighth daughter as a boy.

As reflected in the novel, then, there is not a one-to-one correspondence between pure Qur'anic law and particular Muslim societies. While the Qur'an states that if there is no son and more than one daughter, the daughters inherit two-thirds of the father's wealth, the novel states that only one-third would be inherited by the daughters. The difference between the Qur'anic declaration and the law as presented in the novel is the difference between theory and practice. Qur'anic law is the theory; the reality is that in Muslim lands, various legal systems—Islamic, colonial, bureaucratic, and perhaps republican—operate in piecemeal or amalgamated form. Their application is affected by the social realities of today's Muslim societies. Most are developing countries with rampant illiteracy, entrenched social customs, and limited access to higher education. Discrimination against women in these societies is commonplace.

The status of women in Morocco. According to some scholars, there is strong evidence that Morocco's commitment to wholly integrating women within society falls far below that of nearby Algeria and Tunisia (Griffiths, p. 9). Although the Moroccan constitution guarantees "every child, male and female, the right to primary education in a state-funded school," barely "50% [of female children] reach that mark" (Griffiths, p. 11).

The situation of women in Morocco must be understood against the backdrop of entrenched traditional attitudes as well as colonial notions of gender. Traditionally secluded in harems, Islamic women were kept out of sight of the male world. Harems were abolished in Turkey in 1909, but the practice continued for several years in other Muslim countries. The harem system as such no longer exists in present-day Morocco; however, associated social and psychological attitudes persist. In its sacred usage, the word *haram* in Arabic refers to something that is unlawful and forbidden to the nonfaithful—in other words, something that is to be protected from non-Muslims. One example is the consecrated area around the holy cities of Mecca and Medina, which is closed to all but Muslims. In its secular usage, haram denotes the portion of a man's living quarters in which women, children, and servants are kept in seclusion. In Morocco, especially in rural areas, there are still traditional households in which Moroccan women live in seclusion, speak out only when they attain an advanced age, and never refer to themselves in the singular.

Generally the Moroccan woman in a traditional household has no voice in decisions that affect her life. Her acquiescence to marriage is through a male intermediary who speaks in her place: "Her body censured, her desire repressed, her word forbidden, her image veiled, her reality denied under the mask . . . woman in the Maghreb [Morocco, Tunisia, Algeria] generally ceases to undergo oppression by male society only when she becomes a mother" (Ben Jelloun, *La plus haute des solitudes,* p. 92; trans. J. Erickson). In the novel, the storyteller Fatuma says:

> Yes, I've said nothing, because in this country a woman is used to keeping quiet; if she does speak out, that's an act of violence in itself. I'm old now, which is why I can sit around with you [the other storytellers and audience]. Thirty years ago, or when I was about thirty, do you think I would have dared to be seen with you in a café?
>
> (*Sand Child,* p. 125)

The position of women has also been affected by power relations between France and North Africa. In their historical encounter with North

African society, France and other Western colonial powers often attempted to influence male-female roles and relationships. In Algeria, for example, a campaign initiated by French colonial authorities to unveil the Arab woman rested on the breaking down of traditional indigenous mores. While the act of unveiling may seem "liberating" to Westerners unfamiliar with customs of Muslim societies, one must remember that the French colonizers also brought male chauvinistic attitudes that contributed to the Moroccan woman's being thought of as a second-class citizen. In "the development of women's rights, and the history of social-policy," notes Clare Griffiths, "France trailed far behind the anglophone countries" (Griffiths, p. 9).

In sum, women in Morocco have confronted obstacles to self-affirmation extremely more pronounced than those of their male counterparts. These obstacles arise from the effacement of the woman; she is confronted by an ethos of male superiority in all domains—from education to occupation to marriage. To put it another way, the distinctions and privileges accorded to males in Moroccan society place the woman in a position of inferiority.

The Novel in Focus

Plot overview. Not told in straightforward chronological order, *The Sand Child* unfolds according to the following structural overview. In the introduction, or frame narrative, the protagonist, Ahmed/Zahra, is alive and in seclusion, but it is nearly the end of her life. When the initial storyteller commences Ahmed/Zahra's story, the protagonist has already died (the storyteller talks about a great notebook she left behind). The various storytellers of the novel go back in time, leading us to the point when Ahmed/Zahra leaves home to wander. At the end of the tale four storytellers—Salem, Amar, Fatuma, and the Blind Troubadour—present different, sometimes contradictory, versions of Ahmed/Zahra's fate from the day she leaves home to the end of her life. We surmise that she eventually went into seclusion, which is where we found her at the beginning of the novel.

The plot in detail. *The Sand Child* opens with a speaker who describes in considerable detail an enigmatic person whose facial features have been ravaged by time, and who has voluntarily secluded "himself" from the rest of his family. The person, Ahmed/Zahra, is referred to as "he" at first. The speaker talks about how Ahmed is af-

Jelloun's novel questions the second-class status of women in Morroco.

flicted by the incursions—the sights, sounds, smells—of the outer world and goes on to tell us how he prepares for his impending death. The narrator also alludes to the outline of a story, as told in Ahmed's private and enigmatic journal (*Sand Child*, p. 3).

After five pages, a blank space marks the conclusion of the introduction or frame narrative and signals the beginning of what turns out to be the narrative proper. This opens with the question: "And who was he?" The following words introduce a storyteller who purportedly possesses Ahmed's journal, the secret to his identity. "The secret was there, in those pages, woven out of syllables and images," the storyteller claims as he starts telling Ahmed's tale (*Sand Child*, p. 5).

The tale begins before Ahmed's birth when his father feels a malediction weighing on him because all his offspring are girls. His shame at having only female children grows as each successive birth elicits jeers from his younger brothers who, given his lack of a male child, stand to inherit two-thirds of his wealth. Obsessed by the need for a male heir, the father consults doctors, quacks, healers, and sorcerers. He puts his wife through a frightful regime of spells and cures until she is completely worn out. Despite all these efforts, each new birth brings another girl and, with her birth, despair. The father finally decides to defy fate by making sure the next child is a boy. With his wife's complicity, he arranges for an old midwife to declare the newborn a male, regardless of its gender. At the birth of his eighth child, the midwife announces a boy. The father, though observing that it is a girl, goes through with his plans and rejoices at finally having a male child.

The girl, named Ahmed, is dressed and raised as a boy. She is doted upon, and passed with great ceremony from one stage of masculine development to another, including circumcision in infancy—which the father arranges with the connivance of a barber and blood provided by the father's own slashed finger. Growing up according to the dictates of her father, Ahmed enters fully into the deception that is her life: her chest is bound tightly to prevent her breasts from growing, she sneaks towels from her mother's and sisters' closet when she menstruates, and she strives to emulate men in both speech and bearing. To all intents and purposes, *she* becomes a *he*.

A would-be brother, Ahmed asserts his authority over his sisters and, to his parents' consternation, insists on marrying. Upon the death of his father, he becomes master of the house and takes his cousin Fatima, a lame epileptic, as his wife. He then begins living with her in seclusion from both their families. Fatima accepts a life without sexuality, sensing, and finally learning, Ahmed's secret. Ahmed comes to hate Fatima's presence; meanwhile, she loses her will to live and finally dies through self-neglect. After her death, Ahmed withdraws into his own seclusion.

At one point in the narration of the story thus far, a fight occurs between storytellers. The storyteller of the moment is accused of making everything up, of pretending to read from Ahmed's journal, but reading instead from "a cheap edition of the Koran" (*Sand Child*, p. 49). This first storyteller, not to be confused with the narrator of the frame story, is then replaced by a second storyteller who claims to be Fatima's brother. This storyteller relates the next installment of the story, which begins to appear more and more tenuous. What seems clear is that Ahmed eventually decides to forego his life of deception in order to discover the woman within him, the truth of his/her being. By one account, he/she wanders and finally joins a circus. When a male dancer who masquerades as a woman quits, the circus head, Abbas, proposes that

Ahmed replace him. Ahmed appears on stage dressed first as a man but leaves to reappear as a femme fatale, Lalla Zahra. Zahra becomes the main attraction of the circus.

At this point, when we are more than three-fifths of the way through the story, the latest storyteller disappears and his tale is taken up by three aged persons—Salem, Amar, and Fatuma—who were a part of the audience and now tell their own versions of Ahmed's/Zahra's story. Each person's version of Zahra's last days diverges markedly from the others.

Salem tells how Zahra was brutalized by Abbas, the circus owner. One night, knowing he was about to attack her, she cuts him and, as he bleeds to death, he strangles her. In Amar's story, Zahra escapes from the circus and wanders throughout the country; eventually all trace of her is lost. Amar reads from writings he attributes to her, writings in which she expresses her desire to leave home. But then Amar contradicts what he said earlier by stating that he believes Ahmed/Zahra "never left his room high up on the terrace of the big house," where he/she died a "gentle death" (*Sand Child*, pp. 123-24). Salem objects, saying that since the character of Ahmed/Zahra "is in himself an act of violence . . . only a great act of violence—a suicide with lots of blood—can bring this story to an appropriate end" (*Sand Child*, p. 124). Fatuma, in her turn, tells how she has journeyed through many countries, but admits to having invented those journeys "in a tall, narrow, circular room . . . overlooking the terrace" (*Sand Child*, pp. 127-28). She speaks of a pilgrimage she made to Mecca in the disguise of a man. She tells of learning to be in a dream, "to make of [her] life an entirely invented story," while living in "the illusion of another [male] body" (*Sand Child*, p. 132). While Fatuma never mentions Zahra in her story, she alludes to being Zahra herself, telling her own story, and living now as the old Fatuma.

To these several tales, the Blind Troubadour adds his own version about Ahmed/Zahra's end. He tells of how a woman, probably an Arab, visited him in the library in Buenos Aires where he worked. She gave him a rare Egyptian coin called a *battene* and explained that she had sought him out because he alone was capable of understanding her. She had been wandering, she said, a fugitive wanted "for murder, usurpation of identity, abuse of confidence, and theft of inheritance" (*Sand Child*, p. 141). While the Blind Troubadour tells his tale of the mysterious woman visitor to listeners on the great square in

Marrakech, we come to know a little bit about him. We learn that once he was not blind, but then he lost his sight and decided to travel in search of the unknown woman with whose identity he has become obsessed, the woman whom he calls "a princess who has escaped from a fairy tale" (*Sand Child,* p. 145)

The last chapter tells of the departure of the Blind Troubadour after the first storyteller returns to the square and delivers the final words of the novel. He carries the notebook that supposedly belongs to Ahmed/Zahra and explains that, after he had left them, Ahmed/Zahra appeared to him on a sleepless night and reproached him for betraying her secret. Another time he fell asleep and awakened in a cemetery. The characters he thought he had "invented" appeared and called to him. "Ahmed's father locked me up in an old building and forced me to go back to the square and tell the story in a different way" (*Sand Child,* p. 162). Fatima, Ahmed/Zahra's lame wife, also appeared and said "I am the woman you chose to be your hero's victim" (*Sand Child,* p. 162). She gave him palm dates. After eating them, a dazzling light appeared and the characters vanished.

This first and last storyteller informs his listeners of a visit later from a poor Egyptian woman of Alexandria. She told him that he would be able to tell the story of her uncle who was in fact her aunt, whose true identity was discovered upon his/her death. She proceeded to recount the story of Bey Ahmed and left the storyteller a large notebook containing Bey Ahmed's journal. In his wandering, the storyteller left the book open one night and the pages were washed clean of their writing by the moonlight. He confides to the listeners that "[n]either you nor I would ever know the end of the story"—if they want to know how the story ends, they will have to ask the moon when it is full (*Sand Child,* p. 161).

The Blind Troubadour. Despite the intricacies of a novel that uses multiple storytellers who often contradict one another, the storytellers, according to Marie Fayad, share a common trait: "they all seem to fit into the general Moroccan context of the story, they are part of the multi-faceted, multicolored but predictable crowd that gathers on the square in Marrakech" (Fayad, p. 291). The only exception, which stands out rather boldly, is the Blind Troubadour. He is strange and different not because he is blind, but because he comes from another country, "from afar, from another century, thrown into one tale by another tale" (*Sand Child,* p. 135). "His sudden appearance in the novel is surprising since

he does not seem to have a logical reason for being there" (Fayad, p. 291).

The Blind Troubadour is both mysterious and decipherable—mysterious in that no one knows exactly who he is or why he has suddenly appeared, decipherable in that his character points to his identity as a real person. Although he is never named, numerous allusions link him to the Argentine author Jorge Luis Borges, as pointed out and discussed in print by scholars (John Erickson in 1991 and Marie Fayad in 1993). When the Troubadour is introduced, we are told he is blind, tall and thin, does not seem to carry a cane, and wears a dark suit (*Sand Child,* p. 134). This is almost an exact physical description of the real Borges. In addition, the Troubadour speaks of his vocation as a writer, his life in Buenos Aires, his knowledge of Spanish, and his occupation as a librarian.

Furthermore, as the Troubadour continues to tell his story, he uses words taken from Borges's own writings or interviews. Readers are alerted to Ahmed/Zahara's fate being a type of unresolvable game by the Blind Troubadour's words "The Secret is Sacred but is always somewhat ridiculous," a line imported into *The Sand Child* from the genuine Borges short story "The Sect of the Phoenix" (Erickson, "Writing Double," p. 114). Likewise, the Troubadour says, "I have spent my life falsifying or altering other people's stories. . . . When I was young, I was ashamed to be someone who loved only books, not a man of action" (*Sand Child,* pp. 134-35). Again his words echo those of Borges: "Borges used almost exactly these words when he commented on his debut as a writer of fiction: '[I was] a shy young man who dared not write stories and so amused himself by falsifying and distorting . . . the tales of others'" (Fayad, p. 292).

Perhaps the most intriguing connections to Borges are the use of names and motifs taken from his fiction. The Troubadour's use of the name "Stephen Albert" echoes a character from Borges's story "The Garden of Forking Paths" (*Sand Child,* p. 142). His reference to a coin called the *zahir* recalls Borges's story "The Zahir" (*Sand Child,* p. 138). Likewise, his fascination with things of Arabic origin, his mention of the tales of *The Thousand and One Nights,* his love of *Don Quixote,* and his preponderant interest in esoterica all connect the Troubadour with the real personage of Jorge Luis Borges. Yet the connection is never certain, for many other allusions in the story make pinpointing the Blind Troubadour's identity problematic.

The Blind Troubadour operates on several levels. First, in the event that he is a fictional replica of the real Borges, the Troubadour functions as one of the storytellers, a character in the tale of the first-level narrator who is outside the story. Moreover, the Troubadour functions outside the narrative in his role as a character in other stories. At one point, the Troubadour speaks of himself as coming from and having lived a story in which he is the main character, a magician, who reaches his ultimate goal of dreaming a man only to find out, years later, that he himself is the dream of another (*Sand Child*, p. 136). Here the Troubadour, a character in Ahmed/Zahra's story whom we believe to be the author Jorge Luis Borges, becomes a character in one of Borges's stories, "The Circular Ruins." Thus, the Blind Troubadour is not merely a figure in the story of Ahmed/Zahra, but in other stories as well. He, in other words, brings the world outside the story inside of it.

The Blind Troubadour, then, is the device whereby story levels are displaced, characters put on the same level as their creators, and the authenticity of the main narrative of Ahmed/Zahra called into question. The pivotal figure in the Troubadour's story is an unknown woman visitor who bears a strong resemblance to Ahmed/Zahra, the protagonist of *The Sand Child*.

His visitor speaks of similar episodes in her life, of similar misfortunes and flight, and the Blind Troubadour has a vision in his mind of her tormented father. In a passage omitted from the English translation, the Troubadour even refers to this visitor as being from Morocco (*Sand Child*, p. 144). Yet later, the original storyteller casts doubt on the Troubadour's veracity, saying Ahmed/Zahra is an invented character, based on an Alexandrian woman's uncle/aunt, Bey Ahmed.

Jorge Luis Borges died in June 1986, only a few months after *The Sand Child*'s publication. Given this fact, the figure of the Blind Troubadour may be Tahar Ben Jelloun's way of paying a last tribute to one of the greatest writers of the twentieth century. Much of Borges's fiction worked by "falsifying or altering other people's stories" and by using real characters in fictional stories and fictional characters in real stories (*Sand Child*, p. 134). There is perhaps no better way to pay homage to Borges than to do it in Borgesian fashion, by using Borges, a real person, as a fictional character in a novel (Fayad, p 298). The Blind Troubadour himself states, at one point: "What an odd situation! I felt as if I were in a book, one of those picturesque characters who appear in the middle of a story to throw the reader off the scent" (*Sand Child*, p. 139).

Oral storytelling in *The Sand Child*. The story of Ahmed/Zahra is related by a succession of storytellers in a public square where a crowd gathers to listen. This type of storytelling still exists today in the public squares of cities and towns, such as the famous Square of the Dead in the *medina*, the native quarter, of Marrakech. For an audience that is in large part illiterate, such storytelling provides instruction as well as entertainment. The storyteller passes on to the public the history, legends, myths, moral tales, and popular stories of the past, keeping the people's legacy alive through oral transmission. In *The Sand Child*, Ben Jelloun inserts pauses between the tales of different storytellers, which suggests a parallel with the phrase *qala al-rawi* ("the storyteller said"), a narrative technique used in *The Thousand and One Nights* to indicate the end of a story.

The oral nature of Ben Jelloun's novel does not, however, mean that he has simply transcribed oral narratives. Rather, *The Sand Child* does something much more complex. It takes a European storytelling genre, the novel, and modifies it by using storytelling techniques borrowed from Arabic culture. By employing multiple sto-

JORGE LUIS BORGES

Born in Buenos Aires, Argentina, on August 24, 1899, Jorge Luis Borges became the undisputed giant of Latin American letters, one of the foremost writers of the twentieth century. Shy and bookish, a librarian by profession, Borges looked very much like the Blind Troubadour: tall and thin, wearing dark glasses and a dark suit. At around the age of 55, Borges became completely blind and then began to travel a great deal. Crossing boundaries in his mind as well, Borges reflected on notions of myth, fiction, and reality. He was, in particular, attracted to myths and narratives from Spain and the Arab world, citing both *Don Quixote* and *The Thousand and One Nights* as two of his favorite works of literature. Much of Borges's fiction operates by blurring the distinctions between reality and fiction, whereupon he mingles factual narratives with fictional characters and factual characters with fictional narratives. Complex intellectual levels of organization and storytelling and references to esoteric knowledge also characterize his stories.

rytellers, many of whom speculate and contradict one another, and multiple levels of narrative, the novel confuses the levels, the different storytellers, and ultimately the reader. The demands put upon the reader push illogic and contradiction to the limit. With multiple narrators who contradict one another and speculate about what *they* think happened, we are refused the possibility of getting a definite fix on either the characters or the storytellers. Furthermore, since most of the storytellers are not wholly reliable and themselves figure into the story on some level, one gets the impression that they making up the story as they go along.

One comes to understand that these differing versions, which present glimpses of a fleeting and contradictory reality, demonstrate that all life stories, including so-called objective "history," are in large part invented by storytellers who select what to include in accord with their own aims and desires. Ultimately, the story of Ahmed/Zahra shows how the phenomenon we call "reality" is not merely elusive and unseizable, but in itself fictional. By using unreliable narrators, multiple levels of storytelling, and narrative devices that are deliberately confusing, *The Sand Child* calls attention to its own fictionality, making clear that the story it tells is just that: a story.

Sources and literary context. By the time Tahar Ben Jelloun was 18 and graduating from high school, Algeria, Morocco, and Tunisia were newly independent countries. Their colonial pasts left indelible marks, however. One consequence of the colonial protectorate period in Morocco was the imposition of the French language and culture upon Moroccan subjects. With the exception of religious schools, formal schooling of the population was conducted in French and modeled on France's educational system; thus, most Moroccans who later became writers were educated in French. Struggling to find individual and collective voices that would express the now postcolonial Moroccan experience, these writers confronted the problem of expressing themselves in another culture's language while trying to preserve and express their own culture and beliefs.

One group of young writers and intellectuals congregated around a literary review called *Souffles*. These writers included the journal's founder Abdellatif Laabi as well as Mohammed Khair-Eddine, Abdelkebir Khatibi, Mostafa Nissaboury, and Tahar Ben Jelloun. *Souffles* set out to tackle the problem of postcolonial language. While many of these prominent intellectuals advocated Arabic as the appropriate language of Moroccan literature, this language shift did not occur. However, the nature of Moroccan and North African writing in French began to take a revolutionary turn.

In tackling the dilemma of how to adapt the French language to their own needs and desires, these writers began to violate genres and conventions of the French language. For many, this violation amounted to a more basic rejection of French language and culture than using Arabic would have. The "revolution" spilled over from language to content; their narrative questioned current structures and hierarchies of power—political, religious, social, or cultural. Tahar Ben Jelloun's writing must be understood within this context.

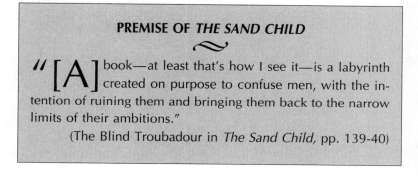

PREMISE OF *THE SAND CHILD*

"[A] book—at least that's how I see it—is a labyrinth created on purpose to confuse men, with the intention of ruining them and bringing them back to the narrow limits of their ambitions."

(The Blind Troubadour in *The Sand Child,* pp. 139-40)

From *The Thousand and One Nights* the novel adopts the notion of the embedded narrative, that is, the enclosure of one story within another. In so doing, *The Sand Child,* much like *The Thousand and One Nights,* creates tales that free themselves from boundaries, gyrating in unforeseen directions and even turning back on themselves. *The Sand Child* attacks the notion of narrative closure typical of the traditional European novel and the reductionist tendency of European philosophy (its preference for rationalism, for example). By leaving the story open-ended, in characteristic North African oral storytelling fashion, the novel rejects the usual denouement of the self-contained story in which everything is neatly tied together. Ben Jelloun reformulates the notion of a novel, countering European notions of storytelling, modifying the novel into a genre that fits with traditional Arabic storytelling and non-Western literature.

Reviews. *The Sand Child* met with a generally favorable reception in France and the English-speaking world. Like other reviewers, Barbara

Harlow commended Ben Jelloun for challenging "the authority of religion and the colonizer [over] women and other subject groups" (Harlow, p. 49). The work, noted Jean-Louise Thatcher, is "sensitive and perceptive" when describing "Ahmed['s] . . . struggle with the feminine side of 'his' nature. The work is also violent, fantastic, convoluted in style, rich in images" (Thatcher, p. 483). Many critics felt that the novel's complexity challenges a reader's understanding. Marie-Noëlle Little likened the storyteller's tale to "a crossing of the desert with its oases and mirages" and compared the novel to tales of *The Thousand and One Nights* that "live longer than the [authors] and embellish our days" (Little, p. 832).

—John Erickson and Faisal Azam

For More Information

'Ali, Abdullah Yusuf, trans. *The Holy Qur'an.* Brentwood, Calif.: Amana Corporation, 1989.

Ben Jelloun, Tahar. *La plus haute des solitudes.* Paris: Éditions du Seuil, 1979.

———. *The Sand Child.* Trans. Alan Sheridan. New York: Harcourt Brace Jovanovich, 1987.

Erickson, John D. *Islam and Postcolonial Narrative.* Cambridge: Cambridge University Press, 1998.

———. "Writing Double: Politics and the African Narrative of French Expression." *Studies in Twentieth-Century Literature* 15, no. 1 (winter 1991): 101-22.

Fayad, Marie. "Borges in Tahar Ben Jelloun's *L'Enfant de sable*: Beyond Intertextuality." *The French Review* 67, no. 2 (December 1993): 291-99.

Griffiths, Claire. "Social Development in Francophone Africa: The Case of Women in Gabon and Morocco." Working Papers in African Studies, no. 211. Boston: African Studies Center, Boston University, 1998.

Harlow, Barbara. "She Took a Wife," review of *The Sand Child,* by Tahar Ben Jelloun. *The New York Times Book Review,* 25 October 1987, p. 49.

Jawad, Haifaa A. *The Rights of Women in Islam: An Authentic Approach.* London: Macmillan, 1998.

Little, Marie-Noëlle. Review of *The Sand Child,* by Tahar Ben Jelloun. *French Review* 1986: 831-32.

Mernissi, Fatima. *Beyond the Veil. Male-Female Dynamics in a Modern Muslim Society.* New York: Schenkman, 1975.

Najib, Ali Ben Salah. *Migration of Labour and the Transformation of the Economy of the Wedinoon Region in Morocco.* Uppsala, Sweden: Uppsala University, 1986.

Thatcher, Jean-Louise. Review of *The Sand Child. The Middle East Journal* 42, no. 3 (summer 1988): 482-83.

Season of Migration to the North

by
Tayeb Salih

Tayeb Salih is among the most respected of contemporary writers in the Arabic world, and perhaps the best-known writer from the Sudan. Not especially prolific, he has produced four novels and a book of short stories in his decades as a writer. He was born in 1929 to a middle-class family in the western part of the Sudan. After studying at Khartoum University and working as a teacher, he ventured abroad, taking a degree in international relations at the University of London. Since the early 1950s he has lived mainly in Europe, working in various bureaucracies, such as the British Broadcasting Corporation and the United Nations Education, Scientific, and Cultural Organization (UNESCO), and returning to the Sudan only for visits. Nevertheless, his ties to the Arabic world remain the key fact of his writing; not only does he concern himself with the condition of the Arab in the modern world, but his works are always published first in the Arabic press. In *Season of Migration to the North* he explores the reassimilation into Sudanese society of two former migrants attempting to make a place for themselves in the fictional village of Wad Hamid.

Events in History at the Time of the Novel

The Sudan: imperial heritage. The modern history of the area now called the Sudan has been shaped by two great imperial forces of the past—Egypt and England. Its northern half, a desert split by the fertile Nile Valley, was enfolded by

---

THE LITERARY WORK

A novel set in the Sudan in the 1960s, with flashbacks to England in the 1930s; published in Arabic (as *Mawsim al-hijra ila al-shamal*) in 1966, in English in 1969.

SYNOPSIS

Two Arabic men who have studied in England find their lives intertwining in mysterious and catastrophic ways.

---

the vast embrace of Islam that spread through this part of the world in the fifteenth century. To this day, the northern half of the country, which includes more than two-thirds of the population, is Arabic-speaking and predominantly Arab; in the southern Sudan, Muslims live alongside Christians as well as those who continue to subscribe to traditional beliefs. In 1820 the Egyptian ruler Muhammad 'Ali invaded the Sudan. By 1826 Egypt had begun establishing administrative control from the new town of Khartoum, but Turkish Ottoman control over Egypt prevented it from reaping the full benefits of its victories in the Sudan for some years. By 1885 Egypt controlled most of the modern Sudan. Although Egyptians and Sudanese were fellow Muslims, the period of domination that followed was neither peaceful nor pleasant. The majority of Sudanese, still devout Muslims, were shocked by what they saw as the laxity and corruption of their foreign masters. The Egyptians, for their part, were more interested in taxing the Sudanese, and in exploiting the rich herds of elephants in the south of the country, than in being effective imperial administrators.

In 1881 conflict turned into open revolt. A Sudanese holy man named Muhammad Ahmad declared a *jihad*, a holy war, against the Egyptians. The Sudanese were not only outnumbered, but also faced troops armed with the latest English weapons; nevertheless, they managed to drive the Egyptians out, winning independence for the Sudan from 1885 to 1898.

SALIH ON THE SUDAN

In a speech delivered at the American University of Beirut in Lebanon in 1980, Salih muses on the influence his native country has on his writing. He notes that, before the Muslim invasion of the late Middle Ages, the country had been predominantly Christian for a thousand years, yet the Muslim religious revolution was almost completely peaceful. He notes also that his home village is halfway between the Arab center of the country, and its southern, largely Nubian people. Speaking to a population that, in 1980s Lebanon, was on the verge of cataclysmic ethnic and religious violence, he sums up the accepting nature of life in his homeland: "The type of Islam in the Sudan, even now, is not ideological, is not fanatical. . . . I believe that if I have contributed anything to modern Arabic literature, it is in my constant plea for toleration, and this I owe entirely to being a Sudanese" (Salih in Amyuni, p. 13).

In the longer term, however, the period of Egyptian rule served mainly to introduce the Sudan to its second imperial master: England. England, which had been closely allied with Egypt since the beginning of the nineteenth century, disliked the prospect of a wholly independent country adjoining the critical Eastern Mediterranean, and their concern may have been justified in view of the fact that independent Sudan was engaged in destabilizing wars for most of its 13 years. In 1896 an Anglo-Egyptian army marched into the Sudan. At the Battle of Omdurman in 1898, the Sudanese suffered about 11,000 dead and 16,000 wounded (Holt, p. 240). The Anglo-Egyptian army's machine gunners had slaughtered the Sudanese, ending their "reconquest" of Sudan. From this point until the 1950s, the Sudan was ruled jointly by Egypt and England. Egypt, a de facto colony of Britain, partnered with it in control of the Sudan. The legal arrangement was called "condominion"; in effect it gave Egypt colonial control over the Sudan, with the rights of levying taxes, arbitrating justice, and the like. Since Egypt's independence was purely nominal, and the country was for all real purposes dominated by England, the Sudan was in effect a colony of a colony. Power and privilege flowed along a predictable route from Khartoum (the Sudanese capital) to Cairo to London. This is the route that the novel's Mustafa Sa'eed follows in his pursuit of education and advancement.

Affiliation with Great Britain brought the same disadvantages and advantages it brought to other British colonies in Africa. The British set up schools and hospitals, built dams, and introduced policies and institutions that gave rise to a wealthy elite in the native population; however, these benefits did not outweigh, for the Sudanese, the humiliation that accompanied foreign control. Fortunately, their route to independence was peaceful and bloodless. First came Egypt's independence. In 1951 Egypt voted to abrogate the treaties that had made it a virtual colony of the United Kingdom. Egypt, in other words, reasserted its sovereignty. The changes in its constitution during this process allowed the Sudanese people to sever their ties to their northern neighbor.

The Sudan became an independent nation on January 1, 1956. As Salih's novel hints, however, the legacy of British colonialism was not so easy to erase as the power's political presence had been.

Women of Islam. The Muslim understanding of women's place in the world is no less confused and contradictory than the Christian conception of it. Just as Christians both revile Eve for man's fall in the Garden of Eden and respect Mary as the mother of Jesus, Muslims have traditionally celebrated women's piety and procreative power, while regarding them as subordinate to men in the affairs of this world. Islam ideology does not offer a unified, unvarying vision of what an ideal woman should do; instead, the religion expects widely varying traits in its female adherents. On one hand, they should be chaste, subservient, and obedient. On the other hand, the prophet Muhammad claimed that they are more pious then men, and that a good wife is the key to a man's salvation.

Despite the prejudiced belief, common in Europe from the seventeenth to the late nineteenth centuries, that Muhammad denied that women have souls, Islam considers men and women spiritual equals. Both are bound to exactly the same spiritual obligations, and the righteous of both sexes will taste the fruits of paradise. However, this fundamental equality does not prevent a strictly ordered hierarchy of genders in this world, with men the more powerful gender in almost every respect in the mid-1900s. Traditionally, men ruled governments and families; they conducted all important trade and received a much more detailed, comprehensive education. Women were almost always confined to the home of their father or husband, and were legally under a man's control, in most cases, from the cradle to the grave. In traditional households the Islamic custom of *purdah*, or seclusion of women, strictly controlled which men a woman would be allowed to interact with, and under what conditions. Theoretically, women were never to be alone in public.

Submission, however, constitutes only half the story of women in traditional Islamic thought. Even as the Qur'an commands women to obey, it orders men to rule justly. Men did not possess unchecked dominion over women; a mistreated wife could obtain a divorce with relative ease. The Qur'an also elevates women in another way; it honors marriage above all other states, and (within a marriage) praises the power of a virtuous wife. "Treat [women] with kindness," says the Qur'an, "for even if you dislike them, it may be that you dislike a thing which Allah has meant for your own abundant good" (Qur'an in Bouhdiba, p. 7). In other words, a woman can be crucial to a man's spiritual life—even if he refuses to acknowledge this truth. In the *hadith* (the collection of his sayings as recorded by his followers), Muhammad asserts that a pious wife represents a greater treasure for a man than gold and silver.

Islam's conception of women created mixed options for individual Muslim women. Social structure kept them, as it kept European women, largely confined to the home, working in domestic occupations. However, this subjugation was tempered by reason, by economic necessity in lower-class families whose females had to work, and by the underlying spiritual equality of man and woman. Even some aspects of Muslim law that seem especially sexist, such as its approval of polygamy, or, more exactly, polygyny, have been in some ways of a benefit to women. Most Muslim countries that allow polygyny require the husband to gain the consent of his cur-

rent wives before wedding again; and, as Wad Rayyes discovers in *Season of Migration to the North*, wives are as free to join together against the husband as to become rivals. Women also benefit from Islam's relatively easy divorce laws. The procedure for divorce does favor males—a man can get a divorce just by renouncing his wife in front of two male witnesses, while a woman must present evidence of mistreatment or neglect. Even with this limitation, though, the unhappy bride still has great latitude for improving her situation.

In sum, Islam as a cultural practice offers both freedoms and restrictions for women. It is telling that neither of the principal Sudanese women in Salih's novel fits the Western stereotype of the meek, veiled, and silent Arab woman; she refuses to suffer male domination silently, even if the

BRAIN DRAIN

The title of Salih's novel raises the issue of migration. In the course of the novel, the narrator migrates to Khartoum for work. The two central figures in the book have also immigrated—to England for extended periods. In fact, migration has haunted the Sudan in various ways both during the Anglo-Egyptian condominion and since. Beginning in the period of British dominance, the best educated and most highly skilled Sudanese were likely to leave their own country, with its struggling, primarily agricultural economy, for promising opportunities abroad. This trend, called "brain drain," has worried Sudanese officials for decades. During colonialism, the most likely destination was England itself. The English created in the Sudan an educational system on English lines; school was conducted in English as soon as possible, and success in learning English was the crucial test for educational advancement. Thus, it only made sense for a Sudanese scholar who had reached the pinnacle of education in his home country to travel to England for further studies. This is what Mustafa does; and, had fate not intervened, he might never have returned to his homeland. Beginning in the early 1970s, a different type of brain drain occurred. Instead of England, well-trained Sudanese professionals sought employment in the better-developed Arab countries, especially Saudi Arabia. As they came from a predominantly Muslim country, they felt at home and were perfectly welcome on the Arabian peninsula; however, the net effect of their departure has been to exacerbate the Sudan's economic woes.

only path to freedom and self-expression entails murder and suicide.

Islamic sexuality. Just as many Westerners have misinterpreted the Qur'an and misunderstood the Islamic conception of women, so have many misinterpreted the Qur'anic conception of paradise. Muhammad's revelation that sexual gratification forms part of the reward for the faithful in the afterlife has seemed strange to many Westerners, raised on the Christian tendency to see sex as sinful, if not coequal with original sin itself. On the other hand, in Muslim eyes, it is the Christian equation of sex and filth that seems odd. "Islam in no way tries to depreciate, still less to deny, the sexual. On the contrary, it attributes a sublime significance to the sexual and invests it with such a transcendental quality that any trace of guilt is removed from it" (Bouhdiba, p. viii). Islam correlates the love between a man and a woman to God's love for humankind; indeed, God's creation of the universe is recreated in the human act of love.

Islam and Christianity both demand that sexual urges be expressed lawfully, but differ in the emphasis they place on this requirement. In Christianity, Paul's famous words—"Better to marry than to burn [with lust]" (1 Cor. 7:9)—present matrimony as a safety valve for people not holy enough to live celibately. The Muslim situation is quite different. Muslims must conduct their sexual lives properly, and the stakes are high: the punishment for adultery can be as severe as whipping or even death by stoning. But such severe punishments are rooted in the very fact that sexual life is vital to the community. In fact, Islam does not place so high a value on celibacy as Christianity—most of the major religious figures in Islamic history were married. Islam holds that husband and wife (or wives) are the building blocks of the whole social structure and, again, the re-enacters of God's grand design. Deviations from the traditional, God-given pattern signal underlying moral perversions that must be eradicated absolutely. In other words, seeking sex outside marriage does not signify simply giving in to one's physical desires; rather, it indicates that one has strayed, fundamentally and completely, from the path ordered by God.

This direct linkage of morality to sexual behavior is crucial in Salih's novel, which explores how psychological maladies can be expressed in sexual compulsions. However, Salih also presents a challenge to the Muslim assumption that marriage sanctifies carnal relations. The two acts of cataclysmic violence that punctuate the text occur, not in adultery or fornication, but rather in the hallowed married bed.

The Novel in Focus

Plot summary. *Season of Migration to the North* intertwines the lives of two Sudanese men: an unnamed narrator, and an older man—Mustafa Sa'eed—whom the narrator encounters in his native village. The novel is structured as a type of duet. While the two men are at dinner one night, Mustafa tells his story, which takes over the narrative for a few chapters. After this digression, the novel returns to the protagonist's story, but it is now concerned with Mustafa, and Mustafa's voice can be heard periodically for the reminder of the book—in flashbacks, in isolated utterances, and in the diaries that the narrator finds in Mustafa's study. The two men share little, except for the crucial fact that both have studied abroad; from this shared experience grows the brief friendship that allows Salih to explore the dynamics of sex, power, and selfhood in the context of colonialism.

The novel opens as the narrator and protagonist returns to his native village after seven years in England. The villagers welcome him home, and the narrator notices a stranger among them—no minor anomaly, since the village is far too small and insignificant for anyone to want to move there. Furthermore, the narrator notices that this newcomer, a man in his late middle age, asks no questions about the Christian world, and only smiles at the narrator's reports of life in England.

His curiosity piqued, the narrator asks around and discovers that the stranger is Mustafa Sa'eed, a man who came to the village a few years back, buying land and eventually marrying the daughter of a local man. He is polite, but distant; no one knows what his past holds, and no one is excessively curious.

The narrator is interested, however, and so readily accepts when Mustafa invites him to dinner. Without getting to know anything about the older man's past, he discovers that Mustafa is indeed highly competent, disciplined, and well-respected among the other members of the village. It is not until Mustafa is drawn, against his will, into a drinking session, that the narrator begins to learn the truth, in a most disconcerting way. Once drunk, Mustafa, whom the narrator has no reason to think is anything other than a simple farmer, begins reciting poetry . . . in English! "I

Sudanese villagers.

tell you that had the ground suddenly split open
and revealed an afreet standing before me, his
eyes shooting out flames, I would not have been
more terrified. All of a sudden there came to me
the ghastly, nightmarish feeling that we—the
men grouped together in that room—were not a
reality but merely some illusion" (Salih, *Season of
Migration to the North*, p. 15). Now Mustafa has,
inadvertently perhaps, revealed that he has
depths of experience that the narrator had not
guessed; it is only a matter of time before he must
explain himself.

The narrator does not have long to wait. Two
nights later, Mustafa invites the young man over
to explain his past. In a long flashback, Mustafa
does just that. He was born in Khartoum and
raised by a mother from whom he is inexplica-
bly distant. From an early age, he felt he was basically bereft of emotion; he was much better at
analyzing than actually feeling. When the British
arrived and set up schools, he was among the
few who volunteered to attend (with his mother's
passive acceptance). He excelled in all areas of
learning; he grew up by following the route from
Khartoum (the periphery of the British empire),
to Cairo (Britain's headquarters in the Middle
East), to London itself. All the while Mustafa was
learning but not feeling, excelling yet taking no
joy in his excellence.

After describing his arrival in London,
Mustafa's narrative becomes more fragmentary
and disjointed. He found London in the exuber-
ant mood that followed World War I. In Bo-
hemian circles he became a much sought-after
exotic specimen. He pursued studies in politics
and economics, meanwhile preoccupying himself with a very different quest: the pursuit of
white women. He describes, in clinical detail, his
methods of seduction and the bedroom that he
decorated to resemble a harem playpen.

> My bedroom was a graveyard that looked onto
> a garden; its curtains were pink and had been
> chosen with care, the carpeting was of a warm
> greenness, the bed spacious, with swansdown
> cushions. There were small electric lights, red,
> blue, violet, placed in certain corners; on the
> walls were large mirrors, so that when I slept
> with a woman it was as if I slept with a whole
> harem simultaneously.
>
> (*Season of Migration*, p. 30)

To conquer his lover, Mustafa traded on his
foreign appeal; he found most of his conquests
among the culturally adventurous, those eager to
taste the East by loving an Arab. Mustafa himself
remained untouched, unperturbed through all of
it. For him, sex was a kind of compulsion, alienated from any kind of emotion. It was, perhaps,
a kind of experiment; he called his bed an oper-

ating table on which he manipulated women into sleeping with him. Even as he tells the story, he expresses no remorse for his deeds, despite the fact that three women—Ann Hammond, Sheila Greenwood, and Isabella Seymour—killed themselves because he did not return their love.

However, it is not the women who killed themselves who end Mustafa's story; that place belongs rather to the woman whom he killed. Jean Morris was the only woman who rejected Mustafa; she called him ugly, a savage bull. He pursued her for three years; sometimes she fled, sometimes she allowed herself to be caught. At last they wed. "I am tired of your pursuing me and of my running before you," she declared. "Marry me" (*Season of Migration*, p. 33). Mustafa does not explain, but the marriage led to tragedy; Jean Morris died by the knife, and Mustafa served seven years in prison because it was he who stabbed her.

Thus ends Mustafa's retelling of his life. In the next chapter the narrator recounts that, later that summer, Mustafa disappears. His body is never found, but everyone assumes that he drowned in the flooding of the Nile, which was especially strong that summer. The narrator continues his life, taking a bureaucratic post in Khartoum, but Mustafa's memory haunts him. On a train ride, he meets a retired bureaucrat who went to school with the brilliant scholar and murderer; at a dinner party, he hears various (erroneous) tales about what happened to this man who was "the first Sudanese to marry an Englishwoman" (*Season of Migration*, p. 55). And the narrator has a more immediate reason to remember Mustafa: the dead man's will makes him the guardian of Mustafa's two sons and (by association) his attractive widow. The way the narrator fills (or rather, fails to fill) this trust shapes the second half of the novel.

It begins innocently enough. On one of his periodic visits to his home village, the narrator overhears a conversation involving his own grandfather, Bint Mahzoud (an often married old woman), Wad Rayyes (a frequently married old man), and a villager named Hajj Ahmed. Their conversation drifts to sex. Readers with any stereotyped beliefs about the modesty of Muslim women will be surprised by the frank earthiness of Bint Mahzoud, who describes her sexual past without demur in front of the men in her company. However, from the perspective of plot, the most important information to come out of this long discussion is that Wad Rayyes, an engineer with an insatiable taste for variety, wants to marry Mustafa's widow, Hosna Bint Mahmoud.

This situation falls between the cracks of Muslim jurisprudence. As a woman, Hosna is presumably under the direction of some man or other; the question is, which man? Mustafa left his sons in the narrator's care, but said nothing about his wife; still, the villagers assume that the narrator will be the one who decides Hosna's fate. Her father endorses the idea of marriage to Wad Rayyes. Mahzoud, the narrator's closest friend, opines that the narrator should marry Hosna himself. However, when he asks Hosna what she wants, she is firm: "'After Mustafa Sa'eed,' she answered immediately, with a decisiveness that astonished me, 'I shall go to no man'" (*Season of Migration*, p. 96). The narrator does not find a resolution; he simply goes back to his job in Khartoum.

He returns to another tragedy. While he is away, Hosna's father forces her to marry Wad Rayyes. Hosna refuses, however, to sleep with her new husband. The tension builds, week by week. Finally, Wad Rayyes attempts to rape her, but she stabs him to death, then kills herself. The villagers, shocked by this terrible atrocity, bury the two bodies and determine never to speak of the crime. Even the narrator is rebuffed in his attempts to find out what has happened, until he persuades Bint Mahzoud to tell him the whole story.

After this, the novel enters its final phase. The narrator visits the now-empty home of Mustafa and Hosna, determined to explore the locked room where Mustafa kept his personal belongings. There, he discovers various artifacts of Mustafa's life: his library, photographs, letters. He reads cryptic comments on scraps of paper. Finally, Mustafa's voice takes over; it is unclear whether this voice is something the narrator remembers from long ago, or if he finds a diary. At any rate Mustafa recounts his tortured marriage to Jean Morris, her flirtations and his infidelities, their mutually destructive manipulations. The story moves inexorably to its conclusion. On a brittle December night, he walks home from work as if in a dream, finds her in bed, and stabs her. Their last words to each other are "I love you" (*Season of Migration*, p. 165).

The novel ends with a brief scene. The narrator leaves Mustafa's house and jumps into the Nile, caught up in an existential crisis. He is on the verge of death, and willing to accept it, when he realizes, "I shall live because there are a few people I want to stay with for the longest possible time and because I have duties to discharge" (*Season of Migration*, p. 168). The last image of the novel is of the narrator screaming for help from the middle of the river.

OTHELLO AND AFRICA

~

When the British conquered a country, they brought not only guns and judges, but also their culture; in fact, the British made claims about their superior culture to justify their conquests. Shakespeare, one of Britain's most compelling claims to a superior culture, became an important secondary symbol of British colonialism. However, Third World intellectuals never patently rejected Shakespeare. Having received a Western-style education, and recognizing Shakespeare's artistic brilliance, they were heavily influenced by the great Renaissance playwright.

For Africa in general, and the Arab world in particular, *Othello* was the central Shakespearean text, for the obvious reason that it dealt most directly with the worlds of the Middle East and North Africa. It was the first Shakespeare play performed in the Middle East—in Turkey in the 1870s—and it continues to preoccupy Arab and African intellectuals to this day. Written at the inception of Britain's colonial adventures (around the time of its first American colonies), the play presents an early European view of the nonwhite world. Othello is a noble Moor, a valiant soldier, and an able commander embraced by the European culture of Venice . . . until he falls in love with, and marries, the white Desdemona. Immediately after the marriage, he is misled by the villainous Iago into believing that his wife is unfaithful. Iago plays on Othello's internalized sense of racial inferiority; the villain makes it seem as if Desdemona could not possibly love a black man. Finally consumed by rage, Othello smothers his wife with a pillow and then kills himself—a recursion into violence presented in the play as a natural tendency in hot-blooded Africans. Shakespeare's play presents a Moor who combines the greatest and the basest in human nature. Perhaps more significant is the fact that *Othello* reveals a European tendency to romanticize Africa, and to view its inhabitants through the lens of racial difference. It is this aspect of the play that Salih's *Season of Migration to the North* explores when the novel refers to Shakespeare's tragedy.

One critic has placed *Season of Migration to the North* in the context of *muaradah,* an Arabic literary tradition in which one text is produced as a response to an earlier text, reversing and questioning the meaning of the original: "It is a re-reading of Shakespeare's *Othello,* a restatement of the tragedy, a reshaping of the tragic figure of the Moor" (Harlow, p. 75). That is, *Othello,* while sympathetic to the Moor, is nevertheless told from a European perspective. Salih's novel tells a similar tale but from inside the African culture that produced the Moors.

The Othello question. No one who is familiar with Shakespeare can read Salih's novel without thinking of *Othello.* This tragedy concerns a Moor (an inhabitant from North Africa) who marries a white woman, eventually becomes insanely jealous, and kills her in her bed. The tragedy of Mustafa and Jean Morris mirrors this situation by Salih's conscious intent; at several key points, he has Mustafa or another character refer to *Othello,* drawing attention to the parallel. Nor are the echoes a simple matter of literary influence or clever referencing; the interplay between these two tragic Moors strikes at the very heart of Salih's great theme, the confrontation of vastly different cultures.

Othello is referred to in several instances in Salih's novel. One of the women who will eventually kill herself for Mustafa begins by asking his race; he replies, "I am like Othello, Arab-African" (*Season of Migration,* p. 38). When Mustafa is put on trial for murdering Jean Morris, his own mind circulates around references to the play. His attorney asserts, "Mustafa Sa'eed, gentlemen of the jury, is a noble person whose mind was able to absorb Western civilization but it broke his heart. These girls were not killed by Mustafa Sa'eed but by the germ of a deadly disease [racism] that assailed them a thousand years ago" (*Season of Migration,* p. 33). In other words, these women see him as strange and exotic and therefore frightening as well as enticing, just as the Europeans in *Othello* see its protaganist. In the novel, Mustafa recalls Othello's anguished confession of guilt, "'Twas I that killed her" (Shakespeare, *Othello* 5.2.131). In reaction to his attorney's plan, Mustafa thinks, "This is untrue, a fabrication. It was I who killed them. I am the desert of thirst. I am no Othello. I am a lie. Why don't you sentence me to be hanged and so kill the lie?" (*Season of Migration,* p. 33). And yet later, the narrator recalls Mustafa saying, "I am no lie. Othello was a lie" (*Season of Migration,* p. 95). The rejection/embracing of the *Othello* analogy reflects Mustafa's own confusion. He is perhaps as much a victim of the "disease" as the woman he kills. In any case, Mustafa sees something of himself in this fictional predecessor.

A BIOGRAPHICAL INFLUENCE

~

One critic has suggested a plausible real-life analogue for some aspects of Mustafa Sa'eed: a Palestinian poet named Tawfiq Sayigh. This poet, who often crossed paths with Salih in London in the 1950s, was in some senses the prototype of the modern Arab nomad; he left Palestine after the founding of the state of Israel, and spent the rest of his life wandering. He edited an influential journal, and helped establish the careers of countless young writers, among them Salih. And, in the late 1950s, he was involved in a violent relationship with an Englishwoman whom his poetry identifies only as K. Many of the passages in his poems to her pick up themes that are also prevalent in *Season of Migration to the North*: the white woman as colonizer; the chase that is love; the intertwining of ardor and disgust; the feeling of utter exile. It seems almost certain, then, that Sayigh supplied part of the genesis for Mustafa; however, he must be seen only in the parts of Mustafa that are tortured and victimized. How Salih felt about the whole man can be seen in his moving testimonial: "His loss was a real tragedy, for Tawfiq Sayigh was a very fine poet and he had a great influence on me and on many other writers of my generation" (Amyuni, p. 14).

It is not difficult to see the similarity, even before he duplicates *Othello*'s tragic irony. Othello won Desdemona's love by telling her stories of his violent life under the desert sun; she was enthralled by this "extravagant and wheeling stranger / Of here and everywhere" (*Othello* 1.1.135-6). Othello genuinely loves his wife; Mustafa adopts the Moor's technique for his own cold-blooded seductions. He tells his prey outrageous stories about his African childhood, adding elephants, crocodiles, and the tragic death of his parents on the Nile. And the women devour these stories, adding embellishments of their own. One renames herself "Sausan," and calls herself his slave girl. Mustafa capitalizes on his ethnic difference, and finds women who are eager to experience the exotic by means of sex.

Salih uses *Othello* to underscore the racism that creates a European fascination with the strange, exotic, and Eastern. This "Orientalism" began in Shakespeare's day and has continued unabated to this day. Of course, Salih's point is that Arabs have no reason to be flattered by European interest in their culture, accompanied as it is by conquest and colonialism. The women Mustafa seduces do not love him; they love the Orient, which they feel they can experience through him.

However, the *Othello* comparison has another valence as well. At the trial, Mustafa's defense attorney "turned the trial into a conflict between two worlds, a struggle of which [Mustafa] was one of the victims" (*Season of Migration,* p. 33). By the early twentieth century, many European intellectuals had come to realize the errors of colonialism, and desired to make amends. Throughout his career in Europe, Mustafa encounters people who view him, not simply as a fellow intellectual, but rather as symbol and test case for the colonial experiment. He is, in short, a token Arab, and the awareness of this position haunts him through his years in London. He self-consciously views himself as an Arab with a singular destiny; he boasts, "I will liberate Africa with my penis" (*Season of Migration,* p. 120). But when his attorney attempts to excuse Mustafa's crime on just this sociological basis, Mustafa objects. He does not want to accept the final indignity of being robbed of his own actions, of being told that he is too powerless even to murder without the impetus of a millenium-old cultural conflict. At this instant, the parallel to Othello assumes a different significance. On her deathbed, Desdemona is asked who killed her, and replies, "Nobody. I myself" (*Othello* 5.2.125).

Othello, already stricken with remorse, spurns this attempt to save him, saying, "She's like a liar gone to burning hell; / 'Twas I that killed her" (*Othello* 5.2.130-31). Similarly, Mustafa detests the plea that he is not responsible for his actions. Even if those actions are horrific—perhaps especially because they are horrific—he wants to be held accountable. To claim that culture-conflict made him do it would be to accept the underlying lie of colonialism: that nonwhites are inferior to, and should be the responsibility of, the white man.

Sources and literary context. Salih has spent most of his adult life in European countries, and was educated in the English manner. It is not surprising, then, that many of the most significant influences on Salih are Western. One critic notes, "He admits to being influenced by a wide spectrum of Western English language writers and poets, such as Swift, Conrad, Faulkner, Shakespeare, and Yeats" (Elad, p. 62). His very choice of the novel form reflects this Western influence, as the novel was imported to the Arab world in the late nineteenth century. The fractured narrative and rich, poetic language reveal a debt to such modernist novelists as James Joyce and William Faulkner.

Within the Arabic context, Salih has stated that he is closest to Yahya Haqqi and the Nobel-Prize winning Egyptian novelist Najib Mahfuz (see **Midaqq Alley**, also covered in *African Literature and Its Times*). It has been said that Mahfuz's career creates the perfect "axis of reference" for the development of the Arabic novel, as his celebrated writings have both shaped and reflected the concerns of other novelists. If this is true, then Salih's novel corresponds to the period of experiment and counter-realism that Mahfuz inaugurated in the middle 1960s, a period in which Arabic writers moved away from the sociopolitical realism of earlier decades.

Finally, Salih has stated that he was very much influenced by Sigmund Freud's *Civilization and its Discontents*. In this seminal work, Freud presents a vision of human beings as torn between an urge to die and an urge to love, so that love and the desire for an end are interwoven. This psychological framework is loudly echoed in the twisted, doomed love affair of Mustafa and Jean Morris.

Reviews. *Season of Migration to the North* was published to great acclaim, and its reputation has grown in the three decades since. Salih calls it "the novel for which for one reason or another I have the reputation that I have" (Salih in Amyuni, p. 14). Frank Birbalsingh writes, "Salih presents migration and the historical events which make it necessary, as symptoms of our shared condition and common fate as human beings who do not fully understand ourselves. The analysis involved in this presentation is what finally confirms the excellence of artistic achievement in *Season*" (Birbalsingh, p. 73). Jareer Abu-Haydar praises the novel's delicacy, likening its use of themes to the movements of a symphony. Eiman El-Nour says, "The novel, traditionally a Western genre, which has been shaped by many a contemporary Arab novelist to reflect an Arab reality, has been given by Salih an additional African dimension" (El-Nour, p. 161). And one Western critic of Arabic literature has called it "among the finest Arabic novels to date" (Allen, p. 21).

—Jacob Littleton

For More Information

Abu-Haydar, Jareer. "A Novel Difficult to Categorize." *Al-Abhath* 32 (1984): 45-54.

Allen, Roger. *Modern Arabic Literature.* New York: Ungar, 1987.

Amyuni, Mona. "Introduction: *Season of Migration to the North.*" *Al-Abhath* 32 (1984): 11-26.

Birbalsingh, Frank. "Season of Migration to the West." *Al-Abhath* 32 (1984): 65-74.

Bouhdiba, Abdelwahab. *Sexuality in Islam.* London: Routledge, 1985.

Elad, Ami. "Fiction and Reality in al-Tayyib Salih's *Dawmat Wad Hamid.*" In *Writer, Culture, Text.* Ed. Ami Elad. Toronto: York University Press, 1993.

El-Nour, Eiman. "The Development of Contemporary Literature in the Sudan." *Research in African Literatures* 28: 3 (fall 1997): 150-61.

Harlow, Barbara. "Sentimental Orientalism: *Season of Migration to the North* and *Othello.*" *Al-Abhath* 32 (1984): 75-80.

Holt, P. M. *The Mahdist State in the Sudan: A Study of Its Origins, Development and Overthrow.* 2nd ed. New York: Oxford University Press, 1977.

Mernissi, Fatima. *Beyond the Veil.* Bloomington: Indiana University Press, 1987.

Salih, Tayeb. *Season of Migration to the North.* Trans. Denys Johnson-Davies. London: Heinemann, 1969.

Shakespeare, William. *The Tragedy of Othello, the Moor of Venice.* Boston: Plays, Inc., 1976.

So Long a Letter

by

Mariama Bâ

~

Born in Dakar, Senegal, in 1929, Mariama Bâ was raised as a Muslim by her maternal grandparents. During school holidays Bâ studied the sacred text the Qur'an under the guidance of the Imam of the main mosque in Dakar. Bâ later became a primary schoolteacher and an activist in the feminist movement in Senegal, in which she participated until her death in 1981. A wife and mother, Bâ married a Senegalese politician, with whom she had nine children. Though the marriage ended in divorce it provided inspiration for her first novel, *So Long a Letter,* noted for its striking depiction of women in Islamic culture and its blistering treatment of polygamy. The novel has been hailed as the most emotionally realistic portrayal of female life in African fiction of the time.

Events in History at the Time of the Novel

Islam in Senegal. In *So Long a Letter* the rituals and observances of Islam form a compelling social backdrop against which the widowed Ramatoulaye struggles to come to terms with her bereavement. In the 1970s, the decade in which the novel closes, more than 80 percent of the Senegalese population was Muslim, while 6 percent was Christian and the remainder worshipped deities indigenous to their particular region (Nelson, p. vii).

The spread of Islam into Senegal and other regions of Africa may have begun as early as the eighth century. Approximately 100 years earlier,

---

THE LITERARY WORK

A novel set in urban Senegal from the 1950s to the 1970s; published in French (as *Une si longue lettre*) in 1979, in English in 1981.

SYNOPSIS

In a letter written to an old friend, a newly widowed schoolteacher reflects upon her life as a Muslim woman in Senegal.

---

in 610 C.E., an Arab merchant—Muhammad—began to preach a series of revelations that he believed came to him from God through the angel Gabriel. Angered by his denunciation of local religious beliefs, the people of Mecca rose up against Muhammad, who fled with his followers to Medina in 622. His flight, called the *hegira,* marked the beginning of a new religious calendar and a new faith, Islam. Islam's effects in the area that eventually became Senegal were not significantly felt until the eleventh century when a ruler of the Tekrur kingdom converted to Islam and persuaded his family and many of his subjects to adopt the new faith. Most mass conversions occurred during the nineteenth and twentieth centuries, as many West Africans turned to the certainties of a strict religious faith to help them cope with the social and political upheaval resulting from colonization by France and Great Britain.

The particular practice of Islam among the Senegalese includes devotion to the prescriptions

A Muslim woman stands in Senegal.

of universal Islam, such as complete submission to the will of God ("Allah"), and the observation of Islamic customs specific to the geographic region and to the ethnic group occupying that region. For example, many Senegalese Muslims observe additional pilgrimages beyond the one all followers of Islam must make to Mecca. Members of Islamic brotherhoods, such as the Muridiya and Tidjaniya, may journey at any time to the home of a spiritual leader or the tomb of a founder. The basic tenets of the Islamic faith, however, remain the same. Devout Muslims prove their dedication to Allah by performing the "five pillars" of Islam: the recitation of the creed "There is no god but God and Muhammad is his prophet"; daily prayers at specific hours of the day; fasting from sunrise to sunset during the ninth lunar month of Ramadan; the giving of alms collected at the beginning of the year and at the end of Ramadan; and the pilgrimage to Mecca, which all Muslims must undertake once in their lives. Approximately 2,000 to 3,000 Senegalese Muslims attempt the journey annually. One who completes the pilgrimage may then use the title *al-Hajj* before his or her name and wear a green turban. In the novel, Modou Fall, Ramatoulaye's husband, obtains a much younger second wife by offering the girl's grasping parents various expensive gifts, including money to finance their pilgrimage to Mecca, where they ac-

quire the titles *al-Hajji* and *al-Hajja.* Also, Islamic precepts dictate Ramatoulaye's practices after she is widowed, from her "purifying baths" to her "changing of mourning clothes every Monday and Friday" and her mandatory grieving period of four months and ten days (Bâ, *So Long a Letter,* p. 8).

Women and Islam. Like Christianity, Islam comprises worship of a sole male deity and confers greater authority upon men than women. Men are the acknowledged heads of their household, to whom their wives and other female relatives must defer upon all matters. For many years marriage and motherhood were still considered the most important goals in the life of a Muslim woman. The ideal was for men to serve as breadwinners, while women raised children and maintained an orderly household. Some modern Muslim women, however, have pursued higher education and found work outside the home. Such work must be deemed acceptable by the religious community. Muslim traditionalists, for example, require that women select jobs appropriate to "the feminine vocation," such as teaching and women's medicine (Jomier, p. 77). In the novel, Aissatou's scheming mother-in-law, Aunty Nabou, rears a young niece in the strictest precepts of Islam, trains her in the domestic arts, then selects an appropriate profession—midwifery—for her, declaring, "The profession you will learn [in the State School of Midwifery] is a beautiful one. . . . [Y]ou will acquire grace for your entry into paradise for helping at the birth of the new followers of Mohammed, the prophet. To tell the truth, a woman does not need too much education" (*So Long a Letter,* p. 30).

Polygamy. The Islamic practice of polygamy—the crux of *So Long a Letter*—dates back to the sixth century and was practiced by Muhammad himself. Proponents of polygamy defend the practice on the grounds of Muhammad's own example, the supposedly greater sexual needs of the male, and the likelihood of war reducing the proportion of men to women in the population. The Qur'an permits polygamy on two conditions—first, the number of wives must not exceed four; and second, the husband must treat all of his wives equally, not favoring one over the others. Women, however, are permitted only one husband at a time, and unlike Muslim men, cannot marry out of their faith. Moreover, while either party is allowed to dissolve the marriage, it is usually easier for a man to obtain a divorce.

After independence in 1960 Senegal passed a new marriage law allowing a couple to choose between monogamy or polygamy (with up to four wives) in a prenuptial contract. Husband and wife appear in court to record the contract, with the woman sometimes learning only at this point that her husband plans on polygamy. Apparently such women often grow so enraged that they force their spouse to settle for monogamy or lose the bride price, the money he paid her family to make her his spouse. Other new marriage laws have followed, mostly to protect women. In 1974 Senegal outlawed repudiation, the failure to honor the marriage contract, legislating that marriages be dissolved only through a divorce granted by the court. Polygamy nevertheless persisted after this date, albeit with some alterations. New difficulties have arisen because of migration from rural areas to cities. School counselors in Dakar report, for example, that the children of polygamous marriages have had a hard time developing a sense of family identity in the city, where they live with their mother in a separate household rather than in a collection of contiguous households, as is the case in a village compound. Their father, rotating among the dispersed households that he heads, is often absent from theirs. Still, women in various parts of Africa continue to attach themselves to polygamous men, either as a first wife, like the protagonists in *So Long a Letter*, or as a subsequent wife. Those who become subsequent wives usually marry men who are middle-aged or older. Rarely do polygamous marriages involve very young men, because of the brideprice and the expense of contributing to more than one household. This helps explain the husbands' belated decision in Bâ's novel to take a second wife; in both cases the men are middle-aged rather than young.

Recently women in a number of African countries have shown a preference for the position of second or even unofficial wife rather than first wife. One reason for such unions is that a woman who lives with a man outside the system can hold on to her own property. Moreover, the first wife "is less and less the envy of today's young women" (Coquery-Vidrovitch, p. 217). Staying single, on the other hand, is not yet a popular option. Most educated urban women of the late twentieth century show a preference for entering into a monogamous or polygamous relationship with a man. They ask, often in vain, that their husbands keep them informed about their plans. Old perceptions still persist. Women have not yet demanded en masse to be treated as equals with the opposite sex. They still regard the man

as superior and the woman as obligated to serve him and bear his children. There have been stirrings, though. A number of educated women who are dissatisfied with the status quo have formed feminist groups, such as Senegal's Yewwu Yewwi ("Women Stand Up"), to contend with tradition-related problems.

In *So Long a Letter*, Ramatoulaye and Aissatou experience polygamy firsthand, when their husbands marry younger wives. Significantly, both husbands fail to honor the Qur'an's second condition of treating their wives equally. Only Assiatou rebels. Her husband, Mawdo, who maintains a separate household with young Nabou, tries to persuade Aissatou to stay in the marriage, but she denounces his reasoning as flawed, even hypocritical: "You want to draw a line between heartfelt love and physical love. I say that there can be no union of bodies without the heart's acceptance, however little that may be" (*So Long a Letter*, p. 31). Unwilling to accept an untenable situation, she leaves Mawdo, taking her children with her.

DEATH, BURIAL, AND MOURNING

Islamic ceremonies involving the dead can be as elaborate as those involving the living. After death the corpse must receive a ritual bath; embalming is not permitted, though the body may be scented before being enveloped in a plain white shroud. According to Islamic law, burial should take place the same day as the death, if at all possible. When the body is interred, it is positioned in the grave so that its head is turned towards Mecca. The family of the deceased also adheres to specific rituals following their bereavement. A three-day mourning period ensues. All of the deceased's relatives live under one roof, receiving visits of condolence and listening to readings from the Qur'an each evening. The full mourning period lasts 40 days, although a widow must remain in seclusion for the even longer interval of four months and ten days. In the novel, Ramatoulaye observes all of the necessary rituals following the sudden death of her husband. The jarring presence of her in-laws and co-wife, Binetou, however, soon has her almost welcoming her mandatory period of solitude: "My heart concurs with the demands of religion. Reared since childhood on their strict precepts, I expect not to fail. The walls that limit my horizon for four months and ten days do not bother me" (*So Long a Letter*, p. 8).

These Senegalese children are playing on the steps in front of a theater advertising a concert by an ensemble from France, former colonial ruler of Senegal.

An independent Senegal. During the nineteenth century, France and Great Britain competed for control over West Africa. By 1895 Senegal had been officially recognized as a French colony, along with French Sudan and Mauritania in the same region. During the early to mid-twentieth century, France consolidated its hold over French West Africa, founding schools, building railroads, and encouraging the cultivation of such lucrative crops as peanuts, maize, and cassava.

Of all the colonies in "Black Africa," Senegal was arguably the most susceptible to French policies of assimilation, in part because the French government granted full citizenship rights to Africans born in the "Four Communes"—Dakar, Gorée, Rufisque, and Saint Louis. These African citizens had the right to "participate in modern electoral politics [and] hold political office (if they met certain educational qualifications)" (Geller, p. 9). Such privileges also allowed them to rise, economically and socially, above the Senegalese of the interior, whom the French regarded as subjects. Although this Senegalese "elite" constituted only about 5 percent of the population, its members made the most of their educational and professional opportunities, hoping to achieve equality with the French. In the

novel, Ramatoulaye vividly recalls how competing French and Senegalese influences shaped "New Africa" and the strain resulting from the attempt to reconcile two vastly different cultures:

> The assimilationist dream of the colonist drew into its crucible our mode of thought and way of life. The sun helmet worn over the natural protection of our kinky hair, smoke-filled pipe in the mouth, white shorts just above the calves, very short dresses displaying shapely legs: a whole generation suddenly became aware of the ridiculous situation festering in our midst.
>
> (*So Long a Letter*, p. 24)

After World War II and the fall of Nazi Germany, France rethought its colonial policies towards black Africans. In 1945, 63 delegates—out of a total 600—representing the African colonies attended the National Assembly. These African delegates included Léopold Sédar Senghor and Lamine Guèye, two Senegalese deputies elected to the French Parliament, who were to play major roles in shaping their country's political development. Senghor, Guèye, and the other African delegates were granted the opportunity to air publicly the grievances and aspirations of their countrymen. The African delegates received "strong support" from the Socialists and Communists; the assembly itself resulted in an evaluation of colonial policy and "a draft plan for the union of France and its colonies" (Nelson, p. 28).

In 1946 French citizenship was extended to the entire population of French West Africa—16 million people in eight colonies (Mauritania, French Sudan [now Mali], Guinea, Upper Volta, Ivory Coast, Dahomey, Niger, and Senegal). Senegal became an overseas territory, with representation in the French parliament and a territorial assembly of its own. Granted, the status of these former colonial subjects was that of second- or even third-class citizens: most of them still did not have the vote. The majority of those who could vote had to do so on a separate roll from the European residents; as a result, African votes were not considered to be worth as much in an election. Moreover, the powers of the new territorial assemblies were only advisory. Not surprisingly, Africans were disappointed by these limited reforms. They began questioning the viability of French assimilationist policies and became increasingly interested in achieving full independence as nations in their own right.

In 1956 the *loi-cadre* reforms led to universal suffrage in Senegal and broadened the powers of the 12 territorial assemblies of French Africa (the eight in West Africa, and four—Gabon, Middle Congo, Chad, and Oubangui-Shari—in Equatorial Africa), setting the stage for self-government among the erstwhile colonies. The federation of French West Africa gradually began to unravel, as more African countries expressed the desire for independence. In 1958 Senegal and the French Sudan formed the Mali Federation, which successfully obtained independence from France on June 20, 1960. Two months later Senegal seceded from the Mali Federation and became recognized as a separate country on August 25, 1960. A congress consisting of all the members of the legislature and of one delegate from each regional assembly and from each regional council unanimously elected Léopold Sédar Senghor as the first president of Senegal, an office he held until his retirement in 1980.

Education. In *So Long a Letter,* Bâ emphasizes, through Ramatoulaye's thoughts and memories, the growing importance of education among native Senegalese. Western schools were first introduced into the region during the nineteenth century, when various Roman Catholic orders founded elementary schools to teach French and manual skills to Senegalese children.

In 1857 Louis Faidherbe, Governor of Senegal, laid a stronger foundation for Western edu-

cation by establishing more schools—for both European and African children—which he later organized into a state school system. Schools in French West Africa frequently served a dual purpose. They trained farmers, teachers, clerks, and interpreters to assist the French in running the colony, and they also introduced French culture to the African people, an important objective during the colonial era. Thus, during the twentieth century, many Senegalese schools—especially in urban areas—adopted an educational system that increasingly resembled that found in French schools. Secondary education for African students received a boost in 1911 with the found-

SENEGAL'S FIRST PRESIDENT

Born in 1906, Léopold Sédar Senghor soon became an influential figure in Senegalese politics and art. The son of a prosperous trader, Senghor at first aspired to the priesthood but realized, at age 20, that his true vocation lay elsewhere. In 1928 he went to Paris on a partial scholarship, continuing his education at the Lycée Louis-le-Grand and the Sorbonne. During his time abroad he met other black intellectuals, including Caribbean poet Aimé Césaire, and developed a deeper appreciation for African culture, which he believed had much to offer the modern world. When World War II broke out in 1939, Senghor was drafted; captured by the Nazis in 1940, he spent two years in a concentration camp, where he wrote some of his finest poems. On his release Senghor joined the French Resistance and, after the war, became increasingly involved in Senegalese politics. In 1948 Senghor, a moderate socialist, founded the Senegalese Democratic Bloc Party, a less radical group than the French Socialist Party, to which he had earlier belonged. During the 1950s Senghor opposed the loi-cadre reforms, which he felt undermined the concept of a federal government in Africa. Attempting to counteract the effects of the loi-cadre, he organized several parties that were committed to the cause of a federal African unity. His efforts contributed to the formation of the Mali Federation in 1958. After Senegal was recognized as an independent republic in 1960, Senghor became its first president. During his 20-year administration, Senghor strengthened political and economic ties between Senegal and its West African neighbors and worked to modernize his country's agriculture. While popular in his prime, he became more revered as he aged, gaining a reputation as "father of his country."

ing of the William Ponty Normal School, which offered separate training programs for prospective teachers and junior administrators in government and business. Closely modeled after French institutions, the William Ponty School consistently maintained high educational standards and boasted a diverse student body from all the French territories in Senegal; many of the school's graduates went on to become part of "Africa's educated elite" (Nelson, p. 157).

In the years following World War II Senegal undertook a new educational agenda: the population as a whole was to receive the basic education necessary to citizens of a Westernized society, while its more gifted students were to be prepared to assume leadership responsibilities in their own communities. During the 1950s schools were expanded and refurbished, enrollment increased, a scholarship program for advanced study abroad was introduced, and an institution of higher learning—later called the University of Dakar—was founded. In the novel, Ramatoulaye, Aissatou, and their contemporaries reap the immediate benefits of these changes. Nostalgically reflecting on her years at secondary school, Ramatoulaye remembers how "we were true sisters, destined for the same mission of emancipation" and eager to participate in "New Africa's" agenda "for the promotion of the black woman" (*So Long a Letter*, pp. 15-16). She reserves special praise for the white headmistress who nourished her students' dreams, aspiring to make them appreciate a multitude of civilizations without renouncing their own. It is because Ramatoulaye has enjoyed such an education that she can sympathize, to some extent, with her bitter co-wife, Binetou, who is pressured into leaving school just before graduation to marry the wealthy Modou.

The Novel in Focus

Plot summary. The novel opens with Ramatoulaye, a middle-aged schoolteacher, writing to her old friend, Aissatou, with the stark news: "Yesterday you were divorced. Today I am a widow" (*So Long a Letter*, p. 1). Ramatoulaye's husband of 30 years, Modou Fall, has succumbed to a sudden heart attack.

Ramatoulaye continues with her letter, describing Modou's interment and the necessary Islamic rituals—the cleansing and clothing of the corpse—accompanying the event. Binetou, Modou's much younger second wife, comes to stay at Ramatoulaye's house for the funeral, but her presence irritates the older woman. Ramatoulaye also resents the way Modou's sisters—newly arrived for the ceremony—seem to consider her 30-year marriage and Binetou's 5-year marriage of equal importance, and hails the eventual departure of them all with relief. Later, a family meeting is held at her house and all of Modou's most intimate secrets are exposed. Ramatoulaye, already embittered by her late husband's abandonment of her and their children after his marriage to Binetou, is further shocked to learn that Modou died heavily in debt. Every penny of Modou's salary—he was a technical adviser in the Ministry of Public Works—was spent to keep Binetou and her grasping mother in luxury. "Lady Mother-in-Law," as Ramatoulaye calls her, demands that payments on Modou's sumptuous new villa, in which her daughter lives, continue out of his estate. Ramatoulaye's own daughter, Daba, counters by accusing Binetou's family of fraudulently removing expensive items from the villa for their own profit. Ramatoulaye is displeased by the wrangling on both sides.

Despairing and angry, she recalls her first meeting with her future husband at a party when she was a young student at the teachers training college: "Modou Fall, the very moment you bowed before me, asking me to dance, I knew you were the one I was waiting for" (*So Long a Letter*, p. 13). After finishing their respective educations, Modou and Ramatoulaye married, despite the objections of Ramatoulaye's mother, who found Modou almost "too perfect for a man" and preferred an older, more reliable suitor, Daouda Dieng, a doctor at the Polyclinique (*So Long a Letter*, p. 14). Meanwhile, Modou's friend, Mawdo Bâ, met and later married Ramatoulaye's best friend, Aissatou.

Both couples settled into married life. Modou and Mawdo thrived in their chosen professions, Ramatoulaye and Aissatou raised their children, and their families enjoyed holidays together. But Aissatou's contentment was marred by the coldness of her husband's family, who felt Mawdo had married beneath him by choosing a goldsmith's daughter for his wife. Aunty Nabou, Mawdo's widowed mother and a princess from the Sine region, was particularly affronted by the marriage and planned to revenge herself on her despised daughter-in-law. One day she traveled back to the Sine and asked her brother to give her one of his daughters to educate. Young Nabou went to live with her aunt, who raised her to be docile and obedient, financed her education as a midwife, then offered her to Mawdo, now middle-aged, as a prospective bride. After Aunty Nabou claimed she would die of shame if her son refused, Mawdo consented to the marriage. Unable to accept the situation or Mawdo's justifications for it, Aissatou left her husband, taking her sons with her. Resuming her education, Aissatou eventually obtained her current appointment as an interpreter to the Senegalese Embassy in the United States, where she enjoyed professional success. Her sons also flourished, despite the separation from their father. Ramatoulaye praised her friend warmly, declaring, "How much greater you proved to be than those who sapped your happiness!" (*So Long a Letter,* p. 31).

Three years after Aissatou's departure, Ramatoulaye was faced with a similar shocking development in her own marriage. The middle-aged Modou secretly began to court Binetou, a beautiful, intelligent girl who was a friend and classmate of his own daughter, Daba. Although Binetou hoped to complete her education, her impoverished mother begged her to accept her suitor, who promised jewels, a car, and other luxuries if she left school to marry him. Ramatoulaye remained in the dark about Modou's plans until after the wedding, when Mawdo, Tamsir (Modou's brother), and the local Imam (religious leader) broke the news to her. Stunned and heartbroken by this disclosure, Ramatoulaye nonetheless decided to remain in her marriage, despite the urgings of her children to break with Modou.

After the marriage Modou moved in with his second wife and her family, avoiding his first wife and their children. He showered the resentful Binetou with expensive gifts and tried to appear younger and more vigorous to her. Alone, Ramatoulaye adjusted to her solitary life, taking on Modou's responsibilities and raising her children single-handedly. Learning of her friend's struggles, Aissatou gave her the gift of a new car. Ramatoulaye learned to drive, obtained her license, and became more independent. But despite her new autonomy, Ramatoulaye missed her husband and her marriage: "The truth is that, despite everything, I remain faithful to the love of my youth. Aissatou, I cry for Modou, and I can do nothing about it" (*So Long a Letter,* p. 56)

In the present, Ramatoulaye endures her fortieth day of mourning but receives an unexpected shock: Tamsir, her brother-in-law, announces his intention to marry her after the mourning period is over. Furious at his presumption, Ramatoulaye violently rejects his proposal, declaring: "You for-

get that I have a heart, a mind, that I am not an object to be passed from hand to hand.... I shall never be the one to complete your collection" (*So Long a Letter,* p. 58). Tamsir is shocked by her outburst but accepts defeat. Later, Ramatoulaye is surprised to receive a visit from her former suitor, Daouda Dieng, now a deputy at the National Assembly and still handsome and prosperous. They soon establish an easy rapport; Daouda reveals that he still loves Ramatoulaye and wishes to marry her. Although she is not in love with Daouda, Ramatoulaye considers accepting his proposal because of his kindness and the promise of financial security. But Daouda also has a wife, and Ramatoulaye ultimately decides that she cannot be part of another polygamous relationship and inflict on another woman the kind of suffering she herself has known. She writes to Daouda, explaining her feelings: "Esteem is not enough for marriage, whose snares I know from experience. And then the existence of your wife and children further complicates the situation. Abandoned yesterday because of a woman, I cannot lightly bring myself between you and your family" (*So Long a Letter,* p. 68). Daouda accepts her decision with regret and ceases to visit. Meanwhile, Modou's estate is finally settled—his new villa goes to his daughter, Daba, who loses no time in evicting Lady Mother-in-Law and Binetou. Ramatoulaye retains ownership of the old villa, and Modou's other effects are divided among his family.

Ramatoulaye occupies her days thinking about her children's futures, especially those of her daughters. Although she tries to keep an open mind about progress, she is still shocked when she catches three of her daughters smoking and suspects they are experimenting with alcohol, too. Moreover, she discovers that another daughter, Aissatou—named for her friend—is three months pregnant. As a devout Muslim, Ramatoulaye is initially angered by this revelation, given Islam's strong stance against premarital sex, but her love for her child ultimately triumphs over her anger. Fortunately, the girl's lover, a law student at the university, intends to marry her after they finish their schooling; his mother will look after the child who is expected, conveniently, during the school holidays. Ramatoulaye is relieved to hear of these plans but wonders what happens to young pregnant girls who are less fortunate. She emphasizes the necessity for sexual education to her younger daughters, although she suspects that they are already more aware of the subject than she was at their age.

In the final segment of her letter, Ramatoulaye anticipates a visit from Aissatou and reveals that, in spite of her tragic experiences, she still believes in "the inevitable and necessary complementarity of man and woman. Love, imperfect as it may be in its content and expression, remains the natural link between these two beings" (*So Long a Letter*, p. 88). Ramatoulaye concludes by assuring Aissatou that she intends to make a new life for herself: "Despite everything—disappointments and humiliations—hope still lives on within me.... The word 'happiness' does indeed have meaning, doesn't it? I shall go out in search of it" (*So Long a Letter*, p. 89).

Women in transition. Although *So Long a Letter* is primarily an account of two women's personal experience of polygamy, it also examines the larger social and historical context surrounding the stories of Ramatoulaye and Aissatou. As literary critic Florence Stratton observes, "Bâ portrays women realistically, grounding her female characters in society and making them subject to historical forces" (Stratton, p. 145). Describing the Senegalese fight for independence, Ramatoulaye writes in her diary-letter: "It was the privilege of our generation to be the link between two periods in our history, one of domination, the other of independence. We remained young and efficient, for we were the messengers of a new design. With independence achieved, we witnessed the birth of a republic, the birth of an anthem and the implantation of a flag" (*So Long a Letter*, p. 25).

Even more specifically, Ramatoulaye and Aissatou represent a generation of women caught between tradition and emancipation, between the often confining customs followed by their mothers and the disconcerting freedoms sought by their daughters. Both women manage to obtain secondary school educations, marry for love in spite of family disapproval, and, with their husbands, attempt to scale the social ladder and become part of the New African elite: "We all agreed that much dismantling was needed to introduce modernity within our traditions. Torn between the past and the present, we deplored the 'hard sweat' that would be inevitable.... We were full of nostalgia but were resolutely progressive" (*So Long a Letter*, pp. 18-19).

Ramatoulaye and Aissatou face a challenge to their progressiveness when, after years of comfortable marriage, their husbands follow Islamic tradition by taking younger, second wives. As literary scholar Nwamaka B. Akukwe observes, tradition overwhelms their progressiveness:

The irony, however, is that having the choice [of whom to marry] alone does not guarantee [Ramatoulaye and Aissatou] freedom, as events in their respective marriages prove. They yearn for the freedom associated with life in a modern world, and they wish to shake off all of the shackles that restrain women in traditional African culture. But they realize that the traditional practices, especially those associated with male privileges, cannot be discarded overnight because they are at the heart of traditional African society.

(Akukwe in Cox, p. 78)

Of the two, only Aissatou has the audacity to break with her past by leaving Mawdo and forging a new life for herself and her sons. Ramatoulaye, by contrast, remains mired in her situation, unable to abandon her marriage or the moral values with which she was reared. Ramatoulaye's children, especially her emancipated eldest daughter, Daba, are deeply dismayed by her decision to remain in the marriage, which proves even more bitter than she had imagined: "I had prepared myself for equal sharing, according to the precepts of Islam concerning polygamic life. I was left with empty hands" (*So Long a Letter*, p. 46). Even Daouda Dieng, Ramatoulaye's former suitor, points out the discrepancy between her arguments for women's rights and the highly traditional life she has led: "You are echoing my own speeches at the National Assembly, where I have been called a 'feminist'.... Women must be encouraged to take a keener interest in the destiny of the country. Even you who are protesting; you preferred your husband, your class, your children to public life" (*So Long a Letter*, p. 62).

In the aftermath of her widowhood, Ramatoulaye remains wryly aware of the contradictions in her life, especially when dealing with her own children. Liberated Daba startles her mother by defining her own marriage as an equal partnership that can be dissolved by either party, leading Ramatoulaye to declare, not altogether approvingly, "She had her own opinions about everything" (*So Long a Letter*, p. 74). Moreover, despite her professed hatred of domineering matriarchs like Aunty Nabou and Lady Mother-in-Law, Ramatoulaye is shocked to find some of her daughters smoking and begins to worry about "the flow of progress" and the dangers of allowing her children too much liberty (*So Long a Letter*, p. 77). The revelation of another daughter's pregnancy also disturbs Ramatoulaye, though she manages to put aside her anger and support her child: "I could not abandon her, as pride would have me do. Her life and her future were at stake, and these were powerful considerations, overriding all taboos and assuming greater importance in my heart and in my mind" (*So Long a Letter,* p. 83). Despite her ambivalence towards the modern world in which she must now live, Ramatoulaye remains determined to complete the transition from spurned wife to independent single woman, as Aissatou has done before her: "It is from the dirty and nauseating humus that the green plant sprouts into life, and I can feel new buds springing up in me" (*So Long a Letter,* p. 89).

Appropriately enough, Ramatoulaye's epiphany corresponds with the growing women's movement in Senegal. During the colonial period most Senegalese women had little formal schooling and remained confined to traditional gender roles as wives and mothers. Moreover, no Senegalese woman could vote until after 1946. After Senegal gained independence, however, enrollment of female students in schools increased, rising from 41,000 in 1961 to 131,000 in 1976 (Gellar, p. 101). During the early 1980s—after *So Long a Letter* first appeared—women constituted approximately one-third of the student population at the University of Dakar (Gellar, p. 192). The postcolonial years also saw the more active involvement of women in politics: in 1963 Caroline Diop became Senegal's first woman deputy in the National Assembly. Changes in the status of women proceeded rapidly in urban areas, like Dakar, where women entered the work force in both skilled and unskilled positions. Meanwhile, educated women, like Mariama Bâ herself and her fellow writer, Aminata Sow Fall, made significant contributions to the cultural and intellectual life of Senegal.

Sources and literary context. While Bâ's novel is not autobiographical, her use of a first-person narrator in *So Long a Letter* has invariably led to speculation from critics, fueled by Bâ's own apparently unhappy marriage. Scholar Florence Stratton points out, however, that there is far more resemblance between Bâ and Aissatou, the narrator's friend and projected recipient of the letter, than between Bâ and Ramatoulaye: "While Bâ treats her conservative heroine (Ramatoulaye) ironically, having her tell her story with subconscious evasion and revelation, she quite explicitly identifies with her radical heroine (Aissatou) who is not only a divorced woman (as Bâ herself was) but also shares Bâ's last name" (Stratton, p. 138). Significantly, Bâ does not specify the ethnic origins of Ramatoulaye and Aissatou, perhaps to emphasize the universality of their plight as

middle-aged women whose solid marriages are threatened by the addition of younger rival spouses. Unlike other African authors, like Elechi Amadi and Flora Nwapa, who present polygamy as an acceptable cultural practice in their respective novels **The Concubine** and **Efuru** (both also covered in *African Literature and Its Times*), Bâ takes a far darker view of the religious practice of polygamy. The balance of power in a Muslim marriage is depicted as being overwhelmingly in the husband's favor. In *So Long a Letter,* "The men enjoy unlimited freedom, choosing and discarding wives as they wish, while the women are expected to keep silent and accept their lot in accordance with the divine will of Allah" (Akukwe in Cox, p. 77). Besides providing an intensely personal exploration of polygamy, Bâ's work earned distinction as the first epistolary novel in African literature. Even today, this particular genre is seldom used. *So Long a Letter* has also been hailed as "the first truly feminist African novel, skillfully weaving the accounts of individual suffering and dilemmas into the exposition of [Bâ's] thesis: the issues of women's status in Senegal today" (Blair, p. 139).

Reviews. *So Long a Letter* has received mixed reactions. The African critic Frederick Ivor Case expressed wonder at the fact that a literary prize (the Noma Award for Publishing in 1981) was conferred upon the novel, a text he considered "of limited value" (Case in Stratton, pp. 134-35). Femi Ojo-Ade, writing for *African Literature Today,* was similarly uncomplimentary, branding Bâ's feminist agenda as "an occidental phenomenon" that offered African women "a fake freedom" because it removed them from the sacred roles of wife and mother, placing them instead in a state of "social and psychological alienation" (Ojo-Ade in Stratton, p. 135). In contrast, the well-known African critic Eldred Jones applauded the work: "Mariama Bâ's novel offers a testimony of the female condition in Africa while at the same time giving that testimony true imaginative depth" (Jones in Stratton, p. 133). Jones also praised *So Long a Letter*'s "maturity of vision and feeling," adding, "[a]s a first novel, it represents a remarkable achievement" (Jones in Stratton, p. 133). Similarly, Victoria Neumark, writing for the *Times Educational Supplement,* praised Bâ as "a Senegalese writer of rare talent," and declared that *So Long a Letter* represented not an outburst of "shrill feminism" but rather, "a study in female dignity" (Neumark, p. 32). Allon White in the *London Review of Books* complimented the tone as well as the text: "The feminism of Senegal—a society in transition but still suffused with religious values—emerges as strongly moralistic, and engaged with paradoxes through which a generation of European feminists have already lived" (White, p. 19). For White, *So Long a Letter* "begins as a profound elegy for [Ramatoulaye's] dead husband" but "ends in hope, and in political courage" (White, p. 19).

—Pamela S. Loy

For More Information

Bâ, Mariama. *So Long a Letter*. Trans. Modupé Bodé-Thomas. Harare: Zimbabwe Publishing House, 1981.

Blair, Dorothy S. *Senegalese Literature: A Critical History*. Boston: Twayne Publishers, 1984.

Coquery-Vidrovitch, Catherine. *African Women: A Modern History*. Trans. Beth Gillian Raps. New York: Westview Press, 1997.

Cox, C. Brian, ed. *African Writers*. Vol. 1. New York: Charles Scribner's Sons, 1997.

Gellar, Sheldon. *Senegal: An African Nation Between Islam and the West*. Boulder, Colo.: Westview Press, 1982.

Jomier, Jacques. *How to Understand Islam*. New York: Crossroad Publishing Company, 1991.

Mazrui, Ali A. *The Africans: A Triple Heritage*. Boston: Little, Brown, and Company, 1986.

Nelson, Harold D. *Area Handbook for Senegal*. Washington, D. C.: Foreign Area Studies, 1974.

Neumark, Victoria. Review of *So Long a Letter*. *Times Educational Supplement*, 15 October 1982, p. 32.

Pedler, Frederick. *Main Currents of West African History 1940-1978*. New York: Barnes & Noble, 1979.

Stratton, Florence. *Contemporary African Literature and the Politics of Gender*. London: Routledge, 1994.

White, Allon. Review of *So Long a Letter*. *London Review of Books*, 2 September 1982, p. 19.

Song of Lawino and Song of Ocol

by
Okot p'Bitek

~

Among Africa's most celebrated poets, Okot p'Bitek is also among the continent's most idiosyncratic writers. Between his birth in 1931 and his death in 1982, p'Bitek was a choirboy, a soccer player, an anthropologist, director of Uganda's national cultural center, and a teacher, in addition to his more famous roles as poet and essayist. p'Bitek is also unusual for the degree to which he rejected the European influence on Africa. He rejected the Christian faith of his parents in the early 1960s, and wrote his most famous works in his native Acoli rather than in English. His essays ruthlessly critique Africans who have fallen under the spell of such European ideas as Christianity or socialism. His scholarly work provides a deeply sympathetic defense of Acoli culture. Both of these purposes are achieved as well in his poems—especially in "Song of Lawino"—which attempt to voice the beliefs and concerns of traditional Acoli culture.

Events in History at the Time the Poems Take Place

The Acoli. *Song of Lawino and Song of Ocol* provides vivid records of the pre-1970s life and customs of the Acoli. Far less numerous than the Buganda or Banyoro peoples, the Acoli reside in the elevated grasslands of northwest Uganda. They are a subgroup of the Luo people, and they speak a Nilotic language (unlike their Bantu neighbors to the South).

Prior to the occupation by the British (formalized by their establishment of the East African

---

THE LITERARY WORK

Two poems set in Uganda in the 1960s; *Song of Lawino* written in Acoli (as *Wer pa Lawino*), translated and published in English in 1966; *Song of Ocol* written in English, published in 1967.

SYNOPSIS

An estranged couple speak of their marital difficulties, which encapsulate the social problems of postcolonial Africa.

Protectorate in 1899), the Acoli pursued subsistence farming and cattle herding. They lived in polygamous, extended families under the leadership of a single male, who dictated plans and divided responsibilities. The various family compounds were loosely knit, first by a village leader who coordinated cooperative activities (such as raids and hunts) and arbitrated interfamily disputes, then by a *Rwot*, or leader of a number of territories, who performed the same functions on a larger scale. Both were hereditary positions. Altogether there were some 30 clans in Uganda before the coming of the British, who consolidated the clans and reduced them to six; the old clans, however, retained strong allegiances that would surface in the postindependence (1962) competition for political posts.

The presence of the British beginning in 1892 wrought changes in Acoli customs. In addition to the conversion of many Acoli to Christianity

Elaborate dances are an important part of Acoli culture.

(sometimes a superficial conversion, as p'Bitek's poems suggests), new leaders were appointed by the British, creating some tension between these and the older sources of authority. The British introduced cotton and tried to force the Acoli to grow it for cash, with mixed results. There was strong resistance to cash farming, though in time Uganda would become a major supplier of cotton to the world.

In Acoli culture, elaborate dances are crucial to social events such as transfers of power and courtship; these dances play a vital role in p'Bitek's poems. Central also to the culture is a pre-Christian religion based on a polytheistic concept—the notion of *Jok*. Jok represents the spirit of individual clans, villages, or wild animals—anything of significance to the life of the Acoli. A Jok can be beneficent or malicious; either way, it is an Acoli's duty to appease the spirits, both good and bad, to ensure success in human endeavors.

When the British withdrew from Uganda in the early 1960s, they left behind traces of colonialism that threatened to fragment Ugandan society. There was a small elite of black Africans, generally Protestants, whom the British had trained to fill government and bureaucratic posts. Educated in the West, these Africans often had little sympathy for the mass of Africans, who lived traditional lives in the villages and in many

cases had adopted Catholicism or perhaps Islam rather than Protestantism. Economically the British left behind a situation that favored trade with the West over the growth of industry in Uganda or trade with other Africa nations. In religion, they left behind a divided populace. The rift between Africans who adhered to traditional African religions (such as the Acoli's polytheistic faith) and those who had converted to Christianity was no less wide than the gap between the Catholic and the Protestant converts or that between the Western-educated elite minority and the illiterate majority. In p'Bitek's poems, Ocol is a Catholic Christian while his wife clings to Acoli beliefs, a difference that mushrooms into one of their deepest tensions. The conflict reflects a larger rift in society as a whole. Around independence, some 34.5 percent of Uganda was Catholic, 28.2 percent Protestant, 5.6 percent Moslem, and the remaining 31.7 percent traditional (Mittleman, p. 68).

The religiously split household was not uncommon in Uganda, with family members often divided along generational lines. For example, Lawino recalls when her Christian-educated mate, Ocol, then still a boy, attacked a traditional healer who had come to his father's house, breaking the sacred drum and sending the old man away. As Christian-educated youths matured into adulthood, matters just grew more complicated. In the 1950s-60s struggle against colonialism, many young Africans who had been born Christian or who had been converted to Christianity rejected this faith as the oppressor's religion. In adulthood, p'Bitek, like his Kenyan friend Ngugi wa Thiong'o (see *Weep Not, Child,* also covered in *African Literature and Its Times*), rejected Christian names as well as Christian beliefs.

To understand the religious situation in British East Africa, one must realize that Christianity was never, for Kenyans or Ugandans, simply a matter of belief. Missionaries first introduced Protestantism and Catholicism to Uganda in the 1870s. While white missionaries thought that they were simply bringing God's light to heathens, Africans saw the new religion quite differently. For Africans, from the highest leaders to the poorest villagers, Christianity was just one more aspect of colonization. With the new religion came education, Western health care, material advantages, and a chance for individual advancement in the new culture of foreign control. Africans chose Christianity for all sorts of reasons, but rarely for a disinterested belief in Jesus Christ. They understood from the start that Christian missions were part of the colonial project. Therefore, they did not see their choice to convert as hypocritical or deceitful, even when they did so without rejecting aspects of their birth religions or their culture that were not Christian at all, such as polygamy.

Most missionaries sensed this, at least in general terms. The first missionary in the land of the Acoli, Albert Lloyd, reports that an Acoli leader invited him with these words: "We have heard long ago that the Bunyoro and Baganda [peoples north of the Acoli] have learned to worship the white man's God but we too want the same.... Do you think we should mind the destruction of our old and worn-out customs and religion if you provided us with good food for our souls?" (Russell, p. 2). However, Keith Russell, a Bishop in Uganda at the time of liberation in 1962, expresses a more practical motivation for embracing the colonial religion:

> The new teaching . . . that he wanted for his people: that he thought in the least of worshipping God—white man's or anyone else's—no; that his people were missing something valuable that others were getting—yes; that this had anything to do with clan ritual, was in any way thought of as a substitute for it—no.
>
> (Russell, p. 3)

Most missionaries in Uganda were keenly aware that their converts' new belief was superficial, that it hinged on material benefits and was liable to be repudiated as soon as Christianity contradicted or outlawed traditional belief. The missionaries showed a reluctance to disturb even polygamy, the most obviously non-Christian aspect of native culture.

Yet over time Christianity created a schism among native-born Ugandans. The disunity tended to result less from Christianity than from its fringe benefits, especially education. In "Song of Lawino," Lawino recalls sneaking away from night school to attend a "get-stuck" dance, where young couples declare their love for each other. Ocol, by contrast, stuck to his studies with diligence. At the end of his course of education, he finds himself alienated from his people, his village, even his wife. Access to Western knowledge makes him intolerant of what he comes to regard as superstition, and he is unable to appreciate Acoli culture. Ocol is representative of a common type in postcolonial Africa: the educated African who feels closer to the traditions and practices of the European invader than to those of his own people. This group imported European goods, followed Western ways, even preferred women who mimicked the styles of white women. They put their faith in Christ, and could be as intolerant as any white priest when considering indigenous theology.

THE LAMB OF GOD

Okot p'Bitek has been loudly critical of Christianity's role in Africa. He asks about missionaries, "Why did these run-away fellows come to Africa to teach Jewish history? Why did they not stay at home in Europe to bring light to that darkest of all continents? If all Europeans hold (and at the moment not many do) that their ancestor was a sinful Jew called Adam, why do they force this ancestorship on Africans?" (p'Bitek, *Artist the Ruler,* p. 61).

Dance and song. p'Bitek's European training was in law and social anthropology, the latter of which turned out to be crucial to his Africanist poetry. Much of his intellectual work was focused on revising European notions of African primitivism; he produced a book critical of Western views of African religion, and produced insightful studies of Luo theology and Acoli oral culture. His work in this last area is critical for understanding *Song of Lawino and Song of Ocol*. As one critic observes, p'Bitek "wrote the Acoli version of *Song of Lawino* in a period in his life when he was daily concerned with Acoli traditional songs, both in his research and in his activities in connection with the Guli festival [of native arts]" (Heron in p'Bitek, *Song of Lawino and Song of Ocol,* p. 5). Acoli folk songs and stories, and the dances at which they were sung, exert a profound and continued influence on p'Bitek's work. In the 1970s he produced a book of traditional songs (*Horn of My Love*) and another of stories (*Hare and Hornbill*). p'Bitek understood that, for Africans, oral culture was not a transitory or meaningless form. In cultures without a written tradition, oral tales and songs were the central forms of artistic expression. Thus, it is far from accidental that he interpolates so many traditional tunes into *Song of Lawino,* or that some of his most vigorous poetry occurs when his speaker describes the dances of the people.

THE CURIOUS ANTHROPOLOGIST

~

One of p'Bitek's most common weapons against colonialism is humor. Making fun of the odd behavior of Europeans in Africa allows him to communicate how strange their presence is, how untenable their goals, without having to assert with anger the evils they introduced to the continent. In one such story, an anthropologist emerges as a ridiculous figure, who ends up hurting himself because of his enthusiasm to delve into African culture:

My old teacher, Professor E. E. Evans Pritchard, used to attend these youthful dances at night among the Shilluk. In the spirit of the social anthropologist he had to be naked as everybody else was. But he always carried a torch. When two lovers left the arena for the nearest private spot, he would follow them, his torch blazing. The Welsh fellow got a thorough beating one night; it left large scars on his legs.

(p'Bitek, *Artist the Ruler,* p. 33)

Acoli dances come in several varieties. *Bwola* and *otole* dances were elaborate political affairs; the first celebrated the coronation of a new leader, and the latter celebrated friendly relations between two neighboring villages. There is also ritual dancing, accompanied by funeral singing, to express both struggle against death, and eventual surrender to it. Finally, there are the *orak* or *larakaraka* dances described so memorably by Lawino; she calls them "get stuck" dances because their primary purpose is romantic.

The scene at a "get stuck" dance is both chaotic and carefully organized, a mixture of social and individual desires. To the beat of different types of drums, a man or woman calls for a given tune, known to all the dancers. Then everyone becomes a soloist at once, singing his or her own song. These songs consist of traditional elements, lines, thoughts, and images, selected and ordered by the individual singer's inspiration. Thus, no song is ever repeated, not in any exact way, but each song is in broad terms familiar to all; they know how to interpret the images chosen. For p'Bitek the miracle of this form is that it allows for individual expression within an affirmative, supportive context of shared participation. Young men sing to their beloved, and the women reciprocate with their own love songs. Insults too are exchanged; romantic advances are made and rejected, or made and reciprocated. The whole drama supports p'Bitek's argument for the unity of culture. For him, it is no use trying to separate artistic expression from social behavior: in a healthy culture, all these elements form a unified whole. In his poetry, Christians like the drunken priest in *Song of Lawino,* who is both aroused and repelled by the naked dancers, and bureaucrats like Ocol, who want to Westernize Africa, threaten the healthy beauty of the dance.

Political factionalism. Uganda was rife with divisions after independence in 1962. Already noted are the religious rivalries. Likewise there were ethnic rivalries, linguistic differences, and political competitions. The two major parties were the Uganda Peoples Congress (UPC), constituted largely of Protestants, and the Democratic Party (DP), comprised mostly of Catholics. In the poems Ocol belongs to the DP, his brother to the UPC. While the UPC enjoyed a large measure of control of government under Prime Minister Milton Obote (1962-72), it was itself riddled with factionalism. All the rivalries were less about establishing a solid footing for the new nation "than about who was going to get the most benefits from independence. Instead of working together to build their new nation, [the politicians] worked against each other. They built disunity instead of unity," in part a result of the fundamental ethnic divisions on which society rested (Davidson, p. 147). Lawino asks in her poem, "Is this the Peace / That Independence brings? / When my husband / Opens a quarrel / With his brother" (p'Bitek, *Song of Lawino and Song of Ocol,* p. 105).

African identity, old and new. In the second section of her song, Lawino addresses her husband: "I do not understand / The ways of foreigners, / But I do not despise their customs. / Why should you despise yours?" (*Lawino and Ocol,* p. 41). This question encapsulates a problem of concern for all Africans after colonialism: how was the newly liberated continent going to think of itself? The old ways, though very far from destroyed, had been complicated forever by Western intervention: African intellectuals, politicians, and ordinary people had to find their own way to fit into the modern world. They had to answer political questions relating to a choice of capitalism, communism, or some third system. They had to resolve social questions—which should take precedence: clan affiliation, regionalism, or pan- African unity? And they had to answer cultural questions—should they opt for loyalty to tradition or for modernization? Behind every question lay the underlying query: how much European thought was appropriate for Africa's future?

Politically, most forward-looking thinkers agreed that Africa had to find its own path. Some, like Ghana's Kwame Nkrumah, advocated a continental unity to survive competition with the superior development of Europe. Nkrumah also advocated what he called "African socialism," an ideal espoused in Kenya and Tanzania as well. Most newly independent African countries chose capitalism. The majority started with some version of democracy, but nearly all ended with military coups and dictatorship.

Culturally, much was made of indigenous African forms. There were numerous debates on how best to promote African ways and African history in Uganda. Discussions ranged from revamping school curricula to teach African languages and history, to promoting the internationally acclaimed African dance troupe, The Heartbeat of Africa. According to a top government aide at the time, Akena Adoko,

Ugandans were demanding
That the table should be turned
That there be revolutions
That the old order of aping
And imitating Europeans
Were fit only for the slaves
. . .

Independence ushered in
The era of expression
Of things purely African:
Our thoughts and our deeds
We had to be ourselves
Whether for better, for worse.
(Adoko in Mittleman, p. 117)

Even those writers—the majority—who chose European genres like the novel attempted to capture a quintessential African voice by incorporating patois, proverbs, and elements of traditional tales. In East Africa especially, key writers chose to write in their own languages as often as in English.

Okot p'Bitek was among the most vocal of those intellectuals who asserted that all of these endeavors were insufficient, timid, and doomed to failure. He argued that European influence must be rooted out wholly, and native forms of culture allowed to flourish without foreign graftings. Obviously, he repudiated all intellectuals who desired a synthesis of European and African; he viewed this as a new form of mental imperialism. Ideas like "African socialism" were nonsense to him; the socialist author Karl Marx had written for a European context that had no parallel in Africa. The same was true for capitalism. Okot p'Bitek also rejected many schools of thought that others found appealing. He rejected the "negritude" movement of French-speaking African intellectuals because he believed its proponents wanted to create an image counter to white hegemony, without first extricating themselves from it. He rejected Frantz Fanon's theory of cultural revolution (see **The Wretched of the Earth,** also covered in *African Literature and Its Times*) because it depended on European psychoanalysis and history. He rejected the teaching of Western works in African universities; he even criticized the exportation of African literature abroad.

p'Bitek's views were markedly radical, and did not become current among the majority of African thinkers. However, the very stridency and intellectual consistency of his position served a crucial purpose: it exposed the depths of European influence on Africa, and identified elements that had to be dealt with in order to eradicate the legacy of colonialism.

The Poems in Focus

Plot summary. *Song of Lawino and Song of Ocol* is divided into two major sections, both of which are further subdivided—*Song of Lawino* into thirteen verse "chapters," *Song of Ocol* into nine. Each chapter revolves around a certain argument, but only loosely; the poet allows his speakers to digress into long, lyrical asides. It is important to note, also, that the two speakers hardly seem to be addressing each other. While the sources of their disagreement are tragically clear, their worldviews and experiences are so different that they cannot be said to understand each other at all. Each starts by addressing the other, but soon slips into speaking to other, larger audiences. Lawino addresses the villagers who she expects to support her charges; Ocol speaks with hostility to the various groups of Africans whom he despises.

Lawino begins her complaint at the personal level. Her first chapter establishes the situation. The husband she loved, and who loved her, now spurns her; he calls her ignorant, dirty, and superstitious. He abuses her mother and her family. The second chapter discusses Klementina (Tina), Ocol's mistress. Lawino disavows jealousy; she says she does not mind her husband's unfaithfulness, only his contempt. If her description of Klementina seems catty or contemptuous, that is only because Tina does exactly what Lawino hates in her husband: she tries to act white. Lawino provides long descriptions of Klementina's painful pursuit of Westernized beauty; her rival dusts her face, cauterizes her hair, starves herself. And the result, Lawino says, is atrocious:

> The beautiful one is dead dry
> Like a stump,
> She is meatless
> Like a shell
> On a dry river bed
>
> (*Lawino and Ocol,* p. 40)

In the third chapter, Lawino begins her defense of her own culture by discussing the significant tradition of the dance. She opens by asserting that she does not know how to dance the dances of white people, then slips into a long and vivid description of an Acoli dance; she stresses its health, emotional openness, and its crucial social function. Because the dancers are naked, Ocol thinks that Acoli dances are immoral; Lawino sees European dances, where dancers violate Acoli taboos such as the interdiction against dancing with blood relatives, as much more immoral. This discussion of dances segues naturally into the next chapter, in which Lawino recalls her youthful beauty, her popularity, and how Ocol courted her. The fifth chapter returns to the subject of physical beauty. Its

title—"The Graceful Giraffe Cannot Become a Monkey"—encapsulates Lawino's argument: European styles of beauty are fine for white women, but look ridiculous on Africans. When Ocol despises her physical appearance, he is rejecting his entire heritage.

In the sixth and seventh chapters, Lawino contrasts European and African styles in two significant aspects of life: cooking and the concept of time. In Chapter Six, she asserts that she cannot work the modern stove and oven that Ocol has bought for her; the food it cooks seems flat and tasteless. She contrasts spiritless stove-food with what she cooks on her native firepit, and the complaint swells into a lyrical description of the important social function of food in Acoli culture; it brings people together and punctuates the day's activities. Chapter Seven extends this critique to the treatment of time. Lawino is frightened by the grandfather clock Ocol has brought into the house; her husband mocks her because she has no conception of time—not even minutes or hours, let alone years or centuries. From Lawino's perspective, however, it is Ocol whose understanding of time is diseased. She sees that he is ruled by his clock. He greets visitors with, "What can I do for you?" rather than letting them get to their purpose in due time; he does not seem to understand that, in Acoli life, people know when to perform a given activity by signs other than what the time is on a clock:

> When the sun has grown up
> And the poisoned tips of its arrows painfully
>   bite
> The backs of the men hoeing . . . This is
>   when
> You take drinking water
> To the workers
>
> (*Lawino and Ocol,* p. 64)

Chapter Eight moves to the topic of Christianity and Lawino's distrust of it. She is, first of all, mystified by the attitude of the missionaries, who demand belief but grow exasperated when Africans are interested enough in the missionaries' ideas to ask questions about them. Next, she recalls the time a drunken priest came to a village dance; for Lawino, this event shows that Christianity provides neither peace nor rest; the priest, who has attempted to repudiate his sexual urges, ends up ogling the naked women at the dance. She closes by criticizing the Christian names Ocol has given to their children. In the next chapter, she extends her critique of Christianity; she wants to understand the faith, but is continually put off by the hostility the priests display to the questions she asks. Chapter Ten concludes Lawino's critique of Christianity by discussing death; her husband, however, rejects the idea that Acoli beliefs can provide emotional or intellectual solace.

In Chapter Eleven, she switches the focus back to earthly matters. Here, she gives a long description of her husband's political beliefs. He is a strident supporter of the Democratic Party, which backs free enterprise and the Church. Yet Lawino notes that, in spite of all his talk of unity and independence, Ocol has rejected his brother. They are locked in a mortal feud because this brother supports the Congress Party, which leans to the left and wishes to disestablish the Church. Both brothers claim to want the best for Uganda. Lawino soberly notes that peace must begin at home; if the brothers did not waste their energy fighting each other, they might have improved material conditions for everyone in the country.

In Chapter Twelve, Lawino vents a long complaint about her husband's books. His library is entirely European, which reveals that Ocol's ideas, like his clothes, are borrowed from whites: "The dogs of white men / Are well trained, / And they understand English!" (*Lawino and Ocol,* p. 115). In the final chapter, Lawino pulls together all her complaints in a simple plea to her husband. She still feels hope; if he rejects Klementina, if he understands how mean and dismissive he has been, he will return to the ways of his people and let the elders perform healing rituals for him.

Ocol's much briefer reply makes it clear at once that he will do no such thing. His first words set the tone: "Woman, / Shut up! / Pack your things / Go!" (*Lawino and Ocol,* p. 120). Indeed, he very quickly stops addressing his wife at all. His first chapter sneers at the wailing and nagging of unhappy wives, but closes on his real theme, which is the destruction of all tradition: "We will obliterate / Tribal boundaries / And throttle native tongues / To dumb death" (*Lawino and Ocol,* p. 124). The next four chapters trace this same theme repeatedly, with only minor variations.

Chapter Two, the briefest, bemoans Africa; Ocol admits the continent means nothing to him but unfathomable blackness and evil.

Chapter Three begins by mocking what he calls "tribal" superstition; he presents ugly images of witch doctors and their vain attempts to save dying children. He boasts that modern politicians will uproot all traditions, and round up and shoot the singers of traditional songs. He closes by dismissing African proponents of negritude and those who attempt to elevate Africa's status by pointing to such ancient monuments as the pyramids in Egypt and the ruins of Great Zimbabwe.

Chapter Four is addressed to African women. He asks what they get from adhering to the old ways, and answers: subjugation, disdain, and a lifetime of labor that wears them down to nothing. He says, "They buy you / With two pots / Of beer; / The Luo trade you / For seven cows" (*Lawino and Ocol,* p. 134).

Chapter Five addresses the men, most particularly the warriors. He mocks the most violent of them for their savagery, and for the fact that their violence could not triumph over the white invaders.

Chapters Six and Seven discuss those whom Ocol believes are Africa's true warriors—those, like himself, who fought for freedom. In this struggle, he says, the so-called warriors were silent as the Western-educated Africans led the struggle. (He uses this fact to justify his wealth and expensive habits, as well.)

In the last two chapters, Ocol makes ever-bolder claims about the future, and passes even more scornful comments on the past. He closes in a grand peroration, dismissing the great empires of Africa's past and boasting, "We will erect monuments / To the founders / Of modern Africa: / Leopold II of Belgium, / Bismarck" (*Lawino and Ocol,* p. 151).

What's lost in translation. p'Bitek first wrote *Song of Lawino* in his native Acoli. The poet reported that he produced a full English version after receiving an enthusiastic response at a conference where he read a small section that he had translated.

The English poem differs from the Acoli version in places. A few details have been added to the English version to clarify meanings that might otherwise not be understood, and some details in the original have been dropped from the English version. Lines that, in the original, read

Timme ducu lutimme Munu-Munu
Ping'o lewic pe mako Munu,
Lukwako dako atyer, calo Munu
Luting'o pong'kor, calo Munu
Wumato taa cigara, calo Munu,
Wa mon, wa co calo Munu,
Wunato lem-wu calo Munu,
Wunato dog-wu calo Munu,
Wunango laa dogwu calo Munu,
Ma dog co nywak ki reng'ng'e pa Munu

are reduced, in English, to

You kiss her on the cheek
As white people do,
You kiss her open-sore lips
As white people do
You suck the slimy saliva
From each other's mouths
As white people do.
(Introduction, *Lawino and Ocol*, p. 6)

G. A. Heron notes that the English version translates only three lines of the Acoli original. In order for an English version of his poem to make sense, p'Bitek had to diminish the effect of repetition with minor variations, which the Acoli original borrowed from folk song. He also found it impossible to mimic the rhyme and meter that are present in the original, so the English version is written in free verse, with relatively short lines. In addition to the very different rules of pronunciation and the immeasurable gulf between the poetic conventions of English and Acoli, p'Bitek had to confront the fact that the original is saturated with Acoli lore and wisdom: songs, proverbs, echoes of stories, and conventional phrases. On almost every page, he encountered a phrase that would echo with meaning for an Acoli reader, but would sound like nonsense to a reader not raised in an Acoli environment.

THE HUNCHBACK

Perhaps the most comical misunderstanding between Christian missionaries and the Acoli is the use of the word "Hunchback" for "God." The Acoli, of course, had their own word for God: Jok. But Acoli religion is primarily functional: it does not concern itself with such concepts as creation. Thus, when early missionaries asked Acoli elders, "Who moulded you?" This question made no sense, since the Acoli knew they were shaped by their mothers. The missionaries, unsatisfied, asked again. p'Bitek writes, "One of the elders remembered that, although a person may be born normally, when he is afflicted with tuberculosis of the spine, then he loses his normal figure, he gets 'moulded.' So he said, 'Rubanga is the one who moulds people.' This is the name of the hostile spirit which the Acoli believe causes the hunch or hump on the back" (p'Bitek, *African Religions*, p. 62). One can imagine the chuckle that Okot, who always appreciated the absurd side of colonialism, enjoyed at the thought of missionaries attempting to convert Acoli people to the worship of Rubanga.

In other words, the problems p'Bitek faced in translating his poem replicated the problem he saw at the core of the modern African experience: an irresolvable tension between native knowledge and imported European culture. Not surprisingly, he uses this tension to his advantage: instead of minimizing how different the two cultures are, he tends to highlight it.

One instance of this is in his use of proverbs. In the English version, p'Bitek explains relatively few of the proverbs to which Lawino refers almost continually. The most significant is the tagline for Lawino's song: "The pumpkin in the old homestead must not be uprooted!" Nowhere does p'Bitek explain the meaning behind the proverb: pumpkins are a special delicacy, around which the homestead garden was built. They symbolize all the values of respect for family and tradition that Lawino defends. "In this proverb . . . Lawino is not asking Ocol to cling to everything in his past, but rather not to destroy things for the sake of destroying them" (Introduction, *Lawino and Ocol*, p. 7). Similarly unexplained phrases occur on nearly every page of the poem: age-mate, husband-in-law, horn, bull, "eating" names (instead of "earning"), get-stuck. In almost all cases, the meaning is made somewhat clear by context. Even the novice reader realizes that "horn" is just that—a horn worn by Acoli men, on which they sound their personal note in hunts, after fights, and at dances. "Bull" is an honorific for people of great spirit. However, these phrases retain an air of mystery for the foreign reader, reminding him or her that Acoli culture is far too deep and rich to understand by reading a single poem.

p'Bitek performs a similar operation on aspects of European culture that are incomprehensible to the Acoli. Christianity is especially strange in Lawino's mouth. For instance, in her Bible class she learned to say, "I accept the hunchback, / The Padre who is very strong, / Moulder of Skyland and Earth" (*Lawino and Ocol*, p. 86). And her version of "Hail Mary:" "Look Mariya, the clean woman/ Mother of the Hunchback/ Pray for us/ Who spoil things/ Full of graciya" (*Lawino and Ocol*, p. 75). "Skyland" is obviously heaven. "Clean" works less well as a translation of "grace," a word for which the Acoli had no equivalent; Lawino also speaks of the "clean ghost" (for "Holy Spirit"). But "hunchback" seems absolutely foreign. By these oddities, minor and amusing in themselves, p'Bitek hopes to underscore the essential absurdity of believing that Christianity has anything to offer the

Acoli. If a person does not even understand the concept of grace, how can he or she possibly pray for it, miss it, or desire it?

In most respects, observes G. A. Heron, *Song of Lawino* is a very literal translation of *Wer pa Lawino*; in many parts of the poem it is difficult to produce a more literal translation" (Heron, p. 43). Sometimes the very literality of the translation leaves the meaning untapped, as with the proverbs in the poem. p'Bitek's translation reveals how much of a poem's meaning depends on cultural context. By refusing to act as a translator of culture as well as of language, he drives home how foreign these two cultures are to each other.

Sources and literary context. Obviously, the most important source for *Song of Lawino and Song of Ocol* is the folk culture of the Acoli. Lawino's song is saturated with Acoli song. When she is not directly quoting songs of the type p'Bitek later printed in *The Horn of My Love*, she is still speaking in the cadences, language, and spirit shaped by Acoli song and dance.

However, it would be naive to claim that p'Bitek is a "purely" Acoli writer, whatever that would mean. The very fact that he produces a printed book indicates that he has been influenced by European culture. In addition, he also uses such Western concepts as individual authorship, rhyme, and division into chapters. But, unlike many African writers, he does not acknowledge specific debt to any European authors, past or present. In his essays, he refers to a remarkably diverse group of European writers, from Horace to John Dewey, but his poetry appears uninfluenced.

A general affinity can be noted between p'Bitek and his friend and contemporary, Ngugi wa Thiong'o. Both rejected Christianity, and favored native over imported languages for writing. However, p'Bitek was unsympathetic to Ngugi's socialism, which he viewed as a foreign borrowing inappropriate to Africa's circumstances.

Events in History at the Time the Poems Were Written

A political role lost. In 1966 Okot p'Bitek was appointed director of the National Cultural Centre in Kampala, the capital of Uganda. He was the first African to head this important cultural position, and he did not fail to make his mark. In his two years as head of the Centre, "Ugandan theatre, poetry, dance, games, painting and sculpture flourished. The Heartbeat of Africa Dance Troupe was formed and toured the world" (p'Bitek, *Africa's Cultural Revolution,* p. 8). In an interview conducted in the 1960s, p'Bitek indicated what he found significant about his work: "The Centre has become a place where people from all walks of life gather to enjoy the facilities and feasts we have to offer. Not only top people as in the old days, but also people who had never set foot in the place before: unemployed people, illiterate artisans and dancers, wives of policemen and others" (p'Bitek, *Africa's Cultural Revolution,* p. 94).

However, in 1968, Okot was dismissed from his post. He had just made a speech in Zambia, where he declared, among other radical ideas, "If at this stage the schools and universities in Africa think that one type of music or dance or drama is more 'civilized' than another . . . then the universities in Africa are citadels of cultural reaction, fit only for demolition" (p'Bitek, *Africa's Cultural Revolution,* p. 14). On his return, he discovered he had been fired. His employers asserted that his speech had not been an issue, and p'Bitek believed them. In any case, he spent the next 11 years in exile.

Reviews. *Song of Lawino and Song of Ocol* produced a great impact upon publication; the warring couple encapsulated, as p'Bitek intended them to, an issue of great concern for the continent. One critic wrote, "It is impossible . . . to discuss our cultural crisis in East Africa, now, without an illustrative reference to the Lawino-Ocol-Tina axis" (Ngugi wa Thiong'o in p'Bitek, *Africa's Cultural Revolution,* p. ix). Not surprisingly, praise was mixed with reservations. Taban lo Liyong, for instance, criticized p'Bitek's refusal to provide the meanings of Acoli proverbs: "The meaning of deep Acoli proverbs are made very, very light by their rendition into English *word for word,* rather than *sense for sense* or *proverb for proverb*" (Liyong, p. 141). Gerald Moore noted that the translation is necessarily flawed: "Rhyme, assonance and tonal variations, the chief ornaments of the original text, are lost" (Moore, p. 53). Okumu pa Lukobo believed that p'Bitek's real purpose should have been to dramatize Lawino's sexual jealousy: "What Lawino has to say would have been better expressed by another Acoli proverb which says *Dako abila ni eye meni* (your first wife is your mother). What Lawino is really concerned with is a personal matter—her rivalry with her husband's mistress Klementina" (pa Lukobo, p. 13). pa Lukobo also complained that both participants are caricatures: Lawino is exaggeratedly naive, and Ocol far more contemptuous than his real-life counterparts. This was a fairly common critique, but others, such as Ngugi, defended p'Bitek from these charges: "[Some critics] turn the fundamental opposition between two value-systems into a mere personal quarrel between Lawino and her husband. We must in fact see the class basis of her attack: Lawino is the voice of the peasantry and her ridicule and scorn is aimed at the class basis of Ocol's behavior" (Ngugi, p. 75).

—Jacob Littleton

For More Information

Davidson, Basil. *Modern Africa: A Social and Political History*. 3rd ed. London: Longman, 1994.

Heron, G. A. *The Poetry of Okot p'Bitek*. London: Heinemann, 1976.

Liyong, Taban lo. *The Last Word: Cultural Synthesism*. Nairobi: East African Publishing House, 1969.

Mittleman, James H. *Ideology and Politics in Uganda: From Obote to Amin*. Ithaca, N.Y.: Cornell University Press, 1975.

Moore, Gerald. "Grasslands Poetry." *Transition* 21, no. 51 (June 1967): 50-54.

Ngugi wa Thiong'o. *Homecoming*. London: Heinemann, 1972.

Ofuani, Ogo. "The Poet as Self-Critic: The Stylistic Repercussions of Textual Revisions in Okot p'Bitek's *Song of Ocol*." *Research in African Literatures* 25, no. 4 (winter 1994): 159-75.

pa Lukobo, Okumu. "Song of Lawino." *Nanga* 2, no. 3 (May 1970): 13-15.

p'Bitek, Okot. *African Religions in Western Scholarship*. Nairobi: Kenya Literature Bureau, [1979?].

———. *Africa's Cultural Revolution*. Nairobi: Macmillan, 1973.

———. *Artist the Ruler*. Nairobi: Heinemann Kenya, 1983.

———. *Song of Lawino and Song of Ocol*. London: Heinemann, 1966.

Russell, Keith. *Men Without God?* London: Heinemann, 1967.

The Story of an African Farm

by
Olive Schreiner

Born in Wittebergen, Cape Colony, in 1855, Olive Emilie Albertina Schreiner was the ninth child of a German missionary, Gottlob Schreiner, and his English wife, Rebecca Lyndall. Home-educated and largely self-taught, she wrote one of the most influential and controversial novels—*The Story of an African Farm*—of the late Victorian era. She spent much of her childhood at various mission stations, and as an adolescent she kept house for her older brothers and sisters. In 1874 Schreiner became a governess, working for several Boer families and writing in her spare time. Her most famous work draws attention to the lives of working-class people, especially women, and she took pains to publish it at a price that its working-class audience could afford. In 1881 Schreiner traveled to Great Britain, hoping to train as a nurse in Edinburgh, Scotland, but having to abandon that plan because of ill health, she resumed writing full-time. *The Story of an African Farm* was published two years later under the pseudonym "Ralph Iron." As *The Story of an African Farm* amply demonstrates, Schreiner—who declared herself a free thinker as an adolescent—questioned the traditional roles of women, the entrenched models of race and class that permeated Victorian culture in South Africa and elsewhere, and the very existence of God.

Events in History at the Time the Novel Takes Place

The British in South Africa. Schreiner does not pinpoint the location of the African farm in her

---

THE LITERARY WORK

A novel set in South Africa during the 1850s and 1860s; published in English in 1883.

SYNOPSIS

Three children living on a remote farm in nineteenth-century South Africa grow up to meet very different fates.

---

novel, but it is most likely situated in Cape Colony, which had been controlled by Great Britain since 1896, where Schreiner herself spent much of her life. At the time the novel begins, the region was inhabited mostly by indigenous peoples and by Afrikaners (then called "Boers," the Dutch term for "farmers"; the group was mainly of Dutch descent). The first official census of the Cape Colony, taken in 1865, reported 180,000 "Europeans" or "whites," 200,000 "Hottentots" and "Others" (designated as "coloured people"), and 100,000 "Kaffirs," a term used at the time to designate the South African blacks, who had become the main labor force in the eastern districts. From 55 to 60 percent of the white population consisted of the Dutch-speaking Afrikaners. They had been settling in the interior of South Africa since the seventeenth and eighteenth centuries, bringing the customs and institutions of their homelands with them, adapting these traditions to their new country. By contrast, few immigrants of British stock settled in South Africa before the nineteenth century. In

1820 the British Parliament, hoping to solve problems of unemployment and social unrest in Great Britain, approved a sum of 50,000 pounds to transport British settlers to South Africa's Zuurveld region and establish them as farmers on lots of approximately 100 acres. The Colonial Office in London selected 4,000 men, women, and children (out of 80,000 applicants) to participate in the settlement scheme. The immigrants were a mixture of English, Scottish, Welsh, and Irish stock. Mostly members of the lower middle class, they generally had more experience as artisans than as farmers, and their inexperience was compounded by the terrain in their new location, which was ill-suited to farming. The result was that more than half of the new settlers abandoned their farms, setting themselves up as merchants and traders instead. Others prospered by raising sheep and selling the wool, as Em's late father appears to have done in the novel. Significantly, the British settlers of 1820—and those who followed them—introduced a new dynamic into colonial society. They did not assimilate with the earlier white settlers, and regarded their Dutch-speaking neighbors with "a marked lack of enthusiasm, if not with barely concealed hostility and contempt" (Schoeman, pp. 323-24). Intermarriage and socializing between the British and the Boers was rare: "Beyond the market square, the two white groups had little contact; living side by side in mutual distrust and incomprehension, each clung to its own language, traditions, and values" (Schoeman, p. 323).

In *The Story of an African Farm,* the hostility between British and Afrikaner is illustrated by the uneasy relationship between Tant' Sannie and the two English girls who are her wards. Passive, compliant Em has little to say about her Afrikaner stepmother, but Em's cousin Lyndall despises the "miserable old woman" as ignorant and superstitious, pointing out: "Your father married her when he was dying, because he thought she would take better care of the farm, and us, than an Englishwoman. He said we should be taught and sent to school. Now she saves every farthing for herself.... She does not ill-use us—why? Because she is afraid of your father's ghost" (Schreiner, *Story of an African Farm,* p. 45). Lyndall's resentment persists into her adulthood. As an adult she mocks Tant' Sannie's practice of marrying husband after husband, and although she attends her wedding to the much younger Piet Vander Walt, Lyndall remains aloof from the festivities, dressing in black and refusing to dance. One may attribute Lyndall's reserve as

much to British disdain for Afrikaner customs as to personal dislike for Tant' Sannie. Gregory Rose, the snobbish young Englishman hired as a farmhand, is even more supercilious, declaring at the reception, "These Boer [Afrikaner] dances are very low things" (*African Farm*, p. 213).

Indigenous people and colonial attitudes. Schreiner never overtly discusses race relations in *The Story of an African Farm.* Such unquestioning acceptance of the status quo in relations with South Africa's indigenous people was representative of its time. As Dan Jacobson observes in his introduction to *The Story of an African Farm*: "A white South African . . . feels no need to ask himself how the black man came to be his inferior; he simply knows the black man is inferior" (Jacobson in Schreiner, p. 7). Schreiner's novel, Jacobson continues, "is about the white people on the farm, not the black; it is far from being the novel of 'race relations' which many people have come to expect every South African novel to be. The black people in it are merely extras, supernumeraries, part of the background" (Jacobson in Schreiner, p. 21). Schreiner's use of contemporary terms for South Africa's indigenous peoples, however, hints at a more complex social system than one might imagine. The term "Hottentot" (a word that many surmise to mean "stutterer," a reference to the distinctive click sounds of the Khoikhoi language) was first applied to the indigenous Khoikhoi people by Dutch settlers led by Jan van Riebeeck, who arrived in the Cape region in 1652. Eventually "Hottentot" also came to refer to the mixed-blood descendants of the Khoikhoi and the Dutch. Consequently, Hottentots were often granted a higher social status than darker inhabitants of the area. In 1828 the Cape governor, General Richard Bourke, passed the Hottentot Charter, making the so-called Hottentots and other free people of color equal to whites before the law.

In the novel, the black residents of the farm reflect the different gradations in social status among nonwhites. Itala Vivan observes that "Schreiner places Africans in three groups: Kaffirs, Hottentots, and Bushmen. . . . [B]y 'Kaffirs' Schreiner means the Bantu people, by 'Hottentots' the KhoiKhoi [sic], and by 'Bushmen' the San people" (Vivan, p. 104). The novel's picture, Vivan confirms, is both historically and anthropologically accurate, since all three groups were living in the Cape area at the time. The whites' attitudes towards the indigenous peoples are likewise authentic. For example, only Tant' Sannie's "yellow Hottentot maid" is permitted, along

An open-pit diamond mine in Kimberley, South Africa.

with her husband, to attend Sunday services in the farm-house: "The Kaffir servants were not there because Tant' Sannie held they were descended from apes and needed no salvation" (*African Farm*, p. 69). Even the adult Lyndall, whom Schreiner depicts as intellectual and enlightened, reveals some condescension when she comments upon a handsome Kaffir she glimpses from a distance: "There is something of the master about him in spite of his blackness and wool" (*African Farm*, p. 227).

Diamonds and industrial development. *The Story of an African Farm* takes place in a rural backwater, far removed from the cities in which significant changes, such as the appearance of the railroad and telegraph, first occur. In fact, fledgling attempts to introduce changes on the farm are frustrated. Bonaparte Blenkins, a greedy overseer, destroys a sheep-shearing machine, an invention of the boy Waldo, then burns the boy's books. Tant' Sannie sees no reason to do things differently from the way her ancestors did them. Near the end of the novel, she laments the very existence of the railroad: "Let them make their steam-waggons and their fire-carriages . . . the destruction of the Lord will follow them. I don't know how such people read their Bibles. When do we hear of Moses or Noah riding in a railway?" (*African Farm*, p. 294).

Even in urban areas nineteenth-century South Africa lagged behind many other nations in terms of immigration and economic development: "By 1870, the United States had a population of over 32 million people of European descent and nearly 53,000 miles of railroad, but in all of Southern Africa there were no more than 70 miles of rail and 250,000 white people" (Thompson, p. 53). The discovery of diamonds and the subsequent mineral revolution, however, laid the foundations for a modern industrial South Africa, accelerating social, economic, and political changes in the area.

In 1867 diamonds were found near the confluence of the Vaal and Harts rivers. Excited settlers converged upon the area to prospect for the precious gems and set up rough mining camps marked by frequent gambling, drinking, and whoring. Given the arduous road conditions and dearth of vegetation, the routes to such excavation sites could be notoriously difficult for miners and livestock alike. Karel Schoeman quotes one contemporary account: "Numerous skeletons of oxen and horns are seen on either side of the road, which becomes ever wider and more denuded of grass and is eroded by thousands of wagon wheels" (Schoeman, p. 249). At one point in Schreiner's novel, Waldo works as a transport-driver to the "Diamond Fields"; his employer's cruelty to the oxen causes him to quit the wagon-train in disgust.

Although diamonds in the Vaal/Harts region were exhausted within a few years, explorers discovered much larger deposits in 1870, near the site of the future town of Kimberley. Four large mines were constructed, and sophisticated machinery, including steam engines, was brought in to excavate the diamonds more effectively than was possible with shovels, buckets, and hand scoopers. In the 1880s, Cecil Rhodes, the future prime minister of South Africa, acquired control first of the De Beers, then the Kimberley mine. By 1891 De Beers Consolidated Mines had established a monopoly over diamond production in the entire region

A GIRL'S BEST FRIEND?

As a young woman of 17, Olive Schreiner actually lived in the diamond fields at New Rush—later the town of Kimberley—for ten months while visiting her older siblings, Theo and Ettie. The family resided in a tent, like many people at the fields, while Theo worked as a digger, but he found no large diamonds to make their fortune. Schreiner, however, was intrigued and inspired by the bustling atmosphere of the camps and began writing stories about diamonds, though these works were never published. Several characters in *The Story of an African Farm* reveal a similar enthusiasm for the gems. As a child, Lyndall boasts that when she grows up, she will be very rich and wear real diamonds in her hair. When Lyndall returns to the farm as a young woman, Em notices "a massive [diamond] ring upon her forefinger" (*African Farm*, p. 184).

The Novel in Focus

Plot summary. *The Story of an African Farm* begins at night as the inhabitants of the farm lie sleeping. The moonlight illuminates the African plain, transforming it into a place of "almost oppressive beauty" (*African Farm*, p. 36). Also illuminated are the sleepers in the house: Tant' Sannie, the Afrikaner woman who runs the farm; her English stepdaughter, Em; and Em's orphaned cousin, Lyndall. In another building, closed off from any light, Otto, the German overseer, also sleeps, but his son, Waldo, is awake. Listening to the loud tick of his father's silver hunting watch, Waldo imagines that "every time it ticked,

a man died!" (*African Farm*, p. 37). The fancy sends him into an agony of religious terror and he grovels on the floor, weeping and praying for the imagined dead.

The next morning the landscape and the people look very different: "The plain was a weary flat of loose red sand sparsely covered by dry karoo bushes, that cracked beneath the tread like tinder, and showed the red earth everywhere" (*African Farm*, p. 38). By daylight, Tant' Sannie is revealed to be homely and coarse, Otto to be childishly simple despite his huge size, and Em to be plain. Lyndall, of "elfin-like beauty," possesses a gravity and concentration beyond her years as she threads beads with her cousin (*African Farm*, p. 36). Meanwhile, Waldo, who works as a shepherd on the farm, drives the sheep out to pasture beyond the *koppjie* (hill). At midday, he builds an altar of stones and lays his lunch on it, praying to God to send fire from heaven to burn his sacrifice. When nothing happens, Waldo is devastated by God's apparent rejection of him and his offering. Two years later, he sits alone on the koppjie at night and confesses that he loves Jesus Christ but hates God. He resigns himself to damnation: "He knew he was certainly lost now; he did not care. If half the world were to be lost, why not he too? He would not pray for mercy any more" (*African Farm*, p. 42).

The year 1862 brings drought and hardship. As the water sinks in the dams, many of the livestock die. That summer Em and Lyndall—now 12 years old—plan their futures. Em contemplates marriage after she turns 17, when the farm, which belonged to her late father, passes to her. But Lyndall intends to go to school. The girls' conversation is interrupted by 14-year-old Waldo, who brings news that an "English stranger"—Bonaparte Blenkins—has arrived.

Tant' Sannie strenuously objects to Bonaparte's presence, but Otto, moved by the man's hard-luck story of having lost his horse and purse on his journey, persuades her to let him stay the night. Bonaparte ingratiates himself to Tant' Sannie through tall tales about his ancestry, pathetic tales about his dead wife, and impassioned, impromptu sermons. Pleased with his protégé's success, Otto bestows a hat and a good black suit on Bonaparte and suggests that he stay on as a paid schoolmaster to Em and Lyndall, an offer the Irishman quickly accepts. The children, however, are not won over by Bonaparte; in fact, Lyndall refuses to return to his schoolroom when he cannot answer one of her questions correctly.

Meanwhile, Bonaparte successfully schemes to supplant Otto as overseer and marry Tant' Sannie; he lies that Otto has confided in him about having sexual liaisons with Tant' Sannie, whereupon she fires Otto, demanding that he be off the farm by morning. In his cabin, Otto sadly packs for his departure, then lies down and dies in his sleep.

With Otto dead, Bonaparte turns his malice on Waldo. As punishment for a trumped-up charge of theft, Bonaparte ties Waldo to a post, horse-whips him until he collapses, then leaves him locked up in the fuel-house all night. The next day, on learning of Waldo's beating and imprisonment, Lyndall defies Tant' Sannie and Bonaparte—neither of whom dares to stop her— by releasing her friend. Soon after, Tant' Sannie witnesses the duplicitous overseer's attempts to court her rich niece, Trana, and, in a rage, overturns a barrel of salt meat on the head of her faithless suitor. The next morning Bonaparte steals away and is never seen on the farm again.

The second half of the novel begins three years later. After weathering various spiritual crises, Waldo takes consolation in nature itself. One summer day, he is carving a grave-post for his father. Em, now 16, brings him lunch and excitedly informs him that an Englishman whom Tant' Sannie has hired to work on the farm is approaching on horseback. Favorably impressed by the stranger's looks and youth, Em hopes that he is bringing letters from Lyndall, who has been in school for several years now.

Alone, Waldo continues to work on his carving when another stranger, "a dark, somewhat French looking little man of eight-and-twenty" rides up to rest for an hour (African Farm, p. 156). The stranger offers to buy the carving but Waldo refuses to sell, explaining that it is for his father's grave. When the stranger identifies himself as "a man who believes nothing, hopes nothing, fears nothing, feels nothing," Waldo is excited to find someone who thinks as he does (African Farm, p. 159). He awkwardly tries to explain the human and animal figures on his carving. The stranger reveals his understanding by relating an allegorical tale of a hunter who must abandon all superstitions, travel through the Land of Absolute Negation and Denial, and climb the mountains of stern reality in search of the snow-white bird, Truth. After years of unsuccessful toil, in his last moments he realizes, "Where I lie down worn out other men will stand, young and fresh. By the steps that I have cut they will climb. . . . They will find her [Truth]

and through me! And no man liveth to himself and no man dieth to himself" (African Farm, p. 168). Then, just as death approaches, a single white feather from Truth drops from the sky onto the hunter's breast and he dies holding it. Profoundly moved by the stranger's understanding, Waldo declares, "All my life I have longed to see you" (African Farm, p. 171). The stranger proceeds to listen closely to the story of Waldo's life, then urges him to stay on the farm and resist the temptations of the outside world until he is certain of his path in life. After giving Waldo a much-handled book whose tenets "may give you a centre round which to hang your ideas, instead of letting them lie about in a confusion," the stranger takes his leave (African Farm, p. 172). Waldo ties his carving to the stranger's saddle before the stranger rides off. They part with a handshake and the hope of meeting again someday.

The focus switches to Gregory Rose, the new farm worker. Snobbish and somewhat effeminate, Gregory pours out his complaints about his life to his sister in England. In one epistle, Gregory confesses his love for Em and his desire to marry her. A tentative courtship ensues. Em, believing herself to be neither pretty nor clever, is moved by Gregory's ardent protestations. After accepting his proposal, she eagerly anticipates her wedding.

Six months later, Lyndall, now a beautiful woman, returns to the farm but, to Em's dismay, is unimpressed by Gregory. After seeing a large diamond ring—inscribed with the initials R. R.— on Lyndall's finger, Em wonders if her cousin has also become engaged but Lyndall quickly denies any such arrangement. Later, she seeks out Waldo and resumes their childhood intimacy, confiding in him about her years at school. She also reveals her intense interest in the position of women and her bitterness towards a society that allows them little scope for their talents beyond marriage and motherhood. Waldo, in turn, confesses that he plans to leave the farm and see something of the world after Gregory becomes master.

Meanwhile, Tant' Sannie, soon to turn over the farm to Em, plans to remarry to a much younger man, a distant relation. Gregory again writes his sister, ostensibly to inform her of Tant' Sannie's wedding, but more genuinely to complain about Lyndall, to whom he has become reluctantly attracted. At Tant' Sannie's wedding, Lyndall spends much of her time with Waldo, reaffirming their unique bond: "When I am with you I never know that I am a woman and you are a man; I only know we are both things that think. Other men . . . are mere bodies to me; but you are a spirit" (*African Farm*, p. 210). The two friends share further confidences and plans for their respective futures. Waldo intends to travel, while Lyndall contemplates becoming an actress. Both agree that work of some kind represents their best hope of fulfillment.

After the wedding Gregory offers to drive Lyndall home. Initially, she refuses, then just as suddenly changes her mind and consents. Em, who has noticed Gregory's attraction to Lyndall, rides home with Waldo and wonders whether she should go through with her own marriage. Shortly after, Waldo embarks on his travels and Em breaks her engagement to Gregory, who soon starts to pursue Lyndall. To his chagrin, Lyndall refuses to take him seriously at first. Later she does an about-face and offers to marry him in name only. Lyndall coldly lays out her terms: "You wish to serve me, and to have nothing in return!—you shall have what you wish. . . . The knowledge that you are serving me is to be your reward" (*African Farm*, p. 232). Gregory agrees to this arrangement. Though hurt by the news, Em conceals her feelings. That night she visits Lyndall in her room to tell her of a disturbing dream. In the dream, Em, a little girl again, enters a large room and sees Lyndall's dead baby laid out upon a bed. Alone again, Lyndall lies awake, wondering about the dream.

Just before the wedding, another stranger—a blond, blue-eyed Englishman—arrives at the farm. Lyndall intercepts him before anyone can meet him and puts him in Waldo's now-deserted cabin. Later, when everyone else is asleep, Lyndall and the stranger talk. He is the lover who gave her the diamond ring and he has come in response to her letter informing him of her marriage to Gregory. The stranger wants to know why Lyndall will marry a foolish farmer whom she does not love, rather than him. Lyndall replies that she will be able to keep Gregory at a distance and thus retain her independence. The stranger urges her to change her mind, but Lyndall refuses. After the stranger continues to importune her, Lyndall makes him another offer, "I cannot marry you . . . because I cannot be tied, but, if you wish, you may take me away with you and take care of me; then when we do not love any more we can say good-bye" (*African Farm*, p. 239). Lyndall's stranger is startled by her proposal but ultimately agrees. They plan to go to the Transvaal in northeastern South Africa,

where no one knows them. Before her departure Lyndall visits Otto's grave and bemoans her sense of isolation and inability to love anything utterly.

Six months later, Gregory, still reeling from Lyndall's abandonment, resolves to search for her. Meanwhile, a gaunt and ragged Waldo, gone for seven months, returns to the farm in the middle of a storm. He asks about Lyndall, but Em avoids answering in any detail. Waldo then composes a letter to Lyndall, relating all of his experiences while he was away. On his travels he worked at several jobs, serving at one point as a transport driver to the diamond fields. But each job was lacking in some way. Feeling isolated and unable to concentrate on anything, Waldo decided to return to the farm. He realizes much of his longing for the old life is tied up in his feelings for Lyndall: "I knew you were not here, but it seemed as though I should be nearer you; and it is you I want" (*African Farm*, pp. 262-63). As Waldo composes these words, Em approaches and gently tells him not to continue: Lyndall is dead.

Gregory returns to the farm and gives Waldo and Em a full account of his search. He tracked Lyndall and her lover through several towns, finally coming to one in which he learned by chance that a young Englishwoman was staying in the hotel. The landlady revealed that the woman arrived alone six months earlier and soon after gave birth to a baby who lived only a few hours. The mother then slipped into a decline. She was not, said the landlady, expected to survive.

After hearing this news, Gregory disguised himself as a woman, shaving his beard and dressing in female clothing. He then offered his services to the landlady as a nurse for the dying woman. On being shown to her bedroom, Gregory was grief-stricken to see Lyndall in such a sorry state. He nursed her tenderly and never revealed his identity. A letter arrived from Lyndall's lover begging her to marry him, but still she refused. During her last days, Lyndall asked to be taken outside to the blue mountain she glimpsed across the plain. Gregory carried her down to a wagon and drove her out to the mountain, where Lyndall regained her faculties long enough to accept her fate.

Back on the farm, Em and especially Waldo are devastated by Gregory's story. After hours of anguish, Waldo finally accepts her death: "It is but the man that dies, the Universal Whole of which he is part re-works him into its inmost self" (*African Farm*, p. 290).

Sometime later, Tant' Sannie, along with her husband and new baby, pays a call on Em to congratulate her on her upcoming marriage to Gregory. Sannie monopolizes the conversation, praising the wedded state, wishing Em many children, and complaining about new inventions like the railway. After her visitors leave, Em goes into the wagon-house to talk to Waldo, who is busy building her a new table. When she offers him money to go abroad and study, Waldo gently refuses. After she leaves, Waldo rests in the sunshine, utterly tranquil, watching a brood of nearby chicks. He appears to fall asleep. When Em returns, she finds the chicks perched on him and thinks Waldo will soon awaken: "But the chickens were wiser" (*African Farm,* p. 301).

Women's choices. *The Story of an African Farm* is structured mainly around the destinies of Em and Lyndall. The Victorian era provided few opportunities for women beyond the traditional roles of wife and mother. Sheltered and protected during childhood, young girls came of age and were duly married off, their husbands assuming the responsibilities as protectors and providers that had once been their fathers'. Despite such legislation as the Divorce Act of 1857, which took jurisdiction over divorces away from the church courts and gave it to a new civil divorce court, and the Married Women's Property Act of 1870, which allowed women to treat as their own the money they inherited or earned from various investments, most women remained dependent on their fathers, husbands, and male relatives for their entire lives.

Unlike men, who were expected to make places for themselves in public life, women remained ensconced in the domestic sphere, tending to their homes and children. During the 1860s, the period during which *The Story of an African Farm* takes place, "woman worship" was a common practice. Victorians idealized the selfless wife who devoted her energies to making her home a haven for her more worldly husband and provided him with a source of "moral inspiration" (Houghton, p. 350). Many women, however, found their pedestals rather confining; even as wives, women's activities were restricted by masculine authority.

Women played no part in public life, attended no public gatherings, and served on no public bodies; they neither signed petitions nor, in normal cirumstances, wrote letters to the press, and they obviously had no franchise, whether locally or nationally. Generally, they spent their lives within the confines of their homes and their families, venturing abroad only for the most ordinary and trivial social events such as receptions, balls, and concerts.
(Schoeman, p. 213)

Even in colonial South Africa, Victorian standards of behavior were maintained with regard to young English girls. Unlike Tant' Sannie who, inured to the rigors of frontier life, enjoys considerable independence and autonomy, Em and Lyndall are hampered by their British heritage. Both are expected to conform to the social standards of Victorian England, despite having grown up in foreign surroundings. Indeed, all English-women living abroad were expected to uphold the standards of their homeland:

[T]he white woman managed to assert the norms of Victorian Britain even in this unlikely new environment.... [T]he settler woman, after her brief liberation from convention, reverted to being a lady. Safely raised on a pedestal and shielded, as under a glass dome, from too much contact with and contamination by everyday realities, she was hemmed in, idealised, and frustrated.
(Schoeman, p. 210)

In the novel, Lyndall becomes bitterly aware of the "hemming in" process when she goes away to a private school. Hoping to gain an education, she is appalled to find that her fellow students' lives are monopolized by such trivial pursuits as painting and needlepoint. Lyndall comments trenchantly on the insidious process leading to the separation between the sexes: "They begin to shape us to our cursed end ... when we are tiny things in shoes and socks. . . . [The curse] finishes its work when we are grown women, who no more look out wistfully at a more healthy life" (*African Farm,* p. 189). Lyndall is even more frustrated by the widespread belief that a socially or an economically advantageous marriage is the only goal to which a woman can or should aspire: "Marriage for love is the beautifullest external symbol of the union of souls; marriage without it is the uncleanest traffic that defiles the world" (*African Farm,* p. 190). Unwilling to lose what independence she has, Lyndall considers a loveless marriage to the weak Gregory, but refuses the proposal of her domineering lover, offering instead to be his mistress. Lyndall maintains her independence, albeit at a hefty price. Her rebellion against the social mores of her time ultimately costs her her life.

Unlike Lyndall, Em embraces the likelihood of marriage and motherhood. Even as a child she displays no ambition but to inherit her farm and eventually marry, declaring, "'I should not like to go to school!" (*African Farm,* p. 45). As a woman Em remains domestic and conventional, though her kindliness and good nature endear her to others. Lyndall compares her cousin to "the accompaniment of a song. She fills up the gaps in other people's lives, and is always number two; but I think she is like many accompaniments—a great deal better than the song she is to accompany" (*African Farm,* p. 231). Em's sole chance to be "number one" arises when an impassioned Gregory first proposes to her: "She had given out so much love in her little life, and had got none of it back with interest. Now one said, 'I love you better than all the world.' One loved her better than she loved him. How suddenly rich she was" (*African Farm,* p. 179). One might expect Em's desires—more modest than Lyndall's—to be easily fulfilled, yet happiness also eludes her when Gregory becomes infatuated with Lyndall. Although Gregory and Em are reconciled after Lyndall's death, Em's romantic views on love and marriage have been permanently altered by Gregory's betrayal. Towards the end of the novel, a wistful Em asks Waldo, "Why is it always so, Waldo, always so? . . . we long for things . . . but we never reach them. Then at last, too late, just when we don't want them any more, when all the sweetness is taken out of them, then

they come" (*African Farm,* p. 296). Em survives while the more audacious Lyndall dies, but neither can be said to have achieved fulfillment. By refusing to bestow a happily-ever-after ending upon either woman, Schreiner illustrates the unhappiness that characterized the lives of many immigrant women on the South African frontier and elsewhere.

Sources and literary context. Although *The Story of an African Farm* is not strictly autobiographical, Waldo undergoes a series of religious doubts and crises similar to those Schreiner herself experienced when (beginning at age 10) she was rejecting Christianity. Schreiner based Waldo's encounter with the nameless Frenchman who "believes nothing" on her chance meeting with John William Bertram, the son of Gottlob Schreiner's predecessor at Wittebergen, in 1871. Traveling to Hermon on business, Bertram stopped in Basutoland where the 16-year-old Schreiner was staying with an aunt. It was a stormy night and Schreiner's aunt's house was the only one within 50 miles. Bertram stayed that night in the house and became acquainted with Schreiner, speaking to her seriously about art, books, and religion. Bertram lent her Herbert Spencer's *First Principles*—the Freethinkers' bible—which introduced Schreiner to an alternative creed that avoided the extremes of "dogmatic Christianity" or "blank atheism" (Schoeman, p. 193). Schreiner was profoundly affected by this brief encounter, claiming that "I always think that when Christianity burst on the dark Roman world it was what that book was to me" (Rive, p. 36). Bertram committed suicide in August 1879 by taking an overdose of morphine. News of his death reached Schreiner shortly after she completed the chapter based on their meeting.

Spencer's *First Principles* appeared in 1862, three years after Charles Darwin published *On the Origin of Species by Natural Selection*. In it, Spencer, an agnostic, argues that human religious feeling is rooted in utter ignorance of the nature of ultimate reality (or the Ultimate Being); all that religious feeling can recognize is that such a reality exists. It is humanity's "highest wisdom and our highest duty to regard that through which all things exist as the Unknowable"; religious inquiry into what this Ultimate Being or reality might be is not just pointless but misguided (Spencer in Boller, p. 48). Spencer pointed out the inconsistencies and absurdities in human religions, while acknowledging that perhaps such religions did respond to an eternal truth.

"THRILLING, LIBERATING, AND HIGHLY SECRET"

~

*T*he *Story of an African Farm* created quite a stir among young Victorian ladies; one historian notes that "virtually every recollection of [working-class student-teacher] life in the last decades of the nineteenth century that I have discovered mentions—with bated breath and great excitement, as a thrilling, liberating, and highly secret experience—reading Olive Schreiner's *The Story of an African Farm*" (Mitchell, p. 37). Enjoyment of the book cut across the social classes. Many an English girl at the turn of the century read it furtively in closets, under the covers, in a deserted corner of the house. What they all found so compelling was the novel's attention to violence, to sex, to disbelief in Christianity, and to the changing attitudes of women to their traditional roles as wives and mothers. Schreiner's novel and its tragic heroine, Lyndall, were important to the rising "new girl" in the late Victorian world, a girl who cast her eyes about for daring alternatives to being a bit-part player in a man's world.

Much of the novel's initial popularity can be attributed to the widespread interest in Africa among the British prompted by the Anglo-Zulu War. Fought in 1879, the war pitted the British against the Zulu (shown here).

Schreiner sums up his influence on her: "He helped me believe in a unity underlying all nature" (Schreiner in First and Scott, p. 59).

A concrete South African literary tradition cannot truly be said to have existed when *The Story of an African Farm* was first published in 1883. Although several works of poetry, including Thomas Pringle's *Ephemerides* (1829), were printed during the early years of British occupancy, the verse was of an uneven quality and showed a strong British influence. Novels dealing with South Africa frequently fell into the "adventure story" category—such as E. A. Kendall's *The English Boy at the Cape* (1835) and Mayne Reid's *The Bush Boys* (1856)—and were directed at younger audiences: "As a land of potential adventure, Africa lent itself ideally to youth literature, and since it was also missionary country it offered the wherewithal for a very effective blend of entertainment and edification" (Schoeman, p. 415). The drawback to such novels, however, was that few adult readers were inclined to take South Africa seriously as a subject for fiction.

The 1870s saw the emergence of a new kind of South African literature, written by authors who lived in and knew the country and whose themes were "less sensational and presented more realistically"(Schoeman, p. 422). Attempts

were made to depict the realities of daily South African life and to convey a sense of the country's unique atmosphere and terrain. Olive Schreiner's *The Story of an African Farm* grows out of that new movement, along with G. H. Close's *The Rose of Rietfontain: A South African Pastoral Romance* (1882) and A. P. B.'s *Rochdale: South African Story of Country Life* (1885). But while the latter titles have been forgotten, *The Story of an African Farm* is considered one of the pivotal texts that helped to establish a South African literary tradition.

Events in History at the Time the Novel Was Written

New opportunities for women. In the novel Lyndall laments the poor quality of the education she received at a finishing school in the 1860s: "They finish everything but imbecility and weakness, and that they cultivate" (*African Farm*, p. 185). Such "schooling," she maintains, leaves women unfit for any kind of useful labor. The following decade, however, saw several developments in the cause of women's rights. In Britain, the women's suffrage movement gained momentum and training programs for nurses and governesses were established. There was also an increased interest in the education of women: Cambridge established a college for women—later called Girton—in 1869. The effects of these social changes soon spread to South Africa; in particular, the education of girls received far more attention. Female pupils in South Africa were formerly taught by unqualified teachers at little one-mistress schools or at home by untrained governesses, the way Schreiner herself had been taught. During the 1870s several seminaries and girls' schools were founded, including the Good Hope Seminary in Cape Town and the Huguenot College at Wellington. In 1877 a girls' school opened in Cradock, where Schreiner had worked as a governess.

The Anglo-Zulu War. During the 1870s, the British Empire sought to expand its territorial holdings in South Africa, annexing the Transvaal in 1877, then setting its sights on Zululand, an independent Zulu state on the Natal border. Sir Theophilus Shepstone, Administrator of the Transvaal and a former Zulu sympathizer, betrayed his allies by persuading the British high commissioner that Zululand's strong military organization—led by King Cetshwayo—represented a threat to peace and order in South Africa. Cetshwayo was ordered by the commissioner to disband his army within 30 days; he responded by mobilizing 30,000 men. British forces invaded Zululand on January 11, 1879, but suffered a major defeat at Insandlwana, where a Zulu army surprised and slaughtered nearly 1,600 British soldiers on the morning of January 22. Humiliated, the British army fought back, invading Zululand again in late May 1879 and this time razing the royal town of Ulundi. Cetshwayo was captured and exiled to Robben Island and Zululand was divided into 13 separate territories to be governed by less powerful Zulu leaders.

While *The Story of an African Farm* never mentions or even foreshadows the Anglo-Zulu War, the event nonetheless influenced the novel's success: "Seen from outside and at a distance, the drama, romance and tragedy of the Anglo-Zulu War stirred the imagination of the world and dominated the image of South Africa in the seventies" (Schoeman, p. 495). Indeed, the Anglo-Zulu War, like the later Boer War (1899-1902), sparked the British public's interest in South Africa, increasing the demand for such works as *The Story of an African Farm*.

Reviews. *The Story of an African Farm* was well received when it first appeared in 1883. Edward B. Aveling, writing for Progress in September 1883, described it as "cosmopolitan and human,"

praising its "portrayal of emotion and of the working of passion" (Aveling in Clayton, p. 67). Aveling also commended author "Ralph Iron"—whom he suspected, correctly, of being a woman—for "her bold outspeaking" and audacity in discussing "political matters" in the novel (Aveling in Clayton, p. 68). Henry Norman, writing for the *Fortnightly Review* in December 1883, likewise found Schreiner's confrontation of such issues as religion, women's rights, and immortality "refreshing," adding, "what is still more surprising and refreshing, she has the right words to say about almost all" (Norman in Clayton, p. 69). An anonymous critic in the *Church Quarterly Review,* however, was disturbed by the novel's apparent advocacy of agnosticism: "*The Story of an African Farm* is one of the most intensely painful books we ever read . . . because of the revelation the work affords of a mind that seems hopelessly diseased" (*Church Quarterly Review* in Clayton, p. 74).

Twentieth-century critics, while noting Schreiner's lack of objectivity and inconsistent characterization, nonetheless acknowledge the novel's peculiar appeal and its importance to South African literature. Uys Krige, writing for *The Cape Argus* in 1955, declares, "Yet—and it is a big yet—notwithstanding all its faults, *The Story of an African Farm* is a most moving book, still after 80 years perhaps the most remarkable novel to have come out of South Africa, of so direct an appeal and so haunting a quality that the reader will not forget it as long as he lives" (Krige in Clayton, p. 77). The book's influence on other women writers in Africa has been strong. Doris Lessing (see **African Laughter,** also covered in *African Literature and Its Times*) writes that she responded to Schreiner's "sense of Africa the magnificent" and that "I had only to hear the title, or 'Olive Schreiner,' and my deepest self was touched" (Lessing in First and Scott, pp. 93-94). Isaak Dinesen, author of **Out of Africa** (also covered in *African Literature and Its Times*) likewise had the book in mind during her stay in British East Africa (now Kenya), and acknowledges her debt to Schreiner.

—Pamela S. Loy

For More Information

Boller, Paul F., Jr. *American Thought in Transition: The Impact of Evolutionary Naturalism, 1865-1900.* Washington, D.C.: University Press of America, 1981.

Clayton, Cherry, ed. *Olive Schreiner.* Johannesburg: McGraw-Hill, 1983.

First, Ruth, and Ann Scott. *Olive Schreiner.* London: André Deutsch, 1980.

Houghton, Walter E. *The Victorian Frame of Mind, 1830-1870.* New Haven, Conn.: Yale University Press, 1957.

Mitchell, Sally. *The New Girl: Girl's Culture in England, 1880-1915.* New York: Columbia University Press, 1995.

Rive, Richard, ed. *Olive Schreiner Letters. Vol. 1: 1871-1899.* Oxford: Oxford University Press, 1988.

Schoeman, Karel. *Olive Schreiner: A Woman in South Africa, 1855-1881.* Trans. Henri Snijders. Johannesburg: Jonathan Ball, 1991.

Schreiner, Olive. *The Story of an African Farm.* Harmondsworth: Penguin, 1971.

Thompson, Leonard. *A History of South Africa.* New Haven, Conn.: Yale University Press, 1990.

Vivan, Itala, ed. *The Flawed Diamond: Essays on Olive Schreiner.* Sydney: Dangaroo, 1991.

Wheatcroft, Geoffrey. *The Randlords: The Exploits and Exploitations of South Africa's Mining Magnates.* New York: Atheneum, 1986.

Sweet and Sour Milk

by

Nuruddin Farah

N uruddin Farah was born in 1945 in the Italian-controlled south of Somalia, to a merchant father, Hassan Farah, and a poetess mother, Aleeli Faduma. As a child Farah became fluent in Somali, Arabic, and Amharic, and then proceeded to learn both English and Italian at school. His exposure to these languages as well as his mother's stature as a recognized poet had a profound impact on Farah. His family moved to Mogadishu in 1963, and Farah later left to study abroad. He received his bachelor's degree in India, and pursued graduate studies in England. On his way home from England in 1976, he placed a casual call to his brother from the Rome airport and learned that his novel *A Naked Needle* had offended the government of Somali dictator Muhammad Siyad (Siad) Barre. He then ran into the Somali minister of justice in the very same airport, who warned him that, if he returned home, he would find himself jailed for the next 30 years. Thus began Farah's long exile from his homeland. He wrote *Sweet and Sour Milk* in Rome, following it with *Sardines* and *Close Sesame,* completing a trilogy known as *Variations on the Theme of an African Dictatorship.* Nuruddin Farah was awarded the Neustadt Prize for Literature in 1998, a prestigious honor considered by many to be second only to the Nobel Prize.

Events in History at the Time of the Novel

Somalia—an overview. Located in East Africa, Somalia (officially the Somali Democratic Re-

---

THE LITERARY WORK

A novel set in and around Mogadiscio (Mogadishu), Somalia, in 1975; published in English in 1979.

SYNOPSIS

Loyaan, a Western educated Somali (Soomaali) dentist, searches for the reason behind his twin brother's mysterious death.

---

public) sits to the east of Ethiopia and Kenya. Its capital, Mogadishu (Mogadiscio in the novel) is on the Indian Ocean. At the time of the novel there were some 4.5 million Somalis spread over 500,000 square miles. Since much of the Somali peninsula is arid and unfit for reliable cultivation, most Somalis are pastoral nomads who herd sheep, goats, cattle, and camels. Somalis in the south and certain portions of the north farm fertile pockets of land, living sedentary lives. The rest of the rural population travels during the year in search of water and pasturage. At the time *Sweet and Sour Milk* was written, a devastating drought, which first began in 1969, was choking the nation. Between October 1974 and May 1975, a total of 16,685 Somalis had died in government relief camps; another 250,000 were still alive in these camps; nearly 20,000 others perished outside the camps (*Facts on File 1975,* p. 503). Uganda, China, and many other nations offered aid in the form of food and medicine. The

Mother and child in a refugee camp in drought-stricken Somalia.

Somali government took the opportunity to change the way of life led by the drought-stricken nomadic people, who were moved from their familiar lands and settled collectively on farms or in fishing villages. This was an extremely bold move—the nomadic Somalis revered their traditions and the change demanded that they detach from their clans and live with nonrelatives.

A Cushitic-speaking people, the Somalis have intermarried over the centuries with Arabs (almost all Somalis are Muslim) and trace their lineage to a mix of traditional African clans and Islamic nobility. The legendary origin of the Somali people is traced back to a single common ancestor, Abu Taalib, uncle of Mohammed—the great prophet of Islam. Legend has it that from Abu Taalib came the few clan families into which all Somalis fall.

Somali clan system. The Northern Somalis are divided into four major clan families: the Dir, Isaaq, Haawiye, and Darood. In Southern Somalia, a large confederacy of clans, called the Raxanwayn, arose in the eighteenth century. A number of other Southern Somali peoples, such as the Jiddu, Funni, and Garree, lie outside this system. The Northern Somalis often group these peoples together as the Digil. The clan-families vary in size—the Darood clan-family, for example, numbers more than one million. Clan family members can count back 30 generations. A subclan might consist of only a few thousand and perhaps count as far back as 10 generations. (Children learn this family history by heart.) Smaller than the subclan is the "dia-paying" group, a juridical-political set of kinspeople that ensures that its members receive *dia* (or compensation) if they are ever wronged. A person thus belongs to a least four major social groupings; the built-in likelihood of unstable allegiances as one negotiates demands of clan-family, clan, subclan, and dia group draws Somalis "into a powerful social fabric of kinship and cultural solidarity while setting them against one another in a complicated maze of antagonistic clan interest" (Laitin and Samatar, pp. 30-31).

> A person . . . gives political allegiance first to his/her immediate family, then to his immediate lineage, then to the clan of his lineage, then to a clan-family that embraces several clans including his own, and ultimately to the nation that itself consists of a confederacy of clan-families. Each level of segmentation defines a person's rights and obligations as well as his/her standing in relation to others. The segmentary law dictates, for example, that two lineages that

are genealogically equidistant from a common ancestor should stand in an adversarial relationship to a third lineage whose genealogical lines fall outside of the common ancestor. The result is a society so integrated that its members regard one another as siblings, cousins, and kin, but also so riven with clannish fission and factionalism that political instability is the society's normative characteristic.

(Laitin and Samatar, p. 31)

This last insight is particularly important in understanding much of the political strife in Somalia, at the time of the novel and otherwise. Farah himself has said that in Somalia, "you are not a person but a member of a clan. My being a Somali matters outside Somalia. But when you are inside, your own clan demands that you become a member of that and not of a large nation" (Farah in Wright, p. 8). *Sweet and Sour Milk* repeatedly alludes to "tribal upstarts" and people who have secured government jobs through their clan connections. At the time the novel was written, Somalia was more or less in the hands of the dictator Siyad Barre's clan (his father was Darood, of the Marehan clan). His immediate family, known as the "Gang of Five" (himself, his first wife, her oldest son, his brother, and his cousin), effectively ruled the nation (Wright, p. 11). In *Sweet and Sour Milk,* Farah writes: "In order to feel well-guarded, well-protected, the General had of late appointed a number of his tribesmen to key army positions" (Farah, *Sweet and Sour Milk,* p. 172).

The central irony here is that Barre had, from the earliest days of his rule, singled out "tribalism" as the root of all evil in Somali culture. In a speech delivered April 29, 1971, he came out squarely against the practice: "We are unanimously agreed that tribalism should have no place in the affairs of the State—in government, the SRC [the Supreme Revolutionary Council], among Secretaries, the Army, Police and the civil servants. We are the servants of our people and our country.... There must be no return to tribalism" (Barre, p. 180). The General insisted that promoting one's "tribesmen" was the sign of a weak leader; by the mid-1970s, however, when *Sweet and Sour Milk* takes place, he himself had succumbed to the temptation of installing his relatives in seats of power.

Political/linguistic landscape. Because the Somalis are a pastoral people, it comes as no surprise that the Somali language was, until quite recently, an entirely oral one. It developed a highly poetic style and expressive diction, and

has produced a vast body of oral literature, including folktales, fables, poetry, and other literary genres. Somali culture is infused with poetry; it deeply influences both public and private life. Clan warfare and vendettas are incited by verse; marriage is contracted and terminated through poetry; and virtually all matters of national importance are discussed through poetic dialogue.

LITERACY IN SOMALIA

On October 21, 1969, Major General Muhammad Siyad Barre led a bloodless coup d'état and seized control of the Somali government. Three years later, on October 21, 1972, the third anniversary of the coup, Barre decreed Latin to be the official script of the hitherto unwritten Somali language.

We have to face and solve once and for all the question of script for our mother language, which goes back historically to our very beginning. It is rich in literature and poetry and can compare with the best languages. Through verbal transmission our ancestors have handed down to us a rich heritage to safeguard and develop. . . . As dedicated revolutionaries we must now ensure that what has been handed down to us over the centuries is no longer lost. . . .

(Barre in Laitin, pp. 120-21)

The resolution of the script crisis enabled Barre's regime to tackle the problem of illiteracy. By 1974 illiteracy had almost disappeared in urban Somalia. However, Somalia is not an urban-dominated nation: in 1978, just before *Sweet and Sour Milk* was published, only 5 percent of Somalis were literate (Wright, p. 143, n. 5).

Nuruddin Farah was raised in this rich poetic tradition. From his mother, Aleeli Faduma Farah, a talented poet, he became aware of the important social function of poetry. He learned how it can enter into political debates in sophisticated ways, becoming epic and satirical but also oblique and allusive. Much of this early knowledge and appreciation for his oral culture informed Farah's later writing, as shown by the manner in which it functions as political critique. Also, each chapter in *Sweet and Sour Milk* begins with a short prose poem that uses natural and pastoral metaphors to set the mood for the action that follows.

As a written language Somali came into existence only in 1972 when Siyad Barre decreed

Latin to be the national script. Before that, various languages—including Arabic, English, and Italian—were used for legal and bureaucratic purposes. Arabic entered Somalia with the first Muslims who immigrated to the area after Islam's birth in the seventh century C.E. As Islam spread and Somalis came to embrace it as their religion, Arabic took hold, and to this day it remains the language of religion.

English and Italian, on the other hand, are more recent colonial additions to the Somali linguistic landscape. Italy entered the colonial game in 1869, gaining a foothold in East Africa through Eritrea and then becoming active in southern Somalia. From 1886 onwards Britain also began to acquire or capture parts of the Somali peninsula for its East Africa sphere of influence.

In addition to Italy and Britain, France and Ethiopia seized parts of traditional Somali territory at this time. Turkey and Egypt showed an active interest in the area as well. The two decades from 1920 to 1940 mark the period of colonial consolidation in Somalia. Of the various colonial powers involved, only Italy made serious efforts to economically develop its territory. Among other things, this included the introduction of the Italian language and bureaucratic systems in southern Somalia. The British introduced the English language in the northern region, called British Somaliland, but did not believe their territory to be economically viable for development.

Somalia's colonial history is important in understanding the rich linguistic milieu in which Nuruddin Farah developed. Being educated in different languages opened up multiple worlds from which Farah learned immensely. *Sweet and Sour Milk* reflects this cultural diversity because it draws on Farah's various linguistic sources. While the novel was originally written in English, Farah constantly employs Somali proverbs, Italian phrases, and knowledge of Arabic. The result is a novel rich in reference to Somali linguistic and cultural history.

"The General": Siyad Barre and the rise of "scientific socialism." In 1960, when Nuruddin Farah was 15 years old, Somalia gained its independence from Britain and Italy. The new state incorporated the two former colonial territories of British Somaliland and the Trust Territory of Somalia under Italian administration (Italian Somaliland). Its boundaries were delineated by Britain, Italy, Ethiopia—which possessed the Somali-speaking Ogaden area—and by France—which retained claim to a small territory on the Gulf of Aden known as French Somaliland (present-day Djibouti). A democratic parliamentary government was established and a national constitution written in 1961 and ratified. Gradually the parliamentary system, a Western-style import, broke down under the temptations of personal gain and clan interests. Historians cite rampant nepotism ("tribalism"), waste, and corruption as the causes for what came next.

Early in the morning of October 21, 1969, a military coup put Somalia into the hands of major General Mohammed Siyad Barre. Six days earlier, Somali president Abdirashid Ali Shermarke had been assassinated by one of his own guards, and, while the ruling party was arguing about who should be his replacement, Barre stepped into the vacuum. He abolished the constitution and the National Assembly, then appointed himself president and head of the Supreme Revolutionary Council (SRC). The SRC announced that it would eliminate corruption and "tribalism," end illiteracy, assure women's rights, and bring about social, economic, and cultural development. It also outlawed all political parties and replaced regional governors and commissioners with army or police officers acting as chairmen of local revolutionary councils.

Barre came from the Marehan subclan of the Darood clan, "the largest and most widely distributed of all the Somali clan-families" (Lewis, p. 6). He was trained by the Italian and Soviet military, and influenced by the successful revolution in Egypt under its leader Gamal Abdul Nasser (also spelled Jamal 'Abd al-Nasir). When Barre first seized power, he seemed to have been an ardent reformer, intent on fostering Somali nationalism and improving the lives of its people. Illiteracy was almost universal, women's rights were minimal, and drought had begun to further impoverish an already poor rural population. On the first anniversary of the coup, Barre proclaimed Somalia to be a socialist state; he had already nationalized all banks, petroleum companies, insurance companies, and import-export companies (Patman, p. 94). In October 1970, he revised history somewhat and claimed that his coup had actually been a socialist revolution and that "scientific socialism"—which in Somali was called *hanti-wadaagga 'ilmi ku dhisan,* or "wealth-sharing based on wisdom"—would now be official policy (Lewis, p. 209).

This meant that the country would be a Marxist-Leninist state in which all means of production and natural resources belonged to the entire society. National products would be distributed according to the contributions of each individual. Somalia, however, had no history of class conflict in the Marxist sense—that is, as a preindustrial, pastoral nation, it possessed no proletariat (working) or bourgeois (middle) classes. Barre substituted tribalism for class and Somalia's socialist goal became self-liberation from distinctions imposed by lineage group affiliation. He stressed that Somalia's brand of socialism, while in keeping with that of countries like the Soviet Union, had to be applied according to the conditions found in Somalia. Thus, the official ideology was composed of three parts: Barre's own conception of community development based on the principle that Somalia should be self-reliant; a form of socialism based on Marxist principles; and Islam, which, according to Barre, was in complete accord with this ideology.

Although Barre proclaimed socialism to be the national ideology, he was pragmatic in its application. He counseled others to regard socialism not as a religion but as a political principle for organizing government and for managing production. In its first few years the new regime began to tackle the socialist objectives it had set for itself, namely social inequality and language reform. The early announcements of the Supreme Revolutionary Council focused on the corruption of the old government. It accused politicians of being ineffectual and of mishandling government funds, and called for accountability. Although the SRC was made up of military and police officers, it relied on a number of civilians to hold ministerial positions. "Appointments, for the first time in the republic's short history, were not carefully scrutinized according to clan affiliation. Merit appeared to be the order of the day" (Laitin and Samatar, p. 79). This would not, however, last very long.

Soviet influence in Somalia. In the 1970s Somalia was at the center of Cold War tensions (the competition between the Soviet Union and the United States for global domination). Interested in keeping a military base on the Indian Ocean and access to the Red Sea, the Soviets had established a presence in northeast Africa, mainly in Egypt and the Sudan; some historians even speculate that the Soviets had sponsored Barre's coup to counter pro-American tendencies in the area. For a variety of reasons, the Soviet presence was threatened beginning in 1971. Somalia stepped in and offered to help the Soviets consolidate their position, partly in hopes of increased Soviet aid. The Soviet Union consequently began pumping military equipment and

personnel, technicians, and money into the Somali economy. The Russian fighter planes that roar across the sky at various points in *Sweet and Sour Milk*, the shadowy Russian doctor who may or may not have given Soyaan a fatal injection, the KGB (Soviet Secret Service) agents who are so greatly feared by those on either side of the revolution—all of these novelistic elements are firmly rooted in historical fact.

> [Beginning in mid-1972] the Soviets supplied miG-15 and miG-17 fighter aircraft, IL-28 bombers, Yak trainer planes, Antonov transport aircraft, T-34 and T-54 tanks, armoured personnel carriers, P-5 torpedo boats and large quantities of automatic guns and artillery. Furthermore, the number of Soviet military advisers and technicians present in Somalia rose from less than a thousand to around 3,600. This was an unusually large figure even allowing for the fact that the mainly Soviet-equipped and Soviet-trained Somali Army increased . . . by almost 50 per cent during this period.
>
> (Patman, p. 117)

THE VICTORY PIONEERS
~

The drums bargained: they would not be silenced. The men who beat them perspired heavily, they sang as they beat; they beat as they sang the praise-songs of the General. They were the griots [storytellers] in green.

"Long live the General. . . . There is no General but the General. . . . Long live the Revolution. . . . The Marxist-Leninist Islamic Revolution. . . . Long, long live the General. . . .

(*Sweet and Sour Milk*, p. 187)

In Farah's novel, the youthful Green Guards parade through the streets of Mogadiscio, calling citizens to sweep the city in preparation for a state visit by Ugandan president Idi Amin Dada. They are modeled on the Victory Pioneers, who also wore bright green unisex shirts, and who maintained law and order. Their insignia was an eye. Founded in the summer of 1972, the organization was based on a similar Soviet organization called the Komsomol. The Victory Pioneers ensured that the revolution was kept within sanctioned bounds, that people participated in volunteer work (like the Revolution of the Brooms in the novel), and that foreigners were monitored while in the country. Special Victory Pioneers branches for women kept an eye on family welfare programs and other community services.

In 1975, the year in which *Sweet and Sour Milk* is set, the Soviet presence in Somalia was strong; this would all change, however, in 1977, when Somalia and Ethiopia battled each other for control of the Ogaden region. Supporting Ethiopia, the Soviets would cut off all aid to the Barre regime.

The decline of human rights. Perhaps more important than the "scientific socialist" ideology espoused by Barre—for Nuruddin Farah at least—was the personal power and control exerted by Barre himself and the mythic image he projected. Following the 1969 revolution, Barre, who is referred to only as "the General" in *Sweet and Sour Milk,* fostered the growth of a cult of personality around his image. He called himself the "Victorious Leader" and had portraits of himself as well as Marx and Lenin displayed in the streets and during public ceremonies. Following the lead of Chinese leader Mao Tse-Tung and Libyan leader Mu'ammar Qaddafi, Barre even produced a little blue and white book containing his epigrams and advice to the populace. Not only was Siyad Barre the person who had synthesized Marxism with Islam; he was also the "Big Man" of Somali tradition, the "warrior often possessing a religious charisma" (Nelson, p. 52).

Such "charisma" and personal power ultimately led to the downfall of democracy and personal freedoms. In addition to abolishing the National Assembly and Somalia's 1960 constitution (which enshrined civil rights), Barre's 1969 revolution extinguished virtually all human rights, turning Somalia into a police state. Barre recreated the law in his own image; his coup marks the abolition of Somalia's Constitutional Court and the High Court of Justice, neither of which were ever reestablished under the regime. Instead, jurisdiction was assumed by the National Security Court, which was under the direct control of the Supreme Revolutionary Council and—it was widely held—under the personal control of Barre.

The overthrow of democratic law went hand-in-hand with the construction of a highly effective internal security machine. Barre's regime, conscious of its origin in a coup d'état, sought foremost to protect and preserve itself against possible domestic threats. After the 1969 coup roughly 60 leaders of the previous government, businessmen, lawyers, and senior military personnel who did not support the coup, were arrested and tried by the National Security Council, which made disruption of peace or the sovereignty of the new socialist nation a crime punishable by death. Following Soviet advice, Barre's regime sought to control political opponents through the use of arrest and imprisonment for broadly defined crimes against the state. On July 3, 1972, Barre caused two Somalis to be executed publicly on charges of plotting his overthrow.

By the mid-1970s Barre's popularity began to decline and his revolution stagnated. As he and trusted members of his clan came to almost completely dominate the government, the regime devoted more time and energy to internal security. Somali intellectuals, artists, and businessmen critical of the regime were increasingly subject to arbitrary arrests and torture. A number of the intelligentsia fled the country. The corruption and tribalism that the regime had set out to eradicate now became an integral part of its politics. While the regime had established a written language and boasted a number of other achievements, in the minds of many none of these compensated for the loss of individual rights and personal freedoms.

The Novel in Focus

Plot summary. As *Sweet and Sour Milk* opens, 29-year-old Soyaan Keynaan lies ill in bed, attended to by his mother, Qumman. Soyaan fell ill after dining with a government minister at the home of his father's second wife, Beydan. Qumman speaks of the possibility that he has been poisoned or perhaps bewitched by an unnamed woman of whom she does not approve. She urges upon her son traditional remedies and refuses to hand him the prescription medicine of Dr. Ahmed-Wellie until Soyaan promises to hear without derision the shaykh who is to come and read to him from the Qur'an. He then briefly recalls a recent day that he spent with his lover, who is, or was, also the mistress of a powerful government official. They speak obliquely of "a strong political statement" that he has written and that she has discovered, a statement that will reappear throughout the novel (*Sweet and Sour Milk,* p. 7).

The novel returns to Soyaan's sickbed, where he is visited by the shaykh and by his father, Keynaan, whom he dislikes. Keynaan is a domestic tyrant, a murderer, and a government informer. The two disagree on national politics: Soyaan protests the Soviet presence in Somalia and the restriction of civil rights, but Keynaan warns him away from protest for his own good. Next, Ladan, Soyaan's younger sister, is introduced; she is sensitive, intelligent, and worried about her brother's political connections and the trouble they have brought him. She reveals that he has spoken feverishly of being jabbed with needles, which he somehow recalls: "these injections, thought he to himself, how they pained!"; also in his fever he mutters "obscenities about the General" (*Sweet and Sour Milk*, p. 12). The family is made complete with the return of Soyaan's twin brother, Loyaan, a rural health official. After calling Loyaan's name three times, Soyaan dies. Loyaan decides to investigate the cause of his twin's demise and to unravel the meaning of Soyaan's life.

Loyaan begins with puzzling clues left to him in Soyaan's diary: "M to the power of 2. I/M comrade-in-project" (*Sweet and Sour Milk*, p. 21). He also obtains a short, antigovernment piece that Soyaan wrote, calling the civil service "clowns," "cowards," and "tribal upstarts," and exposing the dictator's means of internal security: "The methods of the General and the KGB are not dissimilar, I can tell you that. Instructions: Know who do not know you. Plant seeds of suspicion in every thinking brain and hence render it 'unthinking'" (*Sweet and Sour Milk*, p. 33). Soon after, Loyaan finds among Soyaan's things a government directive, which states that any person who spreads information aimed at damaging the sovereignty of the government is liable to death. This paper tips Loyaan off about his brother's political life.

Through Ahmed-Wellie, Soyaan's doctor and friend, Loyaan learns about the abductions, arrests, and tortures that the regime routinely performs. Loyaan does not trust the doctor because the political environment makes trust very difficult. Loyaan's mother repeatedly warns her son not to trust Ahmed-Wellie because he is related to the General by clan ties.

At Soyaan's funeral, the Minister to the Presidency arrives to offer his condolences to the family. He tells Loyaan that, officially, Soyaan's last words were "Labor is honor," but Loyaan knows this to be a lie. When he tells the Minister what actually happened, the Minister replies: "We were given a different version. We prefer that" (*Sweet and Sour Milk*, p. 42). Before the Minister leaves, he asks Loyaan if he has found a memorandum that Soyaan was working on. Loyaan does not know what memorandum is being referred to, but the Minister is insistent on finding this document.

The next morning Loyaan learns that public eulogies are praising Soyaan as a martyr for the

Revolution. A woman with a baby boy comes to see him; the woman turns out to be Soyaan's *mistione* (half-Italian, half-Somali) lover, Margaritta, and the boy, Marco, their son. She invites Loyaan to visit her.

SPEAKING IN CODE

In *Sweet and Sour Milk*, Loyaan is puzzled by the coded message he finds among Soyaan's papers. At the time, Somalia was actually awash in cryptic sayings, because people were aware they were being listened to and watched. Barre's regime itself was known in some circles as M.O.D.: M for Barre's patrilineal clan, the Marehan; O for his mother's clan, the Ogaden; and D for the clan of his favorite son-in-law (who was head of the National Security Service), the Dir. However, no one could speak openly of M.O.D.—Barre had come out aggressively against "tribalism" and to point to the open transgression of this principle by the General himself would have had consequences. Thus, "[w]ith their usual verbal facility, ingenious Somali sophists developed an alternative circumlocution, substituting dates, starting from that of the Glorious Revolution [Barre's coup of October 21, 1969] to represent the major power-holding groups. In this idiom 21 October was used as a synonym for M, 22 October for O and 23 October for D" (Lewis, p. 222).

Later that day Loyaan walks into Mogadiscio to pick up Soyaan's death certificate. On the way he remembers a letter Soyaan wrote to him, revealing his disgust for political corruption and the tyrannical dictator:

> If you ever come to Mogadiscio and you go to the centre of it, you will now find new buildings, new high structures whose ribbons of inauguration have been cut with the very scissors which made the wrist of the nation bleed and this country grow weak.... [H]e [the dictator] breaks the pride of one's dignity; he reduces women to mistresses of his prowess: He is, after all, the General. He constructs showy pieces of tumorous architecture, he gives us monuments of false hope. He creates for the nation heroes of his own choosing.
>
> (*Sweet and Sour Milk*, pp. 71-72)

Unfortunately, Soyaan himself is now being turned into just such a hero. Contrary to everything Soyaan stood for and identified with, he is being hailed as "a living legend of revolutionary vitality" (*Sweet and Sour Milk,* p. 74). When Loyaan returns home, he finds that money has been given anonymously to the family because of Soyaan's "honor"—it appears as though Soyaan's soul is being bought off. Loyaan fights with his mother, Qumman, over Soyaan's new posthumous status; he tries to make her understand that dishonor is being heaped on Soyaan's memory and that history is being rewritten.

Later in the day, Loyaan has dinner with Keynaan, who once worked for the dictator's security forces but was forced to retire after he killed a man in his custody. As punishment, the dictator ordered Keynaan to marry the dead man's widow, Beydan. Keynaan himself functions as a mini-dictator within the family. At the end of their talk, he tells Loyaan that he has forbidden an autopsy of Soyaan's body and has corroborated to a newspaper the government's version that Soyaan's last words were "Labor is honor." As a reward, the government has rehabilitated Keynaan and offered him a position. Loyaan is appalled.

THE TEN SHAYKHS

At his brother's funeral, Loyaan sees a circle of fresh, unmarked graves. Dr. Ahmed-Wellie speculates that these may be "the tombs of the ten sheikhs [or *shaykhs*] . . . the General has executed" (*Sweet and Sour Milk,* p. 40). This was no purely fictional execution. On January 23, 1974, Barre actually had ten religious leaders killed by a firing squad. Muslim holy men, they had openly protested a new liberal law giving equal rights to women in areas such as inheritance and divorce.

The next morning the newspaper carries the interview, and proclaims Soyaan a "carrier of the Revolutionary Torch; the Standard-bearer of Scientific Socialism" whose last words were "Labour is honour and there is no General but our General" (*Sweet and Sour Milk,* p. 97). The article also states that the Supreme Revolutionary Council has decided to name a street after Soyaan and to inscribe his official last words in gold on his tomb. At the registration office for the dead, Loyaan discovers that Soyaan's secretary, a woman named Mulki, was abducted by the government a few days previously, and that the office no longer has any files on Soyaan because, as a hero of the Revolution, he has become state property.

Next Loyaan visits Margaritta, Soyaan's lover. From her he learns the particulars of Soyaan's resistance to the dictatorship: Soyaan was a specialist on the Soviet presence in Somalia, and kept track of the Eastern European teachers, technicians, and doctors in the country. Rumor has it that someone from his mother's clan, a perhaps pro-Western vice president, asked Soyaan to make such investigations. Loyaan also learns that Margaritta has stowed in a bank safe a copy of the elusive memo the Minister wants so badly, and another copy is with a man called Ibrahim Il Siciliano, brother of Mulki. Before Margaritta drops Loyaan home, she shows him the back of a picture on which Soyaan inscribed a poem almost certainly referring to his impending death at the hands of the government. The clues start to make sense: "M to the power of 2" likely refers to Margaritta and Marco, but could also mean "Moscow-Mogadiscio," referring to the alliance between the repressive Soviet and Somali governments. "I/M comrade-in-project" could refer to Ibrahim and Margaritta as comrades in Soyaan's antigovernment life, but could also mean Ibrahim and his sister Mulki. It is apparent that there are still many unanswered questions.

The next day Loyaan visits Ibrahim Il Siciliano. From him he learns that Soyaan was part of a clandestine movement of opposition, a group of ten intellectuals and professionals who took an oath to serve the true interests of Somalia.

The next person Loyaan goes to see is Beydan, one of the last people Soyaan saw before he became ill. From Beydan Loyaan learns that a government official was with Soyaan when she last saw him, and that Soyaan drank beer and took some strange pills. Ahmed-Wellie arrives unexpectedly and takes Loyaan home. On the way, Loyaan learns that Ibrahim has been arrested. When Loyaan arrives at home, he sees Margaritta waiting for him. She tells him that the Minister broke into her bank safe and now has the only accessible copy of the coveted memo.

The next day Loyaan visits the Minister. Loyaan repeatedly questions him about the disappearance of his brother's secretary Mulki, the arrest of her brother Ibrahim, and the motives behind buying Keynaan's lie. Loyaan also probes him about the theft of the memo from Margaritta's safe and finally accuses him and the government outright of poisoning Soyaan. The enraged Minister denies all charges and feigns ignorance.

Later that day Loyaan's afternoon siesta is interrupted by drumming and calls outside. It is the "Rendezvous of the Brooms," a traditional purification ritual that the General has converted to his own purposes: all able-bodied persons are required to "partake in the revolutionary duty of making [their] district clean as glass freshly wiped and washed" (*Sweet and Sour Milk*, p. 188). This is of the utmost urgency because Idi Amin is due to visit in two days.

Loyaan's sister and mother urge him to remain at home; they realize that he is in danger of saying or doing something rash. However, Loyaan no longer cares about the government or any duty to it. As the Green Guards go calling from house to house, Loyaan tells them to keep the racket down and let people sleep. This angers the Green Guards and, after finding out who he is, they order him to be at the Rendezvous. Once there, Loyaan sees that the sweepers are mostly women, as it is deemed "untraditional" for men to take part. When a Green Guard begins to harass a pregnant woman, who has taken a break, Loyaan comes to her aid. Soon after, Security men take Loyaan away for questioning.

Loyaan's masked interrogator tells him that his superiors are upset with the adverse publicity he has brought to Soyaan's name. Loyaan interrogates his interrogator, asking repeatedly why Soyaan was made a hero of the Revolution after his death and why Ibrahim and Mulki have been detained. The masked man replies that Ibrahim was taken in for "anti-Soviet" activities. Then a woman is brought in who claims to be Mulki and says that she has typed no memorandum for Soyaan. "All this is like a badly written farce," Loyaan observes disbelievingly (*Sweet and Sour Milk*, p. 201). At the end of the interrogation Loyaan is told that, rather than being arrested, he has been appointed to Soyaan's government post and that the General has signed a decree appointing him Somalia's Councilor in Belgrade, Yugoslavia. The plane will leave the following evening, after Soyaan's one-week death anniversary.

The next day preparations are made for Soyaan's death anniversary. Goats are slaughtered to feed the guests, and the family cleans and makes arrangements. Ahmed-Wellie comes for a visit. He knows all about Loyaan's departure for Belgrade—but how? Ahmed-Wellie, though pretending to be a friend, appears to be a government informer. Loyaan spends some time with Beydan, who tells him that she has had a prophetic dream in which she dies giving birth to a child that will be named Soyaan. Later that evening, Loyaan meets with Margaritta who tells him she believes that the General had a direct hand in Soyaan's death. After the seventh-day death anniversary, Beydan dies in childbirth and the child is named Soyaan. Loyaan wonders if the child will ever know the truth about his namesake. The novel ends, ambiguously, with a knock on the door at seven in the evening. We never find out what happened to Soyaan.

AN OFFICIAL VISIT

In July 1975 Idi Amin Dada, dictator of Uganda, paid an official visit to Mogadiscio. According to Amin, he came to speak with Barre about the challenges of heading the annual meeting of the Organization of African Unity (OAU), a pan-African body founded in 1963. Barre had chaired the 1974 meeting and Amin was to head the 1975 meeting. Held in Mogadiscio, the 1974 conference had been an exercise in conspicuous opulence. Barre had bought a fleet of European luxury sedans to ferry about leaders and had built an elaborate "People's Palace"—no doubt one of the "showy pieces of tumorous architecture" described in the novel (*Sweet and Sour Milk*, p. 72). All this took place in a very poor nation that had been suffering from drought for six years.

In the novel, Loyaan sees beggars who have been forced out of certain areas by the government in preparation for Amin's visit: "Before any head of state visited . . . the security swept away these ugly sights. . . . This happened . . . a month or two before OAU or Arab League meetings" (*Sweet and Sour Milk*, p. 145).

The foundations of dictatorship. In *Sweet and Sour Milk* Nuruddin Farah critiques the exploitation by Barre's dictatorship of traditional Somali values and culture for unseemly purposes. He suggests that, in its particulars, Barre's regime was essentially Somalian, both responding to and supported by specific Somalian cultural practices. For instance, the General uses an intricate method of surveillance called "Dionysus's Ear." His security service recruits its spies and informers from among the illiterate masses. Everything the informers report is done verbally—nothing is written down. People who are arrested sometimes languish in prisons for years

At the time the novel was written, over 16,000 Somalis had perished in government refugee camps for drought victims; the dead were buried in crude graves like this one.

because there is no record of their being there. Likewise no death certificates are issued for those who perish.

The dissemination of information considered antirevolutionary is punishable by death. While written documents like Soyaan's memorandum are ruthlessly hunted down, the only daily newspaper, a horrendous piece of journalism that gives "no introductory paragraph, no explanation of anything," which "come[s] to a point before [it is] started," is used to rewrite history and proliferate propaganda (*Sweet and Sour Milk*, p. 74). (This is in fact the very newspaper that censored Nuruddin Farah's first and only attempt at fiction in the Somali language in 1973, causing him to flee his own country for fear of reprisals.) The newspaper creates heroes and rewrites history; Soyaan will not be remembered by what he actually did or wrote, but by the official lies told to refashion him into a hero of the Revolution.

For Nuruddin Farah none of these methods would succeed were it not for their use of patriarchy and the authoritarian family unit. In his novel, the father, Keynaan, an ex-torturer and paid informer for the regime, speaks with an absolute authority that reflects that of the dictator: "I am the father. It is my prerogative to give life and death as I find fit. I've chosen to breathe life

into Soyaan [by supporting his transformation into a hero of the Revolution]. And remember one thing, Loyaan: if I decide this minute to cut you in two, I can" (*Sweet and Sour Milk*, p. 94). Keynaan partakes in the rewriting of Soyaan's life, threatens his sons, and beats his wives. That such patriarchal control exists in Somali society explains, for Farah, how a dictator such as Barre could rise to power so successfully. According to one critic, *Sweet and Sour Milk* focuses so much on the workings of families because of the relationship between family and national politics in Somalia:

> [Farah] reveals that, for all the vaunted egalitarianism of Somalia's traditional political institutions, the authoritarian family structure at the roots of the society actually conditions people to and predisposes them towards the tyranny officially endorsed and institutionalized by military regimes.
>
> (Wright, p. 48)

In creating Keynaan's character Farah may have relied on his memory of his own father, whom he has referred to as "despondently despotic, a patriarch willing to submit the world to the authority of his whim" (Farah, "Celebrating Differences," p. 712). For Farah, patriarchy and the authoritarian family lead directly to political dictatorship: "Because we are dictatorial as societies, it follows that we produce grand patriarchs, dictators par excellence" (Farah in Jussawalla and Dasenbrock, p. 56).

What emerges in *Sweet and Sour Milk,* then, is not merely an indictment of the General and his oppressive regime. The novel exposes dictatorial power as it operates at different levels of Somali society and points to the interrelationship of these levels. It also shows that such power is the logical result of a society that emphasizes the supremacy of orality and clan affiliations as well as the authoritarian family unit.

Literary context. Nuruddin Farah was the first Somali novelist, publishing *From a Crooked Rib* in 1970. He is not, however, alone in his treatment of the place of traditional African culture in postcolonial African nations. Although, like most other African cultures, the Somalis' has been oral-based for many centuries, Farah does not try to valorize the oral tradition, like Ngugi wa Thiong'o (*Matigari*) or Ayi Kwei Armah (*Two Thousand Seasons*) or to evoke it as has Okot p'Bitek, Ugandan writer of **Song of Lawino and Song of Ocol** (also covered in *African Literature and Its Times*). Rather, as Derek Wright points out, Farah shows "how indigenous traditions, oral as well as domestic, have themselves been implicated in the new political tribulations and terrors of the independent state" (Wright, p. 52). Furthermore, Farah's characters tend not to be drawn from the same class—peasant and underprivileged—as those in the political works of other African novelists; his heroes and villains are usually from the educated urban elite. Some critics feel that this focus undermines the ability of Farah's writings to promote political change, but others insist that he draws attention to the wide range of Somali society. By writing of the intelligentsia he states what is perhaps not always obvious to a Western audience: that there is, in fact, a Somalian intelligentsia, and that not all Somalis are poor and uneducated. *Sweet and Sour Milk,* as mentioned, became the first in a trilogy by Farah. Certain characters resurface in the subsequent novels, *Sardines* and *Close Sesame.* In *Sardines,* for example, Loyaan reappears, although it is unclear whether he is in prison or exile (an uncertainty that the ambiguous ending of *Sweet and Sour Milk* sets up. In *Close Sesame* Dr. Ahmed-Wellie returns, now as the Somali Minister of Information.

Reviews. Writing for the *New York Times Book Review,* William Ferguson called Farah's trilogy "a chilling exploration of corruption and terror" and praised the "feverishly lyrical" style of the three novels, which he called "a powerful political statement that moves constantly toward song" (Ferguson in Mooney, p. 612). The *Voice Literary Supplement* praised the "intricate moral and physical problems" that Farah sets for his characters (Chua in Mooney, p. 613). Most reviewers of *Sweet and Sour Milk* scrutinized the novel's integration of politics, ethics, and morality:

> In the best scenario, [the political] message is fully integrated into the plot of the novel. Few writers manage to bring off such a wedding with great success, and Farah himself has a tendency to subjugate plot for the sake of his message in some books. But in *Sweet and Sour Milk,* the most artfully constructed novel in his first completed trilogy, Farah has created a major political novel of lasting value.
>
> (McDowell, p. 253)

—Faisal Azam

For More Information

Ahmed, Ali Jimale, ed. *The Invention of Somalia.* Lawrenceville, N.J.: Red Sea Press, 1995.

Alden, Patricio, and Louis Tremaine. *Nurrudin Farah.* New York: Twayne, 1999.

Barre, Siyad. *My Country and My People: Selected Speeches of Jaalle Major-General Mohamed Siyad Barre President of the Supreme Revolutionary Council 1969-1974.* Mogadishu: Ministry of Information and National Guidance, 1974.

Facts on File 1975. New York: Facts on File, 1975.

Farah, Nuruddin. *Sweet and Sour Milk.* Saint Paul: Graywolf Press, 1992.

———. "Celebrating Differences: The 1998 Neustadt Lecture." *World Literature Today* 72, no. 4 (autumn 1998): 709-12.

Jussawalla, Feroza, and Reed Way Dasenbrock. "Nuruddin Farah." In *Interviews with Writers of the Post-Colonial World.* Jackson: University Press of Mississippi, 1992.

Laitin, David D. *Politics, Language, and Thought: The Somali Experience.* Chicago: University of Chicago Press, 1977.

Laitin, David D., and Said S. Samatar. *Somalia: Nation in Search of a State.* Boulder, Colo.: Westview Press, 1987.

Lewis, I. M. *A Modern History of Somalia: Nation and State in the Horn of Africa.* Boulder, Colo.: Westview Press, 1988.

McDowell, Robert. "Nuruddin Farah." In *African Writers.* New York: Charles Scribner's Sons, 1997.

Mooney, Martha T., ed. *Book Review Digest 1993.* New York: H. W. Wilson, 1994.

Nelson, Harold D., ed. *Somalia: A Country Study.* Washington D.C.: Department of the Army, 1982.

Patman, Robert G. *The Soviet Union in the Horn of Africa.* Cambridge: Cambridge University Press, 1990.

Wright, Derek. *The Novels of Nuruddin Farah.* Bayreuth, Germany: Bayreuth University, 1994.

Things Fall Apart

by
Chinua Achebe

~

Chinua Achebe was born in 1930 in Ogidi, Anambra State, Nigeria, to an Igbo family of "devout Christian parents" (Achebe, *Morning Yet on Creation Day,* p. 65). He attended a mission school for his primary education and the elite Government College, Umuahia, for high school. At age 18 Achebe joined the first set of students admitted to Nigeria's premier university, known then as University College, Ibadan, from which he graduated with a degree in English. After college he taught high school before joining the Nigerian Broadcasting Corporation, where he rose to the position of Director of External Broadcasting in charge of foreign services. Along with three other novels by Achebe, *Things Fall Apart* was published while he was in broadcasting. Since leaving radio, Achebe has been a university professor in Nigeria, the United Kingdom, and the United States. Universities across the globe have bestowed honorary doctorates on Achebe, mainly for his work as a novelist. Issued in several editions and translated into the world's major languages, *Things Fall Apart* remains the best selling novel of Africa.

Events in History at the Time the Novel Takes Place

Igbo society around 1850. With the exception of a handful of districts, the Igbo people of southeastern Nigeria were one of a few African societies that did not organize into kingdoms. Unlike Nigeria's Yoruba and Hausa peoples—who constructed large, centrally administered em-

---

> **THE LITERARY WORK**
>
> A novel set in a nineteenth-century precolonial Igbo community in southeastern Nigeria; published in English in 1958.
>
> **SYNOPSIS**
>
> An Igbo man's early social success, brought about by his rigid ethos of hard work, bravery, and resilience, is overturned by a mix of personal weakness and rapid social change. Discovering that his clan is unwilling to battle Christianity and colonialism, the man takes his own life.

---

pires—the Igbo organized their communities into federations of independently governed villages.

Each Igbo village consisted of several clusters of blood relations or families:

> First, a person belonged to the smallest social unit known as *uno,* or house. This was a natural family, consisting of a man, his wife or wives, and their children. The second group was the *umunna,* or lineage, composed of a number of related houses. Finally a group of lineages formed a compact village or town, *obodo.*
>
> (Ohadike, p. xxiii)

The "house" or family consisted of a husband, his wives, and his children. The husband, who was usually the family head, lived in an *obi* (hut), in which he received his guests and housed the family deities. Each wife lived in her own house with her unmarried children. When adult males married, they raised their own homestead, usually in the vicinity of the lineage. Adult females, on the other hand, married into other villages, usually within the federated group, where they become members of other "houses." There had to be no blood ties between marriage partners, a principle that was strictly observed. Adjacent villages with shared strategic interests entered into political agreements. The villages formed a federation that developed its own rules, local deities, festivals, and other features of a civil society, as does the federation of villages of Umuofia in *Things Fall Apart.*

Each political unit beyond the house—the lineage, the village, and the federation of villages—was always an association of equals. Hence, at each level there was no titular head whose word carried more legal weight over and above the rest in the population. Apart from reverence for the wisdom that age is universally presumed to confer on the old, each house was equal in the lineage, each lineage in the village, and each village in the federation. This is not to say, of course, that there were no social and political hierarchies brought about either by developments in the historical experience of groups or achievements in other civil endeavors. A group of lineages might, for example, allot an important priesthood to the lineage or village founded by the oldest of the founding fathers, or give a village of the best warriors certain leeway in security matters.

How were these federations of equals governable in the absence of an elaborate apparatus of state? The communities devised what Don Ohadike calls "cross-cutting ties" to enable all citizens to participate directly as members of groups organized around age, gender, and social achievement. These bodies were "the councils of elders, age-groups, councils of chiefs, women's associations, and secret societies" (Ohadike, p. xxiii).

The council of elders typically consisted of the oldest men in lineages, who settled disputes within their lineage. In matters that affected other lineages and villages, elders of the concerned groups met to resolve the issues, with the oldest man presiding over the deliberations. Old men were granted such authority because they were deemed to be wise with experience and the closest to the ancestors. Elders did not rule by fiat: their opinions carried weight because they reached conclusions only after consulting widely among other adults in the family and by deliberating among themselves.

Society was also divided into age-groups or associations of people born within five-year periods. The groups were named for a memorable event around the time of their birth, a practice that still exists. For example, "the Biafran War age-group" is made up of people born during the civil war of 1967-70, in which millions of Igbo joined the secessionist attempt to break away from Nigeria (Ohadike, p. xxv). Each age-group formulated its rules of association, carried out civil works and other maintenance projects assigned it by the larger community, and promoted good citizenship among its members.

Men (and, in some communities, women) of means were recognized for their achievements through initiation into the group of the titled (or chiefs). The chieftaincy titles were marks of recognition and distinction, arranged in a hierarchy of usually three or four steps that became more exclusive as the rank escalated. Their names and hierarchy varied regionally. Most able-bodied and responsible men could attain the lower titles, while the higher titles were conferred very rarely on truly exceptional individuals. Whereas those who could not progress beyond the lowest titles were not highly regarded, those who earned the higher ones received commensurate public recognition at village deliberations. Untitled men might be described in uncharitable and effeminate terms; certainly they were regarded with some scorn by their age-mates.

Each chieftaincy level had its own signs, symbols, and other paraphernalia of distinction. The highest honor was very exclusive. To qualify for consideration a candidate would have attained all the lower titles, amassed substantial wealth, and be the oldest living male in the extended family on his father's side. Titled men were assigned the front row at communal gatherings. They were the only ones allowed to speak at the council of chiefs or the titled, and their words carried great weight at communal deliberations.

The two most significant women's associations were the *otu umu ada* of women of the same lineage and *otu inyeme di* of women who married into a lineage or town. Through these associations, women influenced decision-making processes in their lineage of birth as well as their lineage of marriage. Like their Yoruba counterparts, women also controlled the distributive trade. The women's equivalent of the men's council of chiefs was the *omu* society, a very select group comprised of wealthy people. Because of the prestige that came with being a member of the omu society, it was looked upon with high regard in the communities.

Igbo women decorate a village shrine in Nigeria.

Secret societies held esoteric knowledge about beliefs, oracular wisdom, and divinatory revelations that bound the lineages and villages together. Among them were diviners, oracular interpreters, and priests of communal deities. They made pronouncements on communal rituals, interpreted the wishes of the gods, and issued judgments on matters that affected the whole society, conducting their affairs with the help of secret codes, signs, and symbols to which only the initiated were privy.

Within the broad sociopolitical institutions summarized here, individuals belonged to more than one group and, in effect, participated in multiple ways in the running of the society. Except for the scorned *osu* caste ("untouchables") of people, who dedicated themselves to the service of deities, it was nearly impossible for an individual to be completely left out of all the pressure groups in the community. The opportunities for meaningful participation in running the affairs of the communities were overwhelmingly democratic.

Igbo worldview. The highly inclusive sociopolitical structure reflects fundamental aspects of the Igbo worldview embedded in the religious understanding of the people. In addition to the supreme deity, there are three types of beings in the Igbo pantheon, all of which play significant roles in the lives of characters in *Things Fall Apart*: gods and goddesses, lineage and village oracles, and spirits attached to individuals. Nature and cosmic deities are recognized and worshiped universally. Prominent among them are Ani, the earth goddess; Amadioha, the god of thunder; and Ekwensu, the god of uncertainty. Every village or federation of villages appoints priests and priestesses to lead the sacrifices to these deities and also to ensure that all infractions of their desires—both the commonly known ones and those revealed through divination—are punished. Lineage and village oracles and deities vary, and are propitiated only by the concerned communities who inaugurated their worship in response to unmet needs and wishes that might have arisen at different points in their history. The priests and priestesses of these deities ensure that all communal taboos are observed, all communal calendars are followed, all oracular messages are delivered, and all necessary sacrifices are promptly carried out. The spirit of the individual, roughly a destiny guide (or guardian angel) in English, is called the *chi*. Unlike destiny or a guardian angel, however, the chi is an entity with whom the living can negotiate a life-path. An all-knowing and all powerful entity like destiny, Achebe says, "is abhorrent to the Igbo imagination" (Achebe, *Morning Yet,* p. 96). Each adult has a representative symbol of his/her chi at the family shrine and only the person designated its owner can pour a libation to this embodiment of individual uniqueness.

Trade, religion, and the British Empire. Igbo land is divided by the largest river basin in West Africa, the Niger. The exploration of that river by the British opened up the interior of Igbo territory to the Europeans early in the nineteenth century. Interest in that territory did not develop fully until after the 1833 abolition of the slave trade throughout the British Empire and the discovery of an alternative trade suited to the expansion of industrial production in England. Palm oil was for a long time the main commodity of that trade. Up to about 1875, before the collapse of the price of palm oil, British trading companies (mainly the Royal Niger Company) established trading posts at port towns like Onitsha and Aboh, and traded with Igbo middlemen and women who organized the interior trade and brought goods to the ports. Chiefs of the Niger River communities collected custom duties and other levies from European traders. Their power waned, though, in the 1880s, when the Royal Niger Company introduced gunboats to patrol the waters. This development made the British traders less dependent on the chiefs for the safe passage of their goods and personnel, and more reluctant to pay the chiefs dues and levies. When disputes arose, the gunboats intervened. Under the guise of restoring order, they routed several Igbo communities.

At about the same time that trading posts were being established, Protestant and Catholic missionaries began to set up permanent camps at Onitsha and Asaba—the largest Igbo towns on either side of the Niger River—from where evangelization of much of the Igboland interior would be coordinated. (The Protestant Church Missionary Society [C. M. S.] founded its first mission in Onitsha in 1857.) The initial success of the missions, originally viewed with some bemused suspicion, is partly attributable to the polytheistic religious outlook of the Igbo communities. As some historians explain, Christianity was just asking for another god to be admitted into the already roomy pantheon. Subsequent events showed that Christianity's monotheism would do heavy damage to the other gods. The Christian faith asked that other deities be renounced, and taught radically new views of life—for example, twins, whom the Igbo regarded as evil, should not be abandoned, and even social outcasts like the osu deserve religious fellowship. In fact, besides a new faith, the missionaries

brought with them methods of education, legal procedures, and so forth, which led to considerable friction between the non-Christians and the converts over the latter's utter disregard for very old traditions: "In Obosi, the chiefs accosted Bishop Crowther and protested the tendency of the Christians to ignore the objects of worship of their forefathers, to kill and eat sacred snakes and fishes, and to pull down objects of worship and shrines" (Ohadike, p. xliv). When violent disagreements broke out, the armed forces of Britain's Royal Niger Company intervened on behalf of the Christians and in several cases sacked the protesting communities.

Military interventions on behalf of British merchants and European missionaries in the last two decades of the nineteenth century culminated in formal colonialism at the turn of the century when, as it usually did in its colonies, Britain moved to formalize the economic domination already established by the Royal Niger Company. Assuming control of the area from the company, the British government declared Igboland a "protectorate" and stood ready, with the power of its superior weapons, to quash all Igbo resistance.

In truth, the British did not have an easy time conquering Igboland. Towns and federations of villages employed different means to forestall foreign rule. According to A. E. Afigbo, some groups, like the Western Igbo Anioma people, simply refused to cooperate and fought long, drawn-out wars waged by secret societies of young men generally called *Ekumeku*—roughly translatable as "invisible," "devastating," "whirlwind," and other terms that suggest stealth and overwhelming power (Afigbo, pp. 14-23). The Ekumeku resistance gave way only after many defeats. Other groups, like the Aro and the Afikpo, attempted diplomatic negotiations to keep the British away, resorting to war only after the attempts failed.

The Novel in Focus

Plot summary. *Things Fall Apart* could be alternatively titled "The Life and Times of Okonkwo." Okonkwo dominates the plot in such a way that his achievements, failures, and death illustrate the ethos and major historical questions of his time. The story begins with a report of Okonkwo's victory at the age of 18 over the most famous wrestler in all the nine villages of Umuofia. Over the next 20 years, through sheer willpower and remarkable forcefulness, he amasses considerable wealth, marries three wives, fathers eleven children, takes two titles, and becomes a very skillful warrior and the representative of his home village in the Umuofia judicial council.

Okonkwo's rise to prominence occupies the first part of the narrative. He is born into crass poverty. His father, Unoka, has no farm to speak of, accumulates debts he does not pay, and fails to take care of his one wife and children. He fits into the class called *efulefu*, or worthless men. Unoka's only passion is music. He shuns men's conversation about wars and stories of blood and gore, and dies ignominiously of a liver disease—called the "swelling"—which is abominable to the earth goddess. His remains are left out in the so-called Evil Forest, a place for those who die abominable deaths, such as Unoka's, and for suicides. The belief is that, because of how they died, these people will not become ancestors and their souls will roam the area without release.

Embarking on his life with no worthy inheritance, Okonkwo has to build his barn from scratch by means of the sharecropping system. This arduous way of accumulating wealth, in which the sharecropper receives only a third of the farm proceeds, is made even more difficult because Okonkwo becomes the practical head of his father's family even while the old man is still alive.

In those formative years Okonkwo develops anxieties that will last throughout his life. He cultivates a fondness for everything his father hates: war, the sight of blood, violence, gruffness, and outstanding physical prowess. He also develops a deep fear of being called an *agbala,* or an effeminate man, an image attached to his father. He therefore detests almost everything his father enjoys: music, merriment, folk tales, and outward display of emotions. As a result of this psychological makeup, he is quick to break things, harsh with his wives and children, and sometimes unkind to less successful men. He "ruled his household with a heavy hand. His wives, especially the youngest, lived in perpetual fear of his fiery temper, and so did his little children . . . his life was dominated by fear, the fear of failure and weakness" (Achebe, *Things Fall Apart,* p. 9).

In the course of the novel, Okonkwo's first significant task as a prominent citizen involves Ikemefuna, a boy given to his federation of villages as part of the reparation paid by the Mbaino people, one of whose kinsmen had killed an Umuofia woman. The boy lives with Okonkwo's

family, in Okonkwo's custody. For the three years the boy lives there he is treated as one of the children and becomes a very good friend of Okonkwo's oldest son, Nwoye. The three years follow the regular rhythm of planting and harvesting until the Oracle decides it is time to sacrifice Ikemefuna. During the three years, Ikemefuna has integrated himself fully into the Okonkwo household, his memories of his own homeland dimming. He even calls Okonkwo "father." Okonkwo too has become fond of Ikemefuna because the boy has exerted a manly influenced on Okonkwo's own first son, whom Okonkwo is beginning to suspect of displaying unmanly traits.

On the eve of Ikemefuna's killing, one of the highly esteemed elders, Ogbuefi Ezeudu, advises Okonkwo not to participate in the ritual killing: "That boy calls you father. Do not bear a hand in his death. . . . Yes, Umuofia has decided to kill him. The Oracle of the Hills and Caves has pronounced it. They will take him outside Umuofia as is the custom, and kill him there. But I want you to have nothing to do with it. He calls you his father" (*Things Fall Apart,* p. 40). Okonkwo, however, does not heed the advice.

The next day, after one of the men has dealt him a deadly blow, Ikemefuna runs to Okonkwo crying, "My father, they have killed me!" At this point, Okonkwo, ever afraid "of being thought weak," draws his machete and cuts the boy down (*Things Fall Apart*, p. 43). Okonkwo returns home profoundly depressed.

The first time Okonkwo ventures out of his compound after the sacrifice, he visits his bosom friend, Obierika, who admonishes him that participating in Ikemefuna's killing was a sacrilege and not an act of bravery: "What you have done will not please the Earth. It is the kind of action for which the goddess wipes out whole families" (*Things Fall Apart,* p. 46). In other words, Okonkwo's participation is akin to killing a member of one's family, an unpardonable violation of the earth.

After a while Okonkwo reinserts himself into the village routine. He participates in the betrothal and settlement of the bride price of one of Obierika's daughters. Shortly thereafter, Okonkwo's routine is disturbed again by the agitation caused by the sickness of Ezinma, his favorite child. Okonkwo is not known to fret over any domestic affairs that do not involve some punishment, but Ezinma is a very special child, who always brings out the softer side of Okonkwo. She among all of his children resembles him most. The only child of his "favorite" wife, Ezinma readily senses her father's feelings quicker than anyone else in the household. He often tells himself, "She should have been a boy" (*Things Fall Apart,* p. 44).

Ezinma is also a special child for another reason: she is an *ogbanje*: "a child who repeatedly dies and returns to its mother to be reborn" (*Things Fall Apart,* p. 150).

OGBANJE CHILD

Ogbanje children are believed to be the transformation of some wayward spirits who invade the womb of pregnant women after promising their fellow spirits to die at the time they are able to cause the greatest sorrow to their human parents. Parents identify ogbanje incarnations by mutilating the corpses of suspected infants in the belief that the scars of the disfigurement will show up in the next incarnation. Once a newborn is so confirmed the parents begin to seek means of making the child stay alive and with them rather than dying early. In the case of Okonkwo's favorite child, Ezinma, her mother, Ekwefi, has been unable to stop nine previous incarnations. Ezinma, the tenth child, lives because her parents finally secure the services of a sharp medicine man who is able to make her give up her *iyi-uwa,* the little piece of rock that symbolizes her association with the spirit world.

Okonkwo's unusual concern for this child illustrates the anxieties of ogbanje parents. The ordinarily unruffled Okonkwo springs into the bush to procure herbs for Ezinma and he follows the priestess of the Oracle of the Hills and the Caves about in the middle of the night to assure himself of the child's safety.

Okonkwo again returns to the public sphere soon after the ogbanje scare. This time he is part of the Umuofia court, the *egwugwu,* which consists of nine members, each representing an Umuofia village. The court justices wear elaborate costumes and masks to conceal their identities; as egwugwu, they are "the spirits of the ancestors, just emerged from the earth" (*Things Fall Apart,* p. 63). In spite of these official guises the community knows the voices and bodies behind the masks: "Okonkwo's wives, and perhaps other women as well, might have noticed that the second *egwugwu* had the springy walk of Okonkwo" (*Things Fall Apart,* p. 64).

The court deliberations show the nonadversarial nature of the Umuofia judicial system. After listening to the parties in a domestic dispute, the lead judge says, "We have heard both sides of this case. . . . Our duty is not to blame this man or to praise that, but to settle the dispute" (*Things Fall Apart,* p. 66). He then delivers the verdict, telling the husband to "Go to your in-laws with a pot of wine and beg your wife to return to you"; he likewise directs the woman's family, "If your in-law brings wine to you, let your sister go with him" (*Things Fall Apart,* p. 66).

A terrible life-altering mishap befalls Okonkwo during the funeral of Ezeudu, one of the highly respected old men in the village (the one who warned Okonkwo, to no avail, about not participating in the sacrifice of Ikemefuna). During the gun salute part of the funeral, which is required for great men like Ezeudu, Okonkwo's gun misfires and kills one of the dead man's children. Although the killing is unintentional, the earth goddess has to be appeased. That night Okonkwo leaves Umuofia with his family in tow. The following morning men from Ezeudu's part of town descend on Okonkwo's property in their war gear. As traditions require, "They set fire to his houses, demolished his red walls, killed his animals and destroyed his barn" (*Things Fall Apart,* p. 87). For the next seven years Okonkwo and his family live in Mbanta, his mother's place of origin, where his uncle and other members of her family welcome him and give him land to farm.

Exile tries Okonkwo almost to a breaking point. He loses his prominent status in Umuofia, hears vexing news of drastic cultural and political changes that he cannot control, and sees that his daughters are maturing rapidly in a place in which he would rather not have them marry. The cultural changes descend on Mbanta in the form of a Christian church, which his oldest son, Nwoye, joins against his father's protest, then renounces his ties to Okonkwo: "He is not my father" (*Things Fall Apart,* p. 101). In regard to politics, Okonkwo mostly remains calm in exile, thinking that Mbanta people are not as strong as his own Umuofia people, who surely would have driven away the Christian scourge.

On his return from exile, Okonkwo learns that conditions back home have not in fact lived up to his expectations. He discovers that, besides possessing a church, Umuofia now answers politically to a queen and her representatives. These representatives have a deadly armed force, make new edicts (like outlawing the tradition of abandoning twins in the Evil Forest), build courts, appoint corrupt court messengers, and decide disputes in strange ways—for example, sending convicts to jail. Okonkwo is surprised that his people have not fought the harbingers of the atrocities. His friend informs him that the time for action has passed:

> It is already too late. . . . Our own men and our sons have joined the ranks of the stranger. . . . If we should try to drive out the white men in Umuofia we should find it easy. There are only two of them. But what of our own people who are following their way and have been given power? They would go to Umuru and bring the soldiers . . . .
>
> (*Things Fall Apart,* p. 124)

There is an uneasy coexistence between the way of life encouraged by the colonial government and Christian missionaries on one hand, and Umuofia traditions on the other. In the midst of this uneasy coexistence, an overzealous Christian convert publicly unmasks an egwugwu during the annual celebration of the earth goddess. Led by the nine egwugwu who administer justice in the land, the Umuofia elders attack the church and raze it, against the protests of the Christians. Two days later the white District Commissioner intervenes. He invites six Umuofia leaders, Okonkwo included, to a meeting at his headquarters to discuss the recent troubles. Before the meeting begins, 12 men, all Igbo operatives in the colonial system, approach the Umuofia elders. Before the elders suspect anything, they are handcuffed, fined 200 bags of cowries, and led to jail, where, despite instructions to treat them with dignity, their heads are shaved clean to utterly humiliate them. The men return home after the village pays the fine.

The novel's final tragedy strikes at the community meeting held after the detention. Okonkwo goes to the meeting fuming and pledges to avenge his humiliation, even if the clan resolves not to fight the abomination of colonialism and Christianity in the land. As the meeting progresses, a court messenger arrives to disperse the gathering. Okonkwo, who is sitting at the edge of the circle, confronts the messenger and asks what he wants. The messenger replies with a taunt: "The white man whose power you know too well has ordered this meeting to stop" (*Things Fall Apart,* p. 144). In response, Okonkwo draws his machete and decapitates the messenger, after which the community disperses in confusion. Then and there Okonkwo realizes

Umuofia is not willing to fight along with him. He promptly returns home and hangs himself.

Later, the District Commissioner arrives to arrest Okonkwo for murder, only to find his corpse dangling from a tree. Because suicide offends the earth goddess and is an abominable form of death in Umuofia, Obierika asks the Commissioner's men, who are from another community, to help them cut down the body. "That man was one of the greatest men in Umuofia," says Obierika. "You drove him to kill himself; and now he will be buried like a dog" (*Things Fall Apart,* p. 147).

The unperturbed Commissioner finds in the death more material for the book he is planning to write about the history of African colonial conquest, which he has euphemistically titled "*The Pacification of the Primitive Tribes of the Lower Niger.*" Okonkwo's illustrious, though tragic, life he plans to reduce to "a reasonable paragraph" about "the man who killed a messenger and hanged himself" (*Things Fall Apart,* p. 147).

Okonkwo: a victim of colonialism? The event that causes Okonkwo's suicide is clearly linked to colonialist meddling in Umuofia affairs. Nonetheless, the tragedy is not that simple, despite the blame laid by Obierika on the District Commissioner. Okonkwo's predilections, mainly his one-sided interpretation of true manliness, also contribute to his undoing. In his determination not to be like his socially unsuccessful father, Okonkwo becomes a great farmer, a renowned wrestler, and a highly decorated citizen. But in trying to escape his father's fate, he ends up a very brash man who shows impatience toward less successful men, denies his emotions, and sometimes even violates sacred tradition, as he does in the novel by beating one of his wives during a designated Week of Peace. Had he remembered his father's deathbed advice that "It is more difficult and more bitter when a man fails *alone,*" he probably would have reconsidered his resolve to fight the white man all by himself (*Things Fall Apart,* p. 18). In Umuofia, as in other Igbo communities, no person, however great, is deemed wiser than the community. In the saddest irony of the story Okonkwo's body will, like his father's, be abandoned in the Evil Forest.

Writing the novel in African English. The cultural context evoked in the story of Okonkwo's rise and fall is not the only feature that distinguishes it as African. *Things Fall Apart* is the first best-selling novel in English in which African characters speak dignified language. It is also perhaps the first in which the narrative voice is attentive to the speech rhythms of its African characters. To the narrator, Okonkwo's fame grows "like a bush-fire in the harmattan," Ikemefuna's rapid growth resembles that of "a yam tendril in the rainy season," the passage of time is measured in "moons and seasons," Obierika's crowded compound during his daughter's marriage ceremony is "as busy as an anthill," and a white man's bicycle is "an iron horse" to the people of Abame, who have never seen one like it (*Things Fall Apart*, pp. 3, 37, 38, 78, 97). All these similes are drawn from local experience, local fauna and flora, and local observations. The harmattan wind that blows over West Africa from October to February dries up vegetation, and extensive wildfires are not uncommon during that season; yams grow luxuriantly during the June and July rains; calendars once revolved around yam cultivation seasons; and thousands of termites living together in colonies make anthills a very busy place.

The novel is also unique in its representation of the speeches of the Igbo people. The elders speak with dignity, they consider the effect of their words before they utter them, and they use proverbs profusely to lend the authority of tradition to their words. Their use of proverbs especially enables the non-English speaking characters to sound authentic in English. The narrative shows that, next to the caffeine-suffused kola nut—he who brings kola brings life [to a conversation], says one proverb—the proverb is the great facilitator of speech. In Igbo culture, as the narrative admits, "proverbs are the palm-oil with which words are eaten" (*Things Fall Apart*, p. 5). Through proverbs speakers appeal to customary precedence ("Eneke the bird says that since men have learned to shoot without missing, he has learned to fly without perching"), state social and philosophical observations ("A child cannot pay for its mother's milk"), and refer to various traditions (*Things Fall Apart*, pp. 16, 117).

The story even tries to capture the dilemma of explaining Okonkwo's rise and fall in two contradictory proverbs, which reflect the Igbo conception of personality: "When a man says yes his chi says yes also" and "A man could not rise beyond the destiny of his chi" (*Things Fall Apart*, pp. 19, 92). The first saying suggests that destiny is self-made, while the second implies that destiny can set the limit to achievement. Okonkwo follows the letter and spirit of the first, but the validity of the second seems to sneak up on him when he least expects it. The resolution lies in another proverb that reflects what Achebe describes as the pervasive duality of Igbo thought, which seems to elude Okonkwo: "Wherever Something stands, Something Else will stand beside it" (Achebe, *Morning Yet*, p. 94). To his peril Okonkwo seems not to know that hard work must be relieved by leisure, gruffness by amiability, rigidity by softness, masculinity by femininity.

Sources and literary context. The main literary instigators of the novel are the British colonialist novels of Africa, whose black characters, in contrast to their European counterparts, live out the white people's racial imaginings. Achebe's famously controversial essay on Joseph Conrad's *Heart of Darkness,* "Colonialist Criticism," shows how such narrative texts depict Africans as beings on whom the contemporary environment has no effect or meaning. They are portrayed as wonderfully barbaric simpletons full of inexplicable superstitions. Their manner of speech is childlike, their worship pathologically heathenish. They seem incapable of deep moral introspection. Critics often refer to the title character of Joyce Cary's *Mister Johnson* as the best realized of such depictions. In contrast to such colonialist representations, *Things Fall Apart* shows religiosity instead of wanton paganism, the characters utter dignified speeches, the society is organized on rational principles, and deep moral conundrums routinely confront the characters.

Events in History at the Time the Novel Was Written

Prelude to independence. In 1958 all African countries, as part of the global decolonization process that took center stage after the end of World War II, were agitating for political independence. Restoring the cultural glories of the colonized people was a major theme of the independence movement. Nationalist leaders, most of whom received their formal liberal education in Western institutions, were appalled by the destruction of traditional values, thought systems, economic production, and cultural institutions that had been wrought by colonialism and by missionaries under the guise of enlightenment and Christian salvation.

On the cultural and ideological front of the independence struggle, artists worked to foreground the precolonial ethos of their people in order to show that, contrary to received wisdom, European civilization and Christianity have not been unmitigated boons to colonized Africans. To use an Achebe expression, the artists looked back to "try and find out where we went wrong, where rain began to beat us" (Achebe, *Morning Yet,* p. 44). This backward glance revealed to the artists that Africans did not learn of God only when Christians came; nor did their idea of governance and society arise in colonialism: "I would be quite satisfied," says Achebe, "if my novels (especially the ones I set in the past) did no more than teach my readers that their past—with all its imperfections—was not one long night of savagery from which the first Europeans acting on God's behalf delivered them" (Achebe, *Morning Yet,* p. 45).

No sphere of life was left untouched by the independence movement. Indigenous churches spread, and churches with foreign affiliations Africanized their liturgies and personnel. Educational institutions reexamined their founding philosophies and reformed their curricula to teach native topics and issues. Individuals changed their Christian names to indigenous ones. Even countries changed their names—Gold Coast, for example, became Ghana. In the French-speaking countries serious attempts at fathoming the essential character of the African way of life resulted in the creation of a philosophy of *négritude,* or the condition of being black.

One of the ironies of the kind of cultural nationalism that inspired the publication and wide acceptance of *Things Fall Apart* is that the text's targets—that is, aspects of the European disruption of African routine—also made possible criticism of the novel. A good number of the cultural critics of Achebe's generation are Christians educated in mission schools. Many of them are monogamists. Most live in cities and work in modern institutions. Their everyday paths do not often cross those of the rural dwellers to whom the precolonial ethos extolled in cultural nationalism still means much. At the time of independence, Igbo society, like that of other African communities, had been changed permanently: traditional shrines existed often in the shadow of huge cathedrals and mosques, traditional rule carried less authority than parliamentary procedures, local laws and customs were being overtaken by national legislation, monogamy had more legal authority than polygamy—all of which reflected not the weakness of traditional practices but the reality of the legacy of close to a century of colonial rule.

Reviews. Upon its release *Things Fall Apart* received Western reviews describing the novel in terms that appear in some cases to reflect the biases of the reviewer's own society. While Pheobe

A group of Catholic boys march in procession in Nigeria.

Adams in the *Atlantic* praised *Things Fall Apart*'s success in conveying the "stately rhythm" of village life "that has come down through the centuries," the *Christian Science Monitor* complimented the novel's expert portrayal of "primitive tribal life" (Adams and *Christian Science Monitor* in Davison, p. 2). In either case, the reviewers acknowledged the as-yet-unparalleled view from inside Igbo life that was imparted by the novel. "Written with quiet dignity," said *Kirkus Reviews,* "that builds to a climax of tragic force, this book about the dissolution of an African tribe, its traditions and values, represents a welcome departure from the familiar 'Me, white brother' genre" (*Kirkus Reviews* in Davison, p. 2). "Patterns of feeling and attitudes of mind," adds the *Times Literary Supplement,* "appear clothed in a distinctively African imagery, written neither up nor down" (*Times Literary Supplement,* p. 341). With similar admiration and a perception of the novel's landmark significance, a reviewer in *Black Orpheus* considered its documentary as well as it artistic import: "This is a piece of history; the reader feels the calamity on every page of the impending collapse of an ancient, self-reliant, purposeful and organised society in which the individual personality is not an end in itself but a contribution to the whole. . . . This was not one village nor even one tribe, but . . . Africa" (Speed, p. 52).

—Adeleke Adeeko

Things Fall Apart

For More Information

Achebe, Chinua. *Morning Yet on Creation Day.* London: Heinemann, 1975.

———. *Things Fall Apart.* London: Heinemann, 1958.

Afigbo, A. E., "Patterns of Igbo Resistance to British Conquest." *Tarikh* 4, no. 3 (1973): 14-23.

Davison, Dorothy P., ed. *Book Review Digest 1959.* New York: H. W. Wilson, 1960.

Henderson, Richard N. *The King in Every Man: Evolutionary Trends in Onitsha Ibo Society and Culture.* New Haven, Conn.: Yale University Press, 1972.

Innes, C. L. *Chinua Achebe.* Cambridge: Cambridge University Press, 1990.

Innes, C. L., and Bernth Lindfors, eds. *Critical Perspectives on Chinua Achebe.* Washington, D.C.: Three Continents Press, 1978.

Ogbaa, Kalu. *Gods, Oracles, and Divination: Folkways in Chinua Achebe's Novels.* Trenton, N.J.: Africa World Press, 1992.

Ohadike, Don C. "Igbo Culture and History." In *Things Fall Apart,* by Chinua Achebe. Portsmouth: Heinemann, 1996.

Review of *Things Fall Apart,* by Chinua Achebe. *Times Literary Supplement,* 20 June 1958, p. 341.

Speed, Diana. Review of *Things Fall Apart,* by Chinua Achebe. *Black Orpheus* 5 (May 1959): 52.

Valley Song

by
Athol Fugard

Born in 1932, Athol Fugard grew up to become the most renowned playwright of South Africa. His career spans four decades of the turbulent history of that racially divided country, during which his plays have made powerful pleas for racial equality and harmony in a land torn by intolerance, resentment, and discrimination. Fugard was the child of a "mixed marriage" of sorts; although his parents were both white, his father was of British descent while his mother was Afrikaner (refers to whites primarily of Dutch descent). Born in the Karoo, the isolated, semidesert farmland in which *Valley Song* is set, Fugard was raised in Port Elizabeth. Despite brief stints in larger cities, and despite worldwide fame, Port Elizabeth has remained his home. His adult years have seen the dismantling of the apartheid policy of racial segregation in South Africa. Fugard has since continued to comment on a political scene that, though more equal, is not much less volatile. Against the backdrop of political change, *Valley Song* examines a family's intergenerational dynamics.

Events in History at the Time of the Play

Apartheid legacy. *Valley Song* is less overtly political than much of Fugard's work: only one speech by the impassioned young heroine, Veronica, directly addresses the political situation in South Africa. Nevertheless, the play cannot be properly understood without some background in the decades-long system of racial

---

THE LITERARY WORK

A one-act play set in the Karoo region of South Africa in the postapartheid era; first produced in Johannesburg, South Africa, in 1995; published in English in 1995.

SYNOPSIS

A coloured (mixed-race) farmer confronts his granddaughter's desire to leave their isolated land for the brighter future of Johannesburg.

---

oppression that ended only a few years prior to the period in which *Valley Song* is set.

Like almost every African country, South Africa is ethnically diverse; what sets South Africa apart are how different its major ethnic groups are. Among its oldest inhabitants are the Khoi and the San (sometimes called "Bushmen"), who are often grouped together as the Khoisan. Later arrivals to the area, also of African origin, include various Bantu-speaking peoples, such as the Zulu, who are taller and darker-skinned than the San or the Khoi. While the Bantu-speakers have numerous subdivisions, the real source of South Africa's ethnic diversity—and difficulty—is the centuries-old influx of Europeans. In the sixteenth century, the expansion of European trade led to the formation of trading posts on South Africa's coast. Europeans from many nations, but most particularly the Netherlands, Germany, and France, immigrated to provide labor, to fight, and to trade. Thousands stayed. Over time, the white immigrants lost a sense of connection to their European birthplaces. Adopting South Africa as their homeland, they developed their own language, Afrikaans (evolved from Dutch), and their own cultural identity. They began to view themselves as Africans—in their own language, as *Afrikaners*. They intermarried with indigenous peoples, helping to found the "coloured," or mixed-race, population treated in Fugard's play.

THE LAWS OF APARTHEID

Apartheid was outlined in several pieces of legislation between 1950 and 1953, whose goal was to severely limit the right of free movement by blacks (that is, Africans, coloureds, and Indians). Most important among the laws were:

Population Registration Act (1950): This act required a person to register his or her race at birth. The essential division was between white and black. Black was broken down into coloured (mixed race); Indian (descendants of workers and slaves brought to the country by the British); and Bantu (Africans), who were further subdivided into specific African peoples. "To determine borderline cases, bureaucrats scrutinized fingernails, peered at nostrils, and tested the curliness of people's hair . . ." (Mallaby, p. 5). Everything about people's lives depended on what their registration papers said in the box labeled "race."

Group Areas Act (1950): This act "racialized" the terrain of the country, establishing places where members of each race were allowed to live. About 86 percent of the land was designated "white," while Africans were confined to crowded, poverty-stricken "homelands," which they could leave, but only with permission, to work in white homes and businesses.

Bantu Education Act (1953): This act limited education of Africans by Christian missions; most education would be provided by government-run schools. Needless to say, the schooling provided was limited in scope. While colonial education elsewhere in Africa aimed at creating a native elite to help run the colony, education for blacks in South Africa aimed only to create a servile, obedient class fit for domestic or factory work.

Less sweeping edicts governed smaller aspects of life. Laws were enacted making sexual relations between races illegal and segregating public places. Above all, though, apartheid rested on the three pillars of 1) registration, 2) land use, and 3) education that were embodied in these three laws.

Thus, South Africa experienced colonialism in a unique way. Its initial European presence was not limited to a few hundred settlers and traders who hoped to profit from the continent's riches while maintaining their allegiance to a European home. Afrikaners intended to stay; indeed, they felt they had nowhere else to go. To make matters worse, the Afrikaners themselves became a colonized people. In 1795 the ascendant British took control of the colony from the Dutch East India Company. Over the next century, English immigrants settled alongside the Afrikaners. Although both parties agreed on the racial oppression of the black population, they agreed on very little else. Tension between them led to the South African War of 1899 to 1902 to decide who would rule the country—the British or the Boers (the label then for Afrikaners, from the Dutch word for "farmer"). The British won the war, then in 1910 united their holdings to the former Afrikaner republics, establishing the Union of South Africa.

Although still technically a colony, the Union of South Africa had internal self-government. Its first order of business was to insure that the country would be governed by whites only. Since they were vastly outnumbered by blacks (meaning Africans, coloureds, and Indians), any sort of democracy would be inimical to white interests. To counteract this danger, the white rulers of the country developed a system called *apartheid*, the Afrikaans word for "separateness." The system rested on the notion that South African society consisted of distinct nations, each of which must live in its own area, or homeland, and that Africans should be able to enter the white homeland only temporarily, as workers. Coloureds would be subject to the same laws as Africans, without ever receiving their own separate homeland.

Apartheid guaranteed the dominance of the white minority in South Africa, but it also guaranteed decades of isolation from the world community and persistent racial unrest at home. South Africa's Africans could not help but note the rising tide of nationalism that was liberating countries across the African continent, and, although the task was much more difficult in their own corner of the continent, they too waged war against the forces of inequality. Aided by other African countries and by leaders around the world, black South Africans agitated for their freedom. Amazingly, apartheid was dismantled more or less peacefully, despite decades of racial violence that seemed to augur violent rebellion.

White members of the South African Conservative Party demonstrate against the release of Nelson Mandela from prison.

By the early 1990s President F. W. de Klerk and his National Party had embarked on a campaign of racial equalization that culminated in the 1994 elections in which, for the first time, the black majority was allowed to vote. Nelson Mandela, whom the South African government had sentenced to life imprisonment in the early 1960s (see **"The Rivonia Trial Speech,"** also covered in *African Literature and Its Times*), was elected President, and the country seemed well on the road to racial harmony.

As Fugard's play reveals, however, South Africa's profound political changes were not instantly matched by changes in the economic and social spheres. Although Africans were now "free," they were still poor; and though whites were no longer solely in power, they still held the great majority of the country's wealth. Black labor unions, political parties, and assistance groups fought against the economic hardships that beset the majority of blacks, but the institutional apparatus of capitalism and private property meant that wealth did not change hands quickly. While the abolition of pass laws and other such policies signified the end of sanctioned police brutality and a loosening of the oppressive state bureaucracy, centuries of unequal development could hardly be reversed in a few short years.

The coloureds: race without identity. By the terms of the Population Registration Act of 1950, a coloured person was defined as "not a White person and not a Bantu [African]" (Van der Ross, p. 5). Islamic Malays brought from Asia to work in South Africa, slaves from Angola, Bantu-speaking peoples, whites of European descent, and even coloureds themselves contributed to the racial mixture, blurring the boundaries that apartheid sought to establish. In a nation obsessed with racial identity, the question of what to do with people of mixed races gave the central government a great deal of trouble. In themselves, South African coloureds reminded the apartheid government of what it most wanted to avoid: free racial mixing. For their part, coloureds received slight benefits, but substantial hindrances, because of their status "between" whites and Africans. They were closer to European culture, and as a result were afforded better schooling and slightly wider opportunities than most Africans. But they were shackled by the same racial oppression as the darker-skinned Africans, and were often unable to find employment.

Coloureds comprise about 10 percent of South Africa's population: about half the percentage of whites, and a small fraction compared to the African majority. Most coloured people live in Cape Province, which includes the Karoo. Historically, the coloured population has experienced a pendulum of freedom and repression. Under Dutch rule from 1652 to 1795, the Khoisan peoples had only limited rights in the Cape Colony. During this time, some whites took Khoisan wives and the coloured population began to form. A number of these people converted to Christianity and passed into white society. Other remained part of the permanent underclass with few rights or privileges.

With the arrival of British colonial officials and missionaries at the turn of the nineteenth century, coloureds were treated a little more equally. Britain was committed to the fight against slavery across the continent, and this commitment affected their administration of the Cape Colony. The pass law system was revoked, and in 1828 Ordinance 50 revoked all limitations on the movement and political freedom of people of mixed race. Then came the abolition of slavery in 1834. Ordinance 50 and the end of slavery led to two separate migrations. The smaller saw great numbers of coloureds and freed slaves moving to cities. The more significant migration was the exodus of Afrikaners, or Boers. The Afrikaner Great Trek began in 1836. Upset at Ordinance 50, and with British rule in general, great numbers of Afrikaners traveled inland to form the Orange Free State and Transvaal. Needless to say, few coloured people joined this trek. Back in Britain's Cape Colony, coloureds enjoyed unparalleled liberty: until 1910, "no distinction was made between Whites and Coloureds in the constitutional development of the Cape and the granting of political rights to citizens" (Cilliers, p. 61).

The joining of British to Afrikaner holdings in 1910 to form the Union of South Africa began a steady erosion of coloured political rights. Coloured people in the Cape retained their rights, but those in the former Afrikaner areas of Transvaal and the Orange Free State had none. Later, in 1948, when the National Party came to power, its leaders began implementing apartheid immediately. Politically, this meant that only in the Cape Province were coloured men allowed to vote—and only for white candidates, since all other races were barred from government. There was an appointed Council of Coloured Affairs, composed for the most part of coloured people, but this council merely advised on crucial issues regarding their constituents. Aside from political discrimination, the coloured population suffered other disadvantages. Residence zones restricted where they could live, for example; pass laws denied them freedom of movement.

In the main, coloured people are oriented toward Europe. The product of sexual unions between Europeans and peoples of Africa, almost all coloureds were born in the shadows of the white culture, which was dominant politically in the coastal areas of the Cape. Their proximity to Europeans tended to erase the coloured connection to other cultures; while Malays, Indians, and Khoisan could maintain their cultures in isolation from Europeans, coloureds generally assumed a Caucasian cultural focus. Thus, the majority speak Afrikaans or English; most are members of the (Afrikaner) Dutch Reformed Church; and most restrict themselves to monogamous marriages. Despite these likenesses, Afrikaners developed a disdain for coloureds and harbored stereotypic images of them as deficient in intelligence, energy, and the like.

After the onset of apartheid in 1948, coloureds became subject to the same discriminatory laws as Africans. In 1966 under the Group Areas Act, their main community, District Six in Cape Town, was declared an all-white zone, as were other areas. "The piecemeal eviction of coloureds from Cape Town's suburbs caused much individual suffering as families were driven to desolate new townships on the sands of the Cape flats" (Ross, p. 137). A decade later, in 1976, blacks demonstrated in Soweto because half their school subjects were to be taught in the Afrikaans language. The police shot to death a 13-year-old African in the incident, after which violence ensued, killing at least 494 Africans, 75 coloureds, 1 Indian, and 5 whites by early 1977 (Thompson, p. 213).

After Soweto, coloureds became more involved in casting off apartheid, as did Africans and Indians. Defiance began to replace the deference customarily paid to whites. In 1984 the government tried to placate the coloureds and Indians with a new constitution mandating three racially separate houses of Parliament: a House of Assembly (178 whites); a House of Representatives (85 coloureds), and a House of Delegates (45 Indians). For the first time coloureds had a say in national politics, but few of them were won over by the ploy. In fact, many coloureds criticized those who participated in the new arrangement. In the end, the attempt to placate the coloured community with their own house of Parliament failed.

The walls of apartheid began to come tumbling down. In 1986 the government repealed

The semidesert farmland of the Karoo.

pass laws, and in 1991 it repealed the Population Registration and Group Areas Acts. This led to the aforementioned 1994 election of Nelson Mandela as President. Overall the whites' National Party received just 20 percent of the vote. However, in the Western Cape Province, in which the Karoo of the play is located, the results were atypical. Here the National Party emerged victorious, winning on the strength of not only the white vote but also 67 percent of the coloured vote (Ross, p. 196). Mandela's party, the African National Congress, "lost heavily in the countryside," where Fugard's play is set; "fear of the ANC as godless and violent . . . worries about jobs . . . and habits of deference all played their part" (Ross, p. 196).

The Great Karoo. Between the coastal regions of the Cape Colony and the Orange River lies a large, elevated plateau of desiccated shrubs and baked red soil. Iron-rich rocks in isolated hillocks called *koppjies* bake in the unforgiving sun. South Africans label this region the Karoo. The Khoisan pastoralists and hunters who were the first to wander this plain called it "Garob" or "Caro," which brought together the senses of "dry," "lifeless," and "infertile." These are still the primary adjectives used to describe the Karoo, although they are not perfectly accurate. The region is indeed an arid semidesert—in fact, some

parts have gone as many as a dozen years without a drop of rain. But the Karoo is not incapable of supporting life. After one of the unpredictable desert rains, new life blossoms everywhere and the Karoo turns green. Such times are short-lived, but the plain's inhabitants have adapted to difficult circumstances. One of the first things to draw Afrikaners to the plain was the hunting: herds of zebra, springbok, and other hoofed creatures were preyed upon by lions, leopards, and other carnivores. As late as 1896 there was a massive *trekbokke*, the spring migration of springbok. However, hunting and human encroachment have now driven the great herds from the Karoo.

Domestic herds have taken their place. Economically, the Karoo is known primarily for its herds of sheep, which provide nearly all of the country's wool and mutton. The leggy, fat-tailed sheep herded by the original Khoisan peoples are still present, joined by large flocks of merino and angora, descendents of livestock imported by European settlers. The wool industry employs well over a million people in South Africa, and certainly gives the lie to the idea that the Karoo is lifeless. Farming also exists, if on a minor scale compared to the importance of sheep herding. The Verwoerd Dam on the Orange River (at the northern border of the Karoo) has helped irrigate the land, which grows pumpkins, potatoes, and beets. In the valleys of the little mountain ranges that dot the Karoo, conditions are more favorable; although, as Fugard's play makes clear, life is still not easy, especially for a poor coloured farmer.

Culturally, the Karoo resembles other semi-arid regions the world over in that it is dismissed by the majority but cherished by those who are charmed by its bleak beauty. On the map, it appears as a scattering of small towns, split by the railroad that runs from the coast to the central Karoo town of Victoria West. Few of these towns have populations in excess of 30,000 (or even 3,000) people. The population is primarily Afrikaner and coloured. There is one sure route to wealth in the Karoo—sheep—but the majority, even of Afrikaners, remain relatively poor and close to the land. Even after the decline of apartheid, social relations have been slow to change. Whites still own most farmland, and towns are divided into two sections: the central area for whites, and a separate "location" for coloured people. Options for coloureds in the region remain limited: farm as a sharecropper on white land, or work in a white home or business. With the elimination of pass laws in 1986, the movement of coloured people was much facilitated. Migration to other areas of South Africa promised more opportunity and less poverty. Thus conditions have fostered an increase in the number of young coloured people who, like Veronica in the play, are eager to escape the limitations of the Karoo. One would expect that others like her have also been similarly opposed by older family members who do not wish to see their way of life die out.

The Play in Focus

Plot summary. *Valley Song* is a slight play. Its scant 50 pages feature only three characters (two played by the same actor) and a handful of scenes that blend into one another and span an uncertain, but relatively short, period of time. The play's focus is on character and psychology; it achieves a delicate drama in the universal tension between young and old, and the painful choices made necessary by the contradictory pulls of dreams and tradition.

The play begins as "Author," a man closely identified with Fugard himself, holds out a handful of pumpkin seeds to the audience. He introduces the setting—a valley of the Sneeuburg Mountains in the Karoo—and the main character, Abraam Jonkers. Jonkers, called "ou Buks"

by the residents of the village where he lives, and "Oupa" by his teenaged granddaughter Veronica, served in the British Army in World War II and has spent his subsequent days as a tenant farmer, tilling his few *akkers* (acres) for a fairly meager living. As the play opens, his landlords (symbolically called the Landmans) have died out or abandoned the property, and Buks farms in peace.

The Author begins singing a song that an Italian prisoner-of-war once taught Buks. The song is "La donne e mobile," which Buks renders "Lae donder mobili." In the course of singing, the Author takes on the role of Buks. Veronica tells him it is time for lunch. They eat and discuss various issues: his wartime experiences, her songs and his. They are very close: all they have is each other, for her mother is dead, as is his wife. Finally Buks admits that he is worried: a white man came by to consider purchasing the property. If he does, he will certainly upset the routine of the Jonkers household. He may even force the old man off his land. Veronica tells him not to worry; many whites have inspected the property, and none have bought it. But Buks feels this man is different; he has already come to see the place three times.

To change the subject, Buks asks Veronica what mischief she has been up to that morning. Instead of diverting him, this reminds Buks of another major worry: Veronica's approaching maturity. The girl complains that she hasn't been up to any mischief, because there is no mischief to be had in the village of Nieu-Bethesda. Bored and longing for adventure and romance, Veronica complains that nothing ever happens. Rather futilely, Buks describes the flowering of pumpkins from seeds as a miracle: "Every year, in these akkers . . . thousands of miracles. And you say nothing happens here?" (Fugard, *Valley Song,* p. 12). But it's hopeless. What Veronica wants is to be a famous singer. Buks points out that she already sings, to the congregation at church and to God. Veronica replies with a song about the Railway Bus, which she hopes will take her to big cities and faraway places.

This song upsets Buks terribly. Prodded by Veronica, he finally tells her the story of her mother, his only child. When she was not much older than Veronica is now, Caroline fell in love with a young man from the village, Harry Ruiters. Ruiters was a troublemaker, a thief, and a fighter. Caroline ran away with him, and did not contact her parents for a year. Then a hospital in Johannesburg called: Caroline was very sick. Buks's wife went to her daughter, and returned with her granddaughter, the infant Veronica. Caroline had died in childbirth.

This story mends the rift in the family, at least for the moment. But when Veronica "leaves" (actually she just retreats upstage), Buks gives a long speech, addressed to his dead wife, in which he vents his frustrations and fears that his life will close with another separation, another tragedy.

After this speech, Veronica takes center stage. Addressing the audience, she describes her "best friend," an alcoholic white woman named Mrs. Jooste. Mrs. Jooste doesn't even know Veronica, but the girl loves her, because Mrs. Jooste watches television all night, with the curtains open. Veronica likes to stand on an apple box and watch along, mimicking the poses and gestures of the singers on the screen. As she pantomimes this procedure, she gets a round of applause from the Author. This startles her, and they begin talking. Veronica tells him her dream of becoming a famous singer, and he counters with the realistic, adult fact that dreams do not always come true. But Veronica will not hear of it. In her mind, to desire something intensely is to guarantee that it will eventually be yours. She has nothing but pity for people with modest dreams, like her friend Alfred Witbooi, who hopes to get a job so he can buy a used bicycle. As this conversation ends, the Author recites Psalm 24: "The Earth is the Lord's and the fullness thereof" (*Valley Song*, p. 25). After this, he changes back into Buks, who sings a hymn in Afrikaans with Veronica.

Time passes. The white man who visited the Landman estate has decided to purchase it, news that reaches Buks and Veronica from the town gossip. Buks is devastated; Veronica, furious. The fear of losing their livelihood prompts the only overtly political discussion in the play. Veronica asks why the country had an election if not to give power back to the people. She wants to write a letter to the government asking for land reform: she has heard that this is happening in other parts of the country. But Buks wants none of it: "Every time they stick their nose in your business you got to pay something" (*Valley Song*, p. 27). He has a more modest plan, to approach the white man and ask to be allowed to continue farming. Besides, if the white man moves in, Buks believes, Veronica can find work tending his house. When he tells his granddaughter this, it reignites their earlier argument; there is nothing in the world Veronica wants less than to do housework for a living. She says as much, and Buks takes this as

an insult to her grandmother, who tended the Landman house her whole life. He scolds his granddaughter into silence.

At this moment Buks returns to the role of Author and delivers a lengthy speech. The Author assumes the persona of the white buyer, then reveals that he decided to purchase the land not *before* but *because* Buks came to him begging to continue farming. The Author also reveals a private vision of a life spent in contented seclusion, a vision that made him decide to purchase the land on the spot. But, he asks, does he really

LAND REFORM IN POST-APARTHEID SOUTH AFRICA

When Veronica plans to write the government asking for land reform, she is not simply indulging in a young woman's fantasy. In 1994 the African National Congress took over the reins of government, intending to rectify the horrible inequality by which whites controlled 86 percent of the nation's land. Establishing the Reconstruction and Development Program (RDP), the ANC gave the RDP the task of managing land reform. It adopted three goals: to secure the position of poor tenant farmers on the land they rented from whites; to restore land stolen from Africans by whites under apartheid; and, most ambitiously, to redistribute 30 percent of the land to nonwhites and to the poor before the year 2000. So far these goals have not been met. The government has been torn between two objectives—eradicating the injustices of apartheid, and avoiding violence or other disruptions to the peaceful transition of power. In light of these objectives, the RDP has been unwilling to force white landowners to give up their land or the property rights they had under apartheid. Also the group employs a number of the same bureaucrats who ran the land system under apartheid (in order to avoid "brain drain" of experienced politicians); not surprisingly, some of these bureaucrats have been slow to enforce the rights of tenant farmers, or to rule in favor of Africans with claims to land owned by whites. The goal of 30 percent redistribution has been the greatest failure so far. The government policy—to match willing sellers with willing buyers—has resulted only in a miniscule transfer, not even one-tenth of the hoped-for 30 percent. Thus Veronica's criticism of the slow process of change is well-founded. When the white Author arrives to buy the Landman house, Buks must bow to his will just as apartheid would have required, begging for the right to scratch out a subsistence on soil he has spent a lifetime working.

own the land? Even if the government gives him the title, is it not Buks's land by the mere fact that he has worked it his whole life and his father worked alongside the first Landman to build the house? This speech is followed, and countered, by Veronica's impassioned soliloquy in which she admits that she hates the land. If the Author suggested that people make the land theirs by working it, Veronica believes the land makes people its slaves. To be a farmer is to become a mere extension of the earth, its perpetually solicitous servant. And she cannot stomach that prospect for herself.

A conversation follows between Veronica and the Author. As Veronica takes her position outside Mrs. Jooste's window, the Author tells her to stop; the old woman has died. They return to the topic of dreams. The Author is explicit about the fact that dreaming big means taking a big risk—if you let yourself dream, and then fail, you are likely to be permanently embittered. Again Veronica refuses to listen. The scene shifts, and she sings to imaginary white people, soliciting donations. Now the stage is set for the final confrontation between the ambitious girl and her weary grandfather.

She walks into the scene as Buks washes himself. She tells him what has just happened at the Post Office. An old white man, Brigadier Pelser, attempted to use the Post Office after it had closed, only to be turned away by the female clerk. He insisted that she serve him, but she refused, saying, "This is not the old South Africa, Brigadier" (*Valley Song*, p. 38). Veronica learned something else at the Post Office: that her grandfather had collected a letter addressed to her. She asks for it, and he hands it over, already opened. He knows it is from her friend in Johannesburg, and he wants to know what it says, but he is unable to find anyone capable of reading it. He tells Veronica to read it to him. At first she lies, pretending it is a simple hello. But soon she breaks down and admits that this friend has agreed to give her a place to stay in the city.

Buks is furious. He tells her that her mother was a thief, stealing his money so she could run away to the city. Veronica says she has her own money; she's been singing for change in the streets of the village. She shows him this money, and he throws it into the darkness. He simply will not let her leave.

The next Sunday in church, Veronica refuses to sing, nor does she pray. Buks attempts to console her with a vision of God: if she can sing to God, no one else should matter. But Veronica is

disconsolate—if she cannot leave the valley, she will never sing again.

The Author returns and delivers a long explanation of Buks's feelings. He is terrified about letting Veronica go, scared of change, and puzzled by the failure of life to give him the simple things he asks for. He feels he has provided abundantly for Veronica, and he cannot understand where he went wrong or why she would want to leave. At the end of this speech, Veronica returns, and the Author becomes Buks again. He mistakes her for her mother, and when this moment of confusion has passed, Veronica tells the simple truth: if he tries to force her to stay, she will run away. She compares her own life to the miracle of pumpkin seeds he discussed earlier. When they blossom, they must follow their destiny. So it is with her—she is blossoming, and has no choice. Reluctantly, and almost with a broken heart, he accepts what he cannot change. On her way out of town, she encounters the Author. He admits that, even when he opposed her on the issue of dreams, he understood her position. Now he gives her his blessing, even as he concedes that a selfish part of him wanted her to stay, and the village to remain just as it was when he first found it.

Veronica leaves, and the Author discloses that the next spring, Buks began the planting as he always had. The land has its consolations; it will always remain, even when people fall apart.

Afrikaner religion. There are two types of tunes in *Valley Song*: the impromptu effusions of Veronica, which express her desire for faraway places, and the hymns (sung in Afrikaans) that Veronica and her grandfather sing together. The former belong to the future; the latter, to the past. Specifically, this past is that of the Dutch Reformed Church, the roots of which go back to the Protestant Reformation in Europe, led by Martin Luther and, later, John Calvin. The Netherlands was largely converted to Reformation Protestantism by the mid-1500s, and the settlers that came from there to South Africa were mostly members of the Dutch Reformed Church.

Theologically the Dutch Reformed Church is Calvinist—that is, it professes that God decided at the moment of creation who was saved and who was damned. Calvinism is widely held to go hand-in-hand with rigid piety and a distrust of secular knowledge and pleasures, but this reputation is not wholly accurate. Many Calvinist groups have been as pleasure-loving and contented as any other people. It is nevertheless true that Calvinism seems like a natural fit for the bleak landscapes of the Karoo; indeed, the Karoo town Calvinia is named for the Swiss theologian. Another influence on the Dutch Reformed Church was pietism, the "heart religion" brought to South Africa by some clergymen. Pietism stresses simplicity, clarity of feeling, and a continual sense of duty to God. Like Calvinism, it tends to distrust matters of the flesh, and to flourish among people removed from cities or other centers of power.

Fugard dramatizes some of the consolations of this type of religion in the piety of Old Buks, for whom God is a continual presence in the natural world of the Karoo. God's power makes the flowering of a simple pumpkin seed a mighty miracle. To Buks, all the austerity and harshness of the Karoo climate are beautiful because they are informed by God's love. Similarly the simple life that Buks wants to live with Veronica is as exalted as the life of a king (or a famous singer), because what really matters is not one's social position, but one's love of God. More than once he attempts to console Veronica by saying that it was God who gave her the power to sing, and only God is an important audience. In his own case, the simple, straightforward rules of Christianity help Buks through all of life's crises. As his father told him,

> You will live your life in three places Abraam— these akkers, our house, and the Church. The rest is unimportant. Here, on the land you must work, and work hard my boy, in your house you must love, love everybody who lives under that roof with you and also your neighbor, and in the Church you must have faith and worship the Almighty.
>
> (*Valley Song,* p. 47)

Buks has always believed that by following these simple guidelines he will be assured of a sweet and happy life.

However, the play shows that happiness is not quite that simple, and especially not in a land as conflicted and turbulent as South Africa. First his daughter and then his granddaughter are pulled from him by the lure of the outside world and repelled by the severity of racially divided life in a semiarid village. For them the Church has no direct consoling power; they look for happiness in things of the world.

When considering the history of the Dutch Reformed Church in its relations with South Africa's coloured people, it is not hard to see why Veronica searched for contentment elsewhere. Originally the *Nederslandse Gereformeerde Kerk* (Dutch Reformed Church) made no separation between its white and its black adherents; slaves who had accepted the creed, and coloured people who had been born into it, worshipped together, on an equal footing with whites from Europe. Although this policy was never fully accepted, it was remarkably forward-looking in its attitude towards race. However, when the British ended slavery, triggering the Afrikaner Great Trek, the issue of race affected religion. While, besides racial policies, the Trekkers had many reasons—political, economic, and social— to flee British rule, they were often appalled by what they saw as a British tendency to elevate blacks to the status of white people.

The Dutch Reformed Church denounced the Trek partly because the Church's leadership was in sympathy with the British. Many Trekkers formed their own churches, with racial purity as a cornerstone. The most important of these was the *Nederduitsch Hervormde Kerk,* founded by Andries Pretorius, the leader of the Trek. These churches officially banned African or coloured membership. Meanwhile, the Dutch Reformed Church could sense the desires of its congregations. Fearing further defections to the more explicitly segregationist churches, the Synod of 1857 finally accepted what it had rejected for years—separate worship for blacks and whites:

> The Synod considers it desirable and according to Holy Scriptures that our heathen members be accepted and initiated into our congregations wherever it is possible, but where this measure, as a result of the weakness of some, would stand in the way of promoting the work of Christ among the heathen people, then congregations set up among the heathen, or still to be set up, should enjoy their Christian privileges in a separate building or institution.
>
> (De Gruchy, p. 32)

The Synod's ruling is remarkably contradictory. On the one hand, it suggests that segregation is necessary, not because Africans are inferior, but because some whites are weak and prejudiced. But, on the other hand, in its adoption of segregationist policies, it conflated coloured people (many of whom had been born into the Church) with so-called heathens. After 1857 coloured people were in the awkward position of attending mission churches (with all the connotations of conversion and difference that the word *mission* has). In other words, the Dutch Reformed Church established missions for coloured people, as it did for the Africans, even though most coloured people already belonged to the church and did not need to be converted. As the child of a Dutch Reformed minister in the Karoo would note over a hundred years later, "The Mission Church was an also-ran compared with its White counterpart. It was much, much smaller, with no steeple, no clock or bells, no church hall, only a vestry" (Barnard, p. 10). In short, the Dutch Reformed Church preached that faith was the only determiner of equality, while practicing a rigid and racialized hierarchy. It is no wonder, then, that some coloured churchgoers became disenchanted with this hypocrisy.

After 1857 the situation only worsened. What had begun as a practical concession to "the weakness of some" was, after the formation of the Union of South Africa in 1910, increasingly understood by Dutch Reformed theologians as an immutable fact based in Holy Scriptures. In 1881 the coloured church was formally separated from the white church; in 1910 another church was created for Africans, and in 1951 a fourth for Indian converts. Theologians argued that racial separation and inequality were based on the Bible.

This complicated, and fundamentally hypocritical, conflation of politics and religion is treated in an understated way in *Valley Song*. The key is the psalm quoted by the Author, and his reflections on it. If the earth belongs to the Lord, the Author asks, does it not also belong to the simple worshipper who has tilled it his whole life? If it is the Lord alone who bestows blessings, would He not be most likely to grant the land, not to the outsider with money, but to the man who most loves the land, and the God he feels is expressed in it? The unstated answer to these questions is obvious. Yet the apartheid government and the Church agreed that land had to be distributed in a racialized way: the white man must keep possession of the major portion (86 percent), so that Africans and coloureds would not capsize white supremacy. Coloured children received few options, little education, and no chance to earn money except by working in a white home or business. No wonder, then, that Veronica takes advantage of her postapartheid freedom; no wonder that this time Buks's religion ends up leaving him confused and alone rather than at ease with the world.

Sources and literary context. Fugard's early work at the University of Cape Town exposed him to the then-voguish ideas of existentialism, especially the existential notion that codes of conduct must be formed by experience, not by preconceived strategies. This is reflected in Buks's struggle to make sense of his experience, which contradicts what traditional Christianity tells him to expect.

Fugard has also been influenced by his work with others in theaters. His collaborations with the Serpents Tail group of actors in Port Elizabeth informed him in the arts of improvisation, dialogue, and political reference. Since the Serpents Tail was a multiracial group, it can be assumed that this work may have helped sharpen his sense of coloured speech patterns. (He has also expressed a debt to his Afrikaans-speaking mother for an awareness of how Afrikaners sound when they speak English.) The intricate and subtle fugue of desires and demands that makes up the core of this eminently psychological play can be attributed to a lifetime of work in close conjunction with actors, trying to get at the heart of what makes characters (especially improvised ones) do what they do.

Finally, *Valley Song* reflects a number of Fugard's abiding concerns. He is said to be at his best when treating "common" people; his most famous plays present the troubles, not of heroes or villains, but of realistic, humble people caught in historical or emotional storms. He is interested, as well, in the turbulent social life of South Africa, an interest that has not waned with the official demise of apartheid. *Valley Song* is Fugard's first answer to the pressing question that faces the country: what next?

Reviews. *Valley Song* was well received at its debut in late 1995; even critics who had disliked Fugard's more recent plays saw it as a return to the high quality of his earlier drama. Howard Kissel called it "[o]ne of his most affecting works" (Kissel, p. 607). Jeremy Gerard praised Fugard's simple but effective characterizations, especially of Veronica, concluding that this is "one of Fugard's smaller plays, but it's got enormous heart" (Gerard, p. 609). In Clive Barnes's estimation, "[t]he play certainly doesn't have the passion of Fugard's earlier plays—pain and anger are easier and more interesting to write about than hope or even reconciliation. Yet it has its own quiet qualities" (Barnes, p. 610).

—Jacob Littleton

For More Information

Barnard, Marius. *Karoo.* Cape Town: Landsowne, 1975.

Barnes, Clive. Review of *Valley Song,* by Athol Fugard. In *New York Drama Critics' Reviews.* 1995: 609-10.

Chidester, David. *Religions of South Africa.* London: Routledge, 1992.

Cilliers, S. P. *The Coloureds of South Africa.* Cape Town: Banier, 1963.

De Gruchy, John. "Settler Christianity." In *Living Faiths in South Africa.* New York: St. Martin's Press, 1995.

Fugard, Athol. *Valley Song.* New York: Samuel French, 1995.

Gerard, Jeremy. Review of *Valley Song,* by Athol Fugard. In *New York Drama Critics' Reviews.* 1995: 609.

Gray, Stephen. *Athol Fugard.* Johannesburg: McGraw Hill, 1982.

Kissel, Howard. Review of *Valley Song,* by Athol Fugard. In *New York Drama Critics' Reviews.* 1995: 607-608.

Mallaby, Sebastian. *After Apartheid: The Future of South Africa.* New York: Times Books, 1992.

Ross, Robert. *A Concise History of South Africa.* Cambridge: Cambridge University Press, 1999.

Thompson, Leonard. *A History of South Africa.* New Haven, Conn.: Yale University Press, 1990.

Van der Ross, R. E. *Myths and Attitudes.* Cape Town: Tafelberg, 1979.

Waiting for the Barbarians

by
J. M. Coetzee

Born in Cape Town, South Africa, in 1940, J. M. Coetzee is probably the best known and most influential South African writer after Nadine Gordimer. Unlike Gordimer, however, Coetzee often avoids strict social realism, instead creating universal, often allegorical fictions that remind us how "oppression and injustice are not limited to South Africa, [and how], in some sense, they are eternal" (Gallagher, p. 10). For this reason Coetzee has been a somewhat controversial figure among African writers, many of whom equate political engagement with a particular kind of realism. Nonetheless, Coetzee has been an outspoken critic of both *apartheid* and political victimization in all its forms. In 1987 Coetzee won the Jerusalem Prize for being "a fighter for human freedom and dignity," and for writing in ways that contribute to "the freedom of the individual in society" (Mitgang in Gallagher, p. 11). *Waiting for the Barbarians,* Coetzee's "contribution to the international discourse on torture in South Africa," is often considered to be his most powerful work (Gallagher, p. 118).

Events in History at the Time of the Novel

Apartheid. *Waiting for the Barbarians* is an allegory in which South Africa is never explicitly mentioned. However, the links between Coetzee's fictional "Empire" and the practices of South Africa's Nationalist government are clear. The novel was written in 1979, at a time when, due to the much-publicized death of Stephen Biko in

---

THE LITERARY WORK

A novel set at an unspecified time in a frontier town in a fictional Empire; published in English in 1980.

SYNOPSIS

When the Empire's security forces enter a quiet frontier town and begin rounding up and torturing the "barbarians" who live nearby, the town magistrate is compelled to terms with the state-sponsored violence.

1977, torture in South Africa had suddenly become the focus of international attention. Biko, whose story is told below, was only one of many revolutionary leaders detained and tortured in South African prisons during the period of Nationalist rule that lasted from 1948 until 1990. This period, characterized by the policy of enforced segregation called *apartheid,* saw the state-sponsored detention and imprisonment of thousands of South Africans who protested the white domination and racial legislation of the Nationalist government. Though reports of the torture of detainees and prisoners in South Africa had circulated since 1948, it was only in the late 1970s that torture became the subject of international discourse and criticism, and that specifics about electric shock treatments and police beatings were revealed to the public. It is in this context that *Waiting for the Barbarians* was written.

Stephen Biko, the martyred leader of South Africa's
Black Consciousness Movement. His death under
suspicious circumstances while in police custody
brought international attention to the brutalities
associated with apartheid.

To understand the practice of torture in South
Africa, it is necessary to understand the history
and ideology surrounding the Nationalist Party
and its policy of apartheid. The Nationalist Party
was voted into power in 1948, after years of increasing concern by Afrikaners (whites mainly of
Dutch descent) over both the "native question"
(race relations) and what they perceived as the
continued threat of British influence in South
Africa. Afrikaner voters wanted concrete solutions to both problems. The electorate, of course,
did not include the black segments of the population (which totaled 80 percent of the population), who were excluded from the vote as from
so much else in South African society. Indeed,
from the very beginning, "the history of white
colonization was one of conquest, plunder, and
dispossession of the indigenous Black peoples
and societies" (Harsch, p. 15). (A note on terminology is in order here. Historians divide South
African society into white, African, coloured [of
mixed descent], and Indian, sometimes using
"black" to refer to all nonwhites.) From the seventeenth and eighteenth centuries on, Dutch and

British settlers had gradually excluded native
Africans from the privileges of power, and when
the two settler groups joined together to form the
Union of South Africa in 1910, there emerged
"one of the most extreme forms of racial segregation in the twentieth-century world" (Beinart
and Dubow, p. 3).

The segregation policies that resulted from
this union included a number of explicitly racial
laws restricting the lives and movements of nonwhites in almost every sphere.

1911 Mines and Works Act: Segregated workers, giving white employees a monopoly on
skilled jobs.

1913 Natives Land Act: Segregated races in
rural areas; reserved 7 percent of land for native Africans (67 percent of population); prohibited them from buying land outside reserves
from non-Africans.

1923 Natives Urban Areas Act: Segregated
races in urban areas; prohibited African purchases of township land.

1936 Representation of Natives Act: Abolished the remnant African franchise, disquali-
fying African voters in Cape Province.

1936 Native Trust and Land Act: Authorized
more land for reserves; increased them to 11.7
percent of the nation by 1939.

(Thompson, p. 163)

As a result of these laws, native Africans were
forced to leave their own lands, live on cramped
reserves, join the labor market, work for low
wages, and carry pass cards (documents of identification used to restrict their movements in urban areas). Black workers could neither strike
nor take jobs designated for white workers. It became official policy to maintain white supremacy
in South Africa—specifically, after 1948, white
Afrikaner supremacy.

Before 1948, however, South Africa's white
British population seemed more supreme than
the often-impoverished Afrikaners, many of
whom felt resentful at "finding themselves at the
mercy of British commerce and culture" (Meredith, p. 19). When United Party co-leader Jan
Smuts led South Africa into World War II—
Britain's war, as many Afrikaners saw it—strident Afrikaners lost patience with more moderate approaches to government, and voted the
virulent, fascist-influenced National Party into
power in 1948, under the campaign slogan of
"apartheid." The National Party promised to return glory to the Afrikaner people. A campaign
manifesto explained:

We can act in only one of two directions. Either we must follow the course of equality, which must eventually mean national suicide for the white race, or we must take the course of apartheid through which the character and the future of every race will be protected.... [T]he [National Party] therefore undertakes to protect the white race properly and effectively against any policy, doctrine or attack which might undermine or threaten its continued existence. At the same time, the Party rejects any policy of oppression and exploitation of the non-Europeans by the Europeans as being in conflict with the Christian basis of our national life, and irreconcilable with our policy.

(Le May, p. 202)

Almost immediately after assuming power the Nationalists began constructing a body of laws, policies, and bureaucracies that would develop into the world's most complex racial system. The system banned interracial marriages and sexual acts between the races. Its laws compelled different racial groups to use separate restaurants, post offices, theaters, buses, and so on; and to use separate entrances and seats in public buildings. As the authorities demarcated separate residential areas for the different racial groups, whole communities were uprooted. Only 11.7 percent of the land was reserved for the African population (nearly 70 percent of the total population) by 1939. As the breakdown shows, the areas demarcated for nonwhite South Africans represented only a small percentage of the country's total land mass; as a result, many nonwhites had no alternative but to build makeshift shantytowns on the outskirts of white-populated cities. Such overwhelming inequality was a standard feature of apartheid legislation. Unlike the separate-but-equal rhetoric in the United States, there was no suggestion that facilities—such as restrooms at a train station—had to be equal or even exist for blacks in South Africa. In fact, in 1953 a legal decision declared that facilities did not have to be equal. The decision is but one example of a host of similar rulings. Between 1948 and 1971 the government enacted about 150 racial laws, affecting every aspect of daily life—three times the number enacted in the four decades preceding the National Party's reign.

Torture and the case of Stephen Biko. Such extreme laws did not go unchallenged. In fact, they provoked continual unrest and protest within oppressed communities. The government retaliated by building an elaborate security force to monitor revolutionary activity. The police, as

well as intelligence officers, were granted more and more power to deal with political troublemakers in whatever ways they felt necessary. A series of harsh laws were passed to restrict political opposition and extend the power of the security forces. Indeed, one of these laws, the Terrorism Act of 1967, granted the security police the power to "hold virtually anyone for as long as they felt necessary, until he had 'satisfactorily replied to all questions' ... or [until] no useful purpose will be served by his further detention" (*Amnesty International Report on Torture*, p. 128). As research by the United Nations (U.N.) Special Committee on Apartheid later confirmed, torture was often an integral part of these detentions:

The conclusion is inescapable that cruelty against opponents of *apartheid* . . . and that torture by the Security police is condoned, if not actually encouraged, by the Government. Allegations of similar tortures have been made from so many centres and have involved so many local officers . . . that there is reason to believe that Security Branch officers have been trained in these methods.

(*Amnesty International Report on Torture*, p. 131)

"IN DETENTION"

Official accounts of prison deaths often blamed suicide or accidents for the deaths of political prisoners. In his poem "In Detention," Christopher van Wyk explores the absurdities of this official rhetoric:

He fell from the ninth floor
He hanged himself
He slipped on a piece of soap while washing
He hanged himself
He slipped on a piece of soap while washing
He fell from the ninth floor
He hanged himself while washing
He slipped from the ninth floor
He hung from the ninth floor
He slipped on the ninth floor while washing
He fell from a piece of soap while slipping
He hung from the ninth floor
He washed from the ninth floor while slipping
He hung from a piece of soap while washing.

(van Wyk in Gallagher, pp. 117-18)

According to the U.N. report and the findings of Amnesty International, these "methods" sometimes included psychological techniques like solitary confinement, but were most often physical and brutal in nature. Allegations were made that there "is an appliance for administering electric shock torture in almost every police station in South Africa" (*Amnesty International Report on Torture,* p. 131). According to Amnesty International, between 1962 and 1971 at least 20 prison deaths in South Africa were believed to have resulted from police torture. Though investigations were sometimes made, neither the police nor government were ever held responsible. As we see over and over again in *Waiting for the Barbarians,* official reports normally concluded that suicide, or accidents, had caused the detainees' deaths.

The press sometimes challenged these official claims; in 1964, for instance, the detainee Suliman Salojee supposedly fell from a window and died during a police interrogation, though, as the press noted, the window in question had been heavily barred. When the same kind of rhetoric was used to explain the mysterious 1977 prison death of Stephen Biko, the charismatic leader of the Black Consciousness Movement, a public outcry followed. "Black consciousness," explained Biko, "is in essence the realisation by the black man of the need to rally together with his brothers around the cause of their subjection—the blackness of their skin—and to operate as a group in order to rid themselves of the shackles" (Biko in Thompson, p. 212). In a series of articles and speeches, a friend of Biko's, the white journalist Donald Woods, blamed Biko's death on the police, who themselves claimed that Biko had died of a hunger strike, despite the fact that Biko had been in prison less than a month. Biko had been one of many arrestees in the Soweto uprisings that began in June 1976 after police opened fire on unarmed student protesters. Hundreds were killed during the 16 bloody months of the uprisings, and thousands more, like Biko, vanished into detention.

In response to the outcry over Biko's death, the South African government banned all Black Consciousness organizations and newspapers, and arrested 47 black and 7 white prominent revolutionary leaders. Afrikaner newspapers repeated the police's explanation of Biko's death and, later, when an autopsy revealed damage to Biko's brain, the newspaper *The Citizen* suggested that Biko had committed suicide by banging his head against the wall.

Eventually, however, due to continued public demand, an inquest was held into Biko's death. The inquest revealed many facts of police brutality and maltreatment of detainees. It was discovered, for instance, that Biko had been kept "naked in isolation and was shackled in leg irons and handcuffs" (Gallagher, p. 114). Donald Woods's wife, Wendy, was present at the inquest. Directly confronted for the first time, like many South Africans, with the mystery of torture, she commented on the security policeman testifying at the inquest:

> These men displayed symptoms of extreme insularity. They are people whose upbringing has impressed upon them the divine right to retain power, and in that sense they are innocent men—incapable of thinking or acting differently. On top of that they have gravitated to an occupation which has given them all the scope they need to express their rigid personalities. They have been protected for years by the laws of the country. They have been able to carry out all their imaginative torture practices quite undisturbed in cells and rooms all over the country with tacit official sanction, and they have been given tremendous status by the government as the men who "protect the state from subversion."
>
> (Woods in Gallagher, pp. 114-5)

Biko's death became symbolic of South African police atrocities, leading to both popular and international protest. When the inquest resulted in the verdict that Biko's death was blameless—that he probably died during a "scuffle" with police—public protest became even more vehement (Gallagher, p. 144). News of Biko's death and the following inquest led the United Nations to declare 1978 as International Anti-Apartheid Year and to levy economic sanctions against South Africa. Antiapartheid protests were heard around the world, with writers in South Africa addressing the issue through their literary works. Like Wendy Woods and others of her time, the Magistrate in *Waiting for the Barbarians* is haunted by the face of the torturer, by his "cells and rooms all over the country" (Woods in Gallagher, p. 115).

The Novel in Focus

Plot summary. *Waiting for the Barbarians* is told from the perspective of the old Magistrate who watches over the affairs of a small frontier settlement on the outposts of the Empire. The Magistrate has held this position comfortably for decades; the town itself is sleepy and quiet, though kept in check by a vague, ever-present fear of the unknown "barbarian" presence existing outside its gates. Though the barbarians function as a scapegoat for the townspeople and rumors of war preparations and attacks circulate continually through the town, the Magistrate knows how little of this talk is based in truth:

> There is no woman living along the frontier who has not dreamed of a dark barbarian hand coming from under the bed to grip her ankle, no man who has not frightened himself with visions of the barbarians carousing in his home, breaking the plates, setting fire to the curtains, raping his daughters. These dreams are the consequence of too much ease. Show me the barbarian army and I will believe.
>
> (Coetzee, *Waiting for the Barbarians*, p. 8)

Unlike the rest of the town, the Magistrate seems to have a basic respect for the "barbarians," who, in his experience, are neither violent nor aggressive. In his spare time he orchestrates excavations of local ruins, unearthing native artifacts. When Colonel Joll arrives in town, the Magistrate tells him how the native inhabitants go about trapping the flocks of geese and ducks that migrate down the lake every year, and suggests that they go together to observe the local custom of fishing at night:

> I suggest that I take him out fishing by night in a native boat. "That is an experience not to be missed," I say; "the fishermen carry torches and beat drums over the water to drive the fish towards the nets they have laid."
>
> (*Barbarians*, p. 1)

Colonel Joll is not interested, however, in learning about the local customs. An official of the ominous-sounding "Third Bureau," he has been sent to the frontier "under emergency powers" (*Barbarians*, p. 1). Convinced that "barbarian tribes" are readying themselves to wage war at any moment, the Empire is preparing a counterattack. The task of Colonel Joll is to interrogate and imprison these barbarians, to figure out "the truth." In other words, Joll is a torturer. He uses a euphemism, "pressure," to describe the way in which he gets to the truth:

> I am speaking of a situation in which I am probing for the truth, in which I have to exert pressure to find it. First I get lies, you see—this is what happens—first lies, then pressure, then more lies, then more pressure ... then the truth. That is how you get the truth.
>
> (*Barbarians*, p. 5)

Waiting for the Barbarians opens with Colonel Joll's arrival in the town. An old native man and a sick young boy suspected of banditry have been captured and locked up in the granary. Colonel Joll goes in to interrogate them, despite the Magistrate's assurance that no raiding party would have included a sick boy and an old man in its ranks, and the prisoners' own insistence that they had been on their way to the doctor. The Magistrate becomes conscious that he is pleading for the two prisoners, and when Colonel Joll tells him that he has "to question them" anyway, and that the Magistrate might find their "set procedures" tedious to watch, the Magistrate retreats to his regular, comfortable routine, leaving Colonel Joll to his business (*Barbarians*, p. 4). Though the Magistrate cannot hear the screaming, he admits that "at every moment that evening as I go about my business I am aware of what might be happening and my ear is even tuned to the pitch of human pain" (*Barbarians*, p. 5). The old man dies during the interrogation. The official report states that the prisoner had attacked the visiting officer and in the subsequent struggle had hit his head against the wall and died. When the Magistrate visits the prisoners later, he sees the old man's corpse still lying on the floor, and the boy lying on some straw, his hands tied in front of him and his body beaten. The Magistrate attempts to care for the boy, by feeding him, instructing the guards to loosen the ties, calling in a doctor, and so on. But the Magistrate knows that he "cannot pretend to be any better than a mother comforting a child between his father's spells of wrath" (*Barbarians*, p. 7). He is not out to be a hero. He comes to abhor the increasing violence around him, but is also excruciatingly aware of his own complicity in it, and of the fascination it holds for him. More than anything, the Magistrate wishes he were able to turn a blind eye to the events around him:

> If I had only handed over these two prisoners to the Colonel, I reflect—"Here, Colonel, you are the specialist, see what you can make of them!"—if I had gone on a hunting trip for a few days, as I should have done, a visit up-river perhaps, and come back, and ... put my seal on his report, with no question about what the word *investigations* meant. . . .
>
> (*Barbarians*, p. 9)

Colonel Joll begins planning raids on the barbarians, hoping to take more prisoners and, in this way, to discover more of the "truth." As the Magistrate attempts to dissuade him, warning him of the difficulties of navigating the terrain and of the inferior quality of their maps, the Colonel consistently replies in neutral, official language, using banal words like "situation" or "investigation" or "procedure" to mask horrible actions: "we will," he says at one point, "locate the encampment of these nomads and proceed further as the situation dictates" (*Barbarians*, p. 12). Throughout the book, the Magistrate attempts to understand and discover what allows such torturers to inflict pain the way they do: "Looking at him I wonder how he felt the first time: did he, invited by an apprentice to twist the pincers or turn the screw or whatever it is they do, shudder even a little to know that at that instant he was trespassing into the forbidden?" (*Barbarians*, p. 12).

Colonel Joll's expedition departs, and within days new prisoners begin arriving. As the townspeople crowd around, the Magistrate recognizes the 12 prisoners as peaceful fishermen. "These are fishing people!" he shouts to a guard, "How can you bring them here?" (*Barbarians*, p. 17). The Magistrate can do nothing but treat the scraggly, harmless barbarian prisoners well until the inevitable day of their torture. When the Colonel and his soldiers return, they reenter triumphant, laughing with excitement and leading a new batch of prisoners "roped together neck to neck" (*Barbarians*, p. 20). The next day, the Colonel begins his interrogations. The Magistrate feels that "the joy has gone from life," and, powerless at home, spends more and more evenings with a young prostitute (*Barbarians*, p. 22). Five days later the prisoners emerge, "sick, famished, damaged, terrified," and the Magistrate orders them to be fed and returned to their homes (*Barbarians*, p. 25).

One barbarian woman, as it turns out, is left behind, having been blinded by her torturers, and having had her feet broken. Her father, also a prisoner, had been tortured and killed in front of her. For the rest of the novel, this woman—with her staring blank eyes and broken body—will hold a strange power over the Magistrate. He takes her into his rooms; feeds, bathes, and warms her; and rubs and washes her broken feet. The care of her feet soon becomes a nightly ritual for him. His feelings and intentions regarding the woman are complicated; while he wants to heal her, he is also fully aware of the sadism coloring his actions, and of the mildly erotic pull her tortured body has for him. As he himself notes, "the distance between myself and her torturers, I realize, is negligible" (*Barbarians*, p. 27). Towards him the woman is passive and submis-

sive, almost indifferent. He tries to imagine what had been done to her, tenderly asking her to describe the torture, and tracing the lines of her scarred body again and again. He goes out to the granary and memorizes the site; he asks the guards to describe those days to him, to tell him about the woman and her father. No matter what he does, however, the woman and her pain remain unfathomable:

> Is this how her torturers felt hunting their secret, whatever they thought it was? For the first time I feel a dry pity for them: how natural a mistake to believe that you can burn or tear or hack your way into the secret body of the other! The girl lies in my bed, but there is no good reason why it should be a bed. I behave in some ways like a lover—I undress her, I bathe her, I stroke her, I sleep beside her—but I might equally well tie her to a chair and beat her, it would be no less intimate.
>
> (*Barbarians*, p. 43)

Even his own motives remain a mystery to the Magistrate; "is it she I want," he asks, "or the traces of history her body bears?" (*Barbarians*, p. 59).

At one point, after several months of living with the barbarian woman in this manner, the Magistrate tells her that he is taking her back to her people. He enlists three men to help them and before spring arrives the five travelers set out on a harrowing journey through the frontier. When they finally meet up with a small group of barbarians, the Magistrate orders the woman to speak to them, to tell them why they have come. Then he tells the woman: "now that I have brought you back, as far as I can, I wish to ask you very clearly to return to the town with me. Of your own choice" (*Barbarians*, p. 71). The woman says no, so the four men head back without her. As they approach their town, they find it much changed; the army has arrived, and the campaign against the barbarians has begun. The Magistrate's office has been taken over by men from the Bureau, one of whom accuses him of "treasonously consorting with the enemy" (*Barbarians*, p. 77). The Magistrate is locked up in the same barracks room in which the barbarians had been held before. He sits in this prison every day, unwashed, neglected, thinking of the woman and her father and of the pain and degradation that the empty walls of the room have witnessed. His mind wanders:

> Somewhere, always, a child is being beaten. I think of one who despite her age was still a child; who was brought in here and hurt before

her father's eyes; who watched him being humiliated before her, and saw that he knew what she saw. . . .

I gave the girl my protection, offering in my equivocal way to be her father. But I came too late, after she had ceased to believe in fathers. . . .

I should never have allowed the gates of the town to be opened to people who assert that there are higher considerations than those of decency.

(*Barbarians*, pp. 80-81)

The Magistrate is deemed an enemy of the state and his tryst with the barbarians, a secret political meeting. In prison for months, supposedly awaiting trial, he sinks into ever-worse degradation, losing all sense of the pride he once had. At a certain point no one cares about him any longer; he has become a joke of a man, and is allowed to roam freely through town, now that he has nowhere to go. Meanwhile, the campaign against the barbarians continues.

As more and more barbarians are arrested, the town's treatment of them becomes more public, more overt. At one point a group of prisoners is beaten horribly as crowds of people look on in excitement, encouraging small children to join in the beatings. The Magistrate himself is tortured publicly; made to wear a dress and hung from a tree, he becomes the butt of laughter to a crowd of onlookers. The soldiers take over the town, the war continues, and suddenly the barbarians gain several victories over the Empire, luring the soldiers, says one of them, "on and on, we could never catch them" (*Barbarians*, p. 147). Unable to make much headway and terrified out of their minds, the soldiers and townspeople begin streaming out of the frontier town and back to the capital. The Magistrate moves back into his rooms, and life becomes almost normal again.

But not really normal. The novel ends with one of the Magistrate's dreams, a dream of children building a snowman:

It is not a bad snowman.
This is not the scene I dreamed of. Like much else nowadays I leave it feeling stupid, like a man who lost his way a long time ago but presses on along a road that may lead nowhere.

(*Barbarians*, p. 156)

The torturer. J. M. Coetzee describes *Waiting for the Barbarians* as being about "the impact of the torture chamber on the life of a man of conscience" (Coetzee in Gallagher, p. 120). The novel itself, while clearly alluding to South Africa

and often seeming to allude to the death of Stephen Biko, is ultimately universal in scope, exploring, in broad terms, the relationship between the oppressor and the oppressed, the torturer and the tortured. But to the novel's Magistrate, it all remains a mystery. He never penetrates the heart of the blinded, broken-footed barbarian woman, nor the soul of the torturer, Colonel Joll:

I look into his clear blue eyes, as clear as if there were crystal lenses slipped over his eyeballs. He looks back at me. I have no idea what he sees. Thinking of him, I have said the words *torture ... torturer* to myself, but they are strange words, and the more I repeat them the more strange they grow, till they lie like stones on my tongue.

(*Barbarians*, p. 118)

As Elaine Scarry points out in *The Body in Pain,* "however near the prisoner the torturer stands, the distance between their physical realities is colossal"; for while the torturer is without pain, the person being tortured is in excruciating pain (Scarry, p. 36). It is this distance that the Magistrate cannot bridge; he cannot access the pain or experience of the tortured (until he is himself tortured), nor can he understand the painlessness of torturing, the way the torturer can perform the acts without his spirit rebelling. As one who lives in the Empire, however, the Magistrate must constantly circle both poles.

Many studies have attempted to shed light on the psychology of torturers, on what allows them to do what they do. While one widely held belief claims that torturers are disturbed, sadistic personalities, more and more people are recognizing that "an understanding of torturers' behaviour is not separable from the wider context in which it occurs—that is, the social and political context" (Foster, p. 167). Thus, they are less likely to be abnormal individuals than they are to be "quite ordinary people in an extraordinary, abnormal situation" (Foster, p. 167). Indeed, a 1974 study by S. Milgram points out that adherence to state authority is key to explaining the acts of the torturer. The torturer is rarely a member of the ruling class: it may be that the ruling class gives the command, but the task of torture itself is generally a sergeant's job. Milgram also found that the torturers' allegiance to the authority commanding him or her would increase in relation to the psychological distance between the torturer and his victim. That is, torturers would obey most loyally if a buffer zone were created between them and the victims—whether that buffer involved being helped by assistants,

J. M. Coetzee

by being under surveillance, or by the existence of some kind of essential separation between them and the victims. As Amnesty International's *Report on Torture* explains, "it seems to be a precondition for torture that the torturer have a world view, no matter how crude, that divides man into the torturable and the non-torturable" (*Amnesty International Report on Torture,* p. 31).

In South Africa, of course, where the white population has always been a small minority (about 20 percent) of the population, the existence of such divisions led to the legislation of racist laws in the first place. It is clear that many white South Africans feared, on some level, being submerged within the "black masses" that crammed into shantytowns outside the fortified cities. Security measures became more and more extreme as the waves of protest among South Africa's nonwhite population became more prevalent; in the minds of the minority, stamping out these movements became important enough to justify the use of torture. Torture, argues one analyst, "survives to this day wherever governments believe themselves, or choose to believe themselves, to be beset by conspiracies and subversion" (Ruthven in Foster, p. 173).

> The Grand Conspiracy is a fantasy in the minds of authorities, born of a paranoid response to the dissidence around them. . . . It is the

reaction of the elite groups, especially in militarised societies, who stand to lose by social change. The Grand Conspiracy becomes a model of repression to be applied to every contingency. [It] takes on an increasingly ideological tone . . . [and] . . . 'foreign' ideas are seen as a source of the poison that is corrupting youth and destroying society.
> (Ruthven in Foster, p. 173)

As Don Foster points out, "the above description captures almost exactly the political and social climate in which torture . . . has developed as an institution in South Africa" (Foster, p. 173). As should be clear, it also describes almost exactly the feeling expressed by Coetzee's title, "waiting for the barbarians."

Sources and literary context. *Waiting for the Barbarians* was one of many South African literary works in the 1970s to explore the question of torture, which "has exerted a dark fascination on many . . . South African writers" (Coetzee in Gallagher, p. 112). Though Coetzee refuses to confirm that the "Empire" in *Waiting for the Barbarians* is analogous to South Africa, it is clear that the sudden worldwide attention on the prevalent use of torture by the South African Police, as well as the image of the much-lionized Biko, shackled and dying, greatly influenced this novel. Other South African treatments of torture include Donald Woods's *Biko,* André Brink's **A Dry White Season** (also covered in *African Literature and Its Times*), Sophia Sepalma's *A Ride on the Whirlwind,* and Mongane Serote's *To Every Birth Its Blood.*

Reviews. *Waiting for the Barbarians* was received with both enthusiasm and criticism; people tended either to admire the style and universal themes of the novel, or censure the novel for failing to engage explicitly enough with South Africa's political situation, a criticism that had been levied against Coetzee's work before. Robert Post saw Coetzee's novels as general "statements of opposition" (Post in Gallagher, p. 11). In contrast, another reviewer faulted *Waiting for the Barbarians* for not being oppositional enough:

> [T]his is a book that will be enthusiastically assimilated into the very system it (vaguely) condemns. In the end it is not a disturbing book, and ultimately it challenges nothing. Coetzee is a fine writer. It's a pity he isn't a bolder one.
> (Menàn Du Plessis in Gallagher, p. 12)

Indeed, in Coetzee's own words, the South African novel often seems to be received in South

Africa with the question "where does this book fit into the political struggle?" (Coetzee in Gallagher, p. 11). In his Jerusalem Prize acceptance speech, he lamented this situation:

> South African literature is an enslaved literature. . . . It is a literature which is not fully human: being more preoccupied than is natural, with power and with the torsions of power, it does not know how to pass from the elementary relations of contestation, of domination, and of subjugation, to the vast and complex human world which extends beyond.
>
> (Coetzee in Gallagher, p. 17)

—Carolyn Turgeon

For More Information

Amnesty International Report on Torture. London: Duckworth, 1975.

Beinhart, William, and Saul Dubow. "Introduction: The historiography of segregation and apartheid." In *Segregation and Apartheid in Twentieth-Century South Africa.* Ed. William Beinhart and Saul Dubow. New York: Routledge, 1995.

Coetzee, J. M. *Waiting for the Barbarians.* New York: Penguin Books, 1980.

Foster, Don. *Detention and Torture in South Africa.* London: James Currey, 1987.

Gallagher, Susan VanZanten. *A Story of South Africa: J. M. Coetzee's Fiction in Context.* Cambridge, Mass.: Harvard University Press, 1991.

Harsch, Ernest. *South Africa: White Rule, Black Revolt.* New York: Monad Press, 1980.

Le May, G. H. L. *The Afrikaners: An Historical Interpretation.* Cambridge, Mass.: Blackwell Publishers, 1995.

Meredith, Martin. *In the Name of Apartheid: South Africa in the Postwar Period.* London: Hamish Hamilton, 1988.

Ranuga, Thomas K. *The New South Africa and the Socialist Vision: Positions and Perspectives Toward a Post-Apartheid Society.* Atlantic Highlands, N.J.: Humanities Press, 1996.

Scarry, Elaine. *The Body in Pain.* Oxford: Oxford University Press, 1985.

Thompson, Leonard. *A History of South Africa.* New Haven, Conn.: Yale University Press, 1990.

A Walk in the Night

by
Alex La Guma

Born in Cape Province, South Africa, in 1925, Alex La Guma belonged to a working-class family in the "coloured"—or mixed race—sector of society. His mother, Wilhemina Alexander, and his father, James La Guma, were a cigarette factory worker and a trade union organizer, respectively. Following in the footsteps of his father, who was himself a leading figure in the black liberation movement, Alex became a member of the Cape Town district Communist party and participated in the drafting of the 1956 Freedom Charter. He would remain involved throughout his life in the struggle for racial equality in his homeland. La Guma played an active role in the Franchise Action Council, which opposed the attempt to disfranchise the coloured population; his own house served as headquarters to the South African Coloured People's Organization. After being placed under house arrest in 1962 because of his writing for *New Age*, a progressive newspaper, he and his wife spent the following years alternating between house arrest and imprisonment under various charges until they left the country for Britain in 1967. *A Walk in the Night,* La Guma's first book, was his attempt to promote Western awareness of the living conditions in his homeland, particularly in the coloured neighborhood of Cape Town's District Six.

Events in History at the Time of the Novella

District Six. La Guma's novella provides an ethnographic record of what once was Cape

---

> ## THE LITERARY WORK
>
> A novella set in Cape Town, South Africa, in the early 1960s; published in English in 1962.
>
> ### SYNOPSIS
>
> Three isolated young men, members of South Africa's oppressed underclass, wander Cape Town at night. Long suppressed anger leads to one youth's inadvertent killing of a drunken white man, initiating a tale of punishment that makes the stories of these separate characters converge.

Town's most populous coloured neighborhood, District Six. This community ceased to exist after 1966, however, when the South African government declared the district an all-white zone. Bulldozers subsequently destroyed all the buildings except for some churches and a mosque.

The razing of District Six struck directly at the symbolic center of coloured consciousness. South Africa's coloured population traces its roots to unions between seventeenth-century Europeans and the indigenous San people (otherwise known as "Bushmen") of the Cape. "Coloured" also denotes offspring of unions between either of these groups and slaves, imported from India, Madagascar, East Africa, and Malaya. Interracial mixing among the groups continues to the present day. It was officially declared illegal under apartheid laws in the late 1940s and

A slum dwelling in District Six, Cape Town.

early 1950s, but those laws were abrogated in the early 1990s.

The historically multicultural district was the closest possible approximation to a homeland for South Africa's coloured population, which had not been given a separate area to call its own. The neighborhood received its name during the electoral divisions of 1867. Given its portside location, it became a first destination for many immigrants to South Africa, a doorstep community for the inner-city industries. The District Six of the early 1960s was a vibrant mix of industry and poverty, in which retailers, shop workers, carpenters, seamstresses, shoemakers, and cabinet makers plied their trades amid exploitative landlords and vicious pawnbrokers. Firsthand recollections of the district invariably place equal emphasis on the neighborhood's vitality and its dangerous squalor.

Though largely comprised of coloured residents, District Six supported an ethnically diverse population. One of the most conspicuous features of *A Walk in the Night* is its faithful replication of the multiple accents and dialects spoken by the black Africans, white Afrikaners (of Dutch and other European ancestry), coloureds, and immigrants from India who intermingle on the streets. Equally noticeable is the author's emphasis on his characters' racial markings. Michael Adonis, for example, is described down to the shades of his hands: "The backs of his hands, like his face, were brown, but the palms were pink with tiny ridges of yellow-white callouses" (La Guma, *A Walk in the Night*, p. 2). This deliberate overemphasis on skin color, which recurs throughout the novella, becomes an ironic commentary on South Africa's myopic focus on race.

Despite its thriving eclecticism, District Six suffered the blight common to urban neighborhoods occupied by coloureds, Indians, or

THE VITALITY OF DISTRICT SIX

〜

Journalist Anthony Hazlitt Heard recalls the vibrancy of District Six, which persisted despite the neighborhood's many social and environmental problems:

Hansom cabs were operated from the centre of the main thoroughfare, Adderley Street. Fresh produce was offered from barrows. Fish horns could be heard above the city noise as vendors hawked the ocean's wares in hilly suburbs. Flower sellers brightened many streetsides. The Grand Parade, where [a statue of] Britain's King Edward VII stood invariably with a sea gull on his head, was an open place of religious, commercial, and political activity.

(Heard, p. 57)

Africans under apartheid policy. This policy, which mandated the entirely separate development of South Africa's different racial communities, guided a number of laws that negatively affected the living conditions of South Africa's nonwhite populations. The Group Areas Act (1950), most importantly, authorized the zoning of neighborhoods according to race, resulting in massive relocations of black and coloured populations. District Six remained heavily populated by the coloured population, though, through the time of the novel. A working class district, it was laden with slum areas.

Coloured majority. In South Africa as a whole in 1960, the coloured population formed a sizeable minority:

Population by Racial Group—1960 South Africa

Black Africans	10,927,922
Whites	3,088,492
Coloured	1,509,258
Asians	477,125

(Western, p. 59)

In Cape Town, however, the racial breakdown differed from these national statistics, including, at the onset of apartheid in 1948, 44 percent coloured, 44 percent white, 11 percent African, and 1 percent Indian (Western, p. 96). District Six was home to many of the coloured residents, whose identity stemmed from their association with the district and from little else. It was a working-class neighborhood, in many parts a slum, but coloured South Africans thought of it as their territory. According to one historian, though they themselves were victimized, even Africans spoke of coloureds as *amalawu*: "a pejorative term implying that they are people without customs and traditions, without pride in themselves. . . . *Place* of origin—home—has become an essential element of self-definition for Coloured people" (Western, pp. 149-50). Their source of pride was to their birthplace, to location. History had conspired to leave them few other options.

After emancipation in 1834, the coloured population passed largely from slavery into servitude; whites confined coloured children to inferior mission schools and paid the coloured worker a lower wage than the white. In the 1890s, Olive Schreiner (see *The Story of an African Farm,* also covered in *African Literature and Its Times*) assessed the plight of this group:

The Half-caste . . . now forms a more or less distinct section of society. . . . Nevertheless, socially his position remains much what it was. Without nationality, tradition, or racial ideals . . . robbed of racial self-respect. . . . He belonged to neither [white nor black]. . . . The Half-caste alone of all created things is at war with his own individuality.

(Schreiner in Western, pp. 15, 16).

Whites conceived of coloureds as illegimate persons, drunks, criminals, weaklings, and liars, which led many coloureds to internalize these stereotypes and develop negative self-concepts. As early as 1923 Schreiner dismissed the theory of "inborn depravity" in them and pointed instead at what she saw as the real culprit in the matter of crime: "In the smaller criminal cases . . . the 'coloured man' figures out of all proportion to the pure-blooded Europeans, Bantus, or Malays. . . . [This is because of] social conditions" (Schreiner in Western, p. 26).

> **FROM THE *CAPE TIMES* ON COLOURED DISTRICTS**
>
> "Almost every house in the districts where the coloured people live is packed tight. Children grow up and marry and in turn have children and are unable to find a place of their own. A family is turned out of an overcrowded house and find shelter with friends for a few days—which grows into weeks, months, years. They sleep in living rooms, in kitchens, in passages, in garages. . . ."
>
> (*Cape Times,* June 20, 1950, in Western, p. 49)

Insecurity—a permanent condition. Beginning in 1950 the Group Areas Act threatened the coloured population with relocation. This threat was all the more fearsome because of the shifting nature of racial classification set in the 1950 Population Registration Act. This act defines a coloured individual in entirely negative terms, specifying only what "coloured" does *not* denote: a person who is neither white, nor a Turk, an Asian, African, a Hottentot (Khoikhoi), a Bushman (San), an American Negro, or a person residing in a native location. Further, the law made a person's classification subject at any moment to change. A light-skinned coloured might be reclassified as white, or a dark-skinned coloured as African, mandating an immediate change of neighborhood, as well as of other rights and privileges.

An anti-pass-law demonstration turned violent when police shot into a crowd of South Africans at
Sharpeville, March 21, 1960.

In short, the primarily coloured residents of
District Six lived in a tense atmosphere. The constant fear of police interrogation and detention
has been suggested as the source for the prevalent mental stress and illness among urban black
Africans and coloureds (Thompson, p. 204). This
psychological oppression was worsened by the
second-class amenities that the government allocated to such regions. During the time in which
La Guma's novella takes place, few tenements in
District Six boasted running water, electricity, or
a sewage system. The neighborhood's unpaved
streets were often muddy and dangerous, and
were seldom lit. Required to reside in a narrowly
zoned area, the district's residents had little say
in the selection of their living quarters; they had
to take what was available. Crime was encouraged by the massive rates of homelessness within
the neighborhood. A 1951 study found that,
across all nonwhite townships, an estimated
167,000 of 314,000 families were without housing (Dubb, p. 442). Danger also came from a
segment of the district's youth known as the
tsotsi, street thugs who identified themselves by
a distinctive slang and style of dress and who
practiced petty acts of theft and violence. This
threat was so widespread that certain areas of the
district were known throughout the 1950s as
"no-goes," areas into which the police would not

venture. In the novella, the tsotsi are represented
by the gang that courts Michael Adonis. Emotionally and socially adrift, Michael eventually
joins their ranks, demonstrating the dangerous
allure of the sense of community offered by such
gangs.

Today, after the razing of District Six, *A Walk
in the Night* serves as a valuable document that
preserves the physical and emotional ambiance
of the neighborhood.

Resistance and protest. A sense of anger suf-
fuses the pages of *A Walk in the Night*—anger at
the substandard living conditions and constant
sense of surveillance outlined above. Indeed, La
Guma wrote at a crucial moment in the history
of resistance to apartheid. Organizations voicing
protest against racial inequalities predate the ascension of the South African Nationalist party
(sponsor of apartheid). Among these organizations were the African National Congress (ANC,
founded 1912) and the Industrial and Commercial Workers Union of Africa (founded 1919),
groups that benefited from significantly improved leadership beginning in 1948. In 1952
the ANC and the South African Indian Congress
began campaigns of passive resistance, encouraging demonstrators to burn their passbooks (a
passbook was a document containing its owner's
photograph, specifying where that person could

live and work). The goal was to invite arrest in the hope of overwhelming the justice system with the sheer number of protestors.

One such demonstration, conducted by the Pan-Africanist Congress (PAC), assembled droves of Africans without passes at police stations on March 21, 1960. In the town of Sharpeville police opened fire on the protestors, killing 67 and wounding 186, an event that has since become known as the Sharpeville Massacre.

The incident was instantly recognized as a pivotal moment in the progression of protest and brutality; March 21 would become a date revered by antiapartheid strugglers, infusing them with a sense of inspiration and rededication. In the immediate wake of the massacre, thousands of Africans and coloureds walked away from their industrial jobs to support the campaign against passes. Other demonstrations followed throughout 1960, including one in which 40,000 coloured workers stayed home, crippling the clothing, building, engineering, leather, and baking industries of the Cape peninsula. This walkout engendered fears for the nation's economic stability, resulting in a stock market run of unprecedented proportions. Though La Guma purposefully refrains from investing the characters of *A Walk in the Night* with any sense of political awareness, resentment against passbook laws is nonetheless evident: "It's getting to get so's nobody can go nowhere," one coloured man remarks to Michael Adonis (*Walk*, p. 9).

The effectiveness of such protests against this integral component of white supremacy created a national mood of panic, indicated by a massive exodus of thousands of white citizens overseas. The extent to which white South Africans were losing faith in their government's ability to negotiate racial tensions was graphically symbolized in the attempted assassination of Prime Minister H. F. Verwoerd by a politically disgruntled white farmer in April 1960. The political importance of Sharpeville and its aftermath is recognized annually, not only by antiapartheid crusaders who mark March 21 with special meetings (the anniversary is today known as the International Day for the Elimination of Racial Discrimination), but also by police, who throughout the 1960s and '70s cordoned off the region around Sharpeville from the night before the anniversary to the day after. In April 1960, in the wake of Sharpeville, the government declared a state of emergency, which led to the arrest of more than 18,000 people and the outlawing of both the PAC and the ANC.

In 1961 South Africa seceded from the British Commonwealth, and antiapartheid protest increased. So did government repression of such protest. In 1962 the new republic's government began to establish the Bantustans—the independent homelands for Africans—by designating the Transkei (an area east of the Kei River) as the homeland for the Xhosa people of South Africa. To forestall unauthorized ethnic intermingling, the police were granted sweeping powers of preventive detention or arrest, initially for 30 days, and later for indefinite periods.

Underground movements gave the government cause for concern; for example, the PAC militant wing known as "Poqo" armed themselves with homemade machetes and staged a number of attacks on police and government officials. Such threats resulted in the passing of the General Law Amendment Act of 1962, which broadened the definition of treason to include such offenses as graffiti—with a minimum penalty of five years in prison and a maximum penalty of death.

International response to Sharpeville. As important as the internal response to the events of March 21, 1960, was the reaction of the international community. In April the United Nations Security Council addressed apartheid directly and called upon the South African government to dissolve it. From then until apartheid's dismantling in 1991, a major component of resistance to apartheid was the publicizing of its horrors to the international community. As the first director of the United Nations Centre Against Apartheid wrote:

> One of the essential contributions of the United Nations in the international campaign against apartheid in South Africa has been the preparation and dissemination of objective information on the inhumanity of apartheid, the long struggle of the oppressed people for their legitimate rights and the development of the international campaign against apartheid.
>
> (Reddy, p. 1)

The United Nations statement stresses the importance of antiapartheid literature; *A Walk in the Night,* with its depictions of brutal, omnipresent police and devastated coloured neighborhoods, is a form of documentation of the conditions that gave rise to protest.

The Novella in Focus

Plot summary. Michael Adonis, a young coloured man, wanders the streets of Cape Town, seething with resentment over his recent firing by a white supervisor. He meets a friend, Willieboy, at a local café, but finds his anger compounded by Willieboy's apparent nonchalance and indifference. A familiar gang of thugs enters the café, and the leader asks Michael whether he has seen a missing member of their gang, whom they need for a "job" they have planned. Michael professes ignorance.

Leaving the café, Michael indulges in the opportunity to help another young man even less fortunate than himself with a small handout. Michael's beneficiary, Joe, expresses his heartfelt thanks, but the emotion is lost on Michael. The anger that clouds all of Michael's perceptions mounts as he is accosted for no apparent reason by two white police officers who question and harass him before letting him go. By the time he returns home, completing a journey through the oppressively filthy and decayed streets of the coloured quarter, Michael's control over his emotions and actions is fast slipping. He encounters a frustratingly drunk and gregarious Irishman who lives across the hallway of his dilapidated tenement, and the results are tragic. The old man insists on portraying himself as a victim—he compares his misery to that of a Shakespearean character, Hamlet's ghost-father, doomed to walk the night. Michael is infuriated at the idea that a white man should feel self-pity, and strikes an irrational blow at the old man, killing him.

Threaded within the narrative of Michael's journey through the city is the similarly aimless wandering in search of a handout undertaken by his acquaintance, Willieboy. His path takes him to Michael's tenement, where he has the misfortune of peeking into the apartment of the slain Irishman. He flees in terror, and in the resulting commotion is assumed to be responsible for the victim's death.

Also threaded within the tales of Michael and Willieboy is the more purposefully destructive path of Constable Raalt, a brutal Afrikaner police officer intent on making the coloured inhabitants of District Six bear the brunt of unspecified problems he has been having with his wife. As he and his partner patrol the streets on the night of the Irishman's death, Raalt notes the relative quiet of the night and observes, "I wish something would happen. I'd like to lay my hands on one of those bushman bastards and wring his bloody neck" (*Walk,* p. 36). Raalt's unreasoning and egotistic brutality is highlighted by the reflections of his more moderately tempered partner, who fears that Raalt's aggressiveness will discredit the white race. Noticing the commotion

at the Michael Adonis tenement, the pair investigate. John Abrahams, a resident who has concluded that cooperation and the path of least resistance are the best guidelines for a coloured man's survival, gives them a description of Willieboy as the suspected murderer.

As for Willieboy, his continued search for a gift of cash or drink takes him next to a bawdy house, an industry that flourished in District Six. Willieboy asks the madam for a bottle of liquor on credit, but his resentment over the coloured prostitutes' entertainment of three American sailors—"what you let the girls mess with these boggers for? They foreigners"—soon ends in his violent ejection from the premises (*Walk,* p. 51).

Meanwhile, the gang of thugs, who have continually been crossing Michael's path in search of their accomplice, encounter him yet again at another café. Tired of waiting, they invite Michael to take their comrade's place at the "job" they have planned. A strange kind of pride in his recent transgression tempts Michael to agree, though he delays giving a final answer. Joe, who has been sitting nearby and is still grateful for Michael's generosity, compassionately attempts to repay the favor by urging him to avoid these thugs and the certain trouble they represent. In his earnestness, Joe reveals the sad family history of his father's abandonment and his mother's consequent desperation. Michael feels a grudging sympathy, but ultimately turns away in embarrassment and chooses to maintain his isolation.

As Michael leaves, Joe runs after him, intent on dissuading him from taking part in the thugs' activities. His efforts are unheeded, however, and Michael soon finds himself welcomed into the gang's meeting. While they plan their escapade, however, the young men are startled by the sound of a gunshot coming from elsewhere in the District.

We soon learn the source of this gunshot. Constable Raalt and his partner, after cruising the city streets for some time, have chanced upon Willieboy, whom Raalt matches with the description supplied by John Abrahams. Raalt's partner urges restraint and observance of proper procedure, but Raalt is eager for confrontation and immediately opens fire. A chase ensues, and the senselessness of the ordeal overwhelms Willieboy with memories of his abusive parents and troubled childhood. Confused and hunted, he gives voice to the sentiment that dominates the consciousness of all the novella's characters: "Always there's somebody to kick you around" (*Walk,* p. 81).

The chase ends when Willieboy falls from a rooftop and Raalt shoots him where he lies. Raalt and his partner feud once again over the propriety of the shooting, and Raalt scorns the proposition of summoning an ambulance. Critically injured, Willieboy slips into delirium, but Raalt insists on the triviality of his injuries and stops for cigarettes on their way to the police station. During this stop, Willieboy dies.

A Walk in the Night concludes with a brief glimpse of each of the other three young men who have figured principally in the plot. Michael Adonis, his conscience now silenced, embarks upon his newfound career of petty crime. John Abrahams spends a sleepless night wracked with guilt over his complicity against his own people. Meanwhile, Joe continues to wander the city streets, longing for the tranquility of nature.

Naturalism and the city in South African literature. *A Walk in the Night* can reasonably be said to feature the city itself as its principal character. Vivid descriptions of the city's filth, iniquity, and poverty dominate each of the narratives in the novella, to the point that the city becomes more than just the backdrop against which events take place. It becomes a force that determines those events, as well as a symbolic representation of the culture's mood, values, and socioeconomic status.

Casting the city as his principal "character" allows La Guma to tell the story of the sense of community that exists among the Cape Town underclass. *A Walk in the Night*'s structure—its sudden alternation among the stories of mostly unrelated characters—seems at first glance to confirm its characters' impressions that there is no cohesion or continuity among these dogged young men. Indeed, the Irishman's Shakespearean quotation—repeated as the novella's inscription—suggests that these individuals are like so many lonely spirits, "[d]oomed for a certain term to walk the night" (*Walk*, p. 26).

Yet by placing the city itself at the center of attention, La Guma provides a convincing connection among these disparate souls. At pubs and cafés it becomes evident that everyone knows everyone else. Echoing gunshots fired in one alleyway are heard in another. Each young man's disoriented path through the District's labyrinthine streets eventually crosses the others'. Historian Leonard Thompson has written that "there is a story to be told by social historians of the ways in which black people not only survived under apartheid but also created their own social and economic worlds" (Thompson, p. 201).

A Walk in the Night tells part of that story, showing the crossethnic cooperation of nonwhites within the city. As evidenced in part by the presence of the Irishman and his coloured wife in Michael Adonis's tenement, the community of District Six defied the principles and practices of racial segregation.

La Guma's focus on environment shows the influence of naturalism, a literary style first employed in the literature of late nineteenth-century France. Naturalism tried to apply to literature the "objective" and "truthful" standards that were held at the time to characterize the natural sciences, and emphasized a dispassionate narrative style, precise attention to physical details, and the influence of environment on human behavior. In its French incarnation naturalism took the lower classes of society for its subject matter, a tradition followed by naturalist writers in Britain and the Americas as well. Naturalist literature portrayed human destiny as subject to forces that were as indifferent as they were inexorable: social pressure, animalistic urges, and the will of Nature itself. Human free will is relatively unimportant in the naturalist world view, as is individual conscience.

DRUM MAGAZINE

Beginning in 1951, *Drum* appeared monthly. It featured large pictures, a beauty queen on the cover, and serious as well as entertaining content. In the articles, black and coloured writers of the decade protested racial policies, prison conditions, and the way African farmers were exploited. Mixed with this protest literature was text on soccer and other entertaining fare, including short stories by new black writers. Published in La Guma's time and after, *Drum* gave voice to defiant African writers whose stories usually dealt with politics indirectly.

A Walk in the Night constitutes a clear example of naturalist writing, though the movement had long since run out in the Americas and Britain by the time La Guma was writing. While the novel itself protests racial policy in South Africa, La Guma's characters do not speak or think of the larger political questions outside their own suffering. Instead, the characters of *A Walk in the Night* are strictly reactive, controlled by their neighborhood's poverty, their poor education, and the savage police force that watches them so closely. Descriptions of the city's locales—pubs, alleyways, bawdy houses, tenements—are just as prominent as those of the actions of the novella's characters, the emphasis being uniformly on decay and shabbiness. In one scene, the grime of a tenement floor is studied minutely:

> On the floors of the tenements the grime collected quickly. A muddied sole of a shoe scuffed across the worn, splintery boards and left tiny embankments of dirt along the sides of the minute raised ridges of wood; or water was spilled or somebody urinated and left wet patches onto which the dust from the ceilings or the seams of clothes drifted and collected to leave dark patches as the moisture dried. A crumb fell or a drop of fat, and was ground underfoot, spread out to become a trap for the drifting dust that floated in invisible particles. . . .
>
> (*Walk,* p. 32)

The naturalist subjugation of individual to environment that La Guma effects throughout the novella creates the impression that the neighborhood is a community of unofficial brotherhoods and unspoken allegiances, a space with its own energy and the power to unite the disparate members of an underclass.

Sources and literary context. *A Walk in the Night* is an example of "protest literature," a literary genre that emerged in 1950s South Africa in the wake of the banning of the ANC and the PAC. Besides La Guma, such African writers as James Matthews, Ezekiel Mphahlele, and Can Themba practiced the form. In fact, all three of these writers published their work in a radical, avant-garde periodical called *Drum.*

Protest literature emphasizes the brutality of the oppressor, the disillusionment and poverty of the oppressed, and the general ugliness of the South African condition. Intended either as a prodding of the white man's guilty conscience or a call to arms for the underclasses, protest literature consistently dramatizes in bold terms the spectacle of horror. La Guma needed to look no further than the familiar environs of Cape Town's District Six for his material; his writing evokes not only the denizens and habitats of this notorious neighborhood, but the very layout of the streets themselves.

Reviews. As suggested by its very name, protest literature is often perceived to be a lesser literary medium, an instance of artistry giving way to politics and unrestrained emotion. *A Walk in the Night,* however, has largely been praised for its finely controlled style and dispassionate detachment. In particular, La Guma's early critics appreciated the novella's vivid imagery and ability to capture the idiosyncrasies of dialect. South African critic Lewis Nkoski, a detractor of ineptly didactic literature, received *A Walk in the Night* warmly, claiming to find in it "real people waging a bloody contest with the forces of oppression" (Nkoski, pp. 164-65). The *Times Literary Supplement* found the novella's political purpose to have an effect that was more appealing than tiresome, and claimed that the novella cannot be read without "saluting the valiant protest which is the author's life-work" (*Times Literary Supplement,* p. 52). *A Walk in the Night,* like other works by La Guma, was banned in South Africa throughout the author's lifetime (1925-85). South Africans were forbidden from quoting La Guma until 1990.

—Jeff Jung

For More Information

Dubb, Allie A. "The Impact of the City." In *The Bantu-Speaking Peoples of South Africa.* Ed. W. D. Hammond. London: Routledge and Kegan Paul, 1974.

Heard, Anthony Hazlitt. *The Cape of Storms: A Personal History of the Crisis in South Africa.* Foreword by Desmond M. Tutu. Fayetteville: University of Arkansas Press, 1990.

La Guma, Alex. *A Walk in the Night and Other Stories.* Evanston, Ill.: Northwestern University Press, 1967.

Nasson, Bill. *Oral History and the Reconstruction of District Six.* Cape Town: Buchu Books, 1990.

Nkoski, Lewis. "Annals of Apartheid." *New Statesman,* 29 January 1965, pp. 164-65.

Reddy, E. S. "Struggle for Liberation in South Africa and International Solidarity." *Notes and Documents* (September 1972): 1.

Review of *A Walk in the Night,* by Alex La Guma. *Times Literary Supplement,* 21 January 1965, p. 52.

Sibeko, David M. "The Sharpeville Massacre." *Notes and Documents* (March 1976): 3-4.

Thompson, Leonard. *A History of South Africa.* New Haven, Conn.: Yale University Press, 1995.

Western, John. *Outcast Cape Town.* Cape Town: Human and Rosseau, 1981.

We Killed Mangy-Dog and Other Mozambique Stories

by
Luís Bernardo Honwana

L uís Bernardo Honwana was born in Lourenço Marques (now Maputo), Mozambique, in 1942. He spent his childhood and early adolescence in the rural area of Moamba where his father served as interpreter for the government. Completing his high school education in Lourenço Marques at age 17, he took up journalism, writing his first short stories for the young people's page in the newspaper *Notícias* and establishing himself as an author of that genre. Honwana was imprisoned by colonial authorities from 1964 to 1967 for his support of the nationalist party FRELIMO (the Front for the Liberation of Mozambique). His short story collection *We Killed Mangy-Dog and Other Stories*—published in 1964, the year he was imprisoned—exposes some of the colonial realities suffered by Africans in Mozambique before independence. In 1970 Honwana traveled to Portugal, where he studied law at the University of Lisbon and was subject to restrictions on his foreign travel. Defying the restrictions, he fled Portugal, eventually joining up with FRELIMO at its headquarters in Dar es Salaam, Tanzania. Honwana became an adviser there to Samora Machel, Mozambique's future first president. After independence in 1975, Honwana became chief of the president's office, then minister of culture. He later moved to South Africa, where he served as UNESCO'S (United Nations Educational, Scientific, and Cultural Organization) regional representative.

THE LITERARY WORK

A collection of seven short stories set in Maputo province in southern Mozambique in the 1950s and 1960s; published in Portuguese (as *Nós Matamos o Cão Tinhoso*) in 1964, in English in 1969.

SYNOPSIS

The seven stories explore the struggle of Africans to survive Mozambique's colonial regime. In the two stories "Dina" and "Nhinguitimo," migrant farm workers strive to cope with the daily injustices of rural life.

Events in History at the Time of the Short Stories

The Salazar regime—mercantilism and assimilation. Honwana's short stories take place during the regime of Dr. António de Oliveira Salazar, the prime minister of Portugal from 1932 to 1968. A civilian economist, Salazar first came to power in 1928, two years after a right-wing officers' coup overthrew an unstable parliamentary government in Portugal. Appointed finance minister to the new, predominantly military, regime, Salazar received a mandate to balance the budget and reduce the country's external debt. He accomplished these objectives and also succeeded in establishing solvent currency, a favorable balance of trade, and surpluses in both the foreign reserves and national budget. Salazar's

António de Oliveira Salazar, Prime Minister of Portugal
from 1932 to 1968.

success was largely attributable to his radical alteration of Portugal's colonial policy: overseas territories were to be made self-supporting while providing Portugal with the surpluses it needed to purchase what it could not produce. Thus, Mozambique and other Portuguese possessions were to increase production and improve marketing of colonial goods.

These aims were reflected in the Colonial Statute of 1930—written by Salazar himself—"which tightened Lisbon's control over the colonies and removed the discretionary powers that had formerly been exercised by colonial authorities" (Nelson, p. 43). The Colonial Statute also promoted the slogan, "One state, one race, one faith and one civilization," conceiving of the provinces as overseas provinces of Portugal; their interests were subordinate to those of the mother country.

In 1932 Salazar became prime minister of Portugal, introducing a civilian government—the *Estado Novo* (New State)—and a new constitution, which took effect the following year and incorporated the principles of the Colonial Statute, reiterating that Portugal and its territories were "one and indivisible" (Nelson, p. 44). Throughout his long administration, Salazar encouraged

colonial production of Portuguese goods and the emigration of white settlers to Mozambique. The latter policy met with only moderate success. During the 1950s, when Honwana's stories take place, there were only about 50,000 Europeans living in Mozambique and they were concentrated in coastal cities and towns along the Zambezi River (Nelson, p. 44).

Salazar also promoted assimilation among Mozambican Africans, who had few legal rights unless they qualified as *assimilados* (assimilated ones). The Colonial Statute of 1930 and the constitution of 1933 encompassed an earlier pronouncement in the *Lei Orgânica das Provincias do Ultramar* (1914), which had established the *Politica Indigena* (Indigenous Policy). Under this legislation, an *indigena* (indigenous inhabitant) was submitted to different judicial and political systems than the colonizers. A legal distinction was thus made between Africans (indigenas) and Europeans (*não indigenas*), the latter having full rights of Portuguese citizenship. Starting in 1927, Africans who could read or write Portuguese, who rejected "tribal" customs, and who were gainfully employed in the capitalist economy could apply for legal recognition as assimilados. Theoretically, assimilados enjoyed all the rights and responsibilities of a Portuguese citizen. Africans and those of mixed race who did not satisfy assimilation criteria were instructed to carry identity cards at all times, fulfill stringent labor contracts, and live outside designated European areas. The indigenas were also denied access to healthcare and education.

Although many Africans applied for assimilado status, few actually received it. Moreover, after 1954 the requirements that an African had to meet in order to qualify as an assimilado became more stringent. For example, a Mozambican who would have achieved assimilado status by previous standards could now be disqualified because he or she did not speak "proper"—as opposed to "colloquial"—Portuguese (Nelson, p. 46). Historian Per Wästberg observed that, as of 1963, only 5,000 Africans had become Portuguese citizens, "less than .1 per cent" of the Mozambican population (Wästberg in Ehnmark and Wästberg, p. 146). In the short stories, the social and legal divisions between whites, assimilados, and indigenas are continually emphasized. In "Dina," Madala, an old African farm laborer, struggles to complete a hard day's work in the fields under the eye of the brutish white overseer, while in "Nhinguitimo," another indigena, Virgula Oito, loses his farm because of a

Portuguese plantation owner's greed. The uneasy position of assimilados in colonial society is similarly conveyed in "Papa, Snake, and I"; Ginho, a young boy from an assimilado family, witnesses the humiliation of his father by a white neighbor, Senhor Castro, who accuses him of poisoning a prized pointer, who actually died of snakebite. Deferential and placatory to Senhor Castro's face, Ginho's father refers to the man as a "son of a bitch" after he leaves (Honwana, *We Killed Mangy-Dog and Other Mozambique Stories*, p. 45).

Local administration in Mozambique. Although Portugal had the final say in decisions affecting its overseas territories, a system of colonial administration in the "province" of Mozambique was first implemented in 1907 and remained virtually intact until Mozambican independence was achieved in 1975. Under this system, the governor general of Mozambique, who resided in the capital of Lourenço Marques (today Maputo), was given the power to act in Mozambique's interests. A provincial council with limited legislative powers was established and the province itself was subdivided into districts and rural jurisdictions. Matters of local government were handled by district governors who were expected to carry out the policies of the governor general. Administrators of rural jurisdictions were responsible for the direct management of African affairs.

At the time of Honwana's stories, Mozambique was divided into nine districts, each possessing its own capital and governor. The district governor was the most important official in the hierarchy, followed sequentially by the administrator, the *chefe de posto,* the *régulos* (traditional African chiefs), the *cipaios* (indigenous policemen), and the interpreters. The administrator, who functioned as a constant, visible representation of the administration among the people of the district, ensured that the colonial laws, especially those pertaining to the indigenas, were carried out effectively. The chefe de posto was in charge of tax collection and managed the economic development within his district. The régulos worked at the disposal of the chefe de posto, and the cipaios served as the police force, which, at times, would be called on by the administrator to punish or torture recalcitrant subjects. Indeed, local administrations were frequently characterized by graft and brutality: "The underpaid and poorly trained Portuguese officials developed a reputation for incompetence, cruelty, and corruption. Because of their frequent use of coercive

measures to effect policy and enforce the law, the whip and the cudgel became the recognized symbols of Portuguese authority among the great mass of rural Africans" (Nelson, p. 43). The administrator in Honwana's story "Nhinguitimo" is portrayed as a shady individual who willingly conspires with Rodrigues to take away Virgula Oita's land on a pretext we never discover.

Agriculture and labor. Despite less than ideal farming conditions—sandy soil and often inadequate rainfall—in many regions of the country, Mozambique was primarily agricultural, its people making their living off the land. The country's agriculture fell into three basic categories: African subsistence farming—cassava, peanuts, vegetables—supplemented by a few cash crops, like cotton and rice; small- and medium-scale farming using European methods and tools, which was practiced by Portuguese immigrants at the government's behest; and large-scale plantation farming, with each estate employing approximately 140,000 people—most of them Africans (Missiaen, pp. 5-7). Cashew nuts, sisal, sugar, and tea were among the principal crops. Cotton was also much in demand; in 1955, 33 percent of Portugal's industrial labor force worked in textile factories, necessitating a steady supply of cotton (Dolney in Saul, p. 216). While most cotton was produced on plantations in northern Mozambique, African subsistence farmers in all regions could be forced by the government to grow cotton in designated areas and to sell the raw cotton to local concession companies at fixed prices that fell far below those of the world market. By the mid-1950s, 500,000 African farmers in Mozambique were engaged in cotton cultivation.

In the short stories, Honwana pays particular attention to the plight of African farm workers. As indigenas, Africans were subjected to forced labor (*chibalo*), curfews, restricted movement, and limitations placed on how they earned a living and even their venues of entertainment. The first and fourth conditions play a major part in Honwana's stories "Dina" and "Nhinguitimo."

The policies and practices of the chibalo system of legalized forced labor changed constantly from the late 1880s until the early 1960s, affecting both rural and urban laborers. During the mid- to late-1950s, the chibalo system decreed four main categories of work: obligatory work; contract work; resocialization work; and forced farming.

At the time of Honwana's stories, the government controlled obligatory work, stating "that

Mozambiquen women pounding grain.

EXCERPTS FROM THE WORK SONG "WHAT KIND OF SHIBALO IS THIS OF *MAGANDANA*?"

~

Work songs such as "What Kind of Shibalo Is This of *Magandana* [evil person]?" were sung in the traditional languages of Mozambique during the long hours of forced labor. These songs created a sort of dialogue among the workers. The lines from this work song reflect the despair and frustration with the indigena reality, specifically the inhumane colonial labor policies and practices of the Portuguese:

> What kind of *shibalo* is this of *Magandana,* ho . . .
> Ho . . . *Magandana,* ho . . .
> —I am dying, my father, ho . . .
> What kind of *shibalo* is this of *Magandana,* ho . . .
> —They don't even let us rest, ho . . .
> What kind of *shibalo* is this of *Magandana,* ho . . .
> —The settlers are trying to kill us, ho . . .
> What kind of *shibalo* is this of *Magandana,* ho . . .
> —Why don't you go back to your country, ho . . .
> We are killing ourselves, *Mangandana,* ho . . .
>
> (Penvenne, p. 210)

African[s] should devote six months of each year to the services of the government or big enterprises (plantations, industries, etc.) or an individual of non African [heritage]" (Martins, p. 64). Significantly, obligatory work policies did not specify how many hours the worker would be required to work per day; rather, the employer decided the number of hours required of all of his workers. The average workday was 12 hours—with a 30-minute lunch break, the *dina* of Honwana's story—but could extend to 18 hours when laborers were employed by particular families. Pay was very low, usually less than 15 *escudos* per day (U.S. $0.50). Workers who "lagged" in production were often punished with physical abuse and torture.

Contract work was imposed by the *Código Rural de Trabalho,* a system in effect since the beginning of Portuguese colonization, which stipulated: "A contractor enters an agreement with the would-be employer and supplies the labor needed by the employer, who then pays the worker in accordance with the agreement" (Martins, p. 66). This policy allowed the contractor to read aloud the "contract" to all of his workers while withholding pertinent information regarding fees to be paid to the contractor. The payment—before subtraction for fees—ranged from 400 to 600 escudos per month ($13-$20 U.S.).

Of the other forms of chibalo, resocialization work was practiced in prisons, on farms, and on roads. The main objective was to "educate" the African worker, transforming him into an individual who could not only fulfill his prescribed duties but also achieve "a higher morality equal to that of the European" (Martins, p. 66). Forced farming, the fourth type of chibalo, was the most commonly practiced policy, affecting the approximately 1 million Africans engaged in subsistence agriculture. Until the *Acto Colonial* in 1961, self-farming Africans had to comply with the following rules:

- Crops for cultivation must include those that would be sold to the government (i.e., cotton, cashew nuts, rice).
- Lands to be cultivated by Africans were determined by the government.
- Africans were obliged always to reside on the land.
- Africans were obliged to pay any tax the government might impose on them.
- Africans' work should cover a period of eight months in any one year.
- An African should build a brick house within three years after being considered an independent farmer.

• An African's failure to abide by these rules would result in the land being taken from him.

(Martins, p. 67)

In his short story, "Nhinguitimo," Honwana depicts just such a scenario as that described in the last stricture when Virgula Oita loses his farm to his greedy employer, Senhor Rodrigues. Significantly, neither the reader nor Virgula himself ever discovers the exact reason that his land is taken from him: "Lodrica [Rodrigues] has shops, tractors, big farms. . . .Why does he want our place? Why?" (*Mangy-Dog*, p. 71).

The Short Stories in Focus

Plot summary. The seven stories comprising *We Killed Mangy-Dog and Other Mozambique Stories* are set in Moamba, a rural area in the Maputo province in southern Mozambique. All but two stories, "Dina" and "The Old Woman," are told from a child's or young adolescent's perspective, and all seven concern the Africans' struggle to survive an unjust and inhumane colonial regime. Both "Dina" and "Nhinguitimo" deal with the social condition of the African laborer within the colonial system.

"Dina" begins as an old field worker, Madala, struggles to complete his tasks while anticipating the break for dina and the relief it would bring from the scorching sun. Fieldwork has left Madala physically and spiritually broken; he suffers "unbearable," "excruciating" pain in the "small of his back," "the muscles in his neck," and the "tendons behind his knee joints" ("Dina" in *Mangy-Dog*, pp. 1-2). His status as a forced-labor worker does not permit him to tend to his aches and pains. Weary and in agony, he must remind himself that he is "not allowed to work kneeling down" ("Dina," p. 4). With the nearby overseer eager to punish those who are not working to his satisfaction, Madala tries with all of his might to conceal his physical pain.

When the overseer allows the workers to break for dina, Madala slowly moves towards the camp where the meal is served; his fellow laborers greet him with respect and deference: "When they saw him approach, they stopped talking about women and put on a more reverent air" ("Dina," p. 6). Madala observes the overseer eating his lunch and drinking wine "with great enjoyment," reminding the old man of his own visits—at the end of the month—to the cantina where he shares wine with his friends ("Dina," p. 8). Although the overseer does not finish his

bottle of wine, Madala notes that he never shares its remains. As the old man watches the overseer, Madala's daughter, Maria, comes to visit him but the overseer interrupts their conversation. Maria encourages her father to go and eat. After Madala gets his food, he observes the overseer talking to Maria in an angry manner. Later, Madala and the other laborers watch as the overseer follows Maria into the field and sexually assaults her. Afterward, a panicky Maria is mainly concerned that her father has witnessed the act, exclaiming to the overseer, "Now Madala saw! . . . Madala saw!" ("Dina," p. 15). But the overseer, unaware that Maria is Madala's daughter, fails to understand the significance of her words. He tosses a silver coin in Maria's lap as payment, then is shocked to learn the truth of Maria and Madala's relationship. A young laborer from the Kraal gang appeals to Madala for encouragement to avenge the rape of Maria: "Madala . . . tell us what we must do! . . . Speak, and we'll finish with all this now" ("Dina," p. 15). Initially beside himself over the discovery that Madala is Maria's father, the overseer suddenly appears to dismiss the fact and recover his domineering manner. As he orders the workers back to the field, he holds out his bottle of wine and beckons to Madala, who takes the bottle and finishes its contents in one gulp. The young man of the Kraal gang spits at Madala's feet and calls him a "dog" ("Dina," p. 18). Ignoring the youth's actions, Madala slowly returns to the field. The overseer commands the youth to return to work, but the youth does not move. The overseer hits him with the bottle, splitting his scalp open with the second blow, then crushes his face with his boots. Meanwhile, Madala and the other laborers resume their labors as though nothing has occurred.

FROM "DINNER" TO "DINA"

Linguistically, *dina* is a corruption of the word "dinner." How did the word find its way into Mozambique? Some Mozambicans, known as *magaíças*, traveled to South Africa to work in its gold mines. Coming from various parts of southern Africa, the miners communicated with one another in a pidgin known as Fanagalô, which contains terms from a number of languages, including English. When the magaíças returned to Mozambique, they introduced Fanagalô terms into their own languages as well as their version of Portuguese.

"Nhinguitimo" (the title refers to the violent storm marking the beginning of the rains) begins with the coming of the storm in the Incomati valley, which lies at the foot of the Libombo mountains. The story is told by an adolescent boy who observes the dynamics of the relationship between a farm owner and black laborer during the extremely humid nights before the arrival of the nhinguitimo. During these humid nights, the "best people" (the administrator, the doctor, the postmaster, the veterinarian, and the stationmaster) are found talking around Rodrigues's counter surrounded by the company of field laborers and village prostitutes.

Virgula Oito, a laborer on Rodrigues's farm, also has his own land "on the other side of Goana, where the administrator had not yet decreed the abolition of the native reserve" ("Nhinguitimo" in *Mangy-Dog*, p. 57). Virgula makes the most of farming his fertile land, planning to make a considerable profit on growing vegetables. He also hopes to build a good life for himself and N'teasee, the girl he intends to marry. During his visits to Rodrigues's store, Virgula unwisely brags about the fertile soil he owns, the abundant crops he produces, and the money he will make from them. Maguiguana and Matchumbutana, two co-workers on Rodrigues' farm, warn Virgula that acquiring as much money as Rodrigues could be dangerous because the whites may become very angry by such an act. Virgula dismisses both men's comments as nonsense, explaining, "But why should you think they'd be angry? . . . I won't kill or steal, I'll eat what I earn from my work, I'll spend my money on my family, I'll pay my taxes, I'll pay my labourers. . . . How could they be angry?" ("Nhinguitimo," p. 62).

Meanwhile, Rodrigues calls the "ownership" and abundance of Virgula's farm to the attention of the administrator. Rodrigues explains to the administrator that his concern derives from "such good rich land being squandered on the blacks" ("Nhinguitimo," p. 62). The administrator asks Virgula about his land, and Virgula explains how his land is large and productive due to its fertile soil. Later Virgula finds out that the administration has taken his land away from him. When one of the laborers asks Virgula, "d'you think it's right, all this business of Lodrica?" ("Lodrica" is a mispronunciation of "Rodrigues"), Virgula begins to laugh maniacally, as thunder clashes and the skies darken; moments later, nhinguitimo strikes, seemingly called into existence by Virgula's lunacy. Later, a mud-spattered Maguiguana enters Rodrigues's store and tells him that

Virgula has gone crazy, killing Machumbutana and some of the other laborers. Rodrigues beckons some of the other men to take up arms and aid him in shooting Virgula before he kills again, exclaiming, "Let's go quickly before something terrible happens in this village! . . . My God!" ("Nhinguitimo," p. 74). Meanwhile, the adolescent narrator of the story is vexed to hear that "a whole lot of super things had been happening and I hadn't even noticed!" and vows to become more aware of what is going on around him ("Nhinguitimo," p. 74).

Violence, resistance, and liberation. Literary scholar David Brookshaw observes that Honwana "was inspired by the moment, the injustices of the colonial system, and the changes that were taking place in Mozambique during the 1950s and 1960s" (Brookshaw in Cox, p. 328). Indeed, Honwana's vivid depiction of "the moment"— epitomized by the daily humiliations suffered by Africans at the hands of their Portuguese oppressors—is arguably the hallmark of his fiction.

Throughout the short stories, Honwana's African characters continually confront the injustices of colonialism; their individual responses to the situation are usually dictated by age and experience. Brookshaw notes that there is often "a clash between an older generation that has been conditioned to accept humiliation and the youths who are disappointed by their elders' inability to react against daily tyranny" (Brookshaw in Cox, p. 322). In "Dina," the youth of the Kraal gang is disgusted when the elderly Madala does nothing to avenge his daughter's rape by the overseer, while in "Papa, Snake, and I," young Ginho wonders why his Papa does not stand up for himself against the white neighbor who wrongfully accuses him of poisoning a dog. Ginho, however, undergoes a similar humiliation in "We Killed Mangy-Dog" when he allows peer pressure—applied by Quim, a Portuguese schoolmate—to persuade him to participate in the shooting of a stray dog that he pities and that Isaura, another schoolmate, loves. In Honwana's stories, however, resistance to one's oppressors is almost invariably met with violent punishment. The overseer beats the recalcitrant Kraal youth senseless in "Dina" while in "Nhinguitimo" Virgula Oita's crazed response to the loss of his land prompts the frightened Portuguese to hunt him down in their turn.

While the impulse to revolt and retaliate is continually frustrated in Honwana's stories, a resistance movement that would eventually change Mozambican history forever was taking shape at the same time. Decades earlier, there had been localized opposition attempts against colonialism, which included social banditry and peasant revolts, but lack of organization among the Africans, and the superior armed strength of the Portuguese police force, doomed most of these protests to failure (Isaacman, p. 101). In the years following World War II, the Mozambican government suppressed through police force and censorship any demonstrations or protests that arose, including "dockers' strikes, unrest in Lourenço Marques in 1948, and protests in Inhambane and other towns to protest labor conditions, inadequate pay, or poor food supplies. Many were killed in riots, and others who took part were imprisoned or suffered reprisals" (Nelson, p. 47).

From the mid-1950s to the mid-1960s, however, various anticolonial political organizations began to form throughout Mozambique. Support for these organizations came mainly from laborers and peasants who had suffered most from the oppressive labor policies and practices implemented by the Portuguese. However, educated African expatriates and Mozambique's "indigenous elite"—who numbered around 30,000 according to the 1955 census—agreed on the necessity for the country's independence from Portugal (Nelson, p. 47). These intellectuals encouraged student associations, regional mutual aid societies, and other social organizations to adopt a political orientation.

In the mid-1950s, a national organization known as NESAM (Nucleus of African Secondary Students of Mozambique) was formed; its members included Eduardo Mondlane, Joaquim Chissano, and Mariano Matsnhe, all future leaders of the liberation struggle. These men generated a wave of interest and activity in the idea of national independence, while encouraging organized resistance to the Portuguese. Other movements dedicated to the cause included UDENAMO (the National Democratic Union of Mozambique), founded in 1959; MANU (the Mozambique African National Union), founded in 1960; and UNAMI (National African Union of Independent Mozambique).

The early 1960s found African workers, peasants, and intellectuals in Mozambique vehemently fighting the atrocities inflicted on them by the Portuguese colonial government. African urban workers staged strikes while peasants resisted the forced labor policy of chibalo. In June 1961, the Portuguese army massacred 600 unarmed peasants protesting unjust labor policies

and practices in the village of Mueda. In response to this incident, representatives from UDENAMO, MANU, and UNAMI met in June 1962 at a conference in Dar es Salaam, a conference that resulted in the formation of a new organization, FRELIMO (the Front for the Liberation of Mozambique). Despite internal stresses and several schisms (the group formerly known as UDENAMO broke away in 1964 and reformed as the National Democratic Union of Munhumutapa), FRELIMO became the dominant organization of the Mozambican liberation movement.

On September 25, 1964, FRELIMO soldiers, aided by the peasants and workers in the surrounding area of the Delgado Province of the north, attacked Chai, a Portuguese administrative post. The soldiers damaged the post, killed one policeman, and wounded several others. This incident marked the true beginning of Mozambique's organized armed struggle against the colonial regime for independence, which was finally achieved in 1975.

Sources and literary context. Honwana drew much of his stories' content from life experiences in his rural childhood home of Moamba. The landscape and people of the region furnished him with themes, characters, and settings. Such real-life places as the Libombo Mountains and the Incomati river valley are referred to in "Nhinguitimo," while Dori, a young girl to whom Honwana dedicated the Portuguese edition of his stories—"a Dori, que é sensível à angústia dos cães" (to Dori, who is sensitive to the anguish of dogs)—served as the model for Isaura in the title story, "We Killed Mangy-Dog."

Honwana's major contribution to Mozambican literature was his development of prose fiction there as a legitimate and respected genre. *Nós Matamos o Cão Tinhoso* was the only book of "African" prose published in Mozambique prior to independence in 1975. Before Honwana's stories appeared in 1964, Mozambican prose fiction was limited to three types: the traditional African folktale delivered in oral form; the European settler's tale, which presented Africa from an outsider's perspective; and the missionary's tale, which had a prevailing moral objective—to lead the pagan African to a better, "civilized," life through religious teachings. Honwana did not draw upon any of these models, but found another source of inspiration in the highly acclaimed protest poetry of José Craveirinha (to whom Honwana also dedicated his collection of short stories) and Noémia Sousa, who both wrote in the 1950s about their dreams of black solidarity and the awakening of Mother Africa. Their simple language and strong rhythms served as a basis for Honwana's own style in depicting the experiences and sufferings of ordinary people under Portuguese colonial rule.

The Depression-era "realist" writings of American writers such as Ernest Hemingway, John Steinbeck, and Erskine Caldwell provided an additional influence on Honwana, especially in relation to social concerns and vivid descriptions of nature.

JOSÉ CRAVEIRINHA: THE POET OF MOZAMBIQUE

José Craveirinha was born in Maputo in 1922. He pursued a career in journalism and proved to be a fierce critic of Portuguese colonialism, resulting in his arrest in 1966. His journalistic prose and creative poetry inspired the nation. Celebrated as the "Poet of Mozambique," Craveirinha is praised for encompassing the collective voice and sentiments of the people of Mozambique in his poetry. Like Senegal's poet-statesman Leopold Senghor, Craveirinha pays homage to Mother Africa and traditional African culture through his use of rhythmic tones and vivid imagery, meanwhile igniting nationalistic sentiments by revealing the injustices that afflict the colonized in Mozambique. In his well-known poem, "Grito Negro" (Black Cry), Craveirinha explores the issue of the exploitation of African coal miners:

> Eu sou cravão!
> Tenho que arder na exploração
> Arder até às crinzas da maldição
> Arder vivo como alcatrão, meu Irmão
> Até não ser mais tua mina
> Patrão!
>
> I am coal!
> I must burn your world of exploitation
> Burn until I become ashes of malediction
> Burn with live heat like tar, my Brother
> Until I am no longer your mine
> Boss!
>
> (Craveirinha in Andrade, p. 180)

Overall, Honwana's prose fiction is viewed as a political act—directed towards an imagined audience consisting of white city dwellers and those living outside colonial Mozambique—that attempts to investigate and expose the daily atroc-

ities taking place in his country. His dedication to the cause of Mozambican liberation in both his life and his art earned him the praise of FRELIMO—a movement he ardently supported—and the reputation as a pioneer of Mozambican literature.

Reviews. Upon its 1964 publication in Mozambique, *Nós Matamos o Cão Tinhoso* was praised by the small group of African intellectuals who were dedicated to using literature (mostly poetry) as a political tool in the struggle for independence. Literary critics speculate on the connection between the publication of *Nós Matamos o Cão Tinhoso*—with its revealing content of the brutal nature of Portuguese colonial rule and practices—and Honwana's subsequent arrest. In *Rádio Moçambique,* José Régio proclaimed Honwana's fiction to be "a genuine form of fresh, spontaneous realism" (Régio, p. 59).

Outside Mozambique, *Nós Matamos o Cão Tinhoso* was very well received after its debut in 1964; within three years, translations of the stories could be found in Nigeria, South Africa, Great Britain, France, the Soviet Union, and the United States. South African novelist Nadine Gordimer (see **Burger's Daughter,** also covered in *African Literature and Its Times*) was so taken with Honwana's short story, "The Hands of the Blacks," that she recommended it to the *New York Times.* In Lisbon, the Portuguese intellectual Amândio César published an enthusiastic review, hailing Honwana as "the youngest revelation in Mozambican prose writing" and drawing particular attention to his "simplistic technique that lends a strange vivacity and authenticity to his testimony" (César, pp. 206-208).

—LaShonda Long and Pamela S. Loy

For More Information

Andrade, Mário. *Antologia Temática de Poesia Africana 1: na noite grávida de punhais.* Lisbon: Sá da Costa, 1975.

César, Amândio. *Parágrafos de literatura ultamarina.* Lisbon: Sociedade de Expans o Cultural, 1967.

Cox, D. Brian, ed. *African Writers.* Vol. 1. New York: Charles Scribner's Sons, 1997.

Ehnmark, Anders, and Per Wästberg. *Angola and Mozambique: The Case Against Portugal.* Trans. Paul Britten Austin. London: Pall Mall, 1963.

Honwana, Luís Bernardo, *We Killed Mangy-Dog and Other Mozambique Stories.* Trans. Dorothy Guedes. London: Heinemann, 1969.

Isaacman, Allen F. *The Tradition of Resistance in Mozambique: The Zambesi Valley, 1850-1921.* Berkeley: University of California Press, 1976.

Martins, Elisio. *Colonialism and Imperialism in Mozambique: The Beginning of the End.* Transcribed and presented by Jospeh Kofi Mensah. Kastrup, Denmark: African Studies, 1974.

Missiaen, Edmond. *Mozambique's Agricultural Economy in Brief.* Washington, D.C.: Economic Research Service, U.S. Deptartment of Agriculture, 1969.

Nelson, Harold. ed. *Mozambique: A Country Study.* Washington, D.C.: Foreign Area Studies, 1984.

Penvenne, Jeanne. *African Workers and Colonial Racism: Mozambican Strategies and Struggles in Lourenço Marques, 1877-1962.* Portsmouth, N.H.: Heinemann, 1995.

Régio, José. *Rádio Moçambique* (Lourenço Marques) 419 (January 1972): 59.

Saul, John S., ed. *A Difficult Road.* New York: Monthly Review, 1985.

Weep Not, Child

by
Ngugi wa Thiong'o

W*eep Not, Child*, the first novel published in English by a black writer from East Africa, launched the career of the most famous of Kenyan novelists. Ngugi wa Thiong'o was born in 1938 into the Gikuyu (also known as the Kikuyu) people of Kenya's central highlands. His childhood coincided with Kenya's struggle for independence through the actions of Jomo Kenyatta's Kenya African Union (KAU) and the violent Mau Mau Rebellion. After independence in 1963 Ngugi emerged as an influential writer and intellectual. Serving as chairman of the English Department at the University of Nairobi in the late 1960s, he successfully agitated for a curriculum focused on African literature. In the late 1970s the author who had led Kenyans in writing in English returned to his native tongue. In 1977 his Gikuyu play *Ngaahika ndeenda* (I Will Marry When I Want; written with Ngugi wa Mirii) was performed by peasants and workers. This highly political drama caused the government to jail Ngugi without trial for over a year. This experience did not intimidate him; since his release, he has continued to write, in Gikuyu and in English, and to comment on the politics of Kenya and the world.

Events in History at the Time the Novel Takes Place

Colonial context. From the beginning Britain's involvement with Kenya differed greatly from its colonial adventures elsewhere in Africa. First, the origins of British interest in East Africa were quite

---

THE LITERARY WORK

A novel set in Kenya in the 1950s; published in English in 1964.

SYNOPSIS

A Kenyan boy comes of age in the turbulent final years of British colonialism.

---

different from those of their interest in West Africa, where they dealt directly with the many local ethnic groups. The British came to Kenya as a result of their longstanding relationship with the Arab sultan of Oman. The Omani Kingdom dominated trade throughout the Middle East and Indian Ocean; almost as a sideline, the sultan held important trading rights in East Africa. The British offered the sultan their military might in exchange for trading privileges in all of these areas.

To protect these trading interests the British sought, and gained, increasing influence over the Omani Kingdom. The death of the powerful Sultan Seyyid Said in 1856 gave the British a perfect opportunity to turn their alliance with Oman into a functional protectorate: using military threat and diplomatic muscle, they picked the next sultan and managed all his affairs. By 1885 the threat of German colonialism in the area convinced the British that indirect rule of East Africa through the Omanis was inefficient; they began to deal directly with the Germans and in 1895 established the British East African Protectorate, which included the island of Zanzibar and Kenya.

GIKUYU LIFE BEFORE THE BRITISH

B efore the British assumed direct control over them, the Gikuyu followed a way of life not much different from that of their ancestors many centuries before. An agricultural people, they devoted themselves to the land and the ancestors who had tamed it. The most important figure in their religion was Murungu, the creator who gave to Gikuyu and Mumbi (the first man and the first woman) all the lands that the Gikuyu people held. The sense of connection to the land was essential to Gikuyu culture; they were enraged when the British expropriated their land and limited them to small reserves.

The Gikuyu owned and worked the land collectively. Every clan or extended family (called a *mbari*) owned and worked a certain amount of land to their own benefit. A few without land of their own, called *ahoi*, were allowed to work on the land of a mbari; the whole social collective of neighboring mbari was governed by a council of elders. The family structure of the Gikuyu was polygamous, or, more exactly, polygynous: a man could marry as often as he could afford to pay dowry, and—since wives worked not only at producing children but also as field laborers—a man's wealth could be said to reside largely in his family.

The incursion of the British disrupted nearly every aspect of Gikuyu society. The British dispossessed the Gikuyu of their land, then appointed Gikuyu chiefs who often enriched themselves by preying on their people. The British also brought Christianity, which found many converts among the Gikuyu, but which also disrupted the rituals that held the people together. In particular, female circumcision and polygyny drew the wrath of Christian missionaries, who made rejection of these practices a prerequisite for baptism. Pushing these issues to the front in the late 1920s and early 1930s, the Christians forced many Kenyans to choose. Many agreed with the Christians and abandoned these traditional ways. But a similarly large number either rejected Christianity or adapted it by blending it with indigenous forms. This early division played a significant part in shaping the Mau Mau Rebellion of the 1950s, which was fought less between the British and Africans than between Africans who supported the British and Africans who wanted the British gone.

Declaring a protectorate in East Africa turned out to be easier than establishing a genuine colonial government there. After 1895 the British faced continual armed struggles against such peoples as the Nandi, the Abagusii, the Turkana, and many others. The Nandi and Abagusii gained prominence for their ferocity in fighting the British, though other groups (the Gikuyu, the Maasai, and the Galla) outnumbered and out-influenced them. To cope with this situation the British colonial administration was divided into two structures. White overseers filled the posts of greatest authority, making all major decisions and shaping the larger path of Kenyan development. However, because qualified colonial administrators were few, and the native Kenyan groups so difficult to manage, the British also attempted to use the power of local chiefs to control the colonized groups. They established a legal structure that allowed those African leaders recognized by the British to decide local matters, administer law, and find laborers for British public works programs. When they encountered peoples such as the Gikuyu, who were ruled by councils rather than chiefs, the British simply created chieftaincies. In this way the British hoped to be able to extract the greatest amount of wealth from Kenya with the least amount of political turmoil.

However, their aims were complicated by another distinctive aspect of the British experience in Kenya: the presence of significant numbers of Europeans who hoped to make Kenya their permanent home (see **Out of Africa,** also covered in *African Literature and Its Times*). The Kenyan highlands, where the Gikuyu people were the dominant group, had a climate far superior—to European tastes—to that of West Africa: temperate, easily arable, and free of malaria. From the 1890s to the 1940s white settlers flooded into Kenya, appropriated land, and forced native Kenyans to work for them. The Kenyans had to cope, therefore, not merely with a miscellany of bureaucrats, traders, missionaries, and soldiers, but with a large group of Englishmen who had come to Kenya not to trade or convert or administer, but to settle.

The British did not have an easy time conquering Kenya; many of the ethnic groups in the region fiercely resisted the colonists' encroachments. Even after the greater unity and more advanced weaponry of the British made it obvious that armed resistance was futile, the region could not really be called subdued. Almost immediately native Kenyans began to clamor for a greater share in government; in less than 20 years from the official British annexation of Kenya, resistance groups pressured the British government to alter fundamentally the nature of the British presence in Kenya.

From the beginning the British settlers in Kenya had a simple aim: they wanted self-governance and a degree of independence from London. Their model was Southern Rhodesia, whose white settlers profited from self-governance blended with a fruitful economic relationship with England. Almost to a person, settlers assumed their natural superiority to the Africans; why should they not rule Kenya? However, in order to persuade England to allow self-governance they had to accomplish certain things. They had to prove that they were economically viable and could survive without assistance. They had to prove they could defend Britain's political interests in the area against the colonial ambitions of her great rival, Germany. Perhaps most importantly, they had to prove themselves capable of managing and controlling the African population. The white settlers of Kenya failed, to varying extents, to accomplish any of these objectives, and they failed particularly miserably in the third. From the beginning the Kenyans protested their condition loudly; in the 1950s protest metamorphosed into mass action and violent rebellion.

Jomo Kenyatta. In 1931 a young Kenyan named Jomo Kenyatta journeyed to England as part of a delegation that planned to air African grievances to the British government. The delegation was largely unsuccessful, but Kenyatta ended up staying in England for 15 years, and this long stay turned out to be anything but a failure. In England Kenyatta associated with other anticolonialist Africans, both from Kenya and elsewhere. In 1944 he was among the 33 founding members of the Kenya African Union (KAU), whose objective was to force the British government to give native Kenyans a much larger share in the colonial government. Two years later, in September 1946, he returned to Kenya and found himself mobbed by enthusiastic supporters everywhere he traveled. In 1947 he was elected president of the KAU and molded what began as a policy-study group for an educated elite into a mass political party. For native Kenyans he was the leader who transcended their division into local groups and pointed the way to freedom; for the white settlers and the British government he was public enemy number one.

The activities of the KAU raised immeasurably the political consciousness of Kenyans. Before the party's birth Kenya's African peoples had remained somewhat isolated from each other; they did not realize that success against the British required intergroup cooperation. Kenyatta's insistence on multigroup leadership underscored the fact that, even if they shared nothing else, all of Kenya's black peoples shared oppression. They would have to work together to expel the British. Perhaps more importantly, Kenyatta stood as a personal symbol of what Kenyans could accomplish: refusing to back down to the British, he proved that military might could be countered by a strong will and firm purpose.

The accomplishments of the KAU are all the more remarkable when one considers that, from the very beginning, the party was split between conservative and radical elements. The conservatives wanted peaceful agitation, gradual reform, and a greater share of self-government within the structures of colonialism. The radical element

THE COLONIAL LAND GRAB

The great Kenyan leader Jomo Kenyatta once said, "If you woke up one morning and found that someone had come to your house, and had declared that the house belonged to him, you would naturally be surprised, and you would like to know by what arrangement" (Kenyatta in Ochieng', p. 119). This was precisely the situation of countless Kenyans in the early twentieth century. By no other arrangement than the power of their guns, the British claimed the Kenyan highlands for themselves. Kenyans living on land that Britain claimed were called squatters and were able to remain only as long as the British allowed it. Worse, the British became both government and landlord. In the former capacity, they levied taxes; in the latter, rent. Both were to be paid not in cash or goods, but in labor—labor on the farms of the new settlers. Thus a Kenyan could find himself legally obligated to work for someone else on land where his ancestors had lived for generations.

The British land laws exempted villages, and a system of reservations for Africans was set up in 1915, concessions that hardly satisfied the African peoples. For centuries Kenya had hosted innumerable visitors: traders from as far away as Arabia and India had passed through. However, when Kenyans realized that the British not only planned to stay but actually claimed to *own* the country, they realized they could not exercise patience. They would have to act to expel the visitors who would not go away.

Jomo Kenyatta.

would settle for nothing less than the immediate end of British colonialism and the introduction of democracy in Kenya. Kenyatta himself had a foot in each camp. On the one hand, he was committed to independence, and even refused to rule out the use of force to achieve it. On the other, he was too canny a politician to eschew attempts to reform British rule from within. Therefore, he continued to work within the system to bring about change. When real violence began in the early 1950s, however, Kenyatta's prominence made him a natural target of British punishment. In a 1952 trial whose significance echoes in Ngugi's novel, Kenyatta was convicted (on flimsy, tainted evidence) of being a leader of the Mau Mau Rebellion.

The Mau Mau Rebellion. The Mau Mau Rebellion is shot through with contradictions and mystery. It would not have happened without the peaceful agitation of the well-organized KAU, yet it was a radical grassroots movement without a single structure of leadership. It began and flourished in the city of Nairobi but is best remembered as a jungle war. It was a war waged against British imperialism, yet it ended up killing more Africans than Englishmen; thousands died violently, the vast majority Kenyan, and many of

those were fighting on the side of the British. Perhaps most paradoxically, this military failure was a political success. Mau Mau was the inversion of a Pyrrhic victory: the rebels lost the battle, but they won the war.

The origins of the name "Mau Mau" are uncertain—suggestions have ranged from a British misspelling of *mumua* (the Gikuyu word for "oath") to a variation of *uma uma,* meaning "out, out," to a variety of others—but the origin of the rebellion can be summed up in one word: frustration. Mau Mau drew its strength from the legions of Kenyans, especially Gikuyus, who agonized over the snail's pace of peaceful reform and the daily indignity of living as squatters in their own country. Conditions on the African reserves were abominable: overcrowded, impoverished, and handicapped by colonial law, Kenyans also had to suffer the sight of British and Indian settlers living in what seemed like wealth and ease.

After World War II this frustration was intensified by the presence of thousands of Kenyan veterans (called *askaris*). Black Kenyans had fought for the British in all phases of the war, gaining experience of the world and a broader perspective on political action. They returned to Kenya to find limited jobs and racial discrimination. Some 15,000 askaris had served as truck drivers in the British Army, and many hoped to continue this line of work but there were only 2,000 trucks in all of Kenya (Ochieng', p. 134). Askaris embodied a dangerous mixture: bitterness at their dismal futures compounded with practical experience in the methods and ends of warfare. From the beginning ex-servicemen played a key role in Mau Mau.

In the late 1940s and very early 1950s, Mau Mau gathered strength as a kind of secret organization. Initiates swore some version of the "Mau Mau Oath," a pledge to fight for Kenyan independence, accompanied by mutations of traditional initiation rights such as drinking the blood of a goat. Late in 1952 the gathering storm broke. Waruhiu, a Kenyan chief staunchly loyal to the British, was assassinated outside Nairobi. This sensational crime (Waruhiu was killed by anti-colonial black men in the uniforms of the colonial police) spurred the colonial government to declare a state of emergency. On the night of October 20, 1952, 187 suspected Mau Mau leaders were arrested, including Jomo Kenyatta. While this move did round up a number of Mau Mau leaders (along with many, like Kenyatta, who were fundamentally uninvolved in the inci-

Suspects of the Mau Mau rebellion in Kenya, 1953.

dent), it did nothing to quell the rebellion be-cause Mau Mau was so widespread. Instead, ar-resting the known leaders left the movement in the hands of younger, more aggressive leaders—like Boro in *Weep Not, Child*.

Mau Mau was less a full-scale war than an ag-gressive guerilla campaign. Rebels hid in the forests and swept out to attack a single settler or an African chief loyal to the British; they stole guns and ammunition in daring raids. This cam-paign of terror profoundly alarmed the white set-tlers and the British government, whose response did not address the underlying grievances that caused the rebellion. Instead, by bombing the forests, stepping up police brutality, and allow-ing the questioning and detention of thousands of innocent Kenyans, the British seemed to prove the Mau Mau's point: the British were a violent invading force and could be driven away only through force. The British Army, supported by a Home Guard composed of loyalist Kenyans, slowly broke the back of the rebellion. Aggres-sive campaigns of bombing, preventive deten-tion, and forced relocation severed the link be-tween the forest Mau Mau and their supporters in Nairobi and the villages; over time, the British were able to strangle the life from the rebellion. With the capture and execution of the great Mau Mau leader Dedan Kimathi in February 1957, the rebellion was effectively over.

Judging by numbers, the Mau Mau failed mis-erably. Close to 15,000 Mau Mau died during the fighting, compared to fewer than 5,000 set-tlers, soldiers, and loyalists. Only about 30 white civilian settlers were killed. In fact, during the rebellion more white settlers died in traffic acci-dents than at the hands of the Mau Mau. But even though the Mau Mau lost the battle, they helped win the war for Kenyan freedom. Their aim had been to frighten whites into leaving the land. They did not accomplish this, but they did effect a long-term shift in British thinking. Forgetting the bloodshed required to conquer Kenya in the late nineteenth century, the British assumed that African peoples were cowardly, unorganized, and easily led. Mau Mau put an end to this way of thinking. If the colony could be held only by the kind of massive expenditure of money and power it took to quell this rebellion, then Kenya was hardly worth the holding. By 1960 the British had agreed to a radical restructuring of Kenyan goverment, one which guaranteed African ma-jority rule. In 1961 Jomo Kenyatta was released from prison. On December 12, 1963, he became the first prime minister of a free Kenya.

The Novel in Focus

Plot summary. *Weep Not, Child* opens as Njoroge, a boy of about nine who lives near the village of Kipanga, is asked by his mother if he would like to attend school. This question opens up a whole new world for Njoroge, who has always dreamed of an education. He enthusiastically agrees. This brief exchange begins a novel that, although short, is vast in scope and rich in incident and character. However, from beginning to end the novel is loosely unified by Njoroge's dogged pursuit of an education. On his first day Njoroge walks to school with Mwihaki, the daughter of Jacobo, his family's landlord. She protects him from the bullying of the older schoolboys, and they begin a friendship that will survive the political events that make their families bitter enemies.

MAJOR CHARACTERS IN THE NOVEL

Njoroge: A Gikuyu schoolboy.

Ngotho: Father of Njoroge; a veteran of World War I and a foreman on Mr. Howlands's farm.

Nyokabi: Mother of Njoroge; Ngotho's second wife.

Njeri: Ngotho's elder wife; mother of Boro and Kamau.

Kamau: Brother to whom Njoroge is closest; a carpenter.

Boro: Njoroge's eldest brother; emotionally scarred by his experience in World War II. Later a rebel.

Jacobo: Kenyan landowner and Ngotho's landlord. Collaborates with the British.

Mwihaki: Jacobo's daughter and Njoroge's closest friend.

Mr. Howlands: A British man rewarded for his service in World War I with land in Kenya. Later tries to suppress the rebellion of the Kenyans.

Jacobo is a man of consequence in the community and a friend of the British colonists. Ngotho, on the other hand, works for Mr. Howlands, a rich British settler, but he is no friend of the colonial regime. He works on Mr. Howlands's farm in order to remain close to the land of his ancestors; at night, he tells his family stories from the religion of the Gikuyu nation to which they belong. These stories prophesy that the British will be forced out and the Gikuyu will resume control of their ancestral lands.

> "Do you think," Ngotho was asked, "that the prophecy will ever be fulfilled?"
> "I don't know. . . . It may not be fulfilled in my lifetime."
>
> (Ngugi wa Thiong'o, *Weep Not, Child*, pp. 29-30)

Ngotho's stories are openly revolutionary, but for one of his sons, Boro, they are not revolutionary enough. Boro served the British in World War II and is permanently embittered by the death of his brother, Mwangi, in the war. Ngotho is confused and hurt by the open disdain Boro shows him. As the novel progresses, Boro withdraws from the family, spending more time with the young men agitating for rebellion in Nairobi. Eventually, he brings these agitators to Kipanga, forcing Ngotho to choose between his job and the struggle for freedom. But at the beginning, he pins his hopes on Njoroge's education: "If Njoroge could now get all the white man's learning, would Ngotho even work for Howlands?" (*Weep Not*, p. 16).

Njoroge does well at school and becomes closer to Mwihaki. The two of them discuss the situation of Kenya with the naive earnestness of children, unaware that their parents are on opposite sides of a great political divide. The only thing Njoroge does not share with Mwihaki are his developing religious and political ideas. He combines the religion told him by his parents with the Christianity taught at school (and Ngugi points out how similar the two are) to develop a sense that his people have a special mission to acquire their freedom. His hopes are pinned on the freedom fighter called "the Black Moses": Jomo Kenyatta. Kenyatta, the great fighter for Kenyan liberty, and eventually the first leader of free Kenya, casts his long shadow over the next, more intense phase of the novel. His return to Kenya from England intensifies the hostility between Kenyans and the British colonists. Agitators brought by Boro to Kipanga spread the word: a general strike is planned. All Kenyans employed by the British are asked to stop working until Africans are given pay equal to that of Europeans and Indians, and until racial discrimination is abolished. The call for a strike means that Ngotho must make a choice. Up till now he has passively waited for Mr. Howlands to leave, using his job as an opportunity to stay close to the land which he is confident will be his again. But Mr. Howlands says that any of his employees who goes on strike will be fired at once. For Ngotho, then, the stakes are unusually high. In spite of the risks, and over the objection of his two wives, he decides to go on strike.

The strife comes to a head on the day Njoroge and Mwihaki learn that they have passed their preliminary examinations. Both rush home, excited to share the news with their families, and both find their families stunned and terrified by horrible events. At a meeting held by the organizers of the strike, Jacobo, who had convinced the British settlers that he was a man of great influence in the Kenyan community, took the stage and attempted to convince the strikers to return to work. The crowd listened in disbelief. But Ngotho was enraged. Years of frustration boil within him, and, seeing Jacobo as the consummate traitor, he rises and attacks him, and is soon joined by the crowd. The intervention of white policemen saves Jacobo's life, and Ngotho is seriously injured.

More significantly, the strike reveals fractures in Kipanga society. When the strike fails Ngotho and thousands of others lose their jobs. Jacobo kicks Ngotho and his family out of their homes, and they are forced to eke out a living on the land of Kamau's former boss, the carpenter Nganga. Superficially, Njoroge's life shows less change. He begins attending his new school, upset by the suffering of his family and confused about his friendship with Mwihaki, daughter of his father's enemy; but he is isolated from the political turmoil of the country. For this is the time of the Mau Mau Rebellion, and the struggle for freedom has turned extremely violent. Njoroge hears of the Mau Mau in stories told by the other schoolboys; he suspects only vaguely how directly his family will be involved in the bloodshed.

After the strike attitudes harden on both sides. Jacobo is made a chief, a Kenyan collaborator in the British attempt to suppress rebellion. Howlands himself, who had been content as a simple farmer, becomes district officer, an official with broad powers to harass suspected revolutionaries. A similar intensification has occurred in Ngotho's family. Boro and his brother Kori have joined the Mau Mau, and Boro pressures their father to follow them. Although sympathetic, Ngotho refuses to take the oath of allegiance from his son, which he considers a violation of his patriarchal authority.

However, his refusal to align himself with the Mau Mau does not save him from harassment. Both Jacobo and Howlands resent Ngotho and focus their energy on him out of proportion to his minimal involvement in the uprising. His wife, Nyokabi, and son, Kori, are arrested for violating curfew; Kori is held in a detention camp. Boro flees permanently to the forest. Open conflict is inevitable.

Meanwhile, Njoroge and Mwihaki meet again in Kipanga, as they have not done since the day of the strike. Somehow their friendship has survived the breach between their families. Their conversations about the turmoil in their country are inconclusive; Njoroge, especially, doubts that their alliance can survive the forces of politics. Nevertheless, this interlude of cautious optimism provides a source of light in a rapidly darkening novel.

EDUCATION IN COLONIAL KENYA

Formal education in colonial Kenya was, at first, provided solely by Christian missionaries. This education was not free and was thus limited to a select few African children, most of whom, like Njoroge's brother Kamau, learned a traditional skill like carpentry. This Christian education tended to disconnect its students from their ethnic roots; many Christian Gikuyu rejected traditional ways altogether, although Njoroge never does.

Despite these shortcomings, European education was very highly valued by the Gikuyu—they understood that it was the only way to gain access to the white man's cultural power. Great sacrifices were made, even by poor families, to send at least one child to school; this child's success or failure would be watched and felt, not just by his family but by the whole village. It is no surprise that one of Jomo Kenyatta's demands was compulsory primary education for all Kenyan children, nor that, in the 1930s, various ethnic groups set up their own independent schools, which provided a British education without Christian disdain for such practices as polygamy and female circumcision.

The structure of Christian education in Kenya basically followed that in Britain. In primary school students learned the basics of reading, writing, and arithmetic. If they passed an exam at the end of primary school, they were sent to intermediate school (equivalent to American junior high school). Both Njoroge and Mwihaki pass this exam, but they are still split up: Njoroge goes to an intermediate school near home, and the more affluent Mwihaki is sent to a boarding school in the country. After intermediate school another exam determined the next step. Those who performed best were sent to secondary school; this is what happens to Njoroge. Mwihaki, who does less well, finds herself at a teacher-training school.

Until the climax of the novel Njoroge's educational career follows that of Ngugi. But while Njoroge is forced by political circumstances to leave his secondary school, Ngugi went on to get university degrees, first in Nairobi and then in England.

Events unravel in short order. Njoroge passes through intermediate school and goes to Siriana Secondary School. Here he discovers another oasis of peace. He strikes up friendships with representatives of all the peoples of Kenya; he even finds common ground with Mr. Howlands's son, whom he had feared as a boy. It turns out that the young white child had been just as terrified of Njoroge as Njoroge had been of him. But soon this place of peace is shattered. Policemen come for Njoroge, and he is interrogated, beaten, and mentally tormented. Mr. Howlands informs him that Jacobo has been murdered. Worse, Ngotho has confessed to the crime, even though everyone knows that Boro was the actual murderer. Ngotho has been tortured nearly to death but will not divulge Boro's hiding place. Finally Ngotho and Njoroge are released. Because of the scandal Njoroge cannot return to school; he returns home with his father, who is dying rapidly. He lives long enough, however, to be reconciled with Boro, who visits his father's deathbed before retreating to the forest.

Two chapters remain, set several months later. Boro has killed Mr. Howlands and been captured. Njoroge, now 19, his dreams of education and a grand future seemingly ruined, is working as a salesclerk in an Indian store in Kipanga. He meets Mwihaki again; their friendship has survived even the murder of her father. She invokes the duty to his people in which he used to believe, but she fails to reinspire him. He pleads with her to leave Kenya with him, and when she refuses, he is desolate. He climbs a hill and ties a noose, intending suicide. The novel ends, not in despair, but with a ray of hope: his two mothers have followed him, and they save him from death. As he allows them to lead him home, he begins to remember his obligations to others, and the novel ends in a simple act of courtesy: "He ran home and opened the door for his two mothers" (*Weep Not,* p. 136).

Adam and Eve, Gikuyu and Mumbi. One of the most riveting episodes of *Weep Not, Child* has Ngotho retelling for his family the Gikuyu story of the creation. The creator, Murungu, saw darkness all over the face of the world; he created a single sacred tree that rose up from the foot of Mt. Kenya. Beneath it he created the first man and woman, named Gikuyu and Mumbi, and he told them: "This land I hand over to you. O man and woman, / It's yours to rule and till in serenity sacrificing / Only to me, your God, under my sacred tree" (*Weep Not,* p. 24). The immediate effect of Ngotho's story is to remind all his fam-

ily that their land has been stolen from them. But the creation story has another effect as well: it underscores the similarities between the Gikuyu's homegrown religion and the imported Christianity that made many converts in Kenya. It also foreshadows the idiosyncratic blend of Christian and Gikuyu themes that Njoroge develops later in the novel: "It did not make much difference that he had come to identify Gikuyu with Adam and Mumbi with Eve. To this God, all men and women were united by one strong feeling of brotherhood" (*Weep Not,* p. 49). Christian education became part of the sweep towards freedom; for example, Ngugi describes Jomo Kenyatta as the Black Moses. An optimism, reinforced by Christianity, that God will eventually right the injustices visited on His people sustains Njoroge through much of the novel. Christianity, it can be concluded, was never for Ngugi simply a tool of colonialism. Britain's staunchest African allies were those Gikuyu who had been deeply Christianized and Westernized. The Christian teachers whom Njoroge encounters are kind and passionate but convinced that white ways are best: the headmaster of one school "brought up his boys to copy and cherish the white man's civilization as the only hope of mankind" (*Weep Not,* p. 115). And even among those Gikuyu who do not reject their traditional customs, Christianity seems to encourage a political passivity that hinders the vigorous fight for freedom. Nevertheless, the novel does not reject Christianity. Ngotho's story is paralleled later in the book by the impassioned sermon of a Christian revivalist. This sermon predicts the imminent return of Jesus but also comments on the political turmoil of Kenya. After they leave the church Njoroge and Mwihake discuss the idea of the end of the world in a passionate blend of theology, personal conviction, and politics. They end up with a kind of cautious optimism, based on the trust that God works in mysterious ways, but always for the ultimate good of His people. This optimism is counterpoised against the violent nihilism of Boro, who states that he believes in nothing but revenge. While it is Boro's active will that brings about political change, Njoroge's quieter drive really propels the novel; it is only when he loses this optimism that he attempts suicide.

Ngugi's own relationship to Christianity is as multifaceted as his first novel's. Like Njoroge, he was in his youth a devout believer, and many critics have seen an autobiographical component to the novel. But by the time he wrote it, and especially later in the 1960s, Ngugi had come to question the role of Christianity in Gikuyu life. He saw that, whatever their stated beliefs, the Christian churches supported the oppressive ruling class. As his interest grew in radicals like Karl Marx and Frantz Fanon (see **The Wretched of the Earth,** also covered in *African Literature and Its Times*), Ngugi rejected anything that might aid this class. More importantly, he came to believe that Christianity forced its adherents to denigrate their Gikuyu heritage: the Church "meant rejection of these values and rituals which held us together: it meant adopting what, in effect, was a debased European middle-class mode of living and behavior" (Ngugi wa Thiong'o in Killam, p. 8). The somewhat accepting view of Christianity evinced in *Weep Not, Child is* replaced in the 1970s with a tendency to denounce Christian influence. This trait must be classed with Ngugi's other attempts to minimize European influences, such as writing in Gikuyu and attempting to refocus college literature departments on African literature. In 1970 he even changed his name. After addressing a Church council with the words, "I am not a man of the Church. I am not even a Christian," Ngugi was confronted by an angry Christian who pointed out that Ngugi still used his Christian name: James. Reflecting on this, Ngugi decided the man was right. He dropped "James" from his name and reverted to the Gikuyu form of his name: Ngugi wa Thiong'o.

Sources and literary context. Ngugi's early work should be placed alongside the first literary fruits of African independence. He is young enough to have felt the influence of slightly older African writers such as Chinua Achebe and Wole Soyinka (see **Things Fall Apart** and **Death and the King's Horseman,** also covered in *African Literature and Its Times*), and shares their concern with defining the African experience and assessing the legacy of colonialism. In Kenya, Ngugi was the first writer to publish in English and has remained Kenya's most famous international author.

Like many African authors, Ngugi received a rigorous, European-style education and has benefited from being positioned between two cultures, the Gikuyu and the British. Even as he has worked to accentuate and enrich his own Gikuyu culture, he has continued to acknowledge a debt to certain English writers, especially D. H. Lawrence and Joseph Conrad. In the late 1960s and early 1970s his work became more stridently political; *Petals of Blood, The Trial of Dedan Ki-* *mathi* and *Ngaahika ndeenda* excoriate Christianity, colonialism, and the political shortcomings of Kenya after independence in terms much harsher than those of his first published work. *Ngaahika ndeenda,* especially, landed him in trouble for just those reasons: this massive three-hour play, put on by peasants in the Kenyan countryside, was performed only once before government officials, upset at its frank treatment of corruption and greed, halted production and arrested Ngugi. He was imprisoned without trial for more than a year.

Despite this arrest, or perhaps because of it, Ngugi has continued to be a powerful, influential voice both within Kenya and outside it. His more recent works have been banned in Kenya, and Ngugi himself has lived in exile (in the United States and Europe) since the mid-1980s; however, the memory of his work continues to inspire many Kenyan authors. For the world at large, Ngugi is the most visible and striking literary representative of Kenya, its first authentic voice.

Events in History at the Time the Novel Was Written

Uhuru and after. *Weep Not, Child* ends at the darkest point in the life of its protagonist and in the life of Kenya. The Mau Mau Rebellion has been crushed; Jomo Kenyatta and many other Kenyan leaders have been imprisoned. It seems as if native Kenyans are powerless to win their freedom, and will have to depend on the dubious generosity of the British interlopers.

However, by the time Ngugi sat to write the book, the situation had turned around completely. From the failed Mau Mau Rebellion, the British had learned that Kenyans would never accept colonial domination peacefully and that they themselves would have to relinquish power. A series of conferences in the late 1950s and early 1960s set the terms by which native Kenyans would be brought into the colonial government, with the eventual aim of *uhuru* (freedom) from Britain. Like many anti-colonial leaders, Kenyatta went almost straight from jail to the state house; he became prime minister in 1962 and, late in 1963, oversaw the final departure of the British. The land laws were overthrown, and white settlers fled in droves.

With independance Kenya had its share of the internal strife experienced by many other newly freed African states. Political freedom was an important step, but it would mean nothing without economic self-sufficiency. Potential conflict between different peoples also loomed, and Kenyatta had to walk a thin line to keep the differences between Gikuyu and Maasai, Nandi and Abagusii from sapping the political life of the country. An even more invidious division, perhaps, had arisen between the small minority of Kenyans who had benefited from England's rule, adopting Christianity and Western dress, and the majority who continued to live traditional African lives. It is in this final area that the importance of Ngugi lies. Beginning with the plays he staged as part of the Independence celebrations in 1964, and more stridently as the years passed, Ngugi has insisted on the unity of all Kenyans in a glorious African culture that needs little from Europeans.

Reviews. Opinions of *Weep Not, Child* vary greatly. The cover of the British edition proclaims it "Ngugi's masterpiece," but this judgment is far from universal. No one denies the novel's historical importance as the first written in English by a black East African. However, many categorize it as a work of Ngugi's youth that bears all the marks of apprenticeship. Charles Larson claims that the characters of the novel "are for the most part underdeveloped" (Larson, p. 365). Ngugi's language has been praised and criticized in equal measure. Peter Nazareth says that "the real problem of Ngugi's language is that one is constantly irritated by its naivete and extreme complexity" (Nazareth, p. 9). But G. D. Killam notes the biblical intensity of Ngugi's style, and observes that this style blossoms in his subsequent novels (Killam, p. 52). There is also a split between critics who see the novel as a flawed, naive attempt to capture the historical truth of the Mau Mau Rebellion and those who see such naiveté as a way of capturing the feelings of being young in troubled times. For the former assessment, W. J. Howard writes: "Very good his-

torical prose fiction has always included an interpretation or a reading of the history. . . . This creative coming to terms with historical fact is absent from *Weep Not, Child*" (Howard in Robson, p. 124). Clifford Robson replies, "Ngugi's work reveals a developing but consistent interpretation—that in a dynamic situation people are often caught up in a complex pattern of events to which they react in unpredictable, irrational ways" (Robson, p. 124).

However, even those critics who dismiss *Weep Not, Child* grant that it is important for two reasons. First, its publication marks a major stage in the development of East African literature. Second, it indubitably shows some glimmer of the promise fulfilled in such later masterpieces as *A Grain of Wheat* and *Petals of Blood*.

—Jacob Littleton

For More Information

Bogonko, Sorobea. *Kenya 1945-1963*. Nairobi: Kenya Literature Bureau, 1980.

Clough, Marshall. *Mau Mau Memoirs*. London: Lynne Renoir, 1998.

Cook, David, and Michael Okenimkpe. *Ngugi wa Thiong'o: An Exploration of His Writings*. London: Heinemann, 1983.

Edgerton, Robert. *Mau Mau: An African Crucible*. New York: Macmillan, 1989.

Killam, G. D. *An Introduction to the Writings of Ngugi*. London: Heinemann, 1980.

Larson, Charles R. *The Emergence of African Fiction*. Bloomington: Indiana University Press, 1972.

Nazareth, Peter. "Ngugi." Iowa Review 7, nos. 2 3 (Summer 1970): 249-62.

Ngugi wa Thiong'o. *Weep Not, Child*. Ibadan, Nigeria: Heinemann, 1964.

Ochieng', William. *A History of Kenya*. Nairobi: Macmillan, 1985.

Robson, Clifford. *Ngugi wa Thiong'o*. London: Macmillan, 1979.

When Rain Clouds Gather

by

Bessie Head

Bessie Head was born in Pietermaritzburg, South Africa, in 1937. Until she was 13 she was raised by a foster family in a poor section of the coloured community in the Cape Province (that is, the community for South Africans of mixed descent). She spent the next six years at St. Monica's Home, an Anglican mission school for coloured girls, where she learned through a shocking revelation from the principal that her white mother had lived and died in a mental asylum because she had sexual relations with an African stable boy. She was made to understand that she herself was being monitored for any sign of mental aberration. After her teacher training education at St. Monica's, Head taught elementary school from 1956 to 1958 in Durban, and then worked for several newspapers in Cape Town, Johannesburg, and Port Elizabeth. Her political involvement as a member of the Pan Africanist Congress led to her brief arrest after anti-pass-law demonstrations that climaxed with police shootings of African protestors in Sharpeville in 1960. She attempted suicide shortly thereafter. The traumatic impact of these experiences was evident in Head's troubled marriage, her sense of alienation in Botswana—where she lived as a refugee from 1964 until she was granted Botswana citizenship in 1979—and her intermittent mental breakdowns. Almost all her writings are based on her personal experiences in these two countries. Her first novel in exile, *When Rain Clouds Gather* examines her decision to live in exile rather than stay and fight the apartheid system inside South Africa.

THE LITERARY WORK

A novel set in eastern Botswana in the 1960s; published in English in 1969.

SYNOPSIS

A young South African refugee settles in a remote village in Botswana and, through participation in an agricultural development project and involvement in the lives of ordinary people, attempts to escape the psychological torture of his experience of apartheid in South Africa.

Events in History at the Time of the Novel

The geopolitics of 1960s Botswana. *When Rain Clouds Gather* is set in the fictional village of Golema Mmidi, in a remote eastern section of Botswana. Golema Mmidi represents Serowe, the village in which Head settled after moving to Botswana in 1964. Known then as the Bechuanaland Protectorate, Botswana, a former British colony, became independent in 1966. Geographically, the country is dominated by the Kalahari sands, and is mostly unsuitable for permanent residence. Regular rainfall may occur over "a ten-year period, followed by ten years of below average rainfall, often accompanied by severe drought. Apart from the peak years of the wet cycle, rain is often highly localized, irregular in amounts, and otherwise unpredictable"

Women fill their buckets from a water tank near Serowe, the village on which Head based her fictional setting of Golema Mmidi.

(Ramsay, p. 2). Consequently, only about 5 percent of the land is arable. Bessie Head uses the nation's constant desire for water as a backdrop for the hopes and aspirations of the people she describes in her novel. Despite the harshness of the land, people constantly look with hopefulness for rain clouds. "Pula," meaning "rain," is the general term of greeting among the Batswana. (*Botswana* refers to the country, *Batswana* to the Tswana people who live in the country, and *Motswana* to an individual member of the community.)

At the time the novel takes place, Botswana had recently gained its independence from the British colonial administration (1966). The Bechuanaland Protectorate was often referred to as an orphaned society to which the British had extended protection, mainly because of the appeals of prominent members of the London Missionary Society and powerful Botswana chiefs, who wanted to prevent other European powers in the surrounding countries—the Dutch, the Germans, and the Afrikaners (or descendents of European, mainly Dutch, settlers in South Africa)—from swallowing their territory. Administratively, the British Empire held Bechuanaland to be part of South Africa, and the protectorate was administered from Mafeking, South Africa.

Few Europeans settled in the region because

of the brutal Botswana climate, and, beside the burdensome task of collecting taxes and maintaining law and order, Britain itself did not see much to covet in the land. It consequently did little to improve the country's infrastructure. Botswana's major usefulness was that it was mostly flat land and thus served as a major transportation link between South Africa and the central African nations.

Historians have argued that the colonial administration's indifference to the future of Botswana led to social and economic underdevelopment, low agricultural productivity, and a legacy of economic dependency on South Africa. This colonial indifference to economic development was also responsible for the poor state of Botswana education in the 1960s. Primary-level education was available to only a few, and, in fact, many local teachers were insufficiently trained. Bessie Head was one of the few expatriates from South Africa willing to work as a teacher in Botswana. To obtain secondary-level education, a select number of native-born Batswana went to South Africa. For a small minority higher education was available in Lesotho and overseas. In 1963 only 45 Batswana were attending institutions of higher education (Parson, p. 58). Thus, with an undeveloped rural economy and a negligible educational system, many people (especially those with skills) sought employment in the more developed nations surrounding Botswana. By 1964, out of a national population of only half a million, the absentee population was estimated at 42,000 (Parson, p. 59).

Botswana's traditional economy is based on herding. Culturally, cattle herding is done by men and boys, who spend a significant part of the year at cattle posts far from home. The raising of crops (such as sorghum, millet, beans, and maize) is done mostly by women, who also gather fruits and vegetables while the men hunt game. Examining the traditional economy of the country in *When Rain Clouds Gather,* Head focuses on agriculture and the need to resist the encroaching desert through technological improvements in farming. The Botswana government also recognized poor agricultural output as one of its major challenges, and initiated large-scale dam construction and irrigated farming projects to overcome cycles of drought (Ramsay, p. 4).

Independence. When the winds of political change blew across Africa in the 1960s, Britain exercised unusual goodwill in the smooth transfer of power to the people of Botswana. Sir Seretse Khama, the son of Sekgoma II of the BaNgwato people, became the first president of the Republic of Botswana. He and his uncle, Tshekedi Khama, former regent of Botswana (1925-50), initially fought to preserve the rights of the traditional rulers of their class; however, in 1956, they both renounced their rights and the rights of their offsprings to *bogosi,* or kingship. Thus, a decade before Botswana achieved independence, they fostered a spirit of democracy in the nation. Botswana's long history of democracy has since become a model for other African nations. Bessie Head succinctly points out in *When Rain Clouds Gather* that some chiefs did not appreciate the changes they were facing, and indeed, relinquishing power to a democratically elected government proved difficult for many traditional rulers. Nonetheless, Seretse and his Botswana Democratic Party (BDP) enjoyed overwhelming support from the people. Seretse is credited with transforming Botswana from a neglected protectorate and tragically impoverished nation to an international model of human rights, stable democracy, and improved economic development (Ramsay, p. 217).

It is generally believed that Britain would not have handed over power so readily to the people of Botswana if the mineral resources for which many agencies had desperately scoured the land had been discovered before 1966. Commercial deposits of diamonds were discovered in 1967, making the mining industry (which in colonial times had explored for copper, nickel, and salt) the most significant foreign exchange earner for the country.

BOTSWANA IN SOUTH AFRICAN POLITICS

Although Botswana leaders were always outspoken about the unjust racial policies of South Africa and made their position clear at the United Nations, at the same time they took a moderate stance in terms of their dealings with the South African government. They were aware that their involvement in South African politics could easily have created an excuse for the South African government to overrun Botswana with the same brutal policies that it enforced in South Africa and Namibia. When South Africa banned the African National Congress (ANC) in 1960, many leading ANC members, including Nelson Mandela (see **"The Rivonia Trial Speech,"** also covered in *African Literature and Its Times*), fled to Botswana for temporary refuge. Botswana also became a convenient location for underground ANC campaigns against the South African government. For example, it was in Botswana that the ANC in exile decided to launch an armed struggle against apartheid in 1961. Neither the Bechuanaland Protectorate nor the independent Botswana banned the ANC, but, they were unwilling to let Botswana become an official base for armed ANC attacks against South Africa (Ramsay, p. 14). Nonetheless, many of Botswana's migrant population in South Africa were active members of the ANC throughout the movement's history.

Botswana, land of exiles. Almost entirely surrounded by the white-dominated countries of South Africa, Rhodesia (now Zimbabwe), and South West Africa (now Namibia), in the 1960s Botswana became a natural refuge for many who were fleeing white oppression. In fact, for the past 200 years warring ethnic groups and violent encounters with Europeans in the more habitable regions of southern Africa led many ethnic groups to take refuge in Botswana. Consequently, although the people of Botswana are deeply traditional, they are at the same time generally tolerant of foreigners.

Geographically and politically Botswana occupies a strategic position in southern Africa.

However, the country is completely landlocked and mostly dependent on South Africa for road outlets for its goods and services. Also, migrant workers from Botswana have found employment in South Africa, serving as a labor reserve in that country's economy. Botswana's economic dependency on rich, powerful neighbors placed it in a difficult position in the 1960s. While Botswana sympathized with and welcomed traumatized refugees, it meanwhile remained intolerant of militant or political expressions that could jeopardize its relations with its neighbors. Botswana adopted the compromise position of staying neutral in the politics of the region. It can be argued that the nation itself underwent a psychological and economic state of exile.

LOADED LANGUAGE—THE SOUTH AFRICAN CONTEXT

*B*anned, *banning*, and, in certain instances, *banished*, are specifically South African terms used for individuals under police surveillance, especially former political prisoners who must remain under house arrest, must not associate with certain people, and must not incite the public through speeches, or even read certain literature. For black South Africans, *banned* could also mean being restricted to a designated homeland (though *banished* is the more appropriate term here). The term, in other words, refers not only to censored material, it also refers to "censored people." Coloured, too, has a different meaning in South Africa than elsewhere. In South Africa, it refers to descendants of mixed unions that involved some combination of whites, local Khoisan, African slaves, and slaves from Southeast Asia.

Apartheid in South Africa. The repressive policies of apartheid in South Africa forced Bessie Head to flee into neighboring Botswana. As she saw it, her nightmarish experience of racial segregation, the unfathomable logic of white hatred, and her own inescapable involvement in South African politics created such tension that living in the country became unbearable. Many of Head's own experiences found their way into *When Rain Clouds Gather*, especially her questioning of political and social life in South Africa.

Although racial segregation had been practiced since Europeans first dominated southern Africa in the late eighteenth century, it was in the twentieth century that it came to involve the exclusion of all non-Europeans from the privileges of citizenship in South Africa. Apartheid, which means "apartness" or its later modification, "separate development," promoted the exploitation of black Africans, coloureds, Indians, and other non-Europeans. Basically, it rested on the white South African notion that the country consisted of separate nations that ought to live in their own distinct areas or homelands, with nonwhites entering the white homeland only temporarily, to work. The term "apartheid" came into common usage in 1948 when the Afrikaner's National Party, led by H. F. Verwoerd, used it as a political platform to win the national election. A "revolutionary, totalitarian doctrine," apartheid "trumpeted separation as the ideal to be applied as consistently and vigorously as possible" (Saunders, p. 17). Economically, socially, and psychologically, apartheid has meant untold suffering for nonwhites. Black South Africans and foreigners from other African countries were put on the lowest social rung, and they were forced to obey repressive legislation, such as the pass laws, which required nonwhites entering white cities to carry papers explaining their purpose for being there. Further, the practice of "petty apartheid," which was similar to the Jim Crow laws of the South in the United States, enforced segregation in public buildings, on public transportation, on beaches, in libraries, on sidewalks, and in social activities such as sporting events.

After her teacher training in 1956, Head entered a world of racial politics that was increasingly tense and conflictual. The late 1950s and '60s witnessed extreme violence on the part of the South African police, and numerous defiance campaigns and strike actions on the part of black resistance movements. The white regime had the full support of the legislative arm of government, which passed many laws further restricting the rights of non-Europeans. In 1956 Parliament sanctioned the removal of the coloured vote. In 1957 it amended the Native Laws Amendment Act, further restricting contact now deemed inappropriate between blacks and whites, such as the free association of persons with the same political or religious beliefs. (Blacks, for example, could no longer attend church in nonblack areas.) Two years later, through the University Education Act, apartheid was introduced to institutions of higher learning. By 1960 political representation for Africans in Parliament was abolished; the same policy was applied to coloured representation in 1968. Blacks and

Aftermath of the Sharpeville Massacre.

coloureds employed numerous strategies to resist such oppressive laws. For instance, women staged mass anti-pass demonstrations at the Union Buildings, Pretoria, in 1956. Groups organized stay-at-home strikes, in which workers refrained from reporting for work. Passive resistance such as the stay-at-home strikes and protest journalism, along with overt resistance such as riots, random attacks on whites, or organized underground campaigns of violence, both played parts in the opposition to white domination.

In response, the government unleashed a reign of terror that included arrests and detentions, with or without trial. Police brutality led to many deaths in police custody, rapes, unprovoked assaults and harassments, and the banning of political parties such as the African National Congress (ANC) and the Pan Africanist Congress (PAC). On March 21, 1960, during a PAC pass-law defiance campaign at Sharpeville that Head helped organize, police shot into the crowd, killing 69 people. Around the world people decried the actions of the South African police, and a few days later the PAC enjoyed a small victory when the pass laws were suspended. However, this apparent victory in fact worked to the advantage of the South African regime, because the government's action made unnecessary an important pass-law campaign that the ANC

had scheduled for March 31, and thus defused the anger that had been growing both in and outside South Africa. The government took the opportunity to place a banning order on the ANC and the PAC after arresting and jailing many of their leaders, and, in April, quickly resurrected the pass laws. The government's determination to continue its apartheid policies was evident in its decision to risk international disrepute rather than share power with non-Europeans. In March 1961 South Africa withdrew its membership in the British Commonwealth and became a Republic two months later. In November 1962 the United Nations voted to impose economic and diplomatic sanctions on South Africa. These measures, however, did not deter the South African government, which became even more repressive after the assassination of H. F. Verwoerd and the election of John Vorster as prime minister in 1966. Formerly in charge of police security, Vorster enacted the Terrorism Act in 1967, advocating indefinite detention without trials, and later, the forced deportation of black Africans to segregated "homelands," the Bantustans. The government also established, among other infrastructures of apartheid, the Bureau of State Security, well-known for its notorious treatment of political prisoners and for its covert attempts to trap activists both inside and outside the country.

Throughout the 1960s many black intellectuals and political activists and white liberals either went underground with their activism or fled the country. Those arrested often spent many years in jail and suffered unspeakable torture. Head's choice of exile over underground sabotage may have stemmed from the psychological tension that came with life as a radical; she has claimed to have "such a delicate nervous balance that when faced with danger or secret activity I tremble violently. The spies of the Boers [Afrikaners] would have long found me out and sent me the parcel bomb" (Head in Eilersen, p. 49). The unhappy political situation in the country; the crisis in her marriage; the nightmare of raising her son in the desperate poverty she and her husband struggled through; and the impossibility of flourishing as a writer in a climate of oppression—all these factors encouraged her to start life over in a foreign land. *When Rain Clouds Gather* captures these years of struggle in South Africa. The main character in the novel epitomizes Head's attempt to abandon the past and to embrace all that was new and free in Botswana.

SOUTH AFRICAN PASS LAWS

The pass laws in South Africa began as early as 1709, when Cape slaves were made to carry passes in order for authorities to monitor their movement and to distinguish the free population from the slaves. Later, the pass law was used to regulate the movement of the native-born Khoikhoi laborers who were attached to farms. By 1911 the Native Labour Regulation Act made it mandatory for male African workers, including foreigners, to carry passes. The pass law became a means of controlling the influx of Africans to the urban areas and of keeping the cost of labor low. Africans continually protested against carrying passes; as early as 1913, for example, African women put up passive resistance against the law. In fact, pass burnings became a form of popular protest. In the 1960s and '70s almost half a million pass-law arrests occurred every year. The special police force and court system that enforced the policy could not always cope with the volume of cases. Consequently, rather than try every case, the government created policies that legitimized the forced deportation of pass-law violators to the Bantustans (Saunders, pp. 133-34).

The Novel in Focus

Plot summary. *When Rain Clouds Gather* opens at the South African border fence with Botswana. The protagonist, Makhaya Maseko, is in the process of disengaging with the past. He feels certain about his desire to leave it behind but is uncertain about the future he wishes to embrace. A young Zulu activist recently out of prison, Makhaya has defied the South African government banning order against him by fleeing the country. His one desire is to live in a free country, although he has no illusions about the quality of freedom he will enjoy in a country as miserably poor as Botswana. Rejecting his political activities—a campaign of violence against the South African government—and his Zulu upbringing, which he holds partly responsible for nurturing people who could allow themselves to be so brutally oppressed by whites, Makhaya opts for a future that might grant him basic human rights. In South Africa he had deliberately courted death by carrying on his person the plans for blowing up buildings; his new goal as a refugee in Botswana is to seek life and nurture it.

However, his experience in South Africa, a land where a black man's identity amounted to that of a black dog, has left Makhaya bitter and distrustful. His dreams about changing the world are reduced to simply satisfying his own personal needs. As he says to an old man who helps him cross the border into Botswana, "I just want to step on free ground. I don't care about people. I don't care about anything, not even the white man. I want to feel what it is like to live in a free country and then maybe some of the evils in my life will correct themselves" (Head, *When Rain Clouds Gather*, p. 10). Makhaya's decision to flee is not based on any "overt political motive," but rather on a strong desire "to calm his jangled black sensibilities" and to come to terms with his personal inner chaos (Heywood, p. 176). He meets an old woman from whom he seeks shelter for the night. Her selfish attitude toward this hapless refugee informs Makhaya that Botswana is no paradise, but a place that has its "vultures" (*Rain Clouds*, p. 14). After he registers as a refugee, Makhaya happens upon Dinorego, a wise old man from Golema Mmidi, who helps him settle down into a quiet search for peace.

The village of Golema Mmidi is a unique refuge for Botswana and South African people who are fleeing tragedies in their lives. Though dry and arid, the village is well suited to Makhaya, who finds this rural community radically different from his urban ghetto existence in

South Africa. Dinorego best expresses this difference when he describes Botswana as "God's country": "God is everywhere around here. People can't steal a thing from you, not even a sixpence. People can't fight, not even to kill an enemy" (*Rain Clouds*, p. 21). Dinorego and the villagers of Golema Mmidi have no concept of the deep-seated hatred that people like Makhaya have felt directed at them from whites and which they had internalized in their struggle to survive apartheid.

After being ruthlessly divorced by her womanizing husband, the elderly Mma Milipede sought refuge in Golema Mmidi. She, like Dinorego, exemplifies an innocent embrace of life in Botswana. She combines ancient wisdom with the Christian religion of the missionaries; so secure are the Batswana in their own identity that foreigners and their new ideas are examined and courageously absorbed into the Batswana way of life. An Englishman, Gilbert Balfour, for example, can afford to live and dream in Golema Mmidi because of his belief that people are open to change and to those things that promote progress. His study of agriculture is an attempt to counteract his stifling middle-class upbringing with the life-giving force of growing things. Gilbert has helped the villagers start a cooperative farming project that is yielding a good return, and his dream is to see Golema Mmidi become an internationally renowned agricultural community.

Gilbert's commitment to the land is evident in his marriage to Dinorego's daughter, the quiet but unpredictable Maria. Makhaya's timely appearance in Golema Mmidi further accelerates Gilbert's dream of a transformed economy for a people who are dirt-poor. Makhaya's philosophical rejection of tribalism and even his disillusionment with politics are appealing to Gilbert, who needs someone willing to invest his energies in the agricultural development of the village. Makhaya's task is to help the women of the village move beyond subsistence farming to cash-crop tobacco farming, since their men are out of the village in faraway cattle posts at this time of year. Without the cooperation of the women, both Gilbert and Makhaya note, the agricultural miracle they envision will die. With the help of Mma Milipede, they enlist the young Motswana widow, Paulina Seboso, who persuades the women of the village to join the new tobacco-growing scheme.

Makhaya's preoccupation with this absorbing world of innocence and growing things is alternately disrupted by the harshness of the land, the often fatal drought conditions, the painful poverty around him, and, worst of all, the African grade of evil personified in the embittered subchief Matenge and the politician Joas Mtsepe. Matenge has been appointed administrator over Golema Mmidi by his brother, Chief Sekoto, who is trying to rid himself of the contentious and greedy subchief. Matenge is disliked by the villagers, for he stands in the way of progress. Having been trained in the old school of masters and slaves, oppressor and oppressed, this traditional ruler regards the change sweeping the country as a disheartening development. Slowly he is losing

---

BESSIE HEAD AND COOPERATIVE FARMS

In 1962 the Botswana Legislative Council introduced the Cooperative Societies Act, which led to the creation of a Department of Cooperative Societies in 1964. British Resident Commissioner Peter Fawcus is credited with promoting the idea of a marketing cooperative movement. Seeing the desperate need for economic independence, the post-Independence government of Seretse Khama established the Botswana Cooperative Bank and the Botswana Agricultural Marketing Board in 1974. The former provided capital for agricultural projects and the latter established a storage, distribution, and marketing system that offered seeds and fertilizers to farmers, and also radically improved the production and management of the agricultural produce of its members. This development policy was aimed at reducing poverty in Botswana's mostly rural population, especially among its poorest farmers, who not only worked the soil under harsh conditions but lacked the tools necessary to improve their agricultural output.

The Bamangwato Development Association (BDA) was one such cooperative farm in the 1960s. It was located at Radisele, about 80 kilometers from Serowe. Bessie Head joined this farm in 1966 as a typist but soon went to work as a harvester for the farm's cash crop experiment in tobacco growing. Like Head, the main character in her novel "turned to agriculture for his salvation" (*Rain Clouds*, p. 81). Many such cooperatives were run by overseas agriculturists and, interestingly, a large number of refugees worked on such farms—in fact, some of the most successful cooperatives largely consisted of refugees. Head's satisfying experience with farming and some of the people she met in the BDA project are vividly sketched in her novel.

his grip on power and his privileged lifestyle, and he fails in his attempts to banish Gilbert and Makhaya, whom he sees as encouraging rebellion through their zealous advocacy of change. Matenge's chief supporter, Joas Mtsepe, who represents the new breed of African nationalists, is also bitter; he is part of the opposition that has lost an election and become a destructive force against all forms of national progress. Mtsepe and Matenge become partners in criticism, connivance, and conspiracy. Matenge's continual juridical onslaught against the villagers meets with successful appeals at the higher court, where Chief Sekoto, who despises his brother, always sides with the appellants. As the chief administrator of the region, Matenge holds power over the villagers but his ruling is always subject to that of the chief.

Matenge's unyielding attachment to tradition finally leads to his self-destruction, when he decides, against his better judgement, to humiliate Paulina for an unstated crime. Paulina speculates that her crime might be that she failed to inform the subchief of the funeral of her son, who died of tuberculosis at a cattle outpost. It is more likely that Matenge is simply jealous of her immense influence over the women of the village and is angry that the tobacco project has been initiated without his permission. In any case, Paulina's tragic loss of her son, Isaac, and the loss of all her cattle to the severe drought do not deter the selfish Matenge. He has also not offered any help or words of comfort to the grieving community of villagers who have suffered the loss of most of their cattle and are now looking for ways to preserve the rest of their herd through the remainder of the unpredictable drought season. His misjudgment in summoning Paulina to court at such a critical time angers the villagers. Assembling in front of Matenge's house, they quietly wait for the subchief to declare his case against Paulina. But Matenge never makes his appearance. Barring the door to his house, he promptly takes his own life. Makhaya is the first to discover Matenge's tragic decision.

By this time in the story, Makhaya has become a welcome member of the community. He remains, however, a "security risk," a former political prisoner who is allegedly violent, and does not know how long he will be able to maintain his place in Golema Mmidi, a village he now loves. From the many ironies and riddles he has witnessed in this remote village, he comes to the conclusion that freedom lies not in rejecting everything but in confronting life in all its con-

tradictions: "you had to concentrate the mind on all that was still alive and treat it as the most precious treasure you had ever been given.... Therefore, he Makhaya, could run so far in search of peace, but it was contact with other living beings that a man needed most" (*Rain Clouds,* pp. 164-66). Makhaya's marriage proposal to Paulina, which she gladly accepts, marks his realization that although life is harsh, its magic lies in creating a world fit to live in, rather than in succumbing to the death wish of the oppressor. Golema Mmidi offers "a means of personal and economic independence and interdependence, where the qualities that count are benign austerity, reverence for the lives of ordinary people ... and, above all, the ability to break out of the prison of selfhood without destroying individual privacy and integrity" (Ravenscott in Heywood, p. 177). In the end, Makhaya learns that a peaceful haven is not a retreat from responsibility but a place one creates through hard work, risk-taking, and involvement in the lives of others.

Women and representation. In her work Bessie Head has always foregrounded the problems of gender relations in Africa. She is one of very few male or female African writers of her generation to not only focus on gender discrimination but also to proffer a solution to the problem of sexism. *When Rain Clouds Gather* highlights the oppressive effects of centuries of male privilege. A woman was something to "buy at some stage, the way you bought a table you were going to keep in some back room and not care very much about" (*Rain Clouds,* p. 124). Makhaya's pronounced sensitivity to apartheid has made him intolerant of the discriminatory practice of female subordination in his Zulu culture. His denunciation of racism is inextricably linked to his rejection of tribalism, male chauvinism, and the sexual and cultural exploitation of women.

Yet, when he crosses the border into Botswana, he is shaken by the reality that female exploitation is not just a South African problem but an African problem. The old woman he encounters while looking for shelter for the night is crude and emotionally hardened from years of labor. Her shrill, discordant voice pierces the pastoral night as she attempts to exact as much money as she can from Makhaya for the miserable shelter she provides. Her hostile response to Makhaya is representative of her bankrupt relationship with men in general. For a fee, she is even willing to offer her underaged granddaughter to Makhaya for a night of sexual pleasure. The young girl, well schooled in servicing men, promptly shows up in Makhaya's hut. Disgusted by child prostitution and the greed of the old woman, Makhaya rejects the offer but hastily gives the girl the money to get rid of her. The old woman exclaims in shocked surprise to the child: "You mean he gave you the money for nothing. . . . This is a miracle! I have not yet known a man who did not regard a woman as a gift from God! He must be mad. . . . Let us lock the door to protect ourselves from the madman!" (*Rain Clouds*, p. 15). Her response links sexual exploitation to the material survival of women, and suggests that male sexual domination of the female body has led to the widespread acceptance of such denigration by women themselves.

It is also important to note that, although South African racism always provides the overarching thrust of this and other major novels written by Head in exile, a feminist portrayal of gender relations seems to be her most expressive way of alluding to racial discrimination. She tackles racism and sexism at once, for example, by having Gilbert marry a black woman, whom he treats with respect. Through this relationship, Head counteracts the novel's scattered references to South African racism; in South Africa, the marriage would have constituted a crime against the state. The almost angelic Gilbert is neither racist nor race conscious; his love-match with Maria is Head's response to myths of white supremacy. Likewise Makhaya's refusal to raise a family in his home country is an indictment of a racist system that denies basic freedoms to black people.

Thus, Head examines two major evils in *When Rain Clouds Gather*—oppressive traditional structures and white racism. Both culminate in the oppression of black women, who traditionally bear an unfair share of family burdens. With the men away at cattle posts most of the year, women must fend for themselves, maintain the homestead, care for the children, and grow all the food necessary for their family's survival. Even when the men return to the village, the women engage in petty jealousy and rivalry because there are indeed too few men to go around. In the 1960s nearly one-third of the Batswana male population had to seek employment outside the country (Parson, p. 58). The labor reserve force that Botswana produced for the South African economy, in particular, led to the breakdown of the family, and to indescribable hardship for its womenfolk. The situation was hardly different in South Africa, where most black women were restricted to designated rural homelands, while their menfolk were employed in cities. Women in urban areas faced sexual exploitation from black men deprived of their families, and from white men whose rape of the nation was often literally enacted in the rape of black women. In this and other ways, black women paid a high price for the oppressive racial and economic policies created by the South African apartheid regime that dominated the region. The moral breakdown has been measured in escalating crime rates, birth rates, prostitution, alcoholism, and other forms of moral destitution in the black and coloured communities.

MISCEGENATION

Interracial marriages are known to have occurred in South Africa since the seventeenth century. Although extramarital relationships were rare, sexual liaisons have always occurred between races, with the children of such illegitimate relationships being regarded as bastards. In 1902 the Cape Morality Act was instituted in an attempt to reduce sexual interaction across racial lines. In particular, white female prostitutes were prosecuted if they had sexual relations with African men. The Immorality Act of 1927 further imposed harsh penalties on all sexual partnership between blacks and whites. In 1949 the National Party legislated the Mixed Marriages Act, forbidding marriages between whites and all other racial groups. An amendment to this act in 1950 forbade sexual relations between whites and coloureds (Saunders, p. 113).

Head's depiction of Gilbert and Maria's interracial marriage is her way of denouncing the South African apartheid laws against miscegenation. Her depiction of Botswana as a country in which race is not such an important issue is borne out by historical fact: the first leader of Botswana, Seretse Khama, married an English woman while studying in England. His marriage almost cost him the privilege of returning to Botswana because both the South African and Rhodesian governments were reluctant to deal with a black leader who was married to a white woman.

For the widow Paulina, the burden of single parenting in such a harsh environment takes its toll in the untimely death of her young son, who is forced to do the work of a grown man. Fortunately for her, Makhaya chooses to become her husband and protector during this tragic season in her life. Although to a large extent their relationship is traditional, Makhaya encourages mutual respect and equality in their dealings with each other. Moreover, Makhaya's attitude to the women in the tobacco project is respectful and generous. He in fact sees generosity of spirit as the key to eliminating gender inequality. Makhaya has one criterion for judging the world:

> generosity, of soul and of mind. Many experiences had led him to the belief that the peace of the world rested with that one word. Because of this, it had become a policy with him to give immediately whatever was asked of him, and he really only felt hatred towards people who consistently displayed selfish attitudes.
>
> (*Rain Clouds*, p. 124)

In essence, *When Rain Clouds Gather* is a romantic, optimistic story that reflects its author's faith in humanity's essential goodness, and her belief that love between individuals can overcome the universal problems of race, class, and gender oppression.

Sources and literary context. "South African literature in exile" has come to mean the use of literature to expose the horrors of apartheid to the international community. According to some critics in the 1970s and '80s, this definition does not include Head. As James Garrett points out in "Writing Community," critics such as Lewis Nkosi, Gillian Stead Eilersen, and Virginia Ola tend to categorize Head's writing as personal rather than political, forgetting that such a separation is impossible in South African thinking and writing:

> Those who stress the "personal and private odyssey of the soul" . . . to the exclusion of the political and social world (and history) in which such odysseys take place are doing Head a great disservice by perpetuating the false dichotomy between the public and private which has been used to dismiss Head's work.
>
> (Garrett, p. 123)

For both black and white South African writers in exile during the apartheid regime, the personal simply was political.

This is particularly true of Head, whose short stories and novels have been predominantly autobiographical in context—that is, they reflect South African reality. Although Head has stated that she modeled Makhaya after a young Zimbabwean refugee who was disillusioned with the political future of Africa, Makhaya and Paulina are, in a way, two sides of the author herself. Paulina's passionate personality reflects Head's own strong desire to live a fulfilled life, and

Makhaya's refugee status, along with his responses to racism and sexism, reflect her attitudes and refugee experience. Like Makhaya, who discovers and develops his potential to love, create, and contribute positively to human society, Head was also able to find access to self-development through her participation in the Bamangwato Development Association, an agricultural project many miles from the village of Serowe. Her soulful journey to define herself, which she explores in all her novels, appears to have been impossible for her in the stifling political climate in South Africa. She wanted to write about innocence and laughter, magical things that could displace the trauma of the past. Indeed, Head found the stimulus for these positive elements in the real-life village of Serowe, which throbbed with the echoes of

> an ancient Africa left almost intact to dream along in its own way. . . . It was this peaceful world of black people simply dreaming in their own skins that I began to slowly absorb into my own. It was like finding black power and black personality in a simple and natural way.
>
> (Head, "Witchcraft," p. 72)

The characters in the novel, according to Head, are representative rather than specific. Thus, Joas Tsepe stands for corrupt politicians, Matenge for greedy chiefs, and Gilbert for European expatriates—all well-known types in Botswana. Gilbert, however, is believed to be closely modeled after Vernon Gibberd, an agriculturist who was the director of the farm project on which Bessie Head worked and who greatly impressed her with his brilliance and energy (Eilersen, p. 100).

Head claims an affinity with Olive Schreiner's pioneering artistic spirit and social critique of South Africa (see *The Story of an African Farm,* also covered in *African Literature and Its Times*). Head, however, is unique in that her "lack of identification with an environment"—with tradition, current customs, or parentage—makes her fearless in her engagement of diverse issues of class, race, religion, feminism, and sociopolitical philosophies (Mackenzie and Clayton, p. 15). Not feeling at home in South Africa or Botswana gives her what some perceive to be an advantage. She lacks the roots that could give her particular prejudices; this rootlessness also makes her writing expansive in its attempt to embrace universal issues. Head's themes of exile and social injustice also fit in with the uniquely South African body of literature that was emerging in the 1960s and '70s on the international scene— works like Alan Paton's ***Cry, the Beloved Country,*** Alex La Guma's ***A Walk in the Night,*** Peter Abrahams's ***Mine Boy,*** and Nadine Gordimer's ***Burger's Daughter*** (all also covered in *African Literature and Its Times*).

Reviews. *When Rain Clouds Gather* is the first book of a trilogy that also includes *Maru* and *A Question of Power.* These texts not only demonstrate Head's increasing artistic maturity but also affirm her strong moral idealism. Her first novel was positively reviewed as an intelligent, passionate, and compelling analysis of the African crisis of dispossession. Head's exploration of the place of women in Africa is considered particularly moving and innovative. In her work, African women emerge "painfully from the chrysalis of tribalist attitudes into a new evaluation of their relationship to men and their position in society" (Borg, p. 696). Although the novel is considered didactic in places, Head's humorous yet ironic distance from the narrative succeeds in blending "the ideal and the actual, especially with regards to the issues of power and identity, [which] has had the effect of making her novels the most ambitious by an African woman" (Brown, p. 161).

—Iyunolu Osagie

For More Information

Borg, Mary. "Victims." *New Statesman* 77 (May 16, 1969): 696.

Brown, Lloyd. *Women Writers in Black Africa.* Westport, Conn.: Greenwood, 1981.

Eilersen, Gillian Stead. *Bessie Head: Thunder Behind Her Ears: Her Life and Writing.* Claremont, South Africa: David Philip, 1995.

Garrett, James. "Writing Community: Bessie Head and the Politics of Narrative." *Research in African Literature* 30, no. 2 (summer 1999): 122-35.

Head, Bessie. *When Rain Clouds Gather.* London: Heinemann, 1986.

———. "Witchcraft." *Ms.,* 4 November 1975, pp. 72-77.

Heywood, Christopher. *Aspects of South African Literature.* London: Heinemann, 1976.

Mackenzie, Craig, and Cherry Clayton, eds. *Between the Lines: Interviews with Bessie Head, Shiela Roberts, Ellen Kuzwayo, and Miriam Tlali.* Grahamstown, South Africa: National English Literary Museum, 1989.

Parson, Jack. *Botswana: Liberal Democracy and the Labor Reserve in Southern Africa.* Boulder, Colo.: Westview Press, 1984.

Ramsay, Jeff, et al. *Historical Dictionary of Botswana.* 3rd ed. Lanham, Md.: Scarecrow Press, 1996.

Saunders, Christopher. *Historical Dictionary of South Africa.* Metuchen, N.J.: Scarecrow Press, 1983.

Woman at
Point Zero

by
Nawal El Saadawi

~

Nawal El Saadawi (also spelled Nawal Sa'-dawi) was born in the Egyptian village of Kafr Tahla in the Nile Delta province of Qalubiyya in 1931. Her high scores on national examinations permitted her to enter the Faculty of Medicine at Cairo University during a time when the student population was still heavily male. She practiced both general medicine and psychiatry, became Director of Health Education for Egypt, edited the popular magazine *Health,* and, having written short stories as a university student, continued to produce fiction. In the 1970s El Saadawi's writing shifted entirely to gender issues. She became known as Egypt's most outspoken critic of the oppression of women and the first to write openly about such aspects of female sexuality as clitoridectomy, incest, and prostitution. Her career shifted from state-funded medical work into full-time research, writing, and activism, when, in reaction to her book *Women and Sex* (1972), she was fired as Director of Health Education and editor of *Health.* Her subsequent research on female neuroses led her to the women's prison in Qanatir, where in 1973 she conducted an interview with the inmate on whom *Woman at Point Zero* is based.

Events in History at the Time the Novel Takes Place

Twentieth-century Egypt—stability and change. During El Saadawi's early life, Egyptians were protesting the colonial presence in Egypt of the

---

THE LITERARY WORK

A novel based on El Saadawi's interview with a woman incarcerated in Egypt's Qanatir prison and executed circa 1973; published in Arabic (as *Imra'ah 'Inda Nuqtat al-Sifr*) in 1979, in English in 1983.

SYNOPSIS

Awaiting execution, Firdaus, a prostitute who has murdered a pimp, relates her experiences as a woman in Egypt to a medical researcher/writer visiting the prison.

British, who would finally be forced out by a revolutionary government in 1952. Egypt had achieved a formal but nominal independence in 1922, under which King Fu'ad I and his son King Faruq ruled with a cabinet and parliament. Britain, however, retained enough influence to oppose cabinets or key politicians and thus dampen the growth of pluralism or effective democracy. The British had occupied Egypt since 1882, ruling it as if it were a colony, though officially it was not. They maintained a military presence there too, to protect their interest in cheap cotton and in revenues from the Suez Canal. Genuine independence and the total withdrawal of foreign forces was a continuous issue in Egypt until the rather surprising 1952 military coup by a group of young army officers, including Gamal Abdul Nasser (also spelled Jamal 'Abd al-Nasir).

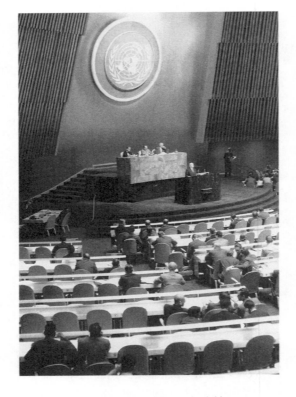

The United Nations General Assembly deliberates a response to Egyptian President Abdul Nasser's nationalization of the Suez Canal in 1956.

The revolution ignited by these officers changed the power structure of Egypt, displacing wealthy property owners as the nation's most influential political force. When first established under President Muhammad Naguib, however, the new regime did not have preformulated platforms or a theoretical framework for future policies. The rebels shipped the king off to Europe; the elite who remained in Egypt would suffer—if not at first, then later under the new regime's populist policies. Meanwhile, the peasants and urban poor appreciated the coup, although because of the inadequacy of reforms and policies like the decision to expand industry, their circumstances would be relieved only at the expense of growing debt and dependency for Egypt.

In 1953 the military officers banned all political parties and abolished the monarchy. The officers were eliminating potential rivals. Their one-time ally, President Naguib, was stripped of his powers, and Nasser became the voice of Egypt, with 'Abd al-Hakim 'Amir in control of the army. Another former ally, the Muslim Brotherhood, a 25-year-old grassroots Islamist party, was repressed by the new regime after a Muslim

Brother tried to assassinate Nasser in 1954. Nasser's government also put down a worker's strike, and moved against the Communist Party and other leftists.

In 1956 Nasser nationalized the Suez Canal in response to the withdrawal of an expected loan from the World Bank that year. The Egyptian masses applauded this seizure of Egypt's largest source of revenue, which had been controlled by foreign powers since its construction under the local ruler, the khedive Isma'il, in the nineteenth century. The ensuing war in Suez, known in Egypt as the Tripartite Aggression, saw the Israelis, French, and British jointly attack Egypt to punish Nasser for the seizure. To Egyptians, the war indicated the hostile intentions of the West against their young government. And in fact the attack met with global condemnation.

Nasser moved further away from the West by announcing a Czech arms deal in September 1955, and by refusing that same year to sign the Washington-sponsored Baghdad pact (to protect Middle Eastern nations such as Iraq and Turkey from Soviet aggression). He would publicly claim a commitment to neutralism, to independence without reliance on the East or the West. But in fact the need to build up Egypt's military base and the army's dominance in politics resulted in Egypt's purchasing weapons from the Eastern bloc and in Russian military advisors arriving to conduct business in Egypt.

Important in this period was Nasser's enunciation of Arab unity. A short-lived (1958-61) union of Egypt and Syria resulted in the United Arab Republic, which would ultimately disintegrate. For a while, many in the region embraced this macro-philosophy, and it complicated the gender issue. If Arabs were to share a unified culture, how would it be possible to allow for the variations in attitudes and practices concerning women in different lands? In some Arab societies, arranged marriages or marriages to first cousins were still preferred, strict separation of the sexes was observed, and women's ability to challenge spousal abuse was extremely limited; in other Arab societies women were moving into the workforce, advancing through education, and challenging some of the legal restrictions imposed on them.

After the short-lived experiment in Arab unity came the defeat of the Arab states in the 1967 so-called Six Day War with Israel. Israel's preemptive strike on June 5, 1967, destroyed much of the Egyptian air force parked on the airfield. Israel emerged victorious not only because of the

Egyptians march through the streets of Cairo in fervent support of President Nasser and the United Arab Republic, a short-lived experiment in Arab unity.

strike but also, among other factors, because of poor training of Egyptian troops, an inadequate budget, and Nasser's refusal to withdraw forces from Yemen. The mix led to Israeli victory in the Sinai, and Israeli occupation of the West Bank and the Golan Heights. The loss was enormous. Arab intellectuals termed the 1967 war the *nakba*—the disaster, a political and cultural crisis, a nadir from which they could descend no further. Suddenly all the slogans in favor of Arab socialism and unity seemed empty, especially the one that promised an eventual reclamation of Palestine. Instead Egypt had experienced a further defeat. There was, however, no vibrant ideology to step into the place of Arab socialism and unity.

The decade following Nasser's death in 1970 brought further disintegration in political and social values. A new economic open-door policy in 1972, the *infitah,* led to the expulsion of Soviet advisors, and the expectation on the part of international aid agencies that Egypt would pursue more "rational" economic policies—that is, embark on privatization, or the transformation of public enterprises into private ones. The policy, involving invitations for Western investment in Egypt, troubled many leftists. Their country had for some years followed a path of neutral self-sufficiency. If the public sector were to be gradually privatized, what would happen to the previously proclaimed commitment to the common citizens?

El Saadawi forged her resistance to oppression, whether it related to gender, or more broadly to authoritarianism, during these decades. The Egyptian public had been regaled with promises that the demise of the ancient regime, and the withdrawal of the lingering British, would bring a new age. Yet women especially did not experience a newly tolerant, materially plentiful existence. Instead they experienced a competition for resources that repeatedly favored men—father over wife and children, uncle over niece, and male employers over female workers, to name a few examples from the novel.

Women in modern Egyptian history. Urban elite women followed a fairly strict code of sexual segregation in the Ottoman Empire of the nineteenth century. In Egypt many upper-class women lived within the boundaries of the harem system, which secluded them from the general male public. Debate stirred here about the need for female education within a modernizing society, about the abuses of polygamy, and about the veiling of women's faces. A woman's honor was theoretically the property of her menfolk, so a high value accrued to virginity. Meanwhile, the custom of paying a brideprice, the amount given to a girl's parents to formalize a union, was sanctioned by religion and custom, which meant that poor women could be "sold." (Wealthy women had more freedom, because they retained control of their own income.)

Women in the countryside were not subject to the Ottoman face veil or practices of female seclusion because their labor was necessary for family subsistence. If girls survived their early childhood, they were circumcised at age six or seven to weaken their sexual urge and ensure virginity. The painful, unsanitary practice involved removing all or part of the clitoris, which resulted in medical and psychological complications. A movement against female circumcision began in the 1920s and '30s, but surveys show that the practice continues even today in countryside and city, among Muslims and Christians.

As Egyptian society progressed from its status under King Faruq to the revolutionary era, to its reorientation to the West under President Anwar Sadat, women and popular ideas about their roles changed. The harem system had declined earlier in the century, and elite women had gained some mobility in the public sphere. By mid-century they enjoyed rights to education and entry into various professions. Discussion about sexual issues would prove more problematic than those about women's rights to study or work, whether such debate touched on female circumcision or the expectation that women would maintain their virginity until marriage or face death at the hands of male relatives. In any case, the condition of women in general changed very slowly, with the lives of peasant women and those of the urban lower class remaining far less altered than among the wealthier. Even elite and middle-class women faced discrimination—although in their case it was alleviated by their financial status and access to legal remedies.

A number of women refused to suffer such discrimination, which gave rise to a generation of female activists who were anything but passive and meek. In the late 1940s and '50s, a second generation of feminists met, wrote, and fought for social reforms. They faced a formidable task. Many in the Arab world still saw monogamous marriage for women, followed by motherhood, to be a religiously sanctioned structure. Certainly it was not something to be abandoned for the free dating and rising divorce rate of the West. Besides, Westerners had imposed their ideas and customs on Egypt from 1882 to 1952. Feminism, said opponents, could be (and was) seen as a weapon directed at Arab-Muslim culture itself.

Women's rights and the Personal Status Code. Since girls married early, it was difficult, especially in past decades, to convince peasant families that there was merit in educating female children. Slowly the outlook changed. In *Woman at Point Zero*, El Saadawi's protagonist, Firdaus, takes advantage of an opportunity to study in Cairo. She also works there, in a factory, where she falls in love with the head of a revolutionary committee. Though a rebel, he proves to be as exploitative as every other male with whom she interacts—from her uncle with his rural roots; to her aged husband, who resents every crumb she eats; to the pimp who usurps her independence as an enterprising prostitute.

The novel mocks the idealism of the 1970s, which failed to address the plight of women. All over Egypt they suffered exploitation, even as the government was touting improved conditions for everyone. When a woman obeyed society's rules, as Firdaus does during her days as an office worker, she suffered inadequate pay. Even in revolutionary circles—women often served as the support base for political parties and revolutionary committees—they failed to receive credit equal to men. At home, domestic violence was rampant in Egyptian society, although it could be mitigated if a women had good relations with her own family and they elected to serve as mediators. Women's rights to divorce, child custody, and relief from an abusive spouse were limited because of prevailing interpretations of *shari'ah,* Islamic law.

Shari'ah formed the basis of the Personal Status Code, the body of law that governed issues of importance to women. Polygamy was permissible for men; they did not have to notify their wives of a divorce or a second marriage; women could not obtain alimony from a divorced husband, though they were entitled to "upkeep" and child support; an outdated custom called *bayt al-ta'ah* (house of obedience) allowed a man to confine his wife to her home prior to divorce; and a woman had to give up custody of her children at specified ages or if she remarried. In 1979 Anwar Sadat's regime enacted important reforms in these policies, but extralegally, without going through set procedure. The reforms were challenged and amended in 1985 to contain less liberal provisions, but in 2000 a new law making divorce easier for women and somewhat harder for men was passed.

Migration and prostitution. The protagonist of *Woman at Point Zero* migrates from the countryside to the city. The problems resulting from her migration reflect realities of mid-twentieth century Egypt, when migrants to Cairo crowded into areas in which they could ill afford to live, only to find little infrastructure and high unemployment in the city.

In other works of Egyptian literature, the countryside is represented as the site of morality and honesty while the city is portrayed as alienating and corrupting. El Saadawi paints a more nuanced portrait. The countryside is not wholly positive—the female protagonist grows up and survives in rural Egypt through luck while siblings die. And the city is not wholly evil; while it represents the loss of her immediate family and is the center of multiple forms of exploitation, it also offers Firdaus the opportunity to obtain an education.

Faced with high unemployment and discrimination in the city, some women chose to become prostitutes, as Firdaus does in *Woman at Point Zero.* In the nineteenth and early twentieth centuries, Egypt saw a multiethnic trade in women, ranging from white foreigners, to Africans, to child prostitutes. Debate raged over the legal means of allowing, controlling, or attempting to curtail the volume of prostitution, which increased at pivotal times, as in World War II, when large numbers of foreign troops, committed to action in the Egyptian desert, retreated to Cairo for rest and recreation.

Of course, women elected to become prostitutes for various reasons. In or out of the trade, society regarded women as objects to serve men. The novel contrasts the protagonist's choice—to

WOMEN AND FEMINISM IN TWENTIETH-CENTURY EGYPT

1899: Qasim Amin's book *The Liberation of Women* (Tahrir al-Mar'ah) ignites public debate.

1909: Bahitha al-Bad'iyya (the pen name of Malak Hifni Nassif) publishes *al-Nisa'iyat,* an anthology of speeches and essays on women.

1919: Veiled women participate in nationalist demonstrations and protests against the British.

1920: Nabawiyya Musa publishes *al-Mar'ah wa al-Amal* (Women and Work).

1922: Egypt is granted nominal independence by Great Britain.

1923: Founding of the Egyptian Feminist Union; Huda Sha'arawi and Saiza Nabarawi, feminist nationalists, cast off their face veils in public.

1944: The Egyptian Feminist Union hosts the Arab Feminist Conference.

1945: Creation of the Arab Feminist Union.

1949: Inji Aflatun, painter and writer, publishes *Nahnu al-Nisa' al-Misriyyat* (We Egyptian Women), which analyzes women's oppression.

1952: Revolution displaces King Faruq.

1954: Amina Sa'id, journalist and feminist, founds *Hawwa,* the first contemporary popular magazine to cater to a broad-based female audience; Durriya Shafiq, philosopher, writer, and founder of the Bint al-Nil (Daughter of the Nile) Union, goes on a hunger strike to protest women's lack of political rights.

1956: Egyptian women achieve suffrage; the Suez War erupts.

1959: Nawal El Saadawi writes *Memoirs of a Female Physician.*

1973: El Saadawi begins her research at Qanatir prison.

1974: Laws introduced for the economic opening of Egypt.

1979: Anwar Sadat's regime enacts reforms of the laws of Personal Status.

1985: Personal Status reforms are amended to reduce freedoms.

2000: New divorce law allowing female-initiated divorce on any grounds is passed.

be a prostitute—with the role society imposes on her, of subservient, respectable wife. Her uncle and his wife are solely concerned with finding a husband who will provide her material support. They search for the standard arrangement, in which a wife trades sexual favors for material support of herself and her offspring. In some ways the prostitute is less oppressed than such a wife—an important point to keep in mind when considering Firdaus's actions in *Woman at Point Zero*. Also crucial is the knowledge that neither Islamic mores nor forces of progress in the 1970s had much impact on prostitution in Egyptian society.

The Novel in Focus

Plot summary. *Woman at Point Zero* opens with the female narrator's account of her efforts to obtain an interview with a female prisoner whose unique demeanor fascinates and troubles the prison doctor, the warden, and eventually, the narrator too. The woman, Firdaus (her name means "paradise" in Arabic), is a prostitute who will soon to be executed for murdering a man who proclaimed himself her pimp. The prison doctor and warden inform the unnamed narrator that Firdaus refuses to speak to her; she has even refused to sign an appeal to the president that would commute her death sentence to life imprisonment. The narrator feels deeply troubled by Firdaus's refusal to be interviewed, but suddenly the prisoner does an about-face. She summons the narrator to her cell, then tells her story. There is a dreamlike quality to the experience, but the narrator reminds us of its factual basis nevertheless:

> But this was no dream. . . . The woman sitting on the ground in front of me was a real woman, and the voice filling my ears with its sound, echoing in a cell where the window and door were tightly shut, could only be her voice, the voice of Firdaus.
>
> (El Saadawi, *Woman at Point Zero*, p. 7)

Firdaus's tale attributes her hatred of men to a lifetime of male oppression. As a child, she experiences a father who beats his wife and neglects his female children, eating when the rest of the family has no food. Without explanation, Firdaus's clitoris is excised, according to the African custom known as female circumcision. Afterward she may no longer roam the fields but must stay home to clean and cook. She is sexually molested by her uncle, whom she nonetheless loves dearly. Firdaus follows him to Cairo, where she attends school.

By this time, as shown by her distaste for her own reflection in the mirror, Firdaus's self-esteem is compromised. She nevertheless loves her studies and her school in Cairo, and is grateful for the opportunity to escape the animalistic destiny she witnessed in the countryside. She keeps house for her uncle, who continues to molest her while serving as her protector, until he marries a woman who resents Firdaus, or, more exactly, resents having to provide for the young woman. Firdaus is transferred to the boarding section of her school, where her passion for reading increases her understanding of the domination of men throughout history. She falls in love with a sympathetic teacher, Ms. Iqbal, the only adult who has shown any unblemished concern for her.

Viewing Firdaus as a useless burden after her graduation, her aunt and uncle marry her off to the elderly Sheikh (or Shaykh) Mahmoud who insists on having sex with her and on scrutinizing her constantly. Firdaus finds him physically revolting—he has an oozing tumor on his chin. When he beats her with his shoe, she runs back to her uncle and aunt, but the aunt dismisses her, stating that "the precepts of religion permitted such punishment" (*Woman at Point Zero*, p. 44). Realizing that her family will not intercede on her behalf, Sheikh Mahmoud beats her more severely, whereupon she runs away. The owner of a coffeehouse offers her temporary shelter, then abuses her too, locking her in his flat, raping her, and sending in his cronies to have intercourse with her.

Once again Firdaus escapes into the streets, and meets a woman, Sharifa Salah el Dine. After surprising Firdaus by asking her who has abused her, the strange woman installs her in her own luxurious apartment on the Nile River. Sharifa teaches Firdaus that in this world dominated by men, she must value herself, must acknowledge her own beauty and degree of education. Serving as a madam, Sharifa collects payments while Firdaus receives male clients. Firdaus acknowledges her own sensuality and enjoyment of material pleasures when living with Sharifa, but cannot enjoy sexual relations. One client, who senses that sex is physically painful to her, vows that he will take her away from Sharifa. Firdaus overhears an argument between this man, a former lover of Sharifa's, and her mistress, followed by violent lovemaking. As has become her pattern, she flees into the streets.

Firdaus next encounters a policeman who threatens her with arrest if she will not have sex with him, and then a stranger rescues her from the streets, sleeps with her, and leaves her ten pounds, the first money she has earned for herself. She now operates independently as a prostitute, describing this period of her life as a time when she owns her own body. Her self-content is ruined when a client speaks of her lack of respectability. Firdaus responds: "My work is not worthy of respect. Why then do you join in it with me?" (*Woman at Point Zero*, p. 71). In pursuit of respectability, Firdaus seeks and eventually obtains a job at an industrial company. She lives miserably on her poor wages but refuses the attentions of men. Eventually Firdaus recognizes that, as a poorly paid employee, she has gained no respect or social status; prostitution is less confining to her than the life of a female employee who is terrified of losing her job.

Firdaus falls in love with a fellow worker, Ibrahim, who is head of a revolutionary committee within the company. She labors incessantly for the committee, only to discover that her lover has become engaged to the company chairman's daughter. Ibrahim's betrayal overwhelms her. With the exception of her crush on Ms. Iqbal, she had not previously loved another human being. Numb with alienation and cynicism, Firdaus picks up a man in the street. "Revolutionary men with principles were not really different from the rest," she reflects. "They used their cleverness to get, in return for principles, what other men buy with their money. Revolution for them is like sex for us. Something to be abused. Something to be sold" (*Woman at Point Zero*, p. 88).

And so Firdaus returns to prostitution. Her financial success brings her to the attention of a head of state and men who wish to marry her. One, a dangerous pimp, Marzouk, seizes control of her business. When she attempts to leave, they argue. He slaps her, and Firdaus stabs him, discovering that her fear of Marzouk, indeed her fear of all men and of the vicious nature of her society, has vanished. She walks again into the street, where she encounters a prince who is her client. She terrifies him by speaking of her ability to kill; he screams until the police arrive. They arrest her and send her to prison.

Firdaus declares to the narrator that she does not fear death and understands that she is intolerable to her captors because her defiance threatens the social order. She utters a final condemnation before she is marched out of the cell to die: "I spit with ease on their lying faces and words, on their lying newspapers" (*Woman at*

Point Zero, p. 103). The narrator leaves with a sense of shame—at her own accommodation to the society that has so dishonorably dealt with Firdaus—and closes with the words: "And at that moment I realized that Firdaus had more courage than I" (*Woman at Point Zero*, p. 108).

The exploited female. At the heart of *Woman at Point Zero* is the feminist critique of Firdaus's world. The power of Firdaus's testimony is twofold. First there are her gendered experiences, from circumcision to abuse, beating, and rape, to her final confrontation with Marzouk, who divides the world into masters and slaves, implying that a woman can be only a slave. Her murder of him might be viewed as a rejection of the role to which he consigns her. Secondly the power of this portrait of one woman's oppression is due to its larger historical validity. Of course, not all mid-to-late twentieth century women sold their bodies to unknown men; some otherwise prostituted themselves to the demands of their families, and many secretly suffered sexual abuse.

Firdaus learns that the gradations of social class and increasing modernization do not seem to affect the treatment of women. She discovers this initially through historical works, and later in her own lived experiences.

> I preferred books about rulers. I read about a ruler whose female servants and concubines were as numerous as his army and another whose only interests in life were wine, women, and whipping his slaves. A third cared little for women, but enjoyed wars, killing, and torturing men.... There was also a ruler so obsessed with plots and conspiracies that he spent all his time distorting the facts of history and trying to fool his people.
>
> I discovered that all these rulers were men. What they had in common was an avaricious and distorted personality, a never-ending appetite for money, sex and unlimited power. They were men who sowed corruption on the earth, and plundered their peoples, men endowed with loud voices, a capacity for persuasion, for choosing sweet words and shooting poisoned arrows. Thus, the truth about them was revealed only after their death, and as a result I discovered that history tended to repeat itself with a foolish obstinacy.
>
> (*Woman at Point Zero*, pp. 26-27)

For Firdaus, the rulers of her own era are no better—nor are the ordinary men whom she encounters in daily life. Westerners frequently attribute women's difficulties in the Arab world to sexist ideas inherent in the religion of Islam, but these views are often based on uninformed ideas about the religion. Likewise, some critics of El Saadawi incorrectly regard her as attacking Islam in her writing. In fact, her views on the causes of patriarchal practices and gender biases in Egypt are nuanced. While she does not exonerate Muslims from suppressing or mistreating women, neither does she consider Islam the root of the problem. Instead she sees several factors as having contributed to sexism—among them, pre-existing customs (from Arab, Nile Valley, or other cultures), perversion of Islamic intents, and the struggling economy. She nevertheless attacks practices adopted by Muslims, such as stricter veiling of women from society, and the extraordinary value attached to virginity. She also opposes female circumcision, arguing that it cannot be justified as an Islamic custom, since Muhammad knew of it but did not recommend the practice.

Sources and literary context. The Azhar, the center of Islamic learning that draws Firdaus and

---

FROM POLITICS TO ALIENATION IN LITERATURE

Nasser's regime refrained from much discussion of the situation of women in Egypt, fearing religious conservative reaction. On one hand, the conservative Muslim Brotherhood, one-time ally of the officers who routed the British, had championed modest dress for women but opposed extending women the vote (which they gained in 1956). On the other hand, Nasser's government wanted to allow for gradual change in women's lives through policies that supported the nationalization of education and health and that heightened productivity, but Nasser did not want to rock the boat with any dramatic changes or open discussions of gender issues. After a Muslim Brother's attempt to assassinate Nasser in 1954, the president cracked down on the Muslim Brotherhood. The crackdown stymied discussion that might otherwise have occurred about the contradiction between Nasser's social policies and current Islamic practices in Egypt. With Nasser's regime came anti-imperialist policies, which were applauded, particularly by the masses, but also the growth of a national bureaucracy as well as repressive measures used to monitor and silence the regime's opponents. Both conditions brought criticism from intellectuals and writers, who suffered censorship and imprisonment. Along with sexual oppression, their suffering is the basis for the extreme alienation from society in El Saadawi's novel.

---

her uncle to Cairo, actually exists. Otherwise the novel's only direct historical allusions are those concerning the socialization of factories and large industries under President Gamal Abd al-Nasser, and El Saadawi's own interview with the protagonist in 1973, which constitutes the framework for the novel.

El Saadawi has explained in an interview that she added only 10 to 20 percent of her own invention to the actual prisoner's story (El Saadawi in Badran and Cooke, p. 402). In 1973, she was collecting case studies in the Qanatir prison as well as local hospitals and clinics, when she met and interviewed the prisoner who served as the model for Firdaus in *Woman at Point Zero*.

El Saadawi had close contact with imprisonment herself. Many of her associates served time for their political views, her husband served a 13-year sentence, and she served a 4-year prison sentence of her own. Since she was jailed for her ideological views and political affiliations, she could relate firsthand to her protagonist's position as a woman punished for refusing to abide by society's rules. El Saadawi's novel is part of an ongoing movement of Egyptian women's writing. A number of her contemporaries have also written about women's erotic and psychological experiences, including, for example, the Egyptian novelist Alifa Rifaat (*Distant View of a Minaret*). El Saadawi has at the same time been part of a broader literary tradition, that of social critique in North Africa and the Middle East. Beyond feminist concerns, her novel has been read as a critique of Egypt's positioning of itself in global affairs.

Events in History at the Time the Novel Was Written

1970s Egypt—spectrum of events. The most important historical events taking place while El Saadawi was writing the novel were the politics of *infitah* (economic opening to the West) in Egypt; the development of Islamic fundamentalism there; and Egypt's increasing economic dependence on international aid agencies and (until 1979) on income from the Gulf states. Some of this income came through governmental aid, but a portion came from tourist revenues. Tensions arose between male tourists from the Gulf and Egyptians because of the association of prostitution and other illegal vices with the entertainment businesses. Tales abounded of Gulf visitors hunting for Egyptian prostitutes, and seeking out little girls to buy from their families.

Feminism in the 1970s. Feminists scored advancements in Egypt from the late 1950s to the 1970s. In 1957 two women won election to the People's Assembly, and from the 1960s to 1979 about a dozen women were either elected or appointed to Parliament. An increasing number of women entered the labor force. Passed in 1959, Law No. 91 prohibited discrimination on the basis of sex; other laws mandated benefits such as maternity leave.

The decade of the 1970s brought advances for women, albeit sometimes cosmetic or temporary, as in the 1979 Personal Status Code reforms. Among the reforms, for example, was a divorced woman's right to retain the family home—an important advance, since previously women lost their residence, and if their families did not want them to return home, often reconciled with objectionable spouses rather than divorce. Women seemed to be gaining ground but a major step backward, from their point of view, was in the offing.

With the growth of Islam in Egypt and other Arab states came what liberal feminists saw as setbacks for women. These setbacks were observable in increased preference for Islamic dress (including long loose gowns and the *hijab*, a covering for the hair) rather than Western fashions, and in the separation of the sexes in local Islamist groups. It was in the 1970s that radical Islamist groups in Egypt gained supporters and overtly opposed the government, which resulted in mass arrests. The groups opposed secular government (the separation of religion and state) in general, and were extremely critical of Anwar Sadat for his enactment, among other things, of the Personal Status reforms. El Saadawi and other feminists were very active during this time in establishing networks to push forward such reforms for women. But opposing Islamist groups mounted a strong backlash against the reforms that would lead to their being reduced.

As the novel was being written, Nawal El Saadawi had assumed the role of feminist activist in a period characterized by an abrupt turning away from the political, social, and economic goals of the earlier decade. Firdaus claims at the end of the novel, "It is my truth that frightens them" (*Woman at Point Zero,* p. 102). El Saadawi seems to be instilling the urgency of Firdaus's statement with her own newfound calling, with the warning tone of a prophet.

Reviews. Banned in Egypt, a number of El Saadawi's works, including *Woman at Point Zero,* were published in Beirut, Lebanon. Her nonfic-

tion had previously attracted an Arab readership and alerted conservatives to the polemics in her work. *Woman at Point Zero* was acclaimed by the Arabic-reading audience and by feminists outside the Arab world for its courage, the power of its prose, and its ideological message. Those who objected to El Saadawi's earlier work criticized the novel from a philosophical perspective, judging its feminist message too strident. Later, as intellectuals moved away from the socialist ideals of the Nasser era, they objected to the work from a literary perspective as well, finding fault with the way it incorporates social critique into fiction at a time when symbolic work was becoming more prevalent and other authors of the region were writing more indirectly to avoid censorship. In the eyes of these critics, El Saadawi's feminist zeal was too overwhelming; she subordinated character, they thought, and therefore language and writing structure, to the "political" novel.

MORE THAN A NOVEL?

Egypt has been frequently represented in sculpture, cartoons, and paintings of the twentieth century as a woman confronting the more sophisticated male powers of the world. Indeed, one reading of *Woman at Point Zero* interprets the work as an allegory that expresses El Sadaawi's Marxist views about Egypt, a land doomed by the world economic system to prostitute itself to outside interests. Such a reading suggests that, had Egypt revolted against Western companies and against contemporary privatization campaigns, the rulers and jailers in modern Egyptian society would have been toppled. Also suggested by such a reading is that Egyptians would have been well advised to resist the corruption prompted by the influential Gulf tourists. Cairo became the playground for vacationing Saudis, Kuwaitis, and others. For their pleasure, nightclubs and casinos lined the long avenue from Cairo University to the pyramids. Men from the Gulf were infamous for harassing Egyptian women and for finding and purchasing very young girls as brides. El Saadawi addresses the issue when Firdaus picks up a "prince" in *Woman at Point Zero.*

Woman at Point Zero has been praised for the same features for which it is criticized. Reviewers compliment its brave discussion of female circumcision and discrimination in Egypt. Fedwa Malti-Douglas locates El Saadawi's work within a tradition that uses the female voice to subvert the rule of patriarchy and its accounting of events. In a more mixed review, Wen-Chin Ouyang recognizes both the artfulness and danger of such a novel: "El Saadawi has a flair for melodrama and mystery. She skillfully tricks us into the world she creates . . . [but] the characters remain symbols and never quite come to life" (Ouyang, pp. 458-59). The reviewer cautions that those who are unfamiliar with the Arabic novel can be led astray by El Saadawi's insistence that her tales are real. She exaggerates, says Ouyang, the portrayal of women as "hopeless, helpless victims" and of men as evil "control freaks," as one would expect of an Arab "novel of ideas," in which the message is the ultimate protagonist and in which women, especially prostitutes, are often symbols of their countries or nations (Ouyang, p. 459). Nevertheless, Ouyang commends El Saadawi for drawing readers in with her "deft use of the first-person narrative," which compels them to live the experience of her female protagonist.

—Sherifa Zuhur

For More Information

Al-Ali, Nadje Sadig. *Gender Writing/Writing Gender: The Representation of Women in a Selection of Modern Egyptian Literature.* Cairo: American University in Cairo, 1994.

Badran, Margot. *Feminists, Islam and Nation: Gender and the Making of Modern Egypt.* Princeton, N.J.: Princeton University, 1995.

Badran, Margot, and Miriam Cooke, eds. *Opening the Gates: A Century of Arab Women's Writing.* London: Virago, 1990.

Ghazoul, Ferial, and Barbara Harlow, eds. *The View from Within: Writers and Critics on Contemporary Arabic Literature.* Cairo: American University in Cairo, 1994.

Malti-Douglas, Fedwa. *Woman's Body, Woman's Word: Gender and Discourse in Arabo-Islamic Writing.* Princeton, N.J.: Princeton University Press, 1991.

Mikhail, Mona. *Images of Arab Women.* Washington D.C.: Three Continents Press, 1979.

Marsot, 'Afaf Lutfi al-Sayyid. *A Short History of Modern Egypt.* Cambridge: Cambridge University Press, 1985.

Ouyang, Wen-Chin. "Nawal al-Sa'dawi, *Woman at Point Zero* and *The Circling Song.*" *International Journal of Middle East Studies* 28, no. 3, (August 1996): 458-59.

Sa'dawi, Nawal. *Woman at Point Zero.* Trans. Sherif Hetata. London: Zed Books, 1983.

Sullivan, Earl. *Women in Egyptian Public Life.* Syracuse, N.Y.: Syracuse University Press, 1986.

Tarabishi, Georges. *Woman Against Her Sex: A Critique of Nawal El Saadawi.* Trans. Basil Hatim and Elisabeth Orsini. London: Saqi Books, 1988.

Zeidan, Joseph T. *Arab Women Novelists: The Formative Years and Beyond.* Albany: State University of New York, 1995.

EL SAADAWI'S CAREER WHEN THE NOVEL WAS WRITTEN

In addition to her writing, El Saadawi became an advisor on women's programs and then moved to the Lebanese office of the United Nations in 1979 to head women's programs in the region. In 1982 she and a group of Arab women from various countries established the Arab Women's Solidarity Association. The group organized a conference of its own, sent a delegation to the United Nation's International Conference on Women, and participated in debate and activism in Egypt concerning the proposed amendments of the laws of Personal Status. As an undeclared war between Islamist militants and the government escalated in the late 1980s and afterwards, El Saadawi's organization was declared illegal and shut down. El Saadawi herself received threats and had to hire an armed guard at her residence. She continued, however, to write. Although censorship of texts on sexual issues has been increasing, her work continues to be read widely in Arabic and in translation.

The Wretched of the Earth

by

Frantz Fanon

Born in 1925, Frantz Fanon grew up in a middle-class black family in the French West Indian colony of Martinique. He was one of the 4 percent of black Martinique children whose families could afford to send them to *lycée* for a European-style secondary education. During World War II, when Martinique was occupied by the Nazis, Fanon fought for the Free French in Europe (the exile forces led by General Charles de Gaulle after France fell to the Nazis in 1940). He later studied psychiatry in Lyon, France. Fanon first went to Algeria as a member of the French colonial administration and, in 1953, became one of the directors of a French psychiatric hospital there. Finding his sympathies turning toward the Algerian Nationalist movement, Fanon joined the Front de Libération Nationale (FLN), which sought to end French colonial rule. He was expelled from Algeria in 1957 by the French government for his participation in an Algerian nationalist strike, and served briefly as the FLN's ambassador to Ghana. Fanon survived a couple of assassination attempts, but fell ill with leukemia in 1961. During his last year he battled the fatal disease while writing, in a fury of anger and passion, *The Wretched of the Earth*. He read the page proofs in September and died in December 1961, at age 36 in a hospital bed in the United States. His body was returned to Algeria and buried in a cemetery of the Algerian revolutionary army.

Events in History at the Time of the Essays

Decolonization: a survey. Fanon drew on his experience as a psychiatrist and revolutionary in

---

THE LITERARY WORK

A collection of essays, parts of which are set in Algeria and other developing nations of Africa, Asia, and Latin America; published in French (as *Les damnés de la terre*) in 1961, in English in 1963.

SYNOPSIS

Drawing on his experiences as a revolutionary in the Algerian war of national liberation (1954-62), psychiatrist Frantz Fanon argues that only violent revolution can free the Third World from colonial rulers. His argument leads into crucial notions about the issues of nation-building and national culture.

Algeria, but his ideas in *The Wretched of the Earth* apply to all colonized nations, especially those in Africa. As demonstrated by the examples Fanon cites in the book, he was well acquainted with the history of colonization and Third World independence movements.

From the sixteenth century to the mid-1970s, European nations held various areas of Asia, Africa, and the Americas as colonial possessions. World War II (1939-1945), however, shifted the balance of power, weakening Europe's two major colonizers, Britain and France, draining them of the financial resources they needed to hold other lands. At the same time, nationalist movements emerged in colonized countries, fueled by the colonized middle classes, who benefited from their education in Europe and their experience in fighting the two World Wars. These privileged classes were able to turn their desire for freedom and independence into national movements that drew strength from changing demographics (mass migrations from the country to the city) and the growth of the urban working classes.

Meanwhile, the United States gained economic and political power and began waging a competition with the Soviet Union for world leadership in the so-called "Cold War," which was played out in violent proxy battles across the Third World. Interested in spreading communism and influencing newly independent nations, the Soviets supported national liberation fronts. The United States, once a colony itself, did not take an openly opposite position. Wary of the threat to capitalism of communist national liberation movements, it neither endorsed nor denounced overt colonialism, but attempted to control new nations by economic, cultural, and tacit means. Fledgling governments and liberation movements received aid from one of the two superpowers in return for a commitment to communism or democracy.

HISTORICAL FRENCH ATTITUDE TO ALGERIANS

"Wherever good water and land are found [in Algeria]," Marshal Bugeaud recommended to the French parliament in 1840, "[European] settlers must be installed without questioning whose land it may be."

(Bugeaud in Davidson, p. 119)

Asian colonies were the first to break free. India declared independence from Britain in 1947, and Indochina from France in 1954. The last bastion of European colonialism was Africa, a continent that remained largely under the rule of Portugal, Britain, and France. In 1957 Ghana became the first African nation to gain its independence. Most African nations followed suit, achieving freedom during the 1960s, except for the Portuguese colonies of Angola and Mozambique, which attained self-rule in the mid-1970s. Revolts against colonial control proved to be grim, bloody affairs. In 1947 more than 70,000 people were killed by the French Army during a peasant revolt in Madagascar. In 1957 the British Army put down the Mau Mau rebellion in Kenya after five years of bloodshed there.

The cost in lives and money of these colonial struggles sapped the will of European powers to hold onto their colonies. At the same time, there was increasing international pressure to end colonial rule, including a condemnation of colonialism by the United Nations General Assembly in 1960, which confirmed the right of people to decide their own sovereignty. The 1960s saw the wholesale dismantling of British and French colonies in Africa; in 1960 alone France granted independence to 16 of its African colonies.

Independence, however, did not free most nations from the colonial legacy. The national borders drawn by European nations in the nineteenth century did not reflect African realities, which meant that a cultural group of people was often split between nations, or one country included more than one people. Attempts to place diverse peoples under the same government created enormous tension and rivalry.

Often, the new nations' economies were left in shambles by the sudden withdrawal of European capital. While they became politically independent, new nations found themselves dependent upon the former colonial powers' economic aid. Exploiting this dependency, the former colonial powers used such aid as leverage to gain political concessions and access to natural resources from the emerging nations. These economically dependent relationships, which continue to this day, are called "neocolonial" because they signify the continuation of colonization by different means.

Algeria: A special case. Even in the nineteenth century Algeria stood out among France's colonies in Africa. Most of the French regarded it not as a separate colony but as an extension of France proper, despite its overwhelmingly Muslim population and the special political bodies by which France governed the area.

On November 1, 1954, the Algerian liberation movement, the FLN, led a nationalist uprising against the French in Algeria. This revolt was the product of over a century of tension between the French (and other European) settlers and the local Algerian Muslims. In June 1830, on a pretext, the French had invaded Algeria with a sizeable force—34,000 strong. French troops behaved with abandon, raping and looting, and desecrating mosques and cemeteries. Their behavior set the tone for the next 100 years, in which the French treated the land as if it were theirs for the taking, with hardly a thought for its local inhabitants.

In the early 1830s some 3 million Algerians

were living on the land. They were a mix of Berbers, Arabs, Jews from Spain and Portugal, and Ottoman Turks. By far, the Muslim Arabs comprised the largest of the groups. After the French invasion, Europeans began immigrating to Algeria; by 1849, 110,000 Europeans (called *colons,* or colonists), including 15,000 French, were living in Algeria. Throughout the remainder of the nineteenth century, French officials systematically legislated Algeria's mostly Muslim population off the land.

By 1940 the European settlers, who comprised just 2 percent of Algeria, owned about a third of its most fertile land, using it to produce wine for export to France, whereas formerly that very land had yielded crops that fed Algeria. Unsurprisingly, the country began suffering a food shortage, with cereal production dropping back to the level of the 1880s, even though the population had tripled. Adding insult to injury, the Europeans invoked racist policies, allowing the use of the most common local language, Arabic, only in Muslim religious schools.

Muslim protest. The roots of the FLN's 1954 uprising reach back to the opposition of 'Abd al-Qadir, who in the 1830s and 1840s controlled as much as two-thirds of Algerian land and led its mostly Muslim inhabitants against the French. His administrative center was Memcen, a city on the Moroccan border; in 1843 'Abd al-Qadir was forced to flee into Morocco, from where he continued to direct raids against the French. He surrendered in 1847, after which the French imprisoned him, despite their assurances that this would not happen; 'Abd al-Qadir was not freed until 1853. Thirty years later, in 1883, this hero of Algerian independence died in Damascus. His standard, which was green and white, was the one under which the FLN fought and is now the Algerian national flag.

In 1871 a second Muslim uprising broke out in Algeria in protest against increasing colonial control of Muslim territory, and the chronic mistreatment of Algeria's Muslim majority during a period of drought and famine. The French retaliated against the uprising, seizing a million acres of productive Muslim-held land, and installing an insulting *indigénat* (or native code) that turned such deeds as "insolence" by a Muslim person into punishable legal offenses. "Insolence" was, of course, defined any way the French wanted to define it. In time the French also imposed highly disproportionate taxes on Muslims in relation to their income, then used the tax revenues to improve life for the Europeans themselves, educat-

Ben Cherif, commander of the Front de Libération Nationale (FLN) forces in Algeria, sits in French custody.

ing their own children and sprucing up their neighborhoods. Some wealthy or elite Muslims received a French education, forming a class of *évolués* ("the cultured"), who, despite their attainment of French ways, were shunned by the European colonists. It was among these Muslims that the nationalist movement took root.

In 1927 *Étoile Nord-Africain,* or "Star of North Africa," became the first group to call for Algerian independence. A Paris-based movement, it was quickly driven underground, but its demands for universal suffrage, land reform, and Arabic education reached thousands. Its leader, Ahmed Messali Hadj, went to Algeria to organize workers there, establishing the *Parti du Peuple Algérien* (PPA; Party of the Algerian People) in 1937.

During World War II (1939-45), Allied Forces used Algeria as a North African base. The Free French commander there, General Henri Giraud, called upon Muslim Algerians to fight for the Allies, which they did. In 1943, 56 prominent Algerians presented the French in Africa with the "Manifesto of the Algerian People," a document that decried Algeria's colonial past and made demands for land, language, and political rights. The French responded by granting full French citizenship to about 60,000 "worthy" Muslims,

French troops in Algeria arrest suspected FLN rebels during a raid.

an unacceptable compromise to the Algerians. The people grew restive.

Allied forces triumphed in Europe on May 8, 1945, V-E (Victory in Europe) Day. In Algeria the day achieved distinction for another reason; Muslims and colonists clashed violently in the town of Sétif, where an Algerian nationalist parade sparked police retaliation. Records indicate that after the police and military crackdown 103 Europeans died at Sétif, in contrast to 45,000 Algerian Muslims. Nearly a decade of political sparring and civil unrest ensued, climaxing in 1954 when the FLN, claiming that progress was impossible without violence, took up arms and declared the War of Independence (November 1).

War of Independence. Pitting itself against the French army and colonists from 1954 to 1962, the FLN waged a guerilla war. At the outset, France declared its intent to defeat the nationalists with force. The French Minister of the Interior, François Mitterand, declared that "Algeria is France," a statement repeated again and again throughout the war (Mitterand in Talbott, p. 39). Smarting from its recent defeat in Indochina, the French army was determined to retain possession of Algeria. By the end of 1956 the 400,000 French troops in Algeria outnumbered the FLN

guerillas by a ratio of 20 to 1. The French army used every means possible to suppress the nationalists, and because of the clandestine nature of the guerilla army, they suspected all Algerians. The press was censored and controlled. Curfews and searches became routine. Civil liberties were suspended. Algerians were jailed without charges, many of them killed indiscriminately. To discourage outside support for the rebels, the French electrified fences at the border and lined them with land mines.

At the same time, the French government attempted to reform the oppressive colonial structures that had sparked the unrest. Their aim was at least partly self-serving—they hoped to recruit Muslims in the general population to their cause and to weaken the rebel's grip on Algeria's rural areas. Ironically the French army, the same army that was killing nationalist combatants and civilians who got caught in the crossfire, helped with the reforms. Its Sections Adminstratives Spéciales (SAS)—a kind of military peace corps—dispensed medical care, oversaw the construction of irrigation systems, advised farmers on improving crop yields, and ran village schools.

In 1956 the FLN moved the war to the capital, Algiers, where the European colonists had congregated. FLN operatives waged violent revolt against the French that included bombings, shootings, and stabbings—an average of 800 shootings and bombings per month in the spring of 1957 (Toth, p. 49). The group had its headquarters in the Casbah, a crowded Algerian ghetto where 80,000 people crammed into tenements, twisting streets, and narrow alleys—a daunting labyrinth that helped FLN rebels elude French patrols. The FLN drew support from petty criminals, hustlers, the unemployed, and the young, whom it transformed, as Fanon discusses, into revolutionary fighters and heroes.

Called the Battle of Algiers, the FLN-sponsored Algerian revolt unnerved the European colonists, who rioted in response to the French government's inability to protect them. Elite French paratroopers, known as *Paras,* were sent to Algiers and took control of the city in January 1957. They conducted massive, indiscriminate round-ups of Algerians, frequently torturing and killing their prisoners in hopes of uncovering the FLN's secret network. Eventually the army broke the guerilla network and killed its leaders; by September 1957 the French army had driven the FLN from the streets of Algiers. Yet despite the defeat, the people still supported the FLN. France was learning that a military win did not mean victory in the war, not if the FLN retained popular support.

The French government regarded victory in Algeria as a political necessity. Its troops often executed their prisoners, officially reporting that they had been killed while attempting to escape. Thousands of Algerian peasants were forcibly moved to resettlement camps to deprive the guerillas of support in the countryside. In France there were protests against the brutal methods of the army, which were compared to those of the Nazis during World War II. The French government persisted, almost blindly, to pursue this course until France itself lost its will to fight.

The Europeans in Algeria contributed to this loss of will. Fearing that de Gaulle (elected French president in 1958) planned to desert their cause, the European minority began conducting terrorist actions inside France, bombing buildings and murdering political foes. Their actions backfired, alienating de Gaulle, who chose to extract France from the war. By then his constituents were criticizing not only the brutality of the army but also the war's staggering financial and human costs. Believing that it was in France's best interest to end the debilitating war, de Gaulle accepted Algeria's independence, and

peace finally arrived in 1962. "It is simply mad to believe that our forced domination has any future whatsoever," wrote de Gaulle. "Decolonization is in our interest and, consequently, our policy" (de Gaulle in Talbott, pp. 153, 204).

Most of Algeria's Europeans subsequently fled the country: only 120,000 of nearly 1,000,000 Europeans remained behind. A final consequence of the war was the fate of the *harkis,* the 150,000 Muslim Algerians who had fought for France. Approximately 30,000 harkis were executed by the FLN after the war, bringing the total number of Algerian fatalities to roughly 1,000,000. In contrast, about 17,500 French died in the war.

FILM: THE BATTLE OF ALGIERS

Italian director Gillo Pontecorvo's internationally acclaimed 1966 film *The Battle of Algiers* presents an accurate, realistic, documentary-style portrayal of the Algerian people's struggle against French colonial oppression. Produced only four years after Algeria gained independence and initially banned by the de Gaulle government, the film uses amateur actors and local crowds on location to portray the war in the Casbah from both the insurgents' and the counter-insurgents' (the French paratroopers') points of view. Petty criminals, hustlers, women, the unemployed, and the young all participate in the war for liberation while the French army cracks down on the revolt by arresting and brutally torturing Algerian suspects. The film supports the tenet Fanon discusses in *The Wretched of the Earth*: only through organized violence can the colonized free themselves from the clutches of the oppressor; the violent struggle transforms the dehumanized masses into human revolutionary agents devoted to freedom and the independence of their nation.

The Essays in Focus

Essay summaries. *The Wretched of the Earth* is divided into five essays: "Concerning Violence," "Spontaneity: Its Strength and Weakness," "The Pitfalls of National Consciousness," "On National Culture," and "Colonial War and Mental Disorders."

Fanon begins by introducing a central philosophical principle: decolonization is a necessary and historical part of a dialectic, the logical process of the struggle of opposites by which history moves into the present and into the future. The dialectic to which Fanon refers begins with the violence of colonization, which calls into existence decolonization.

Since colonization is a violent phenomenon, it begets its antithesis through violence. Thus, "decolonization is always a violent phenomenon" because "colonialism is not a thinking machine, nor a body endowed with reasoning faculties. It is violence in its natural state, and it will only yield when confronted with greater violence" (Fanon, *The Wretched of the Earth,* pp. 35, 61). Violence is thus not an end in itself, but the means to the end of overthrowing colonialism and freeing the oppressed from the psychological and physical shackles of colonialism.

The violence of colonialism—and here "violence" is not only physical, but includes the destruction and eradication of native history, religions, cultures, and traditions—works to make the colonized believe that they are inferior to the colonizer. The revolutionary violence of decolonization is the logical outcome of this process and undoes some of colonization's violence; it works as a creative, cathartic process by which colonized, dehumanized subjects become human again:

> [F]or the colonized people this violence, because it constitutes their only work, invests their characters with positive and creative qualities. The practice of violence binds them together as a whole, since each individual forms a violent link in the great chain, a part of the great organism of violence that has surged upward in reaction to the settler's violence in the beginning.
>
> (*Wretched of the Earth,* p. 93)

Violence is thus necessary because "the 'thing' which has been colonized becomes man during the same process by which it frees itself" (*Wretched of the Earth,* pp. 36-37).

But before the cathartic violence of decolonization unifies the people and breaks the shackles of colonialism, the native turns his aggressiveness inwards. Through tribal feuds, old grudges, and fratricidal warfare, the colonized people release their pent-up aggression on one another. By avoiding the real obstacle and killing one another, the natives prove the colonizers' contention that they are subhuman beasts.

Spirit religions, zombie myths, occult magic, and fatalistic Christianity (brought over by the colonizer as a means of pyschological control) all function to make the natives believe that unseen phantasms and gods are the source of their ills,

and not the colonizer. Their pent-up aggressions are released through dance, seances of spirit possession, exorcism, vampirism, and voodoo, while the real object of armed resistance is again avoided. This further proves to the settlers that the natives are "uncultured" and "backwards" (*Wretched of the Earth,* pp. 55-58). During the struggle for resistance, however, "a marked alienation from these practices is observed" (*Wretched of the Earth,* p. 58). The native begins to see things clearly, and abandons rituals of spirit possessions, magic, and fratricidal violence.

In the rest of the first section of "Concerning Violence," Fanon sketches out how the movement for national liberation occurs, and how the revolution is won. While national bourgeois parties are formed with Western humanistic goals of universal suffrage, democracy, and freedom, these parties simply talk but do not act. They seek through political maneuvering to enrich themselves by replacing the colonizers and reaping the riches from the land. These parties do not aim for revolution, but rather for a compromise with the colonizers in which they will be the only beneficiaries. The real power base of the revolution, however, is the peasant class. The peasants, says Fanon, "have nothing to lose and everything to gain" (*Wretched of the Earth,* p. 61). The peasant takes up arms and fights for national liberation, turning the whole social structure upside down.

Even after the colonizer is finally defeated, the revolution is still far from being won. The native population must beware of the self-interested bourgeois class and greedy dictators taking over. Second, and more importantly, the people must now build the nation out of "cement mixed with [their] blood and anger" (*Wretched of the Earth,* p. 93). After the liberation they must fight more abstract causes of oppression, such as poverty, illiteracy, and underdevelopment. They must, in the third place, beware of foreign domination. In the subsection entitled "Violence in the International Context," Fanon examines the neocolonial economic relationships that evolve and supplant direct colonialism. After independence, the new nation is faced with poverty, hunger, illiteracy, the absence of infrastructure, and the dearth of doctors and engineers. It confronts a "spectacular flight of capital" when it wins independence and its European colonists and investors flee; capitalist monopolies and other private European companies step in to fill the void on the condition "that this money is used to buy manufactured products and machines: in other words, that it serves to keep the factories in the mother country going" (*Wretched of the Earth*, pp. 103-104). These conditions further oppress new nations, which, in order to receive aid, capitulate and become economic vassals of the former colonial masters.

Thus, Fanon argues that the newly independent nations must try to avoid placing themselves in such neocolonial situations and, further, that Europe must pay the new nations reparations for the wealth that it stole from them.

In the second essay, "Spontaneity: Its Strength and Weakness," Fanon examines, in greater depth, some of the key issues touched upon in the first essay—namely, the role of the peasants as the revolutionary power base and the importance of political education in spurring revolutionary consciousness.

Fanon begins by calling attention to the primary weakness of the nationalist parties: the fact that they are a form of organization adopted by the intellectual, bourgeois elite from the mother country "without the slightest modification" (*Wretched of the Earth*, p. 108). The mother country created those parties to carry on the struggle of the working class in a highly industrialized society, unlike that of the colonized society, in which the rural populace predominates. In these colonized societies, the role of the revolutionary and of those in the nationalist parties is "to integrate the people of the countryside, to educate them politically, and to raise the level of their struggle" (*Wretched of the Earth*, p. 117).

Finding themselves committed to a real course of action, revolutionary intellectuals must break with the nationalist parties and throw their lot in with the peasants in the rural areas. After living with them, the revolutionaries will finally understand their wholehearted commitment to revolution. The revolutionary must then work to politically educate and enlighten the peasants.

At this point, Fanon sketches out a brief guide of how the revolution unfolds. His outline corresponds almost exactly to the progression of the Algerian revolution. The revolutionary intellectual takes the revolution to the city, educates the *lumpenproletariat*, and begins waging war. "[T]hat horde of starving men, uprooted from their tribe and from their clan, [these people of the urban slums, this lumpenproletariat] constitutes one of the most spontaneous and the most radically revolutionary forces of a colonized people" (*Wretched of the Earth*, p. 129).

Once the urban rebellion is in full swing, the colonizer strikes back with every method of warfare available. The rebels must therefore change their strategy; they begin at this point to wage a guerilla war. Now, however, political education is crucial in order to turn what seems to be a peasant revolt into a full-fledged revolutionary war. There must be broad-based understanding of the objectives; people need to commit themselves entirely to the struggle for their own liberation and for the freedom of the nation, not because they hate the enemy. "The desire for revenge" cannot sustain a war of liberation (*Wretched of the Earth*, p. 139). If the masses are not properly enlightened, they may end up taking part in the struggle but on the oppressor's side. This was the case of the harkis, the 150,000 Algerian natives who fought for the French, roughly 30,000 of whom were executed after Algeria gained independence.

Once the people understand all of this, they must fight for as long as it takes.

> The war goes on; the enemy holds his own; the final settling of accounts will not be today, nor yet tomorrow, for the truth is that the settlement was begun on the very first day of the war, and it will be ended not because there are no more enemies left to kill, but quite simply because the enemy, for various reasons, will come to realize that his interest lies in ending the struggle and in recognizing the sovereignty of the colonized people.
>
> (*Wretched of the Earth*, p. 141)

This is almost an exact description of the manner in which Algeria gained its independence, not by killing and expelling the French, but by fighting to the point where the French government realized that its interests lay in ending the war and in recognizing Algeria's independence.

Once the people gain their freedom, greedy dictators, politicians, bureaucrats, and the bourgeois class seek to profit at the expense of the people, who must remain vigilant in order to preserve all that they have sacrificed for.

In the third essay, "The Pitfalls of National Consciousness," Fanon examines how national consciousness in many postcolonial nations ends up being "only an empty shell, a crude and fragile travesty of what it might have been" (*Wretched of the Earth*, p. 148). National consciousness becomes a "travesty" primarily because the self-serving middle class fails to "put at the people's disposal the intellectual and technical capital that it has snatched when going through the colonial universities" (*Wretched of the Earth*, pp. 147-49). Instead of striving to develop capacities of production, invention, and labor, all of which are necessary in order to accumulate capital, the national middle class seeks merely to become an intermediary in the economic process. It replaces the former European settlement, occupying positions in the bureaucracy, legal and medical systems, and trade and commerce, and insisting that "all big foreign companies pass through its hands" (*Wretched of the Earth*, p. 152). The national bourgeoisie begins looting the nation's wealth and resources, lining its own pockets with gold while the people suffer. It prostitutes the nation through "tourism," setting up resorts for the Western bourgeoisie, and does not hesitate to invest in foreign banks and countries the profit that it sucks out of its own soil. Similarly, it spends large sums of money on personal pleasures—cars, country houses, and other gratuitous luxuries.

As the national looting continues, ethnic divisiveness, classism, and other developments splinter the people. Certain regions prosper at the expense of the nation. Dictators lull the people with revolutionary rhetoric, while the middle class gets rich. The army grows politically important as discontent multiplies. In the end, national unity exists only during daytime under the watchful eyes of soldiers; at night the people complain of the repressive national party.

In order to avoid this major pitfall, Fanon says that the bourgeoisie in underdeveloped countries should be prevented from installing itself in positions of power. Second, the national party should be decentralized in order to distribute wealth and power evenly through the nation. He suggests moving leaders to locales across the land and shifting the capital of the country to an underdeveloped area. Fanon also contends that the government should take the time to explain its policies, instead of assuming they will not be understood by the people. "[T]he 'time' lost in treating the worker as a human being, will be caught up in the execution of the plan" (*Wretched of the Earth*, p. 154).

In the fourth essay, "On National Culture," Fanon examines the construction of an authentic national culture. The first effort a decolonized people must make in forging a national culture is to rediscover their rich past. "The claim to a national culture in the past does not only rehabilitate the nation and serve as a justification for the hope of a future national culture. In the sphere of psycho-affective equilibrium it is responsible for an important change in the native" (*Wretched of the Earth*, p. 211).

Initially, instead of developing a particular na-

tional culture, the people tend to pursue the notion of a general black African culture. This is beneficial in that it uplifts people who have been dehumanized by racism, but is fundamentally flawed because it simply caters to the erroneous European assumption that Africans are indistinguishable from one another and denies national and cultural differences. The real goal of the people is to forge a genuine national culture that moves beyond the generalizations based on a common race or a shared continent. This national culture is forged out of the fight for liberation when the native intellectual sees clearly the people he seeks to address, and participates in their mutual struggle for freedom.

> The colonized man who writes for his people ought to use the past with the intention of opening the future, as an invitation to action and a basis for hope. But to ensure that hope and to give it form, he must take part in action and throw himself body and soul into the national struggle.
>
> (*Wretched of the Earth*, p. 232)

Ultimately, Fanon says, "the conscious and organized undertaking by a colonized people to reestablish the sovereignty of that nation constitutes the most complete and obvious cultural manifestation that exists" (*Wretched of the Earth*, p. 245).

The final essay, "Colonial War and Mental Disorder," differs from the rest of the book in that it provides patient histories from Fanon's tenure at a psychiatric hospital in Algeria. Here Fanon demonstrates that a colonized people is not just dominated. It is a dehumanized people whose pathologies are produced by the violence of colonialism and by the subsequent violence of decolonization. His patients include fighters on both sides of the conflict, as well as Algerian and European noncombatants.

Fanon ends *The Wretched of the Earth* on a positive, uplifting note, urging the people of the new countries to stop imitating European models of society and to create new ideas of civilization and humankind.

> Let us decide not to imitate Europe; let us combine our muscles and our brains in a new direction. Let us try to create the whole man, whom Europe has been incapable of bringing to triumphant birth.
>
> (*Wretched of the Earth*, pp. 311-13)

Violence and Fanon. Perhaps one of the most consistently misunderstood themes of *The Wretched of the Earth* is Fanon's advocation of violence as the necessary means for national liberation and the restoring of humanity to the colonized.

The colonial situation, says Fanon, is violent from the start. As shown earlier in the entry, the subjugation of the Algerian people began with the raping, looting, and indiscriminate killings inflicted by the French on the Algerians in 1830. During the war for liberation, Fanon learned from victims themselves of the barbaric actions committed by the French who resorted to torture, execution, and "resettlement" of whole villages. When the Algerians began their armed struggle against the colonizers, violence released the tensions of lifetimes of subjugation and oppression. All-out war united the Algerians as never before. The notion of a modern nation is a fairly abstract idea, but physical violence against the French gave the people a concrete cause and goal in which to join together.

Fanon was no stranger to violence himself, having fought for the Free French against the Nazis in World War II. After studying psychiatry, Fanon was sent to Algeria by the French government to work as a member of the French colonial administration. In 1953 he became one of the directors of a French psychiatric hospital outside Algiers that gained a reputation for nurturing the *feda'iyin,* or freedom fighters, who sacrificed themselves for the cause. Here Fanon learned directly of the cruelty and inhumanity of the French. While treating French soldiers and torturers, he simultaneously treated the feda'iyin, many of them secretly because they were being hunted by the French. Fanon himself became a revolutionary in Algeria, where he was injured by explosive mines and narrowly avoided assassination and kidnapping.

Many people misunderstand Fanon's call for violence in the decolonization process. There is a danger of misreading Fanon and thinking he advocates blind violence; a danger of confusing the means with the end. It is important to remember that while Fanon advocates violence, he makes it clear that it is only a vehicle to achieve liberation. Violence against the colonizer unites the people, and serves as a cathartic, creative, humanizing force that enables them to gain back freedom, human dignity, and national sovereignty.

In striving to better understand Fanon's ideas within the general context of decolonization, we must remember that Fanon was not the only Third World revolutionary to promote violence as a liberating force. Ho Chi Minh advocated violence with great success in the Vietminh nationalist movement against France in Indochina. At the start of the conflict in 1946 he exhorted his countrymen: "Those who have rifles will use their rifles; those who have swords will use their swords; those who have no swords will use spades, hoes, or sticks. Everyone must work to oppose the colonialists and save his country!" (Ho Chi Minh, p. 68). In July 1954 the Vietnamese people defeated the French at Dien Bien Phu, a famous victory that inspired colonized people everywhere. As Fanon states, "Not a single colonized individual could ever again doubt the possibility of a Dien Bien Phu; the only problem was how best to use the forces at their disposal, how to organize them, and when to bring them into action" (*Wretched of the Earth,* p. 70).

Likewise Mao Tse-tung, the leader of the Chinese Revolution, maintained that "political power grows from the barrel of a gun"; in fact, he declared, "anything can grow out of the barrel of a gun," including schools, culture, and mass movements (Mao in Schnan, p. 209). Armed strength and violence determines who controls the nation and its future. Mao thus concurs with Fanon's premise that violence unifies the nation and forges a new era.

The example of Mahatma Gandhi is often erroneously used to counter the notion that only violence can bring about freedom and national sovereignty. While Ghandi believed that nonviolence requires greater courage than violence, that "[i]t is the acid test of nonviolence that in a nonviolent conflict there is no rancor left behind and, in the end, the enemies are converted into friends," decolonization in India in fact involved violence (Gandhi, p. 45). Although Ghandi advocated nonviolence as the means to defeat the oppressor, and contributed to the British withdrawal from India, nearly one million Indians were killed after the region was partitioned into Pakistan and India. According to Fanon's philosophy, the British colonizers benefited from Ghandi's nonviolence but the indigenous peoples vented their pent-up aggression against the colonizer by massacring one another in a postindependence bloodbath.

Although Fanon advocates violence as a means to liberation, he also exposes its devastating effects in "Colonial War and Mental Disorders." From the clinical details of individual cases, the true horror of colonial violence and the war for independence comes into focus. Even the dedicated revolutionary must contend with the psychological scars of violence. An FLN fighter, for example, whose own mother was killed, murders a defenseless French woman, then suffers from depression and psychosis. Despite its unflinching examination of such horror, Fanon's final essay is not a counterpoint to the promotion of violence; rather, it demonstrates that Fanon is intimately aware of the cost of violence. It is this cost that lends urgency to Fanon's message about nation building. In his view, the new nation must be forged from the revolutionary principles that were put forth in the struggle for liberation. The evils just defeated—colonialism and oppression—must not be allowed to return in other economic or cultural forms, or the cost of violence will have been too dear.

Sources and literary context. Fanon was influenced by the existentialist movement in France and by its leader, Jean-Paul Sartre, who wrote the preface to *The Wretched of the Earth*. Sartre's writings on philosophy and politics were extremely popular in France during the late 1940s and 1950s, and his support of Fanon helped secure publication of *The Wretched of the Earth*.

Sartre's existentialism maintains that the existence of a person has primacy over the person's essence. An individual is responsible for defining his or her essence—that is, how to live his or her life—even if it conflicts with societal conventions. Fanon applies this idea to colonial society, advocating that individuals take on the collective responsibility to fashion a world of their own making in defiance of the colonial power.

Similarly Fanon also draws upon the ideas of Karl Marx and Georg Wilhelm Friedrich Hegel, ultimately reshaping their ideas into ones of his own. From Hegel, Fanon draws upon the master/slave dichotomy in understanding the structure of the colonized society as being dualistic, one where there is a complete segregation and opposition of both the colonizer and the colonized. Fanon also takes his understanding of decolonization as the necessary outcome of colonialism from Hegel, that is, from Hegel's understanding of history as a continually evolving, dialectical process. From Marx, who was also greatly influenced by Hegel's idea of history, Fanon gets his understanding of modern economics, class struggle in industrial society, and some of his terminology (bourgeoisie, lumpenproletariat).

Fanon developed his ideas over more than a decade. As early as 1952 he published *Black Skin White Masks,* about exploitation on the sugar plantations of Martinique and about the struggles on this French West Indies island. His book

A Dying Colonialism (1959), based on his fieldwork in wartime Algeria, discussed the benefits to be gained by a people sharing stress. *The Wretched of the Earth* capped these years of experience, writings, and thought.

Reviews. Fanon's critics "have never ceased to cry shame" because he embraced violence as beneficial (Perinbam, p. 76). The writer Lewis Coser argued that Fanon is wrong; violence does not have the therapeutic value he assigns to it. Hannah Arendt agreed, considering Fanon's ideas dangerous, even poisonous (Perinbam, p. 76). Yet in the West, *The Wretched of the Earth* was praised by some who recognized its importance as a delineation of the process of decolonization. A review in *Time* magazine compared it to the *Communist Manifesto* and Hitler's *Mein Kampf* in importance. Focusing on Fanon's anti-Western message, the magazine described the work as "not so much a book as a rock thrown through the window of the West" (*Time,* p. 114). Other reviews echoed this one, adding that the work's depth lay in Fanon's blend of theory with his experience in Algeria. Writing for *The New Republic,* Robert Coles explained Fanon's success:

> What distinguishes this book, turns it from a blazing manifesto to an authentic and subtle work of art, is the author's extraordinary capacity to join his sharp social and political sense with the doctor's loyalty to the individual, whatever his particular worth or folly.
>
> (Coles, p. 23)

In the *Nation,* C. C. O'Brien turned the spotlight away from Fanon's attack on the West and toward the Algerian perspective offered in the work: "Fanon forces his readers to see the Algerian Revolution—and by analogy other contemporary revolutions—from the viewpoint of the rebels" (O'Brien, p. 674).

In contemporary scholarship, according to Henry Louis Gates, Jr., "Frantz Fanon has now been reinstated as a global theorist, and not simply by those engaged in Third World or subaltern studies" (Gates, p. 457). Fanon's writing has been used to open discussions on British romantic poets, attack other scholars who seem to be practicing colonial forms of history and interpretation, and has been interpreted and cited by major scholars such as Edward Said, Homi Bhaba, Benita Parry, Albert Memmi, Abdul JanMohammed, and Gayatri Spivak.

Impact. Although Fanon addressed his book to the peoples of the Third World, the audience he reached consisted largely of Western intellectuals. The African peasants and nationalists of whom he writes took little note of his ideas. Yet the negative patterns that he foresaw, the rise of dictators and military power in various nations, quickly came true throughout postcolonial Africa.

In the United States, black activists in the 1960s and 1970s took Fanon seriously, interpreting their own position as analogous to that of the colonized. *The Wretched of the Earth* had an important influence on the founding of the militant Black Panther Party by Huey Newton and Bobby Seale, and won high regard from many in the Black Power movement. Radical civil rights activist and Black Panther leader Stokley Carmichael called Fanon "one of my patron saints" (Carmichael in Caute, p. 103). Like others devoted to raising the consciousness of blacks in America, he paid particular heed to Fanon's idea of violence as a creative force that forges a new man who breaks with Western values.

—John Roleke and Faisal Azam

For More Information

Caute, David. *Frantz Fanon.* New York: Viking, 1970.

Coles, Robert. "What Colonialism Does." *The New Republic,* 18 September 1965, pp. 20-23.

Davidson, Basil. *Modern Africa: A Social and Political History.* 3rd ed. London: Longman, 1994.

Fanon, Frantz. *The Wretched of the Earth.* Preface by Jean-Paul Sartre. Trans. Constance Farrington. New York: Grove Press, 1966.

Gandhi, Mahatma. *The Words of Gandhi.* Ed. Richard Attenborough. New York: Newmarket Press, 1996.

Gates, Henry Louis, Jr. "Critical Fanonism." *Critical Inquiry* 17, no. 3 (spring 1991): 457-70.

Ho Chi Minh. *Ho Chi Minh: Selected Writings, 1920-1969.* Hanoi: Foreign Languages Publishing House, 1977.

O'Brien, C. C. Review of *The Wretched of the Earth,* by Frantz Fanon. *The Nation,* 21 June 1965, p. 674.

Perinbam, B. Marie. *Holy Violence: The Revolutionary Thought of Frantz Fanon.* Washington D.C.: Three Continents Press, 1982.

Review of *The Wretched of the Earth,* by Frantz Fanon. *Time,* 30 April 1965, p. 114.

Schnan, Stuart R. *The Political Thought of Mao Tse-tung.* New York: Frederick A. Praeger, 1963.

Talbott, John. *The War Without a Name: France in Algeria, 1954-1962.* New York: Knopf, 1980.

Toth, Anthony. "Historical Setting." In *Algeria: A Country Study.* 5th ed. Ed. Helen Chapin Metz. Washington, D.C.: Federal Research Division, 1994.

Yaka

by
Pepetela

*P*epetela is the word for "eyelash" in the Umbundu language, and it is a literal translation from the Portuguese of the surname
of Artur Carlos Maurício Pestana, author of *Yaka*.
Originally Pepetela adopted this name while
fighting in the MPLA, or Movimento Popular
para a Libertaç o de Angola (People's Liberation
Movement of Angola). A Marxist-Leninist guerrilla group, the MPLA was formed in the 1950s
to gain Angola's independence from Portugal.
When Angola achieved independence in 1975,
the fledgling nation's poet-president António Au-
gustino Neto called upon patriotic writers to establish a national literature. Pepetela was one of
many who responded to this call. Like the protagonist of *Yaka*, Pepetela was born to parents of
Portuguese descent in the Angolan port city of
Benguela. He was educated in Angola, Portugal,
France, and Algeria, eventually getting his degree
in sociology. In adopting an Umbundu translation of his Portuguese name, the author creates
for himself an identity that melds European and
African elements in a way that is uniquely Angolan. Indeed, Pepetela is known—perhaps most
ambitiously in *Yaka*—for tackling the theme of
Angolanidade, the concept of what it means to be
Angolan, in his literary work. *Yaka*, Pepetela's
fourth novel, won the Angolan national prize for
literature in 1985.

Events in History at the Time the Novel Takes Place

Angola. Angola is a tropical nation below the
equator on the southwestern coast of Africa.
Roughly 14 times the size of Portugal, Angola extends from the Congo River basin in the north

THE LITERARY WORK

A novel set in Angola from 1890 to 1975;
published in Portuguese in 1984, in English in
1996.

SYNOPSIS

Through the influence of a mysterious African
statue, the son of Portuguese settlers in Angola
develops character over the course of his life,
as he comes to understand Africa.

to the edges of the Kalahari Desert in the south.
Angola's coastal lowlands in the west give way to
an ascending series of plateaus, rising eastward
to the nation's inland borders. While the coast is
hot and humid with poor soil, the interior
plateaus offer fertile soil and a healthy climate.
Benguela, where much of the novel takes place,
is a port city midway down the Angolan coast.
The area surrounding Benguela is watered by numerous small streams and rivers, and is homeland to the Ovimbundu people, who constitute
the largest ethnic group in Angola and speak Umbundu. There are seven other major indigenous
groups in Angola. Of these, two are represented
in the novel. The Cuvales, a subgroup of the
Herero of southwest Angola, are herders who
place high cultural value on cattle. The Yaka, or
Jaga, live near the northern border of Angola,
where they migrated sometime in the sixteenth
century. None of these ethnic groups were united
before Portugal began its colonizing efforts in the
fifteenth century; at the time of contact with Europeans in the eighteenth century, the Ovimbundu consisted of some 22 subgroups.

Contact with the Portuguese. Portuguese explorer Diogo Cão landed in Angola in 1482 and struck up friendships with kings in the area of the Congo River basin. These kings welcomed Portuguese traders and missionaries in their lands. In fact. King Affonso I of the Kongo, a subgroup of the Bakongo people who inhabited the northern part of Angola as well as modern Congo, even exchanged ambassadors with King João III of Portugal. Relations between the two nations soured, however, when Portuguese traders, finding no precious metals in the region, turned to the slave trade for profits. African peoples would war against one another to gain prisoners, who would be sold as slaves to the Portuguese, and then shipped, for the most part, to Brazil and the Spanish colonies in the New World. Despite protests from the Portuguese and Kongo kings, the slave trade flourished, with both Portuguese and, to some extent, Africans profiting. Later the Portuguese were joined in the slaving enterprise by England, France, Spain, and Holland, with the trade in human beings continuing well into the nineteenth century. Altogether some 4 million Angolans were taken as slaves while the trade persisted.

In the sixteenth century Portugal attempted a military conquest of the regions south of Kongo lands, in search of a climate healthier than that of the malaria-ridden Congo River basin. The poverty of Portugal limited the ability of Portuguese traders in Angola to purchase slaves, the mainstay of their trade. This was one reason to prefer military conquest—by which slaves could be abducted—to peaceful trade relations—by which slaves had to be purchased. The various African kingdoms managed to resist the Portuguese successfully for a long time, however; as late as the seventeenth century, Portuguese influence in Angola was restricted to Benguela and to a handful of forts in the area around Luanda, a coastal city about 200 miles north of Benguela. Portugal, always on the verge of bankruptcy, desperately sought to exploit Africa and the Americas, but lack of resources made its efforts largely unsuccessful.

Settlement and trade. Relatively few European settlers came to Angola, and those that did were of two types: the *degredados* (exiled convicts) and the poorest of the Portuguese poor. Sometime in the seventeenth century, Portugal began to use Angola as a penal colony where it sent degredados, some of whom were banished from Portugal for political crimes. Portugal's poor left their homeland in large numbers seeking better opportunities overseas, but those who could afford the more expensive passage opted to go to the Americas rather than immigrate to Angola, which was perceived as a dangerous land of degredados, black Africans, and wild animals. Those who did come to Angola were thus the poorest of the poor, and Portugal offered them little or no help in terms of infrastructure.

The Portuguese were mainly interested in trade, which offered the quickest means to make money. These traders proved, for the most part, to be unscrupulous fortune-hunters, who planned to make their money as quickly as possible and return to Portugal with the profits. Likewise, Portuguese settlers in Angola, who were mainly of an urban background, largely avoided agriculture and went into some form of trade, many of them entertaining dreams of someday returning to Europe with wealth earned in Africa.

In the area around Benguela, where the novel is set, the Portuguese entered into trade agreements with Ovimbundu kings, or *sobas,* who would help the Portuguese procure goods from the interior. As in the novel, a few traders would bring caravans from the interior loaded with items such as slaves, ivory, beeswax, hides, and rubber, to the merchants who conducted trade at the port cities. The traders would then exchange the goods from the Angolan interior for European goods brought in ships by Portuguese traders—items of European manufacture such as guns, cloth, tools, and liquor, which were desired by the Ovimbundu. Until the Portuguese abolition of slavery in 1836, Angolan trade was essentially slave trade. In fact, long after slavery was officially proscribed, slaves continued to be shipped out of Angola under the guise of "contract laborers." Eventually slaves were replaced by rubber as the main item of Angolan trade. Angola enjoyed a rubber boom in the 1890s that ended abruptly when cheaper rubber became available from India. Agricultural items such as cotton and coffee soon formed the bulk of Angolan exports, then, in the twentieth century, were superseded by petroleum.

Race in Angola. Angolan society was rigidly stratified according to race over the period in which the novel takes place. At the top of the society were *brancos* (whites), those of European ancestry. Whites born in Europe were termed "first-class whites," while those born in Africa were "second-class whites." Next came *pardos* or *mestiços,* those of mixed African and European ancestry. Soon after the Portuguese established a presence in Angola, they gave rise to a mestiço population. Few Portuguese women would immigrate to Angola before the mid-nineteenth century, so male Portuguese settlers formed relationships with indigenous women, whom many still regarded as inferior beings. Later, as more white women arrived, the mestiço population dwindled and saw a concomitant decline in its rights and status, which was nonetheless significantly above that of *pretos* (blacks), those of purely indigenous ancestry, who were at the bottom of the social hierarchy. Most of the indigenous population were classified as "natives." They might be conscripted into the army or forced labor at any moment, and were not allowed to acquire education beyond two or three years in a village school. In the early 1900s, under Portuguese prime minister António de Oliverira Salazar (governed 1932-68), assimilation became official policy. Those indigenous people who could fluently speak, write, and read Portuguese, who could support themselves and their families, and who had clean police records were eligible to apply to the district governor for status as an *assimilado*. Assimilados gained the right to work at low-status jobs in the government or mission service and, in theory at least, gained freedom from forced labor and conscription. In reality, few indigenous people were given the opportunity to become assimilados, and those that did could lose their status on the merest whim of a colonial official.

The poverty and low status of most Portuguese immigrants to Angola may account in part for the degree of racism in the colony's history. Those who had been at the bottom of Portugal's social hierarchy suddenly found themselves at the top when they came to Angola, simply by virtue of race. With the allure of this sudden promotion came the temptation to do unto others as had been done unto oneself. Also, European notions of race at the time conceived of Africans as at best uncivilized and at worst subhuman. Portugal and the white population of Angola justified the exploitation of the indigenous population of Angola through the then-popular ideology that a European presence in Africa would civilize that continent. According to this view, the forced labor of black Africans was really a humanitarian undertaking, for in working for whites, blacks were helping themselves become more civilized. Likewise, blacks were expected to contribute toward their own "civilization," and were thus exorbitantly taxed on the basis of how many houses or how many children they had. Failure to pay taxes

A watchful soldier stands guard for the People's Liberation Movement of Angola, a Marxist-Leninist guerrilla group fighting for the nation's independence from Portugal.

sometimes led to confiscation of black Africans' lands, which could then be used by immigrant farmers.

Threats to Portuguese control of Angola. Railroads began to crisscross Angola in the late nineteenth century. Three main lines, largely funded with foreign capital, connected the major port cities along the coast and opened up the Angolan interior to Portuguese settlement. In the late 1880s Portugal attempted to claim a vast inland area including Angola, Rhodesia, Malawi, Zambia, and a portion of southern Congo. The Portuguese met with opposition from the British, who were building a railway at the time extending inland from Benguela and wanted the territory for themselves. Eventually Portugal had to settle for the territory of present-day Angola, dissuaded from further expansion by British threats of naval attack. This failure was a blow to Portuguese pride, aggravating the resentment and mistrust of the British that flourished in the Portuguese-Angolan community.

From 1880 to 1915, German explorers and settlers made inroads into southwestern Angola. Germany, which at this time controlled South

West Africa (now called Namibia), a colony bordering Angola to the south, wanted access to a port in south Angola that would be convenient for German copper mines near the border. The boundary between South West Africa and Angola was thus hotly disputed by Germany and Portugal. With the advent of World War I in 1914, German-Portuguese hostilities increased, and Germany began to attack southern Angola. In 1915 German troops surrendered to a combination of Portuguese and South African forces.

Meanwhile, Protestant missionaries of various denominations had also made inroads in Angola. Arriving in the last quarter of the nineteenth century, they discovered that the Catholic missionaries, who preceded them by some three centuries, had made little impact on the indigenous population. While Catholic missionaries remained in the major coastal urban centers, Protestant missionaries penetrated deep into the interior. The Portuguese, who were generally Catholics, regarded the Protestants with mistrust, viewing them as a possibly subversive force among Africans. Indeed, Protestant missionaries sometimes supported Africans in their struggles against Portuguese injustice, and when in the early twentieth century African peoples rose up against Portuguese rule, Protestant missionaries were implicated. In 1902 the Bailundo, a subgroup of the Ovimbundu, conducted one of the greatest of these revolts, the so-called Bailundo Rebellion.

By about 1930, the Portuguese had gained a firmer control over the interior, and rebellions by the indigenous population were no longer a threat, but it was also around this time that Angolans of various racial identities began to develop a consciousness of themselves as Angolans, and as having interests often opposed to the interests of the colonial power, Portugal.

Angolan nationalism. Throughout the twentieth century, various political associations were formed in opposition to the colonial status quo in Angola. Associations with goals of obtaining full rights for indigenous people and assimilados included the Liga Angolana formed in 1913 and Associação Regional dos Naturais de Angola (ANANGOLA) formed in 1929. Restrictions on political activity within Angola were severe; anyone suspected of "subversive" political activity would be arrested and exiled (or worse) by the Portuguese secret political and security police. Because of this, several political associations operated underground or outside the colony, often in Europe. The Angolan Communist Party was

one such group to form in exile in 1956. Later that year, the Movimento Popular de Libertação de Angola (MPLA) was formed in exile. Both the leadership and membership of the MPLA consisted mainly of mestiços and Mbundu, the second largest ethnic group in Angola. The MPLA, which had a Marxist-Leninist orientation, received backing from the Soviet Union and Cuba. In 1957 the Bakongo formed the nationalist party Uni o das Populaçoes do Norte de Angola (UPNA), which later renamed itself Uni o das Populaçoes de Angola (UPA), opening membership to all Angolans.

The bloody year. In February 1961, MPLA forces (numbering 100 to 200) launched an all-out attack against the bases of power in Angola's largest city, Luanda. In small bands, they attacked a police station, a prison, a government office, and a radio station. All the rebels were killed or captured, and seven police officers died in the battle. The hopeless uprising seems to have been intended to draw international attention to the unjust conditions in Angola, which it succeeded in doing. White European settlers felt that the hostilities instigated by a group composed mainly of black Africans constituted a racial attack. Racial hostilities exploded, and the next day a gang of armed European settlers swept through the streets of Luanda killing black Africans indiscriminately. Two months later, the UPA launched an attack on government offices and oppressive cotton plantations in northern Angola. European settlers, including women and children, were massacred, and reports of these atrocities were exaggerated a hundredfold. This led to more massive and indiscriminate reprisals against the indigenous population and marked the beginning of what would be a 14-year armed struggle for Angolan liberation that sometimes took the unfortunate form of a bloody race war. The first few years of this armed struggle saw the formation and reformation of many revolutionary political groups.

Timeline: Angolan Revolutionary Party Politics

1962: UPA (União das Populaçoes de Angola) joins with PDA (Partido Democratico Angolano) to form FNLA (Frente Nacional de Labertaçao de Angola), a largely Bakongo organization with a somewhat narrow ethnic focus.

1962: In Leopoldville in the Congo, the FNLA establishes the Revolutionary Government of Angola in Exile, or GRAE.

1963: GRAE is recognized by the government of Congo-Kinshasa (today's Zaire); the MPLA, a Marxist-Leninist liberation group, mainly of Mbundu and mestiços, denounces GRAE.

1964: A rift occurs in GRAE when its foreign minister, Jonas Savimbi, accuses its prime minister, Holden Roberto, of corruption.

1966: Jonas Savimbi helps form the União Nacional Para a Independencia Total de Angola (UNITA), composed of yet another ethnic group, the Ovimbundu. UNITA drifts towards socialism but stays to the right of MPLA and so receives Portuguese and U.S. backing.

Independence. On April 25, 1974, the Portuguese Armed Forces Movement (AFM) overthrew the Portuguese dictatorship of Marcelo Caetano, and Angolan liberation movements redoubled their efforts, demanding immediate independence. They perceived the weakness of the unstable Portuguese government; the new regime in Portugal lacked the resources to maintain control over its overseas territories. Amid the atmosphere of unrest, right-wing European settlers banded together and conducted new attacks on blacks. Their forces were later augmented by white South African mercenaries who crossed the Namibian border. Africans retaliated with attacks on European settlers.

In the face of such chaos, on July 29, 1974, Portuguese president General Antonio de Spinola made the landmark statement that Portugal recognized the right of her overseas territories to independence. Soon thereafter, the Portuguese government called for a cease-fire in Angola and for an interim government made up of representatives from all the different liberation movements. Independence would come once a popularly elected assembly had framed a constitution for Angola and elections had been held for a new government. The Portuguese army began to withdraw from Angola, and in January 1975 the interim government, with representatives from the MPLA, UNITA, FNLA, and Portugal, was sworn in.

On March 23, 1975, FNLA units attacked MPLA installations in Luanda; a few days later, FNLA troops killed 51 young MPLA recruits in the city. FNLA fighters together with troops from Zaire began to infiltrate the Angolan countryside. On March 28, MPLA, FNLA, and UNITA signed a peace agreement. On July 6, the Angolan constitution was published, but a few days later infighting resumed, and now for the first time the three movements divided Angola into spheres of influence. Some 300,000 terrified white settlers were airlifted out of the country, while thousands more streamed across the borders to Zaire, Zambia, and Namibia, taking what they could and destroying in bitterness what they had to leave behind. November 11, 1975, was the day fixed for Angolan independence, and the departure of the last Portuguese troops. Most white settlers wanted to be out of Angola by then.

Meanwhile, the South African government had started to dispatch troops into Angola in late August 1975, claiming the right to protect the hydroelectric dam that South Africa had built on the Cunene River. Supported by Portugal, South Africa had been training UNITA recruits in camps outside Angolan borders. On October 21, South Africa invaded Angola through Namibia. The MPLA troops were ill equipped to battle a regular army, and by November 11, Benguela and three other major cities had fallen to South African forces. South Africa also sent troops to the north to help the FNLA take Luanda from the MPLA. Unable to resist unaided, the MPLA called on Cuban leader Fidel Castro for help. Castro responded with troops in the thousands, and by the end of March 1976, South African troops had retreated beyond the Namibian border.

On November 11, 1975, Angola had become independent, but there was no new government in place to take over power from the old government. The MPLA set up what they claimed was the rightful government of Angola in Luanda, with MPLA leader Dr. António Agostinho Neto as president. Meanwhile, the FNLA and UNITA together set up their own government for Angola in Ambriz, a coastal town just north of Luanda. Full-scale civil war ensued, from which the MPLA, supported by Cuban troops and Soviet aid, emerged victorious in March 1976.

The MPLA was still in power in Angola in 1984, the year Yaka was published. In the period since independence, the MPLA nationalized education and healthcare and launched an aggressive literacy program in a nation where 95 percent of the population remained illiterate. The United Nations issued a resolution calling for an end to South African attacks on Angola, and for South Africa to pay reparations to Angola for damages inflicted in the invasion of 1975-76. South Africa, however, refused to comply, and MPLA-governed Angola suffered continued attacks by South Africa, UNITA, and FNLA. On December 1, 1976, Angola became the 146th member of the United Nations, despite opposition from the United States on the grounds that there were Cuban troops in Angola.

Angolan children orphaned by the nation's civil war.

The Novel in Focus

Plot summary. *Yaka* spans the lifetime (1890-1975) of its central character, Alexandre Semedo, and treats five generations of his family, from his parents to his great-grandchildren. Alexandre Semedo is the main narrator of his life story, which he frequently addresses to a statue, Yaka, imploring it to supply details or offer explanations. Yaka occasionally makes brief, poetic, riddling intrusions on the narration, which are not heard by Alexandre. Sometimes the novel takes the voice of an omniscient third-person narrator who may or may not be the statue Yaka, which "seemed to see everything" (Pepetela, *Yaka*, p. 16). A few brief passages are narrated by various relatives of Alexandre. The narrative voice often shifts in the midst of a chapter, or even a paragraph. What follows is an account of the basic plot.

Alexandre Semedo is born beneath a tree in the wild Angolan countryside. His father is Oscar Semedo, a law student banished to Angola from Portugal for ax-murdering his former wife, though he claims to be innocent, insisting that he is actually being punished for his republican politics. Alexandre's mother is Esmerelda Semedo, a so-called "second-class white," a white woman born in Angola to Portuguese settler parents. The couple is traveling by oxen-drawn wagon from Capangombe in the Angolan interior to Benguela on the coast to make a new life for themselves. Among their possessions is a statue won by Oscar in a game of cards, a statue made by the Yaka people. En route, Alexandre is born, and his mother's nurse accidentally drops him on the ground where the child's mouth bites the dirt. "Did it bite or kiss it?" the Yaka statue asks (*Yaka*, p. 9).

In Benguela, Oscar Semedo takes the only job available, as assistant in a shop that trades goods brought by Africans from the interior for goods brought in ships from Europe. Oscar's wages are meager, yet he dreams of opening his own shop and earning enough to some day send Alexandre to the university. Senhor Queirós, the owner of the shop where Oscar works, having no children of his own, makes Alexandre his godson.

The slave trade has just been abolished, and Angolan traders no longer ship human chattel overseas, though slavery still exists on the plantations, where the slaves are referred to as "servants" or "boys." As a replacement, Angola's traders have switched to rubber, but now the European purchasers prefer Indian rubber, which can be had at a cheaper price. To compensate for the lower prices at which they must now sell rubber to Europe, the white Angolan traders greatly and disproportionately reduce the rate at which they pay for rubber from the interior. Angered by the obvious underhandedness, the interior traders compensate by focusing their attention on the demand for "servants," for which the market is stable. This leads to unrest among the indigenous population, whose children are being abducted for sale. As anxiety increases, rumors of black uprisings and raids on white settlements spread. The white traders determine that something must be done to quell the blacks, and Oscar Semedo, overcome by fear, agrees to be the white traders' mouthpiece. He writes a letter to the governor demanding complete occupation of the interior and domination of the black population.

Meanwhile, Mutu-ya-Kevela, a Bailundo leader, attempts to organize the other sobas near Benguela to rise together against their white oppressors. Mutu-ya-Kevela is a great leader, and many rally to his cause. Rumors fly through the white populace that a massacre is imminent. Portugal soon responds to the concerns of Benguela traders by sending in troops, but the effort proves unnecessary. Mutu-ya-Kevela is already dead, betrayed by some Catholic priests whose lives he spared. Eventually the truth comes out, and it belies all the wild rumors about the Bailundo leader—no massacre had been planned.

Alexandre, who is now a pimply adolescent, reenacts with his friends the defeat of Mutu-ya-

Kevela. Their one black friend, Tuca, is cajoled into playing the part of the Bailundo leader. One game in which Tuca will not participate is the reenactment of an incident in which white men are said to have avenged the rape of white women by raping black women. The boys take turns raping a 13-year-old black girl, but Tuca does not, because the girl "didn't want it"; the other boys insist that "she enjoyed it just like any black girl" and unlike any white girl, with whom it would be a sin to do such things (*Yaka*, p. 41).

HOW YAKA IMPRESSES CHARACTERS IN THE NOVEL

"My father won this Yaka statue at gambling. He already had it in Capangombe when he got married. My mother always thought it horrible with its transparent resin eyes and three parallel stripes, white, black and red. You know, it's nearly a metre tall and has a man's body, but the face is strange, looking sometimes human and sometimes like an animal. The bulbous nose looks like a drunkard's and gives a mocking look to the whole. . . . It seemed to see everything."
(The character Alexandre Semedo in *Yaka*, p. 16)

"It looks like a clown at a fair, or some pig-headed creature. I've never understood why you like it so much, Senhor Semedo."
(The character Bartolomeu Espinha in *Yaka*, p. 123)

"It was crude, violent, beautiful. A man or a divinity? . . . If a divinity it was nonetheless treated with irony."
(The character Alexandre Semedo in *Yaka*, p. 123)

Senhor Queirós dies suddenly, leaving his shop to Alexandre, with Oscar as manager until the boy comes of age. Lacking the funds to send Alexandre to school, Oscar has the boy work with him in the shop, where, to make ends meet, the two must scrape and even cheat the customers. They find a way to pass the long, tedious days; Oscar teaches Alexandre about the Greeks, and Alexandre develops a lifelong passion for Greek tragedy.

The novel jumps ahead to 1917. Oscar and Esmerelda Semedo have died of disease, and Alexandre has married Donana de Aragão, a servant from Portugal. To satisfy his mother's hopes for him, Alexandre had written to his father's family in Portugal and they had sent one of their servants, for "[w]hat else could the son of an ex-convict born in a land of blacks hope for?" (*Yaka*, p. 68) The couple hate each other but have four children, whom Alexandre names after characters from Greek tragedy: Achilles, Socrates, Orestes, and Euridice. Alexandre has a mestiço daughter too, from a union with a black servant. He gave the mother, Joana, a little money and she and the child moved to another town.

In the local bar around which the social life of Benguela men centers, a white trader brings news from Amboim that a serious rebellion has begun in that region of rich coffee-growing land. There are even rumors that the Germans and Protestants are behind it all. The barber Acácio mocks the bearer of this news, Sô Agripino, making light of the grave reports. Sô Agripino threatens Acacio, and the next morning the barber is found beaten to death in his home. Although Alexandre and many others in the town heard the threats the night before, they say nothing to the authorities, who judge the crime to be a simple burglary.

The news of uprisings in Amboim is confirmed by other reports, and fear spreads among Benguela's inhabitants. People barricade themselves in their houses and go out only if fully armed. The constant fear wears on Alexandre, who decides that the only way to end it is to exterminate all black Africans: "We've got to finish them off. . . . So long as there are blacks we'll live in fear" (*Yaka*, p. 96).

A trader arrives with reports that the nearby town of Catumbela has been taken by rebels who are heading toward Benguela. The governor organizes an army of volunteers, among them Alexandre, who go to Catumbela only to find that the reports are entirely false; there has been no uprising there. Meanwhile, reports continue to arrive from Amboim that whites are being massacred and their estates burned. Alexandre's childhood friend, Tuca, is recruited into the army to go to Amboim to put down the rebellion. The rebellion is quelled, but when Tuca returns, he tells Alexandre a discomfiting story: in Amboim, the orders were to kill everyone in the rebellious villages, even women, children, and the elderly. Why had the villages rebelled? All the fertile land had been seized by white coffee growers, while the blacks had been pushed onto the least desirable land. Then the coffee growers had abducted blacks and turned them into slaves, whipping or even crucifying them if they failed to work hard enough. There had been cases of whites falsely accusing blacks of being rebels just to have them killed and take over their land.

Tuca's story appears to be turning Alexandre's earlier longing for the death of all blacks into a reality, which makes Alexandre so uncomfortable that he quickly puts the story out of his mind.

The novel skips forward to 1940. Alexandre's children are adults with families of their own. Achilles Semedo, Alexandre's eldest son, is a muscular brute of a man, who cares only for soccer and for bullying. He works as an overseer of black laborers, a job in which his bullying skills stand him in good stead. He is married to Gloria and they have three children. Orestes is "peaceful, no good for anything but counting bank notes in the bank of Angola" where he works (*Yaka*, p. 125). Socrates, the so-called intellectual of the family, goes to study law in Lisbon, where he remains (*Yaka*, p. 125). Euridice has recently married Bartolomeu Espinha, a shrewd businessman from Portugal with "no scruples and no education" (*Yaka*, pp. 123-24). Alexandre has purchased a *sapalalo*, a two-story wooden house, in which most of these members of the Semedo family live together.

Achilles, who is always spoiling for a fight, gets caught up in rumors about unrest among blacks in the countryside. Deciding to do something about it, he and some friends undertake a "hunting" expedition into the interior, the real purpose of which is to kill blacks. They see a young black man in the wilderness and open fire on him. Achilles kills the black, Tyenda, the eldest son of a peaceful Cuvale family living nearby. Tyenda's father witnesses the shooting and manages to kill Achilles with a spear, while Achilles's hunting companions flee to the nearest white settlement. They claim that the Cuvales attacked their party for no reason, and demand that the authorities organize a raid to punish the "savages" and avenge Achilles' death (*Yaka*, p. 170).

Meanwhile, Bartolomeu has convinced Alexandre to mortgage the sapalalo and invest the money in a cotton-growing scheme, with Bartolomeu in charge. Now, desperate for additional funds that Alexandre will not give him, Bartolomeu sees an opportunity: he asks to go on the raid against Achilles' Cuvale "killers," knowing that Cuvales are cattle-herders. Bartolomeu bribes the authorities to let him claim the large cattleherd as compensation for Achilles's death. The authorities conduct an air raid against Tyenda's family, bombing people whose only weapons are spears and arrows. The people are killed, their houses burned, and their cattle stolen by Bartolomeu, who uses the proceeds to expand his cotton plantations.

The novel action moves forward to 1961. Donana is dead and, curiously, Alexandre misses her. They have eight grandchildren, all but one in their late teens and twenties. Twenty-year-old Hector is Alexandre's favorite because he chose to study classics in school, and the two can discuss Greek tragedy at length. Ofelia, Alexandre's illicit mestiço daughter by his lover Joana, has a 20-year-old son named Chico. None of the grandchildren is interested in politics.

Bartolomeu has slowly become head of the family, usurping that role from Alexandre and then from Alexandre's sons. Alexandre no longer works in the shop as he can now afford to hire employees; he will not allow any of his children or grandchildren to work there either, believing it to be a "mediocre and castrating life" (*Yaka*, p. 206). By this point, though, his authority has waned. Having been forced by the family to move all his African artifacts, including the Yaka statue, upstairs into his own room, he now spends most of his time there. Alexandre has begun to write his memoirs "in the form of conversations with the Yaka statue"; they change the way he thinks and feels about things, allowing him to step back and become critical (*Yaka*, p. 209). The changes are evidenced when Tuca, exhausted from years of hard labor, comes back to Benguela to die. Alexandre makes critical, sarcastic remarks about the treatment of blacks in Angolan colonial society—remarks he never would have made 20 years earlier.

At the cotton plantation, Bartolomeu conceives a scheme to cheat Moma, a neighboring Ovimbundu soba, of his rich land. A rumor is going around that a Protestant catechist is mobilizing local blacks to rise up and massacre the whites, but the catechist cannot be found. Bartolomeu denounces Moma for harboring the catechist, though he knows the soba is innocent. Various family members join in the raid on Moma's settlement in which Moma is killed and his family evicted from their lands.

Chico, Alexandre's illicit grandson, comes to visit Benguela, and Alexandre invites him to move into the sapalalo. Most of the family treats Chico coldly, angered that Alexandre would bring shame upon them by acknowledging this product of his own indiscretion. On the night of Bartolomeu's raid, a cousin is found in Chico's bed. Chico is driven from the sapalalo and the cousin is shamed.

The novel jumps ahead to 1975. Alexandre has given up on his family and spends most of his time in his room alone. He has heart problems and feigns deafness so as not to have to interact with his family. Only Gloria—Achilles's widow—and her son, Xandinho, with his wife and children still live with Alexandre in the sapalalo. Nationalist guerrillas from "the Movement," Pepetela's euphemism for the MPLA, fly into Benguela and are greeted by a jubilant crowd. Alexandre's great-grandson Joel, an avid supporter of the Movement, has witnessed the guerrillas' arrival. He ecstatically tells the family, who are gathered in the sapalalo, how one guerrilla came out of the airplane face first to kiss the ground of Angola. Alexandre observes Joel's enthusiasm and develops an interest in the boy that he has not felt for any other member of the family. Alexandre's granddaughter Olivia—formerly a fanatic self-flagellant nun, now a devotee of Karl Marx, whose picture hangs in her bedroom—criticizes the Movement for being doctrinally "impure" (*Yaka*, p. 257). She and Joel engage in heated political discussions.

Chico is invited back to the sapalalo. Xandinho in particular makes a point of cultivating the mestiço's friendship. He worries that an inquiry will be conducted into what happened with Moma, and Chico, as the carrier of black blood in the family, is his shield against approbation. Faced with upcoming elections, Xandinho has attempted to join all three political parties: MPLA, FNLA, and UNITA. None would accept him. A former colonial official, Xandinho is convinced that if the MPLA wins, they will massacre all the whites. He eventually has a nervous breakdown.

With independence imminent Bartolomeu fears seizure of his property and wealth, and so determines to move the family to South Africa. Joel does not understand his family's cowardice and lack of faith in the MPLA. He will remain and fight for his country. Alexandre also decides to stay; he has grown to like and respect Joel and is ready to die, except that he wants first to know what the Yaka statue has been trying to communicate to him all his life. "What sense," Alexandre asks of the statue, "would there be in this eighty year dialogue if I die before understanding you?" (*Yaka*, p. 283). South Africa attacks the MPLA to prevent independence. As the troops invade Benguela and approach his two-story wood house, Alexandre takes the Yaka statue out into the yard. He has a heart attack, and as he dies, Alexandre implores the statue one last time to speak. Instead, the Yaka statue shows him an image of the future, of Joel, and then finally does speak to him, telling him that his great-grandson Joel will be a hero, will be adopted by Cuvales, and will win the battle against the South Africans. Angola will be free. As Alexandre dies, he falls to the ground and his mouth bites the Angolan earth once more, as it did the day he was born, and "the earth Alexandre Semedo's mouth bites tastes good to him" (*Yaka*, p. 302).

Connecting with Africa: *Yaka*, Yaka, and Angolanidade. When Alexandre Semedo tastes the African soil at the end of *Yaka*, the circle of his life is complete. Tasting the earth in this novel serves as a metaphor for connecting with the land on other levels. At his birth, Alexandre tastes the earth of Angola, his homeland, unconsciously. He, of course, has no memory of the event, but Yaka, who was tied to the top of the ox-cart, recalls it. On a metaphoric level, Alexandre is connected to Africa simply by virtue of being born there. Yaka knows this, but Alexandre is unable, through most of the novel, to feel this connectedness. He fails, until the very end, to understand Africa. It is only at his death, aided by the Yaka statue, that Alexandre finally makes a conscious connection with his homeland and, as he bites the Angolan soil this time, "the earth . . . tastes good to him" (*Yaka*, p. 302).

This theme of making a connection with Angola, and hence of Angolanidade (what it means to be Angolan), runs through much of Pepetela's writings. The Yaka statue, which is the primary symbol for Angolanidade in the novel, is, according to Pepetela, "pure fiction," yet actual Yaka statuary is a highly developed art form that is peculiarly suited to serving as a symbolic emblem for Angolanidade (*Yaka*, p. ix).

The Yaka (or Jaga) were a warlike people who invaded Angola from lands to the east in the 1560s. They have a fierce reputation. Andrew Battell, an English sailor who became their prisoner near the beginning of the seventeenth century, gave a sensationalist account of their practices, stating that the Yaka were cannibals who increased their number only through abduction from other groups since they killed all their own children. In *Yaka*, Pepetela criticizes Battell's description, scorning this "ingratitude of the Englishman, since they let him live to tell the tale" (*Yaka*, p. ix). Yet perhaps by using the Yaka statue as a symbol of Africanness, an Africanness that is eventually transmitted to the son of European settlers, Pepetela was playing on the practice of the Yaka people of augmenting their own group with children from other groups. This form of incorporation is even more vividly illustrated when Yaka and Alexandre look into the future

and see that Joel will be adopted by a family of Cuvales.

Certain Yaka statues known as *mbwoolo* are particularly relevant to the theme of Angolanidade as it is treated in *Yaka*. Mbwoolo are statues that have powers to curse, protect, and heal. They are frequently set to guard property, the theft of which will result in a curse against the thief through the agency of the mbwoolo. Such curses are hereditary, taking the form of a sickness passed down from one generation to the next of the thief's family until someone in the family gives back the stolen goods or, if this is impossible, undergoes a special ceremony to appease and honor the mbwoolo. When this is done, the mbwoolo cures the sickness and even empowers the formerly cursed family, as the mbwoolo can now be used by them to protect their own property. In the novel, the Yaka statue could be seen as a sort of mbwoolo; in retaliation for their "theft" of African land and resources, it curses the Semedo family with the sickness of fear and alienation that comes from bad conscience.

Each section of the novel is given the name of a part of the body: the mouth, the eyes, the heart, the genitals, and the legs. At the novel's beginning, when Alexandre Semedo is born, Yaka waits "for the unique shower, perhaps without water, that would join mouth to eyes and legs to genitals, still separate in mistrust" (*Yaka*, p. 8). This separation is at once the alienation of the different peoples of Angola from one another, and the falseness of the individual colonist whose actions belie his words, whose religious beliefs are at odds with his cruelty, and whose sexual desire is not linked to his emotions. It seems the thing that will join the divided parts is the one element unnamed by Yaka in this passage: the heart. The central episode in the central section of the novel, entitled "The Heart," is the slaying of Tyenda and the subsequent death of Alexandre's son, Achilles. What is needed to heal Alexandre and his family, and the colonial whites of which they are emblematic, is true compassion, the realization that in killing an African son, one kills one's own son. What is needed to heal Angola is a connection between all the different elements, all the different peoples who make up that nation, through a sense of Angolanidade.

Sources and literary context. Angolan literature has its roots in the spirit of anticolonialism, and, ironically, in the language of the colonial power in Angola, Portuguese. In the second half of the twentieth century, a new national consciousness began to grow in Angola as more and more colonies began to demand and achieve independence in Africa and elsewhere. Journals emerged that combined a progressive nationalist politics with literature that dealt largely with themes of national identity and racial unity. Once Angola achieved independence in 1975, literary fervor increased as the nation's first president, Antonio Agostinho Neto, himself an esteemed poet, called upon writers to become a crucial force in the Revolution, and Pepetela heeded the call. Pepetela cites American authors John Steinbeck, Ernest Hemingway, and John Dos Passos as influences, as well as Brazilian writers in the Portuguese language, José Lins do Rego, Graciliano Ramos, and João Guimarães Rosa. *Yaka* has been judged to contain elements of magic realism, a style that brings supernatural elements—such as the conscious, speaking Yaka statue—into a modern/historical setting.

Events in History at the Time the Novel Was Written

Continuing uncertainty and fear. Although the MPLA succeeded in establishing itself as the governing party of newly independent Angola, the struggle between the rival political parties was not over. UNITA and FNLA moved their bases into neighboring countries from which they conducted guerrilla attacks against the MPLA. FNLA managed to maintain a base in Zaire, but FNLA members were few and their impact was negligible in comparison to that of UNITA. UNITA moved its base across the border into South African-controlled Namibia, and from there carried out guerrilla attacks against southern Angola. South Africa, in retaliation for Angola's open support of South West Africa People's Organization (SWAPO), which was fighting to free Namibia from South African control, lent aid to UNITA, and even attacked Angola with its own troops. Fighting continued into the mid-1980s, when *Yaka* was written, and beyond.

Threatened by such forces, Angola's MPLA government retained 18,000 Cuban troops and accepted aid from the Soviet Union. Angola insisted on a policy of non-alliance, however, not allowing any foreign military bases in its territory and expressing a willingness to cooperate with any nation. Despite this policy, the Western powers did not lend their support; in fact, the United States gave considerable aid to UNITA.

The MPLA also suffered from internal fighting. In May 1977 an internal coup attempt resulted in the deaths of several highly placed party members. Issues of race were a factor; many of those attacked were white or mestiço, and were believed therefore not to have the best interests of the African peoples of Angola at heart.

Constant warfare took its toll on the economy of Angola. In the mid-1980s, nearly half of Angola's budget went into the military. The threat of UNITA attacks in the countryside and the widespread laying of landmines caused the nation's agricultural production to drop. Many skilled and educated Angolans left the country to escape the constant danger and lack of opportunity caused by warfare. *Yaka,* which has been criticized for its sometimes didactic and pamphleteering tone, can perhaps be better understood in light of the danger and uncertainty that continued to be characteristic of Angola at the time the work was written.

Reviews. *Yaka* has met with praise and criticism in fairly equal measure. Reviewers have praised it, in the main, for its wide scope and "richly detailed recounting of Angolan history" (*Publishers Weekly,* p. 74). Literary scholar Hanna Betina Götz declared *Yaka* to be an "important narrative" because "it reenacts the complex historical process of colonization" (Götz, p. 75). On the other hand, Pepetela has been widely criticized for heavy-handedness in his simplistic portrayal of the political situation in Angola. As one reviewer put it, "*Yaka* begins to sound increasingly like a manifesto for the MPLA's beliefs and ideals for the new nation" (Simoes Da Silva, p. 511). Opinions about other elements of the novel have varied as well. Some reviewers simply hated *Yaka*: "The novel promises but never delivers—the pace is slow; the characters creepy and largely unsympathetic, the transitions from first to second person are confusing, and the literary device of Alexandre's Yaka warrior statue as knowing observer throughout the epic is poorly woven into the narrative" (*Publishers Weekly,* p. 74). Others, though maintaining reservations about a certain doctrinaire quality to parts of the novel, praised the satirical representation of Marxism-Leninism in the character of the Marx-worshipping Olivia, and the use of the Yaka statue as a symbol of Angolanidade.

—Kimberly Ball

For More Information

Battell, Andrew. *The Strange Adventures of Andrew Battell of Leigh, in Angola and the Adjoining Regions.* London: The Hakluyt Society, 1901.

Bourgeois, Arthur P. "Mbwoolo Sculpture of the Yaka." *African Arts* 12, no. 3 (May 1979): 58-61.

Götz, Hanna Betina. "Five Generations of Angola's Colonial Erosion and National Birth." *Luso-Brazilian Review* 34, no. 1 (summer 1997): 67-76.

Kaplan, Irving, ed. *Angola: A Country Study*. Washington D.C.: The American University, 1979.

Pepetela. *Yaka*. Trans. Marga Holness. Oxford: Heinemann, 1996.

Review of *Yaka*, by Pepetela. *Publishers Weekly* 243, no. 19 (May 6, 1996): 74.

Simoes Da Silva, Tony. "*Pepetela*." In *Encyclopedia of World Literature in the 20th Century*. Vol. 3. Farmington Hills, Mich.: St. James Press, 1999.

Somerville, Keith. *Angola: Politics, Economics & Society*. London: F. Pinter, 1986.

Wheeler, Douglas L., and René Pélissier. *Angola*. New York: Praeger, 1971.

Index

~

A

'Abbas II   121 (*illus.*)
'Abd al-Nasir, Jamal. *See* Nasser, Gamal Abdul
'Abd al Qadir   505
Abiku children   152–53, 153 (*illus.*), 155
Abolition movement   144–46
Abrahams, Peter, *Mine Boy*   269–77
Achebe, Chinua
    on Armah   21
    on corruption   238 (*sidebar*)
    Things Fall Apart   421–30
    use of Africanized English   287 (*sidebar*)
    use of proverbs   115
Acoli people   387
Adda, Gladys   345
Adultery   283
Afigbo, A. E.   424
African Laughter: Four Visits to Zimbabwe (Doris
    Lessing)   1–11
African National Congress (ANC)   2 (*sidebar*), 3,
    26 (*sidebar*), 26, 28, 347, 348–51, 456, 483
    (*sidebar*)
Afrikaans language   28, 100, 104–5, 444
Afrikaners (Boers)   23–24, 25 (*sidebar*), 59, 97, 98,
    104–5, 348, 397, 432, 444, 484
Age-grade guilds or age-groups   36, 422
Agriculture
    (*See also* Land reform and land ownership issues)
    Bantu   283 (*sidebar*)
    Botswanan   483, 487 (*sidebar*)
    grasshopper storms   321 (*sidebar*), 322
    Mali, Empire of   208
    Mozambiquean   463–65, 464 (*illus.*), 464
        (*sidebar*)
    Nigerian   109, 216, 310

South African   271
    sugar cane   249 (*illus.*)
    by women   283, 298
    Yoruba   328
    Zimbabwean   5, 298
Aidoo, Ama Ata, *Dilemma of a Ghost*   87–95
AIDS (Acquired Immune Deficiency Syndrome),
    Zimbabwe   9 (*sidebar*)
Akan peoples   87
al-Azhar, world's oldest continuous university   125
    (*sidebar*)
Alcohol   108, 272–73
al-Fasi, al-Hassan (Leo Africanus)   212 (*sidebar*)
Algeria: works set in
    Fantasia: An Algerian Cavalcade (Assia
        Djebar)   163–72
    Nedjma (Kateb Yacine)   289–96
    Wretched of the Earth, The (Frantz
        Fanon)   503–13
Algeria (*in chronological order*)
    Keblout and Beni Hilal   124 (*sidebar*), 266,
        294, 295 (*sidebar*)
    'Abd al-Qadir revolt (1830s–40s)   505
    French conquest (1830)   163–64, 168, 291
        (*sidebar*), 504–5
    resistance movements (1830–71)   164–65
    white settlers (mid-1800s)   505
    rebellion against French rule (1940s)   289–91,
        290 (*sidebar*)
    anti-colonial demonstrations in Sétif   289, 292,
        506
    revolution (1954–62)   165–66, 294–28
    war of independence (1954–62)   165–66,
        295–96, 506–7
    role of women in war   166, 171
    independence (1962)   166, 507

E

H

I

J